# Abuse, Neglect, Dependency, and Termination of Parental Rights Proceedings in North Carolina

2019

Sara DePasquale
Jan S. Simmons

Production of this Manual was made possible with funding provided by the U.S. Department of Health and Human Services—Administration for Children and Families, and the Court Improvement Program of the North Carolina Administrative Office of the Courts.

The School of Government at the University of North Carolina at Chapel Hill works to improve the lives of North Carolinians by engaging in practical scholarship that helps public officials and citizens understand and improve state and local government. Established in 1931 as the Institute of Government, the School provides educational, advisory, and research services for state and local governments. The School of Government is also home to a nationally ranked Master of Public Administration program, the North Carolina Judicial College, and specialized centers focused on community and economic development, information technology, and environmental finance.

As the largest university-based local government training, advisory, and research organization in the United States, the School of Government offers up to 200 courses, webinars, and specialized conferences for more than 12,000 public officials each year. In addition, faculty members annually publish approximately 50 books, manuals, reports, articles, bulletins, and other print and online content related to state and local government. The School also produces the *Daily Bulletin Online* each day the General Assembly is in session, reporting on activities for members of the legislature and others who need to follow the course of legislation.

Operating support for the School of Government's programs and activities comes from many sources, including state appropriations, local government membership dues, private contributions, publication sales, course fees, and service contracts.

Visit sog.unc.edu or call 919.966.5381 for more information on the School's courses, publications, programs, and services.

Michael R. Smith, Dean
Thomas H. Thornburg, Senior Associate Dean
Jen Willis, Associate Dean For Development
Michael Vollmer, Associate Dean for Administration

FACULTY

Whitney Afonso
Trey Allen
Gregory S. Allison
David N. Ammons
Ann M. Anderson
Maureen Berner
Frayda S. Bluestein
Mark F. Botts
Anita R. Brown-Graham
Peg Carlson
Connor Crews

Leisha DeHart-Davis
Shea Riggsbee Denning
Sara DePasquale
Jacquelyn Greene
Norma Houston
Cheryl Daniels Howell
Willow S. Jacobson
Robert P. Joyce
Diane M. Juffras
Dona G. Lewandowski
Adam Lovelady

James M. Markham
Christopher B. McLaughlin
Kara A. Millonzi
Jill D. Moore
Jonathan Q. Morgan
Ricardo S. Morse
C. Tyler Mulligan
Kimberly L. Nelson
David W. Owens
William C. Rivenbark
Dale J. Roenigk

John Rubin
Jessica Smith
Meredith Smith
Carl W. Stenberg III
John B. Stephens
Charles Szypszak
Shannon H. Tufts
Aimee N. Wall
Jeffrey B. Welty (on leave)
Richard B. Whisnant

© 2020
School of Government
The University of North Carolina at Chapel Hill

Use of this publication for commercial purposes or without acknowledgment of its source is prohibited. Reproducing, distributing, or otherwise making available to a non-purchaser the entire publication, or a substantial portion of it, without express permission, is prohibited.

Printed in the United States of America

24 23 22 21 20    1 2 3 4 5

ISBN 978-1-56011-979-1

# Contents

*Note: Each Chapter includes a detailed table of contents.*

**Introduction to the Manual**

**About the Authors and Acknowledgments**

**Chapter 1: Overview of the North Carolina Child Welfare System    1-1**

    **1.1   Introduction to Child Welfare   1-2**
- A. Child Welfare Services
- B. Purpose
- C. Overview of a Child Welfare Case in North Carolina
- D. Demographics

    **1.2   Federal-State-County System   1-11**
- A. County-State Structure and Relationship
- B. The County DSS
- C. Federal-State-County Funding
- D. Federal-State Relationship

    **1.3   State and Federal Sources of Authority: Laws, Rules, and Policy   1-19**
- A. North Carolina
- B. Influence of Federal Law

**Chapter 2: The Court, Key People, and the Rights of Children and Parents    2-1**

    **2.1   The Juvenile Court and Officials   2-3**
- A. The Court
- B. Judicial Officials and Staff

    **2.2   Key People: Who's Who in the System   2-7**
- A. Introduction
- B. The People: Explanation of Roles

    **2.3   The Child   2-15**
- A. Introduction
- B. Definitions of Abused, Neglected, or Dependent Juveniles
- C. Rights of the Child
- D. The Child's Guardian ad Litem

    **2.4   Rights of the Parent   2-35**
- A. Protection of Parent-Child Relationship
- B. Notice and Opportunity to Be Heard
- C. DSS Perspective
- D. Representation
- E. Funds for Experts and Other Expenses
- F. Guardian ad Litem for Parent

## Chapter 3: Jurisdiction, Venue, and Overlapping Proceedings    3-1

### 3.1 Summary and Scope of Jurisdiction Issues    3-3
A. Introduction
B. District Court Jurisdiction
C. Continuing and Ending Jurisdiction in Abuse, Neglect, or Dependency Proceedings
D. Terminology Related to Continuing and Ending Jurisdiction

### 3.2 Subject Matter Jurisdiction    3-8
A. Introduction
B. Key Issues in Determining Subject Matter Jurisdiction
C. Issues That Do Not Affect Subject Matter Jurisdiction

### 3.3 Uniform Child-Custody Jurisdiction and Enforcement Act and Parental Kidnapping Prevention Act    3-19
A. Introduction
B. Applicability of the UCCJEA: G.S. Chapter 50A
C. Jurisdictional Basis for Making Custody Determination under the UCCJEA
D. Evidence, Findings, and Conclusions of Law
E. Communication Requirements
F. Hearings
G. Deployed Parents
H. Enforcement of Custody Orders under the UCCJEA
I. Parental Kidnapping Prevention Act: 28 U.S.C. 1738A

### 3.4 Personal Jurisdiction    3-42
A. Introduction
B. Service of Process
C. Consent and Waiver Establishing Personal Jurisdiction
D. Acquiring Personal Jurisdiction in Abuse, Neglect, Dependency Cases
E. Out-of-State Parents in Termination of Parental Rights Cases

### 3.5 Venue    3-49
A. Introduction
B. Proper Venue
C. Transfer of Venue in Abuse, Neglect, or Dependency Cases
D. Transfer of Venue in Termination of Parental Rights Cases

### 3.6 Overlapping Proceedings    3-53
A. Civil Custody Proceedings
B. Juvenile Delinquency and Undisciplined Proceedings
C. Criminal Proceedings
D. Domestic Violence Protection Proceedings

## Chapter 4: Procedural Rules and Orders    4-1

### 4.1 Introduction    4-3
A. Applicability of Rules of Civil Procedure in Juvenile Proceedings
B. Rule Application Analysis

### 4.2 Procedures Regarding the Petition    4-8
A. Contents of Petition

- B. Signature of Attorney or Party
- C. Amended and Supplemental Pleadings
- D. Responsive Pleadings

**4.3 Summons 4-11**
- A. Content and Issuance of Summons
- B. Expiration of Summons

**4.4 Service 4-13**
- A. The Impact of Service
- B. Summons
- C. Notice and Motions

**4.5 Continuances 4-21**
- A. Continuances Disfavored
- B. Abuse, Neglect, Dependency Proceedings
- C. Termination of Parental Rights Proceedings
- D. Considerations

**4.6 Discovery 4-24**
- A. Discovery Generally
- B. The Juvenile Code and Discovery

**4.7 Intervention 4-27**
- A. Abuse, Neglect, Dependency Proceedings
- B. Termination of Parental Rights Proceedings

**4.8 Motions in Juvenile Proceedings 4-30**

**4.9 Judgments and Orders 4-31**
- A. Drafting Orders
- B. Findings of Fact and Conclusions of Law
- C. Entry and Service of the Order
- D. Time Requirements for Orders

## Chapter 5: From Report through Pre-Adjudication in Abuse, Neglect, Dependency Cases 5-1

**5.1 How a Case Enters the System 5-4**
- A. Reporting Suspected Abuse, Neglect, or Dependency
- B. DSS Assessment of Report
- C. DSS Access to Information
- D. Notice to the Reporter
- E. Review by Prosecutor
- F. Law Enforcement Involvement
- G. Interference with DSS Assessment

**5.2 Central Registry and Responsible Individuals List 5-15**
- A. Central Registry
- B. Responsible Individuals List

**5.3 Starting the Abuse, Neglect, Dependency Court Action 5-21**
- A. The Petition
- B. The Summons and Process

**5.4  Parties, Appointment of Counsel, and Guardians ad Litem     5-25**
   A. Parties to the Proceeding
   B. Parents and Other Care Providers
   C. The Child
   D. Department of Social Services

**5.5  Purpose and Requirements of Temporary and Nonsecure Custody     5-34**
   A. Purpose of Temporary and Nonsecure Custody
   B. Temporary Custody
   C. Nonsecure Custody

**5.6  Nonsecure Custody Hearings     5-42**
   A. Summary
   B. Timing
   C. Jurisdictional Inquiry
   D. Nature of Hearing: Evidence and Burden of Proof
   E. Findings and Other Issues at the Hearing on the Need for Continued Nonsecure Custody
   F. Limits on Court's Authority at Nonsecure Custody Stage
   G. Requirements for Court Orders
   H. Nonsecure Custody Order Is Not Appealable

**5.7  Pre-adjudication Hearings, Conferences, and Mediation     5-46**
   A. Pre-adjudication Hearing
   B. Child Planning Conferences
   C. Permanency Mediation

**Appendix 5-1: Table of Differences for Mandated Reporting under G.S. 7B-301 and G.S. 14-318.6     5-49**

**Appendix 5-2: Mandated Reporting Flowchart     5-51**

## Chapter 6: Adjudication of Abuse, Neglect, or Dependency     6-1

**6.1  Summary and Purpose of Adjudication     6-2**

**6.2  The Adjudication     6-3**
   A. Procedure for Adjudication
   B. Timing
   C. Public Access to Hearing
   D. Record of Proceedings
   E. Petition Controls Scope of Adjudication

**6.3  Evidence and Proof     6-6**
   A. Child's Status, Standard, and Burden of Proof
   B. Evidentiary Standards
   C. Evidence at Adjudication
   D. Evidence to Establish Abuse
   E. Evidence to Establish Neglect
   F. Evidence to Establish Dependency

- 6.4 **Adjudication Order**  6-32
  - A. General Requirements
  - B. Findings of Fact and Conclusions of Law

- 6.5 **Consent Orders**  6-33

- 6.6 **Consequences of Adjudication**  6-34
  - A. Continued Jurisdiction and Authority for Disposition
  - B. Impact on Parents and Future Proceedings

## Chapter 7: Dispositional Phase: Initial, Review, and Permanency Planning  7-1

- 7.1 **Introduction and Purpose of Dispositional Phase**  7-4
  - A. Introduction
  - B. Purpose of Disposition
  - C. Significant Legislative Changes regarding Permanency Planning

- 7.2 **Dispositional Hearings**  7-10
  - A. Timing and When Required
  - B. Notice and Calendaring
  - C. Participants
  - D. Open or Closed Hearings
  - E. Evidentiary Standard and Burden of Proof

- 7.3 **Best Interests of the Child**  7-20

- 7.4 **Dispositional Alternatives: Placement and Custody**  7-22
  - A. Dismiss or Continue the Case
  - B. In-Home Supervision and Services
  - C. Parent and Out-of-Home Placement Generally
  - D. DSS Custody
  - E. Custody with a Parent, Relative, Other Suitable Person or Private Agency
  - F. Guardianship
  - G. Verification of Understanding of Legal Significance and Adequate Resources
  - H. Interstate Compact on the Placement of Children

- 7.5 **Visitation**  7-48
  - A. Order Must Address Visitation When Out-of-Home Placement
  - B. Review of Visitation Plan, Notice to Parties, Mediation

- 7.6 **Evaluation and Treatment of Child**  7-53
  - A. Court's Authority to Order Evaluation and Treatment
  - B. Hearing to Determine Treatment Needs and Payment

- 7.7 **Court's Authority over Parents and Others**  7-55
  - A. Treatment and Counseling
  - B. Parenting Classes, Transportation, Remedial Steps, and Other Orders
  - C. Cost Responsibilities
  - D. Failure to Comply with Court Orders
  - E. Court's Authority over DSS
  - F. Court's Authority over Child's GAL
  - G. Limitations on Court's Dispositional Authority

## 7.8 Dispositional Considerations and Findings    7-61
A. Initial Dispositional Hearing
B. Required Criteria for Review and Permanency Planning Hearings
C. Permanency Planning Additional Requirements
D. Initiation of Termination of Parental Rights Proceeding under Certain Circumstances
E. Hearing to Modify or Vacate a Dispositional Order

## 7.9 Reasonable Efforts    7-72
A. Introduction
B. Statutory Definitions: Reasonable Efforts, Return Home, Reunification
C. Required Findings
D. Ceasing Reasonable Efforts

## 7.10 Concurrent Permanency Planning and Outcomes    7-79
A. Concurrent Permanency Planning
B. Achieving a Permanent Plan

## 7.11 Dispositional Orders    7-91
A. Timing
B. General Requirements
C. Consent Orders
D. Status of Jurisdiction

# Chapter 8: Voluntary Placements of Juveniles and Foster Care 18–21    8-1

## 8.1 Introduction    8-1

## 8.2 Voluntary Placement Agreement for a Juvenile    8-2
A. The Agreement
B. Judicial Reviews, Timing, and Duration
C. Purpose and Requirements of Hearing

## 8.3 Foster Care 18–21    8-4
A. Introduction
B. Eligibility and the Agreement
C. Judicial Reviews, Timing, and Parties
D. Requirements of the Hearing

# Chapter 9: Termination of Parental Rights    9-1

## 9.1 Purpose and Overview of Termination of Parental Rights    9-5
A. Overview of Termination of Parental Rights
B. Purpose of the Juvenile Code's Termination of Parental Rights Provisions

## 9.2 Jurisdiction and Procedure    9-6
A. Subject Matter Jurisdiction
B. Personal Jurisdiction
C. Applicability of the Rules of Civil Procedure

## 9.3 Initiation of Proceedings and Standing    9-9
A. Initiation of TPR
B. Standing to File Petition or Motion

9.4 **Counsel and Guardians ad Litem for Parent and Child** 9-14
- A. Counsel for Parent
- B. Guardian ad Litem for Parent
- C. Guardian ad Litem for Child

9.5 **Contents of Petition or Motion** 9-18
- A. Identifying Information
- B. Addressing the UCCJEA
- C. Facts to Support Grounds for Termination
- D. Verification
- E. Request for Relief

9.6 **Hearing for Unknown Parent** 9-22
- A. Preliminary Hearing to Determine Identity of Unknown Parent
- B. Service on Unknown Parent

9.7 **Summons and Notice** 9-24
- A. Introduction
- B. Summons for Proceeding Initiated by Petition
- C. Notice for Proceeding Initiated by Motion in the Cause

9.8 **Answer or Response** 9-29

9.9 **Pretrial and Adjudication Hearing Requirements** 9-30
- A. Pretrial Hearing
- B. Adjudication Hearing

9.10 **Evidence and Proof** 9-35
- A. Evidentiary Requirements and Standards
- B. Events between Filing of Petition or Motion and Hearing
- C. Events after a TPR Is Denied or Reversed
- D. Specific Types of Evidentiary Issues

9.11 **Adjudication: Grounds for Termination of Parental Rights** 9-38
- A. Abuse or Neglect
- B. Willfully Leaving Child in Foster Care for More than Twelve Months without Reasonable Progress
- C. Failure to Pay a Reasonable Portion of the Child's Cost of Care
- D. Failure to Pay Child Support to Other Parent
- E. Father's Actions regarding Child Born Out of Wedlock
- F. Dependency
- G. Abandonment
- H. Murder, Voluntary Manslaughter, and Felony Assault of Child or Parent
- I. TPR to Another Child and Lack of Safe Home
- J. Relinquishment for Adoption
- K. Conception Resulting from Sexually Related Criminal Offense

9.12 **Disposition and Best Interest Determination** 9-73
- A. Overview
- B. Evidentiary Standard
- C. Considerations for Best Interest Determination

## 9.13 Highlighted Federal Laws: ICWA and the ADA    9-81
  A. Compliance with ICWA
  B. ADA Not a Defense to TPR

## 9.14 Orders in Termination of Parental Rights Cases    9-82
  A. Requirements for Order
  B. Entry of Order

## 9.15 Effect of Order and Placement after Termination of Parental Rights    9-86
  A. Severance of Rights and Obligations
  B. Collateral Legal Consequences
  C. Placement and Post-TPR Review Hearings

# Chapter 10: Post-TPR and Post-Relinquishment Reviews, Adoptions, and Reinstatement of Parental Rights    10-1

## 10.1 Post-Termination of Parental Rights Review Hearings    10-2
  A. Circumstances and Purpose
  B. Timing of Hearing
  C. Notice and Participation
  D. Appointment of GAL
  E. Evidence and Considerations for Hearings
  F. The Order

## 10.2 Post-Relinquishment Review Hearings    10-6
  A. Circumstances Requiring Review
  B. Relinquishment for Adoption
  C. Timing and Petition or Motion for Review
  D. Parent's Party Status
  E. Procedure for Hearing

## 10.3 Selected Adoption Provisions    10-12
  A. Introduction
  B. Prospective Adoptive Parents
  C. District Court Jurisdiction When Adoption Is Filed
  D. The Adoption

## 10.4 Reinstatement of Parental Rights    10-18
  A. Introduction
  B. Circumstances for Reinstatement
  C. Hearing Procedures
  D. Criteria and Findings
  E. Interim Hearings and Reasonable Efforts
  F. Orders
  G. Effect of Reinstatement

# Chapter 11: Evidence    11-1

## 11.1 Applicability of Rules of Evidence    11-5
  A. Adjudication
  B. Disposition and Other Proceedings

## 11.2 Child Witnesses   11-9
A. Competency of Child Witnesses
B. Examination of Child Witnesses

## 11.3 Out-of-Court Statements to Refresh, Impeach, or Corroborate   11-17
A. Refreshing Recollection
B. Impeachment
C. Corroboration

## 11.4 Out-of-Court Statements and the Right to Confront Witnesses   11-20
A. Applicability of Confrontation Clause to Criminal and Delinquency Cases
B. Inapplicability of Confrontation Clause to Juvenile Cases

## 11.5 Out-of-Court Statements and the Hearsay Rule   11-22
A. Governing Rules
B. Rationale for Hearsay Rule
C. Components of Hearsay Definition

## 11.6 Hearsay Exceptions   11-25
A. Types of Hearsay Exceptions and Their Rationales
B. Rule 801(d): Admissions of a Party-Opponent
C. Rule 803(2): Excited Utterances
D. Rule 803(3): State of Mind
E. Rule 803(4): Medical Diagnosis or Treatment
F. Rule 803(6): Business Records
G. Rule 803(8): Official Records and Reports
H. Rules 803(24) and 804(b)(5): Residual Hearsay

## 11.7 Prior Orders and Proceedings and Judicial Notice   11-50
A. Generally
B. Definition of Judicial Notice
C. Orders and Other Court Records
D. Findings and Conclusions by Court
E. Documentary Evidence, Court Reports, and Other Exhibits
F. Testimony

## 11.8 Character and Prior Conduct   11-64
A. Generally
B. Theories of Admissibility of Character Evidence
C. Is Character Directly at Issue in Juvenile Cases?
D. Rule 404(b) and "Bad Act" Evidence
E. Rape Shield Law

## 11.9 Lay Opinion   11-70
A. Lay and Expert Testimony Distinguished
B. Examples of Permissible and Impermissible Lay Opinion

## 11.10 Expert Testimony   11-74
A. Revised Evidence Rule 702(a)
B. Three Basic Requirements
C. Other Requirements for Expert Opinion
D. Expert Testimony about Children

E. Expert Testimony about Parents

**11.11 Evidentiary Privileges    11-88**
    A. In Abuse, Neglect, and Dependency Proceedings
    B. In Termination of Parental Rights Proceedings

**11.12 Right against Self-Incrimination    11-91**
    A. Right Not to Answer Incriminating Questions
    B. No Right Not to Take Stand
    C. Drawing Adverse Inference from Refusal to Answer

**11.13 Evidence Procedures    11-93**
    A. Production of Witnesses and Documents
    B. Pretrial Motions in Limine, Objections, and Other Notices
    C. Pre-Adjudication Conference
    D. Objections at Trial

## Chapter 12: Appeals    12-1

**12.1 Scope of Chapter    12-4**

**12.2 Parties and Representation    12-4**
    A. Who Can Appeal
    B. Appellate Representation in Juvenile Proceedings
    C. Role of Trial Counsel
    D. Role of Appellant

**12.3 Identifying Issues for Appeal    12-10**
    A. Preserving Issues for Appeal
    B. Scope of Appellate Review
    C. Appellate Rule 2: Prevent Manifest Injustice
    D. Invited Error
    E. No Swapping Horses

**12.4 Which Orders Can Be Appealed    12-16**
    A. Appealable Orders
    B. When an Appeal Is Moot

**12.5 Notice of Appeal    12-23**
    A. Timing, Manner, and Content of Notice
    B. Service and Proof of Service
    C. Appellate Entry Forms

**12.6 Protection of the Child's Identity in Juvenile Cases – Appellate Rule 42    12-30**

**12.7 Expedited Appeals Process under Appellate Rule 3.1    12-31**
    A. Transcript
    B. Record on Appeal
    C. Briefs

**12.8 Issues on Appeal and Standards of Review    12-34**
    A. Introduction
    B. Sufficiency of Evidence and Findings
    C. Abuse of Discretion

      D. Subject Matter Jurisdiction
      E. Failure to Follow Statutory Mandates and Procedures
      F. Statutory Interpretation

**12.9 Motions to Dismiss and Failure to Comply with Appellate Rules   12-39**

**12.10 Extraordinary Writs, Discretionary Review, and Appeal of Right   12-40**
      A. Writ of Certiorari
      B. Petition for Discretionary Review
      C. Appeal of Right
      D. Writ of Mandamus or Prohibition
      E. Writ of Supersedeas

**12.11 Trial Court's Role during and after Appeal   12-43**
      A. Trial Court's Role pending Appeal
      B. Trial Court's Role after Appeal

## Chapter 13: Relevant Federal Laws   13-1

**13.1 Scope of Chapter   13-3**

**13.2 Indian Child Welfare Act   13-3**
      A. Introduction and Purpose
      B. Applicability
      C. Inquiry at Commencement of Every Proceeding as to "Indian Child" Status
      D. Jurisdiction
      E. Emergency Proceedings
      F. Notice to the Tribe, Parent, Indian Custodian, and Bureau of Indian Affairs
      G. Timing of Court Proceedings
      H. "Active Efforts" Required
      I. Finding of Serious Emotional or Physical Damage
      J. Placement Preferences
      K. Consent to Foster Placement, TPR, and Adoption including Relinquishment
      L. Impact of ICWA Violation

**13.3 Multiethnic Placement Act   13-28**

**13.4 Title VI of the Civil Right Act   13-30**
      A. Introduction
      B. Applicability
      C. Prohibited Discrimination
      D. Requirements
      E. Violations

**13.5 The Americans with Disabilities Act   13-37**
      A. Introduction
      B. Applicability
      C. Prohibited Discrimination
      D. Requirements
      E. Compliance

13.6 **Servicemembers Civil Relief Act**   13-47
    A. Introduction
    B. Applicability
    C. SCRA Requirements

13.7 **Every Student Succeeds Act**   13-53
    A. Introduction
    B. Companion to the Fostering Connections Act
    C. School Selection
    D. Transportation
    E. Designated Points of Contact

13.8 **The Individuals with Disabilities in Education Act**   13-59
    A. Introduction
    B. Part B of IDEA: Children Ages 3-21
    C. Part C of IDEA: Children under 3 Years of Age
    D. Parent: Definition, Role, and Appointment of Surrogate Parent

13.9 **Special Immigrant Juvenile Status and Selected Immigration Resources**   13-80
    A. Introduction and Selected Resources
    B. Special Immigrant Juvenile Status and Obtaining Lawful Permanent Residency

## Chapter 14: Confidentiality and Information Sharing   14-1

14.1 **Juvenile Records**   14-3
    A. Department of Social Services Information
    B. Court Records and Proceedings
    C. DSS Access to Information
    D. The Child's GAL Access to and Disclosure of Information
    E. Designated Agency Information Sharing
    F. Subpoenas

14.2 **Health Records and HIPAA**   14-18
    A. Covered Health Care Providers
    B. Protected Health Information
    C. Duty to Comply with HIPAA
    D. Impact on Abuse, Neglect, Dependency Laws

14.3 **Mental Health Records and G.S. 122C**   14-22
    A. Covered Providers
    B. Confidential Information
    C. The Duty of Confidentiality
    D. Impact on Abuse, Neglect, Dependency Laws

14.4 **Substance Abuse Records and 42 C.F.R. Part 2**   14-25
    A. Covered Programs
    B. Confidential Information
    C. Duty Imposed by Federal Substance Abuse Records Law
    D. Impact on Abuse, Neglect, Dependency Laws

### 14.5 Education Records and FERPA    14-31
   A. Introduction
   B. Consent Required for Disclosure
   C. Exceptions to Consent Requirement
   D. Documentation of Disclosure, Redisclosure, and Use of Information
   E. Complaints and Enforcement

## Appendixes

   **Appendix 1:** Resources and Organizations

   **Appendix 2:** The Chief District Court Judge and Juvenile Court

   **Appendix 3:** JWise: The Automated Information System for North Carolina Juvenile Courts

   **Appendix 4:** Rules of Recordkeeping, Chapter XII

   **Appendix 5:** Case Management for Abuse, Neglect, Dependency, and Termination of Parental Rights Cases in North Carolina Juvenile Courts

## Checklists

   **Checklist 1:** Nonsecure Custody Orders

   **Checklist 2:** Pre-Adjudication

   **Checklist 3:** Adjudication

   **Checklist 4:** Dispositional Findings and Options at Initial, Review, and Permanency Planning

   **Checklist 5:** Initial Disposition

   **Checklist 6:** Review

   **Checklist 7:** Permanency Planning

   **Checklist 8:** Termination of Parental Rights Hearing

   **Checklist 9:** Post-TPR Review Hearing

# Introduction to the Manual

We are pleased to provide the 2019 edition of *Abuse, Neglect, Dependency, and Termination of Parental Rights Proceedings in North Carolina*. This Manual is written for legal professionals involved in these proceedings. The primary purpose of the Manual is to provide easily accessible information about the law, procedures, and concepts that apply to abuse, neglect, dependency, and related termination of parental rights proceedings in North Carolina. This Manual serves the additional goal of making the information uniformly available to a variety of professionals. It is meant to be a useful and reliable reference manual and training tool for judges, social services attorneys, parents' attorneys, guardian ad litem attorney advocates, and others involved in this important and challenging work. Because of the broad intended audience, advocacy materials and perspectives are not included; however, individuals and organizations with a particular advocacy perspective may choose to supplement the Manual with their own materials that are helpful to their work.

This edition is available in an online format and is housed on the UNC School of Government website, with its own "microsite" (or landing page). A reader may download (and print if desired) a pdf version of the complete Manual or any individual chapter. This edition updates the previous editions from 2017, 2015, 2014, and the first edition in 2011. A soft cover, bound copy of the Manual is also available for purchase through the "Publications" section of the UNC School of Government website.

The text of the chapters combines applicable statutes, relevant case citations, additional resources, and practical explanations for particular topics. This 2019 edition includes opinions published by the North Carolina appellate courts through December 31, 2019, and legislative changes made through the 2019 session of the North Carolina General Assembly. Throughout the chapters, "Practice Notes" are set apart to offer insight into practical aspects of a given topic; "Resources" are set apart to alert the reader to resources and tools beyond the Manual; and "AOC Forms" and "NC DHHS DSS Forms" are set apart to notify the reader of applicable forms that are created and updated by the North Carolina Administrative Office of the Courts (AOC) and the North Carolina Department of Health and Human Services Division of Social Services (NC DHHS DSS). The Manual uses cross-references liberally to alert the reader to other parts of the Manual that are relevant to a particular topic.

There is a table of contents at the beginning of the Manual that identifies the location of general topics, and each chapter contains a more detailed table of contents. In the electronic version, readers may search for specific words by using the search function (such as "control f") on their computer or electronic device or the search box on the right navigation bar of the microsite. Web links are present throughout the Manual, typically embedded as a hyperlink in the relevant text. If a link does not work, the reader usually can find the resource by conducting an internet search using the title of the resource.

Appendix materials supplement topics covered in the Manual. Also included are Checklists, which are meant to be used as a tool to help a judge or an attorney identify required findings of fact or jurisdictional issues that should be addressed in the various court orders that apply to these proceedings.

Production of this Manual was made possible with funding provided by the U.S. Department of Health and Human Services – Administration for Children and Families, and the Court Improvement Program of the North Carolina Administrative Office of the Courts. This Manual is copyrighted to the UNC School of Government.

We welcome any corrections, suggestions, or comments. They may be sent to Associate Professor Sara DePasquale at the School of Government, CB #3330, Knapp-Sanders Building, The University of North Carolina at Chapel Hill, Chapel Hill, North Carolina, 27599-3330. You also may reach her by email at sara@sog.unc.edu or by telephone at (919) 966-4289.

*Sara DePasquale*
*Jan Simmons*
December 2019

# About the Authors

**Sara DePasquale** is an Associate Professor of Public Law and Government at the School of Government at the University of North Carolina at Chapel Hill and primary author of this 2019 edition. Before joining the School's faculty, she spent seventeen years practicing law as a civil legal services attorney in Maine, representing low-income individuals and families in family law, education, housing, and public benefits matters. She specializes in child welfare law, with a focus on abuse, neglect, dependency; termination of parental rights; adoption; legitimation; and judicial waiver of parental consent proceedings. She teaches, writes for, and consults with judicial officials, attorneys, and other professionals who are involved in these types of proceedings.

**Jan Simmons** is a research attorney at the School of Government at the University of North Carolina at Chapel Hill. Before coming to the School, she practiced law for eleven years in Chapel Hill, Princeton, New Jersey, and Atlanta, in the areas of bankruptcy and local government law. Her projects include revising *Abuse, Neglect, Dependency, and Termination of Parental Rights Proceedings in North Carolina*, the *North Carolina Clerk of Superior Court Procedures Manual*, and the *North Carolina Trial Judges' Bench Book, District Court Edition*.

# Special Acknowledgements

We specially thank original authors Kella Hatcher, Janet Mason, and John Rubin. The availability of this Manual for all professionals working in child welfare is due to their hard work, commitment, and input.

**Kella Hatcher** was the lead author of the 2011, 2014, and 2015 editions of this Manual. Currently, she is the Executive Director of the North Carolina Child Fatality Task Force. Previously, she worked as Associate Counsel for the North Carolina Guardian ad Litem Program where she authored the *North Carolina Guardian ad Litem Attorney Practice Manual* and served as chair and co-chair of the Juvenile Code Revision Committee for the North Carolina Court Improvement Project.

**Janet Mason** retired from her position as a Gladys Hall Coates Professor at the School of Government in 2015. For over thirty years, she dedicated her career to serving the children of North Carolina by assisting professionals who work in juvenile proceedings in the North Carolina court system. She shared her dedication to and knowledge of this substantive area of the law with the authors (past and present) of this Manual.

**John Rubin** had the original idea to create this Manual, and it was his efforts that made this Manual possible. He is the author of Chapter 11 (Evidence) and has provided moral and technical support to the authors throughout all the various editions of the Manual. He is an Albert Coates Professor of Public Law and Government at the School of Government. He specializes in criminal law and procedure and indigent defense education and teaches, writes for, and consults with indigent defenders, judges, magistrates, and others who work in the court system.

**The North Carolina Court Improvement Program of the North Carolina Administrative Office of the Courts** provided financial support for this Manual, without which this Manual would not have been possible. NC-CIP manager, Kiesha Crawford, and former manager, Lana Dial, also provided logistical and moral support for the various editions. NC-CIP is a federally funded project to improve court practice in child abuse, neglect, and dependency cases. The program's mission is "to improve the performance of North Carolina's Juvenile Courts in abuse and neglect cases so that safety, permanence and wellbeing for each child are achieved in a fair and timely manner." NC-CIP's support for this Manual is one example of its many efforts in that regard. More information about NC-CIP is available on the North Carolina Administrative Office of the Courts website, here.

**Additional Support** for the 2019 and 2017 editions was provided by our School of Government colleagues, Ann Anderson, Mark Botts, Jacquelyn Greene, Cheryl Howell, James Markham, Meredith Smith, Melissa Twomey, and Aimee Wall, who assisted in reviewing content, shared ideas, and provided moral support throughout the update and revision process. Stefanie Panke provided the technical support for the online availability of this Manual. Robby Poore designed the front and back covers. Caitlin Little worked on those numerous finishing details including checking new citations, hyperlinks and internal cross-references.

A special thank you to the following attorneys who reviewed requested content in either the 2017 or 2019 edition: Natalie Bacon, former North Carolina Assistant Attorney General; Margaret Burt, a private practitioner in Rochester, New York who specializes in the Indian Child Welfare Act; Lori R. Gershon, J.D., MPA Candidate 2021; Annick Lenoir-Peek, with the Office of Parent Representation at the North Carolina Office of Indigent Defense Services; LaToya Powell, our former colleague now with the Office of General Counsel at the North Carolina Administrative Office of the Courts; Barbara Parker, Program Manager of the Eastern Band of Cherokee Indians Family Safety; and Reginald O'Rourke, III with the Guardian ad Litem Program at the North Carolina Administrative Office of the Courts.

**A Former Advisory Committee** contributed to the first two editions of this Manual. The Manual benefited immeasurably from the members' time and expertise, as they provided invaluable feedback and insight throughout that drafting process. Members of the committee were Sydney Batch, Frederick R. Benson, Susan K. Button, Rick Croutharmel, Lana Dial, Alice Anne Espenshade, Whitney Fairbanks, Deana K. Fleming, Alisa Huffman, Judge Debra A. Sasser, Wendy Sotolongo, and Jane R. Thompson.

# Overview of the North Carolina Child Welfare System

Chapter 1

# Chapter 1
# Overview of the North Carolina Child Welfare System

**1.1 Introduction to Child Welfare    1-2**
  A. Child Welfare Services
  B. Purpose
    1. Balancing the state's interests with constitutional rights of parents and children
    2. Purposes of North Carolina's Juvenile Code
  C. Overview of a Child Welfare Case in North Carolina
  D. Demographics
    1. National data
    2. North Carolina data

**1.2 Federal-State-County System    1-11**
  A. County-State Structure and Relationship
  B. The County DSS
    1. Governing structure and staff
    2. DSS role and responsibilities
  C. Federal-State-County Funding
  D. Federal-State Relationship
    1. Child and Family Service Review (CFSR)
    2. The IV-E Eligibility Review

**1.3 State and Federal Sources of Authority: Laws, Rules, and Policy    1-19**
  A. North Carolina
    1. The Juvenile Code: G.S. Chapter 7B
    2. The Administrative Code: Title 10A
    3. DHHS Child Welfare Manual
    4. Other relevant North Carolina statutes
    5. Local court rules
  B. Influence of Federal Law
    1. The Child Abuse Prevention and Treatment Act (CAPTA)
    2. The Indian Child Welfare Act (ICWA)
    3. Adoption Assistance and Child Welfare Act
    4. Family Preservation and Support Services Program Act
    5. Multiethnic Placement Act (MEPA-IEP)
    6. Adoption and Safe Families Act (ASFA)
    7. John H. Chafee Foster Care Independence Act
    8. Safe and Timely Interstate Placement of Foster Children Act
    9. Fostering Connections to Success and Increasing Adoptions Act (Fostering Connections)
    10. Preventing Sex Trafficking and Strengthening Families Act
    11. Justice for Victims of Trafficking Act
    12. Family First Prevention Services Act (FFPSA)

## 1.1  Introduction to Child Welfare

### A. Child Welfare Services

Child welfare encompasses child protective, foster care placement, and adoption services. Protective services are intended to protect children who have been alleged to be abused, neglected, or dependent and are established in Chapter 7B of the North Carolina General Statutes[1], which is commonly referred to as "the Juvenile Code." Protective services encompass a myriad of actions, including screening and assessment of reports of a child's suspected abuse, neglect, or dependency; providing casework and counseling to families; and pursuing necessary court action to protect a child. Foster care and adoption services apply to children who require care outside of their families. This type of substitute care is regulated by the State. The State has a duty to assure that the care is quality care that is as close as possible to the nurturing care society expects of a family. *See* Article 1A of G.S. Chapter 131D. The term "child welfare" is not defined in North Carolina law but is used as a general term in statutes, regulations, and state policy that discuss child protective, foster care placement, and adoption services.[2]

In North Carolina, child welfare services are provided by county departments, which are supervised by the North Carolina Department of Health and Human Services (NC DHHS). G.S. 108A-1; 108A-71; 108A-74. The Juvenile Code defines department as "each county's child welfare agency" regardless of what it is named. G.S. 7B-101(8a). A county department is typically a department of social services (DSS) but may be a consolidated county human services agency created pursuant to G.S. 153A-77 or a regional social services department created under G.S. 108A-15.7 through -15.10 that carries out social services functions.[3]

**Note**, for purposes of this Manual, "department of social services" or "DSS" refers to a department as defined by G.S. 7B-101(8a) regardless of how it is titled or structured.

---

**Legislative Note:** Effective March 1, 2019, counties have the option to create a regional social services department that includes more than one county and incorporates all or only selected programs and services, such as child welfare. *See* S.L. 2017-41, Part IV creating G.S. 108A-15.3A through -15.3C (currently, G.S. 108A-15.7 through -15.10).

---

The North Carolina courts are also part of the child welfare system. Court actions alleging a child's abuse, neglect, or dependency are initiated by DSS in district court. Appeals are heard by the North Carolina appellate courts. Adoption proceedings are initiated in superior court

---

[1] Throughout this Manual, the North Carolina General Statutes are referred to as "G.S."

[2] *See, e.g.,* G.S. 131D-10.6A; 108A-74; 7B-101(8a); Title 10A of the North Carolina Administrative Code Subchapter 70G, Section 0402(3); DIV. OF SOC. SERVS., N.C. DEP'T OF HEALTH & HUMAN SERVICES, CHILD WELFARE MANUAL ("NC CHILD WELFARE MANUAL"), available online here.

[3] For information about how the department structure is determined, see G.S. 108A-1 and G.S. 153A-77. For more information on the structures, see AIMEE N. WALL, *Social Services*, CH. 39 *in* FRAYDA S. BLUESTEIN (ed.), COUNTY AND MUNICIPAL GOVERNMENT IN NORTH CAROLINA (UNC School of Government, 2d ed. 2014).

and are special proceedings that are heard by the clerk of superior court, unless a transfer is required to district court. See Chapters 2.1 (district court), 10.3 (adoptions), and 12 (appeals).

The child welfare system is based on an extensive body of state and federal laws that address both procedural and substantive issues. Child welfare services also impact the constitutional rights of children and parents. The various laws, procedures, and constitutional principles are discussed throughout this Manual. For a general discussion of state statutes, regulations, and policies governing child welfare in North Carolina as well as the impact of federal statutes and regulations on North Carolina's laws and policy, see section 1.3, below.

## B. Purpose

A state's child welfare system has the overall important purpose of preventing, identifying, and treating child abuse and neglect.

**1. Balancing the state's interests with constitutional rights of parents and children.** The child welfare system consists of governmental action (in North Carolina, it is a DSS) that involves itself in a family's private life. *See In re Stumbo*, 357 N.C. 279, 294 (2003) (Martin, J. concurring) ("Federal courts…have concluded, either explicitly or implicitly, that constitutional limitations apply to government officials who investigate child abuse.… State appellate courts have reached similar conclusions") and cases cited therein. As a result, constitutional rights of parents and children are affected and a balance between the government's interest in protecting children and the constitutional rights of parents and children must be made. *See* G.S. 7B-100.

Parents have a paramount constitutional right to care, custody, and control of their children. *Troxel v. Granville*, 530 U.S. 57 (2000); *Santosky v. Kramer*, 455 U.S. 745 (1982); *Petersen v. Rogers,* 337 N.C. 397 (1994). However, a parent's right is not absolute. *Petersen*, 337 N.C. 397. The United States Supreme Court has consistently held that a state may interfere with constitutional interests if in so doing it is protecting the public interest and if the regulated behavior is reasonably related to a purpose within the state's competency to effect. Examples that a state has a wide range of power to limit parents' constitutional rights to the care, custody, and control of their children include regulation of child labor and compulsory school attendance laws. *See Prince v. Massachusetts*, 321 U.S. 158 (1944) (child labor); *Pierce v. Society of Sisters*, 268 U.S. 510 (1925) (school attendance).

There is a presumption that a parent acts in his or her child's best interests. *Parham v. J.R*, 442 U.S. 584 (1979); *Price v. Howard*, 346 N.C. 68 (1997). There is also a presumption that the government will not interfere with the parent-child relationship: "[S]o long as a parent adequately cares for his or her children (i.e., is fit), there will normally be no reason for the State to inject itself into the private realm of the family to further question the ability of that parent to make the best decisions concerning the rearing of that parent's children." *In re Stumbo*, 357 N.C. 279, 286 (quoting *Troxel v. Granville*, 530 U.S. 57, 68–69). However, these presumptions may be rebutted, and a state may interfere with a parent's constitutional rights when that parent is unfit or acts inconsistently with his or her protected interests to parent his or her child. *Petersen v. Rogers*, 337 N.C. 397; *Price*, 346 N.C. 68.

For a further discussion of the constitutional rights of parents, see Chapters 2.4 and 7.10.B.5 and for the rights of the child, see Chapter 2.3.

The North Carolina Juvenile Code provides the procedures and parameters for governmental intervention into the parent-child relationship when children are harmed, are at risk of harm, or do not receive minimally adequate care. Whether government intervention is warranted starts with the status or condition of the child – is the child abused, neglected, or dependent. Those conditions are defined by G.S. 7B-101(1) (abuse), (9) (dependency), and (15) (neglect). See Chapters 2.3.B and 6.3.D through F for further discussion of what constitutes abuse, neglect, or dependency.

Governmental intervention is limited by those statutory definitions. If an initial report about a child's circumstances does not satisfy the statutory criteria of abuse, neglect, or dependency, a DSS does not have the authority to interfere with or intervene in the parent-child relationship. *See In re Stumbo*, 357 N.C. 279 (2003) (holding a single, anonymous report of a naked 2-year-old child who was unsupervised in her driveway without any additional information was insufficient to constitute neglect that required DSS involvement with the family). Part of the respective definitions of abuse, neglect, or dependency revolve around the role of the person who creates the child's circumstance: a parent, guardian, custodian, or caretaker. For a discussion of those roles, see Chapter 2.2. The North Carolina Supreme Court recognized that "[n]ot every child who is a victim of serious criminal conduct is necessarily an abused and neglected juvenile under the Juvenile Code. Only when the family fails to provide proper care is DSS empowered to intervene." *In re R.R.N.*, 368 N.C. 167, 169 (2015). As such, DSS is not authorized to intervene in the parent-child relationship when the child's condition results from circumstances created by a person who is not a parent, guardian, custodian, or caretaker. There is an exception, however. Any minor victim of human trafficking shall be alleged to be abused and neglected regardless of how or who created those circumstances. G.S. 7B-101(1)(i), (15)(i); *see* G.S. 14-43.15.

Note that a juvenile may be a victim of a crime other than human trafficking that warrants action from law enforcement rather than DSS involvement with a family. Separate from and in addition to a mandated report to DSS, as of December 1, 2019, any adult who knows or should have reasonably known that a juvenile has been or is the victim of a violent offense, sexual offense, or misdemeanor child abuse must immediately make a report to the appropriate local law enforcement agency. G.S. 14-318.6 (S.L. 2019-245).

**Resource:** For more information about the new mandatory reporting law to local law enforcement, see Sara DePasquale, *BIG NEWS: S.L. 2019-245 Creates a New Universal Mandated Reporting Law for Child Victims of Crimes and Changes the Definition of "Caretaker,"* UNC SCH. OF GOV'T BLOG: NORTH CAROLINA CRIMINAL LAW (Nov. 13, 2019).

Courts that preside over abuse, neglect, dependency, and termination of parental rights (TPR) cases are also bound by the provisions of the Juvenile Code. In determining whether DSS has proved that a child is abused, neglected, or dependent, the court must apply the statutory definitions. See Chapter 6 for a discussion of adjudications. When a court adjudicates a child's condition or status as abused, neglected, or dependent, the adjudication may lead to "an array of possible adverse collateral consequences." *In re R.R.N.*, 368 N.C. at 171. The court proceeds to disposition and looks to the authority it is granted by the Juvenile Code to determine what actions it may order to address the child's circumstances while considering the best interests of the child. *See, e.g.*, G.S. 7B-901; 7B-904. "Collateral consequences" of an adjudication and subsequent disposition may include the temporary removal of the child from the home, a court order to participate in certain services or evaluations, the stigma attached to the adjudication, subjecting a family to ongoing DSS supervision, and for a parent, the possible permanent termination of parental rights. *See In re R.R.N.*, 368 N.C. 167. In a TPR proceeding, the court's focus shifts to whether a ground for termination as specified in the Juvenile Code exists based on the parent's conduct or culpability. If a ground is proved, the court then looks to the child's best interests to determine whether the TPR should be granted. The purpose is not to be punitive but instead looks to a child's safety and well-being. See Chapter 9 (discussing TPR).

**2. Purposes of North Carolina's Juvenile Code.** The Juvenile Code includes stated purposes that provide a big picture perspective that can be helpful. Attorneys and judges may find support for arguments or decisions in the statutory language setting out the purposes of the Juvenile Code or the case law interpreting that language.

G.S. 7B-100 states that the purposes of the Juvenile Code relating to abuse, neglect, dependency, and termination of parental rights must be interpreted and construed so as to implement the following purposes and policies:

1. To provide procedures for the hearing of juvenile cases that assure fairness and equity and that protect the constitutional rights of juveniles and parents;
2. To develop a disposition in each case that reflects consideration of the facts, the needs and limitations of the juvenile, and the strengths and weaknesses of the family;
3. To provide for services for the protection of juveniles by means that respect both the right to family autonomy and the juveniles' needs for safety, continuity, and permanence;
4. To provide standards for the removal, when necessary, of juveniles from their homes and for the return of juveniles to their homes consistent with preventing the unnecessary or inappropriate separation of juveniles from their parents; and
5. To provide standards, consistent with the Adoption and Safe Families Act of 1997 for ensuring that the best interests of the juvenile are of paramount consideration by the court and that when it is not in the juvenile's best interest to be returned home, the juvenile will be placed in a safe, permanent home within a reasonable amount of time.

Specific to abuse, neglect, or dependency dispositions, the purpose is stated at G.S. 7B-900:

> To design an appropriate plan to meet the juvenile's needs and to achieve

the State's objective in exercising jurisdiction. If possible, the initial approach should involve working with the juvenile and the juvenile's family in their own home so that the appropriate community resources may be involved in the care, supervision, and treatment according to the juvenile's needs. The court should arrange for appropriate community-level services to be provided to the juvenile and juvenile's family to strengthen the home situation.

Additional purposes with respect to termination of parental rights are set out in G.S. 7B-1100:

1. To provide judicial procedures for terminating the legal relationship between a juvenile and the juvenile's biological or legal parents when the parents have demonstrated that they will not provide the degree of care which promotes the healthy and orderly physical and emotional well-being of the juvenile.
2. To recognize the necessity for any juvenile to have a permanent plan of care at the earliest possible age, while at the same time recognizing the need to protect all juveniles from the unnecessary severance of a relationship with biological or legal parents.
3. Action which is in the best interests of the juvenile should be taken in all cases where the interests of the juvenile and those of the juvenile's parents or other persons are in conflict.
4. An action to terminate parental rights shall not be used to circumvent the Uniform Child-Custody Jurisdiction and Enforcement Act.

North Carolina appellate courts have helped shape these purposes and have cited them as support for some decisions. For example, the courts have considered the Juvenile Code's stated purposes when determining whether a particular Rule of Civil Procedure furthered those purposes and should apply in juvenile proceedings. *See, e.g., In re B.L.H.*, 190 N.C. App. 142, *aff'd per curiam*, 362 N.C. 674 (2008); *In re S.D.W.*, 187 N.C. App. 416 (2007); *In re L.O.K.*, 174 N.C. App. 426 (2005); see also Chapter 4.1 (discussing the application of the Rules of Civil Procedure). In the case *In re R.R.N.*, 368 N.C. 167 (2015), the supreme court looked to the dual purpose of the Juvenile Code of protecting and promoting the child's best interests while safeguarding the parent-child relationship from state interference. It held a relative who supervised a one-night sleepover and sexually abused the child during that sleepover was a not a "caretaker" who was entrusted with the child's care warranting state intervention with the family who responded appropriately to the child's disclosure. In the case *In re Eckard*, 148 N.C. App. 541, 548 (2002), the court of appeals held explicitly that an order ceasing reunification efforts was "not consistent with the purposes and policies of the statute." Numerous cases have pointed to the Juvenile Code's characterization of the child's best interest as a paramount consideration in juvenile proceedings. *See, e.g., In re A.U.D.*, 832 S.E.2d 698 (N.C. S.Ct. 2019); *In re A.P.*, 371 N.C. 14 (2018); *In re T.H.T*, 362 N.C. 446 (2008); *In re T.R.P.*, 360 N.C. 588 (2006); *In re L.O.K.*, 174 N.C. App. 426 (2005).

## C. Overview of a Child Welfare Case in North Carolina

The following narrative provides an overview of the primary stages and hearings in abuse, neglect, or dependency cases to give a big picture perspective of how these cases flow through North Carolina's child welfare system. Note that there are other hearings associated with these proceedings that are not included in this overview but are explained in the relevant Chapters of this Manual.

- **Assessment after report.** After receiving a report, DSS determines whether an assessment is required, and if it is, DSS conducts the assessment. If DSS finds evidence of abuse, neglect, or dependency, DSS must determine whether to provide protective services to the family, whether to file a petition so that the court can become involved in the case, and whether removal of the child from the home is necessary to protect the child.

- **Immediate removal and nonsecure custody.** If immediate removal is necessary and there is no time to obtain a court order, DSS (or a law enforcement officer) may take a child into temporary custody for up to twelve hours (or if one of those hours falls on a weekend or legal holiday, for up to twenty-four hours) without a court order. At the end of that time period, DSS must return the child or obtain a temporary emergency custody order, which is called a nonsecure custody order.

    A nonsecure custody order may be issued after DSS files a petition in district court and shows that the narrowly defined statutory criteria for nonsecure custody apply. Most initial nonsecure custody orders are issued ex parte. After the initial nonsecure custody order is issued, a hearing on the need for continued nonsecure custody (or the adjudicatory hearing) must be held within seven calendar days unless the parties consent to a continuance for up to ten business days. If the child remains in nonsecure custody the court must hold periodic hearings on the need for continued nonsecure custody at the statutorily prescribed intervals, unless waived by the parties. At these hearings, the court addresses the need for continued nonsecure custody, the child's placement, visitation, and in some cases, medical decision-making pending adjudication.

- **Adjudication and initial disposition.** Abuse, neglect, or dependency petitions are heard in district court by a judge, without a jury. The hearing on the merits involves two stages: (1) *adjudication*, during which the court hears evidence, makes findings, and determines whether allegations in the petition have been proved by clear and convincing evidence that the child is abused, neglected, or dependent; and (2) if the court adjudicates the child to be abused, neglected, or dependent, *disposition*, which is devoted to identifying the needs of the child and the parents, guardians, custodians, or caretakers, considering ways to address those needs, and developing a plan that is in the best interests of the child.

    These two stages have different purposes, standards, and procedures, making it important that the court delineate clearly the end of one stage and the beginning of the other, even if both stages are handled in the same court session. At adjudication, the formal rules of evidence apply, and the burden is on DSS as the petitioner to prove the allegations in the petition by clear and convincing evidence. The court either adjudicates the child to be abused, neglected, or dependent, or dismisses the petition with prejudice. If there is an adjudication, at disposition, the rules of evidence do not apply. The court considers evidence that is finds to be relevant, reliable, and necessary to determine the juvenile's needs and most appropriate disposition. The dispositional hearing may be informal. Although some oral testimony is required, the parties may submit written reports or other evidence concerning their perspectives on the family's needs, how those needs can be met, and what steps should be taken for the child's care and protection. No one party has the burden of proof. The guiding principle for the court's decisions in the dispositional phase is the child's best interests with a focus on the child's health and safety and the need for the child to achieve permanence within a reasonable period of time. After making findings and conclusions, the court may leave the child in the home; place custody with a parent, DSS, a relative, or other suitable person; and make other orders concerning the child or other parties, including provisions addressing visitation, decision-making, treatment or other services, and the payment of child support.

- **Disposition: initial, review, and permanency planning.** Dispositions occur in phases: initial disposition, review, and permanency planning. The Juvenile Code sets forth the maximum time periods within which each type of dispositional hearing must be held. The Juvenile Code does not prohibit the scheduling of the different types of dispositional hearings on the same day.

  The initial dispositional hearing immediately follows the adjudicatory hearing and must be completed within thirty days of the conclusion of the adjudicatory hearing. A review hearing is scheduled within ninety days of the initial dispositional hearing. A permanency planning hearing must be held within one year after the initial order that first removed the child, or within thirty days from an initial dispositional order that determined reasonable efforts for reunification are not required or a finding at a review hearing that reasonable efforts clearly would be unsuccessful or inconsistent with the juvenile's health and safety and need for a safe, permanent home within a reasonable period of time. Periodic review and permanency planning hearings must be held at least every six months absent statutory criteria that allows for a waiver of or longer duration between those hearings.

  For the various dispositional hearings, the rules of evidence do not apply and the court considers evidence it finds to be relevant, reliable, and necessary to meet the juvenile's needs and develop the most appropriate disposition. The applicable standard is the best interests of the child.

  At each review and permanency planning hearing, the court considers and makes findings about a variety of statutory criteria, including what services have been or should be offered, whether the child's placement is appropriate, and whether the child's return home is likely. The presumptive goal in every case is for the child to remain at home safely or, if placed outside the home, to reunify with either parent or with the guardian or custodian from whose home the child was removed by court order.

  At permanency planning hearings, the court must order concurrent permanent plans until one has been achieved, with priority given to reunification unless certain written findings are made by the court. There are six permanent plans: reunification, adoption, guardianship to a non-parent, custody to a non-parent, Another Planned Permanent Living Arrangement (APPLA) (for juveniles who are 16 or 17 years old only), and reinstatement of parental rights. If one of the concurrent permanent plans for the child is adoption, a termination of parental rights (TPR) action may be necessary to implement that plan.

A TPR proceeding is also divided into two stages: adjudication and disposition. At adjudication, the court determines whether a statutory ground for termination of parental rights has been proved by clear, cogent, and convincing evidence. If not, the case is dismissed. If one or more grounds exist, the court moves on to the disposition where it determines whether a TPR is in the child's best interest. The court will terminate parental rights only if it finds both a ground and that it is in the child's best interests. If parental rights are terminated and the child is in the custody of DSS or a licensed child-placing agency, post-termination review hearings must be held at least every six months to examine progress toward achieving the child's permanent plans. In some cases, permanency planning hearings may also be required.

- **The end of the case.** The court retains jurisdiction and can enter orders in the abuse, neglect, or dependency case until the court enters an order that terminates its jurisdiction, a final order of adoption is entered, or the juvenile turns eighteen or is emancipated, whichever occurs first.

---

**Resources:**
For a primer addressing the various stages, time requirements, and applicable rules and standards, with flowchart, see SARA DEPASQUALE, STAGES OF ABUSE, NEGLECT, AND DEPENDENCY CASES IN NORTH CAROLINA: FROM REPORT TO FINAL DISPOSITION (UNC School of Government, 2019).

To learn more about the process, starting with whether to make a report and ending with a final disposition listen to *Beyond the Bench:* Season 02: Homelessness, Neglect, and the Child Welfare System in North Carolina, UNC SCHOOL OF GOVERNMENT, NORTH CAROLINA JUDICIAL COLLEGE (2016) (also available through iTunes and Stitcher). This podcast consists of six episodes, which focus on the different stages of a neglect case and features interviews with district court judges, DSS staff and attorney, a parent attorney, and the child's guardian ad litem team.

---

### D. Demographics

**1. National data.**[4] The U.S. Department of Health and Human Services, via the Children's Bureau, collects and reports data relating to child maltreatment in the United States. For fiscal

---

[4] Information for this section was obtained from CHILDREN'S BUREAU, U.S. DEP'T OF HEALTH & HUMAN SERVICES, "Child Maltreatment 2017" (2017) (based on information gathered from the National Child Abuse and Neglect Data System (NCANDS), which collects annual data that is voluntarily submitted by the fifty states, the District of Columbia, and the Commonwealth of Puerto Rico).

year 2017 (October 1, 2016 through September 30, 2017), child protective services agencies received an estimated 4.1 million referrals of alleged child maltreatment (abuse or neglect) that involved approximately 7.5 million children. Of those reports, 2.4 million, representing 3.5 million children, were screened in (meaning action was taken) from the child protective agency. Of the reports that were screened in, seventeen percent (17%) were substantiated for abuse or neglect having occurred, and those substantiated reports involved an estimated 674,000 children. The vast majority of cases (80%) involved child neglect. Children younger than 1 year old had the highest rate of victimization. A child's death is the most tragic consequence of abuse or neglect and is what child protective services seeks to prevent. Nationally, an estimated 1,688 children died from abuse or neglect in fiscal year 2017, and almost three out of four of those fatalities (72%) were of children younger than 3 years old.

**Resource:** For more statistics and information relating to the reporters, the type of maltreatment, demographics of children, alleged perpetrators, child deaths, and state specific data, see the CHILDREN'S BUREAU, U.S. DEP'T OF HEALTH & HUMAN SERVICES, "Child Maltreatment 2017" (2017).

**2. North Carolina data.**[5] Statistics on North Carolina reports of abuse, neglect, and dependency as well as child placement data are maintained through a joint project of the Jordan Institute for Families at the School of Social Work at The University of North Carolina at Chapel Hill and the Division of Social Services in the North Carolina Department of Health and Human Services.

The data show that in state fiscal year 2016-2017,[6] there were 128,511 investigated reports of abuse, neglect, or dependency. Forty percent (40%) of those children were 5 years old or younger. Findings resulting from investigations or assessments are characterized in nine ways, and one report may result in multiple characterizations.

From July 2016 through June 2017 the data show the following findings:

| Finding | Total Number SFY 2016-2017 |
|---|---|
| • abuse and neglect | 1,161 |
| • abuse | 833 |
| • neglect | 6,557 |
| • dependency | 279 |
| • services needed | 13,420 |
| • services provided, no longer needed | 7,465 |
| • services recommended | 34,740 |

---

[5] Information for this section was obtained from D. F. Duncan, K. A. Flair, C. J. Stewart, J.S. Vaughn, S. Guest, R.A. Rose, and K.M.D. Malley, "Management Assistance for Child Welfare, Work First, and Food & Nutrition Services in North Carolina," (v3.2, 2019) for "Child Welfare." Retrieved on October 11, 2019, from the University of North Carolina at Chapel Hill Jordan Institute for Families website.

[6] The data collected by the UNC Jordan Institute for Families for abuse and neglect findings is complete through fiscal year 2016-2017. Data maintained after that year does not incorporate the data from the small minority of counties that utilized the NCFAST case management system for child welfare.

- unsubstantiated 18,642
- services not recommended 44,414

The data also includes information about children in foster care in North Carolina. During the 2017-2018 state fiscal year, there were 17,828 children who were in foster care in North Carolina at some point during that year. This number reflects the different children who moved into and out of foster care over the course of that year. The data also provides a snapshot in time of the number of children in foster care on the last day of any given month; for example, on August 31, 2019, there were 11,544 children in foster care in North Carolina.

**Resource:** For more information about children alleged or found to be abused, neglected, or dependent (e.g., such as referral source, race, age, gender, ethnicity, number of placements, length of time in foster care, or reason for exit from foster care) on a statewide or individual county basis, see footnote 5 for link to the website data. Note the issue regarding incomplete data for abuse and neglect findings in footnote 6.

## 1.2 Federal-State-County System

### A. County-State Structure and Relationship

North Carolina is in the small minority of states that has a state-supervised, county-administered child welfare system.[7] Each county has either a department of social services (DSS) or a consolidated human services agency that includes social services. *See* G.S. 108A-1. Rather than one centralized state administered system, the 100 different county departments provide child welfare services to families.

The North Carolina Department of Health and Human Services (NC DHHS) is designated as the single state agency responsible for administering or supervising the administration of social services programs under the Social Security Act. G.S. 108A-71. Through its Division of Social Services, NC DHHS provides oversight, technical assistance, and training to the county departments. *See* G.S. 131D-10.6A; 108A-74. The Division of Social Services has a Child Welfare Services section that develops extensive state child welfare policies (published primarily as an online manual, setting out best practice guidelines to be used by DSS staff), provides consultations, and monitors counties' compliance and performance.[8] Starting in 2018, each county DSS is required to enter into a written agreement with NC DHHS (referred to as a memorandum of agreement) that sets out specific mandated performance requirements and administrative responsibilities for all social services programs, including child welfare, with the exception of Medicaid. G.S. 108A-74. An MOU must be executed each year. When a county department is not providing or making reasonable efforts to provide child welfare services in accordance with North Carolina statutes and regulations,

---

[7] "Statutory Changes Will Promote County Flexibility in Social Services Administration" "Final Report" to the Joint Legislative Program Evaluation Oversight Committee, Report No. 2011-03 (May 2011), Program Evaluation Division, the North Carolina General Assembly.

[8] NC CHILD WELFARE MANUAL, available online here.

NC DHHS has the authority to provide technical assistance, withhold state and federal child welfare services administrative funds, create and implement a corrective action plan, and ultimately control service delivery directly or through a contract with a public or private agency. G.S. 108A-74. The procedures for NC DHHS intervention are set forth in G.S. 108A-74.

**Legislative Notes:**
Amendments to G.S. 108A-74 have been made by S.L. 2019-240, Section 12.(d) and are effective July 1, 2020.

S.L. 2017-41 includes several provisions affecting the state's child welfare system. It includes several components related to increasing state supervision through the creation of a new system of regional supervision for local administration. A Social Services Working Group (SSWG) was tasked with making recommendations about the role of NC DHHS and regional supervision of the counties. The two required reports were published in March and December of 2018. The work of the SSWG is available on the UNC School of Government website, on the Social Services microsite, here.

NC DHHS maintains two statewide registries related to abuse, neglect, or dependency: (1) the central registry of abuse, neglect, and dependency cases and child fatalities resulting from alleged maltreatment (central registry) and (2) the responsible individuals list (RIL). G.S. 7B-311. The information maintained in these registries is provided to NC DHHS by the county departments and may be accessed by other county departments. G.S. 7B-311. For more information about these registries, see Chapter 5.2.

NC DHHS is also responsible for approving, periodically reviewing, suspending, and revoking licenses for foster care, residential child care, and adoptive homes. G.S. 131D-10.3; 131D-10.6. The Division of Social Services keeps a registry of all licensed family foster and therapeutic foster homes. G.S. 131D-10.6C.

**Resources:**
For additional information regarding the Division of Social Services, see the "Social Services" home page under "Divisions" on the N.C. Department of Health and Human Services website, here.

For additional information about child welfare programs and services within the Division of Social Services, including child protective services, foster care, etc., see "Child Welfare Services" on the Division of Social Services, N.C. Department of Health and Human Services website.

For information about the structure of child welfare systems in other states, see CHILD WELFARE INFORMATION GATEWAY, U.S. DEP'T OF HEALTH & HUMAN SERVICES, "State vs. County Administration of Child Welfare Services" (2018).

## B. The County DSS

**1. Governing structure and staff.** Each county department has a governing board, which may be a social services board, a consolidated human services board, or a board of county commissioners that has assumed the powers and duties of either a county social services board or consolidated human services board. County social services boards select DSS directors, who hire staff and administer county programs. In counties with a consolidated human services board, the county manager appoints and supervises a county director of human services, who appoints staff only on approval of the county manager. *See* Article I of G.S. Chapter 108A; 153A-77.

Statutes and regulations related to DSS responsibilities usually reference "the director" as the one carrying out DSS responsibilities. The Juvenile Code defines the "director" as the director of the department of social services in the county where the child resides or is found, or the director's representative. G.S. 7B-101(10). The director's duties and authority to delegate responsibilities to staff are set out in G.S. 108A-14. It is therefore understood that most responsibilities belonging to the "director" are carried out through authorized representatives of the director. In this Manual, the term "DSS director" typically refers to the director of a county department of social services or consolidated human services agency and the staff members to whom he or she delegates.

County DSS and human services agencies are departments within county government, and their directors and employees are county employees. However, the director and agency are also guided by and accountable to the state in many respects. State appellate courts have held in several child welfare contexts that the county DSS operates as an agent of the state. *See, e.g., In re N.X.A.*, 254 N.C. App. 670 (2017) (verification requirements for abuse, neglect, dependency petition); *Gammons v. N.C. Dep't of Human Res.*, 344 N.C. 51 (1996) (child protective services); *Vaughn v. N.C. Dep't of Human Res.*, 296 N.C. 683 (1979) (foster care); *In re Z.D.H*, 184 N.C. App. 183 (2007) (appeal in a juvenile case); *Parham v. Iredell County Dep't of Soc. Servs.*, 127 N.C. App. 144 (1997) (adoption).

Individual county DSS agencies may have local policies and procedures developed by the county social services or human services board or director. However, most policies and procedures related to child welfare are determined by statutory requirements, administrative rules adopted by the Social Services Commission (found in 10A N.C.A.C. 70A), and policies adopted by the NC DHHS Division of Social Services.

### Resources:
For more information on social services boards, see JOHN L. SAXON, HANDBOOK FOR COUNTY SOCIAL SERVICES BOARDS (UNC School of Government, 2009).

For further information about social services, see also JOHN L. SAXON, SOCIAL SERVICES IN NORTH CAROLINA (UNC School of Government, 2008).

For information about consolidated human services agencies, see "Consolidated Human Services Agencies (CHSAs)" on the UNC School of Government website.

**2. DSS role and responsibilities.** Child welfare services provided by DSS include intake and assessment of abuse, neglect, and dependency reports; initiation of and participation in court proceedings; provision of reunification and permanency planning services related to those proceedings; foster care and other placement services; and adoption services.

**(a) Protective services.** DSS's responsibility for protective services includes

- screening reports of suspected abuse, neglect, or dependency;
- performing assessments;
- providing casework services; and
- providing other counseling services to parents, guardians, or other caretakers to help those individuals and the court prevent abuse or neglect; improve the quality of child care; be more adequate parents, guardians, or caretakers; and preserve and stabilize family life.

G.S. 7B-300.

**Intake and screening.** DSS has the duty to screen reports of suspected child abuse, neglect, or dependency to determine whether the facts reported, if true, meet the statutory definitions of abuse, neglect, or dependency. *See* G.S. 7B-302; 7B-403. If they do, DSS must determine what type of assessment response is appropriate. *See* G.S. 7B-302(a). See Chapter 5.1 for a discussion of the statutory requirements for the intake and screening process. For DSS policies and procedures related to intake and screening, see DIV. OF SOC. SERVS., N.C. DEP'T OF HEALTH & HUMAN SERVICES, NC CHILD WELFARE MANUAL "CPS Intake," available here.

**Assessment.** A multiple response system (MRS) provides different responsive procedures for different types of situations. A "family assessment" response is used for reports meeting the statutory definitions of neglect and dependency and applies a family-centered approach that focuses on the strengths and needs of the family as well as the child's alleged condition. G.S. 7B-101(11a). A more formal "investigative assessment" response is used for reports containing allegations meeting the statutory definitions of abuse as well as selected reports of neglect or dependency as determined by the director. G.S. 7B-101(11b). At the end of an assessment, DSS determines (or substantiates) whether abuse, neglect, serious neglect, or dependency occurred. Serious neglect is for purposes of placing an individual on the Responsible Individuals List and is not in reference to a child's status. *In re J.M.*, 255 N.C. App. 483 (2017).

If DSS substantiates a report or determines that the family is in need of services, DSS must provide protective services and may file a petition with or without requesting a nonsecure custody order removing the child from the home immediately. *See* G.S. 7B-302(c), (d); 108A-14(a)(11). Without a substantiation or a finding of a need for services, DSS may make appropriate referrals for the family but must close its protective services case. Both types of assessments as well as the statutory requirements of the assessment stage are discussed in Chapter 5.1.B. For an explanation of DSS policies and procedures related to assessments and the multiple response system (MRS), see DIV. OF SOC. SERVS.,

N.C. Dep't of Health & Human Services, Child Welfare Manual "Purpose, Philosophy, Legal Basis and Staffing" and "Assessments," available here.

**Casework and other services.** After substantiation or a finding that a family requires services, DSS is responsible for determining what services would help the family to meet the child's basic needs, keep the child safe, and prevent future harm. DSS must determine and arrange for the most appropriate services, focusing on the child's safety and, in cases where a child has been removed from the home, returning the child to a safe home. Part of the casework requires DSS to make "reasonable efforts" to prevent or eliminate the need for the child's placement outside the home. *See* G.S. 7B-101(18) (defining reasonable efforts). The court may order DSS to provide specific efforts. *See* G.S. 7B-906.2(b). For a discussion of DSS services and related policies and procedures, see Div. of Soc. Servs., N.C. Dep't of Health & Human Services, Child Welfare Manual "In-Home Services," "Permanency Planning," and "Cross Function," available here.

**(b) Child placement services.** A child may be placed in an out-of-home placement through either a voluntary action on the parent's part or by court order. Occasionally a parent and DSS will enter into a voluntary foster care placement agreement. G.S. 7B-910. See Chapter 8 (voluntary placements). If a parent relinquishes a child to DSS (or licensed child-placing agency) for adoption, the agency acquires legal and physical custody of the child and assumes placement responsibility for the child under the adoption law. G.S. 48-3-705. Otherwise, DSS's authority to place children is derived from the following types of court orders giving DSS custody or placement responsibility for children:

- nonsecure custody orders entered before the adjudication hearing;
- initial disposition, review, or permanency planning orders entered after a child's adjudication; or
- termination of parental rights orders that have the effect of vesting or ordering custody and placement responsibility in DSS.

*See* G.S. 7B-507; 7B-905; 7B-906.1(h), (i); 7B-1112(1), (2).

DSS plays a role in the state's foster care licensing process and is responsible for supervising foster care placements. *See* G.S. 108A-14(a)(12). Some of DSS's authority in relation to children in DSS custody is specified by statute. *See, e.g.*, G.S. 7B-505.1; 7B-903.1; 48-3-705. Individual court orders may include provisions relating to the child's placement and DSS's authority and duties. For detailed provisions relating to DSS placement responsibilities, see Div. of Soc. Servs., N.C. Dep't of Health & Human Services, Child Welfare Manual "Cross Function," "Permanency Planning," and "Interstate Compact on the Placement of Children," available here. See also Chapter 7.4 (relating to out-of-home placements in the dispositional phase of the case).

DSS (or the licensed child-placing agency with placement authority for the child) selects the child's prospective adoptive parents. G.S 7B-1112.1. DSS also investigates and supervises adoptive placements. G.S. 108A-14(a)(6) and (13); *see* G.S. 48-3-201 to -207 (preplacement assessment for adoption); 48-2-501 to -504 (report for court in adoption proceeding). *See also* DIV. OF SOC. SERVS., N.C. DEP'T OF HEALTH & HUMAN SERVICES, CHILD WELFARE MANUAL "Adoptions" and "Permanency Planning," available here.

## C. Federal-State-County Funding[9]

Funding for child welfare services that are provided by the county departments of social services comes from a complicated mix of federal, state, and county sources.

Significant federal involvement with the protection of children began with the Social Security Act of 1935, which included funding to states for services ". . . for the protection and care of homeless, dependent, and neglected children." Today, the largest federally funded programs that support state child welfare programs and activities are authorized by the Social Security Act: Title IV-B for the Child Welfare Services and Promoting Safe and Stable Families (formerly known as Family Preservation) programs and Title IV-E for the Foster Care Program, Adoption Assistance Program, and the Chafee Foster Care Independence Program. These programs are administered by the U.S. Department of Health and Human Services. In addition, the Social Services Block Grant (SSBG) is authorized under Title XX of the Social Security Act and funds a wide range of programs that support social policy goals specified in the Social Security Act.

Some sources of the federal funding, such as the Social Services Block Grant (SSBG) under Title XX, are capped at an amount determined by federal legislation. Other sources of federal funding, such as foster care payments provided under Title IV-E, are uncapped, meaning that total funding depends on the number of eligible children in the state. These and other sources of federal funding require some matching funds from the state as well as compliance with numerous program requirements contained in federal laws and regulations.

The state legislature determines how the state and counties share responsibility for the non-federal share of the cost of federally funded programs. The General Assembly appropriates state funds for the state's portion of the non-federal share, allocates federal block grant funds, and appropriates additional state funds for child welfare services and programs.

Counties' primary funding responsibilities for child welfare fall into two categories:

- matching funds and maintenance of effort funds required by the state and
- any amounts above those available from federal and state funds and required matches that are necessary for the county to carry out its statutory duties to provide child welfare services.

Both are the responsibility of boards of county commissioners. A county that fails to provide services due to insufficient county funding could have NC DHHS implement a corrective action plan with the county board of commissioners, DSS board, and DSS director; withhold funding; and eventually take over the county's child welfare programs. G.S. 108A-74.

---

[9] Some of the content for this section was sourced from CHILD WELFARE INFORMATION GATEWAY, U.S. DEP'T OF HEALTH & HUMAN SERVICES, "Major Federal Legislation Concerned With Child Protection, Child Welfare, and Adoption" (2019).

> **Resource:** For a detailed explanation of child welfare funding in North Carolina, see DIV. OF SOC. SERVS., N.C. DEP'T OF HEALTH & HUMAN SERVICES, CHILD WELFARE MANUAL Appendices 1 through 3.7, available here.

## D. Federal-State Relationship

States are primarily responsible for the laws and programs that address the needs of children and families but there are also many federal statutes and regulations that apply to some of the programs and services. Federal funding and the conditions attached to states receiving it have influenced states' child welfare systems, such as the enactment of certain state statutes.

Periodically, the federal Children's Bureau (in the Administration for Children and Families in the U.S. Department of Health and Human Services) reviews North Carolina cases to assess compliance with federal laws. Two significant audits are the Child and Family Services Review (CFSR) and the IV-E Eligibility Review.

**1. Child and Family Service Review (CFSR).**[10] The CFSR evaluates a state's child welfare system with the three-fold purpose of ensuring the state is complying with federal requirements, determining what is actually happening to children and families who are receiving child welfare services, and assisting states in helping children and families achieve positive outcomes. The CFSR measures seven outcomes related to safety, permanency, and well-being and seven systemic factors.

| Safety, Permanency, and Well-being Outcomes | Systemic Factors for the State |
| --- | --- |
| Are children under the care of the state protected from abuse and neglect | Statewide information system |
| Are children safely maintained in their own homes whenever possible and appropriate | Case review system |
| Do children have permanency and stability in their living conditions | Quality assurance system |
| Are the continuity of family relationships and connections preserved for children | Staff and provider training |
| Do families have enhanced capacity to provide for their children's needs | Service array and resource development to meet the needs of children and families |
| Do children receive appropriate services to meet their educational needs | Agency responsiveness to the community |
| Do children receive adequate services to meet their physical and mental health needs | Foster and adoptive parent licensing, recruitment, and retention |

---

[10] The content for this section is sourced from the website for the Children's Bureau, U.S. Department of Health and Human Services, "Child & Family Service Reviews (CFSRs)."

If a state is out of conformance with any of the fourteen measured outcomes, it must submit a Program Improvement Plan (PIP) to identify corrective actions that need to be taken to improve compliance with federal laws. A finding of substantial conformity requires that ninety-five percent (95%) of the reviewed cases be rated as having substantially achieved the outcome. The standards are intentionally set high.

North Carolina has completed three CFSRs (2001, 2007, 2015). Because North Carolina does not have statewide data, the CFSRs were based on a small random sampling of cases from a few counties. Like all other states, North Carolina has not been in substantial conformity with all fourteen outcomes. However, in 2015 although certain strengths were identified, North Carolina was found not to be in substantial conformity with any of the fourteen measured outcomes. North Carolina created a PIP, which went into effect in January 2017.

> **Resources:**
> To view North Carolina's and other states' CFSR reports and PIPs, see "Reports and Results of the Child and Family Services Reviews (CFSRs)" on the Children's Bureau, U.S. Department of Health and Human Services website. The Round 3 CFSR report and PIP are also available on the N.C. Department of Health and Human Services website, searched under "Child and Family Services Performance Improvement Plan," available here.
>
> For information about the CFSR, see "Child and Family Services Reviews" on the website for the Children's Bureau, U.S. Department of Health and Human Services.

**2. The IV-E Eligibility Review.**[11] The on-site IV-E Eligibility Review is conducted every three years to assess compliance with Title IV-E of the Social Security Act. The review determines whether children in foster care meet the eligibility requirements for federal foster care maintenance payments. For this review, sample cases from a few counties are evaluated. Reviewers have access to the child's case records, court orders, placement and payment histories, and provider licensing and safety documentation. The state's "score" is based on the number of cases with errors. There are numerous eligibility factors that are examined, including whether court orders in the sample cases comply with federal requirements, such as those relating to

- judicial determinations of "reasonable efforts" and "contrary to the welfare,"
- voluntary foster care placements (*see* G.S. 7B-910), and
- vesting responsibility for the child's placement and care with the state (or county) agency.

If the state is not in substantial compliance, it must develop and implement a Program Improvement Plan (PIP) to correct the deficiencies, improve performance, and strengthen program operation.

In 2017, North Carolina was in substantial compliance for the period under review. Some areas were noted for needing improvement, such as obtaining judicial determinations of

---

[11] The content for this section is sourced from the website for the Children's Bureau, U.S. Department of Health and Human Services, "Title IV-E Reviews."

"contrary to the welfare" and "reasonable efforts to prevent removal" findings and documenting accurate payment histories to providers.

**Resources:**
To access selected Final Reports for North Carolina's (and other states') IV-E review, see the "Title IV-E State Reports and PIPs" page on the website for Children's Bureau, U.S. Department of Health and Human Services.

For information about the IV-E Eligibility Review, see the website link at footnote 11 and TITLE IV-E FOSTER CARE ELIGIBILITY REVIEW GUIDE (2012). For supplementary information in the Federal Register explaining 45 C.F.R. Parts 1355, 1356, and 1357; Title IV-E Foster Care Eligibility Reviews; and Child and Family Services State Plan Reviews, see 65 Fed. Reg. 4020 (Jan. 25, 2000).

For federal policy in a Q&A format related to Titles IV-B and IV-E, see the CHILD WELFARE POLICY MANUAL under the "Laws and Policies" section of the Children's Bureau, U.S. Department of Health and Human Services website, specifically "7. Title IV-B" and "8. Title IV-E".

## 1.3 State and Federal Sources of Authority: Laws, Rules, and Policy

Although North Carolina's child welfare system is primarily governed by state laws and regulations, those laws and regulations must meet the minimum requirements established by federal laws. Many requirements of relevant federal laws have been integrated into the North Carolina Juvenile Code, and some are explicitly referenced in the Juvenile Code but not codified. Requirements of federal and state laws also are integrated into state regulations and policies.

### A. North Carolina

**1. The Juvenile Code: G.S. Chapter 7B.** North Carolina enacted its first Juvenile Code in 1919. Major rewrites took effect in 1970, 1980, and, most recently, in 1999 when the current Juvenile Code (G.S. Chapter 7B) became effective. The 1919 Juvenile Code applied to juveniles who were neglected, dependent, abandoned, destitute or homeless, delinquent, truant, unruly, wayward, misdirected, disobedient to or beyond the control of their parents, or in danger of becoming any of these things. Over the years these evolved into the current categories of abused, neglected, dependent, delinquent, and undisciplined juveniles.

The 1999 Code was the first to separate within the Juvenile Code provisions relating to juveniles who need protection (abused, neglected, or dependent juveniles) and those whose conduct brings them before the court (delinquent and undisciplined juveniles). The Juvenile Code is organized into five subchapters:

- Subchapter I: abuse, neglect, dependency, and termination of parental rights;
- Subchapter II: undisciplined and delinquent juveniles;

- Subchapter III: juvenile records (including those arising from abuse, neglect, dependency, and termination of parental rights cases);
- Subchapter IV: parental authority and emancipation; and
- Subchapter V: the interstate placement of children.

The Juvenile Code establishes both the procedural and substantive laws that apply to abuse, neglect, dependency, and termination of parental rights cases as well as the legislature's purpose in enacting the Juvenile Code. The legislature amends the Juvenile Code in some respect almost every session—to ensure compliance with federal funding conditions, in response to appellate court decisions, to conform to changes in other laws, or for other reasons.

**Resources:**
The Juvenile Code, along with other North Carolina statutes, may be accessed online at the North Carolina General Assembly website; see "General Statutes" under "Bills & Laws."

For a summary of North Carolina legislation from 1997 through 2005 and its impact on the Juvenile Code, see DIV. OF SOC. SERVS., N.C. DEP'T OF HEALTH & HUMAN SERVICES, CHILD WELFARE MANUAL "Purpose, Philosophy, Legal Basis and Staffing," available here.

For annual summaries of North Carolina legislation, beginning with the 1998 session, see "Legislative Summaries" on the "Legislative Reporting Service" page on the UNC School of Government website.

**2. The Administrative Code: Title 10A.** In North Carolina, binding agency regulations are referred to as "Rules" that are set forth in the North Carolina Administrative Code (N.C.A.C.). The Rules regulating child welfare services are adopted by the Social Services Commission. G.S. 143B-153; *see, e.g.,* G.S. 108A-25(a); 108A-80(d); 7B-311; 131D-10.3; 131D-10.5. The Social Services Commission consists of one member from each of the state's thirteen congressional districts. G.S. 143B-154. Each member is appointed by the Governor for a four-year term. G.S. 143B-154.

Rules regulating health and human services are found in Title 10A of the N.C.A.C. Chapter 70 applies to children's services and consists of sixteen subchapters (Subchapter A through P). Because child welfare services are part of social services, Rules for social services also apply to the extent they do not conflict with federal and state laws. Chapter 69 regulates confidentiality and access to client records (see Chapter 14 of this Manual for a further discussion on confidentiality and information sharing), and Chapters 67 and 68 regulate social services procedures and rulemaking respectively. The Rules are enforced by NC DHHS. G.S. 143B-153(7); *see* G.S. 108A-74.

**Resource:** The N.C.A.C. is available online at the North Carolina Office of Administrative Hearings website, under the "Rules" section. For a table of contents of 10A N.C.A.C. Chapter 70, see Title 10A – Health and Human Services – Chapter 70.

**3. DHHS Child Welfare Manual.** The Division of Social Services at NC DHHS develops policies that comply with state and federal laws and represent best practice guidance. The policies, along with technical assistance and consultation, training for county staff, program reviews, and program improvement plans (when needed), are used by the Division of Social Services as part of its supervision over county departments. DIV. OF SOC. SERVS., N.C. DEP'T OF HEALTH & HUMAN SERVICES, CHILD WELFARE MANUAL "Purpose, Philosophy, Legal Basis and Staffing," available here. Note, however, that the failure to follow the policies does not authorize NC DHHS to withhold state and federal child welfare services administration funds or to assume control of the delivery of services. *See* G.S. 108A-74 (referencing State law and applicable rules adopted by the Social Services Commission). The NC Child Welfare Manual is an extensive resource for anyone who deals with or is interested in abuse, neglect, dependency, and termination of parental rights proceedings in North Carolina.

> **Resource:** The policies and procedures contained in the NC Child Welfare Manual are currently available on the NC DHHS Policies and Manuals website under "Divisional," "Social Services," "Child Welfare Services," "Policy/Manuals."

**4. Other relevant North Carolina statutes.** The Juvenile Code refers to other statutes that apply to abuse, neglect, dependency, and termination of parental rights proceedings.

| G.S. Citation | Substantive Issue |
|---|---|
| G.S. 1A-1 | The North Carolina Rules of Civil Procedure |
| Chapter 8C | The Rules of Evidence |
| Chapter 14 | Certain criminal statutes are incorporated in the definition of abuse and neglect; other criminal statutes relate to when a parent is excluded from being a party in an abuse, neglect, dependency, or adoption proceeding and are included in aggravating factors related to eliminating reasonable efforts at initial disposition |
| Chapter 48 | Adoptions of minor children |
| Chapter 50 | Child custody actions and orders |
| Chapter 50A | The Uniform Child-Custody Jurisdiction and Enforcement Act (UCCJEA) |
| Chapter 108A | Social services law |

Additionally, issues relating to families and children may arise in the context of an abuse, neglect, dependency, or termination of parental rights action that require the attorneys or court to look to other substantive laws that are outside of the Juvenile Code.

Examples include

| G.S. Citation | Substantive Issue |
|---|---|
| Chapter 35A | Incompetency definition and procedures as related to a respondent parent's need for Rule 17 GAL |
| G.S. 8-50.1(b1) | Ordering genetic marker testing when paternity is an issue |
| Chapter 49 | Determining whether paternity is an issue and what efforts have been |

|  | made to establish paternity |
| --- | --- |
| Chapters 50 | Child support and child custody orders help to identify missing parents, determine if paternity is an issue, and identify custodians (if any); applicable as a possible final disposition of the abuse, neglect, or dependency action through G.S. 7B-911 |
| Chapter 110 | Child support and parent locator services to help identify missing parents |
| Chapter 115C | Education issues, including school assignment, decision-making authority for students with disabilities, school discipline |

**5. Local court rules.** In some judicial districts, chief district court judges have adopted local court rules governing the procedures to be followed in juvenile cases. *See* G.S. 7B-700(b); 7B-808(c). To access local rules, see "Local Rules and Forms" on the North Carolina Administrative Office of the Courts website. See also Appendix 2 (Chief District Court Judge) at the end of this Manual.

### B. Influence of Federal Law[12]

Various federal laws provide states with funding for programs related to child welfare services and tie the receipt of that funding to a state's compliance with conditions set out in federal laws and regulations. Compliance with the federal requirements is often assured by the state plan that is submitted to and approved by the U.S. Department of Health and Human Services, *see e.g.,* 42 U.S.C. 622; 42 U.S.C. 671.

The following explains selected components of some of the federal laws that affect child welfare proceedings and have helped shape the North Carolina Juvenile Code and related statutes.

> **Resource:** Information on all of the federal laws mentioned or summarized in this Chapter (and other laws not discussed herein) is available on the Child Welfare Information Gateway, U.S. Department of Health and Human Services website. *See* "Major Federal Legislation Concerned with Child Protection, Child Welfare, and Adoption" and "Timeline of Major Federal Legislation Concerned With Child Protection, Child Welfare, and Adoption."

**1. The Child Abuse Prevention and Treatment Act (CAPTA).** The Child Abuse Prevention and Treatment Act (CAPTA), Pub. L. No. 93-247, 88 Stat. 4, was enacted in 1974 and has since been rewritten through a number of amendments and additions. CAPTA is codified at 42 U.S.C. 5101 *et seq.* and 42 U.S.C. 5116 *et seq.* Effective June 29, 2015, the federal regulations (45 C.F.R. Part 1340) were removed in their entirety by the Administration for Children and Families at the U.S. Department of Health and Human Services after they were found to be obsolete and unnecessary given the major changes to and clarity provided by statute. *See* 80 Fed. Reg. 16577.

---

[12] Some content for this section is adapted or reproduced from CHILD WELFARE INFORMATION GATEWAY, U.S. DEP'T OF HEALTH & HUMAN SERVICES, "Major Federal Legislation Concerned with Child Protection, Child Welfare, and Adoption" (2019).

CAPTA provides funds to states to establish programs to prevent and treat child abuse and neglect. It links federal funding to specific requirements, such as

- **Reporting requirements.** CAPTA requires states to have mandatory child abuse and neglect reporting laws and immunity for people who report abuse or neglect in good faith. North Carolina has a universal mandated reporting law, where any person or institution with cause to suspect a child is abused, neglected, or dependent must make a report to a DSS. G.S. 7B-301. The reporter is immune from civil or criminal liability when acting in good faith, which is presumed. G.S. 7B-309. See Chapter 5.1.A (discussing mandated reporting in North Carolina).

- **Child representation.** CAPTA requires that if a child is alleged to be abused or neglected and the case results in a judicial proceeding, the child must be represented by an appropriately trained guardian ad litem or attorney. In North Carolina, children who are alleged to be abused or neglected must have a guardian ad litem (GAL) appointed to represent them in the court action. Children who are alleged to be dependent only (a status not covered by CAPTA) may have a GAL appointed. G.S. 7B-601. In North Carolina, the child's GAL is a team that consists of a guardian ad litem program staff member, an attorney advocate, and a guardian ad litem volunteer. The state GAL program is a division of the North Carolina Administrative Office of the Courts and is responsible for providing training to those involved with the program. G.S. 7B-1200. See Chapter 2.3.D (discussing the child's GAL).

- **No reasonable efforts.** CAPTA sets forth specific criteria for when reasonable efforts for reunification are not required. In North Carolina, some of the enumerated factors for when reasonable efforts for reunification are not required incorporate criteria specified in CAPTA: the parent has been found by a court of competent jurisdiction to have committed murder or voluntary manslaughter of another child of the parent; aided, attempted, conspired, or solicited to commit such murder or voluntary manslaughter; committed felony assault resulting in serious bodily injury to the child or another child of the parent; committed sexual abuse against the child or another child of the parent; or has been required to register on a sex offender registry. G.S. 7B-901(c)(3). See Chapter 7.8 (discussing findings regarding reasonable efforts at different dispositional hearings) and 7.9 (discussing reasonable efforts).

- **Confidentiality of records.** CAPTA requires that the confidentiality of records be preserved to protect the rights of children, parents, and guardians. Certain disclosures are authorized, such as disclosures to individuals who are the subject of a report, government entities that need the information to carry out their responsibilities to protect children from abuse or neglect, and child fatality and citizen review panels. The Juvenile Code addresses confidentiality of information obtained by DSS, including the circumstances of when it may be shared, in G.S. 7B-302(a1), 7B-2901, 7B-2902, 7B-1413, and 7B-3100. See Chapter 14.1 (discussing confidentiality and access to information).

- **Child fatality review panels and child abuse citizen review panels.** CAPTA requires citizen reviews and child fatality reviews to help determine whether the state is effectively discharging its child protective responsibilities. Article 14 of the Juvenile Code establishes the North Carolina Child Fatality Prevention System. The system is a multidisciplinary review system that consists of state and local components. At the state level, there is the North Carolina Child Fatality Task Force, which develops and analyzes the operation of the child fatality prevention system and makes recommendations regarding laws, rules, and policies governing that system. There is also the North Carolina Child Fatality Prevention Team, which reviews child deaths that are attributed to abuse or neglect or involve a child who had been reported to DSS for suspected abuse or neglect, provides technical assistance to local county teams, and periodically assesses the operations of the child fatality prevention system and makes recommendations to the state Task Force as needed. At the county level, each county has a local Community Child Protection Team (CCPT), which functions as the citizen review panel, and a local Child Fatality Prevention Team (CFPT); in some counties, these teams are blended. The local CCPT reviews selected active child protective cases and cases in which a child died as a result of suspected abuse or neglect when there was a report made to or the family was receiving child protective services from a DSS within the previous twelve months. The local CFPT reviews records of all other child deaths. These local teams report annually to their county commissioners with recommendations, if any, and advocate for system improvements and needed resources where gaps and deficiencies may exist. *See* G.S. 7B-1400 through -1414. In addition to the child fatality prevention system established by the Juvenile Code, North Carolina also has a State Child Fatality Review Team, which provides intensive reviews of child fatalities when the child or family was involved with DSS child protective services in the twelve months preceding the child's death. *See* G.S. 143B-150.20. See Chapter 14.1.A.3(b) (discussing review of child fatalities by these various teams related to access to and disclosure of information).

CAPTA also authorized government research into child abuse prevention and treatment, created the National Center on Child Abuse and Neglect, which has been replaced by the Office on Child Abuse and Neglect, and established the National Clearinghouse on Child Abuse and Neglect Information. CAPTA funds training programs, recruitment of volunteers, and the establishment of resource centers in fields related to abuse and neglect.

---

**Resources:**
For a summary of CAPTA amendments, see CHILD WELFARE INFORMATION GATEWAY, U.S. DEP'T OF HEALTH & HUMAN SERVICES, "About CAPTA: A Legislative History" (Feb. 2019).

Information on some of the legislation reauthorizing and/or amending CAPTA in 1978, 1988, 1992, 1996, 2003, and 2010 to present is available at "Major Federal Legislation Index and Search," on the Child Welfare Information Gateway, U.S. Department of Health and Human Services website.

---

**2. The Indian Child Welfare Act (ICWA).** In 1978, the Indian Child Welfare Act (ICWA), Pub. L. No. 95-608, 92 Stat. 3069, was enacted after Congress found that American Indian children of federally recognized Indian tribes were being inappropriately removed from their families and tribal communities. ICWA is codified as amended at 25 U.S.C.1901 *et seq*. For the first time since its enactment, the U.S. Department of the Interior, Bureau of Indian Affairs adopted federal regulations implementing ICWA, effective December 12, 2016. The regulations are at 25 C.F.R. Part 23.

The purpose of ICWA is to protect the best interests of Indian children and to promote the stability and security of Indian tribes and families by establishing minimum federal standards for the removal of Indian children from their families and the placement of those children in foster or adoptive homes that reflect the unique values of Indian culture. ICWA gives Indian tribes jurisdiction over or the right to intervene in certain types of child custody proceedings involving Indian children, including abuse, neglect, dependency; termination of parental rights; and adoption proceedings. It also imposes specific requirements on state courts that exercise jurisdiction in those proceedings when an Indian child is the subject of the action.

ICWA is specifically referenced in the Juvenile Code at G.S. 7B-505(d) and 7B-506(h)(2). ICWA is also explicitly incorporated in North Carolina adoption laws. *See* G.S. 48-1-108; 48-3-605(f); 48-3-702(b).

For further discussion of ICWA, see Chapter 13.2.

**3. Adoption Assistance and Child Welfare Act.** In 1980, Congress enacted the Adoption Assistance and Child Welfare Act, Pub. L. No. 96-272, 94 Stat. 500, to address problems in the foster care system and the unnecessary separation of children and families. The Act is codified as amended in various sections of 42 U.S.C.

The Act provides federal funds for foster care and adoption assistance. As a condition of receiving funds for foster care, it requires

- **Reasonable efforts.** States are required to make "reasonable efforts" to (1) prevent the need to place children outside their homes or (2) reunify children with their families. "Reasonable efforts" originated with this Act and was the genesis of the reasonable efforts requirements set out in North Carolina's Juvenile Code. *See* G.S. 7B-101(18); 7B-507(a)(2); 7B-901(c); 7B-903(a3); 7B-906.1(e)(5), (f)(3). See Chapter 7.8 (discussing findings regarding reasonable efforts at different dispositional hearings) and 7.9 (discussing reasonable efforts).

- **Periodic reviews**. The Act also requires periodic review of cases of children in foster care every six months, and that a permanent plan be made for every child placed away from home within eighteen months after the child's initial placement. Some of the time requirements in the North Carolina Juvenile Code are based on the Act. See Chapter 7.2.A (discussing timing of dispositional hearings).

- **Placement setting.** A child's case plan must be designed to achieve a placement in the least restrictive, meaning most family like, setting available and in close proximity to the parent's home when it is consistent with the child's best interests and needs. The Juvenile Code requires the court to consider whether it is in the child's best interests to remain in his or her community of residence. G.S. 7B-505(d); 7B-903(a1).

- **Foster home licensure standards.** The Act also establishes standards for foster family homes and for periodic review of those standards. Article 1A of G.S. Chapter 131D and 10A N.C.A.C 70E regulate the licensure of foster homes in North Carolina.

The Act also requires maintenance of a data collection and reporting system about children in care.

**4. Family Preservation and Support Services Program Act.** In 1993, the Family Preservation and Support Services Program Act, Pub. L. No. 103-66, 107 Stat. 312, was enacted. Among its many provisions, the Act strengthened family preservation and support services by focusing on prevention services, such as parent education programs.

It also established the Court Improvement Program. North Carolina received its initial grant for its Court Improvement Program (NC-CIP) in 1995. NC-CIP is based in the North Carolina Administrative Office of the Courts. The purpose of this federally funded program is to improve court practice in child abuse, neglect, or dependency cases. NC-CIP funds have been used to support several different types of initiatives over the years, including

- providing staff to twenty-three judicial districts to provide case management support and/or training and implementing best practices (such as one judge-one family case assignment, child planning conferences, and shared decision-making);
- implementing Family Drug Treatment Courts in four districts; and
- enhancing JWise, which is the information system used to store data on cases of abuse, neglect, or dependency in the North Carolina courts (see Appendix 3).

CIP staff has broadened the program's reach to a more statewide audience for court improvement activities, including trainings for attorneys, judges and other legal professionals involved in child welfare cases and providing financial support for this Manual.

**Resource:** For more information about the Court Improvement Program in North Carolina, see "[Juvenile Court Improvement Program](#)" on the North Carolina Administrative Office of the Courts website.

**5. Multiethnic Placement Act (MEPA-IEP).** In 1994, the Multiethnic Placement Act (MEPA), Pub. L. No. 103-382, 108 Stat. 4056, was enacted as Title V, Part E, subpart 1 of the Improving America's Schools Act, amending Title IV-E of the Social Security Act. In 1996, the Interethnic Adoption Provisions (IEP) of the Small Business Job Protection Act, Pub. L. No. 104-188, 100 Stat. 1744, made significant amendments to MEPA to remove barriers to interethnic adoptions. It is codified in various sections of 42 U.S.C.

MEPA prohibits the delay or denial of a child's foster care or adoptive placement based on the race, color, or national origin of the prospective foster or adoptive parent or child; prohibits the denial of a prospective foster or adoptive parent from becoming such a parent on the basis of race, color, or national origin; and requires the recruitment of a diverse pool of foster and adoptive parents. MEPA is specifically referenced in the Juvenile Code at G.S.7B-505(d) and 7B-506(h)(2). Failure to comply with MEPA is a violation of Title VI of the Civil Rights Act.

For more information about MEPA and Title VI, see Chapter 13.3 and 13.4.

**6. Adoption and Safe Families Act (ASFA).** In 1997, Congress passed the Adoption and Safe Families Act (ASFA), Pub. L. No. 105-89, 111 Stat. 2115. ASFA amended the Adoption Assistance and Child Welfare Act of 1980. It is codified in various sections of 42 U.S.C.

The Juvenile Code refers directly to ASFA in G.S. 7B-100(5), which sets forth the purposes of the Juvenile Code. In addition, many of the ASFA requirements have been integrated into the Juvenile Code. ASFA emphasizes, among other things,

- **The safety of abused and neglected children as the paramount concern.** ASFA provides that when determining reasonable efforts, the child's health and safety must be the paramount concern. In addition, consideration of the "safety of the child" was added to the case plan and review process. Various provisions in the Juvenile Code reference the court's consideration of the child's health and safety. *See, e.g.*, G.S. 7B-507(a); 7B-903(a2); 7B-905.1(a).

  ASFA also requires criminal records checks for foster and adoptive parents who receive federal funds on behalf of a child. Note that the subsequently enacted Adam Walsh Child Protection and Safety Act of 2005 prohibits states from opting out of this provision and additionally requires fingerprinting and a child abuse and neglect registry check of prospective adoptive or foster parents and other adults living in the home. In North Carolina, mandatory criminal history checks are required for foster parents, individuals applying for foster care licensure, and adults who reside in a family foster home. G.S. 131D-10.3A. They are also required for adoptive placements made by DSS, which includes the prospective adoptive parents and all the adults who reside in the home. G.S. 48-3-309.

- **Clarified reasonable efforts.** ASFA requires states to specify situations in which reasonable efforts for reunification are not required because of aggravating circumstances (as defined by the state) or the involuntary termination of the parent's rights to the child's sibling. ASFA further requires that a hearing be held within thirty days after a determination to cease reasonable efforts. It also expanded reasonable efforts to achieve a permanent placement that was not reunification and emphasized children's health and safety. Aggravating circumstances in North Carolina are identified at G.S. 7B-901(c)(1), and the other provisions regarding reasonable efforts that ASFA requires are found at G.S. 7B-901(c)(2) and (d).

  ASFA also allowed for (but did not require) concurrent reasonable efforts to place a child in an adoption or legal guardianship with reasonable efforts for reunification. As of October 1, 2015, in North Carolina, concurrent permanent plans are required until a permanent plan is achieved. *See* S.L. 2015-136, sec. 14, amended by S.L. 2016-94, sec. 12C.1.(h) (effective July 2016). The court must adopt concurrent permanent plans, identify the primary plan and secondary plan, and order DSS to make reasonable efforts toward each plan until a final permanent plan is achieved. G.S. 7B-906.2(a1), (b).

See Chapter 7.8 (discussing findings regarding reasonable efforts at different dispositional hearings); 7.9 (discussing reasonable efforts); and 7.10 (discussing concurrent permanency planning).

- **Participation in case reviews and hearings.** ASFA requires foster parents, pre-adoptive parents, or relatives providing care to a child to be given notice and an opportunity to be heard in any review hearing for the child and clarified that such participation does not make the care provider a party. The Juvenile Code incorporates this provision with respect to review, permanency planning, and post termination of parental rights (TPR) placement review hearings. G.S. 7B-906.1(b); 7B-908(b)(1). See Chapters 7.2.B and C (discussing notice and participation at review and permanency planning hearings) and 10.1.C (discussing notice and participation at post-TPR placement review hearings).

- **Timely permanent placements.** ASFA requires states to initiate court proceedings to free a child for adoption when the child had been in foster care for at least fifteen of the most recent twenty-two months, unless one of several exceptions applied. North Carolina's version of this requirement refers to when a child has been placed out of the home for twelve of the most recent twenty-two months. G.S. 7B-906.1(f). ASFA also requires that the first permanency planning hearing be held no later than twelve months after a child entered foster care, which is reflected in North Carolina's Juvenile Code in G.S. 7B-906.1(a). The concepts of permanence and timeliness for children received increased focus with the enactment of ASFA, which led to the addition of references to the need for the child to have a "safe, permanent home within a reasonable amount of time." *See, e.g.,* G.S. 7B-100(5); 7B-101(18); 7B-906.1(d)(3), (g); 7B-906.2(d)(1). See Chapter 7.2.A (discussing timing of dispositional hearings) and 7.8.D (discussing considerations for initiation of termination of parental rights).

- **Promoted adoptions.** ASFA provided incentive funds to states that increased adoptions. It required states to document and report child-specific recruitment efforts for adoption. States are prohibited from denying or delaying an approved adoptive placement because of the geographic location of the prospective adoptive family.

**7. John H. Chafee Foster Care Independence Act.** In 1999, Congress enacted the John H. Chafee Foster Care Independence Act, Pub. L. No. 106-169, 113 Stat. 1822. It has been amended since its first enactment. The purpose of the Act is to help older children who age out of foster care make the transition from foster care to self-sufficiency. It provides states with more funding for an Independent Living Program for these young adults who are participating in education, training, or services to obtain employment. The Act allows funds to be used to pay for room and board for former foster youth who are 18 years old up to 21 years of age and provides states with the option to extend Medicaid coverage to 18- to 21-year-old young adults who have been emancipated from foster care.

North Carolina has the NC LINKS program, a foster care independence program that focuses on a youth's successful transition from foster care to adulthood. Additionally, as of January 1, 2017, youth who have aged out of foster care may participate in Foster Care 18–21, which is the state's extended foster care program for eligible young adults. *See* G.S. 131D-10.2B; 7B-910.1; 108A-48. See also Chapter 8.3 (discussing Foster Care 18–21).

---

**Resources:**
For more information about Foster Care 18–21, see
- DIV. OF SOC. SERVS., N.C. DEP'T OF HEALTH & HUMAN SERVICES, CHILD WELFARE MANUAL "Permanency Planning," available here.
- Sara DePasquale, *Foster Care Extended to Age 21*, UNC SCH. OF GOV'T: ON THE CIVIL SIDE BLOG (Jan. 11, 2017).

For more information about NC LINKS, see DIV. OF SOC. SERVS., N.C. DEP'T OF HEALTH & HUMAN SERVICES, CHILD WELFARE MANUAL "Permanency Planning," available here.

---

**8. Safe and Timely Interstate Placement of Foster Children Act.** In 2006, the Safe and Timely Interstate Placement of Foster Children Act, Pub. L. No. 109-239, 120 Stat. 508, was enacted. The purpose of the Act was to improve protections for children and to hold states accountable for the safe and timely placement of children across state lines. This Act, along with other measures to expedite interstate placements, set out specific timelines for completion and acceptance of home studies. The Act encouraged states to ratify the Interstate Compact for the Placement of Children (ICPC). North Carolina adopted the ICPC in 1971; it is currently codified at G.S. Chapter 7B, Article 38. Other sections of the Juvenile Code specifically refer to the ICPC for out-of-state placements. G.S. 7B-505(d); 7B-506(h)(2); 7B-903(a1). See Chapter 7.4.H for an explanation of interstate placements and the ICPC.

**9. Fostering Connections to Success and Increasing Adoptions Act (Fostering Connections).** In 2008, Congress passed the Fostering Connections to Success and Increasing Adoptions Act, Pub. L. No. 110-351, 122 Stat. 3949. It is codified in various sections of 42 U.S.C.

A main purpose of the Act was to connect and support relative caregivers. Among many provisions, Fostering Connections promoted and supported funding and programs related to kinship placements, guardianship, and adoptions of foster children; extended and increased adoption incentives; expanded Title IV-E assistance to older youth in foster care and those transitioning out of foster care; required transition plans before a foster child's emancipation; and required case plans that ensured educational stability of children in foster care.

- **Kinship placements.** Fostering Connections requires states to exercise due diligence to identify and provide notice to the child's grandparents and other adult relatives (with exceptions for family or domestic violence) that the child is being or has been removed from the parents. The notice must include options the relative has to participate in the child's care and placement, including services and support available to them if they become a family foster home. The Juvenile Code requires the court to make an inquiry into those efforts at continued nonsecure custody, pre-adjudication, and initial dispositional hearings. G.S. 7B-506(h)(2); 7B-800.1(a)(4); 7B-901(b). The court must order DSS to make diligent efforts and notify relatives of the child's placement in and hearings for nonsecure custody unless the notification would be contrary to the child's best interests. G.S. 7B-505(b). The Juvenile Code refers to "relatives" without defining the term. *See* G.S. 7B-505(b); 7B-800.1(a)(4); 7B-901(b). The Foster Care Bill of Rights also incorporates this requirement of Fostering Connections and specifically refers to grandparents, adult siblings, and other adult relatives. G.S. 131D-10.1(a)(5).

See Chapters 5.6.E (discussing inquiry at nonsecure custody hearing); 5.5.C.3 (discussing nonsecure custody placement); 7.8.A.1 (discussing inquiry at initial dispositional hearing); and 7.4.C.1 (discussing out-of-home placement priority).

- **Siblings**. Fostering Connections requires that reasonable efforts be made to place siblings who are removed from their home in the same placement, unless there is documentation that a joint placement would be contrary to the safety or well-being of any of the siblings. When a joint placement does not occur, frequent visitation or communication should occur. The Juvenile Code does not specifically address sibling placement; however, the Foster Care Bill of Rights does. *See* G.S. 131D-10.1(a)(2). Visitation generally is codified at G.S. 7B-905.1, and the Foster Care Bill of Rights specifically refers to communication measures to maintain contact with siblings when the children are not placed together. *See* G.S. 131D-10.1(a)(10).

- **Educational stability**. Fostering Connections requires that any child of compulsory school age who is receiving federal foster care maintenance or adoption assistance payments be a full-time student, unless the child has completed secondary school or is incapable of attending school full-time because of a medical condition. A child's case plan must address the child's educational stability by providing assurances that when placing the child in out-of-home care, the appropriateness of the child's current educational setting and the proximity of the placement to the child's school were considered. The child is to remain in that school unless it is not in the child's best interests. If the child is required to change schools, the child welfare agency and the school district must assure the child's immediate and appropriate enrollment. Payments to cover the cost of a child's reasonable travel to the school in which the child was enrolled at the time of placement was added to "foster care maintenance payments." Fostering Connections applies to child welfare agencies. In 2015, Congress passed the Every Student Succeeds Act (ESSA), which applies these provisions to educational agencies effective December 10, 2016. See Chapter 13.7 (discussing ESSA).

  The Juvenile Code does not specifically reference a child's school enrollment or attendance; however, the predisposition report provided by DSS to the court should contain educational information. G.S. 7B-808(a). The court also considers whether it is in the child's best interests to remain in his or her community of residence. G.S. 7B-505(d); 7B-903(a1). The Foster Care Bill of Rights promotes allowing a child to remain enrolled in the school he or she attended before being placed in foster care when possible. G.S. 131D-10.1(a)(4).

Note that the Foster Care Bill of Rights sets forth the State's policy regarding a child's placement in foster care but does not create any private cause of action for a violation of its provisions. G.S. 131D-10.1.

**Resources:**
For an explanation of the Act, federal guidance, tools and resources related to its provisions, see
- "Fostering Connections to Success and Increasing Adoption Act of 2008" on the Child Welfare Information Gateway website.
- CHILDREN'S BUREAU, U.S. DEP'T OF HEALTH & HUMAN SERVICES, Program Instruction ACYF-CB-PI-08-05 (Oct. 23, 2008).

For an explanation of the Act's connection to existing North Carolina social services policies and procedures, see NC DHHS Division of Social Services Dear County Directors Letter, CWS-02-09: New Federal Legislation – the Foster Connections to Success and Increasing Adoptions Act of 2008 (March 17, 2009).

**10. Preventing Sex Trafficking and Strengthening Families Act.** In 2014, Congress enacted the Preventing Sex Trafficking and Strengthening Families Act, Pub. L. No. 113-183, 128 Stat. 1919. It makes amendments to Titles IV-B and IV-E of the Social Security Act and is codified in various sections of 42 U.S.C.

The Act has multiple purposes that include

- **A focus on at-risk foster children who may become victims of sex trafficking.** States are required to provide training to caseworkers and develop policies and procedures that identify, document, and determine appropriate services for any child involved in the child welfare system who is believed to be or is at risk of being a sex trafficking victim; to notify law enforcement of instances of sex trafficking; and to locate and respond to children who run away from foster care. The Division of Social Services created the required policy, which can be found at DIV. OF SOC. SERVS., N.C. DEP'T OF HEALTH & HUMAN SERVICES CHILD WELFARE MANUAL "Permanency Planning" and "Cross Function," available here.

**Resources:**
For a further discussion of the law and North Carolina policy, see Sara DePasquale, *Children in Foster Care and Sex Trafficking: New NC Policy to Know About*, UNC SCH. OF GOV'T: ON THE CIVIL SIDE BLOG (Jan. 19, 2016).

For a discussion about identifying and responding to human trafficking involving children and young adults, see Margaret Henderson, Sara DePasquale, Nancy Hagan, and Christy Croft, *Human Trafficking of Minors and Young Adults: What Local Governments Need to Know* (PUBLIC MANAGEMENT BULLETIN No. 2019/18 (UNC School of Government, Dec. 2019).

For more information about the Act, see "Implementing the Preventing Sex Trafficking and Strengthening Families Act to Benefit Children and Youth" (Jan. 14, 2015), available on The Children's Defense Fund website.

- **"Reasonable and prudent parenting standard".** States are required to implement a "reasonable and prudent parent" standard that authorizes foster parents to make decisions that allow children in foster care to engage in "age or developmentally appropriate" activities and specifically references extracurricular and social activities including sleepovers. North Carolina codified the federal definition of "reasonable and prudent parent standard" and includes additional provisions regarding the standard in G.S. 131D-10.2A. The Juvenile Code incorporates this provision in G.S. 7B-903.1(b). The NC DHHS Division of Social Services addresses the reasonable and prudent parent standard in DIV. OF SOC. SERVS., N.C. DEP'T OF HEALTH & HUMAN SERVICES CHILD WELFARE MANUAL "Permanency Planning," available here. See Chapter 7.4.D.4 (discussing the reasonable and prudent parent standard).

- **A focus on older youth.** The Act requires that children in foster care who are 14 years old and older participate in the development and revision of their case plans. The Act also focuses on older youth transitioning out of foster care by limiting a permanent plan of Another Planned Permanent Living Arrangement (APPLA) to 16- and 17-year-old juveniles. It also requires that children who are aging out of foster care receive certain documents that will help them transition to adulthood, including a certified copy of his or her birth certificate, a social security card, health insurance information, medical records, and a driver's license or state ID. The Juvenile Code, at G.S. 7B-912, specifically addresses these provisions. See Chapter 7.8.C.9 (discussing the requirements of G.S. 7B-912) and 7.10.B.6 (discussing APPLA).

- **Contacting parents of siblings.** The Act also expanded who must receive notice of the child's removal and opportunities for those persons to become a possible placement for the child to include parents with legal custody of the child's siblings. North Carolina included and expanded this requirement to "other persons with legal custody" of the child's sibling. *See* G.S. 7B-505(b); 7B-800.1(a)(4); 7B-901(b). See Chapters 5.6.E (discussing inquiry at nonsecure custody hearing); 5.5.C.3 (discussing placement in nonsecure custody); and 7.8.A.1 (discussing inquiry at initial dispositional hearing).

**11. Justice for Victims of Trafficking Act.**[13] In 2015, Congress enacted the Justice for Victims of Trafficking Act, Pub. L. 114-22, effective May 29, 2017. This Act amends CAPTA.

States are required to include procedures to

- identify and assess reports involving suspected child sex trafficking victims;
- provide training for child protective workers;
- make efforts to coordinate law enforcement, juvenile justice, and social services agencies such as runaway and homeless shelters; and
- to the extent possible, collect and report the number of children who are victims of sex trafficking to the National Child Abuse and Neglect Data System.

---

[13] Additional source for the content in this section is from the website for the Children's Bureau, U.S. Department of Health and Human Services, Information Memorandum ACYF-CB-IM-15-05 (July 16, 2015).

Amendments were also made to the Crime Control Act of 1990 to require notification to the National Center for Missing and Exploited Children of each report of a child missing from foster care, including providing a recent photo of the child (if available), and shortened the time to verify and update records on missing children in state law enforcement systems and the National Crime Information Center.

Effective October 1, 2018, North Carolina amended its definitions of "abused juveniles" and "neglected juvenile" to include minor victims of human trafficking. G.S. 7B-101(1)(i), (15)(i). Note that prior to the enactment of the federal law, North Carolina included in its definition of "abused juvenile" a child whose parent, guardian, custodian, or caretaker commits or allows to be committed an offense of human trafficking, involuntary servitude, or sexual servitude against the child. G.S. 7B-101(1)(ii)g. The 2018 amendments expand the former definition of "abused juveniles" by eliminating the condition that circumstances be created by the juvenile's parent, guardian, custodian, or caretaker.

**12. Family First Prevention Services Act (FFPSA).** In 2018, the Family First Prevention Services Act (FFPSA), Pub. L. No. 115-123, 132 Stat. 64, was enacted as Division E, Title VII of the Bipartisan Budget Act of 2018. FFPSA amends various federal laws pertaining to child welfare and is codified in various sections of 42 U.S.C. The stated purpose of the act is to enable States to use Title IV-B and IV-E funding to provide enhanced support to children and families and prevent foster care placements as well as limit payment for placements in congregate care. Some of the FFPSA provisions include

- the expansion of the definition of family reunification services to include services provided to the family after the child has been returned home for a period of 15 months;
- the optional use of funding for up to one year of prevention services related to mental health and substance use issues and in-home parenting for parents and caregivers of children who are "candidate for foster care;"
- a limitation on payment for the placement of children in congregate care in a facility that is not a licensed residential based treatment program to 2 weeks;
- mandatory criminal background and child abuse and neglect registry checks for any adult working in a child care institution, group home, residential treatment center, or other congregate care setting;
- and the implementation of an electronic interstate case processing system for interstate placements.

North Carolina opted to delay implementation of the prevention and congregate care provisions until September 2021 as permitted by the FFPSA. The provisions regarding mandatory background checks for adults working in child care institutions were codified by S.L. 2019-240, Part III-O, Section 25, which created G.S. 108A-133 and G.S. 143B-972, effective November 6, 2019.

**Resource:** For information on the FFPSA implementation in North Carolina, see the "Family First Prevention Services Act" on the NC DHHS website under "Divisions," "Social Services," "Child Welfare Services."

# Chapter 2

# The Court, Key People, and the Rights of Children and Parents

# Chapter 2
# The Court, Key People, and the Rights of Children and Parents

**2.1 The Juvenile Court and Officials    2-3**
    A. The Court
        1. District court is juvenile court
        2. Juvenile court sessions
        3. JWise System
        4. Juvenile Rules of Recordkeeping
    B. Judicial Officials and Staff
        1. Juvenile court judge
        2. Chief district court judge
        3. Juvenile court clerk
        4. Juvenile court case manager or coordinators

**2.2 Key People: Who's Who in the System    2-7**
    A. Introduction
    B. The People: Explanation of Roles
        1. Social services director
        2. Social services caseworkers
        3. Social services attorney
        4. The child or juvenile
        5. The child's guardian ad litem (GAL)
        6. Parent
        7. Parent's attorney
        8. Parent's guardian ad litem
        9. Custodians, guardians, and caretakers
        10. Relatives
        11. Nonrelative kin
        12. Foster parents
        13. Law enforcement
        14. District attorney or prosecutor
        15. Other professionals and their agencies
        16. Persons involved in other court proceedings affecting the family

**2.3 The Child    2-15**
    A. Introduction
    B. Definitions of Abused, Neglected, or Dependent Juveniles
        1. Abused juvenile
        2. Neglected juvenile
        3. Dependent juvenile
    C. Rights of the Child
        1. Right to participate and be heard

2. Best interests and legal rights representation
3. Foster Care Children's Bill of Rights
D. The Child's Guardian ad Litem
 1. Introduction
 2. North Carolina GAL Program establishment and structure
 3. GAL team representation: volunteer, attorney advocate, and staff
 4. Role and responsibilities of the GAL
 5. Fees for child's GAL attorney advocate and experts

## 2.4 Rights of the Parent    2-35
A. Protection of Parent-Child Relationship
 1. Generally
 2. U.S. Supreme Court
 3. North Carolina appellate courts
B. Notice and Opportunity to Be Heard
 1. Entitled to due process
 2. Participation in hearings
C. DSS Perspective
D. Representation
 1. Right to counsel
 2. Appointment of counsel
 3. Waiver of counsel
 4. Withdrawal of counsel
 5. Ineffective assistance of counsel
 6. Payment of counsel and reimbursement of fees
E. Funds for Experts and Other Expenses
 1. Expenses of representation
 2. Standard for obtaining expenses
 3. Parent's ex parte motion
F. Guardian ad Litem for Parent
 1. Circumstances for appointment and legislative history
 2. Privileged communications
 3. Timing and source of GAL appointment
 4. Who may serve as GAL
 5. Determination of incompetence
 6. Role of the parent's GAL
 7. Payment of parent's GAL

## 2.1 The Juvenile Court and Officials

### A. The Court

Abuse, neglect, dependency, and termination of parental rights cases are heard in district court by a judge and not a jury. In practice, the sessions of district court that hear juvenile matters (which include abuse, neglect, dependency, termination of parental rights, delinquency, undisciplined, and emancipation proceedings) are usually referred to as "juvenile court." There is not a separate juvenile court system in North Carolina.

**Note,** as used in this Manual, the term "juvenile court" refers to a district court that hears juvenile proceedings. Juvenile proceedings include those proceedings that are governed by the Juvenile Code (G.S. Chapter 7B). As used in this Manual, the term "juvenile proceeding" typically refers to an abuse, neglect, dependency or termination of parental rights proceeding; however, in some circumstances, the context may require the inclusion of delinquency, undisciplined, and emancipation actions.

**1. District court is juvenile court**. For purposes of abuse, neglect, dependency, and termination of parental rights actions, G.S. 7B-101(6) defines "court" as "the district court division of the General Court of Jurisdiction." There is no definition of "juvenile court" in Subchapter I of G.S. Chapter 7B; however, it is defined in Subchapter II, applying to undisciplined and delinquent juveniles, as "any district court exercising jurisdiction under this Chapter." G.S. 7B-1501(18). The terms "juvenile court" and "district court" are used interchangeably in the Juvenile Code. *See, e.g.,* G.S. 7B-323; 7B-324.

**(a) Juvenile court may be part of a family court district.** In 1998, the legislature authorized the establishment of family courts on a pilot basis, with funding appropriated for three family courts. As of October 1, 2019, there are fifteen family court districts that serve twenty-seven counties. Forty-five percent of the state's population live in a county that is served by a family court district.[1] In these districts, family court case coordinators assist with the assignment and management of cases so that, to the extent possible, all of one family's legal matters are scheduled and heard before the same judge or team of judges who typically receive specialized training to handle complex family matters. Depending on the judicial district, family court matters include abuse, neglect, or dependency; termination of parental rights; domestic violence; child custody and visitation; child support; divorce, alimony, and equitable distribution; and juvenile delinquency and undisciplined proceedings. Some judicial districts that are not designated family court districts model selected family court practices, such as "one family-one judge" or child planning conferences.

**(b) Family Dependency/Drug Treatment Court.** Eight judicial districts have a Family Dependency/Drug Treatment Court (FDTC), which works with parents and guardians who are in danger of losing or have lost custody of their children due to abuse or neglect and

---

[1] N.C. ADMIN. OFFICE OF THE COURTS, CT. PROGRAMS & MGMT. SERVS. DIV., "2016 Annual Report on North Carolina's Unified Family Court Programs" (March 2016).

who have substance abuse issues. Participants receive support in their efforts to overcome substance abuse and to make other changes that will facilitate reunification with their children. FDTCs are grant funded and utilize existing community resources. *See* G.S. 7A-790 *et seq.*

> **Resource:** For more information, see "Family Court" and "Family Dependency/Drug Treatment Courts" on the North Carolina Administrative Office of the Courts website. Use the search box for the term "Family Court."

**2. Juvenile court sessions.** All juvenile proceedings are civil actions in district court, although they are scheduled and heard separately from other civil cases. The court may have special juvenile sessions for cases that are expected to involve lengthy hearings or for other reasons.

**3. JWise System.** JWise is the official court index of juvenile cases. It is an automated computer information system operated by the North Carolina Administrative Office of the Courts (AOC). JWise is used by multiple juvenile court officials and employees to record and access juvenile court information, manage cases, and link case outcomes from different courts. For more detailed information about JWise and other aspects of court administration, see Appendix 3 at the end of this Manual.

**4. Juvenile Rules of Recordkeeping.** The AOC issues rules that govern recordkeeping in the offices of the clerks of superior court. Chapter XII of the Rules of Recordkeeping Procedures for the Office of the Clerk of Superior Court addresses the filing system, access to and expungement of records, and related topics in juvenile proceedings. See Appendix 4 at the end of this Manual.

## B. Judicial Officials and Staff

District court judges and clerks of superior court, often through assistant and deputy clerks, are key participants in every abuse, neglect, dependency, and termination of parental rights (TPR) proceeding.

**1. Juvenile court judge.** A district court judge presides over every juvenile court proceeding, without a jury. Any district court judge may preside over abuse, neglect, dependency, and TPR actions. Assignments of judges to juvenile court are made by the chief district court judge. G.S. 7A-146(1), (7); *see* N.C. R. CIV. P. 40. In judicial districts designated as family court districts, the assignment of one judge to one family is encouraged. Other judicial districts allow for different judges to hear different types of cases for a family or different hearings that are conducted in the same action (e.g., an initial disposition hearing and a permanency planning hearing). Local rules may require or encourage the assignment of one judge to one family, regardless of whether the judicial district is a family court district.

(a) **Specialized training.** Although special training is not a prerequisite for holding juvenile court, the Administrative Office of the Courts (AOC) encourages appropriate training and provides certification to judges who complete an approved series of courses related to juvenile proceedings, satisfy experience requirements set by the AOC, and maintain a certain number of continuing judicial education hours designated as qualified courses for continued juvenile certification. *See* G.S. 7A-147.

---

**Resources:**
The website for the National Council of Juvenile and Family Court Judges is a valuable resource for publications, training opportunities, and technical assistance for juvenile court judges.

For more information about juvenile court certification, see "Juvenile Certification" on the "NC District Court Judges" microsite on the UNC School of Government website.

---

**(b) Recusal.** Recusal of a judge is not addressed in the Juvenile Code, but it is an issue that arises occasionally in abuse, neglect, dependency, and TPR proceedings. Even though the one judge-one family approach to judicial assignments for juvenile court has become more common, the issue of recusal is most likely to come up when a judge hears different proceedings involving the same family. The North Carolina Code of Judicial Conduct addresses recusal (disqualification) in Canon 3. When a party requests recusal by the trial judge, the party must demonstrate that grounds for disqualification exist. *See In re Faircloth*, 153 N.C. App. 565 (2002); *In re LaRue*, 113 N.C. App. 807 (1994). Canon 3 of the Code of Judicial Conduct states in part that a judge should disqualify himself or herself in a proceeding in which the judge's impartiality might reasonably be questioned, including a proceeding in which the judge has a personal bias or prejudice concerning a party or personal knowledge of disputed evidentiary facts concerning the proceedings. *See* N.C. CODE OF JUDICIAL CONDUCT Canon 3(C)(1)(a).

In applying this standard from Canon 3, appellate cases have not found that a judge should be recused simply because he or she presided over another case involving the same children. *See In re Z.V.A.*, 835 S.E.2d 425 (N.C. S.Ct. 2019) (reasoning a statement at the TPR hearing made by the district court judge at the last permanency planning hearing that he was willing to send the child to an out-of-state relative because he did not think the child could be with her parents was merely an explanation of the court's decision about the child's best interests at the time that decision was made, and was not a reflection that the court had reached a conclusion to terminate the parents' rights prior to the TPR hearing; a determination of judicial bias based on this statement would have the illogical consequence of a district court judge never being able to preside over a TPR after ordering a permanent plan that is compatible with the need for a TPR); *In re M.A.I.B.K.*, 184 N.C. App. 218 (2007) (holding that the trial judge who presided over the mother's TPR proceeding was not barred from presiding over the father's TPR proceeding without any showing by the father of "extraordinary circumstances," which, according to local rules, would have been the only basis for recusal of the judge); *In re Faircloth*, 153 N.C. App. 565 (2002) (holding that recusal from a TPR proceeding was not necessary for the sole reason that the judge presided over an abuse, neglect, or dependency proceeding involving the same children); *In re LaRue*, 113 N.C. App. 807 (1994) (holding that the judge did not have to recuse himself from a TPR action because he presided over an earlier review hearing).

When the issue of recusal is not raised at trial, it is not preserved for appellate review. *See In re Z.V.A.*, 835 S.E.2d 425 (N.C. S.Ct. 2019) (although not preserved for appellate review, supreme court exercised discretion under Appellate Rule of Procedure 2 to address respondents arguments raising judicial bias and recusal); *In re D.R.F.*, 204 N.C. App. 138 (2010) (holding that trial judge did not err in failing to recuse himself where the judge had no duty to recuse himself sua sponte; there was no indication of the reason for the judge's earlier recusal in another hearing; and the issue was not preserved for appeal because no motion for recusal was made in the trial court).

> **Resource:** For more information about recusal, see Michael Crowell, *Recusal*, ADMINISTRATION OF JUSTICE BULLETIN No. 2015/05 (UNC School of Government, Nov. 2015).

**2. Chief district court judge.** The chief district court judge has the authority to issue various administrative orders related to juvenile court. For example, the judge may issue an administrative order authorizing someone other than a district court judge to issue nonsecure custody orders or designating a local agency as an agency that is authorized to share confidential information relating to juveniles under G.S. 7B-3100. See Chapters 5.5.C.2 (relating to issuing nonsecure custody orders) and 14.1.E (relating to agency sharing of information). The chief district court judge may also adopt local rules addressing discovery and other procedures in juvenile proceedings. See Appendix 2 (identifying responsibilities of the chief district court judge).

**3. Juvenile court clerk.** The clerk of superior court is responsible for maintaining the official court record and generally designates one or more assistant or deputy clerks to act as juvenile court clerks. Juvenile records include paper filings, audio recordings of hearings, and an automated index of juvenile proceedings (JWise, explained further in Appendix 3). The clerk has specific statutory responsibilities related to juvenile proceedings. For example, the clerk must issue summonses, appoint provisional counsel, notify the local guardian ad litem office of a petition alleging a child's abuse or neglect, and give written notice of hearings. *See, e.g.*, G.S. 7B-406(a); 7B-408; 7B-602(a); 7B-906.1(b), (h). The clerk generally distributes the hearing calendar but does not manage it. The clerk also operates electronic recording systems for juvenile hearings and, when a case is appealed, creates duplicate recordings and delivers them to a transcriptionist.

Note that the clerk of superior court acts as the judicial official presiding over adoptions. G.S. 48-2-100; *see* G.S. 48-2-607(b). See also Chapter 10.3 (discussing adoptions).

**4. Juvenile court case manager or coordinators.** Some judicial districts have court staff whose role is to provide case management for abuse, neglect, dependency, and TPR cases. See Appendix 5, "Case Management for Abuse, Neglect, Dependency, and Termination of Parental Rights Cases in NC Juvenile Courts."

## 2.2 Key People: Who's Who in the System

### A. Introduction

Many people may become involved in an abuse, neglect, or dependency and, if applicable, termination of parental rights (TPR) proceeding, some playing a role inside the courtroom and others functioning in supporting and service roles outside the courtroom. Understanding the roles of these various people in the system is critical and can affect both the proceedings and the quality of advocacy or decision-making in a case.

The tables in a courtroom where the parties sit can get crowded, as three or more sets of people may be participating. These can include a county department of social services (DSS) attorney with the DSS caseworker(s); one or more parents, guardians, custodians, or caretakers and their attorneys; the child's guardian ad litem (GAL) team and perhaps the child himself or herself; and when applicable, a private individual or representatives of a child-placing agency seeking a TPR.

**Note,** for purposes of this Manual, "department of social services" or "DSS" refers to a department as defined by G.S. 7B-101(8a) regardless of how it is titled or structured.

Others who may play a role in the case include relatives, other caretakers or foster parents, professional service providers (related to mental and medical health, education, etc.), and law enforcement officials.

### B. The People: Explanation of Roles

**1. Social services director.** The DSS director has several duties and responsibilities that are established by statute. *See* G.S. 108A-14. Some of those responsibilities relate specifically to child welfare services, such as assessing reports of child abuse and neglect and taking steps to protect such children, supervising children's placements in foster homes, and investigating and supervising adoptive placements. G.S. 108A-14(a)(6), (11) and (12). Laws and regulations related to DSS responsibilities usually reference "the director" as the one carrying out those responsibilities.

Director is defined by the Juvenile Code as the director of the county department of social services in the county where the child resides or is found, or the director's authorized representative. G.S. 7B-101(10); *see In re A.P.*, 371 N.C. 14 (2018). The director's duties and authority to delegate responsibilities to staff are set out in G.S. 108A-14. It is understood that most responsibilities belonging to the director are carried out through an authorized representative of the director. *See In re D.D.F.*, 187 N.C. App. 388 (2007).

**2. Social services caseworkers.** DSS caseworkers screen the report and assess the case and, with others in the department, determine whether to file a petition and/or provide services to the family. Caseworkers carry out many of the statutory responsibilities of the DSS director. Caseworkers are involved in coordinating services for the family, gathering information to present in court, testifying in and making recommendations to the court, and working with and monitoring the family situation until DSS services are no longer needed.

**3. Social services attorney.** The DSS attorney works with the DSS caseworker(s) assigned to a particular case. Because DSS is the petitioner in every abuse, neglect, or dependency case and in some termination of parental rights (TPR) cases, the DSS attorney is responsible for the initial presentation of evidence at many hearings. *See* G.S. 7B-401.1(a). In addition to advising and representing DSS in individual cases, the DSS attorney may provide counsel, advice, and training about court procedures, relevant changes in the law, liability, and other matters. DSS attorneys across the state are a mix of in-house agency attorneys, county or assistant county attorneys, and private attorneys under contract to represent DSS. The source of direction and supervision a DSS attorney receives may vary depending on which arrangement is in place. Because DSS is not a legal entity separate from the county, however, the DSS attorney's ultimate client is the county.

**4. The child or juvenile.** In this Manual the terms "child" and "juvenile" are used interchangeably. The child is the subject of a report of suspected abuse, neglect, or dependency and any resulting petition filed in juvenile court. The child is also the subject of any action seeking to terminate the rights of one or both parents. In both an abuse, neglect, or dependency and TPR court action, the child is a party. G.S. 7B-401.1(f); 7B-601(a); 7B-1104. As defined by the Juvenile Code, a juvenile is anyone under the age of 18 who is not married, emancipated, or in the Armed Forces. G.S. 7B-101(14). In North Carolina, a minor—someone under the age of 18—may become emancipated in one of two ways: marriage or a court order entered in an emancipation proceeding. G.S. 7B-3500 through -3509.

The child may or may not be a source of information relating to the allegations in the petition, and may or may not be called to testify in the adjudication or disposition phases of the case. The child's age and situation, as well as local practice and the court's and parties' preferences, will influence the nature of the child's participation in the case. The Juvenile Code, however, mandates the child's involvement in certain proceedings, starting at age 12. The child's involvement may be as simple as sending notice directly to the child or as complicated as having the court question the juvenile. *See, e.g.*, 7B-906.1(b)(ii); 7B-912(d); 7B-1110(d).

In all abuse and neglect cases and in most dependency and TPR cases the child is appointed a guardian ad litem (GAL), who advocates for the child's best interests and protects the child's legal rights. G.S. 7B-601(a); 7B-1108.

See sections 2.3.C and D, below (explaining the child's rights and GAL representation).

**5. The child's guardian ad litem (GAL).** When a petition alleges that a child is abused or neglected, the court must appoint a GAL for the child; when a petition alleges only that the child is dependent, the court may appoint a GAL. A GAL is also required to represent a child who is the subject of a TPR proceeding in certain circumstances. G.S. 7B-601(a); 7B-1108.

Any time the court appoints a GAL who is not an attorney, the court also must appoint an attorney advocate to protect the child's legal interests. The child's GAL representation is by a team that consists of a GAL volunteer, local GAL program staff, and attorney advocate. The team represents the best interests of the child and protects the child's legal rights. G.S. 7B-601; 7B-1108. See section 2.3.D, below (discussing details related to the N.C. Guardian ad Litem Program and the appointment, role, and responsibilities of GALs). See Chapter 9.4.C (discussing appointment of a GAL in a TPR proceeding).

**6. Parent.** The child's parents are parties to the abuse, neglect, or dependency proceeding involving the child unless a parent's rights have been terminated or the parent has been convicted of first- or second-degree forcible rape, statutory rape of a child by an adult, or first-degree statutory rape that resulted in the child's conception. A parent who has relinquished the child for adoption ordinarily is not a party, but the court may order that he or she be made a party. G.S. 7B-401.1(b). Because abuse, neglect, and dependency cases are about the child, not "against" a parent, and because both parents' rights may be affected by the court's intervention, every effort should be made to serve both parents and involve both parents in the proceeding. A parent who had no involvement in the circumstances leading up to the petition alleging abuse, neglect, or dependency has the same rights in the action as a parent alleged in a petition to have created the child's circumstances.

A parent whose rights are sought to be terminated is named as the respondent in a TPR action.

The term "parent" is not defined in the Juvenile Code but generally is considered to be a child's legal, biological, or adoptive parent. If paternity of a child has not been established legally or if a child has both a legal and a putative father, a determination of paternity in the juvenile proceeding may be necessary. *See* G.S. 7B-506(h)(1); 7B-800.1; 7B-901(b) (requiring the court to inquire about efforts to identify and locate missing parents and to establish paternity if paternity is an issue and authorizing the court to order that specific efforts be made). See Chapter 5.4.B.7 (discussing paternity).

See section 2.4, below (related to parent's rights).

**7. Parent's attorney.** In juvenile proceedings each parent has a statutory right to counsel and to court-appointed counsel if indigent, unless the parent knowingly and voluntarily waives that right. G.S. 7B-602; 7B-1101.1. *See also Lassiter v. Dep't of Social Services*, 452 U.S. 18 (1981) (holding that the Due Process Clause of the U.S. Constitution does not require appointment of counsel for indigent parents in every TPR case and discussing the analysis for determining on a case-by-case basis whether appointment of counsel is constitutionally required). The parent's attorney represents the expressed interests of the parent.

See section 2.4.D, below (discussing court-appointed counsel for respondent parents).

**8. Parent's guardian ad litem.** The Juvenile Code requires the appointment of a guardian ad litem (GAL) pursuant to Rule 17 of the Rules of Civil Procedure for a parent who is an unemancipated minor. The court has discretion to appoint a Rule 17 GAL for an adult parent who is incompetent. A Rule 17 GAL is not the same as the child's GAL appointed under G.S. 7B-601 and has no affiliation with the N.C. Guardian ad Litem Program.

See section 2.4.F, below (discussing GALs for respondent parents in abuse, neglect, or dependency cases), and Chapter 9.4.B (discussing GALs for respondent parents in TPR actions).

**9. Custodians, guardians, and caretakers.** Often people other than a child's parents are responsible for or involved with caring for the child. The Juvenile Code classifies these persons for purposes of determining their legal role and significance in an abuse, neglect, or dependency proceeding as "custodians", "guardians", or "caretakers". It is important to understand the definition of each term to determine which applies in a particular circumstance. *See In re M.S.*, 247 N.C. App. 89 (2016) (holding that stepparent who did not adopt the child or have an order awarding him custody of the child was a caretaker, not a parent or custodian, and thus was not entitled to appeal under G.S. 7B-1002). A custodian, guardian, or caretaker who is a party to the case has many but not all of the same rights as a parent. For example, only parents have a statutory right to appointed counsel if indigent. However, the Office of Indigent Defense Services has a policy addressing the payment of counsel for non-parents when a court appoints an attorney after finding constitutional due process requires such appointment.

> **Resource:** N.C. OFFICE OF INDIGENT DEFENSE SERVICES, "Appointment of Counsel for Non-Parent Respondents in Abuse, Neglect, and Dependency Proceedings" (July 2, 2008).

For more information on the role and status of persons who become custodians and guardians as a result of dispositional hearings, see Chapter 7.4.E and 7.10.B.4 (custodians) and 7.4.F and 7.10.B.3 (guardians).

**(a) Custodian.** The Juvenile Code defines custodian as a person or agency that has been awarded legal custody of the child by a court. G.S. 7B-101(8). The custodian of a child at the time a petition is filed is a party to the abuse, neglect, or dependency action; however, the court may remove a custodian as a party when the court finds both that the person does not have legal rights that may be affected by the action and that the person's continuation as a party is not necessary to meet the juvenile's needs. G.S. 7B-401.1(d), (g). The failure to make both findings before removing a custodian who was a party from the proceeding is reversible error. *In re J.R.S.*, 813 S.E.2d 283 (N.C. Ct. App. 2018) (reversing and remanding the order removing grandparents who were custodians through a Chapter 50 order when the neglect and dependency action was initiated; noting that due to the Chapter 50 custody order awarding legal and physical to grandparents, the district court hearing the juvenile proceeding in its discretion may be prevented from making the first finding required by G.S. 7B-401.1(g)).

A person who was not a party to the case initially but who becomes the child's custodian through an order that awards custody of the child to that person and finds it is the permanent plan automatically becomes a party to the proceeding. G.S. 7B-401.1(d). See Chapter 7.10.B.4 (discussing custody as permanent plan).

**(b) Guardian.** Guardian is not defined in the Juvenile Code. Instead, the statute that addresses the appointment of a guardian specifies the guardian's rights and responsibilities. *See* G.S.

7B-600. In an abuse, neglect, or dependency proceeding, the court may appoint a guardian of the person for the juvenile when no parent appears in a hearing with the juvenile or any time the court finds it would be in the best interests of the juvenile. The guardian operates under the supervision of the court and has the care, custody, and control of the juvenile or may arrange a suitable placement for the juvenile. The guardian also has the authority to consent to certain types of actions for the juvenile that are specified in G.S. 7B-600(a). See Chapter 7.4.F (detailing the appointment and duties of a guardian).

A guardian also includes a guardian of the person or general guardian appointed to the juvenile pursuant to G.S. Chapter 35A by the clerk of superior court. The clerk's authority to appoint a guardian of the person or a general guardian for a minor is limited to when the minor has no natural guardian or pursuant to a standby guardianship. G.S. 35A-1221; 35A-1224(a); 35A-1370 through -1382.

A person who is the child's court-appointed guardian of the person or general guardian at the time the petition is filed is a party to the abuse, neglect, or dependency action. G.S. 7B-401.1(c). The court may remove a guardian as a party when the court finds both that the person does not have legal rights that may be affected by the action and that the person's continuation as a party is not necessary to meet the juvenile's needs. G.S. 7B-401.1(g). The failure to make both findings before removing a guardian(s) who was a party from the proceeding is reversible error. *See In re J.R.S.*, 813 S.E.2d 283 (N.C. Ct. App. 2018) (reversing and remanding the order removing grandparents who were custodians through a Chapter 50 order when the neglect and dependency action was initiated; noting that due to the Chapter 50 order awarded legal and physical custody to the grandparents, the district court hearing the juvenile proceeding in its discretion may be prevented from making the first finding required by G.S. 7B-401.1(g)).

A person who was not a party to the case initially but who is appointed as the child's guardian pursuant to G.S. 7B-600 automatically becomes a party if the court finds the guardianship is the permanent plan for the child. G.S. 7B-401.1(c). See Chapter 7.10.B.3 (discussing guardianship as permanent plan).

**(c) Caretaker.** A caretaker is any person, other than a parent, guardian, or custodian, who has responsibility for the health and welfare of a juvenile in a residential setting. This may be

- a stepparent,
- a foster parent,
- an adult member of the juvenile's household,
- an adult entrusted with the juvenile's care,
- a potential adoptive parent during a visit or trial placement for a juvenile who is in DSS custody,
- a house parent or cottage parent in a residential child care or educational facility, or
- any employee or volunteer of a division, institution, or school operated by the Department of Health and Human Services.

G.S. 7B-101(3).

The definition of caretaker involving an adult member of the juvenile's household was amended by S.L. 2019-245, effective December 1, 2019. Prior to this effective date, a caretaker included an "adult relative entrusted with the juvenile's care," but the relative relationship has now been removed. Regarding the adult relative, the North Carolina Supreme Court addressed how to determine whether an adult relative is "entrusted with the juvenile's care" such that caretaker status attaches warranting government interference with the parent-child relationship in *In re R.R.N.*, 368 N.C. 167 (2015). The supreme court examined the purposes of the Juvenile Code and the definition of caretaker and described the categories of persons identified in the caretaker statute as those with "significant, parental-type responsibility for the daily care of the child." *In re R.R.N.*, 368 N.C. at 170. The trial court (and although not addressed by the supreme court, DSS) must consider the totality of the circumstances and whether the relative has significant parent-type responsibility for the child when determining whether the person alleged to have created the child's circumstances as abused or neglected is a caretaker. Factors to be considered include the duration, frequency, and location of the care provided as well as the level of decision-making authority given to the adult relative by the parent. In applying the totality of the circumstances test to the adult relative, who was the juvenile's stepfather's cousin, the supreme court held that he was not entrusted with the juvenile's care while supervising a one-night sleepover in his home. Although the relative was responsible for ensuring the juvenile's short-term safety, he was not given significant parent-like responsibility of the juvenile and was not a caretaker within the meaning of the statute. *In re R.R.N.*, 368 N.C. 167. To comply with the purposes of the Juvenile Code that same analysis would apply to an adult entrusted with the juvenile's care.

A caretaker is a party to the abuse, neglect, or dependency action only if the petition includes allegations relating to the caretaker, the caretaker has assumed the status and obligation of a parent, or the court orders that the caretaker be made a party. G.S. 7B-401.1(e). A caretaker may be removed as a party when the court finds the person does not have legal rights that may be affected by the action and that the person's continuation as a party is not necessary to meet the juvenile's needs. G.S. 7B-401.1(g). A caretaker does not have all the same rights in the proceeding as a parent, guardian, or custodian. For example, a caretaker does not have standing to appeal any order entered in the abuse, neglect, or dependency action. G.S. 7B-1002(4) (authorizing appeals by a nonprevailing party who is a parent, guardian, or custodian but not a caretaker); *In re M.S.*, 247 N.C. App. 89 (2016) (dismissing appeal brought by stepparent who was a caretaker for lack of standing).

**Practice Note:** Caretakers generally do not have a right to intervene in an abuse, neglect, or dependency action. G.S. 7B-401.1(h); *but see* G.S. 7B-401.1(e1) (addressing foster parents). It is unclear whether the language of G.S. 7B-401.1(e)(iii), which allows for a caretaker to be made a party when ordered by the court, results from a non-party caretaker seeking that status or only from the district court acting sua sponte or in response to a motion made by an existing party in the action.

Prior to January 1, 2016, a "caretaker" also included any person responsible for caring for a child in a child care facility as defined in G.S. 110-86. Now, such person is a "caregiver" who is subject to reports of suspected "child maltreatment" occurring in a child care facility that are made to and investigated by the N.C. Department of Health and Human Services Division of Early Education and Child Development. *See* S.L. 2015-123.

**Resources:**
For more information about determining caretaker status, see Sara DePasquale, *Who Is a "Caretaker" in Child Abuse and Neglect Cases?*, UNC SCH. OF GOV'T: ON THE CIVIL SIDE BLOG (Sept. 2, 2015).

For more information about child maltreatment occurring in a child care facility, see
- Sara DePasquale, *The New Law Addressing Child Maltreatment in Child Care Facilities: It's the State's Responsibility*, UNC SCH. OF GOV'T: ON THE CIVIL SIDE BLOG (Jan. 6, 2016).
- SARA DEPASQUALE, *Suspected Child Maltreatment Occurring in a Child Care Facility* (UNC School of Government, 2016), CH. 13A *in* JANET MASON, REPORTING CHILD ABUSE AND NEGLECT IN NORTH CAROLINA (UNC School of Government, 3d ed. 2013).

**10. Relatives.** Both maternal and paternal relatives may play an important role in the child's life as a resource for support and/or placement. DSS is required to make diligent efforts to notify relatives that the child is placed out of the home and determine whether a relative is willing and able to be an appropriate placement or resource support (e.g., supervise visitation). The court must order placement with a relative who is willing and able to provide proper care and supervision to the child in a safe home unless the court finds it would be contrary to the child's best interests. *See* G.S. 7B-505(b); 7B-506(h)(2); 7B-800.1(a)(4); 7B-901(b); 7B-903(a)(4), (a1). *See also* G.S. 7B-101(19) (definition of "safe home"). If a child is placed with a relative, that relative who is providing care to the child must receive notice of and may be heard in review and permanency planning hearings. G.S.7B-906.1(b)(iv), (c).

Relative is not defined by the Juvenile Code. For guidance, the N.C. Department of Health and Human Services Division of Social Services Child Welfare Manual refers to federal law, which identifies adult grandparents, all parents with legal custody of a sibling of a child, and other adult relatives including those suggested by the parents. Additionally, for relative notification, the Permanency Planning section of the Child Welfare Manual identifies adult relatives and kin suggested by the parents; adult maternal and paternal grandparents, aunts, uncles, siblings, great grandparents, nieces and nephews; and a custodial parent of a sibling. The Cross-Function section of the Child Welfare Manual, for purposes of a conflict of interest, further identifies relatives as birth and adoptive parents, blood and half-blood siblings, grandparents (including great and great-great), aunt and uncle (including great and great-great), nephew, niece, first cousin, stepparent, stepsibling, and the spouse of each of these relatives. *See* DIV. OF SOC. SERVS., N.C. DEP'T OF HEALTH & HUMAN SERVICES, CHILD WELFARE MANUAL, available here.

**11. Nonrelative kin.** The Juvenile Code defines nonrelative kin as (1) an individual having a substantial relationship with the juvenile or (2) for a juvenile who is a member of a State-recognized Indian tribe, an individual who is a member of any State-recognized or federally recognized Indian tribe regardless of whether there is a substantial relationship with the juvenile. G.S. 7B-101(15a). Nonrelative kin may also be referred to as "fictive kin."

The court may consider placing a juvenile with nonrelative kin. G.S. 7B-505(c); 7B-506(h)(2a); *see* G.S. 7B-903(a)(4) (referring to "suitable person"). If a child is placed with nonrelative kin, that nonrelative kin who is providing care to the child must receive notice of and may be heard in review and permanency planning hearings. G.S.7B-906.1(b)(iv), (c).

**12. Foster parents.** Foster parents play a crucial role in an abuse, neglect, or dependency case. They provide substitute care to a child who has been separated from his or her family due to abuse, neglect, or dependency and placed with the foster parents by DSS or the court. The Juvenile Code does not define foster parent; however, the laws governing foster care licensing define a "foster parent" as any individual who is 21 years of age or older and licensed by the State to provide foster care. G.S. 131D-10.2(9a). "Foster care", "family foster care", and "therapeutic foster care" are defined at G.S. 131D-10.2(9), (8), and (14) respectively.

A foster parent is not a party to the abuse, neglect, or dependency proceeding. However, a foster parent may be allowed to intervene when he or she has the authority (or standing) to file a TPR petition (or motion). G.S.7B-401.1(e1). Although not a party, foster parents who are providing care to the child must receive notice of and may be heard in review and permanency planning hearings. G.S. 7B-906.1(b)(iv), (c); *In re J.L.*, 826 S.E.2d 258 (N.C. Ct. App. 2019) (discussing foster parents' participation in the hearing with attorney representation; holding no abuse of discretion). When a child's permanent plan is adoption, if a foster parent who wishes to adopt the child is not selected by DSS, the foster parent has a right to notice of the selected prospective adoptive parent and the right to seek a judicial review of that selection. G.S. 7B-1112.1. See Chapter 10.3.B (relating to selection of prospective adoptive parent).

**Resource:** For more information about the rights and role of a foster parent in the court proceeding, see Sara DePasquale, *What Is the Role of a Foster Parent in the A/N/D Court Action?*, UNC SCH. OF GOV'T: ON THE CIVIL SIDE BLOG (Sept. 30, 2015).

**13. Law enforcement.** It is not uncommon for law enforcement to be the source of reports to DSS of a child's suspected abuse, neglect, or dependency. *See* G.S. 7B-301; 14-204(c); 14-318.6(g) (S.L. 2019-245, effective December 1, 2019). A DSS assessment may reveal facts that DSS is required to report to law enforcement, which then has a duty to initiate a criminal investigation. *See* G.S. 7B-307. See also Chapter 5.1.F (discussing law enforcement involvement in the pre-adjudication stage of a case). At the request of DSS, law enforcement officers are required to assist DSS in the assessment and evaluation of the seriousness of a report. G.S. 7B-302(a), (e). Sometimes law enforcement and DSS coordinate interviews and other aspects of the criminal investigation and social services assessment, and in some counties the agencies have developed protocols to facilitate this type of coordination.

**14. District attorney or prosecutor.** In some circumstances, DSS must notify the prosecutor regarding information it obtains. *See* G.S. 7B-307. Whether criminal charges will be filed is always up to the prosecutor. In addition, the prosecutor may be contacted by the person making the report of a child's suspected abuse, neglect, or dependency to request review of a DSS decision not to file a petition. G.S. 7B-302(g); 7B-305; 7B-306. See Chapter 5.1.E (discussing review by a prosecutor of a DSS decision not to file a petition).

**15. Other professionals and their agencies.** Often various professionals and agencies are involved in evaluating or treating children or parents. Agencies and individuals also may be involved in caring for a child or assisting the parent in addressing issues related to employment, housing, education, etc. Professionals and individuals who speak on behalf of agencies are not parties to the proceedings and generally are not subject to orders of the court absent specific statutory authority. They may be subpoenaed as witnesses or called on to provide affidavits, written reports, or other information. See Chapter 14 (relating to laws governing confidentiality and disclosure of information in abuse, neglect, or dependency cases). If qualified as experts, professionals may also be called on to provide expert opinion testimony. See Chapter 11.10 (relating to expert testimony).

**16. Persons involved in other court proceedings affecting the family.** Parents and children involved in an abuse, neglect, or dependency case may also be involved in juvenile delinquency or undisciplined proceedings, adult criminal court proceedings, domestic violence actions, child support proceedings, or other court actions. In those situations, there may be juvenile court counselors, probation officers, domestic violence counselors, and others with an interest in the abuse, neglect, or dependency case that have information that might assist the juvenile court. See Chapter 3.6 (discussing overlapping proceedings).

## 2.3 The Child

### A. Introduction

An abuse, neglect, or dependency case centers around the child, starting with cause to suspect that the child is abused, neglected, or dependent. For reports that are screened in, DSS completes an assessment that results in its determination as to whether the child is abused, neglected, and/or dependent and if so, whether services and/or court action is needed to protect the child. When court action is taken, in every abuse, neglect, or dependency proceeding, the child is a party and has rights designated in the Juvenile Code. Additionally, the child has constitutional rights, which are recognized by the Juvenile Code but are not specified. In some cases, termination of parental rights (TPR) is necessary. The child is the subject of the TPR proceeding, is a party, and has rights that are impacted in that proceeding as well.

### B. Definitions of Abused, Neglected, or Dependent Juveniles

Children who are the subject of abuse, neglect, or dependency cases must meet the statutory definitions of abused, neglected, or dependent juveniles. Children who do not meet those definitions will not be the subject of a DSS assessment or resulting abuse, neglect, or dependency petition in district court. When a court action is filed, if the court is unable to conclude by clear and convincing evidence that the child is abused, neglected, or dependent, it must dismiss the petition with prejudice, thereby ending both court and DSS involvement. When a court adjudicates a child abused, neglected, or dependent, the action proceeds to disposition, where the child's best interests are the paramount consideration for the court.

See Chapters 5.1 (discussing mandated reporting and the DSS assessment of a report); 5.3.A (discussing the initiation of court action); 6.3 (discussing evidence and proof at an adjudication hearing); and 7 (discussing the various dispositional hearings and options).

The first question for DSS is whether the child meets the statutory criteria of an abused, neglected, or dependent juvenile. One important component of each definition is the role of the adult who creates the child's condition. That role is limited to a parent, guardian, custodian, or caretaker (discussed in sections 2.2.B.6 and 9, above). For both abuse and neglect, there is one exception to the relationship requirement – any minor victim of human trafficking falls under the definition of abuse and neglect. In other words, a minor victim of human trafficking meets the statutory criteria for both abuse and neglect without regard to who created that child's victimization.

1. **Abused juvenile.** An abused juvenile is defined as any juvenile less than 18 years of age who

    - is found to be a minor victim of human trafficking or
    - whose parent, guardian, custodian, or caretaker engages in certain conduct resulting in harm or risk of harm to the child.

    G.S. 7B-101(1).

(a) **Minor victim of human trafficking.** The laws defining human trafficking are codified in North Carolina's criminal statutes – specifically, G.S. 14-43.10 through -43.20. Human trafficking includes both sexual servitude and involuntary servitude; however, there are three separate crimes – human trafficking (G.S. 14-43.11), involuntary servitude (G.S. 14-43.12; *see* G.S. 14-43.10(a)(3) for definition), and sexual servitude (G.S. 14-43.13; *see* G.S. 14-43.10(a)(5) for definition). A "minor" is defined as a person who is younger than 18 years old. G.S. 14-43.10(a)(4). A "victim" is a person who is subjected to human trafficking, involuntary servitude, or sexual servitude. G.S. 14-43.10(a)(6).

Effective October 1, 2018, a minor victim of human trafficking must be alleged to be abused and neglected. G.S. 14-43.15. Any juvenile who is found to be a minor victim of human trafficking is an abused juvenile. G.S. 7B-101(1)(i). There is no required relationship between the juvenile and person who created (or allowed for the creation of) the juvenile's circumstance as a victim of human trafficking, involuntary servitude, or sexual servitude. The role of the parent, guardian, custodian, or caretaker is not considered. This expanded definition of abused juvenile was added to the Juvenile Code as required by the federal Justice for Victims of Trafficking Act (discussed in Chapter 1.3.B.11).

The definition of abused juvenile also includes a juvenile whose parent, guardian, custodian, or caretaker commits or allowed to be committed against the child an offense of human trafficking, involuntary servitude, or sexual servitude. G.S. 7B-101(1)(ii)g.

Under this particular subsection of abused juvenile, the role of the parent, guardian, custodian, or caretaker is relevant. This definition was enacted in 2013 (prior to the federal Justice for Victims Trafficking Act) and was not repealed with the 2018 amendment. Although this more restrictive definition still applies, a juvenile may be alleged to be abused under the more expansive definition of abused juvenile set forth at G.S. 7B-101(1)(i).

---

**Resource**: For more information about minors and human trafficking, see Margaret Henderson, Sara DePasquale, Nancy Hagan, Christy Croft, *Human Trafficking of Minors and Young Adults: What Local Governments Need to Know*, PUBLIC MANAGEMENT BULLETIN No. 2019/18 (UNC School of Government, Dec. 2019).

---

**(b) Conduct by parent, guardian, custodian, or caretaker.** Other than minor victims of human trafficking, conduct that results in a child's status as an abused juvenile as defined by the Juvenile Code includes the action or inaction of a parent, guardian, custodian, or caretaker. The same conduct by someone else may well be deemed abusive in other legal contexts (such as criminal court), but the fact that the harm or risk of harm is caused by the conduct of a parent, guardian, custodian, or caretaker is what makes the child's condition subject to the provisions of the Juvenile Code. While abuse (other than human trafficking) always involves a parent, guardian, custodian, or caretaker, it may involve other people as well. For example, abuse may arise when a parent allows someone else to inflict a non-accidental injury on a child or when a parent creates a substantial risk of serious injury by leaving the child with someone the parent knows to be violent. *See, e.g., In re L.C.*, 253 N.C. App. 67 (2017) (facts involved mother whose infant was severely injured after mother allowed the infant to be in the care of an adult that mother previously agreed the infant would not have contact with due to previous non-accidental injuries to the child while in the presence of this other adult).

**(c) Serious physical injury.** Abuse includes inflicting or allowing to be inflicted on the juvenile a serious physical injury by other than accidental means or creating or allowing to be created a substantial risk of serious physical injury to the juvenile by other than accidental means. G.S. 7B-101(1)(ii)a. and b. The Juvenile Code does not define "serious physical injury." In the criminal context, it is defined as "[p]hysical injury that causes great pain and suffering. The term includes serious mental injury." G.S. 14-318.4(d)(2). Whether the injury is "serious" must be determined on the facts of each case. *See, e.g., In re A.N.L.*, 213 N.C. App. 266 (2011) (holding that respondent mother's decision to enter into a physical altercation with her boyfriend while holding infant created a substantial risk of serious physical injury to the child); *In re C.M.*, 198 N.C. App. 53 (2009) (affirming adjudication of abuse based on head trauma caused by a blow to the head). The Juvenile Code does not require the cause of the serious injuries to be explained. *See In re L.Z.A.*, 249 N.C. App. 628 (2016) (affirming abuse adjudication where the findings of fact established the pre-mobile infant sustained multiple fractures and a subdural hematoma when she was in her parents' sole custody and an expert witness testified were likely the result of non-accidental trauma).

**(d) Cruelty.** Abuse includes using or allowing to be used on the juvenile cruel or grossly inappropriate procedures or devices to modify the child's behavior. G.S. 7B-101(1)(ii)c. This part of the abuse definition has not been relied on often, perhaps because it overlaps with the part of the neglect definition that refers to improper discipline or the part of the abuse definition that refers to serious physical injury or emotional abuse. However, it has been used more recently. In the case *In re H.H.*, 237 N.C. App. 431 (2014), the court of appeals examined this definition of abuse and affirmed the trial court's abuse adjudication after determining that sufficient findings were made that the mother struck her 8-year-old child five times with a belt, leaving multiple bruises on the inside and outside of his legs that were still visible the next day, and the child described "a beating." The statutory criteria looks to the devices or procedures used and not the child's behavior that is sought to be corrected. *See In re F.C.D.*, 244 N.C. App. 243 (2015) (affirming abuse adjudication).

**(e) Sexual abuse and other crimes against the child.** Abuse includes committing, permitting, or encouraging the commission of a violation of any of the following laws related to sexual abuse *by, with, or upon* the juvenile:

- first- or second-degree forcible rape (G.S. 14-27.21; 14-27.22);
- statutory rape of a child by an adult (G.S. 14-27.23);
- first-degree statutory rape (G.S. 14-27.24);
- first- or second-degree forcible sexual offense (G.S. 14-27.26; 14-27.27);
- statutory sexual offense with a child by an adult (G.S. 14-27.28);
- first-degree statutory sexual offense (G.S. 14-27.29);
- sexual activity by a substitute parent or custodian (G.S. 14-27.31);
- sexual activity with a student (G.S. 14-27.32);
- crime against nature (G.S. 14-177);
- incest (G.S. 14-178) (familial relationships include grandparent, grandchild, parent, child, stepchild, legally adopted child, brother, sister, half-brother, half-sister, uncle, aunt, niece, or nephew);
- preparation of obscene photographs, slides, or motion pictures of the juvenile (G.S. 14-190.5);
- employing or permitting the juvenile to assist in a violation of the obscenity laws (G.S. 14-190.6);
- dissemination of obscene material to the juvenile (G.S. 14-190.7; 14-190.8);
- displaying or disseminating material harmful to the juvenile (G.S. 14-190.14; 14-190.15);
- first or second degree sexual exploitation of the juvenile (G.S. 14-190.16; 14-190.17);
- promoting the prostitution of the juvenile (G.S. 14-205.3(b); note that the juvenile is a minor victim of human trafficking; *see* G.S. 14-43.10(a)(4)–(6); 14-43.15);
- taking indecent liberties with the juvenile (G.S. 14-202.1); or
- unlawful sale, surrender, or purchase of a minor (G.S. 14-43.14).

G.S. 7B-101(1)(ii)d.

A juvenile who commits a violation of one of the designated crimes is an abused juvenile when a parent, guardian, custodian, or caretaker permits the juvenile's commission of a designated crime. *In re M.A.E.*, 242 N.C. App. 312 (2015) (originally unpublished July 21, 2015, but subsequently published) (affirming abuse adjudication of older brother (and younger sister) based on findings that older brother sexually abused his sister after respondents learned of the abuse and failed to take appropriate measures to protect the sister).

Harmful conduct that does not fall under one of these laws may constitute abuse under another part of the abuse definition or may be considered neglect.

**Resource:** For information on crimes listed above, see JESSICA SMITH, NORTH CAROLINA CRIMES: A GUIDEBOOK ON THE ELEMENTS OF CRIME (UNC School of Government, 7th ed. 2012) and 2018 CUMULATIVE SUPPLEMENT TO NORTH CAROLINA CRIMES (UNC School of Government, 2019).

**(f) Emotional abuse.** Abuse includes creating or allowing to be created serious emotional damage to the juvenile. Serious emotional damage is evidenced by a juvenile's severe anxiety, depression, withdrawal, or aggressive behavior toward himself or others. G.S. 7B-101(1)(ii)e. Few cases go into court solely on the basis of emotional abuse. This may be because it is difficult to determine the precise cause of a child's behavior and emotional state. The statutory criteria does not require that the juvenile have a formal psychiatric diagnosis of any of the psychological conditions set out in the statute. *In re A.M.*, 247 N.C. App. 672 (2016) (affirming abuse adjudication where findings showed the 16-year-old child had anxiety, felt hopeless, and her coping mechanism was to emotionally withdraw as a result of her mother's behavior toward her).

**(g) Encouraging or approving delinquent acts.** Abuse includes encouraging, directing, or approving of delinquent acts involving moral turpitude committed by the juvenile. G.S. 7B-101(1)(ii)f. "Moral turpitude" is not defined in the Juvenile Code; however, illegality is not equated with moral turpitude. *In re M.G.*, 187 N.C. App. 536, 551 (2007) (rejecting the argument that illegal substance abuse is an act of moral turpitude), *rev'd in part on other grounds*, 363 N.C. 570 (2009). Acts involving moral turpitude include "act[s] of baseness, vileness, or depravity in the private and social duties that a man owes to his fellowman or to society in general." *In re M.G.*, 187 N.C. App. at 551 (quoting *Dew v. State ex rel. N.C. Dep't of Motor Vehicles*, 127 N.C. App. 309, 311 (1997)). Moral turpitude is also considered "[c]onduct that is contrary to justice, honesty, or morality." *In re M.G.*, 187 N.C. App. at 551 (citing BLACK'S LAW DICTIONARY 1030 (8th ed. 2004)). A "delinquent act" is not defined by the Juvenile Code but a "delinquent juvenile" is defined at G.S. 7B-1501(7); *see also* G.S. 143B-805(6) (definition of "delinquent juvenile").

**Legislative Note:** The Juvenile Justice Reinvestment Act (S.L. 2017-57, sec. 16.D.4, amended by S.L. 2019-186) raises the age of criminal responsibility from 16 to 18 years of age for offenses committed on or after December 1, 2019. Juvenile court jurisdiction will apply to juveniles who are younger than 16 years of age when committing a crime or an infraction and to juveniles who are 16 or 17 years of age when committing a crime or an infraction other than a violation of the motor vehicle laws. The definition of "delinquent juvenile" reflects that change, effective December 1, 2019. The legislation is commonly referred to as "raise the age."

**Resources:**
For more information about the new legislation, see
- Jacquelyn Greene, *Raise the Age FAQs*, UNC SCH. OF GOV'T: ON THE CIVIL SIDE BLOG (Oct. 22, 2019).
- JACQUELYN GREENE, JUVENILE JUSTICE REINVESTMENT ACT IMPLEMENTATION GUIDE (UNC School of Government, 2019).

**(h) Failure to prevent harm.** The language "allows to be" in the definition of abuse in various subsections of G.S. 7B-101(1)(ii) means that inaction can constitute abuse. Failure to prevent harm or allowing situations to occur that create a serious risk of harm may be abuse. *See, e.g., In re M.A.E.*, 242 N.C. App. 312 (2015) (originally unpublished July 21, 2015, but subsequently published) (affirming abuse adjudication where respondents permitted older sibling to sexually abuse younger sibling); *In re Adcock*, 69 N.C. App. 222 (1984) (affirming TPR where evidence showed that mother failed to intervene in another adult's abusive conduct toward the child).

For a discussion of case law related to evidence to show abuse, see Chapter 6.3.D.

**2. Neglected juvenile.** A neglected juvenile is one who

- is found to be a minor victim of human trafficking;
- does not receive proper care, supervision, or discipline from the juvenile's parent, guardian, custodian, or caretaker;
- has been abandoned;
- is not provided necessary medical or remedial care;
- lives in an environment injurious to his or her welfare;
- custody of whom has been unlawfully transferred (*see* G.S. 14-321.2, effective for offenses committed on or after December 1, 2016); or
- has been placed for care or adoption in violation of the law.

G.S. 7B-101(15).

In determining whether a child is neglected, it is relevant whether that child lives in a home where another child has died as a result of suspected abuse or neglect or where another child has been subjected to abuse or neglect by an adult who regularly lives in the home. G.S. 7B-101(15). A prior neglect (or abuse) adjudication alone is not determinative or sufficient; instead, the trial court has discretion to determine how much weight to give to evidence of a prior adjudication. *In re J.A.M.*, 822 S.E.2d 693 (N.C. S.Ct. 2019); *In re S.G.*, 835 S.E.2d 479 (N.C. Ct. App. 2019).

Although not in the statute, case law requires that the child experience some physical, mental, or emotional impairment or substantial risk of such impairment as a result of the neglect. *In re J.A.M.*, 822 S.E.2d 693; *In re Stumbo*, 357 N.C. 279 (2003). *See also In re F.S.*, 835 S.E.2d 465 (N.C. Ct. App. 2019); *In re J.R.*, 243 N.C. App. 309 (2015); *In re J.W.*, 241 N.C. App. 44 (2015); *In re A.B.*, 179 N.C. App. 605 (2006); *In re McLean*, 135 N.C. App. 387 (1999) (all emphasizing the need to find some physical, mental, or emotional impairment of the child or a substantial risk of such impairment).

In determining whether the juvenile is neglected, DSS and the court should consider the totality of the evidence. *In re L.T.R.*, 181 N.C. App. 376 (2007).

For additional case law related to evidence to show neglect, see Chapter 6.3.E.

(a) **Lack of care, supervision, or discipline.** A juvenile is neglected if he or she does not receive proper care, supervision, or discipline from the juvenile's parent, guardian, custodian, or caretaker. G.S. 7B-101(15). The effect the conduct has or could have on the child is key to a determination of neglect. *See In re K.J.D.*, 203 N.C. App. 653 (2010) (affirming neglect adjudication of child who was receiving proper care in a kinship placement because the child would be at substantial risk of harm if either parent removed the child from the placement); *In re Everette*, 133 N.C. App. 84 (1999) (vacating an adjudication of neglect because the court failed to make findings that the child was impaired or at substantial risk of impairment due to lack of care, supervision, or discipline). *See also In re J.A.M.*, 822 S.E.2d 693 (N.C. S.Ct. 2019); *In re J.R.*, 243 N.C. App. 309 (2015); *In re J.W.*, 241 N.C. App. 44 (2015); *In re A.B.*, 179 N.C. App. 605 (2006); *In re McLean*, 135 N.C. App. 387 (1999) (all emphasizing the need to find some physical, mental, or emotional impairment of the child or a substantial risk of such impairment). An explicit finding about the detrimental effect of improper care is not required, however, if the evidence supports such a finding. *See In re C.C.*, 817 S.E.2d 894 (N.C. Ct. App. 2018); *In re H.N.D.*, 364 N.C. 597, *rev'g per curiam for reasons stated in the dissent* 205 N.C. App. 702 (2010).

Lack of proper discipline may include improper (i.e., inappropriate) discipline that does not rise to the level of causing serious physical injury or involve the use of cruel or grossly inappropriate procedures or devices (in which case it would be abuse). However, defining what is improper care or discipline is difficult since beliefs about proper care and discipline can vary widely. For a discussion of case law addressing evidence to establish improper care, supervision, or discipline, see Chapter 6.3.E.2.

(b) **Abandonment.** A juvenile who has been abandoned is considered neglected. G.S. 7B-101(15). Abandonment may be the culmination of a parent's long-term failure to perform his or her parental responsibilities. It has been described as "willful or intentional conduct" that "evinces a settled purpose to forego all parental duties and relinquish all parental claims to the child." *Pratt v. Bishop*, 257 N.C. 486, 501 (1962). A parent abandons a child and relinquishes all parental claims when the parent withholds their love, care, and presence; foregoes the opportunity to display filial affection; and does not provide support and maintenance. *In re C.B.C.*, 832 S.E.2d 692 (N.C. S.Ct. 2019); *In re E.H.P.*, 831 S.E.2d 49 (N.C. S.Ct. 2019); *Pratt v. Bishop*, 257 N.C. 486; *see also In re Adoption of Searle*, 82 N.C. App. 273, 275 (1986).

Abandonment also may be a one-time act, such as leaving an infant at a hospital or fire station under North Carolina's infant safe surrender law. *See* G.S. 7B-500 (temporary custody of infant less than 7 days of age). See Chapters 5.5.B.3 (discussing infant "safe surrender" in North Carolina) and 9.11.G (discussing abandonment as a ground for termination of parental rights).

**(c) Lack of medical or remedial care.** A juvenile is considered neglected if he or she is not provided necessary medical or remedial care. G.S. 7B-101(15). The Juvenile Code provides no guidance on the meaning of necessary medical or remedial care, nor does it make reference to parents' religious beliefs as a basis for withholding treatment. Although limited and fact-specific, some case law addresses what does or does not constitute necessary remedial or medical care. See Chapter 6.3.E.2(e) (relating to evidence of lack of remedial or medical care).

**(d) Injurious environment.** A juvenile is neglected if he or she lives in an environment that is injurious to the juvenile's welfare. G.S. 7B-101(15). This may be an environment that puts the child at substantial risk of harm as well as one in which the child actually has been harmed. *See In re Safriet*, 112 N.C. App. 747 (1993). See Chapter 6.3.E.2 (relating to evidence for finding neglect, including cases discussing injurious environment).

**(e) Minor victim of human trafficking.** The laws defining human trafficking are codified in North Carolina's criminal statutes – specifically, G.S. 14-43.10 through -43.20. Human trafficking includes both sexual servitude and involuntary servitude; however, there are three separate crimes – human trafficking (G.S. 14-43.11), involuntary servitude (G.S. 14-43.12; *see* G.S. 14-43.10(a)(3) for definition), and sexual servitude (G.S. 14-43.13; *see* G.S. 14-43.10(a)(5) for definition). A "minor" is defined as a person who is younger than 18 years old. G.S. 14-43.10(a)(4). A "victim" is a person who is subjected to human trafficking, involuntary servitude, or sexual servitude. G.S. 14-43.10(a)(6).

Effective October 1, 2018, a minor victim of human trafficking must be alleged to be abused and neglected. G.S. 14-43.15. Any juvenile who is found to be a minor victim of human trafficking is a neglected juvenile. G.S. 7B-101(15)(i). There is no required relationship between the juvenile and person who created (or allowed for the creation of) the juvenile's circumstance as a victim of human trafficking, involuntary servitude, or sexual servitude. The role of the parent, guardian, custodian, or caretaker is not considered. This definition of neglected juvenile was added to the Juvenile Code as required by the federal Justice for Victims of Trafficking Act (discussed in Chapter 1.3.B.11).

---

**Resource**: For more information about minors and human trafficking, see Margaret Henderson, Sara DePasquale, Nancy Hagan, Christy Croft, *Human Trafficking of Minors and Young Adults: What Local Governments Need to Know*, PUBLIC MANAGEMENT BULLETIN No. 2019/18 (UNC School of Government, Dec. 2019).

---

**(f) Unlawfully placed or transferred.** A juvenile is neglected if he or she (1) has been placed for care or adoption in violation of law or (2) has had his or her custody unlawfully transferred pursuant to G.S. 14-321.2 (effective for offenses committed on after December 1, 2016). G.S. 7B-101(15). No appellate court decisions address these bases for an adjudication of neglect. Possible unlawful adoptive placements include those that violate statutes relating to

- unlicensed group homes (*see* G.S. 131D-10.1 *et seq.*),
- unlawful payments related to adoption (*see* G.S. 48-10-102),
- prohibited activities relating to placement for adoption (*see* G.S. 48-10-101), and
- violation of the Interstate Compact on the Placement of Children (*see* G.S. 7B-3800 *et seq.*).

**(g) Other children.** In determining whether a juvenile is a neglected juvenile, it is relevant whether that juvenile lives in a home where another juvenile has died as a result of suspected abuse or neglect or lives in a home where another juvenile has been subjected to abuse or neglect by an adult who regularly lives in the home. G.S. 7B-101(15). A child need not be physically in the home for the abuse or neglect of another child in the home to be relevant to a neglect determination. *See In re A.B.*, 179 N.C. App. 605 (2006) (holding that a newborn still physically in the hospital may properly be determined to "live" in the home of his or her parents for the purposes of considering whether the abuse or neglect of another child in that home is relevant to the determination of whether the newborn is neglected).

The weight to be given to evidence of neglect of another juvenile in the home is in the trial court's discretion. *In re J.A.M.*, 822 S.E.2d 693 (N.C. S.Ct. 2019); *In re P.M.*, 169 N.C. App. 423 (2005). The fact of prior abuse or neglect of another child, standing alone, may not be sufficient to support an adjudication of neglect; there must be evidence showing a likelihood that the abuse or neglect will be repeated. *See In re J.C.B.*, 233 N.C. App. 641 (2014); *In re S.H.*, 217 N.C. App. 140 (2011). See Chapter 6.3.E.2(b) (addressing evidence involving other children).

**3. Dependent juvenile.** A dependent juvenile is one who is in need of assistance or placement because

- the juvenile has no parent, guardian, or custodian responsible for his or her care or supervision or
- the juvenile's parent, guardian, or custodian is (1) unable to provide for the child's care or supervision and (2) lacks an appropriate alternative child care arrangement.

G.S. 7B-101(9).

Caretaker is not included in this definition and does not factor into a determination as to whether a child is dependent. The definition of dependency includes no reference to the cause of the parent's inability to care for the child or to the temporary or permanent nature of the inability. *Compare* G.S. 7B-101(9) *with* G.S. 7B-1111(a)(6) (TPR ground based on the parent's inability to provide proper care and the child's resulting dependency that addresses causes of the parent's inability and requires a reasonable probability that the parent's incapability will continue for the foreseeable future).

Although the statutory definition uses the singular word parent, the court of appeals has held that a child is not dependent if the child has one parent who can provide proper care or supervision. *In re V.B.*, 239 N.C. App. 340 (2015); *see* G.S. 7B-101 ("the singular includes the plural"). The status of both parents must be taken into account in determining whether a child is dependent. *In re H.H.*, 237 N.C. App. 431 (2014) (where mother left children with their father and placement with father was suitable, it was error for the court to adjudicate the children dependent). Both prongs of the definition must be met for both parents: the parent is unable to provide proper care and supervision and lacks an appropriate alternative child care arrangement. *See In re V.B.*, 239 N.C. App. 340. When an appropriate alternative child care arrangement exists (e.g., an appropriate relative is willing and able to assume responsibility for a child), the child is not dependent, despite the parent's inability to provide proper care. *See, e.g., In re C.P.*, 812 S.E.2d 188 (N.C. Ct. App. 2018); *In re J.D.R.*, 239 N.C. App. 63 (2015); *In re B.M.*, 183 N.C. App. 84 (2007); *In re P.M.*, 169 N.C. App. 423 (2005). The parent must have taken some action to identify the alternative child care arrangement and not merely have gone along with the DSS plan. *In re B.P.*, 809 S.E.2d 914 (N.C. Ct. App. 2018).

When a petition is filed before paternity has been determined, evidence that paternity has been established after the petition was filed may be considered by the court at the adjudicatory hearing when determining whether a child is dependent. If paternity is established, without allegations in the petition or when there are allegations, without evidence at the adjudicatory hearing of the father's inability or unwillingness to care for or make alternative child care arrangements for his child, the child cannot be adjudicated dependent. *In re V.B.*, 239 N.C. App. 340.

For case law related to evidence to show dependency, see Chapter 6.3.F.2.

**Resource:** For more information about the Juvenile Code's definition of abuse, neglect, and dependency, see JANET MASON, REPORTING CHILD ABUSE AND NEGLECT IN NORTH CAROLINA (UNC School of Government, 3d ed. 2013) with 2016 supplemental chapter.

### C. Rights of the Child

Although children's rights in the juvenile justice (delinquency) system have long been recognized by courts and legislatures, children's rights in the context of custody and child protection proceedings are not as clear-cut. The U.S. Supreme Court has recognized that children have constitutional rights but has not defined the nature of a child's liberty interests in preserving family or family-like bonds. *See Troxel v. Granville*, 530 U.S. 57 (2000) (citing *Michael H. v. Gerald D.*, 491 U.S. 110 (1989), as reserving the question) and cases cited in footnote 8. Without defining the nature of those rights, federal courts have recognized that a child has a liberty interest in "his family's integrity and in the nurture and companionship of his parents" although those rights are "attenuated by the fact that, unlike adults, children are always in the custody of either their parents or the state as parens patriae." *Jordan by Jordan v. Jackson*, 15 F.3d 333, 346, 351 (4th Cir. 1994). *See D.B. v. Cardall*, 826 F.3d 721, 740 (4th Cir. 2016) (stating"[j]ust as parents possess a fundamental right with respect to their children, children also enjoy a 'familial right to be raised and nurtured by their parents.' ") (quoting *Berman v. Young*, 291 F.3d 976, 983 (7th Cir. 2002)).

Children are the intended beneficiaries of a child welfare system that aims to keep them safe, protect family autonomy, provide fair procedures that protect their own and their parents' constitutional rights, prevent their unnecessary or inappropriate separation from their parents, and ensure that they have safe permanent homes within a reasonable period of time. G.S. 7B-100. Abuse, neglect, and dependency cases involve the government's interference with constitutionally protected rights that impact families. *See In re T.R.P.*, 360 N.C. 588 (2006) (discussing the gravity of the decision to proceed with a DSS assessment and the potential consequences of filing a petition). Although the intended beneficiaries of DSS action, children have rights in that process.

In North Carolina, children who are the subject of abuse, neglect, dependency, and termination of parental rights (TPR) court actions are parties to the proceedings with both constitutional rights and rights established by the Juvenile Code. *See* G.S. 7B-401.1(f); 7B-601(a); 7B-1104. Some of those rights are explicitly stated legal rights (e.g., the right to a guardian ad litem; the right to access DSS and court records; and the right to keep an abuse, neglect, or dependency hearing open to the public). *See, e.g.,* G.S. 7B-601; 7B-302(a1)(2); 7B-2901(b)(1); 7B-801(b). Other rights, although not strictly speaking "legal rights," are implied and relate to case plans, visitation, placement, and permanency planning. *See Suter v. Artist M.*, 503 U.S. 347 (1992) (holding that the "reasonable efforts" provisions in the federal Adoption Assistance and Child Welfare Act did not create an implied private cause of action on behalf of children).

**1. Right to participate and be heard.** As a party in a juvenile case, the child has a right to participate, but the child's participation differs from that of the respondents. Unlike a respondent parent, guardian, custodian, or caretaker, the child is not issued and served with a summons that directs him or her to appear for a hearing and notifies him or her of possible outcomes or consequences that may be ordered in the action. *See* G.S. 7B-406; 7B-407; 7B-1106. Instead, a copy of the petition and notice of hearing is sent to the local judicial district's guardian ad litem (GAL) office when the petition alleges abuse or neglect. G.S. 7B-408. In a TPR proceeding, if the child is represented by a GAL, the GAL is served with the pleadings and other papers that need to be served. G.S. 7B-1106(a1); *see* G.S. 7B-1106.1(a)(5).

When a GAL is appointed for the juvenile, the child's participation in the proceeding is usually through that GAL. See section 2.3.D, below (discussing the child's GAL). But, a child is not precluded from appearing in court simply because a GAL has been appointed to represent him or her. In some situations, the child must appear at the hearing. For example, the child's testimony may be necessary because he or she is the only witness to an event that must be proved, or if the court is approving a primary permanent plan of Another Planned Permanent Living Arrangement for a 16- or 17-year-old juvenile, the court must first question the juvenile. G.S. 7B-912(c), (d).

At the initial dispositional hearing, the Juvenile Code explicitly gives the child (not the GAL) the right to present evidence and advise the court of what he or she believes is in his or her best interests. G.S. 7B-901(a). At review and permanency planning hearings, the court is required to "consider information from" both the juvenile and the GAL. G.S. 7B-906.1(c). The child's GAL has the right to notice and an opportunity to participate fully in the case. A juvenile who is 12 or older also has a right to individual notice of review and permanency planning hearings and post-TPR placement review hearings. G.S. 7B-906.1(b); 7B-908(b)(1). The court may consider evidence from the juvenile and the juvenile's GAL at post-TPR placement review hearings. G.S. 7B-908(a), (b)(1). A juvenile who is 12 or older must be served with a copy of a TPR order. G.S. 7B-1110(d). When adoption is the child's primary plan, if the child is 12 or older, their consent to the adoption is necessary unless it is waived by the court hearing the adoption proceeding. G.S. 48-3-601(1); 48-3-603(b)(2).

Every juvenile has a right to appeal a final order designated in G.S. 7B-1001. The appeal is taken by the GAL, or if a GAL is not appointed, the juvenile who appeals is then appointed a Rule 17 GAL for the purposes of the appeal. G.S. 7B-1002(1), (2). *See* N.C. R. Civ. P. 17.

**Practice Notes**: With the exception of an appeal, the Juvenile Code is silent as to how a child participates in the proceeding when a GAL is not appointed in those cases where the child is alleged only to be dependent. That child has the same rights to present evidence and be heard that the Juvenile Code establishes for any juvenile who is the subject of the action. As a party, the child also has constitutional due process rights, which require notice and a meaningful opportunity to be heard. *See In re Adoption of K.L.J.*, 831 S.E.2d 114 (N.C. Ct. App. 2019) (in an adoption of minors case, tribal court order not required to be given full faith and credit as the adoption petitioners and children were not afforded due process in the tribal court). If a child appeals an order but is not represented by a G.S. 7B-601 GAL, a Rule 17 GAL is appointed to represent the child in the appeal. When a court is exercising its discretion in deciding whether to appoint a GAL under G.S. 7B-601 for a child alleged to be dependent only, it may want to consider the child's constitutional due process and statutory rights and how those rights will be protected without the GAL appointment. The court may look to the stated purposes of the Juvenile Code, one of which is to "provide procedures for the hearing of juvenile cases that assure fairness and equity and protect the constitutional rights of juveniles…" when making that decision. G.S. 7B-100(1). A similar analysis may be made in a TPR proceeding where the GAL appointment for the child is discretionary under G.S. 7B-1108(c). *See* G.S. 7B-1108.1(a)(2); *In re P.T.W.*, 250 N.C. App. 589 (2016) (noting in footnote 11 that G.S. 7B-1108.1(a)(2) requires the court to affirmatively consider at a pretrial hearing whether a GAL should be appointed to the juvenile).

When a GAL is appointed, the GAL volunteer and attorney advocate use their discretion to determine how involved a child should be in the proceeding, including the circumstances under which it makes sense for a child to attend court hearings or testify. The child, especially an older child, may also be consulted when making that decision. If the child is subpoenaed by another party, the child must appear, but the child's GAL (or another party) may file a motion to quash the subpoena if the circumstances warrant such a motion. See Chapter 11.2 (discussing child witnesses including quashing of a subpoena).

**Resource:** To hear from representatives of the N.C. Guardian Ad Litem Program, a local GAL program, and district court judges discussing how the child's perspective is represented in abuse, neglect, or dependency proceedings, listen to *Beyond the Bench: The Child's Voice in Court*, UNC SCHOOL OF GOVERNMENT, NORTH CAROLINA JUDICIAL COLLEGE (Jan. 12, 2017) (also available through iTunes and Stitcher).

**2. Best interests and legal rights representation.** One of the stated purposes of the Juvenile Code is "[t]o provide standards . . . for ensuring that the best interests of the juvenile are of paramount consideration by the court." G.S. 7B-100(5). North Carolina appellate cases have referred to "best interests" as the "polar star" of the Juvenile Code. *See In re A.P.*, 371 N.C. 14, 21 (2018); *In re T.H.T.*, 362 N.C. 446, 450 (2008); *In re R.T.W.*, 359 N.C. 539, 550 (2005); *In re Montgomery*, 311 N.C. 101, 109 (1984).

For purposes of an abuse, neglect, or dependency case, best interests are not defined. In termination of parental rights (TPR) proceedings, G.S. 7B-1110 identifies six factors a court must consider when determining a child's best interests: the child's age; the likelihood of adoption; whether the TPR will aid in accomplishing the child's permanent plan; the bond between the child and respondent parent; the quality of the relationship between the child and proposed adoptive parent, guardian, custodian, or other permanent placement; and a catch-all "any other relevant consideration."

For a discussion of best interests in the context of the court's dispositional decisions in an abuse, neglect, or dependency case, see Chapter 7.3 and in a TPR proceeding, see Chapter 9.12.

In abuse and neglect and most TPR cases, children have the right to have their best interests represented by a guardian ad litem (GAL) and their legal rights protected by an attorney advocate throughout the course of the case. *See* G.S. 7B-601; 7B-1108. See section 2.3.D, below (discussing GAL appointment and role). The child does not have a right to court-appointed counsel to advocate for his or her expressed interest. However, GALs are trained to consider the child's wishes in determining best interests and to convey the child's wishes to the court even if they contradict the GAL's recommendations.

When a child's express interest is made known to the court either through the child's testimony or the GAL, it is not determinative on the court. The court exercises its discretion when making a best interests of the child determination. *See In re L.M.*, 238 N.C. App. 345 (2014) (holding no abuse of discretion when the court determined it was in the child's best interests to order guardianship rather than reunification, even though the 16-year-old child expressed his desire to be returned home to his mother).

**Resource:** For information on the child's best interests, see CHILD WELFARE INFORMATION GATEWAY, U.S. DEP'T OF HEALTH & HUMAN SERVICES, "Determining the Bests Interests of the Child" (2016).

**3. Foster Care Children's Bill of Rights.** In 2013, the North Carolina legislature enacted a "Foster Care Children's Bill of Rights," which sets out promoted practices while children are in foster care. The law states that a violation of the bill of rights may not be construed as creating a cause of action against DSS or a person or entity providing foster care. The statute sets out eleven enumerated foster care provisions that the General Assembly promotes:

(1) A safe foster home free of violence, abuse, neglect, and danger.
(2) First priority regarding placement in a home with siblings.
(3) The ability to communicate with the assigned social worker or case worker overseeing the child's case and have calls made to the social worker or case worker returned within a reasonable period of time.
(4) Allowing the child to remain enrolled in the school the child attended before being placed in foster care, if at all possible.
(5) Having a social worker, when a child is removed from the home, to immediately begin conducting an investigation to identify and locate all grandparents, adult siblings, and other adult relatives of the child to provide those persons with specific information and explanation of various options to participate in placement of a child.
(6) Participation in school extracurricular activities, community events, and religious practices.
(7) Communication with the biological parents if the child placed in foster care receives any immunizations and whether any additional immunizations are needed if the child will be transitioning back into a home with his or her biological parents.
(8) Establishing and having access to a bank or savings account in accordance with State laws and federal regulations.
(9) Obtaining identification and permanent documents, including a birth certificate, social security card, and health records by the age of 16, to the extent allowed by federal and State law.
(10) The use of appropriate communication measures to maintain contact with siblings if the child placed in foster care is separated from his or her siblings.
(11) Meaningful participation in a transition plan for those phasing out of foster care, including participation in family team, treatment team, court, and school meetings.

G.S. 131D-10.1.

Most of the provisions of the Foster Care Children's Bill of Rights are mandated by federal law or the Juvenile Code. For example, federal law specifically addresses sibling placement and visitation. DSS must make reasonable efforts to place siblings who have been removed from their home in the same placement unless DSS documents that a joint placement would be contrary to the safety or well-being of any of the siblings. When a joint placement is not made, DSS must provide reasonable efforts for frequent visitation or other ongoing interaction between the siblings absent documentation that such contact would be contrary to the safety or well-being of any of the siblings. 42 U.S.C. 671(a)(31).

Both federal law and the Juvenile Code require that DSS make diligent efforts to notify adult relatives of the child's removal and explore the relatives' willingness and ability to be a placement resource for the child. Federal law imposes a time period for notification of within thirty days of the child's removal. See 42 U.S.C. 671(a)(29); 7B-505(b); 7B-506(h)(2); 7B-901(b).

A child's school stability is addressed by the federal Fostering Connections to Success and Increasing Adoptions Act of 2008 and the Every Student Succeeds Act. See Chapter 13.7 for a discussion of those laws related to a child's educational stability.

The federal Preventing Sex Trafficking and Strengthening Families Act required states to adopt a reasonable and prudent parent standard that allows children in DSS custody to engage in normal childhood activities, including extracurricular and community events. The law also requires children who are 14 and older to participate in the development of their case plan. Additionally, a child who will age out of foster care must be provided with copies of his or her social security card, birth certificate, health insurance and medical information, and driver's license or state identification card. The Juvenile Code incorporates these federal mandates in G.S. 7B-903.1(a) and (b) and 7B-912(a) and (b). *See* G.S. 131D-10.2A (definition of "reasonable and prudent parent standard").

### D. The Child's Guardian ad Litem[2]

**1. Introduction.** The foundation of widespread guardian ad litem (GAL) representation for children in abuse and neglect proceedings is the federal Child Abuse Prevention and Treatment Act of 1974 (CAPTA), as amended. CAPTA requires states receiving federal funds for the prevention of child abuse and neglect to provide an appropriately trained GAL for each child involved in an abuse or neglect judicial proceeding. Federal law gives states leeway in exactly how to do this but requires that GAL responsibilities include (1) obtaining first-hand a clear understanding of the child's situation and needs, and (2) making recommendations to the court regarding the child's best interests. 42 U.S.C. 5106a(b)(2)(B)(xiii). See Chapter 1.3.B.1 (discussing CAPTA and its influence on the Juvenile Code).

In some states, GALs are attorneys, and in some they are trained volunteers (often called Court Appointed Special Advocates or "CASA"). Other states, like North Carolina, provide a combination of attorneys and volunteers (supported by GAL program staff) to represent children. GAL representation differs from state to state not only in the structure of the GAL programs, but also in the type of representation provided to children. In some states, representation is focused on the best interests of the child, and in others representation is focused on the child's wishes (or expressed interests). In North Carolina, the GAL represents the best interests of the child but also considers the child's wishes and conveys them to the court.

---

[2] The source for parts of this section is KELLA HATCHER, N.C. ADMIN. OFFICE OF THE COURTS, NORTH CAROLINA GUARDIAN AD LITEM ATTORNEY PRACTICE MANUAL (2007).

**Resources:**
The National Association of Counsel for Children (NACC) addresses the legal protection and representation of children by training and educating child advocates and by affecting policy and legal systems change. The NACC offers training opportunities, memberships, and certifications and produces publications focused on the representation of children.

The National Court Appointed Special Advocate/Guardians ad Litem Association (National CASA/GAL Association) works with state organizations throughout the country that support volunteer GALs advocating for abused and neglected children in court. National CASA provides training and training curricula for programs and advocates; technical assistance to programs; national volunteer recruitment programs; and grant funding to local and state programs.

**2. North Carolina GAL Program establishment and structure.** The North Carolina GAL Program was established by statute in 1983. Current provisions for the implementation and administration of the GAL Program are found in G.S. 7B-1200 through -1204. The GAL Program exists within the state's Administrative Office of the Courts (AOC). The GAL state administrative office oversees local GAL programs that are located in the judicial districts throughout the state; promulgates policy; and provides supervision, training, support, and consultation to local GAL programs.

Every judicial district in the state has at least one local GAL office, and some multi-county districts have more than one office. Each local GAL program has a district administrator responsible for overseeing the program, and each office typically has one or more GAL supervisors. Most local GAL programs have administrative support positions. Local GAL programs handle the recruiting and training of GAL volunteers (using a statewide curriculum), manage the assignment of GAL volunteers to cases, and provide ongoing supervision and support to GAL volunteers. GAL volunteers are screened, must meet specified qualifications, and receive at least thirty hours of pre-service training from GAL staff. After GAL volunteers successfully complete the required pre-service training and background screening, they are sworn in by the court.

Local GAL programs are also responsible for engaging the services of local attorneys, referred to as "attorney advocates," who are appointed by the court and paid from the GAL Program funds. *See* G.S. 7B-601(a); 7B-603(a). Most attorney advocates are independent contractors, but in some judicial districts with large caseloads, the local GAL programs have staff attorneys who are state employees.

**Resources:**
For more information about the North Carolina GAL Program, see the North Carolina Guardian Ad Litem program website, here.

For a more detailed explanation of the GAL Program role, responsibilities, and ethical considerations, see Chapters 8 and 12 *in* KELLA W. HATCHER, N.C. ADMIN. OFFICE OF THE COURTS, NORTH CAROLINA GUARDIAN AD LITEM ATTORNEY PRACTICE MANUAL (2007).

**3. GAL team representation: volunteer, attorney advocate, and staff.** In North Carolina, volunteers usually serve in the role of guardian ad litem (GAL), and if the volunteer is not an attorney, an attorney advocate must be appointed as well. G.S. 7B-601(a). An attorney advocate works as a partner with a GAL volunteer, and both are supported by the local GAL program staff. The attorney advocate, GAL volunteer, and staff act as a team to represent and promote the best interests of the child in abuse and neglect cases and in some dependency and termination of parental rights (TPR) cases.

The North Carolina Supreme Court addressed the concept of GAL team representation when it examined statutes pertaining to GAL representation and stated,

> When read in *pari materia*, these statutes manifest the legislative intent that representation of a minor child in proceedings under sections 7B-601 and 7B-1108 is to be, as DSS argues, by the GAL program established in Article 12 of the Juvenile Code. Under Article 12 volunteer GALs, the program attorney, the program coordinator, and clerical staff constitute the GAL program.

*In re J.H.K.*, 365 N.C. 171, 175 (2011).

**Note,** in this Manual, use of the term "GAL" when referring to the child's GAL (as opposed to a respondent parent's GAL) typically refers to the team appointed pursuant to G.S. 7B-601.

**4. Role and responsibilities of the GAL.**

See Chapter 9.4.C for an additional discussion of the child's GAL in a TPR proceeding.

**(a) Appointment and standing.** The court is required to appoint a GAL for the child in all cases in which a juvenile petition alleges that a child is an abused or neglected juvenile. The court has the discretion to appoint a GAL in cases in which a petition alleges only that a juvenile is dependent. G.S. 7B-601(a). The statute provides no criteria for determining whether a GAL should be appointed in a dependency case; however, any party can bring to the court's attention the potential need for a child to have a GAL. See section 2.3.C.1, above (discussing the child's legal rights including the right to participate in the proceeding).

If the child is represented by a GAL in an abuse, neglect, or dependency case when a TPR petition or motion is filed, that GAL also represents the child in the TPR action unless the court orders otherwise. *See* G.S. 7B-1106(a1); 7B-1106.1(a)(5); 7B-1108(a), (d). In all other TPR cases, the court is required to appoint a GAL for the child only if the respondent parent files an answer or response that denies any material allegation of the TPR petition or motion. G.S. 7B-1108(b). However, in every TPR action, the court has discretion to appoint a GAL for the child at any stage of the proceeding after affirmatively considering at a pretrial hearing whether a GAL should be appointed. G.S. 7B-1108(c); 7B-1108.1(a)(2); *see In re P.T.W.*, 250 N.C. App. 589 (2016).

When the local GAL program receives a copy of a petition alleging abuse or neglect and any notices of hearing, that local program assigns a GAL volunteer, attorney advocate, and staff to the case. *See* G.S. 7B-408; 7B-601(a). Appellate cases have been less concerned with the specifics of how the GAL appointment order reads (i.e., whether it names the program, a volunteer, or a GAL program staff member) than with whether someone was performing the duties of the GAL volunteer and attorney advocate from the time of the required GAL appointment and throughout the case. *See In re A.S.*, 190 N.C. App. 679 (2008) (finding no error where a GAL appointment order did not name a particular person or staff member, but, in fact, a person was performing GAL duties), *aff'd per curiam*, 363 N.C. 254 (2009). Even the lack of an appointment order in the appellate record has been found not to be error as long as the record showed that the GAL carried out his or her duties. *See In re D.W.C.*, 205 N.C. App. 266 (2010); *In re A.D.L.*, 169 N.C. App. 701 (2005).

If a conflict of interest prevents a local GAL program from representing a child, G.S. 7B-1202 authorizes the court to appoint a conflict attorney to represent the child. That attorney may be any member of the district bar. The State and local GAL programs maintain lists of "conflict attorneys" who can represent children in conflict situations.

The GAL volunteer, staff, and attorney advocate have standing to represent the juvenile in all actions related to abuse, neglect, dependency, and termination of parental rights when the team has been appointed. G.S. 7B-601(a). The court of appeals has examined the issue of standing in the context of GAL team representation. Relying on the North Carolina Supreme Court case *In re J.H.K.*, 365 N.C. 171 (2011), the court of appeals held that a TPR petition signed by the GAL program specialist "by and through the undersigned Attorney Advocate" and not by the volunteer GAL directly involved in the action was not improper. *In re S.T.B.*, 235 N.C. App. 290, 293 (2014).

The GAL appointment terminates when the permanent plan has been achieved for the juvenile and is approved by the court, but the court may reappoint the GAL in its discretion or in response to a motion of any party showing good cause for reappointment. G.S. 7B-601(a).

---

**AOC Form:**
AOC-J-207, Order to Appoint or Release Guardian Ad Litem and Attorney Advocate (June 2014).

**Practice Notes:** The AOC form order used for GAL appointments contains space to name a GAL volunteer, attorney advocate, and a GAL staff person. This team appointment ensures that a GAL staff person performs the duties of the GAL any time there is a gap between one GAL volunteer leaving and a new GAL volunteer being appointed.

Individuals working as GAL volunteers or attorney advocates may be appointed only as authorized by statute in abuse, neglect, dependency, and TPR cases. *See* G.S. 7B-601; 7B-1108. There is no statutory authority for GAL volunteers or attorney advocates working under the supervision of the GAL Program to be appointed in delinquency or undisciplined cases or cases in which a GAL is appointed pursuant to Rule 17 of the Rules of Civil Procedure. The GAL Program cannot "consent" to represent a child when the representation is not authorized by statute. In TPR proceedings, the Juvenile Code authorizes the appointment of GALs who are trained and supervised by the GAL Program only when the child is or has been the subject of an abuse, neglect, or dependency petition, but makes an exception if the local GAL program consents to the appointment for good cause. G.S. 7B-1108. Otherwise, a GAL appointed for a child in a TPR case that was not preceded by an abuse, neglect, or dependency case typically is an attorney not connected with the GAL Program.

**(b) Representation.** The GAL volunteer and attorney advocate are responsible for protecting and promoting the best interests of the child, and the attorney advocate is responsible for protecting the child's legal rights as well. G.S. 7B-601(a). This type of representation differs from traditional legal representation in which the focus is on a client's wishes or expressed interests. GALs determine and consider the child's wishes and report those to the court. However, where the GAL's determination of best interests differs from the child's expressed wishes, the GAL advocates his or her perspective but also communicates the child's wishes to the court.

The North Carolina Supreme Court emphasized the concept of GAL team representation in assessing fulfillment of the statutory duties of GAL representation in a case in which the attorney advocate, but not the GAL volunteer, was present at the TPR hearing. In reversing and remanding the decision of the court of appeals that conducting the hearing without the GAL volunteer was error, the supreme court found that the duties of the GAL specified in the statute were in fact fulfilled by the GAL program staff, the attorney advocate, and the volunteer as a team, and that the court of appeals had failed to recognize the concept of GAL team representation. The supreme court held that the GAL volunteer's presence at the hearing was required only if the attorney advocate or the trial court deemed the GAL volunteer's presence necessary to protect the child's best interest. *In re J.H.K.*, 365 N.C. 171 (2011). *See also In re A.N.L.*, 213 N.C. App. 266 (2011) (confirming appropriateness of GAL staff member's appointment as GAL and holding that GAL representation was adequate where attorney advocate but not appointed GAL was present in court for the hearing). The supreme court in *In re J.H.K.*, 365 N.C. 171, distinguished an earlier case, *In re R.A.H.*, 171 N.C. App. 427 (2005), in which the court of appeals found error. In that case, there was an attorney advocate at the TPR hearing but a GAL volunteer was not appointed until after three and a half days of testimony had taken place. The court of appeals held that no one was fulfilling the statutory duty of investigating and determining the best interests of the child and that the GAL volunteer and attorney advocate may not "pinch hit" for one another. The *In re J.H.K.* decision by the supreme court expressly interpreted the Juvenile Code to permit a GAL who is an attorney to perform the duties of both the GAL and the attorney advocate.

**Practice Note:** For clarity, when an attorney is serving in both the role of the GAL volunteer and the attorney advocate, that dual appointment should be clear in the order of appointment.

Appellate courts have rejected the notion of reversing a case for failure to appoint a GAL in a prior proceeding that is not on direct appeal. *See In re J.E.*, 362 N.C. 168 (2008), *rev'g per curiam for reasons stated in the dissent* 183 N.C. App. 217 (2007); *In re O.C.*, 171 N.C. App. 457 (2005).

**(c) Attorneys talking to child.** Just as an attorney should not communicate with a party who is represented by counsel without that counsel's consent, authorization of the child's attorney advocate is required for another attorney to talk to the child. This applies to parents' attorneys, DSS attorneys, prosecutors and law enforcement officers who are acting as agents of prosecutors, and criminal defense attorneys. *See* North Carolina State Bar, RPC 249 (1997) and RPC 61 (1990); 2009 Formal Ethics Opinion 7 (Jan. 27, 2012).

**(d) Duties and responsibilities.** The Juvenile Code sets out specific duties of the GAL, including to

- make an investigation to determine the facts, the needs of the juvenile, and the available resources within the family and community to meet those needs;
- facilitate, when appropriate, the settlement of disputed issues;
- offer evidence and examine witnesses at adjudication;
- explore options with the court at the dispositional hearing;
- conduct follow-up investigations to ensure that the orders of the court are being properly executed;
- report to the court when the needs of the juvenile are not being met; and
- protect and promote the best interests of the juvenile until formally relieved of the responsibility by the court.

G.S. 7B-601. Note that these same duties apply in TPR cases pursuant to G.S. 7B-1108.

In addition, if the child is called to testify in a criminal action relating to abuse, the court may authorize the GAL to accompany the child to court. G.S. 7B-601(b).

Typically, the GAL volunteer has the primary role of communicating with the child, interviewing family and others, collecting and reviewing records, and determining recommendations for the court as to needed services and placement for the child. The attorney advocate receives information from the GAL volunteer and staff and handles the legal aspects of the case, including presenting the GAL volunteer's recommendations in court and advocating the GAL volunteer's position related to the child's best interests. *See In re R.A.H.*, 171 N.C. App. 427 (2005). However, the North Carolina Supreme Court has emphasized the concept of GAL team representation, taking the focus off of which GAL duty is performed by which team member and instead focusing on whether all the duties are in fact performed. *In re J.H.K.*, 365 N.C. 171 (2011).

See Chapter 14.1.D related to the GAL's access to confidential information.

---

**Resource:** Information regarding the complexities of representing children in child protective proceedings is available at "Representing Children" on the Child Welfare Information

Gateway, U.S. Department of Health and Human Services website.

**5. Fees for child's GAL attorney advocate and experts.** GAL volunteers work under the supervision of the GAL Program without compensation. GAL volunteers are paired with attorney advocates who are compensated. In some cases, an attorney is appointed to act as both GAL volunteer and attorney advocate. The child's attorney advocate, regardless of whether he or she is also serving in the role of GAL volunteer, is paid as follows:

- Most often, the attorney advocate is paid by the GAL Program in the Administrative Office of the Courts (AOC), which either contracts with or employs GAL attorneys.
- When the local GAL program has a conflict that precludes representation, a GAL conflict attorney is appointed to represent the juvenile and is paid by the AOC through the GAL Program.

*See* G.S. 7B-603(a); 7B-1202.

Whenever an attorney or GAL is appointed for a juvenile pursuant to G.S. 7B-601, the court may require the juvenile's parent, guardian, or a trustee (if applicable) to pay the fee, but only if a juvenile is adjudicated abused, neglected, or dependent or parental rights are terminated. G.S. 7B-603(a1); 7A-450.1.

While not addressed in the statutes, the way the AOC handles payment for experts for the GAL is similar to the way experts are paid for indigent parents. See section 2.4.E., below. For the GAL Program to use state funds to pay for an expert requested by the attorney advocate, a motion for funds must be made and granted by the court.

**AOC Forms:**
- AOC-J-485, Application for Expert Witness Fee in Juvenile Cases At The Trial Level (Dec. 2017).
- AOC-J-486, Order for Expert Witness Fee in Juvenile Cases At The Trial Level (Dec. 2017).
- AOC-G-200, Civil Case Trial Level Fee Application Order For Payment Judgment Against Parent/Guardian (Aug. 2019).

## 2.4 Rights of the Parent

### A. Protection of Parent-Child Relationship

**1. Generally.** The first stated purpose of the Juvenile Code is to "provide procedures for the hearing of juvenile cases that assure fairness and equity and that protect the constitutional rights of juveniles and parents." G.S. 7B-100(1). Unless a parent's rights have been terminated; the parent has relinquished the child for adoption; or the parent has been convicted of a first- or second-degree forcible rape, statutory rape of a child by an adult, or first-degree statutory rape, and any of those criminal acts resulted in the conception of the child that is the subject of the proceeding, both parents should be named as parties to any abuse, neglect, or dependency proceeding concerning their child. G.S. 7B-401.1(b). That applies to a parent whose identity or whereabouts is unknown and regardless of whether the parent is alleged to have contributed to the child's condition of abuse, neglect, or dependency. An abuse, neglect, or dependency proceeding involves government intervention by a county DSS into constitutionally protected parent-child relationships. A termination of parental rights (TPR) action represents the most severe form of state intervention—asking a court to completely sever the legal relationship between a child and parent.

**2. U.S. Supreme Court.** It is well-settled law that parents have the right to rear their children without the interference of the state. The U.S. Supreme Court has long recognized that parents have a liberty interest in the companionship, custody, care, and control of their children. *See Troxel v. Granville*, 530 U.S. 57 (2000) (declaring a non-parent visitation statute unconstitutional as applied where grandparents were awarded visitation rights based solely on the court's determination of the children's best interest, without a finding of parental unfitness or any special weight given to the parent's determination of the children's best interests). *See also Santosky v. Kramer*, 455 U.S. 745 (1982); *Lassiter v. Dep't of Social Services*, 452 U.S. 18 (1981). This liberty interest, rooted in the Due Process Clause of the Fourteenth Amendment to the U.S. Constitution, continues throughout an abuse, neglect, dependency, and TPR proceeding. *See Santosky v. Kramer*, 455 U.S. 745, 753 (holding procedural due process applies to TPR hearings and stating that the parents' fundamental liberty interest "in the care, custody, and management of their child does not evaporate simply because they have not been model parents or have lost temporary custody of their child to the state").

The Supreme Court also has recognized (in the cases cited above) that the rights of the parent are not absolute. There is a presumption that parents act in their child's best interests, but when a parent is unfit, the state may intervene. *See Troxel*, 530 U.S. 57; *Parham v. J.R.*, 442 U.S. 584 (1979).

Regarding putative fathers, the Supreme Court has held that a biological link between a child and putative father does not establish the constitutional protections of the parent-child relationship. That biological link provides the putative father with the opportunity to develop a relationship with his child and accept responsibility for establishing the parent-child relationship. The putative father must grasp that opportunity before the paramount constitutional rights of parents regarding their children apply to the putative father. *Lehr v. Robertson*, 463 U.S. 248 (1983).

**3. North Carolina appellate courts.** North Carolina case law affirms parents' constitutional liberty interest in the care and companionship of their children and recognizes that the state or other parties who are not parents may interfere with the parent-child relationship only when the parent has acted inconsistently with the parent's superior right as a parent. The general rule in a custody dispute between a parent and a non-parent is that the parent is entitled to custody unless there is proof that the parent is unfit, has neglected the child, or has acted inconsistently with the parent's protected status as a parent. *See Price v. Howard*, 346 N.C. 68 (1997); *Petersen v. Rogers*, 337 N.C. 397 (1994). Only upon finding one of those circumstances by clear and convincing evidence may the court apply a "best interest" test, which applies in custody cases between parents, to determine a child's custody when the contest is between a parent and anyone who is not a parent. *Price*, 346 N.C. 68; *Petersen*, 337 N.C. 397; *Owenby v. Young*, 357 N.C. 142 (2003); *Moriggia v. Castelo*, 805 S.E.2d 378 (N.C. Ct. App. 2017).

The fact that the custody issue arises in an abuse, neglect, or dependency proceeding does not change the rule. *See In re D.A.*, 811 S.E.2d 729 (N.C. Ct. App. 2018) (vacating and remanding for new hearing portion of permanency planning order that awarded *de facto* permanent custody to foster parents because of insufficient findings to support conclusion that father was either unfit or acted inconsistently with his parental rights); *In re E.M.*, 249 N.C. App. 44 (2016) (error to award custody to a non-parent in a permanency planning review order which did not state that the trial court applied the clear and convincing standard when determining whether the parent's conduct had been inconsistent with her constitutionally protected status); *In re D.M.*, 211 N.C. App. 382 (2011) (holding in a dependency case that where neither parent had been found to be unfit and there was no finding that the father acted inconsistently with his constitutional rights as a parent, the trial court erred in awarding permanent custody of the child to the grandmother). *See also In re B.G.*, 197 N.C. App. 570 (2009) (reversing permanency planning order giving custody to relatives where court applied best interest standard without a showing that father was unfit, had neglected the child, or had acted inconsistently with his constitutionally protected status as a parent); *cf. In re T.P.*, 217 N.C. App. 181 (2011) (refusing to consider respondent's argument that trial court erred in applying the best interest standard, because respondent did not raise this objection at trial and constitutional issues not raised and addressed at trial will not be considered for the first time on appeal). Note that majority of the opinions addressing the application of the finding regarding a parent acting inconsistently with his or her parental rights in abuse, neglect, or dependency cases (including the ones cited above) examined permanency planning orders. *Cf. In re S.J.T.H.*, 811 S.E.2d 723 (N.C. Ct. App. 2018) (relying on holding in opinion addressing a permanency planning order; reversing in part the initial dispositional order that did not award custody to the non-removal parent and remanding for new order to address that parent's rights and grant that parent custody unless clear and convincing evidence supports a different dispositional alternative).

Abuse, neglect, and abandonment by a parent constitute conduct inconsistent with the parent's protected status; other conduct must be evaluated on a case-by-case basis as to whether it is inconsistent with a parent's constitutionally protected rights. *Price*, 346 N.C. 68. There is no bright-line test when determining if a parent has acted inconsistently with his or her parental rights. *See In re A.C.*, 247 N.C. App. 528 (2016) (examining the mother's conduct and intentions and holding that she acted inconsistently with her parental rights). The determination is not based on whether the conduct consisted of good or bad acts but rather the court considers the voluntariness of the parent's actions and the relinquishment of exclusive parental authority to a third person. *Mason v. Dwinnell*, 190 N.C. App. 209 (2008). As part of its analysis, the court looks at the parent's intentions. *Mason*, 190 N.C. App. 209; *In re A.C.*, 247 N.C. App. 528. When determining whether a parent is unfit or acted inconsistently with his or her parental rights, "evidence of a parent's conduct should be viewed cumulatively." *Owenby*, 357 N.C. at 147 (2003).

Regarding putative fathers, the court may examine his conduct to determine whether he acted inconsistently with his parental rights by failing to grasp the opportunity to establish a relationship with the child. *Adams v. Tessener*, 354 N.C. 57 (2001) (holding father acted inconsistently with his parental rights when after being informed about the pregnancy and likelihood that he was the father, he did nothing about the pregnancy and impending birth and after the birth, did not inquire about the child or mother). In an adoption proceeding, the North Carolina Supreme Court expanded the putative father's need to grasp the opportunity to acts that would put him on notice of the pregnancy when the opportunity to be on such notice existed. *In re S.D.W.*, 367 N.C. 386 (2014) (holding the putative father did not fall in the class of fathers who may claim a liberty interest in developing a relationship with a child; concluding that even though the mother hid the child's birth from him, he was passive in discovering whether she may have become pregnant with his child despite ample evidence that it was possible).

See Chapter 7.3 and 7.10.B.5 (discussing court opinions addressing the child's best interests standard and need for findings regarding the parent's conduct when ordering custody or guardianship to a non-parent).

**B. Notice and Opportunity to Be Heard**

**1. Entitled to due process.** As a party to the juvenile proceeding, a parent is entitled to procedural due process, including proper service of process, notice of proceedings, and fair procedures. *See Santosky v. Kramer*, 455 U.S. 745 (1982) (holding that a state must provide respondents with fundamentally fair procedures when it moves to destroy weakened familial bonds); *see also In re H.D.F.* 197 N.C. App. 480 (2009) (reversing a neglect adjudication when the required notice of key events in the proceeding was not given to the *pro se* respondent parent). "Due process of law formulates a flexible concept, to insure fundamental fairness in judicial or administrative proceedings which may adversely affect the protected rights of an individual." *In re S.G.V.S.*, 811 S.E.2d 718, 721 (N.C. Ct. App. 2018) (quoting case not cited here).

When one parent is served in an abuse, neglect, or dependency case, the other parent's due process rights are not necessarily violated if he or she is not served before the adjudication and disposition hearings. *In re Poole*, 151 N.C. App. 472 (2002) (in case where mother was served with summons, discussing due process rights of father who was not served and to whom no summons was issued and deciding his rights were adequately protected in light of state's interest in the welfare of children, the child's right to be protected, the father's ability to seek review of the court's order, and the potential for the child's return to his care), *rev'd per curiam for reasons stated in the dissent*, 357 N.C. 151 (2003).

**2. Participation in hearings.** Parents have a right to participate in proceedings in a meaningful way. The summons in an abuse, neglect, or dependency case requires the parent to appear for a hearing at a specified time and place. G.S. 7B-406(a). In a termination of parental rights (TPR) case, the summons or notice includes notice that the parents may attend the hearing. G.S. 7B-1106(b)(6); 7B-1106.1(b)(6). The court of appeals has held that a parent does not have an absolute right to be present at a hearing but "the magnitude of 'the private interests affected by the [termination] proceeding, clearly weighs in favor of a parent's presence at the hearing.'" *In re S.G.V.S.*, 811 S.E.2d at 721 (N.C. Ct. App. 2018) (reversing and remanding for new hearing; holding the magnitude of the interests at stake in a TPR hearing and the trial court's denial of mother's continuance request because mother was previously scheduled to appear in a criminal action in another county at the same time as later scheduled TPR hearing involved a misapprehension of law and substantial miscarriage of justice).

(a) **Incarcerated parent.** When a parent is incarcerated, the parent's attendance may be impossible or require special steps. On application of a party or the attorney for a party who wants the parent to attend or testify, the court may issue a writ to have the parent brought before the court. The closest statutory authority for such a writ, G.S. 17-41, provides for a writ of habeas corpus ad testificandum. Although an application for the writ must state that the person's testimony is believed to be "material and necessary," the same procedure is used when a parent wants to attend but does not plan to testify or has already testified. The court may issue the writ only for someone who is in a facility in North Carolina. If the parent is in a federal facility in this state, the person seeking the parent's attendance should contact that facility directly to determine whether the parent can be brought to court if a writ is issued. A North Carolina court has no authority to effect the attendance of someone who is incarcerated in another state, but parties may explore with an out-of-state facility the possibility of having the incarcerated party participate remotely.

The court's consideration of whether to issue a writ of habeas corpus ad testificandum or take other steps to facilitate a parent's participation in a hearing requires application of the balancing test articulated by the U.S. Supreme Court in *Mathews v. Eldridge*, 424 U.S. 319 (1976). In determining whether due process requires a particular procedure, the court must weigh three factors: (1) the private interests at stake, (2) the risk of deprivation posed by the use (or absence) of the procedure, and (3) the state's interest in providing (or not providing) the procedure. *Mathews,* 424 U.S. at 335. North Carolina courts have applied the test in several juvenile cases. *See, e.g., In re K.D.L.*, 176 N.C. App. 261 (2006) (upholding trial court's denial of incarcerated father's motion to have his deposition taken); *In re Quevedo*, 106 N.C. App. 574 (1992) (holding that father's due process rights were not violated when court denied his motion for transportation to hearing and allowed hearing to proceed in his absence); *In re Murphy*, 105 N.C. App. 651 (holding that the court did not violate the parent's statutory or due process rights by denying a motion for transportation from a correctional facility to the termination hearing), *aff'd per curiam*, 332 N.C. 663 (1992).

Even when the parent does not attend the hearing, other steps to ensure protection of the parent's rights may be appropriate. In *In re Quevedo*, the court said:

> We note that the use of depositions is allowed in civil cases where a witness is unable to attend because of age, illness, infirmity or imprisonment. N.C. Gen. Stat. § 1A-1, Rule 32(a)(4). Therefore, when an incarcerated parent is denied transportation to the hearing in contested termination cases, the better practice is for the court, when so moved, to provide the funds necessary for the deposing of the incarcerated parent.

> The parent's deposition, combined with representation by counsel at the hearing, will ordinarily provide sufficient participation by the incarcerated parent so as to reduce the risk of error attributable to his absence to a level consistent with due process.

106 N.C. App. at 582.

---

**AOC Form:**
AOC-G-112, Application and Writ of Habeas Corpus ad Testificandum (June 2012).

**Resources:**
See the Office of Indigent Defense Services (IDS), Office of Parent Defender, chart, "Participation in Abuse, Neglect, Dependency, and Termination of Parental Rights Proceeding by Incarcerated Parents."

For the North Carolina Department of Public Safety Policy and Procedures related to inmate access to the courts and to their attorneys, see Chapter G, Section .0200 "Court Related Procedures" (Jan. 16, 2018).

---

(b) **Exclusion from courtroom.** Use of the *Mathews v. Eldridge* due process test is not limited to applications for writs to be brought to a hearing. It is also used when parents have been excluded from the proceeding. *See, e.g., In re J.B.*, 172 N.C. App. 1 (2005) (holding that mother could be excluded from the courtroom during the child's testimony); *In re Faircloth*, 153 N.C. App. 565 (2002) (upholding removal of disruptive parent from termination hearing, without providing means for him to testify, based on strong governmental interest and low risk of error).

(c) **Testimony of parties or witnesses in other states.** All abuse, neglect, dependency, and TPR proceedings are subject to the Uniform Child-Custody Jurisdiction and Enforcement Act (UCCJEA), G.S. Chapter 50A. G.S. 50A-511 addresses taking the testimony of parties or witnesses in another state and provides:

> (a) In addition to other procedures available to a party, a party to a child-custody proceeding may offer testimony of witnesses who are located in another state, including testimony of the parties and the child, by deposition or other means allowable in this State for testimony taken in another state. The court on its own motion may order that the testimony of a person be taken in another state and may prescribe the manner in which and the terms upon which the testimony is taken.
> (b) A court of this State may permit an individual residing in another state to be deposed or to testify by telephone, audiovisual means, or other electronic means before a designated court or at another location in that state. A court of this State shall cooperate with courts of other states in designating an appropriate location for the deposition or testimony.
> (c) Documentary evidence transmitted from another state to a court of this State by technological means that do not produce an original writing

may not be excluded from evidence on an objection based on the means of transmission.

## C. DSS Perspective

Recognition of and respect for parents' rights are essential elements of good social work practice. The North Carolina Department of Health and Human Services Division of Social Services' Child Welfare Manual states that parents and other care providers involved in juvenile cases are entitled to

- Be treated in a courteous and respectful manner;
- Know DSS's legal authority and right to intervene in cases of child abuse, neglect, or dependency;
- Know the allegations of abuse, neglect, or dependency reported at the first contact with DSS;
- Know any possible action that DSS may take, including petitioning the court to remove the child in order to ensure safety and protection;
- Know DSS's expectations of the parent/caregiver;
- Know what services they can expect from DSS and other community agencies; and
- Have a family services case plan that is clearly stated, measurable, and specific, that includes time-limited goals, and that is mutually developed by the DSS and the parent/caretaker.

DIV. OF SOC. SERVS., N.C. DEP'T OF HEALTH & HUMAN SERVICES, CHILD WELFARE MANUAL "Purpose, Philosophy, Legal Basis and Staffing" p. 9, available here.

## D. Representation

**1. Right to counsel.** Parents have a statutory right to counsel, and to court-appointed counsel if indigent, in all abuse, neglect, dependency, and termination of parental rights (TPR) proceedings. G.S. 7B-602; 7B-1101.1. A parent's eligibility and desire for appointed counsel may be reviewed at any stage of the abuse, neglect, dependency, or TPR proceeding. A parent's right to counsel includes the right to the effective assistance of counsel. *In re C.D.H.*, 829 S.E.2d 690 (N.C. Ct. App. 2019); *In re Oghenekevebe*, 123 N.C. App. 434 (1996) (holding that the right to counsel provided by then G.S. 7A-289.23 included the right to effective assistance of counsel). See subsection 5, below.

**2. Appointment of counsel.** When an abuse, neglect, or dependency petition is filed, the clerk must appoint provisional counsel for the parent and indicate that appointment on the summons issued to the parent or a separate notice. G.S. 7B-602(a); *see* G.S. 7B-406(b)(2). When a TPR *petition* is filed, the clerk must appoint provisional counsel unless the parent is already represented by appointed counsel, in which case that appointment continues. G.S. 7B-1101.1(a); *see* G.S. 7B-1106(b)(3).

When a TPR *motion* is filed, an attorney appointed to represent the parent in the underlying abuse, neglect, or dependency proceeding will continue to represent the parent in the TPR matter unless the court orders otherwise. *See* G.S. 7B-1106.1(b)(3). The notice to the parent must state that the parent is entitled to appointed counsel if indigent and, if not already represented by an attorney, may contact the clerk to request counsel. G.S. 7B-1106.1(b)(4). Provisional counsel is not appointed; instead, an unrepresented indigent parent must either contact the clerk or request counsel when he or she appears in court. *See* G.S. 7B-1108.1 (providing for pretrial hearing); 7B-1109(b) (requiring the court at adjudication to inquire whether a parent who is present and unrepresented is indigent and wants counsel).

Appointments of counsel are made in accordance with the rules adopted by the North Carolina Office of Indigent Defense Services. G.S. 7B-602(a); 7B-1101.1(a).

When provisional counsel is appointed, the court must confirm the appointment at the first hearing in an abuse, neglect, or dependency proceeding, and at the first hearing after service on the parent in a TPR proceeding, unless the parent

- does not appear at the hearing,
- has retained counsel,
- waives the right to counsel, or
- is not indigent.

G.S. 7B-602(a); 7B-1101.1(a). *See* G.S. 7B-1108.1(a)(1) (retention or release of provisional counsel may be addressed at a pretrial hearing).

In the case *In re D.E.G.*, 228 N.C. App. 381 (2013), the court noted that while G.S. 7B-1101.1(a) requires the court to dismiss provisional counsel when the parent does not appear at the first hearing, counsel who was already representing the parent in the underlying abuse, neglect, or dependency proceeding was not provisional counsel. The provisional counsel statute was inapplicable. The appointed attorney was required to seek leave from the court to withdraw. The court has discretion when deciding whether to allow the attorney's motion to withdraw; however, when an attorney has not provided his or her client prior notice of the intent to withdraw, the court does not have discretion. Instead, the court must either grant a continuance so that the notice may be provided to the client or deny the attorney's request to withdraw. *See also In re M.G.*, 239 N.C. App. 77 (2015) (attorney who represented respondent mother in the underlying proceeding in which the child was adjudicated neglected was not provisionally appointed in the TPR proceeding; trial court erred in allowing respondent's counsel to withdraw without first confirming that respondent had been notified of counsel's intention to do so).

**AOC Form:**
AOC-J-144, Order of Assignment or Denial of Counsel (Abuse, Neglect, Dependency, Termination of Parental Rights; Post-DSS-Placement Review and Permanency Planning Hearings (Delinquent/Undisciplined)) (Oct. 2019).

**3. Waiver of counsel.** Both G.S. 7B-601 (for abuse, neglect, and dependency cases) and 7B-1101.1 (for TPR cases) provide that when a parent qualifies for appointed counsel, the court may allow the parent to proceed without counsel only after examining the parent on the record and making findings of fact sufficient to show that the waiver is knowing and voluntary. Before these provisions became effective on October 1, 2013, the North Carolina Supreme Court held that a parent's waiver of counsel in a juvenile case was not governed by G.S. 15A-1242, which applies only in criminal cases. *In re P.D.R.*, 365 N.C. 533 (2012). Subsequently, the court of appeals held that the trial court must make an inquiry sufficient to determine whether a parent's waiver was knowing and voluntary, the standard now stated in the Juvenile Code. *See In re J.K.P.*, 238 N.C. App. 334 (2014) and *In re A.Y.*, 225 N.C. App. 29 (2013) (both holding that trial court's inquiry relating to the respondent's waiver was adequate to determine that the waiver was knowing and voluntary).

Since amendments made to the Juvenile Code in 1998, a parent does not have a statutory right to self-representation in an abuse, neglect, or dependency proceeding. A parent also does not have a constitutional right to represent him or herself in a juvenile proceeding. The court exercises discretion in deciding whether to allow a parent to waive counsel and represent himself or herself. *See In re J.R.*, 250 N.C. App. 195 (2016) (holding no abuse of discretion when the court denied mother's request to proceed pro se given possibility of criminal charges arising from the same incident and finding that her waiver was not knowing and voluntary because she was influenced and possibly coerced by her abusive boyfriend to waive counsel).

When a respondent parent has a Rule 17 GAL appointed because of his or her incompetency, that GAL's consent to the parent's waiver of appointed counsel should be obtained. *See In re P.D.R.*, 224 N.C. App. 460, 470 (2012) (decided prior to amendment in GAL statute for respondent parent that removed a GAL of assistance based on diminished capacity, holding if respondent had diminished capacity and a GAL of assistance, "then she was free to make her own decision whether to proceed pro se," but if she had a GAL of substitution based on incompetency, "the GAL would act on behalf of respondent mother, making the decision necessary to seek a result favorable to the mother"); *In re A.Y.*, 225 N.C. App. at 38 (decided prior to amendment in GAL statute removing a GAL of assistance based on a parent's diminished capacity, and stating "[b]ecause the GAL was acting only in an assistive capacity, respondent mother had the ability to waive counsel, so long as that waiver was knowing and voluntary"). See section 2.4.F, below (discussing GAL appointment for respondent parent and earlier statutes establishing GAL role as either substitution or assistance).

**AOC Form:**
AOC-J-143, Waiver of Parent's Right to Counsel (Oct. 2019).

**4. Withdrawal of counsel.** Appellate courts have held that an attorney's withdrawal from a case requires: (1) justifiable cause, (2) reasonable notice to the client, and (3) the permission of the court. *In re D.E.G.*, 228 N.C. App. 381 (2013) (citing *Smith v. Bryant*, 264 N.C. 208 (1965)). Whether to permit an attorney to cease representation of a client is within the discretion of the trial court. However, where the client has no notice of the attorney's intent to withdraw, the trial court has no discretion and must either grant a reasonable continuance or deny the motion to withdraw. *In re D.E.G.*, 228 N.C. App. 381. To determine whether circumstances would permit withdrawal when the parent is absent from the hearing, the court must inquire into the efforts made by counsel to contact the parent. *In re D.E.G.*, 228 N.C. App. 381; *see In re M.G.* 239 N.C. App. 77 (2015) (vacating a TPR order and remanding the case because the trial court erred in allowing respondent's counsel to withdraw without first confirming that respondent had been notified of counsel's intention to do so).

**Practice Note:** If an attorney is unable to locate his or her client, the attorney must make reasonable efforts to notify the client of his or her intent to withdraw. This can be done by calling collateral contacts (i.e., family members, employer, landlord), by electronic communication, and by complying with the service requirements of Rule 5(b)(2)(b) of the Rules of Civil Procedure.

**5. Ineffective assistance of counsel.** A parent asserting a claim of ineffective assistance of counsel must show that the attorney's performance (1) was deficient (or fell below an objective standard of reasonableness) and (2) was so deficient that the parent was denied a fair hearing. *In re C.B.*, 245 N.C. App. 197 (2016) (holding assuming arguendo that counsel's performance was deficient, mother was not deprived of a fair hearing); *In re S.N.W.*, 204 N.C. App. 556 (2010); *In re S.C.R.*, 198 N.C. App. 525 (2009). The parent alleging ineffective assistance of counsel has the burden of proving the attorney's performance was below the required standard, and that burden "is a heavy one for [the client] to bear." *In re C.B.*, 245 N.C. App. at 214. An attorney's failure to advocate or remaining silent during the proceeding, is not necessarily ineffective assistance of counsel. *In re C.D.H.*, 829 S.E.2d 690 (N.C. Ct. App. 2019); *In re T.D.*, 248 N.C. App. 366 (2016) (originally unpublished July 19, 2016, but subsequently published).

Several opinions address a respondent parent's ineffective assistance of counsel claim where in the TPR hearing, the respondent did not appear and the respondent's attorney did not participate in the hearing. For such a determination, when the record is insufficient, the court of appeals has held the appropriate remedy is to remand the case back to the trial court to make further inquiries about the reasons for the respondent's absence from the hearing, the attorney's efforts to contact the respondent, and the reasons for the attorney's actions. *In re C.D.H.*, 829 S.E.2d 690 (remanded due to insufficient record for trial court to determine if respondent waived her right to counsel based on her own actions or whether the attorney's performance was deficient); *In re A.R.C.*, 830 S.E.2d 1 (N.C. Ct. App. 2019) (remanded due to insufficient record for trial court to make a determination about the adequacy of the attorney representation, including efforts by attorney to contact mother and adequately represent her at the hearing); *In re S.N.W.*, 204 N.C. App. 556 (2010) (remanded for trial court to determine what efforts counsel made to contact and adequately represent respondent).

If, on remand, the trial court determines the attorney's actions were deficient, the court should then determine whether the deficiencies deprived the parent of a fair hearing. *In re C.D.H.*, 829 S.E.2d 690; *In re A.R.C.*, 830 S.E.2d 1. On remand, the trial court should make the necessary findings in response to the inquiry and determine whether the parent is entitled to a new hearing with the appointment of new counsel. *In re C.D.H.*, 829 S.E.2d 690; *In re S.N.W.*, 204 N.C. App. 556.

As part of the ineffective assistance of counsel cases, the court of appeals has addressed issues related to communication between the attorney and client. In a private TPR action, *In re B.L.H.*, 239 N.C. App. 52 (2015), in which the respondent father asserted ineffective assistance of counsel, the court of appeals concluded that trial counsel did not make sufficient efforts to communicate with the respondent in order to provide him with effective representation and vacated the TPR order, remanding the case for a new hearing. The only action taken by counsel related to communicating with the respondent was to contact the federal prison to learn about its email system. Counsel did not write any letters or send any emails to the respondent and did not engage in any phone conversations with the respondent; he did not present evidence on the respondent's behalf at the hearing and failed to make a cogent argument at the adjudication phase. The court of appeals pointed out that it was not a case where the respondent had failed to cooperate; to the contrary, the respondent acted promptly upon receiving the TPR summons with a response directed to his appointed counsel and timely returned an affidavit of indigency.

In another TPR case, *In re M.T.-L.Y.*, 829 S.E.2d 496 (N.C. Ct. App. 2019), the court of appeals determined that the respondent mother was not denied effective assistance of counsel when the trial court denied her attorney's motion to continue the hearing. A component of effective assistance of counsel involves adequate time for the attorney and client to prepare a defense. Although prejudice is presumed when the court denies a continuance to allow for adequate time to prepare for trial, when the lack of trial preparation is a result of the party's own actions, the trial court does not err when denying a motion to continue. In *In re M.T.-L.Y.*, the court of appeals was not persuaded by the mother's argument that in-person (or face-to-face), rather than phone, text, or email, communication was essential to prepare.

The reviewing court will not second guess an attorney's strategy and trial tactics when determining whether the respondent was denied effective assistance of counsel. There is a "presumption that counsel's conduct falls within the wide range of reasonable professional assistance." *In re M.Z.M.*, 251 N.C. App. 120, 127 (2016). The court examines the attorney's conduct and determines whether there was prejudice to the client or whether the conduct undermined the fundamental fairness of the proceeding. *See In re M.Z.M.*, 251 N.C. App. 120 (holding mother was not denied effective assistance of counsel when her attorney's strategy was to concede the grounds to TPR; attorney did not cross-examine witnesses or present evidence during the adjudication phase but presented evidence and made arguments in the disposition phase).

**6. Payment of counsel and reimbursement of fees.** Counsel appointed for an indigent parent is to be paid a reasonable fee in accordance with rules adopted by the Office of Indigent Defense Services. G.S. 7B-603(b); 7B-1101.1(a). The court may require reimbursement of fees from a parent, but only if (1) the parent is 18 or older and (2) the juvenile is adjudicated abused, neglected, or dependent, or the parent's rights are terminated. The court determines whether the parent should reimburse fees at a dispositional or other appropriate hearing, and the court must take into consideration the parent's ability to pay. If the parent does not comply with the court's order to pay, the court must file a judgment against the parent for the amount ordered. G.S. 7B-603(b1).

**AOC Form:**
AOC-G-200, Civil Case Trial Level Fee Application Order For Payment Judgment Against Payment/Guardian (Aug. 2019).

**Resources:**
The Office of Parent Defender, in the Office of Indigent Defense Services (IDS), assists court-appointed parents' attorneys at both the trial and appellate levels. Information about the office as well as resources for parents' attorneys can be found on the IDS website.

For performance guidelines for representing parents created by the IDS, see N.C. COMM'N ON INDIGENT DEFENSE SERVICES, "Performance Guidelines for Attorneys Representing Indigent Parent Respondents in Abuse, Neglect, Dependency and Termination of Parental Rights Proceedings at the Trial Level" (2007).

For standards of practice in representing parents adopted by the American Bar Association (ABA), see AMERICAN BAR ASS'N, "Standards of Practice for Attorneys Representing Parents in Abuse and Neglect Cases" (2006).

For materials, training, and opportunities to connect with other attorneys, see the ABA Center for Children and the Law website.

Access to resources and organizations focused specifically on parent representation or related topics (for example, fatherhood), can be found by searching those specific terms on the website for the Child Welfare Information Gateway.

### E. Funds for Experts and Other Expenses[3]

**1. Expenses of representation.** Indigent persons entitled to appointed counsel are also entitled to have the state provide them with "necessary expenses of representation." G.S. 7A-450(a), (b). An indigent respondent parent has the right to the services of counsel pursuant to G.S. 7A-451, 7B-602, and 7B-1101.1. Upon a proper showing, the parent also is entitled to funds for the services of expert witnesses or other expenses of representation. Payment for these services is in accordance with Rules of the Office of Indigent Defense Services (IDS). G.S. 7A-454. Under current IDS rules, an indigent parent must apply to the court in which the case is pending for funding (see discussion in subsection 3, below, related to parent's ex parte motion). The parent's attorney must locate an expert and then file a motion using the form AOC-G-309 requesting court approval for expert fees. Fees for types of experts are set out in the form itself.

**AOC Form:**
AOC-G-309, Application and Order for Defense Expert Witness Funding in Non-Capital Criminal and Non-Criminal Cases at the Trial Level (Feb. 2015).

---

[3] Some content for this section is based on Parent Representation Coordinator, N.C. Office of Indigent Defense Services, "Memo on Ex Parte Motions for Experts in AND Cases."

> **Resource:** The Office of Indigent Defense Services maintains a website discussing Forensic Resources, <u>here</u>, which includes a. database of experts in all areas.

It is in the trial court's discretion whether to grant motions to obtain funds for experts and other representation expenses. *See In re D.R.*, 172 N.C. App. 300 (2005) (quoting language from other cases). However, if the indigent person makes the required showing of need, he or she is entitled to funds for expert assistance. *See State v. Parks*, 331 N.C. 649 (1992) (stating the standard). Questions relating to expert assistance arise more often in criminal cases than in abuse, neglect, dependency, and termination of parental rights (TPR) cases. However, all of these cases are decided under the same provisions in Article 36 of G.S. Chapter 7A.

**2. Standard for obtaining expenses.** Case law has established standards for determining whether the fee of an expert or other resource, such as an investigator, is a "necessary expense of representation." Criminal cases establish that the indigent parent must meet a "threshold showing of specific necessity"—that is, a preliminary, but particularized, showing of need. *See State v. Parks*, 331 N.C. 649, 656 (1992) (quoting *State v. Penley*, 318 N.C. 30, 51 (1986)). Juvenile cases have followed that standard. To establish a preliminary, particularized need for funding, a party must show that (1) the person requesting the expert will be deprived of a fair trial without the expert or (2) there is a reasonable likelihood that the expert will materially assist the party in the preparation of his or her case. *See In re J.B.*, 172 N.C. App. 1 (2005) (upholding trial court's denial of parent's motion for expenses for expert in TPR case where parent was unable to show deprivation of a fair trial without the requested expert assistance or material assistance with the requested expert). Particularized need is a "flexible concept" that must be determined on a case-by-case basis. "Mere hope or suspicion that favorable evidence is available is not enough to require that such help be provided[.]" *In re J.B.*, 172 N.C. App. 1, 12 (2005) (quoting *State v. Page*, 346 N.C. 689, 696–97 (1997)).

The court of appeals seemed to apply the standard for obtaining funds for an expert to a motion for funds to conduct a telephone deposition of the child's foster parents. *In re D.R.*, 172 N.C. App. 300 (2005) (holding that trial court did not abuse its discretion in denying motion for funds). Assuming the test for obtaining funding for experts applies to more routine expense requests, as a practical matter the courts may scrutinize these requests less closely. *See In re J.B.*, 172 N.C. App. 1 (affirming trial court's order that denied motion for funds for expert but allowed parent to submit bill for deposition of respondent's therapist and for costs of obtaining therapist's records).

**3. Parent's ex parte motion.** No appellate court decisions address the question of whether, in a juvenile case, a respondent parent's motion for funds for an expert may be made and heard ex parte. It is well established that in criminal cases ex parte hearings on motions for experts are permissible, and even required if requested, on the basis that an open hearing could jeopardize a defendant's Fifth Amendment privilege against self-incrimination, Sixth Amendment right to effective assistance of counsel, or right to privileged communications with his or her attorney. *See State v. Ballard*, 333 N.C. 515 (1993). Although a respondent parent in a juvenile case does not have a Sixth Amendment right to counsel like a defendant in a criminal case, the parent does have due process rights and a statutory right to counsel and to effective assistance of counsel.

**Practice Note:** One possible procedure, given the legal uncertainty regarding ex parte requests, is for respondent's counsel to move to be heard ex parte, giving notice to the other parties of that motion but not of the underlying motion for funds. If the court grants the request to be heard ex parte, counsel would then present the motion for funds ex parte to the court.

## F. Guardian ad Litem for Parent[4]

**1. Circumstances for appointment and legislative history.** The Juvenile Code, in G.S. 7B-602 and 7B-1101.1, either requires or authorizes the court to appoint a guardian ad litem (GAL) for the respondent parent pursuant to Rule 17 of the Rules of Civil Procedure in two circumstances. When the parent is an unemancipated minor, the court *must* appoint a GAL. When the parent is incompetent, the court *may* appoint a GAL. GAL representation for parents has a complex legislative history that is relevant to the interpretation of any case law based on earlier versions of the statute.

Legislation in 2013 substantially changed GAL representation for parents. Before October 1, 2013, the court had the discretion to appoint a GAL for a parent based on incompetence or diminished capacity, and case law established that the GAL's role was one of either substitution or assistance, depending on the basis for the appointment. Those distinctions no longer exist. A GAL for a parent who is not a minor may be appointed only for a parent who is incompetent. *See* G.S. 7B-602(c); *In re T.L.H.*, 368 N.C. 101(2015) (applying G.S. 7B-1101.1). Designated duties of a GAL appointed under G.S. 7B-602 and 7B-1101.1 were also repealed in 2013. *See* S.L. 2013-129, sec. 17 and 32.

**Resource:** For a thorough discussion of the issue of GAL representation of parents, including legislative and case history, see Janet Mason, *Guardians ad Litem for Respondent Parents in Juvenile Cases*, JUVENILE LAW BULLETIN No. 2014/01 (UNC School of Government, Jan. 2014).

(a) **GAL for minor parent.** If the parent is under the age of 18 and not married or otherwise emancipated, the court must appoint a GAL for the parent pursuant to Rule 17 of the Rules of Civil Procedure. G.S. 7B-602(b); 7B-1101.1(b); *see* G.S. 1A-1, Rule 17. If the minor parent reaches age 18 or gets married or becomes emancipated during the course of the proceeding, the GAL should be released unless the court determines that the parent is incompetent.

A minor parent may be "the juvenile" in a separate case involving the minor parent's own status as an abused, neglected, or dependent juvenile. In that proceeding he or she would (or might, if only dependency was alleged) have a GAL appointed pursuant to G.S. 7B-601 like any other juvenile who is the subject of a petition alleging abuse, neglect, or dependency. That G.S. 7B-601 GAL appointment is separate from the Rule 17 GAL appointment for a respondent minor parent.

---

[4] Portions of this section are based on Janet Mason, *Guardians ad Litem for Respondent Parents in Juvenile Cases*, JUVENILE LAW BULLETIN No. 2014/01 (UNC School of Government, Jan. 2014).

**(b) GAL for parent who is incompetent.** On motion of any party or on the court's own motion, the court *may* appoint a GAL for a parent who is incompetent pursuant to Rule 17 of the Rules of Civil Procedure. G.S. 7B-602(c); 7B-1101.1(c). The court determines whether the parent is incompetent. See subsection 5, below.

---

**AOC Form:**
AOC-J-206, Order to Appoint, Deny, or Release Guardian Ad Litem (For Respondent) (Oct. 2013).

---

**2. Privileged communications.** Communications between the GAL and the parent and between the GAL and the parent's counsel are privileged and confidential. G.S. 7B-602(d); 7B-1101.1(d).

**3. Timing and source of GAL appointment.** Any party or the court itself may move for the appointment of a GAL for a respondent parent. If the petitioner (or movant in a termination of parental rights (TPR) case) knows that the parent is incompetent, the petitioner should "make written application" for the appointment of a GAL before or at the time the action is filed. *See* N.C. R. Civ. P. 17(c). There is no statutory limitation on when during a proceeding the motion can or should be made. However, the appellate courts have held that when there is a substantial question as to whether a party in a civil action is competent, the court should address that question "as soon as possible in order to avoid prejudicing the party's rights." *In re J.A.A.*, 175 N.C. App. 66, 72 (2005). *See also In re I.T.P-L.*, 194 N.C. App. 453 (2008) (holding that appointment of a GAL for a respondent was timely when made on motion of the petitioner seventeen days after a TPR petition was filed and three months before the first hearing). The court is not required to conduct an inquiry or a hearing if it determines there is no substantial question about the parent's competency. *See In re T.L.H.*, 368 N.C. 101 (2015), discussed in subsection 5 below.

**4. Who may serve as GAL.** The Juvenile Code does not specify whom the court may appoint as GAL for a parent. Rule 17 of the Rules of Civil Procedure, which is referenced in G.S. 7B-602 and G.S. 7B-1101.1, directs the court to appoint "some discreet person" to serve as GAL when one is required. The only other guidance given by the Juvenile Code as to who may serve as GAL is the following:

- A parent's attorney may not also serve as the parent's GAL. G.S. 7B-602(d); 7B-1101.1(d).
- GALs trained and supervised by the N.C. Guardian ad Litem Program do not serve as Rule 17 GALs. The GAL Program is limited to representing children who are the subject of a petition for abuse, neglect, dependency, or TPR. *See* G.S. 7B-601; 7B-1108(b), (d); 7B-1200.

Neither Rule 17 nor the Juvenile Code requires that the Rule 17 GAL be an attorney, and while courts often appoint attorneys as GALs for parents, the GAL's role in the case is not that of a second or back-up attorney for the parent.

**5. Determination of incompetence.** No specific procedures are articulated in the Juvenile Code or Rule 17 for determining whether to appoint a Rule 17 GAL for the parent. However, it is clear that an actual adjudication of incompetence pursuant to G.S. Chapter 35A is not required. *See* G.S. 35A-1102 (stating that even though Chapter 35A is the exclusive procedure for adjudicating a person incompetent, that does not interfere with the judge's authority to appoint a GAL under Rule 17).

If a court determines there is a substantial question as to a respondent's competence, the court in the juvenile action must conduct a hearing or inquiry on the issue of competence. *See In re D.L.P.*, 242 N.C. App. 597 (2015) (judge has a duty to inquire when made aware of a substantial question as to a litigant's competency); *In re P.D.R.*, 224 N.C. App. 460 (2012); *In re M.H.B.*, 192 N.C. App. 258 (2008); *In re N.A.L.*, 193 N.C. App. 114 (2008) (all decided under prior law). Deciding (1) whether there is a substantial question as to a parent's competence warranting a hearing on the issue and (2) whether the parent is incompetent are both discretionary determinations made by the trial court. *In re T.L.H.*, 368 N.C. 101 (2015); *In re Z.V.A.*, 835 S.E.2d 425 (N.C. S.Ct. 2019). The standard of review for whether an inquiry into the parent's competency should be conducted and for the appointment of the GAL is an abuse of discretion, which results in a ruling that "is manifestly unsupported by reason or is so arbitrary that it could not have been the result of a reasoned decision." *In re T.L.H.*, 368 N.C. at 107 (quoted in *In re Z.V.A.*, 835 S.E.2d. at 428).

A determination of whether there is a substantial question of a parent's incompetency does not require that the parent have a mental health diagnosis. Similarly, if a parent has a mental health diagnosis, that diagnosis is not determinative of incompetency. The trial court's determination of incompetency includes observations of the respondent's behavior in the courtroom, ability to express herself, her understanding of the situation, her ability to assist her counsel, and numerous other factors. *In re T.L.H.*, 368 N.C. 101.

A trial court is given substantial deference when determining whether there is a substantial question as to a parent's competency warranting a hearing or an inquiry on the issue because the court has interacted with the respondent parent. *In re Z.V.A.*, 835 S.E.2d 425; *In re T.L.H.*, 368 N.C. 101. Absent "the most extreme instances," a trial court should not be held to have abused its discretion by not making the inquiry when there is an appreciable amount of evidence that tends to show the respondent is not incompetent. *In re T.L.H.*, 368 N.C. at 108–09 (quoted and applied in *In re Z.V.A.*, 835 S.E.2d. at 429). How a parent appears to be functioning in the case impacts a court's determination of whether there is a substantial question. In *In re T.L.H.*, 368 N.C. 101, the supreme court found there was no abuse of discretion when the trial court did not hold a hearing on the mother's incompetency in a TPR proceeding as the evidence showed the mother appeared to understand the nature of the proceedings and that she understood that she had to manage her own affairs and that there were steps she needed to take to avoid losing her parental rights. In *In re Z.V.A.*, 835 S.E.2d 425, the supreme court held there was no abuse of discretion when the trial court did not conduct an inquiry into the mother's competency despite an indication that she had a mental disability based on an IQ of 64 as mother was able to work, attend school, and complete domestic violence classes that were part of her case plan. In *In re J.R.W.*, 237 N.C. App. 229 (2014), the court of appeals held the trial court was not required to conduct an inquiry as to the mother's competency based on her history of mental health issues because the record established that her mental health issues did not rise to the level of incompetency. For example, the mother had successfully transitioned from shelter to apartment living, had enrolled in a GED program, had appropriate visits with her child, completed a parenting program, and attended all but one hearing where the court had an opportunity to observe her. In its reasoning, the court of appeals pointed out that the statute did not require an inquiry related to competence merely because a parent had a mental health history.

When there is a substantial question of a parent's competency, the court conducts an inquiry or hearing on the issue and the need for a GAL appointment under Rule 17. The parent and his or her attorney must be given notice of the hearing or inquiry. *See Hagins v. Redev. Comm'n of Greensboro*, 275 N.C. 90 (1969). No formal procedure for a hearing to determine incompetence is prescribed, but the court of appeals has offered this guidance:

- when practical, the respondent whose competency is questioned should be present;
- when possible, a voir dire examination of the respondent should take place;
- if the court hears conflicting evidence, the judge should make findings of fact to support its determination.

*Rutledge v. Rutledge*, 10 N.C. App. 427 (1971).

The court's statutory authority to order a pre-adjudication examination of the parent is clear in a TPR proceeding (*see* G.S. 7B-1109(c)), but less clear in the pre-adjudication stage of an abuse, neglect, or dependency case. Although Rule of Evidence 706 and Rule 35 of the Rules of Civil Procedure might provide authority for ordering such an examination, appellate cases have not directly addressed this issue.

In discussing the term "incompetent" in connection with the appointment of Rule 17 GALs for respondent parents, the courts have adopted the definition of "incompetent adult" found in G.S. 35A-1101(7). *See, e.g., In re D.L.P.*, 242 N.C. App. 597 (2015) (decided under current law); *In re A.R.*, 238 N.C. App. 302 (2014); *In re P.D.R.*, 224 N.C. App.460 (2012); *In re A.R.D.*, 204 N.C. App. 500 (2010); and *In re M.H.B.*, 192 N.C. App. 258 (2008) (all decided under prior law). That definition reads as follows:

> Incompetent adult. -- An adult or emancipated minor who lacks sufficient capacity to manage the adult's own affairs or to make or communicate important decisions concerning the adult's person, family, or property whether the lack of capacity is due to mental illness, intellectual disability, epilepsy, cerebral palsy, autism, inebriety, senility, disease, injury, or similar cause or condition.

G.S. 35A-1101(7).

This definition requires more than a mental health diagnosis. Evidence of mental health problems or alleging the ground of incapability based on mental illness for a TPR is not per se evidence of a parent's incompetence to participate in the proceeding. *See In re T.L.H.*, 368 N.C. 101; *In re J.R.W.*, 237 N.C. App. 229.

**6. Role of the parent's GAL.** Appointment of a GAL based on incompetence "will divest the parent of their [sic] fundamental right to conduct his or her litigation according to their [sic] own judgment and inclination." *In re J.A.A.*, 175 N.C. App. 66, 71 (2005) (citation omitted) (decided under prior law). An appointment of a GAL in the juvenile proceeding does not affect the parent's control over any other aspect of his or her life or property. Neither the Juvenile Code nor Rule 17 provides specific guidance as to the role of the parent's GAL. Broadly speaking, the duty of a GAL is "to protect the interest" of the party in the litigation in which he or she is appointed. *Narron v. Musgrave*, 236 N.C. 388, 394 (1952) (quoting *Spence v. Goodwin*, 128 N.C. 273, 274 (1901)). The court of appeals has stated that "Rule 17 contemplates active participation of a GAL in the proceedings for which the GAL is appointed." *In re D.L.P.*, 242 N.C. App. 597, 601 (2015) and *In re P.D.R.*, 224 N.C. App. 460, 469 (2012) (both quoting *In re A.S.Y.*, 208 N.C. App. 530, 538 (2010)). The court of appeals has also said that a GAL's role under Rule 17 is to act "as a guardian of procedural due process for the parent, to assist in explaining and executing her rights . . . to represent the party . . . to the fullest extent feasible and to do all things necessary to secure a judgment favorable to such party." *In re A.S.Y.*, 208 N.C. App. 530, 540 (2010) (citations omitted) (internal quotation marks omitted) (decided under prior law but addressing parent's incompetency and Rule 17). Once a trial court determines that a Rule 17 GAL is required and appoints a GAL to represent a respondent parent in an abuse, neglect, or dependency proceeding, the trial court may not conduct a hearing without the respondent's GAL. *In re D.L.P.*, 242 N.C. App. 597 (vacating adjudication and disposition orders entered after hearings at which respondent's GAL was not present).

The precise nature of a GAL's role will depend on a variety of factors, such as the party's age and maturity, the cause and extent of the party's incompetence, and the nature of the litigation. While a GAL's role may be viewed as one of "substitution," that should not mean depriving the party of the right to participate in and make decisions about the case to the extent he or she is able to do so. The GAL's role should include assisting the parent in understanding the case and in participating to the extent he or she is able, while exercising judgment about and making decisions the parent is unable to make, to protect that parent's interests. The incompetency and guardianship statutes in G.S. Chapter 35A state that "[t]he essential purpose of guardianship for an incompetent person is to replace the individual's authority to make decisions with the authority of a guardian when the individual does not have adequate capacity to make such decisions." G.S. 35A-1201(a)(3). The role of a parent's GAL in a juvenile case can be viewed the same way in the context of the juvenile case.

The following statements referring to guardianship following an adjudication of incompetence seem equally relevant for a parent's GAL:

> Limiting the rights of an incompetent person by appointing a guardian for him should not be undertaken unless it is clear that a guardian will give the individual a fuller capacity for exercising his rights.

> Guardianship should seek to preserve for the incompetent person the opportunity to exercise those rights that are within his comprehension and judgment, allowing for the possibility of error to the same degree as is

allowed to persons who are not incompetent. To the maximum extent of his capabilities, an incompetent person should be permitted to participate as fully as possible in all decisions that will affect him.

G.S. 35A-1201(a)(4) and (5).

A court may address the role of a GAL for the parent in its appointment order, and the GAL, along with the parent's attorney, may seek guidance from the court if they are unsure about the role the GAL should play.

**7. Payment of parent's GAL.** G.S. 7B-603(b) specifies that GALs for parents shall be paid a reasonable fee in accordance with the rules adopted by the Office of Indigent Defense Services. *See* G.S. 7B-1101.1(f). The Juvenile Code does not address fees for a GAL for a parent who is not indigent in an abuse, neglect, or dependency proceeding; however, Rule 17(b)(2) of the Rules of Civil Procedure (under which an appointment of a parent's GAL would be made) states that the court may "fix and tax" the GAL's fee as part of the costs. Regarding a termination of parental rights (TPR) proceeding, G.S. 7B-1101.1(f) states if the parent is not indigent and does not secure private counsel, the fee of a GAL appointed for the parent is a proper charge against the parent. *See also* G.S. 7B-1110(e), which authorizes the court to tax the cost of a TPR proceeding to any party.

# Chapter 3

# Jurisdiction, Venue, and Overlapping Proceedings

# Chapter 3
# Jurisdiction, Venue, and Overlapping Proceedings

**3.1 Summary and Scope of Jurisdiction Issues    3-3**
  A. Introduction
  B. District Court Jurisdiction
  C. Continuing and Ending Jurisdiction in Abuse, Neglect, or Dependency Proceedings
  D. Terminology Related to Continuing and Ending Jurisdiction
     1. Terminate jurisdiction
     2. Waive permanency planning hearings
     3. Caution about "closing a case"

**3.2 Subject Matter Jurisdiction    3-8**
  A. Introduction
  B. Key Issues in Determining Subject Matter Jurisdiction
     1. Proper petitioner
     2. Proper initiation of proceedings
     3. Verified petition
     4. Indian Child Welfare Act
     5. Uniform Child-Custody Jurisdiction and Enforcement Act
     6. Parental Kidnapping Prevention Act
     7. Residence/Location of child
  C. Issues That Do Not Affect Subject Matter Jurisdiction
     1. Defects in or lack of summons
     2. Failure to include certain information in petition
     3. Statutory timelines

**3.3 Uniform Child-Custody Jurisdiction and Enforcement Act and Parental Kidnapping Prevention Act    3-19**
  A. Introduction
  B. Applicability of the UCCJEA: G.S. Chapter 50A
     1. Abuse, neglect, dependency, and termination of parental rights
     2. Inapplicability
     3. Indian Child Welfare Act controls
     4. Foreign countries
  C. Jurisdictional Basis for Making Custody Determination under the UCCJEA
     1. Initial child custody jurisdiction
     2. Modification jurisdiction: exclusive continuing jurisdiction and convenient forum
     3. Temporary emergency jurisdiction
     4. Simultaneous proceedings
     5. Information concerning child's status (affidavit)
  D. Evidence, Findings, and Conclusions of Law
  E. Communication Requirements
     1. Communication between courts
     2. Record of communications between courts

F. Hearings
   1. Judicial cooperation and appearance of parties
   2. Notice and opportunity to be heard
   3. Testimony in another state
G. Deployed Parents
H. Enforcement of Custody Orders under the UCCJEA
   1. Enforcement generally
   2. Temporary visitation
   3. Registration and confirmation of orders from other states
   4. Expedited enforcement procedure
   5. Prosecutor's role
I. Parental Kidnapping Prevention Act: 28 U.S.C. 1738A
   1. Applicability in abuse, neglect, dependency, and termination of parental rights actions
   2. Terms
   3. Jurisdiction
   4. Notice and opportunity to be heard

## 3.4 Personal Jurisdiction   3-42
A. Introduction
B. Service of Process
   1. Who must be served
   2. Proper service
C. Consent and Waiver Establishing Personal Jurisdiction
   1. Making an appearance
   2. Failing to raise the defense
D. Acquiring Personal Jurisdiction in Abuse, Neglect, Dependency Cases
   1. Statutory provisions
   2. Permanent custodians and guardians
E. Out-of-State Parents in Termination of Parental Rights Cases
   1. Juvenile Code requires only service
   2. Appellate cases require minimum contacts in some situations
   3. Service on respondent temporarily in state
   4. Other states
   5. UCCJEA does not require personal jurisdiction

## 3.5 Venue   3-49
A. Introduction
B. Proper Venue
   1. Where to initiate an abuse, neglect, or dependency action
   2. Defining "residence"
C. Transfer of Venue in Abuse, Neglect, or Dependency Cases
   1. Pre-adjudication change of venue
   2. Post-adjudication change of venue
D. Transfer of Venue in Termination of Parental Rights Cases

## 3.6 Overlapping Proceedings   3-53
A. Civil Custody Proceedings

1. Jurisdiction, consolidation, and stays
2. Civil custody as the permanent plan
3. Priority of conflicting orders
4. Termination of parental rights
B. Juvenile Delinquency and Undisciplined Proceedings
1. Simultaneous proceedings
2. DSS custody from delinquency or undisciplined proceeding
3. Representation of the juvenile
C. Criminal Proceedings
1. Evidentiary issues
2. Defendant's participation in an abuse, neglect, or dependency proceeding
3. Access to information and people
4. Timing of the two proceedings
D. Domestic Violence Protection Proceedings

## 3.1 Summary and Scope of Jurisdiction Issues

### A. Introduction

Orders entered by a court that does not have subject matter jurisdiction are void. A court's action with respect to a person over whom the court does not have personal jurisdiction, when personal jurisdiction is required, is not binding on that person. Therefore, an early inquiry should be made in every action as to whether the court has the requisite jurisdiction to proceed.

In abuse, neglect, dependency, and termination of parental rights (TPR) cases

- subject matter jurisdiction generally depends on following the jurisdictional procedures set forth in the Juvenile Code (G.S. Chapter 7B), including the proper initiation of proceedings and compliance with the Uniform Child-Custody Jurisdiction and Enforcement Act (UCCJEA);
- personal jurisdiction generally depends on a statutory basis for exercising jurisdiction and proper issuance and service of process, unless an individual's actions constitute consent to personal jurisdiction, G.S. 1-75.3; 1-75.7; and
- venue addresses where the action is filed, which in juvenile cases depends generally on where the child resides or is present (note that separate from venue, the child's residence or location may also relate to jurisdiction, explained more fully in sections 3.2.B.1 and 7, below).

### B. District Court Jurisdiction

The district court has exclusive original jurisdiction over the following proceedings that are discussed in this Manual:

- any case involving a juvenile who is alleged to be abused, neglected, or dependent;
- proceedings dealing with petitions alleging obstruction of or interference with a DSS assessment required by G.S. 7B-302;
- proceedings on petitions for judicial review of DSS determinations that someone is a "responsible individual";
- proceedings under the Interstate Compact on the Placement of Children (ICPC), Article 38 of the Juvenile Code;
- termination of parental rights proceedings;
- proceedings for reinstatement of parental rights;
- judicial reviews of voluntary foster care placements between the juvenile's parent or guardian and DSS as required by G.S. 7B-910; and
- judicial reviews of voluntary foster care placements between DSS and young adults participating in the Foster Care 18–21 program as required by G.S. 7B-910.1.

G.S. 7B-200(a); *see* G.S. 7B-101(6) (definition of "court").

**Note**, for purposes of this Manual, a "department of social services" or "DSS" refers to a department as defined by G.S. 7B-101(8a) regardless of how it is titled or structured.

The district court also has exclusive original jurisdiction over the following proceedings that are not discussed in this Manual:

- proceedings involving judicial consent for emergency treatment for a juvenile when the juvenile's parent (or other responsible person) refuses to consent for treatment,
- proceedings involving waiver of the parental consent requirement for an unemancipated minor's abortion,
- proceedings involving authorization for an underage party to marry,
- emancipation proceedings, and
- any proceeding in which a juvenile is alleged to be undisciplined or delinquent.

G.S. 7B-200(a); 7B-1600; 7B-1601; *see* G.S. 7B-101(6) (definition of "court").

### C. Continuing and Ending Jurisdiction in Abuse, Neglect, or Dependency Proceedings

The Juvenile Code provides that once jurisdiction is obtained over a juvenile, jurisdiction continues until whichever of the following occurs first:

- jurisdiction is terminated by order of the court,
- the juvenile turns 18, or
- the juvenile is emancipated. (In North Carolina, a juvenile who is 16 or 17 years old may be emancipated by a court order entered under Article 35 of G.S. Chapter 7B; a juvenile who is married is emancipated (G.S. 7B-3509).)

G.S. 7B-201(a).

Absent the juvenile reaching the age of 18, becoming emancipated, or a court order terminating its jurisdiction in the juvenile proceeding, the court continues to have jurisdiction in the case even if a permanent plan for the juvenile is achieved, further court hearings are waived, DSS is relieved of making reasonable efforts, and the respondent's attorneys and juvenile's GAL are released. *In re C.M.B.*, 836 S.E.2d 746 (N.C. Ct. App. 2019) (addressing continuing jurisdiction under G.S. 7B-201 as compared to a civil custody action under G.S. Chapter 50; determining the court never terminated its jurisdiction in the juvenile proceeding pursuant to G.S. 7B-201 or 7B-911); *see McMillan v. McMillan*, 833 S.E.2d 692 (N.C. Ct. App. 2019) (determining court entered order pursuant to G.S. 7B-201(a) expressly terminating its jurisdiction in the juvenile proceeding even though it did not enter an order pursuant to G.S. 7B-911 transferring the case to a G.S. Chapter 50 custody action).

In some actions related to abuse, neglect or dependency, the district court has jurisdiction after the juvenile turns 18. In *In re Patron*, 250 N.C. App. 375 (2016), the court of appeals held that a district court had jurisdiction to review a DSS determination that appellant stepmother was a "responsible individual" even though the juvenile, who was 17 when abused, had turned 18 by the time the petition for judicial review was heard. G.S. 7B-323(e) provides for judicial review of a responsible individual determination "at any time." Note also that a child who ages out of foster care may continue receiving foster care services until he or she turns 21 years of age when meeting the eligibility requirements in G.S. 108A-48(c), and the district court has jurisdiction to review the now young adult's voluntary foster care placement as required by G.S. 7B-910.1. G.S. 131D-10.2B; 7B-200(a)(5a).

The court's jurisdiction in a juvenile proceeding ends when the child becomes the subject of a final order of adoption. G.S. 48-2-102(b); *In re W.R.A.*, 200 N.C. App. 789 (2009). *See* G.S. 7B-908(b) (post–termination of parental rights review hearing no longer required when child is the subject of a final order of adoption).

When the court's jurisdiction terminates, whether automatically or by court order, the court has no authority to enforce or modify any order that was previously entered in the action. G.S. 7B-201(b). Instead, the legal status of the juvenile and the custodial rights of the parties revert to the status they were before the petition was filed, unless an applicable law or a court order in another action provides otherwise. G.S.7B-201(b). The termination of the court's jurisdiction in an abuse, neglect, or dependency proceeding does not affect

- a civil custody order entered pursuant to G.S. 7B-911;
- an order terminating parental rights;
- a pending action to terminate parental rights, unless the court orders otherwise;
- any delinquency or undisciplined proceeding; or
- any proceeding related to a new petition alleging abuse, neglect, or dependency.

G.S. 7B-201(b).

### D. Terminology Related to Continuing and Ending Jurisdiction

Because of the effect of an order that terminates jurisdiction in an abuse, neglect, or dependency action, the language a court uses in its order that addresses the status of the action is critical. There is a significant difference between an inactive case (meaning further hearings are waived) where the court retains jurisdiction and a case where jurisdiction has been terminated. Clarity in a court order is essential so that the parties and the court understand which orders are in effect; whether the court has jurisdiction to hear motions to modify, enforce, or review; or whether a new action is required.

**1. Terminate jurisdiction.** The Juvenile Code refers to the termination of the court's jurisdiction. *See* G.S. 7B-201; 7B-401.1(a); 7B-911(a); 7B-1000(b). The Juvenile Code authorizes different methods for the court to terminate its jurisdiction. One, the court may enter an order under G.S. 7B-201(b) expressly terminating its jurisdiction over the abuse, neglect, or dependency proceeding, which results in the parties returning to their pre-petition status. Second, the court may enter an order pursuant to the requirements of G.S. 7B-911, which requires that the court terminate its jurisdiction in the juvenile proceeding and enter a Chapter 50 custody order, thereby transferring the juvenile proceeding to a civil custody action. When terminating jurisdiction under G.S. 7B-201(b), the court is not required to follow the procedures of G.S. 7B-911. *McMillan v. McMillan*, 833 S.E.2d 692 (N.C. Ct. App. 2019). For a further discussion of G.S. 7B-911, see Chapter 7.10.B.4. Three, when DSS fails to prove at the adjudicatory hearing the child's alleged abuse, neglect, or dependency, the court must dismiss the petition with prejudice. G.S. 7B-807(a). In addition to the procedures of the Juvenile Code, the court may determine it no longer has jurisdiction pursuant to the criteria and procedures of the Uniform Child-Custody Jurisdiction Enforcement Act (UCCJEA) set forth in G.S. Chapter 50A, discussed in section 3.3, below.

When applying G.S. 7B-201 or 7B-911, using the statutory language that "jurisdiction is terminated" in a court order clearly and explicitly addresses the jurisdictional status of the case. *See In re C.M.B.*, 836 S.E.2d 746, 754 (N.C. Ct. App. 2019) (concluding "But unless the trial court determines that the case should remain under the jurisdiction of the juvenile court of Surry County, the trial court's order should clearly terminate the juvenile court's jurisdiction"). There is no room for interpretation as to what the court intended. Without jurisdiction, the court has no authority to act any further in that case. *See McMillan v. McMillan*, 833 S.E.2d 692 (determining court entered order expressly terminating its jurisdiction in the juvenile proceeding pursuant to G.S. 7B-201(a) such that the court had jurisdiction to enter an order in the separate Chapter 50 custody action).

**2. Waive permanency planning hearings.** A court in an abuse, neglect, or dependency action may retain jurisdiction while waiving required permanency planning hearings. G.S. 7B-906.1(k), (n). In contrast to an order that terminates the court's jurisdiction, when permanency planning hearings are waived, a party has the right to file a motion in the cause seeking (1) that an order be modified, vacated, or enforced; (2) a show cause order; or (3) termination of the parental rights (TPR) of a parent over whom the court has personal jurisdiction. G.S. 7B-906.1(n); 7B-905.1(d) (authorizing motion for review of a visitation plan); 7B-1000(a) (authorizing motion to modify or vacate a dispositional order); 7B-904(e) (authorizing motion to show cause); 7B-1102 (authorizing TPR motion). When jurisdiction is retained, the court has the authority to act on the motion. For further discussion about the timing and waiver of required permanency planning hearings, see Chapter 7.2.A.4.

Note, however, that when custody is ordered to a parent and the four criteria of G.S. 7B-401(b), one of which involves a new report about the child, applies, the court does not have authority to act on a motion for review filed by DSS in the existing case. Instead, DSS must file a verified petition in the existing case setting out any new allegations resulting from the new report and assessment. The court must then conduct a new adjudicatory hearing before proceeding to a dispositional hearing where custody may be modified. *In re T.P.*, 254 N.C. App. 286 (2017) (vacating modification of permanency planning order resulting from DSS motion for review when G.S. 7B-401(b) was triggered; holding that motion was not the proper pleading and trial court did not have subject matter jurisdiction to hear motion; G.S. 7B-401(b) requires new petition and subsequent adjudicatory hearing). See Chapters 6 (discussing adjudicatory hearings and adjudication) and 7.2.A.4 (discussing when G.S. 7B-401(b) applies).

**3. Caution about "closing a case".** A court should avoid using the term "closed" because it does not provide clarity about the jurisdictional status of a case. "Closed" is not a statutory term and is subject to varying interpretations about whether the court has terminated its jurisdiction or is retaining jurisdiction while waiving permanency planning hearings.

The court of appeals has said, "[c]losing a case file is not the equivalent of the trial court terminating its jurisdiction." *In re S.T.P.*, 202 N.C. App. 468 (2010) (holding that trial court had jurisdiction to consider DSS's motion to reassume custody years after court entered order that "vested" custody with grandparents and ordered "Case closed"). The court of appeals has also said an order that relieves DSS of further responsibility in a case does not terminate the court's jurisdiction. *Rodriguez v. Rodriguez,* 211 N.C. App. 267 (2011); *see In re C.M.B.*, 836 S.E.2d 746 (N.C. Ct. App. 2019) (in case that was initiated in 2009, court retained jurisdiction in the juvenile proceeding and heard parties' motions filed in 2018; DSS had been relieved in 2011 and did not participate in motions hearings). Earlier cases seem to say the opposite. *See In re D.D.J.*, 177 N.C. App. 441, 444 (2006) ("DSS [did not] include in its brief any citation of statutory or case law authority that would allow the court to act after it had closed the case;" the child's guardian ad litem (GAL) and DSS were released); *In re P.L.P.*, 173 N.C. App. 1 (2005) (concluding that trial court's jurisdiction in earlier action was terminated by trial court's order to "close" case; court also released DSS, child's GAL, and attorneys for respondents), *aff'd per curiam*, 360 N.C. 360 (2006).

When the jurisdictional status of the case is not obvious from the language of the court order, the appellate courts have examined the substance of the order to determine whether the trial court retained jurisdiction. As part of its analysis, the court of appeals has looked to whether the parents are back to their pre-petition legal status.

In *In re S.T.P.*, 202 N.C. App. 468, the court of appeals determined that the respondent parents were not returned to their pre-petition legal status since legal custody was awarded to the maternal grandparents. As a result, jurisdiction was not terminated even though the order said, "case closed." In *In re C.M.B.*, 836 S.E.2d 746, the court of appeals determined the district court did not terminate its jurisdiction in orders entered in 2011 or 2014 and that those orders did not return the respondent mother to her pre-petition status.

In contrast, in *Rodriguez*, 211 N.C. App. 267, the court of appeals held that despite the absence of a specific order terminating its jurisdiction, the contents of the juvenile order amounted to a termination of jurisdiction as contemplated by G.S. 7B-201(a). The order vacated prior custody orders entered in the action, placed the children back in the physical and legal custody of their mother from whose care they were initially removed, ended involvement of DSS and the GAL program, and included no provisions requiring ongoing supervision or court involvement. The order essentially returned the mother to her pre-petition legal status.

When deciding whether a court terminated its jurisdiction, the focus has been on the parents' legal status and not on whether the child has been returned to the parent from whose care he or she was removed. A trial court is not affirmatively obligated to return the child to the removal parent's home before terminating its jurisdiction. *In re A.P.*, 179 N.C. App. 425 (2006) (jurisdiction was terminated when the court placed the child with the non-removal parent and "closed" its case; the parents were returned to their pre-petition legal status as either parent had the option to pursue a G.S. Chapter 50 custody proceeding), *rev'd per curiam for reasons stated in dissenting opinion,* 361 N.C. 344 (2007).

Reference to "closing" a case may be appropriate when referring to a DSS internal administrative action. DSS may "close" a case to document that its involvement in that abuse, neglect, or dependency case has ended. *See, e.g., In re H.D.F.*, 197 N.C. App. 480 (2009) (noting that DSS completed a family assessment and "closed the case"); *In re H.T.*, 180 N.C. App. 611 (2006) (stating that respondents complied with their treatment plan and "their case was closed"). When a court has retained jurisdiction in an abuse, neglect, or dependency action and relieved DSS of further responsibility, an internal DSS administrative action that indicates the case is "closed" does not affect a district court's jurisdiction. *See Rodriguez,* 211 N.C. App. 267. Even if DSS administratively closes its case, it remains a party in the court action until the court's jurisdiction is terminated. G.S. 7B-401.1(a). If a motion is filed in court, DSS should reactivate its case. If DSS does not reactivate its case, the court may order it to do so. *See* G.S. 7B-905.1(d) (visitation); 7B-600(b1)(1) (motion to review guardianship appointment).

---

**Practice Note:** To prevent a misinterpretation of the court's intentions, a court order should state explicitly that the court
- retains jurisdiction over the proceeding even though further hearings are waived (the court may also want to state in the order that any party may file a motion for review) or
- terminates jurisdiction over the proceeding.

---

## 3.2 Subject Matter Jurisdiction

### A. Introduction

Judicial jurisdiction is "[t]he legal power and authority of a court to make a decision that binds the parties to any matter properly brought before it." *In re A.P.*, 371 N.C. 14, 17 (2018) (quoting *In re T.R.P.*, 360 N.C. 588, 590 (2006)). To decide a case, the court must have "[j]urisdiction over the nature of the case and the type of relief sought[;]" otherwise, "the proceedings of a court without jurisdiction of the subject matter are a nullity." *In re T.R.P.*, 360 N.C. 588, 590 (2006) (citations omitted).

The district court has exclusive original jurisdiction over any case involving a juvenile alleged to be abused, neglected, or dependent. G.S. 7B-200(a). The district court also has exclusive original jurisdiction over termination of parental rights cases. G.S. 7B-200(a)(4); 7B-1101. In a particular case, the court may lack subject matter jurisdiction if steps necessary to invoke the court's jurisdiction have not been taken. Subject matter jurisdiction cannot be conferred by consent, waiver, stipulation, estoppel, or failure to object. *In re T.R.P.*, 360 N.C. 588. A lack of subject matter jurisdiction can be raised at any time, including for the first time on appeal. *See In re K.J.L.*, 363 N.C. 343 (2009); *In re T.R.P.*, 360 N.C. 588. A court may conclude that there is no subject matter jurisdiction even when a party challenging jurisdiction asserts an incorrect statutory basis for the lack of subject matter jurisdiction. *In re M.C.*, 244 N.C. App. 410 (2015).

Any order entered by a court that lacked subject matter jurisdiction is void. *See In re T.R.P.*, 360 N.C. 588 (concluding that because trial court lacked subject matter jurisdiction, review hearing order was void ab initio). *See also* N.C. R. Civ. P. 12(h)(3) (dismissal of action).

### B. Key Issues in Determining Subject Matter Jurisdiction

**1. Proper petitioner.** Standing involves a statutory right to bring an action. *In re Baby Boy Scearce*, 81 N.C. App. 531 (1986). The Juvenile Code establishes who may initiate an abuse, neglect, dependency, or termination of parental rights (TPR) action. Standing is a jurisdictional issue and, consequently, it "is a threshold issue that must be addressed, and found to exist, before the merits of [the] case are judicially resolved." *In re S.E.P.*, 184 N.C. App. 481, 487 (2007) (citations omitted). The court does not have subject matter jurisdiction over the action if the petition (or TPR motion) is filed by someone who does not have standing.

**(a) Abuse, neglect, dependency.** An abuse, neglect, or dependency action may only be initiated by a county department. A DSS director, or the director's authorized representative, is the only party authorized to file a petition alleging a juvenile's abuse, neglect, or dependency. G.S. 7B-401.1(a); *In re Van Kooten*, 126 N.C. App. 764 (1997).

In *In re A.P.*, 371 N.C. 14 (2018), the North Carolina Supreme Court examined the issue of standing related to which county DSS had authority under the Juvenile Code to file an abuse, neglect, or dependency petition by looking to the definition of "director." As defined by G.S. 7B-101(10), a "director" is "the director of the county department of social services *in the county in which the juvenile resides or is found* . . . ." (emphasis added). The supreme court reversed the court of appeals decision holding that standing, and therefore subject matter jurisdiction, requires that the child be a legal resident of or found in the county of the DSS that files the petition at the time the petition is filed. The supreme court employed the whole-text canon to interpret the relevant statutes and held that standing was not limited to only DSS directors in the county where the juvenile who was the subject of the action resides or is found. The supreme court reasoned that a limiting interpretation is both contrary to the purpose of the Juvenile Code and "the fundamental principle underlying North Carolina's approach to controversies involving child neglect and custody [is] that the best interest of the child is the polar star." *In re A.P.*, 371 N.C. at 21 (2018).

---

**Resources:**
For a more detailed discussion of the appellate opinions addressing standing, see
- Sara DePasquale, *In re A.P.: A County Director's Standing to File an A/N/D Petition Is Not as Limited as Previously Held by the Court of Appeals*, UNC SCH. OF GOV'T: ON THE CIVIL SIDE BLOG (June 14, 2018).
- Sara DePasquale, *Which County DSS Files the A/N/D Petition: That Is the Jurisdictional Question!*, UNC SCH. OF GOV'T: ON THE CIVIL SIDE BLOG (Sept. 15, 2017).

---

Before DSS may file a petition, it must follow the procedures of G.S. 7B-302(a), (c) and (d). Those procedures require that DSS receives a report of abuse, neglect, or dependency; conducts an assessment that indicates the juvenile is abused, neglected, or dependent; and determines that a petition alleging abuse, neglect, and/or dependency must be filed with the district court. *In re S.D.A.*, 170 N.C. App. 354 (2005) (holding that the trial court lacked subject matter jurisdiction when the county DSS did not follow the proper procedures under G.S. 7B-302 to invoke the court's jurisdiction; the county DSS received a report of abuse and neglect and referred the report to a second county DSS for an investigation; after the second county DSS determined there was no abuse, neglect, or dependency, the first county DSS, without conducting its own investigation, filed a petition); *see also* G.S. 7B-403(a).

**(b) Termination of parental rights.** Persons who have standing to file a termination of parental rights (TPR) petition or motion include

- either parent seeking termination of the other parent's rights, except when the petitioning parent is convicted of
  - first- or second-degree forcible rape occurring on or after December 1, 2004 (G.S. 14-27.21 or 14-27.22; prior to December 1, 2015, G.S. 14-27.2 and 14-27.3),
  - statutory rape of a child by an adult occurring on or after December 1, 2008 (G.S. 14-27.23; prior to December 1, 2015, G.S. 14-27.2A), or
  - first-degree statutory rape occurring on or after December 1, 2015 (G.S. 14-27.24 or after December 1, 2004, under prior language of former G.S. 14-27.2(a)(1)),
  if the rape resulted in the conception of the child who is the subject of the TPR proceeding;
- any judicially-appointed guardian of the person of the child;
- any DSS or licensed child-placing agency to which
  - a court has given custody of the child or
  - a child has been surrendered for adoption pursuant to G.S. Chapter 48 by the parent or guardian of the person of the child appointed by the clerk of superior court under G.S. 35A-1241 (or in another jurisdiction in which the law authorizes

the guardian to consent to the adoption) (*see* G.S. 48-1-101(8) (definition of "guardian");
- any person with whom the child has lived for a continuous period of two years or more immediately preceding the filing of the petition or motion;
- any guardian ad litem appointed to represent the child pursuant to G.S. 7B-601 who has not been relieved of his or her duties; or
- any person who has filed a petition to adopt the child. (Note that petitions for adoption and TPR may be filed concurrently. G.S. 48-2-302(c).)

G.S. 7B-1103(a).

For further discussion about standing to initiate a TPR proceeding, see Chapter 9.3.B.

**2. Proper initiation of proceedings.** Abuse, neglect, or dependency actions are initiated by the filing of a petition. G.S. 7B-405. A TPR proceeding may be initiated either by petition or if there is a pending abuse, neglect, or dependency action, by motion filed in the pending action. *See* G.S. 7B-1101.

The court does not have subject matter jurisdiction in the absence of a valid initiating pleading. *In re T.R.P.*, 360 N.C. 588 (2006); *In re McKinney*, 158 N.C. App. 441 (2003). *See, e.g., In re E.B.*, 834 S.E.2d 169 (N.C. Ct. App. 2019) (disregarding six permanency planning orders that were entered by the trial court and relied upon in a TPR proceeding; trial court lacked subject matter jurisdiction to enter such orders when DSS never filed a proper petition alleging abuse, neglect, or dependency but instead had custody via a relinquishment); *In re S.D.W.*, 187 N.C. App. 416 (2007) (holding that a parent could not initiate a termination action by filing a counterclaim for termination in the other parent's civil action for visitation).

**3. Verified petition.** In abuse, neglect, dependency, and TPR cases, the petition (or TPR motion) must be verified. G.S. 7B-403(a); 7B-1104. A petition or motion that is not properly verified is fatally defective. *In re T.R.P.*, 360 N.C. 588 (2006) (holding that the failure to verify the petition deprived the trial court of subject matter jurisdiction).

**(a) "Verified" defined.** G.S. 7B-403(a) states that a petition alleging abuse, neglect, or dependency must be "verified before an official authorized to administer oaths," and G.S. 7B-1104 says that the petition or motion to terminate parental rights "shall be verified by the petitioner or movant." The Juvenile Code does not define "verification". The appellate courts have looked to Rule 11 of the Rules of Civil Procedure for the definition of verification and have applied Rule 11 to determine whether a verification is sufficient. *See In re N.T.*, 368 N.C. 705 (2016); *In re N.X.A.*, 254 N.C. App. 670 (2017); *In re Triscari Children*, 109 N.C. App. 285 (1993).

Rule 11(b) states that a pleading may be verified by affidavit of a party. The verification by a party must state "in substance" that the contents of the pleading are true to the knowledge of the person making the verification, except as to those matters stated on information and belief, and as to those matters he or she believes them to be true. N.C. R. Civ. P. 11(b).

Rule 11(d) addresses verification when the State or any officer acting in its behalf is a party and allows a pleading to be verified by any person acquainted with the facts. N.C. R. CIV. P. 11(d). When filing a petition alleging abuse, neglect, or dependency, a county DSS is acting as an agent of the State Department of Health and Human Services, and Rule 11(d) applies. *In re N.X.A.*, 254 N.C. App. 670.

Combining the language of the Juvenile Code with the language of Rule 11, proper verification by a party in a juvenile action requires a confirmation of truthfulness

- as to the contents of the petition or motion,
- by an appropriate person with the appropriate signature, and
- sworn to or affirmed before an official who is authorized to administer oaths.

**(b) Proper verification.** In an abuse, neglect, or dependency action, the court is required to hold a pre-adjudication hearing and consider "[w]hether the petition has been properly verified and invokes jurisdiction." G.S. 7B-800.1(5a).

**Director and authorized representative.** G.S. 7B-403(a) requires that a petition alleging abuse, neglect, or dependency "be drawn by the director [and] verified before an official authorized to administer oaths." "Drawn" is not defined in the Juvenile Code, but the court of appeals seems to use the term synonymously with "signed by." *In re D.D.F.*, 187 N.C. App. 388, 395 (2007). In addition, the Juvenile Code states that "the director shall sign a petition" alleging abuse, neglect, or dependency to invoke the jurisdiction of the court. G.S. 7B-302(c), (d). *See* G.S. 7B-403(a). "Director" is defined by the Juvenile Code as "[t]he director of the county department of social services . . . or the director's representative as authorized in G.S. 108A-14," which is a social services statute. G.S. 7B-101(10). Social services law permits a county DSS director to "delegate to one or more members of his staff the authority to act as his representative." G.S. 108A-14(b). One statutory responsibility a director has is to assess reports of suspected child abuse and neglect and take appropriate protective action under Article 3 of G.S. Chapter 7B, which includes filing an abuse, neglect, or dependency petition. G.S. 108A-14(a)(11); *In re D.D.F.*, 187 N.C. App. 388. Based on the statutory duties assigned to the director and executed by caseworkers, the DSS caseworker assigned to the child's case is an authorized representative of the director. *In re D.D.F.*, 187 N.C. App. 388; *In re Dj.L.*, 184 N.C App. 76 (2007).

**Appropriate signature.** The statutory requirement that the petition be verified is a way to ensure that the courts are exercising jurisdiction in cases that impact families and constitutional rights "only when an identifiable government actor 'vouches' for the validity of the allegations." *In re T.R.P.*, 360 N.C. 588, 592 (2006). Verification by a party requires that the petitioner attest that the contents of the petition are true or believed to be true based upon his or her knowledge. N.C. R. CIV. P. 11(b); *In re A.J.H-R.*, 184 N.C. App. 177 (2007). For a proper verification, the petitioner who is verifying the contents of the petition must sign his or her own name before the person authorized to verify the oath and not the name of another individual on whose behalf the action is being commenced. *In re A.J.H-R.*, 184 N.C. App. 177 (DSS caseworker who brought petition on behalf of the director and signed the director's name, followed by her own initials, in one place, and then signed her own first initial and last name in another place, made an insufficient verification; the director should have personally appeared and signed his own name before the person verifying the oath); *In re S.E.P.*, 184 N.C. App. 481 (2007) (insufficient verification when DSS caseworker bought petition on behalf of director and signed the director's name by her own name). For a proper verification by an authorized representative, the representative must sign his or her own name as the petitioner. *See In re D.D.F.*, 187 N.C. App. 388. Although it is best to indicate whether the person signing and verifying the petition is the DSS director or the director's authorized representative, the failure to identify one's role is not a jurisdictional defect. *In re D.D.F.*, 187 N.C. App. 388 (verification sufficient when the record showed the caseworker who signed the petition was assigned to the case; there was no indication she was not an authorized representative); *In re Dj.L.*, 184 N.C. App. 76 (finding no error where the petition was signed and verified by a DSS employee with actual knowledge of the case but did not indicate that the person signing was either the DSS director or an authorized representative; respondent did not assert that the person who signed the petition was not an authorized representative).

The verification of a petition alleging neglect and dependency that was based upon information and belief and was made by a DSS attorney was held to be proper under Rule 11(d). The county DSS was acting as an agent of the State DHHS, and the county DSS attorney was acting as a state official. The DSS attorney's verification showed that he was acquainted with the facts of the case as required by Rule 11(d). *In re N.X.A.*, 254 N.C. App. 670 (2017) (holding that neither Rule 11(b) or (c), requiring personal knowledge of the facts of a case, apply to verification by a state officer; the requirement in Rule 11(d) that a DSS attorney, as an officer of the State, be acquainted with the facts was satisfied; noting that it can be assumed that one becomes acquainted with the facts by reviewing the case materials compiled by the various DSS agents and employees assigned to the case and pointing out that only a person who witnesses the abuse, such as an anonymous reporter, has personal knowledge of the facts).

It is not a jurisdictional defect when the director's or authorized representative's verification is executed before the petition is signed by the department's attorney. *In re M.M.*, 217 N.C. App. 396 (2011) (DSS social worker verified the petition on October 1 before it was signed by the DSS attorney on October 5 and filed with the court on October 7; nothing in the record established that the petition was not in existence when the social worker signed the verification).

A party who signs a proper verification is not required to also sign separately on a signature line if there is a separate signature line, although doing so is the better practice. *In re D.D.F.*, 187 N.C. App. 388.

**Person authorized to administer oaths.** The petition must be verified before a person "authorized to administer oaths." G.S. 7B-403(a). North Carolina law authorizes "any officer competent to take the acknowledgment of deeds, and any judge or clerk of the General Court of Justice, notary public, in or out of the State, or magistrate . . . to take affidavits for the verification of pleadings, in any court or county in the State . . . ." G.S. 1-148; *In re N.T.*, 368 N.C. 705 (2016). *See also* G.S.7A-103(2) (clerk of superior court); 7A-291(1) (district court judge); 7A-292(1), (5) (magistrate); 10B-20(a) (notary).

The petition will include the signatures of

- the petitioner, who is confirming the truthfulness of the contents of the petition, and
- the person who is authorized to administer oaths and is performing the verification.

It is not a jurisdictional defect if the signature of the person authorized to administer oaths is not accompanied by that person's title (or capacity) or full name. The North Carolina Supreme Court, in *In re N.T.*, 368 N.C. 705, rejected a challenge to the verification of a petition where the signature of the person before whom the petition was verified was illegible and no title was stated to explain his or her authority. The court held that the respondent father as challenger had the burden of showing that the petition's facially valid verification was not verified by a person authorized to administer oaths, overcoming the presumption that a public official performing an official duty acts in accordance with the law and his or her authority. Here, the judicial official's signature, made in a conspicuous place designated for the signature of a person authorized to administer oaths, represented the official's authority to act and was presumed to be regular. The respondent failed to challenge the presumption of regularity by evidence or specific allegations to the contrary.

When a notary performs the verification, appellate cases have looked to G.S. 10B-40(d), which addresses verification by a notary, to determine whether the verification was proper. *See In re Dj.L.*, 184 N.C. App. 76 (2007). In an unpublished opinion, the court of appeals held that the presumption of regularity accorded to notarial acts was not overcome when the notary's signature that was dated months before the TPR motion was signed and verified. This was a clerical error that did not deprive the court of subject matter jurisdiction. *In re M.F.*, 828 S.E.2d 752 (N.C. Ct. App. 2019) (unpublished); *see* G.S. 10B-99 (presumption of regularity). A notarization is not synonymous with verification. Verification requires an additional step: the appropriate confirmation of truthfulness. *See In re Triscari Children*, 109 N.C. App. 285 (1993).

**4. Indian Child Welfare Act.** If the abuse, neglect, dependency, or termination of parental rights (TPR) action involves an "Indian child" or if the court has reason to know the child is an "Indian child", the Indian Child Welfare Act (ICWA) applies. 25 C.F.R. 23.103; *see* 25 C.F.R. 23.107. The definition of "Indian child" requires that the child be 17 or younger, unmarried, and either (1) a member of an Indian tribe or (2) eligible for membership in an Indian tribe and the biological child of a member of an Indian tribe. 25 U.S.C. 1903(4). ICWA applies to Indian tribes recognized by the U.S. Secretary of the Interior as eligible for services provided to Indians because of their status as Indians and covers Alaska native villages. 25 U.S.C. 1903(8); *In re A.D.L.*, 169 N.C. App. 701 (2005) (holding that ICWA does not apply to children who are registered members of the Lumbee Tribe, which is a state-recognized but not federally recognized tribe). There are 573 recognized tribal entities; one is located in North Carolina: the Eastern Band of Cherokee Indians. 84 Fed. Reg. 1200 (Feb. 1, 2019).

However, a child who is the subject of a juvenile proceeding in North Carolina may be from an Indian tribe located outside of the state. *See In re Bluebird*, 105 N.C. App. 42 (1992) (child was an Indian child requiring compliance with ICWA based on the putative father being a registered member of the Cherokee Nation of Oklahoma and the child's eligibility for tribal membership).

If the Indian child resides or is domiciled on Indian land or is a ward of tribal court, the Indian tribe has exclusive jurisdiction over the child custody proceeding. 25 U.S.C. 1911(a); *see* 25 C.F.R. 23.110 (dismissal of action by state court); *see also* 25 C.F.R. 23.2 (defining "domicile"); *In re Adoption of K.L.J.*, 831 S.E. 2d 114 (N.C. Ct. App. 2019) (defining "ward of tribal court" and holding the Indian children were not wards of tribal court such that the North Carolina court had subject matter jurisdiction). However, the state court may exercise jurisdiction over that Indian child in an emergency proceeding where the emergency removal or emergency placement of the Indian child is necessary to prevent imminent physical damage or harm to the child. 25 U.S.C. 1922; 25 C.F.R. 23.113. The state court may also exercise jurisdiction over that Indian child when the tribe and state entered into an agreement authorizing the transfer of jurisdiction on a case-by-case basis or allowing for concurrent jurisdiction. 25 U.S.C. 1919. *See In re E.G.M.*, 230 N.C. App. 196 (2013) (acknowledging that an agreement pursuant to 25 U.S.C. 1919 between the State of North Carolina and the Eastern Band of Cherokee Indians would allow for state court jurisdiction but remanding for findings of a determination of subject matter jurisdiction after holding that (1) the agreement was not subject to judicial notice as a "legislative fact", (2) nothing in the trial court record referred to the agreement, and (3) the copy attached to the appellee's brief was not certified or authenticated and could not be validated).

For Indian children who are not (1) residing or domiciled on Indian land or (2) wards of the tribal court, an abuse, neglect, dependency, or TPR action may be commenced in state court; however, the case is subject to transfer to a tribal court. 25 U.S.C. 1911(b); 25 C.F.R. 23.115–23.119. It is important to note that ICWA establishes minimum federal standards that apply to certain types of "child-custody proceedings", which include abuse, neglect, dependency, and TPR actions. *See* 25 U.S.C. 1902 and 1903(1). Failure to comply with certain provisions may result in delays in the proceedings and possibly the invalidation of the court order. 25 U.S.C. 1914; *see In re E.G.M.*, 230 N.C. App. 196 (vacating and remanding permanency planning order for further proceedings consistent with ICWA provisions).

For a discussion about ICWA and what is required in abuse, neglect, dependency, TPR, and adoption proceedings, see Chapter 13.2.

**5. Uniform Child-Custody Jurisdiction and Enforcement Act.** Abuse, neglect, dependency, and termination of parental rights proceedings are child-custody actions for purposes of the Uniform Child-Custody Jurisdiction and Enforcement Act (UCCJEA) codified in G.S. Chapter 50A. The court must have jurisdiction under the UCCJEA, which is discussed in section 3.3, below.

**6. Parental Kidnapping Prevention Act.** The Parental Kidnapping Prevention Act (PKPA) is a federal law found at 28 U.S.C. 1738A and applicable to abuse, neglect, dependency, and termination of parental rights proceedings in North Carolina. The court must have jurisdiction under the PKPA, which is discussed in section 3.3.I, below.

**7. Residence/Location of child.** For an abuse, neglect, or dependency action, the Juvenile Code does not explicitly set forth a jurisdictional requirement that is specific to a child's residence or location. However, the various requirements regarding the residence or location of a child related to DSS's authority to act imply that for subject matter jurisdiction to exist, the child must either reside or be found in North Carolina. *See* G.S. 7B-101(10); 7B-301; 7B-400; 7B-903(a)(6). *Cf.* G.S. 50A-202 (exclusive continuing jurisdiction under the UCCJEA).

Separate from subject matter jurisdiction, there is a venue statute that relates directly to the child's location or residence: G.S. 7B-400. However, venue is not jurisdictional and may be waived. *Zetino-Cruz v. Benitez-Zetino*, 249 N.C. App. 218 (2016). For a discussion of a child's residence and venue, see section 3.5.B, below.

There is a "jurisdiction" statute that specifically makes the child's residence and/or location a jurisdictional requirement for a termination of parental rights (TPR) action. Pursuant to G.S. 7B-1101, the district court in the judicial district where the child (1) resides, (2) is found, or (3) is in the legal or actual custody of a county DSS or licensed child-placing agency at the time the petition or motion is filed has exclusive original jurisdiction to determine the TPR action. "Found" has been interpreted to mean where the child is physically present. *In re J.L.K.*, 165 N.C. App. 311 (2004); *In re Leonard*, 77 N.C. App. 439 (1985).

If none of the three statutory circumstances exist at the time the TPR petition is filed, the district court does not have subject matter jurisdiction to hear the TPR matter. *In re M.C.*, 244 N.C. App.410 (2015). The appellate courts recognize an exception to this jurisdictional requirement when in a TPR proceeding there is an existing abuse, neglect, or dependency proceeding in North Carolina; the child resides outside of North Carolina; and North Carolina is exercising continuing exclusive jurisdiction in the abuse, neglect, or dependency action under the UCCJEA. *In re H.L.A.D.*, 184 N.C. App. 381 (2007), *aff'd per curiam*, 362 N.C. 170 (2008). The court of appeals did not apply this exception when there was an underlying abuse, neglect, or dependency action in North Carolina and the child continued to reside in North Carolina. *See In re J.M.*, 797 S.E.2d 305 (N.C. Ct. App. 2016) (holding that there was a lack of subject matter jurisdiction under G.S. 7B-1101 when the guardians appointed in an abuse, neglect, and dependency proceeding in Durham County filed a petition to terminate parental rights in Durham County when, at the time the petition was filed, the child was not in the custody of the Durham County DSS, was not found in Durham County, and was residing with petitioners in Wake County).

**Resource:** For a further discussion on G.S. 7B-1101, see Sara DePasquale, *It's Complicated: Venue vs Jurisdiction in A/N/D and TPR Actions*, UNC SCH. OF GOV'T: ON THE CIVIL SIDE BLOG (Feb. 22, 2017).

## C. Issues That Do Not Affect Subject Matter Jurisdiction

**1. Defects in or lack of summons.** Lack of a proper summons or problems with issuance of a summons implicate personal jurisdiction, not subject matter jurisdiction. Failure to follow the required procedures with respect to issuance of the summons, defects or irregularities in the contents of the summons, problems with service of the summons, or expiration of the summons will not deprive a court of subject matter jurisdiction. *See In re K.J.L.*, 363 N.C. 343 (2009) (holding that defects in a summons and failure to issue a summons do not deprive a court of subject matter jurisdiction and relate only to personal jurisdiction); *In re J.T.*, 363 N.C. 1 (2009) (preceding *In re K.J.L.* and holding that problems with the summons or service of the summons related to personal, not subject matter, jurisdiction — a holding that did not explicitly disconnect issuance of the summons from subject matter jurisdiction but abrogated a number of appellate decisions that had found a lack of subject matter jurisdiction due to problems with summonses); *In re J.D.L.*, 199 N.C. App. 182 (2009) (holding that failure to serve a summons within the time allowed affects only personal jurisdiction and can be waived). *But see In re P.D.*, 803 S.E.2d 667 (N.C. Ct. App. 2017) (unpublished) (vacating termination of parental rights (TPR) order against a nonresident parent; holding that G.S. 7B-1101 limits the court's authority to exercise jurisdiction in a TPR action involving a nonresident parent by requiring the court to find that (1) it has jurisdiction under the UCCJEA and (2) the nonresident parent was served with process pursuant to G.S. 7B-1106; determining that the statutory jurisdictional requirements regarding proper service of process on the nonresident parent were not satisfied).

Personal jurisdiction is discussed in section 3.4, below. The requirements for the content, issuance, and service of a summons in a juvenile proceeding are discussed in Chapter 4.3 and 4.4.

**2. Failure to include certain information in petition.** While the Juvenile Code sets out requirements for the contents of a petition alleging abuse, neglect, or dependency and for a petition or motion for termination of parental rights (TPR), failure to adhere exactly to the requirements concerning contents may not be a jurisdictional defect when the court can get the necessary information from the record or from the face of the petition and no prejudice is shown. Note that the requirements concerning contents should be distinguished from the jurisdictional requirement of verification, discussed in section 3.2.B.3, above.

(a) **Child's address and "clerical information."** Failure to list the child's address in a dependency petition did not deprive the court of subject matter jurisdiction because it was "routine clerical information" and the court could determine from information provided in the petition whether it had subject matter jurisdiction. *In re A.R.G.*, 361 N.C. 392 (2007).

(b) **Language regarding circumvention of Uniform Child-Custody Jurisdiction and Enforcement Act (UCCJEA).** Failure to include in a TPR petition or motion the statutorily required statement that the pleading was not filed to circumvent provisions of the UCCJEA does not deprive the trial court of subject matter jurisdiction absent a showing of prejudice. G.S. 7B-1104(7) (requiring statement); *In re J.D.S.*, 170 N.C. App. 244 (2005). *See also In re Humphrey*, 156 N.C. App. 533 (2003).

**(c) Affidavit as to child's status.** Information about the child's status, as required by the UCCJEA in G.S. 50A-209(a), must be set out in the petition or motion or in an attached affidavit. Failure to attach the affidavit to an abuse, neglect, dependency, or TPR petition (or motion) does not, by itself, deprive the court of subject matter jurisdiction where the court can get necessary information from the record or direct that the information be provided within a reasonable time and there is no prejudice. *In re A.R.G.*, 361 N.C. 392, 399 (2007) (emphasis in original) (nothing in the statute suggests that the information is jurisdictional; G.S. 50A-209(a) refers to "reasonably ascertainable" information, "requires *both* parties to submit the information[,]" and authorizes the court to stay the proceeding until the information is obtained). *See In re D.S.A.*, 181 N.C. App. 715 (2007) (neglect petition); *In re J.D.S.*, 170 N.C. App. 244 (2005) (TPR petition).

**(d) Custody order.** Failure to attach a custody order, if one exists, to a TPR petition or motion as required by G.S. 7B-1104(5) does not deprive the court of subject matter jurisdiction where the court can get the necessary information concerning custody from the petition itself or from the record and no party is prejudiced by the omission. *See, e.g., In re T.M.H.*, 186 N.C. App. 451 (2007); *In re T.M.*, 182 N.C. App. 566, *aff'd per curiam*, 361 N.C. 683 (2007); *In re W.L.M.*, 181 N.C. App. 518 (2007); *In re B.D.*, 174 N.C. App. 234 (2005). However, failure to attach the custody order has been found to be reversible error when the court is unable to get the needed information concerning custody from the petition or record. *See In re T.B.*, 177 N.C. App. 790 (2006) (when DSS did not attach to the petition a copy of the order giving DSS custody and did not remedy the omission by amending the petition or including the order in the record, DSS failed to establish that it had standing and the trial court lacked subject matter jurisdiction); *In re Z.T.B.*, 170 N.C. App. 564 (2005) (holding that failure to include the custody order, the name and address of the appointed guardian, or a statement declaring that the petitioner had no knowledge of such information rendered the petition facially defective).

**3. Statutory timelines.** The time limits in the Juvenile Code are not jurisdictional. *In re Dj.L.*, 184 N.C. App. 76 (2007). This includes the timeline for initiating a termination of parental rights (TPR) proceeding. *In re B.M.*, 168 N.C. App. 350 (2005) (rejecting the argument that DSS's failure to initiate the TPR proceeding within sixty days after the permanent plan was changed to adoption was a jurisdictional defect; this case was decided under former G.S. 7B-907). See Chapter 4.5.D (explaining delays beyond statutory timelines and remedy of mandamus).

## 3.3 Uniform Child-Custody Jurisdiction and Enforcement Act and Parental Kidnapping Prevention Act[1]

### A. Introduction

The Parental Kidnapping Prevention Act (PKPA), enacted in 1980, is a federal law that requires states to give full faith and credit to other states' child custody orders if the orders comply with the jurisdictional provisions of the federal law. Pub. L. No. 96-611, sec. 6–10. Congress found that the PKPA was necessary because of the increasing number of cases involving child custody and visitation disputes in different state courts that resulted in conflicting and inconsistent resolution of those disputes, which contributed to the seizure, restraint, concealment, and interstate transportation of children by parties involved in the disputes. Pub. L. No. 96-611, sec. 7(a)(1)–(3). The PKPA establishes national standards for state courts to determine which state has jurisdiction over a custody and visitation dispute and what effect should be given to another state's custody order. Pub. L. No. 96-611, sec. 7(b). The relevant federal statute is codified at 28 U.S.C. 1738A.

The Uniform Child-Custody Jurisdiction and Enforcement Act (UCCJEA) addresses the need for uniformity in child custody cases involving multiple states. The UCCJEA is not a federal law; it is a set of uniform statutes that have been adopted by every state but Massachusetts (note that in Massachusetts, the precursor to the UCCJEA, the UCCJA, is in effect). In North Carolina, the UCCJEA is codified at G.S. Chapter 50A.

The UCCJEA was created to harmonize the former UCCJA with the PKPA and the Violence Against Women Act (VAWA). Its purpose is to (1) avoid jurisdictional competition and conflict between different states' courts and the relitigation of custody decisions made by other states, (2) promote cooperation with the different states' courts, and (3) facilitate the enforcement of other states' custody orders. Official Comment to G.S. 50A-101. The UCCJEA establishes a state court's jurisdiction by addressing temporary emergency jurisdiction, jurisdiction to enter an initial child custody order, exclusive continuing jurisdiction, modification jurisdiction, and simultaneous proceedings. In addition, the UCCJEA addresses enforcement of child custody determinations.

The PKPA's full faith and credit provisions and the UCCJEA's jurisdictional requirements seek to ensure that a state is properly exercising subject matter jurisdiction in a child custody proceeding. Subject matter jurisdiction gives the court the authority to act and cannot be conferred by consent on a court that does not have jurisdiction. *In re J.D.*, 234 N.C. App. 342 (2014); *Gerhauser v. Van Bourgondien*, 238 N.C. App. 275 (2014); Official Comment 2 to G.S. 50A-201. An initial question in every abuse, neglect, dependency, and termination of parental rights proceeding is whether the court can properly exercise jurisdiction. Answering this question involves a two-pronged inquiry:

---

[1] Some content for this section is based on *Child Custody*, CH. 4 *in* CHERYL D. HOWELL & JAN S. SIMMONS, NORTH CAROLINA TRIAL JUDGES' BENCH BOOK DISTRICT COURT: VOL. 1, FAMILY LAW (UNC School of Government, 2019).

1. Does the court have jurisdiction under the Juvenile Code?
2. Does the court have jurisdiction under the UCCJEA?

*In re J.H.,* 244 N.C. App. 255 (2015).

The answer to both of these questions must be "yes". In addition, when there is an out-of-state custody order, the North Carolina court should look to the requirements of the PKPA to determine whether that order is entitled to full faith and credit for modification and enforcement purposes. When making a custody determination, the North Carolina court's compliance with the provisions of the PKPA will affect whether the order that court enters is recognized and enforceable in other states.

B. **Applicability of the UCCJEA: G.S. Chapter 50A**

**1. Abuse, neglect, dependency, and termination of parental rights.** The UCCJEA applies to any case in which the court is making determinations related to a child's custody (legal or physical) or visitation. The UCCJEA explicitly defines "child custody proceeding", which includes abuse, neglect, dependency, and TPR actions. G.S. 50A-102(4).

**2. Inapplicability.** The UCCJEA does not apply to adoption, contractual emancipation, authorization of emergency medical care for a child, delinquency, or undisciplined proceedings. G.S. 50A-102(4); 50A-103.

Note, however, that in an adoption proceeding in North Carolina,

- the petition must include any information required by the UCCJEA that is known to the petitioner (G.S. 48-2-304(b)(4)) and
- the court may not exercise jurisdiction if, when the adoption petition is filed, a court in another state is exercising jurisdiction substantially in conformity with the UCCJEA; however, a North Carolina court may exercise jurisdiction when either (1) the other state's court dismisses its proceeding or releases its exclusive continuing jurisdiction before the adoption decree is granted or (2) the other state's proceeding places the child in the custody of an agency, the adoption petitioner, or another custodian that expressly supports an adoption plan when a specific prospective adoptive parent (who is not the adoption petitioner) is unidentified. G.S. 48-2-100(c); *see* S.L. 2019-172.

**3. Indian Child Welfare Act controls.** Custody proceedings pertaining to Indian children are not subject to the UCCJEA to the extent they are governed by the Indian Child Welfare Act. G.S. 50A-104(a). State courts, however, must treat Indian tribes as if they were states for most purposes under the UCCJEA. G.S. 50A-104(b), (c). See Chapter 13.2 for a discussion of the Indian Child Welfare Act.

**4. Foreign countries.** Foreign countries are treated as states for most UCCJEA purposes. The UCCJEA is not applicable if the child custody law of a foreign country violates fundamental principles of human rights. G.S. 50A-105(c). For an example of a court dealing with a foreign country, see *Tataragasi v. Tataragasi*, 124 N.C. App. 255 (1996) (holding that the trial court had emergency jurisdiction despite the father's pending custody action in Turkey).

## C. Jurisdictional Basis for Making Custody Determination under the UCCJEA

Jurisdictional criteria under the UCCJEA differ depending on whether a court is making an initial custody determination, modifying an existing custody order, or dealing with a temporary emergency custody situation.

**1. Initial child custody jurisdiction.** When a court is making an initial child custody determination (meaning there is no court order that addresses custody of the child at issue), the court should look to G.S. 50A-201 to determine if it has jurisdiction. Listed in order of priority, starting with home state, G.S. 50A-201 establishes four different criteria for an initial child custody determination. *See* Official Comment 1 to G.S. 50A-201. These criteria are discussed immediately below. Note that even without initial child custody jurisdiction, a court may exercise temporary emergency jurisdiction, discussed in subsection 3, below.

(a) **Home state.** A North Carolina court has jurisdiction if (1) North Carolina is the child's home state on the date of commencement of the proceeding or (2) North Carolina was the child's home state within six months before the commencement of the proceeding, the child is absent from North Carolina, and a parent or person acting as a parent continues to live in North Carolina. G.S. 50A-201(a)(1).

"Home state" means the state in which a child lived with a parent or a person acting as a parent for at least six consecutive months immediately before the commencement of a child custody proceeding. In the case of a child less than 6 months of age, the term means the state in which the child lived from birth with a parent or person acting as a parent. G.S. 50A-102(7).

A period of temporary absence from a state by a child or parent/person acting as a parent is counted in calculating the six-month statutory period. G.S. 50A-102(7). *See Ellison v. Ramos*, 130 N.C. App. 389 (1998); *Brewington v. Serrato*, 77 N.C. App. 726 (1985). The court of appeals has adopted a "totality of the circumstances" approach for determining whether an absence from a state is a mere temporary absence or a change of residence sufficient to change home state status.

- The almost six months that children spent in Japan prior to the commencement of the child custody action was ruled a temporary absence from North Carolina. *Hammond v. Hammond*, 209 N.C. App. 616 (2011).
- The six weeks that children spent in North Carolina was considered to be a temporary absence from Vermont. *Chick v. Chick*, 164 N.C. App. 444 (2004).
- Ten months spent by children in Georgia pursuant to a temporary custody order was considered to be a temporary absence from North Carolina. *Pheasant v. McKibben*, 100 N.C. App. 379 (1990).
- Military deployment is not necessarily a temporary absence; deployment is one of the circumstances considered by a court when determining whether the absence from a state is temporary. A court may look to the actions taken by a parent after the

commencement of the custody proceeding when determining if a relocation was a temporary absence. *Gerhauser v. Van Bourgondien*, 238 N.C. App. 275 (2014).

**(b) Significant connection and substantial evidence.** A North Carolina court has jurisdiction if there is no home state or if the home state has declined to exercise jurisdiction and

- the child and the child's parents, or the child and at least one parent or a person acting as a parent, have a significant connection with North Carolina other than mere physical presence and
- substantial evidence is available in North Carolina concerning the child's care, protection, training, and personal relationships.

G.S. 50A-201(a)(2).

This type of jurisdiction "is normally referred to as 'significant connection' jurisdiction." *Gerhauser v. Van Bourgondien*, 238 N.C. App. 275, 295 (2014).

A child has no home state when he or she has moved to different states more frequently than every six months or has not lived with a parent or person acting as a parent. *See In re T.N.G.*, 244 N.C. App. 398 (2015) (holding that there was no home state when the child had not lived in South Carolina with a parent or person acting as a parent for six months and had not been living in North Carolina for six months immediately preceding the filing of the neglect petition); *In re M.G.*, 187 N.C. App. 536 (2007) (holding that where children had lived in North Carolina less than six months, it could not be considered their home state), *rev'd in part on other grounds*, 363 N.C. 570 (2009).

The determination of whether jurisdiction exists is made by the court and cannot be consented to by the parties. In its determination, the court generally looks to the facts that exist at the time the action is commenced. *Gerhauser*, 238 N.C. App. 275. There must be both a significant connection to and substantial evidence in the state. *Holland v. Holland*, 56 N.C. App. 96 (1982).

"Substantial evidence" means "more than a scintilla" and includes available evidence from sources in the state that could address each of the aspects of the child's present or future interest, care, protection, training, and personal relationships. *Holland*, 56 N.C. App. at 100. A history of litigation involving custody of the child that was heard in the state is not by itself sufficient to establish that there is a significant connection with or substantial evidence available in that state. *Gerhauser*, 238 N.C. App. 275 (while original custody order was entered in 2003 by North Carolina court and subsequent motions and orders were filed in North Carolina through 2013, neither parents nor children lived in North Carolina since 2009; although there was no home state, North Carolina could not be said to have significant connection simply because past custody proceedings had taken place here). Other factors beyond litigation history must be considered. Examples of when there is a significant connection with and substantial evidence related to the child's care, protection, training, and personal relationships available in the state to establish jurisdiction include evidence showing the following:

- The child, her parents, and her grandparents (who were acting as parents) resided in North Carolina from the time of the child's birth to the filing of the petition, with the exception of a ten-month period when the child and her father were in South Carolina. *In re T.N.G.*, 244 N.C. App. 398 (2015).
- The mother and children were living in, and the mother was also working in, North Carolina during the one-month period from when the family moved to North Carolina and the petition was filed, and the alleged conduct constituting neglect occurred in North Carolina. *In re T.R.,* 250 N.C. App. 386 (2016).

More than one state can have significant connection jurisdiction. *Gerhauser*, 238 N.C. App. 275 (the court of appeals determined that although North Carolina did not have significant connection jurisdiction, Utah and Florida did).

**(c) Convenience and unjustifiable conduct.** A North Carolina court has jurisdiction if all state courts that would have jurisdiction (home state or significant connection) under the above criteria have declined to exercise jurisdiction because a North Carolina court is the more appropriate forum under G.S. 50A-207 (convenience) or because G.S. 50A-208 applies (unjustifiable conduct by the person seeking jurisdiction). G.S. 50A-201(a)(3). While the UCCJEA does not define "unjustifiable conduct", the official comment to G.S. 50A-208 gives the example of one parent abducting a child and establishing a new home state prior to a custody decree. A parent who is a domestic violence victim fleeing for protection is excluded from the definition of "unjustifiable conduct". It is the other state court, not the North Carolina court, that determines whether North Carolina is a more convenient forum and whether the other state will decline to exercise jurisdiction. The North Carolina court cannot exercise jurisdiction under G.S. 50A-201(a)(3) unless a court with home state or significant connection jurisdiction declines jurisdiction. *Gerhauser v. Van Bourgondien,* 238 N.C. App. 275 (2014). In one opinion, the North Carolina Court of Appeals recognized that another "state could not decline to exercise jurisdiction if no one filed a custody proceeding in that state." *Gerhauser,* 238 N.C. App. at 285–86. Note that the provisions regarding inconvenient forum and declining jurisdiction to a more appropriate forum also apply to modification jurisdiction, discussed further in subsection 2, below.

However, when a North Carolina court has home state or significant connection jurisdiction, it can decline to exercise that jurisdiction after determining that North Carolina is an inconvenient forum and another state is a more appropriate forum. G.S. 50A-201(a)(3); 50A-207(a). The issue of an inconvenient forum may be raised by a party or by the court in this state or in another state. G.S. 50A-207(a). When it is raised, there is a list of eight factors the court must consider in determining whether it is an inconvenient forum, but the list is not meant to be exclusive. G.S. 50A-207(b) and Official Comment. The court is required to consider only those factors that are relevant. G.S. 50A-207(b); *Velasquez v. Ralls,* 192 N.C. App. 505 (2008).

Findings about the relevant factors are necessary when the court determines that the current forum is inconvenient. *See Valasquez,* 192 N.C. App. at 509 (the G.S. 50A-207(b) factors "are necessary when the current forum is inconvenient, not when the forum is convenient"); *In re M.M.*, 230 N.C. App. 225 (2013) (reversing order declining jurisdiction and determining that Michigan was a more appropriate forum; North Carolina trial court failed to consider relevant factors in G.S. 50A-207(b), including the likelihood of the recurrence of domestic violence between the respondent parents, the nature and location of the evidence, the relative familiarity of the courts in each state with the case, and the relative financial circumstances of the respondent parents); *In re M.E.*, 181 N.C. App. 322 (2007) (affirming the trial court's determination that Ohio was the more convenient forum after making relevant findings based on evidence that the child had been placed with the father in Ohio for three years, the family had been receiving counseling in Ohio during that time, and the child's therapist and school were in Ohio, among other factors). There must be evidence to support the court's findings of fact regarding the G.S. 50A-207 factors. *In re C.M.B.*, 836 S.E.2d 746 (N.C. Ct. App. 2019) (reversing order when trial court heard only arguments without any evidence to support findings that would support conclusion of inconvenient forum; motion was unverified, there was no sworn testimony, and neither party presented affidavits or documentary evidence). Although most of the factors require evidence, the court of appeals recognized that there are some factors that may be addressed by the court's record without evidence, such as the court's familiarity with the case. *In re C.M.B.*, 836 S.E.2d 746.

The trial court has discretion to determine that another state is a more appropriate forum and to decline to exercise jurisdiction at any time, even if an action has not been commenced in another state at the time the North Carolina court determines the other state is a more appropriate forum. G.S. 50A-207(a); *In re M.E.*, 181 N.C. App. 322, 327–28 (emphasis in original) (affirming trial court's order that determined Ohio was a more convenient forum and stayed the North Carolina proceeding for a specified period to allow the father to bring a custody action in Ohio; a North Carolina court hearing an abuse, neglect, or dependency proceeding has continuing jurisdiction until the child turns 18 (or the court terminates jurisdiction); the action is " 'pending' within the meaning of G.S. 50A-207" such that the court may decline to exercise jurisdiction "*at any time*" it determines it is an inconvenient forum).

The court of appeals discussed a trial court's ability in an abuse, neglect, or dependency case to terminate its jurisdiction when making an analysis of inconvenient forum in *In re C.M.B.*, 836 S.E.2d 746. As a neglect action, *In re C.M.B.* was initiated in 2009. In 2011, a permanent plan was achieved that placed the child in the guardianship of relatives; relieved DSS, the child's guardian ad litem (GAL), and the parents' attorneys; and waived further hearings in the action. In 2014, the North Carolina court entered a consent order in the juvenile action that modified mother's visitation, continued to relieve DSS, and released the child's GAL and mother's attorney. The court never entered an order that terminated its jurisdiction in the juvenile proceeding under G.S. 7B-201(b) or 7B-911. In 2017, the guardians commenced an action in Tennessee where they had been living with the child since 2014. The Tennessee court determined it had jurisdiction as the mother was residing in Virginia. A Tennessee order that transferred jurisdiction to Tennessee and modified mother's visitation was entered. The Tennessee order that transferred jurisdiction to Tennessee had no effect on North Carolina's jurisdiction under the Juvenile Code as "[o]nly North Carolina can terminate its own juvenile jurisdiction." *In re C.M.B.*, 836

S.E.2d at 750. It is the North Carolina court that needs to determine whether it is an inconvenient forum and stay its proceeding (which does not terminate jurisdiction) or enter an order that clearly terminates its jurisdiction in the juvenile action. The other state court's determination that it will "transfer" jurisdiction of the North Carolina juvenile proceeding to that state has no effect on the North Carolina district court's jurisdiction in the juvenile proceeding.

A North Carolina court cannot determine that another state is a more convenient forum and dismiss its case or terminate its jurisdiction in deference to the other state's jurisdiction unless a custody action has been commenced in that other state. Where it is determined that another jurisdiction is a more convenient forum, the trial court must stay its proceedings on the condition that a proceeding be promptly commenced in the other designated state. G.S. 50A-207(c); *In re M.M.*, 230 N.C. App. 225 (reversing trial court order that purported to transfer jurisdiction to another state without properly establishing that North Carolina was an inconvenient forum and without staying the North Carolina case, effectively dismissing the case and leaving the child in legal limbo); *In re M.E.*, 181 N.C. App. 322 (affirming three-month stay of proceedings for father to commence custody action in Ohio, which North Carolina court determined was the more appropriate forum). The court is also authorized to impose any other condition it considers just and proper, such as a temporary custody order. G.S. 50A-207(c) and Official Comment.

> **Resource:** Cheryl Howell, *Child Custody: We Can't "Change Venue" to Another State*, UNC SCH. OF GOV'T BLOG: ON THE CIVIL SIDE (Oct. 28, 2016).

**(d) No other court would have jurisdiction.** A North Carolina court has jurisdiction if no court of any other state would have jurisdiction under any of the criteria in G.S. 50A-201(a)(1), (2), and (3), discussed above. G.S. 50A-201(a)(4). To determine that no other state would have jurisdiction, the North Carolina court would have to apply the criteria discussed above to any potential state that could have jurisdiction and did not decline jurisdiction. If the North Carolina court finds that another state would have jurisdiction, North Carolina does not have jurisdiction. *Gerhauser v. Van Bougondien*, 238 N.C. App. 275 (2014). If the North Carolina court determines that more than one state would have significant connection jurisdiction, it is not required to identify which of those states has the most significant connection. *Gerhauser*, 238 N.C. App. 275.

**2. Modification jurisdiction: exclusive continuing jurisdiction and convenient forum.** A North Carolina court may modify a child custody determination made by a court of another state only if North Carolina has jurisdiction to make an initial custody determination under G.S. 50A-201(a)(1) (home state criteria) or G.S. 50A-201(a)(2) (significant connection jurisdiction) and

- the court of the other state determines that it no longer has exclusive continuing jurisdiction or that North Carolina would be a more convenient forum or
- either the court of the other state or a North Carolina court determines that the child, the child's parents, and any person acting as a parent do not presently reside in the other state.

G.S. 50A-203. Note, there is an exception for temporary emergency jurisdiction, which is discussed in subsection 3, below.

The North Carolina Court of Appeals addressed modification jurisdiction in *In re D.A.Y.*, 831 S.E.2d 854 (N.C. Ct. App. 2019). In that case, there was an initial custody order entered in California that awarded custody of the child to the father. After that order was entered, the father and child moved to and remained in North Carolina, and the mother relocated to Nevada. The father initiated a termination of parental rights (TPR) action in North Carolina, but at the time that the TPR petition was filed, the mother had returned to California and was served in California. Because the mother was presently residing in California at the time that the TPR action was commenced, neither state's court could find that she did not presently reside in the other state – California. As a result, subject matter jurisdiction to modify the California custody order required a determination by a California court that it no longer had exclusive continuing jurisdiction or that North Carolina was a more convenient forum. There was no such determination. There is an Official Comment to G.S. 50A-202 regarding exclusive continuing jurisdiction that states "exclusive continuing jurisdiction is not reestablished if, after the child, the parents, and all persons acting as parents leave the State, the non-custodial parent returns." This comment applies to whether the other state has exclusive continuing jurisdiction and does not apply to a determination of whether the parent presently resides in the other state. Absent a finding by the other state that it no longer has exclusive continuing jurisdiction, the Official Comment does not confer jurisdiction to North Carolina. In *In re D.A.Y.,* the TPR order was vacated and remanded for dismissal for lack of subject matter jurisdiction given that there was no finding by the California court regarding its lack of exclusive continuing jurisdiction.

Once a North Carolina court has made a child custody determination in compliance with G.S. 50A-201 (initial determination) or 50A-203 (modification), North Carolina has exclusive continuing jurisdiction until

- a North Carolina court determines that neither the child, the child's parents, nor any person acting as a parent has a significant connection with North Carolina and that substantial evidence is no longer available in North Carolina concerning the child's care, protection, training, and personal relationships or
- a North Carolina court or a court of another state determines that the child, the child's parents, and any person acting as a parent do not presently reside in North Carolina.

G.S. 50A-202(a).

North Carolina loses exclusive continuing jurisdiction when the child, the child's parents, and any person acting as a parent move out of the state. North Carolina does not regain exclusive continuing jurisdiction to modify its own order if the noncustodial parent moves back to North Carolina. Official Comment 2 to G.S. 50A-202. Instead, a North Carolina court may modify its own custody determination only if it has jurisdiction to make an initial custody determination under G.S. 50A-201. G.S. 50A-202(b) and Official Comment 2. *See also In re D.A.Y.*, 831 S.E.2d 854 (N.C. Ct. App. 2019) (discussing the Official Comment and exclusive continuing jurisdiction).

Both the exclusive continuing jurisdiction and modification jurisdiction statutes refer to where the parties "presently reside." G.S. 50A-202(a)(2); 50A-203(2). "Presently resides" means where someone actually lives and does not refer to a technical domicile. Official Comment 2 to G.S. 50A-202; *In re B.L.H.*, 239 N.C. App. 52 (2015) (North Carolina assumed modification jurisdiction when neither parent nor child was presently residing in Virginia, which was the original decree state; mother and child were residing in North Carolina and father, although asserting that his domicile continued to be Virginia, was presently residing in federal prison in Texas). *See Gerhauser v. Van Bourgondien*, 238 N.C. App. 275 (2014) (although North Carolina had initial custody jurisdiction, it lost exclusive continuing jurisdiction to modify its orders when both parents and the children had not resided in North Carolina for several years and North Carolina did not have significant connection jurisdiction). The determinative period of whether a parent presently resides in the other state is at the time of the commencement of the custody action that seeks to modify another state's custody order. *See In re D.A.Y.*, 831 S.E.2d 854 (N.C. Ct. App. 2019) (at the time the TPR action was commenced in North Carolina, mother was presently residing in California when she returned there after a two-year absence).

The modification and exclusive continuing jurisdiction statutes also address a state court's authority to decide whether exclusive continuing jurisdiction remains with the original decree state. *See* G.S. 50A-202; 50A-203. Either the original decree state or the state where the modification is being sought may determine the criteria that address whether the child, the child's parents, and a person acting as a parent do not presently reside in the original decree state. G.S. 50A-202(a)(2) and Official Comment 1; 50A-203(2) and Official Comment. But only the original decree state has the authority to decide (1) whether it lost exclusive continuing jurisdiction because there is no parent, person acting as a parent, or child with a significant connection to the state and substantial evidence regarding the child's care, protection, training, and personal relationship is no longer available there or (2) that the modification state would be a more convenient forum. G.S. 50A-203(1) and Official Comment. *See* G.S. 50A-202(a)(1) and Official Comment 1; *In re J.W.S.*, 194 N.C. App. 439 (2008); *see also In re D.A.Y.*, 831 S.E.2d 854. Inconvenient forum is also discussed in subsection 1, above.

Before North Carolina exercises modification jurisdiction to modify an order from another state when the child, a parent, or a person acting as a parent presently resides in that other state, there must be an order from the original decree state that says it no longer has jurisdiction. *See* Official Comment 1 to G.S. 50A-202. Without such an order, North Carolina does not have modification jurisdiction as demonstrated by the following cases.

- Where mother was presently residing in California after relocating out of state, North Carolina did not have subject matter jurisdiction to modify the California custody order without a finding by the California court that it no longer had exclusive continuing jurisdiction. *In re D.A.Y.*, 831 S.E.2d 854.
- In the case of *In re J.W.S.*, 194 N.C. App. 439, the trial court's order was reversed for lack of subject matter jurisdiction because, although the court had properly exercised temporary emergency jurisdiction, it had not made a proper determination that it had jurisdiction to modify another state's order. New York maintained exclusive continuing

jurisdiction as the mother was still residing there when the North Carolina action was commenced. The record did not show that the New York court had made a determination that it no longer had exclusive continuing jurisdiction. There was no court order from New York relinquishing jurisdiction; a letter from New York to DSS was not an order directed to the North Carolina trial court.

- Where a New Jersey court had entered multiple child custody orders, the North Carolina trial court did not have jurisdiction to terminate the parental rights of a father who still resided in New Jersey "without an order from the New Jersey court relieving itself of jurisdiction." *In re T.E.N.*, 252 N.C. App. 461, 466 (2017). Although North Carolina was the child's home state, satisfying one condition for modification jurisdiction, the New Jersey court had not determined that it no longer had exclusive continuing jurisdiction or that North Carolina would be a more convenient forum, the second condition for modification jurisdiction. Without the required order, the North Carolina district court had no basis to find that New Jersey had transferred jurisdiction of its proceeding to North Carolina.

- Where an initial custody order was entered in Arkansas, the North Carolina trial court did not have jurisdiction because there was no order from the Arkansas court stating that Arkansas no longer had jurisdiction, Arkansas had not determined that North Carolina would be a more convenient forum, and the children's father continued to reside in Arkansas. *In re N.R.M.*, 165 N.C. App. 294 (2004).

- For purposes of the UCCJEA, an action for termination of parental rights (TPR) is considered an action to modify any existing custody order. *See, e.g., In re K.U.-S.G.*, 208 N.C. App. 128 (2010). The *In re K.U.-S.G.* record reflected that the judge in North Carolina had contacted the court in Pennsylvania, which determined that it did not wish to retain jurisdiction. However, the North Carolina court did not have subject matter jurisdiction to hear the TPR action because the record in the North Carolina action did not have an order from the Pennsylvania court that determined Pennsylvania no longer had exclusive continuing jurisdiction or that it relinquished jurisdiction to North Carolina as a more convenient forum.

- Where an initial custody order was entered in Indiana, the North Carolina court erred in determining that the Indiana court had relinquished jurisdiction, and the North Carolina trial court's order terminating respondent's parental rights was vacated for lack of subject matter jurisdiction. *In re J.D.*, 234 N.C. App. 342 (2014). Where the respondent father continued to reside in Indiana, exclusive continuing jurisdiction remained with Indiana. The Indiana court's denial of the grandparents' motion to intervene in the Indiana custody proceeding was not a relinquishment of jurisdiction, and nothing in the record showed a determination by the Indiana court that it no longer had jurisdiction.

When the North Carolina court obtains an order from another state court that relinquishes its jurisdiction, the North Carolina court is not required to conduct a collateral review of that other state's facially valid order. *In re T.R.*, 250 N.C. App. 386 (2016) (the Illinois docket entry, which contained all of the substantive attributes of a court order and could serve as an order in Illinois, was a sufficient order under the UCCJEA to transfer jurisdiction to North Carolina); *In re N.B.*, 240 N.C. App. 353 (2015) (a New York court order that stated it was "relinquishing jurisdiction to the State of North Carolina" was a sufficient relinquishment of jurisdiction despite respondent mother's argument that the New York order was insufficient under New York law due to its lack of findings indicating the basis for relinquishment of jurisdiction).

**3. Temporary emergency jurisdiction.** A North Carolina court that does not have initial child custody or modification jurisdiction can exercise temporary emergency jurisdiction to make a child custody determination when two prongs are met:

- the child is present in North Carolina and
- the child has been abandoned or it is necessary to protect the child because the child or his or her sibling or parent is subjected to or threatened with mistreatment or abuse.

G.S. 50A-204(a). For purposes of the UCCJEA, abandonment is defined as "left without provision for reasonable and necessary care or supervision." G.S. 50A-102(1).

G.S. 50A-204 requires that certain circumstances exist before emergency jurisdiction can be exercised. The majority of published court of appeals opinions addressing the need for findings to establish the court's jurisdiction under the UCCJEA have held that the court is not required to make specific findings of fact as to the circumstances. *In re N.T.U.*, 234 N.C. App. 722 (2014) (relying on *In re E.X.J.*, 191 N.C. App. 34 (2008), *aff'd per curiam*, 363 N.C. 9 (2009)) (child was found with mother in North Carolina hotel room when mother was arrested and jailed; child was left without any supervision or provision for his care, meeting the criteria of abandonment). *Cf. In re E.J.*, 225 N.C. App. 333 (2013) (stating that to exercise emergency or exclusive jurisdiction, the trial court must make specific findings of fact to support its action). For a further discussion regarding findings, see section 3.3.D, below.

When exercising temporary emergency jurisdiction, the court has the authority to enter temporary orders that are meant to allow a court to protect a child in an emergency situation. Nonsecure custody orders are temporary orders. *See* G.S. 7B-506(a), (e); *In re O.S.*, 175 N.C. App. 745 (2006). The temporary order can protect the child until a state that has jurisdiction to make an initial custody determination or to modify an existing determination enters an order. *See In re Brode*, 151 N.C. App. 690 (2002) (discussing the temporary nature of an order entered pursuant to G.S. 50A-204). The temporary order must specify an adequate period of time for a person to obtain an order in the state with jurisdiction. G.S. 50A-204(c); *In re J.H.*, 244 N.C. App. 255 (2015); *In re E.J.*, 225 N.C. App. 333 (holding that the trial court had temporary emergency jurisdiction to enter nonsecure and continued nonsecure custody orders but not an adjudication order). The North Carolina temporary order will be in effect until an order is obtained from the other state with jurisdiction within the specified period or the period expires. G.S. 50A-204(c). The North Carolina court does not have jurisdiction to enter an adjudication order while exercising temporary emergency jurisdiction. *In re J.H.*, 244 N.C. App. 255; *In re E.J.*, 225 N.C. App. 333; *In re J.W.S.*, 194 N.C. App. 439 (2008).

---

**Resource:** For more on UCCJEA temporary emergency jurisdiction, see Sara DePasquale, *Applying UCCJEA Temporary Emergency Jurisdiction in A/N/D Cases*, UNC SCH. OF GOV'T: ON THE CIVIL SIDE BLOG (March 10, 2017).

**(a) An action in another state with jurisdiction.** If there is an existing custody determination from another state or a custody proceeding has been filed (or is filed) in another state with jurisdiction, the North Carolina court must immediately contact that other state court to address jurisdiction and how to resolve the emergency. G.S. 50A-204(d); 50A-110. See section 3.3.E, below, discussing communication between the courts. The North Carolina court should defer further proceedings in its action until the other state's court makes a determination as to whether it will exercise jurisdiction or that North Carolina is a more appropriate forum. *In re J.W.S.*, 194 N.C. App. 439 (appellate court reversed denial of motion to set aside adjudication order and remanded for trial court to contact New York court regarding jurisdiction; trial court had temporary emergency jurisdiction to enter nonsecure custody orders but did not have jurisdiction, exclusive or temporary, to enter adjudication order); *In re Brode,* 151 N.C. App. 690 (vacating adjudication order that did not defer adjudication on the merits pending notice from Texas court regarding whether it would exercise jurisdiction). *See* G.S. 50A-201. If the other state determines North Carolina is a convenient forum, upon receipt of an order from the other state, North Carolina would then exercise modification jurisdiction, discussed in subsection 2, immediately above.

**(b) No action in other state with jurisdiction.** A North Carolina court that is exercising temporary emergency jurisdiction may acquire initial child custody jurisdiction if (1) it becomes the child's home state, (2) there is not a previous child custody determination made in another state, and (3) a child custody proceeding is not commenced in another state court that has jurisdiction. A temporary order entered in the North Carolina proceeding may become a final order if the order itself so provides. G.S. 50A-204 and Official Comment. In one case, *In re M.B.*, 179 N.C. App. 572 (2006), the adjudication order was entered when the court was exercising temporary emergency jurisdiction, and the respondent father appealed. Before the appeal was decided, the trial court ordered that the adjudication order became a final order after finding that North Carolina had become the child's home state and no custody proceeding had been filed in a state with jurisdiction. The respondent father did not appeal that subsequent order. Without addressing whether an adjudication order can be a temporary order that becomes a final order, the appeal was dismissed as moot. Once initial child custody jurisdiction is obtained, the North Carolina court has the authority to fully act under the provisions of the Juvenile Code and enter adjudication and dispositional orders and hear a termination of parental rights (TPR) action. *See, e.g., In re N.T.U.*, 234 N.C. App. 722 (2014) (holding that North Carolina court acquired home state jurisdiction to hear TPR motion); *In re E.X.J.*, 191 N.C. App. 34 (2008), *aff'd per curiam*, 363 N.C. 9 (2009).

**4. Simultaneous proceedings.** The UCCJEA addresses simultaneous proceedings that are occurring in multiple states and seeks to limit the number of states that exercise jurisdiction over a child. *See* G.S. 50A-206. Simultaneous proceedings involve custody actions for the same child that are commenced and have not been resolved in both North Carolina and another state when both states have jurisdiction substantially in conformity with the UCCJEA and neither state is exercising temporary emergency jurisdiction. G.S. 50A-206(a). The language "jurisdiction substantially in conformity with" the UCCJEA has been interpreted by the North Carolina Supreme Court to mean that when an action has been commenced in another state, the North Carolina court must determine whether the other state has substantially the same type of jurisdiction that North Carolina has (e.g., home state jurisdiction), not whether the other state substantially complied with the statutory prerequisites to determine child custody jurisdiction. *Jones v. Whimper*, 366 N.C. 367 (2013).

Before hearing a child custody proceeding, the North Carolina court must examine all pleadings and information supplied by the parties to determine whether a child custody proceeding has been commenced in another state with jurisdiction substantially in conformity with the UCCJEA. G.S. 50A-206(b). When there is a simultaneous proceedings issue, both state courts cannot act (absent an emergency resulting in a court exercising temporary emergency jurisdiction) because the UCCJEA does not authorize concurrent jurisdiction. *See* Official Comment to G.S. 50A-206. This means that a North Carolina court with jurisdiction to make a custody determination may not be able to act if another state also has jurisdiction and is acting with regard to the same child.

When there are simultaneous proceedings, a "first in time" rule applies when determining which state may exercise jurisdiction in the child custody proceeding. Official Comment to G.S. 50A-206. The court where the first action was filed decides the jurisdictional issue. If at the time a custody proceeding is initiated in North Carolina there was a custody action that had been previously commenced in another state, the North Carolina court may not exercise jurisdiction and must stay its proceeding to communicate with that other state court. G.S. 50A-206(a), (b). North Carolina may exercise jurisdiction only when the other state court terminates or stays its proceeding after determining North Carolina is a more convenient forum. G.S. 50A-206(a); 50A-207. The other state court should terminate its proceeding rather than transfer its action to North Carolina because a separate custody proceeding had been commenced in North Carolina. *See* G.S. 50A-206(a). If the other state court does not determine that North Carolina is a more convenient forum, the North Carolina court must dismiss its proceeding. G.S. 50A-206(b). *Jones v. Whimper*, 366 N.C. 367 (North Carolina court properly dismissed custody action after New Jersey court did not determine that North Carolina was a more convenient forum and instead retained jurisdiction in its custody proceeding, which had not yet been decided and had been commenced when New Jersey was the child's home state, giving New Jersey initial child custody jurisdiction).

There may be a home state when a custody action commences, even though the parties subsequently move out of the state before the action is completed, and a simultaneous issue may arise if a second custody action is filed in another state. *See Jones v. Whimper*, 366 N.C. 367 (New Jersey had home state jurisdiction when action was commenced, even though child and mother did not reside there when North Carolina proceeding was commenced); *see also* Official Comment 2 to G.S. 50A-202 ("Jurisdiction attaches at the commencement of the proceeding"). A simultaneous proceeding issue may arise when there is an existing abuse, neglect, or dependency action that was first initiated in North Carolina but has been inactive due to the waiver of further hearings. *See, e.g., In re C.M.B.*, 836 S.E.2d 746 (N.C. Ct. App. 2019) (discussing retention of jurisdiction under the Juvenile Code, which is a separate jurisdictional analysis from the UCCJEA); *In re M.E.*, 181 N.C. App. 322 (2007) (juvenile action was "pending").

**5. Information concerning child's status (affidavit).** Because jurisdiction under the UCCJEA is determined primarily by the past and present location of the child and any prior custody actions, reasonably ascertainable information that is related to the child's living arrangements, location, and possible involvement in custody or other proceedings must be submitted to the court in each party's initial pleading or in an attached affidavit. *See* G.S. 50A-209(a); *In re A.R.G.*, 361 N.C. 392 (2007). Appellate cases have stated that the better practice is to attach the affidavit as to the child's status to an abuse, neglect, dependency, or termination of parental rights petition (or motion), but failure to file it does not, by itself, deprive the court of subject matter jurisdiction where the court can get necessary information from the record or direct that the information be provided within a reasonable time and there is no prejudice. *See In re A.R.G.*, 361 N.C. at 399 (emphasis in original) (nothing in the statute suggests that the information is jurisdictional; G.S. 50A-209 refers to "reasonably ascertainable" information, "requires *both* parties to submit the information[,]" and authorizes the court to stay the proceeding until the information is obtained); *In re D.S.A.*, 181 N.C. App. 715 (2007); *In re J.D.S.*, 170 N.C. App. 244 (2005); *In re Clark*, 159 N.C. App. 75 (2003).

---

**AOC Form:**
AOC-CV-609, Affidavit as to Status of Minor Child (March 2019).

---

### D. Evidence, Findings, and Conclusions of Law

A statement in an order concluding that the court has subject matter jurisdiction is not binding when it is not supported by findings of fact or evidence in the record. *See In re J.A.P.*, 218 N.C. App. 190 (2012) (holding that the North Carolina court lacked subject matter jurisdiction despite a termination of parental rights order concluding that it had subject matter jurisdiction; there were no findings to support the conclusion and nothing in the record to indicate that the New Jersey court determined that it no longer had exclusive continuing jurisdiction, that North Carolina was a more convenient forum, or that either court determined that the child and parents no longer lived in New Jersey).

Circumstances must exist to support a court's conclusion that it has jurisdiction under the UCCJEA. *In re J.H.*, 244 N.C. App. 255 (2015); *In re E.X.J.*, 191 N.C. App. 34 (2008), *aff'd per curiam*, 363 N.C. 9 (2009). Evidence of those circumstances must be in the record. *In re T.J.D.W.*, 182 N.C. App. 394, *aff'd per curiam*, 362 N.C. 84 (2007); *In re J.B.*, 164 N.C. App. 394 (2004) (vacating and remanding as record was devoid of evidence from which subject matter jurisdiction could be determined).

North Carolina appellate court opinions are split about whether specific findings must be included in the order. One line of opinions holds that findings are not a jurisdictional requirement under the UCCJEA but recognizes that including jurisdictional findings is a better practice. *See In re N.T.U.*, 234 N.C. App. 722 (2014) (trial court properly entered nonsecure custody orders pursuant to temporary emergency jurisdiction because the circumstances in the case supported emergency jurisdiction even though the order did not include findings that the child was abandoned or that temporary emergency jurisdiction was necessary to protect the child from mistreatment or abuse); *In re J.C.*, 235 N.C. App. 69 (2014) (holding that although it is better practice for the court to make jurisdictional findings, the statute requires that certain circumstances must exist, not that specific findings are made; the evidence supported the court's determination that it had jurisdiction under G.S. 50A-201 to adjudicate the child), *rev'd per curiam on other grounds*, 368 N.C. 89 (2015); *In re E.X.J.*, 191 N.C. App. at 40 (holding that "[i]t is immaterial to the question of the trial court's subject matter jurisdiction in granting nonsecure custody to DSS that the trial court did not make the necessary findings;" the record established that temporary emergency jurisdiction existed), *aff'd per curiam*, 363 N.C. 9 (2009); *In re T.J.D.W.*, 182 N.C. App. at 397 (the court properly exercised jurisdiction after determining that North Carolina was the child's home state and that the child and parents no longer lived in South Carolina; the relevant statutes (G.S. 50A-201 and 50A-203(2)) do not require findings of fact but, rather, the circumstances in G.S. 50A-201 must exist and the court must "determine" that the criteria of G.S. 50A-203(2) are met; here, the record supported the court's determination), *aff'd per curiam*, 362 N.C. 84 (2007).

Other cases appear to require specific findings addressing subject matter jurisdiction under the UCCJEA. *See In re E.J.*, 225 N.C. App. 333 (2013) (stating that to exercise emergency or exclusive jurisdiction, the trial court must make specific findings of fact to support its action); *In re J.B.*, 164 N.C. App. 394 (vacating and remanding for specific findings because there were no findings in the order and no evidence to support the court's conclusion that it had subject matter jurisdiction); *Foley v. Foley*, 156 N.C. App 409 (2003) (vacating and remanding because order contained no findings as to jurisdiction but also stating that there was no evidence in the record to support such findings).

### E. Communication Requirements

**1. Communication between courts.** When child custody actions involve more than one state, courts of different states may communicate with one another concerning the proceedings. G.S. 50A-110(a). In certain circumstances, the communication is required and is not discretionary. A North Carolina court must communicate with a court of another state that has made a previous child custody determination or when a child custody proceeding has been commenced in another state when the North Carolina court is exercising temporary emergency jurisdiction (G.S. 50A-204(d)) or when there is a simultaneous proceeding in another state (G.S. 50A-206(b)). There are also circumstances when a North Carolina court may want to contact another state court to see if that court will decline jurisdiction based on significant connection or inconvenient forum. *See* G.S. 50A-201; 50A-203; 50A-207; 50A-208.

The communication must be between trial courts. *In re J.W.S.*, 194 N.C. App. 439 (2008) (holding that the contact made by a North Carolina county DSS attorney with the New York court that had exclusive continuing jurisdiction did not meet the statutory requirements regarding communication); *In re Malone*, 129 N.C. App. 338 (1998) (reversed and remanded for the North Carolina trial court to directly contact the Florida trial court; DSS efforts to contact agencies in Florida were not sufficient). The form of the communication is not specified in G.S. 50A-110, but the Official Comment recognizes the use of modern communication techniques, including telephone and online communication.

The courts may allow the parties to participate in the communication, but participation by the parties is not mandatory. G.S. 50A-110(b) and Official Comment (recognizing that it can be difficult to schedule communication between the courts because of the judges' schedules such that including the parties may be impractical). If the parties are not allowed or are unable to participate, the court must give them an opportunity to present facts and legal arguments before a decision about jurisdiction is made. G.S. 50A-110(b); *In re C.M.B.*, 836 S.E.2d 746 (N.C. Ct. App. 2019).

**2. Record of communications between courts.** A record must be made of all communications, except those concerning scheduling, court records, calendars, or similar matters. Except for communications about such administrative matters, the parties must be informed about communications between the courts and given access to the record. G.S. 50A-110(c), (d). The requirement to make a record of communications between courts is applicable not only to discretionary communications under G.S. 50A-110, but also to "*all* communications [addressed in the UCCJEA.]" *Jones v. Wimper*, 366 N.C. 367, 368 (2013) (emphasis in original). "Record" is defined as "information that is inscribed on a tangible medium or that is stored in an electronic or other medium and is retrievable in perceivable form." G.S. 50A-110(e). An email between the two courts is a record. *In re C.M.B.*, 836 S.E.2d 746.

## F. Hearings

**1. Judicial cooperation and appearance of parties.** Courts may request assistance from and may assist courts of other states. Specifically, a court of one state may request that the court of another state hold an evidentiary hearing, order a person to produce evidence, or order an evaluation related to child custody and may request a certified copy of the record of any such hearing, evidence, or evaluation. A court also may request that the court of another state order a party to a child custody proceeding or any person with physical custody of the child to appear in the proceeding with or without the child. A court may assess travel costs and other expenses incurred through these procedures against the parties. G.S. 50A-112.

**2. Notice and opportunity to be heard.** Before a child custody determination is made, notice and an opportunity to be heard must be given to anyone who would typically be entitled to notice in child custody proceedings in this state, including any parent whose rights have not been terminated and anyone having physical custody of the child. G.S. 50A-205(a). The court may order that the notice given to a party outside the state direct the party to appear in person with or without the child and inform the party that failure to appear may result in a decision adverse to that party. G.S. 50A-210.

**3. Testimony in another state.** A party to a child custody proceeding in another state may offer his or her own testimony or other witnesses' testimony by deposition or other means allowable in North Carolina for testimony taken in another state, in a manner determined by the court. The court may allow a person in another state to be deposed or to testify by phone, audiovisual means, or other electronic means and must cooperate with courts of the other state in designating an appropriate location for the deposition or testimony. G.S. 50A-111.

## G. Deployed Parents

In 2013 the North Carolina legislature adopted the Uniform Deployed Parents Custody and Visitation Act (UDPCVA), creating a new Article 3 in the UCCJEA to address custody and visitation issues when one or both parents are or may be deployed. The Act is codified at G.S. 50A-350 through -396. The definitions of "deploying parent" and "other parent" include a parent of the child or an individual other than a parent with custodial responsibility of a child. G.S. 50A-351(8), (13). Although this Act mostly impacts private custody cases, it appears to apply to an abuse, neglect, or dependency case when the court has entered a permanent plan of custody or guardianship to either a parent or non-parent. The court of appeals recently addressed issues of first impression under the UDPCVA in *Roybal v. Raulli*, 832 S.E.2d 202 (N.C. Ct. App. 2019).

**Resources:**
For more information, see
- "2013 Legislation of Interest to Court Officials," page 68, which was compiled by the UNC School of Government and available on the School of Government website.
- The website of the Uniform Law Commission, use the search box for "Deployed Parents Custody and Visitation Act." See also Chapter 13.6 for a discussion of the federal Servicemembers Civil Relief Act (SCRA).

## H. Enforcement of Custody Orders under the UCCJEA

**1. Enforcement generally.** A North Carolina court must enforce a custody determination made by a court of any other state if the other state exercised jurisdiction in substantial conformity with the UCCJEA or if the custody order was entered under factual circumstances meeting the jurisdictional standards of the UCCJEA. G.S. 50A-303(a). A custody order from one state may be registered and confirmed in another state, with or without a simultaneous request for enforcement, allowing for a "predetermination" of the enforceability of the order. *See* G.S. 50A-305 and Official Comment. A court may grant any relief normally available under its law to enforce a registered child custody determination made by a court of another state. G.S. 50A-306(a). Expedited enforcement of a child custody determination can be sought by filing a petition for enforcement, even if the order has not been registered and confirmed. *See* G.S. 50A-308. A North Carolina court does not acquire jurisdiction to modify another state's custody order merely because the order is registered and confirmed here or because a proceeding to enforce the order is filed here. The court may modify another state's custody determination only pursuant to the UCCJEA's requirements for modification jurisdiction. *See* G.S. 50A-306(b).

**AOC Forms:**
- AOC-CV-660I, Instructions For Registration Of Foreign Child Custody Order (Side 1)/Instructions For Expedited Enforcement Of Foreign Child Custody Order (Side Two) (March 2014).
- AOC-CV-660, Petition For Registration Of Foreign Child Custody Order (Oct. 2006).
- AOC-CV-661, Notice Of Registration Of Foreign Child Custody Order (Dec. 2016).
- AOC-CV-663, Motion To Contest Validity Of A Registered Foreign Child Custody

Order And Notice Of Hearing (Dec. 2006).
- AOC-CV-664, Order Confirming Registration Or Denying Confirmation Or Registration Of Foreign Child Custody Order (Dec. 2006).
- AOC-CV-665, Petition For Expedited Enforcement Of Foreign Child Custody Order (Dec. 2006).
- AOC-CV-666, Order For Hearing On Petition For Expedited Enforcement Of Foreign Child Custody Order (Feb. 2014).
- AOC-CV-667, Warrant Directing Law Enforcement To Take Immediate Physical Custody Of Child(ren) Subject To A Child Custody Order (Oct. 2017).
- AOC-CV-668, Order Allowing Or Denying Expedited Enforcement Of Foreign Child Custody Order (Dec. 2006).

**2. Temporary visitation.** Even if a North Carolina court does not have jurisdiction to modify an order, it may enter a temporary order enforcing (1) a visitation schedule made by a court in another state or (2) visitation provisions in a child custody determination made by another state that did not set out a specific visitation schedule. G.S. 50A-304(a). A temporary order entered by a North Carolina court that sets out visitation provisions that were not included in the other state's child custody determination must specify a period that the court considers adequate for the petitioner seeking enforcement in North Carolina to obtain an order from the appropriate state with jurisdiction. G.S. 50A-306(b). The North Carolina temporary order that sets out a visitation schedule will remain in effect until an order is obtained from the other state with jurisdiction or until the specified period in the North Carolina order expires. G.S. 50A-304(b).

**3. Registration and confirmation of orders from other states.** A custody order from another state may be registered and confirmed with or without a petition for enforcement. G.S. 50A-305(a) and Official Comment (explaining that registration and confirmation allows parties to "predetermine" the enforceability of a custody order before allowing the child to come to the state). A person may register an order by sending two copies of the order, one of which must be certified, to the appropriate court with a letter or other document requesting registration; a statement under penalty of perjury that to the best of the person's knowledge and belief the order has not been modified; and the names and addresses of the petitioner and any parent or person acting as a parent who has been awarded custody or visitation in the order. G.S. 50A-305(a). See G.S. 50A-209(e) for exceptions to the requirement that names and addresses be provided. Upon receipt of the request, the court must register the order and send instructions to the petitioner informing the petitioner of the notice requirements for confirmation. G.S. 50A-305(b).

A person seeking to object to registration must request a hearing within twenty days of service of the required notice. G.S. 50A-305(d). If no request for a hearing is made, the order is confirmed as a matter of law and the court must notify the petitioner and all persons who were served of the confirmation. G.S. 50A-305(e). If a hearing is requested and held, the court must confirm the order unless the person objecting to registration can show that

- the court that issued the order did not have appropriate jurisdiction;
- the order has been vacated, stayed, or modified by a court having appropriate jurisdiction;

or
- the person contesting registration was entitled to notice in the proceeding in the other state but was not given notice in accordance with the statute.

G.S. 50A-305(d).

Confirmation, either as a matter of law or as the result of a hearing, precludes further attack on the validity of the order for any of the reasons that could have been raised in objection to registration. G.S. 50A-305(f). Although a North Carolina court shall enforce a registered order, it may not modify the order without modification jurisdiction. G.S. 50A-306(b).

### 4. Expedited enforcement procedure.

**(a) Petitioner.** A petitioner is a "person" who seeks to enforce another state's child custody determination. G.S. 50A-301(1). The UCCJEA defines "person" as "an individual, corporation, business trust, estate, trust, partnership, limited liability company, association, joint venture, government; governmental subdivision, agency, or instrumentality; public corporation; or any other legal or commercial entity." G.S. 50A-102(12). Based on this definition, DSS may petition for enforcement of another state's child custody determination even though it was not a party to the previous child custody proceeding. *See* Official Comment to G.S. 50A-102 ("The term 'person' has been added to ensure that the provisions of this Act apply when the State is the moving party in a custody proceeding or has legal custody of a child."); *In re Q.V.*, 164 N.C. App. 737 (2004).

> **Practice Note:** A county DSS that receives a request from another state's child welfare agency to pick up a child who has been brought to North Carolina in violation of an order entered in that other state may file a petition for expedited enforcement in North Carolina. Note that depending on the facts, the request by the out-of-state child welfare agency may also be viewed as a report of suspected abuse, neglect, or dependency to the North Carolina county DSS. If DSS screens in that report and an assessment indicates that the child is abused, neglected, or dependent and the criteria for nonsecure custody are met, DSS may file its own petition in North Carolina with a request for a nonsecure custody order. DSS should notify the North Carolina district court of the other state's court action so that the North Carolina court may appropriately enter a temporary emergency order (i.e., nonsecure custody order) when exercising temporary emergency jurisdiction and contact the other state's court to discuss the proper way to address the emergency and jurisdictional issues.

**(b) Petition, timing, and notice.** A petition seeking enforcement of a custody order from another state must be verified. G.S. 50A-308(a). Certified copies of the custody order and of any order confirming the registration of the order must be attached to the petition. G.S. 50A-308(a). The petition must contain all information set out in G.S. 50A-308(b). Upon the filing of the petition, the court must issue an order to the respondent to appear with or without the child at a hearing. The hearing must be scheduled for the next judicial day following service of process, unless that date is impossible, in which case the hearing must be held on the first day possible. The hearing date can be continued only upon the request of the petitioner. G.S. 50A-308(c). The required content of the order that must be sent by the court to the respondent upon the filing of a petition for enforcement is set out in G.S 50A-308(d).

**(c) Hearing.** At a hearing for enforcement, the court must enforce the order by allowing the petitioner immediate possession of the child, unless the respondent can show that the order has not been confirmed (or that the order has been appropriately stayed, modified, or vacated since confirmation) and that

- the issuing court did not have appropriate jurisdiction at the time the order was entered;
- the order has been stayed, vacated, or modified by a court with appropriate jurisdiction; or
- the respondent was entitled to notice in the proceeding in the other state, but notice was not given in accordance with the UCCJEA.

G.S. 50A-310(a).

If the order has been confirmed, the respondent cannot contest enforcement based on any of the grounds that could have been raised in objection to the confirmation at the time of registration. G.S. 50A-305(f).

**(d) Law enforcement involvement.** A party who files a petition to enforce a custody order may also file a verified application for issuance of a warrant to take physical custody of the child. G.S. 50A-311(a). If the court finds from testimony of the petitioner or other witness, and not upon affidavits or verified pleadings alone, "that the child is imminently likely to suffer serious physical harm or be removed from this State," the court may issue a warrant that

- recites the facts on which the court's conclusion of imminent serious physical harm or removal from the state is based,
- directs law enforcement to take physical custody of the child immediately, and
- provides for the child's placement pending final relief.

G.S. 50A-311(a)–(c).

A warrant to take physical custody of a child issued pursuant to G.S. 50A-311 is enforceable throughout North Carolina. An officer executing a warrant that is complete and regular on its face is not required to inquire into the regularity and continued validity of the order and shall not incur criminal or civil liability for its due service. G.S. 50A-311(e).

If the court does not issue a warrant to take custody of a child, the court should not invoke the assistance of law enforcement. *See Chick v. Chick*, 164 N.C. App. 444 (2004) (holding that the trial court erred in ordering law enforcement to assist with enforcing a Vermont custody order when there was no statutory basis for their participation); *In re Bhatti*, 98

N.C. App. 493 (1990) (holding that the trial court lacked statutory authority to order law enforcement to pick up children in an effort to assist in the enforcement of a Georgia custody order).

> **Practice Note:** A court that finds a child is "imminently likely to suffer serious physical harm" is required under North Carolina's reporting law to make a report to DSS if there is cause to suspect that the child is abused, neglected, or dependent as defined in G.S. 7B-101. *See* G.S. 7B-301(a). If DSS finds a risk of immediate harm, the agency may take temporary custody of the child, file a petition, and seek an order for nonsecure custody. See Chapter 5.5. When DSS involvement is appropriate, the court should make a report to DSS rather than directly ordering DSS to assume custody of the child.

**5. Prosecutor's role**. G.S. 50A-315 allows a prosecutor or other appropriate public official to bring an enforcement action on behalf of the court under the circumstances described in that statute. While this has not been a practice in North Carolina, there are circumstances in which prosecutors from other states have become involved.

## I. Parental Kidnapping Prevention Act: 28 U.S.C. 1738A

The Parental Kidnapping Prevention Act (PKPA) governs interstate child custody proceedings simultaneously with the UCCJEA and provides full faith and credit in every state for custody and visitation orders that are entered in conformity with the provisions of the PKPA. *See Potter v. Potter*, 131 N.C. App. 1 (1998). To ensure that its order will be recognized by other jurisdictions, a state court must exercise jurisdiction over a custody proceeding in compliance with the prescribed jurisdictional requirements in the PKPA. *See* 28 U.S.C. 1739A; *Potter*, 131 N.C. App. 1.

**1. Applicability in abuse, neglect, dependency, and termination of parental rights actions.** The PKPA applies to custody and visitation determinations. A "custody determination" is defined as a court order, decree, or judgment that provides for the custody of a child and includes permanent, temporary, initial, and modification orders. 28 U.S.C. 1738A(b)(3). A "visitation determination" is a court order, decree, or judgment that provides for the visitation of the child and includes temporary, permanent, initial, and modification orders. 28 U.S.C. 1738A(b)(9). The PKPA does not reference abuse, neglect, dependency, or termination of parental rights (TPR) proceedings or orders. North Carolina appellate courts have held that the PKPA applies to abuse, neglect, dependency, and TPR proceedings. *In re Brode*, 151 N.C. App. 690, 694 (2002) (citations omitted) (holding that the PKPA applies "to all interstate custody proceedings affecting a prior custody award by a different State, including [abuse,] neglect and dependency proceedings"); *In re Bean*, 132 N.C. App. 363 (1999) (holding that the PKPA applies to TPR action). However, other states are split on the issue of the applicability of the PKPA to abuse, neglect, dependency, or TPR proceedings. *Compare In re Higera N.*, 2 A.3d 265 (Me. 2010) (PKPA does not apply to child protective actions, including TPR actions, which are brought by the state agency seeking to protect a child; a state agency is not a "person" or "contestant" involved in a custody determination; discussing the split in the different state courts). Another state's application of the PKPA to a North Carolina abuse, neglect, dependency, or TPR determination will depend on that state's interpretation of the applicability of the PKPA to those proceedings. A North Carolina court must apply the PKPA to another state's child custody determination, including an abuse, neglect, dependency, and TPR order. *In re J.H.*, 244 N.C. App. 255 (2015).

**2. Terms.** The PKPA has its own applicable terms and definitions. Most of those terms are also used in the UCCJEA and have essentially the same meaning: "child", "home state", "modification/modify", "person acting as a parent", "physical custody", and "State". As explained above, "custody determination" is defined differently in the UCCJEA.

"Contestant" is a term that is used in the PKPA and not in the UCCJEA. A contestant is defined as "a person, including a parent or grandparent, who claims a right to custody or visitation of a child." 28 U.S.C. 1738A(b)(2). Depending on a state's custody and visitation laws, this definition may encompass more people than a parent or person acting as a parent, which is what is used in the UCCJEA. As a result, the PKPA may apply to a proceeding to which the UCCJEA does not apply. Because of the PKPA definition of contestant, a court will need to consider the relevant state's laws regarding who has standing to claim a right to custody or visitation with a child. *See* Official Comment 1 to G.S. 50A-201, Official Comment 2 to G.S. 50A-202 (discussing PKPA). In North Carolina, certain third parties (meaning non-parents) may claim a right to custody or visitation; as a result, a "contestant" in North Carolina may encompass more than a parent or person acting as a parent. *See* G.S. 50-13.1(a) (custody action may be brought by "[a]ny parent, relative, or other person, agency . . . claiming the right to custody"); 50-13.2(b1) (addressing grandparent visitation). For cases discussing third-party custody issues and the required relationship between the third party and the child for standing purposes, see *Estroff v. Chatterjee*, 190 N.C. App. 61, 74 (2008) (facts establishing a relationship "in the nature of a parent and child" are sufficient to find that a third party has standing to bring a custody action) and *Ellison v. Ramos*, 130 N.C. App. 389 (1998) (standing requires a showing that the third party is not a "stranger" to the child).

**3. Jurisdiction.** Through the PKPA, Congress attempted "to create a uniform standard among the states in their exercise of jurisdiction over interstate custody disputes." *In re Brode*, 151 N.C. App. 690, 694 (2002). The PKPA prohibits concurrent jurisdiction by more than one state. *In re Bhatti*, 98 N.C. App. 493 (1990). A state must give full faith and credit to another state's custody order when that state complies with the jurisdictional provisions of the PKPA. 28 U.S.C. 1738A (Title: "Full faith and credit given to child custody determinations"); *Thompson v. Thompson*, 484 U.S. 174 (1988). As a federal law, the PKPA is controlling over any conflicting state custody law. *In re Brode*, 151 N.C. App. 690.

The PKPA is triggered when it has been determined that a prior custody order has been made by another state's court. *In re Brode*, 151 N.C. App. 690. The jurisdictional analysis under the PKPA addresses a state's continuing jurisdiction over child custody proceedings as well as modification and enforcement of other states' custody orders and has substantially the same jurisdictional prerequisites as the UCCJEA.

**(a) Enforcement of out-of-state order.** The PKPA requires that unless an exception applies, a state court must enforce and not modify another state's child custody or visitation determination when that determination was made in accordance with the PKPA. 28 U.S.C. 1738A(a). An order is made in accordance with the provisions of the PKPA when

- the court has jurisdiction under its own state's laws and
- one of the following conditions is met:
    - the state (1) is the child's **home state** when the proceeding was commenced or (2) had been the child's home state within six months before the proceeding was commenced, the child is absent from state, and a contestant continues to live in the state;
    - it appears that no other state has jurisdiction and it is in the child's best interest that the court assume jurisdiction because the child and his/her parents or one contestant have a **significant connection** to the state other than mere physical presence and there is substantial evidence about the child's care, protection, training, and personal relationships available in the state;
    - the child is physically present in the state and has been abandoned or it is necessary in an **emergency** to protect the child because the child, a sibling, or a parent has been subjected to or threatened with mistreatment or abuse;
    - it appears that no other state has jurisdiction or another state has declined jurisdiction because the state at issue is the **more appropriate forum** and it is in the child's best interest that such court assume jurisdiction; or
    - the court has **continuing jurisdiction**.

28 U.S.C. 1738A(c).

Continuing jurisdiction requires that the state (1) continues to have jurisdiction under its own laws and (2) remains the child's or any contestant's residence. 28 U.S.C. 1738A(d). Although "contestant" is broadly defined as a person who claims a right to custody or visitation with the child, it appears that DSS is not a contestant for purposes of the PKPA. *See In re Bean*, 132 N.C. App. 363 (1999) (affirming a trial court's determination that it did not have jurisdiction under the PKPA to terminate a putative father's rights; petitioners were appointed as custodians of the child in a Florida dependency and neglect action where Florida retained jurisdiction; the jurisdictional analysis focused on the putative father's continuing residence in Florida without any discussion of the Florida DSS). *See also* 28 U.S.C. 1738A(b)(2).

**(b) Modification of out-of-state order.** A North Carolina court will have jurisdiction to modify another state's child custody or visitation order when North Carolina has jurisdiction to make a child custody determination and the original state no longer has jurisdiction or has declined to exercise jurisdiction. 28 U.S.C. 1738A(f), (h). In *In re Bean,* 132 N.C. App. 363 (1999), the North Carolina Court of Appeals affirmed a trial court's determination that it did not have jurisdiction under the PKPA to terminate a putative father's rights because Florida had continuing jurisdiction and had not declined to exercise jurisdiction. There was a previous dependency action in Florida where the court awarded long-term custody of the child to her foster parents and retained jurisdiction. The foster parents/custodians moved with the child to North Carolina and eventually initiated a termination of parental rights (TPR) action in North Carolina against the child's putative father who resided in Florida. The father was a contestant in the TPR action and Florida remained his residence. As a result, North Carolina lacked subject matter jurisdiction under the PKPA to proceed with the TPR action.

**(c) Pending custody proceedings.** The PKPA prohibits a state court from exercising jurisdiction in any proceeding for a custody or visitation determination that is commenced during the pendency of a proceeding in a court of another state when that other state court is exercising jurisdiction consistently with the provisions of the PKPA to make a custody or visitation determination. 28 U.S.C. 1738A(g). The PKPA does not define when a proceeding is pending. However, when another state had a dependency proceeding where jurisdiction was retained by that state's court after a permanent plan of long-term custody was achieved, the North Carolina Court of Appeals completed a jurisdictional analysis under the continuing jurisdiction provision, not the pending custody proceedings provision, of the PKPA when determining that North Carolina did not have jurisdiction to hear a TPR action. *In re Bean*, 132 N.C. App. 363 (1999). In conducting a jurisdictional analysis for an inconvenient forum under the UCCJEA, the state court of appeals has held that an abuse, neglect, or dependency proceeding is "pending" because the district court has continuing jurisdiction in that action until the child turns 18. *In re M.E.*, 181 N.C. App. 322, 328 (2007). While not noted in *In re M.E.*, the court's jurisdiction may be terminated by court order. G.S. 7B-201(a); 7B-911; *see In re C.M.B.*, 836 S.E.2d 746 (N.C. Ct. App. 2019) and *McMillan v. McMillan*, 833 S.E.2d 692 (N.C. Ct. App. 2019) (both discussing terminating juvenile court jurisdiction under G.S. 7B-201 and 7B-911). It is unclear whether the holding in *In re M.E.* applies to the PKPA pending custody proceedings provision.

**4. Notice and opportunity to be heard.** Before a custody or visitation determination is made, notice and an opportunity to be heard must be given to the contestants, any parent whose rights have not been terminated, and anyone who has physical custody of the child. 28 U.S.C. 1738A(e). The content and form of the notice are not addressed by the statute. An order entered without notice is not entitled to full faith and credit by another state's court, but one can look to other enforcement remedies that are available under state law. *See* Official Comment to G.S. 50A-205 (discussing the PKPA).

## 3.4 Personal Jurisdiction

### A. Introduction

Personal jurisdiction differs from subject matter jurisdiction. Personal jurisdiction relates to the court's authority (or jurisdiction) over a person rather than over the action. Personal jurisdiction is typically obtained by the issuance and proper service of a summons on a person. *In re K.J.L*, 363 N.C. 343 (2009). Respondent parties to an abuse, neglect, or dependency proceeding are served with a summons issued pursuant to G.S. 7B-406. A respondent parent in a termination of parental rights (TPR) action that is commenced by petition is served with a summons issued pursuant to G.S. 7B-1106. Unlike subject matter jurisdiction, personal jurisdiction may be waived by a failure to timely object or obtained by a party's consent or voluntary appearance. *In re K.J.L.*, 363 N.C. 343. A lack of personal jurisdiction over a party will not deprive the court of subject matter jurisdiction over the action. *In re K.J.L*, 363 N.C. 343. Note, however, that personal jurisdiction for out-of-state parents in a TPR action is more complicated and addressed in section 3.4.E, below.

**B. Service of Process**

**1. Who must be served.**

(a) **Abuse, neglect, dependency.** For an abuse, neglect, or dependency petition, the summons must be issued to and served on each party named in the petition, except the juvenile. G.S. 7B-406(a); 7B-407. Service must occur at least five days before the date of the scheduled hearing unless waived by the court. G.S. 7B-407.

Depending on the circumstances, service may be required on several named respondents. Parties "shall" include the following persons: the child's parents; if the child has a court-appointed guardian or custodian at the time the petition is filed, that guardian or custodian; the child's caretaker (if applicable) when the allegations of the petition relate to the caretaker, the caretaker has assumed the status and obligation of a parent, or the court orders that the caretaker be made a party; and the child. G.S. 7B-401.1(b)–(e), (f). Although the statute does not require service of a summons on the child, the clerk is required to provide a copy of a petition alleging abuse or neglect and any notices of hearings to the local guardian ad litem office immediately after a petition is filed. G.S. 7B-408.

Every petition and summons should name both parents (absent an exception under G.S. 7B-401.1(b)), even if one or both can be identified only as "unknown." Efforts should be made to serve both parents and any other named respondent as expeditiously as possible. However, the court's ability to address the child's circumstances is not dependent on the whether the parents or other named respondents have been served. *See In re K.J.L.*, 363 N.C. 343, 347 (2009) (disavowing interpretation of language in *In re J.T.*, 363 N.C. 1 (2009), to mean that the failure to issue a summons defeats subject matter jurisdiction and explaining that a summons relates to subject matter jurisdiction "only insofar as it apprises the necessary parties that the trial court's subject matter jurisdiction has been invoked and that the court intends to exercise jurisdiction over the case"). The court acquires subject matter jurisdiction and can act to protect the child as soon as a properly signed and verified petition is filed. *See* G.S. 7B-401; 7B-405; *In re T.R.P.*, 360 N.C. 588 (2006).

Although a lack of personal jurisdiction does not defeat a court's subject matter jurisdiction over the proceeding, the North Carolina appellate courts have not addressed whether an abuse, neglect, or dependency case may proceed when there is no personal jurisdiction over any named party. In the juvenile cases decided by the North Carolina Supreme Court that address personal jurisdiction as related to subject matter jurisdiction, the facts in each case involved the trial court having personal jurisdiction over a party who waived any defenses regarding personal jurisdiction. *See In re K.J.L.*, 363 N.C. 343 (holding the failure to issue a summons as a result of the absence of the clerk's signature on the summons did not defeat subject matter jurisdiction in the neglect and dependency case; noting the court had personal jurisdiction over both respondent parents when they appeared at the hearing, waiving defenses implicating personal jurisdiction); *In re J.T.*, 363 N.C. 1 (decided under previous law that required the juvenile in a TPR action be served with a summons; holding summons-related deficiencies implicate personal, not subject matter jurisdiction; noting the children's GAL and attorney advocate waived defenses implicating personal jurisdiction when they made a general appearance by participating in the TPR proceeding without raising objections regarding personal jurisdiction); *see also In re Poole,* 151 N.C. App. 472 (2002) (affirming child's adjudication as dependent and disposition of custody to relatives when only the respondent mother had been served; holding the trial court had subject matter jurisdiction over the action when only one parent was served; noting that the trial court obtained personal jurisdiction over the father when he appeared in the court three years after the child's adjudication), *rev'd per curiam for reasons stated in dissenting opinion,* 357 N.C. 151 (2003).

**Practice Notes:** Although the court may have subject matter jurisdiction to proceed, personal jurisdiction (whether obtained by proper service, a waiver by the respondent, or operation of law) is required for the court to order a specific party to engage in certain actions. *See* G.S. 7B-200(b). The practical effect of an adjudication of a child as abused, neglected, or dependent in a case where personal jurisdiction does not exist over a named respondent is that the court lacks authority to order that named respondent to engage in services or comply with conditions the court has the authority to order under G.S. 7B-904. Separate from the jurisdictional questions, parents and other named respondents have constitutional due process rights. Both of the child's parents and other named respondents should be served whenever possible and as soon as possible. A challenge to the court acting in an abuse, neglect, or dependency proceeding may be raised on constitutional due process grounds. *See In re Poole* 151 N.C. App. at 477 (Timmons-Goodson, J., dissenting) noting "the true issue and nature of respondent's argument… is that of due process"), *rev'd per curiam for reasons stated in dissenting opinion,* 357 N.C. 151; *see also In re H.D.F.* 197 N.C. App. 480 (2009) (reversing a neglect adjudication when the required notice of key events in the proceeding was not given to the *pro se* respondent parent).

At every hearing on the need for continued nonsecure custody, at a pre-adjudication hearing, and at the initial dispositional hearing the court is required to inquire about efforts that have been made to locate and serve a missing parent, and findings of those efforts must be made at continued nonsecure custody and initial disposition. G.S. 7B-506(h)(1); 7B-800.1(a)(3); 7B-901(b). At the pre-adjudication hearing, the court must identify the parties to the proceeding and consider whether all summons, services of process, and notice requirements have been met; this inquiry is not limited to respondent parents. *See* G.S. 7B-800.1(a)(2) and (5).

**(b) Termination of parental rights.** For a termination of parental rights (TPR) proceeding initiated by the filing of a petition, service of the summons is required for

- the parents of the juvenile (except a parent whose rights have already been terminated, who has executed a relinquishment for adoption to DSS or to a licensed child-placing agency that is now irrevocable, or who has consented to adoption by the person petitioning for TPR);
- a judicially-appointed guardian of the person of the child;
- a court-appointed custodian of the child;
- any county DSS or licensed child-placing agency to whom a parent has relinquished the child for adoption; and
- any county DSS to whom a court has given placement responsibility for the child.

G.S. 7B-1106(a).

No summons is required to be issued to or served on the child or the child's guardian ad litem (GAL) if there is one. However, if the child has a GAL, either the GAL or the child's attorney advocate must be served, pursuant to Rule 5 of the Rules of Civil Procedure, with a copy of all pleadings and other papers required to be served. G.S. 7B-1106(a1).

If an attorney has been appointed for a respondent parent in an underlying abuse, neglect, or dependency case, and if that attorney has not been relieved of responsibility, a copy of all pleadings and other papers required to be served on the respondent must also be served on the respondent's attorney pursuant to Rule 5. G.S. 7B-1106(a2).

In the case of an unknown parent, the court shall hold a hearing pursuant to G.S. 7B-1105 and may order service by publication as specified by that statute. For further discussion on a preliminary hearing for an unknown parent, see Chapter 9.6.

**2. Proper service.** Proper service of a summons for an abuse, neglect, or dependency case is addressed in G.S. 7B-407; for termination of parental rights actions, service is addressed in G.S. 7B-1106. Both statutes require service pursuant to Rule 4 of the Rules of Civil Procedure. G.S. 7B-407 (service on parent, guardian, custodian, or caretaker); 7B-1106(a) (service on a respondent person or agency, with an additional requirement for service by publication on a known parent respondent). For details relating to proper service, see Chapter 4.4.

## C. Consent and Waiver Establishing Personal Jurisdiction

When a party has not been served or if there is a defect in service or process, that party's own actions may subject him or her to the court's jurisdiction. Unlike subject matter jurisdiction, challenges to personal jurisdiction must be timely raised by the parties themselves and can be waived. *See* N.C. R. CIV. P. 12(h)(1); *In re J.T.*, 363 N.C. 1 (2009); *In re K.J.L.*, 363 N.C. 343 (2009). The court has personal jurisdiction over a party in an abuse, neglect, or dependency proceeding who has waived service of process. G.S. 7B-200(b).

**1. Making an appearance.** In the case of *In re A.J.M.*, 177 N.C. App. 745 (2006), service was not completed on the mother, but because she was present in court and did not raise an objection regarding insufficient service of process or personal jurisdiction, her actions amounted to a waiver of her right to challenge personal jurisdiction. *See also In re K.J.L.*, 363 N.C. 343 (2009); *In re H.T.*, 180 N.C. App. 611 (2006). However, in another case the court did not view parents as having consented to jurisdiction by appearing at the hearing when the purpose of their appearance was the timely challenge to the sufficiency of process. *In re Mitchell*, 126 N.C. App. 432 (1997). Additionally, a parent who was not served and who did not appear at the hearing was found not to have made a general appearance when his provisionally-appointed counsel, who should have been dismissed, was present during the hearing. *In re C.A.C.*, 222 N.C. App. 687 (2012).

**2. Failing to raise the defense.** A parent may waive the defenses of lack of personal jurisdiction or insufficiency of process or service of process by filing an answer, response, or motion or by appearing at a hearing without raising the defense. *See* N.C. R. Civ. P. 12(b), (h); *In re H.T.*, 180 N.C. App. 611 (2006); *In re J.W.J.*, 165 N.C. App. 696 (2004) (holding that the respondent waived the defense of lack of personal jurisdiction by mailing a handwritten response to the clerk of court and later filing a formal answer without raising the defense); *In re Howell*, 161 N.C. App. 650 (2003).

### D. Acquiring Personal Jurisdiction in Abuse, Neglect, Dependency Cases

**1. Statutory provisions.** The Juvenile Code specifically addresses personal jurisdiction in abuse, neglect, or dependency proceedings in two separate statutes, and the language in each law differs. The general jurisdiction statute, G.S. 7B-200, provides that the court has jurisdiction over a parent, guardian, custodian, or caretaker of a juvenile who has been adjudicated abused, neglected, or dependent if that person has been properly served with a summons pursuant to G.S. 7B-406 or has waived service of process. G.S. 7B-200(b). The referenced summons statute, G.S. 7B-406, requires that the summons advise the parent that upon service, jurisdiction over him or her is obtained and additionally requires the party who is served with the summons to appear for a hearing at the time and place designated in the summons. G.S. 7B-406(a), (c).

The differences in these two statutes relate to the timing of when the court acquires jurisdiction over a party in the proceeding: upon service of the summons or after a juvenile's adjudication. The North Carolina appellate courts have not interpreted the different language used in these two statutes. However, when addressing issues related to personal jurisdiction in abuse, neglect, or dependency proceedings, North Carolina appellate courts appear to look to general principles of personal jurisdiction, which include service of the summons, a party's actions, and whether he or she waived any objection to personal jurisdiction. *See In re K.J.L.*, 363 N.C. 343 (2009); *In re J.D.L.*, 199 N.C. App. 182 (2009). Under general principles of personal jurisdiction, once a party is properly served with a summons or has waived any objection to personal jurisdiction, personal jurisdiction is accomplished; there is no delay. One appellate case specifically recognized that personal jurisdiction was established over the respondent mother when she made a general appearance in the neglect and dependency proceeding at the nonsecure custody hearing, thereby waiving any objection to personal jurisdiction that was based on her not being served with the summons until the day after the adjudication and disposition hearing. *In re S'N.A.S.*, 201 N.C. App. 581 (2009).

Note that a court with personal jurisdiction over a party in an abuse, neglect, or dependency proceeding may only act pursuant to the authority given to it by the Juvenile Code, which varies depending on the stage of the proceeding. For example, a court may not order a parent to engage in services authorized by G.S. 7B-904 until a dispositional (initial, review, or permanency planning) hearing. *See In re A.G.M.*, 241 N.C. App. 426, 433–34 (2015) (citing G.S. 7B-904 when reviewing an adjudication order and stating, "It is also unclear pursuant to what authority the trial court ordered Respondent to engage in therapy."). But a court may order (1) services or other efforts aimed at returning the child to a safe home and (2) visitation with the child that sets forth duration, frequency, and level of supervision as early as nonsecure custody. G.S. 7B-507(a)(5); 7B-506(g1) (incorporating 7B-905.1(a)). Additionally, a discovery request may include a motion for a physical or mental examination of a party, which requires the court to have jurisdiction over the person. *See* G.S. 7B-700(c); N.C. R. Civ. P. 35. Paternity may also be an issue the court addresses in the juvenile proceeding. The court must have personal jurisdiction over any parties it orders to engage in genetic marker testing pursuant to G.S. 8-50.1(b1).

**2. Permanent custodians and guardians.** In the course of an abuse, neglect, or dependency proceeding, the court-ordered permanent plan may award custody or guardianship of the child to a person who was not named as a respondent in the proceeding. *See* G.S. 7B-906.2(a); 7B-903(a)(4) and (5); 7B-600(b). Any person who is awarded custody or guardianship as the child's permanent plan automatically becomes a party to the proceeding. G.S. 7B-401.1(c), (d). The court has personal jurisdiction over that person, who is now a party. G.S. 7B-200(b).

E. **Out-of-State Parents in Termination of Parental Rights Cases**

A court's exercise of personal jurisdiction over a nonresident generally requires both notice and that the individual either have minimum contacts with the state or submit to the court's jurisdiction. *See Int'l Shoe Co. v. Washington*, 326 U.S. 310 (1945). North Carolina has never required that a parent have minimum contacts with the state for a court in the state to act in a custody action involving that parent's child. *See Harris v. Harris*, 104 N.C. App. 574 (1991). The Uniform Child-Custody Jurisdiction and Enforcement Act (UCCJEA) states that personal jurisdiction is not necessary or sufficient to enable a court to make a child custody determination (G.S. 50A-201(c)), and the Juvenile Code requires only that the parent be served properly. Under North Carolina case law, however, in some TPR cases the court may act only if the nonresident respondent has minimum contacts with the state or submits to the court's jurisdiction. The appellate courts have not addressed this conflicting intersection of statutory and case law.

**1. Juvenile Code requires only service.** G.S. 7B-1101 was amended in 2007 to provide that the court has jurisdiction to terminate a parent's rights, without regard to the parent's state of residence, if

- the court finds that it would have jurisdiction to make an initial custody determination or to modify a custody order under the UCCJEA and
- the nonresident parent was served with process pursuant to G.S. 7B-1106, which requires

the issuance and service of a summons upon the filing of a petition to terminate parental rights.

Note that a recent unpublished case found that a defect in the service of process requirement for a nonresident parent related to subject matter jurisdiction, rather than to personal jurisdiction. *In re P.D.*, 803 S.E.2d 667 (N.C. Ct. App. 2017) (unpublished) (vacating TPR after holding that when the requirements in G.S. 7B-1101 applicable to a nonresident parent are not met, a trial court may not exercise subject matter jurisdiction; determining that the requirement regarding service of process was not satisfied).

**2. Appellate cases require minimum contacts in some situations.** In contrast to the statutory criteria for jurisdiction, the court of appeals has held that a court in this state may terminate the rights of an out-of-state parent of a legitimate child (or of a child born out of wedlock if that parent is involved with the child) only if the parent (1) has minimum contacts with North Carolina, (2) submits to the court's jurisdiction, or (3) is served while physically present in the state.

Although TPR proceedings are *in rem*, to satisfy due process a nonresident parent must have minimum contacts with the state before a court here may terminate the parent's rights. *In re Finnican*, 104 N.C. App. 157 (1991), *overruled in part on other grounds by Bryson v. Sullivan*, 330 N.C. 644 (1992); *In re Trueman*, 99 N.C. App. 579 (1990). The North Carolina appellate cases involving minimum contacts in TPR actions involve respondent fathers, and the analysis in these cases focuses on the relationship between the respondent father and child.

In each of the two cases cited above, the child was born during the marriage between the mother (petitioner) and the father (respondent) and was the legitimate child of the marriage. Also in each case, the court of appeals held that the respondent fathers' contacts with North Carolina were insufficient to support the TPR. *In re Trueman*, 99 N.C. App. 579 (the record showed that respondent's only contacts with North Carolina were that his child was brought here by his former wife and was in her custody here and that the respondent's child support payments were sent here by the Wisconsin court that entered the child support order); *In re Finnican*, 104 N.C. App. 157 (the record showed that respondent's only contact with North Carolina was that his child was brought here by his former wife to whom he paid no support). Furthermore, where the nonresident parent had no contacts with North Carolina and made no appearance in the action, the TPR order was void and could be set aside at any time under Rule 60(b)(4) of the Rules of Civil Procedure. *In re Finnican*, 104 N.C. App. 157.

However, when a child is born out of wedlock, the court looks to whether the respondent father "demonstrated a commitment to the responsibilities of parenthood" when determining whether minimum contacts are required. *In re Dixon*, 112 N.C. App. 248, 251 (1993). Minimum contacts are not required when a nonresident father of a child born out of wedlock (1) has failed to demonstrate his commitment to his child and (2) such commitment could have been shown by him taking any of the identified statutory steps to establish paternity, legitimate the child, or provide substantial financial support or care to the child and mother when he had the opportunity to do so. *In re Williams*, 149 N.C. App. 951 (2002); *In re Dixon*, 112 N.C. App. 248. The court's assertion of personal jurisdiction over an out-of-state parent who did not grasp the opportunity to demonstrate his commitment to his child who was born out of wedlock does not offend "traditional notions of fair play and substantial justice." *In re Williams*, 149 N.C. App. at 958; *In re Dixon*, 112 N.C. App. at 252.

Because these holdings are based on the Due Process Clause of the Fourteenth Amendment to the U.S. Constitution, it is unlikely that the 2007 statutory amendment to G.S. 7B-1101 described in subsection 1, above, or the UCCJEA provision described in subsection 5, below, both of which came after these cases were decided, effected any change in the rule established by case law.

The nonresident parent may raise the defense of lack of personal jurisdiction in an answer, response, or motion as provided in Rule 12(b)(2) of the Rules of Civil Procedure.

**3. Service on respondent temporarily in state.** Personal service of process on an out-of-state respondent who is temporarily in the state will confer personal jurisdiction without regard to any other contacts with the state. *Hedden v. Isbell*, 250 N.C. App. 189 (2016) (trial court acquired personal jurisdiction over defendant when she was personally served with the complaint in North Carolina, rendering minimum contacts analysis unnecessary); *see Burnham v. Superior Court*, 495 U.S. 604 (1990) (holding that due process does not bar the exercise of personal jurisdiction over a nonresident defendant based on personal service while the defendant is temporarily in the state).

**4. Other states.** Courts in some states have held that minimum contacts are never required in TPR proceedings on the basis that these cases fall within the "status" exception recognized by the U.S. Supreme Court in *Shaffer v. Heitner*, 433 U.S. 186 (1977). *See, e.g., In re R.W.*, 39 A.3d 682 (Vt. 2011); *In re Termination of Parental Rights to Thomas J.R.*, 663 N.W.2d 734 (Wis. 2003); *S.B. v. State*, 61 P.3d 6 (Alaska 2002).

**5. UCCJEA does not require personal jurisdiction.** The UCCJEA specifically states that "[p]hysical presence of, or personal jurisdiction over, a party or a child is not necessary or sufficient to make a child-custody determination." G.S. 50A-201(c). However, this statute, G.S. 50A-201, addresses subject matter jurisdiction and should not be construed as dispensing with the requirement that parties to a custody action be served. *See* G.S. 50A-108 ("Notice to persons outside of State").

## 3.5 Venue

### A. Introduction

It is not unusual for more than one county to have some degree of involvement in an abuse, neglect, or dependency case. A need for an immediate petition may arise when the child is found somewhere other than his or her county of residence. Families may relocate at some point during the case. A child's placement in another county may occur. One DSS may be asked to handle another county's case due to a conflict of interest.

Venue is the place where the action is located. During the course of an abuse, neglect, or dependency proceeding, there may be a need to transfer venue. The circumstances under which the Juvenile Code permits transfer of venue depends on whether the transfer is pre- or post-adjudication.

Issues of venue should not be confused with jurisdiction. Challenges to venue, unlike challenges to subject matter jurisdiction, must be raised by the parties and can be waived. N.C. R. CIV. P. 12(h).

### B. Proper Venue

**1. Where to initiate an abuse, neglect, or dependency action.** A petition for abuse, neglect, or dependency may be filed in the judicial district in which the child resides or is present. G.S. 7B-400(a). A judicial district may consist of one or more counties. When a petition is filed in a county that is not the child's county of residence, the petitioner must provide a copy of the petition and any notices of hearing to the DSS director in the child's county of residence. G.S. 7B-402(d).

G.S. 7B-400(b) makes clear that when a conflict of interest causes one county DSS to have an assessment conducted by another county DSS, the DSS conducting the assessment may file a petition in either county. *See In re A.P.*, 371 N.C. 14 (2018) (referring to G.S. 7B-400(b)).

**2. Defining "residence".** The Juvenile Code does not specifically define the term "residence", but G.S. 7B-400(a) references G.S. 153A-257, which determines legal residence for social service purposes as follows:

- A minor has the legal residence of the parent or other relative with whom he or she resides. If the minor does not reside with a parent or relative and is not in a foster home, hospital, mental institution, nursing home, boarding home, educational institution, confinement facility, or similar institution or facility, he or she has the legal residence of the person with whom he or she resides. Any other minor has the legal residence of his or her mother or, if the mother's residence is not known, then the legal residence of his or her father, or, if the residence of neither parent is known, of the county in which he or she is found. G.S. 153A-257(a)(1), (3).
- A person has only one legal residence at a time, and a legal residence continues until the person acquires a new residence. G.S. 153A-257(b).
- The director of the Division of Social Services in the state Department of Health and Human Services is authorized to resolve disputes between counties regarding a child's legal residence in an abuse, neglect, or dependency case for purposes of the provision of services. G.S. 153A-257(d).

**Practice Note:** A child's absence from his or her home due to a protection plan or the provision of case management services by DSS will not affect the original venue if it becomes necessary for DSS to file a juvenile petition. G.S. 7B-400(a). For venue purposes, if parents in County A agree to place their child with a relative in County B as part of a protection plan, DSS in County A can file a petition in the judicial district where County A is located, even though the child has temporarily been placed with a relative in County B. DSS in County A may also file the petition in the judicial district where County B is located if the child is present in County B at the time the petition is filed.

## C. Transfer of Venue in Abuse, Neglect, or Dependency Cases

**1. Pre-adjudication change of venue.** Before adjudication, the court may grant a motion for change of venue for good cause. The statute does not provide guidance regarding what constitutes good cause for a pre-adjudication change of venue. Good cause might exist when a petition is filed in the county where the child is found rather than in the child's or another party's (such as the parent, guardian, custodian, or caretaker) county of residence.

When a change of venue is granted, the identity of the petitioner, which is a county DSS, does not change. G.S. 7B-400(c); *see* G.S. 7B-401.1(a). However, the DSS in the county where the action is transferred may seek to intervene as a county DSS that has an interest in the proceeding. G.S. 7B-401.1(h).

**2. Post-adjudication change of venue.** Any time after adjudication, a court may transfer venue to another county (even if the petition could not have been filed there), but only after making numerous findings and communicating with the court in the other judicial district. The court may transfer venue on its own motion or on the motion of a party. G.S. 7B-900.1(a).

**(a) Factors to be considered.** Before ordering that a case be transferred to another county in the post-adjudication phase of the case, the court must consider relevant factors, which may include

- the current residences of the juvenile and the parent, guardian, or custodian and the extent to which those residences have been and are likely to be stable;
- the reunification plan or other permanent plan for the juvenile and the likely effect of a change in venue on efforts to achieve permanence for the juvenile expeditiously;
- the nature and location of services and service providers necessary to achieve the reunification plan or other permanent plan for the juvenile;
- the impact upon the juvenile of the potential disruption of an existing therapeutic relationship;
- the nature and location of witnesses and evidence likely to be required in future hearings;
- the degree to which the transfer would cause inconvenience to one or more parties;
- any agreement of the parties as to which forum is most convenient; and
- the familiarity of the departments of social services, the courts, and the local offices of the guardian ad litem with the juvenile and the juvenile's family.

G.S. 7B-900.1(e).

**(c) Required findings.** After considering the factors set out immediately above, the court may order transfer only if it finds that

- the present forum is inconvenient;
- transfer is in the juvenile's best interest;
- the parties' rights will not be prejudiced by a change in venue; and
- the DSS directors in the two counties have communicated about the case and either
  - the directors are in agreement with respect to each county's responsibility for providing financial support and services in the case or
  - the director of the state Division of Social Services or his or her designee has made that determination pursuant to G.S. 153A-257(d).

G.S. 7B-900.1(a), (b).

**(c) Communication between judges.** Before transferring a case to another judicial district, the court is required to communicate with the chief district court judge or a judge presiding in juvenile court in that district and explain the reasons for the proposed transfer. G.S. 7B-900.1(d).

**(d) Objection by judge to transfer.** If the judge who is contacted about a proposed transfer makes a timely objection, either verbally or in writing, the court proposing the transfer may order the transfer only after making detailed findings of fact that support a conclusion that the juvenile's best interests require that the case be transferred. G.S. 7B-900.1(d).

**(e) Joinder or substitution of DSS as a party and transfer of custody.** When the court transfers a case to a different county, the court is required to join or substitute as a party the DSS director in the county to which the case is being transferred and, if the juvenile is in the custody of DSS in the county where the action is pending, transfer custody to the DSS in the county to which the case is being transferred. These orders may be entered, however, only if the DSS director in the receiving county has been given notice and an opportunity to be heard or has waived the right to notice and a hearing. G.S. 7B-900.1(c).

**(f) Order and clerical procedure.** An order transferring venue of a case must be entered within thirty days after the hearing on the question of transfer. The order must identify the next court action and the date on which the next hearing will be held. The clerk is required to transmit to the court in the other county a copy of the complete record of the case within three business days after entry of the transfer of venue order. The clerk receiving the transferred case is required to promptly assign a file number, ensure that any necessary appointments of new attorneys or guardians ad litem are made, and calendar and give notice of the next court action required in the case. G.S. 7B-900.1(f), (g).

**Practice Note:** An order transferring venue should address whether and when any appointed counsel and guardian(s) ad litem are released. A phone call from the clerk in the first county to the clerk in the county to which the case is being transferred serves as both a courtesy and a way to ensure that the receiving county is aware of the actions that need to be taken when the case file arrives.

### D. Transfer of Venue in Termination of Parental Rights Cases

The termination of parental rights (TPR) statutes do not address venue; instead, the statute that sets forth where the action is commenced is jurisdictional. G.S. 7B-1101 (discussed in section 3.2.B.7, above). Although the Juvenile Code does not address transferring venue in TPR proceedings, the North Carolina Court of Appeals has recognized a respondent parent's right to seek a change in venue. *In re J.L.K.*, 165 N.C. App. 311 (2004) (holding that respondent waived his right to seek a change of venue when he failed to either move for a change in venue or object to venue in his answer pursuant to Rule 12(b) of the Rules of Civil Procedure).

## 3.6 Overlapping Proceedings

It is not unusual for children, parents, or other caregivers involved in abuse, neglect, or dependency proceedings to have some involvement in other court actions. When proceedings overlap, the parties may face challenges with respect to advocacy strategies, and the parties and the court may face procedural issues. Proceedings that may overlap with abuse, neglect, dependency, or termination of parental rights (TPR) proceedings include (but are not limited to) private custody actions, juvenile delinquency and undisciplined cases, adult criminal court actions, and domestic violence proceedings. Statutes and case law provide limited guidance for navigating overlapping proceedings, so they must generally be analyzed on a case-by-case basis.

### A. Civil Custody Proceedings

A civil custody matter may have been decided or may be pending when an abuse, neglect, or dependency proceeding begins, or a civil custody case may be initiated during or as a result of a juvenile case. The relationship between G.S. Chapter 50 civil custody proceedings and abuse, neglect, or dependency proceedings is addressed in both the Juvenile Code and in Chapter 50.

**1. Jurisdiction, consolidation, and stays.** As soon as the court obtains jurisdiction over a juvenile as the result of the filing of a petition alleging abuse, neglect, or dependency, any other civil action in the state in which custody is an issue is automatically stayed as to that issue. G.S. 7B-200(c); 50-13.1(i). Effective October 1, 2019, when there is an automatic stay, the court must ensure that a notice is filed in the stayed action (the civil action) if the county and case file number are made known to the court. G.S. 7B-200(c)(1); *see* S.L. 2019-33.

**AOC Form:**
AOC-J-165, Notice of Stay of Child Custody Issue (Oct. 2019).

Although there is an automatic stay of the civil custody issue, the court hearing the juvenile case has options with respect to consolidation, transfer, and stay of proceedings.

- The court in the abuse, neglect, or dependency proceeding may order that any civil action or claim for custody filed in the same judicial district be consolidated with the juvenile

proceeding. G.S. 7B-200(c)(1), (d). For clarity, orders resulting from consolidated hearings should sufficiently separate the matters considered in the different proceedings by either (1) entering two separate orders that address the separate components of the hearing or (2) subdividing a single order into separate sections to address the evidentiary standard applied, findings of fact, conclusions of law, and appropriate order for each component of the consolidated hearing. *In re R.B.B.*, 187 N.C. App. 639 (2007).
- If the civil custody case is filed in another judicial district, for good cause and after consulting with the court in the other district, the court in the juvenile proceeding may order a transfer of either the civil custody case or the abuse, neglect, or dependency case to allow the proceedings to take place in the same district. G.S. 7B-200(d).
- The court in the abuse, neglect, or dependency proceeding also has the option to proceed in the juvenile case while the civil case remains stayed, or to dissolve the stay of the civil case and stay the abuse, neglect, or dependency proceeding pending a resolution of the civil case. G.S. 7B-200(d).

**2. Civil custody as the permanent plan.** At any dispositional hearing, the court may order the child placed in the custody of a parent, relative, or other appropriate person. G.S. 7B-903(a)(4). When the court awards custody to a parent or non-parent at a dispositional hearing, it should look to the factors set forth in G.S. 7B-911(c) and determine whether the jurisdiction in the abuse, neglect, or dependency proceeding should be terminated and a civil custody order entered pursuant to G.S. Chapter 50. G.S. 7B-911(a). If the court makes the findings and conclusions specified in G.S. 7B-911(c), including that state intervention through a juvenile court action is no longer required, the court may create a civil custody action under G.S. Chapter 50, enter a custody order in that action, and terminate jurisdiction in the abuse, neglect, or dependency proceeding. The order must comply with the various requirements of G.S. 7B-911. *See In re J.K.*, 253 N.C. App. 57 (2017) (reversing and remanding "custody order" that did not make the findings and conclusions specified in G.S. 7B-911(c), did not terminate the juvenile court's jurisdiction, and did not include provisions transferring jurisdiction to a G.S. Chapter 50 matter).

If a civil custody order already exists, the court would modify that order rather than initiate a new action. G.S. 7B-911(b). The custody action and order survive under G.S. Chapter 50 after the court terminates its jurisdiction in the abuse, neglect, or dependency proceeding. G.S. 7B-201(b). Without a Chapter 50 custody order, if the court terminates its jurisdiction in the abuse, neglect, or dependency action, the orders entered in that action are vacated and the parties return to their pre-petition legal status unless a law or valid court order in another civil action (such as a termination of parental rights order) provides otherwise. G.S. 7B-201(b).

For further discussion of a G.S. 7B-911 order, see Chapter 7.10.B.4(a).

**3. Priority of conflicting orders.** If an abuse, neglect, or dependency order conflicts with an order in a civil custody action, the juvenile order controls as long as the court continues to exercise jurisdiction in the juvenile case. G.S. 7B-200(c)(2).

**4. Termination of parental rights.** The initiation of a termination of parental rights (TPR) proceeding does not trigger the automatic stay of a civil action, as it is not a petition alleging abuse, neglect, or dependency. *See* G.S. 7B-200(c). However, a TPR action that is commenced by petition in the same judicial district as an abuse, neglect, or dependency proceeding may be consolidated with that proceeding. G.S. 7B-1102(c). Also, when there is a TPR action (which is a juvenile proceeding) and a civil action or claim for custody, those actions may also be consolidated. G.S. 7B-200(d). *See Smith v. Alleghany County Dep't of Soc. Servs.* 114 N.C. App. 727 (1994) (the facts identify a consolidated TPR and G.S. Chapter 50 custody action).

## B. Juvenile Delinquency and Undisciplined Proceedings

Overlap between the child welfare system and the juvenile justice system is not uncommon. A child who is the subject of an abuse, neglect, or dependency petition may also be the subject of a delinquency or undisciplined petition. Any juvenile who is adjudicated delinquent or undisciplined may be placed in DSS custody at disposition. *See* G.S. 7B-2503(1)c.; 7B-2506(1)c. Before an adjudication in a delinquency or undisciplined proceeding, a juvenile may also be placed in nonsecure custody with a county DSS. G.S. 7B-1902 through -1907. While a juvenile's placement in DSS custody as a result of a delinquency or undisciplined proceeding does not create or require the initiation of an abuse, neglect, or dependency case, it inserts DSS into the delinquency or undisciplined case and requires that certain types of hearings that apply to abuse, neglect, or dependency cases be held in the delinquency or undisciplined proceeding. The Juvenile Code's Subchapter I (abuse, neglect, dependency, termination of parental rights) and Subchapter II (delinquency and undisciplined) have different goals and procedures. The juvenile's entitlement to representation and the nature of the representation differ under the separate systems covered by the subchapters.

**1. Simultaneous proceedings.** When a child is the subject of petitions filed in both delinquency or undisciplined and abuse, neglect, or dependency actions, both the court and key people involved with the juvenile need to be aware of both proceedings. If the juvenile is in DSS custody, then DSS as well as the juvenile's parent should be served with pleadings and notices in the delinquency or undisciplined case. G.S. 7B-1805 through -1807. *See* 7B-1501(6) (defining "custodian" as the "person or agency that has been awarded legal custody of a juvenile by a court"). The court in the delinquency or undisciplined action will have jurisdiction over DSS if DSS has been served with a summons. G.S. 7B-1600(c). Unless excused by the court, when DSS, as the child's custodian, receives notice of a hearing in the delinquency or undisciplined action, a DSS authorized representative must attend that hearing. G.S. 7B-2700.

A juvenile court counselor preparing recommendations for the court in a delinquency or undisciplined case or supervising a juvenile on probation should be in close communication with DSS when the court counselor knows DSS is involved with the juvenile's family. A DSS report to the court at a dispositional hearing in an abuse, neglect, or dependency case would not be complete without addressing the juvenile's involvement in a delinquency or undisciplined matter and, if applicable, the parents' participation in that case. The legislature recognized the need for interagency sharing of information when it enacted G.S. 7B-3100, requiring designated agencies to share information. For more detailed information on access to and sharing of information, see Chapter 14.1.E. For dispositional hearing purposes, a court counselor's presence in an abuse, neglect, or dependency case, and a DSS social worker's presence in a delinquency or undisciplined case, may be critical to the court's ability to obtain complete information and to coordinate services to the child and family.

**2. DSS custody from delinquency or undisciplined proceeding.**

**(a) Nonsecure custody.** The court may order that a juvenile it has jurisdiction over because of a delinquency or undisciplined petition be placed in nonsecure custody if the criteria set forth in G.S. 7B-1903(a) are met. *See* G.S. 7B-1902; 7B-1904. The criteria differ from what a court must find when placing a child alleged to be abused, neglected, or dependent in nonsecure custody. *Compare* G.S. 7B-1903(a) *with* 7B-503(a). The juvenile may be placed in nonsecure custody with a designated person or with a county DSS that may place the child in a licensed foster home, DSS-operated facility, or any other home or facility approved by the court. G.S. 7B-1905(a). There is no statutory requirement that DSS receive notice and have an opportunity to be heard before a nonsecure custody order places the child in DSS custody. *Cf.* G.S. 7B-2503(1)c. and 7B-2506(1)c. (both requiring that DSS receive notice and have an opportunity to be heard before a juvenile is placed in its custody at disposition). Hearings on the need for nonsecure custody are required within seven days of the initial order, within seven business days of the initial hearing, and at intervals of no more than thirty days. G.S. 7B-1906. Procedures governing those hearings and the criteria a court must consider are set forth in G.S. 7B-1906.

**(b) Disposition.** In the dispositional phase of a delinquency or undisciplined case, the court may place a juvenile in the custody of the county DSS where the juvenile resides if the DSS director has been given notice and an opportunity to be heard. *See* G.S. 7B-2506(1)c.; 7B-2503(1)c. The court's placement of a delinquent or undisciplined juvenile in DSS custody does not constitute an adjudication of abuse, neglect, or dependency; instead, the child has been adjudicated delinquent or undisciplined. *See* G.S. 7B-2405; 7B-2409; 7B-2411. The court in the delinquency or undisciplined proceeding does not have subject matter jurisdiction to adjudicate the juvenile abused, neglected, or dependent. As discussed in section 3.2.B.3, above, such an adjudication requires the filing of a properly verified petition by a DSS director that alleges a child's abuse, neglect, or dependency. The juvenile's placement in DSS custody is simply a dispositional alternative in the delinquency or undisciplined case. A juvenile may be placed in DSS custody for reasons that are unrelated to the adequacy of the parent's care but that arose instead from a need for DSS assistance with a specific or specialized placement.

Although there is not a separate abuse, neglect, or dependency action, the court is required to review the juvenile's dispositional placement of DSS custody under G.S. 7B-906.1 (relating to review and permanency planning hearings in abuse, neglect, or dependency cases). G.S. 7B-2503(1)c.; 7B-2506(1)c. Because the only case in which the court is exercising jurisdiction is the delinquency or undisciplined case, the required G.S. 7B-906.1 review hearings occur in the delinquency or undisciplined action, even if local practice is to schedule the hearings for days on which abuse, neglect, or dependency cases are heard. Because this is the delinquency or undisciplined proceeding, the juvenile is represented by the attorney that is retained or appointed pursuant to G.S. 7B-2000(a) and is not represented by a guardian ad litem or attorney advocate. *See* G.S. 7B-601(a); *see also* G.S. 7B-3100(c) (authorizing GAL to share confidential information about the juvenile with the juvenile's attorney in the delinquency or undisciplined action). Effective December 1, 2019, the court's authority over the parents under Article 27 of the Juvenile Code (G.S. 7B-2700 through -2706) in delinquency cases is somewhat different from the court's authority over parents under G.S. 7B-904 in abuse, neglect, or dependency cases. Effective October 1, 2019, a parent who is indigent is entitled to court-appointed counsel for the delinquency or undisciplined G.S. 7B-906.1 review hearings unless that parent makes a knowing and voluntary waiver of that right. G.S. 7B-2506(1)c.; 7B-2503(1)c; *see* S.L. 2019-33. It is not clear which statutes govern G.S. 7B-906.1 hearings resulting from a disposition entered in a delinquency or undisciplined action when it comes to the court's authority to order parents to complete certain acts. See Chapter 7 (discussing G.S. 7B-906.1 hearings and resulting orders).

As with the district court's jurisdiction over the abuse, neglect, or dependency proceeding, when a court obtains jurisdiction over a juvenile who is alleged to be delinquent or undisciplined, the court's jurisdiction continues until the juvenile turns 18 (or is emancipated) or the court orders its jurisdiction terminated. G.S. 7B-1600(b); 7B-1601(b). When the juvenile's probation ends, the court might terminate its jurisdiction. However, if the court's intention is that the juvenile remain in DSS custody, the court must retain jurisdiction in the delinquency action for the custody order to remain in effect.

DSS may discover that a juvenile placed in its custody is abused, neglected, or dependent. In that case, DSS should file a petition, initiating its own separate abuse, neglect, or dependency proceeding. That separate case will proceed as any other abuse, neglect, or dependency action, although nonsecure custody is unlikely to be necessary since the child will have already been placed in DSS custody. When there is no abuse, neglect, or dependency, a petition should not be filed alleging one of those conditions.

**Resources:**
For further discussion about an order placing a juvenile in DSS custody through a delinquency proceeding, see
- Sara DePasquale, *When Does Delinquency Result in Abuse, Neglect, or Dependency?* UNC SCH. OF GOV'T: ON THE CIVIL SIDE BLOG (May 28, 2019).
- Sara DePasquale & Jacquelyn Greene, *Delinquency and DSS Custody without Abuse, Neglect, or Dependency: How Does That Work?*, JUVENILE LAW BULLETIN NO. 2019/02 (UNC School of Government, July 2019).

**AOC Forms:**
- AOC-J-441, Order For Nonsecure Custody (Undisciplined/Delinquent) (Dec. 2017).
- AOC-J-461, Juvenile Level 1 Disposition Order (Delinquent) (Dec. 2019).
- AOC-J-462, Juvenile Level 3 Disposition And Commitment Order (When Delinquent Offense Is The Basis Of The Commitment) (Dec. 2019).
- AOC-J-475, Juvenile Level 2 Disposition Order (Delinquent) (Dec. 2019).
- AOC-J-465, Order to Terminate Supervision (Undisciplined/Delinquent) (Dec. 2017).

**3. Representation of the juvenile.** It is important to recognize the different roles of attorneys for juveniles in delinquency proceedings and of guardians ad litem (GALs) in abuse, neglect, or dependency proceedings. Attorneys representing juveniles in delinquency and undisciplined proceedings are representing the child's rights and wishes — that is, the child's expressed interests. In contrast, GAL attorney advocates in abuse, neglect, or dependency cases (along with the GAL program staff and volunteer) are representing the best interests of the child, which considers but is not centered on the child's expressed interests. Also, GAL attorney advocates are given broad access to confidential information that may not be available to the juvenile's attorney in a delinquency or undisciplined case. Effective October 1, 2019, the GAL attorney advocate may share confidential information with the attorney representing the juvenile in the delinquency or undisciplined action. *See* G.S. 7B-601; 7B-3100(c). See Chapters 2.3.D (relating to the child's GAL) and 14.1.D (relating to GAL access to information).

Representation by an appointed attorney is limited to the type of proceeding for which the attorney is appointed. *See* G.S. 7B-601; 7B-2000(a). The appointment and role of attorneys in delinquency or undisciplined proceedings and in abuse, neglect, or dependency proceedings are separate and distinct. The Juvenile Code does not address whether an attorney could or should represent the same child in both types of proceedings. From an ethical perspective, it would be difficult for an attorney to switch back and forth between expressed interest representation and best interest representation without encountering conflicts of interest. However, GAL attorney advocates and juvenile defense attorneys can and should communicate and exchange information with one another to the extent that such interaction supports and does not interfere with the goals, privileges, and responsibilities of their respective representations. Similarly, a child's attorney in delinquency or undisciplined proceedings should communicate and coordinate with a parent's attorney in an abuse, neglect, or dependency proceeding to the extent that it is prudent.

## C. Criminal Proceedings

Events leading to a petition alleging abuse or neglect also may result in criminal charges. In cases involving abuse, it is not uncommon for a criminal case to be going on simultaneously with a juvenile case. While there is a lack of statutory and case law guidance addressing issues that may arise when criminal and juvenile proceedings overlap, persons involved in both cases need to be able to recognize these issues to prepare for and resolve them in the best possible way.

**1. Evidentiary issues.** If a witness is called to testify in both cases, issues may arise as to how the witness's testimony in one case might affect the other case. If a child witness is involved in both cases, efforts may be made to avoid unnecessarily repetitive or traumatic interviews of and/or testimony by the child. The Juvenile Code specifically allows the court to authorize the child's guardian ad litem (GAL), who is appointed in the abuse, neglect, or dependency proceeding, to accompany the child to court in any criminal action in which the child is called on to testify in a matter relating to abuse. G.S. 7B-601(b). Some types of evidence may be needed for analysis and/or introduction in both cases, and there may be issues concerning logistics (where, when, and with whom the evidence will be) as well as how the introduction of evidence in one case affects the other case. For an analysis of selected evidence issues, see Chapter 11.

**2. Defendant's participation in an abuse, neglect, or dependency proceeding.** An attorney representing a parent (or other respondent) in an abuse, neglect, or dependency proceeding should, with the client's consent, consult any attorney who is representing the client in a related criminal matter. Among other things, the two attorneys should confer and advise the client about the nature and extent of the client's participation in the abuse, neglect, or dependency case; witnesses and evidence that might be relevant to both cases; and the theory of and strategy for each case. In the abuse, neglect, or dependency case, any party could call the respondent parent/defendant as a witness. A witness in an abuse, neglect, dependency, or other civil case may assert his or her Fifth Amendment privilege against self-incrimination and refuse to testify. *Herndon v. Herndon*, 368 N.C. 826 (2016); *In re L.C.*, 253 N.C. App. 67 (2017). Doing so, however, will support an inference that truthful testimony by the witness would have been unfavorable to him or her. *In re L.C.*, 253 N.C. App. 67; *see, e.g., In re Estate of Trogdon*, 330 N.C. 143 (1991). *See also Lovendahl v. Wicker*, 208 N.C. App. 193 (2010) (discussing the relationship between the timing of overlapping civil and criminal proceedings, specifically involving sanctions against the defendant for his refusal to answer deposition questions based on the privilege against self-incrimination). For further discussion of the application of the right against self-incrimination, see Chapter 11.12.

**3. Access to information and people.** In criminal cases, access to information is governed by the statutes and cases governing criminal procedure and discovery. In abuse, neglect, or dependency cases, access to information is governed in part by (1) the confidentiality statutes applicable to information obtained by DSS, including who has access to that information with and without a court order (G.S. 7B-302(a1); 7B-2901(b)); (2) information-sharing and discovery provisions in G.S. 7B-700; (3) the ability of both DSS and the child's GAL to access confidential information pursuant to G.S. 7B-302(e) and 7B-601(c); and (4) access to court records that are withheld from public inspection (G.S. 7B-2901(a)). For a discussion of confidentiality and sharing of information, see Chapter 14. With different standards and procedures for accessing information in criminal court and juvenile court, issues may arise as to what information can be accessed by whom and for what purpose.

Another issue that may arise is an attorney's access to people who are also represented by an attorney. For example, the prosecutor or a defendant's attorney may wish to speak with a child concerning the criminal case, but if the child is represented by a GAL attorney advocate, the attorney advocate's permission is required for another attorney to speak with the child. *See* North Carolina State Bar, RPC 249 (1997) and RPC 61 (1990). Even if a child is not represented (for example, if the child is a witness and not the subject of the abuse, neglect, or dependency action), an attorney who wants to interview the child should consider whether the consent of a parent or guardian or a court order is required and what disclosures must be made to the child. *See* North Carolina State Bar, 2009 Formal Ethics Opinion 7, Interviewing an Unrepresented Child Prosecuting Witness in a Criminal Case Alleging Physical or Sexual Abuse of the Child (Jan. 27, 2012) (ruling that if the prosecuting witness in a criminal physical or sexual abuse case is younger than 14, the prosecutor or defense lawyer may interview the child only with the consent of a parent or guardian or pursuant to a court order).

**4. Timing of the two proceedings.** The criminal process and the juvenile process move independently of one another and often at very different paces. The Juvenile Code permits continuances in juvenile cases only under limited circumstances and specifically prohibits a continuation for the sole reason of awaiting resolution of a pending criminal charge against a respondent arising out of the same occurrence as the juvenile petition. *See* G.S. 7B-803; *In re Patron*, 250 N.C. App. 375 (2016). See also Chapter 4.5 (discussing continuances). In an abuse, neglect, or dependency action, statutory timelines dictate when hearings must be held, regardless of what is happening in the criminal case.

### D. Domestic Violence Protection Proceedings

A parent or child involved in an abuse, neglect, or dependency proceeding may also be involved in a domestic violence protection proceeding that arises before or during the juvenile proceeding. Domestic violence protection proceedings are civil actions brought pursuant to G.S. Chapter 50B.

As defined in G.S. 50B-1(a), "domestic violence" means the commission of one or more of the following acts (but not acts that are in self-defense) upon an aggrieved party or a child who resides with or is in the custody of the aggrieved party, by a person with whom the aggrieved party has or has had a personal relationship:

- attempting to cause bodily injury or intentionally causing bodily injury;
- placing the aggrieved party or a member of the aggrieved party's family or household in fear of imminent serious bodily injury or continued harassment, as defined in G.S. 14-277.3A, that rises to such a level as to inflict substantial emotional distress; or
- committing any act defined in G.S. 14-27.21 through -27.33 (rape and other sex offenses).

A domestic violence protection action may be initiated in an existing G.S. Chapter 50 action or as a new civil action, and the initiating party may be self-represented. G.S. 50B-2(a). The district court has jurisdiction over domestic violence protection actions. G.S. 50B-2(a). Chapter 50B contains an extensive list of remedies the court may order as it deems necessary to protect the aggrieved party or child, including provisions addressing temporary custody and visitation and provisions restricting the defendant's contact with the aggrieved party or child. Any part of a domestic violence protective action that constitutes a claim for custody is automatically stayed when there is an abuse, neglect, or dependency proceeding, starting with the filing of the juvenile petition and continuing until the court no longer has jurisdiction over the juvenile proceeding. *See* G.S. 7B-200(c); *In re V.M.F.*, 218 N.C. App. 455 (2012) (unpublished) (remanding for court hearing the neglect action to consider visitation and citing G.S. 7B-200(b) and (c) in holding that the court was not prohibited from considering visitation because of a domestic violence protection order (DVPO) that contained a visitation provision). As with a civil custody action, the court in the juvenile proceeding may consolidate the actions or dissolve the stay of the civil action and stay the abuse, neglect, or dependency proceeding. G.S. 7B-200(c), (d). In addition, if an abuse, neglect, or dependency order conflicts with the custody and visitation provisions of a DVPO, the juvenile order controls as long as the court continues to exercise jurisdiction in the juvenile case. G.S. 7B-200(c)(2).

**Resources:**
The "Family Violence and Domestic Relations" section of the website for the National Council of Juvenile and Family Court Judges has multiple resources.

VAWnet.org is an online network operated by the National Resource Center on Domestic Violence, with multiple resources on domestic violence on its website.

The National Center for Children Exposed to Violence provides access to statistics, reports, articles, and other internet sites related to children exposed to violence on its website.

The North Carolina Coalition Against Domestic Violence (NCCADV) website has information about resources, information, and statistics related to domestic violence in the state.

# Procedural Rules and Orders

Chapter 4

# Chapter 4
# Procedural Rules and Orders

**4.1 Introduction   4-3**
   A. Applicability of Rules of Civil Procedure in Juvenile Proceedings
      1. Rules apply when explicitly required by the Juvenile Code
      2. A rule or part of a rule will not apply where the Juvenile Code provides a different procedure
      3. Rules or parts of rules apply when required to fill procedural gaps
      4. Rules may not be used to confer rights
   B. Rule Application Analysis

**4.2 Procedures Regarding the Petition   4-8**
   A. Contents of Petition
   B. Signature of Attorney or Party
   C. Amended and Supplemental Pleadings
      1. Amendments in abuse, neglect, or dependency proceedings
      2. Amendments in termination of parental rights proceedings
      3. Supplemental pleadings
   D. Responsive Pleadings

**4.3 Summons   4-11**
   A. Content and Issuance of Summons
      1. Signature of clerk
      2. Timing
      3. Who receives summons
      4. Service requirements when summons is not required
   B. Expiration of Summons

**4.4 Service   4-13**
   A. The Impact of Service
   B. Summons
      1. Service by delivery
      2. Service by publication
      3. Service in a foreign country
   C. Notice and Motions

**4.5 Continuances   4-21**
   A. Continuances Disfavored
   B. Abuse, Neglect, Dependency Proceedings
   C. Termination of Parental Rights Proceedings
   D. Considerations
      1. Party's own actions
      2. Absence of witness
      3. Heavy dockets

4. Time to prepare
5. Delay, prejudice, and the remedy of mandamus

### 4.6 Discovery    4-24
A. Discovery Generally
B. The Juvenile Code and Discovery
   1. DSS sharing of information
   2. GAL sharing of information
   3. Local rules
   4. Discovery methods
   5. Discovery motions
   6. Continuances related to discovery
   7. Redisclosure

### 4.7 Intervention    4-27
A. Abuse, Neglect, Dependency Proceedings
B. Termination of Parental Rights Proceedings
   1. Intervention of right
   2. Permissive intervention
   3. Procedure for intervening

### 4.8 Motions in Juvenile Proceedings    4-30

### 4.9 Judgments and Orders    4-31
A. Drafting Orders
   1. Who drafts the order
   2. Responsibility of the court
   3. Circulating draft orders
   4. Presiding judge must sign order
B. Findings of Fact and Conclusions of Law
   1. Separation of findings of fact and conclusions of law
   2. Findings of fact
   3. Conclusions of law
C. Entry and Service of the Order
   1. What constitutes entry
   2. Serving the order
D. Time Requirements for Orders
   1. Entry of order within thirty days
   2. Clerk's duty to reschedule when entry is late
   3. Remedy for untimely orders is mandamus

## 4.1 Introduction

The first place to look for rules governing the procedures that apply in abuse, neglect, dependency, and termination of parental rights (TPR) actions is Subchapter I of G.S. Chapter 7B. The Juvenile Code (G.S. Chapter 7B) establishes the procedures for these cases. However, there are times when a certain rule of the North Carolina Rules of Civil Procedure applies. This Chapter highlights procedural issues in abuse, neglect, dependency, and TPR cases, with an emphasis on statutes and cases that implicate the Rules of Civil Procedure. The Chapter is not meant to address all aspects of procedure in juvenile cases. Some procedural issues have an impact on jurisdiction and are discussed in Chapter 3. Local rules may also affect procedure and should be consulted.

### A. Applicability of Rules of Civil Procedure in Juvenile Proceedings

The first stated purpose of the Juvenile Code in G.S. 7B-100 is to "provide procedures for the hearing of juvenile cases. . . ." In addition, the legislative intent regarding the termination of parental rights statutes includes a general purpose "to provide judicial procedures for terminating the legal relationship between a juvenile and … [his or her] parents." G.S. 7B-1100(1). When the Juvenile Code provides a procedure, that procedure prevails over the Rules of Civil Procedure. However, a specific Rule of Civil Procedure may apply when it does not conflict with the Juvenile Code and only to the extent that it advances the purposes of the Juvenile Code. *In re E.H.*, 227 N.C. App. 525 (2013); *In re L.O.K.*, 174 N.C. App. 426 (2005).

**1. Rules apply when explicitly required by the Juvenile Code.** The Juvenile Code specifically states that certain Rules of Civil Procedure apply in particular circumstances, in which case those rules must be followed. Rules of Civil Procedure that are referenced in the Juvenile Code include

- **Rule 4** (process),
- **Rule 5** (service and filing of pleadings and other papers); *see In re H.D.F.*, 197 N.C. App. 480, 496 (2009) (emphasis in original) (urging trial courts to check certificates of service to ensure that "*all* parties are served with *all* documents required to be served" after determining that respondent father did not receive notices and, therefore, did not have a meaningful opportunity to participate in the action when his appointed counsel withdrew),
- **Rule 17** (as it pertains to guardians ad litem),
- **Rule 42** (consolidation), and
- **Rule 58** (entry of judgment).

**2. A rule or part of a rule will not apply where the Juvenile Code provides a different procedure.** In juvenile cases many procedures that ordinarily would be governed by the Rules of Civil Procedure are established instead by the Juvenile Code itself. For example, provisions in G.S. 7B-800 relating to amending petitions prevail over Rule 15 of the Rules of Civil Procedure related to amendments. *In re B.L.H.*, 190 N.C. App. 142 (discussing former G.S. 7B-800 and applying it to a TPR petition), *aff'd per curiam*, 362 N.C. 674 (2008).

**3. Rules or parts of rules apply when required to fill procedural gaps.** Where the Juvenile Code does not identify a specific procedure to be used, the Rules of Civil Procedure may be used to fill procedural gaps. *See In re S.D.W.,* 187 N.C. App. 416 (2007) (termination of parental rights proceeding). Some appellate court decisions have held that specific rules apply in abuse, neglect, dependency, and termination of parental rights (TPR) proceedings. In other opinions, the court has referenced or applied a Rule of Civil Procedure without discussion and with no suggestion that the rule's applicability was in doubt. The following rules apply:

- **Rule 7(b).** *In re McKinney,* 158 N.C. App. 441 (2003) (applying Rule 7(b)(1) to determine whether a TPR motion was sufficient to confer jurisdiction).
- **Rule 8.** *In re Dj.L.,* 184 N.C. App. 76, 80 (2007) (applying the rule to construe the petition "as to do substantial justice").
- **Rule 11(a), (b), (d).** *In re Triscari Children,* 109 N.C. App. 285 (1993) (applying Rule 11(a) and (b) when holding verification of a TPR petition is required by statute and verification by the respondent mother, who was the petitioner, was insufficient); *In re Dj.L.,* 184 N.C. App. 76 (2007) (applying Rule 11(b) to determine whether verification of abuse, neglect, or dependency petition was sufficient); *In re N.X.A.,* 254 N.C. App. 670 (2017) (applying Rule 11(d), verification by the State, when holding verification by the DSS attorney of the petition alleging neglect and dependency was sufficient as the county DSS was acting as agent of the State Department of Health and Human Services when implementing the statutory provisions of the Juvenile Code).
- **Rule 12(b), (h).** *In re J.L.K.,* 165 N.C. App. 311 (2004) (applying Rule 12(b)(3) to require respondent to timely object to venue or the right to seek a change of venue is waived); *In re K.G.,* 817 S.E.2d 790 (N.C. Ct. App. 2018) (holding trial court erred when denying Rule 12(b)(6) motion to dismiss dependency petition for failure to state a claim upon which relief may be granted); *In re Quevedo,* 106 N.C. App. 574 (1992) and *In re J.S.K.,* 807 S.E.2d 188 (N.C. Ct. App. 2017) (both applying Rule 12(b)(6) to determine if the TPR petition/motion was sufficient to state a claim upon which relief may be granted); *In re K.J.L.,* 363 N.C. 343 (2009) (discussing Rule 12(h) and waiver of defense of personal jurisdiction when not timely raised).
- **Rule 30.** *In re K.D.L.,* 176 N.C. App. 261 (2006) (discussing incarcerated respondent father's request for deposition and how it could have been taken by telephone). *See In re D.R.,* 172 N.C. App. 300 (2005) (holding no abuse of discretion when court denied respondent's motion for expenses to conduct telephone deposition).
- **Rule 32(a).** *In re Quevedo,* 106 N.C. App. 574 (1992) (where the respondent father in a TPR action was imprisoned in Massachusetts, discussing the rule allowing for the use of depositions at hearing when a witness is unable to attend because of imprisonment).
- **Rule 33.** *In re J.D.,* 234 N.C. App. 342 (2014) (reviewing the factual background of the action, which included interrogatories).
- **Rule 35.** *In re Williams,* 149 N.C. App. 951 (2002) (applying the rule to determine that respondent was not entitled to a mental examination of the child).
- **Rule 41(a)(1)(i).** *In re E.H.,* 227 N.C. App. 525 (2013) (applying the rule to affirm DSS's voluntary dismissal of its action before the adjudicatory hearing).
- **Rule 43(a).** *In re A.M.,* 192 N.C. App. 538 (2008) (applying the rule to require at least some live testimony at a TPR hearing); *see In re S.P.,* 833 S.E.2d 638 (N.C. Ct. App. 2019) and *In re J.T.* 252 N.C. App. 19 (2017) (both holding oral testimony needed at

permanency planning hearing).
- **Rule 45.** *In re A.H.*, 250 N.C. App. 546 (2016) (applying the "unreasonable or oppressive" standard set forth in subsection (c) of the rule to determine whether there was abuse of discretion in quashing a subpoena for the child to testify at hearing).
- **Rule 52(a).** *In re C.M.C.*, 832 S.E.2d 681 (N.C. S.Ct. 2019) (applying Rule 52 to a TPR order when holding the order was a nullity when it was signed by a judge who did not preside over the TPR hearing); *In re D.E.M.*, 810 S.E.2d 375 (N.C. Ct. App. 2018) and *In re T.P.*, 197 N.C. App. 723 (2009) (both applying the rule in a TPR action to require that the court find the facts specially and state its conclusions separately); *In re E.N.S.*, 164 N.C. App. 146 (2004) (referring to Rule 52(a)(1) when determining sufficiency of findings of fact and conclusions of law in a neglect and dependency adjudication order).
- **Rule 59(a).** *In re S.G.V.S.*, 811 S.E.2d 718 (N.C. Ct. App. 2018) (applying Rule 59(a)(1) when reversing and remanding TPR order and order denying Rule 59 motion to reopen the evidence to allow for respondent to present evidence; holding trial court's denial of respondent's motion to continue the TPR hearing or reopen the case to present evidence constituted an irregularity by which a party was prevented from having a fair trial; the court scheduled the TPR hearing at the same time as respondent's previously scheduled criminal hearing in another county and refused to grant a continuance or reopen the evidence due to a misapprehension of the law, which was an unreasonable and substantial miscarriage of justice).
- **Rule 60(a)**. *In re C.N.C.B.*, 197 N.C. App. 553 (2009) (applying Rule 60(a) to prohibit the trial court from making substantive modifications to a judgment versus a correction of a clerical mistake); *In re J.K.P.*, 238 N.C. App. 334 (2014) (court has jurisdiction to correct a clerical mistake, which in this case was the inadvertent checking of a box on an AOC form, pursuant to Rule 60(a) so long as the correction occurs before an appeal is docketed); *In re J.K.*, 253 N.C. App. 57 (2017) (referring to Rule 60(a) and holding when a clerical error is discovered on appeal, remand to the trial court for correction is appropriate so that the record speaks the truth).
- **Rule 60(b).** *In re E.H.*, 227 N.C. App. 525 (2013) (holding that a Rule 60(b) motion was an appropriate means of addressing whether a voluntary dismissal was permissible and looking to G.S. 7B-1001(a) when determining that the order denying the Rule 60 motion was a final order subject to appeal); *In re Saunders*, 77 N.C. App. 462 (1985) (applying Rule 60(b) to reject a motion for relief from a TPR judgment where the respondent did not comply with the time requirements of the rule). Note that a Rule 60(b) motion for relief may only be made with respect to a final order and is not appropriate when an order has been rendered but not entered. *See In re A.B.*, 239 N.C. App. 157 (2015) (where a trial court had granted a Rule 60 motion, the court of appeals noted that it could not analyze the motion in the context of Rule 60 because there had not been an order entered pursuant to Rule 58; the court of appeals treated the motion as a motion to reopen the evidence).
- **Rule 61.** *In re T.M.*, 187 N.C. App. 694 (2007) (applying the rule to find harmless error and reject the argument made by respondent because no prejudice was shown).
- **Rule 63.** *In re Whisnant*, 71 N.C. App. 439 (1984) (holding although the rule allows a judge other than the one who presided at the hearing to sign an order, the circumstances under Rule 63 for a substitute judge to sign the TPR order did not apply to this case).

**4. Rules may not be used to confer rights.** Application of a Rule of Civil Procedure where the Juvenile Code is silent may not be appropriate where it would have the effect of conferring a new procedural right. *See In re B.L.H.*, 190 N.C. App. 142, *aff'd per curiam*, 362 N.C. 674 (2008). Rules that have been held to be inapplicable in juvenile proceedings include the following:

- **Rule 12(c)**. *In re I.D.*, 239 N.C. App. 172 (2015) (originally unpublished Feb. 3, 2015, but subsequently published) (holding that adjudication order entered solely upon allegations in a verified petition amounted to a judgment on the pleadings, which required reversal even though respondent had failed to object); *In re Shaw*, 152 N.C. App. 126 (2002) (holding that default judgment or judgment on the pleadings is inappropriate in an adjudication of neglect); *In re Thrift*, 137 N.C. App. 559 (2000) (holding that judgment on the pleadings is not available in abuse, neglect, or dependency matters because the Juvenile Code requires a hearing).
- **Rule 13**. *In re E.H.*, 227 N.C. App. 525 (2013) (recognizing DSS has burden of proof at adjudicatory hearing for abuse, neglect, or dependency, and respondent parent or child's GAL has no right to seek affirmative relief like that available in a counterclaim); *In re S.D.W.*, 187 N.C. App. 416 (2007) (holding that Rule 13 does not apply to allow a claim for a TPR to be asserted as a counterclaim in a civil custody or visitation action); *In re Peirce*, 53 N.C. App. 373 (1981) (holding that a parent does not have a right to file a counterclaim in a TPR action).
- **Rule 15**. *In re G.B.R.*, 220 N.C. App. 309 (2012) and *In re B.L.H.*, 190 N.C. App. 142, *aff'd per curiam*, 362 N.C. 674 (2008) (both holding in TPR cases that the trial court erred in applying Rule 15(b) to allow amendment of the petitions to conform to the evidence, but holding in *In re G.B.R.* that the error was harmless); *In re M.M.*, 200 N.C. App. 248 (2009) (explains an amendment to a TPR petition that names a previously unknown father is not required and is instead governed by G.S. 7B-1105 and not Rule 15). See section 4.2.C, below (discussing amendments to pleadings).
- **Rule 41(a)(1)**. *In re L.O.K.*, 174 N.C. App. 426 (2005) (holding DSS's voluntary dismissal of its TPR petition after it rested its case and without first obtaining a court order is not a dismissal with prejudice that would preclude DSS from filing a second TPR petition).
- **Rule 55**. *In re I.D.*, 239 N.C. App. 172 (2015) (originally unpublished Feb. 3, 2015, but subsequently published) (reversing abuse and neglect adjudication order; default judgment is inappropriate); *In re Quevedo,* 106 N.C. App. 574 (1992) (Greene, J., concurring) (applying language of TPR statute requiring a hearing to implicitly prohibit default judgment).
- **Rule 56**. *In re J.N.S.*, 165 N.C. App. 536 (2004) (holding that summary judgment as to a ground for TPR is contrary to the procedural mandate of the Juvenile Code requiring the court to hear evidence and make findings); *Curtis v. Curtis*, 104 N.C. App. 625 (1991) (holding that summary judgment procedures are not available in TPR proceedings).

## B. Rule Application Analysis

The language of the Juvenile Code and appellate court decisions that reference or consider specific Rules of Civil Procedure provide the following guidance for determining whether a rule (or part of a rule) applies in a particular circumstance.

**Yes, the rule applies if**

1. the Juvenile Code provides specifically that the rule applies or
2. the Juvenile Code is silent with respect to the procedure the rule covers and applying the rule fills a procedural gap in a way that is consistent with the purposes of the Juvenile Code.

**No, the rule does not apply if**

1. the Juvenile Code provides a different procedure or
2. the rule confers a procedural right that is not contemplated by the Juvenile Code.

**But, there may still be lack of clarity in the application of some rules.** When the Juvenile Code is silent about a procedure and case law provides no guidance, it simply may not be clear whether application of a Rule of Civil Procedure in a juvenile proceeding would fill a procedural gap or confer a new procedural right.

When applicability of a particular rule is unclear, the purpose statements in the Juvenile Code (G.S. 7B-100 and 7B-1100) may provide guidance, since appellate cases have stated that the Rules of Civil Procedure apply to the extent they advance the purposes of the Juvenile Code. *See, e.g., In re A.M.*, 192 N.C. App. 538 (2008) (applying Rule 43(a) to require that some testimony be taken orally in open court because the rule furthered the Juvenile Code's purposes of assuring fairness and equity and developing a disposition that reflects consideration of the facts).

The reasoning by the court of appeals regarding the applicability of part of Rule 41(a)(1), which allows a plaintiff to voluntarily dismiss an action before resting the case, to one proceeding, and the inapplicability of another part of Rule 41(a)(1), which would bar the filing of a second TPR petition, to another proceeding further demonstrates the importance of the purposes of the Juvenile Code. In the case *In re E.H.*, 227 N.C. App. 525 (2013), the court of appeals reasoned that application of Rule 41(a)(1)(i) to allow a department of social services (DSS) to voluntarily dismiss a juvenile petition prior to the adjudicatory hearing advanced the purposes of the Juvenile Code because the legislature entrusted DSS with the duty to determine whether allegations of abuse, neglect, or dependency are credible and what action to take. The court said that requiring the child's guardian ad litem or parent to consent to a dismissal would impermissibly shift this responsibility away from DSS. In addition, allowing DSS to dismiss its own petition after finding that evidence underlying the allegations is too weak to merit proceeding advances the Juvenile Code purpose of avoiding unnecessary periods of family separation and unnecessary burdens on juveniles and their families, while allowing DSS to conserve its limited resources for other juveniles.

**Note,** for purposes of this Manual, "department of social services" or "DSS" refers to a department as defined by G.S. 7B-101(8a) regardless of how it is titled or structured.

Yet in the case *In re L.O.K.*, 174 N.C. App. 426 (2005), the court of appeals held Rule 41(a)(1) was not applicable to bar DSS from filing a subsequent petition to terminate parental rights (TPR) even though DSS had voluntarily dismissed an earlier TPR petition, without obtaining a court order, after presenting evidence and resting its case. The court reasoned that applying Rule 41(a)(1) to preclude a subsequent TPR petition could not be reconciled with a court's continuing jurisdiction over a juvenile under G.S. 7B-201; would be contrary to a child's best interests, which are of paramount consideration under G.S. 7B-100(5); and is antithetical to those best interests because it would result in children being stranded indefinitely in foster care without a permanent plan when they cannot be returned to their parents.

## 4.2 Procedures Regarding the Petition

Abuse, neglect, or dependency actions are initiated by the filing of a verified petition. Termination of parental rights (TPR) actions may be initiated either by verified petition or if there is a pending abuse, neglect, or dependency case, by verified motion.

### A. Contents of Petition

General requirements for the contents of a petition alleging abuse, neglect, or dependency are addressed in Chapter 5.3.A. General requirements for the contents of a TPR petition or motion are addressed in Chapter 9.5. The relationship between petition requirements and jurisdiction is addressed in Chapter 3.2.

Even though the Juvenile Code specifically addresses the required contents of juvenile petitions (and TPR motions), the applicable Rules of Civil Procedure may impose additional requirements. For example, in the case of *In re McKinney*, 158 N.C. App. 441 (2003), an attempt was made to initiate a TPR proceeding by filing a motion in the cause. However, the motion did not include a statement specifically asking that the court terminate parental rights. Because the motion failed to comply with the requirement in Rule 7(b)(1) that the motion set forth the relief or order sought, the court found the motion insufficient to initiate a TPR action.

### B. Signature of Attorney or Party

Rule 11(a) of the Rules of Civil Procedure requires that the petition (as well as all pleadings, motions, and other papers) be signed by (1) at least one attorney of record and state the attorney's address or (2) the party if not represented by counsel. The attorney's signature constitutes certification by the attorney that he or she has read the petition, that to the best of his or her knowledge, information, and belief it is well grounded in fact and is warranted by law or a good faith argument, and that it is not being used for an improper purpose. A petition that is not signed must be "stricken unless it is signed promptly after the omission is brought to the attention" of the attorney or party. N.C. R. Civ. P. 11(a). *See In re L.B.*, 181 N.C. App. 174 (2007) (relying on language in *In re T.R.P.*, 173 N.C. App. 541 (2005), *aff'd* 360 N.C. 588 (2006)), of the possibility that DSS could take remedial action to provide the trial court with subject matter jurisdiction it had been lacking and holding that the trial court gained subject matter jurisdiction to move forward in the action when a DSS representative signed and verified the petition two days after a nonsecure custody order was filed and one day after the summons was issued); *see also In re D.D.F.*, 187 N.C. App. 388, 395–96 (2007) (discussing in Footnote 1 that Rule 11(a) contemplates correcting an omission of a signature and noting "[t]he juvenile code would not prevent this type of minor amendment to a petition").

**Practice Note:** AOC forms may not include space for the attorney's signature, so when AOC forms are used, attorneys must ensure that a signature page is included.

## C. Amended and Supplemental Pleadings

**1. Amendments in abuse, neglect, or dependency proceedings.** The Juvenile Code provides for the amendment of an abuse, neglect, or dependency petition. As a result, the applicable procedure is found at G.S. 7B-800 and not Rule 15 of the Rules of Civil Procedure. The court in its discretion may permit the amendment of a petition. G.S. 7B-800. When allowing an amendment, the court must direct the manner in which the amended petition must be served and specify the time allowed for a party to prepare after the amendment. G.S. 7B-800.

**Practice Note**: Prior appellate decisions prohibiting an amendment from changing the nature of the conditions alleged in the petition (e.g., abuse, neglect, or dependency) are based on the former language of G.S. 7B-800, which contained a limiting provision. That limitation was removed by S.L. 2010-90, sec. 11 and is no longer current law.

**2. Amendments in termination of parental rights proceedings.** The Juvenile Code is silent with respect to amendments to petitions or motions for termination of parental rights (TPR). The court of appeals has held that application of Rule 15(b) of the Rules of Civil Procedure to allow amendments to conform to the evidence is improper in a TPR case because it would superimpose a new right where none was intended by the Juvenile Code. *In re B.L.H.*, 190 N.C. App. 142 (looking to G.S. 7B-800 and applying it to a TPR petition), *aff'd per curiam*, 362 N.C. 674 (2008). This holding differs from several earlier decisions upholding the application of Rule 15(b) in TPR cases. *See, e.g., In re L.T.R.*, 181 N.C. App. 376, 390 (2007) (citing Rule 15(b) in holding that (1) respondent, by not objecting to the evidence, "impliedly consented to the adjudication" of an issue that was not raised by the pleadings, and (2) the trial court did not err in making findings of fact and conclusions of law based on that evidence); *In re Smith*, 56 N.C. App. 142, 147 (1982) (finding no error in the trial court's application of Rule 15(b) to allow a motion to amend the TPR complaint to conform to the evidence).

What these cases have in common is a concern about notice and fairness. The court in *In re B.L.H.*, 190 N.C. App. 142, *aff'd per curiam*, 362 N.C. 674, emphasized (1) that the ground the petition was amended to allege did not exist and could not have been alleged when the petition was filed; and (2) that the original petition did not allege that ground by statutory reference or facts sufficient to put respondents on notice that the ground would be an issue. In *In re Smith*, 56 N.C. App. 142, the court of appeals noted the trial court's finding that the allegations in the pleading had put respondent on notice that the grounds added by the amendment could provide bases for the TPR. The amendment in *In re L.T.R.*, 181 N.C. App. 376, added factual allegations to conform to the evidence, not a different ground, and probably was not even necessary. The court quoted an earlier case in which it said, "[A] party attempting to limit the trial of issues by implied consent must object specifically to evidence outside the scope of the original pleadings; otherwise, allowing an amendment to conform the pleadings to the evidence will not be error, and, in fact, is not even technically necessary." *In re L.T.R.*, 181 N.C. App. at 390 (citations omitted).

More recently, in the case *In re G.B.R.*, 220 N.C. App. 309 (2012), the court of appeals relied on *In re B.L.H.*, 190 N.C. App. 142, *aff'd per curiam*, 362 N.C. 674, in holding that the trial court erred by allowing amendment of the TPR petition to conform to the evidence. The court went on, however, to determine that the respondent had sufficient notice, the erroneous granting of the motion to amend had no effect on the court's ultimate determination, and the error was harmless.

Appellate court decisions addressing amendments to conform to the evidence in TPR proceedings have focused on whether there was sufficient (even if not formal) notice of the allegations in the amended pleading and whether allowing the amendment resulted in prejudice.

**3. Supplemental pleadings.** The Juvenile Code does not address supplemental pleadings in abuse, neglect, dependency, or TPR proceedings, and appellate cases have not directly addressed the applicability in juvenile cases of Rule 15(d) of the Rules of Civil Procedure. Rule 15(d) refers to a supplemental pleading as "setting forth transactions or occurrences or events which may have happened since the date of the pleading" and gives the court discretion to allow a supplemental pleading where there is reasonable notice and on terms that are "just."

Amendments and supplemental pleadings differ primarily with regard to the nature of the additional allegations the party seeks to assert. The facts in a supplemental pleading did not exist when the original pleading was filed. An amended pleading relates to information that existed but was not alleged in the original pleading. Both require a motion and permission of the court. In the case of *Foy v. Foy*, 57 N.C. App. 128 (1982), the court of appeals stated that a plaintiff's motion to amend her complaint was in substance a motion to file a supplemental pleading, which was governed by Rule 15(d). The court acknowledged that whether to allow a party to file a supplemental pleading was within the trial judge's discretion and that such pleadings should be allowed unless they would impose a substantial injustice on the opposing party.

### D. Responsive Pleadings

The Juvenile Code does not address responsive pleadings in abuse, neglect, or dependency proceedings, and the filing of answers in those cases is not required and is rare.

The only provisions in the Juvenile Code for responsive pleadings are in the context of termination of parental rights (TPR) proceedings, where the summons directs the respondent to file an answer to a TPR petition and the notice that accompanies a TPR motion directs the respondent to file a response. G.S. 7B-1106; 7B-1106.1; *see* G.S. 7B-1108(a). See also Chapter 9.8 (discussing details relating to TPR answers and responses). The failure to file an answer or response, however, does not constitute an admission of the allegations and cannot result in a default judgment or judgment on the pleadings. *In re Tyner*, 106 N.C. App. 480 (1992). Filing a responsive pleading in a TPR action that denies any material allegation of the petition or motion does, however, require the court to appoint a guardian ad litem (GAL) for the juvenile unless one has already been appointed under G.S. 7B-601. G.S. 7B-1108.

Appellate cases have rejected attempts to utilize other responsive pleadings, such as counterclaims, in TPR cases, stating that because the Juvenile Code provides procedures that include an answer or response but do not address other types of pleadings, these are the exclusive procedures. *See In re S.D.W.*, 187 N.C. App. 416 (2007); *In re Peirce*, 53 N.C. App. 373 (1981). The court of appeals has also rejected the argument that a counterclaim or cross-claim could be filed by the parent or GAL in an abuse, neglect, or dependency case, reasoning that all authority of the trial court arises out of the juvenile petition, which can be filed only by DSS, and that although the parents and the GAL may present evidence and argument, they have no right to seek affirmative relief. *In re E.H.*, 227 N.C. App. 525 (2013).

## 4.3 Summons

Problems with issuance or service of a summons implicate personal jurisdiction, not subject matter jurisdiction. *In re K.J.L.*, 363 N.C. 343 (2009). For a discussion of the relationship between the summons and subject matter jurisdiction, see Chapter 3.2.C.1.

### A. Content and Issuance of Summons

The Juvenile Code sets out the required contents for the summons in abuse, neglect, or dependency proceedings in G.S. 7B-406 and for termination of parental rights (TPR) proceedings in G.S. 7B-1106. For TPR cases initiated by motion, G.S. 7B-1106.1 sets out similar requirements for the contents of the required notice. For details relating to summonses in abuse, neglect, or dependency proceedings, see Chapter 5.3.B and summonses and notices for TPR proceedings, see Chapter 9.7.

**AOC Forms:**
- AOC-J-142, Juvenile Summons and Notice of Hearing (Abuse/Neglect/Dependency) (Oct. 2013).
- AOC-J-208, Summons in Proceeding for Termination of Parental Rights (March 2012).

**1. Signature of clerk.** Although the Juvenile Code is very specific with respect to the content of summonses in juvenile proceedings, Rule 4(a) and (b) of the Rules of Civil Procedure, relating to the issuance and content of a summons, has been applied to juvenile proceedings as well. In a TPR case, *In re K.J.L.*, 363 N.C. 343 (2009), the North Carolina Supreme Court stated that to be properly "issued," the summons must contain the signature of the clerk, assistant clerk, or deputy clerk as required by Rule 4(b).

**2. Timing.** The Juvenile Code states that the summons must be issued by the clerk immediately after an abuse, neglect, or dependency petition is filed. G.S. 7B-406(a). This is different from the requirement in Rule 4(a) of the Rules of Civil Procedure that a summons be issued within five days of the filing of the complaint. In most situations, the petition is filed with the clerk, who issues the summons at that time. However, a juvenile petition must be accepted for filing by a magistrate in emergency situations when the clerk's office is closed and a petition must be filed to obtain a nonsecure custody order or an order to cease obstruction of or interference with a DSS assessment. G.S. 7B-404. The magistrate's acceptance of the petition constitutes the "filing" of the petition. G.S. 7B-405. A magistrate is not authorized to issue the summons. A petition that is filed with a magistrate must be delivered to the clerk's office for processing as soon as the clerk's office opens. G.S. 7B-404(b). The immediacy requirement for the issuance of a summons applies when the clerk's office opens and processes the petition.

**3. Who receives summons.** When a petition alleges abuse, neglect, or dependency, the summons is issued to each party named in the petition except the juvenile. G.S. 7B-406(a). For a TPR petition, a summons is issued to the respondent parents, except a parent who has irrevocably relinquished the child for adoption or consented to adoption by the petitioner. G.S. 7B-1106(a)(1). For a TPR petition, a summons also must be issued to any court-appointed guardian of the person of the child, legal custodian, a DSS or licensed child-placing agency to whom the child has been relinquished for adoption, and/or any DSS with court-ordered placement responsibility for the child. G.S. 7B-1106(a)(2)–(4).

**4. Service requirements when summons is not required.** Although a summons need not be served on the juvenile or the juvenile's guardian ad litem (GAL), immediately after a petition alleging abuse or neglect is filed, the clerk is required to provide a copy of the petition and any notices of hearings to the local GAL office. G.S. 7B-408. If a child has a GAL when a TPR petition or motion is filed, or if a GAL is appointed for the child during the TPR proceeding, a copy of all pleadings and other papers required to be served (but not a summons) must be served on the GAL or attorney advocate pursuant to Rule 5 of the Rules of Civil Procedure. G.S. 7B-1106(a1).

In a TPR proceeding, if an attorney was appointed for a respondent parent in the underlying abuse, neglect, or dependency proceeding and the attorney has not been relieved of responsibility, a copy of all pleadings and other papers (but not a summons) must be served on the attorney pursuant to Rule 5 of the Rules of Civil Procedure. G.S. 7B-1106(a2).

---

**Practice Note:** The attorney appointed to represent a respondent parent in an abuse, neglect, or dependency action is not relieved from his or her appointment without leave from the court based upon justifiable cause and notice of the intent to withdraw being provided to the parent client. The attorney's representation continues in the TPR action; that attorney is not provisional counsel in the TPR. *See In re D.E.G.*, 228 N.C. App. 381 (2013).

## B. Expiration of Summons

The provisions of Rule 4 of the Rules of Civil Procedure determine the life of a juvenile summons. Rule 4(c) requires that a summons be served within sixty days after the date of issuance but provides that failure to serve the summons within sixty days does not invalidate the summons. When the sixty-day time limit is not met, Rule 4(d) allows an extension of the time for service by obtaining either

- an endorsement on the original summons for an extension of time, but the endorsement must be obtained within ninety days of issuance of the summons; or
- an alias or pluries summons (a summons subsequent to the first), obtained within ninety days of the issuance of the summons.

Failure to obtain an extension may result in lack of personal jurisdiction over the party to whom the summons is directed. However, like other defects in or even the absence of a summons, the expiration of a summons can be waived if the party makes a general appearance or files a responsive pleading and does not raise the issue of personal jurisdiction. *See In re K.J.L.*, 363 N.C. 343 (2009); *In re J.D.L.*, 199 N.C. App. 182 (2009).

Under Rule 4(e), failure to secure an endorsement or an alias or pluries summons within ninety days results in discontinuance of the action with respect to a party who was not served within the sixty-day period. Even after a discontinuance of the action, the petitioner may obtain an extension, an endorsement, or even a new summons, reviving the action. However, the action will be deemed to have commenced when the endorsement, alias or pluries summons, or new summons was obtained. N.C. R. Civ. P. 4(e). At least in juvenile cases, discontinuance of an action under Rule 4(e) does not operate to deprive the court of subject matter jurisdiction, and the court may proceed to exercise personal jurisdiction in the action over a party who makes a voluntary appearance and does not object to insufficiency of service or process. *See In re N.E.L.*, 202 N.C. App. 576, 578 (2010) and *In re J.D.L.*, 199 N.C. App. 182, 187 (2009), in which the court of appeals stated that the supreme court, in *In re J.T.*, 363 N.C. 1 (2009) and *In re K.J.L.*, 363 N.C. 343 (2009), "appear[s] to have rejected the application of Rule 4(e) of the North Carolina Rules of Civil Procedure in all cases under the Juvenile Code."

## 4.4 Service

### A. The Impact of Service

Service of process, unless waived, is necessary for the court to obtain personal jurisdiction over a respondent. Service affects the notice to a respondent party. Notice and a meaningful opportunity to be heard are fundamental requirements for due process under the U.S. and North Carolina Constitutions. *See Armstrong v. Manzo*, 380 U.S. 545 (1965); *Harris v. Harris*, 104 N.C. App. 574 (1991) and cases cited therein. The Juvenile Code specifically directs the court to "protect the rights of the juvenile and the juvenile's parent to assure due process of law." G.S. 7B-802. One of the purposes of the Juvenile Code is to provide procedures that assure fairness and protect the constitutional rights of parents and juveniles. G.S. 7B-100(1).

Although the issuance and service of a summons do not affect the court's subject matter jurisdiction because subject matter jurisdiction is established by statute, defenses implicating personal jurisdiction and challenges on due process grounds may be raised by a respondent. *See In re K.J.L*, 363 N.C. 343 (2009). For further discussion, see Chapter 3.2 (subject matter jurisdiction) and 3.4 (personal jurisdiction). To determine whether a lack of notice unreasonably deprived a parent who was not served of due process, the court balanced the parent's right to custody with the state's interest in the welfare of children and the child's right to be protected by the state from abuse or neglect. *In re Poole*, 357 N.C. 151 (2003), (affirming child's adjudication as dependent when service had not been made on respondent father even though father was entitled to notice of the proceeding; service had been made on respondent mother), *rev'g per curiam for reasons stated in the dissent* 151 N.C. App. 472 (2002).

Appellate cases have discussed the importance of fundamentally fair service procedures when the liberty interests of parents are at stake. *In re K.N.*, 181 N.C. App. 736 (2007), was a case in which service was questionable because although there were signed receipts showing acceptance of service by someone residing at the address on the summons, there was no evidence that the address was where the respondent mother actually lived. The mother arrived in the courtroom after the TPR hearing had concluded, but the court of appeals was not swayed by an argument that her arrival proved she had notice. The court of appeals cited *Santosky v. Kramer*, 455 U.S. 745 (1982), in support of its conclusion that the order should be vacated for lack of fair procedure due to issues of valid service and a twenty-minute hearing with no counsel present for the respondent. Similarly, in the case *In re H.D.F.*, 197 N.C. App. 480 (2009), failure to serve a father whose counsel had withdrawn with notices of hearings and numerous other documents filed in the neglect case was error and required reversal of an adjudication that occurred at a hearing of which the father had not been notified.

## B. Summons

Proper service in a juvenile case is generally the same as proper service in any civil case. The Juvenile Code specifically applies Rule 4 of the Rules of Civil Procedure, which sets out the "[m]anner of service to exercise personal jurisdiction," to service of the summons in abuse, neglect, dependency, and termination of parental rights (TPR) proceedings. G.S. 7B-407; 7B-1106(a). Service must be completed at least five days prior to the scheduled hearing in an abuse, neglect, or dependency action unless the court waives that time requirement. G.S. 7B-407.

**1. Service by delivery.** Service of the summons on a respondent whose whereabouts are known or can be determined is pursuant to Rule 4(j)(1), which provides for the following types of service:

**(a) Personal delivery.** Service can be made by an authorized person's delivery of a copy of the summons and petition to the person or leaving copies at his or her house or usual place of abode with a person "of suitable age and discretion" who lives there. N.C. R. CIV. P. 4(j)(1)a. If DSS knows that a respondent is disabled and under a guardianship of any kind, service must be made on the respondent and guardian. N.C. R. CIV. P. 4(j)(2)b. A minor respondent parent is not considered to be under a disability requiring service also be made on the minor's parent, guardian, person having care or control of the minor, or an appointed Rule 17 guardian ad litem. G.S. 7B-406(a); 7B-1106(a); *see* N.C. R. CIV. P. 4(j)(2)a.

**(b) Delivery by mail or delivery service.** Service can be made by mailing a copy of the summons and petition addressed to the party to be served via registered or certified mail, return receipt requested, or by signature confirmation via the U.S. Postal Service. N.C. R. CIV. P. 4(j)(1)c. and e. In addition to the U.S. Postal Service, mail may be via an approved delivery service (authorized by 26 U.S.C. 7502(f)(2)) with a delivery receipt. N.C. R. CIV. P. 4(j)(1)d. *See In re K.N.*, 181 N.C. App. 736 (2007) (holding that service of TPR summons by certified mail, return receipt requested, was not proper where there was no evidence that respondent lived at the address where the summons was delivered and the return receipt was signed by someone else).

**2. Service by publication.** When service cannot be made by the means described above or the respondent is unknown or missing, service by publication may be permissible. Publication must be once a week for three consecutive weeks. *See* N.C. R. CIV. P. 4(j1) (explaining details of service by publication; the discussion below does not comprehensively cover the requirements of the rule).

**(a) Applicability.** With respect to abuse, neglect, or dependency proceedings, the Juvenile Code states that if service by publication pursuant to Rule 4(j1) of the Rules of Civil Procedure is required, the cost may be charged as court costs. G.S. 7B-407. Note that before October 1, 2013, service by publication required prior court authorization. *See* S.L. 2013-129, sec. 12.

With respect to TPR proceedings, the Juvenile Code deals with unknown parents in G.S. 7B-1105, requiring a special hearing to attempt to ascertain the parent's identity and permitting service by publication when the parent's identity cannot be ascertained. See Chapter 9.6.A and B (discussing details related to a hearing to determine the identity of an unknown parent and special requirements for service by publication). Where the parent's identity can be ascertained but service on the parent cannot be accomplished by other means, service by publication is appropriate but must comply with both the Juvenile Code (G.S. 7B-1106; 7B-1106.1), and Rule 4(j1). *See In re C.A.C.,* 222 N.C. App. 687 (2012); *In re Joseph Children*, 122 N.C. App. 468 (1996) (decided under prior law). Effective October 1, 2017, before service by publication in a TPR proceeding may be made, the court must (1) make findings of fact that the respondent cannot otherwise be served despite diligent efforts made by the petitioner for personal service and (2) approve the form of the notice before it is published. G.S. 7B-1106(a). *See* S.L. 2017-161, sec. 11.

**(b) Diligent efforts.** Diligent efforts, or due diligence, to serve a party by other means is always a prerequisite for serving a party by publication under Rule 4.

The rule requires an affidavit showing "the circumstances warranting the use of service by publication," any information about the party's location, and that after due diligence the party cannot be served personally or by registered or certified mail or designated delivery service. In a neglect case, *In re Shaw*, 152 N.C. App. 126 (2002) (decided under prior law), DSS had attempted service unsuccessfully at the father's last known address. DSS was found to have satisfied requirements for service by publication where it submitted an affidavit stating that the father's address, whereabouts, dwelling house, or usual place of abode was unknown and could not with due diligence be ascertained, and that the father was a transient person with no permanent residence.

A failure to file the required affidavit is reversible error. *In re A.J.C.*, 817 S.E.2d 475 (N.C. Ct. App. 2018) (vacating TPR for lack of personal jurisdiction over respondent; service under Rule 4(j1) was invalid when affidavit filed by DSS only stated that the notice ran for three consecutive weeks (with dates listed) in a specified newspaper and the DSS attorney was the affiant for the affidavit; respondent did not make a general appearance to waive proper service; note this opinion does not address the statutory requirement effective October 1, 2017 that approval from the court must first be obtained prior to service by publication of a TPR on a known parent as set forth in G.S. 7B-1106(a)).

What constitutes "diligent efforts" is not specifically defined by statute or case law. North Carolina cases have rejected having a "restrictive mandatory checklist" for what constitutes due diligence and have said that this issue is fact-specific and must be examined on a case-by-case basis. *See Henry v. Morgan*, 826 S.E.2d 475, 477 (N.C. Ct. App. 2019); *Jones v. Wallis*, 211 N.C. App. 353, 358 (2011); *Emanuel v. Fellows*, 47 N.C. App. 340, 347 (1980). Some cases have stated that to exercise due diligence a party must use all "resources reasonably available" to accomplish service. *See Henry v. Morgan*, 826 S.E.2d at 477, 478; *Jones*, 211 N.C. App. at 357; *Fountain v. Patrick*, 44 N.C. App. 584, 587 (1980). Nevertheless, the court of appeals has rejected the notion that due diligence requires that a party "explore every possible means of ascertaining the location of a defendant." *Jones*, 211 N.C. App. at 359 (holding that due diligence was exercised where service was attempted at defendant's last known address and another address, public records were searched, the internet was searched, counsel for plaintiff went personally to last known address to speak with current residents, determination was made that last known address had been foreclosed, and a copy of the complaint was sent to defendant's attorney to ask that he accept service). When determining whether due diligence was exercised, a court may look at the efforts the petitioner actually made rather than methods the petitioner did not make. *Henry v. Morgan*, 826 S.E.2d 475 (holding a single failed attempt to serve defendant at an address where he did not reside and a general internet search was not due diligence).

In several cases, the court found the diligent efforts requirement was not met where the petitioner failed to check public records to determine the location of the person to be served. *See, e.g., Henry v. Morgan*, 826 S.E.2d 475. In the case of *In re Clark*, 76 N.C. App. 83 (1985) (decided under prior law), it was error for the court to conclude that the father should be served by publication in a TPR proceeding where the petitioning adoption agency did not check public records and the facts indicated that the father would have been easy to locate had the agency made diligent efforts to find him.

Updated information regarding a party's whereabouts must also be considered when making diligent efforts. In *Dowd v. Johnson*, 235 N.C. App. 6 (2014), diligent efforts were not made when a new address for the defendant was specifically provided to the plaintiff's attorney in an email from the defendant's attorney but service was only attempted at the defendant's old address.

**Practice Note:** When the location of a parent is unknown after a diligent search has been completed and service is made by publication, the court in an abuse, neglect, or dependency case should continue to inquire into and enter orders with findings about the efforts to locate and serve the missing parent. This inquiry occurs through the initial dispositional hearing. G.S. 7B-506(h)(1); 7B-800.1(a)(3); 7B-901(b).

**(c) Contents of published notice.** Rule 4(j1) is very specific with respect to the contents of the published notice. In addition, the contents of the notice must comply with Juvenile Code requirements related to summons content. In the case *In re C.A.C.*, 222 N.C. App. 687 (2012), the court of appeals held that service by publication in a TPR case was deficient because it did not include notice of the respondent's right to counsel, required by G.S. 7B-1106(b)(4). Respondent did not appear at the hearing and although provisional counsel did appear, the court of appeals held that provisional counsel's appearance could not be considered a "general appearance" that would waive the deficiency in service. *See also In re Joseph Children*, 122 N.C. App. 468 (1996) (finding error where service by publication did not comply with the Juvenile Code requirement that summons contain information about requesting counsel but further finding the error was not prejudicial) (decided under prior law).

When a parent is served by publication in an abuse, neglect, or dependency case and subsequently a TPR motion is filed, the TPR motion and notice may be served pursuant to Rule 5 (instead of Rule 4) of the Rules of Civil Procedure only if

- the published notice informed the parent that upon proper notice and hearing and a finding based on the criteria set out in G.S. 7B-1111, the court could terminate the respondent parent's parental rights;
- the underlying action was initiated less than two years ago; and
- the court does not order that service be pursuant to Rule 4.

G.S. 7B-1102(b); *see* G.S. 7B-406(b)(4)e.

For TPR cases in which the parent's identity is unknown, G.S. 7B-1105(d) sets out specific requirements for the published notice and directs the court to "specifically order . . . the contents of the notice which the court concludes is most likely to identify the juvenile to such unknown parent." When an unknown parent is served by publication pursuant to G.S. 7B-1105, a summons is not required. G.S. 7B-1105(g).

> **Practice Notes:** Where the name of the parent being served is known, the published notice should contain any known aliases as well as the parent's name. Whether the full name of the other parent (the one not being served by publication) should be included in the notice is not specifically addressed in the Rules of Civil Procedure or the Juvenile Code, but presumably it should be included so that the parent being served by publication can identify the child who is the subject of the action. *See* G.S. 7B-1105(d).
>
> G.S. 7B-1105(d)(3) states that when serving a parent whose identity is unknown, the words "In re Doe" may be substituted for the title of the case. No similar provision exists for other cases in which service by publication is required. While Rule 42 of the Rules of Appellate Procedure protects the child's identity in an appeal of a juvenile order specified in G.S. 7B-1001, nothing in the statutes or in case law addresses protection of the child's identity in a publication notice. G.S. 7B-2901(a) requires the clerk of court to withhold from public inspection records of juvenile cases that are filed in the office and allege abuse, neglect, or dependency.
>
> The hearing on an unknown parent required by G.S. 7B-1105 will be expedited if the attorney has prepared a proposed publication notice that contains facts (such as the place of conception, range of possible dates of conception, and description or nickname of the unknown parent and the known parent) that would help the unknown parent recognize himself or herself. If the court orders service by publication at the conclusion of the hearing, the court can either approve or modify the proposed notice.

**(d) Where to publish.** Publication of notice must be made in a newspaper that is qualified for legal advertising and circulated in the area where the person to be served is believed to be located. If there is no reliable information as to the person's location, publication may be made in a newspaper that is circulated where the action is pending. N.C. R. CIV. P. 4(j1).

When the parent in a TPR proceeding is unknown such that a G.S. 7B-1105 hearing is required, the court order specifies the place or places where the publication is made. G.S. 7B-1105(d).

**(e) Mailing requirement.** If the post office address of the person served by publication is known, or can be ascertained with reasonable diligence, a copy of the notice of service of process by publication must be mailed to the party at or immediately before the first publication. If the post office address cannot be ascertained with reasonable diligence, the mailing may be omitted. N.C. R. CIV. P. 4(j1).

**(f) Affidavit related to service by publication.** Rule 4(j1) requires that once service by publication is completed, an affidavit must be filed with the court showing

- that the publication and mailing (if the party's post office address is known) were done in accordance with the requirements of G.S. 1-75.10(a)(2), which requires an affidavit

- of the publisher or printer specifying the date of the first and last publication, and an affidavit of the person who mailed a copy of the complaint or notice if mailing was required;
- circumstances warranting the use of service by publication and efforts that were made to serve by other means (*see In re Shaw*, 152 N.C. App. 126 (2002) (reaffirming the necessity of including this information on the affidavit and finding this requirement satisfied when the affidavit stated that the respondent's address, whereabouts, dwelling house, or usual place of abode were unknown and could not with due diligence be ascertained because the respondent was a transient person with no permanent residence)); and
- information, if any, regarding the location of the party served.

N.C. R. Civ. P. 4(j1).

**3. Service in a foreign country.** Service in a foreign country is governed by Rule 4(j3) of the Rules of Civil Procedure, which allows service by any internationally agreed means reasonably calculated to give notice, such as those means authorized by the Hague Convention on the Service Abroad of Judicial and Extrajudicial Documents (Hague Convention) or the Inter-American Service Convention when the particular convention applies. N.C. R. Civ. P. 4(j3)(1). Service in a foreign country is a complex issue that this Manual does not attempt to address fully.

Proper service methods vary from country to country and the appropriate method depends on whether a particular country is a party to a particular convention dealing with service. A country may be a signatory to one convention but not another. For example, El Salvador is not a signatory to the Hague Convention but is a signatory to the Inter-American Service Convention. See U.S. Department of State Bureau of Consular Affairs website for El Salvador. Even when a country is a signatory to a convention, it is critical to know whether the country has filed objections or exceptions. Mexico, for example, is a signatory to the Hague Convention, but has filed an objection to alternative service methods, so that service by publication in Mexico is not an option.

Where there is no internationally agreed upon means of service, or applicable agreements allow other means of service, Rule 4(j3)(2) and (3) state that as long as service is reasonably calculated to give notice, it may be

- in the manner prescribed by the law of the foreign country;
- as directed by foreign authority in response to a letter rogatory or letter of request;
- by delivering a copy of the summons and petition to the individual personally (unless prohibited by law of the foreign country);
- through any form of mail requiring a signed receipt, addressed to the party to be served and dispatched by the clerk (unless prohibited by law of the foreign country); or
- by other means not prohibited by international agreement as may be directed by the court.

**Resources:**

For information related to service in a foreign country, see the online resources listed below, many of which include links to more detailed information:
- search "service of process abroad" on the Bureau of Consular Affairs, U.S. Department of State website (use this link to access country-specific information).
- "Service of Process, Foreign Civil Process" on the U.S. Marshals Service, U.S. Department of Justice website.
- Hague Conference on Private International Law website.

For information from the UNC School of Government on this topic, see
- Cheryl Howell, *Service by Publication When Defendant is in Another Country*, UNC SCH. OF GOV'T: ON THE CIVIL SIDE BLOG (Feb. 10, 2017).
- W. Mark C. Weidemaier, *International Service of Process Under the Hague Convention*, ADMINISTRATION OF JUSTICE BULLETIN No. 2004/07 (UNC School of Government, Dec. 2004).
- W. Mark C. Weidemaier, *Service of Process and the Military*, ADMINISTRATION OF JUSTICE BULLETIN No. 2004/08 (UNC School of Government, Dec. 2004).

### C. Notice and Motions

The Juvenile Code addresses the service of only some notices, motions, and orders. G.S. 7B-700(c) requires that discovery motions in juvenile proceedings be served pursuant to Rule 5 of the Rules of Civil Procedure. Rule 5(b) relates to service of "pleadings and other papers," and has been used to fill a "procedural gap" in the Juvenile Code where the Juvenile Code is silent as to service. *See In re D.L.*, 166 N.C. App. 574 (2004). When a motion for termination of parental rights (TPR) is filed in a pending abuse, neglect, or dependency proceeding, while service of the motion and notice generally is pursuant to Rule 5(b), G.S. 7B-1102(b) specifies four circumstances in which service must be pursuant to Rule 4. See Chapter 9.7.C.4 (discussing details related to serving motions and notice to initiate TPR).

Generally, Rule 5 permits service of all pleadings subsequent to the original petition and all other papers to be made

- pursuant to Rule 4, upon either the party or the party's attorney of record;
- by delivering a copy to the party's attorney of record, but if there is no attorney or if the court so orders, to the party;
- by mailing it to the party's attorney of record, but if there is no attorney or if the court so orders, to the party; or
- by filing it with the clerk of court if no address is known for the party or the party's attorney of record.

N.C. R. CIV. P. 5(b).

Although service of the summons on the child is not required, where the child is required to receive notice, acceptance of service by an attorney advocate constitutes proper service on a guardian ad litem (GAL), which constitutes proper service on a child represented by the

GAL. *See In re J.A.P.*, 189 N.C. App. 683 (2008) (decided under former law). However, the Juvenile Code requires that the juvenile who is at least 12 years old be served with certain notices and orders, in addition to service on his or her GAL. *See* G.S. 7B-906.1(b)(ii) and (vi) (notice of review and permanency planning hearings); 7B-908(b)(1) (notice of post-TPR review hearing); 7B-1110(d) (service of TPR order); 7B-1114(d)(1) and (2), (e) (service of motion and notice of hearing to reinstate parental rights).

## 4.5 Continuances

### A. Continuances Disfavored

The Juvenile Code includes specific timelines within which certain hearings must be held, and it speaks directly about the circumstances in which continuances should be permitted. The Juvenile Code provisions are more restrictive than those in Rule 40(b) of the Rules of Civil Procedure and, to the extent they are inconsistent with Rule 40, the Juvenile Code provisions control. Appellate cases related to juvenile proceedings have noted that continuances are generally disfavored, and the burden of demonstrating sufficient grounds for a continuance is on the party seeking the continuance. *See In re J.B.*, 172 N.C. App. 1 (2005); *In re Humphrey*, 156 N.C. App. 533 (2003). A decision to grant or deny a motion for a continuance ordinarily is in the trial court's discretion. *See In re Mitchell*, 148 N.C. App. 483, *rev'd per curiam on other grounds for reasons stated in the dissent*, 356 N.C. 288 (2002).

### B. Abuse, Neglect, Dependency Proceedings

In abuse, neglect, or dependency proceedings, G.S. 7B-803 authorizes the court to continue a hearing, for good cause, for as long as reasonably necessary to

- receive additional evidence, reports, or assessments the court has requested;
- receive other information needed in the child's best interests; or
- allow for a reasonable time for the parties to conduct expeditious discovery.

Otherwise, the court may grant a continuance "only in extraordinary circumstances when necessary for the proper administration of justice or in the best interests of the juvenile." G.S. 7B-803. *See In re R.L.*, 186 N.C. App. 529 (2007) (finding that neither a systemic problem of over-scheduling nor the absence of a respondent or a respondent's attorney at an earlier hearing constituted extraordinary circumstances warranting multiple continuances), *abrogated in part on other grounds by In re T.H.T.*, 362 N.C. 446 (2008). Resolution of a pending criminal charge against a respondent arising out of the same circumstances as the juvenile petition cannot be the sole extraordinary circumstance for granting a continuance. G.S. 7B-803. *See In re Patron*, 250 N.C. App. 375 (2016) (looking to the limitation in G.S. 7B-803 against granting a continuance on the sole basis of a pending criminal charge arising from the same incident in the juvenile matter when determining there was no abuse of discretion in a denial of a motion to stay a judicial review of a placement on the Responsible Individuals List pending resolution of the related criminal charges).

While G.S. 7B-803 does not specify that it applies to dispositional as well as adjudication hearings, appellate cases have generally applied it to any type of hearing in an abuse, neglect, or dependency case. *See, e.g., In re E.K.*, 202 N.C. App. 309 (2010) (analyzing the appropriateness of continuances of a permanency planning hearing according to G.S. 7B-803); *In re C.M.*, 183 N.C. App. 207 (2007) (discussing the continuance of a dispositional hearing in the context of G.S. 7B-803).

### C. Termination of Parental Rights Proceedings

G.S. 7B-1109(d) authorizes the court to continue an adjudication hearing in a termination of parental rights (TPR) proceeding for up to ninety days from the date of the initial petition to

- receive additional evidence,
- allow the parties to conduct expeditious discovery, or
- receive any other information needed in the best interests of the child.

A continuance beyond ninety days may be granted only in extraordinary circumstances when necessary for the proper administration of justice, and the court must enter a written order stating the grounds for granting the continuance. G.S. 7B-1109(d). *See In re D.J.G.*, 183 N.C. App. 137 (2007) (when circumstances warrant it, the judge presiding over the case has discretion to continue the hearing; the hearing had been continued because of the need to appoint respondent mother a new attorney, allow time for responsive pleading and discovery, and sufficient time to hear the case). The burden of showing there are sufficient grounds for a continuance rests on the party requesting the continuance. *In re C.J.H.*, 240 N.C. App. 489 (2015).

The court of appeals has looked to both G.S. 7B-803 and 7B-1109(d) when determining whether a court acted properly in continuing (or denying a motion to continue) a TPR hearing. *In re C.J.H.*, 240 N.C. App. 489 (applying G.S. 7B-803 and 7B-1109 when holding it was not error for the trial court to deny a motion to continue requested by respondent's attorney at the hearing when the respondent chose to start a new job rather than appear at a hearing that he had notice of). *See In re C.M.P.*, 254 N.C. App. 647 (2017) (applying the standard in G.S. 7B-803 to deny respondent's motion to continue a TPR hearing and holding, based on prior case law, that respondent's due process rights were not violated by termination of parental rights at a hearing at which she was not present and there was no abuse of discretion when trial court conducted a full hearing on the petition and allowed respondent's counsel to cross-examine each witness and fully participate); *In re Mitchell*, 148 N.C. App. 483 (applying G.S. 7B-803 to determine that denial of a continuance in a TPR case was proper where nothing in the record indicated that the court requested or needed additional information in the best interests of the children, that more time was needed for expeditious discovery, or that extraordinary circumstances necessitated a continuance, and where it was apparent that mother's absence was voluntary or a result of her own negligence), *rev'd per curiam on other grounds for reasons stated in the dissent,* 356 N.C. 288 (2002).

In the case *In re D.W.*, 202 N.C. App. 624 (2010), the court of appeals reversed an order terminating parental rights, holding that the trial court abused its discretion in denying the mother's motion for a continuance of the adjudication hearing. The appellate court said that "the circumstances of [the] case indicate[d] that justice was impaired by the denial of the continuance." *In re D.W.*, 202 N.C. App. at 625. The court pointed to uncertainty as to whether the mother had notice of the hearing; the mother's diminished capacity, which could have made her absence involuntary; her attendance at all prior hearings; external time constraints that negatively affected the hearing; and the trial court's failure to ascertain the nature of the proceeding before ruling on the motion for a continuance.

### D. Considerations

**1. Party's own actions.** Appellate cases have said that lack of preparation for trial that is due to the party's own actions is not sufficient reason for a continuance. *See In re C.J.H.*, 240 N.C. App. 489 (2015) (finding denial of continuance appropriate when father chose to start new job rather than appear at hearing where his attorney requested a continuance based on father's absence); *In re J.B.*, 172 N.C. App. 1 (2005) (holding that respondent's request for third continuance in TPR case was properly denied where court found that any lack of time to prepare for the hearing related to recent incarceration and was due to respondent's own actions in being arrested for kidnapping the juvenile); *In re Bishop*, 92 N.C. App. 662 (1989) (finding denial of continuance appropriate where respondent had ample time for trial preparation but simply failed to cooperate with her counsel).

**2. Absence of witness.** When a motion to continue is based on the absence of a witness, the motion should be supported by an affidavit containing the facts to be proved by the witness. *In re Lail*, 55 N.C. App. 238 (1981) (decided under prior law).

**3. Heavy dockets.** Avoidance of continuances requires careful attention to scheduling and calendaring in juvenile cases. In a case in which seven of fourteen continuances were attributed to heavy dockets, the court of appeals said: "Given the overall scheme of the juvenile code, which consistently requires speedy resolution of juvenile cases, it is clear that the General Assembly did not contemplate a crowded docket as a circumstance sufficient to warrant delay." *In re R.L.,* 186 N.C. App. 529, 535 (2007), *abrogated in part on other grounds by In re T.H.T.*, 362 N.C. 446 (2008).

**4. Time to prepare.** Although continuances are disfavored, the court's failure to grant a continuance may be reversible error if good cause for the continuance exists and the party is prejudiced by the denial. The burden is on the party seeking a continuance to show good cause. *See In re D.Q.W.*, 167 N.C. App. 38 (2004) (holding that respondent was not prejudiced where he did not explain why his attorney had insufficient time to prepare, what his attorney hoped to accomplish during a continuance, or how preparation would have been more complete if a continuance had been granted). If a continuance is necessary to safeguard a party's constitutional rights, it must be granted. *State v. Jones*, 342 N.C. 523 (1996). G.S. 7B-908(b)(2), when it authorizes the court to appoint a guardian ad litem for the juvenile at an initial post-termination of parental rights hearing, says specifically that "[t]he court may continue the case for such time as is necessary for the guardian ad litem to become familiar with the facts of the case."

**5. Delay, prejudice, and the remedy of mandamus.** The court of appeals has held that where continuances result in the court's failure to meet statutory timelines for conducting hearings, the appropriate remedy is to seek a writ of mandamus. *In re E.K.*, 202 N.C. App. 309 (2010) (acknowledging that delays in the case were "deplorable," the appellate court nevertheless refused to find reversible error and held that the proper remedy for excessive delays in holding hearings is to file a petition for a writ of mandamus during the delay, rather than raise the issue on appeal). The court relied on the supreme court's earlier holding in *In re T.H.T.*, 362 N.C. 446 (2008), that mandamus is the proper remedy for delay in entering orders in juvenile cases. See section 4.9.D.3, below (discussing the elements for seeking mandamus specified in the *In re T.H.T.* case).

**Practice Note:** Most of the cases decided before the holding in *In re T.H.T.*, 362 N.C. 446, that mandamus is the appropriate remedy for delay, analyzed delay issues according to whether prejudice resulted from the delay. These cases were abrogated by *In re T.H.T.*

An order denying a motion for a continuance is interlocutory and not immediately appealable. Nevertheless, a party asserting that the denial of a continuance and a delay in the right to appeal affected a substantial right might pursue an interlocutory appeal or petition for a writ of supersedeas. *See, e.g., Myers v. Barringer*, 101 N.C. App. 168 (1990) (discussing interlocutory appeals and stating that appellant could have sought a writ of supersedeas in response to trial court's order to prosecute). See Chapter 12.10.E for an explanation of a writ of supersedeas.

## 4.6 Discovery

### A. Discovery Generally

G.S. 7B-700 addresses information sharing and discovery in abuse, neglect, dependency, and termination of parental rights proceedings and supersedes the discovery provisions in the Rules of Civil Procedure that differ. Because G.S. 7B-700 applies to all actions under Subchapter I of the Juvenile Code, it also applies when petitions are filed relating to alleged interference with or obstruction of a DSS assessment or for judicial review of a responsible individual determination (both of which are discussed in Chapter 5).

The Juvenile Code encourages a process in which parties access information by means of permissible voluntary information sharing before resorting to discovery motions to obtain information. Parties are permitted to utilize discovery motions pursuant to G.S. 7B-700.

**Practice Note**: The Juvenile Code addresses confidentiality and information sharing in juvenile cases in more than one place (not just in the discovery statute). *See, e.g.,* G.S. 7B-302(a1); 7B-311; 7B-601(c); 7B-700; 7B-2901; 7B-3100. For a discussion of confidentiality and information sharing, see Chapter 14.

## B. The Juvenile Code and Discovery

**1. DSS sharing of information.** The Juvenile Code permits DSS to share with any other party information that is relevant to a pending juvenile action, with these exceptions:

- DSS may not share information that would reveal the identity of a reporter or lead to discovery of the reporter's identity.
- DSS may not share any uniquely identifying information that would lead to the discovery of any other person's identity if DSS determines that disclosure of the information would be likely to endanger that person's life or safety.

G.S. 7B-700(a).

The provisions of G.S. 7B-700 apply to information sharing and discovery requests made by parties in the juvenile proceeding and do not apply to requests for information or discovery made on a DSS by a person or agency who is not a party to the juvenile proceeding, such as a litigant in another action or a government agency investigating a party in the juvenile proceeding. For a discussion about when DSS is authorized to share information to non-parties, see Chapter 14.1.

**2. GAL sharing of information.** The child's guardian ad litem (GAL) is not free to voluntarily share information with other parties but can share information pursuant to either a court order or local rules. G.S. 7B-700(f); 7B-601(c). However, any reports and records the GAL submits to the court must first be shared with the parties in the juvenile proceeding. G.S. 7B-700(f). In addition, the GAL must share information requested by other designated agencies (including DSS) under G.S. 7B-3100 to the extent that information falls within the parameters of that statute. See Chapter 14.1.D and E for further discussion.

**3. Local rules.** The chief district court judge may adopt local rules or enter an administrative order addressing the sharing of information among parties and the use of discovery. G.S. 7B-700(b). Local rules, however, may not contradict statutory requirements. *See In re J.S.*, 182 N.C. App. 79 (2007); *In re T.M.*, 187 N.C. App. 694 (2007). There may also be a local rule or administrative order that addresses the sharing of predisposition reports among the parties. *See* G.S. 7B-808(c).

Note that local rules or administrative orders issued pursuant to G.S. 7B-700 and 7B-808(c) apply to the parties in a juvenile proceeding and may not be directed to agencies or entities that are not parties. Information sharing among agencies is covered by G.S. 7B-3100, and rules issued by the Department of Public Safety authorize a chief district court judge to issue administrative orders designating local agencies that are required to share information pursuant to that statute. *See* 14B N.C.A.C. 11A.0301 and .0302. See Chapter 14.1.E for further discussion of information sharing.

See Appendix 2 at the end of this Manual (discussing responsibilities of chief district court judge relating to local rules, discovery, and information sharing).

**4. Discovery methods.** G.S. 7B-700 makes no reference to the discovery methods or procedures in the Rules of Civil Procedure. However, appellate courts have discussed the use in juvenile proceedings of certain discovery methods that are set forth in the Rules of Civil Procedure. Those methods include depositions, interrogatories, requests for production of documents, and physical/mental examinations. See section 4.1.A, above; *see also In re J.D.*, 234 N.C. App. 342 (2014) (referring to use of request for production of documents in factual summary of the case). A party may also subpoena a witness's attendance at a deposition or command the production, inspection, and copying of designated documents, including electronic records, and tangible things in the possession or control of the person specified in the subpoena. N.C. R. CIV. P. 45; *see In re A.H.*, 250 N.C. App. 546 (2016) (applying Rule 45 when addressing motion to quash subpoena for testimony at hearing). Additionally, a chief district court judge might reference or incorporate certain discovery rules in the judicial district's local rules or in an administrative order issued pursuant to G.S. 7B-700(b). The court of appeals has also referred to Rule 26(b)(1) of the Rules of Civil Procedure, which allows for discovery regarding any matter that is not privileged and is relevant to the subject matter of the pending action. *In re J.B.*, 172 N.C. App. 1 (2005).

**5. Discovery motions.** The Juvenile Code authorizes a motion for discovery and a motion for protective order. G.S. 7B-700(c), (d). As a general rule, discovery orders are reviewed for an abuse of discretion. *In re J.B.*, 172 N.C. App. 1; *Ritter v. Kimball*, 67 N.C. App. 333 (1984).

**(a) Motion for discovery.** Any party may file a "motion for discovery," which appears to be the Juvenile Code's version of a motion to compel. G.S. 7B-700(c). A motion for discovery must contain

- a specific description of the information sought and
- a statement that the requesting party has made reasonable efforts to obtain or cannot obtain the information by means of information sharing permitted by statute, local rules, or an administrative order.

G.S. 7B-700(c).

A motion for discovery must be served on all parties pursuant to Rule 5 of the Rules of Civil Procedure. The court must conduct a hearing and rule on the motion within ten business days of the date the motion is filed. G.S. 7B-700(c). The court is authorized to "grant, restrict, defer, or deny the relief requested" in the motion. G.S. 7B-700(c).

**(b) Motion for protective order.** Any party who has been served with a motion for discovery may seek a protective order to deny, restrict, or defer the discovery. G.S. 7B-700(d). *See In re J.B.*, 172 N.C. App. 1 (holding, in a case decided under prior language of discovery statute, that the trial court did not err in using its authority to "deny or restrict" discovery where it denied a request to interview the child due to the disruption it would cause to the child's therapeutic progress). A protective order should be made pursuant to the requirements of G.S. 7B-700(d) as the Juvenile Code prescribes a procedure that differs from Rule 26(c) of the Rules of Civil Procedure. The court of appeals has consistently held the Rules of Civil Procedure only apply when they do not conflict with the Juvenile

Code and the application of a rule advances the purpose of the Juvenile Code. *In re E.H.*, 227 N.C. App. 525 (2013); *In re L.O.K.*, 174 N.C. App. 426 (2005). *But see In re J.D.*, 234 N.C. App. 342 (2014) (referencing in the factual summary a motion for protective order made pursuant to Rule 26(c), without mentioning G.S. 7B-700(d)).

Pursuant to G.S. 7B-700(d), a party requesting that the discovery be denied, restricted, or deferred must submit the information the party seeks to protect for in camera review by the court. If the court denies or restricts discovery, copies of materials submitted for in camera review must be preserved for potential appellate review. G.S. 7B-700(d).

**6. Continuances related to discovery.** The court may grant continuances in an abuse, neglect, dependency, or termination of parental rights proceeding for a reasonable time to allow for expeditious discovery. G.S. 7B-803; 7B-1109(d). However, any order related to discovery must avoid unnecessary delay and establish expedited deadlines for completion. G.S. 7B-700(c). *See In re J.S.*, 182 N.C. App. 79 (2007) (holding, in a case decided under prior law, that the trial court did not abuse its discretion in denying a continuance where the attorneys failed to make time to examine the records within the time frame set out by the administrative order).

**7. Redisclosure.** Information obtained through discovery or permissible sharing of information may not be redisclosed if the redisclosure is prohibited by state or federal law. G.S. 7B-700(e). *See also* G.S. 108A-80; 7B-3100.

## 4.7 Intervention

### A. Abuse, Neglect, Dependency Proceedings

The Juvenile Code defines precisely who the parties are in an abuse, neglect, or dependency proceeding. *See* G.S. 7B-401.1; 7B-601(a). Someone who is not a party but is providing care for the child, such as a relative or foster parent, is entitled to notice of and an opportunity to be heard at review and permanency planning hearings. G.S. 7B-906.1(b), (c); *see In re J.L.*, 826 S.E.2d 258, 264 (N.C. Ct. App. 2019) (a case where foster parents were not permitted to intervene but court heard their testimony, "which was information the court was required to hear under section 7B-906.1(c)"). The court may also require that notice be given to other persons or agencies. G.S. 7B-906.1(b). At dispositional hearings (initial, review, and permanency planning), the court may consider information from any person or agency that the court finds is relevant, reliable, and necessary to determine the juvenile's needs and the most appropriate disposition. G.S. 7B-901(a); 7B-906.1(c). However, the right to notice and to be heard does not confer party status. G.S. 7B-906.1(b). *See* G.S. 7B-401.1(e1).

Only the following persons or agencies may intervene in an abuse, neglect, or dependency proceeding

- the juvenile's parent, guardian, or custodian;
- another DSS that has an interest in the proceeding;

- a person with standing to initiate a termination of parental rights (TPR) proceeding who seeks to intervene for the sole purpose of filing a TPR motion; or
- a foster parent only if that foster parent has authority (or standing) to file a TPR petition.

G.S. 7B-401.1(e1), (h); 7B-1103(b); *see* G.S. 7B-1103(a) (standing to file TPR).

Although not addressed in the Juvenile Code, when the Indian Child Welfare Act (ICWA) applies to the abuse, neglect, or dependency proceeding, the child's Indian tribe and (if applicable) Indian custodian have a right to intervene at any point in the action. 25 U.S.C. 1911(c); *see* 25 C.F.R. 23.111(d)(6)(ii) and (iii). For a discussion of ICWA, see Chapter 13.2.

**Practice Note:** The intervention statute, G.S. 7B-401.1(h), was enacted by S.L. 2013-129, sec. 9, effective for all actions filed or pending on or after October 1, 2013. Prior to that legislative change, the Juvenile Code did not specifically address intervention in abuse, neglect, or dependency proceedings other than to allow a party with standing to initiate a TPR action to intervene for the purpose of filing a TPR motion in an underlying abuse, neglect, or dependency action. G.S. 7B-1103(b). It was not unusual, however, for relatives or foster parents to make motions to intervene in abuse, neglect, or dependency cases to seek custody of or visitation with a child. The few appellate court decisions that addressed intervention applied Rule 24 of the Rules of Civil Procedure to assess the propriety of the trial court's ruling. *See, e.g., In re T.H.,* 232 N.C. App. 16 (2014). However, since those cases were decided, G.S. 7B-401.1(h) and (e1) were enacted, specifically addressing intervention in abuse, neglect, or dependency proceedings. Parties and the court should look to the Juvenile Code (G.S. 7B-401.1(h) and (e1)) and not Rule 24 when determining whether someone has a right to intervene in an abuse, neglect, or dependency proceeding. *See* S.L. 2016-94, sec. 12C.1(f) removing caretakers from G.S. 7B-401.1(h) (effective July 1, 2016) and S.L. 2015-136, sec. 2 adding G.S. 7B-401.1(e1) to allow a foster parent who has standing to initiate a TPR to intervene (effective for all actions filed or pending on or after October 1, 2015).

**Resource:** Sara DePasquale, *What Is the Role of a Foster Parent in the A/N/D Court Action?* UNC SCHOOL OF GOV'T: ON THE CIVIL SIDE BLOG (Sept. 30, 2015).

While opportunities for intervention in an abuse, neglect, or dependency action are limited, the Juvenile Code makes clear that the restrictions on intervention do not prohibit the court hearing the abuse, neglect, or dependency proceeding from consolidating its case with a civil action that has a claim for custody or visitation. *See* G.S. 7B-200(c)(1), (d); 7B-401.1(h). See also Chapter 3.6.A and D (discussing two types of overlapping civil actions, civil custody proceedings and domestic violence protection proceedings, in which claims for custody are or may be asserted). The Juvenile Code does not address the procedure for how any request to consolidate the two actions would be heard. The court hearing the abuse, neglect, or dependency action makes the decision on consolidation, but a party in the civil action may not be a party or satisfy the criteria to have standing to intervene in the abuse, neglect, or dependency proceeding. In that case, the person would not have standing to file in the abuse, neglect, or dependency action a motion to consolidate the two actions.

Note that a claim for custody or visitation in the civil action is automatically stayed until and unless the court hearing the abuse, neglect, or dependency action consolidates the two proceedings or dissolves the stay. G.S. 7B-200(c)(1). Effective October 1, 2019, the court hearing the juvenile action must ensure that a notice is filed in the stayed action (the civil action) if the county and case file number are made known to the court. G.S. 7B-200(c)(1); *see* S.L. 2019-33.

## B. Termination of Parental Rights Proceedings

The statutory limitations on intervention (in G.S. 7B-401.1(h) and 7B-1103(b)) apply only to intervention in abuse, neglect, or dependency proceedings. The Juvenile Code is silent with respect to intervention in termination of parental rights (TPR) proceedings. Where the Juvenile Code is silent, appellate decisions have applied Rule 24 to analyze whether intervention is permissible. *See, e.g., In re T.H.*, 232 N.C. App. 16 (2014) (holding that intervention pursuant to Rule 24 was permissible in a dependency case as the rule did not conflict with the Juvenile Code and advances its purpose (note that this case was decided before the enactment of G.S. 7B-401.1(e1) and (h), which address intervention in an abuse, neglect, or dependency action)); *In re Baby Boy Scearce*, 81 N.C. App. 531 (1986) (upholding the application of Rule 24 to allow permissive intervention by foster parents, emphasizing the child's best interest).

Assuming that Rule 24 applies in TPR actions, it is important to distinguish between the provisions for intervention of right and those for permissive intervention.

**1. Intervention of right.** Under Rule 24(a), in the absence of an unconditional statutory right to intervene, a person is entitled to intervene by right when

- that person claims an interest in the subject of the action;
- as a practical matter, disposition of the action may impair the person's ability to protect that interest; and
- the person's interest is not adequately represented by existing parties.

The court of appeals applied Rule 24(a) to hold that a child support enforcement agency was entitled to intervene by right in a mother's action to terminate the father's rights. *Hill v. Hill*, 121 N.C. App. 510 (1996) (reversing the trial court's denial of DSS's motion to intervene, because termination of the father's rights would also terminate DSS's ability to seek reimbursement from the father for public assistance the mother would continue to receive). Intervention of right, the court said, "is an absolute right and denial of that right is reversible error." *Hill*, 121 N.C. App. at 511.

When the Indian Child Welfare Act (ICWA) applies to the TPR proceeding, the child's Indian tribe and (if applicable) Indian custodian have a right to intervene at any point in the action. 25 U.C.S. 1911(c); *see* 25 C.F.R. 23.111(d)(6)(ii) and (iii). For a discussion of ICWA, see Chapter 13.2.

**2. Permissive intervention.** Under Rule 24(b) the court may grant a motion for permissive intervention by someone whose claim or defense has a question of law or fact in common with the main action. N.C. R. Civ. P. 24(b). However, because the courts have held that a respondent parent cannot file a counterclaim for custody in a TPR action (*see, e.g., In re Peirce*, 53 N.C. App. 373 (1981)), it seems unlikely that a third party could intervene in a TPR proceeding to pursue a custody claim. Either a party or a nonparty can file a civil action for custody or a motion in a pending civil custody action and seek to have that action consolidated with the TPR action. *See Smith v. Alleghany County Dep't of Soc. Servs.*, 114 N.C. App. 727 (1994) (the facts identify a consolidated TPR and G.S. Chapter 50 custody action).

Should a court find that Rule 24 does apply to allow permissive intervention, in addition to showing a common issue of law or fact, the person seeking to intervene must establish that he or she has standing to assert the claim or defense put forward. *See, e.g., Perdue v. Fuqua*, 195 N.C. App. 583 (2009) (affirming denial of grandmother's motion to intervene in a G.S. Chapter 50 custody proceeding on basis that allegations in her motions to intervene and for custody were insufficient to establish that she had standing to seek custody). In deciding whether to grant a motion for permissive intervention, the court must consider whether allowing intervention will unduly delay or prejudice the adjudication of the rights of the original parties. N.C. R. Civ. P. 24(b). The standard for reviewing an order granting or denying a motion for permissive intervention is abuse of discretion. *In re T.H.*, 232 N.C. App. 16 (2014).

**3. Procedure for intervening.** Intervention, whether permissive or by right, requires a timely application and service on all parties of a motion stating the grounds for intervention. The motion must be accompanied by a pleading that asserts the claim or defense for which the applicant seeks to intervene. N.C. R. Civ. P. 24(c).

---

**Resource:** For information about third party custody and visitation actions, see Cheryl Howell, *Third Party Custody and Visitation Actions: 2010 Update to the State of the Law in North Carolina*, Family Law Bulletin No. 2011/25 (UNC School of Government, Jan. 2011).

---

## 4.8 Motions in Juvenile Proceedings

Unless specified in the Juvenile Code, motions are made according to Rule 7(b) of the Rules of Civil Procedure, Rule 6 of the General Rules of Practice for the Superior and District Courts, applicable Juvenile Code provisions (e.g., G.S. 7B-1102, related to a motion to terminate parental rights), and any pertinent local rules.

Under Rule 7(b) of the Rules of Civil Procedure, a motion may be made orally if it is made during a hearing or at a session for which the case is calendared. Otherwise, motions must be in writing. The motion must state with particularity the grounds for the motion and the relief the moving party is seeking. N.C. R. Civ. P. 7(b)(1). Under Rule 6 of the General Rules of Practice for the Superior and District Courts, a motion must state the specific rule(s) under which the movant is proceeding. Motions must be signed by at least one attorney of record if the party is represented by counsel, stating the attorney's office address and telephone number. N.C. R. CIV. P. 7(b)(2) (certain rules applicable to pleadings apply to all motions provided for by the Rules of Civil Procedure); Rule 6 of the General Rules of Practice for the Superior and District Courts. *See* N.C. R. CIV. P. 11(a). The format of motions is governed by Rule 10 of the Rules of Civil Procedure. *See* N.C. R. CIV. P. 7(b)(2).

Unless the Juvenile Code states otherwise, the filing and service of motions is pursuant to Rule 5 of the Rules of Civil Procedure. The time frame for service of a motion is according to Rule 6 of the Rules of Civil Procedure, which generally requires service no later than five days prior to the hearing. When a motion is based on facts that are not in the record, the court may determine the motion based on affidavits presented by the parties, or the court may require that the matter be heard wholly or partly on oral testimony or depositions. N.C. R. CIV. P. 43(e).

## 4.9 Judgments and Orders

There are provisions contained throughout the Juvenile Code that specifically address orders, including

- the timing for entry of an order,
- required findings of fact and conclusions of law,
- types of available relief that may be ordered (note that the type of relief available is addressed throughout this Manual when discussing specific statutes and topics), and
- service of an order.

Some practices related to orders are addressed by the appellate courts rather than the Juvenile Code.

### A. Drafting Orders

**1. Who drafts the order.** Judges may draft their own orders, but nothing prevents the trial judge from directing the prevailing party to draft an order on the court's behalf. *In re J.B.*, 172 N.C. App. 1 (2005); *see also In re S.N.H.*, 177 N.C. App. 82 (2006) (holding that the trial court did not err in directing the petitioner's attorney to draft an order after enumerating in court specific findings of fact to be included in the order); *In re H.T.*, 180 N.C. App. 611 (2006). Rule 52 of the Rules of Civil Procedure, addressing findings by the court, has not been interpreted to require the judge to manually draft or orally dictate a judgment. *See Johnson v. Johnson*, 67 N.C. App. 250 (1984) (finding no error where the court directed an attorney to prepare proposed findings and conclusions and draft the judgment, and adopted the judgment as its own when tendered and signed); *Walker v. Tucker*, 69 N.C. App. 607 (1984).

**2. Responsibility of the court.** The court of appeals has recognized that district court judges have little or no support staff to assist with preparing orders, which has resulted in judges relying on the attorneys for the parties to assist in preparing the court's order. *In re A.B.*, 239

N.C. App. 157 (2015); *In re J.W.*, 241 N.C. App. 44 (2015). Regardless of who drafts an order, the trial court is ultimately responsible for the order. *In re A.B.*, 239 N.C. App. at 167 (stating "the order is the responsibility of the trial court, no matter who physically drafts the order").

**3. Circulating draft orders.** While it is common practice for attorneys to draft court orders, it is important that draft orders be circulated to all parties before being submitted to the judge. Another party may identify discrepancies between the draft order and that party's understanding of the judge's oral rendition, and a party may elect to submit his or her own proposed findings of fact or amendments to those in the draft order. *See also* North Carolina State Bar, 97 Formal Ethics Opinion 5 (1998) (relating to the need to submit a proposed order to opposing counsel simultaneously with submitting it to the court). In some judicial districts local rules may address the circulation of draft orders.

**4. Presiding judge must sign order.** In almost all instances only the judge who presides at a hearing should sign an order resulting from the hearing. Rule 52 of the Rules of Civil Procedure requires the judge in a non-jury proceeding to find facts, make conclusions of law, and enter judgment accordingly. In the case of *In re Whisnant*, 71 N.C. App. 439 (1984), it was reversible error for a judge other than the one who presided at the hearing to sign the order terminating parental rights. In *In re C.M.C.*, 832 S.E.2d 681 (N.C. S.Ct. 2019), the North Carolina Supreme Court found the reasoning of the court of appeals was sound when vacating TPR orders and holding those orders were a nullity when they were signed by a judge who did not preside over the TPR hearings. The supreme court in *In re C.M.C.* further explained that because *the* judge did not sign the order, resulting in it being a nullity, the order was never entered under Rule 58 of the Rules of Civil Procedure.

Under Rule 63 of the Rules of Civil Procedure, if after the hearing is concluded the judge who presided at a hearing is not able to sign the order – whether by reason of disability, death, resignation, retirement, or any other reason – the chief district court judge can sign the order, but only if the judge who is not available made findings of fact and conclusions of law. *See* Comment to N.C. R. Civ. P. 63; *In re Savage*, 163 N.C. App. 195 (2004) (quotations and citation omitted). If the chief judge of the district is disabled, the order can be signed by any district court judge in the judicial district designated by the director of the Administrative Office of the Courts. N.C. R. Civ. P. 63(2). If the substitute judge concludes that he or she is not able to sign the order for any reason, the judge may grant a new hearing. N.C. R. Civ. P. 63. The substitute judge's action in signing the order is a ministerial, not judicial act, and does not involve decision making. *In re Savage*, 163 N.C. App. 195.

---

**Resource:** For more information about Rule 63, see Ann Anderson, *"To Effectuate a Decision Already Made": The Role of a Substitute Judge Under Rule 63*, UNC Sch. of Gov't: On the Civil Side Blog (Dec. 13, 2017).

## B. Findings of Fact and Conclusions of Law[1]

The Juvenile Code includes a number of specific requirements for the court's findings and conclusions in orders, and these requirements vary depending on the type and stage of the proceeding. In addition, Rule 52 of the Rules of Civil Procedure applies. *See, e.g., In re C.M.C.*, 832 S.E.2d 681 (N.C. S.Ct. 2019). Findings of fact must be based on competent evidence in the record, and conclusions of law must be based on sufficient findings of fact. *In re J.A.M.*, 822 S.E.2d 693 (N.C. S.Ct. 2019); *In re Patron*, 250 N.C. App. 375 (2016); *In re T.H.T.*, 185 N.C. App. 337 (2007), *aff'd as modified*, 362 N.C. 446 (2008). However, "the trial court is not required to make a finding of fact on every single piece of evidence [that] the trial court does not need to resolve material issues." *In re R.D.H., III*, 828 S.E.2d 170 (N.C. Ct. App. 2017).

**1. Separation of findings of fact and conclusions of law.** Rule 52(a) of the Rules of Civil Procedure governs court orders in bench trials and has been applied to juvenile proceedings. *See In re C.M.C.*, 832 S.E.2d 681 (N.C. S.Ct. 2019); *In re D.E.M.*, 810 S.E.2d 375 (N.C. Ct. App. 2018); *In re T.P.*, 197 N.C. App. 723 (2009); *In re J.L.*, 183 N.C. App. 126 (2007). Rule 52(a)(1) specifically requires that findings of fact and conclusions of law be stated separately. Appellate courts have noted that the failure to separate findings from conclusions can hinder appellate review and, in some cases, may prevent the appellate court from determining whether the order is supported by clear, cogent, and convincing evidence, prompting a remand. *See In re T.M.M.*, 167 N.C. App. 801 (2005). See also Chapter 12.8 (explaining the standards of review for findings and conclusions). However, a mislabeled finding of fact or conclusion of law may be reviewed on appeal according to what it actually is rather that what it is incorrectly labelled. *In re J.A.M.*, 251 N.C. Ct. App. 114 (2016), *rev'd on other grounds*, 370 N.C. 464 (2018); *In re M.M.*, 230 N.C. App. 225 (2013).

**2. Findings of fact.** Facts have been described as "things in space and time that can be objectively ascertained by one or more of the five senses . . . [which] in turn, provide the bases for conclusions." *In re M.N.C.*, 176 N.C. App. 114, 121 (2006) (citation omitted). Certain issues related to findings of fact arise repeatedly in appellate cases:

- **Recitation of allegations**. A number of appellate decisions have held that findings of fact must consist of more than mere recitations of the allegations in the petition. *See, e.g., In re O.W.*, 164 N.C. App. 699 (2004) (remanding the case where findings were a mere recitation of the allegations and were not sufficiently specific); *In re Harton*, 156 N.C. App. 655 (2003) and *In re Anderson*, 151 N.C. App. 94 (2002) (both citing Rule 52 and discussing the disfavor of mere recitation in context of a permanency planning order).

  However, in the case *In re J.W.*, 241 N.C. App. 44 (2015), the court of appeals sought to clarify such decisions and held that it is not *per se* reversible error for findings of fact to mirror the wording of a party's pleading. Instead, the determination of whether findings of fact are sufficient depends on an examination of the record of the proceedings and whether they "demonstrate that the trial court, through process of logical reasoning, based on the

---

[1] Some content in this section was sourced or adapted from Janet Mason, *Drafting Good Court Orders in Juvenile Cases*, JUVENILE LAW BULLETIN No. 2013/02 (UNC School of Government, Sept. 2013).

evidentiary facts before it, found the ultimate facts necessary to dispose of the case." *In re J.W.*, 241 N.C. App. at 48 (citations omitted). In its reasoning, the court of appeals acknowledged that trial judges often rely on counsel to assist in drafting orders and stated the need to avoid imposing on counsel the obligation "to eliminate unoriginal prose." *In re J.W.*, 241 N.C. App. at 45. *See also In re A.B.*, 253 N.C. App. 29 (2017) (the ultimate finding as to a parent's reasonable progress must be the result of a process of logical reasoning based on the evidentiary facts found by the court).

Recent cases considering orders containing verbatim recitations of allegations are consistent with *In re J. W.*, 241 N.C. App. 44. *See In re L.C.*, 253 N.C. App. 67 (2017) (considering only those findings that are supported by evidence in the record regardless of whether those findings mirror the allegations in the petition); *In re L.Z.A.*, 249 N.C. App. 628 (2016) (while "several" findings were verbatim recitations of allegations, other substantive findings made after several days of witness testimony did not mirror language in the petition and supported the order's conclusions; moreover, the trial court's discussion of a proposed order with the parties and subsequent modification of a proposed finding demonstrated an independent decision-making process); *In re A.B.*, 245 N.C. App. 35, 44 (2016) (trial court thoughtfully considered the evidence and independently determined the facts even though one of seventy findings contained "unoriginal prose"); *In re M.K.*, 241 N.C. App. 467 (2015) (trial court applied a process of logical reasoning and supported its adjudication of neglect with six substantive findings, even though twelve findings were disregarded as verbatim recitations of allegations).

In *In re A.B.*, 253 N.C. App. 29 (2017), respondent claimed that a TPR order included findings that were copied from prior orders in the case. The findings at issue were viewed as specific findings regarding respondent's progress at each prior hearing, with the court noting that whether the findings were copied from prior orders was "irrelevant" when respondent had not claimed that the findings were not supported by the evidence.

- **Recitation of testimony and sufficient specificity**. Findings must consist of more than mere recitation of the testimony of witnesses, and they must be sufficiently specific to allow an appellate court to review the decision and test the correctness of the judgment. A finding of fact by the court reflects a determination that evidence is credible and sufficiently clear and convincing to permit the court to say that something is a fact. For example, the statement "Dr. Lee testified that the child's injuries could not have been caused accidentally" is a recitation of testimony, whereas the statement "the child's injuries could not have been caused accidentally" is a finding of fact based on the court's determination that the doctor's testimony was credible, clear, and convincing. *See, e.g., In re N.D.A.*, 833 S.E.2d 768 (N.C. S.Ct. 2019) (a recitation of testimony does not constitute a finding of fact; appellate court compelled to disregard that sentence in the challenged finding); *In re L.C.*, 253 N.C. App. 67 (2017) (recitation of testimony does not constitute findings by the court); *In re M.M.*, 230 N.C. App. 225 (2013) (holding that many of the trial court's findings were actually recitations of assertions made by parties and witnesses or even arguments by attorneys); *In re H.J.A.*, 223 N.C. App. 413 (2012) (holding that the trial court's findings of fact were insufficient, although it had recited testimony that might support the required findings).

- **Findings based on reports, documents, and prior orders.** Juvenile proceedings typically involve multiple reports and documents. Depending on the respondent's past history with DSS or the stage of the specific abuse, neglect, or dependency action, the juvenile proceeding may involve prior court orders. A court may consider a prior order but should not merely incorporate the prior order. *In re B.P.*, 809 S.E.2d 914 (N.C. Ct. App. 2018) (in neglect adjudication, trial court properly considered prior orders when making independent findings of fact). In *In re T.N.H.*, 831 S.E.2d 54 (N.C. Ct. App. 2019), the supreme court adopted the court of appeals precedent that a trial court may take judicial notice of findings in a prior court order but may not rely solely on prior court orders and reports. The trial court must take some oral testimony and make an independent determination based on the evidence that is presented at the hearing. *In re T.N.H.*, 831 S.E.2d 54; *see In re J.C.M.J.C.*, 834 S.E.2d 670 (N.C. Ct. App. 2019) (trial court could not rely solely on findings from nonsecure custody order when making adjudicatory findings).

  A report or other document simply attached to an order does not by itself constitute findings of fact. When reports and documents are evidence that the court considered at the hearing, they do not need to be attached to an order. When they (or portions of them) are being incorporated by reference as findings of fact, or the court is finding as a fact that the document exists, they should be attached to the order and the order should specify what the attachment is and why it is being attached. However, the court should incorporate by reference sparingly, and then only if accompanied by the court's own specific findings related to what is incorporated. *See In re R.L.G.*, 816 S.E.2d 914, 921 (N.C. Ct. App. 2018) (incorporation of pre-adjudication order was insufficient for findings of fact and could not support adjudication of neglect; stating "the trial court may not delegate its fact finding duty by relying wholly on DSS reports and prior court orders"); *In re K.L.*, 254 N.C. App. 269, 280 (2017) (incorporated documents "may support a finding of fact; however, merely incorporating the documents by reference is not a sufficient finding of fact"; incorporating by reference findings from previous orders in the case did not result in findings sufficient to support a permanency planning order); *In re H.J.A.*, 223 N.C. App. 413 (2012) (the trial court's order referencing the GAL and DSS reports without making specific findings about those reports was insufficient); *In re A.S.*, 190 N.C. App. 679 (2008); *In re C.M.*, 183 N.C. App. 207 (2007) (finding no error in incorporating reports where the trial court did not simply adopt reports but made separate findings based upon them). A report should not be incorporated by reference without oral testimony from a witness at a hearing that results in the order. *In re J.T.*, 252 N.C. App. 19 (2017) (vacating and remanding orders; holding findings were unsupported by competent evidence when reports were accepted into evidence and then incorporated by reference in the order at a permanency planning hearing where no oral testimony was taken).

- **Findings based on evidence.** Findings of fact must be based on evidence that is actually presented and admitted by the court. *See In re C.W.*, 182 N.C. App. 214 (2007) (finding that the trial court's order and its findings of fact contained information that was neither introduced nor admitted at trial); *In re A.W.*, 164 N.C. App. 593 (2004) (finding error where the trial court based findings of fact for adjudication on a report that was not introduced at adjudication). The issue of what constitutes competent evidence is discussed in Chapter 11, but note that statements by counsel are not evidence and do not support findings of fact. *In re D.L.*, 166 N.C. App. 574 (2004); *In re J.T.*, 252 N.C. App. 19 (2017). Findings of fact based solely on reports without any testimony are not based on competent evidence. *In re S.P.*, 833 S.E.2d 638 (N.C. Ct. App. 2019) (vacating and remanding permanency planning order; holding DSS and GAL reports without testimony were insufficient to support findings; attorney arguments are not testimony); *see also In re C.M.B.*, 836 S.E.2d 746 (N.C. Ct. App. 2019) (holding no evidentiary hearing was ever held when court heard only arguments, no sworn testimony, and motions were unverified). When a case is appealed, the issue of whether there is sufficient evidence to support the findings may be raised regardless of whether that issue was raised in the trial court.

- **Specific findings required by the Juvenile Code.** Many provisions in the Juvenile Code require the court to make very specific findings to support specific types of orders and/or to reflect appropriate consideration of statutory criteria in various stages of the proceedings. When determining what findings must be included in an order, it is important to look at the language of the statute and whether it requires written findings on all/each enumerated factor or only relevant factors. *Compare* G.S. 7B-906.1(n) ("each") *with* G.S. 7B-906.1(d) ("those that are relevant"). In many appellate cases, failure of the trial court to make findings required by the Juvenile Code has led the appellate court to reverse, vacate, and/or remand the trial court's order. *See, e.g.*, *In re D.S.*, 817 S.E.2d 901 (N.C. Ct. App. 2018) (failure to make required finding under G.S. 7B-903(a1)); *In re D.A.*, 811 S.E.2d 729 (N.C. Ct. App. 2018) (failure to make required findings under G.S. 7B-906.2(b) and (d)). This has been especially true when courts fail to make required findings under G.S. 7B-906.1(n) (waiving further review hearings, see Chapter 7.2.A.4 for related cases); and G.S. 7B-906.1(d) and (e) (required findings for review and permanency planning hearings, see Chapter 7.8.B and C for related cases).

---

**Practice Notes**: Older opinions will refer to G.S. 7B-906 (review hearings) and 7B-907 (permanency planning hearings), which were repealed and replaced by G.S. 7B-906.1, effective for all actions filed or pending on or after October 1, 2013. *See* S.L. 2013-129, sec. 26.

There is also a line of appellate decisions that address mandatory findings regarding the cessation of reasonable efforts for reunification pursuant to G.S. 7B-507. Effective for all actions filed or pending on or after October 1, 2015, S.L. 2015-136, sec. 7, 9, and 14 made significant amendments to G.S. 7B-507 by eliminating the language regarding reasonable efforts and adding new language regarding reasonable efforts and reunification to G.S. 7B-901(c) (initial dispositional hearings) and 7B-906.2(b) (concurrent permanency planning).

---

The North Carolina Supreme Court in the case *In re L.M.T.*, 367 N.C. 165 (2013), rejected the argument that findings must include the exact statutory wording, emphasizing practical application of the law so that the best interests of the child are the paramount concern. Examining a permanency planning order for compliance with statutory requirements (then, G.S. 7B-507), the supreme court held that findings of fact do not need to quote the precise language of the statute but must "address the substance of the statutory requirements," noting also that "use of the precise statutory language will not remedy a lack of supporting evidence for the trial court's order." *In re L.M.T.*, 367 N.C. at 165, 168.

**3. Conclusions of law.** The distinction between findings of fact and conclusions of law can be difficult to make. "As a general rule, . . . any determination requiring the exercise of judgment or the application of legal principles" is a conclusion of law, and a "determination reached through 'logical reasoning from the evidentiary facts' " is a finding of fact. *In re A.B.*, 179 N.C. App. 605, 612 (2006) (quoting *In re Helms*, 127 N.C. App. 505, 510 (1997)). Note that an "ultimate finding is a conclusion of law or at least a determination of a mixed question of law and fact" and is different from "findings of primary, evidentiary, or circumstantial facts." *In re N.D.A.*, 833 S.E.2d 768, 773 (N.C. S.Ct. 2019) (citations omitted).

The determination at an adjudicatory hearing of whether the child is an abused, neglected, or dependent juvenile is a conclusion of law because it requires the exercise of judgment and application of legal principles. *See, e.g.*, *In re A.B.*, 179 N.C. App. 605; *In re Helms*, 127 N.C. App. 505. In dispositional orders, determinations of reasonable efforts and best interests are conclusions of law because they require an exercise of judgment. *See In re J.R.S.*, 813 S.E.2d 283 (N.C. Ct. App. 2018) (speaking to best interest determination); *In re Helms*, 127 N.C. App. 505 (speaking to reasonable efforts and best interest determinations). However, the trial court's failure to properly characterize a statement as a finding of fact or conclusion of law is not fatal if the necessary findings and conclusions are present in an order. *In re Helms*, 127 N.C. App. 505.

Conclusions of law must be supported by findings of fact. Where specific findings required by a particular statute are not made or are not specific or strong enough to support the conclusions, appellate courts will not affirm the trial court's order. *See In re B.P.*, 809 S.E.2d 914 (N.C. Ct. App. 2018) (reversing neglect and dependency adjudications when findings of fact did not support conclusions); *In re E.B.*, 805 S.E.2d 390, 393 (N.C. Ct. App. 2017) (concluding "the trial court's vague findings regarding domestic violence lack the required specificity necessary to 'enable an appellate court to review the decision and test the correctness of the judgment' "); *In re I.K.*, 227 N.C. App. 264 (2013) (reversing a permanency planning order where there were inconsistent findings and evidence, including findings that there was a risk of sexual abuse by the father and that the father should have unsupervised visitation); *In re H.J.A.*, 223 N.C. App. 413 (2012) (holding that the trial court erred where findings did not specify which parent particular findings referred to and specific findings required by 7B-907(b), now found in G.S. 7B-906.1, were not made); *In re I.R.C.*, 214 N.C. App. 358 (2011) (holding that trial court erred in failing to link its findings to its conclusion to cease reunification efforts and in neglecting to address G.S. 7B-507(b), now found in G.S. 7B-901(c), requirements). *See also In re O.J.R.*, 239 N.C. App. 329 (2015) (where the trial court's TPR order was reversed and remanded in part due to its failure to make the required findings and conclusions and its lack of findings to support some conclusions).

For findings of fact to support conclusions of law, they must not be inconsistent with those conclusions. In the case *In re A.B.*, 239 N.C. App. 157 (2015), the court of appeals reversed the trial court's order terminating a mother's parental rights where the court's conclusions contradicted its findings and some of its findings contradicted other findings.

> **Practice Note:** While parties may stipulate to facts, they may not stipulate to conclusions of law. *See In re A.K.D.*, 227 N.C. App. 58 (2013). See also Chapter 6.3.C.1 related to stipulations.
>
> **Resource***:* Janet Mason, *Drafting Good Court Orders in Juvenile Cases*, JUVENILE LAW BULLETIN No. 2013/02 (UNC School of Government, Sept. 2013).

### C. Entry and Service of the Order

**1. What constitutes entry.** The Juvenile Code provides for orders to be entered and served in accordance with Rule 58 of the Rules of Civil Procedure. *See* G.S. 7B-1001(b). An order is not entered until it is reduced to writing, signed by the judge, and filed with the clerk pursuant to Rule 5. N.C. R. CIV. P. 58. *See* S.L. 2017-158 sec. 1 and 2 (amending both Rule 5 and Rule 58 regarding filing, effective July 21, 2017); *In re A.U.D.*, 832 S.E.2d 698 (N.C. S.Ct. 2019); *see In re O.D.S.,* 247 N.C. App. 711 (2016) (extensively discussing pre- and post-1994 amendments to Rule 58 of the Rules of Civil Procedure, with applicable case law, and the impact of those amendments on when an order is entered versus orally rendered); *In re Pittman*, 151 N.C. App. 112 (2002). This means that when the judge makes an oral announcement (or rendition) of his or her order in open court, the order does not become enforceable until it is reduced to writing, signed by the judge, and filed with the clerk of court. *See McKinney v. Duncan*, 808 S.E.2d 509 (N.C. Ct. App. 2017); *Carland v. Branch,* 164 N.C. App. 403 (2004); *see also In re O.D.S.,* 247 N.C. App. at ___ (stating "no order or judgment had been entered at that time, and therefore, no party was bound by the judgment").

Because an oral rendition is not an entry of a judgment, it is subject to change, meaning the trial court is not required to adhere to the rendition when making and entering its written order. *In re A.U.D.,* 832 S.E.2d 698 (oral findings made by a trial court are subject to change prior to the entry of the final written order); *In re O.D.S.,* 247 N.C. App. 711 (holding the court was not bound by the oral rendition to terminate parental rights based on neglect when it included both neglect and dependency as grounds to TPR in the written entered order; reasoning it is not bound by the holding in *In re J.C.*, 236 N.C. App. 558 (2014) to the extent *In re J.C* conflicts with prior holdings of the court of appeals or supreme court and can be distinguished from the current case before it).

A court may also consider evidence presented after its oral rendition but before it enters a written judgment. *In re O.D.S.,* 247 N.C. App. 711, and cases cited therein. A trial court's misapprehension of when an order terminating parental rights was entered led to a reversal in the case *In re B.S.O.*, 225 N.C. App. 541 (2013). The trial court has broad discretion to re-open a case and admit additional testimony after the conclusion of the evidence, after argument of counsel, even weeks after the original hearing, or when the "ends of justice require." *In re B.S.O.*, 225 N.C. App. at 543. In *In re B.S.O.,* which cites cases on this principle, the trial court refused to exercise its discretion to take additional evidence because it thought a valid order terminating parental rights had been entered, when in fact the order was not final because it had not been reduced to writing.

> **Resource:** For more information about entering an order versus oral renditions, see Cheryl Howell, *Rule 58 and Entry of Civil Judgments: Statements from the bench are not court orders*, UNC SCH. OF GOV'T: ON THE CIVIL SIDE BLOG (May 3, 2017).

**2. Serving the order.** Rule 58 of the Rules of Civil Procedure requires that the party designated by the judge or the party who prepares the judgment serve a copy of the order on all other parties within three days after the judgment is entered. Service is pursuant to Rule 5 of the Rules of Civil Procedure. Statutory provisions for termination of parental rights (TPR) actions specifically require counsel for the petitioner or movant to serve a copy of the TPR order on the guardian ad litem for the child (if there is one) and on the child if the child is 12 or older. G.S. 7B-1110(d).

Service of the order by mail adds three days to the time within which a party may

- file a motion to amend the findings or the judgment, under Rule 52(b), or
- file a motion for a new trial, under Rule 59.

In addition, the time period for filing these motions is tolled for any period of noncompliance with the service provisions, but not longer than ninety days. N.C. R. CIV. P. 58.

G.S. 7B-1001(b) requires that notice of appeal be given "within thirty days after entry and service of the order in accordance with . . . Rule 58." Thus, the time within which notice of appeal must be given does not begin to run until both entry and service have occurred. For details related to notice of appeal, see Chapter 12.5.

## D. Time Requirements for Orders

When an order is entered impacts the progression of the juvenile proceeding. There are strict time requirements for the entry of orders in the Juvenile Code, which have the purpose of expediting outcomes for children and are consistent with the purpose of the Juvenile Code to achieve safe, permanent homes for children within a reasonable period of time. *In re T.H.T.*, 362 N.C. 446 (2008); *see* G.S. 7B-100(5). Delays in entering orders are directly contrary to the best interests of the children involved. *In re T.H.T.*, 362 N.C. 446; *In re S.Z.H.*, 247 N.C. App. 254 (2016).

**1. Entry of order within thirty days.** Orders for all of the following hearings must be in writing, include appropriate findings of fact, and be entered (signed by judge and filed with clerk) within thirty days of completion of the hearing:

- continued nonsecure custody, G.S. 7B-506(d);
- adjudication of abuse, neglect, or dependency, G.S. 7B-807(b);
- disposition in abuse, neglect, or dependency case, G.S. 7B-905(a);
- review, G.S. 7B-906.1(h);
- permanency planning, G.S. 7B-906.1(h);
- placement on the Responsible Individuals List, G.S. 7B-323(d);
- hearing on unknown parent in a TPR action, G.S. 7B-1105(e);

- TPR adjudication and disposition, G.S. 7B-1109(e); 7B-1110(a);
- post-TPR review hearing, G.S. 7B-908(e1); and
- reinstatement of parental rights, G.S. 7B-1114(*l*).

**2. Clerk's duty to reschedule when entry is late.** For certain orders, the Juvenile Code requires that the clerk schedule a special hearing when the order is not entered within the thirty-day time requirement and requires that an order be entered with ten days after the special hearing:

- adjudication of abuse, neglect, or dependency, G.S. 7B-807(b);
- dispositional order in abuse, neglect, or dependency case, G.S. 7B-905(a);
- review, G.S. 7B-906.1(h);
- permanency planning, G.S. 7B-906.1(h);
- TPR adjudication and disposition, G.S. 7B-1109(e); 7B-1110(a);
- post-TPR review hearing, G.S. 7B-908(e1); and
- reinstatement of parental rights, G.S. 7B-1114(*l*).

The hearings required by these statutes must be scheduled by the clerk at the first session of court scheduled for the hearing of juvenile matters after the thirty-day period expires. The purpose of the hearing is to determine and explain the reason for the delay and to obtain any needed clarification about the contents of the order. If the order is not entered within thirty days after the applicable substantive hearing and the clerk has not scheduled a subsequent hearing to address the delay, a party should file a request for such a hearing with the clerk. *See In re T.H.T.*, 362 N.C. 446 (2008).

**3. Remedy for untimely orders is mandamus.** The appropriate remedy for a trial court's failure to enter a timely order is not a new hearing or an appeal. It is a petition to the court of appeals for a writ of mandamus to require the trial court to proceed to judgment. *In re T.H.T.*, 362 N.C. 446 (2008); *In re S.Z.H.*, 247 N.C. App. 254 (2016) (setting out the remedy of mandamus when a termination order was entered nearly six months after the adjudicatory and dispositional hearing in violation of G.S. 7B-1109(e) and 7B-1110(a)). Application for a writ of mandamus is made pursuant to Rule 22 of the North Carolina Appellate Rules. In describing the remedy of mandamus, the North Carolina Supreme Court specified these required elements:

- the petitioner seeking relief must show a clear legal right to the act requested;
- the respondent must have a clear legal duty to perform the act;
- the duty must relate to a ministerial act, not an act requiring the exercise of discretion (mandamus may be used to compel an official to exercise his or her discretion, but not to direct what the result should be);
- the respondent must have neglected or refused to perform the act and the time to act expired; and
- there must not be an alternative legally adequate remedy.
- 

*In re T.H.T.*, 362 N.C. 446.

When a court fails to enter an order within thirty days of completion of the applicable hearing, schedule a hearing to address the delay, and/or enter an order within ten days following that hearing, a party may petition the court of appeals for a writ of mandamus. *In re T.H.T.*, 362 N.C. 446.

---

**Resource:** For a further discussion see Sara DePasquale, *Tick Tock: Mandatory Time Requirements to Enter A/N/D and TPR Orders*, UNC SCH. OF GOV'T: ON THE CIVIL SIDE BLOG (May 10, 2017).

# Chapter 5

# From Report through Pre-Adjudication in Abuse, Neglect, Dependency Cases

# Chapter 5
# From Report through Pre-Adjudication in Abuse, Neglect, Dependency Cases

5.1 **How a Case Enters the System**    5-4
   A. Reporting Suspected Abuse, Neglect, or Dependency
      1. Failure to report
      2. Manner of report
      3. No privilege; narrow exception for attorneys
      4. Immunity
      5. Other reporting laws
      6. Report may trigger notification to other agencies
      7. DSS determines whether the report indicates abuse, neglect, or dependency
   B. DSS Assessment of Report
      1. Multiple response system
      2. Timing of assessment
      3. Family privacy
      4. Confidentiality
      5. Military affiliation of parent, guardian, custodian, or caretaker
      6. Other juveniles
      7. Immediate removal, protective services
      8. Parent refusing services
      9. Physical abuse may require mental health evaluation
   C. DSS Access to Information
      1. Access to all relevant information
      2. Criminal investigative information
   D. Notice to the Reporter
      1. After DSS receipt of report
      2. After DSS completion of assessment
      3. Right to seek review
   E. Review by Prosecutor
      1. Timing
      2. Substance of review
      3. Outcome of review
   F. Law Enforcement Involvement
      1. DSS to report to law enforcement
      2. The criminal investigation
      3. Abandonment reported
      4. Relationship between DSS and law enforcement
   G. Interference with DSS Assessment
      1. Meaning of interference or obstruction
      2. Requirements for petition for interference
      3. File with clerk or magistrate
      4. Service and notice

5. Hearing
6. Cease interference order
7. Ex parte action and orders
8. Enforceability

## 5.2 Central Registry and Responsible Individuals List    5-15
A. Central Registry
B. Responsible Individuals List
   1. Abuse, serious neglect, responsible individual
   2. Notice to the responsible individual
   3. Placement on the RIL
   4. Right to judicial review
   5. Scheduling the judicial review hearing
   6. The hearing
   7. The court order
   8. Confidentiality

## 5.3 Starting the Abuse, Neglect, Dependency Court Action    5-21
A. The Petition
   1. Proper petitioner
   2. Venue
   3. File with clerk or magistrate
   4. Substance of petition
   5. More than one child
   6. Verification essential
   7. DSS dismissal of petition
   8. Amendment of the petition
B. The Summons and Process
   1. Timing
   2. Substance of summons
   3. Who receives summons
   4. Petition and notice to the child's GAL
   5. Service of petition and summons

## 5.4 Parties, Appointment of Counsel, and Guardians ad Litem    5-25
A. Parties to the Proceeding
B. Parents and Other Care Providers
   1. Parent is a party
   2. Guardians, custodians, and caretakers
   3. Appointment of respondent's counsel
   4. Appointment of guardian ad litem for parent
   5. Significance of uninvolved, missing, or unknown parents
   6. Serving a missing parent
   7. Paternity and putative fathers
   8. Same-sex parents
C. The Child
   1. Child is a party

2. Appointment of a guardian ad litem under G.S. 7B-601
D. Department of Social Services

## 5.5 Purpose and Requirements of Temporary and Nonsecure Custody    5-34
A. Purpose of Temporary and Nonsecure Custody
B. Temporary Custody
  1. Circumstances for temporary custody
  2. Length of temporary custody
  3. Newborn abandonment ("safe surrender")
  4. Medical professionals
  5. Duties of person with temporary custody
C. Nonsecure Custody
  1. Procedure to obtain the initial nonsecure custody order
  2. Criteria for initial and continued nonsecure custody orders
  3. Place of nonsecure custody
  4. Visitation
  5. Medical decision-making
  6. Violent caregivers

## 5.6 Nonsecure Custody Hearings    5-42
A. Summary
B. Timing
  1. The first hearing on continued nonsecure custody
  2. Second and subsequent hearings
  3. Hearings by party request
C. Jurisdictional Inquiry
D. Nature of Hearing: Evidence and Burden of Proof
E. Findings and Other Issues at Hearing on the Need for Continued Nonsecure Custody
F. Limits on Court's Authority at Nonsecure Custody Stage
G. Requirements for Court Orders
H. Nonsecure Custody Order Is Not Appealable

## 5.7 Pre-adjudication Hearings, Conferences, and Mediation    5-46
A. Pre-adjudication Hearing
B. Child Planning Conferences
C. Permanency Mediation

## Appendix 5-1: Table of Differences for Mandated Reporting under G.S. 7B-301 and G.S. 14-318.6    5-49

## Appendix 5-2: Mandated Reporting Flowchart    5-51

## 5.1 How a Case Enters the System

### A. Reporting Suspected Abuse, Neglect, or Dependency

North Carolina has a universal mandated reporting statute. The Juvenile Code requires that any person or institution with cause to suspect that any juvenile is abused, neglected, or dependent, as defined by G.S. 7B-101, or has died as the result of maltreatment, must report the information to the county department of social services (DSS) where the juvenile resides or is found. G.S. 7B-301(a).

**Note,** for purposes of this Manual, "department of social services" or "DSS" refers to a department as defined by G.S. 7B-101(8a) regardless of how it is titled or structured.

The phrase "cause to suspect" is not defined by statute or case law, and a determination of when a concern rises to that level is necessarily subjective. In *Dobson v. Harris*, 352 N.C. 77, 84, n.4 (2000), the supreme court noted that the phrase "gives wide margin to whatever prompts the reporter to notify DSS" and "does not call for scrutiny, analysis, or judgment by a finder of fact." It is reasonable, however, to view "cause to suspect" as more than a vague suspicion. For an individual, the "cause" may be based not only on objective facts and observations, but also on the context in which the concern arises, prior knowledge about a child's situation, and how the child is being affected by the circumstances. *See Rouse v. Forsyth County Dep't of Soc. Servs.*, 822 S.E.2d 100 (N.C. Ct. App. 2018) (discussing cause to suspect in an employment discharge case of a DSS social worker), *review allowed*, 826 S.E.2d 700 (N.C. S.Ct. 2019). There is no obligation on the reporter to attempt to investigate their suspicion. The assessment is performed by DSS.

**Resource:** For a more detailed discussion of the topic of reporting and a county department of social services' response to a report, see JANET MASON, REPORTING CHILD ABUSE AND NEGLECT IN NORTH CAROLINA (UNC School of Government, 3d ed. 2013) with SARA DEPASQUALE, *Suspected Child Maltreatment Occurring in a Child Care Facility* (UNC School of Government, 2016) supplemental Chapter 13a.

**1. Failure to report.** Any person who knowingly or wantonly fails to make a required report or prevents someone else from making a required report commits a Class 1 misdemeanor. G.S. 7B-301(b). *See State v. Ditenhafer*, 812 S.E.2d 896 (N.C. Ct. App. 2018) (noting in a case involving felony obstruction of justice and accessory after the fact charges against a mother whose daughter alleged she was sexually abused by her adoptive father/mother's husband that mother could have been but was not charged with a misdemeanor for failing to report suspected abuse as provided for in G.S. 7B-301), *aff'd in part, rev'd in part and remanded*, 834 S.E.2d 392 (N.C. S.Ct. 2019).

**2. Manner of report.** Reports to a county department of social services may be made orally, by telephone, or in writing. The report should include information the reporter has about

- the juvenile's name, age, address, and present whereabouts;
- the name and address of the juvenile's parent, guardian, custodian, or caretaker;

- the names and ages of other juveniles in the home or facility;
- the nature and extent of the juvenile's condition or injuries resulting from the suspected abuse, neglect, or dependency; and
- any other information the reporter believes might be helpful.

G.S. 7B-301(a).

The law requires the person making a report to provide his or her name, address, and telephone number, but a reporter's failure or refusal to give his or her name does not affect DSS's responsibility to complete an assessment. G.S. 7B-301(a); *see* 10A N.C.A.C 70A.0105(a) (referring to anonymous reports); *In re N.X.A.*, 254 N.C. App. 670, 675 (2017) (stating "a person who reports suspected abuse, neglect, or dependency . . . has the right to remain anonymous"). Note that a reporter's identity (when it is provided to DSS) is subject to confidentiality requirements. See Chapter 14.1.A.3.

**3. No privilege; narrow exception for attorneys.** Child abuse reporting laws were enacted initially to encourage, then require, reporting by doctors and other professionals who, without the statutory mandate, would be prohibited from reporting because of privilege or confidentiality laws. The Juvenile Code (G.S. Chapter 7B) establishes a universal mandate where any person or institution who has cause to suspect a child's abuse, neglect, or dependency must make a report. The Juvenile Code does not recognize privilege as a ground for failing to report, except for one narrow exception. *See* G.S. 7B-310. The statutory exception is for attorneys but only with regard to knowledge an attorney gains from a client during representation in the abuse, neglect, or dependency case. It does not include an exception for an attorney who learns about a client's maltreatment of a child during representation in any other action. However, the U.S. Constitution may require a broader attorney exception to protect the rights of a client who has a constitutional right to the effective assistance of counsel. In addition, this duty to report may conflict with a lawyer's ethical duty to maintain a client's confidences pursuant to Rule 1.6 of the N.C. Revised Rules of Professional Conduct. The North Carolina State Bar Ethics Opinions, RPC 175 (1995) and RPC 120 (1992), address this subject and give the lawyer broad discretion in deciding how to resolve the conflict ethically.

**Resource:** Sara DePasquale, *Mandated Reporting of Child Abuse, Neglect, or Dependency: What's an Attorney to Do?*, UNC SCH. OF GOV'T: ON THE CIVIL SIDE BLOG (Aug. 7, 2015).

For a discussion of privileges in the context of admissibility of evidence, see Chapter 11.11.

**4. Immunity.** Anyone who makes a report, cooperates with DSS in an assessment, testifies in a proceeding resulting from the assessment, provides information or assistance (including medical evaluations or consultations), or otherwise participates in the "program authorized by" the abuse, neglect, or dependency statutes is immune from any civil or criminal liability if acting in good faith. G.S. 7B-309. *See also Dobson v. Harris*, 352 N.C. 77 (2000); *Davis v. Durham City Sch.*, 91 N.C. App. 520 (1988) (decided under an earlier version of the Juvenile Code). In a proceeding involving liability, good faith is presumed, but someone who makes a report "with malice" does not have that protection from liability. *See* G.S. 7B-309; *Kroh v.*

*Kroh*, 152 N.C. App. 347 (2002).

**5. Other reporting laws.** The reporting law discussed in this Manual is in the Juvenile Code: G.S. 7B-301. It applies to everyone, focuses on protecting children, and relates to situations that may result in a district court abuse, neglect, or dependency proceeding. Reports are made to county departments of social services. North Carolina has other laws that require reports involving children be made to different government agencies.

**(a) Reports to law enforcement.** Some laws mandate that reports involving possible child maltreatment be made to law enforcement or punish the making of improper reports in certain circumstances. These laws address

- the duty to report to law enforcement the disappearance of a child under age sixteen (G.S. 14-318.5; 14-318.4(a6));
- failure to notify law enforcement of the death of a child, with the intent to conceal the child's death (G.S. 14-401.22);
- making false or misleading reports to law enforcement relating to the investigation of a child's disappearance or a child victim of a Class A, B1, B2, or C felony (G.S. 14-225);
- the duty of a school principal to report certain crimes that occur on school property to law enforcement (G.S. 115C-288(g)); and
- the duty of physicians and hospitals to report to law enforcement certain wounds, injuries, and illnesses, including any child's recurrent illness or serious physical injury that appears to be the result of non-accidental trauma (G.S. 90-21.20).

**New mandated reporting law.** Effective December 1, 2019, there is a new universal mandated reporting law involving juveniles who are victims of certain crimes. S.L. 2019-245, Part I enacts G.S. 7B-318.6, which requires any adult who knows or should have reasonably known that a juvenile has been or is the victim of a violent offense, sexual offense, or misdemeanor child abuse to report that case to the appropriate local law enforcement agency where the juvenile resides or is found. The definition of juvenile incorporates G.S. 7B-101(14), which is a person who is younger than 18 years of age and is not married, emancipated, or a member of the Armed Forces and further states "[f]or the purposes of this section, the age of the juvenile at the time of the abuse or offense governs." G.S. 14-318.6(a)(1); *see* G.S. 7B-101(14). There are some limited exemptions to the reporting requirement for certain professionals who have a statutory privilege. Absent those professionals covered by the reporting exemption, a person 18 years of age or older who knowingly and willfully fails to make a report to law enforcement or prevents another from doing so is guilty of a Class 1 misdemeanor. For a table comparing this new universal mandated reporting statute, G.S. 14-318.6, and the abuse, neglect, and dependency mandated reporting statute, G.S. 7B-301, see Appendix 5-1 at the end of this Chapter.

---

**Resource:** For a discussion of this new mandated reporting law and questions regarding its interpretation, see Sara DePasquale, *BIG NEWS: S.L. 2019-245 Creates a New Universal Mandated Reporting Law for Child Victims of Crimes and Changes the*

*Definition of Caretaker*, UNC SCH. OF GOV'T: NORTH CAROLINA CRIMINAL LAW BLOG (Nov. 13, 2019).

**(b) Reports of suspected child maltreatment in child care.** Effective January 1, 2016, the Juvenile Code was amended to remove reports and investigations of abuse and neglect occurring in child care facilities from a county DSS to the North Carolina Department of Health and Human Services (DHHS) Division of Child Development and Early Education (DCDEE). *See* S.L. 2015-123. Another universal reporting statute, G.S. 110-105.4(a), was enacted that requires any person with cause to suspect a child has been maltreated or died as a result of maltreatment in a child care facility to make a report to DHHS DCDEE. *See* G.S. 110-105.3(b) (definitions of "child care facilities" and "child maltreatment"). DHHS DCDEE, as the agency that administers the child care licensing system, is responsible for investigating the report and taking appropriate responsive action to the findings of its investigation. *See* G.S. 110-105.3 through -105.6.

**Resources:**
For more information about child maltreatment in a child care facility, see
- Sara DePasquale, *The New Law Addressing Child Maltreatment in Child Care Facilities: It's the State's Responsibility*, UNC SCH. OF GOV'T: ON THE CIVIL SIDE BLOG (Jan. 6, 2016).
- SARA DEPASQUALE, *Suspected Child Maltreatment Occurring in a Child Care Facility* (UNC School of Government, 2016) supplemental CH. 13a *in* JANET MASON, REPORTING CHILD ABUSE AND NEGLECT IN NORTH CAROLINA, (UNC School of Government, 3d ed. 2013).
- The "Complaints" section of the N.C. Department of Health and Human Services Child Development and Early Education website.

For an illustration of the reporting requirements under North Carolina's two universal mandated reporting laws related to a child's suspected abuse, neglect, dependency, or maltreatment, see Appendix 5-2 at the end of this Chapter.

**6. Report may trigger notification to other agencies.** If DSS receives a report that a child was physically harmed in violation of a criminal law by someone who is not the parent, guardian, custodian, or caretaker, the director must make a report to local law enforcement and the district attorney within forty-eight hours. G.S. 7B-307(a). If the report alleges a child has been abused, neglected, or otherwise maltreated while in child care, the DSS director must notify the DHHS DCDEE within twenty-four hours or on the next working day after receiving the report. G.S. 7B-307(a); *see* G.S. 110-105.3(a), (c), (l).

**7. DSS determines whether the report indicates abuse, neglect, or dependency.** When DSS receives a report of suspected abuse, neglect, or dependency, its first task is to determine whether the facts as stated by the reporter, if true, fit within the definitions of abuse, neglect, or dependency in G.S. 7B-101. See Chapter 2.3.B (relating to definitions). If they do not, DSS will "screen out" the report, which requires a two-level review. 10A N.C.A.C. 70A.0105(g); *see* G.S.7B-300 (referring to "screening of reports"). When a report is screened out, DSS does not have a duty or even authority to investigate the matter. *See, e.g., In re Stumbo*, 357 N.C.

279 (2003) (holding that a petition for an order to cease interference with a DSS investigation should not have been granted because the facts reported, even if true, did not fit within the definitions of abuse, neglect, or dependency). When the facts reported do fit the definitions of abuse, neglect, or dependency, DSS will "screen in" the report.

> **Resource:** The state policy for intake and screening of reports of suspected abuse, neglect, or dependency is set forth in the DIV. OF SOC. SERVS., N.C. DEP'T OF HEALTH & HUMAN SERVICES, CHILD WELFARE MANUAL "Intake," available here. The policy contains several intake decision trees based on the reported circumstances (e.g., physical injury, emotional abuse, improper care).

### B. DSS Assessment of Report

When DSS receives a report and determines that information in the report, if true, fits the legal definition of abuse, neglect, or dependency, DSS must conduct an assessment. In the assessment, DSS will ascertain the facts of the case, the extent of any abuse or neglect, and the risk of harm to the juvenile. G.S. 7B-302(a). Effective August 23, 2019, DSS must also collect information about the military affiliation of a parent, guardian, custodian, or caretaker when abuse or neglect has been alleged. G.S. 7B-302(a); *see* S.L. 2019-201, Part III.

**1. Multiple response system.** The multiple response system (MRS) provides for different response procedures for different types of reports. The "family assessment" response is used for reports meeting the statutory definitions of neglect and dependency. This response is a family-centered approach that is protection and prevention oriented and that evaluates the strengths and needs of the child's family, as well as the child's condition. G.S. 7B-101(11a). The "investigative assessment" response is used for reports alleging the statutory definitions of abuse and director selected reports of neglect or dependency. This type of response uses a formal information gathering process to determine whether a juvenile is abused, neglected, or dependent. G.S. 7B-101(11b); *see* G.S. 7B-320(a).

Investigative and family assessments have many procedures in common. Both use a structured decision-making process that requires that more than one person be involved in reaching a decision based on the legal definitions and on documented caretaker behavior that resulted in harm or a risk of harm to the child. An assessment must address and document findings about the frequency and severity of maltreatment, safety issues and risk of future harm, and the need for protection. A family assessment results in a determination of one of the following:

- services needed,
- services recommended (where the child's safety and risk of future harm are not issues),
- services provided and protective services no longer needed, or
- services not recommended.

DIV. OF SOC. SERVS., N.C. DEP'T OF HEALTH & HUMAN SERVICES, CHILD WELFARE MANUAL "Assessments," available here.

At the end of an investigative assessment, DSS either substantiates abuse or serious neglect or does not (sometimes referred to as "unsubstantiated"). A determination by DSS that abuse, neglect, or dependency has occurred triggers specific statutory responsibilities. DSS must determine whether protective services should be provided or whether a petition should be filed to initiate a juvenile court proceeding. *See* G.S. 7B-302(a), (c). In the majority of cases in which the assessment indicates abuse, neglect, or dependency, DSS does not file a petition but provides services to protect the child and may enter into a service agreement or protection plan with the family. These agreements are voluntary and are not legally enforceable. Nevertheless, a parent's failure to comply with a service agreement or protection plan may be relevant later if DSS files a petition alleging abuse, neglect, or dependency. *See* G.S. 7B-302(c); *In re H.L.*, 807 S.E.2d 685 (N.C. Ct. App. 2017).

> **Resource***:* For policies and details of the multiple response system and what is involved in family and investigative assessments, see DIV. OF SOC. SERVS., N.C. DEP'T OF HEALTH & HUMAN SERVICES, CHILD WELFARE MANUAL "Assessments," available [here](.).

**2. Timing of assessment.** When abuse, abandonment, or the unlawful transfer of custody is alleged, DSS must initiate the assessment immediately and at least within twenty-four hours after receiving the report. When neglect (other than abandonment or the unlawful transfer of custody) or dependency is alleged, the assessment must be initiated within seventy-two hours. G.S. 7B-302(a); *see* G.S. 14-321.2 (unlawful transfer of custody).

**3. Family privacy.** As part of the assessment DSS is required to visit the place where the child resides. G.S. 7B-302(a). However, DSS may not enter a private residence for assessment purposes without at least one of the following:

- a reasonable belief that a child is in imminent danger of death or serious physical injury,
- permission of the parent or person responsible for the child's care,
- accompaniment of a law enforcement officer who has legal authority to enter, or
- a court order.

G.S. 7B-302(h).

*See generally Renn v. Garrison*, 100 F.3d 344, 349 (4th Cir. 1996) (holding that DSS workers alleged to have violated family privacy rights were entitled to qualified immunity where there was no showing that their actions exceeded the scope of the North Carolina state child protection statutes in effect at the time, which the court noted "plainly take into account" a family's right to privacy).

**4. Confidentiality.** DSS is required to hold all information it receives, including the identity of the reporter, in strictest confidence. G.S. 7B-302(a1). However, there are a number of exceptions to this requirement. For a discussion of confidentiality and information sharing, see Chapter 14.

**5. Military affiliation of parent, guardian, custodian, or caretaker.** Effective August 23, 2019, as part of its assessment of a report of abuse or neglect, DSS is required to collect information about the military affiliation of the juvenile's parent, guardian, custodian, or caretaker. G.S. 7B-302(a). If DSS finds evidence that a juvenile may have been abused or neglected by a parent, guardian, custodian, or caretaker with a military affiliation, the DSS director must notify the appropriate military authority. G.S. 7B-307(a); *see* G.S. 7B-302(a1)(1) (authorizing the disclosure).

**6. Other juveniles.** DSS must ascertain whether other juveniles who live in the home or who reside in the same facility are in need of protective services or require removal from the home or facility. G.S. 7B-302(b).

**7. Immediate removal, protective services.** If an assessment indicates that a juvenile is abused, neglected, or dependent, DSS must decide whether immediate removal of the juvenile or any other juveniles in the home is necessary for their protection. If immediate removal is not necessary, DSS must immediately provide or arrange for protective services. G.S. 7B-302(c). If immediate removal is necessary, DSS must file a petition and, in some circumstances, may assume temporary custody of the juvenile. G.S. 7B-302(d). See section 5.5.B, below (explaining temporary custody).

**8. Parent refusing services.** After a substantiation or a finding that a family is in need of services, if DSS does not file a petition, it provides or arranges for protective services based on the risks, needs, and strengths of the family identified during the assessment process. If a parent, guardian, custodian, or caretaker refuses to accept the protective services arranged or provided for by DSS, DSS is required to file a petition to protect the juvenile(s). G.S. 7B-302(c).

**9. Physical abuse may require mental health evaluation.** When a child is removed from the home based on physical abuse, DSS must thoroughly review the alleged abuser's background, which includes a criminal history check and review of available mental health records. If the review reveals a history of violent behavior against people, DSS must petition the court to order the alleged perpetrator to submit to a mental health evaluation. G.S. 7B-302(d1).

## C. DSS Access to Information

In making the assessment of the child's status, DSS may consult with any public or private agencies or individuals, including law enforcement officers. G.S. 7B-302(e). See also Chapter 14 (relating to confidentiality and DSS access to information).

**1. Access to all relevant information.** DSS may make a written demand for information or reports, whether or not confidential, that may be relevant to the assessment or to providing protective services, and that information must be provided (to the extent permitted by federal law, described in Chapter 14) unless protected by attorney-client privilege. G.S. 7B-302(e). Refusals of DSS's written demands for information may result in interference proceedings pursuant to G.S. 7B-303, described in section 5.1.G, below.

**2. Criminal investigative information.** If a custodian of criminal investigative information believes release of the information will jeopardize the criminal case or the defendant's right to receive a fair trial, the custodian may seek a court order to prevent disclosure. This kind of action must be set for immediate hearing, and any subsequent proceedings in the action must be given priority by trial and appellate courts. G.S. 7B-302(e).

### D. Notice to the Reporter

**1. After DSS receipt of report.** Within five days of receiving the report, DSS must give written notice to the reporter as to whether the report was accepted for assessment and whether it was referred to a law enforcement agency. The notice is not required if the reporter has asked not to receive notice or has not provided his or her name or contact information. G.S. 7B-302(f).

**2. After DSS completion of assessment.** Within five days after completing the assessment, DSS must give written notice to the reporter as to whether there is a finding of abuse, neglect, or dependency; what, if any, action DSS is taking to protect the child; and whether a petition has been filed. Notice is not required if the reporter has asked not to receive notice or has not provided his or her name or contact information. G.S. 7B-302(g).

**3. Right to seek review.** DSS must inform the reporter of the procedure allowing him or her to request a prosecutor review of the DSS decision not to file a petition. G.S. 7B-302(g).

### E. Review by Prosecutor

When DSS decides not to file a petition alleging abuse, neglect, or dependency, the person who made the report can seek a review of that decision by the prosecutor. G.S. 7B-302(g); 7B-305; 7B-403(b).

**1. Timing.** Request for the review must be made within five days of receiving notice of a DSS decision not to file a petition. G.S. 7B-302(g); 7B-305. The prosecutor must review the DSS decision within twenty days after the reporter is notified of DSS's decision. G.S. 7B-306. The prosecutor notifies the reporter and DSS of the time and place for the review. G.S. 7B-305.

**2. Substance of review.** Once DSS receives notice of the time and place for review from the prosecutor, DSS must immediately transmit a copy of the summary of the assessment to the prosecutor. G.S. 7B-305. The prosecutor's review must include conferences with

- the person making the report,
- the DSS protective services worker,
- the child (if practicable), and
- other persons known to have pertinent information about the child or the child's family.

G.S. 7B-306.

**3. Outcome of review.** At the conclusion of the review, the prosecutor may

- affirm the DSS decision not to file a petition,
- ask an appropriate local law enforcement agency to investigate, or

- direct DSS to file a petition.

G.S. 7B-306.

> **Resource:** For a further discussion of making a report, notice to the reporter, and the prosecutor review, see Sara DePasquale, *A/N/D Reporting: Rights, Protections, and Prosecutor Review*, UNC SCH. OF GOV'T: ON THE CIVIL SIDE BLOG (June 21, 2017).

### F. Law Enforcement Involvement

**1. DSS to report to law enforcement.** If DSS finds evidence that a child may have been abused, as defined in G.S. 7B-101, or receives a report of a crime involving physical harm to a child by someone other than a parent, guardian, custodian, or caretaker, DSS must make immediate oral and subsequent written reports to the district attorney (or designee) and to appropriate local law enforcement within forty-eight hours of when DSS received the report. G.S. 7B-307(a).

**2. The criminal investigation.** Within forty-eight hours of receiving information from DSS, law enforcement must initiate a criminal investigation. If DSS is initiating an assessment, law enforcement's investigation must be coordinated with the protective services assessment. G.S. 7B-307(a). When law enforcement's investigation is complete, the district attorney must determine whether criminal prosecution is appropriate and may request that a DSS representative appear before a magistrate to seek the issuance of a warrant. G.S. 7B-307(a).

**3. Abandonment reported.** When a report alleges that the child is abandoned, the DSS assessment must include a request to law enforcement to investigate through the North Carolina Center for Missing Persons and other national and state resources whether the child is a missing child. G.S. 7B-302(a).

**4. Relationship between DSS and law enforcement.** Complications can arise when DSS and law enforcement are working on separate cases resulting from the same circumstances. DSS and law enforcement may pursue interviewing the same individuals, and sometimes they may conduct interviews jointly. Attention should be given to the circumstances under which *Miranda* warnings are applicable. Even if DSS conducts an interview, if information learned in the interview is used in a subsequent criminal trial, the issue of whether DSS was acting as an "agent" of law enforcement may arise. *See State v. Morrell*, 108 N.C. App. 465 (1993) (holding that a social worker's failure to advise the defendant of her *Miranda* rights caused the defendant's statements in an interview with the social worker to be inadmissible because the social worker became like an agent of the state where the social worker went beyond her role and began working with sheriff's department on the case prior to interviewing the defendant). For a discussion of admissions of a party-opponent, see Chapter 11.6.B.

### G. Interference with DSS Assessment

When someone obstructs or interferes with a DSS assessment, DSS may file an interference petition naming that person as a respondent and asking the court to order that person to cease the obstruction or interference. G.S. 7B-303. The court has exclusive original jurisdiction of proceedings in which a person is alleged to have obstructed or interfered with a DSS assessment. G.S. 7B-200(a)(6).

**1. Meaning of interference or obstruction.** Interference or obstruction includes any of the following:

- refusing to disclose the juvenile's whereabouts,
- refusing to allow DSS to have personal access to the juvenile,
- refusing to allow DSS to observe or interview the juvenile in private (*see State v. Ditenhafer*, 812 S.E.2d 896 (N.C. Ct. App. 2018) (referring to DSS's right to ask mother to leave child's interview and ability to seek an interference order to compel mother's nonattendance if she refused to leave the interview), *aff'd in part, rev'd in part and remanded*, 834 S.E.2d 392 (N.C. S.Ct. 2019),
- refusing to allow DSS access to confidential information and records pursuant to a request under G.S. 7B-302,
- refusing to allow DSS to arrange for an examination of the juvenile by a physician or other expert (*see In re Browning*, 124 N.C. App. 190 (1996), in which a father was not successful in claiming religious beliefs as a reason for refusing to permit a mental health evaluation of his children), or
- other conduct that makes it impossible for DSS to carry out the duty to assess the juvenile's condition.

G.S. 7B-303(b); *see In re J.C.M.J.C.*, 834 S.E.2d 670 (N.C. Ct. App. 2019) (facts in case show that DSS obtained an interference order against respondent parents who refused to cooperate with DSS or allow DSS access to their home and children).

**2. Requirements for petition for interference.** The petition must be verified and

- contain the child's name, date of birth, and address;
- state the basis for initiating an assessment; and
- include a description of conduct alleged to constitute obstruction or interference.

G.S. 7B-303(a).

**3. File with clerk or magistrate.** The interference petition is filed with the clerk of court when that office is open. In an emergency, when an interference order is needed and the clerk's office is closed, the magistrate must accept the petition for filing. A petition accepted by the magistrate must be delivered to the clerk's office for processing as soon as that office opens. G.S. 7B-404. Some judicial districts may have local rules or an administrative order issued by the chief district court judge addressing the appropriate procedure for after-hours filing.

**4. Service and notice.** Service of the interference petition, summons, and notice of hearing must be made "as provided by the Rules of Civil Procedure," on

- the person alleged to have obstructed or interfered with an assessment (the respondent);

- the juvenile's parent, guardian, custodian, or caretaker; and
- any other person determined by the court to be a necessary party.

G.S. 7B-303(c).

**5. Hearing.** The hearing on the interference petition must be held not less than five days after service of the petition and summons on the respondent. G.S. 7B-303(c). The burden of proof at the hearing is on DSS, and the standard of proof is clear, cogent, and convincing evidence. G.S. 7B-303(c). DSS must prove that the respondent both obstructed or interfered with the assessment and did so without a lawful excuse. As part of its case in chief, DSS should prove not only the conduct of the respondent and its effect on the assessment, but also that DSS was acting pursuant to a report that was sufficient to trigger DSS's duty and authority to conduct an assessment. Where the information in the report is not sufficient to constitute abuse, neglect, or dependency, filing an interference petition is improper. *See In re Stumbo*, 357 N.C. 279 (2003).

The scope of the hearing does not extend to the issue of whether the child is abused, neglected, or dependent, and the court does not have jurisdiction to change the child's custody. *See In re K.C.G.*, 171 N.C. App. 488 (2005); *see also In re J.C.M.J.C.*, 834 S.E.2d 670, 678 (N.C. Ct. App. 2019) (stating "findings [of interference by respondent parents] do not support a conclusion that Respondents did 'not provide proper care, supervision, or discipline[,]' or that the children were living in an environment injurious to their welfare").

**6. Cease interference order.** If the court finds at the hearing by clear, cogent, and convincing evidence that the respondent, without lawful excuse, has obstructed or interfered with a required assessment, the court may order the respondent to cease the obstruction or interference. G.S. 7B-303(c).

**7. Ex parte action and orders.** When DSS believes the juvenile needs immediate help or protection, DSS can allege this in the interference petition and seek an ex parte order. G.S. 7B-303(d).

(a) **Standard.** The court may enter an ex parte order to cease obstruction or interference if it finds probable cause to believe that

- the juvenile is at risk of immediate harm and
- the respondent is obstructing or interfering with DSS's ability to assess the juvenile's condition.

(b) **Limitation.** This ex parte order is limited to provisions necessary to enable DSS to conduct an assessment to determine whether the juvenile is in need of immediate protection or assistance.

(c) **Subsequent hearing.** Within ten days of an ex parte order, a hearing must be held to determine whether there is good cause for the order to continue or whether there should be a different order.

**(d) Service on respondent.** The respondent must be served with the ex parte order along with a copy of the interference petition, summons, and notice of hearing.

**8. Enforceability.** An order to cease interference with or obstruction of a DSS assessment is enforceable by civil or criminal contempt as provided in G.S. Chapter 5A. G.S. 7B-303(f). *See In re J.C.M.J.C.*, 834 S.E.2d 670 (N.C. Ct. App. 2019) (referring to the ability of DSS to obtain a contempt order against respondents who fail to comply with an interference order).

**AOC Forms:**
- AOC-J-120, Petition - Obstruction of or Interference with Juvenile Assessment (Abuse/Neglect/Dependency) (Oct. 2019).
- AOC-J-121, Juvenile Summons and Notice of Hearing (Obstruction of or Interference with Juvenile Assessment) (Oct. 2019).
- AOC-J-122, Ex Parte Order to Cease Obstruction of or Interference with Juvenile Assessment (Oct. 2019).
- AOC-J-123, Order to Cease Obstruction of or Interference with Juvenile Assessment (Oct. 2019).

## 5.2 Central Registry and Responsible Individuals List

### A. Central Registry

The Department of Health and Human Services (DHHS) maintains a Central Registry of reports of abuse, neglect, and dependency and child fatalities that are the result of alleged maltreatment. This statewide registry is maintained for study purposes and to identify cases of repeated maltreatment of a child. The data is furnished to DHHS by the county departments of social services which received the reports and completed the assessments. The data is confidential and cannot be used in court "unless based upon a final judgment of a court of law." G.S. 7B-311(a).

The implementing regulations adopted by the Social Services Commission list the organizations and persons who are permitted to access Central Registry data and the limited purposes for which the data may be accessed. 10A N.C.A.C. 70A.0102; *see* G.S. 7B-311(a). A DSS may access the Central Registry to identify whether a child who is currently being assessed for abuse, neglect, or dependency has previously been reported as such or is a member of a family where another child died due to suspected abuse or neglect, but the information is limited to

- the child's name, date of birth, sex, and race;
- the county that investigated or assessed the report;
- the type of maltreatment reported and found, the date of the case decision, and the case decision; and
- the relationship of the perpetrator to the child victim.

10A N.C.A.C. 70A.0102(b)(3).

Confidentiality of Central Registry data is strictly enforced. A person who releases information from the Central Registry to a person who is not authorized to receive the information, and a person who is not authorized to receive the information but who attempts to access it, commit a Class 3 misdemeanor. G.S. 7B-311(c).

**Practice Note:** The Central Registry relates to children who have been reported and found to be abused, neglected, or dependent or who died as a result of suspected abuse or neglect. It is not a registry of perpetrators. Disclosure of information about the perpetrator, other than his or her relationship to the child, is not authorized.

There are two different statewide lists maintained by DHHS that allow for disclosure of information about a perpetrator: the Responsible Individuals List and the Child Maltreatment Registry. *See* G.S. 7B-311(b); 110-105.5. Unlike these two other lists, there is no procedure for a person to discover or challenge information in the Central Registry.

The Child Maltreatment Registry is a statewide registry of caregivers who have been substantiated for maltreating a child in a child care facility. Effective January 1, 2016, DHHS DCDEE is required to maintain this registry, which is a component of the North Carolina's child care licensing system. The names of the caregivers listed in the Child Maltreatment Registry are available to the public. G.S. 110-105.5. See the Division of Child Development and Early Education Public Request Form for Child Maltreatment Registry, available here.

**Resource:** For more information about the DHHS Division of Social Services policy addressing the Central Registry, see DIV. OF SOC. SERVS., N.C. DEP'T OF HEALTH & HUMAN SERVICES, CHILD WELFARE MANUAL "Appendix 1. CPS Data Collection," available here.

## B. Responsible Individuals List

DHHS also maintains a statewide registry of individuals determined by county departments of social services to be responsible for a child being abused or seriously neglected: the Responsible Individuals List (RIL). G.S. 7B-311(b); *see* G.S. 7B-101(18a) (definition of "responsible individual"); 7B-101(19a) (definition of "serious neglect"). The RIL may be accessed by child caring institutions, child-placing agencies, group homes, and providers of child care, foster care, or adoption services to determine a person's fitness to care for or adopt children. G.S. 7B-311(b). County departments of social services and child-placing agencies are providers of foster care or adoption services and have a right to access information on the RIL.

Placement on the RIL has negative consequences for the individual so named. It impacts the individual's ability to adopt, foster, or care for children and obtain and maintain employment in the child care field. *In re W.B.M.*, 202 N.C. App. 606 (2010). As a result, the court of appeals held that procedural due process requires the individual receive notice and have an opportunity to be heard before being placed on the RIL, with an evidentiary standard of at least preponderance of the evidence. *In re W.B.M.*, 202 N.C. App. 606 (holding the 2005 version of the RIL statutory procedures violated due process and were unconstitutional). The

RIL statutory procedures were revised in 2010 after that court of appeals decision. *See* S.L. 2010-90, further amended by S.L. 2013-129. The RIL contains only the names of individuals for whom the procedures in place on or after July 11, 2010 were available. *See* DHHS Division of Social Services Dear County Directors Letter, CWS-23-10: Responsible Individuals List (RIL) Clearance Procedures (Oct. 15, 2010).

**1. Abuse, serious neglect, responsible individual.** When a DSS investigative assessment determines that a child has been abused or seriously neglected, whenever possible DSS also identifies the person(s) responsible for the child's condition. *See* G.S. 7B-320. Abuse is derived from the definition of "abused juvenile" in G.S. 7B-101(1). However, "serious neglect" is distinguished from "neglected juvenile" through different definitions in the Juvenile Code. "Serious neglect" is defined as "[c]onduct, behavior, or inaction of the juvenile's parent, guardian, custodian, or caretaker that evidences a disregard of consequences of such magnitude that the conduct, behavior, or inaction constitutes an unequivocal danger to the juvenile's health, welfare, or safety, but does not constitute abuse." G.S. 101(19a); *compare with* G.S. 7B-101(15) (definition of "neglected juvenile").

**Practice Note**: Petitions alleging that a child is abused or neglected do not allege "serious neglect." A child's adjudication is as a "neglected juvenile" as defined by G.S. 7B-101(15) and is not based on "serious neglect." Serious neglect relates only to placement on the Responsible Individuals List. *In re J.M.*, 255 N.C. App. 483 (2017) (holding a child's adjudication of "serious neglect" was a misapprehension of the law). See Chapters 2.3.B and 6.3.E for a discussion of neglected juvenile.

A responsible individual is defined as "a parent, guardian, custodian, caretaker, or individual responsible for subjecting a juvenile to human trafficking under G.S. 14-43.11 [human trafficking], 14-43.12 [involuntary servitude], or 14-43.13 [sexual servitude], who abuses or seriously neglects a juvenile." G.S. 7B-101(18a) (effective Oct. 1, 2019, S.L. 2019-33 added an individual responsible for subjecting a juvenile to human trafficking or involuntary or sexual servitude). To place someone on the RIL, DSS must identify the individual who caused the abuse or serious neglect. This showing of culpability is not required for a child to be adjudicated as an abused juvenile. *In re Montgomery*, 311 N.C. 101 (1984). A child may be adjudicated abused without DSS proving or the court finding who is responsible. *See In re L.Z.A.*, 249 N.C. App. 628 (2016) (holding abuse adjudication was supported by findings of unexplained non-accidental injuries to the child while the child was in the parents' sole custody); *In re Y.Y.E.T.*, 205 N.C. App. 120 (2010). A RIL placement will not occur when a child is adjudicated abused but DSS does not know who is responsible. When DSS is able to identify the responsible individual, it must take the necessary steps to place that individual on the RIL. *See* G.S. 7B-320; 7B-323.

**2. Notice to the responsible individual.** Upon identifying a person as a "responsible individual," DSS must deliver a written notice to that individual that

- informs the individual whether DSS determined abuse, serious neglect, or both;
- states DSS has identified the person as a responsible individual;
- summarizes substantial evidence supporting DSS's determination, without identifying the

reporter or collateral contacts;
- informs the individual that unless he or she petitions for judicial review his or her name will be placed on the Responsible Individuals List, and describes DHHS's authority to release information on the list; and
- clearly describes steps the person must take to seek judicial review of DSS's determination, with a copy of a petition for judicial review form provided.

G.S. 7B-320(c), (d).

The notice is to be personally delivered by DSS to the individual in an expeditious manner after the investigative assessment is completed. G.S. 7B-320(a). Prior to October 1, 2019, DSS was required to personally deliver the notice to the alleged responsible individual within five working days of the completion of the investigation assessment. *See* S.L. 2019-33. In *In re Harris*, 828 S.E.2d 559 (N.C. Ct. App. 2019), the court of appeals examined under due process grounds the effect of a lengthy delay on notifying the alleged responsible individual of DSS's intent to place the individual on the RIL. In that case, nearly four years after completion of the investigation assessment, DSS notified the individual that he was alleged to be a responsible individual based upon abuse of a child for whom he was a caretaker. The alleged responsible individual timely filed for a judicial review upon receipt of that notice and successfully argued that he should not be placed on the RIL due to the lengthy delay by DSS in providing the notice, which impacted his ability to prepare a defense. The court of appeals affirmed the trial court's order after concluding that the substantial delay in notifying the alleged responsible individual prejudiced his ability to adequately present a defense in an action that impacts his protected liberty interests.

At times, DSS will be unable to complete personal delivery of the notice to the alleged responsible individual. If personal written notice is not given within fifteen days of the DSS determination that a person is a responsible individual and DSS has made diligent efforts to locate the individual, the director must send the notice to the individual by registered or certified mail, return receipt requested, and addressed to the individual at his or her last known address. G.S. 7B-320(b).

**3. Placement on the RIL.** An individual's name may be placed on the Responsible Individuals List only after one of the following:

- the person is properly notified and fails to file a timely petition for judicial review;
- the person files a petition for judicial review and after a hearing the court determines by a preponderance of the evidence that the person is a responsible individual; or
- the person is criminally convicted as a result of the same incident.

G.S. 7B-311(b); *see* G.S. 7B-323(a), (d); 7B-324(a)(1), (a1).

A director may request an ex parte hearing to place the individual on the RIL when the director cannot show that the individual has received actual notice. The director may place the individual on the RIL when the district court judge determines the director made diligent efforts to find the individual. A finding that the individual is evading service is relevant to the court's determination. G.S. 7B-323(a1).

**4. Right to judicial review.** Within fifteen days of receiving the DSS notice determining the person is a responsible individual, the individual may file a petition for judicial review with the district court in the county where the abuse or serious neglect report arose. G.S. 7B-323(a). However, a person is not entitled a judicial review if he or she

- is convicted criminally as a result of the same incident or
- after proper notice, fails to file a timely petition for judicial review.

G.S. 7B-324; 7B-324(a)(1), (a1).

Regarding the first disqualifier, if the alleged responsible individual filed a petition for judicial review prior to any criminal conviction arising from the same incident, the court must dismiss the petition with prejudice if the individual is criminally convicted prior to the court holding the judicial review hearing. G.S. 7B-324(a1) (effective Oct. 1, 2019, *see* S.L. 2019-33); *see* G.S. 7B-324(b) (authorizing court to grant a stay of the judicial review hearing).

Despite the second disqualifier, in extraordinary circumstances or if conducting a review would serve the interests of justice, the court in its discretion may conduct a hearing on a petition for judicial review that is not timely filed. If the individual's name has already been placed on the RIL and the court reverses the DSS determination, the court must order the person's name expunged from the RIL. G.S. 7B-323(e).

G.S. 7B-323(a) sets forth the contents of and service requirements for the petition for judicial review.

**5. Scheduling the judicial review hearing.** The clerk is required to maintain a separate docket for judicial review proceedings; schedule a hearing within forty-five days of the filing of a petition for judicial review or, if there is no juvenile court within that time, for the next session of juvenile court; and send a notice of hearing to the petitioner and the DSS director. G.S. 7B-323(b).

After receiving the notice from the clerk, the DSS director reviews the information from the investigative assessment. If the director determines there is insufficient evidence to support abuse, serious neglect, or that the person is the responsible individual, he or she prepares a statement reversing the DSS determination to place the person on the RIL. The director's statement is delivered to the alleged responsible individual personally or by first-class mail and provided to the clerk for placement in the court file and cancellation of the judicial review hearing. The clerk notifies the petitioner that the hearing is cancelled. G.S. 7B-323(b1).

If a person who files a petition for judicial review also is named as a respondent in an abuse, neglect, or dependency proceeding or a defendant in a criminal case resulting from the same incident, the court may stay the judicial review proceeding. G.S. 7B-324(b). The court exercises discretion in determining whether to grant a stay. *In re Patron*, 250 N.C. App. 375 (2016) (affirming denial of respondent's request for a stay when there was a pending criminal proceeding arising from the same incident).

The district court's jurisdiction to hear the judicial review is based on the age of the victim of the abuse or serious neglect at the time the incident that initiated the DSS investigative assessment occurred. If the victim turns 18 years old after the incident but before the judicial review is heard, the district court has jurisdiction to decide the action. *In re Patron*, 250 N.C. App. 375.

**6. The hearing.** At the request of a party, the court is required to close the hearing to everyone except the parties, witnesses, and law enforcement investigating the same allegations. DSS has the burden of proving by a preponderance of the evidence that the person identified by DSS is a responsible individual who abused or seriously neglected the child. The rules of evidence in civil cases apply, but the court may admit any evidence that is reliable and relevant, such as child medical evaluation reports and child and family evaluation reports that were relied upon by the DSS director when determining whether abuse or serious neglect occurred, if doing so will best serve the general purposes of the rules of evidence and the interests of justice. G.S. 7B-323(b).

At the hearing, the parties have the right to

- present sworn evidence, law, or rules;
- represent themselves or obtain representation by an attorney at their own expense; and
- subpoena witnesses, cross-examine witnesses, and make closing arguments.

G.S. 7B-323(c).

There is no statutory or constitutional right to a jury trial. *In re Duncan, Jr.*, 822 S.E.2d 467, 472 (N.C. Ct. App. 2018) (stating "DSS's placement of a person on the RIL cannot itself constitute anything akin to an action for defamation, and does not provide the 'responsible individual' with any constitutional right to a trial by jury").

**7. The court order.** The court must enter an order within thirty days of the completion of the hearing. The order must contain findings of fact and conclusions of law. If the court concludes DSS did not prove by a preponderance of the evidence both (i) abuse and/or serious neglect and (ii) that the person is a responsible individual, it must order DSS to not place the person's name on the RIL. If the court concludes DSS did meet its burden, it must order DSS to place the individual's name on the RIL. G.S. 7B-311(b)(2); 7B-323(d); *In re Patron*, 250 N.C. App. 375 (2016).

A party may appeal the court's decision under G.S. 7A-27(b)(2), as a final judgment of a district court in a civil action. G.S. 7B-323(f). It is not an order that is appealed under G.S. 7B-1001.

**8. Confidentiality.** Information on the RIL is confidential and may only be accessed by "authorized persons" designated by the rules of the Social Services Commission for the purpose of determining current or prospective employability or fitness to care for or adopt children. *See* G.S. 7B-311(a), (d); 10A N.C.A.C. 70A.0102(c)–(e) and 70A.0104(b)(1) (definition of "authorized persons"). A person who releases information from the RIL to a person who is not authorized to receive the information, and a person who is not authorized to receive the information but who attempts to access it, commit a Class 3 misdemeanor. G.S. 7B-311(c).

**AOC Forms:**
- AOC-J-131, Petition for Judicial Review Responsible Individuals List (April 2018).
- AOC-J-132, Notice of Hearing Judicial Review Responsible Individuals List (Oct. 2013).

**Resources:**
For more information about the DHHS Division of Social Services policy addressing the Responsible Individuals List, see DIV. OF SOC. SERVS., N.C. DEP'T OF HEALTH & HUMAN SERVICES, CHILD WELFARE MANUAL "Appendix 1. CPS Data Collection," available here.

Sara DePasquale, *What Is the Responsible Individuals List and Why Is Someone on It?*, UNC SCH. OF GOV'T: ON THE CIVIL SIDE BLOG (April 27, 2016).

## 5.3 Starting the Abuse, Neglect, Dependency Court Action

### A. The Petition

The petition alleging abuse, neglect, or dependency is the initial pleading in the court action. G.S. 7B-401. The filing of the petition is the means by which DSS commences an abuse, neglect, or dependency proceeding and by which the court obtains subject matter jurisdiction over the case. G.S. 7B-405. See Chapter 3.1–3.3 for a discussion of subject matter jurisdiction.

**1. Proper petitioner.** Only DSS can file a petition alleging abuse, neglect, or dependency. *See* G.S. 7B-401.1(a); 7B-403(a). See Chapter 3.2.B.1 for a discussion of standing.

**2. Venue.** Where to file the petition alleging abuse, neglect, or dependency involves venue. The petition may be filed in the judicial district where the child resides or is present. G.S. 7B-400. Improper venue can be waived, and even if venue is proper, the court can grant a motion for change of venue for good cause. See Chapter 3.5 (discussing venue in detail).

**3. File with clerk or magistrate.** DSS must file the petition with the clerk of court when that office is open. In an emergency, when a nonsecure custody order (or an order to cease obstruction of or interference with a DSS assessment) is needed and the clerk's office is closed, the magistrate must accept the petition for filing. A petition accepted by the magistrate must be delivered to the clerk's office for processing as soon as that office opens. G.S. 7B-404. Some judicial districts may have local rules or an administrative order issued by the chief district court judge addressing the appropriate procedure for after-hours filing.

The court action commences when DSS files the petition with the clerk when the clerk's office is open or when the magistrate accepts the petition for filing when the clerk's office is closed. G.S. 7B-405.

**4. Substance of petition.** The petition must contain

- the juvenile's name, date of birth, and address (*but see In re A.R.G.*, 361 N.C. 392 (2007) (holding that failure to list the juvenile's address did not deprive the trial court of subject matter jurisdiction));
- the name and last known address of each party as designated in G.S. 7B-401.1; and
- facts sufficient to invoke jurisdiction over the juvenile.

G.S. 7B-402(a).

The petition should name and contain information about both parents, even if one of them has no involvement in the circumstances leading to the filing of the petition or is unknown or missing.

The petition or an attached affidavit must also contain information required by the Uniform Child-Custody Jurisdiction and Enforcement Act (UCCJEA) under G.S. 50A-209, as to the places and person(s) the child has lived with over the past five years and any other court actions concerning custody of the child. However, if a party alleges in an affidavit or pleading that the health, safety, or liberty of a party or child would be jeopardized by the disclosure of identifying information, the information must be sealed and may be disclosed to the other party or to the public only pursuant to a court order after a hearing in which the court considers the health, safety, or liberty of the party or child and determines that the disclosure is in the interest of justice. G.S. 50A-209.

See Chapter 3.2.C.2 (discussing problems with petitions that do not impact subject matter jurisdiction).

---

**AOC Forms:**
- AOC-J-130, Juvenile Petition (Abuse/Neglect/Dependency) (Jan. 2019).
- AOC-CV-609, Affidavit as to Status of Minor Child (March 2019).

---

**5. More than one child.** A petition may contain information on more than one child when the children are from the same home and are before the court for the same reason. G.S. 7B-402(a). The petition must contain a separate file number for each child and the clerk must maintain a file for each child regardless of whether more than one child is named in a petition. See Chapter XII, Rules of Recordkeeping Procedure for the Office of the Clerk of Superior Court in Appendix 4. Separate petitions are preferable for children who live together but have different fathers or mothers and where the facts asserted to support the allegations of abuse, neglect, or dependency differ substantially from one child to another.

**6. Verification essential.** The petition must be signed and verified or the petition will be fatally defective and the court will not have subject matter jurisdiction. G.S. 7B-403(a); *In re T.R.P.*, 360 N.C. 588 (2006). See Chapter 3.2.B.3 (discussing in detail verification of the petition, including who may sign and verify).

**7. DSS dismissal of petition.** The Juvenile Code does not address the voluntary dismissal of a petition by DSS, but the court of appeals has held that the voluntary dismissal of a juvenile petition by DSS is permissible. *In re E.H.*, 227 N.C. App. 525 (2013). The court found that the application of Rule 41(a)(1)(i) of the Rules of Civil Procedure to abuse, neglect, or dependency cases advances the purposes of the Juvenile Code and does not conflict with its provisions. The court reasoned that the legislature has entrusted DSS with the duty to determine whether allegations of abuse, neglect, or dependency are credible and what action to take (subject only to limited review by the prosecutor), and that requiring the GAL or parents to consent to a dismissal would impermissibly shift this responsibility away from DSS. The court also discussed the need for judicial efficiency and conservation of limited social services resources.

**8. Amendment of the petition.** The court in its discretion may allow amendment of the petition. If the court allows an amendment, the court must also direct how the amended petition must be served and how much time a party has to prepare after the amendment. G.S. 7B-800. See Chapter 4.2.C (discussing amendments and supplemental pleadings).

## B. The Summons and Process

The summons is the process in an abuse, neglect, or dependency action. G.S. 7B-401(a). See Chapter 4.3 (discussing civil procedure related to summons) and 4.4 (discussing civil procedure related to service).

**1. Timing.** Immediately after the filing of the petition, the clerk issues the summons. G.S. 7B-406(a). Although the court action commences when a magistrate accepts the petition for filing during an emergency when the clerk's office is closed, the magistrate is not authorized to issue the summons. The clerk should issue the summons when the petition is delivered to the clerk's office when it is open for business. *See* G.S. 7B-404.

**2. Substance of summons.** The summons is a printed AOC form that contains the detailed types of notice required by G.S. 7B-406(a) through (c), including

(a) **Notice of hearing.** The summons directs the respondent to appear for a hearing at the time and place stated in the summons. G.S. 7B-406(a).

(b) **Nature of proceedings.** The summons must include notice of the nature of the proceeding. G.S. 7B-406(b)(1).

(c) **Counsel.** The clerk's appointment of provisional counsel for each respondent parent must be indicated on the summons or an attached notice. G.S. 7B-602(a). In addition, the summons must include notice of the right to counsel and information about how a parent may seek the appointment of counsel prior to a hearing if provisional counsel is not identified. G.S. 7B-406(b)(2).

**(d) Court determinations.** The summons must include notice that if the court determines at the hearing that the allegations of abuse, neglect, or dependency in the petition are true, the court will conduct a dispositional hearing to consider the needs of the juvenile and enter an order designed to meet those needs and the objectives of the state. G.S. 7B-406(b)(3).

**(e) Potential outcomes.** The summons must include notice that the dispositional order or a subsequent order

- may remove the juvenile from the custody of the parent, guardian, or custodian;
- may require that the juvenile receive medical, psychiatric, psychological, or other treatment and that the parent participate in the treatment;
- may require the parent to undergo psychiatric, psychological, or other treatment or counseling for the purpose of remedying the behaviors or conditions that are alleged in the petition or that contributed to the removal of the juvenile from the custody of the parent;
- may order the parent to pay for treatment that is ordered for the juvenile or the parent; and
- may terminate the parent's parental rights after proper notice, a hearing, and a finding that grounds for termination exist.

G.S. 7B-406(b)(4).

**(f) Jurisdiction.** The summons must advise the parent that once served, the court has jurisdiction over the parent and that failure to comply with orders of the court may result in a finding of contempt. G.S. 7B-406(c).

**(g) Petition.** A copy of the petition must be attached to each summons. G.S. 7B-406(a).

**3. Who receives summons.** The summons is issued to each party named in the petition, except the juvenile. G.S. 7B-406(a). The petition should name as respondents those parties designated in G.S. 7B-401.1(b) through (e). Unless a statutory exception applies or a parent is deceased, both parents should be named as respondents. *See* G.S. 7B-401.1(b).

**4. Petition and notice to the child's GAL.** Immediately after a petition alleging abuse or neglect is filed, the clerk must provide a copy of the petition and any notices of hearings to the local guardian ad litem (GAL) office. G.S. 7B-408. The court has discretion to appoint a GAL to the child when only dependency is alleged. G.S. 7B-601(a). If a GAL is appointed for an alleged dependent juvenile, a copy of the petition and notice of hearing should be provided to the GAL. The Juvenile Code does not address the provision of notice for a juvenile who is alleged to be dependent only and who is not appointed a GAL, but the juvenile is a party to the court action. *See* G.S. 7B-401.1(f); 7B-601(a). See Chapter 2.3.C and D (discussing the child as a party and the appointment of a GAL).

**5. Service of petition and summons.** Service of the summons and petition is according to Rule 4 of the Rules of Civil Procedure. Unless waived by the court, service must occur not less than five days prior to the date of the scheduled hearing. G.S. 7B-407. See Chapter 4.4 (discussing details related to service).

---

**AOC Forms:**
- AOC-J-141, Notice of Hearing in Juvenile Proceeding (Abuse/Neglect/Dependency) (Jan. 2017).
- AOC-J-142, Juvenile Summons and Notice of Hearing (Abuse/Neglect/Dependency) (Oct. 2013).
- AOC-J-155, Motion and Order to Show Cause (Parent, Guardian, Custodian or Caretaker in Abuse/Neglect/Dependency Case) (Nov. 2000).

---

## 5.4 Parties, Appointment of Counsel, and Guardians ad Litem

### A. Parties to the Proceeding

Abuse, neglect, or dependency proceedings tend to involve many people, and it is important to sort out who the actual "parties" are and what rights those parties have in the proceedings. Relatives, foster parents, other caregivers, service providers, and law enforcement all can become involved in a case, but the Juvenile Code specifically limits parties in an abuse, neglect, or dependency proceeding to: DSS; the juvenile's parents (with limited exceptions); the juvenile's guardian, custodian, and caretaker (when statutory criteria are met); and the juvenile. G.S. 7B-401.1.

For a discussion of key people involved in an abuse, neglect, or dependency case who are not parties, see Chapter 2.1 and 2.2.

### B. Parents and Other Care Providers

**1. Parent is a party.** The juvenile's parent is a party to the case unless

- the parent's right have been terminated;
- the parent has relinquished the child for adoption, unless the court orders that the parent be made a party; or
- the parent has been convicted of first- or second-degree forcible rape, statutory rape of a child by an adult, or first-degree statutory rape and that criminal act resulted in the conception of the child.

G.S. 7B-401.1; *see* G.S. 14-27.21; 14-27.22; 14-27.23; 14-27.24; *see also* G.S. 7B-908(b)(1).

**2. Guardians, custodians, and caretakers.** Guardians, custodians, and caretakers are parties in certain circumstances.

- At the time the petition is filed, any court-appointed guardian of the person or general guardian of the child is a party to the abuse, neglect, or dependency action. In North Carolina, a guardian of the person for the child is appointed either in an abuse, neglect, or dependency action or in a guardianship proceeding before the clerk of court. Note that the clerk's authority to appoint a guardian of the person or a general guardian for a minor is limited to when the minor has no natural guardian or pursuant to a standby guardianship. G.S. 35A-1221; 35A-1224(a); 35A-1370 through -1382. Any person appointed as the child's guardian in the abuse, neglect, or dependency action pursuant to G.S. 7B-600 automatically becomes a party in that action if the court has found that the guardianship is the child's permanent plan. G.S. 7B-401.1(c).
- The child's custodian at the time a petition is filed is a party to the abuse, neglect, or dependency action. A person who is awarded custody in the abuse, neglect, or dependency proceeding automatically becomes a party in that action if the court has found that the custody arrangement is the child's permanent plan. G.S. 7B-401.1(d).
- A caretaker, as defined in G.S. 7B-101(3), is a party only if the petition includes allegations relating to the caretaker, the caretaker has assumed the status and obligations of a parent, or the court orders that the caretaker be made a party. G.S. 7B-401.1(e). Although a foster parent is included in the definition of caretaker, a foster parent who is providing care to the child after the petition is filed is not a party. G.S. 7B-401.1(e1). A foster parent may seek to intervene as a party if the foster parent meets the criteria set forth at G.S. 7B-401.1(e1).

A guardian, custodian, or caretaker who is a party to the case may be removed as a party if the court finds that the person does not have legal rights that may be affected by the action and that the person's continuation as a party is not necessary to meet the juvenile's needs. G.S. 7B-401.1(g). The court must make both findings prior to removing any guardian, custodian, or caretaker as a party. *See In re J.R.S.*, 813 S.E.2d 283 (N.C. Ct. App. 2018) (reversing and remanding the order removing grandparents who were custodians through a Chapter 50 order when the neglect and dependency action was initiated; noting that due to the Chapter 50 custody order awarding legal and physical custody to grandparents, the district court hearing the juvenile proceeding in its discretion may be prevented from making the first finding required by G.S. 7B-401.1(g)). Additionally, a guardian, custodian, or another DSS with an interest in the proceeding who are not named as parties may seek to intervene in the action pursuant to G.S. 7B-401.1(h). See Chapter 4.7.A for a discussion on intervention.

Definitions of "caretaker", "guardian", and "custodian" are addressed Chapter 2.2.B.9. The rights of the parent are addressed in Chapter 2.4.

### 3. Appointment of respondent's counsel.

**(a) Parent.** When a petition is filed, the clerk must appoint provisional counsel for each parent named in the petition and indicate the appointment on the summons or attached notice. At the first hearing, the court must affirm the appointment of counsel unless the respondent parent: (1) does not appear at the hearing, (2) does not qualify for court-appointed counsel, (3) has retained counsel, or (4) makes a knowing and voluntary waiver of the right to counsel. If the court finds at the first hearing that any of those conditions exist, the court must dismiss the provisional counsel. Even after dismissing provisional counsel, however, the court can consider a parent's eligibility and desire for appointed counsel at any stage in the proceedings. The appointment of provisional counsel must be pursuant to rules adopted by the Office of Indigent Defense Services. G.S. 7B-602(a), (a1).

See Chapter 2.4.D (providing further detail related to appointment of counsel, waiver of counsel, withdrawal of counsel, pro se representation, and ineffective assistance of counsel).

**AOC Form:**
AOC-J-143, Waiver of Parent's Right to Counsel (Oct. 2019).

**(b) Guardian, custodian, caretaker.** The Juvenile Code specifies only that a parent has a right to appointed counsel if indigent and, unlike some other states' statutes, is silent with respect to representation of a guardian, custodian, or caretaker. (*See, e.g.,* Ky. Rev. Stat. Ann. § 620.100(1)(d): "the court may, in the interest of justice, appoint separate counsel for a nonparent who exercises custodial control or supervision of the child, if the person is unable to afford counsel . . . ").

The policy of the North Carolina Office of Indigent Defense Services (IDS) states that IDS will pay for representation of an indigent non-parent respondent, pursuant to G.S. 7A-498.3(a)(1), if the judge concludes the respondent is constitutionally entitled to appointed counsel in an abuse, neglect, or dependency proceeding. The IDS policy refers to the respondent's right to due process and the three-prong balancing test established by the U.S. Supreme Court in *Matthews v. Eldridge*, 424 U.S. 319 (1976).

**Resources:**
N.C. OFFICE OF INDIGENT DEFENSE SERVICES, "Appointment of Counsel for Non-Parent Respondents in Abuse, Neglect, and Dependency Proceedings" (July 2, 2008).

Austine Long, *Non-Parents' Right to Counsel in Abuse, Neglect and Dependency Cases*, UNC SCH. OF GOV'T: ON THE CIVIL SIDE BLOG (Feb. 5, 2016).

**4. Appointment of guardian ad litem for parent.** The Juvenile Code, in G.S. 7B-602, addresses the appointment of a Rule 17 guardian ad litem (GAL) for a respondent parent in an abuse, neglect, or dependency proceeding. *See* N.C. R. CIV. P. 17. The court must appoint a Rule 17 GAL for a respondent parent who is an unemancipated minor. G.S. 7B-602(b). The court may appoint a Rule 17 GAL for a respondent parent who is incompetent. G.S. 7B-602(c). The appointment of a GAL and GAL representation for respondent parents is discussed in Chapter 2.4.F.

**5. Significance of uninvolved, missing, or unknown parents.** Even when allegations of a child's abuse, neglect, or dependency relate primarily or solely to one parent, both parents should be named as respondents in the petition and provisional counsel should be appointed for each known parent. Abuse, neglect, or dependency petitions are not filed "against" parents, and a parent who is not involved, whose whereabouts are unknown, or even whose identity is unknown has rights that may be affected by the proceeding. That parent or their relatives may be important resources for the child. All petitions should include information about both parents' identity, location, and involvement or lack of involvement with the child.

The court is required to address the issue of missing or unidentified parents throughout the abuse, neglect, or dependency proceeding, starting with the hearing on the need for continued nonsecure custody (if applicable) and continuing at the pre-adjudication hearing and initial dispositional hearing. The court must make findings of the efforts to locate and serve any missing parents and may order specific efforts be made to determine the identity and location of any missing parent. G.S. 7B-506(h)(1); 7B-800.1(a)(3); 7B-901(b).

**6. Serving a missing parent.** Service of the summons and petition may be made by publication when a party named in the petition cannot be found by diligent effort. G.S. 7B-407; N.C. R. Civ. P. 4(j1). If a missing parent is believed to be in a foreign county, service may be made pursuant to N.C. R. Civ. P. 4(j3). See Chapter 4.4.B.2 (providing more detail on service by publication) and 4.4.B.3 (discussing service in a foreign country).

**7. Paternity and putative fathers.** The Juvenile Code does not define parent. It also does not address the different statuses of fathers: biological father, legal father, and putative father. When paternity has not been established for the juvenile who is the subject of the abuse, neglect, or dependency proceeding, several different possible fathers may be named in the action.

Although these terms are not defined by the Juvenile Code, for purposes of this Manual, a "legal father" is the man who is legally presumed to be the child's father. In North Carolina, if a mother is married at the time of either the child's conception or birth, or between conception and birth, the child is presumed to be the legitimate child of the marriage. This presumption is rebuttable by clear, cogent, and convincing evidence. *See Eubanks v. Eubanks*, 273 N.C. 189 (1968); *In re Papathanassiou*, 195 N.C. App. 278 (2009); G.S. 49-12.1(b). Based on this presumption, the spouse is the "legal father" or "legal parent." For purposes of this Manual, the term "putative father" refers to the person who is believed to be the father of the child but whose paternity is not a recognized legal presumption and has not been legally established by a court determination. A putative father includes a man who has acknowledged the child, either formally or informally, but has not had his paternity adjudicated by a court.

**(a) Mandatory court inquiry and findings on parent's identity and paternity.** Through various stages in an abuse, neglect or dependency action, the court must inquire into the identity and location of missing parents and make findings of efforts made to identify and locate missing parents. The court must also inquire into whether paternity is an issue and make findings of any efforts that have been taken to establish paternity. The court may order specific efforts be taken to identify a missing parent or to establish paternity when paternity is an issue. G.S. 7B-506(h)(1) (continued nonsecure custody hearing); 7B-800.1(a)(3) (pre-adjudication hearing); 7B-901(b) (initial dispositional hearing).

A known parent and other adult caregivers or relatives may have information about the identity and/or location of a missing parent as well as whether paternity has been established. Parents may also be identified through the child's birth certificate, marriage records, affidavits of parentage, and/or court orders. A parent's identity may also be discovered through the IV-D parent locator service.

The North Carolina Department of Health and Human Services is required to "attempt to locate absent parents for the purpose of establishing paternity of and/or securing support for dependent children. The Department is to serve as a registry for the receipt of information which directly relates to the identity or location of absent parents [and] to assist any governmental agency or department in locating an absent parent . . . ." G.S. 110-139(a). DSS or the court may initiate a request for parent locator services. *See* G.S. 110-139(a); 110-139.1. The state's Child Support Enforcement Program (CSE) can obtain information about parents from the Federal Parent Locator Service and through the State Parent Locator Service. If the child support program has not already undertaken efforts to locate an absent parent in an effort to obtain child support from that parent, a county DSS can request location services when the child is receiving protective or foster care services under Title IV-B or Title IV-E of the Social Security Act. 45 C.F.R. 302.35(d). The locator services can be used to obtain information about the location of a parent or putative father in relation to DSS's efforts to keep a child within a family unit, to terminate parental rights, or to facilitate the child's adoption.

**Resource:** Information about North Carolina Department of Health and Human Services (NC DHHS) policies relating to parent locator services are available in the "Locate" section of the NC DHHS Child Support Services Manual. Specific provisions for DSS to request "locate only" services can be found in the "Locate Overview" section of the Child Support Services Manual.

A birth certificate identifies a parent but does not establish paternity and is not definitive. If a mother is married at the time of either the child's conception or birth, or any time between conception and birth, the name of her spouse must be entered on the birth certificate as the father of the child. G.S. 130A-101(e). There are two exceptions to naming the spouse as the child's parent: (1) paternity has been otherwise established by a court, or (2) the child's mother, the spouse, and the putative father complete an affidavit that complies with G.S. 130A-101(e) and includes results of genetic testing confirming the paternity of the putative father. G.S. 130A-101(e); *see* G.S. 12-3(16) (statutory construction of "husband" and "wife" includes any two individuals who are then lawfully married to one another).

**Practice Note:** Although birth certificates sometimes state "refused" for the father's name, G.S. 130A-101 does not allow for such refusal when the legal presumption of the child's legitimacy applies. Marriage and divorce records for the mother may assist DSS in determining whether there is a legal parent who should be named as a respondent parent in the abuse, neglect, or dependency action.

If a mother is unmarried at all times from the date of the child's conception through and including birth, a father's name can be entered on a birth certificate only if both the mother and putative father complete an affidavit acknowledging paternity pursuant to G.S. 130A-101(f). That statute does not include a presumption of paternity resulting from an executed affidavit of parentage, but it does authorize the use of a certified copy of the affidavit of parentage as evidence in an action involving paternity. G.S. 130A-101(f). Note, a presumption of paternity exists for affidavits of parentage that were executed between October 1, 1993 and December 13, 2005. *See* S.L. 1993-333, sec. 1 and S.L. 2005-389, sec. 4. An affidavit of parentage may also be executed for the purpose of establishing a child support obligation. *See* G.S. 110-132.

**AOC Form:**
AOC-CV-604, Affidavit of Parentage (April 2017).
Note, DHHS also has a form Affidavit of Parentage, but as of the date of this Manual, it was not available online.

North Carolina does not maintain a putative father registry. Instead, a man may complete an "Affidavit of Paternity" and file it with NC DHHS, which maintains the affidavit in a central registry. *See* G.S. 7B-1111(a)(5)a.

**NC DHHS DSS Form:**
DSS-6246, Affidavit of Paternity (Oct. 2007).

**Practice Note:** To file an affidavit of paternity or inquire as to whether one has been filed, contact:
North Carolina Division of Social Services
Adoption Review Team
820 S. Boylan Ave.
2411 Mail Service Center
Raleigh, NC 27699-2411
Telephone: 919-527-6370.

(b) **Determining whether paternity is an issue.** The identification of a parent does not necessarily mean the issue of paternity is resolved. The court determines whether paternity is an issue. Examples of when paternity is an issue include when (1) there is a legal father and a putative father; (2) there is more than one putative father; and (3) there is a putative father whose paternity has not been established through a judicial determination even when there is no dispute about him being the father and/or an affidavit of parentage has been executed.

A court may look to other court proceedings to see if paternity has been established. Those actions include

- a special proceeding before the clerk of superior court to legitimate the child (G.S. 49-10; 49-12.1);
- a civil action to establish paternity pursuant to G.S. 49-14;

- a judicial determination of paternity where paternity is an element or issue in the action that is addressed by the court, such as certain child custody, divorce, child support, or a prior abuse, neglect, or dependency proceeding involving the same child;
- a criminal action for nonsupport where parentage must be proved beyond a reasonable doubt as an element of the crime (G.S. 49-2; 49-7; 14-322); or
- a declaratory judgment (G.S. 1-253).

A court may also look to see if a birth certificate has been amended. A birth certificate may be amended pursuant to G.S. 130A-118(b). If the amendment is based on a judicial determination of parentage, the amended birth certificate would be definitive regarding the child's parentage. Note that the court of appeals has held that in the context of a termination of parental rights proceeding, an amended birth certificate creates a rebuttable presumption that the respondent has established paternity either judicially or by affidavit as required by G.S. 7B-1111(a)(5). *In re J.K.C.*, 218 N.C. App. 22 (2012).

**(c) Establishing paternity in the abuse, neglect, dependency action.** While the Juvenile Code requires the court to address the issue of paternity, it does not explicitly provide a procedure for establishing paternity. Although the Juvenile Code does not set forth a specific procedure, paternity may be established in the abuse, neglect, or dependency proceeding. *See, e.g., In re S.J.T.H.*, 811 S.E.2d 723 (N.C. Ct. App. 2018) (at adjudicatory hearing, both father's paternity and child's status as neglected were adjudicated); *In re A.E.C.*, 239 N.C. App. 36 (2015) (at permanency planning hearing, the court ordered paternity testing); *In re V.B.*, 239 N.C. App. 340 (2015) (paternity established at the adjudicatory hearing).

Statutory provisions relating to paternity that apply to abuse, neglect, or dependency proceedings include

- Blood or genetic marker testing. In any civil action in which the question of paternity arises, on motion of a party the court must order the mother, the child, and the "alleged father-defendant" to submit to one or more blood or genetic marker tests. The court may order the party seeking the test to pay for it. *See* G.S. 8-50.1(b1) (setting out procedures and standards for admissibility of test results). An abuse, neglect, or dependency proceeding is a civil action. *State v. Adams*, 345 N.C. 745 (1997). *See In re J.S.L.*, 218 N.C. App. 610 (2012) (holding trial court lacked discretion to deny motion for paternity testing in a TPR case).
- Presumed father or mother as witness. When an issue of paternity of a child born or conceived during a marriage arises in any civil or criminal proceeding, the presumed father or the mother of such child is competent to give evidence as to any relevant matter regarding the child's paternity, including nonaccess to the present or former spouse, regardless of any privilege which may otherwise apply. G.S. 8-57.2. A court may also hear testimony from a mother and/or putative father when paternity is an issue, even if the mother was not married at any time during the child's conception or birth.
- Physical examination of a party. When the physical condition, including the blood group, of a party or a person in the custody of a party is in controversy, a judge of the

court where the action is pending may order the party or the person in the party's custody to submit to a physical examination. N.C. R. CIV. P. Rule 35.

A court's adjudication of one man's paternity directly affects the rights of another man who is presumed to be the child's father. For example, a legal father has recognized rights to the child (e.g., care of the child; the right to inherit from the child). A judicial determination that another man is the father terminates the legal father's rights to the child. As such, the legal father is a necessary party to the proceeding establishing another man's paternity. *In re Papathanassiou*, 195 N.C. App. 278 (2009). The court should not proceed with a paternity adjudication until all necessary parties are named and the court has personal jurisdiction over them. Otherwise, "[w]hen a necessary party to a claim in an action has not been joined, the portion of an order related to that claim is void. A void judgment is in legal effect no judgment. No rights are acquired or divested by it. It neither binds nor bars any one, and all proceedings founded upon it are worthless." *In re T.R.P.*, 360 N.C. 588, 590 (2006) (citations omitted).

**Resources**:
Issues related to paternity are complicated. For a detailed discussion of relevant topics including identifying fathers; determining whether paternity is an issue; establishing paternity in abuse, neglect, or dependency proceedings; and the impact of establishing paternity in those proceedings, along with worksheets for diligent searches and the application of collateral estoppel, see SARA DEPASQUALE, FATHERS AND PATERNITY: APPLYING THE LAW IN NORTH CAROLINA CHILD WELFARE CASES (UNC School of Government, 2016).

For a shorter discussion, see
- Sara DePasquale, *New Book! Fathers and Paternity: Applying the Law in North Carolina Child Welfare Cases*, UNC SCH. OF GOV'T: ON THE CIVIL SIDE BLOG (June 17, 2016).
- Sara DePasquale, *Legitimation versus Paternity: What's the Difference?*, UNC SCH. OF GOV'T: ON THE CIVIL SIDE BLOG (March 23, 2016).

**8. Same-sex parents.** With the exception of one statute addressing a child born during a marriage as a result of heterologous artificial insemination, North Carolina laws do not address artificial reproductive technology. *See* G.S. 49A-1. They also do not address parentage related to same sex-marriages. As a result, many questions regarding the rights and legally recognized status of a same-sex partner or spouse who is not a child's biological parent remain unanswered.

However, some answers are provided to same-sex spouses. The spouse of a parent of a minor child may adopt that child in a stepparent adoption. G.S. 48-4-101; *see* G.S. 48-1-101(18). That stepparent becomes the child's parent as a result of the adoption. *See* G.S. 48-1-106.

Effective July 12, 2017, the law addressing statutory construction in North Carolina, G.S. 12-3, requires that statutes using the terms "husband and wife", "man and wife", "woman and husband", or other terms suggesting a lawful marriage must be construed to include any two individuals who are then lawfully married to each other. Based on this statutory construction, if the mother was married during the period of the child's conception, birth, or anytime in between, the mother's spouse must be named on the child's birth certificate. *See* G.S. 130A-101(e). Note that although the female spouse of the birth mother will be recognized as the child's legal parent, the marital presumption of legitimacy is rebuttable by clear, cogent, and convincing evidence. *See Eubanks v. Eubanks*, 273 N.C. 189 (1968); *In re Papathanassiou*, 195 N.C. App. 278 (2009); G.S. 49-12.1(b). Additionally, the language in the birth certificate statute does not appear to apply to the husband and his spouse since neither one is a mother who conceives and gives birth to the child.

The one artificial insemination statute in North Carolina refers to a husband and wife, which now must be read to mean two lawfully married persons when determining whether the criteria of that statute are met. *See* G.S. 49A-1; 12-3(16); *see also Pavan v. Smith*, 137 S.Ct. 2075 (2017) (reversing decision of Arkansas Supreme Court; holding the Arkansas state law that applies when a married woman conceives a child by artificial insemination and requires her male spouse to be listed on the child's birth certificate applies to a married woman's female spouse).

In those situations where a same-sex spouse or partner is not recognized as a parent, he or she may be named as a respondent guardian, custodian, or caretaker depending on the circumstances and relationship with the child.

**Resource:** Cheryl Howell, *New Legislation Acknowledges Same-Sex Marriage*, UNC SCH. OF GOV'T: ON THE CIVIL SIDE BLOG (Aug. 8, 2017).

## C. The Child

**1. Child is a party.** The Juvenile Code specifically states that the child who is the subject of an abuse, neglect, or dependency proceeding is a party to the case. G.S. 7B-401.1(f); 7B-601(a). However, the child is not always treated the same as other parties in the action, as explained in Chapter 2.3 and other relevant sections in this Manual.

**2. Appointment of a guardian ad litem under G.S. 7B-601.** In cases alleging abuse or neglect, the court *must* appoint a guardian ad litem (GAL) to represent the child. If the GAL is not an attorney, the court also must appoint an attorney advocate. In cases alleging only dependency, the court *may* appoint a GAL to represent the child. G.S. 7B-601. Neither the Juvenile Code nor case law provides criteria for when GALs are appropriate in dependency cases. Although the GAL appointment is discretionary, when deciding whether to appoint a GAL, the court may want to consider the child's constitutional due process rights and how the child, as a party to the proceeding, receives notice and has a meaningful opportunity to be heard in the action. *See* G.S. 7B-100(1) (one purpose of the Juvenile Code is to provide procedures that protect the constitutional rights of juveniles); 7B-601(a) (an attorney advocate assures protection of the juvenile's legal rights); *see also In re P.T.W.*, 250 N.C. App. 589 (2016) (discussing discretionary GAL appointment for a child in a TPR proceeding when holding no abuse of discretion). If the court determines that a GAL under G.S. 7B-601 is not needed, the court may consider whether a Rule 17 GAL for the child should be appointed instead. *See* N.C. R. CIV. P. 17; G.S. 7B-1002(2).

See Chapter 2.3.C and D for a discussion of the rights of the child, including a GAL appointment under G.S. 7B-601.

**AOC Form:**
AOC-J-207, Order to Appoint or Release Guardian ad Litem and Attorney Advocate (June 2014).

### D. Department of Social Services

The director of the county department of social services is the only permitted petitioner in an abuse, neglect, or dependency case and therefore is always a party to the proceeding. G.S. 7B-401.1(a); *see In re A.P.*, 371 N.C. 14 (2018). DSS remains a party until the court terminates jurisdiction in the case. G.S. 7B-401.1(a). However, the Juvenile Code allows for the petitioning county DSS to be substituted by another county DSS when venue is changed to another county after the child's adjudication. The court also has the option of joining the second county DSS rather than substituting the petitioning DSS when granting a post-adjudication change in venue. G.S. 7B-900.1(c). When a pre-adjudication change of venue is granted, the DSS petitioner remains the same. G.S. 7B-400(c). Regardless of whether the action is pre- or post-adjudication, a DSS that is not the petitioner in the abuse, neglect, or dependency action may also seek to intervene in the proceeding when it has an interest in the case. G.S. 7B-401.1(h). In those actions where a county DSS is either joined as a party because of a post-adjudication change of venue or is permitted to intervene, there will be two county departments that are parties to the action.

See Chapter 3.5.C discussing post-adjudication change of venue.

## 5.5 Purpose and Requirements of Temporary and Nonsecure Custody

### A. Purpose of Temporary and Nonsecure Custody

DSS may determine that to protect the child, immediate removal of the child from the home is necessary.

One of the purposes of the Juvenile Code is "[t]o provide standards for the removal, when necessary, of juveniles from their homes and for the return of juveniles to their homes consistent with preventing the unnecessary or inappropriate separation of juveniles from their parents." G.S. 7B-100(4). Another purpose is "[t]o provide for services for the protection of juveniles by means that respect both the right to family autonomy and the juveniles' needs for safety, continuity, and permanence." G.S. 7B-100(2). The language of the statutes addressing temporary custody and nonsecure custody reflects the purpose of protecting the child while putting requirements and time limitations in place to prevent unnecessary or inappropriate placements.

## B. Temporary Custody

Temporary custody is extraordinary state intervention. It allows the state (through DSS or law enforcement) to take physical custody of a child without notice, a hearing, representation, and a court order. Therefore, the statutory grounds for temporary custody are very narrow. Temporary custody is used only briefly to protect a child while a petition or motion is filed, and a court order for nonsecure custody is sought.

**1. Circumstances for temporary custody.** A child may be taken into custody without a court order by law enforcement or DSS, but only if there are reasonable grounds to believe that the child

- is abused, neglected, or dependent and
- would be injured or could not be taken into custody if it were first necessary to obtain a court order.

G.S. 7B-500(a).

When DSS takes a child into temporary custody, it may arrange for the placement, care, supervision, and transportation of the child. G.S. 7B-500(a). When law enforcement takes a child into temporary custody, it should contact DSS immediately as a mandated reporter. *See* G.S. 7B-301.

**2. Length of temporary custody.** Once the juvenile is taken into temporary custody, he or she cannot be held for more than twelve hours — or for more than twenty-four hours if any of the twelve hours falls on a Saturday, Sunday, or legal holiday — unless a petition or motion for review has been filed *and* an order for nonsecure custody has been issued. G.S. 7B-501(b).

**3. Newborn abandonment ("safe surrender").** Certain individuals (health care providers, law enforcement officers, DSS workers, emergency medical workers) must take into temporary custody an infant under 7 days old if the infant is voluntarily delivered to that individual by the infant's parent who does not express an intent to return for the infant. *Any* adult may take such an infant into temporary custody without a court order in the same circumstances. Those who take custody of the infant must do what is necessary to protect the infant and immediately notify DSS or law enforcement. The person taking temporary custody can ask the parent questions about the parents' identities or medical history, but the parent is not required to give any information and must be informed of this. A person who takes custody of an infant in this circumstance is immune from civil or criminal liability if the person acts in good faith. G.S. 7B-500. This is part of North Carolina's "safe surrender" law, which also gives the parent immunity from criminal prosecution for abandonment of an infant in this way if the infant is unharmed. *See* G.S. 14-322.3; 14-318.2(c); 14-318.4(c). While the parent may have immunity from criminal prosecution, safe surrender does nothing to change the juvenile court process and the parent's involvement in that process. G.S. 7B-500(b)–(e). There is no right to anonymity under North Carolina's safe surrender law.

**Resources:**
Janet Mason, *Legal Abandonment of Newborns: North Carolina's Safe Surrender Law*, 75 POPULAR GOV'T 29 (UNC School of Government, 2009).

DIV. OF SOC. SERVS., N.C. DEP'T OF HEALTH & HUMAN SERVICES, CHILD WELFARE MANUAL "Assessments," available here.

For information on safe surrender laws in the various states, see "Infant Safe Haven Laws" on the Child Welfare Information Gateway, U.S. Department of Health and Human Services website.

**4. Medical professionals.** Medical professionals can seek authorization from the court to retain physical custody of a juvenile suspected of being abused when the medical professional examines the juvenile and certifies in writing that the juvenile must remain for medical treatment or that it is unsafe for the juvenile to return home. The medical professional must then make a report to DSS. G.S. 7B-308. This statute is lengthy, with detailed requirements concerning procedures that are in addition to regular provisions concerning reporting and temporary custody.

**Practice Note:** This provision is rarely used by medical professionals, who are more likely to call DSS or law enforcement than to seek authority to assume temporary custody.

**5. Duties of person with temporary custody.** When a law enforcement officer or DSS worker takes a child into temporary custody under G.S. 7B-500, that person must do the following:

- notify the child's parent, guardian, custodian, or caretaker that the child has been taken into temporary custody and advise that person of their right to be present with the child until a determination is made as to the need for nonsecure custody (failure to comply with this requirement is not grounds for releasing the child);
- release the child to the parent, guardian, custodian, or caretaker if the officer or social worker decides continued custody is unnecessary;
- communicate with appropriate DSS personnel who can determine whether a petition should be filed and, if appropriate, can seek an order for nonsecure custody.

G.S. 7B-501(a).

## C. Nonsecure Custody

After a petition alleging abuse, neglect, or dependency has been filed with the district court, when DSS believes it is not safe for the child to remain in the home pending an adjudicatory hearing on the petition, DSS must obtain a nonsecure custody order to remove the child from his or her parent, guardian, custodian, or caretaker. DSS may seek an order for nonsecure custody even when the child was not initially taken into temporary custody as the grounds for nonsecure custody are substantially broader than those for temporary custody.

> **Practice Note:** The Juvenile Code makes distinctions between secure custody, nonsecure custody, custody, and placement. This section refers to nonsecure custody. "Secure" custody is within a locked facility and is available only in cases of delinquent or undisciplined juveniles. *See* Article 19 of G.S. Chapter 7B. A juvenile who is alleged to be abused, neglected, or dependent may not be placed in secure custody. G.S. 7B-503(a). "Nonsecure" custody does not involve a locked facility or placement and, therefore, is not "secure."

**1. Procedure to obtain the initial nonsecure custody order.**

  (a) **Petition.** A petition alleging abuse, neglect, or dependency must have been filed for the court to have jurisdiction to enter a nonsecure custody order. *See In re Ivey*, 156 N.C. App. 398 (2003) (holding that the trial court erred in ordering DSS to assume nonsecure custody of an infant when a petition had been filed naming only the infant's siblings); *see also In re T.R.P.*, 360 N.C. 588, 593 (2006) (stating that "[a] trial court's subject matter jurisdiction over all stages of a juvenile case is established when the action is initiated with the filing of a properly verified petition."); *cf. In re L.B.*, 181 N.C. App. 174 (2007) (holding that the trial court gained subject matter jurisdiction when a DSS representative signed and verified the petition two days after a nonsecure custody order was filed and one day after the summons was issued).

  (b) **Ex parte and notice.** Nonsecure custody orders usually are requested and granted ex parte, after the petition is filed and before the parents have been served or are appointed counsel. *See* G.S. 7B-502(a). Although the statute allows for an ex parte order, when nonsecure custody is being sought at a time when the court is open for business, DSS must notify by telephone an attorney or employee of the attorney's firm that it will be seeking nonsecure custody when (1) DSS has received written notification that a respondent has an attorney for the juvenile matter or (2) the respondent is represented by an attorney in a juvenile proceeding within the same county for another child of the respondent. This notification requirement does not apply to provisional counsel. G.S. 7B-502(a). The statute does not designate how much advance notice must be given; however, some local rules do.

  (c) **Authority to issue a nonsecure custody order.** Any district court judge can issue a nonsecure custody order. In addition, the chief district court judge may delegate the authority to issue nonsecure custody orders to others by filing with the clerk an administrative order designating those persons to whom authority is delegated. G.S. 7B-502(b). The statute does not limit the chief judge's options with respect to whom he or she may designate. The inherent conflict of interest strongly suggests that it should not be an official or employee of the county DSS. It should, however, be someone who understands the context and the extraordinary nature of nonsecure custody orders. Ultimately, the chief district court judge determines who is authorized to issue such orders. Chief judges generally delegate this authority sparingly, and some do not delegate it at all. Entry of a nonsecure custody order by someone with delegated authority accelerates the timing of the first hearing on the need for continued nonsecure custody. See section 5.6.B, below (relating to timing).

**(d) In person or by telephone.** The nonsecure custody order must be in writing and direct an authorized person to take physical custody of the child. G.S. 7B-504. However, a judge (or a person to whom the chief district court judge has delegated authority) may authorize nonsecure custody by telephone when other means of communication are impractical. G.S. 7B-508. Even if authorized by telephone, the order must be in writing and must include

- the name and title of the person communicating by telephone,
- the signature and title of the official entering the written order pursuant to the telephonic authorization, and
- the hour and date of the telephonic authorization.

G.S. 7B-508.

The role of the magistrate or other official completing the written order does not involve the exercise of discretion. He or she simply records who gave the telephonic authorization for nonsecure custody and when that occurred, then signs the order and indicates his or her title. In some judicial districts the same magistrate or official might be authorized by administrative order to actually make the decision about nonsecure custody when it is not possible to contact a judge. Because telephonic authorization may occur when the court is not open for business, each judicial district or county should have clear procedures for ensuring that the petition and nonsecure custody order is delivered to the clerk's office as soon as the office opens.

**(e) Inquires required under federal laws.**

**The federal Servicemembers Civil Relief Act (SCRA).** The SCRA applies to abuse, neglect, or dependency proceedings. DSS must try to determine whether any respondents are in military service. DSS must file an affidavit (or include in its verified petition) information about a respondents' military status before the court can enter an order, including a nonsecure custody order, against any respondent who has not appeared in the action. *See* 50 U.S.C. 3931. If the respondent is in military service, additional protections under the SCRA apply. See Chapter 13.6 (discussing the SCRA).

**The North Carolina Servicemembers Civil Relief Act (NC SCRA).** Effective October 1, 2019, North Carolina has a state SCRA, enacted by S.L. 2019-161 and codified at Article 4 of G.S. Chapter 127B. The NC SCRA incorporates the rights, benefits, and protections of the federal SCRA but extends those rights to (1) members of the North Carolina National Guard who are serving on active duty and (2) members of other states' National Guard members who are serving on active duty who reside in North Carolina. G.S. 127B-26. The NC SCRA also extends rights and protections to a dependent of a servicemember who is engaged in military service. G.S. 127B-29. See Chapter 13.6 (discussing the SCRA).

**Resources:**
For more information about the new NC SCRA, see Ann Anderson, *SCRA is now North*

*Carolina law and its protections are broader*, UNC SCH. OF GOV'T: ON THE CIVIL SIDE BLOG (Oct. 4, 2019).

For more information about the federal SCRA in abuse, neglect, or dependency proceedings, see Sara DePasquale, *The SCRA and Juvenile Proceedings*, UNC SCH. OF GOV'T: ON THE CIVIL SIDE BLOG (April 29, 2015).

**AOC Form:**
AOC-G-250, Servicemember Civil Relief Act Affidavit (Nov. 2019).

**The Indian Child Welfare Act (ICWA).** ICWA requires that at the commencement of every emergency and child-custody proceeding the court inquire of all the participants whether they know or have reason to know the child is an "Indian child" as defined by ICWA. The participants' responses should be made on the record. If the child is an Indian child or there is reason to know the child is an Indian child, ICWA applies until the court determines the child does not meet the definition of an "Indian child." 25 C.F.R. 23.107; *see* 25 U.S.C. 1903(4) (definition of "Indian child"). See Chapter 13.2 (discussing ICWA).

**(f) The initial nonsecure custody order.** An order for nonsecure custody is directed to a law enforcement officer or "other authorized person" to take physical custody of the child. The order, after making certain findings under G.S. 7B-504, may authorize the officer or authorized person to enter private property to take physical custody of the child. An officer or authorized person receiving a nonsecure custody order may execute it according to its terms without inquiring into its validity and will not incur criminal or civil liability for its service. The officer or authorized person is required to give a copy of the order to the child's parent, guardian, custodian, or caretaker. G.S. 7B-504.

The order includes notice of a hearing. See section 5.6.B.1, below, for the timing of the first hearing on the need for continued nonsecure custody.

**AOC Form:**
AOC-J-150, Order for Nonsecure Custody (Abuse/Neglect/Dependency) (Oct. 2019).

**Practice Note:** Nothing in the statute prevents the child's guardian ad litem (GAL) from seeking a nonsecure custody order. Although unusual, this might occur if DSS files a petition but does not seek nonsecure custody and the GAL believes nonsecure custody is necessary.

**Resource:** For a brief discussion on a child's removal and the implications on constitutional rights, see Sara DePasquale, *Initial Removal of a Child from a Home Because of Suspected Abuse, Neglect, or Dependency, Amended G.S. 7B-504*, UNC SCH. OF GOV'T: ON THE CIVIL SIDE BLOG (June 24, 2015).

**2. Criteria for initial and continued nonsecure custody orders.** A nonsecure custody order may only be made if the criteria in G.S. 7B-503(a) are met.

There must be a reasonable factual basis to believe that matters alleged in the petition are true and that

- the juvenile has been abandoned;
- the juvenile has suffered physical injury, sexual abuse, or serious emotional damage;
- the juvenile is exposed to substantial risk of physical injury or sexual abuse because the parent, guardian, custodian, or caretaker has created the conditions likely to cause injury or abuse or has failed to provide, or is unable to provide, adequate supervision or protection;
- the juvenile needs medical treatment to cure, alleviate, or prevent suffering serious physical harm that may result in death, disfigurement, or substantial impairment of bodily functions, and the parent, guardian, custodian, or caretaker is unable or unwilling to provide or consent to the treatment;
- the parent, guardian, custodian, or caretaker consents to a nonsecure custody order; or
- the juvenile is a runaway and consents to nonsecure custody.

There must also be a reasonable factual basis to believe that there are no other means available to protect the child. In making its decision, the court must first consider whether the child can be released to a parent, relative, guardian, custodian, or other responsible adult.

G.S. 7B-503(a).

**3. Place of nonsecure custody.** Any order for nonsecure custody may direct that the child be placed in nonsecure custody with DSS or an individual designated in the order for temporary residential placement in

- the home of a parent, relative, nonrelative kin, other person with legal custody of the child's sibling, or any other home or facility approved by the court and designated in the order;
- a licensed foster home or home authorized to provide foster care; or
- a facility operated by DSS.

G.S. 7B-505(a).

**(a) Preference for placement with relatives.** The court first must consider whether a relative is willing and able to provide proper care and supervision of the juvenile in a safe home. If the court finds that the relative is willing and able to do this, then the court must order placement of the juvenile with the relative unless the court finds that placement with the relative would be contrary to the juvenile's best interests. G.S. 7B-505(b). *See* G.S. 7B-101(19) (definition of "safe home"); *In re L.L.*, 172 N.C. App. 689 (2005) (analyzing an identical requirement for disposition and determining that the trial court's failure to make a finding that it was contrary to the child's best interest to place her with willing relatives before placing her with foster parents was error), *abrogated in part on other grounds by In re T.H.T.*, 362 N.C. 446 (2008). Placement with a relative who lives in another state must comply with the Interstate Compact on the Placement of Children (ICPC). See Article 38 of the Juvenile Code. For more information on the ICPC, see Chapter 7.4.H.

**(b) Nonrelative kin and other persons with legal custody of the child's sibling.** If the court does not place the juvenile with a relative, the court may consider whether nonrelative kin or a person with legal custody of the child's sibling is willing and able to provide proper care and supervision of the juvenile in a safe home, and order such placement if it finds that it is in the juvenile's best interests. G.S. 7B-505(c). "Nonrelative kin" is an individual having a substantial relationship with the juvenile. If the juvenile is a member of a State-recognized Indian tribe, nonrelative kin includes any member of a state or federally recognized tribe, regardless of whether a substantial relationship exists. G.S. 7B-101(15a).

**(c) Consideration of child's community.** In determining placement, the court must consider whether it is in the child's best interest to remain in his or her community. G.S. 7B-505(d).

Note that under federal education and child welfare laws, DSS is required to consider the child's educational stability and make assurances that the placement takes into account the appropriateness of the child's current educational setting and proximity of the placement to the school the child was enrolled in at the time of the placement (school of origin). DSS must ensure the child remains in the school of origin, unless there is a determination that it is not in the child's best interests to do so. See Chapter 13.7 (discussing the Every Student Succeeds Act and the Fostering Connections to Success and Increasing Adoptions Act).

**(d) ICWA and MEPA Considerations.** In placing a juvenile in nonsecure custody, the court must consider the application of the Indian Child Welfare Act (ICWA) and the Multiethnic Placement Act (MEPA). G.S. 7B-505(d). ICWA establishes specific placement preferences, and MEPA prohibits discrimination in the placement of children on the basis of the child's or foster parent's race, color, or national origin. See Chapter 13.2 and 13.3 (discussing ICWA and MEPA).

**(e) ICPC.** Placement of a juvenile with a person, including relatives, outside of this state must be in accordance with the Interstate Compact on the Placement of Children (ICPC). G.S. 7B-505(d); *see* G.S. 7B-3800. See Chapter 7.4.H (discussing the ICPC).

---

**Practice Note:** When a nonsecure custody order is issued ex parte, usually in an emergency, the court is unlikely to have enough information to fully consider potential relatives and kin, unless DSS has some history with the family and is making specific recommendations. These issues will likely receive greater attention at hearings on the need for continued nonsecure custody.

---

**4. Visitation.** Orders on the need for continued nonsecure custody must address visitation. The provisions of G.S. 7B-905.1 apply, which require the court to provide for visitation that is in the child's best interests and consistent with the child's health and safety and may include no visitation. G.S. 7B-506(g1); *see* G.S. 7B-905.1(a). When the child is in the custody or placement responsibility of DSS, the court may order the director to arrange, facilitate, and supervise a visitation plan approved by the court that establishes the minimum frequency and length of visits and whether the visits shall be supervised. G.S. 7B-905.1(b). See Chapter 7.5 (discussing visitation).

**5. Medical decision-making.** When a child is placed in the nonsecure custody of DSS, the director may arrange for, provide, or consent to the child's routine medical and dental care (including treatment for common pediatric illnesses and injuries that require prompt intervention); emergency medical, surgical, or mental health care or treatment; and testing and evaluations in exigent circumstances. G.S. 7B-505.1(a). However, a DSS may not consent to non-routine and non-emergency medical care for a child in its custody without authorization from the child's parent, guardian, or custodian or a court order that authorizes the director to consent to such care after finding by clear and convincing evidence that the care, treatment or evaluation requested is in the juvenile's best interests. G.S. 7B-505.1(c). DSS's consent for a Child Medical Evaluation requires a court order with findings specified in either G.S. 7B-505.1(b) or (c).

For further discussion on consent to medical treatment for a child in DSS custody, see Chapter 7.4.D.3.

**Resource:** Sara DePasquale, *New Law: Consenting to Medical Treatment for a Child Placed in the Custody of County Department*, UNC SCH. OF GOV'T: COATES' CANONS: NC LOCAL GOVERNMENT LAW BLOG (Nov. 6, 2015).

**NC DHHS DSS Forms:**
- DSS-1812, General Authorization for Treatment and Medication (Feb. 2016).
- DSS-1812ins, General Authorization for Treatment and Medication Instructions (Feb. 2016).
- DSS-5143, Consent/Authorization for Child Medical/Child/Family Evaluation (Jan. 2007).

**6. Violent caregivers.** In cases involving allegations of physical abuse, special rules apply to returning a child to the home in which the alleged abuser lives. When a child is removed from a home due to physical abuse, DSS must thoroughly review the alleged abuser's background. This review must include a criminal history check and a review of any available mental health records. If the review reveals that the alleged abuser has a history of violent behavior against people, DSS must petition the court to order the alleged abuser to submit to a complete mental health evaluation by a licensed psychologist or psychiatrist. If DSS files a petition for a mental health evaluation and requests a nonsecure custody order, the court must rule on the petition for an evaluation before returning the child to a home where the alleged abuser is or has been present. *See* G.S. 7B-302(d1); 7B-503(b).

## 5.6 Nonsecure Custody Hearings

### A. Summary

The initial nonsecure custody order is the mechanism for quickly authorizing placement of the child for up to seven calendar days. Keeping the child in nonsecure custody for a longer period requires a hearing and after that, if the child remains in nonsecure custody pending adjudication, opportunities for further hearings. The first hearing on the need for continued nonsecure custody cannot be waived, although it can be continued for up to ten business days with the parties' consent. In hearings to determine the need for continued nonsecure custody, the court must determine whether the criteria for placing a child in nonsecure custody exist *and* must address a variety of additional issues if the child remains in nonsecure custody. In some judicial districts the first hearing on the need for continued nonsecure custody is preceded by an informal meeting or conference of the parties without the judge. Hearings on the need for continued nonsecure custody may be combined with required pre-adjudication hearings (discussed in section 5.7, below). The hearings are open unless the court orders it closed pursuant to G.S. 7B-801 (see Chapters 6.2.C and 7.2.D).

**B. Timing**

**1. The first hearing on the need for continued nonsecure custody**

**(a) When initial nonsecure custody order entered by judge.** The court must conduct a hearing within seven calendar days of when the juvenile is placed in nonsecure custody. As a result, this hearing is often referred to as the "7-day hearing." This initial hearing may be continued for up to ten business days with the consent of the parents, guardian, custodian, or caretaker and the child's guardian ad litem (if appointed), but the court may require the consent of DSS or other parties or deny a request for a continuance. G.S. 7B-506(a).

**(b) When initial nonsecure custody order entered by authorized designee.** If the initial nonsecure custody order was issued by someone designated by the chief district court judge in an administrative order, the hearing must be conducted on the day of the next regularly scheduled session of court in the city or county where the order was entered, but within seven days in any event. G.S. 7B-506(a).

**2. Second and subsequent hearings.** After the first hearing on the need for continued nonsecure custody and pending the adjudicatory hearing, there must be a second hearing on the need for continued nonsecure custody within seven business days of the first hearing and hearings at least every thirty calendar days thereafter. These hearings may be waived with the consent of the juvenile's parent, guardian, custodian, or caretaker and the child's guardian ad litem (if appointed). G.S. 7B-506(e), (f).

**3. Hearings by party request.** In addition to the required hearings, any party may schedule a hearing on the issue of placement. G.S. 7B-506(g). This request can be made even after a party initially waived subsequent continued nonsecure custody hearings.

**AOC Forms:**
- AOC-J-141, Notice of Hearing in Juvenile Proceeding (Abuse/Neglect/Dependency) (Jan. 2017).
- AOC-J-142, Juvenile Summons and Notice of Hearing (Abuse/Neglect/Dependency) (Oct. 2013).

## C. Jurisdictional Inquiry

Early in the nonsecure custody stage, the court should consider information in the "status of child" affidavit filed with or included in the petition pursuant to G.S. 50A-209 and other information related to where the child is living or has lived; whether a custody order relating to the child has ever been entered in another court; and whether any other action involving the custody of the child is pending in any court. The hearing should proceed only after the court concludes that it has jurisdiction under the UCCJEA. See Chapter 3 related to jurisdiction and 3.3 in particular related to UCCJEA requirements. The court also should consider whether proper service of process has occurred or been waived and, if not, whether appropriate efforts are being made to accomplish service of process. Note that G.S. 7B-800.1, addressing pre-adjudication hearings, which may be combined with a hearing on the need for continued nonsecure custody, requires the court to make inquiries related to service, a verified petition, jurisdiction, and other factors prior to the adjudicatory hearing.

## D. Nature of Hearing: Evidence and Burden of Proof

DSS bears the burden to provide clear and convincing evidence that the juvenile's continued placement in nonsecure custody is necessary. The court is not bound by the usual rules of evidence. However, the court must receive testimony and allow the parties to introduce evidence, to be heard, and to examine witnesses. G.S. 7B-506(b). Evidence should be limited to that which relates to the need for continued nonsecure custody prior to adjudication. This hearing should not be a full hearing on the allegations in the petition unless all parties have consented to proceed with an adjudicatory hearing.

For a full discussion of evidence issues in juvenile proceedings, see Chapter 11.

## E. Findings and Other Issues at the Hearing on the Need for Continued Nonsecure Custody

At hearings on the need for continued nonsecure custody, in addition to addressing the criteria authorizing a child's placement in nonsecure custody, the placement and visitation provisions, and medical consent issues (if any), the court must inquire and make findings about

- the identity and location of any missing parent and efforts that have been made to identify, locate, and serve that parent (the court may order specific efforts to determine the identity and location of a missing parent);
- whether paternity is at issue and, if it is, efforts that have been made to establish paternity (the court may order specific efforts to establish paternity);
- whether there are other juveniles in the home and, if there are, DSS's assessment findings and any actions taken or services provided by DSS to protect those children (even though the court does not have jurisdiction over a child who is not named in a petition, *see In re Ivey*, 156 N.C. App. 398 (2003));
- the efforts made to identify and notify relatives as potential resources for placement and support; and unless the court finds it is contrary to the child's best interests, the court must also order DSS to make diligent efforts to notify relatives and other persons with

legal custody of the child's sibling that the child is in nonsecure custody and of any hearings on the need for continued nonsecure custody; and
- if the juvenile is a member of a State-recognized tribe, whether DSS should be ordered to notify the tribe in order to locate relatives or nonrelative kin for placement.

*See* G.S. 7B-506(h); 7B-505(b). See sections 5.4.B.5–7, above (discussing missing parents and paternity), and Chapters 2.2.B.10–11 and 7.4.C.1 (discussing relatives and nonrelative kin).

Additionally, at the first hearing on the need for continued nonsecure custody, the court should inquire about the child's Indian status as required by ICWA. 25 C.F.R. 23.107. Although the law requires the court to make the inquiry at the commencement of the proceeding, when an ex parte request for nonsecure custody is made, DSS is likely to be the only participant present to ask. The first hearing after the parties have been served and where the parties and other participants are present provides the court the opportunity to conduct a full inquiry regarding the child's Indian status, which will implicate whether the court has subject matter jurisdiction and additional procedures that must be followed under ICWA. See Chapter 13.2 for discussion of ICWA.

When an order continues the placement of a juvenile in DSS custody, the court also must adhere to G.S. 7B-507, which requires that the order

- determine whether DSS made reasonable efforts to prevent or eliminate the need for the juvenile's placement,
- make a finding that the child's continuation in or return to his or her own home would be contrary to the child's best interest, and
- specify that the juvenile's placement and care are the responsibility of DSS and that DSS is to provide or arrange for foster care or another placement of the juvenile unless the court orders a specific placement.

Additionally, the court may order services or other efforts aimed at returning the juvenile to a safe home. G.S. 7B-507(a)(5). See Chapter 7.9 (discussing reasonable efforts).

When the hearing on the need for nonsecure custody is combined with a pre-adjudication hearing pursuant to G.S. 7B-800.1, there are additional factors the court is required to consider, which are detailed in section 5.7.A, below.

## F. Limits on Court's Authority at Nonsecure Custody Stage

After making proper findings, the court may order that the child remain in nonsecure custody or return the child to the parent but may not dismiss the petition for reasons other than a conclusion that the court lacks subject matter jurisdiction. *In re Guarante*, 109 N.C. App. 598 (1993). The court at this stage may not award permanent custody to a parent or any other person; that authority exists only after an adjudication that the child is abused, neglected, or dependent. *In re O.S.*, 175 N.C. App. 745 (2006). The court's authority to direct orders to parents under G.S. 7B-904 also exists only after an adjudication. This limitation does not apply to the court's authority to order visitation restricting a parent's access to the child; a complete mental health evaluation of, and payment by, an alleged abuser; and services or other efforts aimed at returning the juvenile to a safe home. G.S. 7B-506(g1); 7B-507(a)(5).

### G. Requirements for Court Orders

An order for continued nonsecure custody must

- be in writing;
- contain findings of fact, including the evidence relied on in reaching the decision and the purpose of continued custody; and
- be entered, meaning signed and filed with the clerk, within thirty days after the hearing.

G.S. 7B-506(d).

See Chapter 4.9 (relating to court orders). See Checklist 1, Nonsecure Custody, at the end of this Manual.

---

**AOC Form:**
AOC-J-151, Order on Need for Continued Nonsecure Custody (Abuse/Neglect/Dependency) (Oct. 2019).

---

### H. Nonsecure Custody Order Is Not Appealable

Nonsecure custody orders are specifically excluded from the list of appealable orders in G.S. 7B-1001. G.S. 7B-1001(a)(4). *See also In re A.T.*, 191 N.C. App. 372 (2008).

## 5.7 Pre-adjudication Hearings, Conferences, and Mediation

### A. Pre-adjudication Hearing

Before the adjudicatory hearing the court must address specific matters in a pre-adjudication hearing, but this hearing may be combined with a hearing on the need for continued nonsecure custody or any pretrial hearing conducted according to local rules.

Under G.S. 7B-800.1, the court must consider the following:

- retention or release of provisional counsel;
- identification of the parties to the proceeding;
- whether paternity has been established or efforts made to establish paternity, including the identity and location of a missing parent;
- whether relatives, parents, or other persons with legal custody of a sibling of the juvenile have been identified and notified as potential resources for placement or support;
- whether all summons, service of process, and notice requirements have been met;

- whether the petition has been properly verified and invokes jurisdiction;
- any pretrial motions, including motions for appointment of a GAL for a parent, for discovery, to amend the petition, or for a continuance;
- any other issue that can properly be addressed as a preliminary matter.

At the hearing, the parties may enter stipulations in accordance with G.S. 7B-807 or enter a consent order in accordance with G.S. 7B-801. G.S. 7B-800.1(c).

## B. Child Planning Conferences

Some judicial districts have "child planning" or "day-one" conferences in cases in which a child is placed outside the home pending an adjudication hearing. These conferences are held soon after a petition is filed and a nonsecure custody order is issued. The parties and their attorneys, as well as others with an interest in the case, are notified and encouraged to attend. To varying degrees, participants share information, identify issues, explore options, discuss resources, resolve problems, and hear recommendations about or agree on such things as child placement, visitation, health and education services, paternity, and child support. Child planning conferences are not provided for by statute and do not involve the judge. They do not take the place of the required hearings on the need for continued nonsecure custody. However, they may expedite those hearings, and sometimes they provide a less adversarial method of resolving issues that otherwise would be addressed at those hearings. They focus more on communication among the parties than on the resolution of legal issues.

Child planning conferences generally seek to

- facilitate the exchange of information, saving the parties time and effort and ensuring that everyone has the same information;
- expedite the delivery of services by identifying needs and appropriate community resources and contacts;
- aid in the early identification and involvement of relatives when appropriate;
- promote a problem-solving rather than adversarial approach to the resolution of issues;
- minimize court delays by coordinating schedules and addressing potential problems that might cause delay; and
- move the case more quickly toward the next stage, minimizing the time the child spends out of the home or speeding the process toward another permanent placement.

In some judicial districts, local court rules establish procedures for these conferences.

Since 2013, G.S. 7B-800.1 has required pre-adjudication hearings to address many of the same issues addressed in child planning conferences.

**Resources:**
Local rules for judicial districts are available on the North Carolina Administrative Office of the Courts website. Use the search box on the AOC website for the term "local rules."

COURT PROGRAMS DIVISION, N.C. ADMIN. OFFICE OF THE COURTS, CHILD PLANNING CONFERENCES BEST PRACTICES AND PROCEDURES FOR JUVENILE ABUSE, NEGLECT AND DEPENDENCY CASES IN NORTH CAROLINA (May 2009).

### C. Permanency Mediation

G.S. 7B-202, in the Juvenile Code, directs the Administrative Office of the Courts to establish, in stages, a statewide Permanency Mediation Program. Only a few districts have implemented permanency mediation. The purpose of the program is to provide mediation services to resolve issues in cases in which a juvenile is alleged to be abused, neglected, or dependent or in which a petition or motion to terminate parental rights has been filed. The goals of permanency mediation include improving the parties' understanding of juvenile proceedings, clarifying the issues for all participants, enhancing the quality of case plans, and reducing the number of court hearings and the amount of relitigation. While each of the programs operates somewhat differently, the primary goal of permanency mediation is to facilitate the permanent placement of children in a timely manner. Cases identified as appropriate for permanency mediation are typically ordered to mediation by the judge at the first court hearing after a child is removed from the home. In other cases, the child's guardian ad litem, a parent's attorney, or DSS may request permanency mediation. G.S. 7B-202 addresses the participants in mediation, confidentiality and privileges with respect to mediation, and the manner in which agreements reached in mediation should be used by the court.

## Appendix 5-1: Table of Differences for Mandated Reporting under G.S. 7B-301 and G.S. 14-318.6

|  | G.S. 7B-301 | G.S. 14-318.6 |
|---|---|---|
| **Who is obligated to report** | Any person or institution | Any person 18 or older |
| **Who is exempt from reporting** | Attorneys who gain knowledge or suspicion from representation in the abuse, neglect, or dependency case (*See* G.S. 7B-310) | Those with privilege as<br>• Attorneys<br>• Licensed psychologists, associates, and employees<br>• Licensed or certified social workers engaged in private social work services<br>• Licensed professional counselors and associates (renamed to licensed clinical mental health counselors, effective 1/1/2020)<br>• Agents of rape crisis centers and domestic violence programs |
| **Standard** | Cause to suspect | Knows or should have reasonably known |
| **Victim** | Juvenile (under 18 years old, not emancipated, married, or in the U.S. Armed Forces) (*See* G.S. 7B-101(14)) | Juvenile (under 18 years old, not emancipated, married, or in the U.S. Armed Forces). "[T]he age of the juvenile at the time of the abuse or offense governs." |
| **What** | • Abuse,<br>• Neglect, or<br>• Dependency<br>(*See* definitions in G.S. 7B-101(1), (9), (15)) | Has been or is the victim of a<br>• Violent offense,<br>• Sexual offense, or<br>• Misdemeanor child abuse |
| **Report made to** | Department of social services in the county where juvenile resides or is found | Appropriate local law enforcement agency in county were juvenile resides or is found |
| **When** | Unspecified | Immediately |
| **How** | Orally, by telephone, or in writing | Orally or by telephone |
| **Information to include** | • Juvenile's name, address, age, and present | • Juvenile's name, address, age, and present whereabouts (if not at home) |

|  |  |  |  |
|---|---|---|---|
|  |  | • whereabouts (if not at home)<br>• Name/address of juvenile's parent, guardian, custodian, or caretaker<br>• Nature and extent of any injury or condition resulting from the abuse, neglect, or dependency<br>• Names and ages of other juveniles in the home<br>• Any other information that may be helpful to establish need for protective services or court intervention | • Name/address of juvenile's parent, guardian, custodian, or caretaker<br>• Alleged perpetrator's name, age, and address<br>• Location of alleged offense<br>• Nature and extent of any injury or condition resulting from the offense<br>• Names and ages of other juveniles present or in danger<br>• Any other information that may be helpful to establish need for law enforcement involvement |
|  | **Reporter Identity** | • Reporter must give name, address, and telephone number but refusal to do so shall not preclude a DSS assessment<br>• Identity is protected and may only be disclosed under criteria of G.S. 7B-302(a1)(1a) or 7B-303(e) | • Reporter must give name, address, and telephone number<br>• Identity is protected and may only be revealed when meeting criteria for 911 or emergency telephone call disclosure under G.S. 132-1.4(c)(4) |
|  | **Immunity for Reporter** | • From civil or criminal liability when reporter in good faith makes a report, cooperates with DSS assessment, testifies in judicial proceeding resulting from report, or participates in child welfare program<br>• Good faith is presumed (*See* G.S. 7B-309) | From civil or criminal liability when reporter in good faith makes a report, cooperates with law enforcement investigation, or testifies in judicial proceeding |
|  | **Violation** | Knowingly or wantonly fails to report or prevents another person from reporting | Knowingly or willfully fails to report or prevents another person from reporting |
|  | **Penalty** | Class 1 misdemeanor | Class 1 misdemeanor |
|  | **Statute of limitations** | Within 10 years of commission of crime (*See* G.S. 15-1(b)(1) amended by S.L. 2019-245, Part II) | Within 10 years of commission of crime (*See* G.S. 15-1(b)(5) amended by S.L. 2019-245, Part II) |

## Appendix 5-2: Mandated Reporting Flowchart

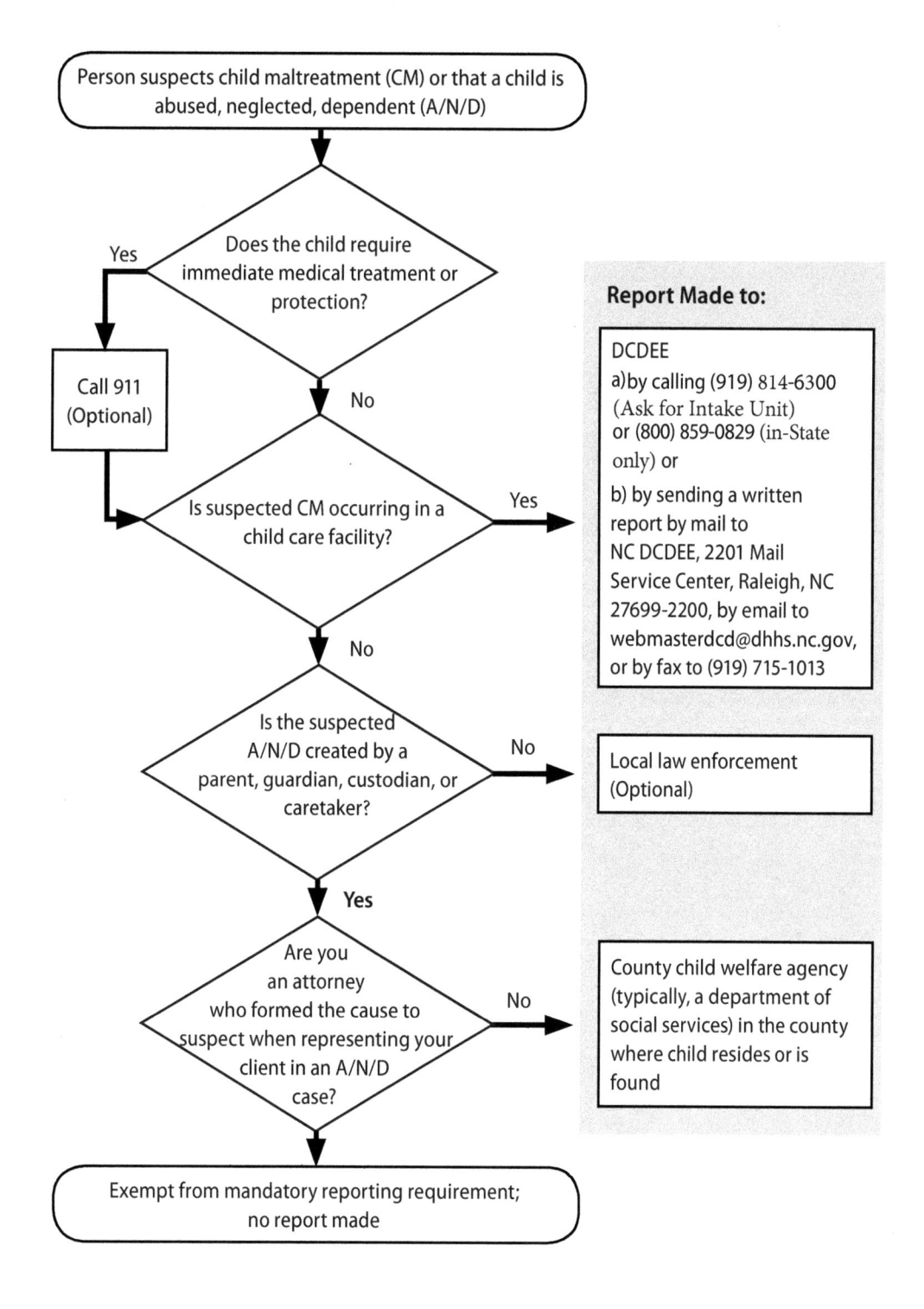

**Person suspects child maltreatment (CM) or that a child is abused, neglected, dependent (A/N/D)**

↓

**Does the child require immediate medical treatment or protection?**
- Yes → Call 911 (Optional)
- No ↓

**Is suspected CM occurring in a child care facility?**
- Yes → Report Made to: DCDEE
  a) by calling (919) 814-6300 (Ask for Intake Unit) or (800) 859-0829 (in-State only) or
  b) by sending a written report by mail to NC DCDEE, 2201 Mail Service Center, Raleigh, NC 27699-2200, by email to webmasterdcd@dhhs.nc.gov, or by fax to (919) 715-1013
- No ↓

**Is the suspected A/N/D created by a parent, guardian, custodian, or caretaker?**
- No → Local law enforcement (Optional)
- Yes ↓

**Are you an attorney who formed the cause to suspect when representing your client in an A/N/D case?**
- No → County child welfare agency (typically, a department of social services) in the county where child resides or is found
- Yes ↓

**Exempt from mandatory reporting requirement; no report made**

# Chapter 6

# Adjudication of Abuse, Neglect, or Dependency

# Chapter 6
# Adjudication of Abuse, Neglect, or Dependency

**6.1 Summary and Purpose of Adjudication   6-2**

**6.2 The Adjudication   6-3**
    A. Procedure for Adjudication
    B. Timing
    C. Public Access to Hearing
    D. Record of Proceedings
    E. Petition Controls Scope of Adjudication

**6.3 Evidence and Proof   6-6**
    A. Child's Status, Standard, and Burden of Proof
    B. Evidentiary Standards
    C. Evidence at Adjudication
        1. Stipulations
        2. Findings of facts must meet statutory definition
        3. Evidence of abuse, neglect, or dependency in other types of hearings
    D. Evidence to Establish Abuse
        1. Definition of abuse
        2. Evidence related to abuse
    E. Evidence to Establish Neglect
        1. Definition of neglect
        2. Evidence related to neglect
    F. Evidence to Establish Dependency
        1. Definition of dependency
        2. Evidence related to dependency

**6.4 Adjudication Order   6-32**
    A. General Requirements
        1. Condition not proved
        2. Condition proved
    B. Findings of Fact and Conclusions of Law

**6.5 Consent Orders   6-33**

**6.6 Consequences of Adjudication   6-34**
    A. Continued Jurisdiction and Authority for Disposition
    B. Impact on Parents and Future Proceedings

## 6.1 Summary and Purpose of Adjudication

"Adjudication" refers both to the hearing at which the court determines the existence or nonexistence of the facts alleged in the petition, and to the court's action when it concludes as a matter of law that a child is an abused, neglected, or dependent juvenile. An adjudication is the court's determination of the child's status as abused, neglected, or dependent. It is not a determination of each individual parent's, guardian's, custodian's, or caretaker's culpability and is not an adjudication of the child's status as to a particular caregiver. *See In re E.X.J.*, 191 N.C. App. 34 (2008), *aff'd per curiam*, 363 N.C. 9 (2009); *In re Q.A.*, 245 N.C. App. 71, 74 (2016) and *In re A.L.T.*, 241 N.C. App. 443, 451 (2015) (both quoting *In re Montgomery*, 311 N.C. 101, 109 (1984)).

The petitioner – DSS – must prove the facts by clear and convincing evidence. The adjudication is a formal trial before a judge, and the rules of evidence apply. A consent order may also be entered, obviating the need for a full formal trial, if the requirements of G.S. 7B-801(b1) are satisfied. Consent orders must include findings of fact that are sufficient to support the conclusion of abuse, neglect, or dependency.

If the alleged facts are proved and the court concludes that they are sufficient to support an adjudication, the child is adjudicated abused, neglected, or dependent. The court may proceed to the dispositional phase of the case to determine the best way to address the family's needs. If the allegations are not proved by clear and convincing evidence, there is no adjudication. The court must dismiss the case with prejudice.

A stated purpose of the Juvenile Code (G.S. Chapter 7B) is to provide hearing procedures that assure fairness and equity and that protect the constitutional rights of juveniles and parents. G.S. 7B-100(1). The Juvenile Code specifically instructs the court to protect the rights of the child and the parent to assure due process at the adjudication hearing. G.S. 7B-802. An important aspect of assuring fairness and protecting rights is appropriately separating the adjudication and disposition phases of the case. While it is permissible for the two phases to take place in one court setting, the purposes, procedures, and standards applicable to the two phases are different.

This Chapter addresses the court's adjudication of the juvenile. All matters that are prerequisites or preliminary to an adjudication hearing are addressed elsewhere in this Manual, such as

- the filing of a proper petition alleging abuse, neglect, dependency (Chapters 5.3.A; 4.2);
- the summons and service of process (Chapters 5.3.B; 4.3; 4.4);
- jurisdiction (Chapter 3);
- appointment of counsel and guardians ad litem for parents (Chapters 2.4.D–F; 5.4.B);
- appointment of guardian ad litem and attorney advocate for child (Chapters 2.3.D; 5.4.C);
- orders for nonsecure custody and hearings on the need for continued nonsecure custody (Chapter 5.5; 5.6);
- discovery and access to information (Chapters 4.6; 14); and
- pre-adjudication hearing and other pretrial conferences (Chapter 5.7).

Dispositional hearings, outcomes, and orders are discussed in Chapter 7.

## 6.2 The Adjudication

### A. Procedure for Adjudication

There are two procedural paths for an abuse, neglect, or dependency adjudication: (1) an adjudicatory hearing and (2) adjudication by consent. *In re R.L.G.,* 816 S.E.2d 914 (N.C. Ct. App. 2018); *In re J.S.C.,* 253 N.C. App. 291 (2017). An adjudicatory hearing involves a judicial process that determines the existence or nonexistence of any of the conditions alleged in the petition. G.S. 7B-802. Allegations in the petition must be proved by clear and convincing evidence. G.S. 7B-805. An adjudication by consent occurs in the absence of an adjudicatory hearing when all the parties have reached an agreement that is sanctioned by the court, and all the criteria of G.S. 7B-801(b1) are satisfied. *See In re R.L.G.,* 816 S.E.2d 914 (N.C. Ct. App. 2018); *In re J.S.C.,* 253 N.C. App. 291. See Section 6.5, below (discussing consent orders).

Most procedural aspects of an adjudication are governed by the Juvenile Code. In some circumstances, a specific Rule of Civil Procedure may apply when it does not conflict with the Juvenile Code and only to the extent that it advances the purposes of the Juvenile Code. *In re E.H.,* 227 N.C. App. 525 (2013); *In re L.O.K.,* 174 N.C. App. 426 (2005). See Chapter 4 (discussing procedures under the Juvenile Code and the applicability of the Rules of Civil Procedure to juvenile cases).

At the adjudication hearing, DSS is the petitioner with the burden of proof. *In re E.H.,* 227 N.C. App. 525. The respondents (parents, guardian, custodian, or caretaker) and the juvenile (usually through a GAL and attorney advocate) have the right to present evidence and cross-examine witnesses. The court may proceed with the hearing even if the respondents are not present. In those circumstances, an adjudication of abuse, neglect, or dependency cannot result from a default judgment or judgment on the pleadings. There must be a hearing where DSS presents evidence and proves its case. *See In re Shaw,* 152 N.C. App. 126 (2002) (default judgment and judgment on the pleadings not available for an adjudication); *see also In re I.D.,* 239 N.C. App. 172 (2015) (originally unpublished Feb. 3, 2015, but subsequently published) (reversing adjudication order and remanding for further proceedings as adjudication amounted to a judgment on the pleadings after the court accepted the verified petition as evidence and DSS put on no evidence at the adjudicatory hearing; immaterial that respondent did not object); *In re K.P.,* 249 N.C. App. 620 (2016) (reversing an adjudication and disposition order and vacating all orders based on the adjudication after determining the adjudication order did not result from a proper adjudicatory hearing or the G.S. 7B-801(b1) requirements for a valid consent adjudication order).

### B. Timing

The adjudication hearing must be held within sixty days from the time the petition is filed unless the court orders that the hearing be continued. G.S. 7B-801(c).

Under G.S. 7B-803, continuances are permissible only

- for good cause, for as long as is reasonably required, to receive
  - additional evidence, reports, or assessments the court has requested or
  - other information needed in the best interests of the juvenile;
- to allow a reasonable time for the parties to conduct expeditious discovery; or
- in extraordinary circumstances when necessary for the proper administration of justice or in the best interests of the juvenile, but resolution of a pending criminal charge against a respondent arising out of the same transaction or occurrence as the juvenile petition may not be the sole extraordinary circumstance.

It is also important to be familiar with any local rules relating to continuances. See Chapter 4.5 (providing more detail and case law related to continuances and the consequences of delay).

Although the Juvenile Code sets forth a sequential hearing process, with an adjudication followed by the initial disposition, review, and permanency planning hearings, it does not prohibit the court from conducting the adjudication, dispositional, and permanency planning hearings on the same day. *In re C.P.*, 812 S.E.2d 188 (N.C. Ct. App. 2018).

### C. Public Access to Hearing

Hearings in abuse, neglect, or dependency cases are open to the public even though the court records are withheld from public inspection. *See* G.S. 7B-801(a); 7B-2901(a). However, the court may determine to close to the public a hearing or part of a hearing. G.S. 7B-801(a), (b). If the juvenile requests that a hearing or part of a hearing be open, it must be open. G.S. 7B-801(b). As long as the juvenile does not request that the hearing or part of the hearing be open, the court considers the circumstances of the case and the following factors when deciding whether to close the hearing or part of the hearing:

- the nature of the allegations in the petition,
- the child's age and maturity,
- the benefit to the child of confidentiality,
- the benefit to the child of an open hearing,
- the extent to which the confidentiality of the juvenile's record pursuant to G.S. 7B-2901 (abuse, neglect, or dependency cases) and 132-1.4(l) (criminal investigations) will be compromised by an open hearing, and
- any other relevant factor.

G.S. 7B-801(a).

Even if a hearing is open, electronic media and still photography coverage of juvenile proceedings is prohibited by Rule 15 of the General Rules of Practice for the Superior and District Courts Supplemental to the Rules of Civil Procedure. Local rules should also be consulted on this issue.

## D. Record of Proceedings

The hearing must be recorded by stenographic notes or electronic or mechanical means. G.S. 7B-806. Audio recording is the means typically used by courts. Recordings of abuse, neglect, or dependency court hearings must be reduced to writing only when a timely notice of appeal has been filed. G.S. 7B-806; 7B-2901(a). Recordings may be erased or destroyed upon written court order after the time for appeal has expired with no appeal having been filed or in accordance with the records retention schedule approved by the director of the Administrative Office of the Courts and the Department of Natural and Cultural Resources. G.S. 7B-2901(a); *see* G.S. 121-5(c). Note that the records retention policies may require that the recordings, which are considered part of the juvenile file maintained by the clerk, be kept longer.

Appellate cases have indicated that gaps in a recording or the accidental destruction of the tape recording is reversible error only if it results in prejudice. *See In re L.B.*, 184 N.C. App. 442 (2007) and cases cited therein. The fact that the recording is of poor quality or inadequate will matter only if the appellant shows specific error (as opposed to probable error) in the recording and that the appellant was prejudiced as a result of the recording problems. *See, e.g., In re L.O.K.*, 174 N.C. App. 426 (2005); *In re Howell*, 161 N.C. App. 650 (2003); *In re Bradshaw*, 160 N.C. App. 677 (2003).

Problems with the recording of a hearing present issues to be dealt with in settling the record on appeal pursuant to Rule 9 of the Rules of Appellate Procedure. When an adequate verbatim transcript is unavailable, there may be ways to reconstruct the testimony, and there is an expectation that an appellant will do everything possible to reconstruct the transcript. *See In re L.B.*, 184 N.C. App. 442 (2007) (rejecting respondent's contention that she was denied due process where electronic recordings were accidentally destroyed, finding that respondent did not do all that she could to reconstruct the transcript and did not show prejudice). For a discussion of appeals, see Chapter 12.

## E. Petition Controls Scope of Adjudication

The court determines whether the conditions alleged in the petition exist. G.S. 7B-802. The conditions – a juvenile's abuse, neglect, or dependency as each term is statutorily defined – are the basis for the petition. *See In re M.G.*, 363 N.C. 570 (2009) (deciding, under former language of G.S. 7B-800, whether the amended petition changed the nature of the conditions alleged, specifically the condition of abuse and looked to all six [now eight] criteria in the definition of abuse).

In conducting the adjudication hearing, the court is required to protect the rights of the juvenile and the parent to assure due process. G.S. 7B-802. The court may consider only matters relating to the conditions alleged in the petition. *See* G.S. 7B-802; 7B-805; 7B-807(a) (referencing matters alleged in petition in relation to adjudication). *See also In re D.C.*, 183 N.C. App. 344 (2007) (holding that it was error for court to allow DSS to proceed on a theory of neglect and to adjudicate neglect when the petition alleged only dependency and the factual allegations did not put respondent on notice as to neglect). A petition is adequate when the facts are sufficient to put the respondent on notice of an alleged condition. *In re K.B.*, 253 N.C. App. 423, 427 (2017) (petition alleging only that child was abused and neglected put respondent on notice that dependency would be at issue when (1) factual allegations attached to the petition encompassed language from the statutory definition of dependency by asserting that respondent "failed to provide proper supervision" and "was unable to provide an alternative placement resource for the child," and (2) an order entering stipulations for adjudication stated in the first sentence that the petition alleged abuse, neglect, and dependency); *In re L.T.R.*, 181 N.C. App. 376 (2007) (rejecting the stepfather's claim that the petition did not put him on notice that the child's bathing routine would be at issue because an attachment to the petition addressed an injury occurring during bathing and the stepfather did not object to evidence of child's bathing routine when it was offered at trial).

Generally, events that occur after the filing of the petition are not to be considered at adjudication because the issue at adjudication is whether the facts alleged in the petition are true. *See In re A.B.*, 179 N.C. App. 605, 609 (2006) ("post-petition evidence is admissible for consideration of the child's best interests in the dispositional hearing, but not an adjudication of neglect"). See also section 6.3.B, below (explaining exception and the separation of evidence for adjudication and disposition).

**Practice Notes:** If after a petition has been filed, DSS learns of additional incidents that were not included in the petition, DSS will need to seek permission of the court to amend the petition under G.S. 7B-800 to include a new condition and/or additional facts. The amendment will put the respondents on notice of the new allegations and/or conditions DSS seeks to prove. If DSS is unable to amend its petition, a second petition alleging the newly discovered incidents may need to be filed.

Regarding consent orders, when parties are negotiating to resolve a case by consent, they should exercise caution to avoid stipulations or agreements that do not accurately reflect the facts of the case or conditions in the petition. For example, if a petition alleges only neglect and the factual allegations relate only to neglect, a consent order adjudicating dependency is improper. Findings and conclusions in an order must be directly related to what is alleged in the petition and what the facts reflect. While parties may view amendment of a petition as a way to address the difference between what is alleged in the petition and what the parties want to agree to, the petition can be amended only with the court's approval. G.S. 7B-800. See Chapter 4.2.C (relating to amendments) and section 6.5, below (relating to consent orders).

## 6.3 Evidence and Proof

This section addresses evidentiary standards, burden of proof, and case law related to the sufficiency of evidence and findings in abuse, neglect, or dependency cases. Additional evidence topics such as hearsay, experts, child witnesses, judicial notice, and other matters related to the admissibility of evidence are addressed in Chapter 11.

## A. Child's Status, Standard, and Burden of Proof

The allegations of the petition must be proved by clear and convincing evidence. G.S. 7B-805; *In re J.A.M.*, 822 S.E.2d 693 (N.C. S.Ct. 2019). Clear and convincing evidence is "stricter than a preponderance of the evidence, but less stringent than proof beyond a reasonable doubt and requires evidence which should fully convince." *In re H.N.D.*, 827 S.E.2d 329, 332 (N.C. Ct. App. 2019) (quoting *In re Mills*, 152 N.C. App. 1, 13 (2002)). DSS is the petitioner and has the burden of proof. *In re E.H.*, 227 N.C. App. 525 (2013); *see In re V.B.*, 239 N.C. App. 340 (2015).

The determination of whether a child is abused, neglected, or dependent is about the circumstances and conditions of the child, not the fault or culpability of the parent, guardian, custodian, or caretaker. *See In re Montgomery*, 311 N.C. 101 (1984); *see also In re Q.A.*, 245 N.C. App. 71, 74 (2016) and *In re A.L.T.*, 241 N.C. App. 443, 451 (2015) (both quoting *In re Montgomery*, 311 N.C. at 109). At adjudication, "the trial court is not required to determine the culpability of each parent as to the children." *In re E.X.J.*, 191 N.C. App. 34, 45 (2008), *aff'd per curiam*, 363 N.C. 9 (2009); *In re J.S.*, 182 N.C. App. 79 (2007). A child may be adjudicated as abused or neglected because of the circumstances created by one respondent only. *See In re A.L.T.*, 241 N.C. App. 443 (2015) (affirming adjudication of neglect based on an injurious environment related to findings about circumstances created by respondent father and holding the lack of findings in the adjudication order about the respondent mother's culpability in contributing to the child's neglect was immaterial). A child may also be adjudicated without there being a finding as to which respondent is culpable for the abuse or neglect. *See In re Y.Y.E.T.*, 205 N.C. App. 120 (2010) (finding that both respondent parents were jointly and individually responsible for their child's injuries where infant suffered non-accidental injuries while in the care of both parents, but a perpetrator could not be identified); *In re R.S.*, 254 N.C. App. 678 (2017) (affirming an adjudication of abuse that found both respondents, who were the sole caretakers of a pre-mobile infant, jointly and individually responsible for the child's serious and unexplained injuries); *In re L.Z.A.*, 249 N.C. App. 628, 638 (2016) (affirming adjudication of abuse and neglect of pre-mobile child with unexplained non-accidental injuries occurring while parents were the child's sole caretakers; trial court noting at disposition its "pause and concern as there has not been any identified perpetrator").

Note that at disposition, identifying the "offending parent" may be an issue for the court in determining whether reasonable efforts for reunification should cease and/or whether reunification is possible and in the child's best interest. *See In re Y.Y.E.T.*, 205 N.C. App. 120, 128 (at disposition, the court ordered parental capacity evaluations with the hope that they would identify who caused the child's injuries and why, which would allow the court to "determine whether reunification could occur with a non-offending parent or if issues could be rectified with an offending parent so that the child could be returned to her home"); *see also In re D.A.*, 811 S.E.2d 729, 733 (N.C. Ct. App. 2018) (vacating and remanding permanency planning order awarding custody to foster parents; stating "the court's findings are unclear of which parent or parents the court assigned responsibility" for the child's unexplained injuries, and "the trial court's findings do not explain how Respondent-father was culpable for [child's] injuries, unfit, or otherwise acted inconsistently with his constitutionally protected status as a parent"). Identification of the offending parent, guardian, custodian, or caretaker is also required for placement on the "Responsible Individuals List" (RIL). See Chapter 5.2.B (discussing the RIL).

In two fairly recent published opinions, the court of appeals has also addressed a child's behaviors and a parent's response to those behaviors and has held the child's behaviors are not the determinative factor in deciding whether the child is abused or neglected. *In re F.C.D.*, 244 N.C. App. 243 (2015) (abuse adjudication affirmed; abuse definition regarding use of cruel or grossly inappropriate procedures to correct a child's behavior does not examine the child's behavior that the procedures and devices were meant to correct); *In re K.G.*, 817 S.E.2d 790, 792 (N.C. Ct. App. 2018) (reversing dependency adjudication; the court is not to look "to the juvenile's willful acts to determine a parent's ability to care for the [child]").

**Resource:** See Sara DePasquale, *When Does Delinquency Result in Abuse, Neglect, or Dependency?*, UNC SCH. OF GOV'T: ON THE CIVIL SIDE BLOG (May 28, 2019).

## B. Evidentiary Standards

The rules of evidence in civil cases apply to adjudication hearings. G.S. 7B-804. In reaching an adjudication decision, the court considers only evidence that is relevant to a determination of the existence or nonexistence of the facts and conditions alleged in the petition. *See* G.S. 7B-802; 7B-807(a). Post-petition evidence should not be considered at the adjudication hearing. *In re A.B.*, 179 N.C. App. 605, 609 (2006) (stating "[p]ost-petition evidence is admissible for consideration of the child's best interest in the dispositional hearing, but not an adjudication of neglect"); *In re J.R.*, 243 N.C. App. 309, 315 (2015) (relying on *In re A.B.* when stating "[t]he fact that respondent-mother had just ten more days to stay at the Salvation Army at the time WCHS filed its petition does not alter our conclusion" that neglect was not proved).

The court of appeals has recognized limited exceptions to the prohibition of considering post-petition evidence at the adjudication. Evidence of a "fixed and ongoing circumstance" that is not a "discrete event or one-time occurrence" may be considered. *In re V.B.*, 239 N.C. App. 340, 344 (2015). In the case of *In re V.B.*, the trial court properly considered evidence that paternity had been established before the adjudication hearing but after the petition alleging dependency (in part based on the respondent father's failure to establish paternity) was filed because paternity was a fixed and ongoing circumstance that was extremely relevant to determining whether the child was dependent.

In cases where the child had been placed with an appropriate alternative caregiver prior to DSS involvement and a petition is filed alleging neglect, the court of appeals has treated these cases like those termination of parental rights cases that allege neglect when the child has not lived with the parent for a substantial period of time prior to the filing of the petition. See Chapter 9.11.A.4 (discussing neglect based on past neglect and likelihood of repetition of neglect). In these types of cases, the trial court looks at the past conditions and the probability of the repetition of neglect that poses a risk of harm to the child. The determinative factors are the child's best interests and "the fitness of the parent to care for the child *at the time of the [adjudication] proceeding*." *In re K.J.D.*, 203 N.C. App. 653, 660 (2010) (emphasis in original) (citations omitted) (affirming adjudication of neglect; mother has not corrected the conditions that led to her placing the child with maternal grandmother); *In re H.L.*, 807 S.E.2d 685 (N.C. Ct. App. 2017) (affirming adjudication of neglect; child was placed with her adult sibling and parents did not correct conditions that required the child's safety placement; parents could not provide proper care); *In re C.C.*, 817 S.E.2d 894 (N.C. Ct. App. 2018) (affirming neglect adjudication; conditions leading to child's placement outside of her home were not corrected at the time of the adjudication hearing); *In re F.S.*, 835 S.E.2d 465 (N.C. Ct. App. 2019) (reversing neglect adjudication; no clear and convincing evidence of current circumstances or future probability of risk of harm to child if immediately returned to mother who had been engaging in services); *In re B.P.* 809 S.E.2d 914, 920 (N.C. Ct. App. 2018) (quoting *In re K.J.D.*; vacating neglect adjudication; there were no findings of risk of harm).

Ordinarily, an adjudication hearing is conducted and the court makes findings and conclusions related to adjudication before proceeding to a disposition hearing. Proceeding in this manner helps to ensure that the appropriate evidentiary standards are applied to the adjudication and disposition phases of the case – the standard at adjudication is clear, cogent and convincing evidence, and at disposition, it is the best interests of the child and placement is discretionary. *In re O.W.*, 164 N.C. App. 699 (2004). However, the Juvenile Code does not require two separate hearings and the appellate courts have held that it is not error for the trial court to consolidate the adjudication and disposition hearings if proper evidentiary standards and rules are applied. *In re O.W.*, 164 N.C. App. 699. If the hearings are consolidated, evidence that relates to facts occurring after the date of the petition (absent a recognized exception), or evidence relating to the needs and interests of the child or parents but not relevant to proving allegations of abuse, neglect, or dependency, may be considered only for the purpose of making dispositional determinations. Predisposition reports may not be submitted to or considered by the court until after adjudication. G.S. 7B-808(a).

Where failure to apply the appropriate evidentiary standards and rules to the separate phases of the case is asserted as error on appeal, appellate courts have refused to find error absent a showing that evidence was improperly considered. *See In re O.W.*, 164 N.C. App. 699. In a nonjury trial, if incompetent evidence is admitted and there is no showing that the judge acted on it, the trial court is presumed to have disregarded it. *See Powers v. Powers*, 130 N.C. App. 37 (1998) (presuming that the judge considered evidence related to post-petition occurrences, which had come in prior to the adjudication determination, only for dispositional purposes); *In re A.L.T.*, 241 N.C. App. 443 (2015) (trial court presumed to have disregarded hearsay statements at neglect adjudication hearing regarding father's inappropriate touching of child when trial court made no findings as to the hearsay evidence in its adjudication order and dismissed sexual abuse allegation against father; trial court was authorized to consider the hearsay evidence at dispositional pursuant to G.S. 7B-901(a)).

## C. Evidence at Adjudication

**1. Stipulations.** Stipulations by a party may constitute evidence at adjudication that the court considers when making its conclusion of law. *See* G.S. 7B-807; *In re R.L.G.*, 816 S.E.2d 914

(N.C. Ct. App. 2018) (pursuant to G.S. 7B-807, factual stipulations may be used in support of an adjudication); *In re L.G.I.*, 227 N.C. App. 512 (2013) (affirming neglect adjudication after reviewing facts which included mother's stipulation to using illegal drugs during pregnancy and child testing positive for morphine at birth and additional evidence of those facts contained in admitted medical records and a court summary).

The Juvenile Code sets forth a specific procedure for how the court accepts stipulated adjudicatory facts. A record of specific stipulated adjudicatory facts must be made by either

- submitting to the court written stipulated facts that are signed by each party stipulating to them or
- reading the stipulated facts into the record, followed by an oral statement of agreement by each party stipulating to them.

G.S. 7B-807(a).

Parties stipulate to facts, not questions of law. *See* G.S. 7B-807(a); *In re R.L.G.*, 816 S.E.2d 914 (N.C. Ct. App. 2018) (determination of whether a juvenile is neglected is a conclusion of law; mother's "admission" that child was neglected was ineffective as support for an adjudication of neglect); *In re A.K.D.*, 227 N.C. App. 58 (2013) (holding that the parties' stipulation that the TPR ground of willful abandonment existed was an invalid stipulation to a conclusion of law). The court of appeals has stated "stipulations as to questions of law are generally held invalid and ineffective, and not binding upon the courts, either trial or appellate." *In re A.K.D.*, 227 N.C. App. at 60 (quoting *State v. Prush*, 185 N.C. App. 472, 480 (2007)).

Stipulations are binding admissions to the court, "preventing the party who agreed to the stipulation from introducing evidence to dispute it and relieving the other party of the necessity of producing evidence to establish" what is stipulated to. *In re A.K.D.*, 227 N.C. App. at 60 (quoting *Thomas v. Poole*, 54 N.C. App. 239, 241 (1981)). Facts stipulated to by a party are presumed to be supported by competent evidence and are binding on appeal. *In re G.T.*, 250 N.C. App. 50 (2016), *aff'd per curiam*, 370 N.C. 387 (2017). When construing a stipulation, the court must attempt to effectuate the intention of the stipulating party as to what facts are being stipulated to so as to avoid giving the stipulation the effect of admitting a fact the party intends to contest. *In re A.K.D.*, 227 N.C. App. 58; *In re I.S.*, 170 N.C. App. 78 (2005).

**2. Findings of facts must meet statutory definition.** A court's determination that a child is an abused, neglected, or dependent juvenile is a conclusion of law. At adjudication, the issue is whether the petitioner has presented clear and convincing evidence to support findings of fact from which the court can conclude that the child is abused, neglected, or dependent as alleged in the petition. However, it is not unusual for courts to refer to "evidence of abuse, neglect, or dependency" as shorthand for the same thing. The facts alleged in the petition and the evidence introduced to establish those facts must relate to the statutory meaning of the alleged status—abused, neglected, or dependent, as defined in G.S. 7B-101(1), (15), or (9). The statutory definitions are especially important given that they do not necessarily conform to common perceptions of what constitutes abuse, neglect, or dependency. See Chapter 2.3.B. (discussing the statutory definitions and case law interpreting them).

**3. Evidence of abuse, neglect, or dependency in other types of hearings.** Abuse, neglect, or dependency are, or are part of, some grounds for termination of parental rights (TPR), so case law addressing evidence to prove abuse, neglect, or dependency sometimes arises from TPR proceedings. However, in the TPR context the court may consider factors that differ from those it considers in an abuse, neglect, or dependency adjudication hearing because the issue in a TPR case is the conduct of the parent while the issue in an underlying adjudication is the condition or status of the child. As a result, some case law concerning evidence to prove abuse, neglect, or dependency as grounds for a TPR may not be directly applicable to abuse, neglect, or dependency adjudications. Some TPR cases do provide guidance regarding whether circumstances meet the definition of abuse or neglect since the definitions are the same in both types of proceedings. *See In re K.J.D.*, 203 N.C. App. 653 (2010) (stating that it is appropriate in examining an adjudication of neglect to look to TPR cases addressing whether circumstances meet the definition of neglect since the definition of neglect is the same in both types of proceedings). See Chapter 9.11.A (discussing abuse and neglect grounds for TPR and cases considering those grounds).

## D. Evidence to Establish Abuse

**1. Definition of abuse.** The Juvenile Code defines an abused juvenile as any juvenile less than 18 years of age

- who is found to be a minor victim of human trafficking under G.S. 14-43.15 or
- whose parent, guardian, custodian, or caretaker
    - inflicts or allows to be inflicted on the juvenile a serious physical injury by other than accidental means;
    - creates or allows to be created a substantial risk of serious physical injury to the juvenile by other than accidental means;
    - uses or allows to be used on the juvenile cruel or grossly inappropriate procedures or devices to modify behavior;
    - commits, permits, or encourages the commission of a violation of laws involving sex and other crimes (the statute lists specific laws) by, with, or upon the juvenile;
    - commits or allows to be committed against the juvenile an offense involving human trafficking, involuntary servitude, or sexual servitude;
    - creates or allows to be created serious emotional damage to the juvenile (serious emotional damage is evidenced by a juvenile's severe anxiety, depression, withdrawal, or aggressive behavior toward himself, herself, or others); or
    - encourages, directs, or approves of delinquent acts involving moral turpitude committed by the juvenile.

G.S. 7B-101(1). See Chapter 2.3.B (discussing the definition of abuse and cases interpreting it).

**2. Evidence related to abuse.** Case law related to evidence for an adjudication of abuse is relatively limited, as compared to case law related to neglect. Since the definition of abuse specifies serious physical injury and grossly inappropriate procedures or devices to modify behavior, circumstances involving child maltreatment more often meet the definition of neglect, in the form of improper care, than abuse. Where a child suffers physical injuries such as bone fractures or brain trauma there may be little dispute about whether the injuries actually occurred or are serious enough to come within the definition of abuse if the circumstances are created by a parent, guardian, custodian, or caretaker. Other situations are less clear regarding what constitutes abuse. Some common issues related to abuse have been discussed in appellate cases.

**(a) Corporal punishment or discipline.** The definition of abuse does not explicitly reference corporal punishment or discipline. If an abuse allegation is based on the inappropriate or excessive use of such discipline by a parent, guardian, custodian, or caretaker, that discipline must satisfy one of the statutory criteria of the abuse definition and be proved by clear and convincing evidence.

**Serious physical injury inflicted by non-accidental means: G.S. 7B-101(1)(ii)a.** Appellate decisions examining the type of injuries sustained from corporal punishment have varied in determining what constitutes abuse. The child's age is taken into consideration. In one case, the court of appeals found that temporary bruising or temporary marks resulting from a spanking were insufficient to rise to the level of "serious injury" on a 13-year-old child. *In re C.B.*, 180 N.C. App. 221 (2006), *aff'd per curiam*, 361 N.C. 345 (2007). However, serious injury constituting abuse was found to have occurred where an almost 4-year-old child was hit with a brush, which left a dark, six-inch bruise on his thigh that lasted well over a week and caused the child to still experience sufficient discomfort to complain of pain several days later, and a doctor testified that it would have taken considerable force to cause such a bruise. *In re L.T.R.*, 181 N.C. App. 376 (2007). The court of appeals noted in *In re L.T.R.* that neither the statute nor case law requires that the injured child receive immediate medical attention to sustain a determination that the injury is serious.

Some cases involving an assessment of injuries resulting from physical discipline are examined in the context of neglect allegations, as opposed to abuse. Because neglect does not require a finding of serious physical injury or cruelty, the analysis is different, making it difficult to compare corporal punishment cases alleged as neglect versus those alleged as abuse. See section 6.3.E.2(f), below (discussing lack of proper discipline as neglect).

**Use of cruel or grossly inappropriate procedures or devices to modify behavior: G.S. 7B-101(1)(ii)c.** This definition of abuse addresses discipline without explicitly referring to the term. The first published appellate opinion that discussed this ground was in 2014. In the case *In re H.H.*, 237 N.C. App. 431 (2014), *overruled by implication in part on other grounds by In re B.O.A.*, 831 S.E.2d 305 (N.C. S.Ct. 2019), the petition alleged abuse under this prong of the abuse definition due to the mother's physical discipline of her 8-year-old son. The court of appeals determined that sufficient findings were made to support the adjudication, including that the mother struck the child five times with a belt, leaving multiple bruises on the inside and outside of his legs that were still visible the next day, and the child described "a beating." In another published opinion, the court of appeals affirmed the adjudication of abuse based on the findings that the child was (1) forced to sleep outside on at least two cold nights in February, (2) bound to a tree, (3) required to conduct a "self-baptism" in a bathtub full of water, (4) ordered to pray while his caretaker held a firearm, (5) struck with a belt all over his body and (6) repeatedly told that he was possessed by a demon to the point that the child began to believe that was true. *In re F.C.D.*, 244 N.C. App. 243 (2015). The court of appeals has held that this definition of abuse focuses on the severity and brutality of the procedures and devices used by the parent, guardian, custodian, or caretaker and does not examine the child's behavior that the procedures and devices were meant to correct. *In re F.C.D.*, 244 N.C. App. 243.

---

**Resources:**
For a further discussion on discipline and abuse under the Juvenile Code, see
- Sara DePasquale, *Parental Discipline: When Is It Abuse and/or a Crime?*, UNC SCH. OF GOV'T: NORTH CAROLINA CRIMINAL LAW BLOG (Nov. 13, 2014).
- Sara DePasquale, *When Parental Discipline Goes Too Far, It's Child Abuse*, UNC SCH. OF GOV'T: ON THE CIVIL SIDE BLOG (May 25, 2016).

---

**(b) Factitious Disorder Imposed on Another (previously, Munchausen Syndrome by Proxy).** Findings of abuse were affirmed where three experts testified that the child was the probable victim of Munchausen syndrome by proxy, which involves a person deliberately causing injury or illness to another person and seeking medical attention for that person, often as a means of gaining attention. During her hospitalization, the child underwent numerous painful and invasive medical procedures to determine the source of symptoms reported by her mother, who one doctor believed had potentially induced the symptoms by either smothering or administering toxin to the child. *In re McCabe*, 157 N.C. App. 673 (2003); *see also In re Greene*, 152 N.C. App. 410 (2002) (affirming TPR on ground of abuse in case in which experts had diagnosed Munchausen syndrome by proxy).

**(c) Serious emotional damage: G.S. 7B-101(1)(ii)e.** Serious emotional damage is evidenced by a juvenile's severe anxiety, depression, withdrawal, or aggressive behavior toward himself, herself, or others. G.S. 7B-101(1)(ii)e. The statute does not require a formal psychiatric diagnosis of any of the psychological conditions set out in the statute. *In re A.M.*, 247 N.C. App. 672 (2016).

- Evidence of serious emotional damage due to the parents' long-standing, acrimonious marital dispute, resulting in chronic adjustment disorder and depression in their children, was sufficient to support a finding of emotional abuse and a conclusion that the children were abused juveniles. *Powers v. Powers*, 130 N.C. App. 37 (1998).
- Evidence of child's emotional withdrawal as a coping mechanism for the child's feelings of hopelessness and anxiety, arising from mother's continued foul, abusive language and maltreatment of child, was sufficient to support an adjudication of abuse based on serious emotional damage. *In re A.M.*, 247 N.C. App. 672.

**(d) Commission of certain sex and other crimes by, with, or upon a child: G.S. 7B-101(1)(ii)d.**

**By a child.** An older sibling who repeatedly sexually abused a younger sibling and the younger sibling victim were both abused juveniles (abuse includes a parent who permits or encourages the commission of certain sex crimes by, with, or upon a child). Evidence supported the findings of abuse by the older sibling, established that respondent parents were aware of the abuse based on the younger sibling's repeated disclosures to them over a period of two years as well as disclosures made to other family members, and showed that the older sibling had been adjudicated delinquent after admitting to multiple counts of second degree sexual offenses against the younger sibling. *In re M.A.E.,* 242 N.C. App. 312 (2015) (originally unpublished July 21, 2015, but subsequently published).

**With or upon a child.**

- Evidence was sufficient to establish abuse where the child had made statements that the father had asked the child to touch his penis, asked her to look at magazines with pictures of naked people, and put his hand on her crotch in bed; and in response to the trial court's question about what she saw when she was in the basement with the child and her father, the child's cousin made a drawing that depicted a man exposing himself. *In re Cogdill,* 137 N.C. App. 504 (2000).
- Evidence was sufficient to support a determination of abuse where the father grabbed the child from behind and fondled her breasts and on another occasion inappropriately touched her in the vaginal area. *In re M.G.,* 187 N.C. App. 536 (2007), *rev'd in part on other grounds,* 363 N.C. 570 (2009).

**(e) Serious physical injury inflicted by non-accidental means: G.S. 7B-101(1)(ii)a.** A child may be adjudicated abused when he or she sustains unexplained non-accidental injuries. *In re L.Z.A.,* 249 N.C. App. 628 (2016). An adult's exclusive custody of a child who suffers non-accidental injuries that were not self-inflicted can support an inference that the adult inflicted the injuries. *State v. Wilson,* 181 N.C. App. 540 (2007). An abuse adjudication may be based on non-accidental injuries without a finding of a pattern of abuse or the presence of risk factors. *In re L.Z.A.,* 249 N.C. App. 628. There is also no requirement to prove abuse beyond a reasonable doubt or to rule out "every remote possibility" of the cause of the injury. *In re L.Z.A.,* 249 N.C. App. at 638. While medical testimony that the child suffered a non-accidental injury may be presented, medical testimony is not required to find that injuries were not accidental. *In re S.G.,* 835 S.E.2d 479 (N.C. Ct. App. 2019). There is no minimum threshold for a serious injury as the determination is dependent on the facts of each case. *In re S.G.,* 835 S.E.2d 479.

Evidence was sufficient to find abuse based on serious physical injury inflicted by non-accidental means.

- Findings that a 3-year-old child had distinct patterned bruising on his forehead and upper eyelid, visible at least four days after the incident, supported the trial court's conclusion of a serious injury. While no medical expert explicitly testified that the injuries occurred through non-accidental means, two medical professionals testified without objection that mother's explanation was inconsistent with the nature of the child's injuries and that the bruising was "definitely consistent with having been hit with a belt buckle", which supported the determination that the injuries were non-accidental. *In re S.G.*, 835 S.E.2d at 484.

- An abuse adjudication based on respondent inflicting or allowing to be inflicted serious physical injury, and by creating a substantial risk of serious physical injury, both by non-accidental means was supported by findings that (1) the child did not experience any substantial injuries when placed in residential care outside the home; (2) the child gave conflicting explanation for injuries sustained after discharge; (3) the extent of the child's injuries and the lack of explanation supported a conclusion of abuse based in part on respondents allowing the child to injure himself; and (4) the child's injuries arose from respondent's failure to maintain the child's prescribed medication, which respondent acknowledged caused behavior problems, and failure to provide adequate supervision of a child known to have significant mental health and behavioral issues. *In re K.B.*, 253 N.C. App. 423 (2017).

- An abuse adjudication was affirmed where there were findings of fact that the child was seen at a hospital for scratches, bruises, swelling, and a skull fracture; a pediatrician concluded that the skull fracture was caused by non-accidental means; the mother's explanations were inconsistent with the injuries; the injuries occurred during the dates the mother had physical custody of the child; and the mother failed to obtain medical attention for the child even though the injuries were obvious and severe. *In re T.H.T.*, 185 N.C. App. 337 (2007), *aff'd as modified on other grounds*, 362 N.C. 446 (2008).

- Non-accidental injury was established where an infant had multiple rib fractures that were several weeks old and in different stages of healing, the parents were the primary caretakers but had not sought medical attention for the child, and there was an undisputed finding that the injury would have caused the child to cry. *In re S.W.*, 187 N.C. App. 505 (2007).

- Evidence was sufficient to show non-accidental injury where doctors testified that the child had suffered a severe blow to the head resulting in extensive bleeding over the surface of the brain within a relatively short time before being brought to the hospital. Doctors could not specify exactly where or how the injury occurred, but three of four doctors testified that the injuries were likely non-accidental. *In re C.M.*, 198 N.C. App. 53 (2009). *See also In re L.Z.A.*, 249 N.C. App. 628 (2016) (abuse adjudication affirmed based on findings that showed pre-mobile infant, while in the sole care of her parents, suffered a skull fracture, subdural hematomas, and an arm fracture that expert witness determined were likely the result of non-accidental trauma).

Evidence was not sufficient to find abuse based on serious physical injury inflicted by non-accidental means.

- Evidence was not sufficient to support a conclusion that a child with unusual fractures had been abused and neglected where medical testimony from eight physicians ranged from conclusions that the child's injuries were due to shaken baby syndrome to "I don't know what happened to this child;" the child's regular pediatrician reported no concerns or "red flags" for child abuse in her dealings with the child's family; there was no evidence that the child's parents were anything other than loving and caring, nor was there any evidence of marital problems between parents or any psychiatric condition that affected their ability to parent the child appropriately. *In re A.R.H.*, 177 N.C. App. 797, 800 (2006).

**(f) Failure to prevent harm.** Failure to prevent harm or allowing situations to occur that would tend to promote harm can be considered abuse. For example, where the mother knew of the father's violent and abusive nature and alcohol abuse, witnessed many incidents where the father would consume alcohol to excess and act out against her and the children, allowed the father to drive the children after he had consumed a large quantity of alcoholic beverages, and failed to take necessary steps to protect the children, the evidence was sufficient to support an adjudication of abuse in that the mother allowed to be created a substantial risk of serious physical injury to the children by other than accidental means. *In re M.G.*, 187 N.C. App. 536 (2007), *rev'd in part on other grounds*, 363 N.C. 570 (2009). *See also In re Y.Y.E.T.*, 205 N.C. App. 120 (2010) (holding that where non-accidental injuries occurred to infant while under the care of both parents and the perpetrator could not be identified, both parents were deemed responsible, either for directly causing the injury or for failing to prevent it); *In re Gwaltney*, 68 N.C. App. 686 (1984) (affirming adjudication of abuse and neglect where evidence showed that mother acquiesced in sexual abuse of the child). *Cf. In re D.A.*, 811 S.E.2d 729, 733 (N.C. Ct. App. 2018) (regarding disposition; permanency planning order awarded *de facto* permanent custody of child adjudicated abused and neglected to foster parents; trial court found that neither parent took responsibility or offered a plausible explanation for the child's injuries; declining to apply *In re Y.Y.E.T* and vacating custody award when there were no findings that child's injuries were non-accidental or that respondent parents were the sole caregivers when injuries were sustained, and the findings were unclear as to which parent or parents the court assigned responsibility).

### E. Evidence to Establish Neglect

**1. Definition of neglect.** The Juvenile Code in G.S. 7B-101(15) defines a neglected juvenile as one who

- is found to be a minor victim of human trafficking under G.S. 14-43.15;
- does not receive proper care, supervision, or discipline from the juvenile's parent, guardian, custodian, or caretaker;
- has been abandoned;
- is not provided necessary medical or remedial care;
- lives in an environment injurious to the juvenile's welfare;
- has had his or her custody unlawfully transferred under G.S. 14-321.2 (effective for offenses committed on or after December 1, 2016); or
- has been placed for care or adoption in violation of the law.

In determining whether a juvenile is neglected, it is relevant whether that juvenile lives in a home where another juvenile has died as a result of suspected abuse or neglect or has been subjected to abuse or neglect by an adult who regularly lives in the home. G.S. 7B-101(15).

The definition in G.S. 7B-101(15) pertains to the adjudication of a juvenile as neglected. The definition of "serious neglect" in G.S. 7B-101(19a) is not to be applied to the adjudication of a juvenile in an abuse, neglect, or dependency case. "Serious neglect" is used only in connection with the placement of an individual on the Responsible Individuals List. *In re J.M.*, 255 N.C. App. 483 (2017). For more on the Responsible Individuals List, see Chapter 5.2.B.

See Chapter 2.3.B (discussing the definition of neglect and cases interpreting the definition).

Some aspects of the definition of neglect are relatively vague, making it especially important for the court and parties to take into account community and cultural values as well as the purposes of the Juvenile Code when determining the meaning of phrases like "proper care [and] supervision", "necessary medical care", or "environment injurious to the juvenile's welfare". However, the statutory definition of neglect has been found to be constitutional and not void for vagueness. *See In re Moore*, 306 N.C. 394 (1982); *In re Huber*, 57 N.C. App. 453 (1982); *In re Biggers*, 50 N.C. App. 332 (1981). Note that these cases dealt with a previous, but similar, version of the definition.

Some of the case law related to what constitutes neglect is in the context of termination of parental rights (TPR) proceedings as opposed to proceedings on petitions alleging neglect. Appellate cases have distinguished neglect in the two types of proceedings, noting that in a TPR case, the child has usually been removed from the parent's home for a significant period of time, but an adjudication resulting from a petition alleging neglect typically occurs immediately after the child has been removed. *In re K.J.D.*, 203 N.C. App. 653 (2010). However, both types of proceedings use the definition of neglect found at G.S. 7B-101(15) and so the court "may look to cases arising in either context to determine if neglect has been demonstrated in the case." *In re K.J.D.*, 203 N.C. App. at 659. See Chapter 9.11.A relating to neglect in the context of TPR cases.

**2. Evidence related to neglect.** Appellate cases typically deal with a trial court's adjudication of neglect that is based on more than one aspect of the definition of neglect (e.g., a combination of lack of proper care, lack of proper supervision, and an injurious environment). In a neglect determination, the evidence must be reviewed on a case-by-case basis considering the totality of the evidence. *In re L.T.R.*, 181 N.C. App. 376 (2007). *See In re J.R.*, 243 N.C. App. 309 (2015).

The following cases highlight some aspects of neglect or factors contributing to neglect that have been discussed by appellate courts.

**(a) Harm or risk of harm.** Although not in the neglect statute, when evaluating evidence to establish neglect, the appellate courts have said that the evidence must show that a child suffers a physical, mental, or emotional impairment or is at substantial risk of such impairment as a result of the parent's, guardian's, custodian's, or caretaker's failure to provide proper care, supervision, discipline, or medical care, or as a result of the child living in an injurious environment. *See In re J.A.M.*, 822 S.E.2d 693 (N.C. S.Ct 2019); *In re F.S.*, 835 S.E.2d 465 (N.C. Ct. App. 2019); *In re K.J.B.*, 248 N.C. App. 352 (2016); *In re J.R.*, 243 N.C. App. 309 (2015); *In re J.W.*, 241 N.C. App 44 (2015); *In re C.B.*, 245 N.C. App. 197 (2016). Actual harm is not required but rather a substantial risk of harm is sufficient. *In re D.B.J.*, 197 N.C. App. 752 (2009). Conduct that may cause or potentially cause injury to the child "may include alcohol or substance abuse by the parent, driving while impaired with a child as a passenger, or physical abuse or injury to a child inflicted by the parent…., exposing the child to acts of domestic violence, abuse of illegal substances, and threatening or abusive behavior toward social workers and police officers in the presence of the children." *In re D.B.J.*, 197 N.C. App. at 755.

When the evidence does not support such a finding, or a finding as to impairment or the risk of impairment is not made, a neglect adjudication is subject to reversal. *See In re B.P.*, 809 S.E.2d 914 (N.C. Ct. App. 2018) (vacating an adjudication of neglect when there was no finding of impairment or risk of impairment to the child and the findings made in the case, relating to mother's mental health, homelessness, and the removal of other children from her care, did not support a conclusion of neglect).

Under G.S. 7B-101(15), the trial court has some discretion in determining if a child is at risk for a particular type of harm given the age and environment in which the child lives. *In re A.L.T.*, 241 N.C. App. 443 (2015). A trial court's failure to make specific findings as to the harm or risk of harm does not require reversal where the evidence supports such findings. *See In re C.C.*, 817 S.E.2d 894 (N.C. Ct. App. 2018); *In re H.N.D.*, 364 N.C. 597, *rev'g per curiam for reasons stated in the dissent* 205 N.C. App. 702 (2010). Evidence that the parent loves or is concerned about his or her child will not necessarily prevent the court from making a determination that the child is neglected. *In re Montgomery*, 311 N.C. 101 (1984).

**(b) Other children living in the home.** Language in G.S. 7B-101(15) about the relevance of abuse or neglect of other children does not mandate a conclusion that a child is neglected when another child in the home has been abused or neglected. *See In re J.A.M.*, 822 S.E.2d 693, 698 (N.C. S.Ct 2019) (a juvenile may not be adjudicated as neglected "solely based upon previous Department of Social Services involvement relating to other children", which in this case referred to termination of respondent mother's rights to six older children; adjudication of neglect affirmed based on findings supported by the evidence of present risk factors and evaluations of past adjudications of other children). The trial court has the discretion to determine the weight to be given to evidence related to abuse or neglect of other children. *See In re J.A.M.*, 822 S.E.2d 693; *In re S.G.*, 835 S.E.2d 479 (N.C. Ct. App. 2019); *In re A.S.*, 190 N.C. App. 679 (2008), *aff'd per curiam*, 363 N.C. 254 (2009). But, there must be evidence to prove that another child was in fact abused or neglected by an adult that regularly lives in the home of the child who is the subject of the neglect proceeding, or that another child died as a result of suspected abuse or neglect. *See In re K.J.B.*, 248 N.C. App. 352 (2016) (reversing adjudication of neglect after determining (1) there was no evidence regarding where another child of the mother's died or that the death was suspected to be from abuse or neglect as the evidence showed the child died of Sudden Infant Death Syndrome, and (2) there was no evidence that respondent mother's rights to two of her other children were terminated because of abuse or neglect or that those children were abused or neglected).

Child who is the subject of the neglect proceeding is a newborn.

- When considering neglect of a newborn, the trial court's decision must be "predictive in nature" as it must assess, based on the historical facts of the case, whether there is a substantial risk of future abuse or neglect. *In re J.A.M.*, 822 S.E.2d 693, 698 (N.C. S.Ct. 2019) (affirming neglect adjudication of newborn).
- Appellate courts have not applied a literal interpretation of the language in G.S. 7B-101(15) that a child "lives in a home" where another child has died as a result of suspected abuse or neglect, or where another child has been abused or neglected by an adult who regularly lives in the home, with respect to newborns who are still in the hospital. Appellant courts have held that the abuse or neglect of siblings or other children in the home, including events that occurred prior to the birth of the newborn, is relevant in assessing the risk to a newborn. *See, e.g., In re A.S.*, 190 N.C. App. 679, *aff'd per curiam*, 363 N.C. 254; *In re A.B.*, 179 N.C. App. 605 (2006); *In re E.N.S.*, 164 N.C. App. 146 (2004).
- Reversible error was found where an adjudication that a newborn was neglected was based on a prior adjudication of a sibling, when the trial court relied solely on prior orders concerning the sibling. The only prior order that could have been properly considered was from a hearing occurring many months earlier, and there was no evidence as to the parents' progress since that time or whether they still denied knowing the cause of the sibling's injuries. *In re A.K.*, 178 N.C. App. 727 (2006).

Consideration of adjudication of one child based in part on another child's adjudication of abuse or neglect at the same adjudicatory hearing.

- When one child is adjudicated abused and neglected at the same hearing in which another child is alleged to be neglected, the trial court has the discretion to consider that adjudication relevant as an "other child in the home" who has been subjected to abuse and neglect. *See In re D.B.J.*, 197 N.C. App. 752 (2009) (conclusion that child was neglected was supported in part by findings that child's sister had been physically abused by an adult who regularly lived in the home). *See also In re C.M.*, 198 N.C. App. 53 (2009) (trial court was permitted, although not required, to conclude at the same hearing that daughter was neglected based on evidence that son was abused and neglected).
- Where a child with serious mental health issues was adjudicated neglected and dependent, the sibling of that child also was neglected when the mother of both children (1) allowed the sibling to be continually exposed to the erratic, troubling, and violent behavior of the child with mental health issues; (2) failed to obtain mental health services for the child in need of those services, which could have mitigated her behavior; and (3) showed no concern for the effect that the behavior of the child with mental health issues had on the sibling. *In re C.B.*, 245 N.C. App. 197 (2016).

Adjudication of neglect as to child who is the subject of the proceeding requires assessment of substantial risk of harm.

- "A court may not adjudicate a juvenile neglected solely based upon previous [DSS] involvement relating to other children… there must be current circumstances that present a risk to the juvenile." *In re J.A.M.*, 822 S.E.2d 693, 698 (N.C. S.Ct. 2019) (affirming neglect adjudication based on historical facts of case that included past adjudications of other children as well as other factors that indicated a present risk to the child).
- Failure to acknowledge responsibility for abuse or neglect of another child can contribute to a conclusion that there is a substantial risk of future abuse or neglect. *See In re N.G.*, 186 N.C. App. 1 (2007), *aff'd per curiam*, 362 N.C. 229 (2008).
- Adjudication of two children as neglected was not supported solely by a finding that another child was abused and neglected. Respondent parents denied responsibility for injuries to the one child, and mother would not agree to keep children from the father, preferring to be with him and have the children stay elsewhere. These findings supported the court's determination that that children were at risk of future harm if they remained with respondents. *In re S.G.*, 835 S.E.2d 479 (N.C. Ct. App. 2019).
- Where one child was adjudicated abused and neglected, the younger sibling was also neglected when she was exposed to her older sibling's abuse and neglect. The court of appeals stated "the exposure of a child to the 'infliction of injury by a parent to another child or parent, can be conduct causing or potentially causing injury' to that child." *In re F.C.D.*, 244 N.C. App. 243, 254 (2015) (citations omitted) (adjudication affirmed; younger sister's exposure to her brother's abuse was distressing and could cause fear and worry that the same would happen to her).

### (c) Lack of proper care or supervision.

Evidence was not sufficient to find lack of proper care or supervision.

- An anonymous call to DSS reporting a naked 2-year-old child playing unsupervised in a driveway was not sufficient, standing alone, to constitute a report of neglect or warrant an investigation by DSS. *In re Stumbo*, 357 N.C. 279 (2003).
- A mother's lack of stable housing, causing frequent moves, did not impede her ability to care for and supervise her child or expose him to an injurious environment. *In re J.R.*, 243 N.C. App. 309 (2015).
- Evidence of the parents' habit of placing an infant on the sofa without surrounding him with pillows or other forms of restraint was not sufficient to establish neglect where there was also evidence that the infant was unable to roll over, was not mobile when placed on the sofa, had never missed any appointments with his pediatrician, was developing appropriately, and had no prior injuries (although other conduct on the part of the father was deemed abuse by the trial court). *In re J.A.G.*, 172 N.C. App. 708 (2005).
- Factual stipulations that mother did not insure child's regular school attendance, that child had missed twenty-five days and was tardy thirty-seven times during one school year, and had failed three core classes, were insufficient to support conclusion that

child was neglected, without findings (i) as to the reasons for the attendance and tardiness issues, or (ii) that the failure to pass core classes was directly related to the child's absences or to mother's failure to provide proper care, supervision, or discipline. *In re R.L.G.,* 816 S.E.2d 914 (N.C. Ct. App. 2018). *See also In re J.C.M.J.C.,* 834 S.E.2d 670 (N.C. Ct. App. 2019) (multiple absences from school, without findings as to the reasons or explaining the degree to which the children were academically behind, were insufficient to show the children were denied an education such that they were neglected).

Evidence was sufficient to find lack of proper care or supervision.

- Mother failed to provide proper care or supervision of a child with emotional difficulties and behavioral issues who sustained "a pattern of injuries [that] any conscientious parent would take into account" and which required more supervision than had been provided. *In re K.B.*, 253 N.C. App. 423, 431 (2017).
- Evidence that a mother had left a 16-month-old child alone in a motel room for more than thirty minutes and that the child was later found by a motel employee after a guest reported continuous crying was sufficient to support an adjudication of neglect. *In re D.C.*, 183 N.C. App. 344 (2007).
- Evidence that while in South Carolina a 9-year-old child shared a bed with two other children, including a 7-year-old male cousin who tried five times to kiss her or touch her private parts, was significant evidence that that child did not receive proper care or supervision, regardless of whether the incidents between the children rose to the level of sexual abuse. *In re T.N.G.,* 244 N.C. App. 398 (2015) (note that respondent father's argument that court could not consider events that occurred outside of North Carolina was rejected).
- Pre-mobile child who suffered a skull fracture, subdural hematomas, and an arm fracture while in the sole care of her parents, which expert witness determined were likely the result of non-accidental trauma, either did not receive proper care or supervision or lived in an injurious environment and suffered a physical impairment as a result. *In re L.Z.A.*, 249 N.C. App. 628 (2016).
- Where findings were that mother had previous problems with drugs and had previously injured the child while abusing drugs, was continuing to use drugs illegally, had hit and kicked the child, refused to cooperate with DSS, and had a friend-like relationship with child that seemed to contribute to the child's defiant behavior (child was diagnosed with oppositional defiant disorder), these findings supported the trial court's conclusion that the child was not receiving proper care and supervision and was living in an injurious environment. *In re J.D.R.*, 239 N.C. App. 63 (2015).
- Findings supported a neglect adjudication based on lack of supervision and substance abuse where mother had an opiate dependency impairing her ability to parent; child was locked out of his house when mother was home, requiring law enforcement assistance to regain access; mother screamed obscenities at DSS in front of children for forty-five minutes; children frequently missed school and mother did not respond to notices related to absences; and baby had not had routine immunizations and also had yeast infection, eczema, and cradle cap. *In re H.D.F.*, 197 N.C. App. 480 (2009).

- Lack of cleanliness or food have been found to be factors contributing to neglect. For example, lack of cleanliness was a primary factor in a finding of neglect where a disabled child who attended a special school was repeatedly coming to school in a "filthy condition" and other children made fun of him, the staff would have to bathe him, and he was not taught hygiene at home. *In re Safriet,* 112 N.C. App. 747 (1993). Finding that a child's home is clean or that the child is well-fed will not prevent a finding of neglect; where there is a finding of physical, mental, or emotional impairment, or risk of impairment, a child may be considered neglected. *See In re Thompson,* 64 N.C. App. 95 (1983).
- Failure to educate a child has been found to be lack of proper care in some circumstances. *See In re McMillan,* 30 N.C. App. 235 (1976) (affirming the determination of neglect where the parents did not send the children to school because school did not teach about Indian culture and heritage, and the parents failed to provide the children with an alternative education); *In re Devone,* 86 N.C. App. 57 (1987) (upholding determination that a child with a mental disability was neglected when the father refused to send the child to school to receive remedial education and special education classes were critical to the child's development and welfare). Note that G.S. 115C-378 describes a school principal's responsibilities in relation to children who are repeatedly absent and sets out circumstances in which a principal is required to notify the district attorney or DSS regarding unlawful absences.
- Evidence of a mother's struggles with parenting skills, domestic violence, anger management, mental illness and a failure to obtain treatment for the illness, as well as her unstable housing situation and history of leaving the child without proper supervision, was sufficient to support an adjudication of neglect because her failure to provide proper care and supervision placed the child at substantial risk of harm. *In re K.D.,* 178 N.C. App. 322 (2006).

**(d) Child placed with alternative caregiver prior to DSS involvement.** A parent's voluntary placement of their child with a caretaker does not automatically preclude an adjudication of neglect based on a lack of proper care or supervision. The court of appeals has treated these cases like those termination of parental rights cases that allege neglect when the child has not lived with the parent for a substantial period of time prior to the filing of the petition. See Chapter 9.11.A.4 (discussing neglect based on past neglect and likelihood of repetition of neglect). In these types of cases, the trial court looks at the past conditions that resulted in the parent placing the child with a caretaker before the petition alleging neglect has been filed and evidence of changed conditions in light of the probability of the repetition of neglect that poses a risk of harm to the child at the time of the adjudication hearing. *See In re K.J.D.,* 203 N.C. App. 653 (2010); *In re B.P.,* 809 S.E.2d 914 (N.C. Ct. App. 2018); *In re C.C.,* 817 S.E.2d 894 (N.C. Ct. App. 2018); *In re H.L.,* 807 S.E.2d 685 (N.C. Ct. App. 2017).

Evidence sufficient to find lack of proper care and supervision.

- On appeal, respondent mother argued that the child should not have been adjudicated neglected, because at the time of the petition the child was in a kinship placement where care was appropriate and the child was safe. The findings supported an adjudication of neglect. The child was placed in kinship care due to both parents' inability to care for the child and this inability continued; the mother continued to engage in assaultive behavior; she had not completed counseling to address anger issues or sought treatment for her mental disorder; and the mother did not have stable housing or a job. The court concluded that the child would be endangered if the mother removed the child from the relative's home, which legally she could do. *In re K.J.D.*, 203 N.C. App. 653 (2010).

- Child placed in a voluntary kinship placement approved by DSS when petition was filed. Evidence was sufficient to support a finding that child would be at a substantial risk of impairment if she was returned to mother's care as conditions that led to the kinship placement, namely, mother's substance abuse and mental health issues and respondent father's incarceration, had not been corrected at the time of the adjudication hearing. *In re C.C.*, 817 S.E.2d 894 (N.C. Ct. App. 2018).
- Child was placed with her adult sibling pursuant to a safety plan with DSS when petition was filed. Supported findings established an altercation where the parents engaged in a tug of war with the child, that parents had failed multiple drug tests, and that child was placed with a safety resource due to parents' drug use. Trial court properly concluded that child was neglected as parents had failed to remedy the conditions that required child's placement pursuant to a safety plan, and failed to address their substance abuse issues while child was in safety placement, such that the parents were unable to provide child proper care. *In re H.L.*, 807 S.E.2d 685 (N.C. Ct. App. 2017).

Evidence not sufficient to find lack of proper care and supervision.

- Before petition was filed, mother placed child with caretakers, whose home was found appropriate by both DSS and the trial court. Mother made placement "on her own, without DSS's input" and child was in that placement when the petition was filed. Findings did not support mother's continuing inability to care for the child or an ultimate finding that the child would be at substantial risk of harm if removed from caretakers and returned to mother. Mother was receiving treatment for her mental health issues and child was in a placement mother arranged for during period of homelessness. *In re B.P.*, 809 S.E.2d 914, 920 (N.C. Ct. App. 2018) (adjudication of neglect vacated and remanded).
- Child was in a placement because of a previous neglect action that was ultimately reversed on appeal. After the mandate in that appeal, a new petition was filed and the child was adjudicated neglected. The court of appeal reversed the second adjudication as there was no clear and convincing evidence of current circumstances indicating a future probability of neglect based on a present risk to the child. Mother had a history of substance abuse and hospitalizations but was engaging in treatment and working with DSS on her plan (during the first neglect case while the appeal of that action was pending). *In re F.S.*, 835 S.E.2d 465 (N.C. Ct. App. 2019).

### (e) Lack of necessary medical or remedial care.

Evidence was sufficient to find neglect based on a lack of necessary medical or remedial care.

- Conclusion of neglect was supported by findings that mother failed to follow the discharge recommendations from a residential care placement to obtain a psychiatrist to manage the child's prescriptions. Mother's failure resulted in the child being without prescribed medication for two weeks, which could result in side effects for the child and which mother acknowledged caused behavior problems. *In re K.B.*, 253 N.C. App. 423 (2017).
- Neglect was established by evidence that the respondent mother delayed seeking medical treatment of significant injuries to her child for two days after the child was injured when left in the care of a person who was barred by a safety plan from having contact with the child. *In re L.C.*, 253 N.C. App. 67 (2017).
- A child was neglected when mother continuously failed to obtain meaningful mental health services for her child. Findings established that the child had serious mental health issues requiring five psychiatric hospitalizations over a period of four months, that the respondent mother minimized and denied the seriousness of the child's condition and at times exacerbated it, and that the mother refused to participate in discharge planning for the child. The child was at a substantial risk of physical, mental, and emotional impairment as a result of lack of medical care. *In re C.B.*, 245 N.C. App. 197 (2016).
- Neglect was established where findings of fact showed that respondents engaged in multiple acts of domestic violence including an incident resulting in an injury to the infant child, after which respondents did not seek medical treatment for the child. Mother also informed a social worker that the child had other serious health issues, but the mother had cancelled medical appointments for the child. *In re A.R.*, 227 N.C. App. 518 (2013).
- Neglect was established where children had never received any medical care, and their younger sister had suffered cardiac arrest as a result of starvation and had to be airlifted to the hospital. *In re S.H.*, 217 N.C. App. 140 (2011).
- Neglect was shown where the mother delayed seeking medical help to find the cause of serious bruising on much of child's body (found to be due to blood disorder) and delayed seeking help for disciplinary, behavioral, and developmental problems displayed by the children. *In re C.P.*, 181 N.C. App. 698 (2007). Similarly, the parent's failure to seek a recommended evaluation to determine whether a child was developing normally and to seek treatment if necessary supported a finding of neglect. *In re Thompson*, 64 N.C. App. 95 (1983).
- Not sending a child to therapeutic day care was considered to be a failure to provide necessary medical or remedial care (along with other circumstances contributing to a finding of neglect). *In re Cusson*, 43 N.C. App. 333 (1979).
- A finding of neglect was supported by evidence showing that the child had a severe speech defect that was treatable and that the mother refused to allow the child to receive the necessary medical and remedial care that would allow the child to develop to her full educational and emotional potential. *In re Huber*, 57 N.C. App. 453 (1982).
- A finding of neglect was supported by evidence that the children did not receive proper medical attention as they did not receive their immunizations or regular medical follow-up, and the 6-month-old infant had never been to a doctor (also

discussing lack of proper nutrition and failure to allow participation in available program that would provide for the children's adequate stimulation and socialization; adjudication was not based on value judgment of mother's socio-economic status). *In re Bell*, 107 N.C. App. 566 (1992).

Evidence was not sufficient to find neglect based on a lack of necessary medical or remedial care.

- Mother's failure to take child to "well care visits", without more, did not support an adjudication of neglect based on lack of medical care. *In re R.L.G.*, 816 S.E.2d 914 (N.C. Ct. App. 2018) (trial court made no findings as the actual numbers of visits missed, the reasons for missing visits, the medical conditions requiring the visits, or any adverse effects on the child's health arising from having missed the visits).

**(f) Lack of proper discipline.** A child who does not receive proper discipline may be a neglected juvenile. Neglect in this form may involve overly severe discipline that does not result in "serious physical injury" or constitute "cruel or grossly inappropriate procedures or cruel or grossly inappropriate devices to modify behavior" within the statutory definition of abuse. Where a parent is using inappropriate discipline, the court may also find that the child is living in an environment injurious to the child's welfare. The variance in appellate analysis of corporal punishment and its impact on a child depends in part on whether the petition alleges the punishment as constituting abuse or neglect. See section 6.3.D.2(a), above (cases analyzing corporal punishment in the context of abuse allegations).

- Evidence contributing to the affirmation of an adjudication of neglect was the fact that the father had beaten a child with various instruments for disciplinary purposes resulting in pain for several days and sustained deep bruising and scarring. *In re S.H.*, 217 N.C. App. 140 (2011).
- Hitting children with a belt as a form of discipline, along with failing to fully comply with a mental health evaluation and resulting therapy and missing arranged visits with the children, was determined to be neglect. *In re A.J.M.*, 177 N.C. App. 745 (2006).
- Evidence was sufficient to withstand a motion to dismiss a neglect petition at the close of petitioner's evidence, where the evidence showed that an 8-year-old child had been left alone for three hours as a form of discipline; she had a cut on her lip and bruising on her face; mother's boyfriend (known for damaging a wall and car in anger) had spanked her and hit her face when she misbehaved; and the mother refused to cooperate with DSS. *In re Gleisner*, 141 N.C. App. 475 (2000) (remanding with instructions for trial court to make proper findings of fact and clear conclusions of law).
- A mother's actions resulting in bruises and other injuries were found to be inappropriately severe discipline establishing neglect. *In re Thompson*, 64 N.C. App. 95 (1983).

**(g) Injurious environment: instability, substance abuse, and domestic violence.** An injurious environment may be an environment that puts the child at substantial risk of harm as well as one in which the child has been harmed. *In re Helms*, 127 N.C. App. 505 (1997); *In re Safriet*, 112 N.C. App. 747 (1993). When all children are subjected to the same circumstances, it is error to adjudicate some but not all of the children neglected based on an injurious environment. *In re Q.A.*, 245 N.C. App. 71 (2016) (when five siblings were without plumbing, electricity, food, and a home while in their grandmother's care, trial court erred when it found two siblings neglected but dismissed the petition as to three other siblings because placement with their father was an option).

Evidence considered when determining whether an injurious environment exists often overlaps with evidence of improper care, supervision, or discipline. *See In re J.C.M.J.C.*, 834 S.E.2d 670 (N.C. Ct. App. 2019) (findings describing respondents' refusal to communicate with DSS and their efforts to obstruct the DSS investigation did not support a conclusion of an injurious environment or improper care, supervision, or discipline); *In re B.P.*, 809 S.E.2d 914 (N.C. Ct. App. 2018) (findings and evidence in the case did not support a conclusion, at the time the petition was filed, that the child was living in an environment injurious to her welfare and was not receiving proper care and supervision); *In re D.L.W.*, 368 N.C. 835 (2016) (adjudication of neglect, as a statutory ground for termination of mother's parental rights, was based on domestic violence that put the children at risk, a lack of consistent and adequate housing, and the parent's inability to meet the minimal needs of the children).

Evidence was sufficient to find neglect based on an injurious environment.

- Child was neglected based on an injurious environment when trial court found that respondent mother failed to take responsibility for her role in the termination of her rights to six other children, denied the need for and thus refused services, and became involved with father of the child when she was aware of his history of domestic violence, even though domestic violence was one of the reasons for removal of her other children. *In re J.A.M.*, 822 S.E.2d 693 (N.C. S.Ct. 2019).
- Children were neglected when the trial court found the mother had taken out a protective order against the father for strangling her and attempting to rape her but she continued to be in contact with him, stated she could not care for the children and asked DSS to place them in foster care but often changed her mind about her children's placement, had a history of problems with her children requiring DSS intervention, behaved inappropriately during some visits with children, and had a history of drug abuse and mental health issues. *In re J.W.*, 241 N.C. App. 44 (2015).
- Findings of fact set out a longstanding and abusive relationship between respondent parents and sufficiently detailed the impact and potential harm father's violence toward mother had on their four children, all of whom were aware of the arguments and physical altercations. Adjudication that all four children were neglected was affirmed. *In re M.K.*, 241 N.C. App. 467 (2015).
- Neglect adjudication of two children was supported by findings that father, when angry, punched holes in walls, engaged in aggressive and violent behaviors in the home, and had struck each child at least once that caused older child to fear father. *In re A.L.T.*, 241 N.C. App. 443 (2015).

- The trial court's findings related to the parents' history of domestic violence and the negative impact of the violence on the children, along with a refusal to develop an in-home services agreement, were sufficient to support the conclusion that the children were neglected. *In re J.C.*, 235 N.C. App. 69 (2014), *rev'd in part per curiam on other grounds,* 368 N.C. 89 (2015).
- Evidence was sufficient to support an adjudication of neglect where respondent mother and her boyfriend had a physical altercation while mother was holding 1-month-old child which caused mother to fall and become injured (child was not injured); mother failed to report the incident to law enforcement when they were called to the scene; mother was being treated for bipolar disorder but did not believe her treatment was working. *In re A.N.L.*, 213 N.C. App. 266 (2011).
- Neglect adjudication supported by stipulated findings of fact that mother used controlled substances during pregnancy, which resulted in child being born with a rapid heartbeat and signs of withdrawal; that mother was belligerent and combative with hospital staff, refused to take her psychiatric medication, had infant removed from her, and was held on an involuntary commitment; and that father was at the hospital following child's birth despite being subject to a domestic violence protective order ordering no contact with mother after he stabbed her, dislocated her jaw, and held a gun on her. *In re G.T.,* 250 N.C. App. 50 (2016), *aff'd per curiam*, 370 N.C. 387 (2017).
- Findings that while in South Carolina, the 9-year-old child was present when adults used marijuana, had to share a bed with a 7-year-old male cousin who tried five times to kiss her or touch her private parts, and was sent to live in different homes with different adult caretakers without any determination by respondent father that the successive caretakers were fit, established that child was at a substantial risk of harm or impairment supporting neglect adjudication. *In re T.N.G.,* 244 N.C. App. 398 (2015) (father's argument that court could not consider events that occurred outside of North Carolina was rejected).
- Evidence of an inability to maintain a secure living situation where mother moved six times during four months and failed to maintain an environment free of drugs, violence, and attempted sexual assaults, supported a conclusion of neglect. *In re Helms*, 127 N.C. App. 505 (1997).
- Evidence of cocaine use during pregnancy, the newborn's positive cocaine test, the mother's refusal to sign a safety plan, and domestic violence between respondents was sufficient to support a conclusion of neglect of the newborn. *In re B.M.*, 183 N.C. App. 84 (2007).

Evidence was not sufficient to find neglect based on an injurious environment.

- Substance abuse by a parent may contribute to a finding of neglect but, without proof of an adverse impact on the child or a substantial risk of harm, is not sufficient itself to support a finding of neglect. *See In re F.S.,* 835 S.E.2d 465 (N.C. Ct. App. 2019); *In re J.C.M.J.C.,* 834 S.E.2d 670 (N.C. Ct. App. 2019); *In re K.J.B.*, 248 N.C. App. 352 (2016); *In re E.P.*, 183 N.C. App. 301, *aff'd per curiam,* 362 N.C. 82 (2007); *Powers v. Powers*, 130 N.C. App. 37 (1998); *In re McDonald*, 72 N.C. App. 234 (1984); *In re Phifer*, 67 N.C. App. 16 (1984).

- Evidence that mother had been hospitalized, or presented to a hospital, ten times for alcohol and substance abuse issues between September 2017 and February 2018, during which time the child was not in her care, did not support a finding of neglect based on an injurious environment. When child is not in mother's care, the trial court must assess and consider the probability of future neglect. Based on testimony from a DSS case supervisor that mother had entered treatment after petition was filed in March 2018, had since had eight negative drug screens, was compliant in her treatment, and was providing proof of her attendance at weekly NA and AA meetings, there was no evidence of current circumstances or a future probability that an immediate return would place the child in an injurious environment. *In re F.S.*, 835 S.E.2d 465 (N.C. Ct. App. 2019).
- A petition for neglect was filed after law enforcement had been called to a home where parents argued in the presence of their four children, the father left home taking the three older children with him, and mother obtained warrants charging father with assault by pointing a gun and communicating threats. The court of appeals affirmed the trial court's decision that DSS failed to prove that the children were neglected: the mother's statements were conflicting and she did not proceed with the case against the father, which the district attorney's office dismissed; the father was not in possession of a firearm when arrested; children had left with father voluntarily; and there was no evidence of domestic violence or that the children were put in danger. *In re H.M.*, 182 N.C. App. 308 (2007).

**(h) Abandonment.** A juvenile who has been abandoned is considered neglected. G.S. 7B-101(15). Abandonment has been described as "willful or intentional conduct" that "evinces a settled purpose to forego all parental duties and relinquish all parental claims to the child," or a "refusal to perform the natural and legal obligations of parental care and support," including withholding "presence, . . . love, . . . [and] the opportunity to display filial affection." *Pratt v. Bishop*, 257 N.C. 486, 501 (1962); *see also In re Adoption of Searle*, 82 N.C. App. 273, 275 (1986); *In re Apa*, 59 N.C. App. 322, 325 (1982); *In re Stroud*, 38 N.C. App. 373 (1978). See generally Chapter 2.6.B.2 (discussing abandonment as a form of neglect). Most appellate cases address abandonment as a ground for termination of parental rights (TPR). To the extent that those cases discuss the definition of abandonment, they may be relevant to abandonment in the context of neglect. See Chapter 9.11.A.7 (cases discussing neglect by abandonment) and 9.11.G (cases discussing evidence to establish abandonment as a TPR ground).

## F. Evidence to Establish Dependency

**1. Definition of dependency.** G.S 7B-101(9) defines a dependent juvenile as one in need of assistance or placement because

- the juvenile has no parent, guardian, or custodian responsible for the juvenile's care or supervision; or
- the juvenile's parent, guardian, or custodian is unable to provide for the child's care or supervision *and* lacks an appropriate alternative child care arrangement.

Note that caretaker is not included in this definition.

When dependency is based on the inability to provide care and supervision and a lack of appropriate alternative child care, both prongs of the definition must be satisfied, and the court must make findings about both prongs. *See In re F.S.*, 835 S.E.2d 465 (N.C. Ct. App. 2019); *In re C.P.*, 812 S.E.2d 188 (N.C. Ct. App. 2018); *In re H.L.*, 807 S.E.2d 685 (N.C. Ct. App. 2017) (reversing adjudication of dependency when order did not include a finding that the parents lacked an alternative child care arrangement and did not address care or supervision by a parent, guardian or custodian); *In re L.C.*, 253 N.C. App. 67 (2017) (vacating and remanding for findings of fact; trial court's failure to make findings addressing both prongs is reversible error; court failed to make findings of either prong).

**2. Evidence related to dependency.** Allegations of dependency are often combined with allegations of neglect and sometimes with abuse as well. Therefore, some appellate cases examining evidence related to dependency often discuss the totality of facts supporting dependency, neglect, and/or abuse. A few cases isolate discussions regarding facts supporting dependency. In one published opinion that related to neglect based on the child having been separated from the parent for a long period of time prior to the petition alleging neglect and dependency being filed, the court of appeals stated "the trial court must consider 'the conditions as they exist at the time of the adjudication as well as the risk of harm to the child from return to a parent' " and "look at the situation before the court at the time of the hearing when considering whether a juvenile is dependent." *In re F.S.*, 835 S.E.2d 465, 473 (N.C. Ct. App. 2019) (quoting *In re B.P.*, 809 S.E.2d 914, 920 (N.C. Ct. App. 2018) (which statement applied to neglect).

### (a) Unable to provide care or supervision (first prong of G.S. 7B-101(9)(ii)).

Appellate court did not find lack of proper care or supervision.

- While acknowledging that chronic alcoholism may impair one's ability to parent, when the trial court made no finding about mother's present inability to supervise the child and evidence was that mother's last alcohol-related hospitalization was prior to the adjudication hearing and that she was presently compliant with her treatment and case plan, "evidence tend[ed] to show an ability or a capability" to parent. *In re F.S.*, 835 S.E.2d at 473.
- Allegations in the petition, taken as true, did not address either prong required for a dependency adjudication and instead "at best" established that the child was delinquent or undisciplined, matters that would be addressed in a pending juvenile delinquency case. *In re K.G.*, 817 S.E.2d 790, 792 (N.C. Ct. App. 2018) (trial court erred in denying respondents' Rule 12(b)(6) motion to dismiss the dependency petition, rejecting argument of DSS and GAL that respondents' failure "to rein in" the child's behavior made them unable to care for the child; court will not look "to the juvenile's willful acts to determine a parent's ability to care for the child").
- Although the statutory definition refers to the singular word "the parent, guardian, or custodian," a child is not dependent when there is one parent who can care for his or her child or make arrangements for appropriate alternative child care. *In re V.B.*, 239 N.C. App. 340 (2015) (reversing dependency adjudication where there were no allegations and no evidence of respondent father's ability to provide proper care or

supervision to the child). *See also* G.S. 7B-101 ("[t]he singular includes the plural…unless otherwise specified").

- An adjudication of dependency will be reversed when the petitioner fails to prove both parents are incapable of providing care for the child or arranging for appropriate alternative child care. *In re J.D.R.*, 239 N.C. App. 63 (2015) (reversing dependency adjudication because there was no evidence and finding of fact about the mother's lack of an appropriate alternative child care arrangement); *In re H.H.*, 237 N.C. App. 431 (2014) (reversing dependency adjudication when before petition was filed the children were living with their father as a result of mother leaving them with him; father was properly caring for the children), *overruled by implication in part on other grounds by In re B.O.A.*, 831 S.E.2d 305 (N.C. S.Ct. 2019); *In re J.A.G.*, 172 N.C. App. 708 (2005) (where an infant suffered head trauma while in the father's care, evidence was insufficient to adjudicate the infant dependent because the mother was capable of providing care and supervision).
- A dependency adjudication based solely on the trial judge's conversations in chambers with child was reversed as there was no evidence presented by petitioner or respondent addressing respondent's ability to provide care or supervision for the child. *In re T.N.G.*, 244 N.C. App. 398 (2015).
- Where the trial court did not find that the father was unable to care for the child and lacked an alternative child care arrangement, a finding that the child was conceived as a result of the father's commission of statutory rape was not sufficient to support a conclusion that the child was dependent. *In re J.L.*, 183 N.C. App. 126 (2007).

Appellate court found lack of proper care and supervision.

- Where the mother had severe psychological problems and the children had psychological problems, learning disabilities, and behavioral and other problems that were not being addressed by the mother and her significant other, the children were adjudicated dependent. *See In re T.B.*, 203 N.C. App. 497 (2010).
- A child was dependent when mother continuously failed to obtain meaningful mental health services for the child when the child was in her custody. Findings established that child had serious mental health issues requiring five psychiatric hospitalizations over a period of four months, and that mother minimized and denied the seriousness of the child's condition and at times exacerbated it and was unable to provide proper care and supervision to the child. *In re C.B.*, 245 N.C. App. 197 (2016).
- Where a child was repeatedly raped by the father, the father agreed to cease contact with her but moved back into home one week later, and the mother would not enforce DSS's safety plan to keep the father away from child, evidence was sufficient to support an adjudication that child was abused, neglected, and dependent. *In re K.W.*, 192 N.C. App. 646 (2008).

### (b) Lacking alternative child care arrangement (second prong of G.S. 7B-101(9)(ii)).

An adjudication of dependency requires evidence and findings establishing that the parent does not have an appropriate alternative child care arrangement. *In re K.D.*, 178 N.C. App. 322 (2006); *In re P.M.*, 169 N.C. App. 423 (2005). An appropriate alternative child care arrangement requires that a parent has taken some action to identify a viable caregiver. *In re C.B.*, 245 N.C. App. 197 (2016); *In re L.H.*, 210 N.C. App. 355 (2011). For a parent to have an alternative caregiver arrangement, "the parent must have taken some action to identify the alternative arrangement" and not merely have gone along with DSS's plan for the child. *In re B.P.*, 809 S.E.2d 914, 920 (N.C. Ct. App. 2018).

Appellate court found a lack of alternative child care arrangement.

- Mother lacked an appropriate alternative child care arrangement for child with serious mental health issues requiring five psychiatric hospitalizations over a period of four months. Mother failed to identify any viable placement alternative outside of placement in her home and refused to participate in and obstructed the development of a hospital discharge plan for the child. *In re C.B.*, 245 N.C. App. 197.
- Evidence was sufficient to support an adjudication of dependency where neither the mother nor the father was able to care for the children, the father's proposed alternate placement was with an aunt to whom he had not spoken in five years, and there was no evidence that the aunt was willing or able to care for the children. *In re D.J.D.*, 171 N.C. App. 230 (2005).
- Where the mother's significant other had been acting in a parental role for twelve or thirteen years, during which the children exhibited multiple problems and had needs that were not met, the significant other could not be considered an appropriate alternate child care arrangement. *In re T.B.*, 203 N.C. App. 497 (2010).
- In a private termination of parental rights case, the respondent mother could not claim that an alternative child care arrangement existed where an unrelated acquaintance had been awarded permanent custody of the child by the court because the acquaintance did not have custody at the respondent's request and the respondent had no ability to decide custody. *In re K.O.*, 223 N.C. App. 420 (2012).
- Where DSS failed to present any evidence on the lack of alternative child care at the adjudicatory hearing and the trial court made no findings as to alternative child care, the adjudication of dependency was reversed. *In re J.D.R.*, 239 N.C. App. 63 (2015); see *In re V.B.*, 239 N.C. App. 340 (2015).

Appellate court did not find a lack of alternative child care arrangement.

- Before petition was filed, mother placed child with caretakers, whose home was found appropriate by both DSS and the trial court. Mother made placement "on her own, without DSS's input" and child was in that placement when petition alleging dependency was filed. There was no lack of an appropriate alternative caregiver arrangement when mother had taken action to identify the caretakers and had not "merely acquiesced in DSS's plan" for the child. *In re B.P.*, 809 S.E.2d 914, 920 (N.C. Ct. App. 2018).

## 6.4 Adjudication Order

For further discussion of technical aspects of orders in juvenile proceedings, including timing and drafting of the order and proper findings of fact and conclusions of law, see Chapter 4.9.

**AOC Form:**
AOC-J-153, Juvenile Adjudication Order (Abuse/Neglect/Dependency) (Oct. 2013).

**Resource:** Janet Mason, *Drafting Good Court Orders in Juvenile Cases*, JUVENILE LAW BULLETIN No. 2013/02 (UNC School of Government, Sept. 2013).

### A. General Requirements

The Juvenile Code requires that an adjudication order

- be in writing;
- contain appropriate findings of fact;
- contain appropriate conclusions of law; and
- be reduced to writing, signed, and filed with the clerk no later than thirty days following the completion of the hearing.

G.S. 7B-807(b). See Chapter 4.9.D (discussing the clerk's responsibility to schedule a special hearing when the order is not entered within thirty days from the completion of the adjudication hearing, as well as the appropriate remedy for untimely orders).

**Practice Note:** Just as it is permissible for more than one child to be named in a petition (when the children are from the same home and are brought to court for the same reason), one order may serve as the order in the case of each child named in the petition. If the findings or conclusions, or both, differ significantly from child to child, or if the adult respondents in each child's case are not the same, the entry of a separate order for each child may be preferable. Any order that is being entered in more than one child's case should clearly indicate which findings relate to which child and must include the file number for each child.

**1. Condition not proved.** If the allegations are not proved by clear and convincing evidence, the court must dismiss the petition with prejudice. If the child is in nonsecure custody, the child must be released to his or her parent, guardian, custodian, or caretaker. G.S. 7B-807(a). If the petition alleges more than one status (abuse, neglect, or dependency) and the court adjudicates one but not another, it must dismiss the allegation that is not proved. *See In re T.B.*, 203 N.C. App. 497 (2010) (holding that trial court erred when it adjudicated children dependent but purported to hold in abeyance its ruling on the neglect allegation, when nothing in the record indicated that a future adjudication hearing was to be scheduled).

**2. Condition proved.** An order that adjudicates a child to be abused, neglected, or dependent must state that the findings of fact are based on clear and convincing evidence. Failure to state the standard of proof in the order is reversible error; however, there is no requirement as to how or where a recital of the clear and convincing standard should be included. *In re O.W.*, 164 N.C. App. 699, 702 (2004) (holding that the statement in the trial court's order that it "concludes through clear, cogent, and convincing evidence. . ." was acceptable).

### B. Findings of Fact and Conclusions of Law

Findings of fact and conclusions of law must be stated in the order separately and specifically. Common issues on appeal include whether the evidence supports the findings of fact and whether the findings of fact support the court's conclusion of law that a child is abused, neglected, or dependent. The topic of what constitutes proper findings of fact and conclusions of law is addressed in detail in Chapter 4.9.B.

Appellate cases have pointed out that in an adjudication order, a conclusion of law that a juvenile is abused, neglected, or dependent is about the status of the child and should not be connected to whose actions resulted in the adjudication. The supreme court has said, "In determining whether a child is neglected, the determinative factors are the circumstances and conditions surrounding the child, not the fault or culpability of the parent." *In re M.A.W.*, 370 N.C. 149, 154 (2017) (quoting *In re Montgomery*, 311 N.C. 101, 109 (1984)); *In re A.L.T.*, 241 N.C. App. 443, 451 (2015) (quoting *In re Montgomery*). Other cases have said the same about adjudications of abuse and dependency – "By determining that a juvenile is abused, neglected or dependent, the court . . . determines the status of the juvenile so that his or her best interests may be ascertained." *In re B.M.*, 183 N.C. App. 84, 87 (2007). *See also In re A.S.*, 181 N.C. App. 706, 714 (2007) (Levinson, J., concurring in part and dissenting in part) (emphasis in original) (stating that it is "*unhelpful and confusing*" for conclusions of law regarding the status of the child to include language such as "as to" [father, mother, guardian] or "because" of [father, mother, guardian]); *In re J.S.*, 182 N.C. App. 79, 86 (2007) (stating "[t]he purpose of the adjudication and disposition proceedings should not be morphed on appeal into a question of culpability regarding the conduct of an individual parent. The question this Court must look at on review is whether the court made the proper determination in making findings and conclusions as to the status of the juvenile").

## 6.5 Consent Orders

An adjudication may result from a consent order in lieu of an adjudicatory hearing. *See* G.S. 7B-801(b1). A consent order is an agreement of all the parties, their decree, entered on the record and sanctioned by the court. *In re R.L.G.*, 816 S.E.2d 914 (N.C. Ct. App. 2018); *In re Thrift*, 137 N.C. App. 559 (2000). It is not a judicial determination representative of the court's judgment but is instead a record of the parties' agreement, which has been approved by the judge. *McRary v. McRary*, 228 N.C. 714 (1948).

The Juvenile Code allows the court to enter a consent adjudication order on a petition alleging abuse, neglect, or dependency only if

- all parties are present or represented by counsel who is present and authorized to consent;

- the child is represented by counsel; and
- the court makes sufficient findings of fact.

G.S. 7B-801(b1); *In re R.L.G.*, 816 S.E.2d 914 (N.C. Ct. App. 2018).

A consent order that conforms to statutory requirements operates as a judgment on the merits and acquires the status of a final judgment. *See In re Thrift*, 137 N.C. App. 559; *Buckingham v. Buckingham*, 134 N.C. App. 82 (1999). If the consent order does not meet the statutory requirements, it is not a valid order. *See In re K.P.*, 249 N.C. App. 620 (2016) (adjudication reversed where there was no adjudication hearing or valid consent order; the order did not contain findings that the parties stipulated to facts or consented to the adjudication; there was no draft consent order or evidence the parties reached a consent agreement); *In re Shaw*, 152 N.C. App. 126 (2002) (reversed and remanded for an adjudicatory hearing after holding the consent of one respondent in the absence of the other respondent's presence was insufficient to dispense with the need to hold an adjudicatory hearing).

Stipulations of fact are not consent orders. *See In re R.L.G.*, 816 S.E.2d at 917 (an adjudication order that "simply contained a stipulation by the parties as to certain facts" pursuant to G.S. 7B-807 was not a valid consent adjudication order under G.S. 7B-801(b1)). The court is not bound by an agreement of the parties where the evidence and facts support a different result. *In re L.G.I.*, 227 N.C. App. 512 (2013) (affirming adjudication of neglect and rejection of the parties' plan of reunification, where the parties had stipulated to facts supporting an adjudication and later the parties indicated that the agreement was contingent on DSS's working toward reunification; the requirements of a consent order had not been met but instead and at most respondent mother stipulated to certain facts).

When there is a proper consent, the adjudication part of a consent order must comply with all requirements for adjudication orders. See section 6.4, above. However, in the case of *In re J.S.C.*, 253 N.C. App. 291 (2017), the court of appeals held that there was no reversible error where a consent adjudication order of abuse and neglect, which was based entirely on stipulated facts, did not state that the adjudicatory findings were based on the clear and convincing evidentiary standard required by G.S. 7B-805. The opinion discussed how an adjudication by consent based entirely on stipulated facts is not an adjudication hearing and so G.S. 7B-805, which addresses the required quantum of proof in an adjudication hearing, does not apply since the court does not engage in the process of fact-finding. The opinion did not address the requirement under G.S. 7B-807(a) that if the court finds from the evidence, including stipulations by a party, that the allegations have been proved by clear and convincing evidence, it "shall so state" because the issue was not timely raised on appeal.

## 6.6 Consequences of Adjudication

### A. Continued Jurisdiction and Authority for Disposition

An adjudication of abuse, neglect, or dependency enables the court to proceed to the dispositional phase of the case in which the court determines the needs of the child and family and makes orders accordingly. An adjudication allows the court to continue exercising jurisdiction over the child and the respondents (if the respondents are properly served or have waived sufficiency of process and/or service of process) until the child reaches age 18 or is emancipated, is adopted, or until the court orders its jurisdiction terminated, whichever occurs first. *See* G.S. 7B-200; 7B-201(a); 48-2-102(b). See Chapter 3.1.C (discussing continuing and ending jurisdiction). Note that the court continues to have jurisdiction over placement review hearings of young adults participating in Foster Care 18–21. G.S. 7B-200(a)(5a); 7B-910.1 See Chapter 8.3 (discussing Foster Care 18–21).

## B. Impact on Parents and Future Proceedings

An adjudication that a child is abused, neglected, or dependent allows the state to intervene in the constitutionally protected parent-child relationship. See Chapter 2.4.A (discussing the protection of parent-child relationships). An adjudication is a prerequisite to disposition, in which the court has the authority not only to remove the child from the home, but also to order the parents to take specific actions to address the causes of the adjudication and, if the child is removed from the home, the reasons for the removal. *See* G.S. 7B-903; 7B-904. See also Chapter 7.7 (relating to disposition and the court's authority over parents).

An adjudication may affect parents in future proceedings. An adjudication that a child is abused or neglected can contribute to a later adjudication that another child living in the same home is neglected because the Juvenile Code makes abuse or neglect of other children living in the home relevant to a determination of neglect. *See* G.S. 7B-101(15). See also section 6.3.E.2(b), above (discussing other children in the home). Also, evidence of an adjudication of abuse, neglect, or dependency can be introduced in a subsequent action to terminate the parents' rights (TPR). See Chapter 9.11.A.4 (discussing the grounds for TPR and the use of prior adjudications of abuse, neglect, or dependency in a TPR proceeding).

The doctrine of collateral estoppel precludes parties from retrying fully litigated issues that were decided in any prior determination and were necessary to the prior determination. *See In re F.S.*, 835 S.E.2d 465, 470-71 (N.C. Ct. App. 2019) (collateral and judicial estoppel precluded DSS from retrying the fully litigated issue that was decided in a proceeding initiated by petition; collateral estoppel did not preclude a "trial court's adjudication of facts from new allegations and events" that took place after entry of an adjudication order in the initial proceeding on 5/15/2017). So, a critical finding of fact in an adjudication order may be adopted by the court and may not be challenged in a subsequent action involving another child of the parent or in a later termination of parental rights action. *See In re N.G.*, 186 N.C. App. 1 (2007), *aff'd per curiam*, 362 N.C. 229 (2008); *In re Wheeler*, 87 N.C. App. 189 (1987). See Chapter 11.7.D.2 (discussing the doctrine of collateral estoppel).

Courts have recognized that an adjudication may have "collateral consequences" that can affect the parent regardless of the dispositional outcome of the case in which the adjudication occurred. In the case *In re A.K.*, 360 N.C. 449 (2006), the North Carolina Supreme Court reversed the court of appeals' dismissal of an appeal as moot. The appeal had been deemed moot because custody of the child was returned to the parent before the court of appeals considered the parent's appeal of an order adjudicating the child neglected and placing the child in DSS custody. The supreme court held that the appeal was not moot because a "neglect adjudication can reasonably result in collateral legal consequences." *In re A.K.*, 360 N.C. at 459 (discussing the potential impact of the adjudication on future proceedings as well as the social stigma involved for the parents in having their child adjudicated abused, neglected, or dependent).

# Chapter 7

# Dispositional Phase: Initial, Review, and Permanency Planning

# Chapter 7
# Dispositional Phase: Initial, Review, and Permanency Planning

**7.1  Introduction and Purpose of Dispositional Phase    7-4**
  A. Introduction
  B. Purpose of Disposition
     1. Exercise jurisdiction to address child's needs
     2. Careful consideration of needs and circumstances
     3. Respect for family autonomy
     4. Preference for placement with relative when no reunification
     5. Fair procedures and protection of rights
     6. Child's best interests
     7. Safe, permanent home within a reasonable period of time
  C. Significant Legislative Changes regarding Permanency Planning

**7.2  Dispositional Hearings    7-10**
  A. Timing and When Required
     1. Initial dispositional hearing
     2. Review hearing
     3. Permanency planning hearing
     4. Waiver of hearings and departure from time requirements
  B. Notice and Calendaring
  C. Participants
  D. Open or Closed Hearings
  E. Evidentiary Standard and Burden of Proof
     1. Rules of evidence
     2. No burden of proof
     3. Reports

**7.3  Best Interests of the Child    7-20**

**7.4  Dispositional Alternatives: Placement and Custody    7-22**
  A. Dismiss or Continue the Case
     1. Dismiss the case
     2. Continue the case
  B. In-Home Supervision and Services
  C. Parent and Out-of-Home Placement Generally
     1. Placement priority: parents and relatives
     2. Child's own community
     3. Required findings
     4. Meaning and impact of "custody" and "placement"
  D. DSS Custody
     1. Notice to GAL of change in placement

2. Court approval for return home and unsupervised visitation
3. DSS authority to consent to child's medical care
4. Reasonable and prudent parent standard
E. Custody with a Parent, Relative, Other Suitable Person, or Private Agency
1. Custody to a parent, relative, other suitable person, or private agency
2. Verification required
3. Return to caregiver with violent history
4. Joint custody is permissible
5. Modification of custody order
6. Consideration of transfer to civil custody action
F. Guardianship
1. Appointment
2. Verification required
3. Role of guardian
4. Duration of the guardianship
G. Verification of Understanding of Legal Significance and Adequate Resources
H. Interstate Compact on the Placement of Children
1. Introduction and purpose
2. State and agency structure
3. Source of requirements and procedures
4. Applicability of ICPC
5. The ICPC and placement with a non-removal parent or relative
6. The ICPC and visitation
7. Summary requirements of the ICPC and Regulations
8. Illegal placements

## 7.5 Visitation    7-48
A. Order Must Address Visitation When Out-of-Home Placement
1. Minimum outline of visits required
2. Cost of supervision
3. Electronic communication
4. No visitation based on child's health, safety, and best interest
5. DSS responsibility; court approval
6. Guardians and custodians
7. Suspension of visitation
B. Review of Visitation Plan, Notice to Parties, Mediation

## 7.6 Evaluation and Treatment of Child    7-53
A. Court's Authority to Order Evaluation and Treatment
B. Hearing to Determine Treatment Needs and Payment
1. County involvement
2. Treatment arrangements
3. Treatment costs
4. Mental illness or developmental disability

## 7.7 Court's Authority over Parents and Others    7-55
A. Treatment and Counseling

1. Participation in child's treatment
2. Evaluations and treatment of parents and others
B. Parenting Classes, Transportation, Remedial Steps, and Other Orders
C. Cost Responsibilities
1. Child support
2. Treatment of child or participating adult
3. Treatment of parent or others
D. Failure to Comply with Court Orders
E. Court's Authority over DSS
F. Court's Authority over Child's GAL
G. Limitations on Court's Dispositional Authority

**7.8 Dispositional Considerations and Findings     7-61**
A. Initial Dispositional Hearing
1. Inquiry as to missing parent, paternity, and relatives required
2. Consideration of G.S. 7B-901(c) factors and reasonable efforts
B. Required Criteria for Review and Permanency Planning Hearings
1. Reunification efforts
2. Visitation
3. Placement
4. Independent living
5. Termination of parental rights
6. Any other criteria
C. Permanency Planning Additional Requirements
1. Returning home
2. Guardianship or custody
3. Adoption
4. Change in current placement
5. Reasonable efforts to implement permanent plan
6. Other criteria
7. Permanent plan
8. Reasonable efforts findings
9. Youth in DSS custody at age 14 and older
D. Initiation of Termination of Parental Rights Proceeding under Certain Circumstances
E. Hearing to Modify or Vacate a Dispositional Order

**7.9 Reasonable Efforts     7-72**
A. Introduction
B. Statutory Definitions: Reasonable Efforts, Return Home, Reunification
C. Required Findings
D. Ceasing Reasonable Efforts

**7.10 Concurrent Permanency Planning and Outcomes     7-79**
A. Concurrent Permanency Planning
B. Achieving a Permanent Plan
1. Reunification
2. Adoption

3. Guardianship
4. Custody
5. Parent's constitutional rights findings before custody or guardianship to non-parent
6. APPLA
7. Reinstatement of parental rights

**7.11 Dispositional Orders    7-91**
   A. Timing
   B. General Requirements
      1. Findings and conclusions
      2. Precise terms
      3. Set next hearing
      4. Compliance with UCCJEA, ICPC, MEPA, and ICWA
   C. Consent Orders
   D. Status of Jurisdiction

## 7.1 Introduction and Purpose of Dispositional Phase

### A. Introduction

In this Manual, the term "dispositional phase" refers collectively to initial dispositional hearings, review hearings, and permanency planning hearings that take place after a child has been adjudicated abused, neglected, or dependent. Initial dispositional hearings, review hearings, and permanency planning hearings share most of the same purposes and procedures. *In re Montgomery*, 77 N.C. App. 709 (1985) (stating that a hearing on a motion for review is in the nature of a dispositional hearing). Yet each type of hearing has distinct purposes and procedures as well.

**Note,** this Chapter discusses all three types of hearings, the applicable procedures, and the outcomes that are available in those different hearings. This Chapter is best understood when read in its entirety, as subsections within the Chapter are not meant to be stand-alone explanations of a topic given the regular use of cross-referencing within this Chapter. Checklists at the end of this Manual identify the required findings and outcome options for orders resulting from each of the three types of dispositional hearings: initial, review, and permanency planning.

Throughout the dispositional phase the court determines and reviews the needs of the child and the family and the best way to meet those needs. The court's guiding principle in the dispositional phase is the child's best interests, which is the paramount consideration or the "polar star" of the Juvenile Code. G.S. 7B-100(5); *In re Montgomery*, 311 N.C. 101, 109 (1984). The court exercises its discretion when determining the child's best interests. *See, e.g., In re J.W.*, 241 N.C. App. 44 (2015) (a neglect proceeding); *In re A.R.A.*, 835 S.E.2d 417 (N.C. S.Ct. 2019) (a termination of parental rights proceeding).

At dispositional hearings of any type, the court may be considering

- whether the child can safely remain at home or be returned home;
- who should have custody of the child;
- where the child should be placed;
- what (if any) visitation is appropriate if the child is out of the home;
- whether to delegate decision-making authority for specific issues involving the child;
- what services the child should receive;
- what services the parents, guardian, custodian, or caretaker over whom the court has personal jurisdiction should receive;
- what directives should be made to the parents, guardian, custodian, or caretaker over whom the court has personal jurisdiction concerning expected changes or accomplishments that would place him or her in a better position to care for the child;
- whether efforts by DSS to reunify the family have been made and whether they should continue; and
- the date of the next hearing.

*See* G.S. 7B-901 through -906.2.

**Note**, for purposes of this Manual, "department of social services" or "DSS" refers to a department as defined by G.S. 7B-101(8a) regardless of how it is titled or structured.

At a permanency planning hearing, the court must also determine the best concurrent permanent plans for the child and the steps necessary to accomplish those plans so that permanence is timely achieved for the child. *See* G.S. 7B-906.2. Permanency options include

- reunification;
- adoption;
- guardianship;
- custody;
- for youth ages 16 or 17, Another Planned Permanent Living Arrangement (APPLA); and
- when there has been a termination of parental rights, reinstatement of those rights.

G.S. 7B-906.2(a).

DSS is required to make reasonable efforts toward those plans. A permanent plan of reunification has priority over other permanent plans, and specific procedures and findings apply when DSS is relieved of making reasonable efforts for reunification and/or reunification as a permanent plan is eliminated by the court. *See* G.S. 7B-906.2(b); 7B-901(c); *see also* G.S. 7B-100(4), (5) (purposes). Note that "reasonable efforts for reunification" and "reunification efforts" appear to be used synonymously throughout the Juvenile Code and case law.

The dispositional hearings may be informal but do require some oral testimony. *In re S.P.*, 833 S.E.2d 638 (N.C. Ct. App. 2019). The court considers evidence that is relevant, reliable, and necessary to determine the child's needs and most appropriate disposition. G.S. 7B-

901(a); *see* G.S. 7B-906.1(c). All parties may submit evidence to the court of their perspectives on what the child's and family's needs are and how those needs can be met.

"Dispositional alternatives" or outcomes related to placement, evaluation, and treatment of the child are addressed in G.S. 7B-903. These dispositional alternatives, which can be combined, are available to the court at any hearing that takes place during the dispositional phase of the case. *See* G.S. 7B-903(a); 7B-906.1(i).

In addressing the child's placement, the priority is to help the family by providing community-level services while the child remains in the home. *See* G.S. 7B-900. However, if the court determines that the child's safety and welfare require that the child be placed outside his or her home (or remain outside the home if the child is already placed outside the home), the court will examine placement alternatives and the best strategy for making it possible for the child to return home safely. *See* G.S. 7B-903. If the court determines that the child cannot be returned home within a reasonable period of time, the court must decide what other placement will provide the child with a safe, permanent home within a reasonable period of time. *See* G.S. 7B-906.1.

Regardless of the child's placement, the court may order evaluations, treatment, or services for the child or parents (or sometimes guardians, custodians, or caretakers) to better understand or address their needs. Dispositional outcomes that require parents or others to participate in evaluations, treatment, or classes, or to take other actions to address the conditions that led to the child's adjudication or removal from home are authorized by G.S. 7B-904 and, indirectly, G.S. 7B-200(b), relating to the court's personal jurisdiction over individuals. The court's authority to enter dispositional orders is not without limits, and the court is not permitted to make dispositional orders that are beyond the scope of the dispositional statutes.

Initial dispositional hearings are addressed in G.S. 7B-901 and review and permanency planning hearings in G.S. 7B-906.1. The initial dispositional hearing is the first hearing in the dispositional phase of the abuse, neglect, or dependency case. It is also the first hearing where the court has the authority to relieve DSS of making reasonable efforts toward reunification. If the child is placed in DSS custody, the court may order DSS cease reasonable efforts toward reunification if the court makes written findings of specified factors set forth in G.S. 7B-901(c). When reunification efforts are ceased at initial disposition, permanency planning is accelerated as a permanency planning hearing must be scheduled within thirty days. G.S. 7B-901(d).

When reunification efforts are not ceased, review hearings are scheduled after the initial dispositional hearing and before a permanency planning hearing (although a review hearing may be combined with a permanency planning hearing). A review hearing provides the court with an opportunity to assess what is happening in the case and to determine whether any changes should be made concerning the disposition. The court does not have authority to cease reunification efforts at a review hearing. *See In re T.W.,* 250 N.C. App. 68 (2016).

A permanency planning hearing is a specific type of review hearing held for the purposes of determining whether the child's return home is likely, identifying concurrent permanent plans for the child, ordering DSS to make reasonable efforts toward each of those plans, and reviewing the progress made in finalizing a permanent plan so that a safe, permanent home for the child may be achieved within a reasonable period of time. *See* G.S. 7B-906.1(g); 7B-906.2.

A permanency planning hearing must be held within twelve months of the initial order that removed custody of the child from a parent, guardian, custodian, or caretaker. Permanency planning hearings must occur sooner when the initial dispositional order ceases reunification efforts or a review order contains a finding that reunification efforts with a parent clearly would be unsuccessful or inconsistent with the juvenile's health or safety and need for a safe, permanent home within a reasonable period of time. In either case, the permanency planning hearing must be scheduled within thirty days. G.S. 7B-901(d); 7B-906.1(d)(3).

Unless the statutory criteria to waive permanency planning hearings are satisfied, permanency planning hearings must be held at least every six months to review the progress in finalizing the permanent plans or to make new permanent plans for the juvenile. *See* G.S. 7B-906.1(a), (k), (n). The achievement of certain permanency outcomes will terminate the court's jurisdiction over the action while other permanency outcomes will result in the court retaining jurisdiction without there being any regularly scheduled permanency planning hearings.

Although the Juvenile Code sets forth this sequential hearing process, it does not prohibit the court from conducting the adjudication, dispositional, and permanency planning hearings on the same day. *In re C.P.*, 812 S.E.2d 188 (N.C. Ct. App. 2018).

**Resources:**
Multiple resources addressing dispositional outcomes for children and issues faced by children and families in foster care, including publications and tools related to specific topics such as physical and mental health issues, child development, child safety, visitation, education, race and ethnicity, substance abuse, older youth, permanency, incarcerated parents, fatherhood, and much more can be found on the following websites:
- The Child Welfare Information Gateway, a service of the Children's Bureau, which is part of the U.S. Department of Health and Human Services Administration for Children and Families.
- The National Council of Juvenile and Family Court Judges.
- The National Conference of State Legislatures.
- The American Bar Association Center on Children and the Law, and also within that website, *ABA Child Law Practice*.

## B. Purpose of Disposition

The Juvenile Code refers specifically to dispositional purposes in both G.S. 7B-100 and 7B-900. Other provisions in the Juvenile Code expand on these purposes. Read collectively, these provisions indicate the following general purposes, which should guide the court in determining dispositional outcomes for any hearing in the dispositional phase. Ultimately, throughout the dispositional phase the court is balancing child safety with family preservation. North Carolina appellate courts have stated, "It is clear from the statutory framework of the Juvenile Code that one of the essential aims, if not the essential aim, of the dispositional hearing and the review hearing is to reunite the parent(s) and the child, after the child has been taken from the custody of the parent(s)." *In re T.W.*, 250 N.C. App. 68, 71 2016) (quoting *In re Shue*, 311 N.C. 586, 596 (1984)).

**1. Exercise jurisdiction to address child's needs.** A stated purpose of disposition is to "design an appropriate plan to meet the needs of the juvenile and to achieve the objectives of the State in exercising jurisdiction." G.S. 7B-900. The court must examine the specific needs and limitations of the child and craft a plan that takes into account the child's need for safety, continuity, and permanence, with a preference for the return of the child to his or her parents and home. *See* G.S. 7B-100(2), (3), (5); 7B-900. In doing so, the court should focus on the conditions that resulted in the adjudication of abuse, neglect, or dependency, with safety as the primary objective. As a corollary, the court also must determine at what point it is no longer necessary or appropriate for the court to continue exercising jurisdiction. *See, e.g.*, G.S. 7B-911.

**2. Careful consideration of needs and circumstances.** A disposition should take into consideration the facts, the child's needs and limitations, and the family's strengths and weaknesses. G.S. 7B-100(2). Juvenile Code procedures require the court to take into account information from multiple sources when making dispositional determinations, and the court has wide latitude to consider relevant, reliable, and necessary evidence for dispositional purposes. G.S. 7B-901(a); 7B-906.1(c).

**3. Respect for family autonomy.** Dispositional plans and orders must respect family autonomy and avoid unnecessary or inappropriate separation of children from their parents. *See* G.S. 7B-100(3), (4). When possible, the initial approach should be for a child to remain at home with appropriate community-level services. G.S. 7B-900.

**4. Preference for placement with relative when no reunification.** When a child must be removed from the home, the court must first consider whether a relative is willing and able to provide proper care for the child in a safe home. *See* G.S. 7B-903(a1); 7B-101(19) (definition of "safe home"). In situations where a child is removed from one parent's home but living in the home of another parent is a possibility, placement with the other parent must be considered before other relatives or other placement options are considered.

**5. Fair procedures and protection of rights.** The procedures set forth in the Juvenile Code are meant to assure fairness and equity as well as protect the constitutional rights of juveniles and parents. *See* G.S. 7B-100(1). See Chapter 2.3 and 2.4 (discussing the rights of children and parents).

**6. Child's best interests.** Applying to all aspects of the Juvenile Code, including dispositions, are standards that ensure that the child's best interests are of paramount consideration for the court. *See* G.S. 7B-100(5). The Juvenile Code also refers to the consideration of the child's "health and safety." *See, e.g.*, G.S. 7B-507(a)(1) and (2); 7B-903(a2), (a3).

**7. Safe, permanent home within a reasonable period of time.** The goal of the dispositional phase is to return the child to his or her home or when that is not possible to a safe, permanent home within a reasonable period of time. The Juvenile Code specifically refers to the federal Adoption and Safe Families Act (ASFA), which has as one focus timeliness to permanency. G.S. 7B-100(5). See Chapter 1.3.B.6 (discussing ASFA and its impact on the Juvenile Code).

## C. Significant Legislative Changes regarding Permanency Planning

In 2013 and 2015 significant changes were made to the Juvenile Code, many of which impact the dispositional phase of abuse, neglect, or dependency proceedings.

Prior to legislative changes in 2013, review hearings were addressed in G.S. 7B-906 and permanency planning hearings in G.S. 7B-907. Both statutes were repealed in 2013 and replaced with G.S. 7B-906.1, which addresses both types of hearings and incorporates most of the language of the two previous statutes. Some cases cited in this Chapter were decided under the earlier statutes that contained language the same as, or similar to, the current statute. *See* S.L. 2013-129.

In 2015, with the enactment of G.S. 7B-906.2, the Juvenile Code mandates concurrent permanency planning in all abuse, neglect, or dependency actions that proceed to a permanency planning hearing. *See* S.L. 2015-136. Prior to October 1, 2015, the Juvenile Code permitted but did not require concurrent reasonable efforts for reunification and another permanent arrangement. *See* former G.S. 7B-507(d) (repealed by S.L. 2015-136, sec. 7). Additionally, the requirements and timing for when the court is authorized to order DSS relieved of providing reasonable efforts for reunification, often referred to as the cessation or elimination of reunification efforts, was changed substantially. Prior to the 2015 legislative changes, G.S. 7B-507 authorized the court in any order that awarded DSS custody of or placement responsibility for the child (e.g., a nonsecure custody, dispositional, review, or permanency planning order) to order that DSS was not required to provide reasonable efforts for reunification. The court was required to first make specific findings designated in former G.S. 7B-507.

Effective for all actions pending or filed on or after October 1, 2015, a court's authority to order the cessation of reasonable efforts changed and is more limited. A court may order the cessation of reasonable efforts for reunification only at the initial disposition or any permanency planning hearing. The criteria a court considers and the required findings a court must make when ceasing reunification efforts differ depending on whether the hearing is the initial dispositional or permanency planning hearing. *See* G.S. 7B-901(c); 7B-906.2(b). See sections 7.8 and 7.9, below (discussing the findings at different hearings and reasonable efforts). Some of the cases cited in this Chapter were decided under the previous statute, which did not distinguish between the type of hearing the order resulted from or when certain findings could be made to support the determination to cease reunification efforts. The majority of cases that have been decided under the current statutes focus primarily on the findings and timing of the findings as those findings relate to the noticed hearing that resulted in the order ceasing reunification efforts. Court of appeals opinions interpreting the new statutory scheme have also bifurcated reunification efforts from reunification as a permanent plan. See sections 7.8.A.2, below (discussing initial dispositional hearing), 7.8.C.8, below (discussing permanency planning hearing), and 7.9, below (discussing the findings at different hearings and reasonable efforts).

## 7.2 Dispositional Hearings

### A. Timing and When Required

There is a sequential process to an abuse, neglect, or dependency proceeding that carries over into the dispositional phase. *See In re T.R.P.*, 360 N.C. 588 (2006). There first must be an adjudication. An initial dispositional hearing follows the adjudication. A review or permanency planning hearing follows the initial dispositional hearing. When a review hearing is held that is not designated as a permanency planning hearing, a permanency planning hearing follows the review hearing. Although the Juvenile Code sets forth this sequential hearing process, it does not prohibit the court from conducting the adjudication, dispositional, and permanency planning hearings on the same day. *In re C.P.*, 812 S.E.2d 188 (N.C. Ct. App. 2018).

The Juvenile Code sets forth the maximum time limits that may expire before each type of hearing must be held; however, a case may proceed faster than the outer time limits designated in the Juvenile Code. The process should not be slower than the statutory maximum time limits. The appropriate remedy for a trial court's failure to conduct hearings in the dispositional phase within the statutory time frames is mandamus, not a new hearing. *See In re T.H.T.*, 362 N.C. 446 (2008); *In re E.K.*, 202 N.C. App. 309 (2010). See Chapter 4.5 (discussing continuances, delay, and remedy for delay) and 4.9.D.3 (discussing the elements for seeking mandamus).

**1. Initial dispositional hearing.** The initial dispositional hearing must be held immediately following adjudication and completed within thirty days after the conclusion of the adjudication hearing. G.S. 7B-901.

**2. Review hearing.** A review hearing must be held within ninety days from the date of the initial dispositional hearing, and within six months thereafter. Depending on when the first permanency planning hearing is scheduled, the review hearing may be replaced with the permanency planning hearing. Review hearings that are scheduled after the initial permanency planning hearing must be designated as permanency planning hearings. G.S. 7B-906.1(a).

In addition, in all cases the court is required to conduct a hearing when a party files a motion seeking review. G.S. 7B-906.1(n); *see also* G.S. 7B-1000. The motion may be made under G.S. 7B-906.1 or 7B-1000. Although the same standard, the child's best interests, applies to hearings under both statutes, different criteria apply. G.S. 7B-1000 authorizes the court to modify or vacate an order in light of changes in circumstances or the needs of the juvenile.

Review hearings under G.S. 7B-906.1 are based on the child's best interests and do not require proof of changed circumstances or the needs of the juvenile before a dispositional order may be modified. *See In re J.S.*, 250 N.C. App. 370 (2016). See section 7.8.E, below (discussing G.S. 7B-1000).

**Practice Notes:** Whether a review hearing that results from a party's motion is held pursuant to G.S. 7B-906.1 or 7B-1000 may depend on what the motion for review asks for and what is contained in the notice to the parties. At the beginning of the hearing, the parties or the court should make clear under what statute(s) the hearing is being held. The type of hearing should also be stated in the court's order. When a motion is filed after the first permanency planning hearing has been held, the hearing on the motion should be designated as a permanency planning hearing. *See* G.S. 7B-906.1(a) (stating "[r]eview hearings after the initial permanency planning hearing shall be designated as permanency planning hearings").

In one statutorily specified circumstance when a child is placed in a parent's custody and a new report is received, DSS will be required to file a new petition in the existing court action rather than a motion for review. *See* G.S. 7B-401(b). See subsection 4(a), below (discussing application of G.S. 7B-401(b)).

**3. Permanency planning hearing.** A type of review hearing called a permanency planning hearing is required within twelve months of the initial order removing custody of the child, which in many cases is a nonsecure custody order issued soon after the petition is filed. *See* G.S. 7B-906.1(a). A permanency planning hearing must be scheduled sooner when the court (1) orders at initial disposition that reasonable efforts for reunification are not required or (2) makes written findings in a review order (that is not a permanency planning order) that reasonable efforts for reunification with either parent clearly would be unsuccessful or inconsistent with the juvenile's health or safety and need for a safe, permanent home within a reasonable period of time. In either case, the court must schedule a permanency planning hearing within thirty days to address the child's permanent plans. G.S. 7B-901(d); 7B-906.1(d)(3).

Hearings after the initial permanency planning hearing are automatically designated permanency planning hearings (taking the place of regular review hearings) and must be held at least every six months unless waived or until the court no longer has subject matter jurisdiction over the action. *See* G.S. 7B-906.1(a), (k), (n); *see also* G.S. 7B-201 (jurisdiction); 7B-911 (transfer to civil custody action). See Chapter 3.1.C (discussing continuing and ending jurisdiction).

**Practice Note:** Permanency planning hearings are also referred to in some districts as "permanency planning review hearings."

**4. Waiver of hearings and departure from time requirements.** The Juvenile Code allows the court to depart from the schedule for review and permanency planning hearings in limited circumstances.

**(a) Custody to a parent.** The court is not obligated to conduct review and permanency planning hearings when custody is placed with a parent. G.S. 7B-906.1(k). No particular findings are required to waive these hearings when custody has been placed with a parent. Although the court is relieved of the duty to conduct periodic review and permanency planning hearings, it has discretion to continue to conduct these hearings as long as it retains jurisdiction over the action. *In re Shue*, 311 N.C. 586 (1984); *In re H.S.F.*, 177 N.C. App. 193 (2006).

When review and permanency planning hearings have been waived because the court has placed custody with a parent, if a new report of suspected abuse, neglect, or dependency is made to DSS, specific procedures under G.S. 7B-401(b) apply. As explained by the court of appeals, there are four criteria that trigger the application of G.S. 7B-401(b):

- the court retained jurisdiction over a child whose custody was granted to a parent;
- the court is not conducting periodic judicial reviews of the child's placement;
- a new report of abuse, neglect, or dependency is received by DSS after review hearings have been discontinued by the court; and
- the DSS director determined, based on an assessment of the new report conducted under G.S. 7B-302, that court action is needed.

*In re T.P.*, 254 N.C. App. 286 (2017).

Once periodic review and permanency planning hearings have been waived, G.S. 7B-401(b) impacts the trial court's subject matter jurisdiction to proceed in the action and limits the court's ability to simply hold a review or permanency planning hearing when the criteria of G.S. 7B-401(b) apply. When all four criteria are met, the court will only have subject matter jurisdiction to modify the dispositional order that awarded custody to the parent based on DSS filing a new petition in the existing action and not a motion for review. DSS sets out the recent allegations of abuse, neglect, or dependency in the new petition. Rather than hold a review or permanency planning hearing on that new petition, the trial court must then conduct a new adjudicatory hearing. If, based on the new petition, the child is adjudicated abused, neglected, or dependent at this second adjudicatory hearing, the court proceeds to a dispositional hearing to modify the existing dispositional order that grants custody to the parent. *See In re T.P.*, 254 N.C. App. 286 (vacating modification of permanency planning order that removed custody of the children from respondent mother resulting from DSS motion for review when G.S. 7B-401(b) was triggered; DSS motion was based on a new report it received and assessed about conditions in the mother's home one week after the court ordered custody to the mother and waived further review hearings; holding the court lacked subject matter jurisdiction to proceed on DSS motion as the proper pleading required by G.S. 7B-401(b) is a new petition filed in the existing case, which would be followed by a subsequent adjudicatory hearing on that petition).

**(b) Custody or guardianship to a non-parent.** When custody or guardianship is awarded to a person who is not the child's parent, the court may waive G.S. 7B-906.1 hearings, require the custodian or guardian to submit written reports to the court in lieu of the hearings, or order hearings less often than every six months if the court finds by clear, cogent, and convincing evidence each of the following factors:

- the child has resided in the placement for (1) at least one year or (2) at least six consecutive months and the court enters a consent order applying the procedures of G.S. 7B-801(b1) (note that this second prong was added by S.L. 2019-33, effective October 1, 2019);
- the placement is stable, and continuing the placement is in the child's best interests;
- neither the child's best interests nor the rights of any party require that review hearings be held every six months;
- all parties are aware that the matter may be brought before the court for review at any time by the filing of a motion for review or on the court's own motion; and
- the court order has designated the relative or other suitable person as the child's permanent custodian or guardian of the person.

G.S. 7B-906.1(n). See Chapter 3.1.D (discussing terminology in court orders when reviews are waived).

The court of appeals held that for purposes of the first condition stated above, the period of "at least one year" means a continuous and uninterrupted period of at least twelve months. *In re J.T.S.*, 834 S.E.2d 637 (N.C. Ct. App. 2019) (vacating portion of permanency planning order that waived review hearings when the first finding was based in part on the children having lived cumulatively with their grandparents for at least one year over the course of their lives). The court of appeals has also held that a child had lived with a relative for a year even though the child had not lived with the same relative for the entire year. *In re T.P.*, 217 N.C. App. 181 (2011) (finding no error with the trial court's combining time spent with two different sets of grandparents to meet the one-year time period). However, *In re T.P.* was decided under a prior statute requiring that the "juvenile has resided with a relative or has been in the custody of another suitable person for a period of at least one year." G.S. 7B-906(b)(1), repealed and replaced with G.S. 7B-906.1(n) by S.L. 2013-129. The court of appeals distinguished *In re T.P.* from the facts of *In re J.T.S.* and stated "[w]e cannot say whether this Court would have reached the same result in *T.P.* under N.C.G.S. § 7B-906.1(n)(1)." *In re J.T.S.*, 834 S.E.2d at 645.

A person who was not initially named as a party in the abuse, neglect, or dependency proceeding but who is later awarded custody of, or appointed guardian for, the child automatically becomes a party to the proceeding when that arrangement is the child's permanent plan. G.S. 7B-401.1(c), (d). Custodians or guardians who are parties may file a motion for review at any time.

Review and permanency planning hearings are not automatically waived when the court appoints a guardian or places the child in the custody of someone other than DSS or a parent. The hearings must continue until all of the conditions in G.S. 7B-906.1(n) are met, and the court makes all the required statutory findings in an order that waives further hearings. Such an order is commonly referred to as having "waived further reviews" (even when the hearing being waived is a permanency planning hearing).

Appellate courts have repeatedly found error where a trial court has waived further review hearings without making all the findings enumerated in G.S. 7B-906.1(n) by clear, cogent, and convincing evidence. *See In re K.L.,* 254 N.C. App. 269 (2017) (holding reversible error when two of the five required findings were not found); *In re E.M.*, 249 N.C. App. 44 (2016) (vacating the order waiving review hearings when neither the order nor the record showed the standard of proof the court applied and the court had made only one of the five required findings); *In re P.A.*, 241 N.C. App. 53 (2015) (holding that it was reversible error for the trial court to waive further review hearings without making findings of fact on each of the five statutory enumerated criteria).

**Practice Note:** When custody is ordered to a parent or non-parent and it seems appropriate for DSS and juvenile court involvement to end, transfer of the abuse, neglect, or dependency proceeding to a Chapter 50 custody action should be considered. If appropriate, the court enters a Chapter 50 custody order and terminates its jurisdiction in the juvenile proceeding pursuant to the criteria and procedures of G.S. 7B-911. See section 7.10.B.4(a) (explaining transfer to a civil custody action).

## B. Notice and Calendaring

DSS is required to make a timely request to the clerk to calendar each review and permanency planning hearing at a juvenile court session. The clerk is required to give fifteen days' notice of the hearing and its purpose to

- the parents,
- the child if 12 or older,
- the guardian,
- the person providing care for the child,
- the custodian or agency with custody,
- the child's guardian ad litem, and
- any other person or agency the court may specify.

G.S. 7B-906.1(b).

For purposes of notice to a person providing care for the child, DSS must either provide the clerk with the name and address of the individual to be given notice or send the notice itself and file with the clerk written documentation that notice of the hearing was sent to the child's current care provider. G.S. 7B-906.1(b).

Unless proper notice was waived, the court cannot enter a permanency planning order at a hearing for which proper notice was not given. Proper notice includes compliance with the fifteen-day time period as well as stating the purpose of the hearing. *See In re H.L.*, 807 S.E.2d 685 (N.C. Ct. App. 2017) (appellate review of father's challenge that trial court should not have conducted a combined dispositional, review, and initial permanency planning hearing was waived when father received multiple notices weeks and months before the hearing that it would be combined and father made no objection); *In re K.C.*, 791 S.E. 2d 284 (N.C. Ct. App. 2016) (originally unpublished Aug. 2, 2016, but subsequently published) (vacating permanency planning review orders and remanding for proper permanency planning hearings when respondent objected after receiving eight days' notice that the hearing initially scheduled as a review hearing would be a permanency planning hearing). *See also In re S.C.R.*, 217 N.C. App. 166 (2011) (holding that trial court erred where it authorized a permanent plan at a disposition hearing without the proper notice required for a permanency planning hearing). However, appellate cases have held that respondents waive any objection to lack of such notice by failing to object at trial. *See In re T.H.*, 232 N.C. App. 16 (2014) (holding that respondent could not claim lack of notice where trial court made a "temporary permanent plan" at adjudication and respondent attended disposition hearing but did not object to a lack of notice at disposition); *In re J.P.*, 230 N.C. App. 523 (2013) (holding that because respondent and counsel attended the disposition hearing in which the trial court announced its intention to enter a permanent plan and they did not object to lack of notice, they waived their right to object).

## C. Participants

At dispositional hearings, in addition to hearing from DSS as the petitioner, the court must give the child and the child's parents, guardian, custodian, or if applicable a caretaker who is a party an opportunity to present evidence and make recommendations about the disposition they believe to be in the child's best interests. *See* G.S. 7B-901(a).

At review and permanency planning hearings, the court is required to consider information from

- the parents,
- the child,
- the guardian,
- any person providing care for the child,
- the custodian or agency with custody of the child,
- the child's guardian ad litem, and
- any other person or agency that will aid in its review.

G.S. 7B-906.1(c).

At any hearing in the dispositional phase, testimony or evidence from persons who are not parties may be considered when the court finds it to be relevant, reliable, and necessary to determine the needs of the juvenile and the most appropriate disposition. G.S. 7B-901(a); 7B-906.1(c). The Juvenile Code states specifically that its provisions should not be construed to make any person providing care to a child a party to the proceeding based solely on receiving notice and having a right to be heard. G.S. 7B-906.1(b). See Chapters 5.4 (discussing parties) and 4.7.A (discussing intervention).

Persons whose presence may not be required (unless subpoenaed by a party) but who could potentially provide useful information to the court because of their involvement with the family or knowledge of or expertise on a particular relevant issue include

- relatives or nonrelative kin,
- counselors/therapists,
- medical or other experts,
- previous foster parents or other caregivers,
- school personnel,
- day care providers,
- law enforcement officers,
- juvenile court counselors,
- probation/parole officers, and
- other service providers.

### D. Open or Closed Hearings

Hearings are presumed to be open unless the court specifically excludes the public. The child has the right to request that the hearing be open, and the court must keep the hearing open when the child (or child's GAL) requests it. G.S. 7B-801(b). Otherwise, the court has discretion to exclude the public from all or part of a hearing, but in deciding to do so must consider the circumstances of the case, including

- the nature of the allegations,
- the age and maturity of the child,
- the benefit to the child of confidentiality,
- the benefit to the child of an open hearing, and
- the extent to which an open hearing would compromise the confidentiality afforded the child's record by G.S. 7B-2901.

G.S. 7B-801(a). See Chapter 14.1 (discussing confidentiality and disclosure of juvenile records).

Rule 15 of the General Rules of Practice for the Superior and District Courts Supplemental to the Rules of Civil Procedure prohibits electronic media and still photography coverage of juvenile proceedings. In some judicial districts local rules may address open hearings.

### E. Evidentiary Standard and Burden of Proof

**1. Rules of evidence.** Hearings in the dispositional phase may be informal, and the court may consider any evidence, including hearsay evidence, it finds to be relevant, reliable, and necessary to determine the child's needs and the most appropriate disposition. *See* G.S. 7B-901(a) (initial dispositional hearing); 7B-906.1(c) (review and permanency planning hearings); *In re J.L.*, 826 S.E.2d 258 (N.C. Ct. App. 2019). Some cases state that the North Carolina Rules of Evidence do not apply to dispositional hearings. *In re J.H.*, 244 N.C. App. 255 (2015) (dispositional hearings are not governed by the rules of evidence); *In re M.J.G.*, 168 N.C. App. 638 (2005) (formal rules of evidence do not apply at dispositional hearings); *In re Montgomery*, 77 N.C. App. 709 (1985) (unlike adjudication hearing, formal rules of evidence do not apply at dispositional hearings). See Chapter 11.1.B (discussing interpretation of this statement).

Although the Rules of Evidence do not apply, the court of appeals has repeatedly held that there must be competent evidence at a permanency planning hearing. Attorney arguments and reports alone are not competent evidence. There must be some oral testimony taken at a permanency planning hearing; otherwise, there is no competent evidence to support the court's findings of fact, resulting in conclusions of law that are made in error. *In re S.P.*, 833 S.E.2d 638 (N.C. Ct. App. 2019) (vacating and remanding permanency planning order that was based solely on DSS and GAL reports without any testimony; attorney arguments are not testimony); *In re J.T.*, 252 N.C. App. 19 (2017) (vacating and remanding permanency planning order as not supported by competent evidence when the court heard no oral testimony from any witnesses and only heard statements made by attorneys and accepted into evidence reports from DSS and the GAL); *In re D.Y.*, 202 N.C. App. 140 (2010) (reversing and remanding permanency planning order that was based solely on DSS and GAL reports, prior court orders, and attorney arguments; trial court failed to hold proper permanency planning hearing because DSS had presented no competent evidence); *In re D.L.*, 166 N.C. App. 574 (2004) (reversing and remanding permanency planning order based on lack of evidence; DSS presented no testimony, just attorney statements and a DSS summary).

Some cases discussing the trial court's rulings on evidentiary issues at dispositional hearings include the following.

- The expert's testimony based on her review of the DSS and GAL reports, listening to the audio recording of the hearing, and explaining her experience and the literature about children who experience loss and trauma from being removed from caregivers, without having personally evaluated the child, was sufficient competent evidence to support the trial court's findings. *In re J.L.*, 826 S.E.2d 258 (N.C. Ct. App. 2019).
- The trial court did not abuse its discretion in refusing to admit hearsay evidence in a permanency planning hearing when there was no explanation as to why the authors of documents were not present to testify, there was no support for the contention that the documents were reliable, and DSS strenuously objected to the documents based on a lack of authenticity and reliability. *In re P.O.*, 207 N.C. App. 35 (2010).
- It was not error for the court to exclude hearsay testimony of mother's sister regarding child's statements about abuse by father because it was cumulative—there was already an abundance of testimony regarding abuse of child by father. *In re J.S.*, 182 N.C. App. 79 (2007).
- It was error for the court to decline to "hear anything else about this thing today" and cut off a party's attempt to introduce evidence regarding best interest where there was no finding that the evidence was incompetent, irrelevant, or cumulative. *In re O'Neal*, 140 N.C. App. 254, 257 (2000).
- It was error for the trial court to base findings on statements made in the dispositional hearing by parties and other individuals who had not been duly sworn; this was not competent evidence. *In re J.N.S.*, 207 N.C. App. 670 (2010).

See Chapters 6.3.B (discussing the handling of different evidentiary standards when adjudication and disposition are combined) and 11 (discussing in detail evidence issues in juvenile proceedings).

**2. No burden of proof.** Juvenile Code provisions related to hearings in the dispositional phase do not place a burden of proof on any party. The essential requirement is that sufficient evidence be presented so that the court can make sufficient findings and a determination regarding the child's best interests. *See In re L.M.T.*, 367 N.C. 165 (2013) (stating that neither the parent nor DSS bears the burden of proof in a permanency planning hearing); *In re Shue*, 311 N.C. 586 (1984) (earlier version of the Juvenile Code did not place any burden of proof upon the parents or DSS during dispositional or review hearings).

**3. Reports.** After an adjudication, the court must proceed to the initial dispositional hearing when it receives sufficient social, medical, psychiatric, psychological, and educational information. G.S. 7B-808(a). Reports containing this type of information may be presented to the court by DSS, the child's guardian ad litem (GAL), and the parent at any type of hearing in the dispositional phase of the proceeding. The admission of a report without any oral testimony as the sole evidence at hearing is insufficient evidence to support the findings. See subsection E.1., above, discussing four published opinions on this issue.

**(a) DSS predisposition reports.** A "predisposition report" is a written report prepared by DSS that provides social, medical, psychiatric, psychological, and educational information, and sometimes recommendations, related to disposition. The court may not receive or consider the predisposition report until the adjudicatory hearing is completed. G.S. 7B-808(a). *Cf.* Chapter 6.3.B (discussing combining of adjudication and disposition hearings while considering certain evidence for dispositional purposes only).

Unless the court makes a written finding that the report is unnecessary, DSS is required to prepare a predisposition report containing

- the results of any mental health evaluation under G.S. 7B-503(b) (ordered by the court when the alleged abuser has a history of violent behavior against people),
- a placement plan, and
- a treatment plan to meet the child's needs.

G.S. 7B-808(b).

**(b) GAL or parent reports.** The Juvenile Code does not require written reports from parties other than DSS. Nevertheless, the child's GAL typically submits written reports to the court as part of the GAL's duties involving the investigation of facts and the child's needs, identification of resources, exploration of dispositional options, and promotion of the child's best interests. *See* G.S. 7B-601; 7B-700(f). This report, submitted to the court in the disposition phase of the case, may address many of the issues addressed in the DSS predisposition report and include the same or different recommendations.

Parents (through their attorneys, if represented by counsel) may submit written reports to the court, describing the parents' circumstances and progress, identifying resources, discussing dispositional alternatives, and making recommendations, including the parents' opinions about the best interests of the child. These reports, like the DSS report, can be given to the court only after adjudication. *See In re A.H.*, 250 N.C. App. 546 (2016) (in a termination of parental rights proceeding, respondent mother did not preserve for appeal the trial court's earlier determination to exclude the parent report made at a hearing on a motion in limine when her counsel did not seek to properly introduce the parent report at the disposition hearing); *see also In re H.M.H.*, 208 N.C. App. 568 (2009) (unpublished) (refers to a parent report admitted as evidence that the court considered at a review hearing).

**Sharing of reports.** Both judicial efficiency and the parties' ability to prepare adequately are enhanced if reports to the court are shared among parties before the day of the hearing. The Juvenile Code requires the GAL to share reports and information with all parties before submitting them to the court, but a time frame for sharing the report is not specified. G.S. 7B-700(f). The court may address deadlines for sharing reports at the pre-adjudication hearing. *See* G.S. 7B-800.1(a)(6)–(7) (court shall consider any discovery motions under G.S. 7B-700 and any other issue that can properly be addressed as a preliminary matter).

The chief district court judge may adopt local rules or issue an administrative order establishing time frames and procedures for the sharing of reports, including how a party's objection to the content of another party's report should be handled. The local rules or administrative order

- may prohibit disclosure of the report to the child if the court determines that disclosure is not in the child's best interests,
- may not prohibit a party entitled by law to receive confidential information from receiving that information, and
- may not allow disclosure of any confidential source protected by statute.

G.S. 7B-808(c). *See* G.S. 7B-700(b). See also Chapter 14.1 (discussing other laws related to sharing information in juvenile cases) and Appendix 2 (discussing the chief district court judge and local rules).

**Court's use of reports.** Although the court may consider reports as evidence, reports alone are insufficient to support a permanency planning order; there must be some testimony at the hearing. See subsection E.1, above, discussing four published opinions on this issue.

When written reports are admitted as evidence, the appellate courts have distinguished between a court's consideration of the reports and a court's incorporation of entire reports into its order as findings of fact. The appellate opinions sometimes characterize broad incorporation as error, but more often they focus on whether the trial court made sufficient independent findings of fact to show that the court did not improperly delegate its fact-finding function by overreliance on outside reports. *See, e.g., In re J.R.S.*, 813 S.E.2d 283 (N.C. Ct. App. 2018) (reversing and remanding permanency planning order for lack of findings to support best interests of the child conclusion as trial court should not delegate its fact-finding duty by merely incorporating DSS and GAL reports); *In re H.H.*, 237 N.C. App. 431 (2014) (holding the incorporation of reports by reference is not the equivalent of a finding); *In re A.S.*, 190 N.C. App. 679 (2008) (explaining that the trial court's finding that the statements in the reports were true did not constitute independent findings and did not tell the appellate court on which statements the court relied), *aff'd per curiam*, 363 N.C. 254 (2009); *In re L.B.*, 181 N.C. App. 174 (2007) (holding that the trial court properly incorporated and made findings of fact based on DSS and guardian ad litem reports).

## 7.3 Best Interests of the Child

The court's decisions related to disposition center on the determination of what is in the child's best interests. North Carolina appellate cases have referred to "best interests" as the "polar star" of the Juvenile Code. *See In re T.H.T.*, 362 N.C. 446, 450 (2008); *In re R.T.W.*, 359 N.C. 539, 550 (2005); *In re Montgomery*, 311 N.C. 101, 109 (1984). See also section 7.1.B, above, discussing purposes of disposition.

As applied to abuse, neglect, or dependency proceedings, there is no specific definition of "best interests" in the Juvenile Code or elsewhere. The determination of best interests is in the trial court's discretion. *In re H.L.*, 807 S.E.2d 685 (N.C. Ct. App. 2017). An appellate court reviews a trial court's best interests determination for an abuse of discretion. *See, e.g., In re B.C.T.*, 828 S.E.2d 50 (N.C. Ct. App. 2019); *In re J.W.*, 241 N.C. App. 44 (2015) (holding no abuse of discretion when the trial court kept the children in DSS custody rather than return the children to respondent mother's custody); *In re D.S.A.*, 181 N.C. App. 715 (2007) (holding that trial court's determination that it was not in child's best interest to be placed in paternal grandparents' custody was not an abuse of discretion).

A determination that a particular disposition is in a child's best interests is a conclusion of law that must be supported by findings of fact based on competent evidence in the record. *See In re B.C.T.*, 828 S.E.2d 50 (holding findings of fact do not support the conclusion of law; child's express preference is not controlling on the court when making a best interests determination); *In re L.M.*, 238 N.C. App. 345 (2014); *In re Helms*, 127 N.C. App. 505 (1997). In an appellate review, the trial court's findings are not viewed in isolation but instead are considered as part of the totality of all the court's findings. *See In re C.P.*, 252 N.C. App. 118 (2017) (affirming permanent plan of guardianship based on child's bests interests; findings of mother's progress should not viewed in isolation and did not contradict other findings that it was not in child's best interests to return home). The court of appeals has stated that "[a] 'conclusory recitation' of the best interests standard, without supporting findings of fact, is not sufficient" as "magic words", without evidence to support findings of fact, to support the related conclusions of law. *In re B.C.T.*, 828 S.E.2d at 58.

What follows are a few of many cases discussing the court's determination of best interests. However, nearly all appellate cases discussing the sufficiency of the evidence to support a dispositional decision either discuss or mention best interests. Many of these are cited in other sections of this Chapter and elsewhere in this Manual.

- Where a sixteen-year-old child had been in and out of foster care during his life, his mother had made some progress, and the child desired to return to his mother, it was not

error for the trial court to conclude that it was nevertheless in the child's best interest to appoint the foster father as the child's guardian. The trial court's findings provided sufficient evidence that the plan for guardianship was in the child's best interest and that the respondent mother could not adequately care for him. *In re L.M.*, 238 N.C. App. 345 (2014).
- There was insufficient evidence to support a conclusion that the change in custody from father to mother was in the child's best interest where the only relevant findings were that the child was not totally happy in her current residence; she missed her animals, her mother, her grandfather, and her stepfather (two of whom had neglected her); and she said she was glad that her biological father was in her life. The appellate court also found fault with an indication from the transcript that the principal basis for the change in custody was the fact that the father was unmarried, citing *Stanley v. Illinois*, 405 U.S. 645 (1972), which explicitly rejected this line of reasoning. *In re H.S.F.*, 177 N.C. App. 193 (2006).
- Evidence of a strong emotional bond between parent and child is critically important but not determinative on the issue of best interest. *In re Shue*, 63 N.C. App. 76 (1983), *aff'd as modified on other grounds*, 311 N.C. 586 (1984).
- Respondent mother asserted that the trial court erred in failing to consider the progress she had made and in ceasing reunification efforts, but the court of appeals found that while the trial court had considered her progress, there was not enough progress for the court to be assured that the children could be safely returned to her care, and the best interests of the children, not the rights of the parents, were paramount. *In re T.K.,* 171 N.C. App. 35, *aff'd per curiam*, 360 N.C. 163 (2005).
- Findings were insufficient to support the best interest determination as to custody outside of respondent's home, where findings were that respondent made diligent efforts to comply with the DSS case plan; both DSS and the GAL noted the absence of safety concerns in the home and recommended custody with respondent; and the trial court's findings that indicated some reservations about custody with the respondent were inadequate to support the best interest determination. *In re J.B.*, 197 N.C. App. 497 (2009).
- Where the trial court had made a finding that return of the child was contrary to the best interests of the child in that conditions leading to removal had not been alleviated, the court of appeals had difficulty determining which "condition" the trial court was referring to. One of the possibilities was the trial court's finding of "sexual deviancy" and that the respondent was bisexual, where the trial court had characterized this lifestyle as "abnormal" and "not conducive to child rearing." The court of appeals rejected such a finding, stating that it is not self-evident that sexual orientation has an adverse effect on the welfare of the child. Even if the court's finding that the parent is bisexual and people who surround her "engage in a similar lifestyle" were supported by evidence, there were no findings linking these circumstances to a negative impact on the child's welfare or on her parents' abilities to care for her. The court of appeals held that these conditions could not be a basis to take custody away from the child's biological parents. *In re M.M.*, 230 N.C. App. 225, 235 (2013) (see also cases cited therein).

## 7.4 Dispositional Alternatives: Placement and Custody

The Juvenile Code refers to placement and custody options as "dispositional alternatives" and enumerates five such options. *See* G.S. 7B-903(a). The court may combine any of those options when it finds the disposition is in the child's best interests. G.S. 7B-903(a). The various dispositional alternatives are available at any dispositional hearing. G.S. 7B-903(a); 7B-906.1(i). Over the course of the dispositional phase of the case, the child's placement is likely to change given the court's consideration of the child's best interests and need for a safe, permanent home within a reasonable period of time and the progress the parents made (or not) in correcting the conditions that led to the child's adjudication and/or removal. *See* G.S. 7B-906.1; 7B-906.2.

> **Resource:** The National Conference of State Legislatures discusses "The Child Welfare Placement Continuum: What's Best for Children?" on its website.

### A. Dismiss or Continue the Case

**1. Dismiss the case.** An adjudication that a child is abused, neglected, or dependent allows the court to exercise jurisdiction to decide and enter dispositional orders. If the court determines at the conclusion of a dispositional hearing that there is no need for the continued exercise of jurisdiction by the court, the court has the option to dismiss the case. G.S. 7B-903(a)(1). In practice, this means that the court enters an order that terminates its jurisdiction in the juvenile proceeding. *See* G.S. 7B-201(a); *McMillan v. McMillan*, 833 S.E.2d 692 (N.C. Ct. App. 2019) (juvenile order expressly terminated its jurisdiction under G.S. 7B-201). With an order that terminates the court's jurisdiction, the legal status of the child and custodial rights of the parties revert to the status that existed before the filing of the petition, unless an applicable law or valid order in another civil proceeding provides otherwise, a Chapter 50 custody order was entered pursuant to G.S. 7B-911, or a termination of parental rights was ordered. G.S. 7B-201(b). See Chapter 3.1.C (relating to ending jurisdiction).

> **Practice Note:** Although dismissal at an initial dispositional hearing is uncommon, it may be appropriate when circumstances since the filing of the petition have changed to the point that there is no longer a need for court involvement (e.g., the parents completed the services agreed upon in the protective services plan such that the child is safe in the parents' care and state intervention is no longer required).

**2. Continue the case.** The court has the dispositional alternative of continuing the case to "allow the parent, guardian, custodian, caretaker or others to take appropriate action." G.S. 7B-903(a)(1). For example, the court may find that the family is on track for addressing the conditions that led to the adjudication and may want to give the family more time to progress before entering a dispositional order or dismissing the case. Similarly, the court might hold a dispositional hearing in which the evidence shows what the needs are, what the parents have accomplished so far, and what remains to be accomplished, then continue the case to a specific time to evaluate the parents' continued progress and determine an appropriate disposition.

Note that this dispositional outcome is different from the continuance of a dispositional hearing. *See* G.S. 7B-803. See section 7.2.A, above (discussing the statutory time requirements for dispositional hearings), and Chapter 4.5 (relating to continuances).

## B. In-Home Supervision and Services

The Juvenile Code sets out a preference for the use of in-home supervision and community-level services by stating that in dispositions "the initial approach should involve working with the juvenile and juvenile's family in their own home." G.S. 7B-900. The court may require that the child be supervised in his or her own home by DSS or another individual who is available to the court, subject to any conditions the court places on the parent, guardian, custodian, or caretaker. G.S. 7B-903(a)(2). When a child remains in the home but is supervised by DSS or another individual, the court may or may not order that DSS or the other individual have legal custody of the child while the parent, guardian, or custodian retains physical custody. If legal custody is ordered to DSS or another individual, that portion of the order would be made under a different dispositional alternative, and the dispositional order would combine the two applicable dispositional alternatives. G.S. 7B-903(a)(2) and (4). In cases where custody is placed with a parent who is subject to supervision, the court is not obligated to conduct periodic review or permanency planning hearings. *See* G.S.7B-906.1(k). However, the court may hold those hearings to receive an update on the family's progress and enter new dispositional orders that may continue or change the existing disposition. See section 7.2.A.4(a), above (discussing waiving review hearings).

Prior to October 1, 2015, this dispositional alternative was codified at G.S. 7B-903(a)(2)a. and contained introductory language about a "juvenile who needs more adequate care or supervision or who needs placement." The court of appeals interpreted that introductory language to be a required finding in the order. *See In re S.H.* 217 N.C. App. 140 (2011) (reversing and remanding dispositional order for failing to include required finding). That introductory language was removed by S.L. 2015-136, sec. 10, and presumably the finding is no longer required under an order entered pursuant to the current G.S. 7B-903(a)(2).

**Practice Notes:** Although permitted by the Juvenile Code, it is uncommon for the court to order someone other than DSS to provide in-home supervision. When that condition is ordered, typically the parent is residing with the person responsible for providing the supervision (e.g., the maternal grandmother, respondent mother, and child reside in the same home, and mother is ordered to be under the supervision of maternal grandmother). The child's guardian ad litem (GAL) cannot serve in the in-home supervisory role, as it is beyond the statutory scope and authority of a GAL's role. *See* G.S. 7B-601.

In-home supervision may be ordered as an initial disposition, but it also may be used later when the court orders the child's return home from foster care or other placement.

## C. Parent and Out-of-Home Placement Generally

Parent and out-of-home placement dispositional alternatives include

- DSS custody with or without placement authority;
- custody with a parent, relative, other suitable person, or private agency offering placement services; or
- appointment of a guardian.

G.S. 7B-903(a)(4)–(6).

Effective for all actions pending or filed on or after October 1, 2015, the dispositional alternatives statute, G.S. 7B-903, was amended with both language changes and a reorganization of the subsections and subdivisions. The prior version of the statute (pre-2015 changes) identified various dispositional alternatives, including the out-of-home placements discussed here, and contained introductory language about a "juvenile who needs more adequate care or supervision or who needs placement." The court of appeals interpreted that introductory language to be a finding the trial court had to make when it ordered one of the dispositional alternatives that followed the language. *See In re S.H.*, 217 N.C. App. 140 (2011) (reversing and remanding dispositional order for failing to include required finding). That introductory language was removed by S.L. 2015-136, sec. 10, and presumably the finding is no longer required under an order entered pursuant to the current G.S. 7B-903(a)(2).

**1. Placement priority: parents and relatives.** Throughout the Juvenile Code it is clear that the preferred placement and permanent plan are the child's remaining in or returning to the child's own home when the child can be safe there. For example, a dispositional order that places or continues the child's out-of-home placement must include findings that the child's continuation in or return to his or her own home would be contrary to his or her health and safety. G.S. 7B-903(a2). The Juvenile Code defines "return home or reunification" as the child's placement "in the home of either parent" or "in the home of the guardian or custodian from whose home the child was removed by court order." G.S. 7B-101(18b). Given the definition of "return home or reunification," when the court makes a placement decision, it is required to consider placement with a parent. *See also* G.S. 7B-100 (in the purposes statute, referring to rights of child and parents and preventing inappropriate separation of child from parents); 7B-906.2(b) (reunification must be a permanent plan absent statutorily required written findings). The appellate courts have also identified the Juvenile Code's prioritization of the child's placement with his or her parents. *See In re T.W.*, 250 N.C. App. 68, 71(2016) and *In re J.D.C.*, 174 N.C. App. 157, 161 (2005) (both quoting *In re Shue*, 311 N.C. 586, 596 (1984) "[i]t is clear from the statutory framework of the Juvenile Code that one of the essential aims, if not the essential aim, of the dispositional hearing and the review hearing is to reunite the parent(s) and the child, after the child has been taken from the custody of the parent(s)").

When placement with either parent is not possible and the court is ordering the child's out-of-home placement, the court must first consider placement with a relative. *See* G.S. 7B-903(a1). Note that the Juvenile Code does not define "parent," and some appellate opinions have referred to parents as relatives. *See In re J.D.R.*, 239 N.C. App. 63, 73 (2015) (stating the "disposition order removed custody from Mother and placed custody with a relative, Father"). As between a parent and relative, parents, not relatives, have paramount constitutional rights to care, custody and control of their children. *See Eakett v. Eakett*, 157 N.C. App. 550, 554 (2003) (stating in grandparent visitation case, "[t]he grandparent is a third party to the parent-child relationship. Accordingly, the grandparent's rights to the care, custody and control of the child are not constitutionally protected while the parent's rights are protected"). See Chapter 2.4.A (discussing constitutional rights of parents).

At the initial dispositional hearing, the court must inquire into efforts made by DSS to identify and notify parents, relatives, or other persons with legal custody of the child's siblings as potential resources for placement or support. G.S. 7B-901(b). *See also* G.S. 7B-506(h)(2) (similar inquiry at the nonsecure custody stage of the case). For a court or DSS to consider placement with the child's relative, the relative must be willing and able to provide proper care and supervision in a safe home. "Safe home" is defined as "a home in which the juvenile is not at substantial risk of physical or emotional abuse or neglect." G.S. 7B-101(19). See section 7.4.D, below (related to custody and placement authority of DSS).

In ordering an out-of-home placement, when there is a willing and able relative with a safe home, the child must be placed with that relative unless the court finds that placement with the relative is contrary to the best interests of the child. G.S. 7B-903(a1). *See In re L.C.*, 253 N.C. App. 67 (2017) (holding failure to make the finding that a relative placement is contrary to the child's best interests will result in a remand; vacating and remanding permanency planning order that did not make required findings about relative that mother identified as possible placement option when DSS was in the process of evaluating the placement). Relative priority applies to initial, review, and permanency planning hearings and placements. *In re E.R.*, 248 N.C. App. 345 (2016); *In re L.L.*, 172 N.C. App. 689 (2005) (decided under previous statute), *abrogated in part on other grounds by In re T.H.T.*, 362 N.C. 446 (2008). Placement with an out-of-state relative requires compliance with the Interstate Compact on the Placement of Children (ICPC). G.S. 7B-903(a1). This requirement may result in a delay and/or the inability to order the placement. *See In re J.D.M.-J.*, 817 S.E.2d 755 (N.C. Ct. App. 2018) (vacating and remanding permanency planning order awarding custody to out-of-state relatives for failure to comply with ICPC as DSS had not received ICPC notice from receiving state); *In re L.L.*, 172 N.C. App. 689 (ICPC home study not approved until review hearing). See section 7.4.H, below (discussing the ICPC).

The following cases are examples of decisions that reviewed the child's out-of-home placement in a non-relative's home.

- In a permanency planning order awarding guardianship to a non-relative, the court did not make any findings about the paternal grandmother who both parents preferred as a placement option. Such a finding is statutorily required before the child is placed with a non-relative. *In re D.S.*, 817 S.E.2d 901 (N.C. Ct. App. 2018) (vacating and remanding order for a new permanency planning hearing).
- When the Indian Child Welfare Act applies, the court is not relieved of its obligation to make the finding under the Juvenile Code that it is contrary to the child's best interests to place the child with a relative when ordering placement with a nonrelative. *In re E.R.*, 248 N.C. App. 345 (2016) (reversing and remanding permanency planning order of guardianship to children's current nonrelative placement provider without making

findings of fact as to why the children's placement with their paternal grandmother was not in their best interests).
- Where the father had not submitted to a paternity test and DSS had not completed a home study of the father's parents, it was not an abuse of discretion for the court to determine that placement with the father's parents was not in the child's best interest, since the child could be subject to removal from that home. *In re D.S.A.*, 181 N.C. App. 715 (2007).
- It was error for the court to place a child with foster parents without finding that it was contrary to the child's best interests to place her with willing relatives. *In re L.L.*, 172 N.C. App. 689 (2005), *abrogated in part on other grounds by In re T.H.T.*, 362 N.C. 446 (2008).
- The trial court did not abuse its discretion in determining that placement with grandparents was not in the child's best interest, where the parents and grandparents were unwilling to consider or explain the source of an infant's serious injuries while in the parents' care, the grandparents were unlikely to deny their daughter access to the child, and it had been recommended that the grandfather attend intensive outpatient substance abuse treatment. *In re B.W.*, 190 N.C. App. 328 (2008).

When placement with a relative is considered, the court must also determine whether it is in the child's best interest to stay in the community where the child lives, discussed in subsection 2, immediately below.

**Practice Notes:** When the court considers whether a relative is "willing and able" to care for a child, it is important for the court to make this determination in relation to the child's specific needs (e.g., special needs) and the relative's ability to meet those needs.

When a child is placed with a relative, depending on the duration of the placement, whether the placement becomes the child's permanent plan, and the location of the placement, a post-adjudication change in venue of the action may be appropriate. See Chapter 3.5.C (discussing change in venue). However, if the relative lives outside of North Carolina, the court cannot transfer the action to another state. When more than one state is involved, the Uniform Child-Custody Jurisdiction Enforcement Act (UCCJEA) applies, and the UCCJEA requires that a court action be initiated in the other state. See Chapter 3.3.C (discussing jurisdictional issues under the UCCJEA).

**Resources:**
For information, resources, statistics, and summaries of state laws that address kinship (relative) placements including foster care licensing and financial assistance, see the Grandfamilies.org website.

CHILD WELFARE INFORMATION GATEWAY, U.S. DEP'T OF HEALTH & HUMAN SERVICES, "Placement of Children with Relatives" (2018).

For additional discussions about the involvement of relatives in an abuse, neglect, or dependency action, see Chapters 2.2.B.10 (identifying relatives), 2.3.C.3 (discussing relatives and the Foster Care Children's Bill of Rights), and 5.5.C.3 and 5.6.E (discussing similar inquiry at and placement priority at the nonsecure custody stage of the proceeding).

**2. Child's own community.** In determining an out-of-home placement, the court must consider whether it is in the child's best interests to stay in the child's own community rather than move elsewhere. G.S. 7B-903(a1).

In addition, federal education and child welfare laws require that DSS consider the child's educational stability and make assurances that the placement takes into account the appropriateness of the child's current educational setting and proximity of the placement to the school the child was enrolled in at the time of the each placement (school of origin). DSS must ensure that the child remains in the school of origin, unless there is a determination that it is not in the child's best interests to do so. For a discussion of the Every Student Succeeds Act and the Fostering Connections to Success and Increasing Adoptions Act as related to school stability, see Chapter 13.7.

**Practice Note:** The court's consideration of community ties is broad and suggests that the court might examine factors such as

- the child's school, the impact of changing schools, and the best interest determination as to whether the child will remain in his or her school of origin;
- ties with or support from siblings, relatives, or friends in the community and the impact that relocating could have on such ties or support;
- the child's current receipt of services from specific individuals or agencies in the community and the impact of disrupting, changing, or losing relationships with particular service providers;
- the child's involvement with specific activities or groups and the impact of changing or losing that involvement (e.g., music, scouts, church, sports, etc.); and
- the location of the parents and the effect of a particular placement on the child's ability to see his or her parents (note that the court is required to address visitation under G.S. 7B-905.1; see section 7.5, below, for a discussion of visitation).

**3. Required findings.** Anytime a dispositional order places or continues the child in an out-of-home placement, the order must contain findings

- that the child's continuation in or return to his or her own home would be contrary to the child's health and safety (G.S. 7B-903(a2));
- whether DSS has made reasonable efforts to prevent the need for the child's placement, based on the child's health and safety as the paramount concern when determining if the efforts were reasonable (note that in cases where reasonable efforts were precluded because of an immediate threat of harm to the child, the order must have a finding that placement is necessary to protect the child) (G.S. 7B-903(a3); *see In re N.B.*, 240 N.C. App. 353 (2015) (holding findings that DSS made reasonable efforts to eliminate the need for an out-of-home placement were supported by evidence of social worker's contact with mother since previous review hearing that showed social worker was involved in scheduling and supervising visits between mother and children and social worker informed mother of children's medical issues and coordinated contact between mother and

- children's therapist)); and
- addressing visitation (G.S. 7B-905.1).

See sections 7.9, below (discussing reasonable efforts), and 7.5, below (discussing visitation).

**4. Meaning and impact of "custody" and "placement".** The term "custody" is not defined in the Juvenile Code and is used in more than one way. "Custody" may refer to a temporary legal arrangement or a more permanent arrangement. Temporary custody, nonsecure custody, and custody granted at disposition are all different. *See, e.g.,* G.S. 7B-500; 7B-505; 7B-903(a)(4). See also Chapter 5.5 (discussing temporary and nonsecure custody).

A custody order entered after adjudication (whether at an initial dispositional, review, or permanency planning hearing) is a dispositional alternative. Only an order entered at a permanency planning hearing can award custody as the permanent plan for the child. *See In re D.C.,* 183 N.C. App. 344 (2007) (decided under prior law) (holding that it was error for the trial court to order a permanent plan of custody when the parent had not received notice that the hearing was a permanency planning hearing). See also section 7.10, below, related to permanent placement options. "Custody" may refer to a civil custody order entered pursuant to G.S. 7B-911 and Chapter 50. See section 7.10.B.4(a), below, relating to civil custody orders.

Although the term "nonsecure custody" is only used in Article 5 of the Juvenile Code, which addresses the pre-adjudication phase of a case, the trial court's use of the term "non-secure custody" at disposition when ordering the dispositional alternative of custody to DSS was not error as the term " 'non-secure custody' merely distinguishes the custody from 'secure custody,' in which the juvenile is placed in a detention facility or other government-supervised confinement." *In re J.W.,* 241 N.C. App. 44, 52 (2015) (rejecting respondent's argument that the court erred in awarding DSS "non-secure custody" at the dispositional hearing; note that the distinction between "nonsecure custody" granted in the pre-adjudication phase of the case under Article 5 of the Juvenile Code and the use of the term "non-secure custody" in the dispositional phase was not addressed).

**Practice Note:** Assumptions tend to be made concerning the authority and duties that accompany an order giving one "custody," but because "custody" does not have one distinct meaning and is not statutorily defined, it is important for the court to make its intentions clear when ordering custody. To avoid problems surrounding the meaning of custody, the court should anticipate questions that might arise with respect to the custodian's authority or duties and specifically address them in the order. Note that "custodian" is defined as "the person or agency that has been awarded legal custody of a juvenile by a court." G.S. 7B-101(8).

Legal custody, physical custody, placement, and placement authority are not the same thing and are not automatically tied to one another. Consider the following:

- The Juvenile Code refers to "custody or placement responsibility" with DSS. *See* G.S. 7B-903.1(b)–(d); 7B-905.1(b); 7B-906.1(f), (*l*). *See also* G.S. 7B-507(a)(4) (an order placing child in nonsecure custody with DSS shall specify that placement and care are DSS's

responsibility unless the court orders a specific placement). Presumably when an order grants custody to DSS without designating a specific placement, DSS has both custody and placement responsibility with the authority to make placement decisions and arrangements for the child's placement. When the order awards custody to DSS and specifies the child's placement, DSS is awarded legal custody without the authority to make decisions related to the child's placement.
- The court may not order physical custody with one person and physical placement without custody with another person. The phrase "physical custody" is used "to refer to the rights and obligations of the person *with whom the child resides.*" *In re H.S.F.*, 177 N.C. App. 193, 202 (2006) (emphasis in original) (quoting 3 Suzanne Reynolds, Lee's *North Carolina Family Law* § 13.2, at 13–16 (5th ed. 2002)). An order granting physical custody to mother and physical placement with paternal grandfather without a grant of custody purported to grant physical custody to a parent who did not reside with the child and physical placement of the child with a person with no custodial rights or the legal ability to make daily decisions regarding the child's welfare. *In re H.S.F.*, 177 N.C. App. 193. However, a person with custody may choose to place the child with a selected caretaker while still retaining custody. In *In re D.L.*, 215 N.C. App. 594 (2011), the court of appeals held the trial court did not abuse its discretion when it sanctioned respondent mother's decision that the children would live with relatives while keeping custody with the respondent mother rather than ordering custody to DSS or the relative caretakers. The court of appeals distinguished *In re D.L.* from *In re H.S.F.* and emphasized that the trial court had not ordered physical placement of the children with the relative but had approved the mother's decision about where the children should be placed.
- Although legal custody is not defined, North Carolina appellate courts have described legal custody as referring "generally to the right and responsibility to make decisions with important long-term implications for a child's best interests and welfare." *In re M.M.*, 249 N.C. App. 58, 61 (2016) (quoting *Peters v. Pennington*, 210 N.C. App. 1, 17 (2011)).
- A court may order joint legal custody to both a parent and another person, with physical custody to the other person. See section 7.4.E.4, below (discussing joint custody).

### D. DSS Custody

The court may order the child to be placed in DSS custody in the county of the child's residence. If the child's residence is in another state, the court may place the child in the physical custody of DSS in the county where the child is found so that DSS can return the child to the responsible authorities in his or her home state. G.S. 7B-903(a)(6).

---

**Practice Notes:** A court in North Carolina cannot "transfer" custody of the child to an agency in another state unless a valid order giving that agency custody is already in place. DSS should contact the appropriate child welfare agency in the other state to discuss the assumption of custody by that agency. However, neither DSS nor the court can force a person or agency in another state to initiate a court action in that state. If a custody action already exists in the child's home state, procedures in G.S. Chapter 50A, the UCCJEA, should be used. The court cannot "transfer" an entire abuse, neglect, or dependency proceeding to another state. See Chapter 3.3 (explaining the UCCJEA).

In an abuse, neglect, or dependency action, if the adjudication occurred somewhere other than the county of the child's legal residence (e.g., a DSS petitioner is the county DSS where the child was found and it filed the court action in its own county) or if the disposition involves placement in a different county, involvement of another county DSS and/or a transfer of venue may be appropriate. See Chapters 3.5.C (discussing transfer of venue) and 4.7 (discussing intervention).

**Resource:** For DSS policies and procedures related to child placement, see DIV. OF SOC. SERVS., N.C. DEP'T OF HEALTH & HUMAN SERVICES, CHILD WELFARE MANUAL "Permanency Planning" and "Cross-Function," available here.

**1. Notice to GAL of change in placement.** When DSS has custody or placement responsibility for a child, it must notify the child's guardian ad litem (GAL) of an intention to change the child's placement unless prevented from giving notice by emergency circumstances. When emergency circumstances exist, DSS must notify the GAL or the attorney advocate within seventy-two hours of a placement change unless local rules require that notification be made sooner. G.S. 7B-903.1(d).

**2. Court approval for return home and unsupervised visitation.** Once the court orders that DSS has custody of or placement responsibility for a child, DSS may not permit unsupervised visitation with or a return of physical custody to the parent, guardian, custodian, or caretaker from whom the child was removed without a hearing at which the court finds that the child will receive proper care and supervision in a safe home. G.S. 7B-903.1(d); *see* G.S. 7B-101(19) (definition of "safe home"). S*ee also In re H.S.F.*, 177 N.C. App. 193 (2006) (holding that it was error for the court to return the child home to the mother without finding that the child would receive proper care and supervision in a safe home); *In re A.S.*, 181 N.C. App. 706 (holding that it was not error for the trial court to limit visitation or refuse to return the children home where the trial court found that the conditions that led to removal from the home were still present and that return to the home would be contrary to the welfare of the children), *aff'd per curiam*, 361 N.C. 686 (2007). See section 7.5, below (discussing visitation).

DSS may not recommend the child's return of physical custody to the removal parent, guardian, custodian, or caretaker without first observing two visits between the child and the removal parent, guardian, custodian, or caretaker. Each observed visit must be at least one hour, and the observations must be at least seven days apart. DSS must provide documentation of the observed visits to the court for the court to consider when DSS is recommending the return of physical custody to the removal parent, guardian, custodian, or caretaker. G.S. 7B-903.1(c). *See* S.L. 2017-41, sec. 10, effective June 21, 2017. Although not in the statute, the state policy requires that the visits occur no more than thirty days before the scheduled permanency planning hearing where DSS will make the recommendation. DIV. OF SOC. SERVS., N.C. DEP'T OF HEALTH & HUMAN SERVICES, CHILD WELFARE MANUAL "Permanency Planning," available here.

> **Practice Note:** The requirement that DSS first observe two visits prior to recommending the child's return to the physical custody of the *removal* parent, guardian, custodian, or caretaker does not apply to the *non-removal* parent, guardian, custodian, or caretaker. Additionally, this requirement only applies to DSS. The child's guardian ad litem, a parent, or any other respondent may recommend and present evidence at a dispositional hearing that supports the child's return of physical custody to the removal parent, guardian, custodian, or caretaker without their having observed any visits. The court will base its decision on what it determines is in the child's best interests based on the evidence presented at the hearing.

**3. DSS authority to consent to child's medical care.** When DSS has custody of a child, unless the court orders otherwise, DSS may arrange for, provide, or consent to the child's

- routine medical or dental treatment or care, including treatment for common pediatric illnesses and injuries that require prompt attention;
- emergency medical, surgical, psychiatric, psychological, or mental health care or treatment; and
- testing and evaluation in exigent circumstances.

G.S. 7B-505.1(a); 7B-903.1(e). *See also In re Stratton*, 153 N.C. App. 428 (2002) (holding that parents whose children were adjudicated neglected and dependent and placed in foster care did not have the authority to object to DSS's decision to immunize the children; decided before the enactment of G.S. 7B-505.1, effective for all cases pending or filed on or after October 1, 2015, which requires DSS to obtain a court order or authorization from the child's parent, guardian or custodian to immunize a child when it is known that the parent has a bona fide religious objection to the standard schedule of immunizations).

For all other medical care or treatment, DSS must obtain consent from the child's parent, guardian, or custodian unless DSS obtains a court order authorizing the director to provide consent. There must be a hearing, and the court must find by clear and convincing evidence that the care, treatment, or evaluation that DSS is requesting the authority to consent to is in the child's best interests. G.S. 7B-505.1(c); 7B-903.1(e). There is a non-exhaustive list in G.S. 7B-505.1(c) of the type of treatment and care that necessitates DSS obtaining a court order authorizing it to consent to that treatment for the child.

When care or treatment is provided to a child in DSS custody, DSS must make reasonable efforts to (1) promptly notify the parent, guardian, or custodian that the care will be or has been provided and (2) give frequent status reports on the care and treatment provided to the child. G.S. 7B-505.1(d); 7B-903.1(e). The parent, guardian, or custodian has a right to copies of any records or results of medical evaluations when the parent, guardian, or custodian requests those records from DSS; however, there is an exception for a Child Medical Evaluation or records prohibited from disclosure by G.S. 122C-53(d). G.S. 7B-505.1(d); 7B-903.1(e). In addition, the health care provider who treats the child must disclose confidential information about the child to the parent, guardian, or custodian and to DSS unless a court order or federal law prohibits such disclosure. G.S. 7B-505.1(f); 7B-903.1(e).

Note that the medical evaluations and treatment discussed in G.S. 7B-505.1 differ from the court's authority to order that the child receive an evaluation and necessary treatment pursuant to G.S. 7B-903(d). See section 7.6, below (discussing court-ordered evaluations and treatment of the child).

---

**Resources:**

For more information about the medical consent statute when children are ordered in DSS custody, G.S. 7B-505.1, see Sara DePasquale, *New Law: Consenting to Medical Treatment for a Child Placed in the Custody of County Department*, UNC SCH. OF GOV'T: COATES' CANONS: NC LOCAL GOVERNMENT LAW BLOG (Nov. 6, 2015).

For information about medical standards of care and best practices related to medical care for children in foster care, see the "Fostering Health NC" section of the North Carolina Pediatric Society website.

**NC DHHS DSS Forms:**
- DSS-1812, General Authorization for Treatment and Medication (Feb. 2016).
- DSS-1812ins, General Authorization for Treatment and Medication Instructions (Feb. 2016).

---

**4. Reasonable and prudent parent standard.** Effective October 1, 2015, North Carolina adopted the federal "reasonable and prudent parent standard" required by the Preventing Sex Trafficking and Strengthening Families Act. See Chapter 1.3.B.10 (discussing the federal law and its impact on North Carolina law). The "reasonable and prudent parent standard" is "characterized by careful and sensible parental decisions that are reasonably intended to maintain the health, safety, and best interests of the child while at the same time encouraging the emotional and developmental growth of a child that a caregiver shall use when determining whether to allow a child in foster care under the responsibility of the State to participate in extracurricular, enrichment, cultural, and social activities." G.S. 131D-10.2A(a); 42 U.S.C. 675(10)(A).

Unless the court orders otherwise, a placement provider for a child in DSS custody (e.g., a relative or foster parent) must use the reasonable and prudent parent standard to provide or withhold permission related to the child's participation in normal childhood activities. The placement provider does not need prior approval from DSS or the court. *See* G.S. 7B-903.1(b); 131D-10.2A(c), (e). Normal childhood activities include overnight activities that are not in the direct supervision of the placement provider for periods up to seventy-two hours; for example, a childhood sleepover. G.S. 131D-10.2A(e); *see* 42 U.S.C. 671(a)(24). If the court determines that it is not in the child's best interests for a placement provider to make these decisions, it shall order alternative parameters for the approval of a child's participation in normal childhood activities. G.S. 7B-903.1(b).

DSS is authorized by statute to make decisions for a child in its custody that are generally made by a child's custodian, unless federal law prohibits DSS from exercising that authority. G.S. 7B-903.1(a); *see* G.S. 131D-10.2A(c); 7B-906.1(*l*). For example, a DSS representative is prohibited from making decisions as the child's parent under the federal Individuals with Disabilities in Education Act (IDEA) regarding special education eligibility and services even though DSS may make other educational decisions, such as which school the child enrolls in. See Chapter 13.7 (discussing the Every Student Succeeds Act regarding school placement decisions) and 13.8 (discussing IDEA). The court may delegate any part of the authority granted to DSS to the child's parent, foster parent, or other individual. G.S. 7B-903.1(a).

At a permanency planning hearing for a child in DSS custody who is at least 14 years old, the court must make an inquiry and specified findings related to the reasonable and prudent parent standard and participation in age- or developmentally-appropriate activities. *See* G.S. 7B-912(a). See section 7.8.C.8, below (discussing required findings at permanency planning hearing).

As part of the recognition and acceptance of the reasonable and prudent parent standard for children in foster care, amendments were made to laws outside of the Juvenile Code to address barriers that existed for teens in foster care who sought to obtain a driver's license. *See* S.L. 2015-135; G.S. 20-11 (application for driver's license); 48A-4 (purchase of automobile insurance).

---

**Practice Note:** It may be helpful at a child and family team meeting to discuss and review "The Reasonable and Prudent Parenting Activities Guide" created by the North Carolina Department of Health and Human Services, Division of Social Services. Through this meeting, the parties may learn whether a disagreement exists warranting court intervention. The court may address the issue raised before it by delegating or limiting a placement provider's or DSS's authority over certain decisions, such as a child's participation in a contact sport, staying overnight at a particular individual's home, or attending a specific religious service. It may be also helpful for the court and others to know what activities the child was engaged in to ensure the child's participation may continue.

**Resources:**
For more information about the reasonable and prudent parent standard, see
- DIV. OF SOC. SERVS., N.C. DEP'T OF HEALTH & HUMAN SERVICES, CHILD WELFARE MANUAL "Permanency Planning," available here.
- Sara DePasquale, *Children in Foster Care, "Normal Childhood Activities," and the "Reasonable and Prudent Parent" Standard*, UNC SCH. OF GOV'T: ON THE CIVIL SIDE BLOG (Oct. 16, 2015).
- The "Reasonable and Prudent Parenting Legislation" on the National Conference on State Legislatures website.

---

### E. Custody with a Parent, Relative, Other Suitable Person, or Private Agency

**1. Custody to a parent, relative, other suitable person, or private agency.** The court may order that the child be placed in the custody of "a parent, relative, private agency offering placement services, or some other suitable person." G.S. 7B-903(a)(4). This gives the court broad authority to place custody with someone other than DSS.

Custody as a permanent placement must be made in the context of a permanency planning hearing. See sections 7.2.A.4, above; 7.8.C, below (discussing permanency planning); and

7.10.B.4, below (discussing custody as permanent plan). As a permanent plan, the best interests of the child standard is not applicable unless the court makes written findings that the parents are unfit, have neglected the child, or have acted inconsistently with their constitutionally protected status as parents. See section 7.10.B.5, below.

However, any time the court orders custody with a parent or other appropriate person, it must determine whether jurisdiction in the juvenile proceeding should be terminated and custody awarded through a Chapter 50 order using the procedure of G.S. 7B-911. If custody is ordered to a parent or to a person the child was living with when the petition alleging abuse, neglect, or dependency was filed, the procedures of G.S. 7B-911 do not require that placement with that parent or person be first designated the child's permanent plan. G.S. 7B-911(c)(2)b. This means the court may terminate its jurisdiction and enter a Chapter 50 custody order prior to a permanency planning hearing. See section 7.10.B.4–5 below, for a discussion of G.S. 7B-911 procedures and findings about parent's constitutional rights before custody to a third party is ordered.

See section 7.3, above (relating to the court's focus on the child's best interests in determining out-of-home placement).

---

**Practice Notes:** When the court retains jurisdiction, DSS remains a party even when custody has been ordered to another person (including the parent) and is responsible for scheduling reviews pursuant to G.S. 7B-906.1(a). *See* G.S. 7B-401.1(a). The court should make clear its expectations with respect to DSS's supervising the child's placement, providing services, and preparing reports for the court.

The Juvenile Code defines a "custodian" as the person or agency who has been awarded legal custody of a child by a court. G.S. 7B-101(8). Before October 1, 2013, the definition of "custodian" also included a person other than the child's parent or legal guardian who assumed the status and obligation of a parent without being awarded legal custody by a court. This part of the definition was removed by S.L. 2013-129, sec. 1. A person who would have satisfied that criteria is now considered a "caretaker." There are some appellate opinions that were decided under the former language of the statute that refer to what is now considered a "caretaker" as a "custodian."

---

**(a) Parent.** The provision allowing custody to a parent may apply in various circumstances, including when

- a child is removed from the home of one parent (the "removal parent") and placement with the other parent (the "non-removal parent") is appropriate;
- the child has been in the custody of someone other than a parent and the court determines that custody should be returned to the parent (but see section 7.4.D.2, above (relating to requirements before DSS may recommend returning physical custody of the child to the removal parent)); or
- one parent needs a court order of custody to establish and protect his or her rights to the child in relation to the other parent.

The Juvenile Code prioritizes reunification with a parent (as discussed in section 7.4.C, above). It is error for the court to fail to consider giving custody to a parent where placement with a parent is a possibility. *See In re S.J.T.H.*, 811 S.E.2d 723 (N.C. Ct. App. 2018) (reversing initial dispositional order granting custody to DSS; remanding to enter new order granting father, the non-removal parent, custody absent findings he acted inconsistently with his parent rights); *In re Eckard*, 148 N.C. App. 541 (2002) (holding that the trial court erred when it refused to consider whether the biological father of the child, who had entered the case late, was a candidate for custody of the child after it ceased reunification efforts with the mother). See section 7.10.B.5, below (discussing the inapplicability of the best interest standard between a parent and non-parent when there is a fit and able parent).

**(b) Relative.** When custody is not ordered to a parent, willing relatives who can provide a safe home are always the preferred out-of-home placement option unless the court finds that the placement is contrary to the child's best interest. G.S. 7B-903(a1); *In re D.S.*, 817 S.E.2d 901 (N.C. Ct. App. 2018); *In re E.R.*, 248 N.C. App. 345 (2016). See section 7.4.C, above (preference for relatives).

**(c) Other suitable person.** The "catch-all" provision in G.S.7B-903(a)(4) permits the court to place custody with "some other suitable person." Nonrelative kin, a person with legal custody of the child's sibling, friends of the family, or others can be given custody of the child if deemed "suitable" by the court. *See* G.S. 7B-800.1(a)(4); 7B-901(b) (court inquiry about notification to other persons with legal custody of the child's siblings as potential resource for placement and support); *see also* G.S. 7B-101(15a) (definition of "nonrelative kin").

**(d) Private agency.** While custody with a "private agency offering placement services" is permissible, it would be rare for the court to order this instead of ordering custody with DSS.

**2. Verification required.** Before the court orders custody to an individual who is not the child's parent, the Juvenile Code requires the court to verify that the person receiving custody of the child understands the legal significance of the placement and will have adequate resources to appropriately care for the child. G.S. 7B-903(a)(4); 7B-906.1(j). See section 7.4.G, below (discussing the verification requirement in greater detail).

**3. Return to caregiver with violent history.** When a child is removed from the home due to physical abuse, DSS must conduct a review of the background of the alleged abuser, and if there is a history of violent behavior against people, DSS must petition the court to order the alleged abuser to submit to a mental health evaluation. G.S. 7B-302(d1); 7B-503(b). When the court has determined the child suffered physical abuse by that person, before it may order the child returned to that person's custody, the court must consider the opinion of the mental health professional who performed the evaluation. G.S. 7B-903(b).

**4. Joint custody is permissible.** The court may order joint custody. In the case of *In re B.G.*, 197 N.C. App. 570 (2009), the trial court awarded joint legal custody of a child to her father and her maternal aunt and uncle, giving physical custody to the aunt and uncle. The court of appeals rejected the father's argument that joint legal custody was not an authorized dispositional alternative after reviewing G.S. 7B-903(a) and finding it allowed the trial court to combine any of the applicable dispositional alternatives and did not prohibit joint legal custody. (The permanency planning order awarding joint custody was reversed, however, because the trial court's findings of fact were insufficient to support application of the best interests standard as there were no findings about whether the father acted inconsistently with his parental rights; see section 7.10.B.5, below (discussing required findings addressing parent's constitutional rights)).

**5. Modification of custody order.** When the court orders custody, the court may modify the order, either based on the child's best interests pursuant to G.S. 7B-906.1 or upon a motion to modify or vacate the order because of changes in circumstances or the needs of the juvenile brought pursuant to G.S. 7B-1000. *See In re J.S.*, 250 N.C. App. 370 (2016). See section 7.8.E, below (discussing G.S. 7B-1000).

**6. Consideration of transfer to civil custody action**. Whenever the court places custody with a parent or other appropriate person, the court is required to determine whether jurisdiction in the juvenile proceeding should be terminated and custody of the child awarded to the parent or other appropriate person under G.S. Chapter 50 civil custody provisions. G.S. 7B-911(a). The court is not required to make a finding about whether jurisdiction in the juvenile proceeding should be terminated and the action transferred to a Chapter 50 custody proceeding. *In re Y.I.*, 822 S.E.2d 501 (N.C. Ct. App. 2018). Transferring the abuse, neglect, or dependency action to a civil custody case pursuant to G.S. 7B-911 is appropriate when the need for intervention through a juvenile court action has ended, but there is a need to have a custody order remain in effect. See section 7.10.B.4(a), below, for details of G.S. 7B-911.

### F. Guardianship

**1. Appointment.** The appointment of a guardian of the person for the juvenile is a dispositional alternative. G.S. 7B-903(a)(5). The court may appoint a guardian of the person when it finds that it would be in the best interests of the child. G.S. 7B-600(a). However, guardianship as a permanent plan may be ordered only in the context of a permanency planning hearing. See sections 7.2.A.4, above; 7.8.C, below (discussing permanency planning); and 7.10.B.3, below (discussing guardianship as a permanent plan). When guardianship is a permanent plan, the best interests standard is not applicable unless the court makes written findings that the parents are unfit, have neglected the child, or have acted inconsistently with their constitutionally protected status as parents. *Cf. In re S.J.T.H.*, 811 S.E.2d 723 (N.C. Ct. App. 2018) (reversing *initial dispositional order* of DSS custody when court did not make findings about father's paramount constitutional rights). See section 7.10.B.5, below.

See sections 7.3, above (relating to the court's focus on best interests in determining out-of-home placement), and 7.4.C.1, above (discussing placement priority and relatives).

**Practice Note:** Guardianship may be ordered as a temporary measure, as a disposition, or as a permanent plan. *See In re E.C.*, 174 N.C. App. 517 (2005) (a guardian may be appointed at any time in an abuse, neglect, or dependency proceeding when the court finds it is in the child's best interests); *see also In re H.L.*, 807 S.E.2d 685 (N.C. Ct. App. 2017) (guardianship is permitted by G.S. 7B-903(a)(5) at the initial disposition). In addition to a dispositional alternative, G.S. 7B-600(a) authorizes the court to appoint a guardian of the child's person when no parent appears at a hearing with the child.

**2. Verification required.** Before the court appoints as a guardian of the child's person an individual who is not the child's parent, the Juvenile Code requires the court to verify that the person who will be appointed as the child's guardian of the person understands the legal significance of the appointment and will have adequate resources to appropriately care for the child. G.S. 7B-903(a)(4); 7B-600(c); 7B-906.1(j). See section 7.4.G, below (discussing the verification requirement in greater detail).

**3. Role of guardian.** "Guardian" is not defined by the Juvenile Code, but the governing statute, G.S. 7B-600, specifies the guardian's roles and responsibilities. A guardian of the person appointed for the child pursuant to G.S. 7B-600

- operates under the supervision of the court, with or without bond;
- files reports only when required by the court;
- has the care, custody, and control of the child;
- may arrange a suitable placement for the child;
- may represent the child in any legal action in any court; and
- may consent to certain actions on the part of the child in place of the parent, including (i) marriage; (ii) enlisting in the military; (iii) enrollment in school; and (iv) necessary remedial, psychological, medical, or surgical treatment.

G.S. 7B-600(a). Note that marriage emancipates the juvenile and results in the termination of the court's jurisdiction in the abuse, neglect, or dependency proceeding. *See* G.S. 7B-3509; 7B-201(a).

**Practice Notes:** In addition to its meaning under the Juvenile Code, the term "guardian" can be used in relation to a person appointed by the clerk of superior court, pursuant to G.S. Chapter 35A, as guardian of the person, guardian of the estate, general guardian, ancillary guardian, or standby guardian of a minor. A guardian appointed under G.S. 7B-600 in an abuse, neglect, or dependency action does not have all of the rights and responsibilities as a guardian appointed for the child pursuant to G.S. Chapter 35A in a proceeding before the clerk of superior court. A G.S. 7B-600 guardian is not a "guardian of the estate" with authority to manage the child's property, estate, or business affairs. *See* G.S. 35A-1202(9); *see also* G.S. 35A-1221 through -1228 (process and criteria for appointment of guardian of estate for a minor). Unlike a guardian of the person appointed by the clerk pursuant to G.S. Chapter 35A, a G.S. 7B-600 guardian does not have authority under the Juvenile Code or the adoption statutes to consent to the child's direct placement adoption or execute a relinquishment to an agency for the child's adoption. *See* G.S. 48-1-101(8) (definition of "guardian").

Additionally, a guardian appointed under G.S. 7B-600 is completely different from the child's guardian ad litem (GAL) appointed pursuant to G.S. 7B-601. See Chapter 2.3.D (discussing the child's GAL). The term "guardian", by itself, does not refer to a GAL appointed pursuant to G.S. 7B-601, G.S. 7B-602, or Rule 17 of the Rules of Civil Procedure. Appointment of a guardian pursuant to G.S. 7B-600 does not substitute for the appointment of a GAL in the abuse, neglect, dependency, or termination of parental rights action.

**4. Duration of the guardianship.** The authority of the guardian continues until the guardianship is terminated by court order; the court terminates its jurisdiction in the abuse, neglect, or dependency action; or the child is emancipated or reaches the age of 18, whichever occurs first. G.S. 7B-600(a); *see* G.S. 7B-201(a) (termination of jurisdiction); Article 35 of G.S. Chapter 7B (emancipation). When guardianship is for a temporary period or is ordered as a disposition that is not the permanent plan, the court may terminate the guardianship based on a determination that it is no longer in the child's best interests. *See* G.S. 7B-600. *See also In re J.D.C.*, 174 N.C. App. 157 (2005) (holding the G.S. 7B-600(b) criteria to terminate a guardianship order that is the child's permanent plan is inapplicable to the termination of a dispositional order that appointed a guardian but was not the child's permanent plan); *In re E.C.*, 174 N.C. App. 517 (2005) (holding only where guardianship is the permanent plan is the court required to make a finding under G.S.7B-600(b) before terminating the guardianship). When guardianship is awarded as the permanent plan for the child, the guardian automatically becomes a party to the case and the guardianship can be terminated only when the certain circumstances specified in G.S. 7B-600(b) are satisfied. *See* G.S. 7B-600(b); 7B-401.1(c) (parties). See section 7.10.B.3, below (discussing details related to guardianship as a permanent plan).

## G. Verification of Understanding of Legal Significance and Adequate Resources

Before placing a child in the custody or guardianship of someone other than a parent, the court must verify that the person receiving custody or guardianship understands the legal significance of the placement or appointment and will have adequate resources to appropriately care for the child. G.S. 7B-903(a)(4) and (5); 7B-600(c). This same determination is required by G.S. 7B-906.1(j) when the court awards custody or appoints a guardian at a review or permanency planning hearing.

The Juvenile Code does not require the court to make specific findings in order to make the verification. *In re J.D.M.-J.*, 817 S.E.2d 755 (N.C. Ct. App. 2018) and *In re N.B.*, 240 N.C. App. 353 (2015) (both citing *In re J.E.*, 182 N.C. App. 612 (2007)). However, appellate cases have required that there be competent evidence in the record to support the court's verification. *See In re J.D.M.-J.*, 817 S.E.2d 755 (vacating custody order; evidence that DSS was in the process of assessing the feasibility of the placement and had no concerns about the proposed custodians' income without proof of the amount of income was too vague and was insufficient to support the findings; nor was there evidence through testimony or a signed guardianship agreement that supported the finding of their understanding of the legal significance of the placement); *In re P.A.*, 241 N.C. App. 53 (2015) (holding that this requirement was not met when there was inadequate evidence in the record as to the proposed guardian's resources; the proposed guardian's own unsworn testimony asserting that her resources were sufficient was simply her subjective opinion and was not evidence of her actual resources); *In re J.E.*, 182 N.C. App. 612 (holding in the context of a permanency planning hearing that the trial court's determination was satisfactory where it had received into evidence and considered a home study conducted by DSS indicating that grandparents had a clear understanding of the enormity of the responsibility of caring for the children, that they were committed to raising the children, and that they were financially capable of providing for the children).

Testimony from the proposed custodian or guardian is not required as the statute does not require that the proposed guardian or custodian demonstrate to the court their understanding; however, it may be a best practice. *In re S.B.*, 834 S.E.2d 683 (N.C. Ct. App. 2019). Competent, reliable, and relevant evidence may include testimony from others, e.g., the social worker, or a court summary/report. *See In re S.B.*, 834 S.E.2d 683 (verification of guardian's understanding based on social worker's testimony and DSS summary submitted to the court was sufficient evidence).

The court's verification that the person receiving custody or guardianship understands the legal significance and their responsibilities applies to each person receiving custody or guardianship. In the case *In re L.M.*, 238 N.C. App. 345, the trial court properly verified this as to the foster father, but not the foster mother, although both were being awarded guardianship. The order of guardianship for the foster father was affirmed, but the order of guardianship for the foster mother was vacated and remanded.

The trial court must make an independent determination based on the evidence that is presented that the resources available to the potential guardian or custodian will be adequate. *In re P.A.*, 241 N.C. App. 53. Effective October 1, 2019, the Juvenile Code was amended to state "the fact that the prospective custodian or guardian has provided a stable placement for the juvenile for at least six consecutive months is evidence that the person has adequate resources." G.S. 7B-906.1(j); *see* G.S. 7B-600(c) (applying to guardianship only); 7B-903(a)(4) (applying to custodian only); S.L. 2019-33. Prior to this amendment, the Juvenile Code did not address any factors for determining whether the proposed guardian or custodian will have adequate resources.

The court of appeals has recognized that the case law examining a trial court's determination of adequate resources has "addresse[d] this situation from numerous angles, none of them precisely on point." *In re N.H.*, 255 N.C. App. 501 (2017). In some cases, the court of appeals has looked to whether there was evidence of monthly income and expenses and whether the income was sufficient to meet the expenses. *See In re K.B.*, 249 N.C. App. 263 (2016) (holding insufficient evidence to make verification); *In re N.H.*, 255 N.C. App. 501 (although a close call, affirming verification of adequate resources); *In re T.W.*, 250 N.C. App. 68 (2016) (reversing order; resources were inadequate). When determining whether the income is adequate, applying for assistance programs or accepting financial support from family members does not preclude a verification of adequate resources. *See In re S.B.*, 834 S.E.2d 683 (N.C. Ct. App. 2019) (finding of adequate resources was based on part-time income, receipt of support from family, and awareness of eligibility to seek child support from child's parents); *In re C.P.*, 252 N.C. App. 118 (2017) (noting proposed guardian's seeking TANF benefits demonstrated his preparation for the financial burden of caring for the child). In other cases, the court has looked to whether the evidence shows that the proposed guardian or custodian will have adequate resources moving forward, rather than allowing the trial court to rely on the past care provided to the child. *See In re N.H.*, 255 N.C. App. 501 (Dillon, J., concurring). The statutory amendments made by S.L. 2019-33 allow for the court's consideration of past care provided to the child but does not preclude the evidence and consideration of current and future resources.

**Practice Note:** The court should consider both income and services available to the child and caregiver. Some caregivers may not be willing to apply for available monetary benefits, such as TANF (Temporary Assistance for Needy Families), because doing so will create a reimbursement obligation for the child's parents and a duty on the part of the caregiver to cooperate with efforts to obtain support from the child's parents. (Note, however, that a caregiver may be excused from the duty to cooperate if he or she can provide evidence to support a claim that doing so would not be in the child's best interest.) Some services and benefits, such as scheduling of mental health or therapy appointments or help with the school IEP (Individual Education Plan) process, may not continue when DSS is no longer the child's custodian. The caregiver may need to apply for other services, such as transportation or day care, which had been provided without cost when the child was in DSS custody and now may become an expense for the caregiver.

**Resource:** For a discussion about appellate opinions addressing the verification of adequate resources (prior to the October 1, 2019 statutory amendments), see Sara DePasquale, *Show Me the Money: Verification of Adequate Resources Required when Ordering Custody or Guardianship to a Non-Parent in an A/N/D Action,* UNC SCH. OF GOV'T: ON THE CIVIL SIDE BLOG (Oct. 25, 2017).

### H. Interstate Compact on the Placement of Children

**1. Introduction and purpose.** The Interstate Compact on the Placement of Children (ICPC) governs the placement of children in foster care, adoptive homes, and institutions across state lines. The ICPC is a binding statutory agreement that has been adopted in all fifty states, the District of Columbia, and the U.S. Virgin Islands. It consists of ten different articles, and in North Carolina, it is codified at Article 38 of the Juvenile Code, G.S. 7B-3800 *et seq.* The district court has exclusive original jurisdiction over ICPC proceedings. G.S.7B-200(a)(1).

The ICPC establishes uniform legal and administrative procedures the states follow when placing children in out-of-state foster care and preadoptive placements. Its purpose is to protect children by having the two involved states (the sending state and the receiving state) work together to ensure appropriate foster care and adoption placements of children across state lines. The ICPC provides a framework for exchanging information, evaluating potential placements and the child's circumstances, and ensuring that the child receives adequate care and protection in the receiving state while the sending state retains jurisdiction over the child. *See* G.S. 7B-3800, Art. 1, Art. V.

This section provides only an overview of the ICPC and is not intended to be a comprehensive guide.

**2. State and agency structure.** Each state has a Compact Administrator. *See* G.S. 7B-3806. A national association of Compact Administrators referred to as the Association of Administrators of the Interstate Compact on the Placement of Children (AAICPC) adopts regulations that are key to interpreting and applying the ICPC. G.S. 7B-3800, Art. VII. There are twelve regulations. Effective October 1, 2019, the AAICPC regulations are enacted into North Carolina law. G.S. 7B-3807. (*See* S.L. 2019-172).

North Carolina's Compact Administrator and staff are located in the Division of Social Services within the state's Department of Health and Human Services (DHHS). The Compact Administrator and staff handle all incoming and outgoing referrals for interstate placements. They oversee the investigation of proposed placements in North Carolina to determine whether the placement is consistent with or contrary to the child's best interests. Effective October 1, 2019, the ICPC office at DHHS has the authority to request necessary supporting or additional information and may treat the ICPC request as expired if that information is not provided to the office within ten business days from the date of the notice for more information. G.S. 7B-3808. *See* S.L. 2019-172.

**3. Source of requirements and procedures.** Requirements and procedures related to the ICPC are determined by the ten ICPC statutory articles found in G.S. 7B-3800 and by G.S. 7B-3808. The North Carolina Administrative Code also includes provisions addressing interstate placement of children under the ICPC. *See* 10A N.C.A.C. Subchapter 70C; 10A N.C.A.C 70H.0301 and .0407(e). In addition, there are the twelve AAICPC regulations, some of which have undergone recent amendments to clarify certain issues. Those regulations have been enacted as law in North Carolina, effective October 1, 2019. G.S. 7B-3807; *see* S.L. 2019-172. In some instances the amended regulations conflict with earlier North Carolina appellate court decisions interpreting the ICPC statute. Finally, the North Carolina DHHS Division of Social Services policies and procedures provide a framework for compliance with the ICPC.

---

**Resources:**
For North Carolina's policies, procedures, and explanations related to interstate placement, see DIV. OF SOC. SERVS., N.C. DEP'T OF HEALTH & HUMAN SERVICES, CHILD WELFARE MANUAL "Interstate Compact on the Placement of Children," available here.

Additional information about the ICPC in North Carolina, including Compact Administrator contact information, can be found on the "North Carolina" page on the ICPC State Pages website. Information for other states can also be found on the ICPC State Pages website by viewing the map and clicking on a particular state.

Information about the ICPC and the AAICPC regulations can be found on the American Public Human Services Association website under "Affinity Groups" "AAICPC".

---

**4. Applicability of ICPC.** The ICPC applies to the interstate placement of a child made by a "sending agency"

- in foster care (which may be a child-caring institution) or
- as a preliminary placement to a possible adoption.

G.S. 7B-3800, Art. III(a); *see* G.S. 7B-3800, Art. II(d) (definition of "placement").

A "sending agency" includes DSS, the court, a child-placing agency, or a person (which may be a parent or guardian). G.S. 7B-3800, Art. II(b).

However, the ICPC does not apply to the sending or bringing of a child into a receiving state by the child's

- parent,
- stepparent,
- grandparent,
- adult sibling,
- adult uncle or aunt, or
- nonagency guardian

when the child is left with any of these relatives or a nonagency guardian in the receiving state. G.S. 7B-3800, Art. VIII. The exclusion from application of the ICPC occurs only when both the person making the placement and the placement recipient belong to the above classes of individuals.

The ICPC also does not apply to

- a juvenile who is adjudicated delinquent but is not being ordered to an out-of-state institution (e.g., the juvenile is placed on probation);
- any child placed in a facility for the sole purpose of education;
- any child placed in a medical facility for the sole purpose of medical care;
- any child placed pursuant to any other interstate compact (e.g., Interstate Compact on Juveniles, Interstate Compact on Mental Health); or
- child placements handled in court cases of paternity, divorce, custody, and probate.

*See* G.S. 7B-3800, Art. II(d) (definition of "placement"), Art. VI.

**5. The ICPC and placement with a non-removal parent or relative.** In 2004 the North Carolina Court of Appeals held that the provisions of the ICPC did not apply at a permanency planning hearing when the court awarded custody to an out-of-state mother. *In re Rholetter*, 162 N.C. App. 653 (2004). In that case the children had been removed from the custody of the father and stepmother in North Carolina, based on adjudications of abuse and neglect, and placed in DSS custody. The court eventually gave custody to the mother who lived in South Carolina, even though two home studies by South Carolina declined to approve the placement. The court of appeals held that the award of full custody to a non-removal parent was not a "placement" under the ICPC. The court found that the language of the ICPC statute was "clear and unambiguous" and that, because the trial court had not placed the children "in foster care or as a preliminary [placement] to adoption," the ICPC did not apply. *In re Rholetter*, 162 N.C. App at 664.

However, in 2011 and 2012, the AAICPC substantially rewrote some of the ICPC regulations, including Regulation 3, which covers definitions, placement categories, applicability, and exemptions. Under Regulation 3, placement categories that require compliance with the ICPC include placements with parents and relatives when the other parent or relative is not making the placement. The definition of "foster care" was also amended to include 24-hour-a-day care provided by the child's parent by reason of a court-ordered placement (and not by virtue of the parent-child relationship). However, the amended regulations exempt the ICPC from a placement with a parent if all of the following apply:

- the parent is not the parent from whom the child was removed;
- the court has no evidence that the parent is unfit;
- the court does not seek any evidence from the receiving state regarding the parent's fitness; and
- the court relinquishes jurisdiction over the child immediately upon placement with the parent.

The language of the AAICPC regulations that include parents in the definition of "foster care" has been rejected by some state courts as contravening the plain meaning of the statutory terms of "foster care" and "adoption" and exceeding the scope of the ICPC statute. Applying the same reasoning as the North Carolina Court of Appeals in *In re Rholetter*, 162 N.C. App. 653, the Connecticut Supreme Court concluded that the ICPC's language, "placement in foster care or as a preliminary to a possible adoption," does not include placement with a noncustodial parent. The court went on to say that "it is reasonable to conclude that the drafters determined that the statute should not be applied to out-of-state parents in light of the constitutionally based presumptions that parents generally are fit and that their decisions are in the child's best interests." *In re Emoni W.*, 305 Conn. 723, 736 (2012). The court went on to state in a footnote that even if the ICPC regulations have the force of law, they are invalid under state law to the extent they impermissibly expand the scope of the Compact itself.

Similarly, the Texas Court of Appeals held the ICPC does not apply to interstate placements of children with their parents. In *In re C.R.-A.A.*, 521 S.W.3d 893 (Tex. App. 2017), the Texas court looked to the Texas version of the ICPC, which specifically refers to out-of-state placements of children into foster care or preliminary to adoptions, and held the unambiguous meaning of the words made the ICPC inapplicable to interstate placements with parents. The Texas court further noted that its conclusion was supported by the state's statutory definitions of "foster care", foster home", and "adoption". The Texas court also stated the regulation contravened the statutory language.

The Indiana Court of Appeals has also held that the child welfare agency and the trial courts should not be applying the ICPC to out-of-state parents given its previous holding that the regulations exceed the scope of the statute limiting the ICPC to foster care and pre-adoptive placements, neither of which applies to parents. In 2018, the Indiana court stated, "So, yet again, we hold as plainly and unambiguously as possible, unless and until the statute is amended, the ICPC does not apply to placement with an out-of-state parent." *Matter of B.L.P.*, 91 N.E.3d 625, 631 (Ind. Ct. App. 2018); *see In re D.B.*, 43 N.E.3d 599 (Ind. Ct. App. 2015).

Maryland joined the states that have held the ICPC does not apply to non-removal parents who lived out of state on the grounds that the regulation as applied to parents (1) impermissibly exceeds the scope of the statute since natural parents do not adopt their own children and foster care involves placement outside of a parent's home and (2) violates the court's constitutional responsibility to safeguard a parent's paramount constitutional rights by transferring the discretion to determine if the parent is fit from the court to a social worker conducting the ICPC home study. *In re R.S.*, 242 Md. App. 338 (2019). Other states have examined the amended regulations and have held the ICPC does not apply to placements with out-of-state parents. *See, e.g., In re S.R.C.-Q.*, 52 Kan. App. 2d 454 (2016); *In re Welfare of Ca.R.*, 191 Wash. App. 601 (2015); *In re Patrick S. III*, 218 Cal. App. 4th 1254 (2013).

There is a split in the state appellate decisions on this issue as other states have reached the opposite conclusion and apply the ICPC to placements with out-of-state parents that do not meet the exception set forth in the AAICPC regulations. The Arizona Court of Appeals found the trial court was a "sending agency" and held that compliance with the ICPC regulations was required for placements with parents and relatives if none of the enumerated exceptions applied. *Arizona Dep't of Econ. Sec. v. Stanford,* 234 Ariz. 477 (Ct. App. 2014). The court reasoned that the ICPC should be "interpreted liberally because the primary purpose of the ICPC is to protect children by making certain they are placed in a safe environment." *Arizona Dep't of Econ. Sec.*, 234 Ariz. at 481–482. The Montana Supreme Court also applied the ICPC to placements with out-of-state parents after noting that "Montana has joined [the ICPC] by statute and for which the Department has adopted by rule the regulations of the Association of the ICPC" when applying AAICPC Regulation 3 to the out-of-state father. *In re J.H.*, 382 Mont. 214, 219 (2016). Other states have held the ICPC applies to out-of-state parents. *See, e.g., Dep't of Children and Families v. C.T.*, 144 So.3d 684 (Fla. Dist. App. 2014); *Dawn N. v. Schenectady County Dep't of Social Services*, 58 N.Y.S.3d 701 (2017).

To date, North Carolina's appellate courts have not addressed the application of the amended AAICPC regulations to an out-of-state parent. However, *In re Rholetter*, 162 N.C. App. 653 (2004), was decided on the language of the statute and did not discuss the AAICPC regulations in effect at the time. If Regulation 3 (covering definitions, placement categories, applicability, and exemptions) applies, the holding in *In re Rholetter* would be contrary to the language of the regulation.

---

**Practice Note:** When the ICPC does not apply, AAICPC Regulation 3 allows a state to request a "courtesy check" of a non-removal parent's home by the receiving state, without invoking the full ICPC home study process. Whether to conduct a courtesy check is in the discretion of the receiving state. When placement with a non-removal parent is made without ICPC compliance or with only a courtesy check, the receiving state has no responsibility for supervising or monitoring the placement.

**Resource:** Sara DePasquale, *A/N/D, ICPC, and Out-of-State Parents: Say What?* UNC SCH. OF GOV'T: ON THE CIVIL SIDE BLOG (Sept. 25, 2015).

The Juvenile Code states that when the court places the child in out-of-home care with a relative outside of North Carolina, that dispositional placement "must be in accordance with the Interstate Compact on the Placement of Children." G.S. 7B-903(a1). AAICPC Regulation 3 makes it clear that the ICPC applies to out-of-state placements with relatives. The North Carolina Court of Appeals has addressed the application of the ICPC to relative placement. Although compliance with the ICPC takes time, it is not mutually exclusive of the preference in the Juvenile Code for relative placement. *In re L.L.*, 172 N.C. App. 689 (2005) (holding the trial court must give out-of-state relatives priority consideration for placement unless it finds such placement is contrary to the child's best interests). See section 7.4.C.1, above (discussing placement priority).

When determining whether the ICPC applies, the court of appeals has looked to whether the dispositional order involves a "placement." In *In re V.A.*, 221 N.C. App. 637 (2012), the court of appeals reversed the dispositional order that awarded legal custody to DSS and placed the child with her maternal great-grandmother in South Carolina when the concurrent permanent plan was reunification and adoption. The court of appeals held the placement fell under the category of both foster care and a placement preliminary to a possible adoption, and in a footnote referred to Regulation 3 regarding foster care. As a result, the placement required strict compliance with the ICPC, which had not happened as the placement had not been approved by South Carolina. In contrast, in *In re J.E.*, 182 N.C. App. 612 (2007), the permanency planning order awarded guardianship, pursuant to G.S. 7B-600, to an out-of-state relative. The court of appeals held the ICPC did not apply because guardianship was not a placement in foster care or preliminary to adoption. The court of appeals also noted that neither G.S. 7B-600 nor the former permanency planning statute (G.S. 7B-907, now G.S. 7B-906.1) refer to the ICPC.

In the most recent case addressing the ICPC, the court of appeals examined both *In re V.A.* and *In re J.E.* and held that the ICPC applied to out-of-state relatives. In *In re J.D.M.-J.*, 817 S.E.2d 755 (N.C. Ct. App. 2018), the trial court, in a permanency planning order, awarded custody of the children to relatives who lived outside of North Carolina. That order was vacated due to the failure to comply with the ICPC; North Carolina had not received the required ICPC notice from the receiving state prior to the entry of the order awarding custody to the out-of-state relatives. In *In re J.D.M.-J.*, the court of appeals further identified a conflict between the two earlier opinions, *In re V.A.* and *In re J.E.*, and followed *In re V.A.* because it relied upon an earlier opinion that had been decided before *In re J.E.* See *In re Civil Penalty*, 324 N.C. 373 (1989) (holding a panel of the Court of Appeals is bound by a prior decision of another panel of the same court addressing the same question, but in a different case, unless overturned by an intervening decision from a higher court); *Graham v. Deutsche Bank Nat'l Tr. Co.*, 239 N.C. App. 301 (2015) (when there is a conflicting line of cases, the older of the two cases must be followed). However, in *In re J.D.M.-J.*, the court of appeals did not address an even older case that was relied upon in *In re J.E.* or the differences in the relative placement, specifically, whether the placement was meant to be temporary (e.g., foster care) or was the achievement of the child's permanent plan (e.g., guardianship or permanent custody).

> **Resource:** For a further discussion of *In re J.D.M.-J.*, see Sara DePasquale, *The ICPC Applies to an Out-of-State Placement with a Relative in an A/N/D Case, But Is There More to Consider?* UNC SCH. OF GOV'T: ON THE CIVIL SIDE BLOG (Aug. 24, 2018).

**6. The ICPC and visitation.** The ICPC applies only to interstate placements of children, not visits. AAICPC Regulation 9 defines a visit according to the purpose, duration, and intention behind a child's stay. The purpose of a visit is to provide the child with a social or cultural experience of a short duration, such as a camp stay or visit with a friend or relative. A stay for such a purpose that is less than thirty days is presumed to be a visit. A stay of more than thirty days is presumed to be a placement. If, however, for a school-aged child, a stay is more than thirty days but less than the duration of a school vacation period (e.g., forty-five days during a summer break), it can be considered a visit and does not require ICPC approval. A stay that does not have a terminal date will be considered a proposed placement and should not occur without ICPC approval. AAICPC Regulation 9.

If, however, the sending state has requested a home study or supervision and sends the child to stay with the proposed caregiver in the receiving state, there is a rebuttable presumption that it is a placement and not a visit.

Note that if a court in North Carolina does not follow the ICPC requirements, another state can decline to monitor the placement or provide services.

**7. Summary requirements of the ICPC and Regulations.** The sending agency is required to "comply with each and every requirement" set forth in G.S. 7B-3800, Art. III.

   **(a) Notice and best interest.** When the ICPC applies, prior to sending or bringing a child from one state to another, the sending agency (which includes the court) must furnish the receiving state with written notice of its intention to send, bring, or place the child in the receiving state. G.S. 7B-3800, Art. III(b) (see the Article for the content of the notice). The receiving state may then request any supporting or additional information it deems necessary. G.S. 7B-3800, Art. III(c); *see* G.S. 7B-3808 (enacted by S.L. 2019-172, effective October 1, 2019). The sending agency may not send or bring the child into the receiving state until the receiving state notifies the sending agency in writing that the proposed placement does not appear to be contrary to the interests of the child. G.S. 7B-3800, Art. III(d).

> **NC DHHS DSS Form:**
> DSS-1837, *Interstate Compact on the Placement of Children Request* (ICPC 100A) (Aug. 2001) with *Instructions*.

   **(b) Social history, case plan, and review.** The sending agency (e.g., a DSS caseworker) must prepare a packet containing items such as the child's social, medical, and educational history; the current status of any court case involving the child; and information about the person being considered for placement in the receiving state. The packet will first be sent to the central ICPC office (in North Carolina, the Division of Social Services at DHHS) in the sending state where it will be examined and, if approved, sent to the receiving state. Once it arrives in the receiving state's central ICPC office, the packet will be examined, and if everything is in order it will be sent to the child welfare agency (in North Carolina, the county DSS) office in the community where the prospective placement is located. *See* "ICPC FAQ" on the Association of Administrators of the Interstate Compact on the Placement of Children section of the American Public Human Services Association website. *See also* AAICPC Regulation 1 for specific requirements; G.S. 7B-3808 (ICPC office's right to request additional information, enacted by S.L. 2019-172, effective October 1, 2019).

(c) **Reports, recommendations, approval or denial.** The local agency receiving the packet will evaluate the prospective home for placement, and a completed home study report will be sent to the central ICPC office in the receiving state. The home study must be completed by the receiving state within sixty days. *See* 42 C.F.R. 671(a)(26)(A); AAICPC Regulation 2(7). The central ICPC office reviews the report, determines whether ICPC requirements have been met, and either approves or denies the recommendation of the report. If the placement is approved, once all plans and agreements have been completed the child is moved to the receiving state. The placement may not be approved if the local agency recommends against the placement or the Compact Administrator determines that a lawful placement cannot be completed, unless the problems can be remedied. The decision to approve or deny the placement should be made as soon as practicable but no later than 180 days from the receipt of the initial request for a home study. AAICPC Regulation 2(8). If a placement is denied, a request for reconsideration may be made by the sending state within ninety days from the date the receiving state signs the denial of the placement. The receiving state has sixty days to complete its reconsideration. AAICPC Regulation 2(9). Whether the placement is approved or denied, there are requirements related to copies of specific documents and reports that must be sent to the sending or receiving state's central office. *See* "ICPC FAQ"; *see also* ICPC Regulation 1.

(d) **Jurisdiction and responsibility for child under the ICPC.** The sending agency retains jurisdiction over the child to determine all matters relating to the custody, supervision, care, treatment, and disposition of the child until the child is adopted, reaches the age of majority, becomes self-supporting, or is discharged with the concurrence of the receiving state. This jurisdiction includes the power to return the child to the sending state or transfer the child to another location. The sending agency also continues to have financial responsibility for the support and maintenance of the child during the period of placement. However, a public agency may enter into an agreement with an agency in a receiving state to provide services as an agent for the sending agency. G.S. 7B-3800, Art. V. Financial responsibility and agreements between agencies are also addressed in G.S. 7B-3801, 7B-3802, and 7B-3803.

**NC DHHS DSS Form:**
DSS-1838, Interstate Compact Report on Child's Placement Status (Aug. 2001) with Instructions.

**(e) Expedited placement procedures.** An issue with the ICPC is the length of time it can take for states to process cases and approve interstate placements. AAICPC Regulation 7 was adopted to allow for expedited ICPC procedures when a judge finds a child meets the criteria for priority ICPC status.

Criteria for an expedited placement decision are

- the child is under the jurisdiction of the court as a result of a DSS action and has been removed from a parent, and
- the out-of-state placement being considered is with the non-removal parent, a stepparent, grandparent, adult aunt or uncle, adult sibling, or guardian, and
    - the child sought to be placed is four years of age or younger (includes older siblings sought to be placed in the same proposed placement);
    - the child currently is placed in an emergency placement;
    - the child is unexpectedly dependent due to sudden or recent incarceration, incapacitation, or death of a parent or guardian; or
    - the court finds that any child in the sibling group sought to be placed has a substantial relationship with the proposed placement resource.

AAICPC Regulation 7(5). See subsection 5, above (discussing whether the ICPC applies to a non-removal parent).

Regulation 7 outlines the manner in which the process is expedited, and includes specific time frames for completing different steps.

**NC DHHS DSS Form:**
DSS-1839, Regulation 7 Form Order For Expedited Placement Decision Pursuant to the ICPC (Feb. 2012).

**8. Illegal placements.** G.S. 7B-3800, Art. IV addresses placements made in violation of the ICPC. Violations are punishable according to the laws of each state involved. In addition, violations constitute grounds for the suspension or revocation of any license, permit, or other authorization under which the sending agency operates.

## 7.5 Visitation

### A. Order Must Address Visitation When Out-of-Home Placement

Anytime custody is removed from a parent, guardian, or custodian, or placement outside the home is continued, the order must address visitation, which may include no visitation, that is in the child's best interest and consistent with the child's health and safety. G.S. 7B-905.1(a). Visitation is only required to be addressed for a parent, guardian, or custodian. *In re S.G.*, 835 S.E.2d 479 (N.C. Ct. App. 2019). It is reversible error to not comply with the visitation statute – G.S. 7B-905.1 – in a disposition order. *See, e.g., In re S.G.*, 835 S.E.2d 479; *In re J.D.M.-J.*, 817 S.E.2d 755 (N.C. Ct. App. 2018); *In re J.R.S.*, 813 S.E.2d 283 (N.C. Ct. App. 2018) (applying to custodians); *In re J.H.*, 244 N.C. App. 255 (2015). An appellate court reviews a visitation order for an abuse of discretion. *In re J.L.*, 826 S.E.2d 258 (N.C. Ct. App. 2019) (order disallowing visitation); *In re Y.I.*, 822 S.E.2d 501 (N.C. Ct. App. 2018) (order setting conditions of visitation); *In re C.S.L.B.*, 254 N.C. App. 395 (2017) (order allowing visitation but delegating judicial function of court to guardians).

---

**Practice Note:** Although the court of appeals has interpreted the language of G.S. 7B-905.1 to require the trial court to address visitation with a parent, guardian, or custodian, the trial court is not precluded from ordering visitation with another person that it believes is consistent with the child's health and safety and is in the child's best interests. For example, the child may have a strong bond with a relative, including a sibling with whom the child is not placed. *See* 42 U.S.C. 671(a)(31) (addressing frequent visitation between siblings who are not placed together).

**Resource**: For state policy on visitation (parent/child family time) and sibling visitation, see DIV. OF SOC. SERVS., N.C. DEP'T OF HEALTH & HUMAN SERVICES, CHILD WELFARE MANUAL "Permanency Planning," available here.

---

The current visitation statute, G.S. 7B-905.1, was enacted by S.L. 2013-129, sec. 24 and applies to all actions pending or filed on or after October 1, 2013. Prior to 2013, visitation was addressed in G.S. 7B-905(c), which had different requirements. Opinions based on the former statute may be based on language that no longer appears in the Juvenile Code. *See In re J.H.*, 244 N.C. App. 255 (2015) (addressing change from G.S. 7B-905(c) to 7B-905.1).

Note that G.S. 7B-506(g1) makes clear that G.S. 7B-905.1 provisions regarding visitation apply to orders for continued nonsecure custody. See Chapter 5.5.C and 5.6 (discussing nonsecure custody and continued nonsecure custody).

**1. Minimum outline of visits required**. Visitation orders must indicate the minimum frequency and length of visits and whether the visits must be supervised. G.S. 7B-905.1(b), (c). All three criteria must be ordered. *See In re S.G.*, 835 S.E.2d 479 (N.C. Ct. App. 2019) (remanding order to address minimum duration of visits); *In re J.D.M.-J.*, 817 S.E.2d 755 (N.C. Ct. App. 2018) (remanding for compliance with G.S. 7B-905.1; order did not contain minimum length, frequency, or whether visits should be supervised); *In re J.H.*, 244 N.C. App. 255 (remanding visitation order to comply with G.S. 7B-905.1(c) after the order appealed from failed to establish the duration of the monthly supervised visits between the child and respondent mother). See subsection 4, below, discussing order of no visitation.

The statutory requirement that visitation orders indicate the minimum frequency and length of visits has been interpreted by the court of appeals to mean that the trial court must provide a framework for the visits (e.g., time, day) but that the order itself does not have to include the particular time and place for visits. *In re N.B.*, 240 N.C. App. 353 (2015) (holding the order complied with G.S. 7B-905.1 when it provided for visits at a minimum of one hour once per month, to be supervised by the family therapist, the date and time of which was to be coordinated with the family therapist).

The minimum outline required by G.S. 7B-905.1 is satisfied when two orders addressing visitation provisions are read together. *See In re L.Z.A.*, 249 N.C. App. 628 (2016) (affirming order of supervised visitation in accordance with the current plan when the current visitation plan was memorialized in the court's previous order that identified the frequency of two days a week, the duration of two hours per visit, and that supervision was required); *In re J.W.*, 241 N.C. App. 44 (2015) (affirming dispositional order that provided for weekly, supervised visits with the child and stated that all prior orders remain in full force and effect; prior order provided for weekly two-hour supervised visits with one child and weekly one-hour supervised visits with the other child; read together, the orders, complied with G.S. 7B-905.1).

The court may not delegate its judicial function of establishing the minimum outline by giving discretion to an individual to reduce or change the terms of the visitation. *See In re C.S.L.B.*, 254 N.C. App. 395 (2017) (holding visitation order complied with minimum outline but improperly delegated the court's judicial function to the court-appointed guardians who were authorized to unilaterally modify the visitation based on their "concerns" about mother's substance use or discord with the children's father during the visits); *In re J.D.R.*, 239 N.C. App. 63 (2015) (holding despite a minimum outline for some of mother's visits, the order impermissibly delegated substantial discretion over other kinds of visitation based on her complying with certain conditions). But where a caretaker who is not entitled to visitation under G.S. 7B-905.1 has an order of no visitation, the trial court did not err when ordering that any contact be recommended by the child's therapist. *In re S.G.*, 835 S.E.2d 479 (N.C. Ct. App. 2019).

**2. Cost of supervision.** Although G.S. 7B-905.1 does not address payment for the cost of supervised visitation, the appellate courts have held that before the court orders a parent to pay for supervised visitation, the trial court must make findings of the cost of visitation and the parent's ability to pay. *See In re J.C.*, 368 N.C. 89 (2015) (vacating and remanding order that made no findings about respondent mother's ability to pay for supervised visitation; without such findings appellate court was unable to review for an abuse of discretion); *In re J.T.S.*, 834 S.E.2d 637 (N.C. Ct. App. 2019) and *In re Y.I.*, 822 S.E.2d 501 (N.C. Ct. App. 2018) (both vacating portion of the order to address who bears the cost of visitation and if responsibility with mother, that she has the ability to pay); *In re E.M.*, 249 N.C. App. 44 (2016) (vacating portion of the order requiring respondent to pay for cost of visitation and remanded for findings of fact regarding cost and respondent's ability to pay).

**3. Electronic communication.** In the case *In re T.R.T*, 225 N.C. App. 567 (2013), the court of appeals held that communication via Skype is a form of electronic communication that cannot take the place of face-to-face visitation required by the Juvenile Code (decided under former statute). In so ruling, the court looked to G.S. 50-13.2(e), after finding the Juvenile Code was silent as to electronic communication. Under G.S.50-13.2(e), electronic communication may supplement visitation and is not a replacement or substitution for custody or visitation. As a result, electronic communication alone is a denial of visitation that requires specific findings. See subsection 4, immediately below (discussing findings when visitation is denied). Additionally, the court of appeals emphasized that electronic communications supplementing visitation between a parent and juvenile must comply with G.S. 50-13.2(e), which provides specific guidelines relating to best interest, availability of equipment, and other factors.

**Practice Note:** In relying on G.S. 50-13.2(e), the court reasoned that while G.S. 50-13.2(a) explicitly limits its application to custody orders entered under G.S. 50-13.2, nothing in subsection (e), dealing with electronic communications, limits its application in that way. Therefore, the court said G.S. 50-13.2(e) is a generic provision that applies to all custody actions. This reasoning raises a question as to whether other subsections of G.S. 50-13.2 could apply to orders under the Juvenile Code when they deal with matters not addressed by the Juvenile Code.

**4. No visitation based on child's health, safety, and best interest.** The Juvenile Code requires that visitation orders be consistent with the health and safety of the child and in the child's best interest. G.S. 7B-905.1(a). While the court must address visitation, it may order no visitation. G.S. 7B-905.1(a). Appellate opinions have required that the court make a finding the parent has forfeited his or her right to visitation or that it is in the child's best interests to deny visits. *See In re J.L.*, 826 S.E.2d 258 (N.C. Ct. App. 2019) (holding no abuse of discretion when court denied visitation; the ultimate finding that visitation was not in the child's best interests and consistent with his health and safety was supported by evidence of respondent's long history with DSS and removal of her other children, minimal progress with her case plan; failure to utilize her visitation; and execution of a relinquishment for adoption); *In re W.H.*, 819 S.E.2d 617 (N.C. Ct. App. 2018) (holding no abuse of discretion when order ceased visitation between father and his sons after considering father's conduct toward his daughters and determining visitation was against all the children's best interests, health, and safety); *In re T.R.T.*, 225 N.C. App. 567 (2013). *See also In re T.W.*, 250 N.C. App. 68 (2016) (holding no abuse of discretion and affirming order that respondent mother have no visitation with the child based on findings that visitation was undesirable, respondent mother was awaiting criminal trial for alleged sexual abuse of child, and she was not compliant with her treatment); *In re J.S.*, 182 N.C. App. 79 (2007) (holding that evidence was sufficient to support the trial court's order for no visitation with the father where evidence showed that the father beat the child two to three times a day causing injuries, thus no amount of contact could be said to be in the best interest of the child or consistent with the health and safety of the child); *In re K.C.*, 199 N.C. App. 557 (2009) (holding that while the court may have failed to make an express finding that visitation with respondent mother would be harmful to the children or that she forfeited her right to visits, any error was invited by respondent mother such that she is not entitled to appeal as she invited the outcome by effectively asking the trial court to not order visitation; noting that the order alluded to numerous findings that related to visitation including her own stated wishes not to see the children, her cancellation of visitation, her refusal to work with DSS toward reunification, and her unwillingness to follow through with agreed-upon recommendations).

**5. DSS responsibility; court approval.** If DSS has custody or placement responsibility for the child, the court may order DSS to arrange, facilitate, and supervise a court-approved visitation plan consistent with the best interests of the child. Although the plan must indicate the minimum frequency and length of visits and whether the visits must be supervised, unless the court orders otherwise, DSS has the discretion to do the following:

- determine who will supervise visits when supervision is required;
- determine the location of visits; and
- change the day and time of visits in response to scheduling conflicts, illness of the child or party, or extraordinary circumstances.

G.S. 7B-905.1(b).

Limited and temporary changes must be communicated promptly to the affected party, and ongoing changes must be communicated in writing to the party, stating the reason for the change. G.S. 7B-905.1(b).

If a child is in the custody or placement responsibility of DSS, the director may not allow unsupervised visitation with the parent, guardian, custodian, or caretaker from whom the child was removed without a hearing at which the court finds that the child will receive proper care and supervision in a safe home. G.S. 7B-903.1(c); 7B-101(19) (definition of "safe home").

**6. Guardians and custodians.** If the child is placed or remains in the custody or guardianship of a relative or other suitable person, any visitation order must specify the minimum frequency and length of the visits and whether the visits must be supervised. The court may authorize additional visitation agreed upon by the respondent and custodian or guardian. G.S. 7B-905.1(c). Determination of visitation rights is a judicial function that cannot be delegated to the child's custodians, guardians, or others. *See In re C.S.L.B.*, 254 N.C. App. 395 (2017) (vacating and remanding visitation order as unilateral right of the guardians to suspend visits based on "concerns" about mother's substance abuse or discord with the children's father during visitation was improper delegation of judicial function); *In re J.D.R.*, 239 N.C. App. 63 (2015) (remanding order related to visitation; although the father did not have complete authority to determine visitation, the degree of delegation given to father by the court to determine visitation by mother went too far); *In re M.M.*, 230 N.C. App. 225 (2013); *In re L.B.*, 181 N.C. App. 174 (2007).

**7. Suspension of visitation.** The court's order concerning visitation may specify conditions under which visitation may be suspended. G.S. 7B-905.1(a). When DSS has custody or placement responsibility, DSS may temporarily suspend all or part of the visitation plan if DSS makes a good faith determination that the plan is not consistent with the child's health and safety. DSS will not be subject to a motion to show cause for the suspension; however, it must expeditiously file a motion for review and request that a hearing be scheduled within thirty days (unless a review or permanency planning hearing is already scheduled to be heard within thirty days of the suspension of visits). G.S. 7B-905.1(b); *see* S.L. 2019-33.

## B. Review of Visitation Plan, Notice to Parties, Mediation

When the court retains jurisdiction in the juvenile proceeding, all parties must be informed of the right to file a motion for review of any visitation plan. G.S. 7B-905.1(d); *In re J.L.*, 826 S.E.2d 258 (N.C. Ct. App. 2019) (vacating portion of order and remanding for compliance with G.S. 7B-905.1(d) as neither the order nor transcript of the hearing revealed that the trial court informed mother of her right to file a motion for review of the visitation plan).

Prior to or at a hearing to review visitation, the court may order DSS or the GAL to investigate and make written recommendations and provide testimony as to appropriate visitation. After a proper motion, notice, and a hearing to review visitation, the court may establish, modify, or enforce a visitation plan that is in the child's best interest. G.S. 7B-905.1(d).

To resolve visitation issues, the court may order the parents, guardian, or custodian to participate in custody mediation where such programs have been established (pursuant to G.S. 7A-494). When the court refers a case to custody mediation, it must specify the issues for mediation, including but not limited to whether visitation must be supervised and whether overnight visitation may occur. Participants in custody mediation may not consent to a change in custody. A copy of any mediation agreement must be provided to the parties and counsel and must be approved by the court. G.S. 7B-905.1(d). Mediation of visitation issues is subject to the provisions of G.S. 50-13.1(d) through (f), which address

- circumstances for dismissal of mediation and having the action heard in court;
- privacy and confidentiality of mediation proceedings as well as inadmissibility in court;
- mediator's authority to interview the child and others; and
- applicability or inapplicability of privilege, immunity, etc.

**AOC Form:**
AOC-J-135, Order and Notice to Mediation in Juvenile Proceeding (Abuse/Neglect/Dependency) (Sept. 2019).

## 7.6 Evaluation and Treatment of Child

### A. Court's Authority to Order Evaluation and Treatment

Regardless of the child's placement and other dispositional plans, the Juvenile Code authorizes the court to order that the child be examined by a physician, psychiatrist, psychologist, or other qualified expert to determine the child's needs. Once the examination is completed, the court must conduct a hearing to determine whether the child needs treatment and, if so, who should arrange and pay for the treatment. G.S. 7B-903(d).

See section 7.4.D.3, above (discussing medical consent for evaluation and treatment of a child placed in DSS custody).

### B. Hearing to Determine Treatment Needs and Payment

After completion of a court-ordered evaluation, the court must have a hearing to determine the child's treatment needs. G.S. 7B-903(d). This hearing may be a stand-alone hearing that only addresses the child's treatment needs or may be combined with an initial dispositional, review, or permanency planning hearing.

**1. County involvement.** Since treatment may involve county services and county finances, the county manager (or other person designated by the chair of the board of county commissioners) of the county of the child's residence must be notified of the hearing and given an opportunity to be heard. G.S. 7B-903(d).

**2. Treatment arrangements.** Subject to G.S. 7B-903.1, if the court finds that the child needs medical, surgical, psychiatric, psychological, or other treatment, the court must permit the parent or other responsible person to arrange for the treatment. However, if the parent declines or is unable to make the necessary arrangements, the court may order the needed treatment and direct the county to arrange for it. The statute requires DSS to recommend a facility that will provide treatment for the juvenile. G.S. 7B-903(d). If the child needs psychological or psychiatric treatment, DSS ordinarily would coordinate with the area authority or managed care organization in planning for the child's treatment, discussed in subsection 4, below.

**3. Treatment costs.** Whether or not the parent arranges for treatment, the court may order the parent or other responsible parties to pay the cost of the child's treatment or care. G.S. 7B-903(d); 7B-904(a). If the court finds that the parent is unable to pay the cost, the court must order the county to arrange and pay for the treatment. G.S. 7B-903(d).

**4. Mental illness or developmental disability.**

**(a) Mental health services.** The Juvenile Code states that if the court determines the child may be mentally ill or developmentally disabled, the court may order DSS to coordinate with the appropriate representative of the area mental health, developmental disabilities, and substance abuse services authority or other managed care organization responsible for managing public funds for mental health and developmental disabilities to develop a treatment plan for the child. G.S. 7B-903(e).

**Practice Notes:** Because the area authority or other managed care organization is not a party to the abuse, neglect, or dependency action, the court should refrain from ordering the area authority or managed care organization to provide services.

Every county falls within the service catchment area of an area authority. The area authority is responsible for providing mental health, developmental disabilities, and substance abuse services that are paid for with Medicaid or State funds. For a child to receive services paid for with these public funds, the child must meet the eligibility requirements for the Medicaid or State benefits program, and the service itself has to be authorized by the area authority following a comprehensive clinical assessment performed by one of the area authority's contracted service providers. Only then will an area authority and its contracted service provider develop a treatment plan. If the child is eligible for publicly-funded services, a representative of DSS may coordinate with the area authority for a clinical assessment to be performed by an area authority contractor and submitted to the area authority with a request for service authorization. If the requested service is denied, both the Medicaid and State-funded programs provide a procedure for appealing the denial of service. (An area authority is often referred to by its employees and contractors, as well as statutory law, as a local management (LME), managed care organization (MCO), and LME/MCO.)

As of the date of this Manual, all Medicaid and state-funded mental health and developmental disabilities services have to be accessed through an area authority and one or more of its contracted service providers. However, the North Carolina General Assembly appears to be moving toward a system where all or some Medicaid services for mental illness and developmental disabilities will be provided through private insurance companies that contract with the state to be an MCO for Medicaid funds. In the event that this policy comes to fruition, the language in G.S. 7B-903(e) will apply to these private MCOs because they will be "a managed care organization responsible for managing public funds for mental health and developmental disabilities."

**(b) Commitment.** The court has no authority to commit a child directly to a state hospital or developmental center for persons with intellectual and developmental disabilities, and any such order is void. If the court determines that the best service for the child is institutionalization, admission should be pursuant to the voluntary consent of the child's parent, guardian, or custodian. However, if the parent, guardian, or custodian refuses to consent to the child's admission, the court's signature may be substituted for the purpose of consent. G.S. 7B-903(e).

If the treatment institution refuses admission to a child referred by the court, or discharges the child prior to the completion of treatment, the institution must submit to the court a written report stating

- the reasons for denying admission or for early discharge,
- the child's diagnosis,
- indications of mental illness or intellectual and developmental disabilities and the need for treatment, and
- the location of any facility known to have an appropriate treatment program for the child.

G.S. 7B-903(e).

**Resource:** Sara DePasquale, *Children in DSS Custody Who Need Treatment in a PRTF: There's a Disconnect*, UNC SCH. OF GOV'T: ON THE CIVIL SIDE BLOG (June 1, 2016).

## 7.7 Court's Authority over Parents and Others

The court has jurisdiction over the parent, guardian, custodian, or caretaker of a juvenile who has been adjudicated abused, neglected, or dependent, if that person has been properly served, has waived service, or has automatically become a party pursuant to G.S. 7B-401.1(c) or (d) by being awarded custody or guardianship as a permanent plan. G.S. 7B-200(b); *see* G.S. 7B-904(d1). See Chapter 3.4 (related to personal jurisdiction).

The court is specifically authorized to direct certain orders to parents, guardians, custodians, and caretakers, but the court's authority is limited by the Juvenile Code. *See* G.S. 7B-904. The court's dispositional authority to impose conditions on the respondents requires "a nexus between the step ordered by the court and a condition [of abuse, neglect, or dependency] that is found or alleged to have led to or contributed to the adjudication" or court order removing custody of the juvenile from the respondent. *In re S.G.*, 835 S.E.2d 479, 486 (N.C. Ct. App. 2019) (quoting *In re T.N.G.*, 244 N.C. App. 398, 408 (2015)). However, the court's authority is not limited to only those issues that directly address the reasons for the child's removal or adjudication but may include services that "could aid 'in both understanding and resolving the possible underlying causes' of the actions that contributed to the trial court's removal decision" or adjudication. *In re S.G.*, 835 S.E.2d at 486 (quoting *In re A.R.*, 227 N.C. App. 518, 522 (2013)). "Put another way, the trial judge in an abuse, neglect, or dependency proceeding has the *authority to order a parent to take any step reasonably required to alleviate any condition* that directly or indirectly contributed to causing the juvenile's removal from the parental home." *In re S.G.*, 835 S.E.2d at 487 (emphasis in original) (quoting *In re B.O.A.*, 831 S.E.2d 305, 312 (N.C. S.Ct. 2019)).

The court's authority to order a respondent to undergo treatment and take steps to remedy the conditions that led to the child's adjudication or removal from the parent's custody exists in the dispositional phase of the proceeding. The court should not order the respondent to undergo treatment or take additional actions in an adjudication order. *See In re A.G.M.*, 214 N.C. App. 426 (2017) (noting that it is unclear pursuant to what authority the court, in an adjudication order, required respondent mother to participate in therapy). But note that G.S. 7B-507 authorizes the court at nonsecure custody to "order services or other efforts aimed at returning the juvenile to a safe home."

### A. Treatment and Counseling

**1. Participation in child's treatment.** If the court finds that it is in the child's best interests, the court may order a parent, guardian, custodian, stepparent, adult member of the child's household, or an adult relative entrusted with the child's care to participate in the child's medical, psychiatric, psychological, or other treatment. G.S. 7B-904(b).

**2. Evaluations and treatment of parents and others.** When in the child's best interests, the court may order a parent, guardian, custodian, stepparent, adult member of the child's household, or an adult relative entrusted with the child's care to undergo treatment or counseling directed toward remediating or remedying behaviors or conditions that indirectly or directly led or contributed to the child's adjudication or to the court's decision to remove the child from that person's custody. G.S. 7B-904(c); *see In re B.O.A.*, 831 S.E.2d 305 (N.C. S.Ct. 2019) (analyzing G.S. 7B-904 in a TPR; holding conditions of removal include all the factors, both those that are indirect and direct, that contributed to the child's removal); *In re A.R.* 227 N.C. App. 518 (2013) (holding that it was within the trial court's authority to order the parents to comply with mental health assessments and recommendations, substance abuse evaluations, and random drug screens, which were reasonably related to aiding the parents in correcting the conditions that led to the children's removal; the children's removal was related to domestic violence and the court-ordered conditions were to assist respondents in understanding and resolving the possible underlying causes of the domestic violence); *In re A.S.*, 181 N.C. App. 706 (holding that the trial court did not abuse its discretion in ordering the father to undergo a psychological evaluation, have a substance abuse assessment, and enroll in parenting classes, where DSS and the GAL recommended evaluations and classes and the trial court found them to be in the best interests of the children), *aff'd per curiam*, 361 N.C. 686 (2007). Additionally, the court may order that the parent or other person comply with a plan of treatment approved by the court in order to maintain or regain custody of the child. G.S. 7B-904(c).

## B. Parenting Classes, Transportation, Remedial Steps, and Other Orders

The court may order a parent, guardian, custodian, or caretaker who has been served with a summons (or has otherwise submitted to the court's jurisdiction) to

- attend and participate in parenting classes, if classes are available in the judicial district where he or she resides;
- provide transportation for the child to keep appointments for any treatment ordered by the court (if the child is in that person's home and to the extent the person is able to provide transportation); or
- take appropriate steps to remedy conditions in the home that led or contributed to the child's adjudication or to the court's removal of custody of the child from that person.

G.S. 7B-904(d1).

The supreme court in *In re B.O.A.*, 831 S.E.2d 305 (N.C. S.Ct. 2019), an appeal of a termination of parental rights based on failure to make reasonable progress to correct the conditions of removal, analyzed the language of G.S. 7B-904(d1)(3) – "take appropriate steps to remedy conditions in the home that led to or contributed to the juvenile's adjudication or to the court's decision to remove custody of the juvenile from the parent, guardian, custodian, or caretaker." In that opinion, the supreme court held that an expansive reading of that language is appropriate, meaning the trial court has authority to order the parent to take steps to alleviate the conditions that directly or indirectly caused the child's removal. The trial court is not limited to those allegations in the petition that immediately led to the child's removal. The supreme court reasoned that a child's removal "is rarely the result of a single, specific incident and is, instead, typically caused by the confluence of multiple factors, some of which are immediately apparent and some of which only become apparent in light of further investigation," and a trial court gains a better understanding of the family dynamic as the case progresses and may modify and update a case plan accordingly. *In re B.O.A.*, 831 S.E.2d at 314. A more restrictive reading (as had been applied by the court of appeals) "would unduly handicap our trial courts in their efforts to rectify the effect of abuse, neglect, and dependency." *In re B.O.A.*, 831 S.E.2d at 314.

The court of appeals applied the holding of *In re B.O.A.* in *In re S.G.*, 835 S.E.2d 479 (N.C. Ct. App. 2019). In that case, respondent parents appealed an initial dispositional order that required them to complete a mental health and substance abuse assessment and follow all recommendations, submit to random drug screens, and obtain and maintain safe and stable housing when the children were removed due to a non-accidental injury (bruising on the forehead and eyelid) to one of the children, respondents' failure to take responsibility for the injury, and mother's willingness to continue to expose the children to the father, putting the children at risk of harm. The court of appeals affirmed the dispositional order, holding there was no abuse of discretion by the trial court as the ordered steps would assist the court and the parties in understanding whether substance abuse and mental health issues were underlying causes of the children's adjudication and removal. In applying the holding of *In re B.O.A.*, the court of appeals noted that its earlier decisions that applied a more restrictive reading, including but not limited to *In re H.H.*, 237 N.C. App. 431 (2014) and *In re W.V.*, 204 N.C. App. 390 (2010), were overruled by the supreme court holding in *In re B.O.A.*, 831 S.E.2d 305.

Without explicitly interpreting the language of G.S. 7B-904(d1)(3), previous appellate cases have applied the more expansive interpretation set out in *In re B.O.A.*, 831 S.E.2d 305. *See In re D.L.W.*, 368 N.C. 835 (2016) (discussing G.S. 7B-904(d1)(3) in a termination of parental rights case; noting the order requiring respondent to create a budgeting plan was appropriate when findings in adjudication order indicated domestic violence, a lack of consistent and adequate housing, and the parents' inability to meet the children's basic needs as reasons for children's removal and adjudication); *In re T.N.G.*, 244 N.C. App. 398 (2015) (holding court did not exceed its dispositional authority in an order directing respondent father to maintain stable employment and obtain a domestic violence offender assessment and follow recommendations when the record established a nexus between the child's court-ordered removal from respondent's custody and the circumstances that led to removal, as set out in an addendum to the petition that alleged respondent was unemployed and unable to care for the child and DSS had concerns about respondent's admitted domestic violence history).

### C. Cost Responsibilities

For a discussion of orders that required a respondent parent to pay the cost of supervised visitation, see section 7.5.A.2, above.

**1. Child support.** If the child is in the legal custody of someone other than a parent, the court may order the parent to pay a reasonable sum to cover (in whole or in part) the support of the child if the court finds that the parent is able to do so. The amount of child support is determined according to G.S. 50-13.4(c) and the Child Support Guidelines. G.S. 7B-904(d). The court must find the parent has an ability to pay support and determine a reasonable sum. *In re A.M.*, 247 N.C. App. 672 (2016) (remanding child support portion of dispositional order for further findings; noting the order contained no findings about the mother's income, ability to work, or ability to pay; the reasonable needs of the children; or an appropriate amount of support). If the child is in the custody of DSS and the court finds that the parent is unable to pay the cost of the child's care, the cost must be paid by the county DSS (unless the child is receiving care in a state or federal institution). G.S. 7B-904(d). The court does not have the authority to order a parent to contact a child support enforcement agency to arrange to pay child support. *In re A.S.*, 181 N.C. App. 706, *aff'd per curiam*, 361 N.C. 686 (2007). However, when a child is placed in foster care, DSS has an obligation to seek support from the child's parents. If support is not addressed in a court order entered in the abuse, neglect, or dependency action, DSS can pursue support through the IV-D child support enforcement program.

**Practice Note:** Child support orders usually are not entered in juvenile court, and child support generally is best dealt with through the IV-D Child Support Enforcement office. The court may order DSS to pursue the establishment, modification, or enforcement of a support obligation through the IV-D office. A parent may volunteer to go to the child support enforcement office. The parent generally is legally responsible for the financial support of a minor child whether or not he or she has a formal support obligation through agreement or court order.

**2. Treatment of child or participating adult.** Regardless of whether the parent arranges for treatment for the child, the court may order the parent "or other responsible parties" to pay for the cost of treatment or care ordered by the court, including treatment in which the parent or others are ordered to participate. G.S. 7B-903(d); 7B-904(a), (b). If the court finds that the parent is unable to pay the cost of the child's treatment, the court must order the county to pay for treatment. G.S. 7B-903(d). See section 7.6, above (evaluation and treatment of child).

**3. Treatment of parent or others.** If the court orders treatment for the parent (or other respondents), the court may order that person to pay the cost of his or her own treatment. If the court finds that the parent or other person is unable to pay, the court may

- order the person to receive treatment currently available from the area mental health program (local management entity) or
- if the court has conditioned the child's legal custody or placement with that person on that person's compliance with treatment, charge the cost of treatment to the child's county of residence.

G.S. 7B-904(c).

### D. Failure to Comply with Court Orders

On motion of a party or on the court's own motion, the court may issue an order for a parent, guardian, custodian, or caretaker who has been served with a summons in an abuse, neglect, or dependency proceeding to show cause why he or she should not be found in contempt (civil or criminal) for willfully failing to comply with a court order. G.S. 7B-904(e). Contempt proceedings are governed by Chapter 5A of the General Statutes.

**AOC Form:**
AOC-J-155, Motion and Order to Show Cause (Parent, Guardian, Custodian or Caretaker in Abuse/Neglect/Dependency Case) (Nov. 2000).

**Practice Note:** Although G.S. 7B-904(e) refers to a parent, guardian, custodian, or caretaker who is served with a copy of the summons, no such limitation appears in G.S. Chapter 5A. The juvenile court may have personal jurisdiction over a respondent who has not been properly served with a summons in the abuse, neglect, or dependency proceeding (e.g., when proper service is waived or a guardian or custodian automatically becomes a party pursuant to G.S. 7B-401.1(c) or (d)). *See* G.S. 7B-200(b). See also Chapter 3.4 (discussing personal jurisdiction).

### E. Court's Authority over DSS

The court's authority over DSS is clear in some circumstances and less clear in others. Throughout the Juvenile Code, the court is authorized to order DSS to take certain actions. For example, when a child is placed outside the home, the court "may order the director to arrange, facilitate, and supervise a visitation plan expressly approved by the court." G.S. 7B-905.1(b). At the nonsecure custody stage, the court may order services or other efforts aimed at returning the child to a safe home, and when the court orders that the child's placement and care are DSS's responsibility, the order states DSS is to provide or arrange for the child's placement. G.S. 7B-507(a)(4) and (5). The court may also grant DSS the authority to make medical decisions for the child for treatment or care that is neither routine nor emergency care pursuant to G.S. 7B-505.1. The court may order DSS to make diligent efforts to notify relatives and other persons with legal custody of the child's siblings of the child's placement in nonsecure custody. G.S. 7B-505(b). At initial disposition and permanency planning, the court may determine whether DSS should continue to make reasonable efforts for reunification. G.S. 7B-901(c); 7B-906.2(b). At permanency planning, the court must order DSS to make efforts toward finalizing the primary and secondary permanent plans and may specify efforts that are reasonable. G.S. 7B-906.2(b). See sections 7.9, below (relating to reasonable efforts), and 7.10, below (discussing concurrent permanent plans). Although there are numerous provisions throughout the Juvenile Code that authorize the court to direct DSS to conduct certain actions, the Juvenile Code is not entirely clear about the court's authority to order DSS to take actions beyond those specifically required or authorized.

### F. Court's Authority over Child's GAL

The Juvenile Code does not specifically address the court's authority over the child's guardian ad litem (GAL). However, the court presumably has the authority to order a GAL to fulfill his or her statutory responsibilities but not to do things beyond the scope of those responsibilities, such as provide transportation or supervise visits. *See* G.S. 7B-601. See also Chapter 2.3.D (relating to the GAL role and responsibilities).

### G. Limitations on Court's Dispositional Authority

The court's authority in juvenile dispositions is limited to statutory options and existing programs or programs for which the funding and machinery for implementation are in place. In the absence of a statute providing otherwise, the court generally has no authority over agencies or individuals who are not parties to the case. Absent a general appearance, due process requires that a person (or organization) who will be subject to a court's order be given reasonable notice and opportunity to be heard before any proceeding that results in entry of an order against that person or a deprivation of that person's rights. *See Helbein v. Southern Metals Co.*, 119 N.C. App. 431 (1995).

- The court could not require DSS to implement the creation of a special type of foster home. *In re Wharton*, 305 N.C. 565 (1982).
- Where there was no alternative education program for an expelled/suspended student, the court could not send the student back to public school absent a voluntary reconsideration of or restructuring of the suspension by the school board to allow for a return to school. *In re Jackson*, 84 N.C. App. 167 (1987).
- In a delinquency case, the court had no authority to order the state to develop and implement specific treatment programs and facilities. *In re Swindell*, 326 N.C. 473 (1990).
- There was no statutory authorization for the court to grant legal and physical custody of a child to the Willie M. Services Section of the Division of Mental Health, Developmental Disabilities and Substance Abuse Services. *In re Autry*, 115 N.C. App. 263 (1994), *aff'd per curiam*, 340 N.C. 95 (1995).
- Although the Juvenile Code allows the court to order a parent to "pay a reasonable sum that will cover in whole or in part the support of the juvenile," the statute does not give the trial court authority to order a parent to contact a child support enforcement agency. *In re A.S.*, 181 N.C. App. 706, *aff'd per curiam*, 361 N.C. 686 (2007); *In re Cogdill*, 137 N.C. App. 504 (2000) (decided under former law).

## 7.8 Dispositional Considerations and Findings

As discussed throughout this Chapter, the court must consider a variety of factors and decide numerous issues during the dispositional stage of an abuse, neglect, or dependency proceeding, with the child's best interests as the paramount consideration. In addition to custody; placement; visitation; decision-making; evaluation and treatment services for the child; payment for services and/or child support; and services for and/or conditions placed on the parent, guardian, custodian, or caretaker, the Juvenile Code places specific requirements on the court regarding inquiries, findings, and possible outcomes at the different dispositional hearings. Different requirements apply to the initial, review, and permanency planning hearings.

Note that significant changes related to the timing and findings of orders eliminating reasonable efforts for reunification resulted from S.L. 2015-136, effective for actions pending or filed on or after October 1, 2015. Before that date, the court had the authority to order the cessation of reasonable efforts based on any statutorily enumerated finding in any order placing or continuing the placement of a child in DSS custody. *See* G.S. 7B-507 prior to S.L. 2015-136. Now, a court may only order the cessation of reasonable efforts for reunification at an initial dispositional hearing or a permanency planning hearing, and the criteria upon which the court may base its order differs in each type of hearing. *See* G.S. 7B-901(c); 7B-906.2(b).

### A. Initial Dispositional Hearing

**1. Inquiry as to missing parent, paternity, and relatives required.** At the initial dispositional hearing, the court is required to

- inquire about the identity and location of any missing parent and whether paternity is an

issue;
- make findings about efforts to locate and serve a missing parent and to establish paternity if paternity is an issue; and
- inquire about efforts made to identify and notify parents, relatives, or other persons with legal custody of the child's sibling as potential resources for placement or support.

G.S. 7B-901(b).

The court may order specific efforts be made to identify and locate a missing parent or to establish paternity. G.S. 7B-901(b).

See Chapter 5.4.B.5–7 (discussing missing or unknown parents and paternity).

**Practice Note:** While the Juvenile Code does not specifically address the issues of missing parents, paternity, or locating relatives in the context of review and permanency planning hearings, the court should address these issues at any hearing where they may have ongoing relevance. *See In re A.E.C.*, 239 N.C. App. 36 (2015) (vacating and remanding TPR order and order ceasing reunification efforts for father who made a late appearance in the case; the facts showed that at a permanency planning hearing, the child's GAL reported mother's husband was not the child's father based on paternity tests conducted in another court; no findings were made at the permanency planning hearing that he was not the father and no inquiries were made into paternity; putative father eventually contacted court and DSS after being notified by mother that he was possible father; his paternity was established; court was required to address reunification efforts with the father).

**2. Consideration of G.S. 7B-901(c) factors and reasonable efforts.** At the initial dispositional hearing, when the court is placing the child in DSS custody, it may order that reasonable efforts for reunification are not required. The court must make written findings of a specific factor identified in G.S. 7B-901(c) before making such an order, and those findings are that a court of competent jurisdiction

- determines or has determined that the parent has committed, encouraged the commission of, or allowed to be committed against the juvenile any of the following aggravated circumstances: sexual abuse, chronic physical or emotional abuse, torture, abandonment, chronic or toxic exposure to alcohol or controlled substances that caused an impairment or addiction in the juvenile, or any other conduct that increased the enormity or added to the injurious consequences of the abuse or neglect (G.S. 7B-901(c)(1));
- has terminated involuntarily the parent's rights to another child (G.S. 7B-901(c)(2)); or
- determines or has determined that a parent committed, or aided, attempted, conspired, or solicited to commit, murder or involuntary manslaughter of the parent's child; committed sexual abuse or felony assault causing serious bodily injury to the parent's child; or has been required to register as a sex offender (G.S. 7B-901(c)(3)).

When the court makes one of those written findings, it must order that reasonable efforts for reunification are not required unless it concludes that compelling evidence warrants continued reunification efforts. G.S. 7B-901(c). When the court determines that reunification efforts are not required, a permanency planning hearing must be scheduled within thirty days. G.S. 7B-901(d). See section 7.2.B, above (discussing timing of dispositional hearings).

---

**Practice and Legislative Note:** Prior to June 25, 2018, the language of G.S. 7B-901(c)(1) and (3) stated "a court of competent jurisdiction *has determined*. . . ." In an appeal challenging the court's authority to make a determination of a specified factor at the initial dispositional hearing, the North Carolina appellate courts held that "has determined" is the present perfect verb tense, which required a previously made determination at a prior hearing or in a prior order. Without a previous determination, the trial court lacked authority to determine, based on evidence presented at the initial dispositional hearing, that a factor existed and reunification efforts were ceased. *In re G.T.*, 250 N.C. App. 50 (2016), *aff'd per curiam*, 370 N.C. 387 (2017). The statute was amended, effective for all dispositional orders effective on or after June 25, 2018, to add the present tense "determines," thus enabling the court to make a finding based on evidence presented at the initial dispositional hearing. *See* S.L. 2018-86.

---

The court's authority to order the cessation of reasonable efforts for reunification and/or eliminate reunification as a permanent plan based upon a G.S. 7B-901(c) factor is limited to the initial dispositional hearing; G.S. 7B-901(c) factors are not applicable at a permanency planning hearing. *See In re T.W.*, 796 S.E. 2d 792 (N.C. Ct. App. 2016) (reversing order ceasing reunification efforts after making a finding of a G.S. 7B-901(c) factor at the permanency planning hearing). Similarly, the more "lenient" requirements of different G.S. 7B-906.2(b) findings, which authorize the court to eliminate reunification efforts, are limited to a permanency planning hearing. The G.S. 7B-906.2(b) findings cannot be applied at the initial dispositional hearing or included in that order. *See In re J.M.*, 255 N.C. App. 483 (2017) (vacating portion of combined initial dispositional and permanency planning order that released DSS from providing reasonable efforts upon finding that those efforts would clearly be unsuccessful or inconsistent with the child's health and safety). An order that follows an initial dispositional hearing implicates the statute governing initial dispositional hearings, G.S. 7B-901(c), and requires the trial court to make a finding of one of the G.S. 7B-901(c) factors before it orders reunification efforts are not required. The requirement that a court find one of the G.S. 7B-901(c) factors cannot be eluded by combining an initial dispositional and a permanency planning hearing in a single order. *In re J.M.*, 255 N.C. App. 483. *See* G.S. 7B-906.2(b). See also section 7.8.C, below (discussing permanency planning hearings and reunification efforts).

The court is only required to make G.S. 7B-901(c) findings when the child is in DSS custody. *See In re H.L.*, 807 S.E.2d 685 (N.C. Ct. App. 2017) (award of guardianship at initial disposition was proper under G.S. 7B-903(a)(5) and did not require the findings of G.S. 7B-901(c)). The court is not required to make findings specified in G.S. 7B-906.1 at an initial dispositional hearing; findings required by that statute apply to review and permanency planning hearings and should be made at the subsequently scheduled hearing. *See In re L.Z.A.*, 249 N.C. App. 628 (2016).

## B. Required Criteria for Review and Permanency Planning Hearings

The court is required to consider the following criteria at review and permanency planning hearings and to make written findings concerning any that are relevant.

**1. Reunification efforts.** The court must consider services offered to reunite the child with either parent (whether or not the child resided with the parent at the time of removal) or with the guardian or custodian from whom the child was removed. G.S. 7B-906.1(d)(1). The court must also consider whether efforts to reunite the child with either parent clearly would be unsuccessful or inconsistent with the child's health or safety and need for a safe, permanent home within a reasonable period of time (regardless of whether the child lived with the parent, guardian, or custodian at the time of removal). G.S. 7B-906.1(d)(3). If the finding that efforts would be unsuccessful or inconsistent with the child's health or safety is made, the court is not authorized by G.S. 7B-906.1(d)(3) to order the cessation of reunification efforts. The finding is the trigger for the court to start the permanency planning process. *See In re T.W.*, 250 N.C. App. 68 (2016). When the court makes the finding, it must schedule a permanency planning hearing within thirty days to address permanent plans for the child. G.S. 7B-906.1(d)(3). See sections 7.9, below (relating to ceasing reunification efforts, including case law on evidence and findings to ceasing reunification efforts), and 7.10, below (discussing concurrent permanent plans).

**2. Visitation.** The court must consider reports on visitation that has occurred and whether there is a need to create, modify, or enforce an appropriate visitation plan according to G.S. 7B-905.1. G.S. 7B-906.1(d)(2). See section 7.5, above (related to visitation).

**3. Placement.** The court must consider reports on the placements the child has had, goals of a foster care placement, and the appropriateness of the foster care plan, as well as the role the current foster parent will play in planning for the child. G.S. 7B-906.1(d)(4). *See also In re L.L.*, 172 N.C. App. 689 (2005) (holding that trial court erred in failing to address the goals for foster care and the role of the foster parents).

**4. Independent living.** If the child is 16 or 17 years old, the court must consider a report on an independent living assessment of the child and, if appropriate, an independent living plan. G.S. 7B-906.1(d)(5). See Chapters 8.3 (discussing Foster Care 18–21) and 1.3.B.7 (discussing the Foster Care Independence Act).

**5. Termination of parental rights.** The court must consider whether and when a termination of parental rights (TPR) should be considered. G.S. 7B-906.1(d)(6). See section 7.8.G, below (explaining when DSS may be required to initiate TPR). See also Chapter 9 (discussing TPR).

**6. Any other criteria.** The court may consider any other criteria it deems necessary. G.S. 7B-906.1(d)(7).

### C. Permanency Planning Additional Requirements

Permanency planning hearings are a type of review hearing with the same requirements as other review hearings, explained in section 7.8.B, immediately above. At permanency planning, the court must adopt concurrent permanent plans and identify a primary and secondary plan until a permanent plan has been or is achieved. G.S. 7B-906.2(a1), (b). See section 7.10.A, below.

The court must consider additional criteria, which are set forth in various statutes, at permanency planning hearings. As the court of appeals noted, the Juvenile Code requires multiple layers of inquiry and resulting findings and conclusions of law. *See In re K.L.*, 254 N.C. App. 269 (2017). While there is a need to address specifically the relevant criteria, appellate courts have not had the expectation that the findings include a formal listing of the factors in the Juvenile Code or that they be expressly denominated as such, where it can be concluded from the findings that the relevant criteria were considered. *See In re T.R.M.*, 188 N.C. App. 773 (2008).

The following statutory criteria must be considered, with findings made of either those that are relevant or every factor listed. The specific statute itself indicates whether findings of all or only relevant enumerated factors must be made. Failure to comply with the applicable statute will result in a remand. *See In re D.A.*, 811 S.E.2d 729 (N.C. Ct. App. 2018) (vacating and remanding permanency planning order for failing to make required G.S. 7B-906.2(d) findings); *In re C.P.*, 812 S.E.2d 188 (N.C. Ct. App. 2018) (reversing and remanding permanency planning order granting guardianship when mandated finding of G.S. 7B-906.1(e)(1) not made); *In re K.L.*, 254 N.C. App. 269 (reviewing whether court made findings required by G.S. 7B-906.1(d), (e), (i), (n) and 7B-906.2(b), (c), (d); reversing and remanding for additional necessary findings). The exact statutory language is not necessarily required. The North Carolina Supreme Court held that the use of the actual statutory language in making findings is best practice, but the statute does not demand that the trial court's order contain a verbatim recitation of its language. *In re L.M.T.*, 367 N.C. 165 (2013) (reversing the court of appeals, which had reversed the trial court, because the order embraced the substance of the statutory provisions; decided under former statute); *In re S.B.*, 834 S.E.2d 683 (N.C. Ct. App. 2019) (applying *In re L.M.T.* and concluding trial court satisfied the statutorily required findings).

**1. Returning home.** The court must consider whether it is possible for the child to be placed with a parent immediately or within the next six months, and if not, why placement with a parent is not in the child's best interest. G.S. 7B-906.1(e)(1). *See also In re C.P.*, 812 S.E.2d 188 (N.C. Ct. App. 2018); *In re I.K.*, 227 N.C. App. 264 (2013); *In re J.V.*, 198 N.C. App. 108 (2009); *In re J.S.*, 165 N.C. App. 509 (2004); *In re Ledbetter*, 158 N.C. App. 281 (2003) (all cases in which the trial court erred by failing to make adequate findings as to why it was not in the child's best interest to return home). However, the child cannot be returned home unless the court finds that the child will receive proper care and supervision in a safe home. G.S. 7B-903.1(c); *see* G.S. 7B-906.1(*l*); *see also* G.S. 7B-101(19) (definition of "safe home"). See section 7.4.D.2, above (relating to court requirements for returning a child home).

Appellate cases have stated that in determining whether it is possible for the child to return home within six months of the permanency planning hearing, the court must look at the progress the parents have made in eliminating the conditions that led to the removal of the child. *In re J.V.*, 198 N.C. App. 108 (2009); *In re T.K.*, 171 N.C. App. 35, *aff'd per curiam*, 360 N.C. 163 (2005). The fact that parents have made some progress does not ensure that the child will be returned home. *See In re T.K.*, 171 N.C. App. 35 (upholding the trial court's determination that while the mother had made progress, the progress was insufficient for the court to be assured that the children could be safely returned to her care and that the best interests of the children, not the rights of the parents, were paramount), *aff'd per curiam*, 360 N.C. 163. Some other issues related to this permanency planning requirement that have been addressed in appellate cases include the following:

- A trial court's finding that the juvenile's return to the home was "improbable," rather than not possible (using a term other than the one in the statute) did not require a remand. Although it is the better practice for the court to use the words of the statute in its findings, the court sufficiently addressed the issue of whether it was possible for the juvenile to be returned home immediately or within the next six months and why it was not in the juvenile's best interests to return home. *In re T.R.M.*, 188 N.C. App. 773 (2008).
- The fact that the court has made guardianship the permanent plan for a child does not eliminate the requirement that the court address whether it is possible for the child to return home. *In re J.V.*, 198 N.C. App. 108 (2009).
- The court reversed and remanded where the trial court's order failed to clarify which findings related to which parent and included insufficient findings to support the ultimate finding (or conclusion) that it was contrary to the child's best interest to be returned to respondent. *In re H.J.A.*, 223 N.C. App. 413 (2012).

**2. Guardianship or custody.** Where the child's placement with a parent is unlikely within six months, the court must consider whether legal guardianship or custody with a relative or some other suitable person should be established and, if so, the rights and responsibilities that should remain with the parents. G.S. 7B-906.1(e)(2). See sections 7.4.C.1, above (placement priority); 7.4.E and F, above (custody and appointment of guardian). The trial court is not required to make findings about whether the respondent parent retains each right or responsibility he or she had before the order granting guardianship or custody. With the exception of visitation, the parent's rights and responsibilities are lost when the court does not provide otherwise in the order that places the child in the custody or guardianship of someone other than a parent. *In re M.B.*, 253 N.C. App. 437 (2017). Before ordering custody or guardianship to a person other than a parent, the court must verify that the potential guardian or custodian understands the legal significance of the placement or appointment and will have adequate resources to appropriately care for the child. G.S. 7B-906.1(j). See section 7.4.G, above (discussing verification requirement).

- A permanent plan placing a child in guardianship with a half-sibling's grandparents was upheld where the child was bonded with the grandparents and lacked interest in visiting the mother, and the mother failed to undergo ordered psychological evaluation, conquer anger problems, and comply with orders to eliminate contact between her child and her sex offender boyfriend. *In re L.B.*, 181 N.C. App. 174 (2007).
- The trial court erred in failing to consider the biological father as a potential candidate for custody because of his late appearance in the case. *In re Eckard*, 148 N.C. App. 541 (2002) (citing G.S. 7B-907(b)(2), now 906.1(e)(2), for the requirement that the father be considered).

- Where the court ordered in a permanency planning hearing that legal guardianship be placed with relatives, even though the court did not explicitly use the term "permanent" in its order or refer to G.S. 7B-600 related to guardianship, it was reasonable to infer from the findings and other provisions of the order that the court intended to establish guardianship as a permanent plan. *In re P.O.*, 207 N.C. App. 35 (2010).

**3. Adoption.** Where the child's placement with a parent is unlikely within six months, the court must consider whether adoption should be pursued and, if so, any barriers to adoption. G.S. 7B-906.1(e)(3). *See In re Z.J.T.B*, 183 N.C. App. 380 (2007) (holding that it was error for the trial court to make no finding as to whether adoption should be pursued).

---

**Practice Note:** When the child to be adopted is age 12 or older, the child's consent to his or her own adoption is required unless the court in the adoption proceeding waives the requirement after finding it is not in the child's best interest to require his or her consent. G.S. 48-3-601(1); 48-3-603(b)(2). The child's desire to be adopted, especially when the child is age 12 or older, may be relevant when considering this factor.

---

**4. Change in current placement.** Where the child's placement with a parent is unlikely within six months, the court must consider whether the child should remain in the current placement or be placed in another permanent living arrangement and why. G.S. 7B-906.1(e)(4). *See In re Z.J.T.B*, 183 N.C. App. 380 (2007) (holding that it was error for the trial court to fail to examine whether the children's placement should change and why); *In re Ledbetter*, 158 N.C. App. 281 (2003) (holding that it was error for the trial court to change a child's custody without adequately explaining in its findings why the change was being made).

**5. Reasonable efforts to implement permanent plan.** At hearings after the initial permanency planning hearing, the court must address whether DSS has made reasonable efforts to implement the permanent plan for the child. G.S. 7B-906.1(e)(5). See section 7.9, below (discussing reasonable efforts).

**6. Other criteria.** The court may consider any other criteria it deems necessary. G.S. 7B-906.1(e)(6). *See In re J.M.D.*, 210 N.C. App. 420 (2011) (holding that even if none of the other statutory criteria were relevant the trial court should have made findings as to "other criteria" relevant to the purpose of the permanency planning hearing).

**7. Permanent plan.** At the conclusion of each permanency planning hearing, the court must make specific findings as to the best permanent plans to achieve a safe, permanent home for the child within a reasonable period of time. G.S. 7B-906.1(g). *See* G.S. 7B-906.2; *In re D.A.*, 822 S.E.2d 664 (N.C. Ct. App. 2018) (holding the trial court erred in failing to adopt a permanent plan as required by G.S. 7B-906.2); *In re T.W.*, 250 N.C. App. 68, 72 (2016) (stating "[o]bviously, a court presiding at a permanency planning hearing will always consider a permanent plan of care for the juvenile and, indeed, must 'adopt concurrent permanent plans and … identify the primary plan and secondary plan.' "). See section 7.10, below, for further explanation of concurrent permanency planning and the options for a permanent plan.

**8. Reasonable efforts findings.** At each permanency planning hearing, unless reasonable efforts to reunify were previously ceased, the court must make a finding about whether DSS's efforts to reunify were reasonable. G.S. 7B-906.2(c). The court may order reunification efforts ceased at the initial disposition or any permanency planning hearing. *See* G.S. 7B-901(c) and section 7.8.A.2, above (related to ceasing reasonable efforts at initial disposition); G.S. 7B-906.2(b); *In re H.L.*, 807 S.E.2d 685 (N.C. Ct. App. 2017) (trial court complied with G.S. 7B-906.2 when ceasing reunification efforts at first permanency planning hearing after finding further reunification efforts would be unsuccessful). In every subsequent permanency planning hearing, the court must make written findings about the efforts DSS has made toward the primary and secondary permanency plans that were in effect before the hearing and determine whether those efforts were reasonable to timely achieve permanency for the child. G.S. 7B-906.2(c); *see In re K.L.*, 254 N.C. App. 269, 282 (2017) (reversing and remanding order that made no findings of whether DSS made reasonable efforts to reunify with respondent mother; noting the record shows "DSS completely disregarded its statutory duty to 'finalize the primary and secondary' plans until relieved by the trial court.").

The court must also make written findings of each of the following four factors regarding the parent, which demonstrates the parent's success or failure toward reunification – whether the parent is

- making adequate progress within a reasonable period of time under the plan;
- actively participating or cooperating with the plan, DSS, and the child's guardian ad litem (GAL);
- remaining available to the court, DSS, and the child's GAL; and
- acting in a manner that is consistent with the child's health or safety.

G.S. 7B-906.2(d). *See In re D.A.,* 811 S.E.2d 729 (N.C. Ct. App. 2018) (vacating and remanding permanency planning order for failing to make required G.S. 7B-906.2(d)(4) finding whether parents acted in a manner inconsistent with the child's health and safety); *In re K.L.*, 254 N.C. App. 269 (reversing and remanding order for additional findings when order did not address mother's progress, shortcomings, or failure to accomplish permanent plan or mother's cooperation or lack thereof with DSS; noting evidence showed DSS offered no assistance to mother). See section 7.9, below (discussing reasonable efforts).

The court's findings of these four factors do not address the ultimate finding of fact to support an order eliminating reunification as a permanent plan under G.S. 7B-906.2(b), which is that reunification efforts clearly would be unsuccessful or inconsistent with the child's health or safety. *See In re D.A.,* 811 S.E.2d at 734 (although addressing findings under G.S. 7B-906.2(d), stating "[t]he order also contains no findings that embrace the requisite ultimate finding that 'reunification efforts clearly would be unsuccessful or would be inconsistent with the juvenile's health or safety' "). A reviewing court will not make ultimate findings on behalf of the trial court or draw inferences. *See In re T.W.*, 250 N.C. App. 68 (2016) (vacating permanency planning order eliminating reunification efforts for failure to make findings under G.S. 7B-906.2(b); remanding for further proceedings). Additional findings are required by G.S. 7B-906.2(b) related to reasonable efforts clearly being unsuccessful or inconsistent with a child's health and safety before the court may cease reunification efforts and/or eliminate reunification as a concurrent permanent plan at a permanency planning hearing. See sections 7.9 and 7.10.A, below, for a discussion of reasonable efforts, those necessary findings, and concurrent permanency planning.

**9. Youth in DSS custody at age 14 and older.** At every permanency planning hearing where the juvenile is 14 years old or older and in DSS custody, the court must inquire and make findings of each of the following:

- the services provided to assist the juvenile in making a transition to adulthood,
- the steps DSS is taking to ensure the placement provider for the juvenile follows the reasonable and prudent parent standard, and
- whether the juvenile has regular opportunities to engage in age- or developmentally-appropriate activities.

G.S. 7B-912. *See* G.S. 7B-906.2(e); 131D-10.2A (reasonable and prudent parent standard). See section 7.4.D.4, above (discussing reasonable and prudent parent standard and normal childhood activities).

When a juvenile is going to age out of foster care, at least ninety days before his or her 18$^{th}$ birthday, the court, at a permanency planning hearing, must inquire as to whether the juvenile has important documentation that will help his or her transition to adulthood and determine the person or entity that will assist the juvenile in obtaining the documents before the juvenile turns 18. The documents include the juvenile's

- birth certificate,
- social security card,
- health insurance information,
- driver's license or other identification card, and
- educational or medical records that are requested by the juvenile.

G.S. 7B-912(b). See also Chapters 1.3.B.10 (discussing the Preventing Sex Trafficking and Strengthening Families Act) and 8.3 (explaining Foster Care 18–21).

---

**Resources:**
For state policy on transition services from foster care to adulthood, including the NC LINKS, TRIP (Transportation Really Is Possible), and Foster Care 18–21 programs, see DIV. OF SOC. SERVS., N.C. DEP'T OF HEALTH & HUMAN SERVICES, CHILD WELFARE MANUAL "Permanency Planning," available here.

For information and resource links applying to older youth in foster care, see the "Supporting Older Youth in Foster Care" section of the National Conference of State Legislatures website.

For materials, training, and tools related to older children in foster care and aging out of foster care, see the "Youth Engagement Project" page of the ABA Center on Children and the Law website.

### D. Initiation of Termination of Parental Rights Proceeding under Certain Circumstances

The court is also required to consider whether a proceeding to terminate parental rights should be initiated so that the child may find permanency outside of his or her parent's home. The Juvenile Code specifies three circumstances in which DSS is required to initiate a termination of parental rights (TPR) proceeding. The circumstances are

- the child is in the custody or placement responsibility of DSS and has been placed outside the home for twelve of the most recent twenty-two months;
- a court has determined that the parent has abandoned the child; or
- a court has determined that the parent has committed murder or voluntary manslaughter of another child of the parent or has aided, abetted, attempted, conspired, or solicited to commit murder or voluntary manslaughter of the child or another child of the parent.

G.S. 7B-906.1(f).

When one of these circumstances exists, DSS must initiate TPR proceedings unless

- the court finds that guardianship or custody with a relative or other suitable person is the permanent plan for the child;
- the court makes specific findings as to why initiation of TPR proceedings is not in the child's best interest; or
- the court finds that reasonable efforts to reunify the family are still required and that DSS has not provided the family with the services DSS deems necessary for reunification.

G.S. 7B-906.1(f).

When a TPR is determined to be necessary to achieve the permanent plan for the child, DSS must file a TPR petition or motion within sixty days of the date the permanency planning order is entered unless the court makes written findings as to why this sixty-day time frame cannot be met. When the court finds the sixty-day time period cannot be met, it must specify the time within which the TPR petition or motion must be filed. G.S. 7B-906.1(m). Note that the sixty-day time requirement is directory, and failure by DSS to file a TPR petition or motion within the sixty days will not deprive the court of subject matter jurisdiction in the TPR proceeding. *See In re T.M.*, 182 N.C. App. 566 (holding that the trial court was not deprived of subject matter jurisdiction when the TPR filing occurred after the sixty-day period and that there was no error where no prejudice was shown from the delay), *aff'd per curiam*, 361 N.C. 683 (2007).

In *In re A.A.S.*, 812 S.E.2d 875 (N.C. Ct. App. 2018), the court of appeals examined the new statutory scheme requiring concurrent permanency planning and stated that G.S. 7B-906.2 "clearly contemplates the use of multiple, concurrent plans including reunification and adoption." *In re A.A.S.*, 812 S.E.2d at 881. The court of appeals distinguished prior cases, including *In re A.E.C.*, 239 N.C. App. 36 (2015), which were decided under the former statutory scheme where concurrent permanency planning was not mandated, and held that the filing of a termination of parental rights to achieve a primary plan of adoption when a secondary plan of reunification remains does not explicitly or implicitly eliminate reunification as a permanent plan.

**Practice Note:** Although the Juvenile Code directs DSS to initiate the TPR action, the child's GAL, a court-appointed guardian of the child's person, or the person with whom the child has resided with for a continuous period of two years or more, has standing to and may initiate a TPR action. *See* G.S. 7B-1103(a)(2), (5), and (6). The timeliness of filing the TPR petition or motion has become increasingly important as of January 1, 2019 due to legislative changes regarding appealable orders under G.S. 7B-1001. If an appeal of an order eliminating reunification as a permanent plan is pending, the trial court continues to exercise jurisdiction in the abuse, neglect, or dependency action (unless otherwise directed by the appellate court) but may not proceed with a TPR action. G.S. 7B-1003. If a child's permanent plan is adoption and a TPR is required, the achievement of that plan will be delayed if there is a pending appeal of an order eliminating reunification as a permanent plan since the TPR action cannot proceed until the appeal is resolved. See Chapter 12.5.A.2 (discussing appeal of an order eliminating reunification as a permanent plan).

**Resource:** Sara DePasquale, *What Can the District Court Do in an A/N/D or TPR Action when an Appeal is Pending?* UNC SCH. OF GOV'T: ON THE CIVIL SIDE BLOG (Aug. 2, 2019).

### E. Hearing to Modify or Vacate a Dispositional Order

The Juvenile Code allows a party to file a motion (or petition) to modify or vacate an order entered in the abuse, neglect, or dependency action. *See* G.S. 7B-1000. Upon such motion (or petition), the court may conduct a review hearing, after providing notice to the parties, to determine whether the order is in the child's best interests. G.S. 7B-1000(a). The applicable standard in the review hearing is either a change in circumstances or the needs of the juvenile. G.S. 7B-1000(a). *See In re A.C.*, 247 N.C. App. 528 (2016).

In *In re A.C.*, 247 N.C. App. 528, the court of appeals addressed the criteria of G.S. 7B-1000. Distinguishing the standard of G.S. 7B-1000 from a motion to modify a G.S. Chapter 50 civil custody order, the court of appeals held that G.S. 7B-1000 allows for a modification based on a change in the needs of the juvenile or a change in circumstances and that the burden is on the moving party to prove the changes that support the modification being sought. The changes must have either occurred or been discovered since the time of the order, but the court may consider historical facts of the case to determine whether a change has occurred. When a change has occurred, the court applies the best interests of the child standard in making any modifications to the order. In *In re A.C.*, the movant alleged a change in circumstances (not the needs of the juvenile), and the trial court properly determined that a substantial change in circumstances existed and a modification of the order was in the child's best interests.

There are exceptions to the application of G.S. 7B-1000(a). When the change being sought is the removal of a guardianship that is the child's permanent plan, the provisions of G.S. 7B-600(b) apply. When custody has been placed with a parent, the court has retained jurisdiction but periodic review and permanency planning hearings have been waived, and DSS receives a new report of abuse, neglect or dependency that warrants court action, DSS must file a new petition in the existing action and not a motion to modify or vacate the order. *See* G.S. 7B-401(b). Under these circumstances, the trial court will not have subject matter jurisdiction to proceed on a motion to modify. *In re T.P.*, 254 N.C. App. 286 (2017) (vacating order modifying permanency planning order based on a DSS motion for review when G.S. 7B-401(b) applied; holding trial court lacked subject matter jurisdiction as proper pleading was not filed and procedure for adjudicatory hearing was not followed). See section 7.2.A.4(a), above (discussing G.S. 7B-401(b)).

## 7.9 Reasonable Efforts

### A. Introduction

In abuse, neglect, or dependency proceedings "reasonable efforts" is a term of art that originated with the federal Adoption Assistance and Child Welfare Act of 1980. Reasonable efforts requirements have been part of the North Carolina Juvenile Code since 1988. *See* S.L. 1987-1090. The Adoption and Safe Families Act (ASFA) was enacted in response to a recognition that the child welfare system was overburdened and moved slowly, that some children were spending what many professionals thought to be an unreasonable portion of their childhoods in foster care, and that efforts to assist parents in correcting conditions that led to a child's removal often were insufficient. The changes also reflected an increased awareness that children's perception of time is different from that of adults. A period of three days, three months, or three years as experienced by judges, attorneys, social workers, and parents is not comparable to that same period in the life of a child. ASFA focused on the child's safety, explicitly addressed permanency for children, included timelines to move a case forward, and made changes to reasonable efforts provisions initially enacted by the Adoption Assistance and Child Welfare Act. See Chapter 1.3.B.3 and 6 (providing more information on the Adoption Assistance and Child Welfare Act and ASFA).

---

**Resources:**
CHILD WELFARE INFORMATION GATEWAY, U.S. DEP'T OF HEALTH & HUMAN SERVICES, "Reasonable Efforts to Preserve or Reunify Families and Achieve Permanency for Children" (2016).

JUDGE LEONARD EDWARDS, REASONABLE EFFORTS: A JUDICIAL PERSPECTIVE (2014), available on the National Council of Juvenile and Family Court Judges website.

For a comprehensive discussion on the reasonable efforts requirements, see the white paper from the YOUTH LAW CENTER, "Making Reasonable Efforts: A Permanent Home for Every Child" (2000). For guidance on what constitutes reasonable efforts, see the material starting on page 66 of this resource.

## B. Statutory Definitions: Reasonable Efforts, Return Home, Reunification

The Juvenile Code defines "reasonable efforts" as DSS's diligent use of

- preventive or reunification services "when a juvenile's remaining at home or returning home is consistent with achieving a safe, permanent home for the juvenile within a reasonable period of time" or
- permanency planning services, to develop and implement a permanent plan for the juvenile, if the court has determined that the juvenile is not to be returned home.

G.S. 7B-101(18).

The Juvenile Code defines "return home or reunification" as "placement of the juvenile in the home of either parent or placement of the juvenile in the home of a guardian or custodian from whose home the child was removed by court order." G.S. 7B-101(18b). This definition was added to the Juvenile Code in 2013 and supersedes the holding of the court of appeals in *In re J.M.D.*, 210 N.C. App. 420 (2011), that a child is returned home only when placed back in the home from which the child was removed.

> **Practice Notes:** The Juvenile Code appears to use the term "reunification efforts" interchangeably with "reasonable efforts" for reunification. There is no definition of "reunification efforts."
>
> Because reunification refers to the child's placement with either parent or with a guardian or custodian from whose home the child was removed, reasonable efforts and reasonable efforts findings must be made with respect to both parents and, if the child was removed by court order from the home of a custodian or guardian, that person as well. *See In re A.E.C.*, 239 N.C. App. 36 (2015).

## C. Required Findings

In any case in which the child is placed in the custody or placement responsibility of DSS, the Juvenile Code requires the court to make findings at each placement stage of the proceeding about whether DSS has made reasonable efforts to prevent the child's need for placement. *See* G.S. 7B-507(a)(2) (nonsecure custody phase); 7B-903(a3) (dispositional phase). A finding that reasonable efforts to prevent the child's placement were precluded by an immediate threat of harm to the child or a finding that reasonable efforts were not made by DSS does not prevent the court from ordering the child's out-of-home placement when the court finds that the child's placement is necessary for his or her protection. G.S. 7B-903(a3); *see* G.S. 7B-507(a)(2). The court must make a finding that the child's continuation in or return to his or her own home would be contrary to the child's health and safety. G.S. 7B-903(a2). Additionally, different findings regarding reasonable efforts are required at different stages in an abuse, neglect, or dependency action as discussed in earlier sections of this Chapter.

Although the child's best interests is the primary standard used throughout the Juvenile Code, some of the statutes related to reasonable efforts refer to the child's health and/or safety as the paramount concern when addressing reasonable efforts. *See* G.S. 7B-507(a)(2); 7B-903(a3); 7B-906.1(d)(3); 7B-906.2(b).

> **Practice Note:** The statute and appellate cases refer to reasonable efforts findings, but the determination as to reasonable efforts is a conclusion of law. *See, e.g., In re E.G.M.*, 230 N.C. App. 196, 211 (2016) (stating "[d]espite its statutory designation as a finding or 'ultimate finding'… the determination that grounds exist to cease reunification efforts under [statutory language that such efforts would clearly be futile or inconsistent with the juvenile's health, safety, and need for a safe, permanent home within a reasonable period of time] is in the nature of a conclusion of law that must be supported by adequate findings of fact."); *In re Helms*, 127 N.C. App. 505, 510–11 (1997) (stating that "reasonable efforts and best interest determinations are conclusions of law because they require the exercise of judgment.").

Beyond the possibility of being reversed on appeal and delaying permanency for a child, the Juvenile Code does not specify consequences for a court's failure to make findings about reasonable efforts or for the failure of a DSS to actually make reasonable efforts. The findings and the efforts themselves are conditions of the state's receipt of federal child welfare funding. Consequences to the state for failing to adhere to reasonable efforts requirements, if they occur, would come from the federal government, which can withhold or recoup funding the state receives under Title IV-E of the Social Security Act if these and other conditions are not met. See Chapter 1.2.C and 1.3.B (providing more information on Title IV-E and other federal programs, as well as state compliance with federal laws).

### D. Ceasing Reasonable Efforts

The court of appeals has noted that the essential aim of dispositional and review hearings is to reunite a child who has been removed from his or her parent's care, and as a result of that purpose, the Juvenile Code limits when a court may order that reasonable efforts to reunify a parent with his or her child are not required. *In re T.W.*, 250 N.C. App. 68 (2016). As of October 1, 2015, the court's authority is limited to the initial dispositional and permanency planning hearings. *See* G.S. 7B-901(c); 7B-906.2(b). Recent appellate opinions involving challenges to orders ceasing reunification efforts have focused on the procedural requirements related to the timing and findings that are required to enter such an order. See sections 7.8.A.2, above (discussing initial dispositional hearing), and 7.8.C.8, above (discussing permanency planning hearing).

A line of recent published opinions by the court of appeals bifurcates the cessation of reunification efforts from the elimination of reunification as a permanent plan, impacting the procedure and timing of when those different actions may be ordered. *See In re M.T.-L.Y.*, 829 S.E.2d 496 (N.C. Ct. App. 2019) (reviewing prior published opinions court of appeals must follow – *In re H.L.*, 807 S.E.2d 685 (N.C. Ct. App. 2017), which permits the trial court to enter order at initial permanency planning hearing that ceases reunification efforts, and *In re C.P.*, 812 S.E.2d 188 (N.C. Ct. App. 2018), which requires reunification be one of the concurrent permanent plans at the initial permanency planning hearing – noting reservations about the decision in *In re C.P.*; following those prior opinions based on *In re Civil Penalty*, 324 N.C. 373 (1989) by affirming initial permanency planning order that ceased reunification efforts and vacating and remanding portion of permanency planning order that failed to include reunification as a primary or secondary plan); *In re C.S.L.B.*, 254 N.C. App. 395, 397 (2017) (stating "Respondent-mother conflates removing reunification as a permanent plan for the children with ceasing reunification efforts" when court awarded guardianship but kept a secondary plan of reunification; vacating portion of order that relieved DSS of further responsibilities and ceased further review hearings as mother continued to have the right to reasonable efforts provided by DSS and the court evaluation of those efforts). See section 7.10.A, below, for further discussion of reunification as a permanent plan.

Other appellate cases involving challenges to orders ceasing reunification efforts have focused on determining whether the trial court made appropriate findings that address the specific requirements of the applicable statute, whether the findings were based on credible evidence in the record, whether the findings supported the court's conclusion of law, and whether the trial court abused its discretion. *See In re I.K.,* 818 S.E.2d 359 (N.C. Ct. App. 2018) (vacating and remanding permanency planning order where evidence could support findings of either parents' reasonable progress or minimal and insufficient progress on their case plans; the findings were not sufficiently specific to allow the appellate court to determine what evidence the trial court relied on to conclude reunification efforts should cease); *In re P.T.W.,* 250 N.C. App. 589 (2016) (affirming order ceasing reunification efforts; findings supporting cessation of reunification efforts were supported by competent evidence – the DSS social worker's testimony and DSS court summary, neither of which were contradicted by respondent mother). The facts and conclusions must be based on evidence *presented at the hearing* that results in an order ceasing reunification efforts. *In re P.T.W.,* 250 N.C. App. 589 (emphasis in original). Note that as of October 1, 2015, the applicable statutes are G.S. 7B-901(c) and 7B-906.2(b); prior to that date, the applicable statute was G.S. 7B-507.

Where court orders have failed to address the specific requirements of the applicable statutes, appellate cases have found reversible error. *See, e.g., In re D.A.,* 811 S.E.2d 729 (N.C. Ct. App. 2018) (vacating and remanding order for additional findings required by G.S. 7B-906.2); *In re K.L.,* 254 N.C. App. 269 (2017) (reversing and remanding order for additional findings required by G.S. 7B-906.1 and 7B-906.2); *In re A.E.C.,* 239 N.C. App. 36 (2015) (vacating and remanding the court's order to cease reunification efforts where that order and the order terminating parental rights failed to determine whether DSS had made reasonable efforts to reunify, whether reunification would be futile, or why placement with the father was not in the child's best interest).

However, the exact statutory language is not necessarily required. The supreme court held that the use of the actual statutory language in making findings is best practice, but the statute does not demand that the trial court's order contain a verbatim recitation of its language. *In re L.M.T.,* 367 N.C. 165 (2013) (reversing the court of appeals, which had reversed the trial court, because the order that ceased reunification efforts embraced the substance of the statutory provisions; decided under former statute); *In re M.T.-L.Y.,* 829 S.E.2d 496 (N.C. Ct. App. 2019) (affirming order ceasing reunification efforts; finding required by G.S. 7B-906.2(b) made when applying *In re L.M.T.*); *In re H.D.* 239 N.C. App. 318 (2015).

In some circumstances, deficiencies with findings of fact that exist in an order eliminating reunification efforts may be cured in a subsequent order terminating parental rights. This may happen when a termination of parental rights (TPR) action is filed within the statutory time period affecting an appeal of an order eliminating reunification such that the appeals of the two orders are heard together. *See In re L.M.T.*, 367 N.C. 165 (reviewing G.S. 7B-1001(a)(5); holding legislature unambiguously instructed the appellate courts to review the appeal of an order ceasing reunification together with an appeal of a TPR order, allowing incomplete findings of fact in the cease reunification order to be cured by findings of fact in the TPR order); *In re M.T.-L.Y.*, 829 S.E.2d 496 (stating TPR order included supplemental findings to support permanency planning order that ceased reunification efforts); *In re J.T.*, 252 N.C. App. 19 (2017) (vacating order ceasing reunification efforts and TPR order; neither order contained sufficient findings to eliminate reunification efforts); *In re D.C.*, 236 N.C. App. 287 (2014) (deficiency in permanency planning order was cured by TPR order). See Chapter 12.4.A.5 (discussing in detail the requirements for an appeal of an order eliminating reunification).

The requirements of the statute authorizing the cessation of reunification efforts based on whether those efforts clearly would be unsuccessful or inconsistent with the child's health, safety, and need for a safe, permanent home have been found to be satisfied where the trial court relates its findings to one of those prongs (sometimes referred to by the court of appeals as "ultimate findings" and other times as a conclusion of law). The court of appeals cannot "simply infer from the findings that reunification efforts would be futile or inconsistent with the juvenile's health, safety, and need for a safe, permanent home." *In re I.R.C.*, 214 N.C. App. 358, 363 (2011) and cases cited therein at 364 (decided under former G.S. 7B-507). *See In re T.W.*, 250 N.C. App. 68 (2016) (quoting *In re I.R.C.*, 214 N.C. App. at 363–64); *see also In re J.P.*, 230 N.C. App. 523 (2013) (holding that the trial court did relate its findings to a conclusion of law setting forth the basis for ceasing reunification efforts; decided under former statute). Note that the former statute authorizing the cessation of reasonable efforts, G.S. 7B-507, was based on a finding that efforts clearly would be "futile" (now replaced with "unsuccessful") or inconsistent with the child's health, safety, "and need for a safe, permanent home within a reasonable period of time" (now referring solely to the child's "health and safety"; however a reasonable period of time is referred to throughout the Juvenile Code).

The following cases address the sufficiency of the evidence and findings to support an order ceasing reunification efforts and have found them sufficient.

- The findings supported conclusion to cease reunification efforts when they showed mother failed to verify with DSS her participation in substance abuse treatment and her employment and living arrangements; did not comply with the family services agreement, visitation schedule, drug testing, or the requirement that she attend her child's medical appointments; violated the safety plan; and tested positive for drugs. Although a parent may partially perform a required condition, that partial performance does not necessarily prevent the court from concluding the performance is inadequate. *In re M.T.-L.Y.*, 829 S.E.2d 496 (N.C. Ct. App. 2019).
- Findings that father had not made progress on his case plan, missed a Child and Family Team meeting (CFT), refused social worker home visits, and visitation had not been

increased supported conclusion to cease reunification efforts. *In re J.A.K.*, 812 S.E.2d 716 (N.C. Ct. App. 2018).
- The findings and evidence showing respondent mother's failure to comply with her case plan, demonstrate sustained parental improvements, and maintain stable housing; substantiation by DSS for sexual abuse of another one of her children who was not the subject of the court action; and lack of awareness of her history of domestic violence with the children's father supported an order ceasing reunification efforts after concluding those efforts would be inconsistent with the child's health, safety, and need for a safe, permanent home within a reasonable time. Although one finding of fact regarding mother's failure to reengage in therapy was not supported by competent evidence, the remaining findings of fact support the court's ultimate decision to cease reunification efforts. *In re P.T.W.*, 250 N.C. App. 589 (2016).
- The findings supported the conclusion of law that a reunification plan with respondent mother would be futile or inconsistent with the child's need for a safe, permanent home within a reasonable period of time where they showed the parent educator who was working with mother was concerned about mother's ability to protect her child and that mother was aware of one of the children's father's sexual abuse of another one of her children, was not prepared for visits and did not interact with and comfort her child at visits, and moved in with a man upon whom she was dependent despite knowing recommendations for reunification would not be made if there were concerns about her living, parenting, and financial situation. *In re E.M.*, 249 N.C. App. 44 (2016).
- Findings in the reunification order that the mother had failed to attend visits or complete her case plan, had pending criminal charges, had not participated in drug screens, and that the children could not go home for at least six months were sufficient to suggest that reunification efforts would be futile. *In re H.D.*, 239 N.C. App. 318 (2015).
- Reviewing the permanency planning order together with the TPR order, the court of appeals found that the detailed findings in the TPR order relating to the respondent mother's drug abuse, failures of treatment, and relapses up until the time of the TPR hearing were sufficient to support cessation of reunification efforts. *In re D.C.*, 236 N.C. App. 287 (2014).
- The supreme court found the findings were sufficient to support the trial court's order ceasing reunification efforts where respondent mother's drug abuse and domestic violence problems were worsening, and she was covering these problems up and refusing to acknowledge them. *In re L.M.T.*, 367 N.C. 165 (2013).
- In the case *In re A.Y.*, 225 N.C. App. 29 (2013), the court of appeals agreed with respondent mother that some findings of fact in an order ceasing reunification efforts were unsupported, but the court determined that they were not material to the trial court's decision, and other findings were sufficient to support ceasing reunification efforts. Supported findings established continuing verbal aggression and significant conflict between the parents, that the parents had not successfully engaged in couples therapy, that the mother had made only limited progress on treatment goals and had a pattern of poor parenting, and that the child had been detrimentally affected.
- An order to cease reunification efforts was upheld where findings were that mother failed to comply with the terms of a case plan regarding the child's sibling, that the father failed to seek necessary medical care despite being prompted, and that both parents had intellectual disabilities. Also, the mother did not understand the reason for DSS

- involvement, and she shared characteristics with parents who have been known to abuse their children. Despite intensive case management offered to respondents, there were missed appointments and an inability to contact or locate the child and mother. Both the mother and father would need ongoing support to effectively parent, and there did not appear to be a person available to supervise the parents if child was placed in their home or the home of a relative. *In re C.M.*, 183 N.C. App. 207 (2007).
- In determining whether to continue reunification efforts or change the permanent plan, it was permissible for the court to consider the cost of providing services deemed necessary for reunification. Here, the court concluded that because the mother would need help twenty-four hours a day to cope with and care for her children, "reunification is possible but not financially practical." *In re J.J.*, 180 N.C. App. 344, 350–51 (2006).

The following cases have found the evidence and findings insufficient to support an order eliminating reunification efforts.

- Findings that respondents made minimal and insufficient progress on case plans addressing substance use, drug screens, and domestic violence were not sufficiently specific to allow for appellate review. There was evidence in the record that could support those findings, but there was also evidence that showed respondents were making reasonable progress on their case plans. It is unclear what evidence the trial court relied on to make its findings. *In re I.K.*, 818 S.E.2d 359 (N.C. Ct. App. 2018) (vacating and remanding permanency planning order).
- Findings that the "home remains an injurious environment" and that "a return home would be contrary to the best interests of the juvenile" do not constitute a finding that reunification efforts would be unsuccessful or inconsistent with the child's health or safety as required by G.S. 7B-906.2(d). *In re D.A.*, 811 S.E.2d 729, 734 (N.C. Ct. App. 2018) (vacating and remanding permanency planning order to determine whether to cease reunification efforts with mother).
- The court of appeals vacated a permanency planning order that ceased reunification efforts with respondent father and as a result vacated the TPR order that was heard together on appeal with the permanency planning order. At the permanency planning hearings, the trial court heard no oral testimony and instead heard statements from the attorneys, which are not evidence, and accepted court reports submitted by DSS and the child's guardian ad litem (GAL). Relying on previous opinions, the court of appeals stated, "reports incorporated by reference in the absence of testimony are insufficient to constitute competent evidence to support the trial court's findings of fact" and determined the findings in the permanency planning order were unsupported by competent evidence and its conclusions of law were in error. In looking to the TPR order, the court of appeals found the TPR order did not cure the deficiencies in the permanency planning order. *In re J.T.*, 252 N.C. App. 19 (2017).
- The court's findings under G.S. 7B-906.2(d) of mother's refusal to engage in treatment, pending criminal charges, failure to attend the permanency planning hearing due to oversleeping, her aggressive behavior toward the proposed guardians at a child and family team meeting, and her acting inconsistently with her parental rights do not address the ultimate finding of fact required by G.S. 7B-906.2(b) to support the cessation of reunification efforts – whether efforts would clearly be unsuccessful or inconsistent with

the child's health or safety. An appellate court will not make that inference. *In re T.W.*, 250 N.C. App. 68 (2016) (vacating permanency planning order and remanding for further proceedings).
- The court of appeals reversed and remanded a permanency planning order that ceased reunification efforts with respondent father, holding that the evidence did not support the trial court's findings related to reunification efforts, and the findings did not support the conclusion that reunification efforts should cease. The findings failed in several respects to meet the requirements of [former statutes] G.S. 7B-907(b) and 7B-507. There was insufficient evidence of risk of abuse by the father; some findings were mere recitations of evidence; some findings were contrary to evidence that the father was not likely to abuse the child; and findings did not explain why the child could not be returned home or why not returning home was in her best interest. *In re I.K.*, 227 N.C. App. 264 (2013).
- Evidence was insufficient to support an order ceasing reunification efforts with respondent mother where DSS recommended reunification; injuries to the child occurred while in the care of someone the mother was no longer seeing; the mother had a low I.Q. but no severe mental health issues that would interfere with her ability to parent; mother understood her poor choices leading to abuse and had grown and matured to a level as to not be a danger to the child; and the mother continued to pay child support, visit the child regularly, stay employed, and comply with her case plan. Also, the trial court had failed to consider changed conditions, which in this case were highly relevant. *In re Eckard*, 148 N.C. App. 541 (2002).

## 7.10 Concurrent Permanency Planning and Outcomes

At the conclusion of the permanency planning hearing, the court must make specific findings required by the various applicable statutes, discussed throughout this Chapter. The court also must make determinations related to the best plans of care to achieve a safe, permanent home for the child within a reasonable period of time. The court has the same dispositional alternatives and authority over parents and others that it has at the initial dispositional and review hearings.

### A. Concurrent Permanency Planning

The Juvenile Code mandates concurrent permanency planning in all actions filed or pending on or after October 1, 2015. *See* S.L. 2015-136, sec. 14. There are six types of permanent plans:

- reunification,
- adoption,
- guardianship with relatives or others,
- custody to a relative or other suitable person,
- Another Planned Permanent Living Arrangement (APPLA) for youth who are 16 or 17 years old, and
- reinstatement of parental rights (when parental rights have been terminated).

G.S. 7B-906.2(a). *See* G.S. 7B-101(18b) (definition of "reunification"); 7B-600 (appointment of guardian); 7B-903(a) (dispositional alternatives); 7B-911 (transfer to a G.S. Chapter 50 custody action); 7B-912(c), (d) (APPLA); 7B-1114 (reinstatement of parental rights); G.S. Chapter 48 (adoption).

At any permanency planning hearing, the court must adopt concurrent permanent plans that the court finds are in the child's best interests. In its permanency planning order, the court must identify the primary and secondary plans and order DSS to make efforts toward finalizing each plan. In its order, the court may also specify the efforts that are reasonable to timely achieve permanency for the child. G.S. 7B-906.2(a), (b). The court of appeals has recognized that G.S. 7B-906.2 "clearly contemplates the use of multiple, concurrent plans including reunification and adoption." *In re A.A.S.*, 812 S.E.2d 875, 881 (N.C. Ct. App. 2018). Concurrent permanency planning must continue until a permanent plan is or has been achieved. G.S. 7B-906.2(a1); *In re S.B.*, 834 S.E.2d 683 (N.C. Ct. App. 2019) (applying G.S. 7B-906.2(a1) and noting a secondary plan is not needed in an order that establishes a permanent plan).

Reunification must be a primary or secondary plan unless

- the court made a G.S. 7B-901(c) finding in an initial dispositional order;
- the court made a G.S. 7B-906.1(d)(3) finding in a review or permanency planning hearing order (effective Oct. 1, 2019; *see* S.L. 2019-33),
- the permanent plan is or has been achieved pursuant to G.S. 7B-906.2(a1) (effective Oct. 1, 2019, *see* S.L. 2019-33), or
- the court, at a permanency planning hearing, makes written findings under G.S. 7B-906.2(b) that reunification efforts clearly would be unsuccessful or would be inconsistent with the child's health or safety.

G.S. 7B-906.2(b). See sections 7.8.A.2; 7.8.C.8; and 7.9, above (discussing reasonable efforts and findings to cease those efforts at initial dispositional and permanency planning hearings).

The court of appeals, in *In re C.P.*, 812 S.E.2d 188 (N.C. Ct. App. 2018), held that the Juvenile Code requires that reunification be part of an initial concurrent permanent plan. This holding was based on a statutory interpretation of the language of G.S. 7B-906.2(b), which stated "reunification shall remain", thereby presupposing the existence of an earlier permanency planning order that included reunification. In an earlier published opinion, the court of appeals also held that reunification efforts could be ceased at the initial permanency planning hearing. *In re H.L.*, 807 S.E.2d 685 (N.C. Ct. App. 2017). In the *In re C.P.* opinion, the court of appeals noted it was bound by the earlier holding of *In re H.L*, even though the panel in *In re C.P.* disagreed with that holding. In later cases, the court of appeals has followed the precedent established by these two opinions (*see In re Civil Penalty*, 324 N.C. 373 (1989)) but recently stated, "To avoid confusion of our DSS workers and trial courts and to promote permanency for children in these cases, we encourage the North Carolina General Assembly to amend these statutes to clarify their limitations." *In re M.T.-L.Y.*, 829 S.E.2d 496, 505 (N.C. Ct. App. 2019). Since *In re M.T.-L.Y.* was published, the statutes relied upon and referenced in *In re C.P.* were amended by S.L. 2019-33 to remove all references to the words "remain" and "subsequent." The interpretation of those two words were the basis for the holding in *In re C.P.* The statutory amendments appear to "effectively abrogate the Court's holding in *In re C.P.*" *In re A.H.A.*, 833 S.E.2d 265, fn. 4 (N.C. Ct. App. 2019) (unpublished).

> **Practice and Legislative Note**: The effective date of S.L. 2019-33 is October 1, 2019. There is no mention as to whether the legislative changes apply to cases pending on or after October 1, 2019 or apply only to cases filed on or after that date.
>
> **Resource:** For a discussion of *In re C.P.* and its impact in practice, see Sara DePasquale, *And Now a Two-Step: Eliminating Reunification as a Permanent Plan in an A/N/D Proceeding*, UNC SCH. OF GOV'T: ON THE CIVIL SIDE BLOG (May 3, 2018).

An order eliminating a reunification as a permanent plan requires findings under both G.S. 7B-906.2(b) and (d). *In re K.L.*, 254 N.C. App. 269 (2017) (reversing and remanding permanency planning order that achieved a permanent plan of custody to make required findings under various statutes, including G.S. 7B-906.2(b) and (d)).

An order eliminating reunification as a permanent plan under G.S. 7B-906.2(b) may be appealed. The statute governing appeals of G.S. 7B-906.2(b) orders eliminating reunification as a permanent plan, G.S. 7B-1001(a)(5), has complex requirements related to the timing and manner of the appeal that depend on whether the appealing party is a parent, custodian, or guardian, and on whether a TPR petition is filed within sixty-five days of the entry and service of the permanency planning order. When reunification continues as a concurrent plan, the order does not meet the criteria of G.S. 7B-1001(a)(5) to allow for an appeal. *In re A.A.S.*, 812 S.E.2d 875 (N.C. Ct. App. 2018) (distinguishing prior cases, including *In re A.E.C.*, 239 N.C. App. 36 (2015), that were decided under former statutory scheme that did not require concurrent permanency planning; holding the filing of a termination of parental rights to achieve a primary plan of adoption when a secondary plan of reunification remains does not explicitly or implicitly eliminate reunification as a permanent plan). These requirements are explained in Chapter 12.4.A.5.

In *In re C.S.L.B.*, 254 N.C. App. 395 (2017), the court of appeals stated that the respondent mother conflated removing reunification as a permanent plan with ceasing reunification efforts. Respondent mother appealed a permanency planning order that awarded the primary permanent plan of guardianship with a relative and retained a secondary plan of reunification. Respondent mother appealed because the order did not contain the findings required by G.S. 7B-906.2(b) to eliminate reunification as a permanent plan. The court of appeals held reunification had not been eliminated as a permanent plan as the order specifically included a secondary permanent plan of reunification. However, the court of appeals agreed with respondent mother that the trial court should not have waived further review hearings as all of the required G.S. 7B-906.1(n) findings were not made. See section 7.2.A.4, above (discussing waiving review hearings). The court of appeals continued its analysis and looked to G.S. 7B-906.2(b) and 7B-906.1(d) and (e) and held the trial court erred in relieving DSS and the child's guardian ad litem (GAL), stating "[m]oreover, by leaving reunification as a secondary permanent plan for the children, Respondent-mother continued to have the right to have [DSS] provide reasonable efforts toward reunifying the children with her, and the right to have the court evaluate those efforts." *In re C.S.L.B.*, 254 N.C. App. at 398 (vacating portion of order) (note that the order met the criteria of G.S. 7B-1001(a)(4) as an order that changed the legal custody of the juvenile).

Note that in *In re C.S.L.B.*, 254 N.C. App. 395, the trial court apparently did not apply, at a permanency planning hearing in August 2016, G.S. 7B-906.2(a1), effective July 1, 2016, which stated "concurrent planning shall continue until a permanent plan has been achieved." Under G.S. 7B-906.2(a1), the trial court was authorized (but was not required) to enter a guardianship order as the achieved permanent plan without a secondary permanent plan being ordered. Additionally, the court of appeals did not address the language of G.S. 7B-601(a), which states the child's GAL appointment "shall terminate when the permanent plan has been achieved for the juvenile and approved by the court." See subsection B, immediately below, for a discussion of achieving a permanent plan.

**Practice Note:** If the court orders a secondary plan, even when a permanent plan has been achieved, under *In re C.S.L.B.*, 254 N.C. App. 395, the court should not relieve DSS from providing reasonable efforts to achieve that secondary plan. If the court would like to relieve DSS from making reasonable efforts toward the secondary plan, it should order the singular plan that is achieved and eliminate any secondary plan as permitted by G.S. 7B-906.2(a1).

**Resources:**
For the state policy regarding permanency planning, see DIV. OF SOC. SERVS., N.C. DEP'T OF HEALTH & HUMAN SERVICES, CHILD WELFARE MANUAL "Permanency Planning," available here.

DSS has a category of services designed for family reunification. For an explanation, policies, and procedures regarding these services, see DIV. OF SOC. SERVS., N.C. DEP'T OF HEALTH & HUMAN SERVICES, CHILD WELFARE MANUAL "Cross Function," specifically "Time Limited Family Reunification Services," available here.

See the following publications by CHILD WELFARE INFORMATION GATEWAY, U.S. DEP'T OF HEALTH & HUMAN SERVICES,
- "Concurrent Planning for Timely Permanence" (2018)
- "Concurrent Planning for Permanency for Children" (2017).
- "Reasonable Efforts to Preserve or Reunify Families and Achieve Permanency for Children" (2016).
- "Supporting Successful Reunifications" (2017).

In addition to the publications, multiple resources related to permanency plans are accessible through the Child Welfare Information Gateway, U.S. Department of Health and Human Services website. See "Concurrent Planning," "Achieving & Maintaining Permanency," "Legal Issues Related to Permanency," "Reunifying Families," and "Concept and History of Permanency in U.S. Child Welfare."

## B. Achieving a Permanent Plan

Permanent placements can be ordered only in the context of permanency planning hearings that are properly noticed as such (unless the party has waived notice). *See* G.S. 7B-906.1(b); *see In re K.C.*, 248 N.C. App. 508 (2016) (originally unpublished Aug. 2, 2016, but subsequently published) (vacating and remanding permanency planning review orders granting custody to paternal grandparents when parent objected at permanency planning hearing to deficient notice but court proceeded with permanency planning hearing). See section 7.2.B, above (discussing notice).

Once a permanent plan is achieved the court is no longer required to order concurrent planning. G.S. 7B-906.2(a1); *In re S.B.*, 834 S.E.2d 683 (N.C. Ct. App. 2019).

**1. Reunification.** Reunification is achieved when the child is placed in the home of either parent (regardless of whether the child was removed from that parent's home) or the guardian or custodian from whose home the child was removed by order of the court. G.S. 7B-101(18b). The permanent plan of reunification may be achieved in a variety of ways. If the court dismisses the case (meaning terminates its jurisdiction), the legal status of the child and the custodial rights of the parties revert to what they were before the court action was commenced (unless there has been a termination of parental rights, a Chapter 50 custody order was entered pursuant to G.S. 7B-911, or an order in another civil action provides otherwise). *See* G.S. 7B-201(b); 7B-807(a); 7B-903(a)(1). If the court does not dismiss the action, achievement of reunification as a permanent plan occurs through a custody order, which is a permissible dispositional alternative. G.S. 7B-903(a)(4). When a custody is awarded to a parent (or custodian or guardian from whom the child was removed), the court must consider whether its jurisdiction should be terminated pursuant to G.S. 7B-911 and a custody order entered pursuant to G.S. Chapter 50. See subsection 4, below (discussing G.S. 7B-911 and transfer to a G.S. Chapter 50 custody action).

If the court does not transfer the juvenile proceeding to a Ch. 50 custody proceeding, it must retain jurisdiction if it intends for the G.S. 7B-903(a)(4) custody order to survive. *See* G.S. 7B-201(b). When the court retains jurisdiction and custody is ordered to a parent, the court is relieved from holding regularly scheduled permanency planning hearings. G.S. 7B-906.1(k). However, a party may file a motion for review at any time, which the court must hold. *See* G.S. 7B-906.1(n). Note that any new report of abuse, neglect, or dependency that results in DSS determining court action is needed must comply with the procedure of G.S. 7B-401(b) apply. *See In re T.P.*, 254 N.C. App. 286 (2017) discussed in section 7.2.A.4(a), above.

**2. Adoption.** For children who cannot return home, placement options have varying degrees of finality or "permanence." An adoption is the permanency option with the greatest degree of legal finality. An adoption is a separate proceeding, initiated by the adoption petitioner. *See* G.S. 48-2-301(a). It is a special proceeding that is heard before the clerk of superior court, unless the action is transferred to district court as a result of a question of fact, request for equitable relief, or equitable defense. G.S. 48-2-100(a); 48-2-601(a1). In some cases, a termination of parental rights (TPR) of one or both parents will be required, and in other cases, relinquishments will be obtained from the necessary persons whose consents are required, allowing the adoption to proceed without a TPR action. *See* G.S. 48-2-603(a)(4). The final decree of adoption results in a complete substitution of the family and establishes a parent-child relationship between the child and adoption petitioner(s). G.S. 48-1-106(a), (b). *But see* G.S. 48-1-106(d) (exception for stepparent adoption). With the final decree of adoption, the child has achieved permanency, and the district court's jurisdiction in the juvenile proceeding terminates with the entry of the final decree. *See* G.S. 48-2-102(b); *In re W.R.A.*, 200 N.C. App. 789 (2009). For a further discussion of adoptions, see Chapter 10.3.

**3. Guardianship.** The court may award guardianship of the person to a non-parent as the child's permanent plan. G.S. 7B-903(a)(5); 7B-906.2(a)(3); 7B-600(b). When the court orders guardianship as a permanent plan for the child and appoints a guardian under G.S. 7B-600, the guardian automatically becomes a party to the proceeding. G.S. 7B-401.1(c). The duties and responsibilities of the child's guardian are discussed in section 7.4.F, above. The guardianship may not be terminated unless the court finds that

- the relationship between the guardian and the juvenile is no longer in the juvenile's best interest;
- the guardian is unfit;
- the guardian has neglected his or her duties; or
- the guardian is unwilling or unable to continue to perform those duties.

G.S. 7B-600(b).

The court must make certain findings before ordering guardianship, as discussed in sections 7.4.F and G, above. Before the court can award guardianship as the permanent plan, it must also make findings about the parent's constitutional rights since guardianship awards care, custody, and control of the child to a non-parent. See subsection 5, below (discussing required findings regarding parent's constitutional rights).

For a guardianship order to remain in effect and be enforced or modified, the court must retain jurisdiction over the abuse, neglect, or dependency action. *See* G.S. 7B-201(b). However, the court may order that periodic judicial reviews of the permanent guardianship order be waived, held less often than every six months, or be substituted by written reports submitted by the guardian to the court in an order that makes all the required G.S. 7B-906.1(n) findings by clear and convincing evidence. See section 7.2.A.4, above (discussing waiving review hearings).

When hearings are waived, a party has a right to file a motion for review. G.S. 7B-906.1(n). If a party files a motion for review under G.S. 7B-906.1 or G.S. 7B-1000 when a permanent plan of guardianship is in place, before conducting a review hearing the court may do one or more of the following:

- order DSS to conduct an investigation and file a written report and give testimony regarding the performance of the guardian,
- utilize the community resources in behavioral sciences and other professions in the investigation and study of the guardian,

- ensure that a guardian ad litem (GAL) for the child has been appointed pursuant to G.S. 7B-601 and has been notified of the pending motion, and
- take any other action necessary to make a determination.

G.S. 7B-600(b).

**Practice Note:** When state intervention through a juvenile court proceeding is no longer necessary, the court should consider entering a custody order (where the court's jurisdiction in the abuse, neglect, or dependency action may terminate upon the entry of a G.S. 7B-911 order that transfers the action to a G.S. Chapter 50 civil custody action, discussed in subsection 4(a), immediately below) rather than a guardianship order, which requires that the court retain jurisdiction in the abuse, neglect, or dependency proceeding.

**4. Custody.** A permanent plan of custody involves an award of custody of the child to someone who is not the child's parent because an order of custody to a parent constitutes the permanent plan of reunification. Because the permanent plan of custody is to a non-parent, the court must make findings regarding the parents' constitutional rights, discussed in subsection 5, below. Additional considerations and criteria the court must consider and satisfy are discussed in sections 7.4.E and G, above.

**(a) Transfer to G.S. Chapter 50 custody action.** When the court places custody with a parent or other appropriate person, the court must determine whether jurisdiction in the abuse, neglect, or dependency proceeding should be terminated and custody awarded pursuant to G.S. Chapter 50. G.S. 7B-911(a). Through G.S. 7B-911, the court is transferring the juvenile proceeding to a G.S. Chapter 50 custody proceeding. Any subsequent action, such as a modification or enforcement action, would occur in the G.S. Chapter 50 proceeding.

The court of appeals has concluded that G.S. 7B-911 does not require the court to make a finding about whether jurisdiction should be terminated in the juvenile proceeding and the matter transferred to a Chapter 50 custody action. *In re Y.I.*, 822 S.E.2d 501 (N.C. Ct. App. 2018). Additionally, a trial court may terminate jurisdiction in the juvenile proceeding without having to follow the transfer requirements of G.S. 7B-911. G.S. 7B-201; *McMillan v. McMillan*, 833 S.E.2d 692 (N.C. Ct. App. 2019) (although trial court intended to transfer juvenile proceeding to Chapter 50 custody action, it never entered a Chapter 50 custody order; trial court did expressly terminate its jurisdiction in the juvenile proceeding under G.S. 7B-201). If the court terminates its jurisdiction in the juvenile proceeding without entering a Chapter 50 order, the parties return to pre-petition legal and custodial status (absent a termination of parental rights order). *See* G.S. 7B-201(b).

The transfer of an abuse, neglect, or dependency proceeding to a G.S. Chapter 50 custody action should occur only when (1) there is a need for a custody order to remain in effect and be enforceable and modifiable and (2) continued state intervention through a juvenile court proceeding is no longer necessary or appropriate. *See* G.S. 7B-911; 7B-201(b). Terminating jurisdiction in the abuse, neglect, or dependency action, by itself, nullifies any custody order entered in that case, and the legal status of the child and custodial rights of the parties revert to the status that existed before the filing of the abuse, neglect, or dependency petition (unless another valid order has been entered or a parent's rights have been terminated). *See* G.S. 7B-201(b). The G.S. Chapter 50 civil custody order will remain in effect and be subject to modification upon a showing of a substantial change in circumstances and enforcement by the district court in the G.S. Chapter 50 action until the child reaches age 18 or is otherwise emancipated.

Under G.S. 7B-911, the juvenile court may enter a new or modify an existing civil custody order and terminate jurisdiction in the abuse, neglect, or dependency case only if the court finds that

- there is not a need for continued state intervention through a juvenile court proceeding and
- placement with the person being awarded custody has been the permanent plan for the child for at least six months, unless that person is a parent or the person with whom the child was living when the petition was filed.

G.S. 7B-911(c)(2). *See In re J.K.*, 253 N.C. App. 57 (2017); *In re J.M.D.*, 210 N.C. App. 420 (2011); *Sherrick v. Sherrick*, 209 N.C. App. 166 (2011).

The court must make the necessary findings under G.S. 7B-911. *See In re J.D.M.-J.*, 817 S.E.2d 755 (N.C. Ct. App. 2018) (vacating and remanding order for court to make findings under G.S. 7B-911(c)(2)); *In re J.D.R.*, 239 N.C. App. 63 (2015) (order terminating jurisdiction was reversed and remanded because the trial court failed to make finding required by G.S. 7B-911(c)(2)a. as to continued state intervention).

The court must also follow the procedures set forth in G.S. 7B-911. *See In re J.K.*, 253 N.C. App. 57 (holding compliance with procedures of G.S. 7B-911 is jurisdictional; remanding order for inclusion of provisions required by G.S. 7B-911 when transferring an abuse, neglect, or dependency proceeding to a G.S. Chapter 50 civil action, creating a new G.S. Chapter 50 action); *see Sherrick v. Sherrick*, 209 N.C. App. 166 (holding procedures of G.S. 7B-911 affect subject matter jurisdiction, which cannot be conferred by consent; holding failure to terminate jurisdiction in juvenile proceeding prevents case from being transferred to a civil custody action such that district court has no jurisdiction to act under G.S. Chapter 50).

If there is no existing civil custody action, the court must instruct the clerk to treat the custody order entered pursuant to G.S. 7B-911 as initiating a civil custody action. The court must designate the parties to the action and determine the most appropriate caption for the action. The filing fees are waived unless the court orders one or more of the parties to pay the filing fee. The order constitutes a custody determination and any motion to enforce or modify the custody order must be filed in the newly created G.S. Chapter 50 action pursuant to the requirements of G.S. Chapter 50. G.S. 7B-911(b).

If the custody order is entered in an existing civil action and the person who is being awarded custody is not a party to that action, the court must order that the person be joined as a party and that the caption be modified accordingly. An order that is filed in an existing action resolves any pending claim for custody and modifies any custody order previously entered in that action. G.S. 7B-911(b).

Any order entered pursuant to 7B-911 must satisfy all the requirements for a civil custody order and should not simply refer to or incorporate a juvenile court order. A modification order must satisfy all requirements for modifying a civil custody order. These requirements include proper findings and conclusions that support the creation or modification of a G.S. Chapter 50 custody order. G.S. 7B-911(c)(1). *See also* G.S. 50-13.2; 50-13.5; 50-13.7; *In re J.B.*, 197 N.C. App. 497 (2009) (holding that the necessary findings were lacking).

**Note,** a thorough description of all of the required contents or characteristics of a valid civil custody order or an order modifying a civil custody order is beyond the scope of this Manual. *See, generally,* G.S. 50-13.1, 50-13.2, 50-13.7, and cases decided thereunder.

Although there are two different actions – the abuse, neglect, or dependency proceeding and the G.S. Chapter 50 case – the court may enter one order for placement in both court files. However, the order must be sufficient to support both the necessary findings terminating jurisdiction in the juvenile proceeding and the initial or modified civil custody order. *See Sherrick v. Sherrick*, 209 N.C. App. 166 (2011); *In re A.S.*, 182 N.C. App. 139 (2007) (holding there is no requirement that there be two separate orders).

**(b) Jurisdiction retained in the abuse, neglect, dependency action.** When the trial court orders custody as a permanent plan pursuant to G.S. 7B-903(a)(4) and determines the criteria of G.S. 7B-911 are not satisfied, it retains jurisdiction over the abuse, neglect, or dependency proceeding. The custody order is effective and can be enforced and modified by the juvenile court while the court continues to exercise jurisdiction in the juvenile action. G.S. 7B-201(b). Review of the custody order will take place periodically pursuant to G.S. 7B-906.1, unless the requirements for waiving reviews in G.S. 7B-906.1(n) are met or the court terminates its jurisdiction. See section 7.2.A.4, above (discussing waiver of reviews). If the criteria for waiving review hearings are met, a custody order in an abuse, neglect, or dependency action can remain in place with little court oversight. Even when reviews are not required, any party may file a motion for review under G.S. 7B-906.1. When the court orders custody as a permanent plan for the child, the custodian automatically becomes a party to the proceeding. G.S. 7B-401.1(d); *see In re M.N.*, 816 S.E.2d 925 (N.C. Ct. App. 2018). A custody order may also be modified pursuant to a G.S. 7B-1000 motion to review or vacate as discussed in section 7.8.E, above.

See also Chapter 3.1.C (discussing continuing or ending jurisdiction) and 3.1.D (discussing terminology related to continuing and ending jurisdiction).

**5. Parent's constitutional rights findings before custody or guardianship to non-parent.**
Parents have paramount constitutional rights to care, custody, and control of their children. See Chapter 2.4.A for a discussion of parents' rights to raise their children and when the state may interfere with those rights.

In the permanency planning stage of an abuse, neglect, or dependency action, before the court may order custody or guardianship with a non-parent, the court must find the parent is unfit, has neglected the child's welfare, or has acted inconsistently with his or her constitutional rights. *See Price v. Howard,* 346 N.C. 68 (1997); *Petersen v. Rogers,* 337 N.C. 397 (1994); *In re B.G.,* 197 N.C. App. 570 (2009) (permanent custody order); *In re D.M.,* 211 N.C. App. 382 (2011) (permanent custody order); *In re R.P.,* 252 N.C. App. 301 (2017) (permanent guardianship order); *In re I.K.,* 818 S.E.2d 359 (N.C. Ct. App. 2018) (permanent guardianship order). This finding is required when the court orders *permanent custody* to a non-parent (in this case, foster parents) even though the previous order, which was not a permanent custody order, had awarded custody to a different non-parent (in this case, DSS). *In re D.A.,* 811 S.E.2d 729 (N.C. Ct. App. 2018) (emphasis on "*permanent custody*" included in opinion). A determination that a parent is unfit, has neglected the child's welfare, or has acted inconsistently with his or her constitutionally protected status must be supported and found by clear and convincing evidence. *Price,* 346 N.C. 68; *Petersen,* 337 N.C. 397; *Owenby v. Young,* 357 N.C. 142 (2003); *In re J.L.,* 826 S.E.2d 258 (N.C. Ct. App. 2019); *In re E.M.,* 249 N.C. App. 44 (2016). That standard requires evidence that fully convinces and is more than preponderance of the evidence but less than beyond a reasonable doubt. *See In re K.L.* 254 N.C. App. 269 (2017) (reversing permanent custody order; holding court's conclusion of parent's unfitness or acting inconsistently with parental rights was unsupported by findings of fact). The finding is required even when the child has been previously adjudicated as neglected and dependent. *See In re R.P.,* 252 N.C. App. 301 (2017) (reversing permanent guardianship order that made no reference to father's constitutionally protected status; rejecting GAL argument that parental conduct leads to an adjudication and constitutes some showing of unfitness); *Rodriguez v. Rodriguez,* 211 N.C. App. 267 (2011) (holding in a custody case between the child's mother and grandparents that a finding that the children had been adjudicated dependent in an earlier proceeding was not, by itself, sufficient to support a conclusion that the mother had acted in a manner inconsistent with her parental status).

There is no bright-line test when determining if a parent has acted inconsistently with his or her parental rights. *See In re A.C.,* 247 N.C. App. 528 (2016) (examining the mother's conduct and intentions and holding that she acted inconsistently with her parental rights). The determination is not based on whether the conduct consisted of good or bad acts but rather the court considers the voluntariness of the parent's actions and the relinquishment of exclusive parental authority to a third person. *Mason v. Dwinnell,* 190 N.C. App. 209 (2008). As part of its analysis, the court looks at the parent's intentions. *Mason,* 190 N.C. App. 209; *In re A.C.,* 247 N.C. App. 528. When determining whether a parent is unfit or acted inconsistently with his or her parental rights, "evidence of a parent's conduct should be viewed cumulatively." *Owenby,* 357 N.C. at 147. The court's conclusion as to whether a parent acted inconsistently with his or her parental rights is a question of law that is reviewable de novo. *See Boseman v. Jarrell,* 364 N.C. 537 (2010); *In re A.C.,* 247 N.C. App. 528.

The best interests of the child standard is not applicable to an order granting permanent custody or guardianship to a non-parent until after the court has found that the parent was unfit or has acted inconsistently with his or her parental rights. *See In re C.P.,* 252 N.C. App. 118 (2017); *In re A.C.,* 247 N.C. App. 528. Note that the best interests of the child standard does apply when the court is deciding custody between two parents, which may be an issue in an abuse, neglect, or dependency proceeding when reunification with either parent is an option and the parents do not reside together.

A parent may waive his or her right to the court finding regarding the constitutionally protected status prior to the court looking to best interests when the parent does not raise the issue before the trial court and had the opportunity to do so. *See In re C.P.*, 812 S.E.2d 188 (N.C. Ct. App. 2018) (holding mother waived her right by failing to raise it at the hearing when she had the opportunity to do so); *In re I.K.*, 818 S.E.2d 359 (N.C. Ct. App. 2018) (vacating and remanding guardianship order; respondents did not waive findings when prevented by trial court from making arguments about constitutionally protected status); *In re R.P.*, 252 N.C. App. 301 (2017) (holding father did not waive his right to the findings as there was not a proper hearing on the issue for the father to raise an objection on constitutional grounds); *In re C.P.*, 252 N.C. App. 118 (2017) (mother failed to preserve the issue when she failed to raise it at permanency planning hearing resulting in guardianship order). Constitutional issues not raised at trial cannot be considered for the first time on appeal. *See In re T.P.*, 217 N.C. App. 181 (2011). See Chapter 12.3 (discussing preservation of issues for appeal).

---

**Practice Note:** North Carolina appellate opinions addressing the issue of parent's constitutional rights before the application of the best interests of the child standard in abuse, neglect, or dependency cases have been applied to appeals of permanency planning orders awarding custody or guardianship to non-parents. However, in *In re S.J.T.H.*, 811 S.E.2d 723 (N.C. Ct. App. 2018), the court of appeals reversed and remanded an initial dispositional order that placed the child in DSS custody rather than with the non-removal parent. In relying on a previously published opinion reviewing a permanency planning order, the court of appeals discussed a parent's constitutional rights and the need for a finding of parental unfitness or actions that are inconsistent with their constitutionally protected status and directed the trial court "to enter a new order addressing respondent's rights and granting him custody unless DSS presents clear, cogent, and convincing evidence which would support another disposition." *In re S.J.T.H.*, 811 S.E.2d at 725.

---

**6. APPLA.** APPLA stands for "Another Planned Permanent Living Arrangement." It is a term that arose from the federal Adoption and Safe Families Act (ASFA). The term is not defined in the Juvenile Code.

APPLA is the least preferred permanent plan as it is only available for children who do not have the option of reunification, adoption, custody, or guardianship. *See* G.S. 7B-912(c). In response to a recognition that APPLA was being used routinely and with young children, restrictions on its use were included in the federal Preventing Sex Trafficking and Strengthening Families Act. See Chapter 1.3.B.10 (discussing that federal law). As a result of that federal law, the Juvenile Code was amended effective for all actions filed or pending on or after October 1, 2015 and for the first time specifically addressed APPLA.

The Juvenile Code identifies APPLA as one of the possible permanent plans for a juvenile in foster care. *See* G.S. 7B-906.2(a)(5). APPLA may be the juvenile's primary permanent plan only when all of the following conditions apply:

- the juvenile is 16 or 17 years old;
- DSS has made diligent efforts to permanently place the juvenile with a parent or relative or in a guardianship or adoptive placement;
- there are compelling reasons that it is not in the juvenile's best interests to be permanently placed with a parent or relative or in a guardianship or adoptive placement; and
- APPLA is the best permanent plan for the juvenile.

G.S. 7B-912(c).

The court must approve APPLA before it becomes a primary permanent plan, and the court must first question the juvenile and make written findings addressing the juvenile's desired permanency outcome. G.S. 7B-912(c), (d). The Juvenile Code does not address when APPLA may become a secondary permanent plan.

A juvenile with a permanent plan of APPLA remains in DSS custody and will age out of foster care. Planning for a successful transition to adulthood and preparing the youth is especially important. The court has authority to specify efforts DSS must make to achieve this permanent plan, and the findings the court makes under G.S. 7B-912 for juveniles who are 14 years old and older may help the court determine what efforts are reasonable and required. *See* G.S. 7B-906.2(b). See section 7.8.C.9 (discussing G.S. 7B-912). When the juvenile ages out of foster care, he or she will be eligible for Foster Care 18–21 if he or she meets the educational, employment, or medical condition/disability criteria of that program. See Chapter 8.3 (discussing Foster Care 18–21).

**Resources:**
For the state policy on APPLA, see Div. of Soc. Servs., N.C. Dep't of Health & Human Services, Child Welfare Manual "Permanency Planning," available here.

For more information about APPLA, see "OPPLA/APPLA" on the Child Welfare Information Gateway, U.S. Department of Health and Human Services website.

**7. Reinstatement of parental rights.** North Carolina is in the minority of states that authorize the reinstatement of parental rights after those rights have been terminated by a court. The Juvenile Code identifies reinstatement of parental rights as a permanent plan for the child. *See* G.S. 7B-906.2(a)(6). Reinstatement is an option in very limited circumstances. Absent a finding of extraordinary circumstances, the reinstatement of parental rights is available for a child who is at least 12 years of age. The child must be without a legal parent, not in an adoptive placement, and unlikely to be adopted within a reasonable period of time. The TPR order must have been entered at least three years before the motion to reinstate parental rights is filed. G.S. 7B-1114(a). The child must be in the custody of DSS. G.S. 7B-1114. The criteria, process, and possible outcomes are governed by G.S. 7B-1114. A reinstatement of parental rights "restores all rights, powers, privileges, immunities, duties, and obligations of the parent as to the juvenile, including those relating to custody, control and support...." G.S. 7B-1114(k). See Chapter 10.4 (discussing reinstatement of parental rights circumstances, procedures, and orders).

---

**Resources:**
For the state policy on reinstatement of parental rights, see 1 DIV. OF SOC. SERVS., N.C. DEP'T OF HEALTH & HUMAN SERVICES, CHILD WELFARE MANUAL "Permanency Planning," available here.

See the "Reinstatement of Parental Rights State Statute Summary" on the National Conference of State Legislatures website.

For articles and other resources with hyperlinks provided, see "Reinstatement of Parental Rights" on the Child Welfare Information Gateway, U.S. Department of Health and Human Services website.

---

## 7.11 Dispositional Orders

### A. Timing

Orders from initial disposition, review, or permanency planning hearings must be reduced to writing, signed, and filed with the clerk within thirty days of the completion of the hearing. G.S. 7B-905(a); 7B-906.1(h). If the order is not entered within thirty days, the juvenile clerk must schedule a hearing at the next juvenile session of court for a determination and explanation of the reason for the delay and for any needed clarification as to the contents of the order. The order must then be entered within ten days of this follow-up hearing. G.S. 7B-905(a); 7B-906.1(h). The appropriate remedy for a trial court's failure to enter a timely order is a petition to the court of appeals for a writ of mandamus to require the trial court to proceed to judgment. *In re T.H.T.*, 362 N.C. 446 (2008). See Chapter 4.9.C (discussing what constitutes entry of the order) and 4.9.D (discussing the effect of and the remedy for delay).

### B. General Requirements

---

**AOC Form:**
AOC-J-154, Juvenile Disposition Order (Abuse, Neglect, Dependency) (Oct. 2015).

**Resource**: See Janet Mason, *Drafting Good Court Orders in Juvenile Cases*, JUVENILE LAW BULLETIN NO. 2013/02 (UNC School of Government, Sept. 2013).

---

This section discusses the specific requirements that apply to any dispositional order. For more information about orders, see Chapter 4.9. In addition to the general requirements, the Juvenile Code has specific requirements that apply to different orders, depending on whether the order is an initial, review, permanency planning, or transfer to G.S. Chapter 50 order and what is actually being ordered (e.g., out-of-home placement). Those specific requirements are discussed in the applicable sections throughout this Chapter. See Checklists at the end of this Manual, which summarize the requirements for initial dispositional, review, and permanency planning orders, respectively.

Generally, the Juvenile Code requires the following for any dispositional order.

**1. Findings and conclusions.** The order must contain appropriate findings of fact and conclusions of law. G.S. 7B-905(a). See Chapters 4.9.B and 12.8.B (relating to defining and separating findings and conclusions as well as the standard of review for findings of fact and conclusions of law).

  **(a) Findings of fact.** The Juvenile Code specifies certain required findings in dispositional orders, depending on the outcomes ordered and the type of dispositional hearing. Failure to include required findings in an order has been found by appellate courts to be reversible error. *See, e.g., In re D.A.,* 811 S.E.2d 729 (N.C. Ct. App. 2018); *In re K.L,* 254 N.C. App. 269 (2017); *In re M.M.,* 230 N.C. App. 225 (2013); *In re H.J.A.,* 223 N.C. App. 413 (2012). However, the North Carolina Supreme Court has held that while the better practice is to include statutory language, an order need not recite the exact language of a statute but must address the substance of the concerns contained in the statute. *In re L.M.T.,* 367 N.C.165 (2013) (affirming an order ceasing reunification efforts under G.S. 7B-507; decided under former statute). Requirements for findings related to specific dispositional outcomes are discussed throughout this Chapter.

  **(b) Conclusions of law.** Determinations of reasonable efforts, best interests, and whether a parent has acted inconsistently with his or her parental rights are conclusions of law because they require an exercise of judgment. *See In re Helms*, 127 N.C. App. 505 (1997). The determinations must be supported by specific findings.

  **(c) Incorporation of reports.** There must be some oral testimony at a dispositional hearing where reports are submitted for those reports to constitute competent evidence that supports a court's findings of fact. *In re S.P.,* 833 S.E.2d 638 (N.C. Ct. App. 2019); *In re J.T.,* 252 N.C. App. 19 (2017). The court cannot simply adopt DSS, GAL, or other reports as its only findings or substitute reports for the court's independent determination. *See In re M.M.,* 230 N.C. App. 225 (2013); *In re Harton*, 156 N.C. App. 655 (2003). Written reports may be incorporated and findings may be based on those reports so long as the court does its own independent review. *See In re C.M.,* 183 N.C. App. 207 (2007) (holding that psychological evaluations and a GAL report were properly incorporated because the court made extensive findings showing that the court made its own determinations with respect to the facts); *In re J.S.,* 165 N.C. App. 509 (2004) (holding that the trial court erred by entering a two-page order that broadly incorporated written reports from DSS and a mental health expert as its findings of fact). *See also In re H.J.A.,* 223 N.C. App. 413 (2012) (noting that recitation of testimony and incorporation of reports without specific findings were insufficient). It is error for the court to generally find statements in reports to be true without specifying the statements in the reports upon which the court is relying. *In re A.S.,* 190 N.C. App. 679 (2008), *aff'd per curiam*, 363 N.C. 254 (2009); *see also In re S.J.M.,* 184 N.C. App. 42 (2007), *aff'd per curiam*, 362 N.C. 230 (2008); *In re Ivey,* 156 N.C. App. 398 (2003). See section 7.2.E.3, above (discussing the court's use of reports). See Chapter 4.9.B.2 (discussing reports and documents in an order).

**(d) Recitation of testimony.** Recitations of the testimony of witnesses do not constitute findings of fact. *In re L.B.*, 184 N.C. App. 442 (2007) (finding no prejudice, however, when the trial court's conclusions were supported by other proper findings). *See also In re M.M.*, 230 N.C. App. 2250 (2013). See Chapter 4.9.B.2 (discussing recitation of allegations or testimony).

**(e) Arguments of counsel not evidence.** Arguments of counsel may not be considered as evidence. *In re J.T.*, 252 N.C. App. 19 (2017); *In re K.S.*, 183 N.C. App. 315 (2007); *In re D.L.*, 166 N.C. App. 574 (2004).

**2. Precise terms.** The court must state with particularity, both orally and in the written order, the precise terms of the disposition. It must include the type of disposition, the duration, and the person responsible for carrying out whatever the disposition requires, as well as the person or agency in whom custody is vested. G.S. 7B-905(a).

**3. Set next hearing.** When custody is removed from a parent, guardian, custodian, or caretaker (and a review hearing as opposed to a permanency planning hearing) is required, the order must direct that a review hearing be scheduled within ninety days from the date of that dispositional hearing and set the date of the review hearing if practicable. G.S. 7B-905(b).

If the court (1) orders the cessation of reunification efforts at an initial dispositional hearing or (2) finds, at a review hearing that is not a permanency planning hearing, that reunification efforts clearly would be unsuccessful or inconsistent with the child's health, safety, and need for a safe, permanent home within a reasonable period of time, the court must schedule a permanency planning hearing within thirty days. If practicable, the order should set the date for the hearing. *See* G.S. 7B-901(d); 7B-906.1(d)(3).

---

**Legislative Note:** Effective October 1, 2017, S.L. 2017-161 amended G.S. 7B-906.1(a) to delete the condition that custody be removed from a parent, guardian, or custodian for the requirement that the court conduct a review hearing within 90 days of the dispositional hearing and within six month thereafter to apply. A corresponding amendment to remove the same language from G.S. 7B-905(b) was not made, so it continues to require that a dispositional order with the condition that custody is removed from a parent, guardian, or custodian direct that a review hearing be scheduled. Practically, it makes sense to include the mandate of G.S. 7B-905(b) when a review hearing is required under G.S. 7B-906.1 rather than limit its inclusion to when custody is removed from a parent, guardian, or custodian.

---

**4. Compliance with UCCJEA, ICPC, MEPA, and ICWA.** All dispositional orders must comply with the

- UCCJEA (Uniform Child-Custody Jurisdiction and Enforcement Act), ensuring that the court has subject matter jurisdiction (see Chapter 3.3);
- ICPC (Interstate Compact on the Placement of Children), which ensures an appropriate process of placing children across state lines (see section 7.4.H, above);

- MEPA (Multiethnic Placement Act), which prohibits the use of a child's or prospective foster or adoptive parent's race, color, or origin to delay or deny placement (see Chapter 13.3); and
- ICWA (Indian Child Welfare Act), ensuring that when an "Indian child" is the subject of the action, placement preferences are followed, active efforts are provided, the burdens of proof required by ICWA are applied, and a qualified expert witness testifies about whether the child's continued custody with a parent or Indian custodian is likely to result in serious emotional or physical damage to the child (see Chapter 13.2).

### C. Consent Orders

Consent orders are permitted only when

- all parties are present or represented by counsel who is present and authorized to consent;
- the child is represented by counsel; and
- the court makes sufficient findings of fact.

G.S. 7B-801(b1). See Chapter 6.5 (providing more detail on consent orders).

### D. Status of Jurisdiction

The Juvenile Code states that one purpose of disposition is to "achieve the objectives of the State in exercising jurisdiction." G.S. 7B-900. The Juvenile Code provides that once jurisdiction is obtained in an abuse, neglect, or dependency proceeding, it continues until terminated by the court or until the juvenile reaches age 18 or is otherwise emancipated, whichever occurs first. G.S. 7B-201(a); *see In re C.M.B.*, 836 S.E.2d 746 (N.C. Ct. App. 2019) (under G.S. 7B jurisdiction, only a North Carolina court can enter order terminating its own jurisdiction). For a full discussion of continuing or ending jurisdiction, including the effect of terminating jurisdiction and why the term "closing" a case is problematic, see Chapter 3.1.C and D.

The court has jurisdiction to modify any disposition made in the abuse, neglect, or dependency proceeding until jurisdiction is terminated. G.S. 7B-906.1; 7B-1000(b). *See also In re H.S.F.*, 177 N.C. App. 193 (2006); *In re J.S.*, 165 N.C. App. 509 (2004).

During an appeal of a dispositional order, the court continues to have jurisdiction to conduct review and permanency planning hearings, unless directed otherwise by an appellate court. G.S. 7B-1003(b). But see Chapter 12.4 and 12.11 (providing details and limitations on what disposition orders may be appealed and how disposition orders and the court's jurisdiction are affected by appeals).

**Resource:** Sara DePasquale, *What Can the District Court DO in an A/N/D or TPR Action when an Appeal is Pending?* UNC SCH. OF GOV'T: ON THE CIVIL SIDE BLOG (Aug. 2, 2019).

**Chapter 8**

**Voluntary Placements of Juveniles and Foster Care 18–21**

# Chapter 8
# Voluntary Placements of Juveniles and Foster Care 18–21

8.1 Introduction 8-1

8.2 Voluntary Placement Agreement for a Juvenile 8-2
   A. The Agreement
   B. Judicial Reviews, Timing, and Duration
   C. Purpose and Requirements of Hearing

8.3 Foster Care 18–21 8-4
   A. Introduction
   B. Eligibility and the Agreement
   C. Judicial Reviews, Timing, and Parties
   D. Requirements of the Hearing

---

## 8.1 Introduction

There are times when foster care services and resources that are available from and provided by a county department of social services (DSS) will be voluntarily sought by a parent, guardian, and/or certain eligible young adults. When the statutory criteria are met, a placement agreement may be entered into between a county DSS and (1) a juvenile's parents or guardian or (2) an eligible young adult. The agreement to provide a foster care placement and services to the family or young adult is not a court order and does not legally transfer custodial rights to DSS. Although court involvement is not required at the time a voluntary agreement is executed and implemented by the participating parties to that agreement, the Juvenile Code (G.S. Chapter 7B) requires that the district court conduct a judicial review of the placement and services provided by DSS. The Juvenile Code provisions focus on the judicial review and are silent as to procedures that apply when executing and implementing a voluntary agreement prior to the judicial review. *See* G.S. 7B-910; 7B-910.1.

**Note,** for purposes of this Manual, "department of social services" or "DSS" refers to a department as defined by G.S. 7B-101(8a) regardless of how it is titled or structured.

This Chapter discusses the two types of voluntary agreements that require a judicial review by the district court:

- a voluntary foster care placement of a juvenile, often referred to as a "voluntary placement agreement" (VPA) and

- a voluntary foster care placement of a young adult who chooses to receive extended foster care by participating in the state's Foster 18–21 program.

*See* G.S. 7B-910; 7B-910.1.

## 8.2 Voluntary Placement Agreement for a Juvenile

### A. The Agreement[1]

Some DSSs occasionally enter into a voluntary placement agreement (VPA) with a juvenile's parents or guardian. Initiation of a VPA does not involve court action; instead, it is a mutual agreement between the DSS and child's parents or guardian. When a VPA is executed, DSS obtains care and placement responsibility for the child based upon the parents' (or parent's) or guardian's consent. *See* 10A N.C.A.C. 70B.0102(a)(3).[2] Custody does not transfer to DSS with the execution of a VPA. *See In re. B.C.T.*, 828 S.E.2d 50 (N.C. Ct. App. 2019) (footnote 7).

A child who is the subject of the VPA receives the same child placement services as a child who is the subject of a court order in an abuse, neglect, or dependency action that grants DSS custody or placement responsibility of the child. The family receives and participates in services; permanency planning review team meetings (PPR) are held; and a permanency planning out-of-home family services agreement (OH-FSA) is completed, which involves the entire family, including the parents (or guardian) and child. The child is placed in an appropriate setting, such as a licensed foster home. Because legal rights do not transfer with the execution of the VPA, there may be provisions that allow the parents or guardian to authorize DSS to consent to certain types of medical and mental health care for the child, such as routine and emergency care. Consent or authorization to consent for other types of services or activities for the child may also be included in the VPA.

Because a VPA is a voluntary foster care placement, it is a child custody proceeding governed by the Indian Child Welfare Act (ICWA). *See* 25 U.S.C. 1903(1); 25 C.F.R. 23.2. If the child who is the subject of the VPA is an "Indian child" as defined by 25 U.S.C. 1903(4), DSS must comply with the applicable provisions of ICWA. The North Carolina Department of Health and Human Services (DHHS) Division of Social Services policy addresses the execution of a VPA when ICWA applies and states that the VPA must be "signed before a judge of competent jurisdiction" and be "accompanied by a judge's certification" that the agreement was fully explained and understood by the parent or Indian

---

[1] The source for some of the content in this section is DIV. OF SOC. SERV., N.C. DEP'T OF HEALTH & HUMAN SERVICES, CHILD WELFARE MANUAL "Cross Function," available here, and the DSS-1789 form. DSS forms can be found here.

[2] Title 10A of the North Carolina Administrative Code (N.C.A.C.) applies to Health and Human Services, and Chapter 70 governs Children's Services. The provisions of 10A N.C.A.C. 70 are the governing rules (or regulations) promulgated by the North Carolina Social Services Commission. See Chapter 1.3.A.2 (discussing the N.C.A.C. and the Social Services Commission).

custodian. DIV. OF SOC. SERV., N.C. DEP'T OF HEALTH & HUMAN SERVICES, CHILD WELFARE MANUAL "Cross Function" (p. 257). The policy discusses additional provisions that should apply when an Indian child is the subject of the VPA. For a discussion of ICWA, see Chapter 13.2.

The VPA designates a period of time that the agreement lasts, but it may be terminated earlier by either party. VPA placements are time limited and must be reviewed by the court if the child does not return to the parent or guardian within ninety days of placement. G.S.7B-910(c); *see* 10A N.C.A.C. 70B.0102(a)(2).

Note that DSS is not precluded from conducting an assessment for abuse, neglect, or dependency and if required, filing a petition in district court thereby initiating an abuse, neglect, or dependency action, during the period a VPA is in effect. A VPA is different from a temporary parental safety agreement (TPSA), which occurs during the period of a DSS assessment for abuse, neglect, or dependency. *In re. B.C.T.*, 828 S.E.2d 50 (N.C. Ct. App. 2019).

**NC DHHS DSS Form:**
DSS-1789, Voluntary Placement Agreement (Oct. 2010).

**Resources:**
Information about Voluntary Placements Agreements (VPA) is not found in one specific section of the DHHS Division of Social Services policy. For some applicable provisions, see DIV. OF SOC. SERV., N.C. DEP'T OF HEALTH & HUMAN SERVICES, CHILD WELFARE MANUAL" Cross Function" and "Permanency Planning," available here.

For information about a Temporary Parental Safety Agreement (TPSA), which differs from a VPA, see DIV. OF SOC. SERV., N.C. DEP'T OF HEALTH & HUMAN SERVICES, CHILD WELFARE MANUAL "Assessments," available here.

## B. Judicial Reviews, Timing, and Duration

The district court has exclusive, original jurisdiction over a judicial review of a voluntary placement agreement (VPA) for a juvenile. G.S. 7B-200(a)(5).

Within ninety days of the child's voluntary placement, the court must conduct a review. An additional review must take place within the next ninety days, and any other review hearings may be conducted on the court's own motion or by motion of the parents, guardian, foster parents, or DSS director. G.S. 7B-910(c). The clerk must provide at least fifteen days' advance written notice of these hearings to the parents or guardian, the juvenile if 12 or older, the DSS director, and any other person the court may specify. G.S. 7B-910(d).

A child may not remain in a voluntary placement for more than six months without DSS filing a petition alleging abuse, neglect, or dependency. G.S. 7B-910(c). *See* 10A N.C.A.C 70B.0102(a)(2).

### C. Purpose and Requirements of Hearing

At the review hearing for a voluntary placement, the court determines whether to (1) approve or disapprove the child's continued placement in foster care on a voluntary basis or (2) direct DSS to petition for legal custody if the placement is to continue. G.S. 7B-910(b). The court must make findings from evidence that is presented as to

- the voluntariness of the placement;
- the appropriateness of the placement;
- whether the placement is in the child's best interests; and
- services that have been or should be provided to the parents, guardian, foster parents, and child either to improve the placement or eliminate the need for the placement.

G.S. 7B-910(a).

---

**Practice Note:** At a review hearing of a voluntary placement, the court does not have jurisdiction to direct orders to the parents, caregivers, or child. The court has jurisdiction to order DSS to file a petition. An indigent parent is not entitled to appointed counsel, and the child is not represented by a guardian ad litem. The voluntary nature of the placement means that the parents or guardian may reassume custody of the child at any time, unless DSS has filed a petition alleging abuse, neglect, or dependency and obtained a nonsecure custody order.

---

## 8.3 Foster Care 18–21

### A. Introduction

Some children will not achieve permanency before aging out of foster care. Others, who were unable to reunify or return home, obtained a permanent safe home at an older age. Effective January 1, 2017, North Carolina offers Foster Care 18–21, a program that provides extended foster care services and benefits to young adults who have aged out of foster care upon turning 18 or found permanency through an adoption or guardianship when 16 or 17 years old. *See* S.L. 2015-241, sec. 12C.9; *see also* 10A N.C.A.C. 70P.0104(6).

Foster Care 18–21 is a voluntary program that assists older youth in foster care in making a successful transition to adulthood. Most of the information about the program is written in the state policy.

---

**Resources:**
For more information about Foster Care 18–21, see
- DIV. OF SOC. SERV., N.C. DEP'T OF HEALTH & HUMAN SERVICES, CHILD WELFARE MANUAL "Permanency Planning," available here.
- Sara DePasquale, *Foster Care Extended to Age 21*, UNC SCH. OF GOV'T: ON THE CIVIL SIDE BLOG (Jan. 11, 2017).

For more information about extended foster care generally and links to additional resources, see
- "Extending Foster Care Beyond 18" on the National Conference of State Legislatures website.
- CHILD WELFARE INFORMATION GATEWAY, U.S. DEP'T OF HEALTH & HUMAN SERVICES, "Extension of Foster Care Beyond Age 18" (Feb. 2017).

## B. Eligibility and the Agreement

The Foster Care 18–21 program is available to young adults who (1) aged out of foster care upon turning 18, (2) were adopted at age 16 or 17, or (3) were placed in a legal guardianship arrangement at age 16 or 17 when guardianship assistance was provided. *See* G.S. 108A-48(c); 108A-49(e); 131D-10.2B. *See also* G.S. 108A-49.1 (foster care and adoption assistance rates); 10A N.C.A.C. 70P.0104(6) (guardianship assistance program). The young adult may choose to participate in the program at any time prior to his or her 21$^{st}$ birthday. G.S. 131D-10.2B(a).

Prior foster care status of a young adult is not the only criteria for participation in the program. A young adult is eligible to participate in the Foster 18–21 program when he or she is

- completing high school or another educational program that leads to an equivalent credential,
- enrolled in an institution that provides post-secondary or vocational education,
- participating in a program or activity designed to promote or remove barriers to employment,
- employed for at least eighty hours a month, or
- incapable of completing the educational or employment requirements because of a medical condition or disability.

G.S. 108A-48(c).

A voluntary placement agreement is entered into between the young adult and the county DSS. *See* G.S. 7B-910.1; 131D-10.2B. A young adult participating in Foster Care 18–21 receives foster care benefits and services designed to assist the young adult in transitioning to independent living and adulthood and includes monthly financial benefits, placement, and case work focused on a transitional living plan. The law requires that if the young adult is residing outside of a foster care facility and is living in a college dormitory or other semi-supervised housing arrangement that has been approved by DSS, DSS must provide monthly supervision and oversight to the young adult. *See* G.S. 108A-48(d). Note that the young adult is of the age of majority and competent to contract for himself or herself. DSS does not have custody of or decision-making responsibility for the young adult.

**NC DHHS DSS Forms:**
- DSS-5097, Voluntary Placement Agreement for Foster Care 18 to 21 (Jan. 2017).
- DSS-5099, Placement Agreement for Foster Care 18–21 (Jan. 2017).

- DSS-5098, North Carolina Monthly Contact Record for Foster Care 18–21 (Jan. 2017).
- DSS-5096a, Part A: Transitional Living Plan for Youth/Young Adults in Foster Care (April 2018).
- DSS-5096b, Part B: Transitional Living Plan – 90 Day Transition Plan for Youth in Foster Care (April 2018).
- DSS-5096c, Part C: Transitional Living Plan – 90 Day Transition Plan for Young Adults in Foster Care 18–21 (Jan. 2017).
- DSS-5096d, Part D: Transitional Living Plan – Helpful Resources for Young Adults (April 2018).
- DSS-5100, Semi-Supervised Independent Living Assessment Tool (Jan. 2017).

### C. Judicial Reviews, Timing, and Parties

The district court has exclusive, original jurisdiction over a judicial review of a placement of a young adult in foster care. G.S. 7B-200(a)(5a). All documents filed in a proceeding to review a voluntary foster placement for a young adult shall establish a new case file and receive a new juvenile file number. There is no associated filing fee for these proceedings. *See* Rule 12.1.2, Chapter XII, Rules of Recordkeeping Procedures for the Office of the Clerk of Superior Court in Appendix 4.

Within ninety days of the execution of the voluntary Foster Care 18–21 agreement, the court must conduct a review. G.S. 7B-910.1(a). Additional review hearings may be held upon the written request of the young adult or DSS director. G.S. 7B-910.1(b). The clerk must provide at least fifteen days' advance written notice of these hearings to the young adult and the DSS director. G.S. 7B-910.1(d).

There are two parties to the judicial review proceeding: the young adult and DSS. G.S. 7B-401.1(i). The young adult, who is no longer a juvenile, is not represented by a guardian ad litem (GAL). G.S. 7B-910.1(c). There is no statutory provision authorizing appointed counsel to represent the young adult.

**AOC Form:**
AOC-J-141, Notice Of Hearing In Juvenile Proceeding (Abuse/Neglect/Dependency) (Jan. 2017).

**Practice Note:** Any GAL appointment in the underlying abuse, neglect, or dependency case that is still in effect when the juvenile turns 18 expires with the termination of the court's jurisdiction in that action. *See* G.S. 7B-200(a). Although no longer in a GAL role, a member of the GAL team may be called as a witness by one of the parties in the judicial review hearing if the GAL has relevant information for the court to consider.

### D. Requirements of the Hearing

At the review hearing, the court must make findings, based on evidence presented at the hearing, of all of the following:

- whether the placement is in the young adult's best interests;
- the services that have been or should be provided to the young adult to improve the placement; and
- if relevant, the services that have been or should be provided to the young adult to further his or her education or vocational ambitions.

G.S. 7B-910.1(a).

# Termination of Parental Rights

Chapter 9

# Chapter 9
# Termination of Parental Rights[1]

9.1 **Purpose and Overview of Termination of Parental Rights**  9-5
    A. Overview of Termination of Parental Rights
    B. Purpose of the Juvenile Code's Termination of Parental Rights Provisions
        1. Procedures
        2. Balancing needs
        3. Child's best interests
        4. No circumvention of UCCJEA

9.2 **Jurisdiction and Procedure**  9-6
    A. Subject Matter Jurisdiction
    B. Personal Jurisdiction
    C. Applicability of the Rules of Civil Procedure

9.3 **Initiation of Proceedings and Standing**  9-9
    A. Initiation of TPR
        1. Only by petition or by motion in pending abuse, neglect, or dependency proceeding
        2. DSS required to initiate TPR in certain circumstances
    B. Standing to File Petition or Motion
        1. Introduction
        2. Either parent
        3. Guardian
        4. DSS or child-placing agency with custody order
        5. DSS or child-placing agency to whom the child has been surrendered for adoption
        6. Person child has lived with for two years
        7. Guardian ad litem for child
        8. Adoption petitioner

9.4 **Counsel and Guardians ad Litem for Parent and Child**  9-14
    A. Counsel for Parent
    B. Guardian ad Litem for Parent
        1. GAL for minor parent
        2. GAL for parent who is incompetent
        3. GAL appointment and role
    C. Guardian ad Litem for Child

9.5 **Contents of Petition or Motion**  9-18
    A. Identifying Information
        1. Title
        2. Child

---

[1] Portions of this Chapter are adapted from JANET MASON, TERMINATION OF PARENTAL RIGHTS IN NORTH CAROLINA (UNC School of Government, 2012).

3. Petitioner or movant
4. Parents
5. Guardian of the person or custodian
- B. Addressing the UCCJEA
    1. No circumvention of UCCJEA
    2. Child status information required by UCCJEA
- C. Facts to Support Grounds for Termination
- D. Verification
- E. Request for Relief

## 9.6 Hearing for Unknown Parent    9-22
- A. Preliminary Hearing to Determine Identity of Unknown Parent
    1. When required
    2. Timing
    3. Notice
    4. Inquiry by court
    5. Order
    6. Amendment of petition to allege identity not required
- B. Service on Unknown Parent
    1. No summons required
    2. Publication
    3. Failure of unknown parent to answer

## 9.7 Summons and Notice    9-24
- A. Introduction
- B. Summons for Proceeding Initiated by Petition
    1. Those entitled to summons
    2. Child and GAL
    3. Contents of summons
    4. Service of summons
    5. Problems with summons
- C. Notice for Proceeding Initiated by Motion in the Cause
    1. Notice required
    2. Those entitled to notice
    3. Contents of notice
    4. Service of motion and notice
    5. Problems with notice

## 9.8 Answer or Response    9-29

## 9.9 Pretrial and Adjudication Hearing Requirements    9-30
- A. Pretrial Hearing
    1. Timing
    2. May be combined with adjudication hearing
    3. Notice
    4. Required considerations

B. Adjudication Hearing
1. Timing
2. General procedures
3. Counsel for parents
4. Examination of child or parent
5. Presence of parent

## 9.10 Evidence and Proof    9-35
A. Evidentiary Requirements and Standards
B. Events between Filing of Petition or Motion and Hearing
C. Events after a TPR Is Denied or Reversed
D. Specific Types of Evidentiary Issues

## 9.11 Adjudication: Grounds for Termination of Parental Rights    9-38
A. Abuse or Neglect
1. Definition of abuse or neglect
2. Constitutional challenge
3. Parental culpability
4. Past neglect and likelihood of repetition of neglect
5. Current neglect
6. Factors related to abuse and neglect
7. Neglect includes abandonment
B. Willfully Leaving Child in Foster Care for More than Twelve Months without Reasonable Progress
1. Constitutional challenge
2. Time period in foster care or placement outside the home
3. Willfulness
4. Reasonable progress to correct conditions that led to child's removal
5. Poverty cannot be basis for TPR
C. Failure to Pay a Reasonable Portion of the Child's Cost of Care
1. Constitutional challenge
2. Ability to pay
3. Willfulness
4. Reasonable portion of cost of care
5. Notice of support obligation irrelevant
6. Child's placement
D. Failure to Pay Child Support to Other Parent
1. Agreement or order and failure to pay must be proven
2. Agreement or order establishes ability to pay
3. Willfulness: parent may rebut ability to pay
E. Father's Actions regarding Child Born Out of Wedlock
1. All prongs of ground required
2. Affidavit of paternity filed with DHHS
3. Substantial financial support or consistent care
4. Knowledge of child's existence
5. Judicial paternity determinations and name on birth certificate
6. Admissibility of paternity test
7. Constitutionality

F. Dependency
   1. Constitutional challenge
   2. Lack of alternative child care required
   3. Evidence of incapability to provide proper care or supervision of the child
   4. Diligent efforts not a prerequisite
   5. GAL for respondent not required
G. Abandonment
   1. Six-month time period
   2. Defining abandonment
   3. Evidence of abandonment
H. Murder, Voluntary Manslaughter, and Felony Assault of Child or Parent
   1. Manner of proof
   2. Standard of proof
   3. Serious bodily injury
I. TPR to Another Child and Lack of Safe Home
J. Relinquishment for Adoption
K. Conception Resulting from Sexually Related Criminal Offense

## 9.12 Disposition and Best Interest Determination    9-73
A. Overview
B. Evidentiary Standard
   1. No burden or standard of proof; court's discretion
   2. Separate hearings not required
   3. Rules of evidence
C. Considerations for Best Interest Determination
   1. Required criteria
   2. Purpose of Juvenile Code
   3. Likelihood that the child will be adopted
   4. Whether the TPR will aid in the accomplishment of the permanent plan for the child
   5. Bond between child and parent
   6. Other relevant considerations
   7. Weighing the factors
   8. Examples of best interest evidence and findings where TPR affirmed
   9. Examples of best interest evidence and findings where TPR was not affirmed

## 9.13 Highlighted Federal Laws: ICWA and the ADA    9-81
A. Compliance with ICWA
B. ADA Not a Defense to TPR

## 9.14 Orders in Termination of Parental Rights Cases    9-82
A. Requirements for Order
   1. Address grounds
   2. Standard of proof
   3. Findings and conclusions
   4. Timing
   5. Service of order on juvenile who is 12 or older
B. Entry of Order

**9.15 Effect of Order and Placement after Termination of Parental Rights    9-86**
  A. Severance of Rights and Obligations
  B. Collateral Legal Consequences
  C. Placement and Post-TPR Review Hearings
     1. When child is in DSS/agency custody
     2. When child is not in DSS/agency custody
     3. Post-TPR review hearings

---

## 9.1 Purpose and Overview of Termination of Parental Rights

### A. Overview of Termination of Parental Rights

Termination of parental rights (TPR) is the state's ultimate interference with the constitutionally protected parent-child relationship, severing all legal ties between the parent and the child. A TPR may occur only when the district court determines that at least one statutory ground for TPR has been proved by clear, cogent, and convincing evidence and the TPR is in the child's best interests.

All TPR proceedings are in juvenile court, before a district court judge without a jury. Informally they are characterized as "private" actions (when initiated by one parent against the other, for example) or as "agency" actions (when the child is in the custody of a department of social services (DSS) or a licensed child-placing agency that initiates the action). If an abuse, neglect, or dependency case is pending and the primary permanent plan for the child is adoption, DSS may be required to initiate a TPR proceeding when a TPR is necessary for the child to be adopted. See Chapter 7.8.D (discussing initiation of TPR under certain circumstances) and 7.10 (discussing various permanent plans).

**Note,** for purposes of this Manual, "department of social services" or "DSS" refers to a department as defined by G.S. 7B-101(8a) regardless of how it is titled or structured.

**Additional Note,** this Manual focuses on abuse, neglect, or dependency cases, some of which require a TPR for the child to achieve a permanent plan of adoption. The various laws and procedures that apply to TPR proceedings related to an abuse, neglect, or dependency action are discussed throughout this Manual. This Chapter is not meant to be a stand-alone explanation of the TPR process in North Carolina and regularly cross-references other Chapters where TPR is discussed. Although a TPR may be initiated and obtained without there ever being DSS involvement with a family, those private TPRs are not the focus of this Chapter.

A TPR proceeding is divided into two stages: adjudication and disposition. At adjudication, the party initiating the proceeding (petitioner or movant) has the burden of proving by clear, cogent, and convincing evidence that one or more of the alleged statutory grounds for termination of parental rights found at G.S. 7B-1111 exist.

If the court adjudicates one or more grounds, the court moves on to disposition where it determines whether TPR is in the child's best interests. At the disposition stage, which is governed by G.S. 7B-1110, there is no burden of proof. After considering additional relevant evidence, the court makes findings of fact and, based on those findings, makes a discretionary determination as to whether the TPR is in the child's best interests.

If the court does not find that grounds for TPR exist or, after adjudicating a ground, determines that TPR is not in the child's best interests, the court must dismiss the action. If the court adjudicates at least one alleged ground and determines TPR is in the child's best interests, the court orders the termination of the respondent parent's rights to the child who is the subject of the action.

If the court terminates parental rights and the child is in the custody of DSS or a licensed child-placing agency, post-termination review hearings must be held at least every six months to examine progress toward achieving the permanent plans for the child. See Chapter 10, discussing post-TPR review hearings and issues related to the child's adoption, including the selection of prospective adoptive parents.

### B. Purpose of the Juvenile Code's Termination of Parental Rights Provisions

Article 11 of the Juvenile Code (G.S. Chapter 7B) governs termination of parental rights (TPR) and reflects the following policies and purposes, as set out in G.S. 7B-1100.

**1. Procedures.** Article 11 provides judicial procedures for terminating the legal relationship between a child and the child's biological or legal parents when the parents have demonstrated that they will not provide the degree of care that promotes the child's healthy and orderly physical and emotional well-being. G.S. 7B-1100(1). *See also In re B.L.H.*, 190 N.C. App. 142, *aff'd per curiam*, 362 N.C. 674 (2008).

**2. Balancing needs.** TPR provisions are meant to recognize the necessity for any child to have a permanent plan of care at the earliest possible age, while also recognizing the need to protect children from the unnecessary severance of the parent-child relationship. G.S. 7B-1100(2). *See also In re L.O.K.*, 174 N.C. App. 426 (2005).

**3. Child's best interests.** If the interests of the child and parents (or others) are in conflict, the child's best interests control. G.S. 7B-1100(3). *See In re Montgomery*, 311 N.C. 101 (1984).

**4. No circumvention of UCCJEA.** TPR provisions in the Juvenile Code may not be used to circumvent the provisions of G.S. Chapter 50A, the Uniform Child-Custody Jurisdiction and Enforcement Act. G.S. 7B-1100(4).

## 9.2 Jurisdiction and Procedure

A termination of parental rights (TPR) occurs exclusively through judicial procedures that are established in the General Statutes. *See In re C.K.C.*, 822 S.E.2d 741 (N.C. Ct. App.

2018) (reversing TPR; holding consent order in Chapter 50 civil custody action between father and grandparents that included a provision that grandmother would file a petition to terminate father's rights that no other party, including father, would oppose is void as against public policy and is neither a properly executed consent or relinquishment under the adoption statutes); *In re Jurga*, 123 N.C. App. 91 (1996) (holding written statement that voluntarily terminated the parents' rights was ineffective and contrary to the statutorily required judicial procedures); *In re J.N.S.*, 165 N.C. App. 536 (2004) and *Curtis v. Curtis*, 104 N.C. App. 625 (1991) (both holding summary judgment not permitted by Juvenile Code). The judicial procedures are set forth in Article 11 of the Juvenile Code. Additionally, under the adoption statutes, a final decree of adoption severs a parent's legal rights to and relationship with their child. G.S. 48-1-106(c); 48-3-607(c); 48-3-705(d).

## A. Subject Matter Jurisdiction

See Chapter 3.1 through 3.3 for a detailed discussion and case law related to subject matter jurisdiction.

The district court has exclusive, original jurisdiction over termination of parental rights (TPR) actions. G.S. 7B-200(a)(4); 7B-1101. In addition to the general jurisdiction statute, G.S. 7B-200, that establishes the district court's jurisdiction over various types of juvenile proceedings, the Juvenile Code has a specific "jurisdiction" statute that applies to TPR proceedings: G.S. 7B-1101. The jurisdictional conditions imposed by G.S. 7B-1101 include

- the child resides in, is found in, or is in the legal or actual custody of a DSS or licensed child-placing agency in the judicial district at the time the TPR petition or motion is filed in district court;
- the court has jurisdiction under the Uniform Child-Custody Jurisdiction Enforcement Act (UCCJEA), specifically G.S. 50A-201, 50A-203, or 50A-204;
- for a nonresident respondent parent, the court has initial custody or modification jurisdiction under the UCCJEA and the court finds process was served pursuant to G.S. 7B-1106 on the nonresident parent.

Failure to comply with the provisions of G.S. 7B-1101 will result in a lack of subject matter jurisdiction. *See, e.g., In re J.M.*, 797 S.E.2d 305 (N.C. Ct. App. 2016) (vacating TPR order for lack of subject matter jurisdiction as child did not reside in, was not found in, and was not in the legal custody of a DSS in the judicial district at the time the action was filed); *In re D.A.Y.*, 831 S.E.2d 854 (N.C. Ct. App. 2019) (vacating TPR order for lack of subject matter jurisdiction under UCCJEA to modify California custody order when mother was presently residing in California after relocating out of state and there was no finding (order) by the California court that it no longer had exclusive continuing jurisdiction); *In re P.D.*, 803 S.E.2d 667 (N.C. Ct. App. 2017) (unpublished) (vacating TPR order for not meeting jurisdictional requirements of G.S. 7B-1101; order did not include finding that nonresident parent was served with process pursuant to G.S. 7B-1106; record shows the service was deficient as summons failed to list respondent-father as the father). *See also* N.C. R. Civ. P. 12(h)(3).

**Resource:** For a further discussion on G.S. 7B-1101, see Sara DePasquale, *It's Complicated: Venue vs Jurisdiction in A/N/D and TPR Actions*, UNC SCH. OF GOV'T: ON THE CIVIL SIDE BLOG (Feb. 22, 2017).

Key factors in determining subject matter jurisdiction in TPR cases include the following, all of which are discussed in detail as referenced below:

- proper petitioner (standing), see section 9.3.B, below, and Chapter 3.2.B.1;
- proper initiation of proceedings, see Chapter 3.2.B.2;
- verification of petition or motion, see Chapter 3.2.B.3;
- compliance with the UCCJEA, see Chapter 3.3;
- location of child, see Chapter 3.2.B.7; and
- compliance with the Indian Child Welfare Act (ICWA), see Chapter 3.2.B.4 and Chapter 13.2 (detailing ICWA application and requirements).

Appellate courts have determined that several specific issues do *not* affect subject matter jurisdiction in TPR cases. These are discussed in detail as referenced below:

- defects in or lack of summons (but note G.S. 7B-1101 requirement for nonresident parent and proper service), see Chapter 3.2.C.1;
- failure to include certain information in petition, see Chapter 3.2.C.2; and
- failure to comply with statutory timelines, see Chapter 3.2.C.3.

Subject matter jurisdiction in a TPR also is not affected by an earlier deficiency in the appointment of a guardian ad litem (GAL) for the child in an underlying abuse, neglect, or dependency proceeding when the child is represented by a GAL in the TPR proceeding. *In re J.E.*, 362 N.C. 168 (2008) (noting the prior orders in the neglect action in which the children were purportedly unrepresented at the hearings are not on appeal), *rev'g per curiam for the reasons stated in the dissent* 183 N.C. App. 217 (2007).

Any order entered by a court that lacks subject matter jurisdiction is void. *See In re T.R.P.*, 360 N.C. 588 (2006) (concluding that because trial court lacked subject matter jurisdiction, review hearing order was void ab initio).

### B. Personal Jurisdiction

Generally, proper service of a summons under G.S. 7B-1106 for termination of parental rights (TPR) confers personal jurisdiction when a TPR proceeding is initiated by petition. (A TPR may also be initiated as a motion in an existing abuse, neglect, or dependency proceeding pursuant to G.S. 7B-1102.) A parent may waive the defenses of lack of personal jurisdiction or insufficiency of process or service of process by making a general appearance or by filing an answer, response, or motion without raising the defense. *See* N.C. R. CIV. P. 12(b), (h). However, some TPR cases involving out-of-state parents present unique issues related to personal jurisdiction.

See Chapter 3.4 for a detailed discussion and case law relating to personal jurisdiction (and for TPRs involving out-of-state parents specifically, see section E).

## C. Applicability of the Rules of Civil Procedure

Where the Juvenile Code provides a procedure, that procedure prevails over the Rules of Civil Procedure. *In re L.O.K.*, 174 N.C. App. 426 (2005). Where the Juvenile Code does not identify a specific procedure to be used in termination of parental rights cases (TPR), the Rules of Civil Procedure may be used to fill procedural gaps. *See In re S.D.W.*, 187 N.C. App. 416 (2007). For example, the TPR statutes do not address venue but the court of appeals has recognized a respondent parent's right to seek a change in venue. *See In re J.L.K.*, 165 N.C. App. 311 (2004) (holding respondent waived his right to seek a change of venue when he failed to either move for a change in venue or object to venue in his answer pursuant to Rule 12(b) of the Rules of Civil Procedure).

Appellate cases that have analyzed the application of specific rules or discussed the Rules of Civil Procedure generally in the TPR context are discussed in detail in Chapter 4.1, and some are referenced in relevant sections of this Chapter.

## 9.3 Initiation of Proceedings and Standing

### A. Initiation of TPR

**1. Only by petition or by motion in pending abuse, neglect, or dependency proceeding.** A proceeding for termination of parental rights (TPR) may be initiated only by (1) filing a petition or (2) filing a motion in a pending abuse, neglect, or dependency proceeding.

(a) **Termination of one's own parental rights not permitted.** Parents cannot unilaterally and extra-judicially terminate their own parental rights. *In re Jurga*, 123 N.C. App. 91 (1996) (affirming dismissal of guardianship of minor action under G.S. Chapter 35A for lack of subject matter jurisdiction when child had natural parents; holding that a written declaration of voluntary termination of parental rights contravened statutory procedures and was ineffective); *see also In re C.K.C.*, 822 S.E.2d 741 (N.C. Ct. App. 2018) (reversing TPR; holding consent order in Chapter 50 civil custody action between father and grandparents that included a provision that grandmother would file a petition to terminate father's rights that no other party, including father, would oppose is void as against public policy and is neither a properly executed consent or relinquishment under the adoption statutes). Note that a parent's consent or relinquishment for adoption results in termination of the parent's rights when the child's adoption is final. *See* G.S. 48-3-607(c); 48-3-705(d).

(b) **TPR cannot be initiated by counterclaim.** A parent cannot initiate a TPR action by filing a counterclaim to terminate parental rights in the other parent's civil action for visitation. *In re S.D.W.*, 187 N.C. App. 416 (2007).

**(c) Initiation of TPR via intervention.** Any person or agency with standing to initiate a TPR may intervene in a pending abuse, neglect, or dependency proceeding for the purpose of filing a TPR motion. G.S. 7B-1103(b).

**2. DSS required to initiate TPR in certain circumstances.** If a termination of parental rights (TPR) is necessary to perfect the primary permanent plan for a child, G.S. 7B-906.1(m) requires that DSS file a TPR petition or motion within sixty days from entry of the permanency planning order unless the court makes findings as to why this sixty-day time frame cannot be met. *See In re A.R.A.*, 835 S.E.2d 417 (N.C. S.Ct. 2019) (facts show that in January 2018, after a permanency planning order was entered that identified adoption as the primary plan and reunification as the secondary plan, DSS filed petition to terminate both parents' rights). If the court finds that the sixty-day time period cannot be met, the court shall specify the time in which any needed TPR petition or motion must be filed. G.S. 7B-906.1(m).

In cases examining DSS's late filing of a TPR action, the court of appeals has held that this statutory sixty-day requirement is "directory" rather than "mandatory" and, therefore, is not jurisdictional. The court of appeals noted that the purpose of the specified time period is to provide for a speedy resolution of a case involving custody of a child and reversing or vacating an order because the action was filed outside the time limit would only cause further delay as a new petition and hearing would be required. The court also looked to whether the failure to timely file a TPR action caused prejudice to the respondent when determining if there was reversible error. *See In re B.M.*, 168 N.C. App. 350 (2005) (decided under former statute; respondents were not prejudiced by late filing); *In re T.M.*, 182 N.C. App. 566, *aff'd per curiam*, 361 N.C. 683 (2007). *See also In re T.H.T.*, 362 N.C. 446 (2008) (holding a writ of mandamus, and not a new hearing, is appropriate remedy to enforce statutory time limits in an appeal involving delay in entry of an order; stating delay is directly contrary to the child's best interests, which is the polar star of the Juvenile Code).

In other circumstances specified in G.S. 7B-906.1(f), DSS is required to initiate TPR proceedings unless the court makes certain findings. These are discussed in Chapter 7.8.D.

**Practice Notes:** Although the Juvenile Code directs that DSS initiate the TPR action, the child's GAL, the child's court-appointed guardian of the person, or the person with whom the child has resided with for a continuous period of two or more years has standing to and may initiate a TPR action. *See* G.S. 7B-1103(a)(2), (5), and (6).

Additionally, the Juvenile Code does not prohibit the commencement of a TPR when the achievement of a secondary permanent plan requires a TPR. Under G.S. 7B-906.2(b), the court must order DSS to make efforts toward finalizing the primary and secondary permanent plans.

### B. Standing to File Petition or Motion

**1. Introduction.** Standing is a jurisdictional issue. *In re J.A.U.*, 242 N.C. App. 603 (2015). The court does not have subject matter jurisdiction if the petition or motion to terminate parental rights (TPR) is filed by someone who does not have standing. *In re Miller*, 162 N.C.

App. 355 (2004). Standing to file a TPR petition or motion is conferred by G.S. 7B-1103, which limits the parties to seven categories of persons or agencies having an interest in the child. *In re N.G.H.*, 237 N.C. App. 236 (2014); *In re E.T.S.*, 175 N.C. App. 32 (2005). The petition, motion, or record must include any document or order pursuant to which the petitioner claims standing. *See In re N.G.H.*, 237 N.C. App. 236, 237 (G.S. 7B-1104(2) requires petitioner to state "the facts sufficient to identify the petitioner or movant as authorized by [G.S.] 7B-1103 to file a petition or motion"); *In re T.B.*, 177 N.C. App. 790, 793 (2006) (the requirement in G.S. 7B-1104(5) that a copy of the order giving petitioner custody be attached to the petition or motion "implicitly recognizes" that a trial court has subject matter jurisdiction only if the record includes the required document).

Only the following persons or agencies have standing to file a TPR petition or motion:

- a parent,
- a child's guardian of the person,
- a DSS or child-placing agency with custody of the child,
- a DSS or child-placing agency to whom the child was surrendered (relinquished) for adoption,
- a person with whom the child has continuously resided for two or more years preceding the filing of the TPR petition or motion,
- a child's guardian ad litem (GAL) appointed in an abuse, neglect or dependency action,
- a person who has filed a petition to adopt the child.

G.S. 7B-1103(a).

**2. Either parent.** Either parent has standing to initiate an action seeking termination of the other parent's rights, except a parent convicted under

- G.S. 14-27.21 or 14-27.22 of first- or second-degree forcible rape occurring on or after December 1, 2004 (formerly codified at G.S. 14-27.2 and 14-27.3),
- G.S. 14-27.23 of statutory rape of a child by an adult occurring on or after December 1, 2008 (formerly codified at G.S. 14-27.2A), or
- G.S. 14-27.24 of first-degree statutory rape (previously G.S. 14-27.2(a)(1)) occurring on or after December 1, 2015 (or December 1, 2004 under previous statute)

when the rape resulted in the conception of the child who is the subject of the TPR proceeding. G.S. 7B-1103(a)(1).

**3. Guardian.** Any judicially appointed guardian of the person of the child has standing to initiate a TPR proceeding. G.S. 7B-1103(a)(2). *See also In re D.C.*, 225 N.C. App. 327 (2013) (affirming the guardians' authority to file for TPR and noting that the statute places no preliminary requirements on guardians before filing); *In re J.A.U.*, 242 N.C. App. 603 (2015) (maternal grandmother with physical and legal custody of child pursuant to a G.S. Chapter 50 custody order was a custodian and lacked standing as a guardian to file a petition to terminate respondent father's parental rights; grandmother also did not meet any other category enumerated in G.S. 7B-1103); *In re B.O.*, 199 N.C. App. 600 (2009) (explaining that the

Juvenile Code does not equate custody and guardianship, and it gives guardians, but not legal custodians, standing to petition for TPR; decided under former definition of "custodian" that also included a person who assumes the status of parent without being awarded legal custody (*see* S.L. 2013-129, sec. 1 amending G.S. 7B-101(8))).

**4. DSS or child-placing agency with custody order.** A TPR proceeding may be initiated by any county DSS or licensed child-placing agency to whom a court has given custody of the child. G.S. 7B-1103(a)(3).

- **(a) Must establish custody order.** Unless the child has been relinquished to DSS for adoption, if DSS does not have court-ordered custody of the child or fails to establish that there is a court order giving DSS custody, DSS will not have standing to initiate a TPR proceeding and the court will not have subject matter jurisdiction. *In re E.X.J.*, 191 N.C. App. 34 (2008), *aff'd per curiam*, 363 N.C. 9 (2009); *In re Miller,* 162 N.C. App. 355 (2004).

  - When DSS did not attach to the petition or remedy the omission by amending the petition or by otherwise including in the record a copy of the order giving DSS custody that was in effect at the time the TPR petition was filed, DSS failed to establish that it had standing. The trial court lacked subject matter jurisdiction. *In re T.B.*, 177 N.C. App. 790 (2006).
  - Custody pursuant to a valid nonsecure custody order is sufficient to confer on DSS standing to file a TPR petition pursuant to G.S. 7B-1103(a)(3). *In re T.M.*, 182 N.C. App. 566, *aff'd per curiam*, 361 N.C. 683 (2007).
  - Where the court had placed the child in the legal custody of relatives before DSS filed its petition, DSS did not have standing to file a TPR petition because it no longer had custody. *In re D.D.J.*, 177 N.C. App. 441 (2006).

  Cases that have considered the failure to attach a custody order, if one exists, to a TPR petition or motion as required by G.S. 7B-1104(5) have found that the failure to attach the order does not deprive the court of subject matter jurisdiction where the court can get the necessary information concerning custody from the petition itself or from the record, and no party is prejudiced by the omission. *See, e.g., In re H.L.A.D.*, 184 N.C. App, 381 (2007), *aff'd per curiam*, 362 N.C. 170 (2008); *In re T.M.H.,* 186 N.C. App. 451 (2007); *In re B.D.*, 174 N.C. App. 234 (2005); and others discussed in Chapter 3.2.C.2.

- **(b) Custody order must be valid.** If the order giving DSS custody is invalid, DSS will not have standing to initiate a TPR proceeding. For example, when the petition in the underlying abuse, neglect, or dependency action was not properly signed and verified, the district court did not have subject matter jurisdiction. The orders entered in that action, including the orders giving DSS custody, were void such that DSS did not have standing to initiate the TPR proceeding. *In re S.E.P.*, 184 N.C. App. 481 (2007). *See also In re A.J.H-R.,* 184 N.C. App. 177 (2007) (holding custody order void for lack of proper verification of petition). See Chapters 3.2.B.3 (discussing verification) and 4.2.B (discussing proper signatures). See also Chapter 3.3 (discussing subject matter jurisdiction under UCCJEA).

**(c) DSS must have court-ordered custody when the petition is filed.** Where the court had placed the child in the legal custody of a couple before DSS filed its petition, DSS did not have standing to petition for termination of parental rights. *In re D.D.J.*, 177 N.C. App. 441 (2006); *In re Miller*, 162 N.C. App. 355 (2004).

**5. DSS or child-placing agency to whom the child has been surrendered for adoption.** A county DSS or a licensed child-placing agency has standing to initiate a TPR proceeding involving a child who has been surrendered to the agency for adoption pursuant to G.S. 48-3-701 by a parent or guardian of the child's person. G.S. 7B-1103(a)(4); *In re E.B.*, 834 S.E.2d 169 (N.C. Ct. App. 2019) and *In re A.L.*, 245 N.C. App. 55 (2016) (in both cases, DSS had standing to file a petition to terminate father's rights pursuant to G.S. 7B-1103(a)(4) based on mother's relinquishment of her parental rights and surrender of the child for adoption pursuant to G.S 48-3-701). *See* G.S. 48-1-101(8) (definition of "guardian" for purposes of adoption limited to appointment under G.S. Chapter 35A).

**6. Person child has lived with for two years.** Any person with whom the child has resided for a continuous period of two years or more immediately preceding the filing of the TPR petition or motion has standing to initiate the TPR proceeding. G.S. 7B-1103(a)(5). The determining factor is the length of time the child has resided with the person and not the relationship between petitioner and the child. *See In re J.A.U.*, 242 N.C. App. 603 (2015) (vacating TPR; holding the court lacked subject matter jurisdiction as petitioner (maternal grandmother) did not have standing when evidence established child had lived with petitioner pursuant to a G.S. Chapter 50 custody order continuously for less than one year at the time the petition was filed); *In re B.O.*, 199 N.C. App. 600 (2009) (holding that the petitioners did not have standing because, when petition was filed, the child had not resided with them for two years and they did not satisfy any other criteria in G.S. 7B-1103 for standing).

Appellate cases have interpreted "residing with" to mean the same as "living with," looking at the number of nights a child spends with a person per year without regard to whether the person has primary, shared, or joint legal custody of the child. *See In re A.D.N.*, 231 N.C. App. 54 (2013) (although the trial court did not make detailed findings as to standing, it did make the ultimate finding that the child had resided with the TPR petitioner for a continuous period of two years before the petition was filed; evidence in the record showed that the child spent an average of eighty-five percent (85%) of his nights with petitioner). The language "continuous period of two years" does not require that the child spend every single night with the person for that period, and a period of temporary absence will not necessarily prevent a determination that the child's stay was "continuous." *In re A.D.N.*, 231 N.C. App. 54 (using the child support guidelines and UCCJEA for guidance and holding that "continuous" allows for a limited number of nights away from the person's home).

**7. Guardian ad litem for child.** A guardian ad litem (GAL) appointed under G.S. 7B-601 to represent the child in an abuse, neglect, or dependency proceeding, who has not been relieved of that responsibility, has standing to initiate a TPR proceeding. G.S. 7B-1103(a)(6). The GAL appointed under G.S. 7B-601 is a team that typically consists of a GAL volunteer, local GAL program staff, and an attorney advocate. The court of appeals has examined the issue of standing in the context of GAL team representation. Relying on the North Carolina Supreme

Court case *In re J.H.K.*, 365 N.C. 171 (2011), the court of appeals held that a TPR petition signed by the GAL program specialist "by and through the undersigned Attorney Advocate" and not by the volunteer GAL directly involved in the action was not improper. *In re S.T.B.*, 235 N.C. App. 290, 293 (2014).

See Chapter 2.3.D (discussing child's GAL).

**8. Adoption petitioner.** Any person who has filed a petition to adopt the child has standing to initiate a TPR proceeding. G.S. 7B-1103(a)(7). *See also* G.S. 48-2-302(c) (providing that a petition for adoption may be filed concurrently with a petition to terminate parental rights). See Chapter 10.3 (discussing selected adoption provisions). Petitioners in a private TPR action failed to establish standing pursuant to G.S. 7B-1103(a)(7) when they did not attach to the TPR petition a copy of the petition for adoption, the TPR petition did not incorporate by reference any adoption petition, and testimony at the TPR hearing did not establish that an adoption petition had been filed. *In re N.G.H.*, 237 N.C. App. 236 (2014).

## 9.4 Counsel and Guardians ad Litem for Parent and Child

### A. Counsel for Parent

The respondent parent has a right to be represented by counsel, and to appointed counsel if indigent, but may knowingly and voluntarily waive the right. G.S. 7B-1101.1(a), (b). For a discussion of the appointment of counsel, see Chapter 2.4.D.

The procedure for appointment of counsel is different for termination of parental rights (TPR) proceedings initiated by petition and TPR proceedings initiated by motion. *See* G.S. 7B-1106(b)(4) (petition); 7B-1106.1(b)(4) (motion). When a respondent parent is represented by appointed counsel in an underlying abuse, neglect, or dependency action that attorney continues to represent the parent in the TPR proceeding unless otherwise ordered by the court. *See* G.S. 7B-1106(a2), (b)(3); 7B-1106.1(b)(3); *In re D.E.G.*, 228 N.C. App. 381 (2013) (attorney representing parent in underlying abuse, neglect, or dependency proceeding was not provisional counsel in TPR proceeding).

When provisional counsel is appointed, the court acts on the status of that provisional appointment at the first hearing in the TPR proceeding after the respondent is served. If provisional counsel is released, the court may reconsider a parent's eligibility and desire for appointed counsel at any stage of the proceeding. G.S. 7B-1101.1(a). Additionally, if a parent appears at the adjudication hearing and is not represented by counsel, the court must conduct an inquiry into whether the parent desires counsel but is indigent and cannot retain counsel. If the court determines that the parent is indigent and desires counsel, the court must appoint counsel and grant the parent an extension of time to permit counsel to prepare. G.S. 7B-1109(b).

All appointments are pursuant to the policies of the Office of Indigent Defense Services (IDS).

**AOC Forms:**
- AOC-J-144, Order of Assignment or Denial of Counsel (Abuse, Neglect, Dependency; Termination of Parental Rights; Post-DSS-Placement Review and Permanency Planning Hearing (Delinquent/Undisciplined)) (Oct. 2019).
- AOC-J-143, Waiver of Parent's Right to Counsel (Oct. 2019).

**Practice Notes:** Appointment of provisional counsel probably is not required for an unknown respondent parent who is not "named in the petition." *See* G.S. 7B-1101.1(a); *see also* G.S. 7B-1105(d) (contents of publication notice do not refer to provisional counsel).

In the process of informing a respondent parent of the right to appointed counsel, the court should explain that even though an attorney is appointed, the respondent may be responsible for some costs. G.S. 7B-603(b1).

Caution should be exercised in appointing one attorney to represent both parents, given the potential for conflicting interests and evidence. *But cf. In re Byrd*, 72 N.C. App. 277 (1985) (holding that the failure to appoint separate counsel for respondent parents was not error, where they did not object when the appointment was made, the record showed that evidence was sufficient to terminate both parents' rights, and there was no indication that the court treated respondents as a couple rather than as individuals).

**Resource:** The Office of the Parent Defender within the North Carolina Office of Indigent Defense Services (IDS) coordinates, assists, and trains parents' attorneys. Information about the office as well as resources for parents' attorneys can be found on the IDS website.

## B. Guardian ad Litem for Parent

In some circumstances the court will either be required or have discretion to appoint a guardian ad litem (GAL) for a respondent parent in a termination of parental rights (TPR) proceeding pursuant to Rule 17 of the Rules of Civil Procedure.

See Chapter 2.4.F (discussing GAL for respondent parent in detail).

**1. GAL for minor parent.** A minor parent's rights may be terminated. *See* G.S. 7B-1101. The minor parent is not deemed to be under a disability. G.S. 7B-1102(b)(2); 7B-1106(a). However, the court must appoint a GAL pursuant to Rule 17 of the Rules of Civil Procedure to represent any parent who is an unemancipated minor. G.S. 7B-1101.1(b).

Appellate courts have not specifically addressed the failure to appoint a GAL for a minor parent in a TPR proceeding, but they have held that failure to appoint a GAL for the child or an adult parent, when the statute required one, was reversible error. *See, e.g., In re R.A.H.*, 171 N.C. App. 427 (2005) (failure to appoint a GAL for a child); *In re B.M.*, 168 N.C. App. 350 (2005) (failure to appoint GAL for parent when former law required appointment). However, when the respondent mother was an adult at the time the TPR was filed, the failure to appoint a GAL to her as a minor parent in an earlier dependency proceeding as required by the applicable statute could not be considered in the TPR proceeding. *In re E.T.S.*, 175 N.C.

App. 32 (2005).

**2. GAL for parent who is incompetent.** On motion of any party or on the court's own motion, the court may appoint a GAL pursuant to Rule 17 of the Rules of Civil Procedure for a parent who is incompetent. G.S. 7B-1101.1(c). Note that legislation in 2013 substantially changed GAL representation for parents and eliminated the role of GALs of assistance based on diminished capacity, now only authorizing GALs of substitution based on incompetency. *See* S.L. 2013-129, sec. 17 and 32.

The court has discretion to determine if there is a substantial question as to whether a respondent is incompetent requiring a hearing to determine the need for a GAL. *In re Z.V.A.*, 835 S.E.2d 425 (N.C. S.Ct. 2019); *In re T.L.H.*, 368 N.C. 101 (2015). When there is a substantial question as to incompetence, the court should address that question as soon as possible. See Chapter 2.4.F.3 and 5 (discussing determination of incompetence for GAL appointment).

**3. GAL appointment and role.** The Juvenile Code prohibits appointing the parent's counsel as GAL for the parent but does not say anything else regarding who should be appointed. *See* G.S. 7B-1101.1(d). In practice, attorneys are often appointed to act as parents' GALs, although there is no requirement that the GAL be an attorney. Rule 17(b)(2) of the Rules of Civil Procedure refers to the appointment of "some discreet person." The role of the parent's GAL is not well defined by either the Juvenile Code or Rule 17. The GAL is required to actively participate in the proceedings for which the GAL is appointed, and when a GAL is appointed in the underlying abuse, neglect, or dependency case, that GAL's responsibilities continue throughout the TPR proceeding as long as the reasons for the appointment still exist. *In re A.S.Y.*, 208 N.C. App. 530 (2010) (holding in a TPR case initiated by motion that it was reversible error for the trial court to excuse the parent's GAL and not appoint another GAL when the parent did not appear for the TPR hearing). See Chapter 2.4.F.6 (discussing role of parent's GAL).

---

**AOC Form:**
AOC-J-206, <u>Order to Appoint, Deny, or Release Guardian Ad Litem (For Respondent)</u> (Oct. 2013).

**Resource:** For a thorough discussion of guardian ad litem representation of respondent parents, including legislative and case history, see Janet Mason, <u>Guardians ad Litem for Respondent Parents in Juvenile Cases</u>, JUVENILE LAW BULLETIN No. 2014/01 (UNC School of Government, Jan. 2014).

---

### C. Guardian ad Litem for Child

The child is a party to the termination of parental rights (TPR) action. G.S. 7B-1104; *see* G.S. 7B-601(a) ("the juvenile is a party in all actions under this Subchapter"). The child's best interests are represented by a guardian ad litem (GAL). See Chapter 2.3.C (discussing the rights of the child including participation in the proceeding).

When there is an underlying abuse, neglect, or dependency proceeding, the GAL representing the child in that proceeding will continue to represent the child in a TPR proceeding, regardless of how it is initiated (petition or motion), unless the court orders otherwise. G.S. 7B-1106(a1); 7B-1106.1(a)(5); 7B-1108(d). The court must appoint a GAL for a child who does not already have one in any TPR case in which an answer or response is filed denying any material allegation of the petition or motion. G.S. 7B-1108(b). Even when not required to do so, the court has discretion to appoint a GAL for the child at any stage of the TPR proceeding to assist the court in determining the child's best interests. G.S. 7B-1108(c). At a pretrial hearing, the court must address whether a GAL should be appointed for the child, if a GAL was not previously appointed. G.S. 7B-1108.1(a)(2). *See In re P.T.W.*, 250 N.C. App. 589 (2016) (footnote 11 discussing G.S. 7B-1108.1).

If the child does not already have a GAL, the court makes a new appointment pursuant to G.S. 7B-601. However, GALs trained and supervised by the GAL Program may be appointed only in cases in which the child is or has been the subject of an abuse, neglect, or dependency petition (i.e., not private TPR cases), unless for good cause the GAL Program consents to the appointment. G.S. 7B-1108(b). See Chapter 2.3.D for an explanation of the GAL Program and GAL team representation. When the GAL Program is not appointed and the GAL who is appointed for the child is not an attorney, an attorney is also appointed. G.S. 7B-1108(b). The supreme court has held that "if the GAL is an attorney, that person can perform the duties of both the GAL and the attorney advocate," which involve both in-court and out-of-court responsibilities. *In re J.H.K.*, 365 N.C. 171, 175 (2011). *Cf. In re J.L.H.,* 217 N.C. App. 192 (2011) (originally unpublished Nov. 15, 2011, but subsequently published) (citing *In re R.A.H.*, 171 N.C. App. 427 (2005) rather than the more recent supreme court case *In re J.H.K.,* 365 N.C. 171) (finding reversible error where the trial court in a private TPR action appointed an attorney advocate but not a GAL for the child as the functions of the two roles are not sufficiently similar).

> **Practice Note:** A court order that appoints an attorney to serve in both roles should specifically state that the attorney is to serve in both the attorney advocate and GAL roles.

Timing of the answer does not impact the requirement that a GAL be appointed. *See In re J.L.S.*, 168 N.C. App. 721 (2005) (holding that although the respondent waited until the day of the hearing to file an answer, the court was required to appoint a GAL for the child). Something less than a formal answer is not likely to trigger the requirement for a GAL. *See In re Tyner*, 106 N.C. App. 480 (1992) (holding that appointment of a GAL for the child was not required, where the court of appeals could not determine from the record when or for what purpose the respondent had filed a letter he later claimed was an "answer").

In the case *In re A.D.N.*, 231 N.C. App. 54 (2013), the court of appeals held that the issue of failure to appoint a GAL for the child when an answer denying a material allegation was filed must be preserved for appeal, and it refused to rule on the failure of the trial court to appoint a GAL because the failure was not objected to at trial. However, in two earlier cases the court of appeals invoked Rule 2 of the Rules of Appellate Procedure to reach the issue, which was not objected to at trial, and in both cases found prejudicial error in the trial court's failure to appoint a GAL for the child when the respondents filed an answer denying a material allegation, triggering the statutory mandate that a GAL be appointed for the child. *See In re Fuller*, 144 N.C. App. 620 (2001); *In re Barnes*, 97 N.C. App. 325 (1990). See Chapter 12.3.C (discussing Appellate Rule 2).

In the case *In re P.T.W.*, 250 N.C. App. 589 (2016), respondent mother did not file an answer denying a material allegation that would have required the trial court to appoint a GAL for the child and also did not preserve for appeal her argument that the trial court abused its discretion by failing to appoint a GAL. However, the appellate court considered the issue and found that the trial court acted within its discretion when it did not appoint a GAL to represent the child's best interests in the TPR proceeding. The trial court heard testimony from petitioner, respondent, and a member of respondent's family and carefully weighed the child's best interests against the evidence presented. The trial court's determination to forego GAL assistance in determining child's best interests was not unreasonable.

The GAL appointment, duties, and payment in a TPR proceeding are the same as for a GAL appointed in an abuse, neglect, or dependency action unless the court determines the child's best interests require otherwise. G.S. 7B-1108(d); *see* G.S. 7B-601.

See Chapter 2.3.D for a full explanation of the child's GAL appointment, role, and duties.

## 9.5 Contents of Petition or Motion

For a discussion of amendments to TPR petitions, see Chapter 4.2.C.2.

### A. Identifying Information

**1. Title.** The petition or motion must be entitled "In Re (*last name of child*), a minor juvenile." G.S. 7B-1104.

Note that in the juvenile record maintained by the clerk, all materials relating to a termination of parental rights proceeding (TPR) are located in a "T" (or "JT") subfolder of the juvenile file, regardless of whether the TPR is initiated by petition or motion and whether it is a private or agency action. Rule 12.1.1, Chapter XII, Rules of Recordkeeping Procedures for the Office of the Clerk of Superior Court (in Appendix 4).

**2. Child.** The petition or motion must include the child's name as it appears on the birth certificate, the date and place of the child's birth, and county of the child's residence or it must state that the information is unknown. G.S. 7B-1104(1).

**3. Petitioner or movant.** The petition or motion must include the petitioner's or movant's name and address and facts sufficient to show that the petitioner or movant has standing to initiate the action. G.S. 7B-1104(2). See section 9.3.B, above (discussing standing).

**4. Parents.** The petition or motion must include the names and addresses of the child's parents. If a parent's name or address is unknown, the petition or motion or an attached affidavit must describe efforts that have been made to determine the name and address. (See section 9.6, below, related to a hearing on an unknown parent.) A parent need not be named in the petition if he or she has been convicted of first- or second-degree forcible rape under G.S. 14-27.21 or 14-27.22, statutory rape of a child by an adult under 14-27.23, or first-degree statutory rape under 14-27.24, and the child who is the subject of the action was conceived as a result of the rape. G.S. 7B-1104(3).

**Practice Note:** The Juvenile Code does not specifically address naming and serving a respondent parent in the TPR action when that respondent parent has been convicted of one of those four enumerated rape offenses and the rape resulted in the child's conception. However, that criminal conviction is one of the grounds to terminate the parent's rights. *See* G.S. 7B-1111(a)(11), discussed in section 9.11.K, below. The parent whose rights are sought to be terminated is a necessary party to the TPR action. In addition, due process requires that the respondent parent have notice and an opportunity to be heard. Presumably, the exclusion of a parent's name and address from the TPR petition (or motion) under G.S. 7B-1104(3) relates to a petition or motion that is not naming that parent as the respondent but is instead seeking to terminate the other parent's rights.

**5. Guardian of the person or custodian.** The petition or motion must include the name and address of any court-appointed guardian of the child's person and of any person or agency to whom a court of any state has given custody of the child. A copy of any related court order must be attached. G.S. 7B-1104(4), (5). See section 9.3.B.4, above (discussing standing and need to attach custody order showing custody in effect at time TPR petition or motion is filed).

In a private TPR action, the petitioner's failure to include a prior custody or "guardianship" order with the petition and failure to include the name and address of any appointed guardian, or a statement declaring the petitioner had no such knowledge, rendered the petition facially defective as there was no information about the guardianship order that was raised by the respondent. *In re Z.T.B.*, 170 N.C. App. 564 (2005).

## B. Addressing the UCCJEA

See Chapter 3.3 (discussing UCCJEA).

**1. No circumvention of UCCJEA.** The petition or motion must include a statement that it has not been filed to circumvent the Uniform Child-Custody Jurisdiction and Enforcement Act (UCCJEA). G.S. 7B-1104(7); *see* G.S. Chapter 50A (UCCJEA). Omission of the statement will not deprive the court of jurisdiction or require dismissal where there is no showing of prejudice. *See In re J.D.S.*, 170 N.C. App. 244 (2005); *In re B.D.*, 174 N.C. App. 234 (2005).

**2. Child status information required by UCCJEA.** Information about the child's status, as required by the UCCJEA in G.S. 50A-209(a), must be set out in the petition or motion or an attached affidavit. Failure to attach the affidavit does not divest the court of subject matter jurisdiction and can be cured by filing the affidavit within a time specified by the court. *In re J.D.S.*, 170 N.C. App. 244 (2005). See Chapter 3.2.C.2(c).

**AOC Form:**
AOC-CV-609, Affidavit as to Status of Minor Child (March 2019).

## C. Facts to Support Grounds for Termination

The petition or motion must include facts sufficient to support a determination that one or more grounds for terminating parental rights exist. G.S. 7B-1104(6). The court cannot adjudicate a ground that is not alleged in the petition. *In re S.R.G.*, 195 N.C. App. 79 (2009). *Cf. In re T.J.F.*, 230 N.C. App. 531 (2013) and *In re A.H.*, 183 N.C. App. 609 (2007), set out below in this section.

G.S. 7B-1104 does not distinguish between the facts that must be alleged in a petition or in a motion to terminate parental rights. Either pleading must comply with the requirement for factual allegations in G.S. 7B-1104(6). *In re J.S.K.*, 807 S.E.2d 188 (N.C. Ct. App. 2017).

> **Practice Note:** The petition or motion should allege specific facts supporting one or more grounds for termination of parental rights that are sufficient to put a respondent parent on notice. While using attachments to petitions may be helpful, it is generally not helpful for them to be used as a substitute for alleging specific facts in the petition or to be voluminous.

Appellate cases discussing this requirement have focused on whether the facts alleged are sufficient to put a party on notice of a ground rather than whether a particular statute number is alleged. Allegations need not be exhaustive or extensive, but they must put a party on notice as to acts, omissions, or conditions that are at issue and must do more than recite the statutory wording of the ground. *In re B.S.O.*, 234 N.C. App. 706 (2014); *In re T.J.F.*, 230 N.C. App. 531 (2013); *In re Hardesty*, 150 N.C. App. 380 (2002). Although appellate cases have focused on the facts alleged rather than the stated grounds, they have also noted that the better practice is to specifically plead a particular ground for termination pursuant to a specific statutory section. *In re B.S.O.*, 234 N.C. App. 706; *In re T.J.F.*, 230 N.C. App. 531.

Cases finding that the pleading provided sufficient notice of a ground for termination.

- The petition did not allege willful abandonment under G.S. 7B-1111(a)(7) but did refer to respondent father's "abandonment" of his children in the context of alleging neglect. This, coupled with allegations that his whereabouts were unknown since his incarceration and deportation approximately eight months prior to the filing of the petitions, was sufficient to put the father on notice of a potential adjudication on the ground of abandonment. *In re B.S.O.*, 234 N.C. App. 706.
- Where the petition alleged only the neglect ground under G.S. 7B-1111(a)(1) but the court adjudicated the abandonment ground under G.S. 7B-1111(a)(7), the court of appeals held that the petition put the father on notice as to abandonment. The petition's language alleged the father's "lack of involvement with or regard for the minor child constitute[d] neglect," and contained several allegations suggesting that the father had foregone his parental responsibilities and withheld his presence, care, and parental affection from the child despite consistently available opportunities for involvement; failure to contact the child in the six months preceding the TPR petition; and failure to provide a reasonable

- amount for the cost and care of the child. *In re T.J.F.*, 230 N.C. App. 531, 533.
- Although the petition did not specifically reference G.S. 7B-1111(a)(6), the allegations gave the respondent sufficient notice that termination of parental rights would be sought on the basis of the parent's inability to provide proper care for the child. *In re A.H.*, 183 N.C. App. 609 (2007). *See also In re Humphrey*, 156 N.C. App. 533 (2003).
- Although the pleading asserted only the barebones legal grounds for terminating parental rights, it was sufficiently detailed because it incorporated by reference the entire juvenile file in the matter, which included all the court orders with facts as to mother's drug use, failure to comply with the orders, and criminal convictions. *In re H.T.*, 180 N.C. App. 611 (2006).
- Bare allegations that the parent neglected the child and willfully abandoned the child for six months did not comply with this requirement, but an attached custody decree incorporated into the petition did contain sufficient facts. *In re Quevedo*, 106 N.C. App. 574 (1992).

Cases finding that the pleading did not provide sufficient notice of a ground for termination.

- Motion filed by DSS to terminate parental rights that "merely recited the statutory grounds" in G.S. 7B-1111(a)(1)–(3) and (a)(6) was insufficient to put respondent mother on notice of the acts, conditions, or omissions at issue. Unlike *In re Quevedo*, 106 N.C. App. 574, above, the TPR motion in this case did not incorporate any prior orders and the custody order attached to the TPR motion did not contain any additional facts that would warrant a determination that a TPR ground existed. *In re J.S.K.*, 807 S.E.2d 188 (N.C. Ct. App. 2017) (trial court erred in denying mother's G.S. 1A-1, Rule 12(b)(6) motion to dismiss).
- When neither the petition nor the affidavit of the DSS social worker that was incorporated by reference mentioned the respondent father's progress or lack thereof in correcting the conditions that led to the child's removal from her mother's home, the TPR was reversed for not providing prior notice that G.S. 7B-1111(a)(2) was a potential ground and an issue in the TPR hearing. *In re L.S.*, 822 S.E.2d 506 (N.C. Ct. App. 2018).
- When the TPR petition did not refer to the ground under G.S. 7B-1111(a)(4) and did not allege respondent's willful failure to pay child support as required by a court order or custody agreement, a TPR order was reversed in part for not providing sufficient notice to respondent father of this ground. *In re I.R.L.*, 823 S.E.2d 902, 906 (N.C. Ct. App. 2019) (petition alleged only that father "[h]as failed to provide substantial financial support or consistent care for the minor child", which the court of appeals noted "may be an assertion under the ground of abandonment").

## D. Verification

G.S. 7B-1104 requires that the petition or motion be verified by the petitioner or movant, and the failure to verify deprives the court of subject matter jurisdiction. *In re T.R.P.*, 360 N.C. 588 (2006) (petition in neglect proceeding); *In re E.B.*, 249 N.C. App. 614 (2016) (motion to terminate parental rights verified by child's guardian ad litem invoked the trial court's jurisdiction); *In re C.M.H.*, 187 N.C. App. 807 (2007); *In re Triscari Children*, 109 N.C. App. 285 (1993) (explaining that a petition that is signed and notarized as subscribed and sworn before me is insufficient to constitute verification).

See Chapter 3.2.B.3 (discussing proper verification).

### E. Request for Relief

A motion or petition that neither contains a prayer for relief nor requests the entry of any order is not a proper pleading, and the court does not have jurisdiction to proceed. *In re McKinney*, 158 N.C. App. 441 (2003). *Cf. In re Baby Boy Scearce*, 81 N.C. App. 531 (1986) (holding that district court had jurisdiction when petition alleged that mother had placed child with DSS, father was unknown, North Carolina was child's home state and no other state had jurisdiction, and child's best interest would be served by court's assuming jurisdiction).

## 9.6 Hearing for Unknown Parent

### A. Preliminary Hearing to Determine Identity of Unknown Parent

**1. When required.** If the name or identity of a parent whose rights are sought to be terminated is unknown, the court must conduct a preliminary hearing to determine that parent's name or identity. G.S. 7B-1105(a). *See also In re M.M.*, 200 N.C. App. 248 (2009). This preliminary hearing on an unknown parent is not required when a parent's identity is known but his or her whereabouts are not. *In re Clark*, 76 N.C. App. 83 (1985). Naming "John Doe" in the alternative does not trigger the need to hold a preliminary hearing on an unknown parent so long as one person is identified as a parent and named as a respondent. *See In re A.N.S.*, 239 N.C. App. 46 (2015) (in a private TPR case, a putative father was named by the petitioner and "John Doe" was named in the alternative; naming "John Doe" in the alternative did not negate the fact that the identity of the father was known and a preliminary hearing was, therefore, not required).

**2. Timing.** The preliminary hearing on an unknown parent must be held within ten days after the petition is filed or if there is no court in the county during that ten-day period, at the next term of court in the county where the petition is filed. G.S. 7B-1105(a). The court must make findings and enter its order within thirty days of the preliminary hearing, unless the court finds that additional time is required for investigation. G.S. 7B-1105(e).

**3. Notice.** Notice of the preliminary hearing need be given only to the petitioner, but the court may direct that a summons be issued directing any other person to appear and testify. G.S. 7B-1105(c).

**4. Inquiry by court.** The court may inquire of any known parent about the identity of the unknown parent and may order the petitioner to conduct a "diligent search" for the parent. G.S. 7B-1105(b).

**5. Order.** If the court determines the parent's identity, the court must enter that finding and direct that the parent be summoned to appear. G.S. 7B-1105(b).

If the parent is not identified, the court must order that the unknown parent be served by publication (see section 9.6.B, below). The court in its order must specify

- the place(s) of publication and
- the contents of the notice the court concludes is most likely to identify the juvenile to the unknown parent.

G.S. 7B-1105(d).

**6. Amendment of petition to allege identity not required.** When the unknown respondent is identified as a result of the preliminary hearing, an amended TPR petition adding him or her as a respondent is not necessary for the court to obtain personal jurisdiction over him or her. Instead, the procedure set forth in G.S. 7B-1105 requires that the court make a finding as to the parent's identity and that the parent be served with a summons as provided for in G.S. 7B-1106. *In re M.M.*, 200 N.C. App. 248, 255 (2009) (determining DSS was not required to amend petition when the parent was identified as a result of the hearing required by G.S. 7B-1105; holding the amended petition, which the appellate court referred to as "no more than a supplemental pleading" clarifying that respondent was the biological father, did not constitute the filing of a new action; rejecting respondent's argument that the judicial determination of his paternity between the filing of the original and amended petitions precluded termination of his parental rights under G.S. 7B-1111(a)(5) for failure to establish paternity).

> **Practice Note:** Although rare, it is possible that respondent mother's identity will be unknown. For example, a mother may safely surrender her infant without disclosing her identity. *See* G.S. 7B-500 (further discussed in Chapter 5.5.B.3).

B. **Service on Unknown Parent**

   1. **No summons required.** No summons shall be required for a parent whose name or identity is unknown and who is served by publication as provided in this section. G.S. 7B-1105(g); *see* S.L. 2018-68 (effective October 1, 2018).

   2. **Publication.** When the court orders that an unknown parent be served by publication, notice must be published in a newspaper qualified for legal advertising under G.S. 1-597 and 1-598 and published weekly, for three successive weeks, in locations specified by the court. After service, a publisher's affidavit must be filed with the court. G.S. 7B-1105(d).

   The published notice must

   - be directed to the mother, father, mother and father of (male) (female) child born at a specified time and place;
   - designate the court, docket number, and name of the case (at the direction of the court, "In re Doe" may be substituted);
   - state that a petition seeking to terminate the parental rights of the respondent has been filed;
   - direct the respondent to answer the petition within thirty days after the specified date of

first publication; (Note that this time period differs from N.C. R. CIV. P. 4(j1), which provides for forty days from the date of first publication of the notice for the defendant to respond.)
- follow the form set out in Rule 4(j1) of the Rules of Civil Procedure; and
- state that parental rights will be terminated if no answer is filed within the time period.

G.S. 7B-1105(d).

> **Practice Note:** In cases involving service by publication on known parents, the court of appeals has said that a notice of publication not only must comply with Rule 4(j1) but also must comply with the requirements for a summons under G.S. 7B-1106. *In re C.A.C.*, 222 N.C. App. 687 (2012); *In re Joseph Children*, 122 N.C. App. 468 (1996) (decided under prior law) (stating that notice of publication must include information related to the respondent's right to counsel since this is required in the summons). It is unclear if these holdings apply to service by publication on an unknown parent. Neither opinion addressed the specific publication notice requirements for an unknown parent set forth in G.S. 7B-1105. Additionally, both these opinions were decided before G.S. 7B-1105(g) was enacted, stating no summons is required for an unknown parent who is served by publication.

For more detail on service by publication, see Chapter 4.4.B.2.

**3. Failure of unknown parent to answer.** If an unknown parent served by publication does not answer within the prescribed time, the court must issue an order terminating the parent's rights. G.S. 7B-1105(f). However, the court of appeals has said that the trial court is never required to terminate parental rights and that default proceedings are not permitted. *See Bost v. Van Nortwick*, 117 N.C. App. 1 (1994); *In re Tyner*, 106 N.C. App. 480 (1992); *see also* G.S. 7B-1110(b) (stating that even if grounds exist, the court may determine that the best interests of the child require that rights not be terminated). See also sections 9.8, below (answers and responses), and 9.12 (best interests).

## 9.7 Summons and Notice

### A. Introduction

Because a TPR may be initiated by a petition or by a motion in an existing abuse, neglect, or dependency proceeding, the Juvenile Code has two different provisions addressing the manner in which a respondent parent is informed of the TPR action. In proceedings initiated by petition, a summons to the parent is required. In proceedings initiated by motion, a specific form of notice is required. The requirements for the summons and the notice are similar but not identical.

**AOC Forms:**
- AOC-J-208, Summons in Proceeding for Termination of Parental Rights (March 2012).
- AOC-J-210, Notice of Motion Seeking Termination of Parental Rights (Sept. 2009).

## B. Summons for Proceeding Initiated by Petition

**1. Those entitled to summons.** When a petition is filed, a summons must be issued and directed to the following persons or agencies who must be named as respondents (note exceptions for the petitioner and as provided for in the case of an unknown parent):

**(a) Parents.** A summons must be directed to the child's parents, except any parent who has irrevocably relinquished the child to a county DSS or licensed child-placing agency for adoption or consented to adoption of the child by the petitioner. G.S. 7B-1106(a)(1).

A copy of all pleadings and other papers that are required to be served on the parent must also be served on a parent's attorney appointed in an underlying abuse, neglect, or dependency action when that attorney has not been relieved of responsibilities. Service on the attorney is pursuant to Rule 5 of the Rules of Civil Procedure. G.S. 7B-1106(a2).

**(b) Custodian or guardian.** A summons must be directed to any judicially-appointed custodian or guardian of the person of the child. G.S. 7B-1106(a)(2) and (3).

**(c) DSS or child-placing agency.** A summons must be directed to any county DSS or licensed child-placing agency to whom a parent has relinquished the child for adoption under G.S. Chapter 48 and to any county DSS to whom a court of competent jurisdiction has given placement responsibility for the child. G.S. 7B-1106(a)(4).

**2. Child and GAL.** No summons is directed to the child or the child's guardian ad litem (GAL). However, if the child has a GAL appointed under G.S. 7B-601 or the court appoints a GAL after the TPR petition is filed, a copy of all pleadings and other papers required to be served must be served on the GAL or the attorney advocate pursuant to Rule 5 of the Rules of Civil Procedure. G.S. 7B-1106(a1).

**3. Contents of summons.** The summons must include the following:

**(a) Child's name.** The child's name must be on the summons. G.S. 7B-1106(b)(1).

**(b) Notice.** The summons must give notice

- that a written answer must be filed within thirty days after service of the summons and petition or the parent's rights may be terminated;
- that any counsel appointed previously and still representing the parent in an abuse, neglect, or dependency proceeding will continue to represent the parent unless the court orders otherwise;
- that if the parent is indigent and not already represented by appointed counsel, the parent is entitled to appointed counsel, that provisional counsel has been appointed

(and is identified on the summons or an attachment), and the court will review the appointment of provisional counsel at the first hearing after the parent is served;
- that after an answer is filed, or thirty days from the date of service if no answer is filed, the petitioner will mail a notice of the date, time, and place of any pretrial hearing and the hearing on the petition;
- that the purpose of the hearing is to determine whether the parent's rights in relation to the child will be terminated; and
- that the parent may attend the termination hearing (see Chapter 2.4.B.2 (discussing cases holding that parent does not have an absolute right to be present at a termination hearing)).

G.S. 7B-1106(b).

**4. Service of summons.** The summons must be served pursuant to Rule 4 of the Rules of Civil Procedure. However, when service by publication is made, G.S. 7B-1106(a) requires an additional step to Rule 4(j1) that involves court action. Before service by publication, the court must make findings of fact that a respondent cannot otherwise be served despite diligent efforts made by petitioner for personal service, and the court must approve the form of the notice before it is published. G.S. 7B-1106(a); *see* S.L. 2017-161, sec. 11 (effective October 1, 2017).

A minor parent is not deemed to be under a disability regarding service. G.S. 7B-1106(a); *see* G.S. 7B-1102(a). However, G.S. 7B-1101.1(b) requires the appointment of a Rule 17 guardian ad litem for any respondent parent under age eighteen who is not married or otherwise emancipated (as discussed in section 9.4.B.1, above). The GAL appointment for the respondent parent is in addition to the appointment of an attorney. G.S. 7B-1101.1(b), (d).

See Chapter 4.4.B for detailed discussion of service of a summons.

**5. Problems with summons.** Failure to issue a summons, or defects or irregularities in the summons or in service of process, relate to personal, not subject matter, jurisdiction and can be waived. *In re K.J.L.,* 363 N.C. 343 (2009). *Cf. In re P.D.,* 803 S.E.2d 667 (N.C. Ct. App. 2017) (unpublished) (applying to out-of-state respondent parent and application of G.S. 7B-1101, discussed in section 9.2.A, above). If not waived, however, these may be grounds for dismissal if the issue raised is a fatal jurisdictional defect as opposed to an irregularity that may be corrected or is not fatally defective. *See, e.g., Hazelwood v. Bailey,* 339 N.C. 578 (1995) (holding defect in summons of listing incorrect county was voidable rather than void and was a nonjurisdictional correctable defect; discussing other cases on the issue).

See Chapters 3.4 (discussing personal jurisdiction, including the manner in which it may be waived); 4.3.B (relating to expiration of the summons and subsequent summonses); and 4.4 (relating to service).

## C. Notice for Proceeding Initiated by Motion in the Cause

**1. Notice required.** Upon filing a motion for termination of parental rights (TPR), the movant must prepare and serve a notice along with the motion. G.S. 7B-1106.1(a). This is not a mere notice of hearing but is a statutorily prescribed notice that resembles a summons. Issuance of a summons is neither necessary nor appropriate when the TPR is initiated by motion. *In re D.R.S.*, 181 N.C. App. 136 (2007).

**2. Those entitled to notice.** The notice must be directed to and served on each of the following who is not a movant:

(a) **Parents.** The child's parents must be given notice unless the parent has irrevocably relinquished the child to a county DSS or licensed child-placing agency for adoption or consented to adoption of the child by the movant. G.S. 7B-1106.1(a)(1).

A copy of all pleadings and other papers that are required to be served on the parent must also be served on a parent's attorney appointed in an underlying abuse, neglect, or dependency action when that attorney has not been relieved of responsibilities. Service on the attorney is pursuant to Rule 5 of the Rules of Civil Procedure. G.S. 7B-1102(b), (b1); *see* G.S. 7B-1106(a2).

(b) **Custodian or guardian.** Any judicially-appointed custodian or guardian of the person of the child must be given notice. G.S. 7B-1106.1(a)(2) and (3).

(c) **DSS or child-placing agency.** Any county DSS or licensed child-placing agency to whom the parent has relinquished the child for adoption under G.S. Chapter 48 and to any county DSS to whom a court of competent jurisdiction has given placement responsibility for the child must be given notice. G.S. 7B-1106.1(a)(4).

(d) **GAL or attorney advocate.** The child's GAL or attorney advocate, who has been appointed under G.S. 7B-601 and not relieved of responsibility, must be given notice. G.S. 7B-1106.1(a)(5).

**3. Contents of notice.** The notice must include the child's name and notice of the following:

- that a written response must be filed within thirty days after service of the motion and notice or the parent's rights may be terminated;
- that any counsel appointed previously and still representing the parent in an abuse, neglect, or dependency proceeding will continue to represent the parent unless the court orders otherwise;
- that the parent, if indigent, is entitled to appointed counsel and, if not already represented by appointed counsel, may contact the clerk immediately to request counsel;
- that when a response is filed, or thirty days from the date of service if no response is filed, the moving party will mail notice of the date, time, and place of any pretrial hearing and the hearing on the motion;
- that the purpose of the hearing is to determine whether the parent's rights in relation to the child will be terminated; and

- that the parent may attend the termination hearing (see Chapter 2.4.B.2 (discussing cases holding that parent does not have an absolute right to be present at a termination hearing)).

G.S. 7B-1106.1(b).

**4. Service of motion and notice.** When a motion for termination of parental rights (TPR) is filed in a pending abuse, neglect, or dependency proceeding, service of the motion and notice generally is pursuant to Rule 5(b); however, G.S. 7B-1102(b) specifies four circumstances in which service must be pursuant to Rule 4.

**(a) When Rule 4 service is required.** The motion and notice must be served pursuant to Rule 4 of the Rules of Civil Procedure if

- the person or agency to be served was not served originally with a summons;
- the person to be served was served originally by publication that did not include notice substantially in conformity with G.S. 7B-406(b)(4)e. (that after proper notice and a hearing an order in the case may terminate respondent's parental rights);
- a period of two years has elapsed since the date of the original action; or
- the court orders that service be made pursuant to Rule 4.

G.S. 7B-1102(b); 7B-1106.1(a).

**Practice Note:** These factors do not affect whether a TPR can be initiated by motion. They relate only to the method by which a motion and notice must be served.

**(b) When Rule 5(b) service is appropriate.** The motion and notice may be served pursuant to Rule 5(b) of the Rules of Civil Procedure, except in the circumstances explained above where service pursuant to Rule 4 is required. G.S. 7B-1106.1(a) (service of the motion and notice shall be as provided in G.S. 7B-1102(b)); 7B-1102(b). Rule 5 requires that service be made on a party's attorney of record if there is one. Service directly on the party is required only if ordered by the court or if the party has no attorney of record. When a party has an attorney of record, service only on the party is not sufficient; the party's attorney must be served. N.C. R. CIV. P. 5(b). See Chapter 4.4.C for additional information related to service of motions and notice under Rule 5 of the Rules of Civil Procedure.

- Respondents' contention that more than two years had passed since initiation of the proceeding, thus triggering a requirement for service pursuant to Rule 4, was not supported by the record. Service of the motion and notice pursuant to Rule 5 was proper. *In re H.T.*, 180 N.C. App. 611 (2006).
- Because Rule 5 service was permissible, service on respondent's attorney was proper. *In re H.T.*, 180 N.C. App. 611 (decided under an earlier version of Rule 5 that allowed service on either the party or the attorney).
- Service pursuant to Rule 5 was proper when the motion was filed within two years after filing of the most recent neglect petition. *In re P.L.P.*, 173 N.C. App. 1 (2005), *aff'd per curiam*, 360 N.C. 360 (2006).

**(c) Minor parent not under disability.** A minor parent is not deemed to be under a disability regarding service. G.S. 7B-1102(a); 7B-1106(a). However, G.S. 7B-1101.1(b) requires the appointment of a Rule 17 guardian ad litem for any respondent parent under age eighteen who is not married or otherwise emancipated in addition to the appointment of an attorney. *See* G.S. 7B-1106(a2) (Rule 5 service on attorney appointed to respondent parent in an underlying abuse, neglect, or dependency proceeding who has not been relieved).

**5. Problems with notice.** Problems with notice do not affect subject matter jurisdiction. *See In re C.S.B.*, 194 N.C. App. 195 (2008). Failure to comply with the notice requirement may constitute reversible error, however. *See In re D.A.*, 169 N.C. App. 245 (2005) (holding that where respondent objected to some aspects of the notice, the issue was preserved for appeal and failure to give proper notice was prejudicial error); *In re Alexander*, 158 N.C. App. 522 (2003) (holding that failure to give the respondent notice that complied with G.S. 7B-1106.1 was prejudicial error). The respondent waives any defect in the notice or service of the notice by failing to make a timely objection. *See In re C.S.B,* 194 N.C. App. 195; *In re J.S.L.*, 177 N.C. App. 151 (2006); *In re Howell*, 161 N.C. App. 650 (2003).

## 9.8 Answer or Response

Any respondent may file an answer to a termination of parental rights (TPR) petition or written response to a motion. G.S. 7B-1108(a). The answer or response must be filed within thirty days after service of the summons and petition or motion (or within the time determined by Rule 4(j1) if service is by publication). *See* G.S. 7B-1106(b)(2); 7B-1106.1(b)(2); 7B-1107. Only a district court judge may grant an extension of time in which to file an answer or response. G.S. 7B-1108(a).

If a county DSS that is not the petitioner or movant is served with a TPR petition or motion, DSS must file a written answer or response and is deemed a party to the proceeding. G.S. 7B-1106(c); 7B-1106.1(c).

A respondent's answer to a petition or response to a motion must admit or deny the allegations and provide the name and address of the respondent or respondent's attorney. G.S. 7B-1108(a). Denial of any material allegation triggers the requirement that a guardian ad litem (GAL) be appointed for the child if one is not already in place. G.S. 7B-1108(b). See section 9.4.C, above (discussing appointment of a GAL in TPR proceedings), and Chapter 2.3.D (discussing the child's GAL).

Regardless of whether the respondent files an answer or response, and regardless of whether the respondent admits or denies allegations in the petition or motion, the court must hold a TPR hearing. When the respondent does not file an answer or response, the court at the hearing may examine the petitioner or movant or others on facts alleged in the petition or motion and may issue an order terminating the respondent's parental rights. *See* G.S. 7B-1107. Absence of an answer denying material allegations of the petition does not authorize a "default type" order terminating parental rights, since the statute requires a hearing on the petition. *In re Tyner*, 106 N.C. App. 480 (1992).

The parent's failure to file an answer or response or to ask for counsel before the hearing does not constitute waiver of the right to counsel (*Little v. Little*, 127 N.C. App. 191 (1997)), nor does it remove the court's responsibility under G.S. 7B-1109(b) to inquire at the adjudicatory hearing about and potentially appoint counsel for the parent. See section 9.4.A, above.

## 9.9 Pretrial and Adjudication Hearing Requirements

### A. Pretrial Hearing

**1. Timing.** Unless all respondents have filed answers or responses, the pretrial hearing should be held only after the time for filing an answer or response has run.

**2. May be combined with adjudication hearing.** The court must conduct a pretrial hearing in every termination of parental rights case but may combine the pretrial and adjudicatory hearings. If the pretrial and adjudicatory hearings are combined, no separate order is required for the pretrial hearing. G.S. 7B-1108.1(a).

**3. Notice.** Written notice of the pretrial hearing is required. The notice must include the date, time, and place of the hearing and be mailed by the petitioner or movant to the respondent after an answer or written response has been filed or if there is no answer or response, thirty days after service of the summons or notice. *See* G.S. 7B-1106(c); 7B-1106.1(c); 7B-1108.1(b).

**4. Required considerations.** At a pretrial hearing the court must consider the following:

- retention or release of provisional counsel;
- whether a guardian ad litem for the juvenile should be appointed if not already appointed;
- sufficiency of the summons, service, and notice;
- any pretrial motions;
- issues, including any affirmative defense, raised by an answer or response;
- any other issue that can be addressed properly as a preliminary matter.

G.S. 7B-1108.1(a).

### B. Adjudication Hearing

**1. Timing.** A hearing on a termination of parental rights (TPR) petition or motion must be held within ninety days after the petition or motion is filed unless the court orders that it be held at a later time. G.S. 7B-1109(a).

(a) **Continuance.** For good cause, the court may continue an adjudication hearing up to ninety days from the date of the initial petition (or motion) to receive additional evidence, allow parties to conduct expeditious discovery, or to receive any other information needed in the best interests of the child. The court may grant a continuance that extends beyond that ninety-day period only in extraordinary circumstances, when necessary for the proper administration of justice, and must issue a written order stating grounds for the continuance. G.S. 7B-1109(d). Granting or denying a motion for a continuance is in the trial court's discretion and is reviewed for an abuse of discretion. However, motions to continue based on a constitutional right present a question of law and are fully reviewable on appeal. *In re C.M.P.*, 254 N.C. App. 647 (2017).

Continuances are generally disfavored, and the burden is on the party seeking the continuance to show the statutory criteria for the continuance is satisfied. *In re C.D.A.W.*, 175 N.C. App. 680 (2006). See subsection 5(b), below, and Chapter 4.5.C (discussing continuances in TPR proceedings in greater detail).

**(b) Delay and prejudice.** After the supreme court's holding that mandamus is the appropriate means to address a trial court's failure to enter an order within the statutory thirty-day time period (*see In re T.H.T.*, 362 N.C. 446 (2008)), the court of appeals reached the same conclusion with respect to delay in holding a hearing. *In re E.K.*, 202 N.C. App. 309 (2010) (refusing to find reversible error but acknowledging that delays in the case were "deplorable"). Note that prior to *In re T.H.T.*, numerous appellate cases had held that failure to comply with the statutory time requirements could be reversible error, but only if an appellant showed prejudice resulting from the delay. See Chapter 12.10.D for required elements for seeking mandamus.

**2. General procedures.** The Juvenile Code sets out most procedural aspects of the adjudicatory hearing, but where it does not, case law and the Rules of Civil Procedure provide additional requirements and/or guidance.

**(a) Bench trial.** The adjudicatory hearing is before a judge, without a jury. G.S. 7B-1109(a). There is no constitutional right to a jury trial in termination of parental rights (TPR) proceedings. *In re Clark*, 303 N.C. 592 (1981); *In re Ferguson*, 50 N.C. App. 681 (1981).

The fact that a judge acquires knowledge of evidentiary facts from an earlier proceeding does not require the judge to be disqualified from presiding over a TPR hearing. *In re Z.V.A.*, 835 S.E.2d 425 (N.C. S.Ct. 2019) (judge's statement at an earlier proceeding did not disqualify the judge from hearing a later TPR proceeding; the statement, when viewed in the context of the child's permanent plan having been changed to adoption and DSS having been ordered to file a TPR petition at the earlier hearing, was an explanation of the steps previously taken after determining those actions were in the child's best interest at the time); *In re M.A.I.B.K.*, 184 N.C. App. 218 (2007) (holding that the judge who presided over action to terminate one parent's rights was not precluded from presiding over later hearing to terminate other parent's rights); *In re Faircloth*, 153 N.C. App. 565 (2002); *In re LaRue*, 113 N.C. App. 807 (1994) (holding that the fact that judge conducted review, found that children should remain with DSS, and recommended that TPR be pursued was not sufficient to show bias). See Chapter 2.1.B.1 (discussing recusal).

**(b) Consolidation with underlying case.** When a TPR proceeding is initiated by petition in the same judicial district in which there is pending an abuse, neglect, or dependency proceeding involving the same child, the court on its own motion or motion of a party may consolidate the actions pursuant to Rule 42 of the Rules of Civil Procedure. G.S. 7B-1102(c). Court orders resulting from consolidated hearings should sufficiently separate the matters considered in the different proceedings. *See In re R.B.B.*, 187 N.C. App. 639 (2007).

**(c) Combined adjudication and disposition.** The TPR proceeding has two phases: the adjudication phase and the disposition phase. *In re D.L.W.*, 368 N.C. 835 (2016). Although different evidentiary standards apply at the adjudicatory phase, which determines whether a statutory ground for termination of parental rights exists and is governed by G.S. 7B-1109, and the dispositional phase, which determines whether termination of the parent's rights is in the child's best interest and is governed by G.S. 7B-1110, it is not necessary for the two phases to be conducted at two separate hearings. *In re F.G.J.*, 200 N.C. App. 681 (2009); *In re Carr,* 116 N.C. App. 403 (1994). However, to ensure that a parent's constitutional rights to his or her child are not violated by an order to terminate parental rights based solely on the child's best interest, the court must conduct two separate inquiries, even though the two inquiries may be conducted in the same hearing. *In re S.Z.H.,* 247 N.C. App. 254 (2016).

**(d) Reporting.** The hearing is reported as provided for in civil trials. G.S. 7B-1109(a); 7A-198. Current practice statewide is to use electronic recording.

If equipment fails to function, the record must be reconstructed. To show prejudicial error from an equipment failure, a party must show (1) prejudice from the loss of specific testimony and (2) what the content of any gaps or lost testimony was. *In re Caldwell*, 75 N.C. App. 299 (1985). *See also In re Clark*, 159 N.C. App. 75 (2003). The fact that a recording is incomplete or unintelligible, by itself, is not a ground for reversal. There is a presumption of regularity in a trial, and the appellant must make a specific showing of probable error during the faulty or missing part of the recording. *In re Howell*, 161 N.C. App. 650 (2003); *In re Bradshaw*, 160 N.C. App. 677 (2003) (noting that the respondent took no steps to reconstruct the record and alleged only general prejudice).

**3. Counsel for parents.** The court must inquire whether parents are present and, if so, whether they are represented by counsel or desire counsel. If a parent appears, is not represented, has not waived counsel, desires counsel, and is indigent, the court must appoint counsel for the parent, according to the rules of the Office of Indigent Defense Services, and grant an extension of time to permit counsel to prepare. *See* G.S. 7B-1109(b); 7B-1101.1(a), (a1). See section 9.4.A, above, and Chapter 2.4.D (providing additional details and cases related to appointment of counsel).

**4. Examination of child or parent.** The court, upon finding reasonable cause, may order that the child be examined by a psychiatrist, a licensed clinical psychologist, physician, a public or private agency, or other expert, to ascertain the child's psychological or physical condition or needs. The court may order a parent similarly examined if the parent's ability to care for the child is an issue. G.S. 7B-1109(c).

**5. Presence of parent.** A parent has a right to attend all hearings in a proceeding to terminate that parent's rights. The court of appeals has held that this right is not absolute; however, "the magnitude of 'the private interests affected by the [termination] proceeding, clearly weighs in favor of a parent's presence at the hearing.'" *In re S.G.V.S.*, 811 S.E.2d 718, 721 (N.C. Ct. App. 2018) (reversing and remanding for new hearing; holding denial of mother's continuance request and motion to reopen the evidence when mother was previously scheduled to appear in a criminal action in another county at the same time as the later scheduled TPR hearing involved a misapprehension of law and substantial miscarriage of justice).

In very limited circumstances the court can proceed in the absence of a parent who wants to be present. The most common circumstance involves parents who are incarcerated. The court must take steps to ensure that the absent respondent's due process rights are protected. *See In re Murphy*, 105 N.C. App. 651 (denial of respondent's motion to be brought to the hearing from a state correctional facility did not violate respondent's state statutory rights or his state or federal due process rights), *aff'd per curiam*, 332 N.C. 663 (1992).

For more detailed information on this topic, see Chapter 2.4.B, discussing the parent's right to notice and opportunity to be heard, including the right to participate and limitations on that right.

---

**Resource**: For the North Carolina Department of Public Safety Policy and Procedures related to inmate access to the courts and to their attorneys, see Chapter G, Section .0200 "Court Related Procedures" (Jan. 16, 2018).

---

(a) **Modified setting for testimony by child.** The trial court can modify the setting in which the child testifies. The court may allow the child to testify outside the presence of the parent, but the court must make appropriate findings as to the need for doing so and must utilize appropriate procedures. *See In re J.B.*, 172 N.C. App. 1 (2005) (holding that respondent's due process rights were not violated when the court excluded her from the courtroom during the child's testimony, where respondent was in a room with her guardian ad litem, could hear the proceedings, and had a video monitor and telephone contact with her attorney); *In re Williams*, 149 N.C. App. 951 (2002) (holding that the trial court did not err in allowing the child to testify in closed chambers without the father present because all attorneys were allowed to be present and the court made findings about this type of setting being in the child's best interest). For a more detailed discussion of modified settings for testimony, see Chapter 11.2.B.1.

(b) **Continuance and failure of parent to appear.** Note that the court of appeals has looked to both G.S. 7B-803 and 7B-1109(d) when determining whether a court acted properly in continuing (or denying a motion to continue) a termination of parental rights (TPR) hearing.

Appellate cases have acknowledged the trial court's discretion to determine whether to hold a TPR hearing when the parent is not present or continue the hearing to secure the parent's presence. The court has discretion to proceed with the hearing, however, only if the respondent has been properly notified. *See In re K.N.*, 181 N.C. App. 736 (2007) (reversing a TPR order where the respondent entered courtroom shortly after the hearing and rebutted the presumption of proper service).

Whether to grant a continuance is in the trial court's discretion. When deciding a motion to continue, the court's main consideration is whether substantial justice will be furthered by granting or denying the motion. *In re C.D.A.W.*, 175 N.C. App. 680 (2006) (denying the motion for a continuance was not error where the respondent chose to attend a drug treatment program rather than attend the hearing after repeatedly rejecting earlier opportunities to undergo drug rehabilitation), *aff'd per curiam*, 361 N.C. 232 (2007).

A case-by-case analysis has been found more appropriate than the application of rigid rules. *In re D.W.*, 202 N.C. App. 624 (2002) (denial of absent mother's motion to continue was an abuse of discretion).

- When absent respondent's motion to continue was not based on a constitutional right and where the trial court conducted a full hearing on the petition, heard testimony, and allowed respondent's counsel to cross-examine each witness and to otherwise fully participate in the hearing, respondent was not prejudiced by denial of a motion to continue. *In re C.M.P.*, 254 N.C. App. 647 (2017) (respondent had notice of the hearing and indicated to counsel that she would attend, failed to give counsel or the court notice of or a reason for her absence, and counsel did not argue that more time was needed to prepare).
- In a private TPR case in which the respondent father knew about the hearing but failed to appear, the trial court did not abuse its discretion in denying an oral motion to continue that was made by the father's attorney at the start of the hearing. Also, after learning in the middle of the hearing that the father could be present the next day, it was not an abuse of discretion for the trial court to allow direct examination of the petitioner's witness with the father's counsel present but continue the hearing until the next afternoon so that the respondent father could be present for cross examination of that witness and the remainder of the hearing. *In re C.J.H.*, 240 N.C. App 489 (2015).

The court of appeals has addressed a respondent parent's failure to appear for a TPR hearing in the context of a Rule 60(b) motion based on "excusable neglect." Excusable neglect is a question of law that is fully reviewable on appeal and depends on what may be reasonably expected of a party in paying proper attention to his or her case given all the surrounding circumstances. *Mitchell County Dep't of Soc. Servs. v. Carpenter,* 127 N.C. App. 353 (1997), *aff'd per curiam*, 347 N.C. 569 (1998). In two cases, the court of appeals held the respondents' failure to appear for the TPR hearing was not excusable neglect given the receipt of proper notice of the hearing and the failure to act prudently. *See In re Hall*, 89 N.C. App. 685 (1988) (holding no excusable neglect when respondent, after being served with the summons, failed to give her defense the attention a person of ordinary prudence would give important business; noting her poor financial situation does not account for her failure to call or write court authorities (including legal counsel) or DSS for assistance or to appear for the hearing because she was worrying about finding work; ignorance of the judicial process is not excusable neglect); *Mitchell County Dep't of*

*Soc. Servs. v. Carpenter*, 127 N.C. App. 353 (holding trial court did not abuse its discretion in denying Rule 60(b) motion as respondent paying proper attention to her case would have made transportation arrangements sooner or would have contacted her attorney when she discovered her transportation was not available; noting the record did not show her husband assured her he would transport her, lulling her into missing her court date when he refused to transport her), *aff'd per curiam*, 347 N.C. 569.

## 9.10 Evidence and Proof

Evidentiary issues are discussed in greater detail in Chapter 11.

### A. Evidentiary Requirements and Standards

At the adjudicatory hearing, the court must take evidence, find the facts, and adjudicate the existence or nonexistence of any alleged ground(s) for termination of parental rights (TPR). G.S. 7B-1109(e). The rules of evidence in civil cases apply. G.S. 7B-1109(f). The standard of proof is clear, cogent, and convincing evidence, and the burden of proof is on the petitioner or movant. G.S. 7B-1109(f); 7B-1111(b). *See In re N.D.A.*, 833 S.E.2d 768 (N.C. S.Ct. 2019); *In re Pierce*, 356 N.C. 68 (2002); *In re Young*, 346 N.C. 244 (1997). There is no distinction between "clear, cogent and convincing" and "clear and convincing" evidence. *In re Belk*, 364 N.C. 114, 122 (2010); *In re Montgomery*, 311 N.C. 101, 109 (1984) ("clear and convincing" and "clear, cogent and convincing" describe the same evidentiary standard). Clear and convincing evidence is "stricter than a preponderance of the evidence, but less stringent than proof beyond a reasonable doubt and requires evidence which should fully convince." *In re H.N.D.*, 827 S.E.2d 329, 332 (N.C. Ct. App. 2019) (quoting *In re Mills*, 152 N.C. App. 1, 13 (2002)).

At disposition, on the other hand, there is no burden of proof on any party, and the court exercises its discretion, based on findings supported by the evidence, to determine whether TPR is in the child's best interest. *See* G.S. 7B-1110(a); *In re C.W.*, 182 N.C. App. 214 (2007). See also section 9.12.B, below (discussing the evidentiary standard at disposition).

A court's TPR order cannot be based solely on documentary evidence. In the case of *In re A.M.*, 192 N.C. App. 538 (2008), the court of appeals looked to G.S. 7B-1109(e), requiring the trial court to "take evidence" in conjunction with the purpose of the Juvenile Code (G.S. 7B-100(1), (2)), to determine that Rule 43(a) of the Rules of Civil Procedure was applicable to TPR proceedings. Rule 43(a) requires that "[i]n all trials the testimony of witnesses shall be taken orally in open court." Therefore, the petitioner was required to present some live testimony (even if minimal), and the court could not terminate parental rights based solely on documentary evidence (prior court orders and DSS and GAL reports). *See also In re N.B.*, 195 N.C. App. 113 (2009) (holding that DSS's case in chief consisting solely of the DSS social worker's report and statements by counsel and the testimony by only the respondent mother, which refuted DSS's allegations, was insufficient since DSS, as petitioner, carried the burden to prove the grounds of neglect or dependency; there was no testimony to support its assertion that parental rights should be terminated). The court of appeals has also held that summary judgment is not available in a TPR because of the requirement of G.S. 7B-1109(e) that the court "take evidence." *In re J.N.S.*, 165 N.C. App. 536 (2004).

While a party may stipulate to facts from which the court can make conclusions, parties may not stipulate to a conclusion of law such as the conclusion that grounds for termination exist. *See In re A.K.D.*, 227 N.C. App. 58 (2013) (holding in a private TPR case that the father's stipulation to the abandonment ground was invalid). See Chapters 6.3.C.1 (relating to stipulations for an adjudication in abuse, neglect, or dependency proceeding) and 11.7.D.5 (relating to stipulations made in prior proceedings).

The court may not rely on a consent order (or agreement between the parties) that a TPR will not be opposed as proof of an adjudicatory ground and the child's best interests determination. Such an agreement is both void as against public policy and avoids the judicial process that requires a determination of whether a ground to TPR exists and whether the TPR is in the child's best interests. *In re C.K.C.*, 822 S.E.2d 741, 745 (N.C. Ct. App. 2018) (reversing TPR; holding consent order in Chapter 50 civil custody action between father and grandparents that included a provision that grandmother would file a petition to terminate father's rights, which no other party, including father, would oppose is void as against public policy and is neither a properly executed consent or relinquishment under the adoption statutes (quoting *Foy v. Foy*, 57 N.C. App. 128, 131 (1982) ("In essence, the parental rights of a parent in his child are not to be bartered away at the parent's whim."))).

### B. Events between Filing of Petition or Motion and Hearing

An evidentiary issue that arises in termination of parental rights (TPR) proceedings is the significance of events that occur between the time the TPR petition or motion is filed and the time of the TPR hearing. Several TPR grounds refer to a specified period of time immediately preceding the filing of the TPR petition or motion, and when adjudicating those grounds, the court is limited to considering that specific time period. *See* G.S. 7B-1111(a)(3), (4), (5), (7). Note, however, that relevant evidence of events occurring after the filing of the petition or motion is admissible at the disposition stage when determining whether TPR is in the child's best interests. *In re Pierce*, 356 N.C. 68 (2002); *In re J.A.O.*, 166 N.C. App. 222 (2004).

In cases involving the abuse and neglect ground in G.S. 7B-1111(a)(1), the appellate courts have regularly referred to the determination of "whether [abuse or] neglect authorizing the termination of parental rights existed at the time of the hearing." *In re J.W.*, 173 N.C. App. 450, 455 (2005), *aff'd per curiam*, 360 N.C. 361 (2006). *See also In re D.L.W.*, 368 N.C. 835, 843 (2016) (termination of rights on this ground "requires a showing of neglect at the time of termination hearing"); *In re M.P.M.*, 243 N.C. App. 41, 48 (2015) (finding of neglect for purpose of terminating parental rights "must be based on evidence showing neglect at the time of the termination proceeding"), *aff'd per curiam*, 368 N.C. 704 (2016); See also section 9.11.A, below (discussing abuse and neglect grounds for TPR). When current neglect or abuse cannot be shown because the parent and child have been separated for a long period of time, the court must determine whether there is past neglect or abuse and a probability of a repetition of abuse or neglect in light of the fitness of the parent to care for the child at the time of the TPR proceeding. *See In re Z.V.A.*, 835 S.E.2d 425 (N.C. S.Ct. 2019) and *In re*

*Ballard*, 311 N.C. 708 (1984) (both relating to neglect); *Alleghany County Dep't of Soc. Servs. v. Reber*, 75 N.C. App. 467 (1985) (relating to abuse), *aff'd per curiam*, 315 N.C. 382 (1986). See section 9.11.A.4 and 5, below (discussing time periods).

When TPR is sought on the basis of willfully leaving the child in foster care or placement outside the home for more than twelve months without making reasonable progress to correct conditions that led to the child's removal pursuant to G.S. 7B-1111(a)(2), the court may consider evidence relating to the *parent's progress* up to the time of the hearing. *In re A.B.*, 253 N.C. App. 29 (2017) (holding the period for evaluating the nature and extent of a parent's reasonable progress extends up to the TPR hearing). *See In re Pierce*, 356 N.C. 68, 75 n.1 (2002) (decided on an earlier wording of the statute that included a second twelve-month period where the parent must make progress, but noting that under a 2001 amendment that removed that second twelve-month time period, "there is no specified time frame that limits the admission of relevant evidence pertaining to a parent's 'reasonable progress' or lack thereof"); *In re C.L.C.*, 171 N.C. App. 438, 447 (2005) (noting that after deletion of the second-twelve month period in G.S. 7B-1111(a)(2) "[t]he focus is no longer solely on the progress made in the 12 months prior to the petition"), *aff'd per curiam*, 360 N.C. 475 (2006). However, the evidence must show that the *child's placement* for more than twelve months resulted from a court order and the twelve months expired before the filing of the TPR petition or motion. *In re A.C.F.*, 176 N.C. App. 520 (2006) (reversing TPR order when the requisite time period had not expired before TPR motion was filed; holding removal began with the first nonsecure custody court order and not the voluntary placement agreement entered into by the parent months earlier). See section 9.11.B.2 and 4, below (discussing time periods).

## C. Events after a TPR Is Denied or Reversed

As explained throughout this Manual, there are multiple court proceedings and hearings that may arise from a family's involvement with DSS. Some cases will involve a termination of parental rights (TPR) action naming one or more respondent parents. The district court must deny a TPR motion or dismiss a TPR petition if it determines that none of the alleged grounds were proved or that the TPR is not in the child's best interests. G.S. 7B-1110(b), (c). In those cases where the TPR is granted, the parent has a right to appeal. G.S. 7B-1001(a1); 7B-1002(4). One possible result of an appeal is a reversal of the TPR decision. A denial of a TPR motion, dismissal of a TPR petition, or reversal on appeal of a TPR order does not automatically preclude the filing of a second TPR action based on the same or other ground.

The law of the case doctrine applies when "a question before an appellate court has previously been answered in an earlier appeal in the same case[.]" *In re S.R.G.*, 200 N.C. App. 594, 597 (2009). The appellate court's answer to the question on appeal becomes the law of the case in subsequent proceedings in the trial court and in a subsequent appeal. *In re S.R.G.*, 200 N.C. App. 594. However, "the law of the case doctrine does not apply when the evidence presented at a subsequent proceeding is different from that presented on a former appeal." *In re K.C.*, 812 S.E.2d 873, 874 (N.C. Ct. App. 2018) (citations omitted) (affirming second TPR based on abandonment, after reversal of first TPR based on abandonment by neglect; the operative facts supporting the ground in the second TPR were based on new events – the six-month period immediately preceding the filing of the second TPR). In *In re K.C.*, the court of appeals recognized that time does not stand still and stated, "the prior opinion of this Court does not mean that respondent is immune from termination of her parental rights based upon abandonment for the rest of the child's minority. . . ." *In re K.C.*, 812 S.E.2d at 874.

The court of appeals also discussed the law of the case as well as res judicata in *In re S.R.G.*, 200 N.C. App. 594 (2009). The court of appeals reversed a second TPR order based on neglect that was entered by the trial court after the first TPR based on abandonment was reversed. The second TPR was entered on remand and was based on the same (first) petition. The court of appeals held that the re-litigation of a ground alleged but not previously determined in the first proceeding was barred and stated, "[a] new [TPR] petition, based on circumstances arising subsequent to the original termination hearing, would have constituted a new action, and would not have been barred by the doctrine of res judicata." *In re S.R.G.*, 200 N.C. App. at 599. *See also In re F.S.*, 835 S.E.2d 465, 471 (N.C. Ct. App. 2019) (stating in a neglect, not a TPR action that "[t]he doctrine of collateral estoppel does not preclude the trial court's adjudication of facts from new allegations and events which transpired after the [previous] adjudication" of neglect that was reversed).

### D. Specific Types of Evidentiary Issues

Chapter 11 discusses in detail the following types of evidentiary issues commonly arising in TPR proceedings:

- judicial notice of earlier proceedings, see Chapter 11.7;
- collateral estoppel and res judicata, see Chapter 11.7.D.2;
- medical, mental health, substance abuse, and other records, see Chapter 11.6.E and F (see also Chapter 14.2–4);
- opinions and expert testimony, see Chapter 11.9–10;
- testimony by children, see Chapter 11.2;
- character and prior acts, see Chapter 11.8;
- privileges, see Chapter 11.11;
- hearsay and hearsay exceptions, including out-of-court statements by children, see Chapter 11.5–6.

## 9.11 Adjudication: Grounds for Termination of Parental Rights

A termination of parental rights (TPR) proceeding consists of two phases: the adjudication phase and the disposition phase. At the first phase – adjudication – the court determines, based on clear, cogent, and convincing evidence, whether a statutory ground to terminate a parent's rights exists. *See In re A.R.A.*, 835 S.E.2d 417 (N.C. S.Ct. 2019); *In re D.L.W.*, 368 N.C. 835 (2016). Clear and convincing evidence is "stricter than a preponderance of the evidence, but less stringent than proof beyond a reasonable doubt and requires evidence which should fully convince." *In re H.N.D.*, 827 S.E.2d 329, 332 (N.C. Ct. App. 2019) (quoting *In re Mills*, 152 N.C. App. 1, 13 (2002)).

The Juvenile Code, at G.S. 7B-1111(a), sets out eleven statutory grounds for terminating parental rights. A finding of any one of the eleven grounds is sufficient to support a TPR order. *In re B.O.A.*, 831 S.E.2d 305 (N.C. S.Ct. 2019); *In re T.N.H.*, 831 S.E.2d 54 (N.C. S.Ct. 2019); *In re E.H.P.*, 831 S.E.2d 49 (N.C. S.Ct. 2019). The grounds for TPR require the court to focus on the parent's individual conduct and make a determination, based on the evidence presented, about the parent's actions as those actions relate to the alleged statutory ground(s) to terminate that parent's rights. *See In re D.T.N.A.*, 250 N.C. App. 582 (2016). The focus on the parent's culpability at the TPR adjudication differs from the focus on the child's status, rather than the parent's culpability, at the abuse, neglect, or dependency adjudication.

### A. Abuse or Neglect

A parent's abuse or neglect of a child within the meaning of G.S. 7B-101 is grounds for termination of that parent's parental rights. G.S. 7B-1111(a)(1).

**1. Definition of abuse or neglect.** Abuse or neglect of the child that is the subject of a TPR proceeding must meet the same statutory definition that would apply in an underlying abuse or neglect proceeding. *See* G.S. 7B-101(1) (definition of "abused juvenile"); 7B-101(15) (definition of "neglected juvenile"). See Chapter 2.3.B.1 and 2 for details on the definitions of abuse and neglect.

The North Carolina Supreme Court has interpreted the ground that a parent has abused or neglected the child to require "a showing of neglect at the time of the termination hearing, or if the child has been separated from the parent for a long period of time, there must be a showing of past neglect and a likelihood of future neglect by the parent." *In re D.L.W.*, 368 N.C. 835, 843 (2016) (citing *In re Ballard*, 311 N.C. 708, 713–15 (1984)).

The court of appeals has recognized that there is a substantive difference between the quantum of proof of neglect required for a TPR and that required for a child's adjudication as neglected and removal of the child from a parent's custody. *In re Evans*, 81 N.C. App. 449 (1986). Parental rights may not be terminated for a risk of neglect based on the risk of future harm to the child. *In re Evans*, 81 N.C. App. 449 (distinguishing required proof for TPR from a child's adjudication as a neglected juvenile in an appeal of an adjudication of a juvenile as neglected); *In re Phifer*, 67 N.C. App. 16 (1984) (holding that the parent's behaviors including abuse of alcohol, without proof of those behaviors having an adverse impact on the child, was insufficient for adjudication of the neglect ground for TPR; discussing threat of harm that might happen at some time in the future is insufficient to support TPR on neglect ground).

**2. Constitutional challenge.** This ground is not unconstitutionally vague. *In re Moore*, 306 N.C. 394 (1982) (decided under an earlier version of the Juvenile Code). The statute does not apply only to the poor and thus violate equal protection. *In re Wright*, 64 N.C. App. 135 (1983) (decided under an earlier version of the Juvenile Code).

**3. Parental culpability.** In an underlying abuse or neglect proceeding the issue is whether the child is an abused or neglected juvenile, and the court is not adjudicating parental culpability. In a TPR proceeding, however, the issue is whether a particular parent abused or neglected the child. A parent's culpability may be found even when the court cannot determine which parent was the perpetrator of the child's abuse or neglect when the court finds that both parents were jointly and individually responsible as the child's sole care providers. *See In re Y.Y.E.T.*, 205 N.C. App. 210 (2010) (affirming TPR on ground of abuse and neglect, based on finding that both parents were responsible for their 4-month-old infant's non-accidental serious injury as one or both parents inflicted the injury and protected each other by refusing to identify the perpetrator, or one caused the injury and the other failed to prevent it; rejecting respondents' argument that an individual must be identified as the perpetrator as against public policy as it would encourage individuals to deny responsibility for and knowledge of harm to a child and interfere with the court's ability to serve the child's best interests).

**4. Past neglect and likelihood of repetition of neglect.** When a child has been separated from his or her parent for a long period of time such that it cannot be shown that a parent is neglecting the child at the time of the termination hearing, the petitioner (or movant) must prove (1) prior neglect of the child by the parent and (2) a likelihood of future neglect of the child by the parent. *In re M.A.W.*, 370 N.C. 149 (2017).

**(a) Past neglect: prior adjudication admissible but not required.** A prior adjudication of abuse or neglect is not a precondition to a TPR proceeding based on those grounds. *See, e.g., In re R.B.B.*, 187 N.C. App. 639 (2007) (a court may find that the parent abused or neglected the child in the TPR adjudicatory hearing without the child having been previously adjudicated abused or neglected); *In re Williamson*, 91 N.C. App. 668 (1988) (holding that an earlier adjudication of dependency was not inconsistent with a finding that the parent neglected the child for purposes of TPR); *In re Z.D.*, 812 S.E.2d 668 (N.C. Ct. App. 2018) (there was no prior adjudication of neglect but the court's finding that respondent mother left son with a woman she had just met earlier that day and did not return to the woman's home to get him supported the trial court's ultimate finding that respondent had previously neglected her son; note the TPR was reversed for insufficient findings to support grounds).

When there is a prior adjudication, evidence of that prior adjudication of abuse or neglect is admissible in a TPR proceeding, but that order alone is unlikely to be sufficient to support a TPR when the parents have been deprived of custody for a significant period of time before the TPR proceeding. *See In re M.A.W.*, 370 N.C. 149 (2017); *In re Ballard*, 311 N.C. 708 (1984). The North Carolina Supreme Court has recognized that a TPR for neglect cannot be based solely on past conditions that no longer exist but also cannot be based on evidence of current neglect when, after a child's adjudication as neglected, the child has been removed from that parent's custody. Instead, the trial court must consider (1) evidence of neglect prior to removal, including a prior adjudication of neglect, (2) evidence of changed circumstances since the prior adjudication, and (3) whether there is a likelihood of future neglect if the child is returned to the parent. *In re M.A.W.*, 370 N.C. 149; *In re D.L.W.*, 368 N.C. 835 (2016); *In re Ballard*, 311 N.C. 708. The trial court considers the parent's circumstances and fitness to care for the child at the time of the termination hearing. *In re Z.V.A.*, 835 S.E.2d 425 (N.C. S.Ct. 2019); *In re Ballard*, 311 N.C. 708.

The supreme court's reasoning also applies to prior abuse. *See Alleghany County Dep't of Soc. Servs. v. Reber*, 75 N.C. App. 467 (1985) (applying reasoning in *In re Ballard* to prior abuse), *aff'd per curiam*, 315 N.C. 382 (1986); *In re Beck*, 109 N.C. App. 539 (1993) (holding that the court did not err in admitting the prior order finding the child to be abused, since the court did not rely solely on that order in finding the child neglected for TPR purposes); *see also In re McMillon*, 143 N.C. App. 402 (2001); *In re Wheeler*, 87 N.C. App. 189 (1987) (holding that a prior adjudication of abuse was collateral estoppel on the question of whether the father had abused the children, the parties were estopped from relitigating that issue, and the court did not rely solely on the prior adjudication in terminating parental rights).

**(b) Likelihood of repetition of neglect.** To predict the probability of a repetition of neglect, the court looks to the historical facts of the case to assess whether there is a substantial risk of future abuse or neglect. *In re M.P.M.*, 243 N.C. App. 41 (2015), *aff'd per curiam*, 368 N.C. 704 (2016). The court must also look to evidence of changed conditions and "the fitness of the parent to care for the child *at the time of the termination proceeding.*" *In re Z.V.A.*, 835 S.E.2d 425, 430 (N.C. S.Ct. 2019) (emphasis in original); *In re Z.D.*, 812 S.E.2d 668, 675 (N.C. Ct. App. 2018) (petitioners' evidence in a private TPR as to mother's conduct primarily occurring at least six months prior to the termination hearing lacked "temporal proximity" and did not support a finding that mother was incapable of providing proper care at the time of the termination hearing and that there was a likelihood of repetition of neglect).

The order must set out the process by which the court reasoned and adjudicated the facts in support of the conclusion that the respondent was likely to neglect the child upon return to respondent's custody. *In re L.L.O.*, 252 N.C. App. 447 (2017). Failure to include the required finding of fact about the probability of the repetition of neglect is not harmless error. *See In re L.L.O.*, 252 N.C. App. 447 (vacating and remanding portion of an order without the required finding when evidence in the record supported, but did not compel, a finding of neglect); *In re E.L.E.*, 243 N.C. App. 301 (2015) (reversal was required when necessary finding as to probability of repetition of neglect was not made even though there was evidence in the record to support a finding).

When there is an underlying abuse, neglect, or dependency case, a parent's failure to make progress in completing a case plan is indicative of a likelihood of future neglect. *In re M.J.S.M.*, 810 S.E.2d 370 (N.C. Ct. App. 2018) (although mother made some progress on her case plan, it was sporadic and inadequate; her lack of significant progress supported court's determination of likelihood of future neglect); *In re C.M.P.*, 254 N.C. App. 647 (2017) (children were removed because of domestic violence (DV), unstable housing and employment, and inappropriate supervision, all of which were addressed in respondent mother's case plan; the finding of a high probability of the repetition of neglect was supported by evidence that during the three years the children had been removed, mother had not completed a DV assessment and had been arrested on assault charges related to another DV incident, mother's employment remained unstable based on a history of losing jobs, and mother had not obtained independent housing; mother's failure to make progress on the case plan was indicative of a likelihood of future neglect).

A parent's substantial compliance with a case plan may constitute evidence of changed conditions at the time of the TPR hearing that could support a determination of a low probability of future neglect. *See In re J.K.C.*, 218 N.C. App. 22 (affirming denial of TPR on ground of neglect; holding that in spite of a prior adjudication of neglect and the father's incarceration, there was not a substantial probability of a repetition of neglect and he had not willfully left the children in foster care without making progress, given his substantial compliance with the DSS case plan, keeping in contact with DSS, completing courses available to him in prison, and sending gifts to the children through his mother); *In re Shermer*, 156 N.C. App. 281 (2003) (holding that the evidence was insufficient to establish that an incarcerated parent abandoned or neglected the children, where the father wrote to and called his sons while in prison and made progress on a case plan after his release; there was no evidence of a likelihood of repetition of prior neglect because the earlier neglect was due solely to the mother's failure to provide proper care and supervision).

However, completion of a case plan does not preclude a court's conclusion that the ground of neglect exists. *See In re M.P.M.*, 243 N.C. App. 41 (2015) (affirming TPR based on neglect; despite complying with his case plan by attending ten therapy sessions and interacting appropriately during supervised visits with his daughter, father had not demonstrated at the time of the TPR hearing that he had learned how to keep daughter safe in the future; conclusion of a likelihood of repetition of neglect was supported by findings about the severity of respondent's and mother's abuse of the child's siblings, respondent's dishonesty about his role in the abuse, and respondent's dishonesty as to his continued contact with child's abusive mother and his continued belief that mother did not pose to a risk to daughter), *aff'd per curiam*, 368 N.C. 704 (2016).

Cases involving prior neglect adjudications in which parental rights were terminated include

- *In re Z.V.A.*, 835 S.E.2d 425 (N.C. S.Ct. 2019) (clear, cogent, and convincing evidence supported the district court's findings that father was willing to leave the child alone with mother who was unfit to parent the child by herself, that respondents displayed constant marital discord during supervised visits with the child, and respondents intended to remain together; these findings supported the conclusion that father's rights were subject to termination under G.S. 7B-1111(a)(1)).
- *In re M.A.W.*, 370 N.C. 149 (2017) (respondent father's incarceration during the prior neglect adjudication is neither a sword nor a shield in the TPR action; prior neglect supported by findings of respondent's long history of substance abuse and criminal activity and awareness of mother's substance abuse issues that he knew would result in DSS involvement; likelihood of repetition of neglect supported by respondent's inconsistent visitation with and failure to provide any care, discipline, or supervision to child, denial of social worker's access to his home, and failure to complete clinical assessment after his release from prison despite his successfully participating in substance abuse treatment and parenting courses while incarcerated). *See also In re C.L.S.*, 245 N.C. App. 75, 78, *aff'd per curiam*, 369 N.C. 58 (2016) (citations omitted) (stating that "[i]ncarceration alone ... does not negate a father's neglect of his

child").

- *In re D.L.W.*, 368 N.C. 835 (2016) (likelihood of neglect existed based on injurious environment where in underlying abuse and neglect case, mother was ordered to participate in domestic violence counseling based on findings that parental domestic violence placed the children at risk and that one child had intervened when the parents were arguing, and findings in the order terminating mother's parental rights included findings from the underlying neglect adjudication order and new findings of domestic violence incidents between the parents after the children's removal and mother not articulating an understanding of what she learned in domestic violence counseling).
- *In re A.A.S.*, 812 S.E.2d 875 (N.C. Ct. App. 2018) (earlier neglect adjudication established a history of past neglect; competent evidence supported findings as to future neglect, specifically, that mother needed an additional support person to assist her in safely parenting but was unable to identify any such support person, she repeatedly failed drug screens, DSS had to intervene during supervised visitations because of her inappropriate behavior, and she had not complied with her case plan).
- *In re B.S.O.*, 234 N.C. App. 706 (2014) (affirming the trial court's order finding that there was a high probability of a repetition of neglect where the mother had failed to address the issues that had led to the children's removal and to the original neglect adjudication: improper supervision, domestic violence, unhealthy relationships, mental health issues, and unstable living arrangements).

Cases involving prior neglect adjudications in which parental rights were not terminated include

- *In re C.N.*, 831 S.E.2d 878 (N.C. Ct. App. 2019) (reversing a conclusion of neglect when mother had made some progress on her case plan by completing parenting classes, the assessments, re-engaging in services, recently submitting to drug testing, being employed, and obtaining stable housing and transportation; opinion also noted that there was no evidence or findings to indicate that the reason for child's removal, which was the child spilling Mr. Clean on herself causing chemical burns, were likely to be repeated).
- *In re G.B.R.*, 220 N.C. App. 309 (2012) (reversing termination of father's rights where petition alleged neglect as grounds; father had been incarcerated and evidence at the hearing focused primarily on his incarceration but failed to address circumstances since his release or show a likelihood of a repetition of neglect, showing instead that while incarcerated father wrote many letters to the children and took a number of courses, including a "father accountability" class; since release, he had employment, his own apartment and insurance, and did not drink alcohol or use any medication).
- *In re J.G.B.*, 177 N.C. App. 375 (2006) (holding that the neglect ground was not established where DSS took custody soon after the child's birth and the child was adjudicated only dependent; there must be evidence of prior neglect while in respondent's custody and a likelihood of repetition of neglect).

Other cases addressing the neglect ground to TPR when there was not a prior adjudication of neglect include

- *In re Z.D.*, 812 S.E.2d 668, 675 (N.C. Ct. App. 2018) (reversing TPR; evidence in a private TPR did not support ultimate finding that there was a reasonable probability that child would be neglected if returned to respondent's care when (i) "ambiguous" findings did not address respondent's mental health at the time of the termination hearing or the impact her mental health issues had on the child and (ii) a finding used the subjective terms "concerning" and "disturbing" to describe mother's behavior during visitation, without further explanation of the behavior and how it impacted mother's ability to care for her son at the time of the termination hearing).
- *In re C.G.R.*, 216 N.C. App. 351 (2011) (affirming TPR; holding that evidence of neglect of child who was removed at birth while mother was incarcerated was sufficient: prior to the child's birth the mother had been living in a home used for drug dealing with her other child who was adjudicated neglected; since release from prison the mother chose to live with co-defendants in the drug raid that was the source of her arrest; she had numerous short-term jobs and residences resulting in an unstable living and employment situation, all of which resulted in a substantial risk of impairment to the child).
- *In re C.W.*, 182 N.C. App. 214 (2007) (reversing TPR; holding that there was not sufficient evidence of neglect at the time of the hearing where the incarcerated father sent cards, letters, and money to the children and tried to stay in contact with them during incarceration, and DSS had never developed a case plan with the father).
- *In re Young*, 346 N.C. 244 (1997) (reversing and remanding TPR; child had been in custody of others for over a year at time of termination proceeding but there was no prior adjudication of neglect; evidence of mother's prior neglect was not sufficient evidence of neglect at the time of the termination proceeding as the probability of repetition of neglect was not shown from evidence that mother made considerable positive changes to her lifestyle).

**5. Current neglect**. The ground of neglect may also be proved by showing the parent has neglected the child at the time of the filing of the TPR petition or motion. When determining whether neglect exists, the court "may consider . . . a parent's complete failure to provide the personal contact, love, and affection that [exists] in the parental relationship." *In re A.J.M.P.*, 205 N.C. App. 144, 149 (2010) (quoting *In re Apa*, 59 N.C. App. 322, 324 (1982)). Note that a number of reported cases addressing current neglect involve incarcerated parents.

- *In re N.D.A.*, 833 S.E.2d 768, 775 (N.C. S.Ct. 2019) (noting that the absence of findings that applied the two-prong test of past neglect and likelihood of future neglect in the TPR order suggests the trial court considered whether respondent father was currently neglecting the child for purposes of the TPR).
- *In re R.B.B.*, 187 N.C. App. 639 (2007) (affirming TPR on ground of abuse and neglect; TPR hearing was consolidated with adjudicatory hearing on an abuse and neglect petition).
- *In re Bradshaw*, 160 N.C. App. 677 (2003) (affirming private TPR; holding that, although the incarcerated parent's lack of contact with the child was beyond his control, other

evidence and findings of respondent father's infrequent correspondence with mother (petitioner) regarding child and failure to pay any support despite having small income supported the conclusion that the neglect ground existed).
- *In re A.J.M.P.*, 205 N.C. App. 144 (upholding adjudication of the neglect ground where incarcerated parent had never written to child, sent child anything, paid support despite have some ability to do so, or challenged a court order that ceased his visitation rights; court of appeals reiterated that incarceration alone is not sufficient to establish a ground for TPR).
- *In re C.L.S.,* 245 N.C. App. 75 (child was adjudicated neglected and dependent based on mother's stipulations to allegations in DSS petition and while father's identity was still unknown; father's paternity was later established, father was incarcerated, and father's rights were terminated; TPR of father upheld based on evidence at the time of the TPR hearing that father had neglected the child by failing to provide love, support, affection, and personal contact to the child between the time paternity was established and the TPR hearing; evidence that before incarceration father did not want to pursue reunification and missed appointments with the social worker and post-incarceration that father would not sign a case plan, meet the child, or provide financial support was sufficient to support termination), *aff'd per curiam,* 369 N.C. 58 (2016).

**6. Factors related to abuse and neglect.** The following appellate cases have discussed factors that relate to neglect or abuse in the context of termination of parental rights. See also Chapters 6.3.D and E (discussing evidence for neglect and abuse, outside the context of TPR) and 2.3.B.1 and 2 (discussing the definitions of abuse and neglect).

**(a) Not limited to physical necessities.** For a finding of neglect, it is not necessary to find a failure to provide the child with physical necessities. *In re Black*, 76 N.C. App. 106 (1985); *In re Apa*, 59 N.C. App. 322 (1982).

**(b) Parent's love and concern not determinative.** Determinative factors are the child's circumstances and conditions; the fact that the parent loves or is concerned about the child will not necessarily preclude adjudication of the neglect ground. *In re Montgomery*, 311 N.C. 101 (1984). *See also In re T.J.C.*, 225 N.C. App. 556 (2013) (holding that despite findings that the parents loved their children and the children loved their parents, the parents' ongoing domestic violence was sufficient to support a finding of neglect).

**(c) Nonfeasance as neglect.** Parent's nonfeasance, as well as malfeasance, can constitute neglect. *In re Adcock*, 69 N.C. App. 222 (1984) (holding that mother's failure to intervene or protect child from another person's physical abuse was neglect). *See also In re D.A.H.–C.*, 227 N.C. App. 489 (2013) (finding sufficient evidence of neglect where despite mother's participation in classes, she continued to cohabit and associate with people violent toward her and her children, failing to protect them from abuse and neglect and creating a substantial risk of future neglect).

**(d) Participation in previous action.** It was error to admit evidence of father's failure to participate in the underlying neglect proceeding when there was no evidence that he was served in that action. *In re Mills*, 152 N.C. App. 1 (2002).

**(e) Relinquishment of another child.** The trial court did not err in admitting evidence of mother's surrender of her rights to another child, since the way another child in the same home was treated and that child's status clearly were relevant to whether there could be an adjudication of the neglect ground. *In re Johnston*, 151 N.C. App. 728 (2002); *see also In re Allred*, 122 N.C. App. 561 (1996).

**7. Neglect includes abandonment.** The definition of "neglected juvenile" includes a juvenile "who has been abandoned." G.S. 7B-101(15). The ground of abandonment as neglect under G.S. 7B-1111(a)(1) is separate from the ground of abandonment set forth at G.S. 7B-1111(a)(7) (discussed in section 9.11.G, below). Although "abandonment" has the same meaning under both statutory grounds, the determinative time period the trial court examines when adjudicating the existence or nonexistence of each ground differs.

Termination of parental rights for neglect based on abandonment requires a determination that the conduct of the parent "demonstrates a 'willful neglect and refusal to perform the natural and legal obligations of parental care and support.' " *In re N.D.A.*, 833 S.E.2d 768, 775 (N.C. S.Ct. 2019) (quoting *Pratt v. Bishop*, 257 N.C. 486, 501 (1962). The North Carolina Supreme Court recognizes that "willful" does not appear in G.S. 7B-101(15), but abandonment based on neglect "is inherently a willful act." *In re N.D.A.*, 833 S.E.2d at 776, n.2. Willfulness is a question of fact. *See In re N.D.A.*, 833 S.E.2d 768.

To terminate a parent's rights pursuant to G.S. 7B-1111(a)(1) for neglect based on abandonment, the trial court must find that a parent has engaged in conduct "which manifests a willful determination to forego all parental duties and relinquish all parental claims to the child as of the time of the termination hearing." *In re N.D.A.*, 833 S.E.2d 768 (agreeing with the application by the court of appeals in *In re C.K.C.*, 822 S.E.2d 741 (N.C. Ct. App. 2018) of this standard to neglect by abandonment). When the trial court's order does not include findings addressing the willfulness of the parental conduct, the order will be vacated. *See In re N.D.A.*, 833 S.E.2d 768 (findings did not address whether father, who was incarcerated when DSS first became involved up to the adjudication hearing, had the ability to contact petitioner or the child, to exercise visitation, or pay child support).

The determinative time period is not specified by G.S. 7B-1111(a)(1); however, the appellate courts have held that there must be evidence of neglect at the time of the TPR hearing. *In re C.K.C.*, 822 S.E.2d 741 (quoting *In re Young*, 346 N.C. 244 (1997)). When considering neglect by abandonment, the court may examine the parent's conduct over an extended period of time. *In re N.D.A.*, 833 S.E.2d 768, 776 (considering whether father had the ability to contact the petitioner in a private TPR during a period from 2014 through December 2016, during most of which father was incarcerated). Unlike the ground of abandonment under G.S. 7B-1111(a)(7), neglect in the form of abandonment does not require findings regarding the six-month period immediately preceding the filing of the petition. In some cases, however, these time periods may overlap. For example, the determination that respondent father had not willfully abandoned his children pursuant to G.S 7B-1111(a)(7) because he sought sole custody of the children during the determinative six-month period under that ground was relevant to the determination in the same TPR proceeding that considered whether he neglected the children by abandonment. *In re C.K.C.*, 822 S.E.2d 741 (N.C. Ct. App. 2018) (reversing TPR; father's attempt to regain custody of his children precluded a determination that father neglected the children by abandonment pursuant to G.S. 7B-1111(a)(1) as his attempt to obtain custody of the children did not show he intended to forego all parental duties and relinquish all parental claims to his children).

## B. Willfully Leaving Child in Foster Care for More than Twelve Months without Reasonable Progress

Willfully leaving the child in foster care or placement outside the home for more than twelve months without showing to the satisfaction of the court that reasonable progress under the circumstances has been made in correcting the conditions that led to the child's removal is grounds for termination of parental rights (TPR). Parental rights may not be terminated for the sole reason that a parent is unable to care for his or her child because of poverty. G.S. 7B-1111(a)(2).

This statutory ground, G.S. 7B-1111(a)(2), requires a two-part analysis: (1) that the child has willfully been left by the parent in foster care or placement outside the home for over twelve months and (2) that as of the time of the TPR hearing, the parent has not made reasonable progress under the circumstances to correct the conditions that led to the child's removal. *In re Z.D.*, 812 S.E.2d 668 (N.C. Ct. App. 2018); *In re L.L.O.*, 252 N.C. App. 447 (2017).

**1. Constitutional challenge.** This ground is not unconstitutionally vague. *In re Moore*, 306 N.C. 394 (1982) (decided under an earlier version of the Juvenile Code).

**2. Time period in foster care or placement outside the home.** G.S. 7B-1111(a)(2) requires that a parent has willfully left the child in foster care or placement outside the home for more than twelve months. The language "for more than twelve months" has been interpreted to require that the twelve-month period expire by the date a motion or petition to terminate parental rights is filed. *In re A.C.F.*, 176 N.C. App. 520 (2006); *In re J.G.B.*, 177 N.C. App. 375 (2006) (twelve-month period is calculated from the date the child is left in foster care or placement outside the home until the date that a TPR motion or petition is filed). This interpretation provides parents "with at least twelve months' notice" to correct the conditions that led to their child(ren)'s removal before having to respond to a pleading seeking to terminate their parental rights. *In re A.C.F.*, 176 N.C. App. at 527.

The period of one year in foster care or other placement must be pursuant to a *court order*. *In re A.C.F.*, 176 N.C. App. 520 (emphasis in original). A child has not been "removed" when a parent can withdraw his or her consent at any time, such that time a child spent in a placement pursuant only to a voluntary protection plan (e.g., a temporary safety placement) cannot be counted as part of the twelve-month period. *In re A.C.F.*, 176 N.C. App. 520 (reversing TPR; child was not left in foster care for more than twelve months when removal occurred by nonsecure custody order and TPR motion was filed ten months later, even though separation between child and parent occurred with a voluntary protection plan months before entry of the nonsecure custody order). However, time spent outside the home pursuant to a civil custody order can be counted, as can time spent with guardians appointed pursuant to G.S. 7B-600. *See In re L.C.R.*, 226 N.C. App. 249 (2013) (where a neglect matter had been transferred to a

G.S. Chapter 50 civil custody action pursuant to G.S. 7B-911); *In re D.H.H.*, 208 N.C. App. 549 (2010) (rejecting the father's argument to count only the time prior to guardianship, stating that this ground and G.S. 7B-600 are independent and noting the ground does not require the child be in DSS custody).

The court order requiring that a child be removed from the home and which starts the clock on the twelve-month period can be a nonsecure custody order as in *In re J.A.K.*, 812 S.E.2d 716 (N.C. Ct. App. 2018). The twelve-month time period in foster care placement applies when the respondent in the TPR was the "non-removal parent" and did not appear in the underlying abuse, neglect, or dependency action until after the child's adjudication and almost one year after the nonsecure custody order was issued. *In re J.A.K.*, 812 S.E.2d 716 (rejecting argument of respondent father that the statutory period began when father first appeared at a hearing with counsel).

It is not necessary that the period of time in foster care be continuous. *In re Taylor*, 97 N.C. App. 57 (1990) (holding that trial period during which children were placed with parents did not defeat this ground).

**3. Willfulness.** Appellate cases have emphasized and shaped the meaning of the term "willful" in this ground.

  **(a) Fault not required.** Willfulness, for purposes of this ground, is something less than willful abandonment and does not require a showing of parental fault. *In re J.A.K.*, 812 S.E.2d 716 (N.C. Ct. App. 2018) (willfulness exists when the respondent has an ability to show reasonable progress but is unwilling to make the effort; it does not require a showing of fault); *In re C.R.B.*, 245 N.C. App. 65 (2016); *In re A.W.*, 237 N.C. App. 209 (2014); *In re N.A.L.*, 193 N.C. App. 114 (2008); *In re Bishop*, 92 N.C. App. 662 (1989) (holding that the evidence was sufficient to support a finding of willfulness even though the parent had made some effort and some progress). *Cf. In re Fletcher*, 148 N.C. App. 228 (2002) (affirming termination of mother's rights, but not the father's, on this ground). It is not a prerequisite for a TPR that the parent whose rights are at issue caused the conditions that resulted in the child's placement. *In re A.W.*, 237 N.C. App. 209 (affirming termination of father's rights pursuant to G.S. 7B-1111(a)(2) where the child was placed in DSS custody and removed from his mother's care before paternity was established, but father made almost no efforts to obtain custody despite the repeated attempts by DSS to help him do so).

  **(b) Parent's ability.** For willfulness to attach, evidence must show a parent's ability (or capacity to acquire the ability) to overcome the factors that resulted in the child's placement and that the parent was unwilling to make the effort. *In re L.L.O.*, 252 N.C. App. 447 (2017); *In re H.D.*, 129 N.C. App. 318 (2015). *See In re C.C.*, 173 N.C. App. 375 (2005) (holding that the evidence and findings were not sufficient to establish that respondent "willfully" left the children in care); *In re Baker*, 158 N.C. App. 491 (2003) (affirming TPR where the evidence of willfulness included parents' refusal to inquire about or complete parenting classes, sign a reunification plan, or use mental health services).

(c) **Minor parent.** In the case of a minor parent, the court must make specific findings showing that the parent's age-related limitations have been adequately considered in relation to willfulness. *In re J.G.B.*, 177 N.C. App. 375 (2006); *In re Matherly*, 149 N.C. App. 452 (2002).

(d) **Incarcerated parent.** A parent's incarceration, standing alone, neither requires nor precludes a finding that the parent willfully left the child in foster care. The parent's failure to contact DSS or the child is evidence of willfulness. *In re Harris*, 87 N.C. App. 179 (1987); *see also In re Shermer*, 156 N.C. App. 281 (2003) (holding that evidence was insufficient to find willfulness where the incarcerated father wrote to his sons while in prison and informed DSS that he did not want his rights terminated); *Whittington v. Hendren*, 156 N.C. App. 364, 369–70 (2003) (affirming TPR where the court found that "[e]ven though the respondent was incarcerated, he could have made more of an effort to maintain contact with his child," and respondent had foregone the opportunity to attend the TPR hearing).

(e) **Some effort does not preclude a finding of willfulness.** The fact that a parent makes some efforts does not preclude a finding of willfulness. *See, e.g.*, *In re A.B.*, 253 N.C. App. 29 (2017) (a trial court may find willfulness when a parent has made some attempt to regain custody but has failed to make reasonable progress or exhibit a positive response to the efforts of DSS); *In re A.W.*, 237 N.C. App. 209 (2014) (upholding TPR on this ground where although the father did visit the child seven times in six months, the father made almost no efforts to get the child placed in his custody despite repeated efforts from DSS to engage and assist him in doing so); *In re D.C.*, 225 N.C. App. 327 (2013) (upholding TPR where a three-year-old child had been removed from the home due to serious injuries sustained by a dog attack in the home, the dog was immediately destroyed, and the mother's home had no dogs and was deemed "clean and tidy," but the mother still did not understand the nature of the child's injuries or the trauma he experienced; she failed to set up appointments with the child's therapist; and she waited three and a half years before filing a motion for review to seek help with visitation); *In re J.L.H.*, 224 N.C. App. 52 (2012) (upholding TPR on this ground where respondent mother had participated in some services but failed to participate with her own mental health treatment and was inconsistent in participating with her daughter's therapy); *In re D.H.H.*, 208 N.C. App. 549 (2010); *In re B.S.D.S.*, 163 N.C. App. 540 (2004); *In re Tate*, 67 N.C. App. 89 (1984); *but see In re Nesbitt*, 147 N.C. App. 349 (2001) (reversing TPR because there was insufficient evidence that mother failed to make reasonable progress; noting that even if she had, there was no evidence any failure was willful).

### 4. Reasonable progress to correct conditions that led to child's removal.

(a) **Conditions that led to the child's removal.** In *In re B.O.A.*, 831 S.E.2d 305 (N.C. S.Ct. 2019), the North Carolina Supreme Court interpreted the phrase "those conditions that led to the removal of the juvenile" appearing in G.S. 7B-1111(a)(2). As part of its analysis, the supreme court looked to other relevant statutory provisions, including the trial court's authority over parents at disposition in an abuse, neglect, or dependency action under G.S. 7B-904(d1)(3). At disposition, the trial court may order a parent to take appropriate steps to remedy the conditions that led to the child's adjudication or removal from the parent's custody. A parent's compliance with a judicially adopted case plan is relevant when determining if grounds to terminate that parent's rights exist pursuant to G.S.7B–1111(a)(2). See Chapter 7.7.A and B (discussing the court's authority over parents and others at disposition).

In looking at the language of "conditions of removal," the supreme court held that an expansive reading is appropriate and reversed the court of appeals, which limited its interpretation of conditions of removal to that which was alleged in the abuse, neglect, or dependency petition. The supreme court reasoned that a child's removal "is rarely the result of a single, specific incident and is, instead, typically caused by the confluence of multiple factors, some of which are immediately apparent and some of which only become apparent in light of further investigation," and a trial court gains a better understanding of the family dynamic as the case progresses. *In re B.O.A.*, 831 S.E.2d at 314. The supreme court held that "conditions of removal" encompasses all factors directly or indirectly contributing to the child's removal, which allows the courts to recognize the complexity of issues that must resolved in abuse, neglect, or dependency cases. In applying the more expansive interpretation of conditions of removal, the supreme court affirmed the TPR after determining there was a nexus between the court-ordered case plan and the complex series of interrelated factors causing the child's removal and that respondent mother failed to make reasonable progress on her case plan. The supreme court noted that its holding did not mean a trial judge has unlimited authority or that "conditions of removal" has no meaning.

**(b) What constitutes reasonable progress by a parent.** Extremely limited progress is not reasonable, but perfection is not required for a parent to reach the reasonable progress standard. *In re C.N.*, 831 S.E.2d 878 (N.C. Ct. App. 2019); *In re S.D.*, 243 N.C. App. 65 (2015); *see In re A.B.*, 253 N.C. App. 29, 33 (2017) (quoting *In re J.S.L.*, 177 N.C. App. 151, 163 (2006)) ("a parent's failure to fully satisfy all elements of the case plan goals is not the equivalent of a lack of 'reasonable progress'."). The supreme court has observed that "a trial court has ample authority to determine that a parent's 'extremely limited progress' in correcting the conditions leading to removal adequately supports a determination that a parent's parental rights in a particular child are subject to termination." *In re B.O.A.*, 831 S.E.2d at 314 (affirming TPR). The supreme court also has found that a parent's limited progress in correcting conditions that led to removal will support a termination of rights under G.S. 7B-1111(a)(2) when findings showed, among other things, "that mother waited too long to begin working on her case plan." *See In re I.G.C.*, 835 S.E.2d 432, 435 (N.C. S.Ct. 2019) (affirming TPR), discussed in subsection (d), below.

Whether a parent is in a position to actually regain custody of the child at the time of the TPR hearing is not relevant in determining whether the parent has made reasonable progress to correct the conditions that led to removal. *In re L.C.R.*, 226 N.C. App. 249 (2013) (transfer of neglect order to a civil custody order was immaterial to showing of reasonable progress; holding respondent is not required to regain custody to defeat TPR on this ground, and conditions resulting in removal do not need to be completely corrected;

**(c) Time period for a parent's reasonable progress.** The period for evaluating the nature and extent of a parent's reasonable progress extends up to the hearing on the TPR motion or petition. *See In re I.G.C.,* 835 S.E.2d 432 (N.C. S.Ct. 2019) (affirming TPR; considering respondent mother's progress up to time of termination hearing); *In re D.L.W.*, 368 N.C. 835 (2016) (affirming TPR; one finding addressed mother's lack of housing at the time of the termination hearing); *In re A.B.*, 253 N.C. App. 29 (2017) (vacating and remanding TPR order that contained no findings as to mother's conduct or circumstances after the last review hearing up to the TPR hearing; respondent mother and social worker presented testimony upon which findings up to the time of the hearing could be based); *see also In re Pierce*, 356 N.C. 68, 75 n.1 (2002) (decided on an earlier wording of the statute that included a second twelve-month period where the parent must make progress, but noting that under a 2001 amendment that removed that second twelve-month time period, "there is no specified time frame that limits the admission of relevant evidence pertaining to a parent's 'reasonable progress' or lack thereof"); *In re C.L.C.*, 171 N.C. App. 438, 447 (2005) (noting that after deletion of the second-twelve month period in G.S. 7B-1111(a)(2) "[t]he focus is no longer solely on the progress made in the 12 months prior to the petition"), *aff'd per curiam*, 360 N.C. 475 (2006).

**(d) Findings must support court's conclusion as to a parent's reasonable progress.** The ultimate finding as to a parent's reasonable progress must be the result of a process of logical reasoning based on the evidentiary facts found by the court. *In re A.B.*, 253 N.C. App. 29 (2017).

A conclusion that a parent has not made reasonable progress to correct conditions is not supported by findings when the order contains inconsistent findings and conflicting evidence that were not resolved by the trial court. *See In re L.L.O.*, 252 N.C. App. 447 (2017) (vacating and remanding a TPR order based on G.S. 7B-1111(a)(2) that did not resolve conflicting evidence); *In re A.B.*, 253 N.C. App. 29 (vacating and remanding a TPR order based on G.S. 7B-1111(a)(2) when respondent mother and DSS social worker presented conflicting material evidence on willfulness and reasonable progress that was not resolved in the court's order).

Cases where the findings support the conclusion that parent failed to make reasonable progress to correct conditions that led to child's removal.

- Findings that respondent mother lacked an understanding of, or did not accept responsibility for, the circumstances leading to children's removal was supported by evidence that mother continued to live with father during the juvenile proceeding and placed more importance on their relationship than the safety of the children. Father did not comply with his case plan and denied responsibility for domestic violence and other conditions that led to children's removal. Mother blamed the children and others for the father's return to the home, and she continued to defend father. While mother made some progress on her case plan, she did not comply with the requirement that she provide a safe and stable home environment for the children. *In re A.R.A.*, 835 S.E.2d 417 (N.C. S.Ct. 2019).

- Respondent mother's limited achievements in correcting conditions were "well-documented" by findings that "showed that mother had waited too long to begin working on her case plan." *In re I.G.C.*, 835 S.E.2d 432, 435 (N.C. S.Ct. 2019). Findings that related to mother's conduct after she agreed to the case plan included that mother did not complete the recommended substance abuse or domestic violence programs and that she missed multiple drug screens, tested positive on two occasions, and committed two DWI offenses. Findings relating to mother's conduct after reunification efforts ceased up to the date of the TPR hearing included that mother did not maintain stable employment or stable housing for six months and moved frequently, signaling instability. Mother's progress at the TPR hearing "was not the level of progress required by her class plan." *In re I.G.C.*, 835 S.E.2d at 435.
- Respondent father's case had two main components: attend parenting classes and stabilize housing and income. Findings showed limited progress in that father completed parenting classes but failed to obtain independent and appropriate housing. Completion of one component did not rebut failure on the other component. *In re J.A.K.*, 812 S.E.2d 716 (N.C. Ct. App. 2018).

Case where findings did not address, or did not sufficiently address, the parent's progress or lack of progress in correcting conditions that led to child's removal.

- Primary condition that led to child's removal was respondent mother's mental health, but other conditions were mother's drug use and DSS's concern for the child's care and well-being. The trial court made no findings at the time of the termination hearing as to mother's progress or lack of progress in correcting her drug use or the conditions of her home. The following findings were insufficient to support the ultimate finding of lack of reasonable progress: findings as to mother's mental health lacked detail in describing what a mental illness "episode" was, how frequently mother had such episodes, and how the episodes "left her incapable of properly caring for [her son]"; and findings describing mother's behavior during visits with her child as "consistently concerning" and "disturbing" lacked any particularity in what behavior it was referring to and how that behavior impacted mother's ability to care for her son. Moreover, testimony of mother's psychiatrist tended to show that mother had made significant progress in addressing her mental health issues, and other evidence showed she had stable housing and income and was not using drugs. *In re Z.D.*, 812 S.E.2d 668, 673 (N.C. Ct. App. 2018).

**5. Poverty cannot be basis for TPR.** The Juvenile Code explicitly prohibits the termination of a parent's rights for the sole reason that he or she is unable to care for his or her child because of poverty. G.S. 7B-1111(a)(2). North Carolina appellate courts have examined this issue in a limited number of cases.

- Findings in the underlying neglect adjudication order indicated that a lack of consistent and adequate housing and an inability to meet the children's minimal needs led in part to their removal. Findings in the TPR order that mother refused to comply with a case plan requirement that she create a budgeting plan, her inability to account for where her earnings went, multiple evictions for nonpayment of rent despite being employed, her loss of employment after being incarcerated because of a domestic violence incident, and her driving without a valid driver's license resulting in charges, demonstrated mother's failure to correct the conditions that led to the children's removal and that her failure "was not simply the result of poverty." *In re D.L.W.*, 368 N.C. 835, 846 (2016).

- Father's argument that his inability to obtain housing due to poverty was directly rebutted by the court's finding that his actions were not solely the result of poverty. *In re J.A.K.*, 812 S.E.2d 716 (N.C. Ct. App. 2018)

- The trial court found that mother met five of the requirements for reunification but concluded that she had failed to make reasonable progress when she had not complied with three other requirements: resolve pending criminal charges, obtain a psychological evaluation and follow recommendations, and maintain employment sufficient to meet both her and her child's needs. The order terminating mother's rights was reversed when evidence as to those three requirements indicated that (1) at the time of the hearing mother's criminal charges could have been resolved in a week's time by plea for time served, (2) mother had submitted to a psychological evaluation and attended therapy as recommended by her therapist, which was for "individual counseling services" and not "intensive individual counseling" as found by the trial court, and (3) while mother's monthly income from a part-time job was insufficient to meet her and her child's needs, G.S. 7B-1111(a)(2) does not allow parental rights to be terminated on the sole basis of poverty. *In re S.D.*, 243 N.C. App. 65 (2015).

- When reviewing a TPR based on failure to make reasonable progress under G.S. 7B-1111(a)(2), the court of appeals examined whether the father's rights were terminated solely because of poverty even though the father did not present this issue on appeal. The court of appeals affirmed the TPR noting the father's failure to obtain custody of his daughter has nothing to do with poverty but was instead due to his own inaction. *In re A.W.*, 237 N.C. App. 209 (2014).

### C. Failure to Pay a Reasonable Portion of the Child's Cost of Care

When a child has been placed in the custody of DSS, a licensed child-placing agency, a child-caring institution, or foster home, and the parent has willfully failed to pay a reasonable portion of the cost of the child's care for a continuous period of six months immediately preceding the filing of the petition or motion, although physically and financially able to do so, a ground for terminating parental rights (TPR) exists. G.S. 7B-1111(a)(3).

**1. Constitutional challenge.** The ground is not unconstitutionally vague. *In re Moore*, 306 N.C. 394 (1982) (decided under an earlier version of the Juvenile Code); *In re Clark*, 303 N.C. 592 (1981) (decided under an earlier version of the Juvenile Code).

**2. Ability to pay.** A finding that the parent is able to pay a reasonable portion of the cost of the child's care or support is essential to termination on this ground. *In re Ballard*, 311 N.C. 708 (1984) (deeming it essential that the court find that a parent has the ability to pay support before terminating for nonsupport on this ground); *In re Clark*, 303 N.C. 592 (1981) (a parent's ability to pay is the controlling characteristic in determining what constitutes a reasonable portion of the cost of the child's care).

The court must make specific findings that the parent was able to pay some amount greater than what he or she paid (including more than zero if nothing was paid) during the relevant time period but is not required to find a specific amount of support that would have constituted a reasonable portion under the circumstances. *In re N.X.A.*, 254 N.C. App. 670 (2017) (holding no error in ordering TPR; mother paid no support, had annual income of $10,000 to $13,000, claimed her children as dependents for tax purposes resulting in a significant tax refund, and had the ability to pay some amount greater than zero).

An order terminating a parent's rights on this ground will be reversed if the required finding as to the parent's ability to pay is not included. *In re Clark,* 151 N.C. App. 286 (2002) (incarcerated father paid no child support and was not ordered to do so; when there was no finding that father had the ability to pay an amount greater than zero, conclusion that respondent father failed to pay a reasonable portion of his child's care was error).

When a court orders child support, it has determined the reasonable portion of the cost of the child's care based on the parent's ability to pay and the child's needs. When a TPR is based on a parent's willful failure to pay a reasonable portion of the cost of the child's care, and there is an order for child support, the TPR petitioner (or movant) is not required to independently prove the respondent parent's ability to pay. *In re S.T.B.*, 235 N.C. App. 290 (2014) (holding that the trial court's findings that (1) the father failed to pay any amount of his $50/month child support obligation and (2) the court was unaware of any disability that would prevent the father from paying some amount of support were sufficient to establish the father's ability to pay some amount greater than zero); *In re A.L.*, 245 N.C. App. 55 (2016) (affirming TPR of father who only made two child support payments and who was subject to a child support order; father's ability to pay was established by (1) child support enforcement orders, (2) findings that father had signed a memorandum of understanding on two occasions acknowledging that he had the ability to pay the support ordered, and (3) evidence that father was employed as a mechanic and a truck driver with at least $600/month in disposable income).

A parent cannot assert lack of ability or means to contribute to support when the opportunity to do so is lost due to the parent's own misconduct. *In re Tate*, 67 N.C. App. 89 (1984) (parent was not excused from contributing support after she voluntarily quit her various jobs and made no payments, explaining to social worker that she did not feel she had to pay the ordered amount of $10/month because another mother with a child in foster care was not paying support); *In re Bradley,* 57 N.C. App. 475 (1982) (father was removed from prison work-release program after violating program rules by returning from the program intoxicated).

**3. Willfulness.** As used in G.S. 7B-1111(a)(3), the term " 'willfully'. . . imports knowledge and a stubborn resistance . . . one does not willfully fail to do something which is not in his power to do." *In re Matherly*, 149 N.C. App. 452, 455 (2002) (quoting *In re Moore,* 306 N.C. 394, 411 (2002)). See *In re J.K.C.*, 218 N.C. App. 22 (2012) (finding that the father could not be found to have willfully failed to pay child support because he had attempted to do so but was told by child support enforcement agency that it could not be arranged because he did not make enough income). In the case of a minor parent, the findings must show adequate consideration of respondent's age-related limitations. *In re Matherly*, 149 N.C. App. 452.

**4. Reasonable portion of cost of care.** A finding as to the cost of foster care can establish the child's reasonable needs. *In re Montgomery*, 311 N.C. 101 (1984). Determination of a reasonable portion of the cost of the child's care depends on the parent's ability to pay. *In re A.L.*, 245 N.C. App. 55 (2016); *In re Manus*, 82 N.C. App. 340 (1986). Appellate cases have held that this ground can be adjudicated only if there is clear and convincing evidence that respondent is able to pay some amount greater than zero. *See In re J.E.M.*, 221 N.C. App. 361 (2012) (finding that zero support was not a reasonable portion of the cost of care when respondent father was gainfully employed from time to time and was physically and financially able to make some payments); *see also In re T.D.P.*, 164 N.C. App. 287 (2004), and cases cited therein (finding this ground was met even though respondent's prison wages ranged from forty cents to one dollar per day), *aff'd per curiam*, 359 N.C. 405 (2005).

Where a mother was earning approximately $300 per weekend, occasional small sums she gave to the foster parents and children (such as $1, $10, or $20) could not be deemed to be active financial support. Total expenditures by social services in caring for the mother's five children exceeded $315,000. *In re B.S.O.*, 234 N.C. App. 706 (2014).

**5. Notice of support obligation irrelevant.** Neither the absence of notice of the support obligation nor the father's lack of awareness that support was required of him was a defense to termination on this ground. *In re Wright*, 64 N.C. App. 135 (1983).

**6. Child's placement.** Parental rights may be terminated pursuant to G.S. 7B-1111(a)(3) only if the child has been placed in the custody of a DSS, a licensed-child placing agency, a child-caring institution, or a foster home.

In the case *In re E.L.E.*, 243 N.C. App. 301 (2015), the court of appeals examined what qualifies as a "foster home" for purposes of this TPR ground. It looked to the definition of "foster home" in G.S. 131D-10.2(8), which requires that a child be placed in the home by a child-placing agency or that foster care is being provided full-time for two or more children who are unrelated to the adult members of the household by blood, marriage, guardianship, or adoption. In this case, the child was placed with her great aunt and uncle, who were the TPR petitioners. Although initially placed with petitioners by DSS in a neglect action, the trial court ultimately awarded custody of the child to petitioners and transferred the juvenile action to a civil custody action. Because petitioners had custody pursuant to a civil custody order and were related to the child, neither criteria of "foster home" was met, thus, mother's rights could not be terminated pursuant to G.S. 7B-1111(a)(3).

A child may be placed in the custody of a DSS by court order or by operation of law through the execution of a relinquishment pursuant to G.S. Chapter 48. *See In re A.L.*, 245 N.C. App. 55 (2016) (holding child was in custody of county DSS when mother relinquished her parental rights and surrendered the child to DSS for adoption as authorized by G.S. 48-3-701 and 48-3-703); *see also* G.S. 48-3-705(b), (c) (consequences of relinquishment related to custody of child).

## D. Failure to Pay Child Support to Other Parent

Where one parent has custody of the child pursuant to a court order or custody agreement of the parents, and the other parent (respondent), for one year or more immediately preceding the filing of the petition or motion, has willfully failed without justification to pay for the child's care, support, and education as required by the court order or custody agreement, failure to pay support is grounds for termination of parental rights (TPR). G.S. 7B-1111(a)(4). The petition or motion to terminate for failure to pay child support must put respondent on notice of this ground by referring to G.S. 7B-1111(a)(4) and/or alleging a willful failure to pay support as required by a court order or other agreement. *See In re I.R.L.*, 823 S.E.2d 902, 906 (N.C. Ct. App. 2019) (when TPR petition did not include any of the foregoing, an order was reversed for not providing sufficient notice in a private TPR proceeding to respondent father of the ground in G.S. 7B-1111(a)(4); petition alleged only that father "[h]as failed to provide substantial financial support or consistent care for the minor child").

**1. Agreement or order and failure to pay must be proven.** The existence of a child support agreement or order as well as the parent's failure to pay the amount must be established by clear, cogent, and convincing evidence. *See In re I.R.L.*, 823 S.E.2d 902, 905 (N.C. Ct. App. 2019) (although both parents testified in a private TPR proceeding about a support order entered the year the child was born for $50/month, findings were insufficient to support termination for failure to pay child support when the termination order contained no findings indicating that a child support order existed or that respondent father had failed to pay support "as required by" a child support order); *In re J.M.K.*, 820 S.E.2d 106 (N.C. Ct. App. 2018) (in a private TPR proceeding, conclusion that ground in G.S. 7B-1111(a)(4) existed was reversed when there was no evidence of a child support order); *In re D.T.L.*, 219 N.C. App. 219 (2012) (holding that this ground could not be proven where the petition did not allege that there was a decree or custody agreement requiring respondent to pay and no such evidence was introduced at trial); *In re Roberson*, 97 N.C. App. 277, 281 (1990) (stating "[i]n a termination action pursuant to this ground, petitioner must prove the existence of a support order that was enforceable during the year before the termination petition was filed").

**2. Agreement or order establishes ability to pay.** The order or support agreement may be used to establish what the parent should have reasonably paid. However, there is no requirement that petitioner independently prove or that the court find as a fact respondent's ability to pay support during the relevant time period since the existence of the agreement or order must be established, and it is based on the parent's ability to pay. *See In re J.D.S.*, 170 N.C. App. 244 (2005); *In re Roberson*, 97 N.C. App. 277 (1990).

**3. Willfulness: parent may rebut ability to pay.** Even though the existence of an agreement or order creates a presumption that the parent has the ability to pay support, the parent may present evidence to prove he or she was unable to pay child support to rebut a finding of willful failure to pay. *See Bost v. Van Nortwick*, 117 N.C. App. 1 (1994) (reversing TPR; overwhelming evidence showed inability to pay due to alcoholism and financial status); *In re Roberson*, 97 N.C. App. 277 (1990) (affirming TPR; father's evidence of emotional difficulties was insufficient to rebut evidence that his failure to pay was willful); *see also In re J.D.S.*, 170 N.C. App. 244 (2005) (affirming TPR; findings support conclusion that respondent willfully failed to pay support as required by an order entered by a Nevada court in that he only made one partial payment and had significant arrears at time of the TPR hearing).

### E. Father's Actions regarding Child Born Out of Wedlock

Grounds for termination of parental rights (TPR) exist where the father of a child born out of wedlock has not, before the filing of the TPR petition or motion,

- filed an affidavit of paternity in a central registry maintained by the North Carolina Department of Health and Human Services (DHHS),
- legitimated the child pursuant to G.S. 49-10 or 49-12.1 (special proceedings before the clerk of superior court) or filed a petition to do so,
- legitimated the child by marriage to the mother,
- provided substantial financial support or consistent care with respect to the child and mother, or
- established paternity through G.S. 49-14 (civil action to establish paternity), G.S. 110-132 (affidavits of parentage executed by putative father and mother for purposes of child support), G.S. 130A-101 (affidavits of parentage for purposes of registration of child's birth signed by the mother and putative father or by the mother, her husband, and the putative father when there is genetic marker testing of paternity), G.S. 130A-118 (amendment of child's birth certificate based on parents' marriage after the child's birth or a court order relating to parentage), or other judicial proceeding.

G.S. 7B-1111(a)(5).

**1. All prongs of ground required.** Petitioner must prove that respondent failed to take any of the listed actions. *See, e.g., In re S.C.R.*, 198 N.C. App. 525 (2009); *In re M.A.I.B.K.*, 184 N.C. App. 218 (2007) (both decided under prior law). The court must make findings of fact based on clear, cogent, and convincing evidence addressing each of the statutorily required elements in G.S. 7B-1111(a)(5)a.–e. G.S. 7B-1109(f); *In re L.S.*, 822 S.E.2d 506 (N.C. Ct. App. 2018) (DSS offered no evidence that the children were born out of wedlock or that respondent father had failed, before the filing of the TPR petition, to act as required by G.S. 7B-1111(a)(5)a., b., c., or e.; a minimal proffer of evidence as to G.S. 7B-1111(a)(5)d. had been made at trial but was not sufficient to support an adjudication); *In re J.M.K.*, 820 S.E.2d 106 (N.C. Ct. App. 2018) (reversing TPR when only three of the five subsections were addressed in the order).

**2. Affidavit of paternity filed with DHHS.** The petitioner or movant must inquire of DHHS to determine whether an affidavit of paternity has been filed. DHHS's certified reply must be presented to and considered by the court. G.S. 7B-1111(a)(5)a. The inquiry is made to

Division of Social Services
Adoption Review Team
820 S. Boylan Ave.
2411 Mail Service Center
Raleigh, NC 27699-2411
Telephone: 919-527-6370.

**3. Substantial financial support or consistent care.** The Juvenile Code does not define "substantial financial support" or "consistent care"; however, these terms have been discussed by the North Carolina Court of Appeals. Looking to the dictionary definition of "consistent", the court of appeals stated " 'consistent' means with 'regularity, or steady continuity throughout: showing no significant change, unevenness, or contradiction.' " *In re A.C.V.*, 203 N.C. App. 473, 478 (2010) (quoting WEBSTER'S THIRD NEW INTERNATIONAL DICTIONARY UNABRIDGED 484 (1976)). In applying the definition, the court of appeals determined the father failed to provide consistent care to the mother, when during her pregnancy, he only made a few phone calls and attended some parenting classes and an ultrasound. *In re A.C.V.*, 203 N.C. App. 473.

Regarding "substantial support", the court of appeals held that in a TPR action, the father must have provided the support directly to the mother and child, and at a minimum he should have provided support that was requested of him: gas money, medical co-pays, and general financial support during the pregnancy. *See In re A.C.V.*, 203 N.C. App. 473 (distinguishing the TPR statute from a similar consent to adoption statute (G.S. 48-3-601(2)b.4.II) that uses the word "for" rather than "to"). The court of appeals has also held that a finding regarding the respondent father's ability to pay is not required. *See In re J.D.S.*, 170 N.C. App. 244 (2005); *In re Hunt*, 127 N.C. App. 370 (1997). Cases have not addressed whether the respondent could defeat that prong of the ground by proving that he lacked the ability to provide substantial support or consistent care.

**4. Knowledge of child's existence.** The fact that the father of a child born out of wedlock does not know of the child's existence is not an automatic defense to a TPR under this ground. North Carolina appellate courts have analyzed this issue in the contexts of this TPR ground and a similarly worded adoption statute, G.S. 48-3-601 (persons whose consent is required for adoption). Interpreting these statutes, the appellate courts have held that a father's lack of knowledge that he has a child is not a bar to termination of his rights and does not prevent an adoption from proceeding without his consent. *See A Child's Hope, LLC v. Doe*, 178 N.C. App. 96 (2006) (affirming TPR where mother deceived father, claiming that she had miscarried, and father knew of child's existence only when served with TPR petition); *In re T.L.B.*, 167 N.C. App. 298 (2004) (affirming TPR where father claimed not to have known of child's existence).

The issue of whether and how a father's lack of knowledge of the child's existence impacts his parental rights has also been analyzed in the constitutional context. The North Carolina Supreme Court analyzed the particular facts surrounding a putative father's attempt to protect his parental rights when he learned of his child's existence, of which the mother intentionally had not informed him, six months after the child's birth. The court concluded that the father's constitutional rights would not be violated by allowing a pending adoption to proceed without his consent. *In re Adoption of S.D.W.*, 367 N.C. 386 (2014). In doing so, the supreme court did not address the analysis undertaken by the court of appeals, which had reversed the trial court and remanded out of concern that the statute regarding who must consent to adoption may be unconstitutional. The supreme court also did not examine prior North Carolina cases addressing the issue (such as *In re Baby Girl Dockery*, discussed below).

Instead, the court focused on "the extent to which a natural father's biological relationship with his child received protection under the Due Process Clause," the question articulated by the U.S. Supreme Court in *Lehr v. Robertson*, 463 U.S. 248, 258 (1983). *In re Adoption of S.D.W.*, 367 N.C. at 391. Using *Lehr* as the "backdrop" for analysis, the supreme court stated that North Carolina's statutory framework recognized that a concern for a biological father's interest exists only in those men who have "grasp[ed] the opportunity [to develop a relationship with their offspring] and accept[ed] some measure of responsibility for the child's future." *In re Adoption of S.D.W.*, 367 N.C. at 394 (quoting *Lehr*, 463 U.S. at 262). According to *Lehr*, however, statutes designating the class of biological fathers entitled to notice may be unconstitutional (1) if they omit too many responsible fathers, or (2) if the qualifications for notice are beyond the control of an interested putative father. Pursuant to this second prong, the North Carolina Supreme Court then examined whether obtaining notice of the child's birth was beyond the putative father's control, concluding that it was not, and emphasizing the facts in the case:

> [The biological father] . . . demonstrated only incuriosity and disinterest. He knew that [the mother] was fertile because she already had a child when they met. He knew that, despite [the mother's] purported use of birth control, he had impregnated her once, leading to an abortion. He assumed that her subsequent birth control methods would be effective without making detailed inquiry. He and [the mother] continued an active sex life, even after they broke up. From [the father's] perspective, the sex was unprotected and contraception was wholly [the mother's] responsibility. The burden on him to find out whether he had sired a child was minimal, for he knew how to contact [the mother]. All the while, [the child] continued to live and bond with his adoptive parents.

*In re Adoption of S.D.W.*, 367 N.C. at 395.

The supreme court held that the father was not deprived of due process: the father "had the opportunity to be on notice of the pregnancy and . . . he failed to grasp that opportunity by taking any of the steps that would establish him as a responsible father," therefore falling outside "the class of protected fathers who may claim a liberty interest in developing a relationship with a child." *In re Adoption of S.D.W.*, 367 N.C. at 396.

In a subsequent adoption case, *In re Adoption of B.J.R.*, 238 N.C. App. 308 (2014), the court of appeals examined this same adoption statute, G.S. 48-3-601, in the context of a father's claim that his consent should have been required for his child's adoption and that his due process rights were violated by the determination under the adoption statutes that his consent was not required. Although in this case the father knew of the child's existence and filed a G.S. Chapter 50 custody action with a request for genetic testing prior to the filing of the adoption petition, the court of appeals cited both *Lehr* and *In re Adoption of S.D.W.* in reasoning that the 17-year-old father's actions, many of which were consistent with his desire to develop a relationship with the child, were not sufficient to meet the statutory criteria in G.S. 48-3-601, nor sufficient to demonstrate that he had "grasped the opportunity" to develop a relationship with his child such that he had a constitutionally protected right of parentage.

It is worth noting that in both the *In re Adoption of S.D.W.* and *In re Adoption of B.J.R.* opinions, the appellate courts' holdings were very fact-specific. It is likely that the outcome of future cases addressing similar issues will likewise depend to a great extent on the facts surrounding a putative father's circumstances. For example, the court of appeals in *In re R.D.H.*, III, 828 S.E.2d 170, 174 (N.C. Ct. App. 2017), a TPR based on neglect, stated, "[w]hile there may be certain situations where a man should 'know' he is likely the father of a child, this is not one of them." The evidence in this case showed the mother and respondent did not have a relationship but instead had meetings that were sexual in nature, and the child was named after a different man that the mother identified as the potential father.

In an earlier case, *In re Baby Girl Dockery*, 128 N.C. App. 631 (1998), the court of appeals rejected a putative father's constitutional challenge to an order refusing to allow him to intervene in an adoption proceeding, even though his failure to act sooner was due in part to his lack of knowledge of the child's existence. The court held that the statutory scheme making his consent unnecessary violated neither due process nor equal protection and was "a reasonable means of addressing the legitimate state concern that only those persons who have, in addition to a biological link, a parental relationship of care and provision for a minor child be afforded the right to the requirement of consent before his or her parental rights are severed by such child's adoption." *In re Baby Girl Dockery*, 128 N.C. App. at 635. Other cases addressing the constitutionality of this ground but unrelated to the issue of knowledge of the child's existence, are discussed in subsection 7, below.

**5. Judicial paternity determinations and name on birth certificate.** For purposes of the ground to terminate parental rights under G.S. 7B-1111(a)(5), the petitioner must prove the respondent father has not "established paternity through G.S. 49-14, 110-132, 130A-101, 130A-118, or other judicial proceeding." This means the father has not

- judicially established his paternity in a civil action to establish paternity (G.S. 49-10), a declaratory judgment (G.S. 1-253), or other civil or criminal action where paternity is an element of the claim (e.g., criminal nonsupport (G.S. 49-2; 14-322) or custody (G.S. 50-13.1));
- executed an affidavit of parentage along with the child's mother within ten days of the child's birth (G.S. 130A-101) or as part of a child support case (G.S. 110-132); or
- sought an amendment of the child's birth certificate as provided for in G.S. 130A-118.

This prong of the TPR ground, G.S. 7B-1111(a)(5)e., was enacted by S.L. 2013-129, sec. 35, effective for all actions pending or filed on or after October 1, 2013. Prior to its enactment, the court of appeals held in a TPR action based on G.S. 7B-1111(a)(5) that there is a rebuttable presumption that respondent father took the required legal steps necessary to establish paternity if he is named on the child's amended birth certificate. *In re J.K.C.*, 218 N.C. App. 22 (2012). *Cf. Gunter v. Gunter,* 228 N.C. App. 138 (2013) (unpublished) (mother could not rely on holding in *In re J.K.C.* to support her argument that husband's name on child's birth certificate judicially established his paternity of the child).

See Chapter 5.4.B.7 for further discussion of paternity, putative fathers, and birth certificates.

---

**Practice Note:** Although the statutory language in G.S. 7B-1111(a)(5)e. refers to the establishment of paternity, some of the identified statutes have the legal effect of acknowledging paternity but do not establish paternity. For example, G.S. 130A-101 provides for the execution of an affidavit of parentage for the purposes of registering the child's birth, to be executed within ten days of the child's birth. As a result of a properly executed affidavit, the father's name will be listed on the child's birth certificate. However, G.S. 130A-101(f) does not include a presumption or adjudication of paternity but instead provides that "a certified copy of the affidavit shall be admissible in any action to establish paternity."

**Resources:**
Issues related to paternity are complicated. For a detailed discussion of relevant topics, see SARA DEPASQUALE, FATHERS AND PATERNITY: APPLYING THE LAW IN NORTH CAROLINA CHILD WELFARE CASES (UNC School of Government, 2016).

For a shorter discussion, see
- Sara DePasquale, *New Book! Fathers and Paternity: Applying the Law in North Carolina Child Welfare Cases,* UNC SCH. OF GOV'T: ON THE CIVIL SIDE BLOG (June 17, 2016).
- Sara DePasquale, *Legitimation versus Paternity: What's the Difference?,* UNC SCH. OF GOV'T: ON THE CIVIL SIDE BLOG (March 23, 2016).

---

**6. Admissibility of paternity test.** A TPR action is a civil action where the issue of paternity may be raised as an element of the claim or defense. When paternity is at issue and paternity testing is sought, the court must order paternity testing. *See* G.S. 8-50.1(b1); *In re J.S.L.*, 218 N.C. App. 610 (2012) (private TPR action holding G.S. 8-50.1(b1), the evidence statute requiring paternity testing when requested at "the trial of any civil action in which the question of parentage arises" applies; reversing the trial court's adjudication of this ground, where the father had denied paternity and requested testing, and the trial court denied his request).

Even if paternity test results show a high likelihood that the respondent is not the child's father, the court may consider those results only if they are properly introduced into evidence. The results of testing ordered under G.S. 8-50.1(b1) create a rebuttable presumption, and respondent must be allowed an opportunity to rebut the presumption. *In re L.D.B.*, 168 N.C. App. 206 (2005) (reversing order regarding paternity and TPR when court excluded named respondent from TPR action based on test results, which were not admitted into evidence, that showed a zero probability of parentage; concluding the respondent's right to offer evidence regarding the allegations in the TPR petition, including whether he is actually the child's parent, is inherent in due process protections that require an adequate opportunity to be heard).

**7. Constitutionality.** The court of appeals, in *In re A.C.V.*, 203 N.C. App. 473 (2010), affirmed an order terminating a teenage father's rights to his newborn child based on G.S. 7B-1111(a)(5). The court expressed concerns about the constitutionality of applying this ground to the facts of the case. Noting that none of the trial court's 123 findings indicated that the father was unfit to parent the child or that his home was unsuitable, the court said, "It is difficult, under the circumstances of this case, to conclude that [the father's] constitutional rights were assured through the application of section 7B-1111(a)(5)." *In re A.C.V.*, 203 N.C. App. at 482. The court affirmed the TPR order on the basis that it was bound by cases such as *Owenby v. Young*, 357 N.C. 142 (2003) (stating that a finding of any ground for termination under G.S. 7B-1111 will result in forfeiture of a parent's constitutionally protected status) and *A Child's Hope, LLC v. Doe*, 178 N.C. App. 96 (2006). See also the discussion of constitutional issues related to this ground in subsection 4, above.

## F. Dependency

Where the parent is incapable of providing for the proper care and supervision of the child, such that the child is dependent as defined by G.S. 7B-101(9), there is a reasonable probability that the parent's incapability will continue for the foreseeable future, and the parent lacks an appropriate alternative child care arrangement, a ground for termination of parental rights (TPR) exists. The parent's incapability may be the result of substance abuse, intellectual disability, mental illness, organic brain syndrome, or any other cause or condition that renders the parent unable or unavailable to parent the child. G.S. 7B-1111(a)(6).

To adjudicate the ground in G.S. 7B-1111(a)(6), the court must find that the parent (1) does not have an ability to provide care or supervision to the child and (2) lacks an available alternative child care arrangement for the child. *In re Z.D.*, 812 S.E.2d 668 (N.C. Ct. App. 2018); *In re D.T.N.A.*, 250 N.C. App. 582 (2016).

**1. Constitutional challenge.** This ground does not violate the equal protection clause or deny due process. *In re Montgomery*, 311 N.C. 101 (1984) (decided under an earlier version of the Juvenile Code).

**2. Lack of alternative child care required.** This ground cannot be established without findings supporting a conclusion that the parent lacks an appropriate alternative child care arrangement. *In re N.B.*, 200 N.C. App. 773 (2009); *see also In re C.N.C.B.*, 197 N.C. App. 553 (2009). For a parent to have an appropriate alternative child care arrangement, the parent must have taken some action to identify viable alternatives; it is not enough that the parent merely goes along with a plan created by DSS. *In re L.H.*, 210 N.C. App. 355 (2011). *See also In re K.O.*, 223 N.C. App. 420 (2012) (holding that respondent mother could not claim she had an alternative child care arrangement with an unrelated acquaintance where this acquaintance had been awarded permanent custody of the child by the court, the acquaintance did not have custody at the mother's request, and the mother had no ability to decide custody).

Alternative child care arrangements suggested by the parent are not "appropriate" if they cannot be approved by DSS. In the case of *In re N.T.U.*, 234 N.C. App. 722 (2014), three alternative placements were provided to DSS by an incarcerated respondent mother, but none could be approved by DSS: one was incarcerated, one physically disciplined another child in front of DSS, and another demonstrated a lack of interest in the child. *See also In re L.R.S.*, 237 N.C. App. 16 (2014) (child care arrangement suggested by mother was not shown to be viable).

A finding that respondent father had never offered another child care placement was contradicted by evidence in the case file. The father had recommended a cousin for placement in the underlying dependency case, and that cousin was approved by the court but not utilized by DSS because respondent believed the child remaining in his foster care placement was better for the child. *In re D.T.N.A.*, 250 N.C. App. 582 (2016) (order terminating father's parental rights pursuant to G.S. 7B-1111(a)(6) reversed).

**3. Evidence of incapability to provide proper care or supervision of the child.** This ground cannot be established without findings supporting a conclusion that the parent does not have the ability to provide care or supervision to the child. The parent's incapability must be proved by clear and convincing evidence. G.S. 7B-1111(b) (petitioner or movant has the burden to prove the facts justifying termination by clear and convincing evidence). *See, e.g., In re Scott*, 95 N.C. App. 760 (1989) (holding that the physician's testimony about a mother with a personality disorder did not provide clear and convincing evidence to support the trial court's findings and termination order); *see also In re Small*, 138 N.C. App. 474 (2000) (holding that the finding that the respondent was incapable of providing proper care to her children was not supported by clear and convincing evidence); *In re D.T.N.A.*, 250 N.C. App. 582 (2016) (holding evidence did not support the court's findings that respondent father was incapable of providing proper and supervision because he had failed to comply with his case plan, engaged in poor decision making, was unable to provide for the child's daily needs, and used drugs; court's finding that assumed the respondent's refusal to take drug tests would have resulted in positive results is not supported by the record, which included judicial notice of the court file that contained permanency planning orders where the court found the respondent had negative drug screens as part of his criminal probation and a court report that stated respondent had tested negative for illegal substances; further holding even if drug use was proven, the petitioner has the burden of showing that abuse prevents the parent from providing proper care and supervision for the child, and there was no such evidence).

The cause of the parent's incapability to provide proper care and supervision may be based on any cause or condition and is not limited to certain types of conditions. *See In re L.R.S.*, 237 N.C. App. 16 (2014) (affirming TPR where respondent's incapability was based on her incarceration; explaining 2003 amendment to G.S. 7B-1111(a)(6) that removed limiting conditions for basis of parent's incapability). Note that before statutory amendments in 2003, this ground required that the parent's incapacity be due to substance abuse, "mental retardation" (now diagnosed as "intellectual disability"), mental illness, organic brain syndrome, or any other similar cause or condition. In 2012, the court of appeals relied on an older case that examined the former language of the statute and held that this ground was not established where there was no evidence that the father, who was incarcerated, was incapable of providing care and supervision due to a condition specified in the statute or any other similar cause or condition. *In re J.K.C.* 218 N.C. App. 22 (2012) (looking to *In re Clark*, 151

N.C. App. 286 (2002)). To the extent the court of appeals relied on *In re Clark*, that reliance was misplaced. *See In re L.R.S.*, 237 N.C. App. 16 (2014) (discussing significance of the change in the statutory language related to the *In re Clark* and *In re J.K.C.* opinions).

Termination under this ground does not require that the parent's incapability be permanent or that its precise duration be known, only that there is a reasonable probability that such incapability will continue for the foreseeable future. *In re H.N.D.*, 827 S.E.2d 329, 335 (N.C. Ct. App. 2019) (affirming TPR; determination of a reasonable probability that mother's incapability to provide proper care and supervision would continue for the foreseeable future was based on mother's stated intent to keep father in her and the children's lives "in spite of the enduring pattern of violence [m]other has suffered" during their troubled history together); *In re N.T.U.*, 234 N.C. App. 722 (2014) (affirming TPR order where the respondent mother had been incarcerated for three years on charges relating to homicide and bank robbery and had not received a trial date, the child had been in DSS custody for two-thirds of his life, and none of the alternative child care arrangements suggested by respondent could be approved for placement); *see also In re L.R.S.*, 237 N.C. App. 16 (2014) (where child had been in DSS custody since the age of two months due to mother's pretrial incarceration and subsequent conviction on federal charges resulting in a sentence of 38 months, the trial court properly found there was a reasonable probability that the incapability would continue for the foreseeable future; statute no longer requires incapability continue throughout child's minority).

A mental health evaluation conducted a year before a termination hearing can support a termination of parental rights based on dependency when "the persistence of [the] personality problems" is characterized as "not easily amendable to change" and there is a lack of mental health treatment. *In re A.L.L.*, 254 N.C. App. 252, 267 (2017) (citations omitted) (affirming TPR based on two prior mental health assessments that showed mother's longstanding mental health conditions and her repeated failures to follow treatment recommendations necessary to care for her children). *Cf. In re Z.D.*, 812 S.E.2d 668 (N.C. Ct. App. 2018) (reversing TPR; evidentiary findings in a private TPR proceeding were insufficient to support the ultimate finding that respondent mother had a current incapability that would continue for the foreseeable future; findings as to mother's mental health and parenting ability related to mother's history rather than her progress (or lack of progress) over the fifteen months prior to the termination hearing and included no specific findings regarding her condition, mental health, and alleged incapability at the time of the hearing; mother's psychiatrist testified that mother was participating and committed to her treatment and had been symptom free for over a year).

In the case of a minor parent, the court must adequately address the parent's capacity (or lack thereof) and whether his or her transition to adulthood would cure the basis of the incapacity. *In re Matherly*, 149 N.C. App. 452 (2002) (reversing and remanding TPR; noting respondent was 15 years old when her child was first placed in DSS custody, 17 years old when the TPR petition was filed, and as an unemancipated minor was legally unable to establish her own residence as required by the case plan).

**4. Diligent efforts not a prerequisite.** The court will not read into G.S. 7B-1111(a)(6) a requirement that DSS make "diligent efforts" to provide services to parents before proceeding to seek termination of parental rights; any such requirement must come from the legislature. *In re Guynn*, 113 N.C. App. 114 (1993).

**5. GAL for respondent not required.** Before a 2005 amendment, the trial court was required to appoint a guardian ad litem (GAL) for the parent when the ground for termination in G.S. 7B-1111(a)(6) was alleged, and a number of cases were reversed because the court failed to appoint a GAL. Under current law, appointment of a GAL for the parent is discretionary and based upon a determination that the parent is incompetent. Note that appointment of GAL for a minor respondent parent is mandatory. G.S. 7B-1101.1(b)–(f). See section 9.4.B, above, and Chapter 2.4.F (relating to GAL appointments for parents).

## G. Abandonment

Where the parent has willfully abandoned the child for at least six consecutive months immediately preceding the filing of the petition or motion, a ground for termination of parental rights (TPR) exists. G.S. 7B-1111(a)(7). Additionally, a parent's rights may be terminated on this ground where the parent voluntarily abandoned an infant under North Carolina's "safe surrender" law and at least sixty consecutive days have passed immediately preceding the filing of a TPR petition or motion. *See* G.S. 7B-500, discussed in Chapter 5.5.B.3.

Abandonment is also included in the definition of "neglected juvenile" and may also be the basis to TPR on the ground of neglect pursuant to G.S. 7B-1111(a)(1). *See* G.S. 7B-101(15) (definition of "neglected juvenile"); *In re T.J.F.*, 230 N.C. App. 531 (2013). See also section 9.11.A, above, and specifically subsection 7.

**1. Six-month time period.** The critical period for a finding of abandonment of a juvenile (unrelated to the safe surrender of an infant) is at least six consecutive months immediately preceding the filing of a TPR petition or motion. G.S. 7B-1111(a)(7). *See In re Young*, 346 N.C. 244, 252 (1997) (reversing TPR order on the basis that the mother's conduct during the relevant six-month period did not manifest "a willful determination to forego all parental duties and relinquish all parental claims to the child"); *In re S.Z.H.*, 247 N.C. App. 254 (2016) (reversing TPR order when both petitioner and respondent in private TPR proceeding testified that respondent called child during approximately half of the relevant six-month period and asked to attend child's birthday party which was to occur during that time). However, the trial court may consider the respondent's conduct outside this six-month window for the purpose of evaluating the respondent's credibility and intentions. *See In re D.E.M.*, 254 N.C. App. 401 (2017) (looking back to months before relevant six-month period for TPR ground when determining that mother's actions of failing to visit, contact, or provide for the child were willful), *aff'd per curiam*, 370 N.C. 463 (2018); *In re C.J.H.*, 240 N.C. App. 489 (2015) (it was appropriate for the trial court to examine the respondent's history of sporadic contact with the child outside the six-month period to evaluate whether his requests for visitation within the six-month period were made in good faith). While a trial court may consider a parent's conduct outside the six-month period to evaluate the parent's credibility and intentions, actions of the parent outside the six-month period will not preclude the trial court from finding willful abandonment pursuant to G.S. 7B-1111(a)(7) if the parent "did nothing to maintain or establish a relationship with [the child] during the determinative six-month period." *In re C.B.C.,* 832 S.E.2d 692, 697 (N.C. S.Ct. 2019).

**2. Defining abandonment.** The supreme court has defined abandonment as a parent's willful or intentional conduct evincing a settled purpose to forego all parental duties and relinquish all parental claims. *Pratt v. Bishop,* 257 N.C. 486 (1962) (adoption case); *In re Young,* 346 N.C. 244 (1997) (in private TPR case, abandonment may be implied from parental conduct which manifests a willful determination to forego all parental duties and relinquish all parental claims). *See also In re C.B.C.,* 832 S.E.2d 692 (N.C. S.Ct. 2019) and *In re E.H.P.,* 831 S.E.2d 49 (N.C. S.Ct. 2019) (both private TPR cases adopting definition set out in *In re Young*). Abandonment also has been defined as willful neglect and refusal to perform natural and legal parental obligations of care and support. If a parent withholds the parent's presence, love, care, and opportunity to display filial affection, and willfully neglects to lend support and maintenance, the parent relinquishes all parental claims and abandons the child. *Pratt,* 257 N.C. 486; *In re N.D.A.,* 833 S.E.2d 768, 773 (N.C. S.Ct. 2019) and *In re E.H.P.,* 831 S.E.2d 49, 52 (N.C. S.Ct. 2019) (both quoting *Pratt*).

An integral part of abandonment is willful intent, which is a question of fact. *In re N.D.A.,* 833 S.E.2d 768 (N.C. S.Ct. 2019); *Pratt,* 257 N.C. 486; *In re C.B.C.,* 832 S.E.2d 692, 695 (quoting *Pratt*). For purposes of abandonment, willfulness requires "more than an intention to do a thing, there must also be purpose and deliberation." *In re E.B.,* 834 S.E.2d 169, 174 (N.C. Ct. App. 2019) and *In re D.M.O.,* 250 N.C. App. 570, 572–73 (2016) (both quoting *In re S.R.G.,* 195 N.C. App. 79, 84 (2009)). Willful intent for abandonment under G.S. 7B-1111(a)(7) is "something greater" than the willful intent necessary for leaving a child in foster care without making reasonable progress under G.S. 7B-1111(a)(2). *In re D.M.O.,* 250 N.C. App. at 576.

Because willful intent is integral to a determination of abandonment and is a question of fact, there must be evidentiary findings to support an ultimate finding of willful intent. *In re D.M.O.,* 250 N.C. App. at 573; *In re I.R.L.,* 823 S.E.2d 902, 905 (N.C. Ct. App. 2019) (quoting *In re D.M.O.*). In *In re I.R.L.,* a private TPR proceeding, the finding of willfulness was "especially important" because during the relevant six-month period, respondent father was subject to a domestic violence protection order that prohibited contact with mother, who had custody of the 3-year-old child. When the termination order did not address the willfulness of father's conduct, the findings did not support termination for abandonment, even though the order included findings that during the relevant six-month period, father knew the child's location but had not seen, visited, or inquired about the child, or provided any substantial financial support for the child. *In re I.R.L.,* 823 S.E.2d at 905 (noting that, given the child's age, "any communication with, gifts to, or requests to visit" the child would necessarily have been directed to mother, which would have violated the no-contact provision of the DVPO).

That a prior petition to terminate a parent's rights on the ground of willful abandonment was denied does not preclude a trial court in a second termination proceeding on the same ground from finding that the same parent has willfully withheld love, care and affection from the child during the relevant six-month period. *In re C.B.C.*, 832 S.E.2d 692 (N.C. S.Ct. 2019) (2016 TPR petition on ground of willful abandonment denied; 2018 petition on same ground allowed).

**3. Evidence of abandonment.** Evidence of abandonment was sufficient in the following cases:

- Findings demonstrated that during the determinative six-month period (the last three months of which father was incarcerated), respondent father did not pursue a relationship with the child as he sent no cards or letters other than a birthday card sent from prison after service of the petition to terminate his rights, did not contact the child's custodians to inquire about the child's well-being despite having their contact information and not being prohibited from doing so by the custody order, did not seek to modify the custody order, and had not paid support from pre-incarceration earnings. The supreme court went on to note that other findings demonstrated that father had had no contact with the child or her custodians for nearly a year before the filing of the petition despite having "the ability to make at least some contact," all of which supported the conclusion of willful abandonment. *In re C.B.C.*, 832 S.E.2d 692, 696 (N.C. S.Ct. 2019).
- In a private TPR proceeding, respondent father's argument that he was forbidden by a temporary custody judgment from contacting his children was rejected as there was sufficient evidence that supported the trial court's determination of abandonment. Father admitted having had no contact with his children during the determinative six-month period and for several years after entry of the temporary custody judgment. Although father was incarcerated for most of the determinative six-month period, he filed a motion to suspend his obligation to pay child support during his incarceration but made no effort to modify the custody judgment to allow contact with his children. *In re E.H.P.*, 831 S.E.2d 49 (N.C. S.Ct. 2019).
- Unchallenged findings supported the trial court's conclusion of abandonment. Before the relevant six-month period, father stated that he was "just going to allow [his] sister to handle" the child's care and placement. During the relevant-six month period, father moved to California without telling DSS, failed to attend permanency planning hearings and a child support hearing, did not request a single visit despite weekly visits being authorized, and did not make any Skype calls to the child before the TPR petition was filed, despite having an opportunity to do so. *In re E.B.*, 834 S.E.2d 169, 174–75 (N.C. Ct. App. 2019).
- The trial court's order terminating parental rights for willful abandonment was affirmed where during the six months in question, the respondent did not provide timely and consistent financial support for the child; before the six-month period in question, the respondent did not pay sufficient support until ordered to do so and then did not pay consistently; and the respondent failed to make a good faith effort to visit the child or to maintain or reestablish a relationship with the child. The respondent's last-minute efforts at financial support and visitation did not undermine the trial court's conclusion of abandonment. *In re C.J.H.*, 240 N.C. App. 489 (2015).
- The trial court's conclusion of willful abandonment was supported by its findings showing that during the six-month determinative period the father made no effort to

remain in contact with his children or their caretakers and neither provided nor offered anything toward their support. The father's single phone call during the six-month period could not be deemed material enough to potentially change the outcome. Although the father had been jailed and then deported during that time, the court of appeals analyzed deportation similarly to incarceration, stating that like incarceration, deportation should serve as "neither a sword nor a shield in a termination of parental rights decision." *In re B.S.O.*, 234 N.C. App. 706, 711 (2014) (quoting *In re P.L.P.*, 173 N.C. App. 1, 10 (2005)). In comparing deportation and incarceration, the court of appeals in *In re B.S.O.*, stated that a deported parent has more opportunities than an incarcerated parent to support a child. A deported parent can communicate with a child, earn money that is sent to support a child, and even pursue legal action to attempt to have the child returned to his or her custody. In *In re D.M.O.*, 250 N.C. App. 570 (2016), the court of appeals notes that an incarcerated parent has fewer opportunities to show affection and have contact with a child than a deported parent.

Evidence of abandonment was not sufficient in the following cases:

- In a private TPR case, father's unchallenged testimony showed that he unsuccessfully attempted to make arrangements to visit the child. The trial court made no determination regarding father's credibility or findings about whether father, who was incarcerated, had the <u>ability</u> to contact the child or petitioner, or pay financial support during the relevant period. The lack of findings addressing father's ability, which went to father's intent/willfulness, did not support a determination of willful abandonment under G.S. 7B-1111(a)(7). *In re N.D.A.*, 833 S.E.2d 768, 776 (N.C. S.Ct. 2019).
- During the relevant six-month period, father filed a motion to modify a G.S. Chapter 50 custody order and requested sole custody of his children who were in the custody of their maternal grandmother. Father's act in seeking sole custody demonstrated that he did not intend to forego all parental duties and relinquish all parental rights to the children. The trial court erred in concluding that father's rights should be terminated pursuant to G.S. 7B-1111(a)(7). Additionally, the trial court's reliance on a consent order entered in a Chapter 50 custody action between father and grandparents that included a provision that grandmother would file a petition to terminate father's rights that no other party, including father, would oppose was error because that order is void as against public policy and is neither a properly executed consent or relinquishment under the adoption statutes. *In re C.K.C.*, 822 S.E.2d 741, 745 (N.C. Ct. App. 2018).
- In a private TPR case, findings that mother failed to visit child, attend his sports games, or contact petitioner father during the relevant six-month period were not sufficient to establish mother's actions were willful when mother was incarcerated all but 33 of the 180 relevant days and struggled with addiction issues for which she received treatment during the same relevant period. No findings addressed how mother's incarceration, addiction issues, or participation in a drug treatment program while in custody might have affected her opportunities to exercise visitation, communicate with her child, or attend games, or whether mother had made the effort or had the ability to exercise any of those rights but failed to do so during the relevant period. *In re D.M.O.*, 250 N.C. App. 570 (2016) (additionally, on remand, the trial court was instructed to resolve material conflicts in the evidence presented by mother and father as to her efforts to communicate

- with father and contact the child during the relevant period).
- Finding that father had failed to provide a plan for the child and failed to comply with his own case plan was unsupported by evidence and other findings that father substantially complied with his case plan. Additional findings that respondent worked part-time and supplemented that income by playing music, was current in his monthly child support obligation, made his home appropriate for a child by cleaning it and relinquishing his pit bulls, attended the majority of visits with the child, and successfully completed a parenting program did not show an intent to willfully forego parental duties and did not support conclusion that father willfully abandoned his child. *In re D.T.N.A.*, 250 N.C. App. 582 (2016).
- In a private TPR case, the trial court's finding of willful abandonment during the six months immediately preceding the filing of the TPR petition was not supported by the evidence because the respondent was under a court order not to have contact with the children during the six-month period, and he filed a civil action seeking visitation, which showed he did not intend to forego his role as a parent. *In re D.T.L.*, 219 N.C. App. 219 (2012).
- Evidence was not sufficient to establish the abandonment ground where the court's findings did not "clearly show that the parent's actions [were] wholly inconsistent with a desire to maintain custody of the child." *In re S.R.G.*, 195 N.C. App. 79, 87 (2009) (finding that the mother had visited eleven times during the relevant six-month period); *see also In re S.Z.H.*, 247 N.C. App. 254 (2016) (evidence showed respondent contacted child the first half of the relevant six-month period and attempted to communicate with child after that but was stopped by petitioner from doing so).
- Although the father had not visited or asked for visits during the relevant six months and had not regularly sent cards or gifts, the appellate court held that findings did not support willful abandonment because the father had been instructed by his attorney in the criminal case not to contact the child or mother, the DSS protection plan provided for no contact, and he had been making support payments during the relevant six-month period. *In re T.C.B.*, 166 N.C. App. 482 (2004).

Evidence of the following circumstances is insufficient, standing alone, to determine abandonment:

- Neither a parent's history of alcohol abuse nor a parent's incarceration, standing alone, necessarily negates a finding of willfulness for purposes of abandonment. *In re McLemore*, 139 N.C. App. 426 (2000); *In re C.B.C.*, 832 S.E.2d 692 (N.C. S.Ct. 2019) (speaking to incarceration); *In re D.M.O.*, 250 N.C. App. 570, 575 (2016) (quoting *McLemore*, 139 N.C. App. at 431) ("[I]ncarceration, standing alone, neither precludes nor requires a finding of willfulness" in the context of abandonment).
- Failure to pay support, in itself, does not constitute abandonment. *Bost v. Van Nortwick*, 117 N.C. App. 1 (1994). However, the fact that a parent paid some support during the relevant six-month period may not preclude a finding of willful abandonment. *In re Adoption of Searle*, 82 N.C. App. 273 (1986).

## H. Murder, Voluntary Manslaughter, and Felony Assault of Child or Parent

Grounds for termination of parental rights exist where the parent has

- committed murder or voluntary manslaughter of another child of the parent or other child residing in the home;
- aided, abetted, attempted, conspired, or solicited to commit murder or voluntary manslaughter of the child, another child of the parent, or other child in the home;
- committed a felony assault that results in serious bodily injury to the child, another child of the parent, or other child residing in the home; or
- committed murder or voluntary manslaughter of the child's other parent; provided, the court must consider whether the killing was committed in self-defense or in defense of others, or whether there was substantial evidence of other justification.

G.S. 7B-1111(a)(8).

**1. Manner of proof.** Petitioner has the burden of proving the criminal offense by either (1) proving the elements of the offense or (2) proving that a court of competent jurisdiction has convicted the parent of the offense, whether by jury verdict or any kind of plea. G.S. 7B-1111(a)(8).

**2. Standard of proof.** The ground of a parent's commission of voluntary manslaughter of another child requires proof of the elements of the offense by clear and convincing evidence, not beyond a reasonable doubt. *In re J.S.B.*, 183 N.C. App. 192 (2007).

**3. Serious bodily injury.** To prove that respondent committed a felony assault resulting in serious bodily injury by proving that respondent was convicted of the offense, a petitioner would have to show a conviction under G.S. 14-32.4(a) (assault inflicting serious bodily injury) or perhaps G.S. 14-318.4(a3) (felony child abuse inflicting serious *bodily* injury). A conviction under G.S. 14-318.4(a) (felony child abuse inflicting serious *physical* injury) would not be sufficient. As defined in G.S. 14-318.4(d)(1), "serious bodily injury" (1) creates a substantial risk of death; (2) causes serious permanent disfigurement, coma, a permanent or protracted condition that causes extreme pain, or permanent or protracted loss or impairment of the function of any bodily member or organ; or (3) results in prolonged hospitalization. *See In re T.J.D.W.*, 182 N.C. App. 394, *aff'd per curiam*, 362 N.C. 84 (2007); *State v. Downs*, 179 N.C. App. 860 (2006); *State v. Hannah*, 149 N.C. App. 713 (2002).

To prove felony child abuse inflicting serious bodily injury under G.S. 14-318.4(a3), the state must show that defendant is the parent of the child, the child was not yet sixteen years old, and defendant intentionally and without justification or excuse inflicted serious bodily injury. *State v. Bohannon,* 247 N.C. App. 756 (2016). In *Bohannon,* all elements were undisputed except whether the child's injury, a subarachnoid hemorrhage, constituted a serious bodily injury as defined in G.S. 14-318.4(d)(1). Based on the definition set out above, the trial court properly denied defendant's motion to dismiss based on testimony of three experts who treated the child as to the impact of bleeding on an infant's developing brain, which could be life-threatening and would require further monitoring.

## I. TPR to Another Child and Lack of Safe Home

Grounds for termination of parental rights (TPR) exist where a court of competent jurisdiction has terminated the parent's rights with respect to another child of the parent and the parent lacks the ability or willingness to establish a safe home. G.S. 7B-1111(a)(9). *In re J.D.A.D.*, 253 N.C. App. 53 (2017) (interpreting G.S. 7B-1111(a)(9) to require a two-part analysis before terminating parental rights: (1) that there was an involuntary termination of parental rights to another child of the respondent parent and (2) that the respondent parent has an inability or unwillingness to establish a safe home). A "safe home" is defined in G.S. 7B-101(19) as "a home in which the juvenile is not at substantial risk of physical or emotional abuse or neglect." *See In re T.N.H.*, 831 S.E.2d 54 (N.C. S.Ct. 2019).

Whether parental rights to another child have been terminated by a court is often undisputed, leaving the appellate court to determine whether the evidence established that respondent lacked the ability or willingness to establish a safe home.

The following cases found sufficient evidence to support termination for lack of a safe home:

- *In re T.N.H.*, 831 S.E.2d 54 (N.C. S.Ct. 2019) (the record in the case supported findings that respondent's parental rights to another child were terminated by court order, that respondent was incarcerated at the time of the termination hearing with an unknown release date, respondent had a history of unstable housing and had failed to complete her case plan, that child was sexually abused while in respondent's care, respondent did not believe child was sexually abused and failed to report the abuse, and respondent did not understand the resulting trauma suffered by the child or his mental health needs).
- *In re D.J.E.L.*, 208 N.C. App. 154 (2010) (evidence of respondent mother's history with domestic violence with multiple individuals was sufficient to establish that she lacked the ability or willingness to establish a safe home).
- *In re L.A.B.*, 178 N.C. App. 295 (2006) (evidence that, among other things, mother's housing at all times since child's birth was transient was sufficient).
- *In re V.L.B.*, 168 N.C. App. 679 (2005) (evidence of mother's chronic mental health problems, her failure to pursue treatment, and her intention to personally care for respondent father whose mental and physical problems required round-the-clock care demonstrated that respondents could not provide a safe home).

Respondent father's incarceration, while relevant, was not sufficient by itself to support a conclusion to terminate parental rights based on his inability to establish a safe home. *In re J.D.A.D.*, 253 N.C. App. 53 (father's incarceration was the only rationale in the adjudicatory findings supporting termination; evidence was presented that father had not been approved for visitation, provided minimal financial support, continued to abuse illegal substances, and failed to obtain treatment, but there were no adjudicatory findings as to those issues, warranting reversal of the TPR order).

## J. Relinquishment for Adoption

One ground for termination of parental rights addresses situations in which a child is being adopted in another state, the relinquishment or consent to adoption occurred in North Carolina, and the consent or relinquishment is not sufficient under the law of the state in which the adoption is taking place. This ground exists when the child has been relinquished to DSS or licensed child-placing agency or placed for adoption with a prospective adoptive parent, and

- the parent's consent to or relinquishment for adoption is irrevocable (except for fraud, duress, or other circumstances set out in G.S. 48-3-609 and 48-3-707);
- termination of the parent's rights is required for the adoption to occur in another jurisdiction where an adoption proceeding has been or will be filed; and
- the parent does not contest the termination of parental rights.

G.S. 7B-1111(a)(10).

### K. Conception Resulting from Sexually Related Criminal Offense

A ground for termination exists when the parent has been convicted of a sexually related offense under G.S. Chapter 14 that resulted in the conception of the child. G.S. 7B-1111(a)(11). This ground became effective October 1, 2012. *See* S.L. 2012-40. The effective date did not specify the offenses to which the law applies, but it would appear at a minimum to cover offenses committed on or after that date.

The law does not define "sexually related offense." Given the context, it most clearly covers offenses where vaginal intercourse is an element of the crime, such as rape or incest. Most of North Carolina's rape statutes explicitly state that a person convicted of the crime has no rights to custody of or inheritance from or any rights related to the child under G.S. Chapter 48 (adoptions) and Chapter 7B (juvenile proceedings). G.S. 14-27.21(c) (first-degree forcible rape); 14-27.22(c) (second-degree forcible rape); 14-27.23(d) (statutory rape of a child by an adult); 14-27.24(c) (first-degree statutory rape). *But see* G.S. 14-27.25 (statutory rape of a person who is 15 years of age or younger, which does not include such a provision). *See also* G.S. 7B-401.1(b); 7B-1103(c); 7B-1104(3). See section 9.4.A.4, above, discussing naming parents in TPR petition or motion.

Less clear is whether the law also covers crimes that may be committed through either vaginal intercourse or some other sexual act, such as sexual activity by a substitute parent or custodian under G.S. 14-27.31, or even those that never include vaginal intercourse as an element, such as indecent liberties with a child under G.S. 14-202.1. To determine whether those offenses resulted in the conception of a child would require a factual determination going beyond the elements of the conviction offense—a practice deemed proper in some related contexts, but improper in others. *Compare State v. Arrington*, 226 N.C. App. 311 (2013) (trial court not limited to the elements of the offense when determining whether kidnapping involved a minor victim and thus required sex offender registration), *with State v. Davidson*, 201 N.C. App. 354 (2009) (trial court limited to the elements of the crime of conviction when determining whether the crime meets the definition of an aggravated offense for satellite-based monitoring purposes). The appellate courts have yet to consider the question as applied to G.S. 7B-1111(a)(11).

## 9.12 Disposition and Best Interest Determination

### A. Overview

Termination of parental rights (TPR) proceedings involve two stages: the adjudication stage and dispositional stage. *In re D.L.W.*, 368 N.C. 835 (2016). The dispositional stage only occurs if the court concludes a TPR ground has been proved by clear, cogent, and convincing evidence; otherwise, the court dismisses the petition or denies the motion after making appropriate findings of fact and conclusions of law. *See* G.S. 7B-1110(c); 7B-1111(b).

After an adjudication that one or more TPR grounds exist, the court is never required to order the termination parental rights. Rather, the court must determine whether TPR is in the child's best interest. G.S. 7B-1110(a). If the court concludes that TPR is not in the child's best interests, the court must dismiss the petition or deny the motion after making findings of fact and conclusions of law supporting its determination. G.S. 7B-1110(b). The TPR petition or motion will be granted when the court determines both a ground has been proved and TPR is in the child's best interests.

### B. Evidentiary Standard

**1. No burden or standard of proof; court's discretion.** At disposition, no party has a burden of proof. All parties may present evidence, and the court makes findings of fact and a discretionary determination as to whether it is in the child's best interest to terminate parental rights. *See In re A.R.A.*, 835 S.E.2d 417 (N.C. S.Ct. 2019) (at the dispositional stage, the court must consider whether termination of parental rights is in the child's best interests); *In re E.H.P.*, 831 S.E.2d 49, 54 (N.C. S.Ct. 2019) (trial court's findings, demonstrating that it duly considered the G.S. 7B-1110(a) factors, were a "valid exercise of its discretion" to determine that TPR of father was in children's best interest); *In re H.N.D.*, 827 S.E.2d 329, 332 (N.C. Ct. App. 2019) (upon determining that termination is in the child's best interest, the trial court "may terminate the parent's rights in its discretion"). While G.S. 7B-1109(f) requires that findings in an adjudication order be based on clear, cogent, and convincing evidence, there is no like requirement for findings in dispositional orders. *See In re Z.L.W.*, 831 S.E.2d 62 (N.C. S.Ct. 2019).

Although appellate courts refer to the trial court's discretionary decision as to best interest, they also say that a best interest determination is a conclusion of law. *See, e.g., In re J.R.S.*, 813 S.E.2d 283 (N.C. Ct. App. 2018) (in dispositional orders, determinations of best interests are conclusions of law because they require an exercise of judgment); *In re M.N.C.*, 176 N.C. App. 114 (2006). Unlike a conclusion of law regarding an adjudicatory ground that is reviewed de novo, the court's best interest determination at the dispositional stage of a TPR proceeding is reviewed by appellate courts only for an abuse of discretion. *See In re A.R.A.*, 835 S.E.2d 417 (N.C. S.Ct. 2019); *In re A.U.D.*, 832 S.E.2d 698 (N.C. S.Ct. 2019); *In re L.M.T.*, 367 N.C. 165 (2013). An "[a]buse of discretion results where the court's ruling is manifestly unsupported by reason or is so arbitrary that it could not have been the result of a reasoned decision." *In re A.U.D.*, 832 S.E.2d 698, 700–01 (N.C. S.Ct. 2019) (quoting *In re T.L.H.*, 368 N.C. 101, 107 (2015)).

**2. Separate hearings not required.** Although the court applies different evidentiary standards at the adjudicatory stage, which determines whether a statutory ground for termination exists, and the dispositional stage, which determines whether termination of the parent's rights is in the child's best interest, there is no requirement that the two stages be conducted at two separate hearings. *In re F.G.J.*, 200 N.C. App. 681 (2009); *In re White*, 81 N.C. App. 82 (1986). However, to ensure that a parent's constitutional rights to his or her child are not violated by an order to terminate parental rights based solely on the child's best interest, the court must conduct two separate inquiries, even though the two inquiries may be conducted in the same hearing. *In re S.Z.H.*, 247 N.C. App. 254 (2016).

**3. Rules of evidence.** At disposition, the court may consider any evidence, including hearsay evidence, that the court finds to be relevant, reliable, and necessary to determine the best interests of the juvenile. G.S. 7B-1110(a). As the trier of fact, the court determines the weight and credibility to give to evidence. *In re K.G.W.*, 250 N.C. App. 62 (2016) (affirming trial court's decision that respondent's expert witness not testify, after an offer of proof resulted in court determining witness did not have any evidence to offer it, as trier of fact, that would be credible and persuasive).

## C. Considerations for Best Interest Determination

**1. Required criteria.** In making a determination regarding the child's best interest, the court is required to consider the following criteria and make written findings regarding those that are relevant:

- the child's age;
- the likelihood that the child will be adopted;
- whether termination will help achieve the permanent plan for the child;
- the bond between the child and the parent;
- the quality of the relationship between the child and the proposed adoptive parent, guardian, custodian, or other permanent placement;
- any other relevant consideration.

G.S. 7B-1110(a); *In re A.U.D.*, 832 S.E.2d 698, 702 (N.C. S.Ct. 2019) (emphasis in original) (stating that "[i]t is clear that a trial court must *consider* all of the factors in section 7B-1110(a)"); *In re A.R.A.*, 835 S.E.2d 417, 424 (N.C. S.Ct. 2019) (quoting *In re A.U.D*).

The trial court must consider and make findings about any of the factors that are relevant and is not required to make written findings on all six factors. *See In re A.R.A.*, 835 S.E.2d 417; *In re A.U.D.*, 832 S.E.2d 698. The North Carolina Supreme Court has recently stated that "a factor is 'relevant' if there is 'conflicting evidence concerning' the factor, such that it is 'placed in issue by virtue of the evidence presented before the [district] court[.]' " *In re A.R.A.*, 835 S.E.2d at 424 (agreeing with court of appeals and quoting *In re H.D*, 239 N.C. App. 318, 327 (2015)). The court of appeals has also stated that a relevant factor is one that has "an impact on the trial court's decision[.]" *In re S.Z.H.*, 247 N.C. App. 254, 265 (2016) (citations omitted). When there is no conflicting evidence as to a factor, the trial court's failure to make a written finding was not reversible error "under the unique circumstances" in

*In re A.U.D.*, 832 S.E.2d at 703 (when there was no conflict in the evidence as to the likelihood of adoption, that no bond existed between respondent and the children, and that there was no permanent plan in the private termination proceeding, to remand for findings on uncontested issues would elevate form over substance and delay permanence for the children).

**Practice Note:** The North Carolina Supreme Court considers it the better practice to make written findings as to statutory factors identified by a petitioner and encourages trial courts to make written findings as to all G.S. 7B-1110(a) factors in the dispositional portion of a TPR order to preclude an argument that a written finding was not made on a relevant factor. *In re A.U.D.*, 832 S.E.2d 698 (footnote 4 encouraging written findings).

Cases considering whether the factors considered by the court were relevant include

- *In re A.R.A.*, 835 S.E.2d 417 (N.C. S.Ct. 2019) (there was no conflicting evidence regarding the likelihood of the child's adoption; with no potential adoptive parent at the time of the TPR hearing, the district court was not required to make a finding about the quality of the relationship between child and proposed adoptive parent).
- *In re T.H.*, 832 S.E.2d 162 (N.C. Ct. App. 2019) (without conflicting evidence concerning efforts by DSS to contact respondent mother during her incarceration about DSS's reunification efforts, no findings were required under G.S. 7B-1110(a)(6)).
- *In re D.H.*, 232 N.C. App. 217 (2014) (emphasis in original) (rejecting the mother's argument that the court erred in making no findings regarding four of the factors, holding that two of the factors were not relevant—age because it was not raised as relevant *in this case*, and quality of a relationship with proposed placement because there was no proposed placement—and that the court did in fact make findings on the other two factors).
- *In re H.D.*, 239 N.C. App. 318 (2015) (quoting *In re D.H.*, 232 N.C. App. 217, and stating that one of the statutorily enumerated factors is relevant if there is conflicting evidence concerning that factor).

**Practice Note:** Some appellate cases addressing whether the trial court handled these criteria appropriately were decided under a previous version of the statute that required the court to consider the criteria but did not require written findings. In *In re J.L.H.*, 224 N.C. App. 52, the court of appeals specifically stated that such cases (*e.g., In re S.R.*, 207 N.C. App. 102 (2010); *In re S.C.H.*, 199 N.C. App. 658 (2009)) are superseded by the new version of the statute requiring written findings.

Although written findings on the relevant statutory criteria are required, recitation of the statutory language is not required where findings indicate the criteria were considered. In the case *In re D.C.*, 236 N.C. App. 287 (2014), the respondent mother challenged the court's finding of best interest, arguing that factors 3, 4, and 5 of G.S. 7B-1110(a) were not properly considered by the court. The court of appeals rejected this argument, in part noting that although the trial court did not use the word "bond" that is contained in factor 4, it did find that the child was over five years old and had been in foster care for over two years, which indicated that he did not have a strong bond with his mother since he would barely, if at all, have remembered her. Best interest was also supported by the findings related to the child's positive relationship with his prospective adoptive family and their desire to adopt him. *See also In re L.M.T.*, 367 N.C. 165 (2013) (findings need not recite the exact statutory language but must address the substance of the statutory requirements).

**2. Purpose of Juvenile Code.** The child's best interests, not the rights of the parents, are paramount. When the child's and parents' interests conflict, the child's best interests control. G.S. 7B-1100(3). *See also In re Montgomery*, 311 N.C. 101 (1984); *In re C.A.D.*, 247 N.C. App. 552 (2016).

A purpose of the Juvenile Code is to provide standards to ensure that the best interests of a child are of paramount consideration and when it is not in the child's best interest to be returned home, that the child will be placed in a safe, permanent home within a reasonable time. G.S. 7B-100(5). Another purpose is to provide standards for the removal and return of a child in a manner that prevents the unnecessary or inappropriate separation of children from their parents. G.S. 7B-100(4). Recent cases have considered these purposes when making a best interest determination.

- After considering the purposes in G.S. 7B-100, an order determining that termination of respondent father's rights was not in the child's best interest was affirmed. The supreme court reviewed the fundamental principles that the child's best interest is the polar star and of paramount consideration and the process of the trial court, which included weighing the competing purposes, considering the dispositional factors in G.S. 7B-1110(a)(1)–(5), and other relevant circumstances as allowed by G.S. 7B-1110(a)(6). Even though evidence would have supported a contrary decision, the trial court's decision was not arbitrary nor manifestly unsupported by reason. *In re A.U.D.*, 832 S.E.2d 698 (N.C. S.Ct. 2019).
- The trial court's conclusion that termination of respondent father's rights was in the children's best interest was affirmed, even though the trial court had found a strong bond between respondent and the children. The supreme court considered the stated policies in G.S. 7B-100(4) and (5) when rejecting father's argument that the trial court should have considered other dispositional alternatives that would have allowed a relationship with father. *In re Z.L.W.*, 831 S.E.2d 62 (N.C. S.Ct. 2019).

**3. Likelihood that the child will be adopted.** While G.S. 7B-1110(a)(2) requires the court to consider the child's adoptability, the court is not required to find that the child is adoptable before terminating parental rights. *See In re Norris*, 65 N.C. App. 269 (1983) (decided under an earlier version of the Juvenile Code). Lack of an adoptive placement for the child does not bar termination of the parent's rights. *In re A.H.*, 250 N.C. App. 546 (2016) (likelihood of adoption of child with autism was good even though foster parents did not wish to adopt him because they did not want to adopt any child; evidence showed child was high functioning, had transitioned to mainstream classes, all but one of which he had recently passed, was doing well with his foster parents, and was very likeable); *see In re A.R.A.*, 835 S.E.2d 417 (N.C. S.Ct. 2019) (TPR affirmed; addressing best interests factors where at the time of TPR hearing there was no potential adoptive parent identified for the child).

Child's likelihood of adoption was not affected by the prospective adoptive parents' failure to meet a procedural requirement in the adoption statute regarding standing when the procedural requirement could be waived by the court hearing the adoption proceeding. *In re D.E.M.*, 254 N.C. App. 401 (2017), *aff'd per curiam*, 370 N.C. 463 (2018). In that case, the TPR petitioners had custody of their grandchild pursuant to a civil custody order. Before filing a petition to adopt, G.S. 48-2-301(a) requires that a child be "placed" with the prospective adoptive parent by direct placement or by placement by an agency. Respondent argued that petitioners did not have the ability to adopt because the child had not been placed with them in accordance with G.S. 48-2-301(a). This argument was rejected as G.S. 48-2-301(a) expressly authorizes waiver of the placement requirement for cause. Moreover, petitioners had raised the child since he was eighteen months old, he was thriving in their home, and the GAL supported the adoption, making adoption likely.

Consideration of the child's adjustment in a foster or preadoptive home is appropriate. *In re T.M.*, 182 N.C. App. 566, *aff'd per curiam*, 361 N.C. 683 (2007); *In re V.L.B.*, 168 N.C. App. 679 (2005); *see also In re H.D.*, 239 N.C. App. 318 (2015) (finding that the trial court had properly considered the factor of adoptability in concluding that TPR was in the child's best interest).

In the case *In re A.B.*, 239 N.C. App. 157, 169–70 (2015), the court of appeals interpreted the trial court's order in part as having improperly "tipped the 'best interest' scales" in favor of TPR instead of guardianship or custody based on the availability of financial benefits conferred on the potential adoptive parents. The court of appeals noted that while the financial circumstances of potential adoptive parents could be relevant in determining the likelihood of adoption, therefore making it a relevant factor in analyzing best interest, in this particular case the factor of financial assistance to the potential adoptive parents was used to outweigh the close emotional bonds between the children and their mother and her efforts to regain custody, raising questions about the internal consistencies of the order.

If adoption is a remote possibility, termination of the parent's rights may be an abuse of discretion. *In re J.A.O.*, 166 N.C. App. 222 (2004) (holding that termination was an abuse of discretion where the chance of a troubled teen being adopted was small and there was possible benefit to the child from a continued relationship with his mother and relatives). *Cf. In re A.L.L.*, 254 N.C. App. 252 (2017) (appellate court rejected mother's contention that as in *In re J.A.O.*, the likelihood of her two children's adoption was low so her rights should not have been terminated; distinguishing *In re J.A.O.* based on documentary evidence presented by the children's GAL that with therapy the children in *In re A.L.L.* would be adoptable).

When a child who is 12 or older is being adopted, his or her consent to the adoption is required unless the court hearing the adoption waives that requirement after finding it is not the child's best interest. G.S. 48-3-601(1); 48-3-603(b)(2). The child's desire to be adopted, especially when the child is 12 or older, may be relevant to whether the child is likely to be adopted.

See Chapter 10.3 (discussing selected adoption provisions).

**4. Whether the TPR will aid in the accomplishment of the permanent plan for the child.** A finding that termination of both respondents' parental rights was necessary to accomplish the best permanent plan for the juveniles, which was adoption, satisfied the best interest criteria in G.S. 7B-1110(a)(3). *In re T.H.,* 832 S.E.2d 162 (N.C. Ct. App. 2019).

The North Carolina Supreme Court determined this factor is not relevant in a private TPR because there is no permanent plan within the meaning of G.S. 7B-1110(a)(3). *In re A.U.D.,* 832 S.E.2d 698 (N.C. S.Ct. 2019).

**5. Bond between child and parent.** The bond between parent and child set out in G.S. 7B-1110(a)(4) is just one factor to be considered under G.S. 7B-1110(a) and a trial court may give greater weight to other G.S. 1110(a) factors. *In re Z.L.W.,* 831 S.E.2d 62 (N.C. S.Ct. 2019).

**6. Other relevant considerations.**

**(a) Court's obligation as to findings.** A trial court is not required to make findings of fact on all the evidence that is presented or to state every option that it considered when determining a disposition under G.S. 7B-1110. *In re A.L.L.,* 254 N.C. App. 252 (2017) (reviewing mother's argument about a lack of detailed findings of "any relevant consideration" under G.S. 7B-1111(a)(6)).

**(b) Availability of relatives.** The court may, but is not required to, consider the availability of placement with a relative. *In re C.A.D.,* 247 N.C. App. 552 (2016); *In re M.M.,* 200 N.C. App. 248 (2009).

**(c) GAL information and opinion.** A primary function of the child's guardian ad litem (GAL) is to provide the court with information relevant to the child's best interest. In carrying out his or her duties under G.S. 7B-601, the GAL may offer evidence and/or a report at the disposition stage of a TPR proceeding. The GAL's opinion about the child's best interest, however, may not be a proper consideration for the court. In the case of *In re Wheeler,* 87 N.C. App. 189 (1987), respondent asserted as error the admission of a GAL's lay opinion that termination was in the children's best interest. The appellate court stated that the proper analysis of the admissibility of an opinion by a lay or expert witness is whether it is helpful to the trier of fact and found that the helpfulness of the GAL's lay opinion was questionable. Although the court found error in the admission, in view of the abundance of other evidence supporting the trial court's decision and remarks of the judge indicating that he did not rely on this testimony, the admission was not prejudicial.

The trial court is not bound by a GAL's recommendation. *In re A.U.D.,* 832 S.E.2d 698 (N.C. S.Ct. 2019) (rejecting petitioner's argument that the trial court erred by not giving proper consideration to a report and recommendation of the child's GAL that respondent's parental rights be terminated; the trial court considered the GAL's report and recommendation but elected not to follow the recommendation).

**(d) Parents' religion.** Questions and testimony about the parents' religious beliefs and practices are not necessarily constitutional error. *In re Huff,* 140 N.C. App. 288 (2000) (finding no error where the inquiry was brief, related primarily to practices that might affect the child and not to the parents' beliefs, was directed to the father rather than to an expert or minister, and did not result in any findings by the court).

**(e) Efforts of DSS.** A finding that DSS made diligent efforts to provide services to a parent is not a condition precedent to terminating a parent's rights. *In re J.W.J.*, 165 N.C. App. 696 (2004); *In re Frasher*, 147 N.C. App. 513 (2001). Findings under G.S. 7B-906.2(b), which address reasonable efforts, apply to permanency planning hearings and are not required at a TPR hearing. *In re T.H.*, 832 S.E.2d 162 (N.C. Ct. App. 2019).

**(f) Compliance with case plan not relevant.** The court of appeals has stated that "compliance with the case plan is not one of the factors the trial court is to consider in making the best interest determination." *In re Y.Y.E.T.*, 205 N.C. App. 120, 131 (2010).

**7. Weighing the factors.** The appellate courts have stated that the trial court may give greater weight to some factors over others. *In re Z.L.W.*, 831 S.E.2d 62 (N.C. S.Ct. 2019) (affirming TPR; trial court's determination that other factors outweighed children's bond with respondent was not an abuse of discretion); *In re T.H.*, 832 S.E.2d 162, 166 (N.C. Ct. App. 2019) (stating that the "court is entitled to give greater weight to certain factors over others in making its determination concerning the best interests of the child").

**8. Examples of best interest evidence and findings where TPR affirmed.**

- The conclusion that termination of respondent mother's rights was in the child's best interest was not arbitrary or unsupported by reason based on findings that the child was nine years old and termination would aid in achieving the permanent plan of adoption, that adoption would be more likely once child became available for adoption, that the child's need for permanence outweighed any bond between the child and mother, that child was doing well in his therapeutic placement, having formed a strong bond, and mother no longer participated in child's therapy and had not called to ask about child's welfare. *In re A.R.A.*, 835 S.E.2d 417 (N.C. S.Ct. 2019).
- Reviewing an order in which the trial court set out five of the six G.S. 7B-1110(a) factors, the supreme court affirmed the best interest determination based on unchallenged trial court findings of a high probability of adoption, that termination of father's rights would help achieve the primary plan of adoption, that while children had a bond with father, that bond had diminished during the lengthy period the children were in foster care, during which a reciprocal bond between the children and the prospective adoptive parents formed, as well as other factors which included the court's deep concern about father's lack of progress toward mental health and substance abuse treatment, and domestic violence counseling. *In re Z.L.W.*, 831 S.E.2d 62 (N.C. S.Ct. 2019).
- Trial court made detailed findings of the dispositional criteria in G.S. 7B-1110(a), which included a strong likelihood that the children would be adopted by their stepfather, with whom the children were extremely bonded, and the lack of a bond with respondent father. Also supporting the best interest determination were findings that father's home was extremely unstable and that his conduct demonstrated that he would not promote the physical and emotional well-being of the children. *In re E.H.P.*, 831 S.E.2d 49 (N.C. S.Ct. 2019).

- It was not abuse of discretion for the trial court to conclude that TPR was in the children's best interest where there was extensive evidence regarding domestic violence, lack of necessary medical care for the children, drug abuse, and criminal activity by respondent; neglect of the children during visits with respondent involving lack of feeding and bathing; respondent's failure to obtain a job and pay child support; and respondent's struggle with mental illness. The trial court also found that the respondent had made little progress toward correcting conditions leading to removal, which would subject the children to irreparable harm if returned to respondents. The trial court additionally found that there was a minimal bond between the children and respondent, that the children were of tender age, and that the children were likely to be adopted and had begun to adjust to their potential adoptive home. *In re L.M.T.*, 367 N.C. 165 (2013).
- It was not an abuse of discretion for the court to determine that TPR was in older child's best interest when there were no present viable candidates for guardianship or custody; adoption was more likely than guardianship or custody to achieve true permanence; mother's interactions with past foster placements made the possibility of another stable placement unlikely; TPR of mother would result in more available placement options; and evidence supported finding that the likelihood of adoption was good when child was autistic but high functioning and had made recent progress in school. That current caretakers did not want to adopt did not impact child's adoptability when their decision was not specific to older child but was because they did not want to adopt any child. *In re A.H.*, 250 N.C. App. 546 (2016).
- Although the mother had made progress in doing what the trial court ordered and emphasized her bond with the children, she stated repeatedly that she could not handle the responsibility of parenting the children. *In re C.L.C.*, 171 N.C. App. 438 (2005), *aff'd per curiam*, 360 N.C. 475 (2006).
- Although there was some improvement in the mental condition of a mother diagnosed with borderline personality disorder, after almost two years of DSS efforts, she could not demonstrate that she was capable of providing adequately for the child's needs. One expert testified about the negative effect of further delay in obtaining a permanent placement for the child given his age and close bond with the foster family. *In re Brim*, 139 N.C. App. 733 (2000).

### 9. Examples of best interest evidence and findings where TPR was not affirmed.

- In private TPR proceeding involving twins, the first five factors in G.S. 7B-1110(a) were either not applicable or did not favor respondent father. Findings established that the children were approximately six months old when placed with prospective adoptive parents (PAPs); remained in their care throughout the proceedings; were strongly bonded; and the likelihood of adoption by the PAPs was high. There was no bond between father and the children as father had been incarcerated since their birth and being a private termination, there was no permanent plan. The determination that it was not in the children's best interest for father's rights to be terminated was affirmed based on other relevant considerations, specifically, that mother solely relinquished the children to the adoption agency; father was not afforded an opportunity to care for the children before the relinquishment; he proactively attempted to establish paternity; he sought to have the aunt, who has previously appropriately cared for the children, obtain custody until his

release from prison; and he engaged in services while incarcerated that resulted in self-improvement. *In re A.U.D.*, 832 S.E.2d 698 (N.C. S.Ct. 2019).
- The child was 14 years old and had mental and physical health problems and violent tendencies that made adoption very unlikely; the mother had made reasonable attempts to correct conditions that led to filing of a petition; and the reasons she stopped visitation were the child's transfer to a distant hospital, the mother's lack of transportation, and DSS's request to suspend visitation due to an increase in the child's violent behavior. *In re J.A.O.*, 166 N.C. App. 222 (2004).
- The father, a recovering alcoholic, had stopped drinking, attended Alcoholics Anonymous, and was employed; the children were settled in a new family unit with the custodial parent and her financially stable husband; and both the GAL and a court-appointed psychologist expressed the opinion that the father's rights should not be terminated. *Bost v. Van Nortwick*, 117 N.C. App. 1 (1994).

## 9.13 Highlighted Federal Laws: ICWA and the ADA

### A. Compliance with ICWA

The Indian Child Welfare Act (ICWA) is a federal law the sets forth minimum federal standards that must be complied with for certain child custody proceedings and is governed by 25 U.S.C. 1901 *et seq.* and new federal binding regulations, effective December 12, 2016, codified at 25 C.F.R. Part 23. A termination of parental rights (TPR) is considered a child custody proceeding for purposes of ICWA. 25 U.S.C. 1903(1). Under ICWA, the court must make an inquiry of all participants at the commencement of every TPR action (including private TPRs) as to whether any participant knows or has reason to know the child is an "Indian child" as defined by ICWA. 25 C.F.R. 23.107(a); *see* 25 U.S.C. 1903(4) (definition of "Indian child"). When there is reason to know but insufficient evidence for the court to determine that the child is an Indian child, the court must treat the child as an Indian child and comply with ICWA requirements until and unless it is determined on the record that the child does not meet the definition of "Indian child". 25 C.F.R. 23.107(b)(2). The court must also confirm on the record through a report, declaration, or testimony that DSS or another party in the proceeding has used due diligence to identify, work with, and obtain verification from the tribes of which there is reason to know the child (1) may be (or is) a member or (2) is eligible for membership and a biological parent is a member. 25 C.F.R. 23.107(b)(1). *See In re L.W.S.*, 255 N.C. App. 296, 298 n.4 (2017) (in appeal of TPR order entered before application of federal regulation, noting under new federal regulations "it seems to be the case that the burden has shifted to state courts to inquire at the start of a proceeding whether the child at issue is an Indian child, and, if so, the state court must confirm that the agency used due diligence to identify and work with the Tribe and treat the child as an Indian child unless and until it is determined otherwise").

When ICWA provisions apply, the following issues are implicated: the court's subject matter jurisdiction if the child resides or is domiciled within an Indian reservation or is a ward of tribal court; a proper ICWA notice to the parent, Indian custodian (if applicable), child's Indian tribe, and regional office of the Bureau of Indian Affairs; the right to intervene; the provision of "active efforts"; required findings based on a beyond a reasonable doubt standard and qualified expert testimony; and placement preferences.

See Chapter 13.2 (discussing ICWA and its requirements in detail).

### B. ADA Not a Defense to TPR

The Americans with Disabilities Act (ADA) prohibits discrimination on the basis of a physical or mental disability. In a case of first impression, the North Carolina Court of Appeals held in *In re C.M.S.*, 184 N.C. App. 488 (2007), that the ADA did not preclude termination of the respondent's (who had an intellectual disability) rights. The court of appeals reviewed other state courts' treatment of the issue and adopted the rule followed by other states that termination of parental rights (TPR) proceedings are not services, programs, or activities within the meaning of Title II of the ADA, and the ADA is not a defense to a TPR. At the same time, the court of appeals found that the requirements for and the trial court's findings about reasonable efforts constituted compliance with the ADA.

See Chapter 13.5 (discussing the ADA).

## 9.14 Orders in Termination of Parental Rights Cases

See also Chapter 4.9 (discussing orders in juvenile cases).

### A. Requirements for Order

**1. Address grounds.** The court must find facts and adjudicate the existence or nonexistence of the grounds alleged in the petition or motion. G.S. 7B-1109(e); 7B-1110(c). *In re O.D.S.*, 247 N.C. App. 711 (2016) (G.S. 7B-1109(e) requires that a trial court address every ground brought forth in a TPR petition or motion and make a determination in its order for every ground alleged, whether petitioner proved that ground or failed to prove it). The trial court's failure to address an alleged ground at all constitutes a conclusion that it does not exist. *In re S.R.G.*, 200 N.C. App. 594 (2009).

**2. Standard of proof.** With respect to the adjudication, the order must recite the clear, cogent, and convincing evidence standard of proof. G.S. 7B-1109(f) (all findings of fact shall be based on "clear, cogent, and convincing" evidence); 7B-1111(b) (petitioner or movant has the burden to prove the facts justifying termination by "clear and convincing" evidence). The two standards in G.S. 7B-1109(f) and 7B-1111(b) are used interchangeably and are synonymous. *In re Faircloth*, 153 N.C. App. 565 (2002) (comparing the two statutes); *see In re Belk*, 364 N.C. 114, (2010); *In re Montgomery*, 311 N.C. 101, (1984) ("clear and convincing" and "clear, cogent and convincing" describe the same evidentiary standard). Clear and convincing evidence is "stricter than a preponderance of the evidence, but less stringent than proof beyond a reasonable doubt and requires evidence which should fully convince." *In re H.N.D.*, 827 S.E.2d 329, 332 (N.C. Ct. App. 2019) (quoting *In re Mills*, 152 N.C. App. 1, 13 (2002)).

Adjudicatory orders that failed to include the standard of proof set out in either G.S. 7B-1109(f) or 7B-1111(b) have been reversed. *See In re Matherly*, 149 N.C. App. 452, 454 (2002) (the burden in G.S. 7B-1111(b) to prove by clear and convincing evidence the facts establishing a ground for termination applies "throughout the adjudicatory process"; TPR order which failed to state that findings as to termination grounds were made by clear, cogent and convincing evidence was reversed); *In re Church*, 136 N.C. App. 654 (2000) (failure to state that the proper standard of proof was applied was not harmless error). *See also In re D.R.B.*, 182 N.C. App. 733 (2007) (holding that the TPR order was deficient where it did not state the standard of proof pursuant to which the court made adjudicatory findings as required by G.S. 7B-1109(f) and did not indicate which ground(s) the court was adjudicating).

However, there is no requirement as to where or how the standard is recited in the order. *In re J.T.W.*, 178 N.C. App. 678 (2006), *rev'd per curiam on other grounds*, 361 N.C. 341 (2007); *see In re A.B.*, 245 N.C. App. 35 (2016) (emphasis in original) (order that did not state that *all* findings were based on clear, cogent, and convincing evidence as required by G.S. 7B-1109(f) was affirmed; trial court used the correct standard when it orally indicated the standard it was applying, one of the seventy findings stated the appropriate standard, and there was no other contradictory standard in the order).

**3. Findings and conclusions.** The order must include findings of fact and conclusions of law. *See* G.S. 7B-1109(e); 7B-1110(b), (c). Findings of fact are determinations from the evidence concerning facts averred by one party and denied by another. Conclusions of law are findings by a court as determined through the application of rules of law. *In re Johnston*, 151 N.C. App. 728 (2002).

Rule 52 of the Rules of Civil Procedure also requires the court, in any action tried without a jury, to "find the facts specially and state separately its conclusions of law thereon." *See In re Anderson*, 151 N.C. App. 94 (2002) (discussing application of Rule 52 to adjudicatory facts; note this case has been distinguished by *In re J.W.*, 241 N.C. App. 44 (2015) regarding facts that recite the allegations in petition). "[W]hile Rule 52(a) does not require a recitation of the evidentiary and subsidiary facts required to prove the ultimate facts, it does require *specific findings* of the ultimate facts established by the evidence, admissions, and stipulations which are determinative of the questions involved in the action and essential to support the conclusions of law reached." *In re T.N.H.*, 831 S.E.2d 54, 59 (N.C. S.Ct. 2019) (quoting *Quick v. Quick*, 305 N.C. 446, 451–52 (1982)).

See Chapters 4.9.B (discussing findings of fact and conclusions of law) and 12.8.B (discussing the difference between findings and conclusions, including the different standard of review on appeal).

(a) **Findings based on clear, cogent, and convincing evidence.** Findings in the adjudication order must be based on clear, cogent, and convincing evidence. G.S. 7B-1109(f); *see* G.S. 7B-1111(b) (burden of proof). *See also In re Young*, 346 N.C. 244 (1997) (reversing TPR based on neglect and abandonment grounds on the basis that there was not clear, cogent, and convincing evidence to support trial court's findings); *In re Montgomery*, 311 N.C. 101 (1984); *In re C.W.*, 182 N.C. App. 214 (2007) (reversing TPR where none of the grounds was supported by clear and convincing evidence and a number of findings were supported by no evidence). *See also In re O.J.R.*, 239 N.C. App. 329 (2015) (one factor leading to reversal of TPR was the lack of competent evidence to support some findings).

**(b) Sufficiently specific findings.** Findings must be sufficiently specific. *See In re T.P.*, 197 N.C. App. 723 (2009) (holding that insufficient findings of fact required reversal where the findings mainly quoted statutory language and were not adequate for meaningful appellate review); *In re Locklear,* 151 N.C. App. 573 (2002) (holding that where findings did little more than restate the statutory grounds and discuss DSS's efforts to reunify, the order was not sufficient to establish a ground for termination). It is not necessarily reversible error for a trial court's finding of fact to mirror the language of the petition. *In re A.B.,* 245 N.C. App. 35 (2016) (affirming TPR that found DSS substantially proved facts alleged in paragraphs a-k of the TPR petition and an additional finding mirrored language in the petition when other findings of fact demonstrated the trial court made an independent determination of the facts, rather than merely reciting allegations in the petition).

**(c) Conclusions.** The court's adjudication of the existence or nonexistence of grounds alleged in the petition or motion is a conclusion of law and must be based on the findings of fact. *See, e.g., In re S.R.G.,* 200 N.C. App. 594 (2009) (holding that failure to address an alleged ground constitutes a conclusion that it does not exist); *In re L.C.,* 181 N.C. App. 278 (2007); *In re T.M.H.,* 186 N.C. App. 451 (2007); *see also In re D.L.W.*, 368 N.C. 835 (2016) (upholding the trial court's TPR order as to mother on the basis of neglect because the findings in the order supported the conclusion that there would be a repetition of neglect based on the juveniles living in an environment injurious to their welfare); *In re O.J.R.*, 239 N.C. App. 329 (2015) (TPR order in private case was reversed and remanded in part due to lack of adequate conclusions and findings).

With respect to best interest, the court is required to consider specific criteria pursuant to G.S. 7B-1110(a) and make specific findings regarding those criteria that are relevant. See section 9.12.C, above. The court's determination that terminating the parent's rights is or is not in the child's best interest is a conclusion of law that must be supported by the findings. *See In re M.N.C.*, 176 N.C. App. 114 (2006).

**4. Timing.** The order must be entered within thirty days following completion of the hearing. If the order is not entered within thirty days, the juvenile clerk is required to schedule a hearing at the first session of juvenile court after the thirty-day period, for an explanation of the reason for the delay and to obtain any needed clarification about the contents of the order. The court must enter the order within ten days after this hearing. G.S. 7B-1109(e). Where the court fails to enter a timely order, the appropriate remedy is a petition to the court of appeals for a writ of mandamus to require the trial court to proceed to judgment, not a new hearing. *In re T.H.T.*, 362 N.C. 446 (2008); *In re S.Z.H.,* 247 N.C. App. 254 (2016) (setting out the remedy of mandamus when a TPR order was entered nearly six months after the adjudicatory and dispositional hearing in violation of G.S. 7B-1109(e) and 7B-1110(a)); see also Chapter 4.9.D.3 (discussing mandamus as the remedy). Failure to comply with statutory timelines does not deprive the trial court of jurisdiction. *See In re C.L.C.*, 171 N.C. App. 438 (2005), *aff'd per curiam*, 360 N.C. 475 (2006).

**5. Service of order on juvenile who is 12 or older.** The juvenile is a party to the TPR proceeding. G.S. 7B-1104; 7B-601(a). Although the juvenile may be represented by a guardian ad litem (GAL), the juvenile, if 12 or older, must be served with a copy of the TPR order. G.S. 7B-1110(d); *see* G.S. 7B-1108 (GAL appointment). Service on the juvenile is in addition to service on the juvenile's GAL when a GAL is appointed. The juvenile has a right to appeal any order that grants or denies the TPR. G.S. 7B-1001(a)(6) (appealable orders); 7B-1002(1), (2) (standing to appeal). See Chapter 12 (discussing appeals).

## B. Entry of Order

An order is entered when it is reduced to writing, signed by the judge, and filed with the clerk pursuant to Rule 5. N.C. R. CIV. P. 58. An order that fails to indicate it was filed with the clerk (e.g., a file-stamp or other mark to indicate a filing date) is not entered. *McKinney v. Duncan*, 808 S.E.2d 509 (N.C. Ct. App. 2017) (dismissing appeal for lack of subject matter jurisdiction in the appellate court when the underlying orders were never entered as they were devoid of any proof of filing with the clerk). *Cf.* N.C. R. CIV. P. 5(e)(3) (addressing failure to affix a date or file stamp on an order by authorizing the clerk to enter the order or judgment nunc pro tunc to the date of filing). *See* S.L. 2017-158 sec. 1 and 2 (amending both Rule 5 and Rule 58 regarding filing, effective July 21, 2017).

Specific provisions of the Juvenile Code require that orders in TPR proceedings be reduced to writing, signed by the judge, and entered, and G.S. 7B-1001(b) explicitly refers to Rule 58 of the Rules of Civil Procedure for entry and service of orders. *See* G.S. 7B-1109(e); 7B-1110(a). The judge who presides over the TPR hearing is the judge who must sign the order; otherwise, the order does not comply with Rule 58 and is not entered. *In re C.M.C.*, 832 S.E.2d 681 (N.C. S.Ct. 2019) (holding TPR order signed by a judge who did not preside over the TPR hearing was a nullity).

There is no requirement in G.S. 7B-1109 that the trial court render a decision in open court. *In re O.D.S.*, 247 N.C. App. 711 (2016). But, when the judge makes an oral announcement (or rendition) of his or her order in open court, the order does not become enforceable until it is reduced to writing, signed by the judge, and filed with the clerk of court pursuant to Rule 5. *See McKinney v. Duncan*, 808 S.E.2d 509 (N.C. Ct. App. 2017); *Carland v. Branch*, 164 N.C. App. 403 (2004); *see also In re O.D.S.*, 247 N.C. App. 711, 722 (stating "[n]o order or judgment had been entered at that time, and therefore, no party was bound by the judgment").

Because an oral rendition is not an entry of a judgment, it is subject to change, meaning the trial court is not required to adhere to the rendition when making and entering its written order. *In re A.U.D.*, 832 S.E.2d 698 (N.C. S.Ct. 2019) (oral findings made by a trial court are subject to change prior to the entry of the final written order); *In re O.D.S.*, 247 N.C. App. 711 (holding the court was not bound by the oral rendition to TPR based on neglect and could include both neglect and dependency as grounds to TPR in the written entered order; reasoning it is not bound by the holding in *In re J.C.*, 236 N.C. App. 558 (2014), to the extent *In re J.C* conflicts with prior holdings of the court of appeals or supreme court and can be distinguished from the current case before it).

A court may also consider evidence presented after its oral rendition but before it enters a written judgment. *In re O.D.S.,* 247 N.C. App. 711, and cases cited therein. A trial court's misapprehension of when an order terminating parental rights was entered led to a reversal in the case *In re B.S.O.,* 225 N.C. App. 541 (2013). The trial court has broad discretion to reopen a case and admit additional testimony after the conclusion of the evidence, after argument of counsel, even weeks after the original hearing, or when the "ends of justice require." In *In re B.S.O.,* which cites cases on this principle, the trial court refused to exercise its discretion as to whether to take additional evidence, because it thought a valid order terminating parental rights had been entered, when in fact the order was not final because it had not been reduced to writing.

See Chapter 4.9.A and C, discussing the following:

- what constitutes entry of order;
- requirement that the presiding judge sign the order;
- judge's authority to direct a party to draft the order, and fact that draft orders should be circulated and are the court's responsibility even if drafted by a party; and
- service of signed orders on parties.

For a discussion of appeals of TPR orders, see Chapter 12.4.A.

**Resource:** Janet Mason, *Drafting Good Court Orders in Juvenile Cases*, JUVENILE LAW BULLETIN No. 2013/02 (UNC School of Government, Sept. 2013).

## 9.15 Effect of Order and Placement after Termination of Parental Rights

### A. Severance of Rights and Obligations

An order terminating parental rights (TPR) completely and permanently severs all rights and obligations of the parent to the child and the child to the parent. G.S. 7B-1112. However, the child's right of inheritance does not terminate until a final order of adoption is entered. G.S. 7B-1112. In addition, any child support arrears remain after termination of parental rights, even though the parent is no longer liable for ongoing support obligations. *See* G.S. 48-1-107; 7B-1112; *see also Michigan v. Pruitt*, 94 N.C. App. 713 (1989) (holding that even though support obligation ceased when adoption became final, support arrears owed prior to adoption were still owed).

When parental rights have been terminated, parents no longer have any constitutionally protected interest in their children. *In re Montgomery,* 77 N.C. App. 709 (1985). After a TPR, the parent is not entitled to notice of adoption proceedings and may not object to or participate in them. G.S. 7B-1112; *see* G.S. 48-2-401. A parent whose rights have been terminated does not have standing to seek custody of the child as an "other person" under G.S. 50-13.1(a) when DSS has custody of the child both before and after the TPR petition was filed. *Krauss v. Wayne County Dep't of Soc. Servs.*, 347 N.C. 371 (1997) (examining language of former TPR statute and holding it is a narrow statute that provides an exception to the broad language regarding standing of G.S. 50-13.1(a); note that the language of the former statute is substantially the same as the current G.S. 7B-1112(1)).

A termination of parental rights does not necessarily terminate a grandparent's rights to visitation. While mother had no constitutionally protected interest in the child after termination of her rights in a private TPR proceeding, termination of mother's rights did not extinguish a grandmother's court-ordered visitation rights. Grandmother was a party after intervening in an earlier custody proceeding between the child's parents and was awarded visitation rights. Grandmother/intervenor's visitation rights existed independently of mother's parental and custodial rights such that grandmother/intervenor could seek to enforce those rights through contempt proceedings after mother's rights were terminated. *Adams v. Langdon*, 826 S.E.2d 236 (N.C. Ct. App. 2019).

> **Resource:** See Cheryl Howell, *Grandparent visitation: termination of parent's rights does not terminate grandparent's court ordered visitation*, UNC SCH. OF GOV'T: ON THE CIVIL SIDE BLOG (Apr. 10, 2019).

In very limited circumstances, a parent's rights may be reinstated. See Chapter 10.4 (discussing the criteria and procedure for reinstatement of parental rights).

## B. Collateral Legal Consequences

A TPR order may have an effect on an individual's parental rights in the future as to any other children the individual has or may have. For example, if the parent has another child that has been adjudicated abused, neglected, or dependent and is in DSS custody, the order terminating the parent's rights to a different child may be a basis for relieving DSS from making reasonable efforts to reunify the parent with the child who is the subject of the abuse, neglect, or dependency action at initial disposition. *See* G.S. 7B-901(c)(2). See also Chapter 7.8.A.2 (discussing G.S. 7B-901(c) factors and reasonable efforts) and 7.9 (discussing reasonable efforts). A TPR order is also one part of a two-prong ground to terminate parental rights to another child of the parent. *See* G.S. 7B-1111(a)(9), discussed in section 9.11.I, above.

These collateral legal consequences have been held to satisfy the exception to the mootness doctrine in an appeal. *In re Baby Boy*, 238 N.C. App. 316 (2014) (because of the potential collateral consequences, appeal of an order terminating respondent mother's rights was not moot even though the child's adoption had been finalized by the time the appellate court considered mother's appeal of the TPR order).

For more on collateral consequences arising from a TPR order, see Chapter 12.4.B.2.

## C. Placement and Post-TPR Review Hearings

**1. When child is in DSS/agency custody.** If the child had been placed in the custody of (or relinquished for adoption by one parent to) a county DSS or licensed child-placing agency and is in the custody of that agency (which includes a DSS) when the TPR petition or motion is filed, upon entry of a TPR order that agency acquires all rights for placement of the child that the agency would have acquired, including the right to consent to adoption, had the parent relinquished the child to the agency pursuant to G.S. Chapter 48, except as otherwise provided in G.S. 7B-908(d). G.S. 7B-1112(1). *See also In re I.T.P-L.*, 194 N.C. App. 453 (2008) (holding that the trial court did not have subject matter jurisdiction to order the child placed with a relative following termination because the statute gives DSS exclusive placement authority when the child was in DSS custody when TPR petition or motion was filed); *In re Asbury*, 125 N.C. App. 143 (1997). Statutory changes made after these cases were decided create narrow exceptions. Until the child is placed with prospective adoptive parents as selected in G.S. 7B-1112.1, the court at a post-TPR review hearing may order a placement different from the one proposed as long as the court considers DSS's recommendations and finds that the placement is in the juvenile's best interest. G.S. 7B-908(d1). See Chapter 10.3.B (discussing selection of prospective adoptive parents).

**2. When child is not in DSS/agency custody.** When the child is not in DSS or another agency's custody when the TPR petition or motion is filed, the court may place the child in the custody of the petitioner or movant, some other suitable person, a county DSS, or a licensed child-placing agency, as may appear to be in the child's best interests . G.S. 7B-1112(2).

**3. Post-TPR review hearings.** After termination of parental rights, the court must conduct review hearings under G.S. 7B-908(b) at least every six months until the child is the subject of a final order of adoption, if

- the child is in the custody of DSS or another licensed child-placing agency and parental rights have been terminated pursuant to a petition or motion by one of the persons or agencies with proper standing under G.S. 7B-1103(a)(2) through (6); or
- one parent's parental rights have been terminated by court order and the other parent's parental rights have been relinquished under G.S. Chapter 48.

A parent whose rights have been terminated continues to be a party for purposes of post-TPR review hearings only if

- an appeal of the TPR order is pending and
- a court has stayed the TPR order pending the appeal.

G.S. 7B-908(b)(1).

See Chapter 10.1 (discussing post-TPR review hearings).

# Post-TPR and Post-Relinquishment Reviews, Adoptions, and Reinstatement of Parental Rights

Chapter 10

# Chapter 10
# Post-TPR and Post-Relinquishment Reviews, Adoptions, and Reinstatement of Parental Rights

**10.1 Post-Termination of Parental Rights Review Hearings   10-2**
   A. Circumstances and Purpose
      1. Circumstances
      2. Purpose
   B. Timing of Hearing
   C. Notice and Participation
      1. Timing and procedure for notice
      2. Persons entitled to notice
      3. Right to participate and party status
   D. Appointment of GAL
   E. Evidence and Considerations for Hearings
      1. Evidence
      2. Sources of information
      3. Required considerations and findings
   F. The Order
      1. Contents
      2. Timing

**10.2 Post-Relinquishment Review Hearings   10-6**
   A. Circumstances Requiring Review
   B. Relinquishment for Adoption
      1. Who may relinquish
      2. Types of relinquishment
      3. Right to counsel
      4. Revocation
      5. Rescission
      6. Voiding the relinquishment
      7. Consequences of relinquishment
      8. Compliance with ICWA
   C. Timing and Petition or Motion for Review
   D. Parent's Party Status
   E. Procedure for Hearing

**10.3 Selected Adoption Provisions   10-12**
   A. Introduction
   B. Prospective Adoptive Parents
      1. DSS responsibility and discretion to select
      2. Notice of adoptive parent selection to GAL and foster parent
      3. Review hearing on selection
      4. Placement with prospective adoptive parent(s)

5. Prospective adoptive parent is petitioner
C. District Court Jurisdiction When Adoption Is Filed
   1. Adoption is a special proceeding
   2. Jurisdiction in a G.S. Chapter 7B action
D. The Adoption
   1. The determination
   2. Notice of decree
   3. Effect of decree

## 10.4 Reinstatement of Parental Rights    10-18
A. Introduction
B. Circumstances for Reinstatement
C. Hearing Procedures
   1. Notification to child and appointment of GAL
   2. Service of motion
   3. Former parent not a party and not entitled to appointment of counsel
   4. Timing
   5. Pre-hearing reports
   6. Participants
   7. Evidence and standard for review
D. Criteria and Findings
E. Interim Hearings and Reasonable Efforts
F. Orders
G. Effect of Reinstatement

---

# 10.1 Post-Termination of Parental Rights Review Hearings

### A. Circumstances and Purpose

**1. Circumstances.** Review hearings that take place after termination of parental rights (TPR) are required when the child is in the custody of a department of social services (DSS) or another licensed child-placing agency and

- parental rights have been terminated pursuant to a petition or motion by one of the following persons or agencies with proper standing under G.S. 7B-1103(a)(2) through (6):
  - a court–appointed guardian of the person of the child,
  - a DSS or licensed child-placing agency with custody of the child pursuant to a court order or resulting from an executed relinquishment,
  - a person with whom the child has lived continuously for at least two years immediately preceding the filing of the action, or
  - a guardian ad litem appointed to represent the child pursuant to G.S. 7B-601 who has not been relieved of that responsibility; or
- one parent's rights have been terminated by court order and the other parent's rights have been relinquished under G.S. Chapter 48.

G.S. 7B-908(b). *See* G.S. 48-3-705(b)(1) (legal and physical custody vests with the agency to whom the child is relinquished); 48-1-101(4) (definition of "agency").

**Note,** this hearing is commonly referred to in practice as a "post-TPR review hearing" and will be referred to as such in this Manual. For purposes of this Manual, a "department of social services" or "DSS" refers to a department as defined by G.S. 7B-101(8a) regardless of how it is titled or structured.

**Additional Note,** throughout this Chapter the word "agency" is sometimes used as shorthand for "DSS or licensed child-placing agency." "Agency" is defined in G.S. 48-1-101(4) and refers to a public or private entity that is licensed or otherwise authorized by law to place children for adoption and specifically includes a county department of social services. Sometimes the statutes, especially G.S. 7B-1112.1, refer only to DSS when it is clear from the context that a provision applies equally to a licensed child-placing agency. In those instances, this Chapter uses "agency."

**2. Purpose.** The purpose of post-TPR review hearings is to ensure that when a child is in the custody of a DSS or licensed child-placing agency every reasonable effort is being made to provide for permanent placement plans for the child that are consistent with the child's best interests. G.S. 7B-908(a). See Chapter 7.3 (discussing the child's best interests), 7.9 (explaining reasonable efforts) and 7.10 (discussing permanent plans).

> **Practice Note**: G.S. 7B-908 does not appear to limit post-TPR review hearings to those situations where a child is placed in the custody of an agency by a court order entered in an abuse, neglect, or dependency proceeding. A child may be placed in the custody of a licensed child-placing agency, including DSS, by (1) operation of law upon an executed relinquishment or (2) an order entered in a termination of parental rights action. *See* G.S. 48-3-705(b); 7B-1112. However, G.S. 7B-908(d) references concurrent permanent plans set forth at G.S. 7B-906.2, and that statute applies to abuse, neglect, or dependency actions.

**B. Timing of Hearing**

The first post-TPR review hearing must be conducted within six months of the date of the hearing at which parental rights were terminated pursuant to the circumstances stated in section 10.1.A.1, above. Thereafter, hearings must be conducted at least every six months until the child is adopted. G.S. 7B-908(b). Once there is a decree of adoption, any calendared review hearings must be cancelled, and the clerk must provide notice of the cancellation to all persons previously notified of the hearing. G.S. 7B-908(e).

A post-TPR review hearing may also be combined with an interim hearing on a motion to reinstate parental rights pursuant to G.S. 7B-1114 (discussed in section 10.4, below). G.S. 7B-1114(h).

**C. Notice and Participation**

**1. Timing and procedure for notice.** Notice must be given by the clerk between fifteen and thirty days prior to each post-TPR review hearing. DSS must either provide the clerk with the name and address of the person providing care for the child or file written documentation with the clerk that DSS has sent notice of the hearing to the child's current care provider. G.S. 7B-908(b)(1).

**2. Persons entitled to notice.** Notice must be given to

- the child, if the child is 12 years of age or older;
- the child's legal custodian or guardian;
- the person who is caring for the child;
- the child's guardian ad litem (GAL), if there is one; and
- any other person or agency the court specifies.

G.S. 7B-908(b)(1).

Based on due process grounds, while not required by G.S. 7B-908(b)(1), notice should be given to a parent whose rights have been terminated, if there is a pending appeal of the order terminating the parent's rights and a court has stayed the TPR order while the appeal is pending. In that case, the parent remains a party. G.S. 7B-908(b)(1).

**AOC Form:**
AOC-J-141, Notice of Hearing in Juvenile Proceedings (Abuse/Neglect/Dependency) (Jan. 2017).

**3. Right to participate and party status.** Unless otherwise directed by the court, only the following persons may participate in the post-TPR review hearing:

- the child (regardless of age);
- the child's legal custodian or guardian;
- the person who is caring for the child; and
- the child's GAL, if there is one.

G.S. 7B-908(b)(1); *see* G.S. 7B-908(a).

A person is not made a party to the proceeding simply because he or she is entitled to notice and an opportunity to be heard at the post-TPR review hearing. G.S. 7B-908(b)(1).

A parent whose rights have been terminated is not a party unless there is a pending appeal of the order terminating the parent's rights and a court has stayed the TPR order pending the appeal. G.S. 7B-908(b)(1). When these criteria are met such that the parent is a party, due process requires that the parent have a right to notice and the opportunity to meaningfully participate in the post-TPR review hearing.

### D. Appointment of GAL

If a guardian ad litem (GAL) was appointed previously to represent the child in the TPR proceeding, the GAL will continue to represent the child for purposes of post-TPR review hearings. If a GAL was not appointed previously, the court has the discretion to appoint a GAL at the first post-TPR review hearing and may continue the case to give the GAL time to prepare. G.S. 7B-908(b)(2).

E. **Evidence and Considerations for Hearings**

**1. Evidence.** The court may consider any evidence, including hearsay that the court finds to be relevant, reliable, and necessary to determine the needs of the child and the most appropriate disposition. G.S. 7B-908(a).

**2. Sources of information.** The court may consider information from DSS, the licensed child-placing agency, the child's GAL, the child, the person providing the child's care, and any other person or agency the court determines is likely to aid in the review. G.S. 7B-908(a).

**3. Required considerations and findings.** The court must consider the following four factors and make written findings regarding those that are relevant.

(a) **Adequacy of the plan.** The court must consider the adequacy of the permanency plans developed by DSS or a licensed child-placing agency for a permanent placement in the child's best interests and the efforts made by the agency to implement those plans. G.S. 7B-908(c)(1).

(b) **Adoption listing.** The court must consider whether the child has been listed for adoptive placement with the NC Kids Adoption and Foster Care Network or any other child-specific recruitment program, or whether there is an exemption to listing that the court finds is in the child's best interest. G.S. 7B-908(c)(2).

(c) **Previous efforts.** The court must consider any previous efforts made by DSS or the child-placing agency to find a permanent placement for the child. G.S. 7B-908(c)(3).

(d) **Best interest**. The court must consider whether the current placement is in the child's best interest. G.S. 7B-908(c)(4).

**Practice Note:** The court is not limited to these considerations, but these factors are the minimum the court must consider.

F. **The Order**

**1. Contents.** In its order, the court, after making findings of fact,

- must adopt concurrent permanent plans and identify the primary and secondary plan in accordance with G.S. 7B-906.2(a)(2) through (6) (note that reunification as a permanent plan is not a designated option but reinstatement of parental rights (discussed in section 10.4, below) is);
- may specify efforts necessary to accomplish a permanent placement that is in the best

interests of the child; and
- if a child is not placed with prospective adoptive parents as selected in G.S 7B-1112.1, may order a placement that the court finds to be in the child's best interest after considering the agency's recommendations.

G.S. 7B-908(d), (d1). See section 10.3.B, below, regarding the selection of prospective adoptive parents. See Chapters 7.10 (discussing concurrent permanency planning) and 9.15.C (discussing the court's authority related to child placement upon entering TPR order).

**2. Timing.** The order must be reduced to writing, signed, and entered (filed with the clerk) within thirty days of the completion of the hearing. G.S. 7B-908(e1) (effective October 1, 2019 by S.L. 2019-33); *see* N.C. R. CIV. P. 58 (entry of order). If the order is not entered within thirty days, the juvenile clerk must schedule a hearing at the next juvenile session of court for a determination and explanation of the reason for the delay and for any needed clarification as to the contents of the order. The order must then be entered within ten days of this follow-up hearing. G.S. 7B-908(e1). The appropriate remedy for a trial court's failure to enter a timely order is a petition to the court of appeals for a writ of mandamus to require the trial court to proceed to judgment. *In re T.H.T.*, 362 N.C. 446 (2008). See Chapter 4.9.C (discussing what constitutes entry of the order) and 4.9.D (discussing the effect of and the remedy for delay).

## 10.2 Post-Relinquishment Review Hearings

### A. Circumstances Requiring Review

The Juvenile Code (G.S. Chapter 7B) requires the court to conduct periodic reviews of cases in which a child is in the custody of a DSS or licensed child-placing agency after a relinquishment for adoption has been made to that DSS or a child-placing agency by a

- parent,
- G.S. Chapter 35A guardian for the child (or other state's equivalent), or
- guardian ad litem appointed for an incompetent parent pursuant to G.S. 48-3-602 (discussed in section 10.2.B.1(d), below).

G.S. 7B-909(a). *See* G.S. 48-1-101(8) (definition of "guardian").

### B. Relinquishment for Adoption

Relinquishment of a child for adoption is governed by G.S. 48-3-701 through -707. This section is meant to provide general information on relinquishment and does not comprehensively address requirements and procedures for relinquishment.

**1. Who may relinquish.** A parent may relinquish all parental rights and a guardian appointed pursuant to G.S. Chapter 35A may relinquish all guardianship powers, including the right to consent to adoption, to a DSS or licensed child-placing agency. G.S. 48-3-701(a); 48-1-

101(4) (definition of "agency"); 48-1-101(8) (definition of "guardian").

- **(a) Married parents living together.** If the parents are married to each other and living together, the parents must act jointly in relinquishing a child to an agency. G.S. 48-3-701(a).

- **(b) Mother.** The mother of a child may execute a relinquishment at any time after a child is born but not sooner. G.S. 48-3-701(b).

- **(c) Father or possible biological father.** A relinquishment may be executed by a man whose consent is required under G.S. 48-3-601 either before or after the child is born. G.S. 48-3-701(b). For a discussion of cases related to whether a man's consent for adoption is required based on his knowledge (or lack thereof) of the child's existence, see Chapter 9.11.E.4.

- **(d) Incompetent parent.** If a parent has been adjudicated incompetent, the court must appoint a guardian ad litem (GAL) for the parent and, unless the child already has a guardian, a GAL for the child to investigate whether the adoption should proceed. The investigation must include an evaluation of the parent's condition and any reasonable likelihood that the parent will be restored to competency, the relationship between the child and the parent, alternatives to adoption, and any other relevant fact or circumstance. If the court determines after a hearing that it will be in the child's best interest for the adoption to proceed, the court is required to order the parent's GAL to execute a consent or relinquishment on behalf of the incompetent parent. G.S. 48-3-602.

  > **Practice Note:** The GAL appointed pursuant to G.S. 48-3-602 is appointed by the clerk of superior court who has jurisdiction over the adoption proceeding. *See* G.S. 48-2-100(a); 1-7 (when "court" means clerk). The GAL for purposes of executing a relinquishment on behalf of a parent who has been adjudicated incompetent is not the Rule 17 GAL appointed by the district court in the juvenile proceeding, unless the clerk of court also appoints that person as the GAL for the incompetent parent pursuant to G.S. 48-3-602.

- **(e) Minor parent.** A parent who is younger than 18 years old has the legal capacity to execute a relinquishment of (as well as a consent to) his or her child for adoption and is fully bound by such relinquishment. G.S. 48-3-605(b); 48-3-702(b). There is an additional procedure that applies for a minor parent executing a relinquishment relating to the minor parent's identity. The minor parent's identity may be identified to the person authorized to administer oaths or take acknowledgements by (1) methods of identification permitted by G.S. Chapter 10B or other applicable law or (2) an affidavit of a teacher, licensed professional social worker, health service provider, adult relative (of the minor), or if none of these persons are available, an adult the minor has known for more than two years. G.S. 48-3-605(h).

- **(f) Guardian**. A child's guardian may execute a relinquishment of guardianship powers, including the right to consent to adoption, at any time. G.S. 48-3-701(a), (c). In the adoption context, "guardian" refers only to an individual

- appointed in a proceeding under G.S. Chapter 35A to exercise the powers conferred by G.S. 35A-1241 (including a standby guardian whose authority has commenced) or
- appointed in another jurisdiction, according to the law of that jurisdiction, who has the power to consent to adoption under the law of that jurisdiction.

G.S. 48-1-101(8).

**2. Types of relinquishment.** A child may be relinquished only to a county DSS or a licensed child-placing agency, not to an individual. *See* G.S. 48-3-201(b), (c). The relinquishment is effective only when accepted by the agency. *See* G.S. 48-3-702(c). A relinquishment may be "general," allowing the agency full discretion to choose the adoptive parent, or "designated," meaning that the parent consents only to the child's adoption by the person(s) the parent designates in the relinquishment form. G.S. 48-3-703(a)(5); 48-3-704. In a designated relinquishment, the parent indicates whether he or she wants to be notified if the adoption by the designated person(s) cannot be completed. After a parent is notified that the adoption cannot be completed, the parent has ten days from the date he or she receives that notice to revoke the relinquishment. If the parent elects not to be notified or does not timely revoke the relinquishment after being notified, the designated relinquishment becomes a general relinquishment, and the agency may place the child with a prospective adoptive parent it selects. G.S. 48-3-704.

**NC DHHS DSS Form:**
DSS-1804, Relinquishment of Minor for Adoption by Parent or Guardian or Guardian ad Litem of the Mother/Father (Nov. 2019).

**3. Right to counsel.** Parents must be advised of their rights to seek legal advice from an attorney before they execute a relinquishment (or consent), and notice that the parent has been informed of this right must be included in the relinquishment (or consent). G.S. 48-3-702(b1)(5); 48-3-703(a)(12)c. (relinquishment); 48-3-605(c)(5); 48-3-606(14)c. (consent) (effective October 1, 2019 by S.L. 2019-172). Although a parent has the right to be advised by an attorney, a parent who is indigent does not have a right to court-appointed counsel for purposes of the relinquishment process, with one exception.

Effective October 1, 2019, the Juvenile Code explicitly addresses a parent's relinquishment to DSS when that parent is a respondent in an abuse, neglect, dependency, or termination of parental rights action – G.S. 7B-909.1. *See* S.L. 2019-33. When that parent has either retained an attorney or when his or her provisional attorney (appointed pursuant to G.S. 7B-602(a) or 7B-1101.1(a)) has been confirmed by the court, before the relinquishment is executed, DSS must

- give notice by any reasonable and timely means to the parent's attorney, or if the attorney is unavailable to the attorney's law partner or employee, that it has made arrangements for the parent to execute a relinquishment at a specific date, time, and location; and
- advise the parent of their right to seek the advice of their attorney before executing the relinquishment and to have their attorney present when executing the relinquishment.

G.S. 7B-909.1.

This new statute codifies the holding of a 1994 published opinion by the court of appeals – *In re Maynard*, 116 N.C. App. 616 (1994). In that case, the court of appeals affirmed the decision made by the district court hearing a neglect proceeding to set aside a relinquishment that was executed by the respondent mother. The respondent mother was represented by court-appointed counsel as the result of a petition alleging that her children were neglected in part because of her mental illness. During the course of the neglect proceeding, DSS asked respondent to sign a relinquishment for adoption but, after conferring with her attorney, she declined and notified the court of her interest in having her children returned to her. Later, during supervised visitation but without her attorney present or being informed of the discussions, DSS asked respondent mother to sign a relinquishment, which she did. Respondent's attorney did not become aware of the relinquishment until after the revocation period expired, and as a result, filed a motion to set aside the relinquishment. Because an adoption petition had not been filed, the district court hearing the neglect proceeding had jurisdiction to hear the motion. Because the signing of the relinquishment occurred following and as a consequence of a neglect proceeding in which the respondent was entitled to and had not waived her right to counsel, the court of appeals held that the signing of the relinquishment was directly related to the neglect proceeding and based on the findings of fact by the trial court, the respondent was entitled to counsel when she signed the relinquishment forms.

**Practice Note:** In addition to notifying the parent of their right to consult with and have their attorney present, in most instances DSS should involve its own attorney before continuing any discussion with the parent about relinquishment.

**4. Revocation.** A relinquishment may be revoked within seven days, except that a second identical relinquishment is irrevocable. A revocation must be in writing and either delivered to the agency that accepted the relinquishment within seven days or sent to the agency by registered mail or overnight delivery service (as long as the revocation is placed in the mail or with the overnight delivery service by the seventh day). *See* G.S. 48-3-706(a), (d). *See In re Adoption of Baby Boy*, 233 N.C. App. 493, 505 (2014) (the birth mother attempted a revocation on the eighth day that was treated by the agency as ineffective; in addressing an appeal on a different issue regarding the relinquishment, the court of appeals stated "there was a valid relinquishment in this matter, which the birth mother failed to timely revoke").

When interpreting the statutes addressing consent and the purpose of the adoption chapter, as a matter of first impression, the court of appeals held that the seven-day revocation period does not begin to run until an original or copy of the signed consent is actually delivered to the parent. *In re Ivey*, 810 S.E.2d 740 (N.C. Ct. App. 2018) (affirming trial court's order dismissing adoption based on findings that mother timely revoked her consent when she did so within seven days of her receipt of the consent rather than within seven days of when she signed the consent, which was weeks earlier). The statutory language relied upon by the court of appeals included the requirement that the parent executing the consent has "been given an original or copy of his or her fully executed" consent. G.S. 48-3-605(c)(3). This same language is included in the companion procedures for relinquishment statute – G.S. 48-3-

702(b1)(3).

> **NC DHHS DSS Form:**
> DSS-1805, <u>Revocation of Relinquishment for Adoption by Parent, Guardian, or Guardian ad Litem of the Mother/Father</u> (Nov. 2014).

**5. Rescission.** A relinquishment may be rescinded at any time by mutual agreement of the parent and the agency to which the child was relinquished, but only if the child has not been placed with a prospective adoptive parent. G.S. 48-3-707(a)(2). After a child has been placed with a prospective adoptive parent but before the entry of the adoption decree, a relinquishment may be rescinded if agreed upon by the agency, the person relinquishing the child, and the prospective adoptive parent. G.S. 48-3-707(a)(3).

**6. Voiding the relinquishment.** Before a final adoption decree is entered, a relinquishment becomes void if the parent establishes by clear and convincing evidence that the relinquishment was obtained by fraud or duress. G.S. 48-3-707(a)(1). A relinquishment also can be voided for fraud or duress after a final order of adoption is entered, but only if a parent moves to set aside the adoption within six months of the time the fraud or duress reasonably should have been discovered. G.S. 48-2-607(c).

If the court finds, on motion of DSS or a child-placing agency, that a consent or relinquishment that is necessary for the child's adoption cannot be obtained from a parent and that no further steps are being taken to terminate that parent's rights, the court may void the relinquishment by the other parent upon finding that it is in the child's best interest. Before voiding the relinquishment, the court must require the agency to give at least fifteen days' notice to the relinquishing parent whose rights will be restored. That parent then has a right to be heard on whether the relinquishment should be voided and his or her plan to provide for the child if the relinquishment is voided. If the relinquishing parent cannot be located with due diligence, notice of the hearing must be sent by U.S. mail, return receipt requested, to the address of the parent given in the relinquishment. G.S. 7B-909(b1); *see* G.S. 48-3-707(a)(4).

**7. Consequences of relinquishment.** A relinquishment vests legal and physical custody of the child in the agency and empowers the agency to place the child for adoption consistent with the manner specified in the relinquishment (designated or general, discussed in subsection 2, above). G.S. 48-3-705(b). *See In re A.L.*, 245 N.C. App. 55 (2016) (holding the relinquishment executed by the mother gave DSS custody). Custody of the child vests in the agency by operation of law such that there is no court order. However, after the expiration of the revocation period, the agency to whom the child was relinquished may apply ex parte to the clerk of superior court for an order that finds the child has been relinquished to the agency and confirms that the agency has legal custody of the child for purposes of obtaining a certified copy of the child's birth certificate, Social Security number, or federal or state benefits for the child. G.S. 48-3-705(e).

A parent who relinquishes a child gives up his or her custodial rights, the right to consent to the child's adoption, and unless the parent has filed an action to set aside the relinquishment for fraud or duress, the right to notice of the adoption petition being filed. G.S. 48-3-705(c);

48-2-401(b)(3). A parent who has relinquished the child for adoption is not required to be a party in the abuse, neglect, or dependency action; however, the court may order that the parent be a party. G.S. 7B-401.1(b)(2). A relinquishment does not terminate parental rights and does not affect the child's right to inherit or the parent's support obligation, which continues until the final decree of adoption. *See* G.S. 48-3-705(d); *Stanly County Dept. of Social Services ex rel. Dennis v. Reeder*, 127 N.C. App. 723 (1997). All parental rights and duties terminate when the final decree of adoption is entered. G.S. 48-3-705(d); 48-1-106(c).

**8. Compliance with ICWA.** For relinquishments involving an "Indian child," the requirements of the Indian Child Welfare Act (ICWA) must be complied with, and those requirements differ from the procedures set forth in G.S. Chapter 48. G.S. 48-3-605(f); 48-3-702(b); *see* 25 U.S.C. 1901 *et seq.*; 25 U.S.C. 1903(4) (definition of "Indian child"). For example, a relinquishment cannot be made until ten days after the child's birth and any relinquishment executed before then is invalid. 25 C.F.R. 23.125(e). A relinquishment must be executed and recorded before a court of competent jurisdiction. 25 U.S.C. 1913(a); 25 C.F.R. 23.125; *see* G.S. 48-3-605(g); 48-3-702(b). A relinquishment may also be withdrawn at any time before the adoption decree is final. 25 U.S.C. 1913(c); 25 C.F.R. 23.125(b)(2)(iii) and 23.128(b). For a discussion of ICWA, see Chapter 13.2 (for relinquishments specifically, see section K).

## C. Timing and Petition or Motion for Review

When a child has not been adopted within six months following a relinquishment, the DSS or child-placing agency with custody of the child must promptly file a petition for post-relinquishment review or, if the court is exercising jurisdiction over the child, a motion for post-relinquishment review. The post-relinquishment review hearing must be conducted within thirty days following the filing of the petition or motion unless the court directs otherwise. After the first review, the court must continue to conduct reviews every six months until a final decree of adoption is entered or the relinquishment is voided under G.S. 7B-909(b1). G.S. 7B-909(a), (c).

**AOC Form:**
AOC-J-140, Motion for Review (Abuse/Neglect/Dependency) (Oct. 2013).

If the form is used as a petition for review, the user should change the title from "Motion" to "Petition."

## D. Parent's Party Status

A parent who relinquished the child for adoption is not a party to the post-relinquishment review hearing. A parent whose rights have been terminated is considered a party only if an appeal of the order terminating that parent's rights is pending and a court has stayed the order pending the appeal. G.S. 7B-909(c).

## E. Procedure for Hearing

The procedure for post-relinquishment review hearings is the same as for post-TPR review hearings, explained in section 10.1, above. If the proceeding involves an "Indian child" or if the court has reason to know the child is an "Indian child," the Indian Child Welfare Act (ICWA) applies. 25 C.F.R. 23.103; *see* 25 C.F.R. 23.107. See Chapter 13.2 (discussing ICWA).

## 10.3 Selected Adoption Provisions

### A. Introduction

Adoption procedures and requirements are primarily contained in Chapter 48 of the General Statutes. This Manual does not attempt to explain adoption law but does seek to explain the relationship between juvenile court proceedings and adoption proceedings.

As discussed in Chapter 7.10 of this Manual, adoption is one of six possible permanent plans for a child who is the subject of an abuse, neglect, or dependency proceeding. If the court determines that adoption is a permanent plan, DSS has responsibilities related to placing the child for adoption as well ensuring that necessary relinquishments, consents, and/or termination of parental rights (TPR) orders are obtained. *See, e.g.*, G.S. 48-3-201(d); 7B-1112.1. The responsibilities of the child's guardian ad litem (GAL) to protect and promote the child's best interests remain intact during the adoption process and include participating in the adoption selection process and having standing to initiate a TPR proceeding. G.S. 7B-1112.1; 7B-1103(a)(6). Unless waived by the court presiding over the adoption proceeding, a child who is 12 or older consents to his or her own adoption. G.S. 48-3-601(1); 48-3-603(b)(2). A parent who has executed a valid relinquishment or whose rights have been terminated has no role in the adoption process. *See* G.S. 7B-1112; 48-3-703(a)(10); 48-3-705(b), (c). The role of the district court in an adoption proceeding is limited.

The Indian Child Welfare Act (ICWA) applies to adoption proceedings. G.S. 48-1-108. ICWA sets forth specific procedures that must be followed, including the court inquiring into whether the participants know or have reason to know the child is an "Indian child" and additional requirements for consents, relinquishments, termination of parental rights, and placement preferences. *See, e.g.*, 25 C.F.R. 23.103 and 23.107. See Chapter 13.2 (discussing ICWA).

---

**Resources:**
In addition to G.S. Chapter 48, resources for adoption information include the following:
- Subchapter 70M of Title 10A of the North Carolina Administrative Code, "Adoption Standards" (sections 10A N.C.A.C. 70M.0101 to 10A N.C.A.C. 70M.0604).
- The DHHS policies and procedures related to DSS adoption services, found in DIV. OF SOC. SERVS., N.C. DEP'T OF HEALTH & HUMAN SERVICES, CHILD WELFARE MANUAL "Adoptions," available here.
- CHERYL D. HOWELL, JAN S. SIMMONS, NORTH CAROLINA TRIAL JUDGES' BENCH BOOK DISTRICT COURT: VOL. 1, FAMILY LAW (UNC School of Government 2019). In particular, see Chapter 8 "Adoption."

- SARA DEPASQUALE, FATHERS AND PATERNITY: APPLYING THE LAW IN NORTH CAROLINA CHILD WELFARE CASES (UNC School of Government 2016). In particular, see Chapter 7 "A Child's Permanent Plan of Adoption: The Process and the Role of Fathers."
- Website for the North American Council on Adoptable Children, a resource for publications, training, support, and a wide range of information related to adoption.
- "Adoption" on the Child Welfare Information Gateway website, with resources on aspects of domestic and international adoption.

## B. Prospective Adoptive Parents

**1. DSS responsibility and discretion to select.** DSS (or a licensed child-placing agency) with legal and physical custody of the child has the sole responsibility and discretion for the selection of specific adoptive parents, unless a designated relinquishment has been executed and accepted. G.S. 48-3-203(a), (d); 7B-1112.1. The agency is required to consider any current placement provider who wants to adopt the child. G.S. 7B-1112.1. The agency may consult with the child's parent. *See* G.S. 48-3-203(b), (d)(2). The agency may also consult with the child. If the child is 12 or older, he or she must consent to the adoption, unless the court hearing the adoption action waives this requirement after finding it is not in the child's best interests. G.S. 48-3-601(1); 48-3-603(b)(2).

The child's GAL may consult with and request information from DSS (or the child-placing agency) regarding the selection process. G.S. 7B-1112.1. If the GAL requests information related to the selection, the agency must provide the information within five business days. G.S. 7B-1112.1. The GAL's duties to see that the child's interests and needs are being met (*see* G.S. 7B-601) extend to involvement in the child's placement for adoption. *See In re N.C.L.*, 89 N.C. App. 79 (1988) (confirming the GAL's duty and right to inquire into DSS's handling of the child's adoption and the authority of the court to order DSS to turn over information requested by the GAL); *Wilkinson v. Riffel*, 72 N.C. App. 220 (1985) (affirming trial court's order that DSS disclose confidential information, specifically the children's adoptive placement, to the GAL, who has the right to confidential information that she believes is relevant to the case and had an ongoing duty to conduct follow-up investigations and report to court when the child's needs are not being met) (both opinions were decided under the former law).

**Practice Notes:** In practice, DSS and the GAL often communicate openly throughout the process of selecting an adoptive placement, sharing information and discussing concerns as they arise. Such open communication may avoid a motion for review that could delay and complicate the adoption.

Although the GAL has an ongoing duty in the abuse, neglect, dependency, or termination of parental rights action until he or she is relieved or the court's jurisdiction terminates, the GAL has no statutorily defined responsibilities or authority in the adoption proceeding. It is possible the GAL could be called as a witness in an adoption hearing. If the adoption proceeding is contested, the court in that action may appoint an attorney or GAL to represent the child's interests in that action. G.S. 48-2-201(b).

**2. Notice of adoptive parent selection to GAL and foster parent.** While the GAL and foster parents have no authority with respect to the selection of adoptive parents, the agency is required to notify the GAL and the foster parents of the prospective adoptive parent selection within ten days after the selection is made and before the filing of the adoption petition. G.S. 7B-1112.1. The statute does not designate whether that notice must be in writing. But, the agency must provide the foster parents who are not selected with a copy of a motion for judicial review of adoption selection. G.S. 7B-1112.1.

**AOC Form:**
AOC-J-140, Motion for Review (Abuse/Neglect/Dependency) (Oct. 2013).

**3. Review hearing on selection.** After receiving notice of who the agency selected as prospective adoptive parents, if the GAL disagrees or the foster parents who want to adopt the child were not selected, either may file a motion for judicial review. The motion for judicial review must be filed with the district court within ten days of the agency's notification of who was selected. The case should be scheduled for hearing on the next juvenile calendar. Foster parents do not acquire party status solely based on their right to receive notice and to be heard by filing a motion.

At a hearing on a motion to review the selection, the court must consider the agency's and GAL's recommendations and other facts related to the selection of adoptive parents. The court determines whether the proposed adoptive placement is in the child's best interests. G.S. 7B-1112.1.

**Practice Note:** The judicial review is governed by G.S. 7B-1112.1, which has limiting language. The court is determining whether the proposed adoptive placement that was selected by DSS is in the child's best interests. The statutory language does not authorize the court to decide that a different specific placement should have been selected or to order a new selected placement.

**4. Placement with prospective adoptive parent(s).** An agency may acquire the authority to place a child for adoption and consent to the child's adoption only by means of a relinquishment or by termination of parental rights (TPR) when the child is in the agency's custody. G.S. 48-3-203(a); *see* G.S. 48-3-601(3)a. (consent by agency). When a parent executes a relinquishment to an agency, legal and physical custody of the child vest with the agency, and the agency may place the minor for adoption as specified in the relinquishment. G.S. 48-3-705(b). When a child is in DSS custody at the time a TPR petition or motion is filed, entry of a TPR order gives DSS all of the rights for adoptive placement of the child that the agency would have if the parents had relinquished the child to it, except as otherwise provided in G.S. 7B-908(d)[1]. G.S. 7B-1112(1). Cases based on the law as it read before October 1, 2011, held that the trial court did not have subject matter jurisdiction to order the

---

[1] S.L. 2017-161, sec. 9, amends G.S. 7B-908(d) and creates G.S. 7B-908(d1), which addresses the court's authority to order a placement for a child who has not been placed with prospective adoptive parents selected by G.S. 7B-1112.1. G.S. 7B-1112(1) was not simultaneously amended to refer to G.S. 7B-908(d1), and the failure to do so appears to be an oversight.

child placed with a relative following TPR, because the statute gave DSS exclusive placement authority. *See, e.g., In re I.T.P-L.*, 194 N.C. App. 453 (2008); *In re Asbury*, 125 N.C. App. 143 (1997). That continues to be true once DSS places the child for adoption. However, until the child is placed with prospective adoptive parents as selected in G.S. 7B-1112.1, the court at a post-TPR review hearing may order a placement different from the one proposed by DSS, as long as the court considers DSS's recommendations and finds that the placement it is ordering is in the child's best interest. G.S. 7B-908(d1). See Section 10.1, above (discussing post-TPR review hearings).

If the child must be moved from his or her current placement to the home of the prospective adoptive parents, the agency may not move the child until after the time for the GAL or foster parent to file a motion for review of the selection of prospective adoptive parents has expired and a motion has not been filed. G.S. 7B-1112.1.

When DSS has custody or placement responsibility for a child, DSS may not place the child with the prospective adoptive parents until a criminal history investigation, determination of the individual's fitness for having responsibility of children's safety and well-being, and determination of whether other individuals who reside in the home are fit to have the child live with them are completed. G.S. 48-3-203(d1); 48-3-309. There must also be a favorable preplacement assessment. G.S. 48-3-203(d); *see* G.S. 48-3-301 through -309. The Interstate Compact on the Placement of Children (ICPC) applies to interstate placements of children in pre-adoptive homes. G.S. 48-3-207; 7B-3800. See Chapter 7.4.H (discussing the ICPC).

Unless the court orders otherwise, when an agency makes an adoptive placement, the agency retains legal custody but not physical custody of the child until the adoption decree becomes final. The agency may delegate responsibility for the child's care and support to the adoption petitioner. G.S. 48-3-502(a). The agency may notify the parent when a placement has been made. G.S. 48-3-203(c).

Before an adoption is final, the agency may petition the court for cause to dismiss the adoption proceeding and restore its full legal and physical custody of the child. The basis for the court's determination is the best interests of the child. G.S. 48-3-502(b); *see* G.S. 48-2-604(a).

**5. Prospective adoptive parent is petitioner.** A prospective adoptive parent has standing to file a petition when the child has been placed with him or her pursuant to G.S. 48-3-201 through -207 unless the court has waived the placement requirement for cause. G.S. 48-2-301(a); *see In re D.E.M.*, 254 N.C. App. 401, 411 (2017), *aff'd per curiam,* 370 N.C. 463 (2018) (stating, "N.C. Gen. Stat. § 48-2-301(a) expressly authorizes a waiver of the requirement of an adoption placement 'for cause'."). There is no summons in an adoption proceeding; instead, the petitioner serves notice that the adoption petition was filed pursuant to G.S. 48-2-401 through -407.

## C. District Court Jurisdiction When Adoption Is Filed

**1. Adoption is a special proceeding.** An adoption proceeding is separate from an abuse, neglect, dependency, or termination of parental rights proceeding that is before the district court, even when the child's primary permanent plan in the abuse, neglect, or dependency action is adoption.

An adoption is a special proceeding before the clerk of superior court. G.S. 48-2-100(a). However, the district court may acquire jurisdiction over the adoption proceeding if

- the proceeding must be transferred by the clerk pursuant to G.S. 48-2-601(a1) and G.S. 1-301.2(b) or
- a final order entered by the clerk is appealed pursuant to G.S. 48-2-607(b).

An adoption proceeding must be transferred to district court when an issue of fact, equitable defense, or request for equitable relief is raised before the clerk. G.S. 48-2-601(a1); 1-301.2(b). The proceeding remains a separate special proceeding from the juvenile action. When the action is transferred, the district court judge may hear and determine all the matters in the adoption proceeding, unless it appears to the judge that justice would be more efficiently administered by the district court disposing of only the matter that resulted in the transfer and remanding the special proceeding to the clerk. G.S. 1-301.2(c).

**2. Jurisdiction in a G.S. Chapter 7B action.** If a child who is the subject of an adoption petition is also the subject of a pending abuse, neglect, dependency, or termination of parental rights proceeding (TPR), the district court having jurisdiction under G.S. Chapter 7B retains jurisdiction in the juvenile proceeding until the final order of adoption is entered. The district court may waive jurisdiction for good cause. G.S. 48-2-102(b).

An adoption hearing or disposition on the petition occurs at least ninety days after and within six months of when the adoption petition is filed, unless the court presiding over the adoption proceeding waives these time requirements for cause. G.S. 48-2-603(a)(1); 48-2-601(c). A hearing may be continued on the court's own motion for further evidence. G.S. 48-2-603(c). While an adoption is pending, a permanency planning, review, post-TPR review, or post-relinquishment review hearing may be required or requested pursuant to G.S. Chapter 7B. The district court has jurisdiction over those hearings. See sections 10.1 and 10.2, above (discussing post-TPR and post-relinquishment review hearings) and Chapter 7 (discussing dispositional hearings, including review and permanency planning hearings).

A TPR may be necessary for the adoption to be achieved. An adoption petition and TPR action may be filed concurrently. G.S. 48-2-302(c). The adoption petitioner has standing to initiate a TPR action. G.S. 7B-1103(a)(7). The district court has jurisdiction to hear the TPR action, and the clerk of superior court has jurisdiction to hear the adoption proceeding. G.S. 7B-200(a)(4); 48-2-100(a). When the adoption is a result of a placement made by DSS or a licensed child-placing agency (an "agency placement"), a TPR stays the adoption proceeding. *See* G.S. 48-2-402(c); *In re Adoption of S.D.W.*, 367 N.C. 386 (2014). A TPR is not required to be stayed when an adoption for the same child is pending, even if there is a pending appeal of an order entered in the adoption proceeding. In the case of *In re Adoption of Baby Boy*, 233 N.C. App. 493 (2014), the trial court found the mother's relinquishment for adoption of her baby boy void, and the adoptive parents appealed the order. While that appeal was pending, the adoptive parents filed a TPR petition, and the district court terminated the mother's parental rights. In an appeal from the TPR order, in *In re Baby Boy*, 238 N.C. App. 316 (2014), the court of appeals affirmed the TPR order and held that G.S. 7B-1003 prohibits the district court from exercising jurisdiction over a TPR proceeding when there is a pending appeal of an order designated in G.S. 7B-1001 only. The trial court may exercise jurisdiction over a TPR proceeding while an appeal of an adoption order, entered pursuant to G.S. Chapter 48, is pending. For a discussion of the trial court's jurisdiction to proceed with a TPR action during pendency of appeal in an adoption case or in other cases, see Chapter 12.11.A.3.

### D. The Adoption

**1. The determination.** An adoption is resolved after a hearing, but if the adoption is uncontested, the court may dispose of the petition without a formal hearing. G.S. 48-2-601. There are several factors that must be found before the adoption may be granted, including

- by a preponderance of the evidence, that the adoption will serve the adoptee's best interest;
- each necessary consent, relinquishment, waiver, or termination of parental rights order has been obtained;
- each petitioner is a suitable adoptive parent; and
- unless waiving the placement requirement for cause, that the child has been in the petitioner's physical custody for at least ninety days.

G.S. 48-2-603(a); 48-2-606(a)(7). *See* G.S. 48-3-601 and 48-3-603 for whose consent is or is not required.

If the court denies the petition, custody of the child reverts to the agency or person who had custody immediately before the filing of the petition. G.S. 48-2-604(c). Post-TPR or post-relinquishment reviews would continue.

**2. Notice of decree.** Within ten days of receiving notice of a final decree of adoption, the agency must file with the court hearing the post-TPR or post-relinquishment reviews and serve on the child's GAL (if any) written notice of the entry of adoption. The adoption decree itself should never be filed in the district court file. The clerk must cancel any review hearings and provide notice of the cancellation to those required to receive notice of the hearings. G.S. 7B-908(e).

The agency may notify the parent when an adoption decree is issued. G.S.48-3-203(c).

**Practice Note:** The Juvenile Code requirements that adoption petitions, motions, and decrees should never be filed in the juvenile case likely relate to the confidentiality provisions contained in G.S. Chapter 48 and have the effect of protecting adoption information from unintended inspection. While certain individuals are permitted access to the juvenile file pursuant to G.S. 7B-2901(a), the adoption file can be opened only by order of the court presiding over the adoption proceeding pursuant to G.S. 48-9-102(b) and 48-9-105.

**3. Effect of decree.** A final decree of adoption has the legal effect of a complete substitution of families for the adoptee. G.S. 48-1-106(a); *but see* G.S. 48-1-106(d) (exception for stepparent adoption). However, a child's grandparent has visitation rights when the grandparent has a substantial relationship with the child and the child is adopted by a relative or stepparent. G.S. 48-1-106(f); 50-13.2(b1); 50-13.2A; 50-13.5(j).

The relationship of parent and child is established between the adoption petitioner and adoptee. G.S. 48-1-106(b). The relationship of parent and child is severed between the adoptee and the biological or previous adoptive parent of the adoptee, except for a stepparent adoption, where the relationship between the parent who is the stepparent's spouse and the child continues. G.S. 48-1-106(c), (d).

If there is an underlying abuse, neglect, or dependency proceeding, the district court's jurisdiction is terminated upon the final decree of adoption. G.S. 48-2-102(b); *In re W.R.A.*, 200 N.C. App. 789 (2009).

## 10.4 Reinstatement of Parental Rights

### A. Introduction

As discussed in Chapter 7.10 of this Manual, reinstatement of parental rights is one of six possible permanent plans for a child who is the subject of an abuse, neglect, or dependency proceeding. This permanent plan is an option in very limited circumstances and requires that there was a termination of parental rights for one if not both of the child's parents. The criteria and procedures to reinstate parental rights are codified at G.S. 7B-1114.

> **Resource:** For the state policy, see DIV. OF SOC. SERVS., N.C. DEP'T OF HEALTH & HUMAN SERVICES, CHILD WELFARE MANUAL "Permanency Planning," available here.

### B. Circumstances for Reinstatement

Circumstances in which the procedure is available are narrow:

- A motion to reinstate parental rights may be filed only by a child whose parent's rights have been terminated, the child's guardian ad litem (GAL) attorney advocate, or a department of social services (DSS) that has custody of the child.
- The child must be at least 12 years old or, if the child is younger than 12, the motion must allege extraordinary circumstances requiring consideration of the motion.
- The child must not have a legal parent, must not be in an adoptive placement, and must not be likely to be adopted within a reasonable time.
- The order terminating parental rights must have been entered at least three years before the motion is filed, unless the court has found or the child's GAL attorney advocate and the DSS with custody stipulate that the child's permanent plan is no longer adoption.

G.S. 7B-1114(a).

Although it is not stated explicitly, the statute read as a whole limits its application to children who are in the custody of DSS.

## C. Hearing Procedures

**1. Notification to child and appointment of GAL.** If a parent contacts DSS or the child's GAL about reinstatement of the parent's rights and a motion can be filed under G.S. 7B-1114(a), DSS or the GAL must notify the child that the child has a right to file a motion for reinstatement of parental rights. G.S. 7B-1114(b). DSS and the child's GAL attorney advocate also have standing to bring a motion. When a motion to reinstate parental rights is filed, the court must appoint a GAL for the child if the child does not have one. The appointment, duties, and payment of the GAL and GAL attorney advocate are the same as in G.S. 7B-601 and 7B-603. G.S. 7B-1114(c). See Chapter 2.3.D (discussing the child's GAL).

**2. Service of motion.** The party filing the motion (the child, DSS, or the GAL attorney advocate) must serve it on each of the following who is not the movant:

- the child,
- the child's GAL or GAL attorney advocate,
- the DSS with custody of the child, and
- the former parent whose rights the motion seeks to have reinstated.

G.S. 7B-1114(d).

**3. Former parent not a party and not entitled to appointment of counsel.** Although the former parent must be served, he or she is not a party. The former parent is not entitled to appointed counsel if indigent but may retain counsel at his or her own expense. G.S. 7B-1114(d).

**4. Timing.** The party filing the motion must ask the clerk to calendar a preliminary hearing on the motion for reinstatement of parental rights within sixty days of the filing of the motion and must give at least fifteen days' notice to those who were required to be served and to the child's placement provider (who is not made a party by virtue of receiving notice). G.S. 7B-1114(e). At the conclusion of the preliminary hearing, the court must either dismiss the motion or order that the child's permanent plan become reinstatement of parental rights. If the motion is not dismissed at the preliminary hearing, the court must conduct interim hearings at least every six months until the motion is granted or dismissed. G.S. 7B-1114(h). The court must grant or dismiss the motion within twelve months from the date the motion was filed unless the court makes written findings about why that cannot occur and specifies a time frame for entering a final order. G.S. 7B-1114(j). After an order reinstating parental rights is entered, the court is not required to conduct further reviews. G.S. 7B-1114(k).

Note that the phrase "preliminary hearing" is used in this statute to refer to the first hearing on a motion to reinstate parental rights, and the phrase "interim hearing" (see section 10.4.E, below) is used to refer to subsequent periodic hearings.

**5. Pre-hearing reports.** At least seven days before the preliminary hearing, DSS and the child's GAL must provide the court, the other parties, and the former parent with reports that address a list of factors specified in section 10.4.D, below. G.S. 7B-1114(f); *see* G.S. 7B-1114(g).

**6. Participants.** At the preliminary hearing and any subsequent hearing on the motion, the court must consider information from the DSS that has custody of the child, the child, the child's GAL, the child's former parent whose parental rights are the subject of the motion, the child's placement provider, and any other person or agency that may aid the court in its review. G.S. 7B-1114(g). Although the child's former parent and current placement provider are entitled to notice and may be heard at the hearings, they are not parties to the proceeding. G.S. 7B-1114(d), (e).

**7. Evidence and standard for review.** The court may consider any evidence, including hearsay evidence, that the court finds to be relevant, reliable, and necessary to determine the needs of the child and whether reinstatement of parental rights is in the child's best interest. G.S. 7B-1114(g).

### D. Criteria and Findings

The court must consider the following criteria and make written findings regarding those that are relevant:

- efforts that were made to achieve adoption or a permanent guardianship;
- whether the parent whose rights the motion seeks to have reinstated has remedied the conditions that led to the child's removal and termination of the parent's rights;
- whether the child would receive proper care and supervision in a safe home if placed with the parent;
- the child's age, maturity, and ability to express his or her preference;
- the parent's willingness to resume contact with the child and to have parental rights reinstated;
- the child's willingness to resume contact with the parent and to have parental rights reinstated;
- services that would be needed by the child and the parent if the parent's rights were reinstated;
- any other criteria the court deems necessary.

G.S. 7B-1114(g). *See* G.S. 7B-101(19) (definition of "safe home").

### E. Interim Hearings and Reasonable Efforts

Interim hearings may be combined with post-TPR review hearings (discussed in section 10.1, above). At each interim hearing the court must assess whether the plan of reinstatement of parental rights continues to be in the child's best interest and whether DSS has made reasonable efforts to achieve that permanent plan. G.S. 7B-1114(h).

## F. Orders

After every hearing, whether preliminary or interim, the court must make findings of fact and conclusions of law and may

- enter an order for visitation under G.S. 7B-905.1 or
- order that the child be placed in the former parent's home and supervised by DSS either directly or, when the former parent lives in a different county, through coordination with the DSS in that county, or by other personnel available to the court, subject to any conditions the court specifies.

G.S. 7B-1114(i). See Chapter 7.5 (discussing visitation under G.S. 7B-905.1).

If the court places the child with the former parent, the order must state the child's placement and care remain the responsibility of the DSS with custody and that DSS is to provide or arrange for the child's placement. G.S. 7B-1114(i).

Orders from any type of reinstatement of parental rights hearing must be entered within thirty days following the completion of the hearing. If an order is not entered within that time, the clerk must schedule a subsequent hearing at the next session of juvenile court to determine and explain the reason for the delay and to obtain any needed clarification as to the contents of the order. The order must be entered within ten days of the subsequent hearing. G.S. 7B-1114(*l*). Where the court fails to enter a timely order, the appropriate remedy is a petition to the court of appeals for a writ of mandamus to require the trial court to proceed to judgment, not a new hearing. *In re T.H.T.*, 362 N.C. 446 (2008). See Chapter 4.9.D.3 (discussing mandamus as the remedy).

## G. Effect of Reinstatement

An order reinstating parental rights restores all rights, powers, privileges, immunities, duties, and obligations of the parent to the child, including those relating to custody, control, and support. G.S. 7B-1114(k). A parent whose rights are reinstated is not liable for child support or the cost of services provided to the child after the termination of parental rights order and before the order reinstating parental rights. G.S. 7B-1114(n). Reinstatement of parental rights does not vacate or otherwise affect the validity of the original order terminating those rights. G.S. 7B-1114(m).

**Practice Note:** When a parent's rights are reinstated, a permanent plan for the child has been achieved. *See* G.S. 7B-906.2(a), (a1). The statute governing reinstatement of parental rights does not address the status of the underlying abuse, neglect, or dependency action. The court should consider whether jurisdiction in the abuse, neglect, or dependency proceeding should continue such that jurisdiction over the proceeding is retained or whether the case may be dismissed with the reinstatement of parental rights and child's return to a parent's custody and control. *See* G.S. 7B-903(a)(1). If the court retains jurisdiction, it is not obligated to conduct periodic permanency planning hearings under G.S. 7B-906.1 because custody is with a parent; however, the court may continue to hold those hearings. *See* G.S. 7B-906.1(k). In addition, any party may file a motion for review in the abuse, neglect, or dependency action. *See* G.S. 7B-906.1(n); 7B-1000. However, if reviews have been waived and DSS receives a new report of abuse, neglect, or dependency, completes an assessment, and determines court action is needed, DSS must file a new petition rather than a motion for review. G.S. 7B-401(b). *See In re T.P.*, 254 N.C. App. 286 (2017). See Chapter 7.2.A.4(a) (discussing waiving permanency planning hearings).

# Chapter 11

# Evidence

# Chapter 11
# Evidence[1]

**11.1 Applicability of Rules of Evidence     11-5**
  A. Adjudication
     1. Applicability of rules
     2. Reliance on criminal cases
     3. Evidence issues involving children
     4. Local rules affecting evidence
  B. Disposition and Other Proceedings

**11.2 Child Witnesses     11-9**
  A. Competency of Child Witnesses
     1. General rule
     2. Procedure for determining competency
     3. Application of standard
     4. Unavailability distinguished from incompetency
     5. Quashing of subpoena for child
  B. Examination of Child Witnesses
     1. Remote testimony
     2. Excluding bystanders during child's testimony
     3. Excepting witnesses from sequestration order
     4. Oath for child witness
     5. Leading questions
     6. Written testimony
     7. Use of anatomical dolls to illustrate testimony
     8. Use of own terms for body parts
     9. Questioning by court
     10. Positioning on witness stand
     11. Recesses

**11.3 Out-of-Court Statements to Refresh, Impeach, or Corroborate     11-17**
  A. Refreshing Recollection
  B. Impeachment
  C. Corroboration

**11.4 Out-of-Court Statements and the Right to Confront Witnesses     11-20**
  A. Applicability of Confrontation Clause to Criminal and Delinquency Cases
     1. General rule

---

[1] This Chapter is by School of Government faculty member John Rubin. His work in this area owes its start to Ilene Nelson, former administrator of North Carolina's Guardian ad Litem program, and Janet Mason, former School of Government faculty member, who many years ago began thinking and writing about how evidence principles apply in juvenile cases.

2. Applicability to statements made to law-enforcement personnel, social workers, medical personnel, and others
   B. Inapplicability of Confrontation Clause to Juvenile Cases

## 11.5 Out-of-Court Statements and the Hearsay Rule    11-22
   A. Governing Rules
   B. Rationale for Hearsay Rule
   C. Components of Hearsay Definition
      1. Oral or written assertion of fact
      2. Made outside current proceeding
      3. Offered for truth of assertion

## 11.6 Hearsay Exceptions    11-25
   A. Types of Hearsay Exceptions and Their Rationales
   B. Rule 801(d): Admissions of a Party-Opponent
      1. Criteria
      2. Potential constitutional, statutory, and other bars
      3. Application of admission exception to common situations in juvenile cases
   C. Rule 803(2): Excited Utterances
      1. Criteria
      2. Statements by children
   D. Rule 803(3): State of Mind
      1. Criteria
      2. Examples
   E. Rule 803(4): Medical Diagnosis or Treatment
      1. Criteria
      2. First requirement: declarant's understanding and motivation
      3. Child declarants
      4. Examination protocols
      5. Identity of listener
      6. Statements to medical professional by parent of child obtaining treatment
      7. Second requirement: pertinence to diagnosis and treatment
      8. Mixed purpose examinations
      9. Identification of perpetrator
      10. Videotape of examination
      11. Anatomical dolls
      12. Basis of opinion
   F. Rule 803(6): Business Records
      1. Criteria
      2. Method and circumstances of preparation
      3. Observations, statements, and other information within a record
      4. Opinions within business records
      5. Objections to business records
   G. Rule 803(8): Official Records and Reports
   H. Rules 803(24) and 804(b)(5): Residual Hearsay
      1. Comparison of rules
      2. Unavailability
      3. Notice, trustworthiness, probative value, and other criteria

4. North Carolina opinions on residual hearsay in juvenile cases

## 11.7 Prior Orders and Proceedings and Judicial Notice   11-50
   A. Generally
      1. Ambiguity in judicial notice principles in juvenile cases
      2. Suggested approach
   B. Definition of Judicial Notice
      1. Generally
      2. Judicial notice of prior proceedings
   C. Orders and Other Court Records
      1. Summary
      2. Judicial notice of record entries
   D. Findings and Conclusions by Court
      1. Summary
      2. Collateral estoppel
      3. Prior adjudication findings and conclusions
      4. Prior findings and conclusions from non-adjudication proceedings
      5. Formal concessions; stipulations of fact
   E. Documentary Evidence, Court Reports, and Other Exhibits
      1. Summary
      2. Juvenile cases on documentary evidence
   F. Testimony
      1. Summary
      2. Hearsay nature of prior testimony

## 11.8 Character and Prior Conduct   11-64
   A. Generally
   B. Theories of Admissibility of Character Evidence
      1. Character directly in issue
      2. Character to show conduct
      3. Credibility
      4. Opening the door
   C. Is Character Directly at Issue in Juvenile Cases?
   D. Rule 404(b) and "Bad Act" Evidence
      1. Applicability of rule
      2. Basic requirements for admission of other acts under Rule 404(b)
      3. Form of proof; prior criminal proceedings
   E. Rape Shield Law

## 11.9 Lay Opinion   11-70
   A. Lay and Expert Testimony Distinguished
      1. Rule 602 and the requirement of personal knowledge
      2. Rule 701 and the allowance of inferences if rationally based on perception and helpful
   B. Examples of Permissible and Impermissible Lay Opinion
      1. Shorthand statements of fact, including statements about mental and emotional condition
      2. Lay opinion requiring special expertise

3. Guilt of another person
4. Truthfulness of another person's statements

## 11.10 Expert Testimony    11-74
A. Revised Evidence Rule 702(a)
B. Three Basic Requirements
   1. Generally
   2. Scientific, technical, or other specialized knowledge that will assist trier of fact
   3. Qualified as an expert
   4. Three-pronged reliability test
C. Other Requirements for Expert Opinion
   1. Rule 403 balancing
   2. Degree of certainty of opinion
   3. Permissible topics and purposes
D. Expert Testimony about Children
   1. Credibility
   2. Legal conclusions
   3. Identity of perpetrator
   4. Physical injuries and their causes
   5. Battered child syndrome
   6. Opinion about abuse if no or inadequate evidence of physical injuries
   7. Psychological syndromes
   8. Characteristics of abused children
   9. Delayed disclosure
   10. Repressed memory
   11. Suggestibility of children
   12. Examination of child by respondent's expert
E. Expert Testimony about Parents
   1. Generally
   2. Polygraph evidence

## 11.11 Evidentiary Privileges    11-88
A. In Abuse, Neglect, and Dependency Proceedings
   1. Effect of broad negation of privileges in G.S. 7B-310
   2. Effect of specific negation of privileges in G.S. Chapter 8
   3. Attorney-client and clergy-communicant protections
   4. Protections against disclosure of confidential information
B. In Termination of Parental Rights Proceedings

## 11.12 Right against Self-Incrimination    11-91
A. Right Not to Answer Incriminating Questions
B. No Right Not to Take Stand
C. Drawing Adverse Inference from Refusal to Answer

## 11.13 Evidence Procedures    11-93
A. Production of Witnesses and Documents
B. Pretrial Motions in Limine, Objections, and Other Notices

C. Pre-Adjudication Conference
D. Objections at Trial
   1. Timely objection
   2. Grounds for objection
   3. Evidence for limited purpose
   4. Motion to strike
   5. Offers of proof
   6. Importance of complete recordation

___

This Chapter addresses common evidence issues that arise in abuse, neglect, dependency, and termination of parental rights proceedings (referred to in this manual as juvenile proceedings or juvenile cases). It is not intended to be a complete guide to all of the evidence issues that the court or parties may need to address. The Chapter draws on several sources on evidence, and the reader is encouraged to consult those sources for additional information and legal authority. Sources on North Carolina law include:

- KENNETH S. BROUN ET. AL., BRANDIS & BROUN ON NORTH CAROLINA EVIDENCE (8th ed. 2018) (hereinafter BRANDIS & BROUN);
- ROBERT P. MOSTELLER ET AL., NORTH CAROLINA EVIDENTIARY FOUNDATIONS (3d ed. 2014) (hereinafter MOSTELLER); and
- Jessica Smith, *Evidence Issues in Criminal Cases Involving Child Victims and Child Witnesses*, ADMINISTRATION OF JUSTICE BULLETIN No. 2008/07 (UNC School of Government, Dec. 2008).

General sources on evidence law include:

- ROBERT P. MOSTELLER ET AL., MCCORMICK ON EVIDENCE (8th ed. 2020) (hereinafter MCCORMICK);
- JOHN E. B. MYERS, MYERS ON EVIDENCE OF INTERPERSONAL VIOLENCE: CHILD MALTREATMENT, INTIMATE PARTNER VIOLENCE, RAPE, STALKING, AND ELDER ABUSE (6th ed. 2015) (hereinafter MYERS); and
- EDWARD J. IMWINKELRIED ET AL., COURTROOM CRIMINAL EVIDENCE (6th ed. 2016) (hereinafter IMWINKELRIED).

Other sources are noted where applicable.

## 11.1 Applicability of Rules of Evidence

### A. Adjudication

**1. Applicability of rules.** This Chapter focuses primarily on adjudication hearings in abuse, neglect, and dependency cases and termination of parental rights (TPR) proceedings. In both types of adjudication hearings, the North Carolina Rules of Evidence apply. *See* G.S. 7B-804 (so stating for abuse, neglect, and dependency cases); G.S. 7B-1109(f) (stating that the rules of evidence apply to adjudication hearings in TPR proceedings); *In re A.L.T.,* 241 N.C. App. 443 (2015) (recognizing that rules of evidence apply at adjudication hearing on abuse, neglect, and dependency); *In re F.G.J.,* 200 N.C. App. 681 (2009) (applying the rules of evidence in assessing the admissibility of evidence at a TPR adjudication); *see also* N.C. R. EVID. 1101(a) (stating that the rules of evidence apply to all actions and proceedings in the North Carolina courts except as otherwise provided by statute or rule).

The courts have stated that in cases heard by a judge without a jury, it is presumed in the absence of some affirmative indication to the contrary that the trial judge, having knowledge of the law, is able to distinguish between competent and incompetent evidence (that is, admissible and inadmissible evidence) and base findings on competent evidence only. *See In re F.G.J.,* 200 N.C. App. 681, 686–87 (2009); *In re L.C.,* 181 N.C. App. 278, 284 (2007). This principle may relax the formality of bench trials, but it does not lessen the importance of correctly applying the rules of evidence. The court's findings still must be based on competent, substantive evidence. *See Little v. Little,* 226 N.C. App. 499 (2013) (holding that although appellate court generally presumes that trial court disregarded incompetent evidence, the only evidence supporting the trial court's finding in action for domestic violence protective order was inadmissible hearsay; therefore, admission of the inadmissible evidence was not harmless error).

In addition to understanding whether evidence is competent, it is important to differentiate between evidence offered for a substantive or nonsubstantive purpose. *See In re K.W.,* 192 N.C. App. 646, 651 (2008) (distinguishing between substantive and impeachment evidence); 1 BRANDIS & BROUN § 3, at 6 (substantive evidence is evidence that "tends, directly or circumstantially, to prove a fact in issue"). The different purposes for which evidence may be offered are noted in this Chapter where applicable.

The question of whether evidence is admissible differs from whether the evidence is sufficient to satisfy the petitioner's burden of proving the allegations by clear and convincing evidence or, in a TPR case, by clear, cogent, and convincing evidence. This Chapter does not address the sufficiency, as opposed to the admissibility, of evidence at adjudication.

**Note:** To preserve questions about evidentiary rulings for appellate review, parties ordinarily must give the trial judge an opportunity to rule correctly by making timely and specific objections—that is, by objecting to inadmissible evidence or, if the evidence is admissible for a limited purpose, by requesting that the evidence be limited to that purpose. 1 BRANDIS & BROUN § 19, at 95–96. For a further discussion of objections, offers of proof, and other preservation requirements, see section 11.13, below.

**2. Reliance on criminal cases.** A growing body of appellate decisions addresses evidence issues in juvenile proceedings. To fill in gaps, the discussion in this Chapter refers to criminal cases, particularly criminal cases involving children. Constitutional requirements for the two types of proceedings differ, but for the most part North Carolina's evidence rules apply equally to criminal and civil cases.

**3. Evidence issues involving children.** Many of the evidence issues in juvenile proceedings concern children. These issues fall into three basic categories, discussed in the indicated sections of this Chapter:

- testimony by children, which may involve questions about their competency as witnesses and accommodations to assist them in testifying (see section 11.2, below);
- testimony about statements made by children, which primarily involves questions about the admissibility of hearsay (see section 11.6, below) and the permissible use of their statements for nonsubstantive purposes (see section 11.3, below); and
- testimony in the form of an opinion about children, primarily expert testimony (see section 11.10, below).

**4. Local rules affecting evidence.** Many districts have local juvenile court rules. Attorneys and judges who participate in juvenile cases should familiarize themselves with those rules. Local rules for each district are available on the Administrative Office of the Courts website.

Some local rules contain evidence provisions not contained in the North Carolina Rules of Evidence. For example, to encourage treatment and other services, Local Rule 7 relating to civil juvenile cases in the Twelfth Judicial District restricts the admission at adjudication of evidence of treatment services provided after the filing of a petition as well as statements made by the respondent when receiving such services. *See* Twelfth Judicial District, District Court, Family Court Division, Juvenile Case Management Plan, I. Civil Cases (Apr. 2016).

Local rules are authorized by G.S. 7A-34 and Rule 2(d) of the General Rules of Practice for the Superior and District Courts Supplemental to the Rules of Civil Procedure, if they are supplementary to, and not inconsistent with, acts of the General Assembly. Few cases have addressed the extent to which local rules may modify evidence and other procedures and, absent additional clarification by the appellate courts, the parties should follow local rules on evidence. *See In re T.M.*, 187 N.C. App. 694, 697–701 & n.2 (2007) (because the respondent father failed to object to medical records by the deadline in the then-applicable Twelfth Judicial District local rules [deleted from the current version of the rules], the trial court admitted the records at the adjudication hearing over the respondent's objection that DSS had not established a proper foundation; the Court of Appeals did not specifically decide whether the local rules provided an appropriate basis for overruling the respondent's objection because the respondent could not show prejudice, but noted that the local rule was not intended to be an evidentiary rule but instead was designed to promote the efficient administration of justice); *see also In re J.S.*, 182 N.C. App. 79 (2007) (upholding, in a two-to-one decision, a local administrative discovery order requiring respondents to review DSS records within ten working days after receiving notice that records are available for review).

## B. Disposition and Other Proceedings

The Juvenile Code relaxes the rules of evidence for most juvenile hearings other than adjudication. *See* G.S. 7B-506(b) (relating to nonsecure custody), 7B-901 (relating to disposition), 7B-906.1(c) (relating to review and permanency planning), 7B-1110(a) (relating to disposition in TPR proceedings), 7B-1114(g) (relating to reinstatement of parental rights).

For a further discussion of the applicability of the rules of evidence in particular proceedings, consult the applicable section of this manual. See Chapters 5.6.D (nonsecure custody), 7.2.E.1 (dispositional phase: initial, review, and permanency planning), 10.1.E (disposition in termination of parental rights proceeding), 10.4.C.7 (reinstatement of parental rights).

In light of these provisions, some cases have observed that the rules of evidence do not apply in such proceedings. *See In re J.H.*, 244 N.C. App. 255 (2015) (noting that dispositional hearing may be informal and court may consider written reports and other evidence about needs of juvenile); *In re M.J.G.*, 168 N.C. App. 638, 648 (2005). This means that the rules of evidence do not exclude some evidence that would be inadmissible at adjudication. The rules of evidence still play some role, however.

First, the parties have the right to present and have considered evidence that is competent (i.e., admissible) and relevant under the rules of evidence, subject to the court's discretion to exclude cumulative evidence. *See In re Shue*, 311 N.C. 586, 598 (1984) (error not to hear competent, relevant, non-cumulative evidence); *In re J.S.*, 182 N.C. App. 79, 84–85 (2007) (not error to preclude evidence as cumulative); *In re O'Neal*, 140 N.C. App. 254, 256–57 (2000) (error to refuse to allow respondent to offer evidence); *see also* G.S. 7B-506(b) (at hearing to determine need for continued custody, "the court shall receive testimony and shall allow . . . the right to introduce evidence, to be heard in the person's own behalf, and to examine witnesses").

Second, privileges apply to a limited extent at both adjudication and disposition. See section 11.11, below.

Third, while the court may consider hearsay and other evidence that ordinarily would be inadmissible under the rules of evidence, the court may consider only such evidence that it finds to be "relevant, reliable, and necessary." G.S. 7B-901; *see also In re K.G.W.*, 250 N.C. App. 62 (2016) (trial court had discretion to exclude respondent's expert testimony on ground that testimony would not assist trier of fact); *In re J.N.S.*, 207 N.C. App. 670, 679–80 (2010) (holding that unsworn testimony was not proper at disposition hearing); *In re P.O.*, 207 N.C. App. 35, 39–41 (2010) (holding that the trial court did not abuse its discretion in excluding certain hearsay evidence at a permanency planning hearing).

Although not binding, the rules of evidence remain a helpful guide to determining reliability and relevance. *See State v. Greene*, 351 N.C. 562, 568 (2000) (so noting for criminal sentencing proceedings, at which the rules of evidence do not apply); *State v. Stephens*, 347 N.C. 352, 363–64 (1997) (stating that although the rules of evidence are relaxed at sentencing, the rules should not be totally abandoned). The principal evidence rules that advance reliability and that may provide guidance to the trial court in its consideration of evidence are those limiting hearsay (discussed in sections 11.5 and 11.6, below) and opinion testimony (discussed in sections 11.9 and 11.10, below) and those requiring that witnesses have personal knowledge of the matters to which they testify (discussed in sections 11.6.F.3 (business records) and 11.9.A (lay opinion), below). On the question of relevance are rules related to admission of character evidence (discussed in section 11.8, below) as well as the general requirement of relevance expressed in Evidence Rule 401.

> **Note:** Because the rules of evidence do not bar the introduction of otherwise inadmissible evidence at disposition hearings, questions have arisen over whether orders and other matters from such hearings are admissible at later adjudication hearings, at which the rules of evidence apply. For a discussion of this issue, see section 11.7, below.

## 11.2 Child Witnesses

The common law imposed a variety of grounds for disqualifying witnesses from testifying. Most of these disabilities have been removed by the current rules of evidence, which allow anyone to be a witness, including a child, who meets the standard of competency. *See* 1 BRANDIS & BROUN § 131, at 506.

### A. Competency of Child Witnesses

**1. General rule.** Evidence Rule 601(a) provides that every person is considered competent to be a witness except as otherwise provided in the rules. *See also State v. DeLeonardo*, 315 N.C. 762, 766 (1986) (recognizing the requirements of Rule 601).

Rule 601(b) disqualifies a person as a witness if the person is incapable of (1) expressing himself or herself so as to be understood or (2) understanding the duty of a witness to tell the truth. *See also State v. Gordon*, 316 N.C. 497, 502 (1986) (stating that Rule 601(b) is consistent with prior North Carolina case law). In jurisdictions such as North Carolina, where every person is considered competent to testify unless shown otherwise, the party challenging a witness's competence probably has the burden of establishing incompetence. *See* MYERS § 2.13[B].

There is no fixed age under which a person is considered too young to testify. *See, e.g., State v. Eason*, 328 N.C. 409, 426 (1991).

**2. Procedure for determining competency.** The trial court must determine the competency of a witness when the issue "is raised by a party or by the circumstances." *Eason*, 328 N.C. at 427. Evidence Rule 104 states that the trial court is not bound by the rules of evidence, except those related to privileges, when determining preliminary questions such as the competency of a person to be a witness. *See State v. Fearing*, 315 N.C. 167, 173 (1985) (recognizing applicability of Rule 104 to competency determinations); see also section 11.11, below (discussing limitations on assertions of privilege in juvenile proceedings).

No particular procedure is required for determining competency, but the trial court must make an adequate inquiry into the issue, which generally must include personal observation of the witness by the trial court. *See State v. Spaugh*, 321 N.C. 550, 553–55 (1988) (explaining that the primary concern is not the particular procedure used by the trial court, but that the trial court exercise independent discretion in deciding competency after observation of the child). A stipulation by the parties is insufficient to support a finding of incompetency. *Fearing*, 315 N.C. at 174 ("[T]here can be no informed exercise of discretion where a trial judge merely adopts the stipulations of counsel that a child is not competent to testify . . . ."); *State v.*

*Pugh*, 138 N.C. App. 60, 64–67 (2000) (trial court disqualified a 4-year-old from testifying without making an adequate inquiry because the court's brief questions were not sufficient to determine the competency of the witness).

Although statutory changes enacted in 2011 allow judges to rely on stipulations to support adjudicatory findings in abuse, neglect, and dependency proceedings (*see* G.S. 7B-807(a)), this change does not authorize stipulations as to a witness's competency, a conclusion of law. *See generally State v. Forte*, 206 N.C. App. 699, 707–08 (2010) (stating that trial court's findings "and its conclusion that [the witness] was competent" established that the court exercised its discretion in declaring the witness competent); *see also In re A.K.D.*, 227 N.C. App. 58 (2013) (holding that trial court could not rely on parties' stipulation of a ground for TPR, a conclusion of law).

Typically, a voir dire of the witness should be conducted before the witness testifies. *Fearing*, 315 N.C. at 174. The court may hear testimony from parents, teachers, and others familiar with the child, but such testimony is not required. *See State v. Roberts*, 18 N.C. App. 388, 391–92 (1973) (so stating).

The court also may observe the child while the child testifies. *See Spaugh*, 321 N.C. at 553–55 (finding that the trial court's observation of the witness while she testified was adequate without a separate voir dire). If the court waits until the child testifies and then finds the child incompetent, the child's preceding testimony may need to be disregarded. *See generally State v. Reynolds*, 93 N.C. App. 552, 556–57 (1989) (in a case involving a jury trial, stating that the better practice is to determine competency before the witness begins to testify); MYERS § 2.13[C] ("If, during a child's testimony, the judge determines that the child is incompetent, the court may order the child's testimony stricken . . . .").

In criminal cases, the courts have held that the defendant's Confrontation Clause rights are not violated by being excluded from a voir dire hearing to determine a child's competency. *See Kentucky v. Stincer*, 482 U.S. 730 (1987) (finding no violation where children were found competent to testify and the defendant had the opportunity to cross-examine at trial); *State v. Jones*, 89 N.C. App. 584 (1988) (finding no violation where the defendant could view the hearing via closed-circuit television and communicate with his attorney), *overruled on other grounds*, *State v. Hinnant*, 351 N.C. 277 (2000). For a further discussion of the issue of excluding a party during a child's testimony, see section 11.2.B.1, below.

If the court finds that a child is incompetent to testify, the party seeking to call the child should make an offer of proof about the substance of the child's testimony to preserve the issue for appeal. *See In re M.G.T.-B.*, 177 N.C. App. 771 (2006) (declining to address the propriety of the trial court's decision to quash a subpoena for a child based on incompetency because the respondent made no offer of proof and therefore failed to preserve the issue for appellate review); *see generally* 1 BRANDIS & BROUN § 18, at 83 (substance of what a witness would say should appear in the record).

**3. Application of standard.** Most appellate decisions have held that the trial court did not abuse its discretion in finding a child witness competent to testify. Most of these cases involve criminal prosecutions, in which the State called a child who was a witness to or victim of a crime, but the legal principles appear to be equally applicable to juvenile proceedings. For summaries of the facts of several such cases, see Jessica Smith, *Evidence Issues in Criminal Cases Involving Child Victims and Child Witnesses*, ADMINISTRATION OF JUSTICE BULLETIN No. 2008/07, at 5–7 (UNC School of Government, Dec. 2008); *see also In re Clapp*, 137 N.C. App. 14, 19–20 (2000) (upholding the finding of competency of a child witness in a juvenile delinquency case); *In re Quevedo*, 106 N.C. App. 574, 584–85 (1992) (in a termination of parental rights proceeding, it was not error for a 10-year-old child to testify; the trial judge and attorneys questioned her about the duty to tell the truth, and any inability she had to remember all of the events went to the weight, not admissibility, of the testimony).

A witness may be found incompetent if, although able to understand the duty to tell the truth, the witness is incapable of expressing himself or herself so as to be understood. *See State v. Washington*, 131 N.C. App. 156, 159–60 (1998) (upholding the finding of incompetency of a witness with cerebral palsy based on her impaired ability to speak, which made her difficult to understand); *see also* MYERS § 2.05 (suggesting that an interpreter can be used for child witnesses whose speech is difficult to understand).

**4. Unavailability distinguished from incompetency.** The standard for incompetency under Rule 601 is not the same as for unavailability under North Carolina's hearsay rules. A person may be found unavailable to testify, based on a physical or mental illness or infirmity, for purposes of admitting a hearsay statement. *See* N.C. R. EVID. 804(a)(4). The potential detriment to the mental health of a child witness from testifying may establish the child's unavailability for purposes of admitting hearsay, but it is not sufficient alone to establish that the child is incapable of expressing himself or herself or understanding the obligation to tell the truth. *See In re Faircloth*, 137 N.C. App. 311 (2000) (explaining the difference between competency and unavailability and holding that the trial court erred in relying on the unavailability standard in disqualifying children from testifying). The court in *Faircloth* noted that other mechanisms are available to protect the mental health of a child witness who is required to testify. For a discussion of such accommodations, see section 11.2.B, below.

Hearsay statements of a child witness found to be incompetent to give live testimony are still admissible if they meet the requirements of a hearsay exception. If the hearsay exception requires that the declarant be unavailable, such as the residual hearsay exception, a child witness who is found to be incompetent would be considered unavailable to testify. Such a finding, however, may raise questions about whether the child's out-of-court statements are sufficiently trustworthy to be admissible under the residual hearsay exception. See section 11.6.H.2, below.

**5. Quashing of subpoena for child.** Some cases, cited below, indicate that trial courts have sometimes quashed subpoenas for child witnesses on the ground that the child is incompetent to testify, that testifying would be harmful to the child's mental health, or that the child has no relevant information to offer. In one case, the Court of Appeals addressed the merits of the motion to quash and upheld the trial court's order; the other opinions did not address the merits.

Incompetency may be a permissible ground for quashing a subpoena, but the court would need to conduct an adequate inquiry into the child's competency before ruling, including personally observing the child as discussed in subsection 2, above (discussing procedures for assessing competency). The inquiry also would need to be sufficiently close in time to when the child would be expected to testify. *See generally State v. McRae*, 58 N.C. App. 225, 227 (1982) (trial court did not err in denying the defendant's motion to quash a subpoena for two children who were in the car at the time of the alleged kidnapping; motion, in effect, asked the court to declare the children incompetent before they were asked to testify).

Potential harm to a child's mental health has been held not to be a ground for finding a child incompetent and precluding the child from testifying. It may provide a basis for one or more accommodations during the child's testimony, discussed in section B., below. In *In re A.H.*, 250 N.C. App. 546 (2016), the court went further and upheld the quashing of a subpoena, finding that the potential harm to the child supported the GAL's objection that the subpoena was "unreasonable and oppressive." The court was careful to clarify that the issue on appeal was whether quashing the mother's subpoena of her child violated her right to present evidence at the disposition phase of the termination proceeding; the mother did not challenge the adjudication phase of the proceeding, admitting that the trial court correctly found grounds for termination. The court also observed that the GAL presented comprehensive evidence about the child's mental health condition and extreme distress at the prospect of testifying.

Ordinarily, the relevance of a witness's testimony is determined when the witness testifies; the ordinary burden of testifying in a legal proceeding does not outweigh the right of a party to subpoena witnesses. If the objecting party raises concerns about the child's mental health or other extraordinary burdens, the subpoenaing party may need to forecast the testimony of the child to show that its relevance outweighs the potential burdens.

The improper quashing of a subpoena, if issued by a respondent, may infringe on the respondent's constitutional right to present evidence and call witnesses on his or her behalf, applicable in criminal cases through the Sixth Amendment, in civil cases under the Due Process Clause, and under the corresponding provisions of the North Carolina Constitution. *See Washington v. Texas*, 388 U.S. 14, 18–19 (1967) (right to compel attendance of witnesses is "in plain terms the right to present a defense" under the Sixth Amendment and is a fundamental element of due process of law); *State v. Rankin*, 312 N.C. 592 (1985); *see generally In re L.D.B.*, 168 N.C. App. 206, 208–09 (2005) (respondent's right to present evidence in a TPR case "is inherent in the protection of due process"). In *In re A.H.*, 794 S.E.2d at 878–79, above, the court found that quashing of the respondent's subpoena did not violate the respondent's due process rights.

If the trial court quashes a subpoena, the party who subpoenaed the witness must make an offer of proof to preserve the issue for appeal unless the significance of the evidence is otherwise obvious from the record. *Id.* at 876–77.

Cases raising, although not resolving, the merits of motions to quash subpoenas for child witnesses in juvenile cases include:

- *In re M.G.T.-B.*, 177 N.C. App. 771 (2006) (based on a telephone conversation with the child's therapist and without observing or examining the child, the trial court found the child incompetent and quashed a subpoena for the child; the Court of Appeals declined to address the propriety of the trial court's determination of incompetence where the respondent made no offer of proof as to the potential testimony of the child and therefore failed to preserve the issue for appellate review).
- *In re C.N.P.*, 199 N.C. App. 318 (2009) (unpublished) (noting, but not ruling on, the trial court's decision to quash a subpoena in response to a DSS motion alleging that the children had little information to offer at the termination hearing and that testifying in front of their mother would have a negative impact on their mental health).
- *In re A.A.P.*, 193 N.C. App. 752 (2008) (unpublished) (holding that the trial court abused its discretion in quashing subpoenas for children where its decision was based substantially on the fact that it had already made its disposition decision before hearing evidence).

### B. Examination of Child Witnesses

The courts have approved several accommodations for child witnesses who testify. Some are intended to reduce the potential harm to child witnesses from testifying about sensitive matters, others to assist children in communicating information more clearly.

**1. Remote testimony.** In appropriate cases, a child witness may testify remotely—that is, via closed circuit television or other audio-visual equipment by which the child testifies in one room and the respondent views the testimony from another room. The system can be either "one-way" where the witness is not in the party's presence and cannot see the party but the party can see the witness, or "two-way" where the witness is not in the party's presence but the witness and party can see and hear each other over audio-video monitors. Generally, in cases involving child witnesses, the testimony is by one-way closed-circuit television. One-way remote testimony has been permitted in both juvenile proceedings and criminal and delinquency proceedings. The standards differ somewhat, but the two key considerations are (a) the need for remote testimony and (b) the procedure for testifying.

Interest has grown in two-way remote systems for taking witness testimony, without an in-person appearance by the witness, as a possible way to comply with a defendant's confrontation rights in criminal cases. Whether two-way remote testimony would be permissible for reasons other than those permitted for one-way remote testimony is beyond the scope of this Chapter. *See generally* Jessica Smith, *Remote Testimony and Related Procedures Impacting a Criminal Defendant's Confrontation Rights*, ADMINISTRATION OF JUSTICE BULLETIN No. 2013/02 (UNC School of Government, Feb. 2013); *see also State v. Seelig*, 226 N.C. App. 147 (2013) (allowing two-way remote testimony for seriously ill witness who lived in another state); *In re S.H.*, 206 N.C. App. 761 (2010) (unpublished) (finding that trial court did not abuse its discretion in denying respondent mother's motion to testify by telephone where she did not have funds or means to travel from West Virginia to hearing in North Carolina); G.S. 50A-111 (authorizing court in child custody proceeding, defined as including abuse, neglect, dependency, and TPR proceedings, to take testimony by telephone, audiovisual means, or other electronic means from witness residing in another state).

(a) **Showing of need.** The showing of need for the taking of remote testimony by a child witness may be lower in juvenile cases than in criminal or delinquency cases. In criminal cases, the Confrontation Clause applies. *See Maryland v. Craig*, 497 U.S. 836 (1990); *see also In re Stradford*, 119 N.C. App. 654 (1995) (applying the Confrontation Clause to remote testimony in a delinquency proceeding and upholding its use on proper findings). The court must find both that the child witness would suffer serious emotional distress by testifying in the defendant's presence and that the ability of the witness to communicate with the trier of fact would be impaired by doing so. G.S. 15A-1225.1, enacted by the General Assembly in 2009, codifies these requirements for remote testimony by child witnesses in criminal and delinquency cases. In *State v. Jackson*, 216 N.C. App. 238 (2011), the Court of Appeals addressed the permissibility in a criminal case of a child testifying remotely, pursuant to G.S. 15A-1225.1, in light of the U.S. Supreme Court's Confrontation Clause decision in *Crawford v. Washington*, 541 U.S. 36 (2004). The Court of Appeals held that *Crawford* did not overrule earlier decisions holding that a child may testify remotely in a criminal case when the court finds a sufficient showing of need and uses appropriate procedures for taking the child's testimony. Face-to-face confrontation is not required. *Accord State v. Lanford*, 225 N.C. App. 189 (2013).

In juvenile cases, the more flexible due process standard applies to remote testimony. *See In re J.B.*, 172 N.C. App. 1, 20–22 (2005). In juvenile proceedings, the cases have looked at whether "'the excluded party's presence during testimony might intimidate the witness and influence his answers, due to that party's position of authority over the testifying witness.'" *In re J.B.*, 172 N.C. App. at 21 (quoting *In re Barkley*, 61 N.C. App. 267, 270 (1983)). The cases also consider the emotional impact on the child. *See In re J.B.*, 172 N.C. App. at 21–22 (noting a counselor's testimony that testifying in front of the mother would have a very negative impact on the child); *see also* N.C. R. EVID. 616 (authorizing remote testimony by witnesses with developmental disabilities or mental retardation in civil cases if testifying in the presence of a party or in an open forum would cause serious emotional distress and impair the witness's ability to communicate with the trier of fact).

(b) **Procedures for testifying.** The procedures for taking remote testimony appear to be comparable in civil and criminal cases. The court must ensure that the defendant or respondent has the ability to confer with counsel, to cross-examine the witness fully, and to see and hear the witness while he or she is testifying. *See State v. Phachoumphone*, 810 S.E.2d 748 (N.C. Ct. App. 2018) (finding that trial judge failed to follow the procedural requirements for remote testimony); *In re J.B.*, 172 N.C. App. at 22 (finding that these procedures had been followed); G.S. 15A-1225.1 (requiring these procedures in criminal and delinquency cases); *compare Coy v. Iowa*, 487 U.S. 1012 (1988) (holding that placement of a screen obscuring the defendant's view of child sexual assault victims during testimony in a criminal case violated the defendant's Confrontation Clause rights).

May the court in a juvenile proceeding exclude a respondent parent without allowing the parent to view the witness via closed-circuit television or other device? Some cases have found it permissible if the parent's counsel is present and is allowed to question the witness. *See In re Williams*, 149 N.C. App. 951, 960 (2002); *In re Barkley*, 61 N.C. App. 267, 270 (1983). Failing to allow a parent to view a witness's testimony, when the parent is otherwise permitted to participate in the proceedings, may create a risk of error, however. In an unpublished opinion, *In re B.P.*, 183 N.C. App. 154 (2007), the trial court heard testimony of a 17-year-old witness in chambers with the parent's attorney present and able to question the witness, but the parent was not able to view the witness and the testimony was not recorded. Focusing on the lack of recordation, the Court of Appeals found that the procedure violated the parent's due process rights. *See also In re Nolen*, 117 N.C. App. 693, 696 (1995) (finding no prejudice in the failure to record in-chambers testimony where the respondent failed to argue any error in the unrecorded testimony).

---

**Note:** To obtain closed circuit television equipment, contact the North Carolina Administrative Office of the Courts.

---

**2. Excluding bystanders during child's testimony.** G.S. 7B-801(a) authorizes the court to close to the public any hearing or part of a hearing in a juvenile proceeding after considering the factors listed in the statute. Thus, during a child's testimony the court may have grounds to exclude from the courtroom those not involved in the hearing of the case. *See also* Michael Crowell, *Closing Court Proceedings in North Carolina* at 2–3 (UNC School of Government, Nov. 2012) (discussing qualified right of public access under Art. I, § 18 of the N.C. Constitution, which provides that "[a]ll courts shall be open," and grounds for excluding public). The hearing may not be closed, however, if the juvenile requests that it remain open. *See* G.S. 7B-801(b); Chapters 6.2.C, 7.2.D (further discussing the circumstances in which a hearing may be closed to the public).

In criminal cases, the courts have upheld the exclusion of bystanders in rape and sex offense cases during the testimony of the child victim. *See State v. Burney*, 302 N.C. 529 (1981) (holding that it was permissible for the court to exclude everyone from the courtroom during a child victim's testimony except court personnel and those engaged in the trial of the case); *State v. Godley*, 234 N.C. App. 562 (2014) (recognizing that to balance interests of State with defendant's constitutional right to public trial, court must employ four-part test; closing of courtroom during victim's testimony did not violate defendant's rights); *State v. Smith*, 180 N.C. App. 86 (2006) (trial court acted within its discretion in closing the courtroom in a statutory sex offense case; although the trial court did not hold a hearing or make findings on the issue, the defendant did not object to the closing of the courtroom); *see also* G.S. 15-166 (authorizing the trial judge to close the courtroom in such cases); *compare State v. Jenkins*, 115 N.C. App. 520 (1994) (trial court erred in closing the courtroom without making proper findings).

**3. Excepting witnesses from sequestration order.** Evidence Rule 615 authorizes the judge to exclude potential witnesses during the testimony of other witnesses. It also empowers the judge to permit a person to be present in the interest of justice.

In criminal cases, judges have used this authority to permit the parent of a victim to remain in the courtroom although the parent may later be a witness. *See State v. Dorton*, 172 N.C. App.

759, 765–66 (2005); G.S. 15A-1225 (stating this authority for criminal cases). In juvenile cases, no exception to a sequestration order is necessary to allow a parent to be present because a parent is a party and generally has the right to be present during the testimony of other witnesses. The juvenile court may find it appropriate to except other witnesses from a sequestration order and allow them to be present although they may testify later. *See State v. Stanley*, 310 N.C. 353, 356–57 (1984) (upholding an order allowing a social services worker and juvenile court officer to be present); *State v. Weaver*, 117 N.C. App. 434, 436 (1994) (upholding an order allowing a social worker and a therapist to be present).

**4. Oath for child witness.** Evidence Rule 603 provides that every witness must testify under oath or affirmation. The commentary states that the wording of the rule is intended to provide flexibility in dealing with, among others, child witnesses. No special verbal formula is required as long as the oath or affirmation is administered to the witness in a way "calculated to awaken his conscience and impress his mind with his duty" to tell the truth. N.C. R. EVID. 603; *see also State v. Beane*, 146 N.C. App. 220, 223–26 (2001) (not plain error for the trial court to permit a child to testify without taking an oath; although the child did not understand the significance of taking an oath, the child promised to tell the truth).

**5. Leading questions.** Several cases have upheld leading questions of child witnesses. *See State v. Higginbottom*, 312 N.C. 760, 767–68 (1985) (finding leading questions of a child witness to be permissible based on the principle that a party may ask leading questions if the witness has difficulty in understanding questions because of immaturity, age, infirmity, or ignorance or if the inquiry is into a subject of a delicate nature such as sexual matters); *State v. Ammons*, 167 N.C. App. 721, 729 (2005) (finding leading questions of a child witness to be permissible on the ground that a party may ask leading questions if the examiner, without stating the particular matters required, seeks to aid the witness's recollection or refresh his or her memory when the witness's memory is exhausted).

**6. Written testimony.** In addition to allowing leading questions, the court has allowed a child witness to write down particularly sensitive testimony while on the witness stand and the prosecutor to read the statement to the jury. *State v. Earls*, 234 N.C. App. 186 (2014) (testimony was that the defendant had placed his penis in her vagina).

**7. Use of anatomical dolls to illustrate testimony.** The use of anatomically-correct dolls to illustrate a child's testimony has been upheld. *See State v. Fletcher*, 322 N.C. 415, 421 (1988); see also section 11.6.E.11, below (discussing the admissibility of statements to medical personnel while using anatomical dolls).

**8. Use of own terms for body parts.** Child witnesses have been permitted to use terms with which they are familiar when referring to body parts. *See State v. Watkins*, 318 N.C. 498 (1986) (7-year-old child's testimony that the defendant stuck his finger in her "coodie cat" and her indication of her vaginal area through use of anatomically correct dolls constituted sufficient evidence of penetration to support conviction of first-degree sexual offense).

**9. Questioning by court.** Evidence Rule 614(b) permits the trial judge to question witnesses, and cases have upheld the trial judge's questioning of a child witness to clarify confusing or contradictory testimony. *See State v. Ramey*, 318 N.C. 457, 463–65 (1986) (not improper for the trial court to ask questions of an 8-year-old witness where the questions were intended to clarify the child's answers on a delicate subject; the questions did not violate G.S. 15A-1222, applicable to criminal jury trials, as the questions did not express an opinion by the judge); *see generally In re N.D.A.*, 833 S.E.2d 768 (N.C. S.Ct. 2019) (finding that Evidence Rule 614(b) permits trial judge to question witnesses and that judge's questioning in this case did not show lack of impartiality).

**10. Positioning on witness stand.** The physical location or positioning of a child witness may be adapted in aid of the child's testimony. *See State v. Reeves*, 337 N.C. 700, 727 (1994) (permissible for the trial court to allow a child to sit on her stepmother's lap while testifying; the trial court warned the stepmother not to suggest to the child how the child should testify and, after the testimony was completed, made a finding that the stepmother had followed the court's instructions).

**11. Recesses.** The court may order a recess if a child witness becomes upset while testifying. *See State v. Higginbottom*, 312 N.C. 760, 769–70 (1985); *State v. Hewett*, 93 N.C. App. 1, 14 (1989).

## 11.3 Out-of-Court Statements to Refresh, Impeach, or Corroborate

A witness's prior out-of-court statements may be used in the circumstances discussed below to refresh the witness's recollection, impeach the witness, or corroborate the witness's testimony.

When an out-of-court statement is offered for one of these purposes, it is not subject to the restrictions on the admission of hearsay, discussed in sections 11.5 and 11.6, below. It also is not considered substantive evidence. *See State v. Williams*, 341 N.C. 1, 9–11 (1995) (holding that prior inconsistent statement offered to impeach is not substantive evidence); *State v. Bartlett*, 77 N.C. App. 747, 752 (1985) (prior inconsistent statement offered to impeach is not substantive evidence and may not be considered in determining whether the State produced sufficient evidence to withstand a motion to dismiss in a criminal case).

### A. Refreshing Recollection

A witness may refer to a writing or object during or before testifying to refresh his or her recollection. The writing or object, including a prior statement, is not itself admitted into evidence (except as permitted on cross-examination) and does not establish any particular fact; rather, it is a prompt for testimony that may be admissible. *See* 1 BRANDIS & BROUN § 172, at 659.

If the witness refers to a writing or object during his or her testimony, the adverse party has a right to have the writing or object produced; if the witness refers to a writing before testifying, production is in the judge's discretion. *See* N.C. R. EVID. 612(a), (b). If entitled to have the writing or object produced, an adverse party may cross-examine the witness about it and may offer into evidence those portions that relate to the witness's testimony. *See* N.C. R. EVID. 612(c).

If a writing does not refresh a witness's recollection, it may be admissible under the hearsay exception for past recollection recorded. To be admissible on this ground, the writing must satisfy the criteria in Evidence Rule 803(5). That hearsay exception appears to arise infrequently in juvenile cases. *See generally State v. Harrison*, 218 N.C. App. 546 (2012) (discussing differences between refreshing recollection and past recollection recorded); *see also State v. Harris*, 253 N.C. App. 322 (2017) (allowing videotape of witness interview as past recollection recorded under Evidence Rule 803(5)).

### B. Impeachment

A witness may be impeached with his or her prior statements that conflict with the witness's testimony. Prior inconsistent statements to impeach are admissible for the purpose of assessing the credibility of the witness about the testimony he or she has given, not as substantive evidence of the facts asserted in the statements. *See* 1 BRANDIS & BROUN § 159, at 584–85 (collecting cases).

A party may impeach his or her own witness with prior inconsistent statements. *See* N.C. R. EVID. 607. It is impermissible, however, to impeach one's own witness as a subterfuge for getting otherwise inadmissible statements before the trier of fact. Thus, a party may not call a witness to the stand, knowing that the witness will not reiterate a prior statement the witness made, for the purpose of impeaching the witness with the prior statement. *Compare State v. Hunt*, 324 N.C. 343, 349–51 (1989) (so holding and finding impeachment improper in this case), *with State v. Williams*, 341 N.C. 1, 9–11 (1995) (reiterating holding of *Hunt* but finding impeachment permissible in this case).

If the impeachment does not concern a collateral matter, a party also may offer extrinsic evidence of the witness's prior statements—for example, a party may call other witnesses to attest to the prior statements. If the matter is collateral, the cross-examiner is bound by the witness's answer. *See, e.g., State v. Gabriel*, 207 N.C. App. 440 (2010); *State v. Riccard*, 142 N.C. App. 298 (2001). Generally, a matter is not collateral if it relates to "material facts in the testimony of the witness"; it is collateral if it relates to immaterial facts. *See* 1 BRANDIS & BROUN § 161, at 589–94.

### C. Corroboration

Under North Carolina law, if a person testifies, a party may offer prior consistent statements of that person to corroborate his or her testimony. The purpose of such evidence is to bolster the credibility of the witness's testimony. As with prior statements to impeach, discussed in section B., above, the prior statement itself is not substantive evidence and does not establish the particular fact or event. 1 BRANDIS & BROUN § 165, at 609–11; *see also State v. Bates*, 140 N.C. App. 743 (2000) (trial court erred in admitting a child's statements under the medical diagnosis and treatment exception; the statements could not later be treated as mere corroborative evidence because the trial court treated them as substantive and did not limit their use).

North Carolina's approach to admitting prior consistent statements is more permissive than the approach taken elsewhere. In many jurisdictions, a prior consistent statement of a witness is admissible to corroborate the witness only after the witness's credibility has been challenged. North Carolina has effectively eliminated the requirement that the witness's credibility be challenged before a prior consistent statement may be admitted. *See* 1 BRANDIS & BROUN §§ 162–65.

To be admissible to corroborate a witness's testimony under North Carolina law, the prior consistent statement must be consistent with the witness's trial testimony. Variations between the prior statement and in-court testimony, including new information if it adds weight or credibility to the testimony, do not necessarily make the prior statements inconsistent and inadmissible as corroboration. *See id.* § 165, at 605–08 & nn.503–04.

A prior consistent statement may be established by examination of the witness and, if the matter is not collateral, by extrinsic evidence. *See id.* § 163, at 598; *see also State v. Yearwood*, 147 N.C. App. 662, 667–68 (2001) (permitting a videotape of a therapy session with a child to corroborate the child's in-court testimony).

**Note:** The above principles do not justify admission of out-of-court statements of someone other than the witness whose testimony is being corroborated. The prior statements must be those of the witness. *See State v. Freeman*, 93 N.C. App. 380, 387–88 (1989) (determining that a witness's testimony could not be corroborated by an extrajudicial statement of another person that was not otherwise admissible); 1 BRANDIS & BROUN § 165, at 611–12 & n.510.

If a witness's out-of-court statement is admissible as substantive evidence under a hearsay exception, other out-of-court statements by the witness may be admissible to corroborate (or impeach) the hearsay statement under Evidence Rule 806, which states that "[w]hen a hearsay statement has been admitted in evidence, the credibility of the declarant may be attacked, and if attacked may be supported, by any evidence which would be admissible for those purposes if declarant had testified as a witness." The rule explicitly requires that the credibility of the hearsay declarant be attacked before evidence supporting credibility may be admitted, which may be stricter than North Carolina's approach to prior statements that corroborate a witness's live testimony. Some North Carolina cases have allowed out-of-court statements to corroborate statements admitted under a hearsay exception, but they have not specifically referred to Rule 806 or described its requirements. *See State v. Chandler*, 324 N.C. 172, 182 (1989) (without referring to Rule 806, the court finds that a child's statements to others were admissible to corroborate the child's testimony from a previous trial, which was admitted as substantive evidence under a hearsay exception); *In re Lucas*, 94 N.C. App. 442, 450 (1989) (court follows *Chandler* in allowing a child's out-of-court statements to be admitted for the nonsubstantive purpose of corroborating other statements by the child admitted under a hearsay exception [note that the analysis of the applicability of the hearsay exception in this case is no longer good law after *State v. Hinnant*, 351 N.C. 277 (2000), discussed in section 11.6.E, below]).

## 11.4 Out-of-Court Statements and the Right to Confront Witnesses

### A. Applicability of Confrontation Clause to Criminal and Delinquency Cases

**1. General rule.** The Confrontation Clause of the Sixth Amendment regulates the admissibility of out-of-court statements against the defendant in a criminal trial. In *Crawford v. Washington*, 541 U.S. 36 (2004), the U.S. Supreme Court adopted a stricter interpretation of the Confrontation Clause, holding that the State may not offer into evidence an out-of-court "testimonial" statement except in one of the following circumstances:

- the declarant who made the statement is subject to cross-examination at the current trial,
- the declarant was subject to adequate cross-examination before trial, or
- a narrow exception applies (e.g., the defendant forfeited the right to confront the witness by the defendant's own wrongdoing).

In light of *Crawford*, for an out-of-court statement to be admitted against the defendant in a criminal case, it must first be determined whether the statement satisfies the constitutional requirements of the Confrontation Clause and then be determined whether the statement satisfies North Carolina's evidence rules, including North Carolina's rules on hearsay (discussed in sections 11.5 and 11.6, below). For a discussion of *Crawford* and subsequent case law, see Jessica Smith, *A Guide to* Crawford *and the Confrontation Clause*, NORTH CAROLINA SUPERIOR COURT JUDGES' BENCHBOOK (UNC School of Government, July 2018).

The Confrontation Clause, as interpreted in *Crawford*, also applies to juvenile delinquency trials. *See State ex rel. J.A.*, 949 A.2d 790 (N.J. 2008); *In re N.D.C.*, 229 S.W.3d 602 (Mo. 2007); *People ex rel. R.A.S.*, 111 P.3d 487 (Colo. App. 2004); *see also In re Stradford*, 119 N.C. App. 654 (1995) (applying the Confrontation Clause in determining the appropriateness of testimony of child witnesses by closed-circuit television in a delinquency proceeding).

**2. Applicability to statements made to law-enforcement personnel, social workers, medical personnel, and others.** The courts have explored the meaning of "testimonial" statements in light of *Crawford* in various contexts. Some patterns have emerged:

- Statements collected by or generated by law enforcement personnel are ordinarily considered testimonial because, except in emergency situations, they are ordinarily gathered for purposes of prosecution.
- Statements obtained by social workers in child welfare cases have been found to be testimonial in various circumstances, regardless of whether the social workers were formally affiliated with law enforcement.
- For a statement to medical personnel to be considered testimonial, there generally must be a more affirmative showing of a law-enforcement purpose or connection. *See also Ohio v. Clark*, ___ U.S. ___, 135 S. Ct. 2173 (2015) (holding that statement by child to teacher was not testimonial; in so holding, court relies in part on young age of child and states that mandatory reporting statutes alone do not convert a conversation between a teacher and student into a law enforcement mission); *accord State v. McLaughlin*, 246 N.C. App. 306

(2016) (mandatory duty to report child abuse under North Carolina law did not make statements to nurse testimonial).
- Statements to family and friends have usually not been found to be testimonial.

See Jessica Smith, *Evidence Issues in Criminal Cases Involving Child Victims and Child Witnesses*, ADMINISTRATION OF JUSTICE BULLETIN No. 2008/07, at 14–31 (UNC School of Government, Dec. 2008); Robert P. Mosteller, *Testing the Testimonial Concept and Exceptions to Confrontation: "A Little Child Shall Lead Them,"* 82 IND. L. J. 917, 944–65 (2007).

## B. Inapplicability of Confrontation Clause to Juvenile Cases

Because *Crawford* involved interpretation of the Sixth Amendment Confrontation Clause, which applies only in criminal (and delinquency) cases, the holding in Crawford does not apply to juvenile cases (that is, abuse, neglect, dependency, and termination of parental rights proceedings). *See In re D.R.*, 172 N.C. App. 300 (2005) (admission of statements by a child to DSS workers and others did not violate the Sixth Amendment right to confrontation, which does not apply to a proceeding to terminate parental rights, a civil action). Therefore, the admissibility of out-of-court statements in juvenile cases depends primarily on North Carolina's hearsay rules, discussed in sections 11.5 and 11.6, below.

The Due Process Clause of the Fourteenth Amendment still affords the respondent the right to confront the witnesses against him or her. It is unclear whether the Due Process Clause provides respondents with greater protections than under North Carolina's hearsay rules. *See generally In re Pamela A.G.*, 134 P.3d 746, 750 (N.M. 2006) (Confrontation Clause, as interpreted in *Crawford*, does not apply in an abuse and neglect case, but the Due Process Clause requires that "parents be given a reasonable opportunity to confront and cross-examine a witness, including a child witness"; no violation found where the parents failed to show how admission of a hearsay statement of a child and lack of cross-examination increased the risk of erroneous deprivation of their relationship with the child); *Commonwealth v. Given*, 808 N.E.2d 788 (Mass. 2004) (in a proceeding to commit the respondent as a sexually dangerous person, the trial court admitted a police report containing allegations by a victim against the respondent about a prior offense; the court held that the Confrontation Clause does not apply to civil commitment proceedings and that the constitutional test for admissibility of hearsay is whether the evidence is reliable under the Due Process Clause); *Smallwood v. State Dep't of Human Resources*, 716 So. 2d 684, 691 (Ala. Civ. App. 1998) (recognizing a due process right to confront witnesses in a civil proceeding to revoke a daycare license on the ground of child abuse and finding that hearsay statements were not admissible where the administrative law judge made no findings that the hearsay had "particularized guarantees of trustworthiness" or were "of a type relied upon by reasonably prudent persons in the conduct of their affairs"); *In re A.S.W.*, 834 P.2d 801 (Alaska 1992) (recognizing a due process right to confront witnesses in a civil child protection proceeding and finding that the hearsay rules adequately protected the parent's right).

## 11.5 Out-of-Court Statements and the Hearsay Rule

### A. Governing Rules

Evidence Rules 801 through 806 set forth North Carolina's rules on the admissibility of hearsay. These rules apply in both criminal and civil cases, to statements by children and other witnesses, and to both oral and written statements. (If the statement is written, the offering party may need to satisfy other requirements, such as the rules on authentication.) The North Carolina rules governing hearsay are as follows:

- Rule 801 defines "hearsay" and the terms "statement" and "declarant," which are components of the definition of hearsay. The rule also excepts admissions of a party-opponent from the restrictions on hearsay.
- Rule 802, entitled the "hearsay rule," sets forth the basic principle that hearsay is inadmissible except as otherwise provided by statute or rule.
- Rule 803 sets forth numerous exceptions to the hearsay rule, which apply whether the declarant is available or unavailable as a witness.
- Rule 804 sets forth five exceptions to the hearsay rule, which apply only if the declarant is unavailable as a witness. The term "unavailability" is defined in the rule.
- Rule 805 provides that hearsay within hearsay is admissible if each part of the statement is admissible under an exception to the hearsay rule.
- Rule 806 provides for attacking or supporting the credibility of a hearsay declarant when hearsay has been admitted in evidence. See section 11.3.C, above (discussing potential application of this rule to corroborating statements).

### B. Rationale for Hearsay Rule

The often-repeated hearsay principle is that an out-of-court statement offered for the truth of the matter asserted is inadmissible unless it satisfies an exception to the hearsay rule. The reason for this phrasing, particularly its focus on whether the statement is offered for its truth, lies primarily in the importance of cross-examination. *See* 2 BRANDIS & BROUN § 193, at 789 (rationale that most fairly explains the hearsay rule and offers a common justification for exceptions to the rule is the importance of cross-examination). The following observations highlight the relationship between the purpose for which a statement is offered and the importance of cross-examination.

- "We are interested in the declarant's credibility only when the out-of-court statement is being used to prove the truth of the assertion. In that circumstance, the evidence's value depends on the *credibility of the out-of-court declarant*." MOSTELLER § 11-1, at 11-5 (emphasis added). The opponent therefore has the need to cross-examine the declarant to inquire into possible problems with the declarant's perception, memory, or sincerity, which the trier of fact then may weigh in determining whether to accept the declarant's statement as true. The statement is nevertheless admissible if it satisfies one of a number of hearsay exceptions, discussed in section 11.6, below.
- "On the other hand, if the proponent does not offer the out-of-court declaration for its truth, the opponent does not need to cross-examine the declarant. If the declaration is

logically relevant on some other theory, the evidence's value usually depends on the *credibility of the in-court witness*." MOSTELLER § 11-1, at 11-5 (emphasis added). The opponent still needs to cross-examine the in-court witness to determine whether the witness heard and remembered the statement correctly and is telling the truth about what he or she heard. The statement is not considered hearsay and does not require a hearsay exception to justify its admission.

Examples of statements offered for the truth and for other purposes are provided in section C.3, below.

## C. Components of Hearsay Definition

Hearsay is "a statement, other than one made by the declarant while testifying at the trial or hearing, offered in evidence to prove the truth of the matter asserted." N.C. R. EVID. 801(c). This definition contains three components, discussed in subsections 1 through 3, below.

**1. Oral or written assertion of fact.** The statement must be an assertion of fact. For example, if a child said to her mother, "Daddy hit me," the child's statement would be an assertion of that fact. In contrast, if the mother overheard the child say, "Ouch" or "Don't" in interacting with the father, the statement might not be an assertion of fact. "Ouch" is an exclamation, "don't" is a command or imperative; neither explicitly asserts a particular fact. But, if offered to elicit an implicit assertion of fact—that is, that the father hit the child, prompting her exclamation or imperative—the statement still might be considered an assertion of fact. *See* MOSTELLER § 11-2(A)(1), at 11-6 to 11-8 (imperative statement is not hearsay unless the proponent's purpose is to elicit an assertion embodied in the statement).

Because the distinction between an assertion of fact and other utterances can be difficult to draw, cases have sometimes assumed that an arguably non-assertive utterance is hearsay and then found an exception. *Compare State v. Mitchell*, 135 N.C. App. 617, 618–19 (1999) (testimony that the inmate told the defendant to "hurry" or "leave" as she was departing from the jail was not inadmissible hearsay; the statement was a directive not offered for the truth of the matter asserted), *with State v. Smith*, 152 N.C. App. 29, 35–36 (2002) (holding that victim's statements to the defendant, "Shut up" and "Hush," were admissible under the present sense impression hearsay exception in Evidence Rule 803(1)).

**2. Made outside current proceeding.** The hearsay rule is typically thought of as applying to out-of-court statements. This component of the definition actually covers a broader range of statements. Statements that are made other than while the person is testifying at the current trial or hearing, including statements made in previous court proceedings or in previous hearings in the same case, constitute hearsay (assuming they meet the other components of the definition of hearsay) and must meet a hearsay exception to be admissible. *See* N.C. R. EVID. 804(b)(1) (providing a hearsay exception for testimony of a witness at another hearing in the same or a different proceeding); see also section 11.7.F.2, below (discussing this hearsay exception).

**3. Offered for truth of assertion.** The last and most often considered component of the definition of hearsay is that the statement must be offered for the truth of the matter asserted. If a child said to her mother, "Daddy hit me"—and the proponent offered that statement to show that the father in fact hit the child—it would be considered as offered for the truth of the matter asserted and would be inadmissible unless within a hearsay exception.

Statements containing a factual assertion are not necessarily offered for their truth, however. Examples are discussed below. If a statement is not offered for its truth, two additional considerations come into play. First, the purpose for which the statement is offered must be relevant to the issues in the case. Second, consideration of the statement is limited to the purpose for which it is offered.

**(a) To show resulting state of mind of person who heard statement.** One common nonhearsay purpose is to show the state of mind of the person who heard the statements. For example, suppose the mother testifies that shortly before the father allegedly struck the child, she heard the child tell her father, "I broke those things." If the purpose of offering the mother's statement was not to show the child actually broke the items but rather to show the father's resulting state of mind, the statement would not be offered for the truth of the matter asserted—that the child broke the items—and would not constitute hearsay. *See* 2 BRANDIS & BROUN § 195, at 794–99 (declarations of one person may be admitted to prove the state of mind of another person who heard them); *see also State v. McLean*, 251 N.C. App. 850 (2017) (not error to allow witness's testimony that jailer told her that defendant was in adjacent cell; statement was not offered to prove its truth but rather to explain why the witness was afraid to testify); *In re S.N.*, 180 N.C. App. 169, 174–75 (2006) (social worker's testimony about what a drug counselor told the respondent about the terms of his case plan was properly allowed to show the respondent's knowledge of the case plan and was not offered for the truth of matter asserted); *State v. Chapman*, 359 N.C. 328, 354–55 (2005) (where the defendant left the house in response to a phone call, the statements in the phone call were admissible not for their truth but to explain the defendant's subsequent actions).

**(b) To explain why police or DSS undertook investigation.** A question that has arisen in both criminal and juvenile cases is whether a statement reciting misconduct of a defendant or respondent is admissible if it is offered not to show the truth of the statement—that is, that the misconduct actually occurred—but rather to show why the police or DSS investigated the matter or took some other action. Decisions have found that when offered for the latter purpose, the statement is not offered for its truth and does not constitute hearsay. *See In re F.G.J.*, 200 N.C. App. 681, 687 n.2 (2009) (noting that statements for this purpose were not hearsay); *In re Mashburn*, 162 N.C. App. 386, 390 (2004) (out-of-court statements of children were admissible to show why DSS initiated an investigation and were not offered for their truth); *see also State v. Treadway*, 208 N.C. App. 286, 290 (2010) (child's statement to grandparent admissible for nonhearsay purpose of showing why grandparent told parents, who then sought medical treatment).

The cases suggest that when offered for this purpose the statements should be limited in detail because of the potential prejudice of the statements. *See* 1 IMWINKELRIED § 1004, at

10-24 to 10-30; *State v. Harper*, 96 N.C. App. 36, 39–40 (1989) (statements were permissible for the nonhearsay purpose of explaining an officer's conduct in investigating drug transactions; the substance of the statements by informants who were guiding the officer was limited to telling the officer to wait, to go ahead, and where to go); *cf. State v. Hueto*, 195 N.C. App. 67, 69–71 (2009) (statement that a witness was told that a child had been sexually assaulted was offered for the nonhearsay purpose of explaining why the witness called the police; the defendant objected on hearsay grounds only and waived any objection that the testimony was irrelevant or, if relevant, that the testimony's probative value was outweighed by its prejudicial effect under Evidence Rule 403).

## 11.6 Hearsay Exceptions

### A. Types of Hearsay Exceptions and Their Rationales

There are three basic categories of exceptions to the hearsay rule, each based on a somewhat different rationale. The discussion in the following sections deals with the hearsay exceptions within each category most likely to arise in juvenile cases. The three basic categories are:

- Rule 801 admissions of a party-opponent, discussed in section 11.6.B, below;
- Rule 803 exceptions, discussed in sections 11.6.C through H, below; and
- Rule 804 exceptions, discussed in section 11.6.H, below.

The rationale for allowing an admission of a party-opponent is unique. It is not based on considerations of reliability (as with Rule 803 exceptions) or on considerations of need (as with Rule 804 exceptions). Rather, the exception is "a product of the adversary litigation system; the opponent can hardly complain that he or she does not have an opportunity to cross-examine himself or herself." MOSTELLER § 11-3, at 11-20 to 11-21 (also noting that because of this unique rationale, the Federal Rules of Evidence treat admissions of a party-opponent as nonhearsay).

The hearsay exceptions in Rule 803 are recognized because they deal with statements that carry a greater inference of reliability or sincerity in light of the circumstances in which they were made. MOSTELLER ch. 11 pt. 3, at 11-39. Because the overriding reason for allowing such statements is their greater reliability, they are admissible whether the witness is available or unavailable.

The hearsay exceptions in Rule 804 depend to a greater degree on a showing of necessity for the evidence contained in the statement. MOSTELLER ch. 11 pt. 4, at 11-83. Therefore, in addition to meeting the criteria for a particular exception, the proponent must show that the declarant is unavailable.

### B. Rule 801(d): Admissions of a Party-Opponent

**1. Criteria.** Evidence Rule 801(d) excepts admissions by a party-opponent from the prohibition on hearsay. To satisfy the exception, the statement must have been made by a party to the case, and it must be offered against the party by the party's opponent. *See State v. Rainey*, 198 N.C. App. 427, 432 (2009) (reciting the requirements of Rule 801(d)). Juvenile cases involve various parties to which this exception may apply, discussed in subsection 3, below.

A number of cases state generally that the party's statement also must be against the party's interest. *See, e.g., State v. Lambert*, 341 N.C. 36, 50 (1995) (stating that an admission of a party-opponent is a statement of pertinent facts that, in light of other evidence, is incriminating); *In re J.J.D.L.*, 189 N.C. App. 777, 782 (2008) (stating the same principle in a delinquency case). A showing that the statement is against the party's interest does not appear to be required under this exception, however. *See* 2 BRANDIS & BROUN § 199, at 814–15.

The statement still must be relevant to be admissible. *See* 2 BRANDIS & BROUN § 199, at 818 (observing that the general requirements of relevance and materiality apply to admissions); *State v. Hutchinson*, 139 N.C. App. 132, 135–37 (2000) (defendant's statement that he committed burglaries after the charged offense was admissible; the statement was an admission of a party-opponent, and the subsequent burglaries were admissible under Evidence Rule 404(b) to show the defendant's motive and intent).

**2. Potential constitutional, statutory, and other bars.** Constitutional and statutory principles may bar the use of statements (as well as other evidence) obtained from a respondent during an investigation of alleged abuse, neglect, and dependency. These issues primarily arise in criminal and delinquency cases when the State offers the statement against the defendant or juvenile respondent. For the statement to be admissible, the State must comply with constitutional as well as hearsay requirements. MOSTELLER § 11-3(A)(2), at 11-23. In civil proceedings, including abuse, neglect, dependency, and termination of parental rights proceedings (juvenile proceedings), constitutional and statutory grounds for exclusion are considerably more limited but still may arise depending on the violation and the nature of the proceeding. The discussion below briefly considers potential grounds, in both criminal and juvenile cases, for excluding statements and other evidence obtained in an investigation of alleged abuse, neglect, and dependency.

(a) ***Miranda* warnings.** In criminal cases, a person in custody is entitled to *Miranda* warnings before being questioned by law-enforcement officers or their agents. Ordinarily, a DSS representative is not required to give *Miranda* warnings because DSS is not considered a law enforcement or prosecutorial agency. *See generally State v. Martin*, 195 N.C. App. 43, 48 (2009). If, however, a DSS representative is working so closely with law enforcement as to be considered an agent of law enforcement, the representative must give an in-custody defendant *Miranda* warnings before questioning. *See State v. Morrell*, 108 N.C. App. 465 (1993) (determining that a social worker was acting as a law enforcement agent).

In juvenile cases, *Miranda* violations by law enforcement or their agents ordinarily do not provide grounds for excluding evidence of a statement that was made without the required warnings. *See In re Pittman*, 149 N.C. App. 756 (2002) (holding that because an abuse and neglect proceeding is civil, an alleged *Miranda* violation by a law enforcement officer did not bar the use of the respondent's statements in that proceeding).

**(b) Due process and involuntary statements.** In criminal cases, a statement is inadmissible as a matter of due process if the statement was involuntary in the totality of the circumstances and the statement was causally related to some official, coercive action by law enforcement officers, their agents, or other government officials. *See Colorado v. Connelly*, 479 U.S. 157 (1986); *In re Weaver*, 43 N.C. App. 222, 223 (1979) (stating in a delinquency case that although a DSS representative was not required to give *Miranda* warnings to a juvenile before questioning, the juvenile's statement still must have been voluntarily and understandingly made); *see also generally* 2 WAYNE R. LAFAVE ET AL., CRIMINAL PROCEDURE § 6.2(c), at 721 (4th ed. 2015).

A threat to take away a person's children may be considered coercive and, in the totality of the circumstances, render a statement involuntary. *See People v. Medina*, 25 P.3d 1216 (Colo. 2001) (detective's threat to have children removed from the defendant's family, in the totality of circumstances, rendered the defendant's statement involuntary and inadmissible in a criminal case); *compare Morrell*, 108 N.C. App. at 474–75 (finding that the defendant made the statements without threats, promises, or duress by the social worker and that the statements were voluntary); *Commonwealth v. Roberts*, 376 N.E.2d 895 (Mass. App. Ct. 1978) (defendant's confession to a social worker was not the product of physical or psychological coercion).

In juvenile cases, involuntary statements in violation of due process also appear to be inadmissible. *See generally Bustos-Torres v. I.N.S.*, 898 F.2d 1053 (5th Cir. 1990) (*Miranda* warnings are not required before questioning of a person about information used to deport him or her because deportation proceedings are civil, not criminal, but deportation proceedings still must conform to due process standards and involuntary statements are inadmissible).

**(c) Fifth Amendment privilege against self-incrimination.** In criminal cases, the Fifth Amendment privilege against self-incrimination bars use of statements if the person was compelled to answer by the threatened loss of rights for refusing to answer. This principle comes from the line of U.S. Supreme Court cases known as the "penalty cases." *See Debnam v. N.C. Dep't of Correction*, 334 N.C. 380 (1993) (public employee may be discharged for failing to answer a public employer's questions, but the Fifth Amendment right against self-incrimination bars the use of statements in a criminal case that were obtained from an employee under the threat of discharge for not answering); *State v. Linney*, 138 N.C. App. 169, 177–81 (2000) (holding that an attorney was not compelled to give statements to a State Bar investigator and therefore the attorney's statements were not inadmissible in a later criminal prosecution); *see also Baltimore City Dep't of Social Services v. Bouknight*, 493 U.S. 549, 562 (1990) ("In a broad range of contexts, the Fifth Amendment limits prosecutors' ability to use testimony that has been compelled."); *McKune v. Lile*, 536 U.S. 24 (2002) (plurality finds that adverse consequences faced by a prisoner for refusing to make an admission required for participation in a sexual abuse treatment program were not so severe as to amount to compelled self-incrimination).

For a discussion of the application of the Fifth Amendment privilege in juvenile proceedings, see section 11.12, below.

**(d) Right to counsel.** In criminal cases, once a defendant's Sixth Amendment right to counsel attaches, law enforcement agents may not question the defendant, whether he or she is in or out of custody, without a proper waiver. *See generally Montejo v. Louisiana*, 556 U.S. 778 (2009). Questioning by a DSS representative after attachment of the Sixth Amendment right to counsel is not a violation if the representative is not acting as an agent of law enforcement. *See State v. Nations*, 319 N.C. 318, 325 (1987). The filing of a civil abuse and neglect petition does not constitute the initiation of criminal proceedings and so has been held not to trigger the Sixth Amendment right to counsel; therefore, questioning by a law enforcement agent does not make statements inadmissible on that ground in a criminal case. *See State v. Adams*, 345 N.C. 745 (1997) (also finding that the admission of statements in a criminal case did not violate the statutory right to counsel afforded to a defendant in an abuse and neglect case).

In juvenile cases, the respondent does not have a Sixth Amendment right to counsel, but a violation of the respondent's due process and statutory rights to counsel in those proceedings may warrant exclusion in some circumstances. The principal case on this issue is *In re Maynard*, 116 N.C. App. 616, 619–21 (1994), in which the respondent mother had been appointed counsel in a juvenile case and had stipulated through counsel that the children were dependent. During the pendency of review hearings, DSS workers talked with the respondent about surrendering her children for adoption and obtained her written surrender, without notice to or the presence of her appointed counsel. The court found a right-to-counsel violation and nullified the surrenders, analogizing the respondent's right to counsel in a juvenile case to a defendant's right to counsel in a criminal case and stating that once the respondent invokes the right to counsel, he or she has the right to have counsel present during any questioning unless he or she waives the right. It is unclear whether the courts would be willing to extend this principle beyond official concessions by the respondent, as respondents often must coordinate directly with DSS employees about the respondents' children and the issues that led to the court proceeding.

**(e) Fourth Amendment issues.** In criminal cases, searches and seizures in violation of the Fourth Amendment often require exclusion of the evidence obtained. Generally, actions by government officials, whether by law enforcement officers or other government actors, are subject to Fourth Amendment restrictions. *See New Jersey v. T.L.O.*, 469 U.S. 325, 335 (1985); *see generally* 1 WAYNE R. LAFAVE, SEARCH AND SEIZURE § 1.8(d), at 417–18 (5th ed. 2012). However, if they are not for law enforcement purposes, actions by child protection workers, such as DSS workers, are subject to relaxed requirements. *See generally* 5 WAYNE R. LAFAVE, SEARCH AND SEIZURE § 10.3(a) (5th ed. 2012) (discussing the application of the Fourth Amendment to investigations and other actions by child protection agencies); *see also* G.S. 7B-302(h) (regulating entry by DSS workers into private residences for assessment purposes).

In civil cases, violations of the Fourth Amendment or of statutory search and seizure restrictions ordinarily do not require exclusion of the evidence obtained. *See Quick v. N.C. Div. of Motor Vehicles*, 125 N.C. App. 123, 127 n.3 (1997) (holding in a license revocation proceeding that the exclusionary rule did not bar evidence obtained as the result of an allegedly illegal arrest). *But cf. In re Freeman*, 109 N.C. App. 100 (1993) (raising but not resolving the applicability of the exclusionary rule to a search in a teacher dismissal case); *I.N.S. v. Lopez-Mendoza*, 468 U.S. 1032, 1050–51 (1984) (holding in deportation proceedings, which are considered civil, that the exclusionary rule ordinarily does not bar evidence obtained in violation of the Fourth Amendment, but recognizing that an exception may exist for "egregious violations"); *United States v. Janis*, 428 U.S. 433 (1976) (applying a balancing test to determine whether the exclusionary rule should apply in a civil proceeding).

It does not appear that North Carolina has specifically addressed the issue in juvenile cases, but generally courts have been unwilling to exclude evidence in such cases based on Fourth Amendment violations. *See* 1 WAYNE R. LAFAVE, SEARCH AND SEIZURE § 1.7(e), at 333–35 (5th ed. 2012) (observing that the application of the Fourth Amendment to civil proceedings varies, but that generally courts are unwilling to exclude evidence for Fourth Amendment violations in child welfare cases); *cf. In re Beck*, 109 N.C. App. 539, 543–44 (1993) (sheriff's department seized materials from the respondent's home pursuant to a search warrant in a criminal case and, after the criminal charges were dismissed, transferred the materials to DSS, which later offered the materials as evidence in a TPR case; the court found no violation of the respondent's rights by the transfer of the materials to DSS, but the propriety of the initial seizure by the sheriff was not at issue).

**(f) Settlement efforts.** Other bars to admission of a respondent's statement also may exist. *See* N.C. R. EVID. 408 (stating that evidence of conduct or statements made in compromise negotiations is not admissible); Local Rule 7.3 of Twelfth Judicial District, District Court, Family Court Division, Juvenile Case Management Plan, I. Civil Cases (Apr. 2016) ("Statements made by respondents after the filing of the petition about or during treatment or services are inadmissible during the adjudicatory hearing except those made during court ordered assessments and evaluations."); *see also* Jessica Smith, *Criminal Evidence: Pleas and Plea Discussions*, NORTH CAROLINA SUPERIOR COURT JUDGES' BENCHBOOK (UNC School of Government, Mar. 2015) (discussing Evidence Rule 410 and the admissibility of plea discussions).

**3. Application of admission exception to common situations in juvenile cases.** In criminal cases, the admissibility of a defendant's statements is complicated by the constitutional issues discussed in subsection 2, above, but application of the hearsay exception for admissions is relatively straightforward because ordinarily there is a single defendant against whom the statement is offered. The reverse is the case in juvenile proceedings. Some common scenarios are as follows:

**(a) Offered by DSS against respondent.** In juvenile proceedings, a statement of a respondent is admissible as an admission of a party-opponent when offered by DSS against that respondent. *See In re S.W.*, 175 N.C. App. 719, 723 (2006) ("In termination of parental rights proceedings, the party whose rights are sought to be terminated is a party adverse to DSS in the proceeding"; therefore, DSS could offer the statement of the mother against the mother); *In re Hayden*, 96 N.C. App. 77, 80–81 (1989) (mother's statements to social workers about the father's conduct were admissions by her that the child was subject to conduct in her presence that could be found to be abusive and neglectful and therefore were admissible against the mother as admissions of a party-opponent); *see also State v. Wade*, 155 N.C. App. 1, 14–15 (2002) (in a criminal sex offense prosecution, the child victim testified that the defendant father said to her it would be her word against his and no one would believe her; the statement was admissible against the defendant father as an admission of a party-opponent).

**(b) Offered by DSS against different respondent.** The statement of one respondent parent is not necessarily admissible as an admission of a party-opponent when offered by DSS against another respondent parent. *See* 2 BRANDIS & BROUN § 204, at 831 (there is no presumption that spouses are authorized agents for each other and that the statement of one is admissible against the other); *cf. In re F.G.J.*, 200 N.C. App. 681 (2009) (mother's statements were admissible against her; father waived objection as to the admission of her statements against him).

Grounds may exist, however, for attributing the statement of one respondent to another. *See* 2 BRANDIS & BROUN §§ 200–08 (discussing various theories for admissibility, such as agency); *State v. McLemore*, 343 N.C. 240, 247–48 (1996) (defendant husband told his wife to tell his father and the police that he had shot his mother; the wife was acting as an agent of the defendant husband and the statement was admissible as an admission of a party-opponent).

Even if not attributable to other respondents, statements by one respondent may still be relevant to an issue to be decided in the case. For example, a statement by the mother that the father struck the child may be admissible to show the status of the child as abused. *See In re J.M.*, 255 N.C. App. 483 (2017); *see generally In re M.G.*, 187 N.C. App. 536, 549 (2007) (stating that the issue to be decided is whether abuse occurred, not whether the mother committed the abuse), *rev'd in part on other grounds*, 363 N.C. 570 (2009). In contrast, at a proceeding to terminate the father's rights, at which the father's fault is at issue, the mother's statement would not be admissible against the father as an admission of a party-opponent (unless a ground existed for attributing the mother's statement to the father).

**(c) Offered by one respondent against another respondent.** The statement of one respondent, for example, the statement of a respondent father, is not necessarily admissible as an admission of a party-opponent when offered by another respondent, for example, by a respondent mother. The respondent father's statement would appear to be admissible only when truly offered *against* the respondent father and not for the respondent mother's benefit. *See* 1 IMWINKELRIED § 1102, at 11-2 & n.3 (discussing the issue in the context of one co-defendant offering a statement of another co-defendant).

**(d) Statement of child.** The statement of a child is not admissible as an admission of a party-opponent when offered by either DSS or a respondent. Treating a child's statement as an admission under this exception would effectively negate the prohibition on hearsay involving statements by children and render the other hearsay exceptions unnecessary. Although a child is designated as a party to a juvenile case (*see* G.S. 7B-401.1(f); G.S. 7B-1104), the child's statement is generally not offered against the child but rather for the benefit of the offering party. *See generally* 1 IMWINKELRIED § 1102, at 11-2 & n.3; *cf. State v. Shoemaker*, 80 N.C. App. 95, 100 (1986) (statement by a complaining witness is not admissible as an admission of a party-opponent because a complaining witness is not a party to a criminal case).

**(e) Statement of DSS worker.** The statement of a DSS worker is admissible against DSS as an admission of a party-opponent when offered by a respondent against DSS. *See* N.C. R. EVID. 801(d)(D) (stating that this exception includes a statement by an "agent or servant concerning a matter within the scope of his agency or employment, made during the existence of the relationship"); *State v. Villeda*, 165 N.C. App. 431, 436–37 (2004) (holding that since a law-enforcement officer was an agent of the government, his statements were admissible against the state in a criminal case as an admission of a party-opponent).

In *State v. Phillips*, 365 N.C. 103, 128–29 (2011), the Supreme Court noted that it had not yet considered whether the statement of a law-enforcement officer is admissible against the State in a criminal case as an admission of a party-opponent. The court did not resolve the issue, finding that any error by the trial court did not constitute plain error. The comment in *Phillips* may signal a willingness by the Supreme Court to consider the approach taken in some jurisdictions that a law enforcement officer's statements are not necessarily attributable to the government in a criminal case. *See, e.g., United States v. Kampiles*, 609 F.2d 1233, 1246 (7th Cir. 1979) (citations omitted) ("Because the agents of the Government are supposedly disinterested in the outcome of a trial and are traditionally unable to bind the sovereign, their statements seem less the product of the adversary process and hence less appropriately described as admissions of a party."). Such an approach, if adopted in North Carolina, would have less applicability to statements by DSS workers acting on behalf of DSS, the party bringing the case. *See generally In re N.X.A.*, 254 N.C. App. 670 (2017) (discussing authority of DSS representatives to verify petition as agents of the State).

## C. Rule 803(2): Excited Utterances

**1. Criteria.** Rule 803(2) excepts from the prohibition on hearsay an excited utterance, defined as "[a] statement relating to a startling event or condition made while the declarant was under the stress of excitement caused by the event or condition." The courts have recognized that this definition requires that two conditions be satisfied. There must be:

- a sufficiently startling experience suspending reflective thought, and
- a spontaneous reaction, not one resulting from reflection or fabrication.

*State v. Fullwood,* 323 N.C. 371, 387 (1988) (the defendant's statement that his girlfriend had stabbed him, when the statement was made in the emergency room one hour after stabbing, was not an excited utterance; the trial court properly could conclude that the defendant had time to manufacture the statement and did not make it spontaneously), *vacated on other grounds,* 494 U.S. 1022 (1990).

Factors to consider in determining whether a statement meets these criteria include:

- the time lapse between the event and statement;
- whether the statement was made at or away from the scene or the event;
- whether the statement was spontaneously uttered or in response to an inquiry;
- the appearance of the declarant;
- the nature of the event and statement; and
- the declarant's conduct after the event.

**2. Statements by children.** When considering whether a child's statement satisfies the spontaneity requirement, the North Carolina courts have been more flexible about the length of time between the event and the child's statement. In *State v. Smith,* 315 N.C. 76, 86–90 (1985), a rape prosecution, the court held that out-of-court statements by 4-year-old and 5-year-old victims to their grandmother were excited utterances although made two to three days after the rape. The conversation began when the grandmother visited the home, apparently for the first time after the rape, and one of the children volunteered to the grandmother, "I have something to tell you . . . . I want you to come in the room. I am scared . . . . I want to tell you what Sylvester done [*sic*] to me." The court reviewed several cases and other authorities and noted the special characteristics and circumstances of young children that may prolong stress and spontaneity, which the court stated are the critical factors in evaluating whether a statement qualifies as an excited utterance. The court held that those factors remained present notwithstanding the lapse in time between the event and statements.

Based on this rationale, several North Carolina cases have admitted as excited utterances statements by children that were not contemporaneous with the event but were made within a few days thereafter. In a termination of parental rights case, *In re J.S.B.,* 183 N.C. App. 192, 199–200 (2007), a 9-year-old child's statement that she saw her mother whip and hit her brother was found to be an excited utterance. Although the statement was made during an interview by a detective at the police station sixteen hours after the incident, the court found that the stress and spontaneity were prolonged because of intervening events—the child had watched the mother's boyfriend attempt CPR on the brother, emergency technicians had come to the house, and the child's brother died—and because of the child's demeanor when she made the statements to the detective—the child was teary-eyed and very withdrawn while talking to the detective and was seen in the victim assistance room "basically in a corner in like a ball, like a fetal position." *See also State v. McLaughlin,* 246 N.C. App. 306 (2016) (admitting statement by 15-year-old victim of sexual abuse); *In re Clapp,* 137 N.C. App. 14, 20–21 (2000) (in a juvenile delinquency case, a 3-year-old child's statement to her mother that the juvenile had licked her private parts was admissible; the child told her mother about the act immediately after the juvenile left the house). *But see State v. Blankenship,* 814 S.E.2d 901 (N.C. Ct. App. 2018) (statement by child to grandparents after they picked up the child from defendant's house was not excited utterance; delay did not bar admission of statements but State presented insufficient evidence that the child was under stress when she made the statement; later statements to others also did not satisfy exception); *State v. Carter*, 216 N.C. App. 453, 462–63 (2011) (statement by child to social worker was not admissible as excited utterance; record contained no evidence of child's behavior or mental state at time of statement), *rev'd on other grounds*, 366 N.C. 496 (2013); *State v. Thomas*, 119 N.C. App. 708, 712–17 (1995) (statements by the victim to her kindergarten friends four or five days after alleged sexual abuse were excited utterances, but the friends' statements to their mothers relating the victim's statements were not excited utterances). For additional summaries of cases applying the excited utterance exception to statements by children, see Jessica Smith, *Evidence Issues in Criminal Cases Involving Child Victims and Child Witnesses*, ADMINISTRATION OF JUSTICE BULLETIN No. 2008/07, at 34–36 (UNC School of Government, Dec. 2008).

### D. Rule 803(3): State of Mind

**1. Criteria.** Rule 803(3) excepts from the hearsay rule "[a] statement of the declarant's then existing state of mind, emotion, sensation, or physical condition . . . but not including a statement of memory or belief to prove the fact remembered" (unless it relates to a will). *See In re Hayden*, 96 N.C. App. 77, 81 (1989) (respondent father offered testimony of his wife that the child said to her that the child had burned herself on the previous day; statement was inadmissible under this exception because Rule 803(3), by its terms, excludes "a statement of memory or belief to prove the fact remembered or believed"); *see also State v. Blankenship*, 814 S.E.2d 901 (N.C. Ct. App. 2018) (statement by child to grandparents was not admissible as present sense impression under Evidence Rule 803(1); record did not show when sexual misconduct occurred in relation to statements and thus did not show that child made the statement while perceiving the conduct or immediately thereafter).

The exception does not appear to arise very often in juvenile cases. The exception arises more in criminal cases in which the State seeks to offer a deceased victim's statements about his or her feelings toward the accused. *See generally* 2 BRANDIS & BROUN § 217, at 880–83; *see also State v. Hipps*, 348 N.C. 377, 392 (1998) ("Evidence tending to show the state of mind of a victim is admissible as long as the declarant's state of mind is a relevant issue and the potential for unfair prejudice in admitting the evidence does not substantially outweigh its probative value"; the court found that a murder victim's statement that she feared the defendant was relevant to show the status of the victim's relationship with the defendant); *State v. Lesane*, 137 N.C. App. 234, 240 (2000) ("[O]ur courts have created a sort of trichotomy in applying Rule 803(3). Statements that recite only emotions are admissible under the exception; statements that recite emotions and the facts underlying those emotions are likewise admissible; but statements that merely recite facts do not fall within the exception."). *But see State v. Jones*, 137 N.C. App. 221, 227 (2000) (stating, in a case decided the same day as *Lesane*, that "our courts have repeatedly found admissible under Rule 803(3) a declarant's statements of fact that indicate her state of mind, even if they do not explicitly contain an accompanying statement of the declarant's state of mind").

**2. Examples.** A declaration of intent, such as a threat, is a type of declaration of state of mind. *See* 2 BRANDIS & BROUN §§ 218–19. Threats by a party, when offered against that party, are also admissible as admissions of a party-opponent, discussed in section 11.6.B, above. Threats also can be analyzed as non-hearsay evidence of a verbal act. *See State v. Weaver*, 160 N.C. App. 61, 64–66 (2003) (the statement of a bribe was evidence of a verbal act and was not offered for the truth of the matter asserted but rather to prove the statement was made).

Diary entries may or may not be admissible under this exception depending on whether they consist of mere factual recitations or express the writer's then-existing state of mind. *Compare State v. Hardy*, 339 N.C. 207, 227–30 (1994) (holding that diary entries that consisted of mere factual recitations, written in a calm and detached manner after the events occurred, were inadmissible under the state of mind exception), *with State v. King*, 353 N.C. 457, 474–78 (2001) (holding that diary entries that stated the victim's frustration with the defendant and her intent to end their marriage were admissible under this exception).

### E. Rule 803(4): Medical Diagnosis or Treatment

**1. Criteria.** Rule 803(4) excepts from the hearsay rule statements made for the purpose of medical diagnosis or treatment. In *State v. Hinnant*, 351 N.C. 277 (2000), the North Carolina Supreme Court reexamined the requirements of this exception. *Hinnant* involved a criminal prosecution for rape and other sexual acts. The State offered the hearsay statements of the defendant's 5-year-old niece, who met with a clinical psychologist specializing in child abuse approximately two weeks after the alleged abuse and initial medical examination. In finding the statements inadmissible, the court held that the proponent of statements under this hearsay exception must establish that:

- the declarant made the statements understanding that they would lead to medical diagnosis or treatment, and
- the statements were reasonably pertinent to diagnosis or treatment.

**2. First requirement: declarant's understanding and motivation.** The *Hinnant* decision modified or at least clarified North Carolina law by emphasizing the importance of the first requirement of the medical diagnosis and treatment exception, which depends on the declarant's motivation for making the statements. The court found that a statement made for purposes of medical diagnosis and treatment is treated as inherently reliable and is excepted from the hearsay rule (assuming the second requirement is also satisfied) when the declarant is motivated "to tell the truth in order to receive proper treatment." *Id.* at 286. The proponent of the statement therefore "must affirmatively establish that the declarant had the requisite intent by demonstrating that the declarant made the statements understanding that they would lead to medical diagnosis or treatment." *Id.* at 287.

The discussion in subsections 3 through 6, below, discusses some of the issues raised by this requirement.

**3. Child declarants.** The requirement of a treatment motive applies to children as well as adult declarants. *Id.* at 287–88. Although acknowledging the occasional difficulties in determining a child's intent, the court found that trial courts could make this determination by considering the objective circumstances surrounding the examination, including whether the purpose of the examination was explained to the child, the person to whom the child was speaking (a medical professional versus another person), the setting of the interview (a child-friendly room versus a doctor's examination room), the nature of the questions (leading versus non-leading), and the time of the examination in relation to the incident (whether medical attention was sought immediately or delayed). The court added, however, that corroborating physical evidence cannot be used to establish the declarant's treatment motive. *Id.*

In *Hinnant*, the court found that the proponent failed to establish that the child declarant had a treatment motive in talking with the clinical psychologist. Although the clinical psychologist testified that she interviewed the child to obtain information for the examining physician, there was no evidence that the purpose of the interview was explained to the child. In addition, the interview was conducted in a "child-friendly" room, not a medical environment, and consisted entirely of leading questions, which in the court's view further undermined the reliability of the child's responses. *Id.* at 289–90.

**Note:** Because a child's intent for purposes of this exception may be determined from the circumstances surrounding the statements, neither a psychological examination nor a voir dire examination of the child is required. *See State v. Carter*, 153 N.C. App. 756, 760–61 (2002) (so holding in reliance on *Hinnant*).

**4. Examination protocols.** In a number of cases immediately after *Hinnant*, the court found that examination protocols involving children, particularly for mental health examinations, did not show that the child understood the purpose of the interview and did not meet the requirements for the medical diagnosis and treatment exception. *See State v. Waddell*, 351 N.C. 413 (2000) (holding on facts similar to *Hinnant* that the child's statements to a psychologist were inadmissible under the medical diagnosis and treatment exception); *State v. Bates*, 140 N.C. App. 743 (2000) (to same effect); *State v. Watts*, 141 N.C. App. 104 (2000) (child's statements to nurse, child medical examiner, and child mental health examiner were inadmissible under the medical diagnosis and treatment exception; the nurse, who examined the child shortly after the alleged incident, testified that the child seemed unaware of why she was there, and the examination by the two doctors took place three months later); *see also State v. Blankenship*, 814 S.E.2d 901 (N.C. Ct. App. 2018) (observing that it was a "close call" whether child had required intent under *Hinnant* where record did not indicate that nurse impressed importance of truth telling, child did not understand why she was at hospital, and nurse did not make it clear to child why she needed treatment; court does not decide issue because other, substantially identical statements were properly admitted).

The frequency of such cases has declined, as examiners have changed their protocols to communicate the purpose of the examination more clearly to child patients. *See, e.g., State v. Lewis*, 172 N.C. App. 97 (2005) (holding that the *Hinnant* requirements were satisfied where the interviews were at a medical center by a registered nurse, the children signed a form stating they understood that the nurse would share information with the doctor, and the nurse testified that she explained to the children that she would share information with the doctor, who would perform a medical examination).

**5. Identity of listener.** Cases before *Hinnant* admitted statements by children to family members and others who were not medical personnel if, following the statements, the children received treatment. *See, e.g., In re Lucas*, 94 N.C. App. 442, 446–47 (1989) (in a pre-*Hinnant* case, a child's statements to her mother resulted in medical attention and were therefore found admissible under the medical diagnosis or treatment exception).

*Hinnant* observed that statements made to a family member or other person who is not a medical professional may be admissible under the medical diagnosis and treatment exception, but the proponent must affirmatively show that the child made the statement understanding that it would lead to treatment. *See Hinnant*, 351 N.C. at 288. To the extent that pre-*Hinnant* cases did not require such a showing, they are no longer good law. *See also In re T.C.S.*, 148 N.C. App. 297 (2002) (per *Hinnant*, a doctor's testimony about a child's statements to a social worker, which the social worker relayed to the doctor, was inadmissible, even though the statements were used by the doctor for purposes of diagnosis); *State v. McGraw*, 137 N.C. App. 726 (2000) (per *Hinnant*, statements made to a person other than a medical doctor may constitute statements for purposes of medical diagnosis or treatment, but there was nothing to indicate that the child made statements to her mother with the understanding that they would lead to medical diagnosis or treatment). *But see In re Clapp*, 137 N.C. App. 14 (2000) (in a decision issued shortly after *Hinnant*, the court found that a child's statements to a doctor at an emergency room were for purposes of medical diagnosis and treatment; the court also stated, without explanation, that the medical diagnosis and treatment exception allowed the doctor to testify to the child's statements to her mother prior to the emergency room visit).

The participation in an examination of a person who is not a medical professional does not necessarily remove the child's statement from the coverage of the exception. *See State v. Thornton*, 158 N.C. App. 645 (2003) (statements by a child to a social worker were admissible where the social worker was part of the team conducting the medical and psychological evaluation at a medical center, the interview was the same day as the physical examination, and the social worker explained to the child that she worked with the doctor, whose office was in the same building and doors apart); *State v. Stancil*, 146 N.C. App. 234 (2001) (child's statements to a physician, nurse, and social worker at a hospital were admissible under the medical diagnosis and treatment exception; the father took the child to the hospital within hours of the incident, the interviews were for the purpose of diagnosis, and the child testified that she went to the hospital because the defendant had "hurt her privacy"), *aff'd as modified on other grounds*, 355 N.C. 266 (2002).

**6. Statements to medical professional by parent of child obtaining treatment.** In *In re J.M.*, 255 N.C. App. 483 (2017), the court found that Evidence Rule 803(4) allowed the mother's statements to medical professionals that she had observed the father punch the child who was being examined, hold him upside down by the ankles, and do other physical acts. (The mother was not recounting statements the child had made to her, discussed in subsection 5, above.) The court held in this case that the parent had the same incentive to obtain appropriate medical care for the child and that neither the evidence rules nor *Hinnant* required that the declarant be the patient. The court also found that the statements were pertinent to diagnosis and treatment, the second requirement for admissibility.

**7. Second requirement: pertinence to diagnosis and treatment.** North Carolina cases, before and after *Hinnant*, have given the term "diagnosis" a relatively narrow construction. Diagnosis, without the possibility of subsequent treatment, is not covered by the exception. *See* 2 BRANDIS & BROUN § 217, at 885–86. *Hinnant's* emphasis on the declarant's treatment motivation reinforces the requirement that for the exception to apply, diagnosis must be connected to treatment. *See Hinnant*, 351 N.C. at 289 ("If the declarant's statements are not pertinent to medical diagnosis, the declarant has no treatment-based motivation to be truthful.").

Statements made to a medical professional for the purpose of preparing for trial, although diagnostic, do not meet this treatment requirement and are not admissible under the exception. *See State v. Stafford*, 317 N.C. 568 (1986) (witness's statements to a pediatrician concerning symptoms she had experienced earlier were not made for the purpose of diagnosis or treatment but rather for the purpose of preparing and presenting the State's "rape trauma syndrome" theory at a rape trial; the statements did not qualify under the medical diagnosis and treatment exception); *State v. Reeder*, 105 N.C. App. 343 (1992) (holding that since the examination was for the purpose of determining whether the child was sexually abused and not for purposes of diagnosis or treatment, the child's statements to the doctor were inadmissible under this exception).

The courts also have scrutinized statements, particularly to nonphysicians, after the declarant is no longer in need of immediate medical attention. *See Hinnant*, 351 N.C. at 289–90 (finding that statements to a clinical psychologist two weeks after a medical examination were not pertinent to medical diagnosis and treatment); *State v. Smith*, 315 N.C. 76, 85–86 (1985) (determining that statements to rape task force volunteers after a medical examination were not pertinent to medical diagnosis and treatment); *see also State v. Reeder*, 105 N.C. App. 343, 351–54 (1992) (determining that statements by child to physician at an examination over a year after the incident were not pertinent to diagnosis and treatment and were not admissible); Robert P. Mosteller, *Testing the Testimonial Concept and Exceptions to Confrontation: "A Little Child Shall Lead Them,"* 82 IND. L.J. 917, 956–57 (2007) (expressing skepticism about the purpose of later examinations in analyzing whether statements are for purposes of treatment or prosecution [the discussion concerns the Confrontation Clause, which is applicable to criminal cases only, but the analysis is similar]).

Statements to psychological professionals for the purposes of mental health treatment are not necessarily excluded from the hearsay exception if the proponent makes an adequate showing of both prongs. *Compare State v. Kidd*, 194 N.C. App. 374 (2008) (unpublished) (upholding admission of child's statement to licensed clinical social worker, which led to mental health treatment); *In re N.M.H.*, 183 N.C. App. 490 (2007) (unpublished) (upholding admission of statements by child to family therapist for purposes of treatment); *with State v. Carter*, 216 N.C. App. 453 (2011) (excluding statement by child to social worker who conceded that she was not qualified to give medical diagnosis or treatment), *rev'd on other grounds*, 366 N.C. 496 (2013); *State v. Hilton*, 194 N.C. App. 821 (2009) (unpublished) (holding that trial court erred in admitting children's statements to licensed clinical counselor who was providing therapy to children; record failed to show that children had requisite treatment motivation at time of statements).

Additional issues involving this second requirement are discussed in subsections 8 and 9, below.

**8. Mixed purpose examinations.** Statements made by a patient during an examination with a mixed purpose—for example, for treatment and potentially for use in criminal investigation or other legal proceedings—are still admissible under the medical diagnosis and treatment exception if the requirements of *Hinnant* are satisfied. *See State v. Isenberg*, 148 N.C. App. 29, 36–39 (2001) (determining that, although the child was examined after a request by law enforcement, the examination was for treatment purposes and the child's statements to the pediatric nurse and physician who conducted the physical examination of the child were admissible under the medical diagnosis and treatment exception). *But see State v. Lowery*, 219 N.C. App. 151 (2012) (defendant's statements were not admissible under this exception where his primary objective was to obtain diagnosis of mental illness to use as defense even though defendant may have wanted continued treatment of any diagnosed condition), *remanded on other grounds*, 748 S.E.2d 527 (2012). When an examination involves mixed purposes, this factor also may bear on whether the statements are admissible in a criminal case under the Confrontation Clause, discussed in section 11.4.A, above.

**9. Identification of perpetrator.** North Carolina cases have allowed under the medical diagnosis and treatment exception a child's statement to a medical professional identifying the perpetrator of sexual abuse. The same may apply to child victims of physical abuse. The courts have reasoned that the identification of the perpetrator is pertinent to continued treatment of possible psychological problems and is not merely a statement as to "fault," which ordinarily is not pertinent to diagnosis and treatment. *See State v. Aguallo*, 318 N.C. 590, 596–97 (1986) (allowing statement); *State v. Lewis*, 172 N.C. App. 97 (2005) (allowing statement); *State v. Reeder*, 105 N.C. App. 343, 351–54 (1992) (disallowing statement because the examination was not for the purpose of diagnosis and treatment but rather to determine whether sexual abuse had occurred); *see also In re Mashburn*, 162 N.C. App. 386 (2004) (in a neglect case, the trial court allowed, under the medical diagnosis and treatment exception, a statement by a child to a doctor that her mother did not believe the child about sexual abuse; the dissent argued that the statement was not reasonably pertinent to medical diagnosis and treatment and should not have been admitted); Robert P. Mosteller, *The Maturation and Disintegration of the Hearsay Exception for Statements for Medical Examination in Child Sexual Abuse Cases*, LAW & CONTEMPORARY PROBLEMS, Winter 2002, at 47, 94–95 (supporting the admissibility of such statements under the medical diagnosis and treatment exception when made at initial medical examinations, but expressing skepticism about the treatment purpose when such statements are elicited at later examinations).

**10. Videotape of examination.** A videotape of a child's statements during an examination is admissible under the medical diagnosis and treatment exception if it satisfies the *Hinnant* requirements. *See State v. Burgess*, 181 N.C. App. 27, 34–35 (2007) and cases cited therein (upholding the admission of a videotape of an interview with a nurse before an examination by a physician; also noting that the trial court had denied admission of a videotape made six days later at which a detective was present); *cf. State v. McLaughlin*, 246 N.C. App. 306 (2016) (finding that admission under medical diagnosis and treatment exception of videotape of interview of child by nurse did not violate defendant's confrontation rights; court finds that primary purpose of interview was health of child, not use at trial). Videotaping of an examination may suggest that the examination has a mixed purpose, discussed in subsection 8, above, and the proponent may need to show that the examination included a substantial treatment purpose. *See* Robert P. Mosteller, *Testing the Testimonial Concept and Exceptions to Confrontation: "A Little Child Shall Lead Them,"* 82 IND. L.J. 917, 957 (2007) (formality of videotaping may indicate that an examination is for the purpose of preserving evidence for prosecution, and proponent should produce firm evidence of a substantial medical purpose).

A videotape also must be adequately authenticated. *See* MOSTELLER § 5-6, at 5-88 to 5-89; § 5-9(B), at 5-107 to 5-108 (authenticity of an audio recording may be established by someone who heard the conversation and indicates the recording is an accurate reproduction of the conversation; authenticity of a video recording may be similarly established by a person who was present when the activity occurred; if such a witness is not available, authenticity may be shown by proof of the circumstances of the recording, such as the operator's qualifications, working condition of the equipment, etc.); *see also* G.S. 8-97 (allowing videotape as substantive evidence with a proper foundation); *State v. Mason*, 144 N.C. App. 20, 24–27 (2001) (assessing adequacy of foundation for admission of videotape in criminal case).

The courts also have allowed videotapes to corroborate a witness's statement (see section 11.3.C, above); under the hearsay exception for past recollection recorded (see section 11.3.A, above); and under the residual hearsay exception (see section 11.6.H, below).

**11. Anatomical dolls.** Statements by children to medical personnel while employing anatomical dolls have been found admissible in cases alleging sexual abuse. *See State v. Bullock*, 320 N.C. 780, 781–83 (1987). The person who examined the child may use anatomical dolls in his or her testimony to illustrate how the child used the dolls during the examination. *See generally State v. Chandler*, 324 N.C. 172 (1989) (allowing such testimony [note, however, that the substantive use of the children's statements in this case likely would not qualify under the medical diagnosis and treatment hearsay exception as interpreted in the later *Hinnant* decision]).

The improper use of anatomical dolls by an interviewer may undermine the basis for admitting a child's statements under the medical diagnosis and treatment exception. *See Hinnant*, 351 N.C. at 290 (quoting *State v. Harris*, 808 P.2d 453, 459 (1991)) (child did not have a treatment motive and her statements were not inherently reliable where the entire interview consisted of a series of leading questions during which the interviewer pointed to anatomically correct dolls and asked whether anyone had or had not performed various acts with the child; "'[i]nherent in this type of suggestive questioning is the danger of planting the idea of sexual abuse in the mind of the child'"). The proper use of anatomical dolls, in contrast, has been found to bolster the reliability of a child's statements. *See State v. Wagoner*, 131 N.C. App. 285, 290 (1998) (finding that the use of anatomical dolls bolstered the trustworthiness of a child's out-of-court statement, which supported admission of the statement under the residual hearsay exception). (The residual hearsay exception is discussed in section 11.6.H, below.)

Statements by a child to a medical professional about sexual abuse while employing anatomical dolls, without adequate physical evidence of abuse, are insufficient to support the admission of expert testimony that the child has been sexually abused. *See State v. Delsanto*, 172 N.C. App. 42 (2005); *State v. Dixon*, 150 N.C. App. 46, 51–54 (2002), *aff'd per curiam*, 356 N.C. 428 (2002). For a further discussion of the admissibility of expert opinion in such cases, see section 11.10.D.6, below.

**12. Basis of opinion.** Statements of children to medical professionals that do not satisfy the medical diagnosis and treatment exception may still be admissible as the basis of an expert's opinion. *See* 2 BRANDIS & BROUN § 217, at 884. If admitted on that ground, the statements are not substantive evidence of the facts asserted in the statement.

### F. Rule 803(6): Business Records

**1. Criteria.** Rule 803(6) excepts from the hearsay rule entries made in the regular course of business. This exception requires inquiry into: (1) the method and circumstances of the preparation of the record; and (2) the information contained within the record. This exception applies to hospital and medical records, among others. The cases also analyze DSS records under this exception.

---

**Note:** Pursuant to the statutory requirements for juvenile proceedings, documentary evidence alone is insufficient to support an order terminating parental rights. Some live testimony is required. *In re N.B.*, 195 N.C. App. 113, 118 (2009) (reversing termination order where "petitioner presented no oral testimony to carry its burden of proof"); *In re A.M.*, 192 N.C. App. 538, 541 (2008) (also relying on Rule 43(a) of the N.C. Rules of Civil Procedure in holding in a termination case that one or more witnesses must be "sworn or affirmed and tendered to give testimony"); *see also* Chapter 9.10.A.

The same principle applies in abuse, neglect, and dependency proceedings. *See In re J.T.*, 252 N.C. App. 19 (2017) (statements by attorneys are not considered evidence and do not satisfy requirement for taking of evidence); *In re D.Y.*, 202 N.C. App. 140, 141–43 (2010) (reversing a permanency planning order where no witnesses testified and the order was based solely on written reports, prior orders, and attorneys' oral arguments); *In re D.L.*, 166 N.C. App. 574 (2004) (holding that the trial court's findings in a permanency planning order were not supported by competent evidence where DSS offered a written summary but no oral testimony).

---

**2. Method and circumstances of preparation.** The requirements as to the method and circumstances of the creation of business records are familiar ones: The record must be made at or near the time of the event, it must be prepared by someone with a business duty to the organization (typically, an employee of the organization), it must have been made in the regular course of business, and the regular practice of the business must have been to make such records. *See generally* 2 BRANDIS & BROUN § 225.

**(a) Establishment of foundational requirements.** The witness who testifies in court to the method and circumstances of the preparation of a business record is not required to be the maker of the record. The rule requires only that the foundation be shown by the testimony of the custodian of the business's records or other qualified witness. Thus, if the employee who made the record is not available to testify, another employee familiar with the circumstances of the creation of the record and the business's procedures may testify to the method and circumstances of the record's preparation. *See In re Smith*, 56 N.C. App. 142, 148 (1982) (upholding the admission of a DSS report based on the testimony of a social worker who did not work on the report but who testified that it was made in the regular course of business, etc.); *accord In re C.R.B.*, 245 N.C. App. 65 (2016).

**(b) Records within records.** DSS records often include records from other organizations, such as records from other county DSS agencies, private drug labs, and police and sheriff departments. See Chapter 14.1 (discussing DSS access to information of other agencies). A proper foundation, including authenticity, must be shown for both the DSS record and the records from other organizations within the DSS record. The requirements are relatively easy to satisfy, but the mere sharing of the information with DSS may be insufficient. *See* 2 BRANDIS & BROUN § 243, at 985 & n.39 ("Copies that are neither certified as correct nor authenticated in any other recognized manner are not admissible.").

The foundation may be established by live testimony of a custodian or employee of the outside organization. If the record of the outside organization is an official record or report, the foundation may be shown, without live testimony, by a proper certification from an official with the outside organization attesting to authenticity and by the court's taking of judicial notice of the legal requirements for preparation of the record. *See* MOSTELLER § 5-4, at 5-77 to 5-78 (authenticity of a public record may be established by an attesting certificate), § 11-5, at 11-44 to 11-46 (court may take judicial notice of the statute, regulation, or custom requiring a public official to prepare the record and, if the attested copy is fair on its face (complete with no erasures), the document's face creates a permissive inference that the official followed the proper procedures in preparing the particular record). The hearsay exception for official records is discussed further in section 11.6.G, below.

In some circumstances, a DSS employee may be able to lay the foundation for an outside organization's records, but the extent to which the courts would allow that possibility may be limited. *See In re S.D.J.*, 192 N.C. App. 478, 482–84 (2008) (permitting a DSS employee to establish the foundation for a drug test report prepared by an outside lab where the DSS employee collected the sample, ordered the report, and filed the results with her office); *see also State v. Hicks*, 243 N.C. App. 628 (2015) (allowing officer to lay foundation for record from federal database showing defendant's purchases of pseudoephedrine, a methamphetamine precursor); *State v. Sneed*, 210 N.C. App. 622, 628–31 (2011) (not plain error for trial court to admit under Rule 803(6) printout from National Crime Information Center (NCIC) about stolen gun; court rejected defendant's argument that State was required to present testimony from a custodian of records for NCIC, finding that adequate foundation was laid through testimony of local police officer who used the database in his regular course of business).

Evidence Rule 803(6) now allows the use of an affidavit to establish the foundation for business records, without live testimony. The revised rule applies to records of nonparties, such as records obtained by DSS from an outside, nonparty organization. The proponent must give advance notice to all other parties of the intent to offer the evidence by affidavit. *See generally* Jonathan Holbrook, *Rule 803(6): Please Hold for the Next Available Representative . . .*, UNC SCH. OF GOV'T: NORTH CAROLINA CRIMINAL LAW BLOG (Mar. 13, 2018) (discussing affidavit procedure).

Another mechanism for attesting to business records, without live testimony, is North Carolina Rule of Civil Procedure 45(c)(2), which provides that the custodian of hospital medical records or public records may submit an affidavit attesting to the records in response to a subpoena duces tecum. *See In re J.B.*, 172 N.C. App. 1, 17–18 (2005) (relying on the rule to admit mental health records). Opposing parties may still contest the admissibility of specific information within records offered by affidavit.

**(c) Records prepared in anticipation of litigation.** Exclusion is not automatically required of records prepared in anticipation of litigation. Thus, a DSS record that meets the requirements for admission as a business record is not necessarily inadmissible even though it is prepared in part in anticipation of legal proceedings. A record prepared specially for litigation purposes, however, would likely not satisfy the business record exception because it would not be prepared in the regular course of business. *See generally Palmer v. Hoffman*, 318 U.S. 109 (1943) (holding that a railroad company's preparation of an accident report for use in defending against potential litigation was not made in the regular course of the company's business within the meaning of the exception). Also, if the court finds a record untrustworthy, even though it otherwise satisfies the requirements of the business records exception, the court has the discretion to exclude it. *See* N.C. R. EVID. 803(6) (stating that business records are admissible "unless the source of information or the method or circumstances of preparation indicate lack of trustworthiness"); *State v. Wood*, 306 N.C. 510, 513–16 (1982) (factor in evaluating the reliability of a business record is whether it was prepared ante litem motam, that is, before a lawsuit was brought); MOSTELLER § 11-4(B), at 11-41 (court may exclude records that otherwise meet the business records exception if they are suspect or unreliable).

---

**Note:** By statute, predisposition reports are not admissible at the adjudication hearing in an abuse, neglect, or dependency proceeding. *See* G.S. 7B-808(a); *see also In re Quevedo*, 106 N.C. App. 574, 584 (1992). Such a report would likely not satisfy the business records exception in any event because, by its terms, it is prepared for the court's use and thus likely would not be considered a record prepared in the regular course of business.

---

**3. Observations, statements, and other information within a record.** Two basic requirements, described below, apply to information recorded within a record. Both must be satisfied for information within a business record to be admissible.

**(a) Knowledge of fact or event.** First, the entry in a record must be based on information provided by a person with knowledge of the fact or event. The employee who enters the information in the record (or the witness who testifies to the making of the record) need not have personal knowledge of the facts or events in the record, but the person who provided the information must have had personal knowledge. N.C. R. EVID. 803(6) commentary; *Donavant v. Hudspeth*, 318 N.C. 1, 9 (1986) (evidence of practice is sufficient to establish prima facie that a record was prepared from personal knowledge; in this case, however, the record showed that the information in the report was not based on personal knowledge, and the information was therefore not admissible under the business records exception). For example, if a DSS employee's report states, "The respondent had no food in the house on the day of the investigation," the employee must have personal knowledge, or have received the information from someone with personal knowledge, of that fact.

**(b) Business duty.** Second, the person who provided the information entered in the record must have a business duty to report the information. Information provided by third parties who do not have a duty to the business is generally inadmissible unless it qualifies under another hearsay exception. For example, in the above example about lack of food in the house, if the DSS employee received the information from the respondent's neighbor, even a neighbor claiming to have personal knowledge of the condition of the respondent's house, the information would not be admissible under the business records exception because the neighbor does not have a business duty to DSS. To be admissible, the neighbor's statement would have to qualify under another hearsay exception. *See* 2 BRANDIS & BROUN § 225, at 911 n.481 (stating that "the underlying theory of the exception [is] that the business environment encourages the making of accurate records by those with a duty to the enterprise"); *State v. Reeder*, 105 N.C. App. 343, 351–54 (1992) (statement by a child in a medical report identifying the defendant as the perpetrator was not admissible under the business records exception because it was hearsay within hearsay; the statement did not independently meet the medical diagnosis and treatment exception because the examination was not for that purpose). *But see State v. Scott,* 343 N.C. 313 (1996) (intake form of home for abused women and children, filled out by a resident after she arrived, was properly admitted even though the resident had no business duty in filling out the form; decision criticized by Brandis & Broun, in the above citation, as contrary to the underlying theory of the business records exception).

The obligation to report abuse, neglect, and dependency, in G.S. 7B-301, likely does not constitute a business duty to DSS for the purpose of qualifying a private person's statements to DSS under the business record exception. Reporting by a private person is not in the regular course of the person's responsibilities to DSS, as required by the rule.

**4. Opinions within business records.** Ordinarily, statements in business records are factual in nature, but Evidence Rule 803(6) also allows appropriate "opinions . . . or diagnoses." At a minimum, the opinion must meet the requirements for admissibility of opinion testimony, discussed in sections 11.9 and 11.10, below. *See In re J.S.B.*, 183 N.C. App. 192 (2007) (determining that the opinion in an autopsy report as to the cause of death as well as observations were admissible under the public records hearsay exception, which is similar to the business records exception); *State v. Galloway*, 145 N.C. App. 555, 565–66 (2001) (statement by a doctor in a hospital record that the patient had psychiatric problems was not admissible because the sources of information on which the doctor based the opinion were not reliable and the doctor was not qualified to render a psychiatric opinion).

In some circumstances, courts may be reluctant to admit opinions contained in business records even if they satisfy the minimum requirements for admission. According to Imwinkelried, the modern trend is to allow such evidence if the subject matter of the opinion is relatively simple and noncontroversial—for example, an entry in a hospital record listing physical symptoms such as blood pressure. The courts may be reluctant to admit an opinion within a business record if the opponent has a substantial need to cross-examine the declarant of the opinion, which is a function of two factors. The first factor is the opinion's complexity or subjectivity. When the opinion is highly evaluative, "the policy underlying the hearsay rule mandates that we afford the opponent an opportunity to cross-examine." IMWINKELRIED § 1220, at 12-59 to 12-60. The second factor is the importance of the issue in the case. "The more central the issue in the case, the more likely the court is to hold that the opponent is entitled to confront a witness rather than a document." *Id.* at 12-60; *see also* 2 MCCORMICK § 293, at 481–82 (federal version of Rule 803(6) [which is comparable to North Carolina's version] allows opinions and diagnoses within business records, but such statements may be inadmissible if they lack trustworthiness or their probative value outweighs their prejudicial effect under Evidence Rule 403; courts also may be reluctant to permit a verdict based on an opinion in a business record without allowing the opponent the opportunity to cross-examine the person who gave the opinion).

**5. Objections to business records.** The rules of evidence do not contain any special requirement for objecting to business records. A party may do so before trial by motion in limine or at trial by objection. Some local rules may contain a time limit on objecting, however. *See In re T.M.*, 187 N.C. App. 694, 697–701 & n.2 (2007) (because the respondent father failed to object to medical records by the deadline in the then-applicable Twelfth Judicial District local rules [deleted from the current version of the rules], the trial court admitted the records at the adjudication hearing over the respondent's objection that DSS had not established a proper foundation; the Court of Appeals did not specifically decide whether the local rules provided an appropriate basis for overruling the respondent's objection because the respondent could not show prejudice, but noted that the local rule was not intended to be an evidentiary rule but instead was designed to promote the efficient administration of justice); *In re J.S.*, 182 N.C. App. 79 (2007) (upholding, in a two-to-one decision, a local administrative discovery order requiring respondents to review DSS records within ten working days after receiving notice that records are available for review).

If the method and circumstances of preparation of the record do not satisfy the business records exception (for example, the record was not prepared in the regular course of business), the opponent may object to the entire record. If specific information within a business record is not admissible (for example, the information is hearsay from a person without a business duty to the organization or is inadmissible opinion), the opponent should object specifically to each item of information. Otherwise, the issue may be waived on appeal for failing to bring the objectionable evidence specifically to the attention of the trial court. See section 11.13.D, below.

## G. Rule 803(8): Official Records and Reports

Rule 803(8) excepts public records and reports from the hearsay rule. The use of the term "public" is somewhat misleading because the record does not need to be public in the sense that members of the public have a right to view it. For that reason, commentators refer to this exception as covering "official" records and reports.

The foundational requirements for official records are similar to those for business records, discussed in section 11.6.F, above. Because of this overlap, the exception has not arisen very often in juvenile or other North Carolina cases. *See In re J.S.B.*, 183 N.C. App. 192 (2007) (trial court allowed the admission of an autopsy report under the business records exception, while the appellate court upheld admission under the public records exception). For a brief discussion of laying a foundation for the admission of official records, see section 11.6.F.2(b), above (discussing official records within other records).

The principal reason for having a separate exception for official records appears to come from criminal cases. The exception prohibits the use of law enforcement reports and other investigative reports by the State against the defendant in a criminal case. *See* N.C. R. EVID. 803(8) & commentary (rule states this limitation and the commentary elaborates that if investigative reports are not admissible under the public records exception, they also are barred under the business records exception); *State v. MacLean*, 205 N.C. App. 247, 250–51 (2010) (holding that ministerial matters, such as fingerprints or photographs, are not subject to this limitation); John Rubin, *Evidence Rule 803(8) and the Admissibility of Police Reports*, UNC SCH. OF GOV'T: NORTH CAROLINA CRIMINAL LAW BLOG (Mar. 7, 2017) (discussing whether police reports inadmissible under Rule 803(8) may be admitted under other hearsay exceptions); 2 MCCORMICK § 296, at 497–501 (discussing the meaning of the limitation).

This limitation does not apply to the use of law enforcement reports in civil proceedings. As under the business records exception, however, hearsay within a law enforcement report or other official record still must satisfy another hearsay exception to be admissible. *See Wooten v. Newcon Transportation, Inc.*, 178 N.C. App. 698, 703–04 (2006) (finding a 911 report admissible in a civil workers' compensation proceeding where the report met the public records exception and the statements from a caller within the report met the present sense impression hearsay exception).

## H. Rules 803(24) and 804(b)(5): Residual Hearsay

Rules 803(24) and 804(b)(5) create a catch-all or "residual" exception to the hearsay rule, allowing the admission of a statement that does not satisfy an enumerated hearsay exception if the statement meets certain criteria.

**1. Comparison of rules.** Rules 803(24) and 804(b)(5) each create an exception for residual hearsay. The rules are identical, requiring that the proponent satisfy six requirements (discussed in subsection 3, below), except that Rule 804(b)(5) also requires that the declarant be unavailable to testify for his or her statement to be admissible. Although not explicitly a requirement for admission under Rule 803(24), unavailability is still a factor affecting admissibility under that rule. *See, e.g., In re F.S.*, 835 S.E.2d 465 (N.C. Ct. App. 2019) (trial judge erred in allowing social worker to testify about notes of child's statements to therapist and former social worker under Rule 803(24) where, among other things, DSS made no showing of unavailability of child, therapist, or former social worker). The cases state that the inquiry into the trustworthiness and probative value of a statement, two of the six requirements for admission under both rules, may be less strenuous under Rule 804 because, if the declarant is unavailable to testify, the need for admitting the evidence may be greater. *See* 2 BRANDIS & BROUN § 241, at 964; *State v. Garner*, 330 N.C. 273, 284 (1991); *see also State v. Smith*, 315 N.C. 76, 91–92 (1985) (cautioning that the trial judge must carefully scrutinize evidence when offered under Evidence Rule 803(24)). The cases also indicate that the availability of the witness remains a factor under the other requirements for admissibility. *See State v. Hollingsworth*, 78 N.C. App. 578, 580 (1985) (to be admissible under Rule 803(24) or 804(b)(5), evidence must be more probative than other evidence reasonably available; the availability of a witness is therefore a crucial factor under either exception because usually live testimony will be more probative on the point for which it is offered); *State v. Nichols*, 321 N.C. 616, 624–25 & n.2 (1988) (reason for the declarant's unavailability to testify is relevant to whether the statement is sufficiently trustworthy, a key factor under both residual exceptions).

**2. Unavailability.** Rule 804(a) lists five grounds for a finding of unavailability. Those most likely to arise in cases involving child witnesses in juvenile cases are as follows.

**(a) Physical or mental illness or infirmity.** Rule 804(a)(4) provides that unavailability includes situations in which the declarant is unable to testify because of a then-existing physical or mental illness or infirmity. Before finding a child witness unavailable on this basis, the court may need to determine whether various accommodations would enable the child to testify (discussed in section 11.2.B, above). If a witness is incompetent to testify, then the witness is unavailable within the meaning of Rule 804(a)(4). *In re Clapp*, 137 N.C. App. 14, 20 (2000).

A finding of incompetency to testify may bear on whether the witness's out-of-court statements are sufficiently trustworthy to be admissible under either residual hearsay exception. *Compare State v. Stutts*, 105 N.C. App. 557 (1992) (holding that a child's out-of-court statements were inadmissible under the residual hearsay exception where the trial court found the child unavailable as a witness on the ground that the child could not tell truth from fantasy), *with State v. Wagoner*, 131 N.C. App. 285, 290–91 (1998) (determining that the child's incompetence to testify satisfied the unavailability requirement but did not render her out-of-court statements too untrustworthy to be admitted under the residual hearsay exception).

Other cases addressing unavailability under Rule 804(a)(4) include: *State v. Carter*, 338 N.C. 569, 590–92 (1994) (trial judge did not err in finding the witness unavailable where the witness refused to testify and the witness's former psychiatrist testified that compelling her to testify would exacerbate her depression for which she had previously been hospitalized and could lead to suicide); *State v. Chandler*, 324 N.C. 172, 178–81 (1989) (4-year-old child victim was unavailable to testify when she was so overcome with fear that she was unable to respond to the prosecutor's questions even after the court allowed the mother to sit with the child while she attempted to testify).

Juvenile cases addressing unavailability under Rule 803(24) include: *In re F.S.*, 835 S.E.2d 465 (N.C. Ct. App. 2019) (trial judge erred in allowing social worker to testify about notes of child's statements to therapist and former social worker under Rule 803(24) where, among other things, DSS made no showing of unavailability of child, therapist, or former social worker); *In re W.H.*, 819 S.E.2d 617 (N.C. Ct. App. 2018) (trial judge's finding of trustworthiness was not contradicted by its basis for finding the daughters unavailable—that testifying would traumatize them and would cause them confusion and that there was a risk that they would not be truthful out of guilt and fear).

**(b) Refusal to testify.** Rule 804(a)(2) provides that a witness is unavailable if he or she persists in not testifying despite being ordered to do so by the court. As with other witnesses, for this ground of unavailability to apply the court must specifically order the child witness to testify and the child must refuse to do so. *See State v. Linton*, 145 N.C. App. 639, 645–47 (2001) (so holding). Hostility to the questions or questioner does not amount to a refusal to testify. *State v. Finney*, 358 N.C. 79, 80–84 (2004) (so holding).

**(c) Lack of memory.** Rule 804(a)(3) provides that a witness is unavailable if he or she testifies to a lack of memory about the subject matter of the out-of-court statement. This exception contemplates that the witness, including a child witness, take the stand and be subject to cross-examination. N.C. R. EVID. 804 commentary. If the witness remembers the incident or matter to which the statement refers, a lack of memory as to the details of the incident or matter does not make the witness unavailable. *See State v. Miller*, 330 N.C. 56, 60–62 (1991) (trial court erred in finding witnesses unavailable for lack of memory and admitting their statements under the residual hearsay exception where the witnesses testified that they remembered the incident; the witnesses were not unavailable for not being able to remember all of the details of the incident or for disagreeing with the detective's account of their out-of-court statements). The rationale for this ground of unavailability is that when the witness does not remember the subject matter of the statement, testimony about that subject is effectively "beyond reach." N.C. R. EVID. 804 commentary. One case has found that a lack of memory about the details of the out-of-court statement, as opposed to the subject of the statement, rendered the witness unavailable. This approach may not be in accord with the requirements of the rule. *See State v. Brigman*, 178 N.C. App. 78, 87–90 (2006) (holding that it was not an abuse of discretion for the trial court to find the children unavailable and to admit their statements where the children testified on voir dire that they had told their foster parents about the things the defendant had done to them but they could not remember what they said).

**3. Notice, trustworthiness, probative value, and other criteria.** For a statement to be admitted under Rule 804(b)(5), six conditions must be satisfied (in addition to the declarant being unavailable). The six conditions also apply to Rule 803(24) (although unavailability of the declarant is not an explicit requirement, as described in subsection 1, above). Under both rules, the trial judge must make findings on all six requirements. *See State v. Dammons*, 121 N.C. App. 61, 64 (1995) (requiring the trial court to make these six determinations for statements offered under Rule 804(b)(5)); *In re Gallinato*, 106 N.C. App. 376, 377–78 (1992) (error for the court not to make the findings under Rule 803(24); the rationale for this requirement is to ensure that the trial court undertakes serious and careful consideration of admissibility).

**(a) Conditions.** The six conditions that must be satisfied are:

- The proponent must give the adverse party written notice of intention to offer the statement and its particulars, including the name and address of the declarant, sufficiently in advance of offering the statement to provide a fair opportunity to meet the statement.
- The statement must not be specifically covered by any other hearsay exception.
- The statement must have circumstantial guarantees of trustworthiness equivalent to those of the specifically listed exceptions.
- The statement must be offered as evidence of a material fact.
- The statement must be more probative on the point for which it is offered than any other evidence procurable by reasonable efforts.
- Admission of the statement will best serve the purposes of the rules of evidence and the interests of justice.

*See State v. Smith*, 315 N.C. 76 (1985) (setting forth the six-part test).

**(b) Notice.** The cases have stressed the importance of proper notice, although they have allowed relatively short notice when the circumstances showed that the adverse party had sufficient time and information to meet the statement. *See State v. Carrigan*, 161 N.C. App. 256, 260–62 (2003) (noting that some North Carolina cases have found notice given at the beginning of trial to be sufficient when notice was effectively given earlier through oral notice or discovery; finding in this case that the proponent did not give sufficient notice when he first notified the other side of his intent to offer evidence under the residual hearsay exception at the beginning of trial); *In re Krauss*, 102 N.C. App. 112 (1991) (respondent had sufficient notice of content of children's statements offered under Rule 803(24); DSS had provided names and addresses of witnesses and some notes of expert to whom children made some statements); *In re Hayden*, 96 N.C. App. 77, 82 (1989) (holding evidence inadmissible under Rule 803(24) because no notice was given); *see also* 2 BRANDIS & BROUN § 241, at 969 & n.763 (collecting cases).

**(c) Trustworthiness.** In considering whether a statement has sufficient guarantees of trustworthiness, courts consider various factors. *See Idaho v. Wright*, 497 U.S. 805 (1990) (noting that courts have considered the spontaneity of statements, consistent repetition, the mental state of the declarant, the use of terminology unexpected of a child of similar age, and the lack of motive to fabricate); *State v. Isenberg*, 148 N.C. App. 29, 35–36 (2001) (quoting *State v. Wagoner*, 131 N.C. App. 285, 290 (1998)) (court should consider among other factors: "'(1) assurances of the declarant's personal knowledge of the underlying events, (2) the declarant's motivation to speak the truth or otherwise, (3) whether the declarant has ever recanted the statement, and (4) the practical availability of the declarant at trial for meaningful cross-examination'"). (The last factor was interpreted in *State v.*

*Nichols*, 321 N.C. 616, 624–25 & n.2 (1988), as requiring consideration of the reason for the witness's unavailability.)

A finding of trustworthiness is particularly important because it overcomes the presumption of unreliability of statements that are not within a specific hearsay exception. *State v. Dammons*, 121 N.C. App. 61, 65 (1995).

For application of the trustworthiness factor in cases involving child witnesses in North Carolina, see *State v. Deanes*, 323 N.C. 508 (1988) (upholding a finding that statements had sufficient circumstantial guarantees of trustworthiness); *State v. Blankenship*, 814 S.E.2d 901 (N.C. Ct. App. 2018) (trial judge erred in failing to make finding on trustworthiness, but appellate court conducted own review of the record and found sufficient guarantees of trustworthiness to allow admission of child's statements under Rule 804(b)(5)); *In re M.A.E.*, 242 N.C. App. 312 (2015) (trial judge found that certain statements were sufficiently trustworthy and admissible, including videotaped statements, and others were not; Court of Appeals upholds admission of statements); *State v. Brigman*, 178 N.C. App. 78 (2006) (upholding admission); *State v. Isenberg*, 148 N.C. App. 29, 35–36 (2001) (upholding admission); *State v. Wagoner*, 131 N.C. App. 285, 289–90 (1998) (child's incompetence to testify satisfied the unavailability requirement but did not render her statements to a social worker too untrustworthy to be admitted); *State v. Holden*, 106 N.C. App. 244, 251–52 (1992) (distinguishing *Stutts*, below, and finding that the trial court's isolated statement that the child seemed unable to understand the consequences of not telling the truth did not undermine the finding that the statements were sufficiently trustworthy to be admissible); *State v. Stutts*, 105 N.C. App. 557 (1992) (holding that the child's statements were inadmissible under the residual hearsay exception where the trial court found the child unavailable as a witness on the ground that the child could not tell truth from fantasy).

**4. North Carolina opinions on residual hearsay in juvenile cases.** The following published opinions in juvenile cases address the admissibility of statements under the residual hearsay exception in Evidence Rule 803(24).

*In re F.S.*, 835 S.E.2d 465 (N.C. Ct. App. 2019): Trial judge erred in allowing social worker to testify about notes of child's statements to therapist and former social worker under Rule 803(24). DSS made no showing of unavailability of child, therapist, or former social worker, and trial judge made no findings about trustworthiness or other conditions for admission.

*In re W.H.*, 819 S.E.2d 617 (N.C. Ct. App. 2018): DSS sent written notice of intent to offer daughters' statements from one week to seven months before various hearings; notice was adequate under Rule 803(24). Trial judge made sufficient findings of trustworthiness despite failing to address daughters' recantation at one of interviews. Trial judge's finding of trustworthiness was not contradicted by its basis for finding the daughters unavailable—that testifying would traumatize them and would cause them confusion and that there was a risk that they would not be truthful out of guilt and fear.

*In re M.G.T.-B*, 177 N.C. App. 771 (2006): Any error in admitting child's statements under Rule 803(24) was harmless, as evidence was sufficient to support finding of neglect.

*In re Gallinato*, 106 N.C. App. 376 (1992): Trial judge's failure to make findings to support admission of statements under Rule 803(24) required reversal.

*In re Krauss*, 102 N.C. App. 112 (1991): Respondent had sufficient notice of content of children's statements offered under Rule 803(24). DSS had provided names and addresses of witnesses and some notes of expert to whom children made some statements.

*In re Hayden*, 96 N.C. App. 77 (1989): Respondent failed to comply with notice requirement for admission of statements under Rule 803(24), and trial judge properly excluded child's statements.

## 11.7 Prior Orders and Proceedings and Judicial Notice

### A. Generally

**1. Ambiguity in judicial notice principles in juvenile cases.** Numerous North Carolina appellate decisions, discussed in this section, state that the trial court in a juvenile case may take judicial notice of prior proceedings in the same case. As one juvenile case observed, however, the extent to which the trial court actually may rely on prior proceedings is unclear. *See In re S.W.*, 175 N.C. App. 719, 725 (2006). The most troublesome question is the extent to which a trial court at an adjudication hearing, such as an adjudication hearing in a TPR case, may rely on prior abuse, neglect, and dependency proceedings, including disposition and review hearings at which the rules of evidence do not apply. Juvenile decisions on judicial notice have not clearly answered that question.

Many decisions, discussed further below, have bypassed close analysis of the permissible reach of judicial notice by relying on the presumption that the trial court disregarded any incompetent evidence in the judicially noticed matters and made an independent determination of the issues in the current proceeding. *See, e.g., In re D.M.R.*, 230 N.C. App. 598 (2013) (unpublished) (stating these principles and finding it immaterial that court copied language from its prior order because there were sufficient, properly supported findings to show grounds for termination); *In re J.W.*, 173 N.C. App. 450, 455–56 (2005) (stating these principles), *aff'd per curiam*, 360 N.C. 361 (2006); *In re J.B.*, 172 N.C. App. 1, 16 (2005) (to same effect).

Likewise, in determining whether the trial court's findings of fact were supported by competent evidence, several decisions have recited, without elaboration, that the trial court took judicial notice of aspects of prior proceedings. Although judicially noticed matters may provide support for a trial court's findings, *see, e.g., In re G.T.*, 250 N.C. App. 50 (2016), *aff'd per curiam*, 370 N.C. 387 (2017), these decisions did not evaluate whether the taking of judicial notice was proper. Some trial courts, in an effort to avoid possible error, have added a general qualification when taking judicial notice—for example, one trial court added "the caveat that the court 'affords each such document the appropriate weight, taking into consideration the differing standards of proof which govern the hearing from which a particular Order was generated.'" *In re X.L.S.,* 806 S.E.2d 706 (N.C. Ct. App. 2017) (unpublished); *see also In re I.S.D.,* 797 S.E.2d 384 n.7 (N.C. Ct. App. 2017) (unpublished) (trial court took judicial notice of all orders in the case file "to the extent allowed by the North Carolina Court of Appeals").

Although many juvenile decisions do not resolve which aspects of prior proceedings are appropriate subjects of judicial notice, other juvenile decisions, discussed below, suggest that the appellate courts may limit consideration of prior proceedings. The remainder of this section suggests an approach consistent with those cases and established principles of judicial notice.

**2. Suggested approach.** To determine the extent to which the trial court may rely on prior proceedings, three basic questions should be addressed:

- First, what are the different aspects of prior proceedings that potentially could be considered? Prior proceedings may consist of orders and other entries in the court's records, findings and conclusions by the court, reports and other documentary evidence offered by the parties, and testimony by witnesses.
- Second, what are the appropriate legal principles governing consideration of the different aspects of prior proceedings? While the juvenile cases have relied primarily on the doctrine of judicial notice, other doctrines, such as collateral estoppel and the rules on hearsay, may be more appropriate in some instances.
- Third, what is the impact of the information from prior proceedings? Some information may be binding, other information may be admissible but not binding, and other information may be inadmissible if the opposing party objects.

The discussion below addresses the different aspects of prior proceedings and suggests the appropriate treatment for each. The discussion leans more heavily on decisions outside the juvenile context than in other parts of this Chapter because those decisions more closely analyze the requirements for judicial notice and other doctrines regulating reliance on prior proceedings. The discussion also attempts to order the North Carolina decisions according to the categories identified below. The decisions themselves do not always characterize the information in that way. The approach below reflects the author's analysis of the controlling principles under North Carolina law. First, however, the discussion describes the doctrine of judicial notice because the juvenile decisions so often refer to it in considering prior proceedings.

---

**Note:** The discussion in this section concerns whether information from prior proceedings may be considered at adjudication. Because the rules of evidence do not apply at disposition and other non-adjudication hearings, a court at those hearings may have greater latitude in considering prior proceedings, just as it has greater latitude at non-adjudication hearings in considering evidence that would be inadmissible at adjudication. *See, e.g., In re R.A.H.,* 182 N.C. App. 52, 59–60 (2007) (at a permanency planning hearing, the court could take judicial notice of findings from a previous disposition hearing); *In re Isenhour,* 101 N.C. App. 550,

552–53 (1991) (in a custody review hearing under previous Juvenile Code provisions, the court could take judicial notice of matters in the file in considering the history of the case and conducting the current hearing); *see also State v. Smith*, 73 N.C. App. 637, 638–39 (1985) (at resentencing in a criminal case following appeal, at which rules of evidence did not apply, the court could consider evidence offered at the prior sentencing hearing).

### B. Definition of Judicial Notice

**1. Generally.** Evidence Rule 201 contains the general definition of judicial notice. It covers "adjudicative facts," meaning it allows a court to take judicial notice of a fact for the purpose of adjudicating the issues in the current case. N.C. R. EVID. 201(a) & commentary. The term "adjudicative fact" should not be confused with facts adjudicated in a previous proceeding, which may or may not be the proper subject of judicial notice (discussed in section 11.7.D, below).

For a fact to be subject to judicial notice, it must "be one not subject to reasonable dispute." N.C. R. EVID. 201(b). A fact is not subject to reasonable dispute if it either is "generally known within the territorial jurisdiction of the trial court" or "is capable of accurate and ready determination by resort to sources whose accuracy cannot reasonably be questioned." *Id.* For example, a court may take judicial notice of the time that the sun set on a particular date. *See State v. McCormick*, 204 N.C. App. 105 (2010); *see also In re N.J.M.G.*, 822 S.E.2d 326 (N.C. Ct. App. 2019) (unpublished) (Court of Appeals took judicial notice that Duplin County is two counties away from New Hanover County and is separated by Pender County). The fact to be noticed also must be relevant to the issues in the case as provided in Evidence Rule 401, the general rule on relevance.

The court may not take judicial notice of a disputed fact. *See Crews v. Paysour*, 821 S.E.2d 469, 473 n.1 (N.C. Ct. App. 2018)). It may not take judicial notice of a matter that is not generally known within the territorial jurisdiction of the trial court. *See In re E.G.M.*, 230 N.C. App. 196 (2013) (in case involving Indian Child Welfare Act, court declines to take judicial notice of memorandum of agreement purporting to give state court subject matter jurisdiction). Nor may it take judicial notice of a matter that is not capable of accurate and ready determination by resort to sources whose accuracy cannot reasonably be questioned. *See State v. Anthony*, 831 S.E.2d 905 (N.C. Ct. App. 2019) (improper to take judicial notice of studies offered by State about alleged risk of recidivism of sex offenders).

When a court takes judicial notice of a fact on the ground that it is not subject to reasonable dispute, evidence of the fact need not actually be offered in the current proceeding. Further, in a civil case, the taking of judicial notice of a fact removes the fact "from the realm of dispute," and evidence to the contrary "will be excluded or disregarded." 1 BRANDIS & BROUN § 24, at 116–17; *see also* N.C. R. EVID. 201(g) ("In a civil action or proceeding, the court shall instruct the jury to accept as conclusive any fact judicially noticed").

A party is entitled on timely request to be heard about the propriety of the taking of judicial notice. *See State v. Anthony*, 831 S.E.2d 905 (judicial notice improper where matters were not offered in evidence or presented to the defendant or trial judge and were only discussed in argument). If not notified ahead of time, a request to be heard may be made after judicial notice is taken. N.C. R. EVID. 201(e).

**2. Judicial notice of prior proceedings.** North Carolina decisions often have observed that a trial court may take judicial notice of its prior proceedings.

In cases outside the juvenile context, judicial notice has usually been limited to matters of record, such as the date of filing of an action (discussed in section 11.7.C, below). These decisions are consistent with the approach to judicial notice in Evidence Rule 201 because they involved facts that were not subject to reasonable dispute and that required no further proof. Isolated decisions outside the juvenile context have departed from this approach, allowing the trial court to consider evidence offered in prior proceedings, but these cases do not appear to reflect the general approach to judicial notice; rather, they appear to have involved an effort by the court to fill inadvertent gaps in the evidence in those cases. The decisions also do not appear to impose the usual consequences of judicial notice because they treat the evidence as competent in the current proceeding but not as beyond dispute. *See, e.g., Long v. Long*, 71 N.C. App. 405, 408 (1984) (court could take judicial notice in an alimony suit of information about the husband's expenses from an order for alimony pendente lite [note that the decision may be superseded by later decisions, discussed in section 11.7.D.4, below]); *In re Stokes*, 29 N.C. App. 283 (1976) (court could take judicial notice of an order in an earlier delinquency case involving the same juvenile to show his age and the court's jurisdiction over the juvenile); *Mason v. Town of Fletcher*, 149 N.C. App. 636 (2002) (in a case in which the parties disputed the width of a right-of-way, the court could take judicial notice of a prior case involving the same parties and could consider evidence from that case about the width of the right-of-way).

In juvenile cases, the courts also have approved the taking of judicial notice of prior proceedings, relying on Evidence Rule 201. In most instances, however, the decisions do not appear to have used judicial notice in the sense meant under that rule. *See, e.g., In re J.W.*, 173 N.C. App. 450, 455–56 (2005) (referring to Evidence Rule 201 but suggesting that the noticed matters were disputed and subject to further proof by stating that the trial court was presumed to have disregarded any incompetent evidence and had to make an independent determination), *aff'd per curiam*, 360 N.C. 361 (2006).

---

**Note:** If the taking of judicial notice of prior proceedings is impermissible in part, the objecting party may need to specify the objectionable part; an objection to the taking of judicial notice of all of the proceedings may be insufficient. *See generally* 1 BRANDIS & BROUN § 19, at 96 (so noting for objections to testimony or documents that are inadmissible in part). If the judge sustains an objection to the taking of judicial notice of all of the proceedings, the offering party would need to specifically reoffer the unobjectionable parts of the proceedings. *Id.*

A party requesting judicial notice of prior proceedings may waive objection to the matters noticed. *See generally In re D.T.N.A.*, 250 N.C. App. 582 (2016) (in reversing order terminating parental rights, court noted that permanency planning order, of which trial court took judicial notice, included findings that respondent's multiple drug screens were all negative); *see also Riopelle v. Riopelle*, 833 S.E.2d 258 (N.C. Ct. App. 2019) (unpublished) (trial judge did not err in relying on prior orders where all parties, including respondent, stipulated and agreed to taking of judicial notice by judge).

## C. Orders and Other Court Records

**1. Summary.** This section addresses information entered or appearing in the court's records, such as the date of filing of a case or an order requiring a party to take certain action. It does not address findings and conclusions within a prior order; nor does it deal with reports or other evidence introduced in prior proceedings, which although they become part of the court file are not record entries in the sense discussed in this section.

A juvenile court may take judicial notice of prior orders by a court and other entries in court records in the sense used here. In a TPR case, for example, it would be appropriate for a trial court to take judicial notice of a prior permanency planning order changing the permanent plan from reunification to adoption. The fact of the prior order and the directives within it are not subject to reasonable dispute and require no further proof to establish them, as contemplated by Evidence Rule 201.

**2. Judicial notice of record entries.** North Carolina decisions have routinely approved the taking of judicial notice of entries in court records. Decisions have done so, for example, to determine the chronology of litigation, such as the timeliness of a summons or the filing of an appeal. *See, e.g., In re McLean Trucking Co.*, 285 N.C. 552, 557 (1974) (court could determine the chronology of litigation by taking judicial notice of docketed records); *Gaskins v. Hartford Fire Ins. Co.*, 260 N.C. 122, 124 (1963) (court could determine whether a complaint was filed within the time permitted for submitting a claim of loss by taking judicial notice of the filing date of the complaint); *Massenburg v. Fogg*, 256 N.C. 703, 704 (1962) (docketing of appeal); *Harrington v. Comm'rs of Wadesboro*, 153 N.C. 437 (1910) (issuance of summons); *In re M.G.S.*, 803 S.E.2d 665 (N.C. Ct. App. 2017) (unpublished) (appellate court took judicial notice that another state's law assigns role of terminating parental rights to courts); *In re S.D.*, 243 N.C. App. 65, 70 n.3 (2015) (appellate court took judicial notice of official records showing that father was serving active time in prison during period in question); *State v. King*, 218 N.C. App. 384 (2012) (appellate court could take judicial notice of clerk's records showing amount of fine and costs paid by defendant); *Slocum v. Oakley*, 185 N.C. App. 56 (2007) (in determining a motion to dismiss the plaintiffs' lawsuit for failure to prosecute, the court could take judicial notice of the plaintiffs' previous dismissal of a related case and other documents in the court's files showing the failure to prosecute the prior case).

Decisions also have allowed judicial notice of the entry of orders to show the existence of the order and its terms. *See, e.g., State v McGee*, 66 N.C. App. 369 (1984) (magistrate's contempt order was properly admitted in evidence because the court could have taken judicial notice of the order, without its being offered into evidence, to determine whether the magistrate had the authority to hold the defendant in contempt; contempt order was reversed, however, where the State relied solely on statements in the magistrate's order and offered no independent evidence of acts of contempt).

Juvenile decisions likewise have allowed judicial notice of the entry of orders and other record entries in prior proceedings. These decisions are consistent with North Carolina decisions on judicial notice outside the juvenile context. *See, e.g., In re D.K.*, 227 N.C. App. 649 (2013) (unpublished) (trial court took judicial notice of decretal portions of prior orders and made findings about respondent's failure to comply); *In re D.B.G.*, 222 N.C. App. 854 (2012) (unpublished) (stating that trial judge could take judicial notice of prior orders since it is presumed that judge disregarded incompetent evidence; court found that judge relied on prior orders primarily for procedural history); *In re F.H.*, 209 N.C. App. 470 (2011) (unpublished) (taking judicial notice of terms of prior visitation order); *In re A.S.*, 203 N.C. App. 140 (2010) (Court of Appeals stated that it could take judicial notice of its prior decision in finding that the trial court on remand relied on a finding that the Court of Appeals had disavowed); *In re S.W.*, 175 N.C. App. 719, 725–26 (2006) (court could take judicial notice of the entry of prior orders terminating the mother's parental rights to three other children); *In re Stratton*, 159 N.C. App. 461, 462–63 (2003) (court could take judicial notice of a termination order to determine whether the current appeal was moot); *In re Williamson*, 67 N.C. App. 184, 185–86 (1984) (court could take judicial notice of a custody order to determine whether the current appeal was moot).

A number of juvenile decisions state generally that the trial court may take judicial notice of prior orders, but they do not identify the parts of the order being noticed or the purpose for which they could be used. *See, e.g., In re S.D.J.*, 192 N.C. App. 478, 487–88 (2008) (stating generally that a court may take judicial notice of prior orders, but also stating that the court is presumed to have disregarded incompetent evidence within the noticed matters). These decisions provide little guidance on the appropriate scope of judicial notice.

### D. Findings and Conclusions by Court

**1. Summary.** This section deals with findings and conclusions from a prior proceeding, such as a determination at an adjudication hearing that a child is neglected or a finding at a review hearing that a parent is not making progress on certain matters. While judicial notice can establish that a particular record *is* the record of prior proceedings (as discussed in the preceding section), the applicable doctrine for considering findings and conclusions from orders in that record is ordinarily *not* judicial notice in the sense meant by Evidence Rule 201. *See generally U.S. v. Zayyad*, 741 F.3d 452, 464 (4th Cir. 2014) ("[f]acts adjudicated in a prior case, or in this instance, a prior trial in the same case, do not meet either test of indisputability in [Federal Evidence] Rule 201(b)") (citation omitted); 1 STEPHEN A. SALTZBURG ET AL., FEDERAL RULES OF EVIDENCE MANUAL § 201.02[3], at 201-8 to 201-9 (11th ed. 2015) (explaining that a court may take judicial notice that a judgment was entered or that findings of fact were made, but "the truth of these . . . findings are not proper subjects of judicial notice"); N.C. R. EVID. 201 commentary (noting that N.C. Evidence Rule 201(b) is substantively the same as Federal Evidence Rule 201(b)).

The applicable doctrines and their impact appear to be as follows:

- The court may consider findings and conclusions from orders in prior proceedings if collateral estoppel applies, in which case the findings and conclusions are binding in a

later proceeding. Collateral estoppel applies to findings from prior adjudication hearings but not to findings from non-adjudication hearings.
- Under the rules of evidence, when collateral estoppel does not apply, prior judgments and orders ordinarily are not admissible as evidence of the facts found. Nevertheless, North Carolina opinions in juvenile cases may allow a court at adjudication to consider findings of fact from prior non-adjudication hearings. The opinions are unclear, however, about the circumstances in which such findings may be considered and the weight that may be given them.
- Formal concessions in prior proceedings, such as stipulations of fact, are likely binding in later proceedings against the party who made the concession or entered into the stipulation.

**2. Collateral estoppel.** The doctrines of res judicata and collateral estoppel permit consideration of findings from prior proceedings because their very purpose is to preclude a party from relitigating claims or issues decided in prior proceedings. Most relevant to juvenile cases is the doctrine of collateral estoppel (or issue preclusion), which bars the parties "'from retrying fully litigated issues that were decided in any prior determination and were necessary to the prior determination.'" *In re N.G.*, 186 N.C. App. 1, 4 (2007) (quoting *In re Wheeler*, 87 N.C. App. 189, 194 (1987)), *aff'd per curiam*, 362 N.C. 229 (2008).

When applicable, the effect of collateral estoppel is comparable to judicial notice, removing the matter from further dispute, but it is misleading to use the term "judicial notice" because it does not adequately identify the requirements for collateral estoppel. *See generally In re C.D.A.W.*, 175 N.C. App. 680, 686–87 (2006) (respondent objected to the court's taking of judicial notice of prior findings, but the court observed that the "basis of respondent's objection is that petitioner should not have the benefit of collateral estoppel with respect to previous findings of fact not determined by the requisite standard of proof required in a termination of parental rights proceeding"; the respondent showed no prejudice in this case), *aff'd per curiam*, 361 N.C. 232 (2007). It would be appropriate, however, for a court to take judicial notice of a prior order for the purpose of establishing the prerequisites of collateral estoppel. *See Eagle v. Johnson*, 159 N.C. App. 701 (2003) (so holding for related doctrine of res judicata).

**3. Prior adjudication findings and conclusions.** Juvenile cases have recognized that the trial court may rely on a prior determination of abuse or neglect in a later TPR case to show the occurrence of prior abuse or neglect. The prior finding or determination is conclusive as to the condition of the child at that time (although it is not conclusive on the question of whether the parents' rights should be terminated because the court still must consider the circumstances since the time of the adjudication as well as the relevant actions or inactions of each parent). *See In re N.G.*, 186 N.C. App. 1, 4–5 (2007), *aff'd per curiam*, 362 N.C. 229 (2008); *In re A.K.*, 178 N.C. App. 727 (2006) (based on collateral estoppel, the court could rely on a prior adjudication of neglect of one child of the parents in determining in a later case whether another child of the same parents was neglected; the prior adjudication was insufficient alone, however, to establish that the second child was neglected); *see also In re D.N.M.G.*, 245 N.C. App. 130 (2016) (unpublished) (holding that it was proper for trial court in termination of parental rights proceeding to rely on neglect adjudication and supporting findings; court rejects argument that trial court erroneously applied findings from review proceedings to prove grounds for termination, finding that trial court received unrebutted live testimony at termination hearing); *In re G.N.*, 217 N.C. App. 399 (2011) (unpublished) (father was estopped from contesting adjudication of neglect based on consent order; father's counsel signed order and did not object to order when offered at later proceeding).

Collateral estoppel also applies to adjudications adverse to DSS. *See In re F.S.*, 835 S.E.2d 465 (N.C. Ct. App. 2019) (DSS was collaterally estopped from arguing that mother's hospitalizations showed risk of harm to child where issue was fully litigated and court's previous findings showed no nexus of harm or substantial risk of harm; collateral estoppel did not preclude trial judge from adjudicating subsequent allegations and events).

Some cases explicitly refer to the doctrine of collateral estoppel, while others state that a determination of abuse or neglect is admissible in a later proceeding. *See, e.g., In re Ballard*, 311 N.C. 708, 713–14 (1984); *In re J.H.K.*, 215 N.C. App. 364, 368 (2011); *In re Brim*, 139 N.C. App. 733, 742 (2000); *In re Byrd*, 72 N.C. App. 277, 279 (1985). The result appears to be the same. The prior determination at adjudication establishes the matter found for purposes of the subsequent proceeding. *See In re Wheeler*, 87 N.C. App. 189, 194 (1987) (noting similarities in the two approaches).

When collateral estoppel applies, a court may rely on the ultimate conclusion reached in the prior proceeding (for example, that a child was abused) as well as subsidiary findings (for example, that a parent had engaged in a sexual act with the child). *See id.* (prior finding of sexual abuse of children by father had been fully litigated and was necessary to adjudication of abuse).

**4. Prior findings and conclusions from non-adjudication proceedings.** Perhaps the most perplexing aspect of judicial notice in juvenile cases is the treatment of prior findings and conclusions from non-adjudication proceedings. The issue requires consideration of collateral estoppel principles, rules of evidence, and juvenile caselaw.

(a) **Collateral estoppel inapplicable.** The decisions discussed in 3., above, indicate that for collateral estoppel to apply to findings from a prior proceeding, the findings must have been based on clear and convincing evidence, the standard applicable to findings at adjudication. *See In re N.G.*, 186 N.C. App. 1, 9 (2007) (holding that the doctrine of collateral estoppel permits trial courts to rely only on those findings of fact from prior orders that were established by clear and convincing evidence), *aff'd per curiam*, 362 N.C. 229 (2008); *In re A.K.*, 178 N.C. App. 727, 731–32 (2006) (to same effect).

Under this principle, collateral estoppel would not apply to findings from non-adjudication hearings at which the clear and convincing evidence standard does not apply. *See also In re K.A.*, 233 N.C. App. 119, 125–28 & n.4 (2014) (trial court erred in abuse, neglect, and dependency proceeding by applying doctrine of collateral estoppel to prior civil custody proceedings because proceedings involved different burdens of proof—preponderance of the evidence in civil custody case versus clear and convincing evidence at adjudication in abuse, neglect, and dependency case; court also rejected argument that juvenile decisions allow trial judge to take judicial notice of facts in prior disposition orders subject to lower evidentiary standard, stating that taking judicial notice of the existence of an order or a disposition in an order "is not the same thing as taking judicial notice of each of the facts resolved in that order"); *In re J.S.B.*, 183 N.C. App. 192, 202–03 (2007) (judgment in a civil action is not admissible in subsequent criminal prosecution although exactly the same questions are in dispute because, among other reasons, the standard of proof in the civil action is lower).

Collateral estoppel likely would not apply even if the trial court at a non-adjudication hearing applied a clear and convincing evidence standard of proof. The court's decisions in *In re N.G.* and *In re A.K.*, cited above, reflect an unwillingness to accord collateral estoppel effect—that is, to bar a party from litigating an issue—based on findings from non-adjudication hearings. Collateral estoppel principles do not apply to bar a party from litigating an issue unless he or she had a full and fair opportunity to litigate that issue in a prior proceeding. *See Allen v. McCurry*, 449 U.S. 90, 95 (1980) (recognizing that "the concept of collateral estoppel cannot apply when the party against whom the earlier decision is asserted did not have a 'full and fair opportunity' to litigate that issue in the earlier case"); *Blonder-Tongue Lab., Inc. v. Univ. of Ill. Found.*, 402 U.S. 313, 329 (1971) (recognizing due process basis for the requirement); *In re N.G.*, 186 N.C. App. at 4 (recognizing that doctrine of collateral estoppel operates to preclude parties from retrying "fully litigated issues"), *aff'd per curiam*, 362 N.C. 229 (2008). Because of the reduced procedural protections at non-adjudication hearings, findings from those hearings would not appear to be an appropriate basis for collateral estoppel even if the trial court found that clear and convincing evidence supported the findings. *See In re J.C.M.J.C.*, 834 S.E.2d 670 (N.C. Ct. App. 2019) (questioning reliance at adjudication on findings from prior nonsecure custody hearing; although subject to the clear and convincing standard of proof, nonsecure custody hearing lacks the procedural safeguards for adjudications); *see also Wells v. Wells*, 132 N.C. App. 401, 409–15 (1999) (in an alimony case, collateral estoppel did not preclude wife from relitigating at the final alimony hearing issues ruled on in interim postseparation support hearing in the same case; the court notes the relaxed rules of evidence, the lack of a right to appeal, and other characteristics distinguishing interim and final hearings); *accord Langdon v. Langdon*, 183 N.C. App. 471, 474 (2007).

---

**Note:** The cases do not distinguish between TPR proceedings by petition, which initiates a new case, and TPR proceedings by a motion in the cause, which is part of an ongoing case; however, the result would appear to be the same. In both instances the findings from prior non-adjudication hearings would not appear to be binding at adjudication. *See also* 18 JAMES WM. MOORE ET. AL., MOORE'S FEDERAL PRACTICE § 134.20[1], at 134-52.3 (3d ed. 2018) (collateral estoppel principles apply to relitigation of an issue after final judgment; doctrine of the law of the case is similar for issues decided at various stages of the same litigation).

---

**(b) Hearsay restrictions.** If collateral estoppel does not apply, findings and conclusions within a prior judgment are ordinarily inadmissible in a later proceeding subject to the North Carolina Rules of Evidence. The principal reason is that they are a form of hearsay—

statements made outside the current proceeding, offered as evidence of the truth of those statements. See section 11.5.C, above (discussing the definition of hearsay). "It is chiefly on this ground that, except where the principle of *res judicata* [or the related principle of collateral estoppel] is involved, the judgment or finding of a court cannot be used in another case as evidence of the fact found." 2 BRANDIS & BROUN § 197, at 805; *see also Reliable Props., Inc. v. McAllister*, 77 N.C. App. 783, 787 (1985) ("North Carolina law has long prohibited the use of a previous finding of a court as evidence of the fact found in another tribunal. This practice remains the same under the new evidence code."); *cf. Bumgarner v. Bumgarner*, 231 N.C. 600, 601 (1950) (facts found on a motion for alimony pendente lite, a preliminary proceeding in an alimony action, "are not binding on the parties nor receivable in evidence on the trial of the issues").

Findings from a previous judgment are admissible in a later proceeding if the judgment comes within a hearsay exception. *See generally* N.C. R. EVID. 802 ("Hearsay is not admissible except as provided by statute or by these rules."). North Carolina's evidence rules contain one hearsay exception for prior judgments. *See* N.C. R. EVID. 803(23) & commentary (exception applies to "[j]udgments as proof of matters of personal, family or general history, or boundaries, essential to the judgment, if the same would be provable by evidence of reputation"; the commentary notes the need for having an exception because judgments generally cannot be used to prove facts essential to a judgment except where the principle of res judicata applies).[2]

Because this hearsay exception ordinarily would not apply in juvenile cases, findings from non-adjudicatory hearings, such as nonsecure custody or disposition hearings, would not

---

[2] When it enacted the rules of evidence, North Carolina chose not to include a second hearsay exception, patterned after Federal Rule of Evidence 803(22), for criminal convictions. The federal hearsay exception allows use of a judgment of conviction to prove "any fact essential to sustain the judgment" in the circumstances described in the exception. Because North Carolina omitted this exception, a criminal conviction is generally not admissible in a later case to establish the facts of the offense underlying the conviction unless principles of res judicata or collateral estoppel apply. *See* N.C. R. EVID. 803 commentary (noting that exception (22) is reserved for future codification because North Carolina did not adopt the equivalent of the federal hearsay exception for judgments of conviction); *Carawan v. Tate*, 53 N.C. App. 161, 164 (1981) (holding that evidence of conviction of assault was not admissible in a civil action to establish the commission of the assault), *aff'd as modified on other grounds*, 304 N.C. 696 (1982); *see also* 2 BRANDIS & BROUN § 197, at 805 n.74 (collecting cases). *But see Little v. Little*, 226 N.C. App. 499 (2013) (finding it unnecessary to determine whether plaintiff in action for domestic violence protective order could rely on non-mutual offensive collateral estoppel as basis for using defendant's prior assault conviction to establish that defendant engaged in acts of domestic violence against her; judge in criminal case entered prayer for judgment continued, which was not final judgment); *Burton v. City of Durham*, 118 N.C. App. 676 (1995) (allowing defendant city in civil rights action to rely on non-mutual defensive collateral estoppel as basis for using plaintiff's prior conviction of assault on officer to preclude plaintiff from relitigating certain issues).

Other grounds may still allow use of a criminal conviction or aspects of it. For example, the fact of conviction, as opposed to the facts underlying the conviction, may be used to impeach a witness or, in juvenile cases, to show a basis for abuse designated in the Juvenile Code. See section 11.8.D.3, below (discussing this basis of admissibility of a prior conviction). A guilty plea, being an admission, generally would be admissible in a later civil action against the party who entered the plea. See section 11.6.B, above (discussing hearsay exception for admissions of party-opponent); *see also* Michael G. Okun & John Rubin, *Employment Consequences of a Criminal Conviction in North Carolina*, POPULAR GOV'T, Winter 1998, at nn.64–66 and accompanying text (1998) (discussing the admissibility of a guilty plea as opposed to a conviction). But see section 11.8.D.3, below (explaining that when a party is relying on Evidence Rule 404(b) to show another crime, wrong, or act, the proponent generally may not rely on a criminal conviction).

appear to be admissible under the rules of evidence at an adjudicatory hearing. This result would not preclude a party from offering testimony or other admissible evidence on the issues that were the subject of non-adjudicatory findings—for example, evidence of the condition of a parent's home or evidence that a parent had or had not taken certain steps directed by the court.

**(c) A different theory of admissibility.** A number of juvenile cases state that a court may take judicial notice of findings from non-adjudicatory hearings, such as disposition hearings. *See, e.g., In re M.N.C.*, 176 N.C. App. 114, 120–21 (2006) (in a TPR case, permitting the court to take judicial notice of prior findings on the respondent's progress in completing remedial efforts ordered at prior review hearings); *In re Johnson*, 70 N.C. App. 383, 388 (1984) (in a TPR case, noting that the trial court reviewed prior orders detailing the parents' lack of progress between the initial juvenile petition and TPR order). The decisions do not hold that such findings have collateral estoppel effect. Nor do they appear to use the term judicial notice in the sense meant by Evidence Rule 201—that is, as establishing the prior findings as conclusive for purposes of the later proceeding. At most, the cases may allow a court at adjudication to consider prior non-adjudicatory findings. In other words, the findings may be admissible but not binding or determinative; however, the matter is not settled.

The North Carolina Supreme Court's recent decision in *In re T.N.H.*, 831 S.E.2d 54 (N.C. S.Ct. 2019), illustrates this possibility. There, the Court held that at adjudication (in this instance, a TPR adjudication) a trial court may take judicial notice of findings from prior disposition orders (in this instance, about the respondent's lack of progress following a determination of neglect). The Court held that the trial court may do so even though the prior findings are based on a lower standard of proof than in the current proceeding. As in other juvenile cases referring to judicial notice, the decision raises several questions. First, the circumstances in which a court may consider prior non-adjudicatory findings is unclear. As in other juvenile cases, *T.N.H.* falls back on the often-stated principle that the trial judge is presumed to have disregarded incompetent evidence and relied on competent evidence only. Second, the weight that may be given prior non-adjudicatory findings, to the extent admissible, is unclear. The Court in *T.N.H.* states that the trial court may rely in its TPR findings on prior disposition findings but recognizes that the trial court still must make an independent determination. Reviewing the evidence in support of the TPR findings in *T.N.H.*, the Court upheld them in light of other permissible evidence, including prior stipulations by the respondent (binding on the respondent, as discussed in 5., below), findings from a prior adjudication (subject to collateral estoppel, as discussed in 3., above), and live testimony by a social worker and respondent at the TPR adjudication hearing. Last, the legal basis for admitting prior non-adjudicatory findings is unclear. *T.N.H.* relies on previous juvenile decisions stating that a trial court may take judicial notice of prior orders but, as in the cited decisions, does not articulate a rationale for admitting non-adjudicatory findings at a proceeding that is otherwise subject to the rules of evidence.

Another recent decision recognizes that basing adjudicatory findings on prior non-adjudicatory findings may be "problematic." *In re J.C.M.J.C.*, 834 S.E.2d 670, 677 (N.C.

Ct. App. 2019). There, the Court of Appeals found that the trial court's findings of fact from a nonsecure custody hearing were the sole evidentiary support for the great majority of its findings in a later adjudication order of neglect. Unlike the hearings in *T.N.H.*, the clear and convincing evidence standard applies at nonsecure custody hearings. Nevertheless, the Court found it significant that the usual rules of evidence do not apply at nonsecure custody hearings and the respondent has no right to appeal. The Court observed:

> There is thus no way to ensure that the findings in the "First Seven Day Hearing Order" [the nonsecure custody order] were based on evidence admissible for purposes of an adjudication. To allow the trial court to find adjudicatory facts simply by taking judicial notice of its prior findings in the nonsecure custody order risks insulating adjudicatory findings from appellate review and undermines the procedural safeguards for adjudications. *Id.*

The Court in *J.C.M.J.C.* questioned whether the trial court made the required independent determination of the facts and concluded in any event that the findings did not support the trial court's conclusions of law. *Id.* at 677 & n.8, *see also In re N.J.H.*, 820 S.E.2d 137 (N.C. Ct. App. 2018) (unpublished) (finding it improper for trial judge to incorporate findings from review hearings into order terminating parental rights without making an independent finding that they were supported by clear and convincing evidence).

Other opinions have considered these issues, but they also do not provide clear answers about the appropriate treatment of non-adjudicatory findings. *See In re Ballard*, 63 N.C. App. 580, 590 (1983) (Wells, J., dissenting) (dissent suggests that under due process requirements, a party might be permitted to offer prior findings as some evidence of issues previously heard, subject to rebuttal or refutation; dissent does not address impact of rules of evidence, and it is unclear whether the prior findings in question were made at an adjudicatory or non-adjudicatory hearing), *rev'd on other grounds*, 311 N.C. 708 (1984); *In re T.F.L.*, 243 N.C. App. 506 (2015) (unpublished) (observing that prior findings and orders were "broadly corroborative" of testimony at termination hearing); *In re C.M.G.*, 243 N.C. App. 505 n.2 (2015) (unpublished) (trial court found that different standard of proof at permanency planning hearing went to weight, not admissibility, of order; appellate court did not resolve issue, stating that trial court is presumed to have disregarded incompetent evidence in taking judicial notice of findings in prior orders).

**5. Formal concessions; stipulations of fact.** Formal concessions of a party during litigation, such as stipulations of fact, are considered "judicial admissions." *See In re I.S.*, 170 N.C. App. 78, 86 (2005); *see also* G.S. 7B-807(a) (allowing court to find from evidence, including stipulations, that allegations in abuse, neglect, and dependency proceeding have been proven by clear and convincing evidence). They remain in effect for the duration of the case, ordinarily "preventing the party who agreed to the stipulation from introducing evidence to dispute it and relieving the other party of the necessity of producing evidence to establish the stipulated fact." *In re I.S.*, 170 N.C. App. at 86 (quoting *Thomas v. Poole*, 54 N.C. App. 239, 241 (1981)); *see also In re T.N.H.*, 831 S.E.2d 54 (N.C. S.Ct. 2019) (respondent bound at

TPR proceeding by stipulations from earlier neglect adjudication); *In re A.K.D.*, 227 N.C. App. 58 (2013) (stipulation is judicial admission and binding, but stipulation as to question of law is generally "invalid and ineffective"); 2 BRANDIS & BROUN § 198, at 809–12 (describing effect of formal concessions and stipulations and circumstances in which they may not be binding).

If a stipulation is from a previous case, it may not preclude a party from litigating the issue in a subsequent case. For purposes of this discussion, however, whether an abuse, neglect, and dependency proceeding is considered a part of or separate from a later TPR proceeding may be inconsequential. In *In re Johnson*, 70 N.C. App. 383, 387–88 (1984), the court considered a prior abuse, neglect, and dependency case to be part of the same "controversy" as a later TPR case and held that a stipulation from the prior proceeding was a binding judicial admission in the later proceeding. If an abuse, neglect, and dependency case is considered separate from a TPR case, a stipulation from the prior case may still bar relitigation of the issue in the subsequent case based on the principle of "judicial estoppel." *See, e.g., Bioletti v. Bioletti*, 204 N.C. App. 270, 275 (2010) (doctrine of judicial estoppel, which applies to the same *or* related litigation, prevents a party from asserting a legal position inconsistent with one taken earlier in litigation). At the least, a stipulation from a prior case may constitute an "evidential admission," which is not conclusive in a later case but is still admissible. *See* 2 BRANDIS & BROUN § 203, at 829; *UNCC Props., Inc. v. Greene*, 111 N.C. App. 391, 395 (1993) (statement contained in an answer from another proceeding was evidential, not judicial, admission).

### E. Documentary Evidence, Court Reports, and Other Exhibits

**1. Summary.** This section deals with evidence offered in prior proceedings, including reports presented to the court. No established doctrine allows the trial court in one proceeding to take judicial notice of documentary evidence and other exhibits received in prior proceedings. The documentary evidence must satisfy the rules of evidence applicable to the current proceeding. Juvenile decisions, however, appear to allow the trial court to consider documentary evidence from prior proceedings, if admissible in the current proceeding, without the evidence being physically reoffered.

**2. Juvenile cases on documentary evidence.** Juvenile cases have stated that the trial court may take judicial notice of the underlying case file, including reports submitted to the court in prior disposition hearings. *See, e.g., In re W.L.M.*, 181 N.C. App. 518 (2007). It does not appear, however, that the decisions mean that the information in the reports is conclusively established, as under the traditional approach to judicial notice, or even that the information is admissible in the later proceeding. *See id.* (relying on the presumption that the trial court disregarded incompetent evidence in the files). Rather, it appears that the decisions mean that reports and other evidence received in a prior proceeding do not necessarily have to be physically reoffered into evidence to be considered by the trial court. *See generally In re J.M.*, 190 N.C. App. 379 (2008) (unpublished) (stating that the court at an adjudication hearing may consider prior proceedings but must evaluate the proceedings in accordance with the rules of evidence).

If this construction is correct, a party still may object to a court report and other documents that were received in a prior proceeding. Thus, a party may object to a document on the ground that the document does not meet the requirements for admission under the hearsay exception for business records or another hearsay exception. See section 11.6.F.2, above (discussing the requirements for business records and observing that reports to the court likely do not satisfy the requirements). If the document is admissible, a party also may have grounds to object to information within the document. See section 11.6.F.3, above (discussing admissibility of information within a business record).

## F. Testimony

**1. Summary.** This section addresses testimony from prior proceedings, including testimony from adjudication and non-adjudication hearings. Testimony from prior proceedings is hearsay if offered for the truth of the matter asserted in the testimony. It is improper for a trial court to admit testimony from a prior proceeding unless the testimony satisfies a hearsay exception or is offered for a purpose other than its truth, such as impeachment of a witness's current testimony by his or her prior inconsistent testimony.

**2. Hearsay nature of prior testimony.** A witness's testimony from a prior proceeding, if offered for its truth, is a form of hearsay because it consists of statements made outside the current proceeding. See section 11.5.C, above (discussing the definition of hearsay). Even when the testimony is admissible at the prior proceeding—for example, the testimony recounted the witness's own observations and did not consist of hearsay statements—the prior testimony itself is hearsay when offered for its truth and is inadmissible at a later proceeding unless it satisfies a hearsay exception.

Evidence Rule 804(b)(1) governs "former testimony" and applies to testimony given "at another hearing of the same or a different proceeding." The rule creates an exception for former testimony if two basic conditions are satisfied. First, the witness must be unavailable at the current proceeding. *See* N.C. R. EVID. 804(a) (stating the definition of unavailability); see also section 11.6.H.2, above (discussing unavailability). Second, the party against whom the former testimony is now offered must have had an opportunity and similar motive to develop the testimony at the prior proceeding. Testimony from a prior non-adjudication hearing, such as a review hearing, may not satisfy this second requirement because the rules of evidence do not apply at such hearings, limiting the opposing party's ability to address the testimony, and because the purposes of review hearings and adjudications differ, which may bear on the opposing party's incentive to address the testimony.

If the testimony at the prior proceeding was given by a person who is a party in a later proceeding—for example, a parent—the testimony would be admissible against that party as an admission of a party-opponent. *See In re K.G.*, 198 N.C. App. 405 (2009) (unpublished) (holding that statements made by respondent-parents at a prior hearing on a domestic violence protective order were admissible as admissions of party-opponents at adjudication in a neglect case). This exception would not permit a party to offer the party's own prior testimony at a later proceeding—for example, DSS could not rely on this exception to offer the prior testimony of one of its employees. See also section 11.6.B.3, above (discussing the application of the exception to admissions).

Decisions recognize that judicial notice is not a proper device for considering prior testimony. *See Hensey v. Hennessy*, 201 N.C. App. 56, 68–69 (2009) (in case involving domestic violence protective order, trial court could not take judicial notice of testimony from prior criminal proceedings; the facts that were subject of testimony must not reasonably be in dispute); *In re J.M.*, 190 N.C. App. 379 (2008) (unpublished) (testimony from a previous proceeding, when offered for truth of matter asserted, is hearsay and is not admissible at proceeding at which the rules of evidence apply unless it satisfies a hearsay exception; judicial notice may not be used as substitute for complying with hearsay restrictions on admissibility of former testimony).

## 11.8 Character and Prior Conduct

### A. Generally

"Character comprises the actual qualities and characteristics of an individual." 1 BRANDIS & BROUN § 86, at 279. Thus, a person may have a violent character or a law-abiding character or a truthful one. Three basic types of evidence are potentially admissible to show a person's character:

- specific acts by the person,
- opinion about the person, and
- the person's reputation in the community.

The admissibility of these different types of character evidence depends on the theory under which the evidence is offered. The theory of admissibility also controls other rules regulating character evidence, such as whether a party may elicit character evidence on cross-examination only or may offer extrinsic evidence as well.

The rules on character evidence rarely have been addressed in appellate decisions in juvenile proceedings, perhaps because evidence of a type similar to character evidence is admitted for noncharacter purposes. The discussion below first addresses the different theories of admissibility for character evidence and then discusses the theories of admissibility that potentially apply in juvenile proceedings. The discussion also addresses (in section 11.8.D, below) the admissibility of prior conduct for noncharacter purposes under Evidence Rule 404(b).

### B. Theories of Admissibility of Character Evidence

**1. Character directly in issue.** One theory of admissibility of character evidence is that a person's character is directly in issue. This theory applies in a narrow range of cases, "as in litigation to determine the custody of children when the fitness of one or both parents is in issue, or when the issue is the good moral character of an applicant for admission to the bar."

1 BRANDIS & BROUN § 86, at 279. When character is directly in issue, specific acts, lay opinion, and reputation are admissible. *See* N.C. R. EVID. 405(a), (b).

Evidence about character is still subject to general evidence requirements. Thus, the evidence must be relevant to the character issue to be decided—for example, marijuana use in high school may be considered irrelevant to fitness to practice law. *See generally* 1 BRANDIS & BROUN § 100, at 357 (observing that evidence of specific instances of conduct should be confined to those relevant to the trait at issue). The witness also must be qualified to testify about the matter. To testify to specific acts, the witness must have personal knowledge of the acts. To give an opinion about a person's character, the witness must know the person. To testify to reputation, the witness must know the person's reputation in the community. (Reputation testimony is a form of hearsay because the witness is testifying to what others in the community think about the person, but it is excepted from the hearsay rule by Evidence Rule 803(21). *See* 1 BRANDIS & BROUN § 96, at 335.) Opinion and reputation testimony also must be about matters of character, not factual information about a person's conduct. *See State v. Collins*, 345 N.C. 170, 173–74 (1996); *State v. Moreno,* 98 N.C. App. 642, 645–46 (1990) (explaining that "not using drugs" is a character trait akin to "sobriety," but "not dealing in drugs" is evidence of a fact and is not a character trait); *see also* JOHN RUBIN, THE ENTRAPMENT DEFENSE IN NORTH CAROLINA 70–71 & n.46 (UNC School of Government, 2001) (discussing the admissibility of opinion and reputation testimony). Testimony on character is subject to exclusion under Evidence Rule 403 if its probative value is substantially outweighed by the danger of prejudice, confusion of the issues, or considerations of undue delay or needless presentation of cumulative evidence. *See also* 1 MCCORMICK § 186, at 1132 (observing that the "pungency and persuasiveness" of character evidence declines as one moves from the specific to the general).

**2. Character to show conduct.** A second theory of admissibility is when character evidence is offered to show a person's conduct on a particular occasion. Ordinarily, character is inadmissible to prove conduct. *See* N.C. R. EVID. 404(a) ("Evidence of a person's character or a trait of his character is not admissible for the purpose of proving that he acted in conformity therewith on a particular occasion" except as otherwise provided).

Narrow exceptions exist. In a criminal case, the defendant may offer evidence of a pertinent trait of his or her own character or of the victim, and in rebuttal the State may offer evidence of that person's character. *See* N.C. R. EVID. 404(a)(1), (2) (describing this ground for admitting character evidence); N.C. R. EVID. 405(a) (describing the method of proving character for this purpose); *see also State v. Walston*, 367 N.C. 721 (2014) (holding in criminal case that trial court did not err in excluding opinion testimony about defendant's respectful attitude toward children because it was not sufficiently tailored to charges of unlawful sex acts; cites other decisions), *rev'g* 229 N.C. App. 141 (2013); *State v. Wagoner*, 131 N.C. App. 285, 292–93 (1998) (holding that evidence of the defendant's general psychological makeup was not a pertinent character trait in a prosecution for sexual assault). In either a civil or criminal case, a party also may offer evidence of a habit or routine practice of a person or organization to prove that the person or organization acted in conformity with that habit or practice. *See* N.C. R. EVID. 406.

**3. Credibility.** A third theory of admissibility is when character evidence is offered on a witness's credibility. *See* N.C. R. EVID. 404(a)(3). This theory is also an exception to the general rule that character may not be offered to prove conduct. In this instance, character evidence bears on the witness's conduct on the stand—that is, whether the witness is telling the truth. Under this theory, evidence is limited to the witness's character for truthfulness or untruthfulness. *See* N.C. R. EVID. 405(a), 607, 608, 609. Under these rules, a lay witness may give an opinion about the character for truthfulness of another person, including a child, if the person's character for truthfulness has been attacked, but neither a lay nor an expert witness may testify that a person is telling or told the truth. Compare sections 11.9.B.4, 11.10.D.1, below (discussing this limit on opinion testimony).

**4. Opening the door.** Last, character evidence may be offered when a party opens the door through the testimony he or she offers. The admissibility of evidence under this theory depends on the circumstances of the case. *See, e.g., State v. Garner*, 330 N.C. 273, 287–90 (1991).

### C. Is Character Directly at Issue in Juvenile Cases?

It does not appear that any North Carolina cases have addressed the issue in juvenile cases, but character is likely directly at issue at disposition in both abuse, neglect, and dependency cases and termination of parental rights cases. *See generally* MYERS § 8.02[B]. The focus of the dispositional phase is the best interest of the child, which necessarily is bound up with a determination of the parent's fitness. *See Adoption of Katharine*, 674 N.E.2d 256, 258 (Mass. App. Ct. 1997).

One writer posits that the character of the parent also could be considered at issue at adjudication because the petitioner is seeking to prove what happened in the past to protect the child in the future and evidence of parental character is relevant in this regard. *See* MYERS § 8.02[B]. The argument is not an exact fit, however, with the issues to be resolved at adjudication in North Carolina juvenile cases.

When the basis of alleged abuse is a discrete incident—for example, that a parent inflicted serious physical injury or committed a criminal act of a sexual nature—the issue to be decided is whether the incident occurred. In that kind of case, the rules prohibit evidence of the parent's character to show that the incident occurred (although evidence of the parent's past conduct may be admissible for a noncharacter purpose under Evidence Rule 404(b), discussed in section D., below).

When the allegations involve a broader inquiry into a parent's conduct—for example, when the basis of alleged neglect is that the juvenile has not received proper care or supervision or lives in an environment injurious to the juvenile's welfare—the question is closer. *See In re Mark C.*, 8 Cal. Rptr. 2d 856, 861–62 (Ct. App. 1992) (observing that the legislature intended to place character at issue "to some extent" when the allegation is that a caretaker's abuse of one child endangers another child). The North Carolina courts have permitted evidence of a parent's past conduct and behavior in a number of such cases, but they have not specifically analyzed whether the evidence is permissible because the parent's character is directly "in issue" or because the conduct is simply relevant evidence of the alleged abuse or neglect. *See* Chapter 6.3.D and 6.3.E (discussing cases showing evidence that may support a finding of abuse or neglect). The North Carolina courts may be reluctant to premise the admission of evidence of prior conduct on the theory that the parent's character is directly in issue because such an approach would permit a broad range of opinion and reputation testimony (discussed in section 11.8.B.1, above), not just evidence of specific conduct and behavior. If the basis of admissibility is relevance, evidence of past conduct would be admissible to the extent relevant to the type of abuse or neglect alleged. This would not necessarily be true for opinion or reputation testimony unless admissible on another ground.

### D. Rule 404(b) and "Bad Act" Evidence

**1. Applicability of rule.** Evidence Rule 404(b) prohibits evidence of a person's crimes, wrongs, or acts when offered "to prove the character of a person in order to show that he acted in conformity therewith." In other words, it prohibits evidence of other "bad acts" to show that a person had a propensity to commit the current act and therefore committed the act. Rule 404(b) permits evidence of other acts, however, if offered for a noncharacter purpose—that is, if the act is offered for a purpose other than the person's propensity to commit the current act. In juvenile cases, Rule 404(b) comes into play primarily when the basis of abuse or neglect is a person's alleged commission of a particular act, such as the infliction of serious injury or commission of a sex act against a child, and the issue is whether other acts by that person are admissible.

Rule 404(b) may not be the correct vehicle for analyzing "bad act" evidence when the alleged basis of abuse or neglect necessarily involves a broader inquiry into the parent's conduct. In such cases, a parent's prior conduct may be admissible without regard to Rule 404(b), either because the prior acts themselves are relevant evidence of abuse or neglect or because the parent's character is directly in issue, as discussed in section C., above. *See In re Deantye P.-B.*, 643 N.W.2d 194, 198–99 (Wis. Ct. App. 2002) (court observes that the "other acts" evidence statute in Wisconsin [which is similar to North Carolina's Rule 404(b)] prevents "fact finders from unnecessary exposure to character and propensity evidence in the context of determining whether a party committed an alleged act"; that concern is not applicable when a fact finder must determine "whether 'there is a substantial likelihood' that a parent will not meet conditions for the return of his or her children," which necessarily involves consideration of a "parent's relevant character traits and patterns of behavior"); *In re Allred*, 122 N.C. App. 561, 563–65 (1996) (respondent argued that Rule 404(b) barred evidence of prior orders finding neglect of her other four children; the court found that the evidence was relevant and admissible without determining whether the evidence needed to satisfy the other relevant purpose requirement of Rule 404(b)).

If Rule 404(b) applies, evidence of other acts would be admissible if offered for a noncharacter purpose relevant to the alleged basis of abuse or neglect. *See In re Termination of Parental Rights to Teyon D.*, 655 N.W.2d 752, 759–60 (Wis. Ct. App. 2002).

**2. Basic requirements for admission of other acts under Rule 404(b).** Numerous criminal cases have addressed the applicability of Rule 404(b). Review of those cases is beyond the scope of this discussion. Certain basic principles have emerged, which presumably would apply to juvenile cases.

- Rule 404(b) is considered a rule of inclusion in North Carolina, allowing evidence of other acts if offered for a relevant purpose and excluding the acts if their only probative value is to show the defendant's propensity to commit the act in question. *State v. Coffey*, 326 N.C. 268, 278–79 (1990). This formulation means that the list of possible relevant purposes in Rule 404(b)—motive, identity, knowledge, and the like—is not exhaustive. The proponent may offer evidence of other acts for purposes not specifically listed in Rule 404(b) as long as the purpose is relevant to an issue to be decided in the case and is not to show the defendant's character.
- The courts have set an outer limit on relevance, excluding other acts that are too dissimilar or too remote in time in relation to the current act. *See, e.g., State v. Al-Bayyinah*, 356 N.C. 150, 154–55 (2002).
- In prosecutions for sexual offenses, the courts have been "markedly liberal" in finding evidence of other sex acts to be for a relevant noncharacter purpose. *Coffey*, 326 N.C. at 279 (citation omitted). For a discussion of such cases, see Jeff Welty, *Special Evidentiary Issues in Sexual Assault Cases: The Rape Shield Law and Evidence of Prior Sexual Misconduct by the Defendant*, ADMINISTRATION OF JUSTICE BULLETIN No. 2009/04 (UNC School of Government, Aug. 2009).
- Evidence of other acts may be excluded if the probative value of the evidence is substantially outweighed by its prejudicial effect under Evidence Rule 403. *See State v. Smith*, 152 N.C. App. 514, 528 (2002) (trial court must engage in Rule 403 balancing in determining whether to admit evidence under Rule 404(b)); *see also State v. Hembree*, 368 N.C. 2 (2015) (cautioning trial courts to subject 404(b) evidence to strict scrutiny because of its dangerous tendency to mislead and raise spurious presumption of guilt; conviction reversed).
- If admitted for a noncharacter purpose, the factfinder must restrict consideration of the evidence to that purpose and not consider it for inadmissible purposes. *See* N.C. R. EVID. 105; *State v. Watts*, 370 N.C. 39 (2017) (reversing conviction for trial court's failure to instruct jury to limit its consideration of evidence admitted under Rule 404(b)).

**3. Form of proof; prior criminal proceedings.** A proponent must show the commission of other acts by admissible evidence. Thus, the proponent must offer live testimony by a person with personal knowledge of the acts or by hearsay within an exception, such as an admission by a party-opponent. *See* 1 IMWINKELRIED § 903, at 9-3. The other act need not have been the subject of a criminal proceeding. By its terms, Rule 404(b) applies to other "crimes, wrongs, or acts." When the other act has been the subject of criminal proceedings, however, the cases have limited the evidence that may be offered about the proceedings.

The other act may not be established by an arrest, indictment, or other charge. *See* 1 BRANDIS & BROUN § 98, at 351–52 (discussing this bar in the context of impeachment of a witness); *cf. State v. Bryant*, 244 N.C. App. 105 (2015) (recognizing that G.S. 15A-1221(b) prohibits entry of indictment, arrest warrant, and other charging documents into evidence).

Nor may the other act ordinarily be shown by the bare fact of conviction. *See* 1 BRANDIS & BROUN § 94, at 303–04; *State v. Wilkerson*, 356 N.C. 418 (2002), *rev'g per curiam for the reasons stated in the dissent* 148 N.C. App. 310 (2002) (dissent, adopted by the Supreme Court, states this rule and notes exceptions); *State v. Bowman*, 188 N.C. App. 635 (2008) (discussing exceptions but finding them inapplicable in the circumstances of the case). The proponent ordinarily must prove the acts underlying the charge or conviction through admissible evidence (as well as show that the acts are relevant to an issue to be decided in the case and not for character). *See also* Phil Dixon, *Rule 404 and Evidence of Prior Incarceration*, UNC SCH. OF GOV'T: NORTH CAROLINA CRIMINAL LAW BLOG (Feb. 21, 2017) (discussing *State v. Rios*, 251 N.C. App. 318 (2016), which held that the bare fact of incarceration is improper propensity evidence).

The existence of a criminal conviction is admissible, however, when the fact of the conviction itself is a basis for a finding of abuse or a ground for termination of parental rights. *See* G.S. 7B-101(1)d. (providing that the commission of a violation of specified statutes, such as first-degree rape under G.S. 14-27.2, is abuse); G.S. 7B-1111(a)(1) (providing that a juvenile is deemed abused for the purpose of a termination of parental rights proceeding if the court finds the juvenile to be abused within the meaning of G.S. 7B-101); *Curtis v. Curtis,* 104 N.C. App. 625, 628 (1991) (holding that the father's conviction of first-degree sexual offense against the minor child provided a basis for a finding of abuse).

An arrest or conviction also may be admissible if not offered to show commission of an act but for another purpose, such as why a parent was physically unable to care for a child. *See In re Termination of Parental Rights to Teyon D.*, 655 N.W.2d 752, 759–60 (Wis. Ct. App. 2002) (offenses and sentences were admissible to show why the mother had been unable to take responsibility for her children). A conviction also may be used to impeach a witness's testimony under Evidence Rule 609. *See also* Phil Dixon, *Cross-Examination on Pending Charges*, UNC SCH. OF GOV'T: NORTH CAROLINA CRIMINAL LAW BLOG (Oct. 31, 2017) (discussing right of defendant to cross-examine State's witnesses about pending charges to show bias).

For a further discussion of the admissibility of prior proceedings, see section 11.7, above.

### E. Rape Shield Law

Evidence Rule 412 modifies the customary rules on character evidence and evidence offered for noncharacter purposes in rape and sex offense cases, barring evidence of opinion and reputation testimony on character and allowing evidence of specific acts in limited instances. By its terms, the rule applies only to criminal cases, but the North Carolina courts have held that a trial court may (although apparently is not required to) apply the rule's restrictions to juvenile cases. *In re K.W.*, 192 N.C. App. 646, 648–49 (2008). Asking questions about matters covered by the rape shield law, without following the procedures in the law, could result in sanctions. *State v. Okwara*, 223 N.C. App. 166 (2012) (upholding finding of contempt against defense counsel).

For a discussion of North Carolina's rape shield law, see Jeff Welty, *Special Evidentiary Issues in Sexual Assault Cases: The Rape Shield Law and Evidence of Prior Sexual Misconduct by the Defendant*, ADMINISTRATION OF JUSTICE BULLETIN No. 2009/04 (UNC School of Government, Aug. 2009). Cases since release of that bulletin have recognized additional circumstances in which prior sexual conduct may be admissible if relevant; the evidence need not fall within one of the rule's enumerated exceptions. *See, e.g., State v. Martin*, 241 N.C. App. 602, 610 (2015); Shea Denning, *The Rape Shield Statute: Its Limitations and Recent Application*, UNC SCH. OF GOV'T: NORTH CAROLINA CRIMINAL LAW BLOG (Aug. 17, 2017). The trial court may exclude the evidence under the balancing test in Evidence Rule 403. *See State v. West*, 255 N.C. App. 162 (2017).

## 11.9 Lay Opinion

### A. Lay and Expert Testimony Distinguished

Two evidence rules distinguish the scope of lay and expert testimony.

**1. Rule 602 and the requirement of personal knowledge.** Evidence Rule 602 provides that a witness, other than an expert witness, may not testify to a matter unless the witness has personal knowledge of the matter. If a lay witness purports to describe facts that he or she observed, but the description actually rests on statements of others, the testimony is objectionable on the ground that the witness lacks personal knowledge of those matters. If the lay witness testifies directly to the statements of others, the admissibility of the testimony is then assessed in accordance with the rules on hearsay. 1 MCCORMICK § 10, at 72–73. An expert witness, in contrast, may base an opinion on facts or data that are not within his or her personal knowledge and are not admissible in evidence, if of a type reasonably relied on by experts in the particular field.

**2. Rule 701 and the allowance of inferences if rationally based on perception and helpful.** Evidence Rule 701 provides that a lay witness's testimony in the form of an opinion or inference is permitted if it is:

- rationally based on the perception of the witness and
- helpful to a clear understanding of the witness's testimony or a determination of a fact in issue.

These requirements both loosen and limit the scope of lay opinion testimony, allowing lay testimony in the form of an opinion but subject to greater restrictions than applicable to experts. The requirement that the opinion be based on the witness's "perception" reiterates that the testimony must be based on firsthand knowledge or observation. N.C. R. EVID. 701 commentary (so stating); *Duncan v. Cuna Mut. Ins. Soc'y*, 171 N.C. App. 403, 407–08 (2005) (generalized observations and opinions by a licensed social worker and substance abuse counselor about methadone use and abuse were not admissible because they were not based on personal knowledge and not offered as expert opinion). The rule loosens the distinction between fact and opinion, allowing the latter if "rationally" based on the witness's perception, but it does not permit opinion testimony that goes beyond rational inferences and requires special expertise. The requirement that the opinion be "helpful" does away with any notion that the opinion must be "necessary" to be admissible, while giving the court discretion to exclude opinion testimony that is unhelpful. *See* N.C. R. EVID. 701 commentary (so stating); *see generally* 2 BRANDIS & BROUN § 175, at 676; *see also In re Wheeler*, 87 N.C. App. 189, 195–97 (1987) (in a case involving termination of a father's parental rights, the court questioned the helpfulness and therefore the admissibility of the mother's opinion that adoption would be best for the children and the GAL's opinion that termination was in the children's best interest [for a discussion of the inadmissibility of opinions in the form of a legal conclusion, see section 11.10.D.2, below]).

## B. Examples of Permissible and Impermissible Lay Opinion

**1. Shorthand statements of fact, including statements about mental and emotional condition.** Many cases recognize that lay witnesses may testify in the form of a "shorthand expression of fact." *See generally* MOSTELLER § 10-2(A), at 10-2 (testimony under "the collective fact or shorthand rendition doctrine" is permissible because there are certain sorts of opinions and inferences that lay witnesses commonly draw, and it would be impractical to require that they describe in detail the subsidiary facts supporting their opinion); *State v. Davis*, 368 N.C. 794, 798 n.4 (2016) (reaffirming that such testimony is permissible).

Among other matters, a lay witness may testify about the mental or physical state of another person based on the witness's observations. *See, e.g., State v. Dills*, 204 N.C. 33 (1933) (finding it permissible for a witness to testify that the defendant was "drunk"); *State v. Wade*, 155 N.C. App. 1, 13–14 (2002) (quoting *State v. Brown*, 350 N.C. 193, 203 (1999)) (witness could testify to the "'instantaneous conclusions of the mind'" as to the defendant's mental state, "'derived from observation of a variety of facts presented to the senses at one and the same time'"; included in the witness's testimony was an opinion that the defendant was a "molester at heart," which gave the court "pause," but in light of other evidence the court found that the jury would probably not have reached a different result absent this testimony); *State v. Wagner*, 249 N.C. App. 445 (2016) (allowing witness's testimony in sexual assault case that she should have picked up on "red flags," which court characterized as shorthand label for unusual conduct that witness had observed by defendant with victim); *State v. Pace*, 240 N.C. App. 63 (2015) (allowing as shorthand statement of fact testimony by victim's mother about changes she observed in her daughter after assault); *State v. Kelly*, 118 N.C. App. 589, 594–97 (1995) (lay opinion on the emotional state of another is permissible and, in a case involving allegations of sexual abuse, parents could testify that their children seemed embarrassed or frightened or displayed other emotions); *see also State v. Waddell*, 130 N.C. App. 488, 500–502 (1998) (assuming the witness was not testifying in the capacity of an expert, she could give lay opinion that the child demonstrated oral and anal intercourse by manipulations of anatomical dolls; her testimony was a shorthand statement of fact), *aff'd as modified*, 351 N.C. 413 (2000) (child's statements to the witness were not admissible under the medical diagnosis and treatment exception, discussed in section 11.6.E, above).

**2. Lay opinion requiring special expertise.** Lay opinion about another's mental or emotional state (or other matters) may not cross into areas requiring scientific knowledge or other special expertise. *See State v. Solomon*, 815 S.E.2d 425 (N.C. Ct. App. 2018) (defendant's testimony about the relationship between his own mental disorders and criminal conduct was not relevant without additional foundation; such evidence required expert witness in compliance with rules of evidence); *State v. Storm*, 228 N.C. App. 272 (2013) (licensed clinical social worker could testify to her observations of defendant, but could not testify as lay witness that he "appeared noticeably depressed with flat affect," which was psychiatric diagnosis for which witness was not offered as expert); *State v. Kelly*, 118 N.C. App. at 594–97 (parents could not testify to behavioral patterns and characteristics of sexually abused children, which went beyond the perception of a non-expert); *State v. Hutchens*, 110 N.C. App. 455, 459–61 (1993) (family counselor who was not qualified as an expert could not give an opinion about the behavioral patterns of sexually abused children); *State v. Bowman*, 84 N.C. App. 238 (1987) (police officer, who had not been qualified as an expert, could not give an opinion that an 8-year-old child did not have sufficient information about sexuality to fantasize allegations of sexual abuse); *cf. State v. King*, 235 N.C. App. 187, 190–92 (2014) (although trial court did not formally qualify witness as expert in pediatric medicine and evaluation and treatment of child sex abuse, qualification was implicit in trial court's admission of witness's testimony about common behaviors of children who have suffered sexual abuse).

The North Carolina courts have stated that if a lay witness, "'by reason of opportunities for observation . . . is in a position to judge . . . the facts more accurately than those who have not had such opportunities,'" the witness's testimony may be admitted as lay opinion. *State v. Lindley*, 286 N.C. 255, 257–58 (1974) (citations omitted). Under this rationale, a witness may give what has been termed "skilled lay observer testimony." MOSTELLER, § 10-2(B), at 10-5 to 10-6. For example, by virtue of previous opportunities for observation, a witness who has become familiar with a person's voice or handwriting may give an opinion identifying the voice or handwriting. *Id.*

Some decisions have taken this principle further and have allowed, as lay opinion, testimony by someone with special training and experience in the subject. *See State v. Smith*, 357 N.C. 604, 610–13 (2003) (in a case in which a nurse did not have sufficient knowledge, training, or experience to testify as an expert about the effects of valium, it was nevertheless permissible for her to give a lay opinion about the typical effect of valium and her observation about whether the defendant exhibited those effects); *State v. Wallace*, 179 N.C. App. 710, 714–15 (2006) (based on his experience and training, a detective could give as lay opinion that if a child gives the same exact story each time, the child has been coached but in most cases the story will not be exactly the same each time; the court also found this testimony did not amount to improper opinion on the victim's credibility, discussed in subsection 4, below); *State v. Friend*, 164 N.C. App. 430, 437 (2004) (in a case in which an officer was not proffered as an expert witness, it was permissible for the officer to give a lay opinion about fingerprinting techniques and why it is rare to find useful prints).

These decisions may no longer be good law in light of amended Evidence Rule 702, which requires greater scrutiny of expert opinion. In *State v. Davis*, 368 N.C. 794 (2016), the State called a psychologist and mental health counselor as witnesses, who testified about their experiences treating victims of sexual abuse and the problems that victims experience, such as depression and anxiety. The Court of Appeals held that the testimony did not constitute expert opinion because it involved the witnesses' own experiences and observations. The Supreme Court reversed, recognizing that "when an expert witness moves beyond reporting what he saw or experienced through his senses, and turns to interpretation or assessment 'to assist' the jury based on his 'specialized knowledge,' he is rendering an expert opinion." *Id.* at 798. The outcome in *Davis* was that the testimony was subject to the discovery requirements on disclosure of expert opinion. *Accord State v. Broyhill*, 254 N.C. App. 478 (2017). These decisions also mean that such testimony is not admissible as lay opinion; it must satisfy the requirements for the admission of expert opinion under Evidence Rule 702, discussed further in section 11.10, below. *See also* John Rubin, *A Rare Opinion on Criminal Discovery in North Carolina*, UNC SCH. OF GOV'T: NORTH CAROLINA CRIMINAL LAW BLOG (May 3, 2016) (discussing implications of *Davis*).

A stricter dividing line between expert and lay opinion may prevent parties from avoiding the reliability requirements for experts by offering expert testimony "in lay witness clothing." *See* MOSTELLER § 10-2(B), at 10-6; *see also State v. Armstrong*, 203 N.C. App. 399, 411–15 (2010) (defendant argued that testimony by witness who was head of the Forensic Test for Alcohol Branch of the North Carolina Department of Health and Human Services was expert testimony "masquerading" as lay testimony and was inadmissible; while court found that defendant overstated its holdings, court agreed that witness provided expert testimony and that testimony was inadmissible because State did not comply with discovery requirements governing expert testimony); *State v. Moncree*, 188 N.C. App. 221, 225–27 (2008) (SBI agent's "extensive education and training in forensic analysis makes it difficult to imagine how he was able to separate his education, training, and experience" from his determination about the substance found in the defendant's shoe; court concludes that the agent testified as an expert, not a lay, witness and that the State violated criminal discovery requirements by failing to notify the defendant of its intent to offer expert testimony).

**3. Guilt of another person.** Neither a lay nor an expert witness may testify that a person is guilty of a particular act. *See State v. Warden*, 836 S.E.2d 880 (N.C. Ct. App. 2019) (testimony that DSS had substantiated sexual abuse by defendant constituted improper vouching for credibility of victim's allegations); *State v. Martinez*, 212 N.C. App. 661 (2011) (holding that trial court improperly admitted testimony by DSS social worker that DSS had substantiated claim that sex offense occurred); *State v. Giddens*, 199 N.C. App. 115 (2009) (child protective services investigator improperly testified that DSS had substantiated that abuse had occurred and that the defendant was the perpetrator), *aff'd per curiam*, 363 N.C. 826 (2010); *State v. Kelly*, 118 N.C. App. at 596 (stating general principles); *see also* 2 BRANDIS & BROUN § 190, at 779–80. *But cf. State v. Black*, 223 N.C. App. 137 (2012) (where defendant cross-examined children about their testimony at prior DSS hearing, it was permissible for State to ask DSS worker to explain what prior hearing was and why it took place).

**4. Truthfulness of another person's statements.** Neither a lay nor an expert witness may testify that a witness is telling the truth. *See State v. Robinson*, 355 N.C. 320, 334–35 (2002) (witness may not give an opinion vouching for the veracity of another witness); *Giddens*, 199 N.C. App. 115 (witness may not vouch for the credibility of the victim); *State v. Gobal*, 186 N.C. App. 308, 318–19 (2007) (detective could testify that a witness became less nervous during an interview but not that the witness was therefore telling the truth; vouching for the veracity of a witness is not opinion that is helpful under Evidence Rule 701), *aff'd per curiam*, 362 N.C. 342 (2008); *State v. Owen*, 130 N.C. App. 505, 515–16 (1998) (finding exclusion proper for this reason); *see also* N.C. R. EVID. 701 commentary (explaining that if testimony amounts "to little more than choosing up sides, exclusion for lack of helpfulness is called for by the rule").

Opinion testimony about another person's statements may be admissible if it does not amount to a comment on the person's credibility, but the line may be difficult to draw. *See, e.g., State v. Orellana*, 817 S.E.2d 480 (N.C. Ct. App. 2018) (detective's observation about victim's demeanor during questioning—that she seemed thoughtful, was trying to recollect, and seemed genuinely affected by what had occurred—was not improper vouching but rather was instantaneous conclusion and admissible as shorthand statement of fact); *State v. O'Hanlan*, 153 N.C. App. 546, 562–63 (2002) (permitting the testimony of a detective who was not offering an opinion that the victim had been assaulted, kidnapped, and raped, but was explaining why he did not pursue as much scientific testing in a case in which the victim survived and was able to identify the assailant); *State v. Love*, 100 N.C. App. 226, 231–32 (1990) (mother permitted to testify that she believed her child when the mother had testified that at first she did not believe the child and that the child had lied to her in the past; in this context, the testimony was helpful to the jury in understanding the mother's testimony), *dismissal of habeas corpus rev'd on other grounds sub nom.*, *Love v. Freeman*, 188 F.3d 502 (4th Cir. 1999) (unpublished); *State v. Murphy*, 100 N.C. App. 33, 40–41 (1990) (upholding as permissible lay opinion the testimony of a school guidance counselor that a child's statements to others about sexual abuse were consistent with statements to the counselor). *But see, e.g., State v. Ramey*, 318 N.C. 457, 467 (1986) (improper for a detective to give opinion that a child did not make any inconsistent statements to her; the opinion was not helpful and not admissible as lay opinion); *State v. Carter*, 216 N.C. App. 453 (2011) (upholding exclusion of testimony of social worker that victim was "overly dramatic," "manipulative," and exhibited "attention seeking behavior," which court found to be inadmissible commentary on child's credibility), *rev'd on other grounds*, 366 N.C. 496 (2013).

When character evidence is admissible, a lay witness (but generally not an expert witness) may give an opinion on a witness's character, including character for truthfulness. See section 11.8.B.3, above.

## 11.10 Expert Testimony

This section reviews the basic requirements for expert testimony as well as testimony specifically about children and parents. The discussion begins by addressing the impact of the 2011 changes to the North Carolina Rules of Evidence on expert testimony.

### A. Revised Evidence Rule 702(a)

In 2011, the North Carolina General Assembly revised North Carolina Rule of Evidence 702(a), one of the key rules governing the admissibility of expert testimony. In essence,

North Carolina adopted the federal *Daubert* test for evaluating the admissibility of expert testimony, adopted by the U.S. Supreme Court in *Daubert v. Merrell Dow Pharmaceuticals, Inc.*, 509 U.S. 579 (1993), and later incorporated into Federal Rule of Evidence 702(a). The North Carolina General Assembly's adoption of this approach requires greater scrutiny of expert testimony by North Carolina courts and possibly reconsideration of subjects of expert testimony previously considered to be admissible.

The revision applies to criminal and civil actions arising on or after October 1, 2011. *See also Sneed v. Sneed*, 820 S.E.2d 536 (N.C. Ct. App. 2018) (applying Rule 702 to expert testimony in child custody case). In felony criminal cases, the courts have construed the effective-date language as making the change applicable to cases in which the indictment was filed on or after October 1, 2011. *State v. Gamez*, 228 N.C. App. 329 (2013). Thus, the revised rule applies to acts underlying an indictment issued on or after October 1, 2011, even if the acts occurred before October 1, 2011.

In *State v. McGrady*, 368 N.C. 880 (2016), the court considered the requirements of revised Rule 702(a), which states:

> (a) If scientific, technical or other specialized knowledge will assist the trier of fact to understand the evidence or to determine a fact in issue, a witness qualified as an expert by knowledge, skill, experience, training, or education, may testify thereto in the form of an opinion, or otherwise, if all of the following apply:
> (1) The testimony is based upon sufficient facts or data.
> (2) The testimony is the product of reliable principles and methods.
> (3) The witness has applied the principles and methods reliably to the facts of the case.

The earlier version of the rule did not include the criteria in (1) through (3), above.

The court in *McGrady* held that the amended rule incorporates the federal *Daubert* standard for admission of expert testimony. 368 N.C. at 884. The court recognized that the requirements of the rule are stricter than the approach articulated in *Howerton v. Arai Helmet, Ltd.*, 358 N.C. 440 (2004), which had rejected the *Daubert* test. The general thrust of *Howerton* was that trial courts had to assess the reliability of expert testimony but did not have to be as exacting as under the federal rules of evidence. *See Howerton*, 358 N.C. at 464 (stating that North Carolina's approach was "less mechanistic and rigorous" than federal approach). The court in *McGrady* observed that the basic structure of the inquiry under the amended rule is not new, but it specifies new components and requires trial courts to scrutinize expert testimony with greater "rigor" before admitting it. *McGrady*, 368 N.C. at 892.

The court noted that the adoption of the stricter *Daubert* approach did not necessarily abrogate all North Carolina precedent on expert testimony. Previous cases may still be good law if they do not conflict with the *Daubert* standard. *Id.* at 888.

## B. Three Basic Requirements

**1. Generally.** The *Daubert* test, as incorporated in Evidence Rule 702(a), has three main parts, discussed below. Expert testimony must satisfy each part to be admissible, although the inquiry may overlap and proposed testimony may satisfy or fail different parts for similar reasons.

In determining whether expert testimony is admissible, the trial court does a preliminary inquiry under Evidence Rule 104(a). Under that rule, the trial court is not bound by the rules of evidence except with respect to privileges. In fulfilling this gatekeeping function, the trial court is not required to follow particular procedural requirements, although questions of admissibility are often resolved at in limine hearings before trial or voir dire hearings at trial. *McGrady*, 368 N.C. at 892–93; *accord State v. Walston*, 369 N.C. 547 (2017). The trial court should assess the reliability of expert testimony under the *Daubert* test whether or not there is an objection. *See State v. Hunt*, 250 N.C. App. 238 (2016); Jeff Welty, *Must a Trial Judge Act as a Gatekeeper Even if Not Asked to Do So?*, UNC SCH. OF GOV'T: NORTH CAROLINA CRIMINAL LAW BLOG (June 13, 2017).

**2. Scientific, technical, or other specialized knowledge that will assist trier of fact.** First, as specified in Evidence Rule 702(a), "the area of the proposed testimony must be based on 'scientific, technical or other specialized knowledge' that "will assist the trier of fact to understand the evidence or to determine a fact in issue." *McGrady*, 368 N.C. at 889. This step is a relevance inquiry, but it requires more than that the expert testimony be relevant within the usual meaning of Evidence Rule 401, which gives the basic definition of relevance. To assist the trier of fact, "expert testimony must provide insight beyond the conclusions that jurors can readily draw from their ordinary experience." *Id.* at 889, 894–95 (trial court did not abuse discretion in self-defense case in finding that defense expert's proposed testimony about pre-attack cues and use of force variables would not assist jury); *see also State Daughtridge*, 248 N.C. App. 707 (2016) (medical examiner's testimony that victim's death was homicide, not suicide, was based on non-medical information provided to him by law enforcement officers, not on medical information; trial court erred in allowing testimony under *Daubert* test, as the medical examiner was not in a better position than the jury to draw this conclusion).

---

**Note:** Expert testimony need not be scientific in nature to be governed by the revised rule. Expert testimony may be based on "scientific, technical, or other specialized knowledge," N.C. R. EVID. 702, which means that the trial judge must assess the reliability of the testimony whether it is in a scientific or other field. *See Kumho Tire Co. v. Carmichael*, 526 U.S. 137 (1999) (recognizing that *Daubert* principles require the trial court to assess the reliability of expert testimony in nonscientific fields).

---

**3. Qualified as an expert.** Second, as specified in Evidence Rule 702(a), "the witness must be 'qualified as an expert by knowledge, skill, experience, training, or education.'" *McGrady*, 368 N.C. at 889. Expertise may come from practical experience or academic training as long as the witness has "enough expertise to be in a better position than the trier of fact to have an opinion on the subject." *Id.* at 889, 895–96 (finding that trial court did not abuse discretion in self-defense case in finding that defense expert was not qualified to offer expert testimony on the stress responses of the sympathetic nervous system); *see also State v. Godwin*, 369 N.C. 604 (2017) (record need not contain express finding that witness is qualified as expert if trial court implicitly recognized the witness as an expert by overruling objection to witness's qualifications and allowing testimony).

**4. Three-pronged reliability test.** Third, the testimony must satisfy the three-pronged test for reliability specified in Evidence Rule 702(a), which is new to the rule:

> (1) The testimony [must be] based upon sufficient facts or data. (2) The testimony [must be] the product of reliable principles and methods. (3) The witness [must have] applied the principles and methods reliably to the facts of the case.

These requirements constitute the reliability inquiry under *Daubert. McGrady*, 368 N.C. at 890.

*Daubert* articulated several factors that bear on reliability in the context of scientific inquiry, such as the known or potential rate of error of the theory or technique. Other reliability factors to consider generally include, among others, whether the expert unjustifiably extrapolated from an accepted premise to an unfounded conclusion and adequately accounted for alternative explanations. 368 N.C. at 890–91. The court in *McGrady* noted that the factors identified in *Howerton* for evaluating the reliability of expert testimony, such as the use of established techniques and independent research by the expert, may also be useful in determining whether the proposed testimony satisfies this third prong. *Id.* at 891.

In *McGrady,* the court found that the trial court did not abuse its discretion in a self-defense case in finding that the proposed expert testimony about reaction times was not sufficiently reliable under this test. *Id.* at 897. Other cases applying the three-pronged test include: *State v. McPhaul*, 808 S.E.2d 294 (N.C. Ct. App. 2017) (finding that trial court erred in allowing latent fingerprint testimony where evidence did not show that expert applied principles and methods reliably to facts of case as required under third prong of test); *State v. Babich*, 252 N.C. App. 165 (2017) (finding that trial court erred in allowing retrograde extrapolation testimony in impaired driving case where testimony was not based on sufficient facts or data about defendant; testimony failed "fit" test under *Daubert* because analysis was not properly tied to facts of case); *see also State v. Younts,* 254 N.C. App. 581 (2017) (proponent of horizontal gaze nystagmus (HGN) testimony was not required to show reliability of principles and methods under second prong of *Daubert* test because the General Assembly, by enacting Evidence Rule 702(a1) specifying the conditions for admissibility of HGN testimony, obviated the need for that part of the *Daubert* showing).

Cases decided under the previous version of the rule, although not explicitly employing the *Daubert* reliability test, may involve similar considerations. For example, earlier cases have excluded expert testimony when the theory or principles were unreliable, the second prong of the reliability inquiry under the amended rule. *See, e.g., State v. Berry*, 143 N.C. App. 187, 202–06 (2001) (barefoot impression analysis inadmissible); *State v. Spencer*, 119 N.C. App.

662, 663–68 (1995) (penile plethysmograph results inadmissible). Earlier cases also considered to some extent whether the testimony was based on sufficient facts or data and whether the witness applied the principles and methods reliably to the facts, the first and third prongs of the reliability inquiry under the amended rule. *Compare State v. McCall*, 162 N.C. App. 64, 72–73 (2004) (expert's opinion about the general characteristics and symptoms of sexually abused children was admissible; the expert relied on facts and data of a type reasonably relied on by experts even though the expert had not examined the child), *with State v. Grover*, 142 N.C. App. 411 (2001) (expert's opinion that a child was sexually abused was improperly admitted; among other things, psychological testing was contrary to that of sexually abused children in that the answers to a 54-question trauma symptom checklist administered to the child showed that the child was not in the clinical range for any symptoms), *aff'd per curiam*, 354 N.C. 354 (2001).

### C. Other Requirements for Expert Opinion

**1. Rule 403 balancing.** The trial court has the inherent authority to exclude evidence, including expert testimony, under Evidence Rule 403, which provides that otherwise admissible evidence may be excluded if its probative value is substantially outweighed by other factors, such as the danger of unfair prejudice. The revisions to Evidence Rule 702 did not alter the trial court's discretion in this regard. *State v. McGrady*, 368 N.C. 880 (2016); *see also State v. King*, 366 N.C. 68 (2012) (in case decided before adoption of *Daubert* test, holding that although trial court found that expert testimony about repressed memory met requirements for admissibility, trial court had discretion to exclude it under Evidence Rule 403), *modifying and aff'g* 214 N.C. App. 114 (2011).

**2. Degree of certainty of opinion.** North Carolina cases have not required that an expert state his or her opinion with complete certainty but only to the degree of certainty that he or she believes. *See, e.g., In re C.M.*, 198 N.C. App. 53, 60 (2009) (doctor testified that "he could not say with 'absolute certainty' as to whether [the child's] injuries were accidental or non-accidental, but that there were 'a number of factors' that made him think that it was 'likely that this was a non-accidental injury'"; this testimony and other evidence constituted clear and convincing evidence to support the finding that the child's injuries were inflicted by non-accidental means).

When too speculative or equivocal, expert testimony has been excluded. *See State v. Clark*, 324 N.C. 146, 160 (1989) (finding that the testimony was so speculative and conjectural that it would not have assisted the trier of fact). Even if admissible, an uncertain opinion may be insufficient to support a finding. *See* 2 BRANDIS & BROUN § 189, at 776; *State v. Robinson*, 310 N.C. 530, 533–34 (1984) (holding that an expert's testimony that the insertion of a male sexual organ "could" have caused the vaginal condition was insufficient to support a rape charge).

The revisions to Rule 702(a) do not appear to affect this part of the analysis. *See State v. Babich*, 252 N.C. App. 165 (2017) (observing that when there are some facts that support an expert's testimony—in this case, about retrograde extrapolation—"the issue then becomes one of weight and credibility, which is the proper subject for cross-examination or competing expert witness testimony"; in this case, however, the expert's testimony was inadmissible because it was based on a speculative assumption and not on any actual facts); *see also* MOSTELLER § 10-3(D), at 10-53 (discussing approaches of different jurisdictions about the required degree of certainty—for example, some require that the expert be "reasonably certain," others require a "reasonably probable" opinion).

**3. Permissible topics and purposes.** The North Carolina courts have found that certain topics are improper areas for expert testimony—for example, the credibility of a witness, identity of the perpetrator, or conclusions about abuse in the absence of evidence of physical injuries (discussed in section 11.10.D.1, 3, and 6, below). These rulings could be construed as establishing additional limits on expert testimony, or they could be construed as applying the previous or current criteria for evaluating the reliability of expert testimony (described in section 11.10.B, above), although not all of the cases explicitly use that approach in finding the testimony impermissible.

Some opinions, although admissible, may be admissible for a limited purpose only—for example, to corroborate or explain (as discussed in section 11.10.D.7 through 10, below)—and therefore may not constitute substantive evidence or be sufficient to support a finding.

For a discussion of subjects of expert testimony that may arise occasionally in juvenile cases, such as DNA evidence, see Jessica Smith, *Criminal Evidence: Expert Testimony*, NORTH CAROLINA SUPERIOR COURT JUDGES' BENCHBOOK (UNC School of Government, Aug. 2017).

### D. Expert Testimony about Children

The following cases have addressed the admissibility of expert testimony on the indicated topics. Most were decided before the revisions to Evidence Rule 702(a). Where cases have considered the revisions to Evidence Rule 702(a), the discussion so indicates.

**1. Credibility.** An expert may not testify that a child is believable or is telling the truth. Several cases have applied this principle. *See State v. Aguallo*, 318 N.C. 590 (1986) (holding that it was improper under Evidence Rules 405 and 608 for the expert to testify that the child was believable, and ordering a new trial), *on appeal after remand*, 322 N.C. 818 (1988) (holding that it was not an impermissible comment on the child's truthfulness for an expert to testify that physical injuries were consistent with what the child had told the expert); *State v. Heath*, 316 N.C. 337 (1986) (holding that it was improper for the prosecutor to ask the expert whether the child had a mental condition that would cause her to make up a story about the sexual assault and for the expert to testify that the child had no record of lying); *State v. Brigman*, 178 N.C. App. 78 (2006) (expert improperly testified about the child's credibility when she testified about the child's disclosure that the defendant had "put his hand in his bottom and it hurt" and added "where a child not only says what happened but also can tell you how he felt about it is pretty significant because it just verifies the reliability of that disclosure"); *compare State v. Baymon*, 336 N.C. 748 (1994) (an expert witness may not testify that a child is believable or is not lying, but otherwise inadmissible evidence may become admissible if the door has been opened by the opposing party's cross-examination of the witness; because the defendant's cross-examination of the doctor suggested that the child had been coached by others, the doctor could testify that she did not perceive that the child had been coached or told what to say); *State v. Thaggard*, 168 N.C. App. 263 (2005) (noting *Baymon* but finding that the State improperly elicited the expert's opinion on credibility on direct examination); *see also State v. Ryan*, 223 N.C. App. 325 (2012) (reading *Baymon* as holding that expert testimony that a child had not been coached is admissible and not an impermissible comment on credibility; also holding under *Baymon* that defendant's opening statement, cross-examination of other witnesses, and general cross-examination questions of expert did not open door to testimony by expert that child's story was not fictitious, which is inadmissible testimony on credibility).

The courts have applied this principle in cases decided after the amendment of Evidence Rule 702. *See State v. Warden*, 836 S.E.2d 880 (N.C. Ct. App. 2019) (testimony that DSS had substantiated sexual abuse by defendant constituted improper vouching for credibility of victim's allegations); *State v. Crabtree*, 249 N.C. App. 395 (2016) (expert's testimony was improper comment on child's credibility; opinion does not discuss *Daubert* test), *aff'd per curiam*, 370 N.C. 156 (2017).

An expert also may not testify about the character of a particular child (or other person) for truthfulness. *See* N.C. R. EVID. 405(a) (so stating); *compare* section 11.8.B.3, above (discussing admissibility of lay opinion on character). Experts have been allowed to testify generally, however, that children do not lie about sexual abuse. *See State v. Worley*, 836 S.E.2d 278 (N.C. Ct. App. 2019); *State v. Oliver*, 85 N.C. App. 1 (1987); *see also State v. Speller*, 102 N.C. App. 697, 702 (1991) (holding that it was permissible for the state's expert to testify that mothers of abused children generally do not believe their children). For a discussion of expert testimony on the suggestibility of children, see section 11.10.D.11, below.

Expert testimony about a child's statements also may be admissible if it does not amount to a comment on the child's credibility, but the line may be difficult to draw. *See* 1 BRANDIS & BROUN § 96, at 332–33 ("courts have found numerous ways to permit expert comment on truthfulness, particularly of child witnesses, under various guises"); *State v. O'Hanlan*, 153 N.C. App. 546, 555 (2002) ("[T]he cases dealing with the line between discussing one's expert opinion and improperly commenting on a witness' credibility have made it a thin one."). The expert's testimony must be examined in each case to determine whether it crosses the line into impermissible opinion about credibility. *Compare, e.g., State v. Frady*, 228 N.C. App. 682 (2013) (trial court erred in allowing expert to testify that child's disclosure was consistent with sexual abuse; this testimony essentially expressed an opinion that the child was credible, which is impermissible), *with State v. Dew*, 225 N.C. App. 750 (2013) (finding that expert's testimony was devoid of direct comment on credibility).

**2. Legal conclusions.** An expert may testify about the ultimate issue to be decided in the case but not in the form of a legal conclusion. *See State v. Smith*, 315 N.C. 76, 100 (1985) (stating this principle and finding that it was permissible for an expert to testify that injuries were caused by a male sex organ or object of similar size or shape but that it would have been improper for the expert to testify that the victim had been raped, a legal conclusion).

**3. Identity of perpetrator.** An expert may not testify that a particular person is the perpetrator or is guilty. *See State v. Figured*, 116 N.C. App. 1, 8–9 (1994) (explaining that such testimony is improper under Evidence Rules 405, 608, and 702); *accord State v. Ryan*, 223 N.C. App. 325, 734 S.E.2d 598 (2012); *State v. Brigman*, 178 N.C. App. 78, 91 (2006).

An expert may testify, however, that a child said that a particular person was the perpetrator if the statement is admissible under the hearsay exception for statements for purposes of medical diagnosis or treatment. See section 11.6.E.9, above (discussing this issue).

**4. Physical injuries and their causes.** A qualified expert has been permitted to give an opinion about the cause of injuries, such as "injuries were caused by insertion of blunt object," "injuries were intentionally inflicted, not accidental or self-inflicted," or possibly even "injuries were caused by sexual abuse." (The last phrase is not preferred because it approaches a legal conclusion, but the admission of such testimony has been found not to be error when used as a shorthand statement of matters that have already been described specifically.) *See, e.g., State v. Jacobs,* 370 N.C. 661 (2018) (trial judge erred in refusing to allow expert to testify about presence of STDs in victim and absence of same STDs in defendant, which supported inference that defendant did not commit charged crime); *State v. Kennedy*, 320 N.C. 20, 32–33 (1987) (permitting testimony by a medical expert that injuries were not self-inflicted or accidental); *State v. Smith*, 315 N.C. 76, 99–100 (1985) (permitting testimony by a medical expert that injuries were caused by a male sex organ or an object of similar size and shape); *State v. Pearce*, 296 N.C. 281, 285–86 (1979) (explaining that testimony by the victim that she was "raped" was a shorthand reference to otherwise detailed testimony and permissible); *State v. Orellana,* 817 S.E.2d 480 (N.C. Ct. App. 2018) (permissible for nurse to testify that erythema, or redness, in vaginal area could be caused by and was consistent with touching, improper hygiene, or other causes); *State v. Dye*, 254 N.C. App. 161 (2017) (in case decided after the revisions to Evidence Rule 702, the court held that it was permissible for an expert to testify that the results of a physical examination were suspicious of vaginal penetration and sexual abuse; the court cited *McGrady* but did not apply the *Daubert* test); *State v. Ryan*, 223 N.C. App. 325 (2013) (not error to allow expert to give opinion that child had been sexually abused in light of physical evidence of an unusual deep hymenal notch, along with the presence of bacterial vaginosis that by itself could have other causes); *State v. Goforth*, 170 N.C. App. 584, 589–91 (2005) (hymenal tissues of the children reflected penetrating trauma and was sufficient physical evidence to support the doctor's opinion of repeated sexual abuse); *State v. Fuller*, 166 N.C. App. 548, 561 (2004) (court found that a SANE (sexual assault nurse examiner) nurse was properly qualified as an expert to offer an opinion about her examination of the child at the hospital emergency room; the court also found that the SANE nurse and doctor were properly permitted to testify that physical findings concerning the victim were consistent with vaginal penetration and someone kissing the child's breast); *State v. Dick*, 126 N.C. App. 312 (1997) (permitting a medical expert to testify that injuries were very likely the result of sexual mistreatment); *In re Hayden*, 96 N.C. App. 77, 82 (1989) (permitting a doctor to give an opinion that burns on a child were not accidental); *see also State v. Ford*, 314 N.C. 498, 503–04 (1985) (in a case in which a child had contracted gonorrhea in the throat, permissible for an expert to testify about how venereal disease is transmitted); *cf. State v. Perry*, 229 N.C. App. 304 (2013) (rejecting defendant's argument that state of medical science had changed and did not support expert's opinion that child's brain injuries were caused by intentional acts and not accidental; court found no information in record concerning state of current medical science or degree to which significant doubt had arisen regarding the way brain injuries occur).

**5. Battered child syndrome.** Experts have been permitted to testify that a child suffers from battered child syndrome, which is a diagnosis that a pattern of physical injuries was the result of physical abuse and not accidental. *See* Robert P. Mosteller, *Syndromes and Politics in Criminal Trials and Evidence Law*, 46 DUKE L.J. 461 (1996) (distinguishing battered child syndrome from other types of syndrome testimony not involving physical injuries); *see also State v. Stokes*, 150 N.C. App. 211, 225–27 (2002) (upholding the admission of expert testimony about battered child syndrome), *rev'd on other grounds*, 357 N.C. 220 (2003).

**6. Opinion about abuse if no or inadequate evidence of physical injuries.** If there is no evidence or inadequate evidence of physical injuries, an expert may not testify that a child was the victim of sexual or physical abuse. This view culminated in *State v. Stancil*, 355 N.C. 266 (2002), in which the court held that a doctor should not have been permitted to testify that a child was the victim of sexual abuse based on two examinations of the child in which no physical evidence of sexual abuse was observed and on the doctor's review of an in-depth interview of the child by a psychologist.

Numerous cases have followed *Stancil*. *See State v. Towe*, 366 N.C. 56, 61–64 (2012) (finding that admission of testimony amounted to plain error); *State v. Casey*, 823 S.E.2d 906 (N.C. Ct. App. 2019) (granting motion for appropriate relief and new trial); *State v. Black*, 223 N.C. App. 137 (2012) (holding that clinical social worker's testimony that child was sexually abused was improper where there was no physical evidence to support testimony); *State v. Treadway*, 208 N.C. App. 286, 292–95 (2010) (to same effect); *State v. Delsanto*, 172 N.C. App. 42, 45–47 (2005) (holding it was error to allow a doctor's opinion that the child was sexually abused where the only physical manifestation of injury was the child's statement of pain, which is subjective and not independently verifiable); *State v. Couser*, 163 N.C. App. 727, 729–32 (2004) (holding it was error to allow the state's medical expert to offer an opinion that the victim had suffered "probable sexual abuse" where the physical evidence consisted of two abrasions on either side of the introitus, which the expert admitted could have been caused by something other than sexual abuse); *State v. Bush*, 164 N.C. App. 254, 258–60 (2004) (in the absence of physical evidence, it was plain error to allow a doctor's opinion that the victim had been sexually abused; the opinion was not rendered admissible by the doctor's testimony that physical evidence is not always present and that its absence is absolutely consistent with abuse of a prepubertal child); *In re Morales*, 159 N.C. App. 429 (2003) (expert opinion that sexual abuse had occurred was improper absent any evidence of physical injury, but admission of the testimony was not prejudicial because the judge did not rely on it). *But see In re B.D.*, 174 N.C. App. 234 (2005) (assuming that the interpretation of evidence rules in criminal cases applies to termination of parental rights proceedings, the court found that they did not bar admission of experts' opinions of sexual abuse based on the child's statements, reports from other sources of sexualized behavior, and his medical history; the court's opinion does not refer to physical injuries other than bruising on the lower legs of the child).

This prohibition is based on concerns about scientific reliability and vouching for the credibility of the child. It applies to opinions of both medical and psychological experts. Earlier decisions allowing an expert to testify that a child was the victim of sexual abuse in the absence of physical injuries are no longer good law. *See, e.g., State v. Bailey*, 89 N.C. App. 212, 219 (1988) (allowing expert in the field of social work specializing in child development and family relations to give opinion that a child had been sexually abused based on several interviews with child; case decided before *Stancil*).

Experts have been permitted to testify that the absence of physical evidence of abuse does not establish that no abuse occurred. In *State v. Jennings*, 209 N.C. App. 329, 333–35 (2011), the court held it was permissible for an expert to testify that the lack of physical evidence of sexual abuse did not mean that the victim had not been sexually abused. The expert testified that had there been a tear in the victim's hymen, it would have healed by the time of the expert's medical examination a year after the alleged sexual abuse. The court found that this testimony did not amount to an impermissible opinion, without supporting physical evidence, that the victim had been sexually abused. *See also State v. Peralta*, 836 S.E.2d 254 (N.C. Ct. App. 2019) (to same effect); *State v. Pierce*, 238 N.C. App. 537 (2014) (to same effect).

Experts must remain cautious, however, about crossing the line into impermissible testimony that sexual abuse occurred. *See State v. Towe*, 366 N.C. 56 (2012) (admission of doctor's expert testimony that victim fell into the category of children who had been sexually abused but showed no physical symptoms of such abuse was improper); *State v. Davis*, 828 S.E.2d 570 (N.C. Ct. App. 2019) (nurse improperly permitted to testify that lack of physical indicators was consistent with someone reporting a sexual assault; testimony did not aid trier of fact as required by Evidence Rule 702(a)).

**7. Psychological syndromes.** With a proper foundation, qualified experts have been permitted to testify that a child suffered from post-traumatic stress syndrome. *See State v. Stancil*, 355 N.C. 266 (2002). Such opinion testimony has been found admissible, without evidence of physical injuries, to explain or corroborate only, not as substantive evidence that sexual abuse occurred. *See State v. Hall*, 330 N.C. 808, 817 (1992) (explaining that such testimony is admissible to assist the jury in understanding behavior patterns of sexually abused children and to aid the jury in assessing the complainant's credibility); *State v. Hicks*, 239 N.C. App. 396 (2015) (testimony about PTSD was not admitted as substantive evidence but rather to rebut inference, elicited on cross-examination, that victim's psychological problems were caused by something other than sexual assault); *State v. Brigman*, 178 N.C. App. 78, 92–93 (2006) (holding that it was error to admit expert testimony about PTSD for substantive purposes); *see also* Robert P. Mosteller, *Syndromes and Politics in Criminal Trials and Evidence Law*, 46 DUKE L.J. 461 (1996) (psychological syndrome evidence has not been proven to be diagnostic—that is, to establish cause—but it may be useful in explaining typical human behavior in response to certain conditions).

Testimony about child sexual abuse accommodation syndrome, if based on a proper foundation, has likewise been found admissible to corroborate or explain. *See State v. Stallings*, 107 N.C. App. 241, 248–51 (1992).

**8. Characteristics of abused children.** Testimony about the characteristics of abused children is expert testimony, subject to the requirements for expert opinion. *See State v. Davis*, 368 N.C. 794 (2016) (recognizing that such testimony is subject to expert disclosure requirements in discovery).

With a proper foundation, qualified experts have been permitted to testify, without identifying a particular syndrome and without evidence of physical injuries, that a child exhibited characteristics consistent with sexual abuse. *See State v. Stancil*, 355 N.C. 266 (2002); *State v. Davis*, 828 S.E.2d 570 (N.C. Ct. App. 2019) (nurse improperly permitted to testify that lack of physical indicators was consistent with someone reporting a sexual assault; nurse's testimony was not based on any science or other medical knowledge but rather on assumption that all people she examined were telling the truth about being sexually abused); *State v. Khouri*, 214 N.C. App. 389 (2011) (allowing such testimony); *State v. Chavez*, 241 N.C. App. 562 (2015) (finding no error in admission of doctor's testimony that victim's "cutting behavior" was common among children who have been sexually abused); *State v. Couser*, 163 N.C. App. 727, 729–32 (2004) (it was error to allow a medical expert's opinion under this principle; the expert testified that the victim had suffered "probable sexual abuse" when there was insufficient physical evidence to support the opinion given and there was no evidence to support that the victim's behavior or symptoms were consistent with being sexually abused); *State v. Wade*, 155 N.C. App. 1 (2002) (it was permissible for a professional psychologist, who had treated the child on a weekly basis for ten months, to testify that the child exhibited characteristics consistent with sexual abuse; the two-judge concurrence found that the psychologist's testimony that the child had in fact been sexually abused was improper in the absence of evidence of physical injuries but that the admission of the testimony was not plain error).

The courts have held that an expert may give this opinion testimony without examining the child as long as the expert is otherwise qualified to give the testimony. *State v. Ragland*, 226 N.C. App. 547 (2013) (expert interviewed but did not physically examine child); *State v. McCall*, 162 N.C. App. 64 (2004) (expert did not interview or examine child and based her opinion on DSS report, police reports, and interviews by medical personnel of child).

The courts have held that the expert's testimony must concern the characteristics of sexually abused children and not cross into impermissible opinion about whether a child is credible or, in the absence of physical evidence, whether sexual abuse occurred. *See State v. Frady*, 228 N.C. App. 682 (2013) (trial court erred in allowing expert to testify that child's disclosure about incident was consistent with sexual abuse; testimony neither addressed characteristics of sexually abused children nor spoke to whether child exhibited symptoms consistent with those characteristics).

As with syndrome testimony, the cases have indicated that an opinion about symptoms or characteristics is admissible to explain or corroborate but not as substantive evidence. *See State v. Kennedy*, 320 N.C. 20, 31–32 (1987) (such testimony "could help the jury understand the behavior patterns of sexually abused children and assist it in assessing the credibility of the victim"); *State v. Hall*, 330 N.C. 808, 817 (1992) (reaffirming *Kennedy*); *State v. Ewell*, 168 N.C. App. 98, 102–05 (2005) (testimony about profiles and symptoms of abused children is permissible to inform the jury that the absence of physical evidence is not conclusive, but it was error to allow testimony by a doctor that it was "probable" that the child was a victim of sexual abuse); *State v. Kelly*, 118 N.C. App. 589, 595 (1995) ("Explanations of the symptoms and characteristics of sexually abused children are admissible only through expert testimony for the limited purpose of assisting the jury in understanding the behavior patterns of abused children."); North Carolina Pattern Jury Instruction—Criminal 104.96 (June 2011) (pattern jury instruction limits such evidence to corroboration or impeachment); *see also State v. Ware*, 188 N.C. App. 790, 798 (2008) (licensed clinical social worker was sufficiently qualified as an expert to give an opinion that it was common for children who have been abused by a parental figure to "have a dilemma" about reporting the abuse). *But see State v. Isenberg*, 148 N.C. App. 29, 39–40 (2001) (court rejected the defendant's argument that the trial court erred in failing to give an instruction limiting the jury's consideration of an expert's testimony to corroborative, not substantive, purposes because the defendant did not ask for a limiting instruction at trial; the court also stated that the defendant was not entitled to a limiting instruction when the testimony is about the general characteristics of abused children, not about a specific profile or syndrome, relying on *State v. Richardson*, 112 N.C. App. 58 (1993) [note, however, that the court in *Richardson* found the testimony permissible because it was *not* offered for the substantive purpose of showing that a sexual assault occurred]).

**9. Delayed disclosure.** Applying revised Evidence Rule 702, the court in *State v. Shore*, 814 S.E.2d 464 (N.C. Ct. App. 2018), found it permissible for the trial court to allow the State's witness to testify as an expert in clinical social work, specializing in child sexual abuse cases. The witness testified that it was not uncommon for children to delay disclosure of sexual abuse. She explained some of the reasons for such delays, such as fear and self-guilt; she was not allowed to testify about why the alleged victim in this case delayed in reporting abuse. The court found that the witness's testimony was based on sufficient facts and data under Rule 702(a)(1) and her testimony was the product of reliable principles and methods under Rule 702(a)(2). Prior cases have reached a similar result. *State v. Purcell*, 242 N.C. App. 222 (2015) (medical doctor testified as to why children may delay reporting sexual abuse and did not opine on child's credibility); *State v. Carpenter*, 147 N.C. App. 386 (2001) (to same effect). Like testimony about other characteristics of abused children, discussed in subsection 8, above, such testimony is to explain or corroborate, not as substantive evidence.

**10. Repressed memory.** In *State v. King*, 366 N.C. 68 (2012), *modifying and aff'g* 214 N.C. App. 114 (2011), the North Carolina appellate courts addressed the admissibility of testimony about repressed memory—that is, testimony about delayed recall of traumatic events such as sexual abuse.

The Court of Appeals in *King* considered the scope of the trial court's discretion under *Barrett v. Hyldburg*, 127 N.C. App. 95 (1997), which held that testimony about repressed memories by an alleged victim of sexual abuse is admissible only if (1) the testimony is accompanied by expert testimony explaining the phenomenon of memory repression, and (2) the expert testimony has sufficient scientific assurance of reliability that the repressed memory is an indicator of what actually transpired in the past. The State argued that because *Barrett* requires that evidence of delayed recall of traumatic events be accompanied by expert testimony about repressed memory, the trial judge abused his discretion in excluding the

State's expert testimony on the subject. The majority of the Court of Appeals held that *Barrett* did not obviate the gatekeeping function of trial judges to assess the reliability of expert testimony or remove their discretion to weigh the admissibility of evidence under N.C. Rule of Evidence 403. The majority upheld the trial court's determination that even if the State's expert testimony about repressed memory technically satisfied the requirements for admission of expert testimony [under the then-applicable *Howerton* test], the testimony was inadmissible under Evidence Rule 403 because its probative value was substantially outweighed by the danger of unfair prejudice, confusion of the issues, and misleading the jury.

The Supreme Court in *King* affirmed the Court of Appeals' ruling that the trial court did not abuse its discretion by excluding the State's expert testimony on repressed memory under Evidence Rule 403. The court stated further: "We promulgate here no general rule regarding the admissibility or reliability of repressed memory evidence under either Rule 403 or Rule 702." 366 N.C. at 77. The Supreme Court disavowed the part of the Court of Appeals' opinion that concluded, in reliance on *Barrett v. Hyldburg*, 127 N.C. App. 95 (1997), that all testimony based on recovered memory must be excluded unless it is accompanied by expert testimony. The Supreme Court agreed with the holding in *Barrett* that a lay witness may not express the opinion that he or she has experienced repressed memory. The court stated, however, that *Barrett* "went too far" when it added that even if the witness in that case had avoided use of the term "repressed memory" and simply testified that she suddenly remembered traumatic incidents from her childhood, such testimony had to be accompanied by expert testimony. 366 N.C. at 78. The Supreme Court concluded that a lay witness may not testify that memories were repressed or recovered but may testify, in essence, that for some time period he or she did not recall, had no memory of, or had forgotten the incident. The court added that a defendant facing a witness who claims to have recently remembered long-ago events could seek to present an expert to address or refute the witness's purported sudden recall, thereby requiring the trial court to determine the admissibility of the witness's testimony.

**11. Suggestibility of children.** In *State v. Walston,* 244 N.C. App. 299 (2015), *rev'd on other grounds*, 369 N.C. 547 (2017), the North Carolina Court of Appeals and North Carolina Supreme Court considered the admissibility of expert testimony offered by the defendant about the suggestibility of children, including the alteration or creation of memories through questioning, gestures, or other suggestive acts. The opinions recognize that such testimony is permissible if, as with other expert testimony, the trial court determines that the testimony meets the criteria for admissibility under amended Evidence Rule 702. The Court of Appeals in *Walston* cautioned that an expert testifying about suggestibility may not express an opinion about the credibility of the particular child in the case. *See also State v. Carter*, 216 N.C. App. 453 (2011) (upholding exclusion of testimony by social worker on respondent's behalf that victim was "overly dramatic," "manipulative," and exhibited "attention seeking behavior," which court found was inadmissible commentary on child's credibility, was not about the profiles of abused children, and was not a subject on which the witness was qualified to render an opinion), *rev'd on other grounds*, 366 N.C. 496 (2013); *cf. State v. Peralta*, 836 S.E.2d 254 (N.C. Ct. App. 2019) (upholding exclusion of testimony that mother talked about sexual acts in front of child; court finds that testimony was too speculative to show that mother's comments were the origin of child's ability to graphically describe sex acts against her); *State v. Steen*, 826 S.E.2d 478 (N.C. Ct. App. 2019) (finding that trial judge's exclusion of defense expert testimony about "induced confabulation," if error, was not reversible error; judge allowed expert to define the condition, explain how it could affect memories of a person with amnesia after a traumatic injury, and testify that witness in this case was at risk of condition based on her injuries, but judge prohibited expert from testifying as to relationship between questions asked by officers and potential for confabulation regarding identification of defendant as attacker).

**12. Examination of child by respondent's expert.** In *Walston*, in 11., above, the Supreme Court held that the Court of Appeals was correct in holding that the respondent's expert was not required to examine or interview the children as a condition of giving expert testimony. The Supreme Court stated, "Such a requirement would create a troubling predicament given that defendants do not have the ability to compel the State's witnesses to be evaluated by defense experts." 369 N.C. at 553. The opinions recognized that prior cases did not establish a per se requirement of an examination but rather held that the trial court did not abuse its discretion in excluding the proffered testimony on the facts of the case. *See State v. Robertson*, 115 N.C. App. 249, 260–61 (1994). The Supreme Court determined that the trial court did not abuse its discretion in excluding the proffered testimony on the facts of this case on the grounds that it did not meet the requirements for expert testimony under Rule 702 as well as the balancing test under Rule 403 (probative value of testimony weighed against danger of unfair prejudice, confusion of issues, or misleading of jury). *See also In re J.L.*, 826 S.E.2d 258 (N.C. Ct. App. 2019) (permissible for trial judge at permanency planning hearing to allow non-party foster parent to call expert witness to testify about attachment relationship and impact of removing child from foster home without having examined child); *In re K.G.W.*, 250 N.C. App. 62 (2016) (recognizing that expert witness need not personally examine person before being permitted to testify as expert about person's condition, but holding that trial court did not abuse discretion in finding that respondent's expert testimony would not be helpful where expert had not worked with juvenile and had no experience in juvenile cases).

E. **Expert Testimony about Parents**

**1. Generally.** The following cases involve expert testimony about parents. All were decided before the adoption of revised Evidence Rule 702.

*State v. Faulkner*, 180 N.C. App. 499, 507–09 (2006) (permissible for a developmental and forensic pediatrician to testify, in rebuttal of the defense claim that child abuse is over diagnosed, about the profile of normal caretaker behavior as one of the indicators of whether a child's injuries are accidental or inflicted).

*Tate v. Hayes*, 127 N.C. App. 208 (1997) (substance abuse counselor was properly allowed to testify that the mother had a substance abuse problem in reliance on the "Sassy" [*sic*] test, which is accepted by the State of North Carolina for substance abuse assessments and is of a type reasonably relied on by experts in that field).

*In re Carr*, 116 N.C. App. 403, 408 (1994) (trial court did not err in refusing to allow an expert witness to testify about the mother's mental health and parenting capacity where the witness was an expert in clinical social work specifically dealing with adolescents and there was no evidence she was an expert in mental health issues).

*In re Chasse*, 116 N.C. App. 52, 59–60 (1994) (trial court erred in refusing to allow a psychologist to testify about the treatment of adult sexual offenders because of his lack of clinical experience with adults; "[h]is acknowledged expertise in the field of adolescent sex offenders and his study of the 'entire psychological literature, which included the review articles on treatment of adult sexual offenders,' made him better qualified than the trial court to render an opinion on the length and efficacy of adult sexual offender therapy . . . .").

*In re Byrd*, 72 N.C. App. 277, 280–81 (1985) (in a termination of parental rights proceeding, it was not error to admit expert testimony of witnesses tendered as experts in juvenile protective services, infant development, and permanency planning; although the witnesses should have refrained from giving an opinion about whether parental rights should be terminated [a legal conclusion and therefore an improper subject of expert testimony, as discussed in section 11.10.D.2, above], the substance of the testimony was that the child was in need of a permanent placement and a stable home environment).

*In re Pierce*, 67 N.C. App. 257, 260 (1984) (trial court did not err in permitting a social worker to give an opinion as to the parents' capacity to provide a stable home environment; although the proponent did not tender the social worker as an expert and the better practice is for the proponent to do so, the record was clear that the trial court treated the witness as an expert).

*In re Peirce*, 53 N.C. App. 373, 384–85 (1981) (trial court did not err in finding that a social worker was sufficiently qualified to give an expert opinion about whether the parents' actions were indicative of good parenting skills; although the proponent did not tender the social worker as an expert and the better practice is for the proponent to do so, the record was clear that the trial court treated the witness as an expert).

**2. Polygraph evidence.** The North Carolina Supreme Court has held that polygraph evidence is inherently unreliable and therefore inadmissible at trial. *State v. Grier*, 307 N.C. 628 (1983) (also expressing concern that jury would be unduly persuaded by polygraph evidence); 1 BRANDIS & BROUN § 113, at 416–18; *see also State v. Spencer*, 119 N.C. App. 662 (1995) (penile plethysmograph results were not sufficiently reliable to provide basis for expert opinion that defendant was not sexually aroused by children, thereby making it less likely that he committed the acts charged).

## 11.11 Evidentiary Privileges

Several statutes address the applicability of evidence privileges in juvenile proceedings. The statutes are not entirely consistent, but taken together they override most evidentiary privileges. The few privileges not overridden appear to apply to disposition as well as adjudication proceedings. *See generally* MOSTELLER § 8-2, at 8-3 (general rule is that privileges apply in any proceeding in which testimony can be compelled unless there is an exception overriding the privilege).

## A. In Abuse, Neglect, and Dependency Proceedings

**1. Effect of broad negation of privileges in G.S. 7B-310.** G.S. 7B-310 is the broadest of the statutes on evidentiary privileges in juvenile cases, providing that no evidentiary privilege other than the attorney-client privilege is ground "for excluding evidence of abuse, neglect, or dependency in any judicial proceeding (civil, criminal, or juvenile) in which a juvenile's abuse, neglect, or dependency is in issue nor in any judicial proceeding resulting from a report submitted under this Article." Because of its reference to abuse, neglect, and dependency, this statute applies at least to all hearings in abuse, neglect, and dependency cases.

**2. Effect of specific negation of privileges in G.S. Chapter 8.** Various communications are protected from compelled disclosure in court proceedings by G.S. Chapter 8, Article 7 (Competency of Witnesses). Several but not all of those statutes provide that a particular protection created by that Chapter is not a ground for excluding evidence of abuse or neglect in judicial proceedings. Thus, G.S. 8-53.1 states that the protection for physician-patient and nurse-patient communications is not a ground for excluding evidence of abuse or neglect of a child under age 16. Similar, although not identical language, appears in G.S. 8-53.3 (psychologists), G.S. 8-53.10 (peer support group counselors), and G.S. 8-57.1 (spouses). *See State v. Godbey*, 250 N.C. App. 424 (2016) (by operation of G.S. 8-57.1, marital privilege did not apply in criminal prosecution for indecent liberties with child); *State v. Knight*, 93 N.C. App. 460, 466–67 (1989) (by operation of G.S. 8-53.3, the psychiatrist-client privilege did not apply in a criminal prosecution for a sexual offense against a child); *see also* G.S. 8-57.2 (negating spousal privilege for paternity determinations).

No such language accompanies other privileges in G.S. Chapter 8. *See, e.g.,* G.S. 8-53.4 (school counselors), 8-53.5 (marital and family therapists), 8-53.7 (private social workers). The absence of limiting language in those statutes is likely of no consequence in abuse, neglect, and dependency proceedings (except possibly for communications between clergy and communicants, discussed next) because G.S. 7B-310 is so broad that it likely overrides the incomplete treatment in G.S. Chapter 8. *See generally State v. Byler*, 167 N.C. App. 109 (2004) (unpublished) (reading G.S. 7B-310 and G.S. 8-53.1 together).

**3. Attorney-client and clergy-communicant protections.** G.S. 7B-310 explicitly protects information subject to the attorney-client privilege. The privilege may be asserted as grounds for excluding evidence—including evidence of abuse, neglect, or dependency—in any court action. In its technical sense, the attorney-client privilege protects only communications between attorney and client, but the statute likely protects information gained in the course of the attorney-client relationship and subject to attorney work product and confidentiality obligations. *See* N.C. REVISED RULES OF PROF'L CONDUCT R. 1.6 & comment (providing that a lawyer shall not reveal information acquired during the professional relationship with a client). A narrower reading could infringe on the respondent's constitutional and statutory right to counsel.

> **Note:** For purposes of the duty to report suspected child abuse, neglect, or dependency, G.S. 7B-310 does not protect all information that is subject to the attorney-client privilege. The exemption states that it applies only to knowledge or suspicion the attorney gains from the client during representation in the abuse, neglect, or dependency case. *See* N.C. State Bar Ethics Opinion, RPC 175 (1995) (ruling that a lawyer ethically may exercise discretion as to whether to reveal confidential information pursuant to the child abuse, neglect, and dependency reporting law). The right to counsel guaranteed by the U.S. and N.C. Constitutions may require a broader attorney exception, however. See Chapter 5.1.A.2.

G.S. 8-53.2 recognizes a privilege for clergy-communicant communications and does not indicate any circumstances negating the privilege. G.S. 7B-310, however, does not exempt clergy-communicant communications from the broad override of privileges in that statute. Nevertheless, the protections for religion in the First Amendment of the U.S. Constitution and Art. I, Sec. 13 of the North Carolina Constitution may protect such communications. *Cf. In re Huff*, 140 N.C. App. 288, 294–99 (2000) (discussing the applicability of these limits on the questioning of parents about religious practices); *see also* JANET MASON, REPORTING CHILD ABUSE AND NEGLECT IN NORTH CAROLINA at 61–62 (UNC School of Government, 3d ed. 2013) (discussing application of reporting requirement to confidential communications with clergy).

**4. Protections against disclosure of confidential information.** G.S. 7B-310 overrides "privileges" only. In its technical sense, a privilege protects a witness from being compelled to testify in court proceedings or bars a witness from testifying without another person's consent. Many other provisions of law, while not establishing a "privilege" not to testify, make information confidential, such as provisions on mental health and substance abuse records, school records, and the like. *See* 1 BRANDIS & BROUN § 125, at 462 ("There are many statutes that while perhaps short of creating a privilege in the technical sense, provide, to varying extent, for confidentiality of specified records, reports or information."). G.S. 7B-310 probably should be interpreted as providing that confidentiality provisions are likewise not grounds for excluding evidence of abuse, neglect, and dependency.

Confidentiality laws still may pose barriers to admissibility in the sense that, to obtain protected information, a party must comply with the particular statute or other law governing production and disclosure of the information. GALs and DSSs have broad access to confidential information, but some information may have special state and federal law protections allowing disclosure only if certain conditions are met. See Chapter 14.1 (discussing access to confidential information); *see also In re J.S.L.*, 177 N.C. App. 151, 156–57 (2006) (admission of mental health records was proper where the respondent failed to request an in camera review of the records when the records were ordered disclosed and lodged only a general objection when the records were offered in evidence). Once obtained, the records still must satisfy the applicable evidence rules, such as authenticity and hearsay requirements, to be admissible. See, e.g., section 11.6.F, above (discussing the admissibility of business records).

## B. In Termination of Parental Rights Proceedings

G.S. 7B-1109(f) addresses termination of parental rights proceedings, providing that "[n]o husband-wife or physician-patient privilege shall be grounds for excluding any evidence regarding the existence or nonexistence of any circumstance authorizing the termination of parental rights." The impact of this language, which is narrower than in G.S. 7B-310 (discussed in section 11.11.A, above), appears to be as follows:

- By its terms, G.S. 7B-1109(f) disallows the husband-wife and physician-patient privilege as grounds for excluding evidence in termination of parental rights proceedings.
- The provisions in G.S. Chapter 8 that override specific privileges, in addition to the two privileges specified in G.S. 7B-1109(f), apply to termination of parental rights proceedings as well. *See* G.S. 8-53.1 (nurses), 8-53.3 (psychologists), 8-53.10 (peer support group counselors).
- G.S. 7B-310 may preclude the assertion of other privileges in termination of parental rights proceedings when asserted to exclude evidence of abuse, neglect, or dependency. A counter-argument can be made that G.S. 7B-1109(f), which applies specifically to termination of parental rights proceedings, supersedes the more general G.S. 7B-310.

## 11.12 Right against Self-Incrimination

### A. Right Not to Answer Incriminating Questions

Under the Fifth Amendment of the U.S. Constitution and Art. I, Sec. 23 of the North Carolina Constitution, a person has the right not to "incriminate" himself or herself—that is, not to give testimony that might make the person subject to criminal prosecution under state or federal law. *See* 1 BRANDIS & BROUN § 126, at 463. The Fifth Amendment privilege is the same in civil and criminal cases in the sense that a witness called to testify in either type of case, including in juvenile proceedings, has the right to refuse to answer questions that might incriminate him or her in future criminal proceedings. *See In re L.C.*, 253 N.C. App. 67 (2017) (so holding in abuse and neglect proceeding). A court may not override the assertion of the privilege and compel a witness to testify unless the court finds no possibility that answering might tend to incriminate the witness. *See* 1 BRANDIS & BROUN § 126, at 480. This right is not inconsistent with the statutes discussed in section 11.11, above, which negate most evidentiary privileges but do not appear to apply to constitutional rights. *See also* G.S. 7B-802 (providing that in an adjudicatory hearing, the court must protect the rights of the juvenile and the juvenile's parent to assure due process of law). To the extent inconsistent, those statutes must yield to constitutional protections. *See generally In re Davis*, 116 N.C. App. 409, 412–13 (1994) (recognizing the right of the respondent in a termination of parental rights case to refuse to answer questions that might subject her to criminal responsibility).

The judge may, but is not required to, advise a witness of his or her right not to answer incriminating questions. *See State v. Poindexter*, 69 N.C. App. 691, 694 (1984) (finding no requirement that the court advise a pro se defendant of the defendant's Fifth Amendment right); *State v. Lashley*, 21 N.C. App. 83, 84–85 (1974) (same); 1 MCCORMICK § 131, at 840–41 (generally, a witness has no right to a warning, but the judge is not barred from alerting the witness to the right against self-incrimination). The Court of Appeals has found that this rule has been altered by statute for juvenile delinquency proceedings. *See In re J.R.V.*, 212 N.C. App. 205 (2011) (holding that G.S. 7B-2405 requires the judge to advise a juvenile alleged to be delinquent of his or her privilege against self-incrimination before permitting the juvenile to testify).

For a further discussion of Fifth Amendment principles, see Robert L. Farb, *[Fifth Amendment Privilege and Grant of Immunity](#)*, NORTH CAROLINA SUPERIOR COURT JUDGES' BENCHBOOK (UNC School of Government, May 2014).

## B. No Right Not to Take Stand

The Fifth Amendment protection differs in criminal and civil proceedings in that a criminal defendant has the right to refuse to take the stand and may not be called as a witness by the State, the court, or another party. *See Jones v. State*, 586 A.2d 55 (Md. Ct. Spec. App. 1991) (co-defendant may not call another defendant as a witness at their joint trial). In contrast, in a civil proceeding such as a juvenile proceeding, a respondent does not have the right to refuse to take the stand, and one party may call another party to testify. *See* 1 BRANDIS & BROUN § 126, at 478–79; *see also In re Davis*, 116 N.C. App. at 412–13 (DSS was free to call the respondent mother as a witness, without a subpoena, where the mother was present at the termination of parental rights proceeding).

In *In re L.C.*, 253 N.C. App. 67 (2017), the court distinguished between a witness who voluntarily takes the stand and a witness who is compelled to take the stand. When a witness voluntarily takes the stand, the Fifth Amendment does not provide a shield to questions about matters that the witness puts in issue. When a witness is compelled to take the stand, as in this case in which DSS called the respondent parent as a witness, the witness's right to assert the Fifth Amendment is preserved until asked a question that would be incriminating. Therefore, a compelled witness who answers some questions about the matter in question does not waive the right to refuse to answer later questions that call for incriminating information. The court in *L.C.* distinguished *Herndon v. Herndon*, 368 N.C. 826 (2016), a case in which the defendant voluntarily took the stand. In *Herndon*, the Supreme Court found that the defendant was a voluntary witness and the Fifth Amendment was not available in response to questions within the scope of matters that the defendant put in dispute on direct examination.

**Note:** Although *L.C.* treats a party called by the opposing party as a compelled witness—and holds that the witness may wait until an incriminating question is asked before asserting the Fifth Amendment privilege—the safer course is for the witness to assert the privilege as soon as he or she is asked about any aspect of the matter in question. Such a course may avoid disputes about whether the witness failed to timely assert the privilege and waived the Fifth Amendment privilege. *See generally Minnesota v. Murphy*, 465 U.S. 420 (1984). An early assertion of the privilege also may protect against disclosure of information that could be used in a later prosecution.

## C. Drawing Adverse Inference from Refusal to Answer

In a civil proceeding, the Fifth Amendment does not forbid the drawing of an adverse inference against a party who refuses to answer in reliance on the privilege. *See In re Estate of Trogdon*, 330 N.C. 143, 151–52 (1991) (finder of fact in a civil case may use a witness's invocation of the Fifth Amendment privilege against self-incrimination to infer that truthful testimony would have been unfavorable to the witness); *accord McKillop v. Onslow County*, 139 N.C. App. 53, 63–64 (2000); *see also In re B.W.*, 190 N.C. App. 328, 338–39 (2008) (permitting the trial court to rely on, among other things, the mother's silence at the disposition hearing in support of its decision to cease reunification efforts). (The court's general statement in *In re B.W.* that the Fifth Amendment does not apply is correct in the limited sense that a court may draw an adverse inference from silence.)

A refusal to answer, and an adverse inference from the refusal, apparently may not be the sole basis for an adverse action against the party refusing to answer. There must be some other evidence to support the adverse action. *See Baxter v. Palmigiano*, 425 U.S. 308, 318 (1976) (suggesting this result in finding that an inmate's refusal to answer questions was not treated as a final admission of guilt of a disciplinary infraction). *But see* 1 MCCORMICK § 136, at 862–63 (discussing later U.S. Supreme Court cases that may cast doubt on whether the automatic imposition of an adverse action for a refusal to answer is necessarily improper).

## 11.13 Evidence Procedures

This section briefly reviews the procedures for offering and objecting to evidence. For the most part, the procedures are not unique to juvenile cases. Counsel should consult local rules in their district to determine whether additional or different requirements apply. For local rules, see Local Rules and Forms on the North Carolina Court System webpage.

### A. Production of Witnesses and Documents

The parties have the right to subpoena witnesses and documents to juvenile hearings in accordance with Rule 45 of the North Carolina Rules of Civil Procedure. A party or other person or organization receiving a subpoena has the right to object to or move to quash a subpoena as provided in that rule. For a brief discussion of motions to quash a subpoena to testify for a child witness, see section 11.2.A.5, above. For a further discussion of subpoena procedure, see John Rubin & Aimee Wall, *Responding to Subpoenas for Health Department Records*, HEALTH LAW BULLETIN No. 82 (UNC School of Government, Sept. 2005) (bulletin addresses subpoenas for health department records but describes procedures generally applicable to subpoenas for documents, including subpoenas for confidential information).

The parties may have the right to obtain records without a subpoena. See Chapter 14.1 (discussing access to documents and other information). But, without a witness or other evidence establishing a foundation for the record, the party offering the record may not be able to establish its admissibility.

## B. Pretrial Motions in Limine, Objections, and Other Notices

A party may, but generally is not required to, make a motion in limine to obtain a preliminary ruling on the admissibility of evidence. If a party makes a motion in limine to exclude evidence and the court denies the motion, the party who made the motion still must object when the evidence is offered at trial to preserve the issue for appeal. In 2003, the General Assembly amended Evidence Rule 103 to do away with the requirement that a party object at trial if the court had already denied a motion in limine. The appellate courts found this revision invalid on the ground that it conflicts with North Carolina Appellate Rule 10(b)(1), which has been consistently interpreted as providing that an evidentiary ruling on a pretrial motion is not sufficient to preserve the issue for appeal and that the objection must be renewed at trial. *See State v. Oglesby*, 361 N.C. 550, 553–55 (2007). Likewise, if the court grants a motion in limine to exclude evidence, the party still must offer the evidence at trial and, if the court excludes the evidence, make an offer of proof to preserve the issue for appeal unless the record otherwise shows what the substance of the excluded evidence would have been. *See In re A.H.*, 250 N.C. App. 546 (2016).

A party may request a voir dire hearing to determine whether a witness's testimony is admissible—for example, whether a witness is qualified as an expert, see section 11.10, above, or a witness is competent to testify. See section 11.2, above. A voir dire hearing may be conducted before or during trial.

Some local rules provide that objections are waived if not raised before the hearing. For a brief discussion of these rules, see section 11.1.A.4, above.

A party who intends to offer hearsay under the residual hearsay exception must give notice as required by that exception. See section 11.6.H.3, above.

## C. Pre-Adjudication Conference

Local rules for pre-adjudication conferences may require the parties to exchange witness lists and exhibits that they intend to offer at the adjudication hearing. Counsel should consult their local rules to determine the effect of failing to produce an exhibit as required at the pre-adjudication conference. *See also* G.S. 7B-800.1 (requiring pre-adjudication hearings in abuse, neglect, and dependency proceedings); G.S. 7B-1108.1 (requiring pretrial hearings in termination of parental rights cases). For a discussion of pre-adjudication conferences, see Chapter 5.7.

## D. Objections at Trial

The North Carolina appellate courts have strict waiver rules requiring that a party timely and specifically object to the admission of evidence to preserve the issue for review on appeal. *See, e.g., In re E.M.*, 249 N.C. App. 44 (2016) (respondent failed to preserve issue for appeal by failing to object to evidence). The North Carolina appellate courts have declined to extend to juvenile cases the plain error doctrine, which allows review of errors to which a party did not object at trial if injustice would otherwise result. *See, e.g., In re B.D.*, 174 N.C. App. 234,

245 (2005) (declining to adopt the plain error doctrine in termination of parental rights proceedings); *In re Gleisner*, 141 N.C. App. 475, 479 (2000) (to same effect for neglect proceeding). The failure to make appropriate objections, however, may amount to ineffective assistance of counsel. *In re S.C.R.*, 198 N.C. App. 525, 531 (2009).

Even if a proper objection is made, it is presumed that the trial court did not rely on incompetent evidence unless it affirmatively appears to the contrary. *See, e.g., In re A.L.T.*, 241 N.C. App. 443 (2015) (the trial court was presumed to have disregarded hearsay evidence because it made no findings pertaining to the evidence in support of its adjudication order). However, "'this presumption is weakened when, over objection, the judge admits clearly incompetent evidence.'" 1 BRANDIS & BROUN § 5, at 14–15 (quoting *State v. Davis*, 290 N.C. 511, 542 (1976)).

In brief, to preserve an evidentiary issue fully for review on appeal, a party must do the following.

**1. Timely objection.** Evidence Rule 103(a) provides that the party opposing the introduction of evidence must make a timely objection to the evidence in question. Generally, to be timely, the objection must be made when the evidence is first offered and must be repeated thereafter each time the evidence is offered. *See In re Morales*, 159 N.C. App. 429 (2003) (parents waived their objection to the admission of a social worker's opinion that the daughter was sexually abused where a physician later gave the same opinion without objection). The party making the objection also must obtain a ruling from the court on the objection. N.C. R. APP. P. 10(a).

A party is not required to repeat an objection if the court allows a standing, or line, objection to a particular line of questions. *See* N.C. R. CIV. P. 46. To ensure that a line objection is preserved, the party should ask the trial court's permission for a standing or line objection to the particular evidence. If a question within a line of questioning is objectionable on additional grounds, the party must object to that question on the additional ground.

A party is not required to object to each question if the initial ground for objection is that the witness is incompetent or otherwise disqualified from testifying. *Id.*

**2. Grounds for objection.** The opposing party must state all grounds for the objection, including any constitutional grounds. *See In re K.D.*, 178 N.C. App. 322, 326 (2006) ("A party may not assert at trial one basis for objection to the admission of evidence, but then rely upon a different basis on appeal."); N.C. R. APP. P. 10(a)(1) ("[A] party must have presented to the trial court a timely request, objection, or motion, stating the specific grounds for the ruling the party desired the court to make if the specific grounds were not apparent from the context.").

**3. Evidence for limited purpose.** The party offering evidence is not required to specify the purpose for which it is offered unless the evidence is challenged. *See State v. McGraw*, 137 N.C. App. 726, 730 (2000) (explaining that the better practice is for the offering party to specify the purpose, but it is not required). It is therefore incumbent on the opposing party to raise the issue and, if the evidence should be considered for a limited purpose only, request that the evidence be considered for that purpose only. *See In re A.S.*, 190 N.C. App. 679, 688–89 (2008) (holding that since the respondent did not object to the admission of the report or request that its use be limited, the report could be treated as substantive evidence), *aff'd per curiam*, 363 N.C. 254 (2009).

**4. Motion to strike.** If a party's question is not objectionable but the witness's answer is improper, the opposing party must make a timely motion to strike. *See* 1 BRANDIS & BROUN § 19, at 90.

**5. Offers of proof.** If evidence is excluded, the proponent of the evidence must make an offer of proof to preserve the issue for appeal unless the record otherwise shows what the substance of the excluded evidence would have been. *See* N.C. R. EVID. 103(a); *In re Montgomery*, 77 N.C. App. 709, 713 (1985); *see generally* 1 BRANDIS & BROUN § 18, at 78–83. This requirement applies to evidence a party offers and also when a witness is not permitted to testify. *See* 1 BRANDIS & BROUN § 18, at 83 (explaining that the substance of what an excluded witness would say should appear in the record).

The trial court must allow a party's request to make an offer of proof. *See In re A.H.*, 250 N.C. App. 546, 559-61 (2016). The preferred, and most complete, approach is to make a formal offer of proof by eliciting the testimony from the witness on the record or, if the evidence is an exhibit, by filing the document with the trial court. *See State v. Martin*, 241 N.C. App. 602, 605 (2015). The trial court may deem an informal offer of proof to be appropriate, in which the party forecasts the evidence that would have been presented. To be sufficient, an informal offer of proof must include a specific forecast of the testimony and must be made with particularity. *Id.* at 605–06 (describing informal offer of proof).

**6. Importance of complete recordation.** When conversations or proceedings take place at the bench or in chambers, extra steps may need to be taken to ensure that the conversations or proceedings, including any objections, appear in the record. A party may request the court to have the conversations or proceedings recorded or, if not recorded at the time, to summarize them for the record afterward.

---

**Resource:** For a fuller discussion of preserving the record for appeal, see JULIE RAMSEUR LEWIS & JOHN RUBIN, NORTH CAROLINA DEFENDER MANUAL, Vol. 2, Trial, Appendix B: Preserving the Record on Appeal (UNC School of Government, 2d ed. 2012). The discussion focuses on criminal cases, but many of the principles also apply to juvenile cases. See also Chapter 12.3 (discussing preservation of the record for appeal).

# Appeals

Chapter 12

# Chapter 12
# Appeals

**12.1 Scope of Chapter    12-3**

**12.2 Parties and Representation    12-4**
    A.  Who Can Appeal
        1.  Parties on appeal
        2.  Joinder of parties
        3.  Relationship of DHHS and county DSS as parties
        4.  Nonparticipating party
    B.  Appellate Representation in Juvenile Proceedings
        1.  Appellate representation for DSS
        2.  Appellate representation for parents
        3.  Appellate representation for children
        4.  Appellate representation for guardians or custodians
    C.  Role of Trial Counsel
    D.  Role of Appellant

**12.3 Identifying Issues for Appeal    12-10**
    A.  Preserving Issues for Appeal
        1.  Objection, grounds, and ruling required
        2.  Issues automatically preserved for appeal
    B.  Scope of Appellate Review
        1.  Issues identified in briefs
        2.  The contents of the record
    C.  Appellate Rule 2: Prevent Manifest Injustice
    D.  Invited Error
    E.  No Swapping Horses

**12.4 Which Orders Can Be Appealed    12-16**
    A.  Appealable Orders
        1.  No jurisdiction
        2.  Order determining the action
        3.  Initial disposition and underlying adjudication order
        4.  Order changing custody
        5.  Order eliminating reunification as a permanent plan
        6.  Order granting or denying a termination of parental rights
        7.  Order deciding placement on the Responsible Individuals List
    B.  When an Appeal Is Moot
        1.  Exception based on collateral legal consequences of abuse, neglect, dependency adjudication
        2.  Exception based on collateral legal consequences of termination of parental rights

## 12.5 Notice of Appeal    12-23
- A. Timing, Manner, and Content of Notice
    1. Timing and manner generally
    2. Timing and manner of appeal of order eliminating reunification as a permanent plan
    3. Signatures
    4. Contents
- B. Service and Proof of Service
- C. Appellate Entry Forms

## 12.6 Protection of the Child's Identity – Appellate Rule 42    12-30

## 12.7 Expedited Appeals Process under Appellate Rule 3.1    12-31
- A. Transcript
- B. Record on Appeal
    1. Appellant's proposed record
    2. Appellee's response or lack thereof
    3. Settling the record when there is disagreement
    4. Problem with recording
- C. Briefs
    1. Time limits for briefs
    2. No-merit briefs

## 12.8 Issues on Appeal and Standards of Review    12-34
- A. Introduction
- B. Sufficiency of Evidence and Findings
    1. Generally
    2. Review of findings of fact and conclusions of law at adjudication
    3. Review of dispositional findings
- C. Abuse of Discretion
- D. Subject Matter Jurisdiction
- E. Failure to Follow Statutory Mandates and Procedures
- F. Statutory Interpretation

## 12.9 Motions to Dismiss and Failure to Comply with Appellate Rules    12-39

## 12.10 Extraordinary Writs, Discretionary Review, and Appeal of Right    12-40
- A. Writ of Certiorari
    1. Review of trial court
    2. Review of court of appeals
- B. Petition for Discretionary Review
- C. Appeal of Right
- D. Writ of Mandamus or Prohibition
- E. Writ of Supersedeas

## 12.11 Trial Court's Role during and after Appeal    12-43
- A. Trial Court's Role pending Appeal
    1. Enforcement of or motion to stay order

2. Continued court involvement in non-TPR appeals
3. Cannot proceed to TPR during appeal of the underlying matter
4. Continued court involvement in TPR appeals
5. Order requirements pending appeal disposition
6. Rule 60 of the Rules of Civil Procedure
- B. Trial Court's Role after Appeal
  1. Modification of order
  2. Carrying out appellate mandate

## 12.1 Scope of Chapter

This Chapter addresses general characteristics of appeals in abuse, neglect, dependency, and termination of parental rights (TPR) cases and issues that trial attorneys and trial court judges encounter in connection with these appeals. This Chapter does not comprehensively discuss appellate procedure.

The Juvenile Code addresses certain aspects of appeals, including who can appeal, which orders can be appealed, and notice of appeal. However, appeals in abuse, neglect, dependency, and TPR proceedings are governed primarily by the Rules of Appellate Procedure (Appellate Rules). Appellate Rule 3.1 applies to appeals of orders designated by G.S. 7B-1001.

**Practice Note:** Effective January 1, 2019, significant changes were made to G.S. 7B-1001, the statute designating which juvenile orders may be appealed, and to the Rules of Appellate Procedure. Two of those significant changes include (1) the right to appeal certain orders directly to the North Carolina Supreme Court and (2) the requirement that all documents for appeals of any order designated in G.S. 7B-1001 must be filed electronically unless an exception is granted for good cause. G.S. 7B-1001(a), (a1); N.C. R. APP. P. 3.1(a), (i). This efiling requirement applies to appeals of orders before the North Carolina Court of Appeals and the North Carolina Supreme Court.

**Resources:**
The "Appellate Reporter" page of the North Carolina Administrative Office of the Courts (AOC) website includes the following links:
- "Court Rules," which includes the current codification of the NORTH CAROLINA RULES of APPELLATE PROCEDURE and recent orders of the North Carolina Supreme Court amending those Rules.
- "Opinions" decided by the North Carolina Supreme Court and Court of Appeals.

The "Supreme Court" page of the AOC website includes the following links:
- "eFiling and Document Library" (note all appeals of juvenile orders governed by Appellate Rule 3.1 require efiling unless an exception is granted for good cause).
- "Calendar of Oral Arguments" and "Dockets."
- Under "Additional Resources,"

- o THE GUIDEBOOK: CITATION, STYLE, AND USAGE AT THE SUPREME COURT OF NORTH CAROLINA (June 11, 2019) (note change to citation format of North Carolina appellate cases when there is no state reporter cite).
- o The North Carolina Court of Appeals Legal Standards Database (last revised July 26, 2016), with sections on "Appellate Process", "Evidentiary Matters", and "Juvenile Proceedings").

For more information about the amendments to both appeals of juvenile orders and applicable appellate rules, see Sara DePasquale, *Big Changes to Appeals of A/N/D – TPR Orders Designated in G.S. 7B-1001*, UNC SCH. OF GOV'T: ON THE CIVIL SIDE BLOG (March 25, 2019).

## 12.2 Parties and Representation

### A. Who Can Appeal

**1. Parties on appeal.** G.S. 7B-1002 limits who has standing to appeal an order designated in G.S. 7B-1001 to

- the juvenile, acting through a guardian ad litem (if one has not been appointed under G.S. 7B-601, the court must appoint a Rule 17 GAL for purposes of the appeal);
- a county department of social services (DSS);
- a parent, guardian, or custodian who is not a prevailing party (for a discussion of parent, guardian, and custodian, see Chapter 2.2.B); and
- any party who sought but failed to obtain a termination of parental rights.

*See In re M.N.*, 816 S.E.2d 925 (N.C. Ct. App. 2018); *In re J.C.B.*, 233 N.C. App. 641 (2014). See also section 12.4, below, for a discussion of appealable orders under G.S. 7B-1001.

**Note,** for purposes of this Manual, a "department of social services" or "DSS" refers to a department as defined by G.S. 7B-101(8a) regardless of how it is titled or structured.

Standing is jurisdictional, and a party invoking the jurisdiction of the appellate court has the burden of proving that he or she has standing to file an appeal. *In re J.L.*, 826 S.E.2d 258 (N.C. Ct. App. 2019); *In re T.B.*, 200 N.C. App. 739 (2009). A motion to dismiss an appeal must be made by motion under Appellate Rule 37 and should not be raised for the first time in a brief to the appellate court; this includes a motion to dismiss based on a lack of standing. *In re J.L.*, 826 S.E.2d 258 (deciding the issue of standing because it is jurisdictional despite it being raised for first time in a brief).

Whether an appellant has standing to appeal arises most commonly when a party in the abuse, neglect, or dependency proceeding fails to prove his or her standing pursuant to G.S. 7B-1002(4) as a parent, guardian, or custodian who is a nonprevailing party. That failure to prove standing results in the dismissal of the appeal. *See In re T.H.*, 232 N.C. App. 16

(2014); *In re J.C.B.*, 233 N.C. App. 641 (2014); *In re T.B.*, 200 N.C. App. 739; *In re A.P.*, 165 N.C. App. 841 (2004). A party that is designated by G.S. 7B-1002 as a "proper party" for appeal has standing to appeal even when he or she has not been served with the initiating petition and has not appeared at the hearing resulting in the order being appealed. *See In re E.J.*, 225 N.C. App. 333 (2013) (holding the respondent mother who was not served with the neglect and dependency petition and did not appear at the hearing had standing to appeal the adjudication and initial dispositional order because G.S. 7B-1002(4) makes it clear that a parent is a proper party to appeal).

(a) **Parent.** The Juvenile Code does not define "parent" and does not address the status of a putative father. Yet, a child's parents should be identified and named as respondent parties in an abuse, neglect, or dependency proceeding, unless a statutory exception applies. *See* G.S. 7B-401.1(b); 7B-506(h)(1); 7B-800.1(a)(3); 7B-901(b).

The legal relationship and rights of a biological parent to his or her child are severed by the child's adoption. G.S. 48-1-106(c). *But see* G.S. 48-1-106(d) (exception in a "stepparent adoption" for the spouse of the adoption petitioner who is the child's biological parent). Except for a stepparent adoption, a biological (or adoptive) parent of a child who has been adopted has no parental rights and therefore no standing to appeal as a parent. *In re T.H.*, 232 N.C. App. 16 (2014).

(b) **Stepparent.** In *In re M.S.*, 247 N.C. App. 89 (2016), the court of appeals held that a stepparent who had not adopted the child was not a parent after it examined the Juvenile Code and applicable adoption statute. The Juvenile Code distinguishes between a parent and stepparent by including stepparent in the definition of "caretaker." By definition, a caretaker is a person who is not the child's parent. G.S. 7B-101(3). Further supporting the distinction between parent and stepparent, the adoption statute defines stepparent as an individual who is the spouse of a child's parent but who is not the child's legal parent. G.S. 48-1-101(18).

A stepparent may become a parent, with standing to appeal, upon the stepparent's adoption of the child. *See* G.S. Chapter 48, Article 4. A stepparent who has a court order awarding him or her guardianship or legal custody of the child becomes the child's guardian or custodian with standing to appeal as a guardian or custodian. *See* G.S. Chapter 35A (guardian); 7B-600 (guardian); 7B-101(8) (definition of "custodian"). Absent an adoption or court order for legal custody or guardianship, a stepparent is a caretaker and lacks standing to appeal.

(c) **Caretaker**. A "caretaker" is defined at G.S. 7B-101(3) and is any person who is not the child's parent, guardian, or custodian but has responsibility for the child's health and welfare in a residential setting. A caretaker does not have standing to appeal a juvenile order, and an appeal taken by a caretaker will be dismissed. *See* G.S. 7B-1002; *In re M.S.*, 247 N.C. App. 89 (2016) (dismissing appeal; holding the caretaker stepfather lacked standing to appeal adjudication and disposition order). See Chapter 2.2.B.9(c) (discussing caretaker).

**(d) Nonprevailing or aggrieved party.** G.S. 7B-1002(4) requires that a parent, guardian, or custodian be a nonprevailing party in the order that is being appealed. A prevailing party is one in whose favor the judgment was entered. *In re J.L.*, 826 S.E.2d 258 (N.C. Ct. App. 2019); *In re T.B.*, 200 N.C. App. 739 (2009). When the trial court grants the party's request, that party is a prevailing party and as such lacks standing to appeal. *See In re T.B.*, 200 N.C. App. 739 (dismissed respondent's appeal of an order that granted the relief requested by the respondent, which was to not award permanent custody to the paternal grandparents and to order visitation with her).

In some cases, the court of appeals has looked to G.S. 1-271, which refers to an "aggrieved" party, when determining if the appellant is a nonprevailing party. In those cases, the court of appeals has held that only an "aggrieved party" may appeal from an order, and an aggrieved party is one whose rights have been directly and injuriously affected by the trial court's action. *In re C.A.D.*, 247 N.C. App. 552 (2016). A party authorized by G.S. 7B-1002 to appeal a final juvenile order does not have standing if he or she is not an aggrieved party. *See In re C.A.D.*, 247 N.C. App. 552 (holding respondent mother lacked standing to appeal the permanency planning order designating adoption as the plan and placing the children in the custody of DSS instead of relatives, as mother could not claim injury on behalf of the relatives who neither claimed they were injuriously affected by the order nor appealed); *In re B.D.*, 174 N.C. App. 234 (2005) (respondent parents in a termination of parental rights (TPR) action were not aggrieved parties that were directly and injuriously affected by the alleged failure of the court to properly serve the child who was the subject of the TPR action; decided under previous statutory language requiring the child to be served).

Whether a party is aggrieved appears to depend upon whose interests or grievances are being asserted – the interests of the party appealing or the interests of someone other than the party appealing. The appealing party must assert their own interests versus the interests of someone else. *See In re J.L.*, 826 S.E.2d 258 (N.C. Ct. App. 2019); *In re D.S.*, 817 S.E.2d 901 (N.C. Ct. App. 2018); *In re C.A.D.*, 247 N.C. App. 552. Three recent court of appeals opinions examined standing based on nonprevailing or aggrieved party status when in each case, a parent appealed the order that placed the children with someone other than who the appellant parent supported. The court of appeals looked to whether the parent's preferred proposed placement provider was a party with the ability to independently appeal the order but did not do so. In the first case, *In re C.A.D.*, 247 N.C. App. 552, the court of appeals held that the respondent mother was not an aggrieved party and did not have standing to appeal the trial court's order designating adoption as a permanent plan and placing the child in DSS custody instead of with the maternal grandparents because the grandparents, who could have appealed that order, did not do so and did not allege they were injured by the court order.

In the two most recent opinions, the court of appeals distinguished the facts of *In re C.A.D.* and held that each respective appellant parent was an aggrieved party with standing to appeal when the potential placement providers who were not selected by the trial court were not parties in the action and could not have independently appealed the order. In *In re J.L.*, 826 S.E.2d 258, the court of appeals held that the appellant mother had standing as a nonprevailing party when the order granted guardianship to the current foster parents instead of where mother preferred – the home where the child's half-siblings resided and had been adopted. The mother was asserting her interest in having her child placed with his half siblings when that prospective placement provider was not a party and could not have independently appealed the order. In *In re D.S.*, 817 S.E.2d 901, the court of appeals held that the appellant father was an aggrieved party and had standing to appeal. The father was asserting his own interests that were affected by the order that granted guardianship to a nonrelative without first considering a viable placement with the child's paternal grandmother. Paternal grandmother was not a party who could have independently appealed the order.

**2. Joinder of parties.** Any two or more parties whose interests are the same may pursue or respond to an appeal jointly. Parties who are appealing may join initially or after taking separate appeals. After joinder, the parties proceed as a single appellant or appellee. N.C. R. APP. P. 5.

**3. Relationship of DHHS and county DSS as parties.** Even though the North Carolina Department of Health and Human Services (DHHS) is not routinely involved in appeals of abuse, neglect, dependency, or termination of parental rights proceedings, in two related cases the court of appeals granted DHHS's motions to dismiss the appeals by the counties' DSS. DHHS was an intervening party in the underlying actions that resulted in the orders on appeal, one of which was an appeal of the order allowing DHHS to intervene. In granting DHHS's motions to dismiss, the court of appeals held that "there is an agency relationship between DHHS and the counties' DSS . . . . It is axiomatic that the principal controls the agent . . . . DHHS is the principal to both DSS divisions. Each county's DSS must act as instructed by its principal." *In re Z.D.H.*, 184 N.C. App. 183, 186 (2007); *In re J.L.H.*, 184 N.C. App. 180, 183 (2007).

**4. Nonparticipating party.** When one party to an abuse, neglect, dependency, or termination of parental rights proceeding appeals, another party may choose not to participate in the appeal. For example, where both parents participate in the proceeding at the trial level and only one appeals a judgment, the other parent may or may not elect to participate in the appeal. *See, e.g., In re A.R.A.*, 835 S.E.2d 417 (N.C. S.Ct. 2019); *In re B.C.T.*, 828 S.E.2d 50 (N.C. Ct. App. 2019). Rule 26(b) of the Appellate Rules requires that copies of all papers filed by a party must be served on all other "parties to the appeal," which would seem to indicate that nonparticipating parties need not be served. However, because a party's decision not to participate in an appeal is typically not marked by a specific declaration or the filing of a specific document to make it clear that he or she is not a "party to the appeal," failure to serve nonparticipating parties in some circumstances could be problematic. Attorneys may view service on nonparticipating parties as the best approach. Attorneys who represent nonparticipating parties in the underlying trial sometimes are allowed to withdraw, in which case papers would be served directly on the party. If a party is unrepresented, he or she should be served at his or her last known address.

### B. Appellate Representation in Juvenile Proceedings

**1. Appellant representation for DSS.** Appellate representation for the county DSS is the responsibility of the individual county. An appeal may be handled by the attorney who represented DSS at trial, another DSS attorney, or an attorney retained or contracted by DSS specifically to represent it in the appeal. Unlike the Office of the Parent Defender at the Office of Indigent Defense Services or the North Carolina Guardian ad Litem Program, there is no state agency or program that provides or coordinates appellate representation to the counties' DSS. The North Carolina Department of Health and Human Services assumes no responsibility for county DSS representation.

**2. Appellate representation for parents.** The statutory entitlement to counsel for indigent parents continues through any stage of the proceeding, including appeals. *See* G.S. 7B-602(a); 7B-1101.1(a); 7A-451(b) (entitlement to services of counsel continues through any "critical stage"). When notice of appeal is given, a respondent is not required to execute and serve a new affidavit of indigency, and the trial court is not required to make a new determination of eligibility for appointed counsel. *See In re D.Q.W.*, 167 N.C. App. 38 (2004); *see also* G.S. 7A-450(c) (allowing but not requiring question of indigency to be redetermined at any stage of the action or proceeding). However, if the trial court determines it is appropriate, the trial court may review a party's financial status and eligibility for appointed counsel at any time. *See* G.S. 7B-602(a); 7B-1101.1(a); *In re D.Q.W.*, 167 N.C. App. 38. Respondents who are not indigent must bear the cost of their own appellate representation.

For parents who are indigent, appellate representation is coordinated by the Office of Indigent Defense Services (IDS) and handled by the Office of the Parent Defender. The appeal is assigned to an assistant appellate defender or a private attorney who has completed mandatory training and been accepted for placement on the "7B appellate roster." Once appellate entries are completed and signed by the trial judge, the Office of the Parent Defender completes a Notice of Appointment that contains the name and contact information of the assigned appellate attorney. This notice is mailed to the juvenile clerk for filing in the district court file and copies are sent to the parties' attorneys and the transcriptionist.

**Resource:** The Office of the Parent Defender of the N.C. Office of Indigent Defense Services maintains on its website, information on appealing juvenile matters, including sample as well as interactive fillable appellate forms and a brief bank. See the "Training & Resources" and "Information for Counsel" sections of the website.

**3. Appellate representation for children.** When children participate in appeals through their guardians ad litem, representation is handled by the Guardian ad Litem Services Division (the GAL Program) of the North Carolina Administrative Office of the Courts (AOC). When the GAL Program is notified by the AOC of an appeal, the case is either assigned "in house" to the GAL Appellate Counsel or Associate Counsel or assigned to an attorney in the GAL pro bono attorney program coordinated by the GAL Program. Occasionally, the trial attorney advocate handles the appeal. When the case is assigned, an Order of Appointment of Appellate Counsel is forwarded to the local GAL program in the judicial district where the appeal originated, for signature by the trial judge. This appointment order is filed in the juvenile court file and served on the parties' attorneys and the transcriptionist.

> **Resource:** The Guardian ad Litem Services Division of the N.C. Administrative Office of the Courts maintains on its website, resources for attorneys.

**4. Appellate representation for guardians or custodians.** Indigent respondents who are not parents do not have a statutory right to court-appointed counsel. *See* G.S. 7B-602(a); 7B-1101.1(a) (addressing only an indigent parent's right to appointed counsel). North Carolina appellate courts have not addressed the question of whether there is any circumstance in which an indigent respondent who is not a parent would be entitled to court-appointed counsel. IDS, which is responsible for providing representation for indigent parent respondents, defers to the courts on that question and provides by policy that IDS will pay for representation "[i]f a judge concludes that due process requires appointment of counsel for a particular indigent non-parent respondent in an abuse, neglect, or dependency proceeding." N.C. OFFICE OF INDIGENT DEFENSE SERVICES, "Appointment of Counsel for Non-Parent Respondents in Abuse, Neglect, and Dependency Proceedings" (July 2, 2008).

## C. Role of Trial Counsel

The Rules of Appellate Procedure specifically address the role of trial counsel when a different attorney will be handling the appeal in an abuse, neglect, dependency, or termination of parental rights case. Appellate Rule 3.1(h) states that trial counsel for an appealing party has a duty to assist appellate counsel in preparing and serving a proposed record on appeal.

> **Practice Note:** The role and division of responsibilities between trial counsel and appellate counsel in the early stage of an appeal depend on the arrangements made between the attorneys themselves as well as the policies of their respective agencies. Trial counsel should advise the client about appeal rights, timelines, required actions to perfect an appeal, and the effect of the appeal; file the notice of appeal and any appropriate motions before appellate counsel becomes involved; and respond to requests for information from appellate counsel.

> **Resources:**
> For information related to the responsibilities of respondents' trial counsel in relation to appeals, see
> - N.C. COMM'N ON INDIGENT DEFENSE SERVICES, "Performance Guidelines for Attorneys Representing Indigent Parent Respondents in Abuse, Neglect, Dependency and Termination of Parental Rights Proceedings at the Trial Level" (2007).
> - N.C. OFFICE OF INDIGENT DEFENSE SERVICES, "Division of Responsibility between Trial and Appellate Counsel Who Are Proceeding Under Appellate Rule 3.1" (2009).
>
> Note, both documents predate the 2019 amendments to the Rules of Appellate Procedure and amendments made to the Juvenile Code since their respective publications.

### D. Role of Appellant

An appellant may proceed with an appeal without attorney representation. An unrepresented appellant must file and serve the notice of appeal in the time and manner required. N.C. R. APP. P. 3.1(b) (referring to G.S. 7B-1001(b) and (c)). The appellant, regardless of whether he or she is represented, must sign the notice of appeal. G.S. 7B-1001(c); N.C. R. APP. P. 3.1(b) (referring to G.S. 7B-1001(b) and (c)). For a further discussion of notice of appeal, see section 12.5, below.

## 12.3 Identifying Issues for Appeal

### A. Preserving Issues for Appeal

**1. Objection, grounds, and ruling required.** To preserve an issue for appellate review, in the trial court a party must

- make a timely request, objection, or motion;
- state specific grounds for the desired ruling (unless the specific grounds are apparent); and
- obtain a ruling on the request, objection, or motion.

N.C. R. APP. P. 10(a). *See also In re J.T.S.,* 834 S.E.2d 637 (N.C. Ct. App. 2019) (holding that respondent mother failed to preserve for appellate review issues regarding visitation terms and a guardianship appointment when she consented to those terms at the hearing); *In re E.M,* 249 N.C. App. 44 (2016) (holding that respondent failed to preserve the issue for appellate review as no timely objection or motion to strike was made to challenge reports and documentary exhibits that were never formally offered into evidence but were repeatedly referred to during trial); *In re K.A.,* 233 N.C. App. 119 (2014) (holding that the issue of the trial court's misapplication of the doctrine of collateral estoppel was properly objected to and therefore preserved for appeal); *In re A.D.N.,* 231 N.C. App. 54 (2013) (acknowledging the respondent's claim that the trial court failed to appoint a GAL for the child although required to do so but declining to address the issue because it was not raised at trial).

A constitutional issue not raised at the trial level will not be considered for the first time on appeal. *See, e.g., In re C.M.P.,* 254 N.C. App. 647 (2017) (holding respondent mother failed to preserve the issue of whether the trial court's denial of her motion to continue violated her constitutional right to effective assistance of counsel); *In re C.P.,* 252 N.C. App. 118 (2017) (declining to address respondent mother's argument, not raised in the trial court, that her constitutional rights were violated by award of guardianship to a non-parent without finding that respondent was unfit or had acted inconsistently with her constitutionally protected status); *In re T.P.,* 217 N.C. App. 181 (2011) (declining to address the trial court's finding that the respondent parent had acted inconsistently with her constitutionally protected parental status).

The supreme court in *Dogwood Dev. & Mgmt. Co. v. White Oak Transp. Co.,* 362 N.C. 191, 195 (2008), explained that this appellate rule requirement to make an objection in the trial court "plays an integral role in preserving the efficacy and integrity of the appellate process" because it allows a trial court to correct an error that is timely brought to its attention, thereby preventing unnecessary appellate review and new trials caused by errors.

See Chapter 11.13.B and D for an additional discussion relating to preservation of evidentiary issues for appeal (including motions in limine; specific, continuing, and timely objections; and offers of proof).

**2. Issues automatically preserved for appeal.** Certain issues are preserved as a matter of law even if no objection was made in the trial court, including but not limited to

- lack of subject matter jurisdiction (N.C. R. App. P. 10(a)),
- whether the judgment is supported by the findings of fact and conclusions of law (N.C. R. App. P. 10(a)), and
- questions directed to a witness by the trial court (N.C. R. Civ. P. 46(a)(3)).

Additionally, case law has preserved in some cases the right to appeal a decision in which the trial court failed to follow a statutory mandate that resulted in prejudice to a party, even though an objection was not made at trial. *See State v. Ashe*, 314 N.C. 28 (1985) (addressing trial court actions contrary to statutory mandate); *State v. Hernandez*, 188 N.C. App. 193, 204 (2008) (quoting *State v. Golphin*, 352 N.C. 364, 411 (2000)) (allowing consideration of an issue on appeal although not objected to at trial, because "[w]hen a trial court acts contrary to a statutory mandate, no objection is necessary to preserve the error"); *In re Taylor*, 97 N.C. App. 57, 61 (1990) (reviewing the trial court's failure to conduct a special hearing in a termination of parental rights case despite respondent's failure to object at trial, and stating that "[w]hen … a judge acts in contravention of a statute to the prejudice of a party, the right to appeal is preserved notwithstanding the failure to enter an objection").

However, even when an appellate issue involves a statutory mandate, appellate courts will not necessarily consider the issue on appeal when it is not objected to at trial. For example, appellate cases have recognized the statutory mandate to appoint a guardian ad litem (GAL) for the child in certain circumstances but have not always been willing to consider the issue of failing to appoint a GAL when no objection was made at trial. *See In re A.D.N.*, 231 N.C. App. 54 (2013) (refusing to rule on the issue of the failure to appoint a GAL for the child in a termination of parental rights case when an answer denying a material allegation was filed since there was no objection at trial).

## B. Scope of Appellate Review

With few exceptions only those issues properly preserved at trial may be presented as issues on appeal. The issue of subject matter jurisdiction can be raised for the first time on appeal and may be raised by the appellate court sua sponte. *See, e.g., Rodriguez v. Rodriguez*, 211 N.C. App. 267 (2011) (the court of appeals on its own motion raised the issue of the juvenile court's exclusive jurisdiction).

**1. Issues identified in briefs.** Appellate courts will only review issues properly preserved at trial if presented and discussed in briefs. A brief must contain an argument with the contentions as to each issue presented. Issues not presented and discussed in a party's brief are deemed abandoned. N.C. R. APP. P. 28(a), (b)(6). *See In re Ivey,* 810 S.E.2d 740 (N.C. Ct. App. 2018) (referring to Appellate Rule 28(a) in footnote 2 when noting the appeal of second order identified in the notice of appeal was abandoned when there was no argument in the brief addressing that second order); *In re A.H.*, 250 N.C. App. 546 (2016) (respondent mother appealed the trial court's quashing of her subpoena for her son's testimony at the TPR hearing; in the trial court, respondent did not specify whether her son's testimony was to be presented at the adjudication or disposition phase of the hearing but in her appeal, respondent did not challenge the adjudication; as a result, the court of appeals limited its analysis to the dispositional phase). *See also In re J.D.R.*, 239 N.C. App. 63 (2015) (although mother appealed from more than one order, because the brief only addressed the disposition order, appellate review was limited to that issue). Issues are also presented in the record on appeal, but failure to present an issue in the record will not prevent a party from arguing the issue as long as it is presented and discussed in a brief. N.C. R. APP. P. 10(b).

Cases citing Appellate Rule 28(b)(6) have required a party to an appeal to assert, in his or her brief, specific (as opposed to general) determinations of the trial court as issues to be reviewed by the appellate court. For example, one cannot assert that there is insufficient evidence for the trial court's findings generally, or errors in the trial court's conclusions generally. Rather, a brief must assert a particular finding of fact for which there is insufficient evidence or a particular conclusion of law for which there are insufficient findings to properly present an issue for review by the appellate court. *See, e.g., In re A.H.*, 183 N.C. App. 609 (2007) (holding that although respondent assigned error to various findings, under the former appellate rule that required assignments of error, they were not argued in her brief and were deemed abandoned); *In re J.M.W.*, 179 N.C. App. 788 (2006) (refusing to review two of the grounds for termination of parental rights because appellant failed to argue them in her brief); *In re P.M.*, 169 N.C. App. 423 (2005) (holding that where the appellant failed to specifically argue in her brief that specified findings were unsupported by evidence, the appellate court would consider only whether the findings supported the conclusions of law).

The brief itself is not a source of evidence, meaning representations made in a brief that do not relate to matters in the record cannot be considered by the court. *See In re A.B.*, 239 N.C. App. 157 (2015) (counsel's representations in a brief that attempted to explain an error in drafting a court order could not be considered evidence on appeal).

**2. The contents of the record.** The scope of the court's review also depends on the contents of the record on appeal. The contents, format, and requirements for the record on appeal are addressed in Appellate Rule 9.

The record must demonstrate that the trial court had subject matter jurisdiction. In *In re J.C.M.J.C.*, 834 S.E.2d 670 (N.C. Ct. App. 2019), the court of appeals dismissed the respondents' appeal when the record did not contain copies of the underlying juvenile petitions; the petitions commence the action to establish subject matter jurisdiction with the trial court. (Note that the court of appeals reviewed the respondent's arguments by granting a writ of certiorari (discussed in section 12.10.A., below)).

The record must also contain anything necessary for the appellate court to review all issues presented on appeal, without including unnecessary documents from the court file. *See In re B.C.T.*, 828 S.E.2d 50 (N.C. Ct. App. 2019) (court of appeals could not address appellant's argument about the applicability of a G.S. 7B-910 hearing to review a voluntary placement agreement when the record did not include documentation about the agreement and its terms). In the absence of a transcript from the hearing resulting in the order that is being appealed, the appellate court is obligated to treat the trial court's findings as supported by competent evidence. *In re A.L.L.*, 254 N.C. App. 252 (2017). However, when the hearing transcript and remainder of the record are insufficient for the appellate court to address an ineffective assistance of counsel claim, the appropriate remedy is a remand to the trial court to determine the adequacy of the attorney representation. *In re A.R.C.*, 830 S.E.2d 1 (N.C. Ct. App. 2019); *In re C.D.H.*, 829 S.E.2d 690 (N.C. Ct. App. 2019).

The court of appeals has stated, "[i]t is the appellant's duty to include any information necessary for review of the issues raised on appeal." *In re B.C.T.*, 828 S.E.2d 50, 57 (N.C. Ct. App. 2019). Appellate Rule 9(b)(5)(a) allows a responding party to "supplement the record on appeal with any items that could otherwise have been included pursuant to this Rule 9" when "the record on appeal as settled is insufficient to respond to the issues presented in an appellant's brief or the issues presented in an appellee's brief pursuant to Rule 10(c) . . . ." These supplemental materials, however, cannot contain documents or issues that were not before the trial court in the case being considered. *See In re M.G.*, 239 N.C. App. 77 (2015) (admonishing counsel for filing supplemental materials containing documents from another case not before the trial court in the present case and raising issues never considered by the trial court).

**Practice Note:** In an unpublished opinion, the court of appeals admonished all counsel about the unnecessarily large volume of the record on appeal. The court of appeals devoted part of its opinion to discussing the waste of time and resources, pointing out that the record was 770 pages, consisting of what appeared to be copies of everything in the trial record. *In re J.J.*, 199 N.C. App. 755 (2009) (unpublished).

## C. Appellate Rule 2: Prevent Manifest Injustice

The appellate court, pursuant to Appellate Rule 2, may suspend or vary the requirements or provisions of the Appellate Rules and consider issues that are not properly preserved or presented for review, either to "prevent manifest injustice to a party" or to "expedite decision in the public interest." Rule 2 may be invoked upon application of a party or sua sponte. However, the supreme court has recognized that Appellate Rule 2 is an "extraordinary step" that should be "invoked 'cautiously'" in "exceptional circumstances." *Dogwood Dev. & Mgmt. Co. v. White Oak Transp. Co.*, 362 N.C. 191, 196 (2008).

Rule 2 has been applied in appeals of orders entered in abuse, neglect, dependency, and termination of parental rights (TPR) actions. *See, e.g., In re Z.V.A.*, 835 S.E.2d 425 (N.C. S.Ct. 2019) (electing sua sponte to invoke Rule 2 to address respondent-parents' arguments that the trial judge should have recused himself from hearing the TPR when the issue was not preserved at trial); *In re D.A.*, 820 S.E.2d 873 (N.C. Ct. App. 2018) (invoking Rule 2 to respondent father's appeal to expedite a decision in the public interest; suspending the mandatory service requirement of Rule 3.1(d) when all efforts by the appellant's attorney to serve his client were unsuccessful); *In re S.B.*, 166 N.C. App. 488 (2004) (invoking rule sua sponte after determining potential for manifest injustice to respondent father in a TPR proceeding when he was not appointed a guardian ad litem); *In re O.W.*, 164 N.C. App. 699 (2004) (invoking the rule to decide issue of consolidation of neglect and abuse adjudicatory hearing and disposition hearing).

The court of appeals has also declined to invoke Rule 2 in juvenile proceedings. *See, e.g., In re P.T.W.*, 250 N.C. App. 589 (2016) (determining application of rule was not necessary to prevent manifest injustice to respondent mother or child on the issue of the trial court abusing its discretion in failing to appoint a GAL for the child in a TPR proceeding where respondent mother willfully failed to make progress on her case plan); *In re E.T.S*, 175 N.C. App. 32 (2005) (declining to invoke rule upon request of respondent mother in a TPR proceeding on evidentiary issue she failed to object to at trial).

The North Carolina Supreme Court recently made clear that application of Appellate Rule 2 by an appellate court should not be automatic, even when there is precedent for its application. In *State v. Campbell*, 369 N.C. 599 (2017), the supreme court reviewed a decision allowing review pursuant to Rule 2 of a fatal variance issue not raised at trial. After citing an earlier appellate decision that invoked Rule 2 to review a similar fatal variance argument, the court of appeals, without further discussion or analysis of Rule 2, addressed the merits of defendant's argument and reversed his conviction. The supreme court reversed and remanded as the process by which an appellate court determines whether a case is one of the "rare 'instances' " appropriate for application of Rule 2 that requires an individual analysis "made in light of the *specific circumstances of individual cases and parties*, such as whether 'substantial rights of an appellant are affected.' " Moreover, "precedent cannot create an automatic right to review via Rule 2" because the decision to suspend a rule of appellate procedure is "always a discretionary determination to be made on a case-by-case basis." *Campbell*, 369 N.C. at 603 (emphasis in original).

The individual analysis required by the appellate court that may result in seemingly conflicting decisions when determining whether to apply Appellate Rule 2 is demonstrated in three court of appeals decisions addressing the trial court's failure to appoint a GAL for the child who was the subject of a TPR action, when that issue was not objected to in the trial court. In two cases the court of appeals invoked Appellate Rule 2 to reach the merits of the issue, and in both cases found prejudicial error in the trial court's failure to appoint a GAL for the child when the respondents filed an answer denying a material allegation, triggering the statutory mandate that a GAL be appointed. *See In re Fuller*, 144 N.C. App. 620 (2001) (determining child who is intended beneficiary of statute requiring appointment of GAL to represent his best interests was unrepresented and the 9-year-old child was not present at the hearing to object to the trial court's failure to appoint him a GAL); *In re Barnes*, 97 N.C. App. 325 (1990) (unrepresented 22-month-old child, who is a party to the proceeding, was unable to make objection to trial court's failure to appoint statutorily mandated GAL; fundamental fairness required the child be represented by counsel when the respondent was represented by counsel). In contrast, the court of appeals did not invoke Appellate Rule 2 to decide the merits of the same issue, finding the rule was inapplicable to the case as there was no manifest injustice to the respondent mother or the child who was not appointed a GAL. *In re A.D.N.*, 231 N.C. App. 54 (2013) (determining respondent mother repeatedly chose substance abuse over her 2-year-old child during his lifetime and almost entirely abdicated responsibility for him to petitioner, the child's paternal grandmother).

### D. Invited Error

A party is not entitled to appellate relief when they invite the trial court to make an error they are now complaining of – this is the doctrine of "invited error." This doctrine "applies to 'a legal error that is not a cause for complaint because the error occurred through the fault of the party now complaining.' " *In re R.L.G.*, 816 S.E.2d 914, 919 (N.C. Ct. App. 2018) (citations omitted). The court of appeals has examined the invited error doctrine in juvenile appeals.

In one case, the court of appeals determined invited error applied such that the respondent mother was not entitled to relief on appeal. In *In re K.C.*, 199 N.C. App. 557 (2009), respondent mother was not entitled to review of a disposition order that did not include a visitation plan as required by the Juvenile Code. Respondent mother invited the error when the trial court did what she essentially asked it to do, which was to not order visitation. The disposition order included findings that the mother had cancelled visits, had no plans to see her children, stated she did not wish to see or work with the children, and was not interested in working with DSS toward her reunification with the children until the children's problems were resolved.

In another case, *In re R.L.G.*, 816 S.E.2d 914, the court of appeals determined there was no invited error. At the adjudicatory hearing, respondent mother's stipulation to facts about her child's school attendance and performance and missed medical appointments was not an invitation for the trial court to adjudicate her child neglected. There was no indication in the record that respondent mother requested that the trial court adjudicate or remove her daughter.

### E. No Swapping Horses.
The North Carolina appellate courts have stated that parties are not allowed to "swap horses between courts in order to get a better mount," meaning parties cannot take different positions or make different arguments at trial and on appeal. *In re B.C.T.*, 828 S.E.2d 50, 61 (N.C. Ct. App. 2019); *In re I.K.*, 227 N.C. App. 264, 266 (2013) (quoting *Weil v. Herring*, 207 N.C. 6, 10 (1934)). A party who changes its position has a responsibility to notify the affected courts and explain a change in position to justify its actions. *In re B.C.T.*, 828 S.E.2d 50 (DSS did not acknowledge that its position at trial was the child's return to his mother and release of DSS from the case when arguing on appeal that the disposition order continuing the child in DSS custody should be affirmed); *In re I.K.*, 227 N.C. App. 264 (DSS did not acknowledge its position regarding the continuation of

reasonable efforts changed – requesting the continuation of those efforts with respondent father at trial and seeking affirmation of the order ceasing those efforts on appeal).

The court of appeals has noted that a change in position by DSS is particularly concerning because the primary goal of the Juvenile Code, which includes the duties of a DSS, is to protect an abused, neglected, or dependent child's best interests. *In re B.C.T.*, 828 S.E.2d 50; *In re I.K.*, 227 N.C. App. 264. In the most recent opinion, the court of appeals stated, "DSS is not obligated to adopt a different position on appeal just to oppose the appealing parent if it has previously determined that a parent has a safe and appropriate home and the child should be returned to the parent." *In re B.C.T.*, 828 S.E.2d at 61.

## 12.4 Which Orders Can Be Appealed

### A. Appealable Orders

The Juvenile Code specifies the types of final orders in abuse, neglect, dependency, and termination of parental rights cases that may be appealed by an aggrieved party who has standing to appeal. *See* G.S. 7B-1001(a), (a1). Significant changes were made to G.S. 7B-1001, the statute designating which juvenile orders may be appealed, and the Rules of Appellate Procedure, both of which became effective on January 1, 2019.

> **Resource:** For more information about the changes to G.S. 7B-1001 and the Rules of Appellate Procedure, see Sara DePasquale, *Big Changes to Appeals of A/N/D – TPR Orders Designated in G.S. 7B-1001*, UNC SCH. OF GOV'T: ON THE CIVIL SIDE BLOG (March 25, 2019).

**1. No jurisdiction.** Any order finding a lack of jurisdiction may be appealed directly to the court of appeals. G.S. 7B-1001(a)(1). A party may not appeal an order under G.S. 7B-1001(a)(1) by claiming a jurisdictional defect, the trial court must have found that it lacked jurisdiction to decide the matter before it. *See In re A.T.*, 191 N.C. App. 372 (2008) (rejecting the appellant's assertion that an order denying a motion to modify a payment provision in a nonsecure custody order was related to a lack of jurisdiction and therefore appealable).

**2. Order determining the action.** Any order that in effect determines the action and prevents a judgment from which appeal might be taken, including the involuntary dismissal of a petition, may be appealed directly to the court of appeals. G.S. 7B-1001(a)(2). In the case *In re E.H.*, 227 N.C. App. 525 (2013), the trial court denied the GAL's Rule 60 (of the Rules of Civil Procedure) motion for relief from DSS's voluntary dismissal of its petition, and the GAL appealed. The court of appeals held that the trial court's order denying the Rule 60 motion was appealable because it (1) terminated jurisdiction by refusing to set aside the voluntary dismissal and (2) determined the action and prevented a final judgment on the merits.

Orders made during the pendency of an action that do not dispose of the case are interlocutory. Interlocutory orders are not immediately appealable unless the failure to grant an immediate review would affect a substantial right. *See* G.S. 1-277(a). The burden is on the appellant to establish that a substantial right will be affected, with the test being whether the right itself is substantial and the deprivation of that right would cause injury if not corrected before appeal from the final judgment. *See In re J.G.*, 186 N.C. App. 496 (2007) (and cases cited therein) (holding that the trial court's order affecting DSS's right to choose how to dispose of funds it received as a representative payee for Social Security benefits affected a substantial right and was immediately appealable). *See also In re A.R.G.*, 361 N.C. 392 (2007) (analyzing a previous version of G.S. 7B-1001 and holding that respondent's appeal was properly dismissed because the order was interlocutory and did not affect a substantial right).

**3. Initial disposition and underlying adjudication order.** An initial disposition order and the adjudication order upon which it is based may be appealed directly to the court of appeals. G.S. 7B-1001(a)(3). An appeal of the adjudication order cannot be made prior to the entry of the initial dispositional order. *See In re P.S.*, 242 N.C. App. 430 (2015). An adjudication order and any temporary dispositional order entered after the adjudication but before the initial dispositional hearing are not final orders and, therefore, are not appealable. *In re P.S.*, 242 N.C. App. 430 (dismissing appeal of adjudication order that included a temporary disposition pending the initial dispositional hearing); *In re C.M.*, 183 N.C. App. 207 (2007) (dismissing respondent father's appeal of a temporary dispositional order).

Although the orders are appealed together, an appellant may choose to only raise challenges to one of those orders. *See, e.g., In re B.C.T.*, 828 S.E.2d 50 (N.C. Ct. App. 2019) (respondent mother's notice of appeal included both the adjudication and disposition orders, but her brief did not include any arguments challenging the adjudication order). When the orders are appealed, if the adjudication order is challenged and reversed or vacated, the disposition order must also be reversed or vacated. *In re M.N.*, 816 S.E.2d 925 (N.C. Ct. App. 2018) (orders reversed); *In re R.L.G.*, 816 S.E.2d 914 (N.C. Ct. App. 2018) (orders vacated). Further, when an adjudication order is reversed or vacated and issues with the dispositional order are raised, the appellate court is not required to address those issue since the dispositional order must also be reversed or vacated; however, the appellate court may choose to proceed with a review. *In re S.C.R.*, 217 N.C. App. 166 (2011) (choosing to briefly address two issues respondent raised with the dispositional order so as to prevent repetition on remand).

**4. Order changing custody.** Any final order, other than a nonsecure custody order, that changes the legal custody of a juvenile may be appealed directly to the court of appeals. G.S. 7B-1001(a)(4). The appellate courts have examined what constitutes a change in legal custody when considering whether the order is an appealable order.

Legal custody involves "the right and responsibility to make decisions with important and long-term implications for a child's best interest and welfare" and includes the "right to control [one's] children's associations." *In re M.M.*, 249 N.C. App. 58, 61, 62 (2016) (citations omitted). An order that changes the decision-making responsibilities or imposes a new restriction on who a child may have contact with is a change in legal custody and is an appealable order. *In re M.M.*, 249 N.C. App. 58 (holding a permanency planning order that continued joint legal custody between respondent parents but added a provision that prohibited contact between the child and the maternal grandfather was an order that changed legal custody and was subject to appeal).

A temporary dispositional order entered prior to the initial dispositional hearing is analogous to a nonsecure custody order and is not an appealable order based on a change in legal custody. *In re P.S.*, 242 N.C. App. 430 (2015). *See also In re J.V.*, 198 N.C. App. 108 (2009) (stating that a permanency planning order that awarded guardianship to the child's relatives modified the child's custody from DSS to the relatives and was immediately appealable under G.S. 7B-1001(a)(4)).

In analyzing an earlier version of this Juvenile Code provision, which included in the list of appealable orders "any order modifying custodial rights" (and did not include a provision addressing the appeal of an order ceasing reunification efforts, discussed immediately below), the supreme court considered a father's argument that the trial court's determination that it was in the child's best interest to pursue a termination of parental rights (TPR) cut him off as a possible placement and therefore modified custodial rights. *In re A.R.G.*, 361 N.C. 392 (2007). The supreme court rejected this argument, after looking at the definition of "custody" and "legal custody" in Black's Law Dictionary (8th ed. 2004) as " 'the care, control, and maintenance of a child awarded by a court to a responsible adult' or awarded 'to the state for placing the child in foster care if no responsible relative or family friend is willing and able to care for the child.' " *In re A.R.G.*, 361 N.C. at 396. The supreme court held there was no modification of the father's custodial rights after finding that throughout the case the trial court had ordered that legal custody of the child remain with DSS, the father had never been awarded custody, and there had not yet been an order terminating parental rights.

**5. Order eliminating reunification as a permanent plan.** An order entered under G.S. 7B-906.2(b) that eliminates reunification as a permanent plan may be appealed by a parent, guardian, or custodian with whom reunification is not the permanent plan. G.S. 7B-1001(a)(5); (a1)(2); *see* G.S. 7B-101(18b) (definition of "return home or reunification"). However, the procedure for, timing of, and appellate court that reviews the G.S. 7B-906.2(b) order depends upon whether the appellant is a parent, guardian, or custodian with whom reunification was eliminated as a permanent plan. An appeal by a guardian or custodian is made directly to the court of appeals. The procedure of an appeal by a parent is unusual – it requires a delay in timing and the proper preservation of the right to appeal. Whether the parent's appeal of an order eliminating reunification as a permanent plan is made directly to the court of appeals or to the North Carolina Supreme Court depends on whether a termination of parental rights (TPR) action is timely commenced and whether the TPR is granted. *See* G.S. 7B-1001(a)(5), (a1)(2). See also section 12.5.A, below (discussing the timing and manner of an appeal of an order eliminating reunification as a permanent plan).

The G.S. 7B-906.2(b) order is relatively new, as this statute was enacted in 2015 and replaced G.S. 7B-507(c) regarding reunification and reunification efforts. *See* S.L. 2015-136, sec. 7, 14 (effective for all actions pending or filed on or after October 1, 2015). The differences in these two statutes are significant and impact which orders may be appealed under G.S. 7B-1001(a)(5) and (a1)(2).

Pursuant to G.S. 7B-906.2(b), the trial court must order concurrent permanent plans; identify the primary and secondary plan; and unless certain findings were made, designate reunification as a primary or secondary plan. The court is not required to order concurrent planning once a permanent plan is or has been achieved. G.S. 7B-906.2(a1); S.L. 2109-33; *see* G.S. 7B-906.2(a) (referring to one or more permanent plans).

The court eliminates reunification as a permanent plan by entering an order pursuant to G.S. 7B-906.2(b) that either (a) does not designate reunification as a primary or secondary plan or (b) achieves a permanent plan other than reunification and either chooses to stop concurrent planning or identifies a secondary plan that is not reunification. Regardless of how reunification is eliminated as a permanent plan, the G.S. 7B-906.2(b) order may be appealed under G.S. 7B-1001(a)(5) or (a1)(2). Only the first permanency planning order that eliminates reunification under G.S. 7B-906.2(b) may be appealed; a later permanency planning order that merely continues the permanent plans that did not include reunification is not an order that eliminates reunification as a permanent plan and is not an appealable order under G.S. 7B-1001. *In re J.A.K.*, 812 S.E.2d 716 (N.C. Ct. App. 2018) (dismissing respondent father's appeal of an October permanency planning order that merely continued the concurrent permanent plans of adoption and guardianship ordered in April).

G.S. 7B-1001(a)(5) and (a1)(2) focus on the elimination of reunification as a permanent plan under G.S. 7B-906.2(b) and not the cessation of reunification efforts. In interpreting G.S. 7B-906.2(b), the court of appeals has distinguished between eliminating reunification as a permanent plan and ceasing reunification efforts. *See In re C.P.*, 812 N.C. App. 188 (N.C. App. 2018) (affirming portion of permanency planning order that ceased reunification efforts and vacating portion of order that eliminated reunification as a concurrent permanent plan); *In re C.S.L.B.*, 254 N.C. App. 395, 397 (2017) (stating in case that established the primary plan of guardianship and kept a secondary plan of reunification, "[r]espondent mother conflates removing reunification as a permanent plan for the children with ceasing reunification efforts"). If the G.S. 7B-906.2(b) order ceases reunification efforts but includes reunification as a primary or secondary plan, that order may not be appealed under G.S. 7B-1001(a)(5) or (a1)(2) because reunification is still a concurrent permanent plan and has not been eliminated. *See In re A.A.S.*, 812 S.E.2d 875 (N.C. Ct. App. 2018) (holding permanency planning order with a primary plan of adoption and a secondary plan of reunification did not meet the criteria of G.S. 7B-1001(a) designating orders that may be appealed); *cf. In re C.S.L.B.*, 254 N.C. App. 395 (permanency planning order achieved the primary permanent plan of guardianship and continued to identify a secondary plan of reunification; note the order did change legal custody of the juvenile with the appointment of a permanent guardian and was likely reviewed on appeal pursuant to G.S. 7B-1001(a)(4)).

Additionally, a permanency planning order that includes reunification as a secondary plan but directs DSS to commence a termination of parental rights (TPR) action to achieve the primary permanent plan of adoption does not implicitly or explicitly eliminate reunification as a permanent plan and is not an appealable order under G.S. 7B-1001(a). *In re A.A.S.*, 812 S.E.2d at 881 (recognizing new statutory framework "clearly contemplates the use of multiple, concurrent plans including reunification and adoption" and noting prior cases holding an implicit cessation of reunification efforts were decided under the former statutory scheme).

See Chapter 7.8.C.8 (discussing reasonable efforts findings); 7.8.D. (discussing the initiation of a TPR under certain circumstances); 7.9.D (discussing ceasing reasonable efforts); and 7.10.A (discussing concurrent permanent plans and reunification).

The former statute, G.S. 7B-507(c), which was replaced by G.S. 7B-906.2, authorized the trial court to order the cessation of reunification efforts in any order that awarded custody or placement responsibility of the child to DSS (e.g., nonsecure custody, disposition, review, permanency planning). The order ceasing reunification efforts under G.S. 7B-507(c) was an appealable order under the prior statutory language of G.S. 7B-1001(a)(5) at any stage in the abuse, neglect, or dependency proceeding and did not address or require the elimination of reunification as a permanent plan.

Beware that older case law addresses the cessation of reasonable efforts under G.S. 7B-507(c) and does not address an appeal of an order eliminating reunification as a concurrent permanent plan under G.S. 7B-906.2(b). The court of appeals has acknowledged the differences in the statutory framework for permanency planning when deciding issues addressing reunification as a permanent plan and reunification efforts and distinguishing earlier cases that were decided under the former statutes. *See In re A.A.S.*, 812 S.E.2d at 880 (stating "*In re A.E.C.*[, 239 N.C. App. 36 (2015)] and the other cases cited by Respondent-Mother were decided prior to 1 October 2015, when N.C. Gen. Stat. § 7B-906.2 was enacted[;]" *see also In re C.S.L.B.*, 254 N.C. App. 395 (2017) (reunification remained a permanent plan such that findings about reunification efforts were not required; differs from *In re N.B.*, 240 N.C. App. 353 (2015), which involved an order that awarded guardianship as the permanent plan, effectively ceasing reunification efforts and thus requiring statutory findings regarding reunification efforts); *In re R.S.B.*, 818 S.E.2d 644 (N.C. Ct. App. 2018) (unpublished) (noting that *In re A.E.C.*, *In re N.B.*, and *In re A.P.W.*, 225 N.C. App. 534 (2013), which held an order that designates a permanent plan of adoption and directs DSS to file a TPR petition implicitly ceases reunification efforts making the order appealable, were all decided under former version of the statute, before the enactment of G.S. 7B-906.2).

**6. Order granting or denying termination of parental rights.** Any final order terminating parental rights or denying a petition or motion to terminate parental rights may be appealed directly to the North Carolina Supreme Court. G.S. 7B-1001(a1)(1); 7A-27(a)(5) (effective for all appeals filed on or after January 1, 2019).

**7. Order deciding placement on the Responsible Individuals List**. An appeal of a district court order deciding whether an individual is placed on the Responsible Individuals List (RIL) is appealed under G.S. 7A-27(b)(2), not G.S. 7B-1001. G.S. 7B-323(f). Because it is not an order designated in G.S. 7B-1001, Appellate Rule 3.1 does not apply. Appellate Rule 42, which protects the minor's identity, applies when the alleged responsible individual committed a sexual offense against the juvenile, or a motion to seal the entire matter or just the juvenile's identity was made and granted by the appellate court. See Chapter 5.2.B for a discussion of the Responsible Individuals List.

## B. When an Appeal Is Moot

As a general rule, courts will not answer moot questions, and a case or issue "is 'moot' when a determination is sought on a matter which, when rendered, cannot have any practical effect on the existing controversy." *In re D.S.*, 817 S.E.2d 901, 905 (N.C. Ct. App. 2018); *In re M.B.*, 253 N.C. App. 437, 439 (2017). The appellate court will decide a case only if the controversy giving rise to the appeal continues at the time of appeal. *In re A.K.*, 360 N.C. 449 (2006); *see In re D.S.*, 817 S.E.2d 901.

In the following cases, the court of appeals declined to address certain issues that were raised in appeals of orders entered in abuse, neglect, or dependency cases after concluding that the challenged issues had been rendered moot.

- Mother's appeal of a permanency planning order that eliminated reunification and ceased reunification efforts was rendered moot when the trial court subsequently terminated mother's parental rights (TPR), and the TPR order was affirmed. In the TPR order, the trial court, after a hearing, made independent findings of fact and conclusions of law that did not rely on the permanency planning order appealed from, contained extensive findings of fact and conclusions of law that were not in the permanency planning order, and included findings of then-current conditions. *In re H.N.D.*, 827 S.E.2d 329 (N.C. Ct. App. 2019) (relying on *In re V.L.B.*, 164 N.C. App. 743 (2004)).
- The argument that the permanency planning order that awarded guardianship to an out-of-state resident without first complying with the Interstate Compact on the Placement of Children was rendered moot when the guardian moved back to North Carolina. Respondent did not argue any exception to the mootness doctrine. *In re M.B.*, 253 N.C. App. 437 (2017).
- Respondent mother's appeal of the permanency planning order only was moot when she did not also appeal the accompanying order that terminated the court's jurisdiction in the neglect proceeding and the resulting Chapter 50 custody order that was entered pursuant to G.S. 7B-911. Those two orders (the Ch. 50 civil custody and 7B termination of jurisdiction orders) would remain in effect. The respondent mother did not raise an exception to the mootness doctrine. *In re J.S.*, 250 N.C. App. 370 (2016).
- Respondent's appeal was moot because the order being appealed had been subsequently modified in a review hearing. Any determination of the issues on appeal would have no practical effect. No exceptions to the mootness doctrine applied. *In re A.S., III.*, 229 N.C. App. 198 (2013).
- Appeal of permanency planning order was dismissed as moot when the juvenile reached the age of 18 while the appeal was pending. Under G.S. 7B-201, the trial court's jurisdiction terminates when the juvenile turns 18. *In re B.G.*, 207 N.C. App. 745 (2010).
- The part of the mother's appeal challenging the trial court's finding that returning custody of the child to her was not in the child's best interest was moot when the trial court apparently had entered a subsequent order returning custody to the mother. *In re H.D.F.*, 197 N.C. App. 480 (2009).

The court of appeals has also determined challenged issues in appeals of juvenile orders were not moot and were properly before the court for appellate review. In *In re D.S.*, 817 S.E.2d

901 (N.C. Ct. App. 2018), the court of appeals rejected the arguments of DSS and the child's GAL that respondent father's challenge to the permanency planning order, which granted guardianship of the child to a non-relative without first addressing the statutory placement preference with a relative, the child's grandmother, was moot due to a subsequent order that ceased all contact between the child and grandmother. Although the trial court ceased contact between the child and grandmother, it never addressed the statutory requirement to consider priority placement with a relative over a non-relative. The reasoning behind the decision to cease the contact with the grandmother may be relevant to the priority placement preference with a relative, but it is an evidentiary matter that does not render the issue moot. Because there may be a practical effect on the case when the trial court addresses the statutory placement priority, the issue is not moot.

In other cases, if the continued existence of the judgment itself may result in adverse collateral legal consequences for the appellant, the validity of the judgment continues to be a live controversy and an appeal from that judgment is not moot. *In re A.K.*, 360 N.C. 449 (2006).

**1. Exception based on collateral legal consequences of abuse, neglect, dependency adjudication.** A parent's regaining custody during a pending appeal challenging an abuse, neglect, or dependency adjudication does not render the case moot because there are collateral legal consequences for the parent. *In re A.K.*, 360 N.C. 449 (reversing and remanding court of appeals dismissal of respondent father's appeal as moot). Possible collateral legal consequences include (1) the use of an abuse or neglect adjudication to support a determination that another child with whom the parent resides is neglected (*see* G.S. 7B-101(15) definition of "neglected juvenile") and (2) the admissibility of the adjudication in any future termination of parental rights proceeding involving the same child that alleges abuse or neglect as the ground (*see* G.S. 7B-1111(a)(1)). *In re A.K.*, 360 N.C. 449.

**2. Exception based on collateral legal consequences of termination of parental rights.** The termination of a parent's rights to one child may be a ground for termination of that parent's rights to another child if that parent lacks the ability or willingness to establish a safe home for the other child. G.S. 7B-1111(a)(9). The court of appeals has held that the collateral consequence arising from a possible future application of G.S. 7B-1111(a)(9) makes an appeal of a TPR order not moot. *See In re Baby Boy*, 238 N.C. App. 316, 319 (2014) (appeal of an order terminating respondent mother's parental rights was not moot when the order was entered while an appeal of the child's adoption based on the validity of mother's relinquishment was pending (*see In re Adoption of Baby Boy*, 233 N.C. App. 493 (2014)) and subsequently held valid after the TPR was granted, thus finalizing the adoption; even though the TPR appeal would have no practical effect on the child's parentage, the TPR order "may have an effect on respondent's parental rights in the future as to any other children she has or may have"); *In re C.C.*, 173 N.C. App. 375 (2005) (refusing to dismiss as moot a mother's appeal from a TPR order, when the child took his own life after notice of appeal was given, because a TPR may form the basis of a subsequent proceeding to terminate the parent's rights in relation to another child); *In re J.S.L.*, 218 N.C. App. 610 (2012) (trial court erred when it denied respondent putative father's motion for paternity testing and terminated respondent's parental rights; that respondent's parental rights had been terminated did not render moot his appeal of the denial of the motion for paternity testing because of the collateral legal consequences of a TPR order; if testing did not establish paternity, the trial court would be required to dismiss the TPR petition).

Although not addressed in these appellate decisions, another collateral consequence of a TPR is the cessation of reunification efforts with that parent if another child of the parent is adjudicated abused, neglected, or dependent. Under G.S. 7B-901(c)(2), the court is authorized at the initial dispositional hearing to relieve DSS of providing reunification efforts to a parent if the trial court finds that a court of competent jurisdiction has involuntarily terminated that parent's rights to another child.

## 12.5 Notice of Appeal

### A. Timing, Manner, and Content of Notice

**1. Timing and manner generally.** A notice of appeal is filed with the clerk of superior court and must be given in writing within thirty days after entry and service of the order pursuant to Rule 58 of the Rules of Civil Procedure. G.S. 7B-1001(b); N.C. R. APP. P. 3.1(b). A judgment is not entered until it is reduced to writing, signed by the judge, and filed with the clerk of court. N.C. R. CIV. P. 58. The judge who presided over the hearing is the judge who must sign the order; otherwise, the order does not comply with Rule 58 and is not entered. *In re C.M.C.*, 832 S.E.2d 681, 684 (N.C. S.Ct. 2019) (holding termination of parental rights (TPR) order signed by a judge who did not preside over the TPR hearing was a nullity; stating, "[i]n view of the fact that no viable adjudication and termination orders were actually entered... "). An order that fails to indicate it was filed with the clerk (e.g., a file stamp or other mark to indicate a filing date) is not entered. *McKinney v. Duncan*, 808 S.E.2d 509 (N.C. Ct. App. 2017) (dismissing appeal for lack of subject matter jurisdiction in the appellate court when the underlying orders were never entered as they were devoid of any proof of filing with the clerk). *Cf.* N.C. R. CIV. P. 5(e)(3) (addressing failure to affix a date or file stamp on an order) (enacted by S.L. 2017-158, effective July 21, 2017). See Chapter 4.9.C (discussing entry and service of orders and Rule 58).

Rule 58 of the Rules of Civil Procedure requires that the parties be served within three days of the entry of the judgment. If the party has been served as required, within three days of the entry of the judgement, the thirty-day time period to appeal starts from the date of the entry of the judgment. N.C. R. APP. P. 3(c)(1). The three-day period does not include weekends and legal holidays when the courthouse is closed. N.C. R. CIV. P. 6(a). If service is not made within three days of the judgment's entry, the thirty-day time period starts with the date of service; additional time is not added for service by mail. N.C. R. APP. P. 3(c).

The court of appeals has held that actual notice that an order has been entered substitutes for proper service under Appellate Rule 3(c), making the service requirements inapplicable. *See Brown v. Swarn*, 810 S.E.2d 237 (N.C. Ct. App. 2018) and cases discussed therein. Actual notice to a party occurs by an email of the order to that party even though email is not a valid method of service under Rule 4 of the Rules of Civil Procedure. *Magazian v. Creagh*, 234 N.C. App. 511 (2014) (dismissing appeal as untimely after holding plaintiff received actual notice of the order by email within three days of the entry of the judgment, thus requiring the notice of appeal to be filed within thirty days of entry of the judgment and not thirty days from the date the email was received). The court of appeals has further held that when seeking a dismissal of an appeal based on untimeliness when there is not a certificate of service of the judgment in the record, the *appellee* has the burden to show that the appellant (the party appealing) received actual notice of the judgment's entry more than thirty days before the appeal was taken. *Brown v. Swarn*, 810 S.E.2d at 240 (emphasis in original).

> **Resource:** For a discussion of the thirty-day time period to appeal a civil judgment, see Ann Anderson, *Appeal Deadlines and Tolling Under Rule 3(c)(2): Don't Be So Sure!*, UNC SCH. OF GOV'T: ON THE CIVIL SIDE BLOG (April 6, 2016).

Notice of appeal given within thirty days after the oral rendering of judgment in open court, but before entry of judgment, is timely. *See In re J.L.*, 184 N.C. App. 750 (2007) (holding that the trial court erred in dismissing the respondent's appeal for failure to timely give notice of appeal, when the respondent filed a written notice of appeal after the court rendered its judgment but before the court entered its written judgment); *In re S.F.*, 198 N.C. App. 611 (2009) (holding that notice of appeal was timely where respondent filed the notice nine days after the court orally announced the decision to terminate parental rights, even though the court's written order was not entered until more than a month later). A notice of an appeal from an orally rendered judgment in open court does not vest jurisdiction in the appellate court until that judgment is entered pursuant to the requirements of Rule 58. *In re O.D.S.*, 247 N.C. App. 711 (2016). When a notice of appeal has been filed from an orally rendered judgment made in open court, a second notice of appeal must be filed if the judgment that is written and entered does not generally conform to the judgment that was orally rendered. *In re O.D.S.*, 247 N.C. App. 711.

Any necessary amendment to the notice of appeal must also be filed within the thirty-day time limit. *See In re K.C.*, 199 N.C. App. 557 (2009) (dismissing appeal by right of the adjudication and disposition orders when the amended notice of appeal, the only notice that referenced the disposition order, was filed more than thirty days after the order was entered; granting writ of certiorari to hear appeal).

**2. Timing and manner of appeal of order eliminating reunification as a permanent plan.**
Reunification is one of six possible permanent plans for a child who is the subject of an abuse, neglect, or dependency action. G.S. 7B-906.2(a). The Juvenile Code defines reunification as the child's placement in the home of either parent or in the home of a guardian or custodian from whose home the child was removed by court order. G.S. 7B-101(18b). Under G.S. 7B-906.2(b), when a court orders concurrent permanent plans, reunification must be designated as a primary or secondary permanent plan unless certain findings are made. See Chapter 7.8.A.2, 7.8.C.8, and 7.10.A (relating to types of dispositional hearings addressing findings at initial dispositional hearing under G.S. 7B-901(c) and permanency planning hearings under G.S. 7B-906.2). An order entered under G.S. 7B-906.2(b) that eliminates reunification as a permanent plan is an appealable order (as discussed in section 12.4.A.5, above), but the

requirements for an appeal vary depending on the circumstances.

(a) **Immediate appeal for custodian or guardian before the court of appeals.** A custodian or guardian who is a party may appeal a G.S. 7B-906.2(b) order that eliminates reunification with the custodian or guardian as a permanent plan directly to the court of appeals. G.S. 7B-1001(a)(5)b. The notice of appeal must be given within thirty days after entry and service of the order as set forth in Rule 58 of the Rules of Civil Procedure. G.S. 7B-1001(b).

(b) **Delayed appeal for parent.** Instead of an immediate appeal of an order eliminating reunification with a parent as a permanent plan entered under G.S. 7B-906.2(b), a parent must wait a minimum of sixty-five days from the entry and service of that order before filing a notice of appeal. *See* G.S. 7B-1001(a)(5)a.2.; (a1)(2)b. The purpose of the delay is to allow for the commencement and resolution of a termination of parental rights (TPR) action (if such an action is necessary) and when a TPR is ordered, to combine the appeals of the G.S. 7B-906.2(b) order with the appeal of the TPR order.

**Written notice to preserve right to appeal required**. The parent must preserve the right to appeal the G.S. 7B-906.2(b) order in writing within thirty days of the order being entered and served. G.S. 7B-1001(a)(5)a.1., (a1)(2)a., (b) . After a designated period of time passes, the parent must then file a notice of appeal of the G.S. 7B-906.2(b) order. G.S. 7B-1001(a)(5)a.3., (a1)(2)c. The timing of the filing of the notice of appeal depends on whether there is a subsequent TPR motion or petition that is filed with the district court to commence that action within sixty-five days of the entry and service of the G.S. 7B-906.2(b) order.

Note that a G.S. 7B-906.2(b) order may meet the criteria of another type of order designated in G.S. 7B-1001, such that an appeal is made under that other provision of G.S. 7B-1001. The court of appeals determined that an appeal of an order that changed legal custody of the child and ceased reasonable efforts under a former statute (G.S. 7B-507) was immediately appealable under G.S. 7B-1001(a)(4), allowing appeal of any order, other than a nonsecure custody order, that changes legal custody of the child. *In re E.G.M.*, 230 N.C. App. 196 (2013) (order appealed from changed custody from respondent mother to DSS in addition to ceasing reasonable efforts; distinguished from *In re D.K.H.*, 184 N.C. App. 289 (2007), which dismissed appeal without prejudice as order did not change custody of child and did not meet criteria under G.S. 7B-1001(a)(5)a.–c., noting father could refile at later time as permitted by G.S 7B-1001(a)(5); decided under former statutes).

**A TPR is not filed within sixty-five-day time period – court of appeals review.** If a TPR petition or motion is not filed within sixty-five days of entry and service of the G.S. 7B-906.2(b) order eliminating reunification as a permanent plan, a parent who has given written notice preserving the right to appeal that order may appeal directly to the court of appeals at that time. G.S. 7B-1001(a)(5)a. A parent must wait the designated time period (effective January 1, 2019, sixty-five days, which is shortened from the previously designated 180 days) before filing the notice of appeal when a TPR petition or motion has not been filed during that designated time period. G.S. 7B-1001(a)(5)a.1, 2. *See In re D.K.H.*, 184 N.C. App. 289 (2007) (decided under former statutes; dismissing father's appeal of order ceasing reunification efforts where the father filed notice of appeal before the required 180 days had passed; dismissal was without prejudice since father had given proper notice of his intent to appeal). Once the sixty-five days have elapsed, the thirty-day time period to file the notice of appeal under G.S. 7B-1001(b) starts to run. G.S. 7B-1001(a)(5)a.3. The notice of appeal must be filed within those thirty days, making the time period between sixty-six and ninety-five days after entry and service of the G.S. 7B-906.2(b) order. G.S. 7B-1001(a)(5)a.3; *see In re A.R.*, 238 N.C. App. 302 (2014) (dismissing respondent's appeal for being untimely as the notice of appeal was filed more than 210 days after entry of the order ceasing reunification efforts; decided under the former applicable statutes).

**Combined with TPR appeal – North Carolina Supreme Court review.** When a TPR action is filed within sixty-five days of entry and service of the G.S. 7B-906.2(b) order eliminating reunification as a permanent plan and there is a subsequent appeal of the order granting the TPR, the appeal of the G.S. 7B-906.2(b) order may be made directly to the North Carolina Supreme Court, together with the appeal of the TPR order. G.S. 7B-1001(a1); *see* G.S. 7A-27(a)(5) (direct appeal of TPR to supreme court). All of the following conditions must have occurred:

- the right to appeal the G.S. 7B-906.2(b) order was timely preserved in writing;
- the TPR motion or petition has been heard and granted;
- the TPR order is appealed in a proper and timely manner; and
- a separate notice of appeal of the G.S. 7B-906.2(b) order is filed within thirty days of entry and service of the TPR order.

G.S. 7B-1001(a1)(2) (effective Jan. 1, 2019).

In the case, *In re L.M.T.*, 367 N.C. 165 (2013), the North Carolina Supreme Court interpreted the former language in G.S. 7B-1001(a)(5)a. (when it referred to an appeal of an order ceasing reunification efforts under G.S. 7B-507(c)) that stated the G.S. 7B-507 order shall be reviewed "together with an appeal of the termination of parental rights [TPR] order." The supreme court held that "together" means that the two orders are considered as a whole and are not reviewed separately. This supreme court holding reversed the court of appeals holding that the permanency planning order ceasing reunification efforts when reviewed alone was insufficient and, therefore, was reversed and remanded. The supreme court held that both the permanency planning order and the TPR order when read together were sufficient and stated that even if the permanency planning order was deficient, it should have been reviewed in conjunction with the TPR order to determine whether the statutory requirements were met. Insufficient findings of fact in the cease reunification order may be cured by the findings of fact in the TPR order. The supreme court reasoned that this interpretation of "together" advances one of the purposes of the Juvenile Code – to provide for the child's best interests within a reasonable amount of time. Of note, the language of G.S. 7B-1001(a2) states, "the Supreme Court shall review the order eliminating reunification *together* with an appeal of the order terminating parental rights." (emphasis supplied).

G.S. 7B-1001 is silent as to a parent's right to appeal a G.S. 7B-906.2(b) order eliminating reunification when a TPR is initiated within the sixty-five-day period and is denied. The lack of designation in G.S. 7B-1001 appears to mean that the order is not an appealable order. A party wishing to appeal that G.S. 7B-906.2(b) order may need to petition for a writ of certiorari (discussed in section 12.10.A., below). *See In re Doe*, 126 N.C. App. 401 (1997) (holding a minor may petition the appellate court for a writ of certiorari to review a superior court order denying a judicial waiver of parental consent for abortion when the statute does not provide an appeal of right to the appellate courts).

---

**Resources:**

For more information about the appeal process for these juvenile orders, see Sara DePasquale, *Big Changes to Appeals of A/N/D – TPR Orders Designated in G.S. 7B-1001*, UNC SCH. OF GOV'T: ON THE CIVIL SIDE BLOG (March 25, 2019).

For a discussion of the effect on the district court's authority when the TPR is not filed within the designated time period and an appeal of the G.S. 7B-906.2(b) order is pending, see Sara DePasquale, *What Can the District Court Do in an A/N/D or TPR Action when an Appeal is Pending?*, UNC SCH. OF GOV'T: ON THE CIVIL SIDE BLOG (Aug. 2, 2019).

**Practice Note:** Beware. The court of appeals has interpreted former versions of G.S. 7B-1001 when challenges have been made about the manner of the notice and/or lack of written notice for either the preservation of or notice to appeal the order ceasing reunification efforts. *See, e.g., In re A.E.C.*, 239 N.C. App. 36 (2015) (dismissing writ of certiorari as moot; holding father, who did not preserve the right to appeal the orders that ceased reunification efforts by giving a timely notice of appeal of those orders, did properly preserve his right to challenge those orders when he raised them as an issue in his appeal of the TPR order). Given the different statutory language currently in effect, it is likely the court of appeals would distinguish those prior holdings as having been interpreted under the former statutory language. *See In re A.A.S.*, 812 S.E.2d 875, 880 (N.C. Ct. App. 2018) (stating "*In re A.E.C.*[, 239 N.C. App. 26 (2015)] and the other cases cited by Respondent-Mother were decided prior to 1 October 2015, when N.C. Gen. Stat. § 7B-906.2 was enacted").

---

**3. Signatures.** The Juvenile Code requires that the notice of appeal be signed by both the appealing party and counsel for the appealing party, if any. G.S. 7B-1001(c); N.C. R. APP. P. 3.1(b) (incorporating G.S. 7B-1001(c)). *See In re A.S.*, 190 N.C. App. 679 (2008) (dismissing the appeal for failure of the mother to sign the notice of appeal, but granting her writ of certiorari). For an appeal by a juvenile, the notice of appeal must be signed by the guardian ad litem (GAL) attorney advocate. G.S. 7B-1001(c); N.C. R. APP. P. 3.1(b) (incorporating G.S. 7B-1001(c)). The appeal statute, G.S. 7B-1001, does not contemplate an appeal by a juvenile who is not represented by a GAL attorney advocate. However, G.S. 7B-1002(2), which designates proper parties for an appeal, requires that the court appoint a Rule 17 GAL to a juvenile who makes an appeal and has not had a G.S. 7B-601 GAL appointed. Neither statute addresses who signs the notice of appeal for the juvenile who does not have a G.S. 7B-601

GAL. *See* Chapters 2.3.D and 9.4.C (discussing the child's GAL).

The Juvenile Code also does not specify who must sign the written notice to preserve the right to appeal a G.S. 7B-906.2(b) order that eliminates reunification as a permanent plan. The sole instruction is found in G.S. 7B-1001(b), which states "notice to preserve the right to appeal shall be given in writing by a proper party as defined in G.S. 7B-1002." *See* N.C. R. APP. P. 3.1(b) (incorporating G.S. 7B-1001(b)) Whether "given" means the signature of that party is unclear. The safest approach is to follow the same signature requirements for a notice of appeal. *See* G.S. 7B-1001(c); N.C. R. APP. P. 3.1(b) (incorporating G.S. 7B-1001(c)).

For both the notice of appeal and the notice to preserve the right to appeal, it is unclear whether the signature of a Rule 17 GAL of substitution for a respondent parent may sign for that parent. The issue has not been addressed by the court of appeals. *See In re L.B.*, 187 N.C. App. 326 (2007) (dismissing the appeal based on the insufficient signature of appellant parent when the parent's GAL of assistance signed the notice of appeal instead of the parent; analyzing an earlier version of the GAL appointment statute, G.S. 7B-1101.1, which allowed for a GAL of assistance without any reference to Rule 17 of the Rules of Civil Procedure and contained limiting language of the GAL's role), *aff'd per curiam*, 362 N.C. 507 (2008); *In re A.S.Y.*, 208 N.C. App. 530, 537 & n.5 (2010) (emphasis in original) (although an amended G.S. 7B-1101.1(c) specifically refers to Rule 17, the determination of this case relating to duties of a respondent parent GAL *during* the TPR did not require the court of appeals "to touch upon or otherwise disturb the ultimate question determined by the *L.B.* Court, that a notice of appeal signed by the GAL but not the parent is insufficient to grant jurisdiction of the appeal to this Court"). Because the sufficiency of a Rule 17 GAL's signature is not altogether clear, the safer practice is for both the GAL and the respondent parent to sign the notice of appeal along with the attorney when possible. See Chapter 2.4.F (discussing GALs for respondent parents).

**4. Contents.** The notice of appeal must specify the party or parties taking the appeal and must designate the judgment or order from which the appeal is taken and the court to which the appeal is taken. N.C. R. APP. P. 3(d). *See In re D.W.C.*, 205 N.C. App. 266 (2010) (dismissing argument on appeal related to the underlying neglect case where respondent mother alleged error with the GAL appointment in both the TPR and underlying neglect cases but only referenced the TPR order in her notice of appeal).

Special rules related to the protection of the child's identity apply to the notice of appeal and are explained in section 12.6, below.

## B. Service and Proof of Service

Appellate Rule 26(c) addresses the manner of service of the notice of appeal, which may be made in a variety of ways. Service may be made pursuant to Rule 4 of the Rules of Civil Procedure on a party or the party's attorney of record. Service also may be made by delivering a copy of the notice to the party or the attorney. Delivery of a copy means handing it to the attorney or to the party or leaving it at the attorney's office with a partner or employee. Service also may be made by mailing a copy to the recipient's last known address, or, if no address is known, by filing it with the clerk. Service by mail is complete upon deposit of a properly addressed, postage paid envelope or package in a post office or official depository of the United States Postal Service or, for those having access to such services, upon deposit with "the State Courier Service or Inter-Office Mail." When a document relating to an appeal is filed electronically to the electronic filing site, service also may be accomplished electronically to the other counsel's correct and current email address or by any other manner described in this section.

> **Practice Note:** Appellate Rule 3.1(i), which applies to appeals of juvenile orders designated in G.S. 7B-1001, requires that all documents be filed electronically unless an exception is granted for good cause.
>
> **Resources:**
> For more information on service by mail, see "Mail Service Center" on the North Carolina Department of Administration website, which provides information about the state Mail Service Center, including explanations of state courier mail and inter-office mail.
>
> For more information on efiling, see "North Carolina Supreme Court and Court of Appeals Electronic Filing Site and Document Library" on the North Carolina Appellate Courts website.

The notice of appeal filed with the court must contain an acknowledgment of service signed by the person who was served or a certificate of service from the person who made the service. N.C. R. APP. P. 26(d). Failure to file proof of service with the notice of appeal, when not waived by the party entitled to be served, is grounds for dismissal of the appeal. *See Blevins v. Town of West Jefferson*, 361 N.C. 578 (2007) (failure to include certificate of service was waived when the appellee did not raise the issue and participated without objection in the appeal), *aff'g per curiam for the reasons stated in the dissent* 182 N.C. App. 675 (2009); *In re A.C.*, 182 N.C. App. 759 (2007) (dismissing appeal; by filing a motion to dismiss before participating in the appeal without objection, DSS did not waive the defect); *In re C.T.*, 182 N.C. App. 166 (dismissing appeal when DSS and GAL did not waive the proof of service requirement), *aff'd per curiam*, 361 N.C. 581 (2007). The failure to show proof of service affects personal jurisdiction, not subject matter jurisdiction. *In re S.F.*, 198 N.C. App. 611 (2009) (exercising discretion to grant appellant's petition for writ of certiorari and hear the appeal when the appellant did not include a certificate of service in his timely notice of appeal; finding the appellate court had subject matter jurisdiction over appeal and DSS and GAL had actual notice of the appeal).

When parties are joined in an appeal, service on any one of the joined parties is sufficient. N.C. R. APP. P. 26(e).

### C. Appellate Entry Forms

Appellate entry forms are North Carolina Administrative Office of the Courts (AOC) forms typically filled out by the clerk of court when notice of appeal has been given. The form is signed by the judge and orders the clerk to furnish copies of the file to the parties, orders assignment of a transcriptionist, and orders appointment of Indigent Defense Services (IDS) appellate counsel when appropriate. The forms also include contact information for persons involved in the appeal and address costs, any need for a translator or interpreter, and the dates of the hearings for which recordings should be sent to the transcriptionist.

**AOC Forms:**
- AOC-J-160, Appellate Entries in Abuse, Neglect, Dependency, or Termination of Parental Rights Proceeding (Jan. 2019) (for use by respondents).
- AOC-J-161, Appellate Entries for DSS/GAL in Abuse, Neglect, Dependency, or Termination of Parental Rights Proceeding (Jan. 2019) (for use by TPR petitioners, DSS, or child's GAL).

## 12.6 Protection of the Child's Identity – Appellate Rule 42

The January 1, 2019 amendments to the Appellate Rules created Appellate Rule 42, which protects the identities of children in certain appeals and keeps items that were sealed in the trial court under seal in the appellate court. Prior to January 1, 2019 the protection of a juvenile's identity was addressed throughout the Appellate Rules, rather than being contained in one designated rule as it is now with Appellate Rule 42.

Through Appellate Rule 42(b)(1), items filed with the appellate courts in an appeal under G.S. 7B-1001 (designated juvenile orders) are under seal. Appellate Rule 42(b)(3) also seals items filed with the appellate courts for appeals involving a sexual offense that was committed against a minor. This appears to include appeals of orders involving placement on the Responsible Individuals List (RIL) when the abuse or serious neglect of the juvenile consists of a sexual offense. *See* G.S. 7B-101(1) (definition of "abused juveniles"), (18a) (definition of "responsible individual"), (19a) (definition of "serious neglect"); 7B-323(f) (referring to appeal under G.S. 7A-27(b)(2)). Appellate Rule 42 also applies to extraordinary writs filed in these designated cases when the right to appeal has been lost. N.C. R. APP. P. 42(b)(4). For appeals of orders not designed in Appellate Rule 42(b) (e.g., an appeal of an RIL placement that does not involve a sexual offense), counsel may motion the appellate court to seal the item. N.C. R. APP. P.42(c).

Pursuant to Appellate Rule 42(d), documents filed with the appellate courts that are under seal must state at the top of the first page

> UNDER SEAL AND SUBJECT TO PUBLIC INSPECTION ONLY BY ORDER OF A COURT OF THE APPELLATE DIVISION.

Appellate Rule 42 requires that the juvenile's name not be used in any brief, motion, or petition. Instead, counsel must use initials or a pseudonym that each counsel has agreed on, and a stipulation of the agreement must be included in the record on appeal. N.C. R. APP. P. 42(b). At oral argument, counsel must use the minor's initials or pseudonym. N.C. R. APP. P. 30(a)(2).

## 12.7 Expedited Appeals Process under Appellate Rule 3.1

Appellate Rule 3.1 sets out an expedited process for appeals of abuse, neglect, dependency, and termination of parental rights (TPR) orders designated in G.S. 7B-1001. The timelines and the process move the case through the appellate system much quicker than the average appellate case. The appeals are decided on the record and briefs, unless oral argument is ordered by the appellate court reviewing the challenged order. N.C. R. APP. P. 9(a); 30(f).

### A. Transcript

The Appellate Rules require the clerk of superior court to complete the Expedited Juvenile Appeals Form within one business day of the filing of the notice of appeal. The court reporting manager at the North Carolina Administrative Office of the Courts (AOC) must assign a transcriptionist within five business days after the clerk completes the form. The transcriptionist must deliver the transcript electronically to each party to the appeal within forty days of receiving the assignment. If there is an order that the appellant is indigent, the cost is at the State's expense. If there is no such order, the appellant has ten days from when the transcriptionist is assigned to contract for the transcript of the proceedings. N.C. R. APP. P. 3.1(c). The record on appeal must include a verbatim transcript if one is available. *See In re J.A.K.*, 812 S.E.2d 716 (N.C. Ct. App. 2018) (noting neither the transcript from the permanency planning hearing nor a narrative of the hearing was included in the record on appeal; requiring appellate court to deem findings as conclusive).

Motions for extensions of time to prepare and deliver transcripts are "disfavored and will be allowed by the appellate courts only in extraordinary circumstances." N.C. R. APP. P. 3.1(g).

> **Practice Note:** The printing and distribution of transcripts and copies of transcripts (electronic and hardcopy) is handled exclusively by the AOC. It is against AOC policy for parties to share a copy of the transcript or for one party to make a copy for another party, as this creates problems with billing transcription costs.

### B. Record on Appeal

Regarding time limits discussed below, three days shall be added to time limits when service is by mail or email (if permitted by appellate rule). N.C. R. APP. P. 27(b).

**1. Appellant's proposed record.** The appellant must prepare a proposed record on appeal and serve it on all other parties to the appeal within fifteen days after delivery of the transcript. N.C. R. APP. P. 3.1(d). The contents and requirements for the record on appeal are contained in Appellate Rule 9.

The appellate courts have stated that "[t]he burden is on the appellant to 'commence settlement of the record on appeal. . . . .' " *In re J.A.K.*, 812 S.E.2d 716, 719 (N.C. Ct. App. 2018) (quoting *Sen Li v. Zhou*, 252 N.C. App. 22, 27 (2017) (quoting *State v. Berryman*, 360 N.C. 209, 216 (2006))).

> **Practice Notes:** Appellate counsel prepares the record on appeal based on information contained in the Appellate Entries Form, which is prepared by the clerk of superior court when notice of appeal is given. See AOC Forms in section 12.5.C, above.
>
> If two or more appellate counsel are working jointly (e.g., one counsel for each parent), the ten-day period for service of the proposed record on appeal begins after the last attorney receives the transcript.

**2. Appellee's response or lack thereof.** An appellee has ten days after being served with the proposed record to respond by serving on all other parties to the appeal one of the following:

- notice of approval of the proposed record (this settles the record on appeal);
- specific objections or amendments to the proposed record, which triggers Appellate Rule 11(c) (Settling the Record on Appeal); or
- a proposed alternative record, which triggers Appellate Rule 11(c) (Settling the Record on Appeal).

N.C. R. App. P. 3.1(d).

If all appellees do not respond to the proposed record on appeal within the ten-day time limit, the proposed record becomes the settled record on appeal. The appellant then has five business days from the last date on which the appellees could have responded to file the settled record. N.C. R. App. P. 3.1(d). Note that a party could still file a motion to amend the record pursuant to Appellate Rule 9(b)(5).

**3. Settling the record when there is disagreement.** The parties to the appeal must follow the procedures of Appellate Rule 11(c) to settle the record when specific objections or amendments to the proposed record or a proposed alternative record is made by an appellee. N.C. R. App. P. 3.1(d). The procedures of Appellate Rule 11(c) include an agreement, a supplement to the printed record, or a court order after a judicial settlement has been requested and held with the judge from whose order the appeal was taken. Within fifteen days of the record being settled through an Appellate Rule 11(c) procedure, the appellant must file the settled record. N.C. R. App. P. 12(a).

**4. Problem with recording.** The fact that the recording is incomplete or of poor quality will require a new hearing in the trial court only if specific error during the missing or unintelligible portion of the recording is alleged or prejudice to the appellant as a result of the recording problems is shown. *See, e.g., In re Bradshaw*, 160 N.C. App. 677 (2003); *In re Howell*, 161 N.C. App. 650 (2003).

### C. Briefs

**1. Time limits for briefs.** The appellant's brief must be filed within thirty days after the record on appeal has been filed with the appellate court, and the appellee's brief must be filed within thirty days after appellee is served with appellant's brief. Copies of briefs must be served on all other parties of record. N.C. R. App. P. 13(a)(1). Three days may be added to time limits when service is by mail or email (if permitted). N.C. R. App. P. 27(b).

Motions for extensions of time to file briefs are disfavored and are allowed only in extraordinary circumstances. N.C. R. App. P. 3.1(g).

**2. No-merit briefs.** Appellate Rule 3.1(e) allows counsel for an appellant to file a "no-merit" brief in appeals taken pursuant to G.S. 7B-1001. An appeal of an order designated in G.S. 7B-1001 that is based on a no-merit brief was first permitted in 2009 with the adoption of Appellate Rule 3.1(d) by the North Carolina Supreme Court and is similar to an *Anders* review, a rule adopted by the U.S. Supreme Court that applies to criminal appeals. *See In re L.E.M.*, 831 S.E.2d 341 (N.C. S.Ct. 2019); *see also Anders v. California*, 386 U.S. 738 (1967).

Note that prior to the January 1, 2019 amendments to the Appellate Rules, no-merit briefs were permitted by former Appellate Rule 3.1(d), now Appellate Rule 3.1(e). In one opinion, the North Carolina Supreme Court noted, "[w]hile the language addressing no-merit briefs as set out in Rule 3.1(e) differs in certain respects from that formerly contained in Rule 3.1(d), the two provisions are substantially similar." *In re L.E.M.*, 831 S.E.2d 341, 344, n.1.

(a) **When a no-merit brief may be filed.** A no-merit brief is permitted when appellate counsel concludes that there is no issue of merit on which to base an argument for relief. N.C. R. App. P. 3.1(e).

(b) **Contents of no-merit brief.** A no-merit brief must identify any issues in the record on appeal that arguably support the appeal and state why those issues lack merit or would not alter the ultimate result. N.C. R. App. P. 3.1(e).

(c) **Duty to appellant and appellant's *pro se* brief.** When the appellant's counsel files a no-merit brief, he or she must provide the appellant with a copy of the brief, the transcript, the printed record on appeal, and any Appellate Rule 11(c) supplement or exhibits that have been filed with the appellate court. The appellant's counsel also must advise the appellant in writing that the appellant has the option of filing a *pro se* brief and that it is due within thirty days of when the no-merit brief was filed. Counsel must attach to the no-merit brief evidence of this required communication with his or her client. N.C. R. App. P. 3.1(e).

As advised by his or her appellate counsel, the appellant may file a *pro se* brief. However, the appeal may not be dismissed on the basis that the appellant failed to file a *pro se* brief. *See In re L.E.M.*, 831 S.E.2d 341 (reversing dismissal of appeal by court of appeals; holding appellate court must conduct an independent review of the issues identified in the no-merit brief; overturning *In re L.V.*, 814 S.E.2d 928 (N.C. Ct. App. 2018), which dismissed the appeal after concluding no issues were argued or preserved for review when the appellant did not file a *pro se* brief).

(d) **Mandatory appellate court review.** In *In re L.E.M.*, 831 S.E.2d 341, the North Carolina Supreme Court addressed, as a case of first impression, whether Appellate Rule 3.1(d) (now (e)) requires appellate courts to conduct an independent review of the no-merit brief when the appellant does not file a *pro se* brief. The supreme court held that the rule mandates an independent review of the issues raised in the no-merit brief. The supreme court reasoned its holding was consistent with both the language and purpose of Appellate Rule 3.1(d) and "furthers the significant interest of ensuring that orders depriving parents of their fundamental right to parenthood are given meaningful appellate review." *In re L.E.M.*, 831 S.E.2d at 345. In its decision, the supreme court overruled the holding of the court of appeals in *In re L.V.*, 814 S.E.2d 928 (dismissing appeal when appellant did not file a *pro se* brief on the basis that no issues were argued or preserved for review) and abrogated the court of appeals' decisions in *In re I.B.*, 822 S.E.2d 472 (N.C. Ct. App. 2018); *In re I.P.*, 820 S.E.2d 586 (N.C. Ct. App. 2018); and *In re A.S.*, 817 S.E.2d 798 (N.C. Ct. App. 2018), all of which relied upon *In re L.V.* The effect of the holding of *In re L.E.M.* also abrogates the additional following court of appeals decisions: *In re T.H.*, 832 S.E.2d 162 (N.C. Ct. App. (2019) and *In re D.A.*, 820 S.E.2d 873 (N.C. Ct. App. 2018).

> **Practice Note:** The Office of Indigent Defense Services and the Guardian ad Litem Services Division of the North Carolina Administrative Office of the Courts may have policies related to no-merit briefs that should be consulted by appellate counsel prior to filing a no-merit brief.

## 12.8 Issues on Appeal and Standards of Review

### A. Introduction

Specific issues on appeal from abuse, neglect, dependency, and termination of parental rights proceedings are addressed in the appellate cases discussed throughout this Manual. This section is not a comprehensive presentation of issues on appeal but addresses some general categories of issues in which the appeals in these cases tend to fall and discusses standards of review used for various issues.

### B. Sufficiency of Evidence and Findings

**1. Generally.** Issues dealt with frequently in appeals of abuse, neglect, dependency, and termination of parental rights (TPR) cases are whether the evidence is sufficient to support the findings of fact and whether the findings of fact are sufficient to support the trial court's conclusions of law. *See, e.g., In re I.G.C.*, 835 S.E.2d 432 (N.C. S.Ct. 2019); *In re B.O.A.*, 831 S.E.2d 305 (N.C. S.Ct. 2019); *In re L.M.T.*, 367 N.C. 165 (2013).

"[A]ny determination requiring the exercise of judgment or the application of legal principles is more properly classified a conclusion of law." *In re Adoption of C.H.M.*, 371 N.C. 22, 28 (2018) (quoting *State v. Sparks*, 362 N.C. 181, 185 (2008)). "Any determination reached through 'logical reasoning from the evidentiary facts' is more properly classified a finding of fact." *In re Helms*, 127 N.C. App. 505, 510 (1997) (citations omitted); *see also In re A.B.*, 179 N.C. App. 605, 612 (2006) (quoting *Helms*). However, appellate courts have repeatedly found a trial court's misclassifications of conclusions of law and findings of fact to be inconsequential, stating that if a contested finding of fact is more accurately characterized as a conclusion of law, it is treated as a conclusion of law on appeal. *See In the Adoption of*

*C.H.M.*, 371 N.C. 22; *In re B.W.*, 190 N.C. App. 328 (2008); *In re R.A.H.*, 182 N.C. App. 52 (2007). Conclusions of law are reviewed de novo. *In the Adoption of C.H.M.*, 371 N.C. 22; *In re C.B.C.*, 832 S.E.2d 692 (N.C. S.Ct. 2019).

Where a finding is properly supported by competent evidence, the finding is binding on appeal, even if there is evidence that would support a finding to the contrary. *See In re B.O.A.*, 831 S.E.2d 305 (N.C. S.Ct. 2019); *In re J.A.M.* 370 N.C. 464 (2018) (citations omitted). Where a party fails to except to findings of fact on appeal, they are deemed supported by competent evidence and are conclusive on appeal. *See State v. Sparks,* 362 N.C. 181; *In re C.M.P.*, 254 N.C. App. 647 (2017); *In re L.A.B.*, 178 N.C. App. 295 (2006). When facts are challenged as unsupported and the appellate record does not contain a verbatim transcript when one is available or a narrative of the hearing, the appellate court must deem the findings of fact as conclusive. *In re J.A.K.*, 812 S.E.2d 716 (N.C. Ct. App. 2018). Erroneous findings that are not necessary to the determination do not constitute reversible error. *In re C.B.*, 245 N.C. App. 197 (2016).

**2. Review of findings of fact and conclusions of law at adjudication.** The standard of review for adjudications in abuse, neglect, or dependency cases is whether the findings of fact are supported by clear and convincing evidence. *In re J.A.M.*, 822 S.E.2d 693 (N.C. S.Ct. 2019); *R.S.*, 254 N.C. App. 678 (2017). *See* G.S. 7B-805. The standard of review in a TPR proceeding is the same. *See* G.S. 7B-1109(f) (requiring adjudicatory findings be based on clear, cogent, and convincing evidence); G.S. 7B-1111(b) (requiring facts justifying termination be proved by clear and convincing evidence); *In re C.B.C.*, 832 S.E.2d 692 (N.C. S.Ct. 2019) (citing G.S. 7B-1109 when addressing standard of review of TPR adjudication). There is no distinction between "clear, cogent, and convincing" and "clear and convincing" evidence. *See In re Belk*, 364 N.C. 114 (2010); *In re Montgomery*, 311 N.C. 101 (1984). The appellate court then reviews whether the conclusions of law are supported by adequate findings of fact. *See In re In re C.B.C.*, 832 S.E.2d 692 (TPR); *In re R.S.*, 254 N.C. App. 678 (abuse, neglect, dependency).

**3. Review of dispositional findings.** The standard of review that applies to findings of fact in disposition, review, permanency planning, and TPR disposition orders is whether the findings are supported by "competent" or "credible" evidence. *See In re S.P.,* 833 S.E.2d 638 (N.C. Ct. App. 2019); *In re J.T.,* 252 N.C. App. 19 (2017); *In re B.W.*, 190 N.C. App. 328 (2008); *In re C.M.*, 183 N.C. App. 207 (2007). Appellate courts will review dispositional (or best interest) conclusions of law according to an abuse of discretion standard (described in section 12.8.C, below). *See In re E.H.P.*, 831 S.E.2d 49 (N.C. S.Ct. 2019); *In re D.L.W.*, 368 N.C. 835 (2016). Nevertheless, the trial court must consider and make findings about relevant statutory factors. For example, when a child in an abuse, neglect, or dependency proceeding is going to be ordered in an out-of-home placement, and the court finds a relative is willing and able to provide proper care and supervision of the child in a safe home, the court must place the child in that home unless the court finds the placement would be contrary to the child's best interests. G.S. 7B-903(a1); *In re D.S.*, 817 S.E.2d 901 (2018); *In re E.R.*, 248 N.C. App. 345 (2016). In a TPR case, the court must consider the dispositional factors set out in G.S. 7B-1110(a) and make written findings about those that are relevant. *See In re A.R.A.*, 835 S.E.2d 417 (N.C. S.Ct. 2019); *In re A.U.D.*, 832 S.E.2d 698 (N.C. S.Ct. 2019).

## C. Abuse of Discretion

The appellate court will disturb certain rulings by the trial court only if it finds that the trial court abused its discretion. An "[a]buse of discretion results where the court's ruling is manifestly unsupported by reason or is so arbitrary that it could not have been the result of a reasoned decision." *In re A.U.D.*, 832 S.E.2d 698, 700–01 (N.C. S.Ct. 2019) (quoting *In re T.L.H.*, 368 N.C. 101, 107 (2015)).

Abuse of discretion as a standard of review is most commonly applied to errors alleged in the disposition phase of the case when the court is making discretionary determinations related to the child's best interest. *See, e.g., In re Z.L.W.*, 831 S.E.2d 62 (N.C. S.Ct. 2019) (reviewing whether TPR was in child's best interest); *In re S.G.*, 835 S.E.2d 479 (N.C. Ct. App. 2019) (affirming trial court's case plan and order of visitation once per month; vacating and remanding monthly visitation order to address length of visits); *In re C.P.*, 252 N.C. App. 118 (2017) (affirming guardianship order); *In re J.W.*, 241 N.C. App. 44 (2015) (affirming disposition order that did not return the child to respondent mother's custody).

Abuse of discretion is also the standard applied in the review of other discretionary determinations, such as whether to grant a continuance or appoint a guardian ad litem for a parent. *See, e.g., In re Z.V.A.*, 835 S.E.2d 425 (N.C. S.Ct. 2019) and *In re T.L.H.*, 368 N.C. 101 (both holding that trial court did not abuse its discretion when determining there was not a substantial question about a respondent parent's incompetency requiring the court to conduct an inquiry); *In re C.D.A.W.*, 175 N.C. App. 680 (2006) (holding that trial court did not abuse its discretion by denying mother's motion for a continuance so that she could enter a drug treatment facility), *aff'd per curiam*, 361 N.C. 232 (2007). A trial court may abuse its discretion not only by making a decision that is arbitrary or unreasoned, but also by failing to exercise its discretion at all. *See, e.g., In re B.S.O.*, 225 N.C. App. 541 (2013) (holding court's refusal to exercise discretion based on a misapprehension of the law requires reversal and remand).

Evidentiary rulings are also reviewed for an abuse of discretion. *See In re W.H.*, 819 S.E.2d 617 (2018) and *In re M.A.E.*, 242 N.C. App. 312 (2015) (originally unpublished July 21, 2015, but subsequently published) (both stating admission of evidence under the residual hearsay exception, Rule 803(24) of the Rules of Evidence, is within the discretion of the trial court); *In re A.H.*, 250 N.C. App. 546 (2016) (reviewing decision to quash subpoena for child's testimony as unduly burdensome for an abuse of discretion); *In re Faircloth*, 137 N.C. App. 311 (2000) (a trial court's decision that a witness has the requisite knowledge or training to testify as an expert is within the exclusive province of the trial court and is reviewed for an abuse of discretion).

## D. Subject Matter Jurisdiction

A lack of subject matter jurisdiction can be raised at any time, including for the first time on appeal; parties cannot waive or consent to subject matter jurisdiction. *In re K.J.L.*, 363 N.C. 343 (2009); *In re T.R.P.*, 360 N.C. 588 (2006). Whether a court has subject matter jurisdiction is a question of law reviewable de novo on appeal. *In re D.A.Y.*, 831 S.E.2d 854

(N.C. App. 2019); *In the Adoption of K.L.J.*, 831 S.E.2d 114 (N.C. Ct. App. 2019); *In re J.H.*, 244 N.C. App. 255 (2015). Orders entered by a court that lacks subject matter jurisdiction are void. *See In re T.R.P.*, 360 N.C. 588 (concluding that because trial court lacked subject matter jurisdiction, review hearing order was void ab initio); *In re E.B.*, 834 S.E.2d 169 (N.C. Ct. App. 2019) (in TPR, disregarding as void six permanency planning orders with requirements imposed on father; trial court lacked subject matter jurisdiction to enter such orders when no petition for abuse, neglect, or dependency had ever been filed); *In re A.G.M.*, 241 N.C. App. 426 (2015) (noting that all orders entered in trial court before it had subject matter jurisdiction under the UCCJEA were void ab initio).

Common issues that impact subject matter jurisdiction in abuse, neglect, dependency, and termination of parental rights (TPR) actions include standing, proper verification of the initiating pleading, the Uniform Child-Custody Jurisdiction Enforcement Act, and compliance with certain jurisdictional provisions in the Juvenile Code. Note that deficiencies in the issuance and service of a summons relate to personal jurisdiction and do not affect the court's subject matter jurisdiction. *In re K.J.L.*, 363 N.C. 343 (2009).

For a discussion of subject matter jurisdiction and personal jurisdiction in abuse, neglect, dependency, and TPR proceedings, see Chapter 3.

### E. Failure to Follow Statutory Mandates and Procedures

Often appeals assert error based on the trial court's failure to comply with mandates or procedures set out in the Juvenile Code or, when applicable, the Rules of Civil Procedure.

For example, the Juvenile Code sets out specific criteria the court must address in its findings in orders resulting from review and permanency planning hearings, and a common issue on appeal is whether the court made all of the required findings. *See, e.g., In re J.L.*, 826 S.E.2d 258 (N.C. Ct. App. 2019) and *In re J.D.M.-J.*, 817 S.E.2d 755 (N.C. Ct. App. 2018) (both reversing visitation portion of dispositional orders for noncompliance with G.S. 7B-905.1); *In re J.R.S.*, 813 S.E.2d 283 (N.C. Ct. App. 2018) (reversing order removing custodians as guardians when findings under G.S. 7B-401.1(g) were not made); *In re D.S.*, 817 S.E.2d 901 (N.C. Ct. App. 2018) (vacating and remanding for a hearing when findings about relative placement were not made in permanency planning order as required by G.S. 7B-903(a1)); *In re K.L.*, 254 N.C. App. 269 (2017) (reversing and remanding permanency planning order eliminating reunification and waiving further permanency planning hearings because it failed to make findings required by G.S. 7B-906.1(d), (n) and 7B-906.2(b)–(d)); *In re J.K.*, 253 N.C. App. 57 (2017) (reversing and remanding "custody order" that did not make required findings under G.S. 7B-911); *In re P.A.*, 241 N.C. App. 53 (2015) (holding that when waiving further permanency planning hearings, the failure to make written findings of fact satisfying each of the enumerated criteria in G.S. 7B-906.1(n) is reversible error). Note that earlier cases refer to findings required by G.S. 7B-906 and 7B-907, which have been replaced by G.S. 7B-906.1.

When making required statutory findings of fact, the trial court need not quote the exact statutory language; instead, the findings must embrace the substance of the statutory requirements. *In re L.M.T.*, 367 N.C. 165 (2013); *In re M.T.-L.Y.*, 829 S.E.2d 496 (N.C. Ct. App. 2019); *In re H.D.*, 239 N.C. App. 318 (2015). The appellate courts have noted that the best practice, however, is to use the actual statutory language. *In re L.M.T.*, 367 N.C. at 167 ("trial courts are advised that use of the actual statutory language would be the best practice").

Even if the appellate court finds error in failing to follow statutory mandates, it may decline to disturb the lower court's ruling unless there is a showing that the error was prejudicial. *See In re H.T.*, 180 N.C. App. 611, 613 (2006) ("[I]n general, technical errors and violations of the Juvenile Code will be found to be reversible error only upon a showing of prejudice"). The Juvenile Code prescribes timelines for conducting hearings and for the entry of orders. After numerous appellate court decisions analyzing whether a trial court's delay in holding a hearing or entering an order was prejudicial, the North Carolina Supreme Court held that the proper remedy for a court's failure to follow the timelines is a petition for a writ of mandamus, rather than an assertion of error on appeal. *In re T.H.T.*, 362 N.C. 446 (2008); *see also In re E.K.*, 202 N.C. App. 309 (2010). For a discussion on the time requirements for orders, including the remedy, see Chapter 4.9.D. See also section 12.10.D, below (discussing writ of mandamus).

### F. Statutory Interpretation

Appeals of juvenile orders have also focused on the interpretation of statutory language. Some of these appeals focus on language that has been in effect for several years but is now being raised for the first time on appeal, while other appeals focus on the meaning of recent statutory amendments made to the Juvenile Code. The North Carolina Supreme Court has discussed how courts should construe statutory language.

A statute's meaning is controlled by legislative intent, which is first determined by the statute's plain language and then from legislative history and "the spirit of the act and what the act seeks to accomplish." *In re B.O.A.*, 831 S.E.2d 305, 311 (N.C. S.Ct. 2019) (citations omitted). Courts have the "duty to give effect to the words actually used in a statute and not to delete words used or to insert words not used." *In re B.O.A.*, 831 S.E.2d at 311 (citations omitted). Additionally, "[w]hen the language of a statute is clear and without ambiguity, it is the duty of this Court to give effect to the plain meaning of the statute." *In re B.O.A.*, 831 S.E.2d at 311; *see In re T.R.P.*, 360 N.C. 588 (2006) (holding that a verified petition is required for subject matter jurisdiction as statute's reference to verification of the petition is unambiguous). A whole-text view of the statutes should be employed rather than an interpretation that focuses on isolated provisions of a statute. The North Carolina Supreme Court has stated, "[p]erhaps no interpretive fault is more common than the failure to follow the whole-text canon, which calls on the judicial interpreter to consider the entire text, in view of its structure and of the physical and logical relation of its many parts." *In re A.P.*, 371 N.C. 14, 18 (2018) (citations omitted). By not employing a holistic interpretation, the result of the interpretation may be more limiting or narrow than what the legislature intended. *See In re B.O.A.*, 831 S.E.2d 305 (reversing court of appeals opinion that gave more restrictive rather than expansive interpretation of statutory phrase "conditions of removal"); *In re A.P.*, 371 N.C. 14 (reversing court of appeals opinion that county director lacked standing to file a petition when focus was on one term in a statute, rather than the whole of the Juvenile Code).

In abuse, neglect, dependency, and termination of parental rights cases, the appellate courts have also considered the purposes of the Juvenile Code, which are set forth at G.S. 7B-100. Through various opinions the appellate courts have repeatedly recognized that "the fundamental principle underlying North Carolina's approach to controversies involving child neglect and custody [is] that the best interest of the child is the polar star.' " *In re A.P.*, 371 N.C. at 21 (quoting *In re M.A.W.*, 370 N.C. 149, 152 (2017)). *See* G.S. 7B-100(5). When applying the whole-text canon, courts consider this principle when interpreting a statute in the Juvenile Code. *See, e.g., In re A.P.*, 371 N.C. 14. The North Carolina Supreme Court has also considered other provisions of G.S. 7B-100 when construing the meaning of a statute. *See, e.g., In re R.R.N.*, 368 N.C. 167 (2015) (recognizing the dual purpose of the Juvenile Code in promoting a child's best interests and safeguarding the parent-child relationship from needless state interference when interpreting the "caretaker" statute).

## 12.9 Motions to Dismiss and Failure to Comply with Appellate Rules

A motion to dismiss an appeal may be made under Appellate Rule 25 if a party fails to comply with the Rules of Appellate Procedure. If a party gives notice of appeal but then fails to take actions required by the Appellate Rules to move forward with the appeal, another party may move to dismiss the appeal. Motions to dismiss must be supported by affidavits or certified copies of docket entries that show the failure to take timely action or otherwise perfect the appeal. Before the appeal is filed in an appellate court, motions to dismiss for failure to take timely action are made to the trial court, and the Rules of Civil Procedure relating to motions practice apply. After an appeal is filed in the appellate court, motions to dismiss are made to that court, and Appellate Rule 37 sets out the procedure for the motion. N.C. R. APP. P. 25(a). A motion to dismiss should not be raised for the first time in a brief to the appellate court; this includes a motion to dismiss based on a lack of standing. *In re J.L.*, 826 S.E.2d 258 (N.C. Ct. App. 2019) (deciding the issue of standing because it is jurisdictional despite it being raised for first time in a brief).

The motion to dismiss must be granted unless

1. compliance or waiver of compliance is shown on the record;
2. the appellee consents to the untimely action; or
3. the court for good cause permits the action to be taken out of time.

N.C. R. APP. P. 25(a).

In determining whether failure to comply with the Appellate Rules warrants dismissal, the appellate court will engage in an analysis of the appropriate remedy for noncompliance, looking at whether the noncompliance is substantial or gross; which, if any sanction should be imposed; and if dismissal is the appropriate sanction, whether the circumstances of the case justify suspension of the rules under Appellate Rule 2 to reach the merits of the appeal.

*Dogwood Dev. & Mgmt. Co. v. White Oak Transp. Co.*, 362 N.C. 191 (2008). See section 12.3.C, above (discussing Appellate Rule 2). The supreme court "stress[ed] that a party's failure to comply with nonjurisdictional [appellate] rule requirements normally should not lead to dismissal of the appeal." *Dogwood Dev. & Mgmt. Co. v. White Oak Transp. Co.*, 362 N.C. at 198.

The appellate court may also issue sanctions for failure to comply with the Appellate Rules. N.C. R. APP. P. 25(b). *See also, e.g., In re T.M.*, 180 N.C. App. 539 (2006) (sanctioning appellate counsel and requiring him to personally pay the costs of the appeal because he submitted a brief in which the one-page statement of facts was almost entirely naked argument and contained no citations to the record, in contravention of the Appellate Rules, and counsel had previously been admonished by the court for Appellate Rules violations).

## 12.10 Extraordinary Writs, Discretionary Review, and Appeal of Right

The supreme court and the court of appeals have jurisdiction to issue prerogative writs, including mandamus, prohibition, certiorari, and supersedeas. G.S. 7A-32.

### A. Writ of Certiorari

A petition for a writ of certiorari, filed in the appellate courts, is a means by which a party may seek appellate review when other means do not exist.

**1. Review of trial court.** In civil cases a writ of certiorari may be issued by either the court of appeals or the North Carolina Supreme Court to permit review of a decision of the trial court when

- the right to appeal has been lost for failure to take timely action or
- no right of appeal from an interlocutory order exists.

N.C. R. APP. P. 21(a)(1). *See, e.g., In re C.M.C.*, 832 S.E.2d 681 (N.C. S.Ct. 2019) (granting writ of certiorari to review termination of parental rights order when notice of appeal was filed with court of appeals rather than supreme court); *In re B.C.T.*, 828 S.E.2d 50 (N.C. Ct. App. 2019) (granting writ of certiorari to allow mother to appeal civil custody order regarding one child entered under G.S. 7B-911 when notice of appeal only referenced disposition order regarding different child); *In re S.Z.H.*, 247 N.C. App. 254 (2016) (treating a notice of appeal that was untimely by one day as a petition for writ of certiorari; issuing a writ to review the merits of the appeal); *In re K.C.*, 199 N.C. App. 557 (2009) (granting respondent mother's petition for writ of certiorari to hear appeal of initial disposition order that was dismissed for untimeliness when appeal was untimely due to no fault of mother's, amended notice of appeal was filed as soon as trial counsel realized his mistake in failing to include disposition order in notice of appeal of adjudication, and given the importance of issues that involve the relationship between parents and children).

The appellate court exercises its discretion when deciding whether to grant a petition for writ of certiorari. *See In re J.A.K.*, 812 S.E.2d 716 (N.C. Ct. App. 2018) (exercising discretion to deny petition for writ of certiorari; dismissing appeal).

**2. Review of court of appeals.** A writ of certiorari may be issued by the North Carolina Supreme Court to permit review of a decision of the court of appeals when

- the right to appeal or petition for discretionary review has been lost by failure to take timely action or
- no right of appeal exists.

N.C. R. App. P. 21(a)(2).

Requirements for filing, content, service, and responses are contained in Appellate Rule 21.

B. **Petition for Discretionary Review**

Under Appellate Rule 15, a party may petition the supreme court in writing to certify a cause for discretionary review by the supreme court, either prior to or after the court of appeals rules on a matter, upon any grounds specified in G.S. 7A-31. Under G.S. 7A-31(a), discretionary review may also be initiated by the supreme court on its own motion.

The grounds for granting a petition for discretionary review are as follows:

- Where the court of appeals has not yet made a determination and in the opinion of the supreme court
    - the subject matter of the appeal has significant public interest or is important in overseeing the jurisdiction and integrity of the court system;
    - the cause involves legal principles of major significance to the jurisprudence of the State;
    - delay in final adjudication is likely to result from failure to certify and thereby cause substantial harm; or
    - the work load of the courts of the appellate division is such that the expeditious administration of justice requires certification.

    G.S. 7A-31(b).

- Where the court of appeals has already made a determination and in the opinion of the supreme court
    - the subject matter of the appeal has significant public interest;
    - the cause involves legal principles of major significance to the jurisprudence of the State; or
    - the decision of the court of appeals appears likely to be in conflict with a decision of the Supreme Court.

    G.S. 7A-31(c). *See, e.g., In re A.P.*, 371 N.C. 14 (2018) (granting discretionary review of court of appeals opinion that applied a restrictive interpretation of "director", based on which the court of appeals held that standing and subject matter jurisdiction in a neglect and dependency action were lacking).

Interlocutory determinations by the court of appeals, including orders remanding the cause for a new trial or for other proceedings, will be certified for review by the supreme court only upon a determination by the supreme court that failure to certify would cause a delay in final adjudication that would probably result in substantial harm. G.S. 7A-31(c); N.C. R. App. P. 15(h).

Requirements for filing, content, service, and responses for the motion and briefs are set out in Appellate Rule 15.

## C. Appeal of Right

A party has a right to appeal a court of appeals decision to the North Carolina Supreme Court when

- there is a dissent in the court of appeals decision or
- the case directly involves a substantial question under the United States or North Carolina Constitutions.

G.S. 7A-30.

Requirements for filing, content, service, the record and briefs are set out in Appellate Rule 14.

## D. Writ of Mandamus or Prohibition

A writ of mandamus is used to compel a trial court (or any governmental official) to perform a required ministerial act or a mandatory duty.

In describing the remedy of mandamus, the North Carolina Supreme Court specified these required elements:

- the petitioner seeking relief must show a clear legal right to the act requested;
- the respondent must have a clear legal duty to perform the act;
- the duty must relate to a ministerial act, not an act requiring the exercise of discretion (mandamus may be used to compel an official to exercise his or her discretion but not to direct what the result should be);
- the respondent must have neglected or refused to perform the act and the time to act has expired; and
- there must not be an alternative legally adequate remedy.

*In re T.H.T.*, 362 N.C. 446 (2008).

For example, the North Carolina Supreme Court has held that mandamus is the appropriate remedy for the trial court's failure to act within statutory timelines set out in the Juvenile Code. *In re T.H.T.*, 362 N.C. 446. See Chapter 4.9 for an explanation of the statutory time requirements related to entering certain orders in abuse, neglect, dependency, and termination of parental rights proceedings, including the remedy of mandamus.

A writ of prohibition is the converse of mandamus and is used to preclude a court from exceeding its jurisdiction in matters it does not have the power to hear or determine.

Requirements for filing, content, service, and response for mandamus and prohibition are set out in Appellate Rule 22.

> **Resource:** For more on a writs of mandamus and of prohibition, see JULIE RAMSEUR LEWIS & JOHN RUBIN, NORTH CAROLINA DEFENDER MANUAL, Vol. 2, Trial (UNC School of Government, 2d ed. 2012). In particular, see Chapter 35 "Appeals, Post-Conviction Litigation, and Writs."

### E. Writ of Supersedeas

A writ of supersedeas may be sought to stay the execution or enforcement of any judgment, order, or other determination of a trial court when the judgment is not automatically stayed by the taking of the appeal or when a petition for mandamus, prohibition, or certiorari has been filed and

- a stay order has been sought and denied in the trial court or
- extraordinary circumstances make it impracticable to obtain a stay from the trial court.

N.C. R. APP. P. 23(a)(1).

Requirements for filing, content, service, and response for supersedeas are set out in Appellate Rule 23.

## 12.11 Trial Court's Role during and after Appeal

### A. Trial Court's Role pending Appeal

The Juvenile Code specifically addresses the trial court's ability to enforce orders and exercise jurisdiction in an abuse, neglect, dependency, or termination of parental rights (TPR) proceeding when there is a pending appeal. The specific statute, G.S. 7B-1003, controls over G.S. 1-294, the general statute addressing jurisdiction of a trial court upon perfection of an appeal. *In re M.I.W.*, 365 N.C. 374 (2012).

**1. Enforcement of or motion to stay order.** During an appeal of an order entered in an abuse, neglect, dependency, or TPR proceeding, the trial court may enforce the order unless a stay is ordered by the trial court or the appellate court. G.S. 7B-1003(a).

A motion in the trial court for a stay when an appeal is taken is governed by Rule 62(d) of the Rules of Civil Procedure. If the trial court denies or vacates a stay, a motion may be made to the appropriate appellate court for a temporary stay and a writ of supersedeas in accordance with Appellate Rule 23. N.C. R. APP. P. 8(a). See section 12.10.E, above (writ of supersedeas). When extraordinary circumstances make it impracticable to move for a stay in the trial court, an application for a temporary stay and writ of supersedeas may be made to the appellate court. N.C. R. APP. P. 8(a).

**2. Continued court involvement in non-TPR appeals.** Unless the appellate court orders otherwise, when an appeal is pending in an abuse, neglect, or dependency case, the trial court must continue to exercise jurisdiction, conduct hearings (except TPR proceedings, discussed in subsection 3, immediately below), and enter orders related to custody and placement that it finds to be in the child's best interests. G.S. 7B-1003(b).

**3. Cannot proceed to TPR during appeal of the underlying matter.** G.S. 7B-1003(b)(1) prevents the trial court from exercising jurisdiction and conducting hearings in a TPR action when an appeal from an underlying abuse, neglect, or dependency action is pending. The North Carolina Supreme Court has held that G.S. 7B-1003(b)(1) prohibits the trial court from exercising jurisdiction over a TPR proceeding until after the issuance of a mandate by the appellate court in the underlying appeal; however, once the appeal has been resolved, the trial court may act on a TPR motion that was filed during the pendency of the appeal. *In re M.I.W.*, 365 N.C. 374 (2012) (TPR motion was filed while appeals of disposition order were pending, but trial court did not act on TPR motion until after the appellate mandate affirming the order had issued and after the time within which a petition for discretionary review could have been filed). In making its ruling, the supreme court reasoned that G.S. 7B-1003 did not divest the trial court of jurisdiction altogether, but rather prohibited the exercise of jurisdiction before the appellate mandate resolving the appeal has issued, and that issuance of the mandate returned the power to exercise jurisdiction to the trial court. *But see In re P.P.*, 183 N.C. App. 423 (2007) (vacating TPR order; TPR petition was filed during an appeal of a permanency planning order that resulted in that order being vacated and remanded but trial court proceeded with the TPR hearing after the appeal was resolved and before complying with the mandate remanding the case; even though the TPR hearing and entry of the TPR order occurred after resolution of the appeal and G.S. 7B-1003(b)(1) prohibits proceeding with TPR hearings "pending disposition of an appeal," the legislature could not have intended the language in G.S. 7B-1003(b)(1) to allow a result that avoids the effects of the appeal).

The prohibition in G.S. 7B-1003(b)(1) against proceeding in a TPR case during the pendency of an appeal applies to appeals from orders designated in G.S. 7B-1001 and does not apply to appeals of orders entered in related cases arising outside of the Juvenile Code. *In re Baby Boy*, 238 N.C. App. 316 (2014) (holding district court had jurisdiction to hear the TPR petition during an appeal of an adoption order that found the mother's relinquishment was void because G.S. 7B-1003 does not apply to orders outside of G.S. Chapter 7B, and the adoption order was entered pursuant to G.S. Chapter 48).

**4. Continued court involvement in TPR appeals.** While an appeal is pending in a TPR case, the court may enter temporary orders related to custody and placement that it finds to be in the child's best interest. G.S. 7B-1003(b), (c). However, "the trial court has no authority—even in the underlying abuse, neglect, and dependency action—to enter any orders other than ones affecting the custody and/or placement of the juvenile." *In re K.L.*, 196 N.C. App. 272, 273 (2009). The court of appeals in *In re K.L.* stated that TPR proceedings initiated by motion in the abuse, neglect, or dependency action are governed by G.S. 7B-1003(b), and TPR proceedings that are initiated by petition and commence a new action are governed by G.S. 7B-1003(c), but both provisions only allow the court to enter temporary orders affecting the custody and placement of the child that it finds to be in the child's best interest when the TPR appeal is pending.

**5. Order requirements pending appeal disposition.** Pending disposition of the appeal, orders must meet certain requirements:

- Any order entered during an appeal that places or continues placement of a child in foster care must comply with G.S. 7B-903.1, which addresses decision-making authority of a county DSS, participation in normal childhood activities, DSS notice to the child's GAL when a change in the juvenile's placement is required, and DSS responsibilities before a child may have unsupervised visitation or be returned to the home of the parent, guardian, custodian, or caretaker from whom the child was removed. G.S. 7B-1003(e); 7B-903.1(a), (b), (c), (d).
- When the court has found that the child has suffered physical abuse by someone with a history of violent behavior, the court must consider the opinion of the mental health professional who performed the required evaluation on the person before returning the child to the custody of that person pending resolution of the appeal. G.S. 7B-1003(d); *see* G.S. 7B-503(b) (evaluation).

---

**Resource:** For a further discussion of the district court's role when an appeal is pending, see Sara DePasquale, *What Can the District Court Do in an A/N/D or TPR Action when an Appeal is Pending?*, UNC SCH. OF GOV'T: ON THE CIVIL SIDE BLOG (Aug. 2, 2019).

---

**6. Rule 60 of the Rules of Civil Procedure.** Rule 60(a) of the Rules of Civil Procedure permits the trial court to correct clerical mistakes and errors in its order arising from oversight or omission up to the time an appeal is docketed in the court of appeals, but the court may not make substantive changes to the order. *In re C.N.C.B.*, 197 N.C. App. 553 (2009) (holding that the trial court could not add a finding that was essential to adjudication of a ground for termination); *In re J.K.P.*, 238 N.C. App. 334 (2014) (court has jurisdiction to correct a clerical mistake, which in this case was the inadvertent checking of a box on the AOC form, pursuant to Rule 60(a) so long as the correction occurs before an appeal is docketed).

Rule 60(b) of the Rules of Civil Procedure permits the trial court to relieve a party from a final judgment, order, or proceeding for the six reasons set out in the statute. When a Rule 60(b) motion is made while an appeal is pending, a request may be made of the trial court to indicate how it would rule on the motion if an appeal were not pending, along with a request to the appellate court to delay consideration of the appeal until the trial court has considered the Rule 60(b) motion. *See In re L.H.*, 210 N.C. App. 355 (2011) (discussing this procedure pursuant to *Bell v. Martin*, 43 N.C. App 134 (1979), *rev'd on other grounds*, 299 N.C. 715 (1980)).

### B. Trial Court's Role after Appeal

**1. Modification of order.** On affirmation of an order by the appellate court, the trial court may modify its original order as the court finds to be in the child's best interest to reflect the child's adjustment or changed circumstances while the case was on appeal. If modification is ex parte, the court must notify interested parties within ten days to show cause why the modifying order should be vacated or altered. G.S. 7B-1003(c); 7B-1004.

These statutes do not create a right to another review proceeding; they give the trial court discretion to modify or vacate the original order due to changed circumstances. When a party moves to modify or vacate the order, the trial court has discretion to hear or decline to hear evidence. *In re Montgomery*, 77 N.C. App. 709 (1985).

**2. Carrying out appellate mandate.** The trial court is bound by the mandate of the appellate court but may not act until the mandate issues. The mandate of the court, which consists of certified copies of its judgment and opinion and any direction as to costs, is issued by transmittal from the clerk of the appellate court to the clerk of the trial court. Unless otherwise ordered, mandates are issued twenty days after the written opinion of the court has been filed with the clerk. N.C. R. APP. P. 32. The mandate issues on the date that the appellate court transmits the mandate to the trial court, not on the day the trial court receives it. *State v. Singletary*, 810 S.E.2d 775 (N.C. Ct. App. 2018).

Generally, failure to follow an appellate mandate on remand is error. *See In re S.R.G.*, 200 N.C. App. 594 (2009).

- The trial court erred when it failed to carry out the mandate of the court of appeals to make findings according to G.S. 7B-907(b). *In re J.M.D.*, 210 N.C. App. 420 (2011) (decided under previous statute).
- The trial court erred when it ignored the mandate of the court of appeals to hold a new termination of parental rights (TPR) hearing, but the error was not prejudicial when the court, instead, held a permanency planning hearing. *In re R.A.H.*, 182 N.C. App. 52 (2007).
- The trial court committed reversible error when it failed to carry out the mandate of the court of appeals by holding a TPR hearing instead of a permanency planning hearing after remand of the permanency planning order. *In re P.P.*, 183 N.C. App. 423 (2007).

A trial court on remand should also be aware of "the law of the case doctrine" that applies when a question before an appellate court has previously been answered in an earlier appeal in the same case, constituting the law of the case both in subsequent proceedings in the trial court and on a subsequent appeal. *See In re S.R.G.*, 200 N.C. App. 594 (court of appeals reversed a TPR order based on abandonment, one of three grounds alleged by DSS, and remanded for further consideration consistent with its opinion; the law of the case doctrine precluded the trial court on remand from finding one of the other grounds alleged in the petition based on the trial court's previous failure to find that ground). The law of the case doctrine does not apply to a second TPR proceeding that alleges the same ground but is based on different facts because the doctrine "does not apply when the evidence presented at a subsequent proceeding is different from that presented on a former appeal." *In re K.C.*, 812 S.E.2d 873, 874 (N.C. Ct. App. 2018) (citations omitted) (holding law of case doctrine did not apply when fifteen months had passed between the first TPR hearing (the order of which was reversed on appeal) and the filing of the second TPR petition that contained allegations of events that occurred after the first TPR was filed). See Chapter 9.10.C (discussing events that occur after a TPR has been denied or reversed on appeal).

When an appellate court remands a case to the trial court, the opinion may give the court specific directions or it may say "for further action consistent with this opinion," or "for additional findings." *See, e.g., In re S.R.G.*, 195 N.C. App. 79, 88 (2009) (remanding "for further action consistent with this opinion"); *In re L.C.*, 253 N.C. App. 67, 81 (2017) (remanding "for additional findings on these issues"). Within the parameters of the appellate court's mandate, the trial court often has discretion as to how to proceed once the mandate issues. When an appellate court remands a case for additional findings, for example, unless the opinion says otherwise the trial court has discretion as to whether to conduct a further hearing and hear additional evidence. *See In re J.M.D.*, 210 N.C. App. 420 (2011) (rejecting respondent's argument that the trial court erred in refusing to allow her to present evidence on remand, stating that whether to receive new evidence on remand is within the discretion of the court, and in this case there was no abuse of discretion). When a remand allows for a trial court to exercise discretion in determining whether to receive additional evidence, the trial court is not obligated to hear new evidence. *In re A.B.*, 245 N.C. App. 35 (2016) (holding no abuse of discretion when trial court did not hear additional evidence regarding the child's best interests).

An order resulting from a mandate that reverses and remands the order that was appealed must be an entirely new and complete order. *In re A.R.P.* 218 N.C. App. 185 (2012). In *In re A.R.P.*, the court of appeals explained that a reversal is " 'an appellate court's overturning of a lower court's decision[,]' and '[i]n the legal context, 'overturn' means to invalidate.' " 218 N.C. App. at 188 (citations omitted). Because the appealed order is invalidated, the order after remand cannot supplement findings of fact and conclusions of law in the order that has been reversed, and doing so results in an incomplete order. *In re A.R.P.* 218 N.C. App. 185.

When an entire order is vacated and remanded, the entire order is void and of no effect and the posture of the case returns to the order that was entered before the vacated order. *In re D.S.*, 817 S.E.2d 901 (N.C. Ct. App. 2018). Similarly, when a portion of the order is vacated, those portions of the order become void and have no effect. *In re D.S.*, 817 S.E.2d 901. Whether an order is vacated and remanded in part or in full will determine what the court must consider and include in the order entered after remand.

# Chapter 13

# Relevant Federal Laws

# Chapter 13
# Relevant Federal Laws

**13.1 Scope of Chapter    13-3**

**13.2 Indian Child Welfare Act    13-3**
- A. Introduction and Purpose
- B. Applicability
  1. Proceedings covered by ICWA
  2. Proceedings not covered by ICWA
  3. "Indian Child"
- C. Inquiry at Commencement of Every Proceeding as to "Indian Child" Status
  1. Reason to know child is an "Indian child"
  2. Burden of establishing "Indian child" status
- D. Jurisdiction
  1. Exclusive tribal court jurisdiction
  2. Concurrent jurisdiction in tribal and state court, intervention by tribe, transfer
- E. Emergency Proceedings
- F. Notice to the Tribe, Parent, Indian Custodian, and Bureau of Indian Affairs
  1. Right to intervene in a state court action
  2. Voluntary and adoption proceedings
- G. Timing of Court Proceedings
- H. "Active Efforts" Required
- I. Finding of Serious Emotional or Physical Damage
- J. Placement Preferences
- K. Consent to Foster Care Placement, TPR, and Adoption including Relinquishment
- L. Impact of ICWA Violation

**13.3 Multiethnic Placement Act    13-28**

**13.4 Title VI of the Civil Rights Act    13-30**
- A. Introduction
- B. Applicability
- C. Prohibited Discrimination
- D. Requirements
  1. Compliance
  2. Outreach
  3. Language access
- E. Violations
  1. Complaint
  2. North Carolina findings

**13.5 The Americans with Disabilities Act    13-37**
- A. Introduction
- B. Applicability

1. Public entities
2. Disability defined
C. Prohibited Discrimination
D. Requirements
    1. Access and opportunity
    2. Exceptions
    3. Application to abuse, neglect, dependency, and TPR proceedings
    4. Notice of applicability
E. Compliance
    1. Filing a complaint
    2. Violations related to child welfare

## 13.6 Servicemembers Civil Relief Act    13-47
A. Introduction
B. Applicability
    1. Servicemember defined
    2. Military service defined
C. SCRA Requirements
    1. The SCRA affidavit
    2. Additional SCRA requirements when respondent is in military service

## 13.7 Every Student Succeeds Act    13-53
A. Introduction
B. Companion to the Fostering Connections Act
C. School Selection
D. Transportation
E. Designated Points of Contact

## 13.8 The Individuals with Disabilities Education Act    13-59
A. Introduction
B. Part B of IDEA: Children Ages 3–21
    1. Qualifying disability
    2. Services for children 3 to 21 years of age
    3. Decision-making by the IEP Team
    4. Procedural safeguards
C. Part C of IDEA: Children under 3 Years of Age
    1. Children substantiated as abused or neglected
    2. Qualifying disability
    3. Early intervention services (EI)
    4. Individualized family service plan (IFSP)
    5. The IFSP Team
    6. Procedural safeguards
D. Parent: Definition, Role, and Appointment of Surrogate Parent
    1. Parent's role
    2. Parent defined
    3. Determining parent
    4. Appointment of a surrogate parent

**13.9 Special Immigrant Juvenile Status and Selected Immigration Resources    13-80**
    A. Introduction and Selected Resources
    B. Special Immigrant Juvenile Status and Obtaining Lawful Permanent Residency
        1. Introduction
        2. Eligibility for SIJS
        3. The application process
        4. Impact on parents

---

## 13.1 Scope of Chapter

Many federal laws affect abuse, neglect, dependency, or termination of parental rights (TPR) proceedings. Some of those federal laws relate specifically to child welfare and require the states to comply with certain requirements, particularly when related to eligibility for and receipt of federal funding for child welfare activities. For a discussion of selected federal child welfare laws and the impact of those laws on North Carolina's Juvenile Code (G.S. Chapter 7B), see Chapter 1.3.B.

Other federal laws apply to abuse, neglect, dependency, or TPR cases because of an issue that is present in a particular case and is addressed by a federal law. When working with children and families, many issues arise that require county departments of social services (DSS), the attorneys, and the courts to look to federal substantive laws that are outside the scope of North Carolina's Juvenile Code. Examples include federal education laws and federal entitlement and/or anti-discrimination laws.

**Note**, for purposes of this Manual, "department of social services" or "DSS" refers to a department as defined by G.S. 7B-101(8a) regardless of how it is titled or structured.

This Chapter identifies and discusses selected federal laws that the parties, the attorneys, and the courts encounter most frequently in abuse, neglect, dependency, and TPR cases. The Chapter does not attempt to address all the federal laws that may relate to an abuse, neglect, dependency, or TPR case or to provide a comprehensive discussion of the laws that are included here. Instead, this Chapter provides an overview of selected federal laws and includes links to additional resources when a greater explanation of a particular federal law is needed.

## 13.2 Indian Child Welfare Act

### A. Introduction and Purpose

The Indian Child Welfare Act (ICWA), Pub. L. No. 95-608, 92 Stat. 3069, was enacted in 1978 and is codified at 25 U.S.C. 1901–1963. Federal regulations, effective December 12, 2016 and found at 25 C.F.R. Part 23, were promulgated by the Department of Interior Bureau of Indian Affairs (BIA). The regulations in Subpart I, which apply to ICWA implementation in state court proceedings, do not apply to proceedings that were initiated prior to December 16, 2016 but do "apply to any subsequent *proceeding* in the same matter or subsequent proceedings affecting the custody or placement of the same child." 25 C.F.R. 23.143 (emphasis added). The 2016 regulations are the first binding federal regulations implementing ICWA since its enactment in 1978. Complementary Guidelines for Implementing the Indian Child Welfare Act were issued by the BIA on December 16, 2016 (Guidelines, 2016). *See* 81 Fed. Reg. 96476. Although the Guidelines, 2016 are not binding, they explain the ICWA statute and regulations and provide examples of best practices for implementing ICWA.

**Cautionary Note:** Both federal and state appellate opinions interpreting ICWA for proceedings that occurred before December 12, 2016, will not address the federal regulations and may be superseded by those regulations. Some opinions refer to the BIA Guidelines that were in effect before December 2016 (Guidelines, 1979 and Guidelines, 2015), which were replaced by Guidelines, 2016.

ICWA was enacted in response to the disproportionately large numbers of American Indian and Alaska Native children who were removed from their families and communities by public and private child welfare and adoption agencies and placed in non-Indian foster and adoptive homes and institutions. *See* 25 U.S.C. 1901(4). One of Congress's findings in enacting ICWA is that "there is no resource that is more vital to the continued existence and integrity of Indian tribes than their children." 25 U.S.C. 1901(3). The purpose of ICWA is "to protect the best interests of Indian children and to promote the stability and security of Indian tribes and families by the establishment of minimum Federal standards for the removal of Indian children from their families and the placement of such children in foster or adoptive homes which will reflect the unique values of Indian culture." 25 U.S.C. 1902.

Because ICWA establishes minimum federal standards, when a provision in ICWA provides a higher standard of protection to the Indian family than is provided by state law, the standard under ICWA prevails. *In re E.G.M.*, 230 N.C. App. 196 (2013). When state law or another federal law has a higher standard of protection than ICWA provides to the rights of the Indian child's parent or Indian custodian, the state or other federal law applies. 25 U.S.C. 1921.

## B. Applicability

ICWA applies whenever an "Indian child" is the subject of a "child custody proceeding" or an "emergency proceeding" as those terms are defined by the Act. 25 C.F.R. 23.103(a). *See In re A.D.L.*, 169 N.C. App. 701 (2005). Note that the child's status as an "Indian child" is based upon political affiliation (or citizenship) with a federally recognized tribe and not merely on the child's or parent's ancestry. Guidelines, 2016, B.1 (p. 10). See subsection 13.2.B.3, below discussing "Indian child."

The federal regulations are clear that the qualifying condition for whether ICWA applies to a child custody or emergency proceeding is the child's status as an Indian child. When the child is determined to be an "Indian child," the court may not consider other factors (e.g., a parent's or child's participation in tribal culture or activities, the relationship between the child and parent including whether the parent ever had custody of the child, or the child's blood quantum) to decide whether ICWA applies. 25 C.F.R. 23.103(c).

**1. Proceedings covered by ICWA.** ICWA applies to "emergency proceedings" and "child custody proceedings." For purposes of ICWA, "child custody proceedings" are defined at 25 U.S.C. 1903(1) as proceedings that *may result in a*

- foster care placement,
- termination of parental rights (TPR),
- preadoptive placement, or
- adoptive placement.

Foster care placement results from any action that removes an Indian child from his or her parent (whose rights have not been terminated) or Indian custodian for temporary placement in a foster home or institution or the home of a guardian or conservator where the parent or Indian custodian cannot have the child returned upon demand with a simple verbal request. 25 U.S.C. 1903(1)(i); *see* 25 C.F.R. 23.2 (definition of "foster-care placement" and "upon demand"). If a child is placed in foster care or another out-of-home placement as a result of a status offense, which in North Carolina is an undisciplined juvenile proceeding, that proceeding is a child custody proceeding under ICWA. 25 C.F.R. 23.2; *see* G.S. 7B-1501(27) (definition of "undisciplined juvenile"); 7B-1902 through -1907 (nonsecure custody criteria, orders, placement, and hearings); 7B-2503(1)b. and c. (out-of-home placement dispositional alternatives for undisciplined juveniles).

**"Parent"** is defined under ICWA as a biological or adoptive parent (including adoptions under tribal law or custom) of an Indian child but does not include an unwed father who has not acknowledged or established paternity. 25 U.S.C. 1903(9); 25 C.F.R. 23.2. An unwed father could establish or acknowledge paternity by state law or tribal law or custom. *See* 25 U.S.C. 1911(d) (full faith and credit); 25 U.S.C. 1903(12) (definition of "tribal court").

An **"Indian custodian"** is any Indian person with legal custody under state law or tribal law or custom of an Indian child or to whom temporary physical care, custody, and control of the Indian child has been transferred by the parent. 25 U.S.C. 1903(6); 25 C.F.R. 23.2. The definition of "Indian custodian" is broader than the definition of "custodian" under the Juvenile Code. *See* G.S. 7B-101(8).

A preadoptive placement is the temporary placement of an Indian child in a foster home or institution that is made after a TPR, but it is not the permanent adoptive placement. 25 U.S.C. 1903(1)(iii); 25 C.F.R. 23.2.

An adoptive placement is the permanent placement of an Indian child for adoption, including an action that results in a final adoption decree. 25 U.S.C. 1903(1)(iv); 25 C.F.R. 23.2. An adoptive placement occurs in all adoption proceedings, including private, agency, and stepparent adoptions.

> **Practice Note:** The same child may be the subject of multiple child custody proceedings because an action that may result in one of the four possible outcomes (foster care, preadoptive, or adoptive placements or a TPR) is a separate child custody proceeding from an action that may result in a different outcome. 25 C.F.R. 23.2. For example, an adoption proceeding involving Child A is a separate child custody proceeding from a TPR action involving Child A, just as TPR action involving Child A is a separate child custody proceeding from an abuse, neglect, or dependency action involving Child A. The same child may be the subject of each of these three different child custody proceedings, which in this example, are adoption, TPR, and foster care proceedings. The applicable ICWA provisions apply to all three proceedings.

ICWA distinguishes between voluntary and involuntary child custody proceedings and emergency proceedings.

- An involuntary proceeding is a child custody proceeding in which the parent (1) does not consent to the foster care, preadoptive, or adoptive placement or the TPR or (2) consents to the foster care, preadoptive, or adoptive placement when under threat of the child's removal by DSS or court action. 25 C.F.R. 23.2.

- Voluntary proceedings are those child custody proceedings that are not involuntary proceedings and are freely consented to by either or both parents or the Indian custodian without any threat of removal by DSS. 25 C.F.R. 23.2. One example of a voluntary proceeding is an initial voluntary foster care placement agreement entered into between the parent and DSS without the threat of a DSS removal or need for a petition alleging abuse, neglect, or dependency. *See* G.S. 7B-910. ICWA applies to a voluntary proceeding that prohibits the parent (or Indian custodian) from regaining custody of the child upon demand with a simple verbal request. 25 C.F.R. 23.103(a)(1)(ii). For example, parents who execute a consent for a direct placement adoption vest legal and physical custody of their child to the prospective adoptive parent(s) such that the parents may not regain custody of their child with a simple verbal request. *See* G.S. 48-3-607(b). Similarly, parents who execute a relinquishment of their child to a child-placing agency (this may include a DSS when child protective services are not involved) vest legal and physical custody of their child with that agency such that the parents may not regain custody of their child with a simple verbal request. *See* G.S. 48-3-705(b). See section 13.2.K, below (discussing ICWA requirements for consents and relinquishments for adoption)

- An emergency proceeding is any court action that involves an emergency removal or placement of an Indian child. 25 C.F.R. 23.2; *see* 25 U.S.C. 1922; 25 C.F.R. 23.113. See section 13.2.E, below.

Although ICWA applies to voluntary and involuntary child custody and emergency proceedings, different provisions of the Act will apply depending upon the type of proceeding. *See* 25 C.F.R. 23.103(a) (setting out the proceedings to which ICWA does/does not apply) and 23.104 (table listing sections of the ICWA regulations as applied to the type of child custody proceeding).

**2. Proceedings not covered by ICWA.** ICWA does not apply to

- actions involving custody, including divorce, between the child's parents;
- voluntary placements chosen by either or both parents (or the Indian custodian), made of their free will and without a threat of removal by DSS, and subject to the parent (or Indian custodian) regaining custody of the child upon demand by a simple verbal request;
- juvenile delinquency proceedings and criminal prosecutions of juveniles as adults (*see* G.S. 7B-2200; 7B-2200.5; 7B-1604(b) regarding adult prosecution); and
- tribal court proceedings.

25 U.S.C. 1903(1); 25 C.F.R. 23.103(b).

**3. "Indian Child".** ICWA applies to an "Indian child," which is defined at 25 U.S.C. 1903(4) and 25 C.F.R. 23.2 as an unmarried child under the age of 18 who is either

- a member of a federally recognized Indian tribe or
- eligible for membership in an Indian tribe *and* the biological child of a member of an Indian tribe.

Each federally recognized tribe establishes its own membership criteria and decides membership issues for the child and biological parent. Enrollment in a tribe may open and close at any time set by the tribe, and the standards for enrollment can change. The tribe's determination is conclusive; the court may not substitute its own determination as to whether a child or parent is a member of the tribe or whether the child is eligible for membership in the tribe. 25 C.F.R. 23.108(a), (b). However, the court determines whether the child is an Indian child triggering the application of ICWA based on the information that is provided to it regarding the child's membership status or the biological parent's membership status *and* the child's eligibility for membership. The court may rely on facts or documentation (e.g., tribal enrollment documentation) that indicates tribal membership or eligibility for membership. 25 C.F.R. 23.108(c). The child's status as an "Indian child" is based upon political affiliation (or citizenship) with a federally recognized tribe and not merely on the child's or parent's ancestry. Guidelines, 2016, B.1 (p. 10).

(a) **Federally recognized Indian tribes.** ICWA applies to federally recognized Indian tribes, meaning those tribes (including Alaska native villages) that are recognized by the Secretary of the Interior as eligible for services that are provided to Indians. 25 U.S.C. 1903(8).

There are 573 federally recognized tribes in the U.S., one of which is located in North Carolina: the Eastern Band of the Cherokee Indians (EBCI). There are over 13,000 enrolled members of the EBCI and most of those members live on the Qualla Boundary, which is located in Jackson, Cherokee, Graham, Haywood, and Swain counties.[1] Although there is only one federally recognized tribe in North Carolina, an Indian child who is the subject of a child custody proceeding under ICWA may be from any federally recognized

---

[1] Information obtained from the Eastern Band of Cherokee Indians, Public Health and Human Services website.

tribe regardless of where that tribe is located. According to the 2010 U.S. Census, seventy-eight percent (78%) of the American Indian and Alaska Native population do not live on tribal lands.[2]

---

**Resources:**
The Bureau of Indian Affairs (BIA) maintains a list of federally recognized Indian tribes, organized by region, with an ICWA point of contact designated for each tribe and region. As of the date of this Manual, the most recent notice was published in the Federal Register on February 1, 2019. *See* 84 Fed. Reg. 1200-01.

The BIA also maintains a Tribal Leaders Directory (organized through a map) with contact information for the tribes on the BIA website.

**Practice Note:** Family Safety is the agency of the Eastern Band of Cherokee Indians (EBCI) that handles cases that involve children who are Indian children in the Cherokee community. Family Safety may be able to assist a participant in a state child custody or emergency proceeding by checking with the enrollment office to determine whether the child is an "Indian child," whether the Family Safety program is or will be working with the family, and whether tribal court action will be taken. The contact information for Family Safety is 117 John Crowe Hill Drive, Cherokee, North Carolina 28719; Telephone: (828) 359-1520. Any contact with Family Safety is separate from the notice that must be sent to the tribe pursuant to 25 U.S.C. 1912(a) and 25 C.F.R. 23.11, discussed in section 13.2.F, below.

---

**(b) State recognized tribes not covered by ICWA.** ICWA does not apply to tribes that have only state recognition. *In re A.D.L.*, 169 N.C. App. 701 (2005) (holding ICWA did not apply to children were who registered members of the state recognized Lumbee tribe). There are seven state recognized tribes in North Carolina to which ICWA does not apply. Those tribes are the

- Coharie Tribe,
- Haliwa-Saponi Indian Tribe,
- Lumbee Tribe of North Carolina,
- Meherrin Indian Tribe,
- Occaneechi Band of the Saponi Nation,
- Sappony, and
- Waccamaw Siouan Tribe.

*See* G.S. Chapter 71A (Indians); 143B-407(a).

---

[2] "The American Indian and Alaska Native Population: 2010," U.S. Census Bureau 2010 Census Brief (Jan. 2012). Note that the data presented is not limited to only those American Indians who are members of or are eligible for membership in a tribe and does not distinguish between state and federally recognized tribes.

**Resources:**
For information about the Indian Tribes in North Carolina, see "Tribes" under the "Commission of Indian Affairs" section of the N.C. Department of Administration website.

The National Conference of State Legislatures maintains a list, organized by state, of both federal and state recognized tribes on its website. Checking this site will assist in determining whether the tribe falls under ICWA protections as a federally recognized tribe or whether the tribe is not protected by ICWA as a state only recognized tribe.

Even though ICWA is inapplicable to tribes with only state recognition, North Carolina's Juvenile Code provides for special placement consideration and notice in the pre-adjudication phase of an abuse, neglect, or dependency proceeding for children who are members of a tribe recognized by North Carolina. The court may consider the role of "nonrelative kin," which for child members of a North Carolina recognized tribe includes any member of a state or federally recognized tribe, even when there is not a substantial relationship between the child and the adult tribal member. G.S. 7B-101(15a). At a hearing for nonsecure custody, the court may consider "nonrelative kin" as a placement option if the court is not placing the child with a parent or relative and placement with a nonrelative kin is in the child's best interests. G.S. 7B-505(c) and 7B-506(h)(2a). The court may order DSS to notify the child's North Carolina recognized tribe of the need for nonsecure custody for the purpose of locating relatives or nonrelative kin for placement options for the child. G.S. 7B-505(c); 7B-506(h)(2a). See Chapter 5.5.C.3 (discussing nonsecure custody placement) and 5.6.E (discussing inquiry and findings).

Although nonrelative kin are not explicitly referenced as a placement option for dispositional alternatives after a child's adjudication as abused, neglected, or dependent, the court may order that the child be placed in the custody of a "suitable person" if it determines that placement is in the child's best interests. G.S. 7B-903(a)(4). A suitable person may be a nonrelative kin. However, when a child is not placed with a parent, relatives have priority. G.S. 7B-903(a1) requires the court to place the child with a relative who is willing and able to provide proper care and supervision to the child in a safe home unless the court finds such placement would be contrary to the child's best interests. See Chapter 7.4.C.1 (discussing out-of-home placement priority).

The North Carolina Department of Health and Human Services (NC DHHS) Division of Social Services must collaborate with the Department of Administration Commission of Indian Affairs, and the North Carolina Association of County Directors of Social Services to develop effective processes to accomplish a number of goals, including

- identifying a reliable process through which Indian children in the child welfare system can be identified;
- enabling state-recognized tribes to receive reasonable notice when Indian children are being placed in foster care or adoptive placements or otherwise enter the child protective services system, and to be consulted on policies and matters related to the placement of Indian children in foster care or adoption;

- identifying and recruiting North Carolina Indians to become foster care and adoptive parents; and
- teaching cultural, social, and historical perspectives associated with Indian life to appropriate child welfare workers and foster and adoptive parents.

G.S. 143B-139.5A; *see* G.S. 143B-404 through -411 (State Commission on Indian Affairs).

**NC DHHS DSS Forms:**
- DSS-5335, Consent to Explore American Indian Heritage (with Instructions) (June 2011).
- DSS-5336, Fostering Connections/Tribal Relative Search (with Instructions) (June 2011).

These forms may assist in determining whether a child is a member of any tribe, including a North Carolina recognized tribe, and in finding relatives of that child.

### C. Inquiry at Commencement of Every Proceeding as to "Indian Child" Status

Under the regulations, an inquiry at the commencement of every emergency and child custody proceeding must be made by the court to determine whether the child is an Indian child. The inquiry is made of all the participants, including the attorneys, in the proceeding as to whether he or she knows or has reason to know that the child is an Indian child. The responses should be made on the record. The court must instruct the parties to inform it of information a party subsequently receives that provides reason to know the child is an Indian child. 25 C.F.R. 23.107(a).

For example, the court inquiry may result in the discovery that the child is not an Indian child for purposes of ICWA because neither biological parent is a member of a tribe but the child is eligible for membership. The child may be eligible for certain benefits and services if he or she becomes an enrolled member of an Indian tribe. As a result, the child's guardian ad litem, parent, guardian, or custodian or DSS may take responsibility for pursuing the child's membership. If the child becomes a member of a federally recognized tribe during the proceeding, the court must be notified as ICWA will then apply since the child will satisfy the criteria of "Indian child." *See* 25 U.S.C. 1903(4); *In re C.P.*, 181 N.C. App. 698 (2007); Guidelines, 2016, B.1 (p. 11).

**AOC Forms:** These form orders include sections addressing the ICWA inquiry:
- AOC-J-150, Order for Nonsecure Custody (Oct. 2019).
- AOC-J-151, Order on Need for Continued Nonsecure Custody (Oct. 2019).

**NC DHHS DSS Form:** This form may assist DSS in determining Indian child status. DSS-5335, Consent to Explore American Indian Heritage (with Instructions) (June 2011).

**Practice Notes:** Because the court must inquire at the beginning of every abuse, neglect, or dependency; termination of parental rights; and adoption proceeding whether the participants know or have reason to know whether the child is an Indian child, DSS should explore the child's Indian heritage with the child and family before the specific court action is initiated. DSS may find it helpful to ask parents, guardians, custodians, and/or caretakers and the child (if appropriate) to complete the DSS form or a family tree that specifically includes information about Native American heritage and tribal enrollment information. If the parent is driving a vehicle with an Eastern Band of Cherokee license plate, that could be an indication that the child is an Indian child. To obtain this special license plate, a tribal identification card must be shown to the Division of Motor vehicles. G.S. 20-79.4(b)(72).

**1. Reason to know child is an "Indian child."** The regulations address when a court has reason to know a child is an Indian child. Identified factors are when

- the court is informed by a participant in the proceeding, officer of the court involved in the proceeding, or Indian tribe that the child is an Indian child or that it has discovered information indicating the child is an Indian child;
- the child gives the court reason to know he or she is an Indian child; or
- the court is informed that
    - the child, the child's parent, or Indian custodian is domiciled or resides on an Indian reservation or in an Alaska Native village;
    - the child is or has been a ward of a tribal court; or
    - either parent or the child possesses an identification card indicating membership in an Indian tribe.

25 C.F.R. 23.107(c); *see In re Adoption of K.L.J.*, 831 S.E.2d 114 (N.C. Ct. App. 2019) (defining "ward of tribal court").

When there is reason to know but insufficient evidence for the court to determine that the child is an Indian child, the court must treat the child as an Indian child and comply with ICWA requirements until and unless it is determined on the record that the child does not meet the definition of "Indian child" at 25 U.S.C. 1903(4). 25 C.F.R. 23.107(b)(2). The court must also confirm on the record through a report, declaration, or testimony that DSS or another party in the proceeding has used due diligence to identify, work with, and obtain verification from the tribes of which there is reason to know the child (1) may be (or is) a member or (2) is eligible for membership *and* a biological parent is a member. 25 C.F.R. 23.107(b)(1). See section 13.2.F, below (discussing notice requirements to the tribe and regional BIA office). The information from the tribe will allow the court to determine whether the child is an Indian child. *See* 25 C.F.R. 23.108(c).

In *In re A.P.*, 818 S.E.2d 396 (N.C. Ct. App. 2018), the court of appeals addressed whether the trial court had reason to know that the child was an Indian child such that the mandatory notice provisions of ICWA applied. See section 13.2.F., below (discussing notice requirements). The court of appeals cited 25 C.F.R. 23.107(c)(2), which states the court has reason to know a child is an Indian child if "[a]ny participant in the proceeding . . . informs the court that it has discovered information indicating that the child is an Indian child." It then looked to opinions that were decided before the federal regulations were enacted and that concluded the ICWA notice requirements to the tribes were required when there was a suggestion that the child had Indian heritage. The court of appeals reasoned it was better to err on the side of caution and send the notice even when it was unlikely that the child was an Indian child. Based on those opinions, the court of appeals concluded in *In re A.P.* that the trial court had reason to know the child was an Indian child when the respondent mother's attorney notified the court at the adjudicatory hearing that there was an indication the mother and child had potential Cherokee and Bear Foot heritage.

Because there was reason to know the child was an Indian child, the court of appeals held that the trial court was required to direct DSS to send a notice under ICWA and remanded for the trial court to order that DSS comply with the notice provisions and other mandatory ICWA requirements. In its remand, the court of appeals stated that if no response to the notice was received, the mother had the burden to prove ICWA applied (discussed in subsection 2, immediately below). If a response was received confirming that the child is an Indian child, the trial court must determine if it has subject matter jurisdiction under ICWA (discussed in section 13.2.D, below) and, if so, comply with ICWA and the tribe's wishes. Although the court of appeals focused on the notice provisions of ICWA, the regulations state that when the trial court has reason to know the child is an Indian child, it must treat the child as such until it is determined on the record that the child does not meet the definition of Indian child – this means all the provisions of ICWA apply during that time. *See* 25 C.F.R. 23.107(b)(2).

**2. Burden of establishing "Indian child" status.** Anyone may raise the question of whether ICWA applies to the proceeding because the child is an Indian child. The burden starts with an inquiry by the district court. *See* 25 C.F.R. 23.107(a); *In re L.W.S.*, 255 N.C. App. 296 (2017). However, the burden of proof may ultimately be with the party raising the child's Indian child status and thus the applicability of ICWA.

In cases decided before the 2016 federal regulations, North Carolina appellate decisions addressing child custody proceedings held that the party who seeks to invoke ICWA has the burden of showing that the Act applies. *In re Williams*, 149 N.C. App. 951 (2002) (affirming the trial court's decision to deny a motion to dismiss a TPR proceeding for lack of subject matter jurisdiction where the respondent father merely mentioned his Indian heritage in his motion to dismiss and his testimony but provided no supporting evidence, such as documentation or testimony from a tribal representative, to prove ICWA applied); *In re C.P.*, 181 N.C. App. 698 (2007) (holding ICWA did not apply when respondent raised the issue that she and the children might be members of the Pokagen Band of Potawatomi Indians; the tribe did not respond to the ICWA notice sent by DSS and the period of time for the tribe to respond under ICWA had been exceeded; and respondent did not meet her burden of proof to show that ICWA applied).

The first North Carolina appellate decision to address the 2016 regulations is *In re L.W.S.*, 255 N.C. App. 296 (2017), even though the regulations did not apply since the termination of parental rights action concluded before the effective date of the regulations. The court of appeals found the respondent father did not timely raise or meet his burden of proving ICWA applied, but it referenced the new 2016 regulations. In footnote 4, the court of appeals stated "it seems to be the case that the burden has shifted to state courts to inquire at the start of a proceeding whether the child at issue is an Indian child, and, if so, the state court must confirm that the agency used due diligence to identify and work with the Tribe and treat the child as an Indian child unless and until it is determined otherwise." *In re L.W.S.*, 255 N.C. App. 296, 298 n.4 (2017).

Reading the regulations and appellate opinions together, the trial court has the burden of making the inquiry, and if there is reason to know the child is an Indian child, the petitioner has the burden of notifying the tribe and regional office of the BIA. The tribe should address the child's status in a response to the notice. The regulations do not address what happens when a tribe or the BIA fails to timely respond to the notice requesting information about the child's membership status, which includes the child's eligibility for membership when a biological parent is a member of a tribe. See section 13.2.F, below, discussing the ICWA notice.

The length of time a trial court must wait for the tribe to respond is not specifically addressed in the regulations. However, the court of appeals has addressed the timing issue in two opinions: *In re A.P.*, 818 S.E.2d 396 (N.C. Ct. App. 2018), and *In re C.P.*, 181 N.C. App. 698 (2007). In both opinions, the court of appeals looked to the time requirements under ICWA for when a hearing can be held after notice is received by the tribe. Under ICWA, the trial court may not hold a hearing until at least ten days after the tribe receives notice, and if requested, the trial court must grant a continuance of an additional twenty days. 25 U.S.C. 1912(a). Combined, the time period is thirty days. If the tribe fails to timely respond, the burden to introduce evidence showing the child is an Indian child is on the party who is asserting ICWA applies. *See In re A.P.*, 818 S.E.2d 396 (DSS must send notice; respondent mother must meet her burden if no response received); *In re C.P.*, 181 N.C. App. 698 (holding the trial court complied with ICWA when the length of time granted by two continuances exceeded thirty days; the court did not abuse its discretion in denying a third continuance and determining ICWA did not apply when the tribe had still not responded and the respondent mother offered no additional evidence showing the child was an Indian child).

When considering the evidence, the trial court makes "a judicial determination as to whether the child is an 'Indian child'." 25 C.F.R. 23.108(c). If the child is an Indian child, ICWA applies. 25 C.F.R. 23.107. The determination requires that the court decide whether the evidence provided is sufficient to prove that the child meets the criteria of an "Indian child" under 25 U.S.C. 1903(4). The court of appeals has identified documentation or testimony from a tribal representative as examples by which a party can prove ICWA applies, and while recognizing there are other methods of proof, it has stated the "equivocal testimony of the party seeking to invoke the Act, standing alone, is insufficient to meet this burden." *In re Williams,* 149 N.C. App. 951, 957 (2002); *see In re C.P.,* 181 N.C. App. 698 (holding mother did not meet her burden of proof when the only evidence was her word, without any supporting documentation, that she and the children were tribal members). *See also* 25 C.F.R. 23.108(c) (court may rely on facts or documentation such as tribal enrollment documentation that indicates tribal membership or eligibility for membership when determining whether the child is an Indian child).

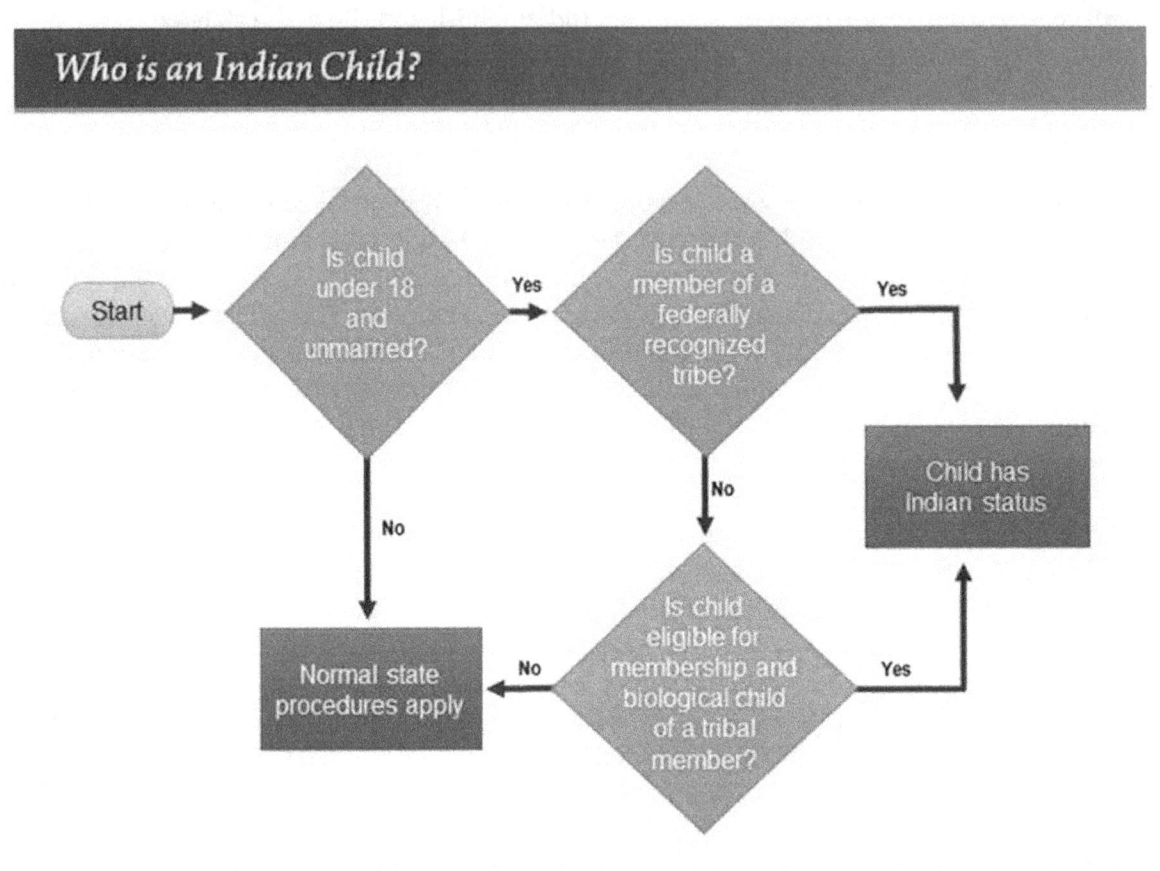

## Who is an Indian Child?

```
Start → Is child under 18 and unmarried?
  No → Normal state procedures apply
  Yes → Is child a member of a federally recognized tribe?
    Yes → Child has Indian status
    No → Is child eligible for membership and biological child of a tribal member?
      No → Normal state procedures apply
      Yes → Child has Indian status
```

[3]

### D. Jurisdiction

**1. Exclusive tribal court jurisdiction.** The tribal court has exclusive jurisdiction of a child custody proceeding when an Indian child

- resides or is domiciled on a reservation (even if visiting elsewhere) or
- is a ward of the tribal court (regardless of where the child resides or is domiciled).

25 U.S.C. 1911(a); *see* 25 C.F.R. 23.2 (definition of "domicile"); *see also Mississippi Band*

---

[3] Image reproduced from the "Resources for Caseworkers" section of the National Indian Child Welfare Association website.

*of Choctaw Indians v. Holyfield*, 490 U.S. 30 (1989) (vacating an adoption decree after holding the state court did not have jurisdiction when the Indian children's domicile was the reservation).

When a tribal court has exclusive jurisdiction of a child custody proceeding, the state court must expeditiously notify the tribal court of its pending dismissal of the state court action based on the jurisdictional issue, dismiss the state court action, and ensure the tribal court is sent all the information, including court pleadings and any record, regarding the state court action. 25 C.F.R. 23.110(a).

The court of appeals addressed the issue of exclusive jurisdiction of a tribal court in *In re Adoption of K.L.J.*, 831 S.E.2d 114 (N.C. Ct. App. 2019). In this North Carolina adoption proceeding, ICWA applied because the two children who were the subject of the proceeding are members of the Cheyenne River Sioux Tribe. The children had also been the subject of child custody proceedings in the tribal court where their parents' rights were terminated and custody was ordered to a "paternal aunt," after which the case was dismissed by the tribal court. The "aunt," as custodian, placed the children with the adoption petitioners in North Carolina and ultimately sought a G.S. Chapter 35A guardianship for the children with the petitioners through the North Carolina courts. The guardians subsequently initiated adoption proceedings in North Carolina. After notice of the adoption proceeding was sent to the Tribe and to the "aunt," the "aunt" intervened and raised subject matter jurisdiction under ICWA as an issue. The district court determined it had subject matter jurisdiction and granted the adoptions. The court of appeals affirmed.

The court of appeals held that the exclusive jurisdiction provision of ICWA did not apply because the criteria of 25 U.S.C. 1911(a) did not exist. In its opinion, the court of appeals focused on whether the children were wards of the tribal court giving that court exclusive subject matter jurisdiction over the adoption proceedings since the children did not meet the jurisdictional criteria of residing or being domiciled within the reservation. Recognizing that ICWA does not define "ward of tribal court," the court of appeals adopted the definition of "ward of the state" from Black's Law Dictionary. As applied to ICWA, an Indian child is a "ward of tribal court" when he or she "is housed by or provided protections and necessities from the tribe" and when that stops, the Indian child "will cease being its ward for purposes of 25 U.S.C. § 1911(a)." *In re Adoption of K.L.J.*, 831 S.E.2d at 117. The court of appeals held the children were not wards of the tribal court; they lived outside of the reservation and were not provided protections and necessities from the tribe after custody was ordered to the "aunt."

The "aunt" raised a second issue related to full faith and credit of a tribal court order as part of her argument that the North Carolina court lacked subject matter jurisdiction under ICWA. The court of appeals held that the district court did not err when it failed to give full faith and credit to a tribal court order that concluded the children were wards of the tribal court – an order the "aunt" obtained two days before the adoption hearing.

ICWA requires every state to give full faith and credit to an Indian tribe's judicial proceedings that are applicable to Indian child custody proceedings to the same extent that the state gives full faith and credit to judicial proceedings of any other entity. 25 U.S.C. 1911(d). The case law in North Carolina addressing foreign judgments requires compliance with the Uniform Enforcement of Foreign Judgements Act (UEFJA). In applying UEFJA to the tribal court order, the "aunt" as the party seeking to enforce that order was required to "file a properly authenticated foreign judgment with the office of the [C]lerk of [S]uperior [C]ourt in any North Carolina county along with an affidavit attesting to the fact that the foreign judgment is both final and unsatisfied in whole or in part. . . ." *In re Adoption of K.L.J.*, 831 S.E.2d at 118 (citations omitted). The "aunt" did not comply with this requirement; she only provided an unauthenticated faxed copy that was purportedly entered by the tribal court. Additionally, the court of appeals determined there was a lack of due process for the adoption petitioners and the children, who were not given notice of or an opportunity to participate in the alleged hearing in tribal court.

> **Practice Note:** As *In re Adoption of K.L.J.* demonstrates, ICWA does not automatically divest a North Carolina court of subject matter jurisdiction over a child custody proceeding. *See also In re J.H.S.*, 808 S.E.2d 624 (N.C. Ct. App. 2018) (unpublished) (tribe intervened in N.C. neglect and dependency and TPR actions involving two Indian children). North Carolina courts lack subject matter jurisdiction when either (1) the Indian child resides on the reservation, (2) the Indian child is domiciled on the reservation, or (3) the Indian child is a ward of a tribal court. If there is any doubt, addressing the following questions on the record is one way to determine which court has subject matter jurisdiction:
>
> - Where does the child reside; is it a reservation?
> - Where is the child's domicile (where is the domicile of the child's parents or if applicable Indian custodian or guardian, *see* 25 C.F.R. 23.2 (defining "domicile")); is it a reservation?
> - Is the child a ward of tribal court? Has the child ever been the subject of a child custody proceeding in a tribal court? If so, what is the status of that proceeding? Is there an order? What does the order provide? Has the order been modified? If so, in what court (the tribal court or a state court)?
> - If the tribal court has exclusive jurisdiction, does an exception (as discussed immediately below) apply?

(a) **Exception to tribal court's exclusive jurisdiction: emergency removal.** Although a tribal court has exclusive jurisdiction of a child custody proceeding, a state court may act in an emergency proceeding, which is any court action that involves the emergency removal or emergency placement of an Indian child. *See* 25 U.S.C. 1922; 25 C.F.R. 23.2 and 23.113. To protect an Indian child who resides or is domiciled on a reservation but is temporarily located off the reservation from imminent physical damage or harm, ICWA allows for the emergency removal of that child from his or her parent or Indian custodian or emergency placement in a foster home or institution under applicable state law. See section 13.2.E, below, for a discussion of emergency proceedings.

(b) **Exception to tribal court's exclusive jurisdiction: agreement between tribe and state.** Another exception to a tribe's exclusive jurisdiction of a child custody proceeding is when the state and tribe enter into an agreement that relates to the care and custody of

Indian children and jurisdiction over child custody proceedings. The agreements may provide for the orderly transfer of jurisdiction on a case-by-case basis and allow for concurrent jurisdiction between the courts of the state and the tribe. Any agreement may be revoked by a party with 180 days written notice. 25 U.S.C. 1919. The North Carolina Court of Appeals has held that it will not take judicial notice of an agreement between the tribe and state because it is a "legislative fact" that is not subject to judicial notice. *In re E.G.M.*, 230 N.C. App. 196 (2013) (remanding the case for findings on a determination of subject matter jurisdiction under ICWA where the Indian child's domicile was that of her parents' on EBCI tribal land and the agreement was not introduced into evidence). As a result, the memorandum of agreement must be admitted as evidence in each state court case where an Indian tribal court would have exclusive jurisdiction.

**Practice Notes:** Prior to 2015, the Eastern Band of Cherokee Indians (EBCI) entered into a memorandum of agreement (MOA) with the NC DHHS Division of Social Services and four county departments of social services located within Judicial District 30 (Cherokee, Swain, Jackson, and Graham). The MOA deferred the exclusive jurisdiction of child welfare cases involving an Indian child of the EBCI from the EBCI tribal court to the North Carolina courts. In 2015, the memorandum of agreement was revoked, and the EBCI tribal court began to exercise exclusive jurisdiction in child welfare cases involving an Indian child of the EBCI who resides or is domiciled on the Qualla Boundary and Tribal Trust Lands or is a ward of the EBCI tribal court.

It is important that the petitioner (or movant in a TPR) and the state court determine whether the state court has jurisdiction to proceed in an abuse, neglect, dependency; termination of parental rights; and/or adoption action. For all federally recognized Indian tribes, the ICWA point of contact is named in the Designated Tribal Agents for Service of Notice in the Federal Register. That person should have information on whether the tribe exercises exclusive jurisdiction. *See* 84 Fed. Reg. 20387-02 (May 9, 2019).

**2. Concurrent jurisdiction in tribal and state court, intervention by tribe, transfer.** In cases where the tribal court does not have exclusive jurisdiction, meaning that the child is not (1) residing or domiciled on a reservation or (2) a ward of a tribal court, state and tribal courts have concurrent jurisdiction. Both the state court and the tribal court have subject matter jurisdiction, and the state action may proceed.

**(a) The tribe's right to intervene in a state court action.** The Indian child's tribe has the right to intervene at any time in a state court proceeding for foster care or termination of parental rights. 25 U.S.C. 1911(c). *See In re J.H.S.*, 808 S.E.2d 624 (N.C. Ct. App. 2018) (unpublished) (tribe intervened in N.C. neglect and dependency and TPR actions involving two Indian children); *see also In re C.P.*, 181 N.C. App. 698 (2007) and *In re A.R.*, 227 N.C. App. 518 (2013) (both addressing the tribe's right to intervene under ICWA). The right of the Indian child's tribe to intervene in the state court proceeding under ICWA is in addition to the intervention statute in North Carolina's Juvenile Code applying to abuse, neglect, or dependency proceedings. *See* G.S. 7B-401.1(h) (right to intervene; Indian tribe is not included as a party who may intervene).

**(b) Transfer of ICWA case to tribal court.** The parent, the Indian custodian, or the Indian child's tribe may request (orally or in writing) that the state court transfer jurisdiction of a proceeding for foster care placement or termination of parental rights to the tribal court at any stage in the proceeding. 25 U.S.C. 1911(b); 25 C.F.R. 23.115. A transfer request must be granted unless (1) either parent objects (including a non-Indian parent), (2) the tribal court declines jurisdiction, or (3) the state court finds "good cause to the contrary." 25 C.F.R. 23.117.

In making a good cause determination, the state court cannot consider

- whether the proceeding is at an advanced stage if the child's parent, Indian custodian, or tribe did not receive notice of the child custody proceeding until an advanced stage;
- prior proceedings involving the child where a request for transfer was not made;
- whether the transfer could affect the child's placement;
- the child's cultural connection to the tribe or its reservation; or
- the socioeconomic conditions or negative perceptions of tribal or BIA social services or judicial systems.

25 C.F.R. 23.118(c).

**Practice Note:** Family Safety is the EBCI agency that handles child welfare cases for the tribe. Family Safety receives Title IV-E funding and is independent of any North Carolina state agency, including the North Carolina Department of Health and Human Services. If a state court case is transferred to the EBCI tribal court, Family Safety is the agency responsible for proceeding with the tribal court action and working with the family. DSS is no longer involved. The contact information for Family Safety is 117 John Crowe Hill Drive, Cherokee, North Carolina 28719; Telephone: (828) 359-1520.

### E. Emergency Proceedings

ICWA distinguishes an emergency proceeding from a child custody proceeding and establishes different procedures for the two types of proceedings. An emergency proceeding is "any court action that involves an emergency removal or emergency placement of an Indian child." 25 C.F.R. 23.2. In North Carolina, an emergency removal and emergency placement result from a nonsecure custody order. *See* G.S. 7B-502 through -508.

The procedures, findings, and time requirements that apply to emergency proceedings are set forth at 25 C.F.R. 23.113. An emergency removal or emergency placement requires the court to find that the removal or placement "is necessary to prevent imminent physical damage or harm to the child" and must terminate when the removal or placement is no longer necessary to prevent imminent physical harm or damage to the child. 25 C.F.R. 23.113(a), (b)(1). This standard differs from the criteria required for a nonsecure custody order. *See* G.S. 7B-503. Hearings during the emergency proceeding, which in North Carolina are hearings on the need for continued nonsecure custody, must determine whether the removal or placement is no longer necessary to prevent imminent physical damage or harm to the child. 25 C.F.R. 23.113(b); *see* G.S. 7B-506. When the court determines that emergency removal or placement is no longer necessary to prevent imminent physical damage or harm to an Indian child, the emergency proceeding must be terminated, by either transferring the case to tribal court, commencing a child custody proceeding, or returning the child to his or her parents or Indian custodian. 25 C.F.R. 23.113(b)(4), (c). The emergency proceeding should not last longer than thirty days. 25 C.F.R. 23.113(e).

**AOC Forms:** The AOC form orders for nonsecure custody and continued nonsecure custody include sections addressing the finding of imminent physical damage or harm to the Indian child when that finding is required under ICWA.
- AOC-J-150, Order for Nonsecure Custody (Oct. 2019).
- AOC-J-151, Order on Need for Continued Nonsecure Custody (Oct. 2019).

**Practice Note:** In North Carolina, a child custody proceeding is commenced when the petition alleging abuse, neglect, or dependency is filed with the district court. G.S. 7B-405. The ICWA regulations do not address emergency removals and placements that are part of a child custody proceeding when the state court has concurrent jurisdiction to hear the action and do not specify which requirements apply. Unlike child custody proceedings, emergency proceedings allow for immediate court action to protect a child from imminent harm. Emergency proceedings do not require (i) formal notice to the Indian child's tribe, parent, and Indian custodian and the ten-day time period before a hearing may be scheduled (see sections 13.2.F and G, below), (ii) the provision of active efforts to prevent the breakup of the Indian family before a placement may be made (see section 13.2.H, below), (iii) testimony from a qualified expert witness about the child's likelihood of experiencing serious emotional or physical damage from continued custody with a parent or Indian custodian (see section 13.2.I, below), or (iv) the use of placement preferences (see section 13.2.J, below). However, those requirements will apply when the emergency proceeding is terminated and the child custody action proceeds. Section C.3 of the Guidelines, 2016 briefly discusses the termination of the emergency proceeding and the initiation of a child custody proceeding, where the child's actual placement does not change.

## F. Notice to the Tribe, Parent, Indian Custodian, and Bureau of Indian Affairs

In any involuntary foster care placement or termination of parental rights (TPR) proceeding to which ICWA applies, the party seeking the placement or TPR must send notice and a copy of the petition (for each proceeding) by registered or certified mail, return receipt requested, to

- the parents;
- the Indian custodian, if applicable; and
- the Indian child's tribe, the tribes to which the child may be a member, or the tribes that the child may be eligible for membership of if a biological parent is a member.

25 U.S.C. 1912(a); 25 C.F.R. 23.11(a) and 23.111.

The content of the notice is specified in 25 C.F.R. 23.111(d). Copies of the notices must be sent to the appropriate BIA Regional Director by either registered or certified mail, return receipt requested or personal delivery. 25 C.F.R. 23.11(a).

If the identity or location of the parents, Indian custodian, or tribes in which an Indian child is a member or eligible for membership cannot be determined, but there is reason to know the child is an Indian child, notice must be sent to the appropriate BIA Regional Director. That notice should include as much information as is known regarding the child's direct lineal ancestors. The purpose of this notice is to seek assistance from the BIA in identifying and notifying the tribes to contact and in identifying, locating, and notifying the child's parents and Indian custodian (if applicable). 25 U.S.C. 1912(a); 25 C.F.R. 23.11(c), (d) and 23.111(e). Within fifteen days of receiving the ICWA notice, the BIA will make reasonable documented efforts to locate and notify the child's tribe and parents or Indian custodian of the proceeding and send a copy of the notice it provides to the state court. 25 C.F.R. 23.11(c); *see* 25 U.S.C. 1912(a). If the BIA is unable to locate the parents or Indian custodian or verify that the child meets the criteria of an Indian child within the fifteen-day period, the BIA must inform the state court of such and include the additional time it will need. 25 C.F.R. 23.11(c).

An original or copy of each notice together with return receipts or other proof of service is filed with the court. There is no provision for service by publication. However, the regulations recognize notice may be sent by email or personal service. These alternative methods do not replace the requirement that notice be sent by registered or certified mail, return receipt requested. 25 C.F.R. 23.111(c). As a practical matter, although email will not substitute for the formal notice ICWA requires, email or telephone contact may result in a faster response to the issue of whether the child is an "Indian child" and timely assistance in identifying placement options and services.

**Resources:**
To determine the ICWA point of contacts for the BIA Regional Directors and the various federally recognized tribes, see the annual Designated Tribal Agents for Service of Notice in the Federal Register. The most recent version as of this writing is 84 Fed. Reg. 20387-02 (May 9, 2019). If a tribe has not designated a tribal agent for service of an ICWA notice, contact the tribe to be directed to the appropriate office or person. 25 C.F.R. 23.105(b). The BIA maintains a Tribal Leaders Directory with contact information for tribes on its website.

For child custody proceedings in North Carolina, notice is sent to the

Eastern Regional Director
Bureau of Indian Affairs
545 Marriott Drive, Suite 700
Nashville, TN 37214
Telephone: (615) 564-6500; Fax: (615) 564-6701.

In North Carolina, the tribe will often (but not always) be the Eastern Band of Cherokee Indians (EBCI). The EBCI designated tribal agent for receiving the required ICWA notice is

Jenny Bean, Family Safety Supervisor
Eastern Band of Cherokee
P.O. Box 666
Cherokee, NC 28719.
Telephone: (828) 359–6149; Fax: (828) 359–0216; Email: jennbean@nc-cherokee.com.

**Practice Note:** Tribes may have names in common, requiring notice to be provided to more than one tribe if a specific tribe is not identified. For example, if a participant has reason to know the child is Cherokee without additional information regarding a region or tribe, notice should be given to the Eastern Band of Cherokee Indians in North Carolina, the Cherokee Nation in Oklahoma, and the United Keetoowah Band of Cherokee Indians in Oklahoma.

**1. Right to intervene in a state court action.** The parent, Indian custodian, and tribe have the right to intervene in any involuntary foster care placement or termination of parental rights, and the notice must inform them of that right. 25 U.S.C. 1912(a); 25 C.F.R. 23.11(a), 23.111(d)(6)(ii) and (iii). *See In re C.P.*, 181 N.C. App. 698 (2007) and *In re A.R.*, 227 N.C. App. 518 (2013) (both addressing the tribe's right to intervene under ICWA); *see also In re J.H.S.*, 808 S.E.2d 624 (N.C. Ct. App. 2018) (unpublished) (tribe intervened in N.C. neglect and dependency and TPR actions involving two Indian children). The right of the Indian custodian to intervene in the state court proceeding under ICWA is in addition to the to the statutory right to intervene in North Carolina's Juvenile Code. *See* G.S. 7B-401.1(h). Under ICWA, an indigent parent or Indian custodian has the right to court-appointed counsel in any removal, placement, or TPR proceeding. 25 U.S.C. 1912(b); 25 C.F.R. 23.111(d)(6)(iv), (g). An Indian custodian will have the right to court-appointed counsel even though the statutory right to appointed counsel in an abuse, neglect, dependency, or TPR proceeding under North Carolina's Juvenile Code is limited to parents. *See* G.S. 7B-602; 7B-1101.1.

**2. Voluntary and adoption proceedings.** The notice requirements do not explicitly apply to adoption proceedings or voluntary proceedings. But, if there is reason to believe the child is an Indian child, the state court must ensure that the party seeking placement has taken reasonable steps to verify the child's status, which may include contacting the tribe(s) of which the child is believed to be a member or eligible for membership when a biological parent is a member of the tribe. 25 C.F.R. 23.124(b). Because parents, Indian custodians, and the Indian child's tribe have certain rights and protections under ICWA, regardless of whether the proceeding is voluntary, involuntary, or an adoption (e.g., placement preferences), it may be prudent to provide the notice.

## G. Timing of Court Proceedings

An involuntary proceeding for foster care placement or termination of parental rights may not be held until ten days after the required notice is received by the parent or Indian custodian and the tribe or BIA Regional Director. The parent, Indian custodian, and tribe may request additional time to prepare, and the request must be granted for up to twenty additional days, resulting in a total of thirty days from receipt of the notice. 25 U.S.C. 1912(a); 25 C.F.R. 23.112.

## H. "Active Efforts" Required

Before ordering an involuntary foster care placement or a termination of parental rights (TPR), the court must find that "active efforts" have been made to provide remedial services to prevent the breakup of the Indian family and that those efforts proved unsuccessful. 25 U.S.C 1912(d); 25 C.F.R. 23.120. Active efforts are defined at 25 C.F.R. 23.2 and consist of thorough, active, affirmative, and timely efforts that are intended primarily to maintain or reunite an Indian child with his or her family and are provided in a manner consistent with the prevailing social and cultural conditions and way of life of the Indian child's tribe. Active efforts are conducted in partnership with the Indian child, parents, extended family members, Indian custodians, and the tribe. Eleven specific examples of active efforts are included in the definition; one example is that DSS not only identify appropriate services for the parent but actively assist the parent in obtaining the services. 25 C.F.R. 23.2. Active efforts must be documented in detail in the court record. 25 C.F.R. 23.120(b).

Active efforts are different from reasonable efforts, which are required by the federal Adoptions and Safe Families Act (ASFA) and are included in North Carolina's Juvenile Code. See Chapters 1.3.B.6 (discussing ASFA, reasonable efforts, and the Juvenile Code) and 7.9 (discussing reasonable efforts). The North Carolina Court of Appeals addressed whether a court, in a case where ICWA applies, may order the cessation of reasonable efforts before the final stage of a case. *In re E.G.M.,* 230 N.C. App. 196 (2013). The court of appeals looked to the standards regarding reasonable efforts and the cessation of those efforts and held that the order ceasing reasonable efforts as authorized by the Juvenile Code (and ASFA) does not conflict with the minimum federal standards established by ICWA regarding active efforts. ICWA does not prohibit a trial court from ordering the cessation of reasonable efforts in an abuse, neglect, or dependency action, before a TPR proceeding is commenced if the court finds that "[s]uch efforts clearly would be futile" or are "clearly inconsistent with the juvenile's health, safety, and need for a safe, permanent home within a reasonable period of time." *In re E.G.M.,* 230 N.C. App. at 210 (citing G.S. 7B-507(b)(1) (note the statutory language regarding the required findings was amended by S.L. 2015-136 as of October 1, 2015, when G.S. 7B-507(b) was replaced with G.S. 7B-901(c) and 7B-906.2(b))). In examining court opinions from other states, the court of appeals stated there was a consensus that "although the state must make 'active efforts' under the ICWA, it need not 'persist with futile efforts.' " *In re E.G.M.,* 230 N.C. App. at 210 (citations omitted). In addressing the required ICWA finding, both before ordering a foster care placement and before terminating parental rights, that "active efforts" to prevent the disruption of the Indian family "proved unsuccessful," the court of appeals stated if those efforts were ceased at the time of the foster care placement, the trial court may cite the pre-foster-care active efforts when making the necessary findings at the TPR proceeding. *In re E.G.M.,* 230 N.C. App. 196.

## I. Finding of Serious Emotional or Physical Damage

No Indian child may be placed in foster care or be the subject of an order terminating parental rights (TPR) unless the court determines that continued custody by the parent or Indian custodian is likely to result in serious emotional or physical damage to the child. For foster care placements, the determination must be supported by clear and convincing evidence; for TPR, the evidence supporting the determination must be beyond a reasonable doubt. The evidence must include testimony from one or more "qualified expert witnesses" (QEW). 25 U.S.C. 1912(e), (f); 25 C.F.R. 23.121(a), (b); *see In re J.H.S.*, 808 S.E.2d 624 (N.C. Ct. App. 2018) (unpublished) (affirming TPR; holding expert's opinion along with the evidence presented at the TPR hearing supported trial court's determination under ICWA standards; discussing qualification of expert and expert's opinion testimony; noting respondent's failure to timely object to the expert's testimony at the hearing). The qualified expert testimony on which the court's finding is made must be part of the hearing that results in the foster care placement and cannot be based on testimony heard at an earlier hearing. *In re E.G.M.*, 230 N.C. App. 196 (2013) (holding that the requirement of qualified expert testimony was not met when the expert testimony was given at the disposition hearing and not at the permanency planning hearing that resulted in the order placing the child in DSS custody).

To satisfy the requirements of ICWA, the evidence must show a causal relationship between the particular conditions in the home and the likelihood that continued custody with a parent or Indian custodian will result in serious emotional or physical damage to the child. 25 C.F.R. 23.121(c). Evidence only showing family or community poverty, single parenthood, inadequate housing, substance abuse, nonconforming social behavior, isolation, or custodian's age without a causal relationship to the child's likelihood of suffering serious emotional or physical damage will not be sufficient under the applicable evidentiary standards. 25 C.F.R. 23.121(d).

The ICWA statute does not define qualified expert, but the regulations state that the person should be qualified to testify to the prevailing social and cultural standards of the Indian child's tribe. This person may be designated by the tribe as being so qualified. 25 C.F.R. 23.122(a). The social worker who is regularly assigned to the Indian child may not be the qualified expert in a proceeding related to that child. 25 C.F.R. 23.122(c). Any party, or the court, may request that the tribe or the appropriate BIA regional office assist in locating a qualified expert. 25 C.F.R. 23.122(b). The Guidelines, 2016 point out that the federal regulation does not limit qualified experts to only those persons with particular knowledge of the Indian child's tribe and gives an example of an expert on the sexual abuse of children as being qualified to testify to whether the child's return to a parent who has a history of sexually abusing the child is likely to result in serious emotional or physical damage to the child. Note that the North Carolina Court of Appeals addressed the qualifications of an expert in *In re E.G.M.*, 230 N.C. App. 196, but the Guidelines, 1979 that were relied upon were replaced with the federal regulations and Guidelines, 2016.

In addressing the requirement that serious emotional or physical damage to the child must be proved beyond a reasonable doubt in a TPR proceeding, the North Carolina Court of Appeals held that that burden of proof is not required to prove the ground to TPR. ICWA creates a dual burden of proof, where the ICWA requirement must be satisfied separately from the requirements in the Juvenile Code, which establishes the standard of clear and convincing evidence to prove an alleged ground. *In re Bluebird*, 105 N.C. App. 42 (1992); *see* G.S. 7B-1109(f); 7B-1111(b).

## J. Placement Preferences

An Indian child placed in foster care or a preadoptive placement must be in the least restrictive setting that approximates a family and considers sibling attachment; is within reasonable proximity to the child's home, extended family, or siblings; and allows the child's special needs (if any) to be met. Listed in order of priority, preference must be given, in the absence of good cause to the contrary, to

- a member of the child's extended family;
- a foster home licensed, approved, or specified by the child's tribe;
- an Indian foster home approved by a non-Indian authority; or
- an institution for children approved by a tribe or operated by an Indian organization that has a program that is suitable to meet the child's needs.

25 U.S.C. 1915(b); 25 C.F.R. 23.131; *see* 25 U.S.C. 1903(2) (definition of "extended family member"); 25 C.F.R. 23.2 (definition of "Indian foster home") and 23.124(c) (application of placement preferences to voluntary proceedings).

For an adoptive placement, ICWA requires that absent good cause to the contrary, the placement preference for an Indian child is made in the following order:

- a member of the child's extended family,
- other members of the child's tribe, or
- another Indian family.

25 U.S.C. 1915(a); 25 C.F.R. 23.130(a); *see* 25 C.F.R 23.124(c) (application of placement preferences to voluntary proceedings).

A tribe may designate by resolution a different placement preference order. When an Indian child's tribe has a different placement preference order, the agency or state court making the placement must follow the tribe's placement preferences so long as the placement is the least restrictive setting appropriate to the child's needs. 25 U.S.C. 1915(c); 25 C.F.R. 23.130(b).

The court may also consider the placement preference of the Indian child or parent, but their preferences are not determinative. 25 U.S.C. 1915(c); 25 C.F.R. 23.130(b), (c); *see* 25 C.F.R. 23.132(c)(1) and (2) (good cause to deviate from placement preference based on request of parent or child).

The placement preferences must be applied at the initial and any subsequent change to a foster care, preadoptive, or adoptive placement absent a determination by clear and convincing evidence made on the record that good cause exists not to apply the preferences. 25 C.F.R. 23.129(c); *see* 25 U.S.C. 1916(b); 25 C.F.R. 23.132. Note that the Juvenile Code prioritizes placement with the child's relative, which aligns with ICWA's first preferred placement priority – an extended family member. *See* G.S. 7B-506(h)(2); 7B-903(a1); 25 U.S.C., 1903(2) (definition of "extended family member"). Note also that "relative" is not defined in the Juvenile Code. At nonsecure custody and every dispositional stage, when the court does not place the child with a parent and there is a relative who is willing and able to provide proper care and supervision to the child in a safe home, the court may only place the child outside of that relative's home if it makes findings that the placement with the relative is contrary to the child's best interests. G.S. 7B-506(h)(2); 7B-903(a1). This finding is required even when ICWA applies. *In re E.R.*, 248 N.C. App. 345 (2016) (reversing and remanding the guardianship order placing the Indian children with their sibling in a non-relative's home without making the required findings under the Juvenile Code about placement with the children's paternal grandmother). See Chapter 7.4.C.1 (discussing relative placement).

Good cause to deviate from the ICWA placement preferences is addressed in 25 C.F.R. 23.132. Placement in a non-Indian foster home or preadoptive home that is licensed by a non-Indian licensed authority is not included in the placement preferences and requires a determination that good cause to deviate from the preferences exists. The office of the clerk of superior court, the district court, and the superior court are all courts of competent jurisdiction to determine whether there is good cause to deviate from a placement preference. G.S. 48-3-605(g)(ii). The requirements in the 2016 federal regulations regarding the application of placement preferences differ from the holding in *Adoptive Couple v. Baby Girl*, 570 U.S. 637 (2013) that the preferences for an adoptive placement are not applicable if an alternative adoptive party has not formally sought to adopt the child.

### K. Consent to Foster Care Placement, TPR, and Adoption including Relinquishment

ICWA sets forth specific procedures for when a parent or Indian custodian voluntarily consent to a foster care placement, a termination of parental rights (TPR), or the child's adoption (which includes both a consent to and relinquishment of a child for an adoption under North Carolina law). The consent must be in writing and recorded before a court of competent jurisdiction. In North Carolina, a court of competent jurisdiction for a judicial proceeding to accept a voluntary consent to or relinquishment for an adoption includes the office of the clerk of superior court, the district court, and the superior court. G.S. 48-3-605(g); *see* G.S. 48-3-702(b). The court must (1) explain to the parent or Indian custodian the terms and consequences of the consent and the limitations on the withdrawal of the consent and (2) certify that the terms and consequences were fully explained and understood by the parent or Indian custodian. 25 U.S.C. 1913(a); 25 C.F.R. 23.125(a)–(c). The contents of a consent to a foster care placement are addressed in 25 C.F.R. 23.126, and the consent to the voluntary foster care placement may be withdrawn at any time, for any reason, resulting in the return of the child to the parent or Indian custodian. 25 C.F.R. 23.125(b)(2)(i) and 23.127(a). A voluntary consent to a TPR or an adoption may be withdrawn for any reason at any time before the entry of the applicable final decree (TPR or adoption), and the child is returned to the parent or Indian custodian when the consent or relinquishment to adoption is withdrawn. 25 C.F.R. 23.125(b)(2)(ii)–(iii) and 23.128(a), (b).

There are several important differences between adoption procedures under ICWA and North Carolina law. When ICWA applies, its provisions supersede the procedures under state law. G.S. 48-1-108; *see* G.S. 48-3-605(f) (consent must meet the requirements of ICWA); 48-3-702(b) (relinquishment must meet requirements of ICWA). Some of the differences between the adoption laws and procedures under ICWA and the North Carolina statutes include the following:

- Under ICWA, adoption consents may not be given until ten days after the child's birth; any consent given before then is invalid. 25 U.S.C. 1913(a); 25 C.F.R. 23.125(e). In contrast, North Carolina law allows the father to consent pre-birth and the mother to consent immediately after birth. G.S. 48-3-604.

- Under ICWA, adoption consents may be revoked at any time for any reason before the final decree of adoption. 25 U.S.C. 1913(c); 25 C.F.R. 23.125(b)(2)(iii) and 23.128(b). In contrast, North Carolina law provides for a seven-day revocation period of a consent or relinquishment. G.S. 48-3-608(a) (consent); 48-3-706(a) (relinquishment); *see In re Ivey*, 810 S.E.2d 740 (N.C. Ct. App. 2018) (holding seven-day period for revocation starts to run when the parent who signed the consent receives an original or copy of the consent he or she executed). After the seven-day time period to revoke a consent or relinquishment under North Carolina law has expired, a revocation may be made under ICWA by filing a written document with or testifying before the court. 25 C.F.R. 23.128(c). The court must promptly notify the person or agency who arranged for the voluntary preadoptive or adoptive placement of the parent's withdrawal of consent, and the child must be returned to the parent or Indian custodian as soon as practicable. 25 C.F.R. 23.128(d).

- The adoption of an Indian child resulting from a consent or relinquishment that was obtained through fraud or duress can be challenged for up to two years after a final adoption decree is entered by filing a petition in state court to vacate the decree. The court must give notice to the parties in the adoption proceeding and the Indian child's tribe and hold a hearing. If the court finds the consent or relinquishment was obtained through fraud or duress, the adoption must be vacated and the child returned to the parent. 25 U.S.C. 1913(d); 25 C.F.R. 23.136. North Carolina law limits the right to void a consent or relinquishment for fraud or duress to the period before entry of the adoption decree. G.S. 48-3-609(a)(1); 48-3-707(a)(1).

- After an adoption of an Indian child, the court must notify the biological parent or prior Indian custodian and the Indian child's tribe when the adoption decree has been vacated or set aside or the adoptive parent has voluntary terminated his or her parental rights. The notice must be sent by certified or registered mail, return receipt requested. When the biological parent or prior Indian custodian receives the notice, he or she may petition the court in a proceeding under 25 U.S.C. 1912 for the return of custody of the Indian child, which must be granted absent a showing that it is not in the child's best interests. 25 U.S.C. 1916(a). A biological parent or Indian custodian may execute a revocable written waiver to his or her right to receive such notice and file it with the court. 25 C.F.R. 23.139(c). This issue is not addressed in North Carolina law.

- Within thirty days of a state court entering a final decree of adoption, it must provide a copy of the decree along with other required information designated in 25 C.F.R. 23.140(a), marked "Confidential," to the Bureau of Indian Affairs, Chief, Division of Human Services, 1849 C Street NW, Mail Stop 3645 MIB, Washington, DC 20240. This issue is not addressed in North Carolina law.

- Upon the application of an Indian adoptee who has reached age 18, the court entering the final decree must inform the adoptee of the tribal affiliation of his or her biological parents and provide any other information necessary to protect any rights resulting from tribal membership. 25 U.S.C. 1917; 25 C.F.R. 23.138. This issue is not addressed in North Carolina law.

### L. Impact of ICWA Violation

Violations of certain (not all) ICWA provisions may result in the action being invalidated; specifically, violations of 25 U.S.C. 1911 (jurisdiction, transfer, intervention), 1912 (notice, time for proceeding, appointment of counsel, active efforts, findings about serious damage to the child), and 1913 (consents, withdrawal of consent, voluntary TPR). A petition to invalidate a proceeding for foster care placement or a termination of parental rights may be brought in any court of competent jurisdiction by

- the Indian child who is or was the subject of the suit,
- a parent or Indian custodian from whose custody the child was removed, or
- the Indian child's tribe.

25 U.S.C. 1914; 25 C.F.R. 23.137(a). *See In re A.R.*, 227 N.C. App. 518 (2013) (recognizing tribe's right to seek invalidation of court's action).

The petitioner alleging a violation of a provision of 25 U.S.C. 1911, 1912, or 1913 is not required to show that their rights were violated. 25 C.F.R. 23.137(c). ICWA does not establish a time period in which a petition to invalidate an action must be filed. If a petition to vacate is based on a jurisdictional challenge, in unrelated cases, the North Carolina appellate courts have held that subject matter jurisdiction can be raised at any time. *See, e.g., In re T.R.P.*, 360 N.C. 588 (2006). If the petitioner shows that a provision of 25 U.S.C. 1911, 1912, or 1913 was violated, the court must determine if it is appropriate to invalidate the action. 25 C.F.R. 23.137(b).

---

**Resources:**
The U.S. Department of the Interior Bureau of Indian Affairs (BIA) website includes a section on ICWA that includes many resources, some of which are
- Guidelines for Implementing the Indian Child Welfare Act (Dec. 2016).
- Five different ICWA Quick Reference Guides: Voluntary Proceedings, Tribes, State Agencies, State Courts, and Active Efforts.
- Sample Consent and Withdrawal of Consent forms.
- Sample Notice (of child custody proceeding for Indian child) form.
- The ICWA regulations (Final Rule) and FAQ.
- Designated Tribal Agents for Service of Notice.

DIV. OF SOC. SERVS., N.C. DEP'T OF HEALTH & HUMAN SERVICES, CHILD WELFARE MANUAL "Cross Function", available here. The manual contains a link to DSS-5291, Indian Child

Welfare Act Compliance Checklist, but this checklist was last updated in April 2008 and will not reflect changes in the law (including the 2016 regulations) since then.

ICWA Quick Reference Guide: Involuntary Proceedings (Dec. 2016) on the American Bar Association website.

NATIONAL COUNCIL OF JUVENILE AND FAMILY COURT JUDGES, INDIAN CHILD WELFARE ACT JUDICIAL BENCHBOOK (Reno, NV 2017).

The National Indian Child Welfare Association website includes a section "About ICWA" and resources "For Families & Service Providers" on its website.

**Note**, as of the date of this Manual, some of the information provided by the various sources listed below have not been updated to reflect the December 2016 federal regulations and BIA Guidelines, 2016.
- The Native American Rights Fund includes information on ICWA on its website.
- The National Indian Law Library has a "Research Guides" section that includes information on Indian Child Welfare on its website.
- The "Indian Child Welfare Act" section of the National Child Welfare Resource Center for Tribes website.
- The National Council of Juvenile & Family Court Judges website includes information on ICWA.

## 13.3 Multiethnic Placement Act

The Howard M. Metzenbaum Multiethnic Placement Act (MEPA), Pub. L. No. 103-382, sec. 551–554, 108 Stat. 4056, was enacted in 1994 and was amended by the Removal of Barriers to Interethnic Adoption provisions (IEP), Pub. L. No. 104-188, sec. 1808, 110 Stat. 1755, 1903, in the Small Business Job Protection Act of 1996 (collectively referred to here as "MEPA-IEP").

MEPA-IEP is an anti-discrimination law that focuses on race, color, and national origin. It conditions federal funding, specifically Titles IV-B and IV-E funding, on compliance with its provisions. MEPA-IEP is designed to

- prevent discrimination in the placement of children in foster care or for adoption on the basis of race, color, or national origin;
- decrease the length of time that children wait to be adopted; and
- facilitate the identification and recruitment of a diverse pool of foster and adoptive parents.

Two provisions in the North Carolina Juvenile Code specifically require compliance with MEPA-IEP when making an out-of-home placement of a child in an abuse, neglect, or dependency proceeding. *See* G.S. 7B-505(d); 7B-506(h)(2).

Under MEPA-IEP, states and other entities involved in foster care or adoption placements that receive federal financial assistance are prohibited from

- delaying or denying a child's foster care or adoptive placement on the basis of the child's or the prospective parent's race, color, or national origin or
- denying to any individual the opportunity to become a foster or adoptive parent on the basis of the prospective parent's or the child's race, color, or national origin.

42 U.S.C. 671(a)(18); *see* 42 U.S.C. 674(d)(2); 42 U.S.C. 1996b.

Race and ethnicity are not factors to be considered by agencies or the court when making placement decisions. However, federal policy recognizes that placements of children are based on protecting the child's best interests. A child's best interests may allow for an individualized determination of facts and circumstances to address the child's individualized needs where special circumstances may indicate the consideration of race or ethnicity is required in a specific case. Any such rationale is subject to strict scrutiny. Generalizations about the needs of children of a particular race or ethnicity, or about the abilities of prospective parents of one race or ethnicity to care for a child of another race or ethnicity, may not be used in making placement decisions. *See* CHILDREN'S BUREAU, U.S. DEP'T OF HEALTH & HUMAN SERVICES, Information Memorandum ACYF-CB-IM-98-03 (May 8, 1998).

MEPA-IEP does not affect the requirements of the Indian Child Welfare Act (ICWA) in child custody and emergency proceedings that involve an "Indian child" (as defined by ICWA). 42 U.S.C. 674(d)(4); 42 U.S.C. 1996b(3); *see* 25 U.S.C. 1901 *et seq.* (ICWA). ICWA includes placement preferences designated by the Indian child's tribe or by the ICWA statute and regulations, discussed in section 13.2.J, above. However, ICWA only applies to an "Indian child" of a federally recognized Indian tribe and does not apply to children of state only recognized tribes. The placement of a child who is a member of a state only recognized Indian tribe is subject to MEPA-IEP. See section 13.2, above (discussing ICWA).

MEPA-IEP also requires states to diligently recruit foster and adoptive parents who reflect the racial and ethnic diversity of the children in the state who need foster and adoptive homes. 42 U.S.C. 622(b)(7). A state's compliance with this provision is part of the federal Child and Family Service Review (CFSR). See Chapter 1.2.D.1 (discussing the CFSR). The North Carolina Department of Health and Human Services (NC DHHS) Division of Social Services policy addresses recruitment plans pursuant to MEPA-IEP (see Resources, below).

Compliance with MEPA-IEP is a civil rights issue, and noncompliance is deemed a violation of Title VI of the Civil Rights Act. 42 U.S.C. 1996b. Any individual child, parent, relative, or (prospective) foster or adoptive parent who has been aggrieved by a violation of MEPA-IEP can bring a civil rights action. For more information about Title VI, see section 13.4, below, and specifically 13.4.E for complaints. Additional sanctions for noncompliance include corrective action, a reduction in federal funding, and the repayment of federal funds. 42 U.S.C. 674(d)(1) and (2). The U.S. Department of Health and Human Services Office for Civil Rights may investigate a possible violation and take corrective action and impose penalties as provided for in 45 C.F.R. 1355.38. An aggrieved individual also has a right to sue in state or federal court within two years of an alleged MEPA-IEP violation. 42 U.S.C. 674(d)(3).

> **Resources:**
> The NC DHHS Division of Social Services child welfare policies address
> - MEPA-IEP at DIV. OF SOC. SERVS., N.C. DEP'T OF HEALTH & HUMAN SERVICES, CHILD WELFARE MANUAL "Cross Function" (which is cross referenced in "Permanency Planning") and "Adoptions," available here.
> - The impact of cultural diversity at DIV. OF SOC. SERVS., N.C. DEP'T OF HEALTH & HUMAN SERVICES, CHILD WELFARE MANUAL "Cross Function" and "Permanency Planning," available here.
>
> See NC DHHS Division of Social Services Dear County Director Letter, CWS-10-2017: North Carolina's New Diligent Recruitment and Retention Plan (June 15, 2017), with four attachments, found on the NC DHHS website under "DSS 'Dear County Director' Archive."
>
> For federal policy in a Q&A format related to recruitment, enforcement, compliance, and guidance on MEPA-IEP, see the CHILD WELFARE POLICY MANUAL under the "Laws and Policies" section of the Children's Bureau, U.S. Department of Health and Human Services website, specifically "4. MEPA/IEAP".
>
> For guidance on the application of MEPA (1994) to child welfare services, see the "Protection from Discrimination in Child Welfare Activities" section of the U.S. Department of Health and Human Services website.
>
> For a comprehensive guide to MEPA, as well as common questions and checklists for implementation, see JOAN HEIFETZ HOLLINGER & THE ABA CENTER ON CHILDREN AND THE LAW, NATIONAL RESOURCE CENTER ON LEGAL AND COURT ISSUES, A GUIDE TO THE MULTIETHNIC PLACEMENT ACT OF 1994 AS AMENDED BY THE INTERETHNIC ADOPTION PROVISIONS OF 1996 (1998), available on the American Bar Association website.
>
> For additional guidance, see the training powerpoint, Ensuring the Best Interests of Children Through Compliance with the Multiethnic Placement Act of 1994, as amended, and Title VI of the Civil Rights Act of 1964, by the U.S. Department of Health and Human Services, Administration for Children and Families and the Office for Civil Rights.

## 13.4 Title VI of the Civil Rights Act

### A. Introduction

Section 601 of Title VI of the Civil Rights Act of 1964 (Title VI), Pub. L. No. 88-352, 78 Stat. 252, prohibits discrimination on the basis of race, color, or national origin by any program or activity that receives federal financial assistance. 42 U.S.C. 2000d *et seq.* Federal regulations implementing the provisions of Title VI are found at 28 C.F.R. 42.101 *et seq.* and 28 C.F.R. 50.3. Additional federal regulations applying Title VI nondiscrimination requirements for programs receiving federal financial assistance through the U.S. Department of Health and Human Services (U.S. DHHS) (e.g., Titles IV-B and IV-E funding) are found at 45 C.F.R. Part 80.

This section provides a general overview of Title VI and its application to child welfare programs and services in North Carolina. There is a focus on national origin discrimination as related to language access for those individuals with no or limited English proficiency (LEP) who are involved in an abuse, neglect, dependency, or termination of parental rights case. Section 13.3, above, discusses the Multiethnic Placement Act as amended (MEPA-IEP), which prohibits discrimination in the placement of children in foster care and adoptive homes and in the opportunity for an individual to become a foster or adoptive parent because of the race, color, or national origin of the child or the prospective parent. Violations of MEPA are Title VI violations.

**Resources:**
For guidance on the application of Title VI to child welfare services, see
- Title VI Child Welfare Joint Guidance Letter (Oct. 2016) by the U.S. Department of Justice and the U.S. Department of Health and Human Services, Administration for Children and Families and Office for Civil Rights, available on the U.S. Department of Health and Human Services website.
- The "Protection from Discrimination in Child Welfare Activities" section of the U.S. Department of Health and Human Services website.

For more general information about Title VI, see CIVIL RIGHTS DIVISION, U.S. DEPARTMENT OF JUSTICE, TITLE VI LEGAL MANUAL, available on the U.S. Department of Justice website.

## B. Applicability

Title VI applies to any public or private agencies that receive any federal financial assistance. Federal financial assistance may be received directly or indirectly through a grant, contract, or subcontract but is not limited to monetary disbursements such as grants or loans. Federal financial assistance includes grants, donations, or permission to use federal property or an interest in the property (this may include equipment) without any or with nominal or reduced consideration; a federal contract for the provision of assistance; or the detail of federal personnel. 28 C.F.R. 42.102(c); 45 C.F.R. 80.2, 80.4(a)(2), and 80.13(f); *see* 28 C.F.R. Part 42, Subpart C, Appendix A (list of financial assistance provided by the U.S. Department of Justice); 45 C.F.R. Part 80, Appendix A (list of financial assistance provided by U.S. DHHS). As a condition to approval, every application for federal financial assistance must contain an assurance that the applying program will comply with Title VI requirements. 28 C.F.R. 42.105; 45 C.F.R. 80.4(a).

As applied to child welfare, recipients of federal financial assistance include the North Carolina Department of Health and Human Services, county departments of social services, child-placing agencies, the court system, and programs within the North Carolina Administrative Office of the Courts such as the N.C. Guardian ad Litem Program and Indigent Defense Services. Examples of less obvious recipients of federal financial assistance that provide services to families involved in the child welfare system include medical, mental health, and substance abuse treatment providers and a local management entity/managed care organization (LME/MCO) (e.g., receipt of Medicaid funding); the school system (e.g., Title I funding); domestic violence programs; shelters and public housing programs; parent education programs; and visitation centers.

Title VI states "no person" shall be discriminated against because of race, color, or national origin. 42 U.S.C. 2000d. This universal language provides protection to the various participants in a child welfare case, including the child, parents, guardians, custodians, caretakers, relatives, placement providers (including foster parents and kinship and nonrelative kinship placements), prospective adoptive parents, the child's guardian ad litem (GAL), DSS employees, etc. Title VI applies to both U.S. citizens and non-citizens. CIVIL RIGHTS DIVISION, U.S. DEPARTMENT OF JUSTICE, , Section V.A. Therefore, unless a specific program conditions eligibility requirements on U.S. citizenship or a specific immigration status (e.g., Medicaid), Title VI protections apply to a non-citizen who is accessing programs or benefits, including child protective and child welfare services, and prohibit discrimination on the basis of race, color, or national origin.

Covered services and activities may include protective services: screening of reports, assessments, casework, and counseling services. *See* G.S. 7B-300. Covered services also include court-related activities, such as mediation and hearings, and actions resulting from a court order, such as the child's removal and placement, visitation, conditions imposed on a party, and a party's participation in treatment, parent education, or similar programs. Title VI protections apply to an individual who is participating in services required by DSS or court order when those contracted service providers receive any federal financial assistance. The prohibition against discrimination on the basis of race, color, or national origin extends to services purchased or otherwise obtained by the grantee (for example, DSS contracting with a community service provider). 45 C.F.R. 80.5(a).

### C. Prohibited Discrimination

Title VI prohibits discrimination on the basis of race, color, or national origin. The federal regulations list examples of specific discriminatory actions that are prohibited, which include

- denying a service or participation in a program,
- providing a different service or a service in a different manner from that provided to others,
- subjecting an individual to separate (or segregated) treatment,
- restricting an individual in any way from enjoying a service that others enjoy, or
- treating an individual differently when determining what criteria or conditions must be satisfied to be provided a service.

28 C.F.R. 42.104; 45 C.F.R. 80.3(b); *see* 45 C.F.R. 80.5(a).

There are three types of discrimination:

- intentional discrimination resulting in disparate treatment,
- disparate impact (or effect) resulting from executing facially neutral actions or policies (*see Lau v. Nichols*, 414 U.S. 563 (1974)), and
- retaliatory actions or discrimination directed against an individual for the purpose of interfering with a Title VI right or because the person complained or participated in any manner in an investigation or proceeding involving an alleged Title VI violation (*see* 45 C.F.R. 80.7(e)).

**Resource:** For a discussion of the three types of discrimination, see Section VI (Proving Discrimination - Intentional Discrimination), Section VII (Proving Discrimination – Disparate Impact), and Section VIII (Proving Discrimination – Retaliation) of the Title VI Legal Manual by the Civil Rights Division of the U.S. Department of Justice.

### D. Requirements

**1. Compliance.** The U.S. DHHS must provide assistance and guidance to recipients of its federal financial assistance to help those recipients voluntarily comply with Title VI requirements. 45 C.F.R. 80.6(a). The recipient must also keep and submit compliance reports to the U.S. DHHS and allow U.S. DHHS officials or designees to access information that may be necessary to determine whether the recipient is complying with Title VI. Confidentiality does not bar access, and redisclosure is not authorized unless it is necessary in a formal enforcement proceeding or otherwise authorized by law. 45 C.F.R. 80.6(b), (c); *see* 45 C.F.R. 80.7 (compliance investigations). Similar compliance and access to information provisions apply to federal financial assistance provided by responsible departments other than the U.S. DHHS. *See* 28 C.F.R. 42.106. *See also* 28 C.F.R. 50.3 ("Guidelines for the enforcement of Title VI, Civil Rights Act of 1964"). See section 13.4.E, below (discussing the North Carolina Department of Health and Human Services Voluntary Compliance Agreement entered into with the U.S. DHHS after a compliance review and the North Carolina Administrative Office of the Courts letter of finding of a violation).

**NC DHHS DSS Forms:**
- DSS-1464, Statement of Assurance of Compliance with Title VI of the Civil Rights Act of 1964 For Agencies, Institutions, Organizations or Facilities (March 2006).
- DSS-1464a, Statement of Assurance of Compliance with Title VI of the Civil Rights Act of 1964 For Other Agencies, Institutions, Organizations or Facilities (July 2014).

**2. Outreach.** Recipients must make available to participants, beneficiaries, and other interested persons information about anti-discrimination provisions and their applicability to the programs the recipient provides in a manner that will notify the persons of the Title VI protections. 28 C.F.R. 42.106(d); 45 C.F.R. 80.6(d).

**3. Language access.** Discrimination on the basis of national origin may occur when a person or group is denied a meaningful opportunity to participate in the program or service because of language access issues. *See Lau v. Nichols*, 414 U.S. 563 (1974) (holding minority group of 1,800 students of Chinese ancestry who speak, read, write, and understand Chinese and not English were denied a meaningful opportunity to obtain education generally obtained by the majority of English-speaking students in the school system where English language instruction was not provided; further holding minority group of students were discriminated against under Title VI on basis of national origin; requiring school district to take affirmative steps to rectify language deficiency). Recipients of federal financial assistance must provide meaningful access to persons with limited English proficiency (LEP) who apply for and/or receive benefits and services from the recipient, and the federal agency must give those recipients guidance on how to do that. *See* Executive Order 13166 (65 Fed. Reg. 50121). See also Resources, below.

Federal guidance by both the U.S. Department of Justice (U.S. DOJ) and U.S. DHHS specifies a four-factor test for recipients of federal financial assistance to use when determining what steps to take to provide LEP individuals with meaningful access to programs and activities. The four factors are

- the number or proportion of LEP persons from a particular language group eligible to be served or encountered by the program,
- the frequency with which the LEP persons come (or may come) into contact with the program,
- the nature and importance of the program, activity, or service provided by the program to the people's lives, and
- the resources available to the grantee/recipient and costs.

The four-factor analysis may result in different language assistance measures being provided for different types of programs or activities. Regarding the third prong and the importance of the program to the people's lives, child welfare services involve government intervention in a family's life that impacts constitutional rights of parents and children and may ultimately result in a termination of parental rights, which legally severs the parent-child relationship. See Chapter 2.4.A (discussing parent's constitutional rights) and 2.3.C (discussing the rights of the child).

There are two main language assistance measures: oral interpretation and written translation (of all, part, or a summary of a document, with distinctions identified for "vital documents"). The type and level of language assistance measures depend on what is determined to be necessary and reasonable under the four-factor analysis. Regardless of the level or type of language assistance provided, it is critical that it be of high quality, accurate, and timely. Once a determination of appropriate language assistance measures is made, the agency should provide notice to persons with limited English proficiency (LEP), in a language those persons will understand, of the availability of the language assistance measures that are at no cost to the individual. Examples of notices include signs and posters, outreach documents, a telephone voice mail menu, outreach to community-based organizations and stakeholders (including schools and churches), and notices in non-English newspapers and on non-English radio and television programs. Specific examples for courts are included in Appendix A, section C.1 of the U.S. DOJ Guidance, referenced in Resources, below.

**Practice Notes:** Regarding language access, it is important to ask the individual what is his or her primary language rather than assume the language he or she speaks based upon a country of origin. For example, Guatemala has over twenty official languages, one of which is Spanish but other common Mayan languages include K'iche, Q'eqchi, Kaqchikel, Mam, and Ixil. See "GUATEMALA: New Law Recognises Indigenous Languages" (IPS, May 3, 2003) on the Inter Press Service News Agency website.

A parent attorney, child's guardian ad litem, or other respondent in the court proceeding may need to file a motion to translate documents and/or provide an interpreter. Additionally, if a respondent or the child believes DSS is not providing accurate and/or timely language access services, he or she may raise the issue with the court and seek a provision in an order that specifies the language access service to be provided as a necessary measure or possibly as part of DSS's provision of reasonable efforts.

**AOC Form:**
AOC-G-107, Motion and Appointment Authorizing Foreign Language Interpreter/Translator (March 2007).

**NC DHHS DSS Forms:**
- DSS-1463, Title VI, Federal Civil Rights Act of 1964 (Explanation) (Nov. 1982).
- DSS-10001, Language Access Services Agreement (For Limited English Proficiency (LEP) Customer And Sensory Impaired Customer) (June 2005) with Instructions (Dec. 2014).

**Resources:**
For federal guidance, including a discussion on requirements related to interpreters and document translation, see
- Guidance to Federal Financial Assistance Recipients Regarding Title VI Prohibition Against National Origin Discrimination Affecting Limited English Proficient Persons, 68 Fed. Reg. 47311 (Aug. 8, 2003), by the U.S. Department of Health and Human Services and available on its website.
- Guidance to Federal Financial Assistance Recipients Regarding Title VI Prohibition on National Origin Discrimination Affecting Limited English Proficient Persons, 67 Fed. Reg. 41457 (June 18, 2002), by the U.S. Department of Justice and available on its website.
- Title VI Child Welfare Joint Guidance Letter (Oct. 2016) by the U.S. Department of Justice and the U.S. Department of Health and Human Services, Administration for Children and Families and Office for Civil Rights, available on the U.S. Department of Health and Human Services website.

For information about language access services in state courts, see
- U.S. DEPARTMENT OF JUSTICE, CIVIL RIGHTS DIVISION, FEDERAL COORDINATION COMPLIANCE SECTION, LANGUAGE ACCESS IN STATE COURTS (Sept. 2016).
- The "Language Access: Resource Guide" section on the National Center for State Courts website.
- The "Office of Language Access Services" on the North Carolina Administrative Office

of the Courts website.

For information and resources addressing language access issues, including demographic information by state, frequently asked questions, complaint information, training materials, language access cards, recipients of federal financial assistance, and more, see LEP.gov, a federal interagency website.

### E. Violations

**1. Complaint.** Any person who believes he or she was discriminated against on the basis of race, color, or national origin by a recipient of federal financial assistance from the U.S. DHHS may file a written complaint with the U.S. DHHS. The person must file the complaint within 180 days from the date of the alleged discrimination, unless the U.S. DHHS extends the time for filing. 45 C.F.R. 80.7(b). The same provisions apply to alleged discrimination by recipients receiving federal financial assistance from other federal departments, where the complaint would be filed with the responsible department. *See* 28 C.F.R. 42.107(b). The complainant's identity is confidential except to the extent necessary to carry out the investigation and any resulting hearing or judicial proceeding. 45 C.F.R. 80.7(e); 28 C.F.R. 42.107(e).

The responsible department investigates the complaint, and the investigation should include a review of the practices and policies, the circumstances of the alleged noncompliance, and other relevant factors. 45 C.F.R. 80.7(c); 28 C.F.R. 42.107(c). The possible outcomes of an investigation are (1) the recipient complied with Title VI (meaning there was no discrimination) and the responsible department informs the recipient and complainant in writing or (2) the recipient failed to comply with Title VI (meaning there was discrimination) and the responsible department informs the recipient and when possible, resolves the matter informally. 45 C.F.R. 80.7(d); 28 U.S.C. 42.107(d).

When the matter involving discrimination by a recipient of financial assistance from the U.S. DHHS cannot be resolved informally, the U.S. DHHS may take action to effect compliance, including withholding funding and referring the matter to the Department of Justice with a recommendation for enforcement proceedings. 45 C.F.R. 80.8. Before funding is withheld, a hearing is required. *See* 45 C.F.R. 80.8 through 80.11. For matters involving other responsible departments, the provisions of 28 C.F.R. 42.107 through 42.111 apply. Other available options to obtain compliance include court enforcement and administrative action. *See* 28 C.F.R. 50.3 ("Guidelines for the enforcement of title VI, Civil Rights Act of 1964").

**2. North Carolina findings.** Effective in 2003, the North Carolina Department of Health and Human Services (NC DHHS) entered into a Voluntary Compliance Agreement with the U.S. DHHS Office for Civil Rights. *See* OCR Reference NO: 04-01-700. The agreement occurred after a 2001 compliance review was conducted by the U.S. DHHS, which raised concerns about Title VI discrimination on the basis of national origin related to persons' with limited English proficiency (LEP) lack of meaningful access to programs and services at the county social services and health departments. NC DHHS policy requires that each county DSS develop a Title VI/LEP compliance plan. NC DHHS has a Title VI compliance attorney in the Office of General Counsel, who works with a Title VI Advisory Committee, and provides assistance to county departments of social services in meeting their obligations under Title VI.

In 2012, the U.S. Department of Justice Office of Civil Rights issued a letter of finding to the North Carolina Administrative Office of the Courts (AOC) of a Title VI violation based on failing to provide individuals with limited English proficiency with meaningful access to state court proceedings and operations. The AOC has been working to voluntary correct the violations and comply with Title VI requirements.

**Resources:**
For information about NC DHHS language access services, see its website and search for "Title VI – Limited English Proficiency," which includes the complaint procedure and forms.

See the following NC DHHS Division of Social Services Dear County Directors Letters (available on the NC DHHS website, under "DSS 'Dear County Director' Archive", here, by year):
- FAEP-14-2004: Civil Rights Assurance with Attachment (Sept. 15, 2004).
- PM-PC-01-2005: Language Services Agreement for Limited English Proficiency (LEP) (Aug. 2, 2005).
- PM-PC-01-2006: Language Services Agreement for Limited English Proficiency (LEP) (Jan. 23, 2006).
- PM-PC-01-2007: Title VI Nondiscrimination Statement (Jan. 3, 2007).
- PM-PC-02-2008: Update Limited English Proficiency Plan (April 22, 2008) with Attachment.
- PC-03-11: Civil Rights Assurance (April 1, 2011).
- DIR-01-2012: Office of Civil Rights (OCR) Title VI Compliance Review of the NC Division of Social Services (DSS) (May 7, 2012).
- PC-02-201: All Program Civil Rights Complaints (Oct. 1, 2012).

See the "Office of Language Access Services" on the North Carolina Administrative Office of the Courts website for information on available services including requesting an interpreter or other language access services; a language access benchcard; an online complaint form; the standards applying to language access services in the courts; and interpreter recruitment, training, and certification.

## 13.5 The Americans with Disabilities Act

### A. Introduction

The Americans with Disabilities Act (ADA), 101 Pub. L. 336, 104 Stat. 327, was enacted in 1990 and prohibits disability-based discrimination with the purpose of ensuring that individuals with disabilities have full and equal opportunities to participate in all aspects of society. In 2008, Congress made significant amendments to the ADA to ensure the broad coverage of the Act's protections and to explicitly reject narrow and restrictive court interpretations of who is a person with a disability protected by the Act (ADAAA), 122 Stat. 3553. The ADA is codified at 42 U.S.C. 12101 *et seq.* Federal regulations implementing the provisions of the ADA in state and local government services are found at 28 C.F.R. Part 35. Note that North Carolina also has its own "Persons with Disabilities Protection Act," which is codified at G.S. Chapter 168A. The state law is not discussed in this Manual.

The ADA is a comprehensive federal civil rights law that protects persons with physical or mental disabilities from discrimination in various areas including employment, public services, and public accommodations and services operated by private entities. There are five titles to the ADA. The discussion in this Manual is limited to a general overview of, with links to various resources for, Title II, Public Services (codified at 42 U.S.C. 12131 through 12134), and its application to child welfare agencies and the state court system in North Carolina. Note that a private entity involved with the child welfare system may be covered by Title III of the ADA (42 U.S.C. 12181 through 12189).

The U.S. Department of Justice (U.S. DOJ) and U.S Department of Health and Human Services (U.S. DHHS) recognize a 2012 report from the National Council on Disability that found parents with disabilities are disproportionately and often inappropriately involved in the child welfare system with permanent separation from their children as an outcome. Stereotypes about dangerousness or deficient parenting abilities, lack of individualized assessments, and failure to provide services were identified as negatively affecting parents with disabilities.[4] The ADA applies to parents with disabilities. It also applies to children with disabilities and current and prospective foster and adoptive parents (including relatives) with disabilities. For a discussion of early intervention and special education eligibility and services for infants, toddlers, and children who have qualifying disabilities, see section 13.8, below (discussing the Individuals with Disabilities Education Act).

There is another federal law that prohibits discrimination on the basis of disability: Section 504 of the Rehabilitation Act of 1973 (Section 504). *See* 29 U.S.C. 794; *see also* 45 C.F.R. Part 84 (regulations implementing Section 504 regarding federal financial assistance administered by U.S. DHHS). Section 504 has the same definitions and prohibitions as Title II of the ADA, but its application is conditioned on the receipt of any federal financial assistance, which is not a criterion under the ADA. The discussion in this Manual is limited to the ADA; however, the protections and remedies that are discussed may be available under both laws.

**Resources:**
For guidance on the application of the ADA to child welfare services, see
- Protecting the Rights of Parents and Prospective Parents with Disabilities: Technical Assistance for State and Local Child Welfare Agencies and Courts under Title II of the Americans with Disabilities Act and Section 504 of the Rehabilitation Act (Aug. 2015) by the U.S. Department of Justice, Civil Rights Division and U.S. Department of Health

---

[4] NATIONAL COUNCIL ON DISABILITY, "Rocking the Cradle: Ensuring the Rights of Parents with Disabilities and Their Children" (2012).

and Human Services, Administration for Children and Families and Office for Civil Rights.
- The "Protection from Discrimination in Child Welfare Activities" section of the U.S. Department of Health and Human Services website.
- The Disability Fact Sheet, "Your Rights as a Person with a Disability in the Child Welfare System," available on the U.S. Department of Health and Human Services Office for Civil Rights website.

For information, generally, about the ADA, see "Information and Technical Assistance on the Americans with Disabilities Act," including the TITLE II TECHNICAL ASSISTANCE MANUAL, at ADA.gov, a website that is part of the U.S. Department of Justice Civil Rights Division.

For information about the ADA in the court system, see the "Access and Fairness" "ADA" section of the National Center for State Courts website.

The Child Welfare Information Gateway provides information and resources related to children and parents with disabilities in the child welfare system on its website, specifically in sections addressing "Children & Youth with Disabilities in the Child Welfare System," "Permanency for Children With Disabilities," "Services for Parents with Disabilities," and "Reunification with Parents Affected by Behavioral or Physical Health Issues."

## B. Applicability

**1. Public entities.** Title II of the ADA applies to "public entities," which is defined as any state or local government and their departments and agencies. 42 U.S.C. 12131(1); 28 C.F.R. 35.104. This includes the North Carolina Department of Health and Human Services, every county department of social services (DSS), and the state courts. Note that the federal government is not included in the definition of "public entity".

**2. Disability defined.** Protections under Title II of the ADA apply to a "qualified individual with a disability," defined as "an individual with a disability who, with or without reasonable modifications to rules, policies, or practices, the removal of architectural, communication, or transportation barriers, or the provision of auxiliary aids and services, meets the essential eligibility requirements for the receipt of services or the participation in programs or activities provided by a public entity." 42 U.S.C. 12131(2).

The ADA defines disability in three ways. An individual

- has a physical or mental impairment that substantially limits one or more major life activities (e.g., hearing, vision, mobility, cognitive skills, communication, daily activities of self-care, or the operation of a major bodily function such as the immune system, normal cell growth, digestive, bowel, bladder, neurological, respiratory, circulatory, endocrine, and reproductive functions),
- has a record of such an impairment, or

- is regarded (or perceived) as having such an impairment (regardless of whether the individual has an impairment).

42 U.S.C. 12102; 28 C.F.R. 35.108.

The definition of disability is meant to be construed broadly so as to give expansive coverage of the protections of the Act. 28 C.F.R. 35.101(b) and 35.108(a)(2)(i). Determining whether an individual has a disability should not require extensive analysis, and "the primary object of attention in cases brought under the ADA should be whether entities covered under the ADA have complied with their obligations and whether discrimination has occurred, not whether the individual meets the definition of 'disability.' " 28 C.F.R. 35.101(b).

There is an exception to the definition of an "individual with a disability", which is when an individual is currently using illegal drugs, and the public entity (e.g., DSS) is acting on the basis of the individual's current drug use. 42 U.S.C. 12210(a); 28 C.F.R. 35.104. However, an individual may be disabled when he or she has been successfully rehabilitated or is participating in a supervised rehabilitation program and is not currently using illegal drugs. 42 U.S.C. 12210(b); 28 C.F.R. 35.131(a). The ADA does not "encourage, prohibit, restrict, or authorize" drug testing. 28 C.F.R. 35.131(c)(2). "Illegal use of drugs" means using, possessing, or distributing drugs (defined in schedules I through V of the Controlled Substances Act) in a manner that is unlawful under the Controlled Substances Act or other federal law. 42 U.S.C. 12210(d); *see* 21 U.S.C. 812 *et seq.* (Controlled Substances Act). It does not include using drugs when taken under the supervision of a licensed health care professional or when used as authorized by federal law. 28 C.F.R. 35.104.

**Practice Note:** A disability may not be obvious or known. In some cases, it will be clear. For example, the disability may be included in the allegations of the juvenile petition (e.g., dependency), or an individual may inform DSS or the court of his or her disability or of the child's disability. When it is less obvious, information is available to both the court and DSS that may assist in determining whether the individual has a disability, such as an individual's receipt of SSI, an Individual Educational Program (IEP) (discussed in section 13.8, below), medical records, or the results of any evaluations (past or current). In other cases, the disability will not be not known or suspected initially but will be discovered during the course of the child welfare case.

## C. Prohibited Discrimination

The ADA recognizes the numerous ways that an individual with a disability may be discriminated against, including intentional exclusion or segregation, barriers that have a discriminatory effect, overprotective rules or policies, the failure to make modifications to practices and facilities, and the provision of lesser services or opportunities. 42 U.S.C. 12101(a)(5). *See* 28 C.F.R. 35.130.

Title II of the ADA uses broad language to address the various types of discrimination experienced by individuals with disabilities by requiring that "no qualified individual with a disability shall, by reason of such disability, be excluded from participation in or be denied the benefits of the services, programs, or activities of a public entity, or be subjected to discrimination by any such entity." 42 U.S.C. 12132; *see* 28 C.F.R. 35.149 (related to accessibility of facilities). Retaliatory discrimination against a person who made a complaint or assisted or participated in an investigation or proceeding of a complaint is explicitly prohibited. A person who aids or encourages another to exercise rights under the ADA is also protected by the ADA. 42 U.S.C. 12203; 28 C.F.R. 35.134. In addition to the individual with a disability, a person who has a relationship with or associates with another person who has a disability may not be discriminated against as a result of that relationship or association. 28 C.F.R. 35.130(g).

The federal regulations list examples of specific discriminatory actions that are prohibited at 28 C.F.R. 35.130. Such actions include denying the opportunity to participate, affording an opportunity that is not equal to that of others, providing different or separate benefits or services, or limiting a qualified individual with a disability of any advantage or opportunity enjoyed by others who receive the benefit or service.

### D. Requirements

**1. Access and opportunity**. A qualified individual with a disability must have an equal opportunity to participate in programs or services provided by the public entity. *See* 28 C.F.R. 35.130(b). This means the parent, child, relative, foster parent, etc. must be able to participate equally in the programs provided by DSS and the state courts. Title II provisions apply to all the activities and programs of the public entity, which includes the state court system, county DSSs, and the North Carolina Department of Health and Human Services. *See* 28 C.F.R. 35.102. It also includes services or activities provided through a contract or other arrangement with the public entity (e.g., a private agency under contract with DSS). 28 C.F.R. 35.130(b)(3). As related to child welfare and DSS, the ADA applies to protective services: screening of reports, assessments, casework, and counseling services. *See* G.S. 7B-300. In addition, DSS provides reasonable efforts to parents and others so that a permanent plan for the child is achieved. *See, e.g.*, G.S. 7B-101(18); 7B-507(a)(2) and (5); 7B-903(a3); 7B-906.2(b). Adoption and foster care services are provided by DSS as well. *See* G.S. 108A-14(a)(6), (12), and (13). The ADA also applies to the court proceedings that arise from an abuse, neglect, or dependency petition.

The North Carolina Court of Appeals noted in an abuse, neglect, or dependency case that the "two principles that are fundamental to Title II of the ADA and Section 504 are: (1) individualized treatment; and (2) full and equal opportunity." *In re S.A.*, 806 S.E.2d 81, n.2 (N.C. Ct. App. 2017) (unpublished) (quoting *In re Hicks*, 890 N.W.2d 696, 705 (Mich. Ct. App. 2016)).

There are numerous provisions under Title II of the ADA that require a public entity to accommodate individuals with a disability in various ways, including policy or procedural modifications, facility design and relocation of inaccessible programs, and effective communication methods. *See* 28 C.F.R. 35.130. The public entity may not impose a surcharge on the individual or group of individuals with a disability for the costs of any anti-discrimination measures it must take to serve that individual or group. 28 C.F.R. 35.130(f).

Services, programs, and activities must be provided in the most integrated setting that is appropriate to the needs of the qualified individual with a disability. 28 C.F.R. 35.130(d). Although made available, the individual with a disability is not required to accept the accommodation provided for under the ADA. 28 C.F.R. 35.130(e).

When necessary to avoid discrimination on the basis of a disability, the public entity must make reasonable modifications to policies, practices, or procedures (except when the individual meets the definition of disability solely on the basis of a perceived disability). 28 C.F.R. 35.130(b)(7). A reasonable modification is determined on an individualized basis by examining "whether a specific modification for a particular person's disability would be reasonable under the circumstances as well as necessary for that person…." *PGA Tour, Inc. v. Martin*, 532 U.S. 661, 688 (2001). Note that in addition to the ADA, North Carolina has codified provisions addressing service animals, which may require a modification of a policy that prohibits animals from a facility, at G.S. Chapter 168.

Programs and facilities must be readily accessible to individuals with a disability (e.g. wheelchair accessible). 28 C.F.R. 35.149 through 35.151; *see* 28 C.F.R. Part 35, Appendix A (providing section-by-section analysis of Title II revisions made in 2010).

The public entity must take steps to ensure that its communications with persons with disabilities are as effective as communications with others. This may require the provision of auxiliary aids and services, such as a qualified sign language interpreter, effective telecommunication systems for individuals with hearing or speech impairments, and audio recordings and/or large print materials for persons who are blind or have impaired vision. *See* 28 C.F.R. 35.160 through 35.163 and 35.130(f); *see* 42 U.S.C. 12103(1) and 28 C.F.R. 35.104 (definition of "auxiliary aids and services"). In North Carolina, G.S. Chapter 8B regulates interpreting services for deaf persons in judicial proceedings, including juvenile proceedings, when needed for any party or witness. North Carolina licensure requirements for interpreters and transliterators for individuals who are deaf, hearing impaired, or dependent on manual modes of communication are codified at G.S. Chapter 90D.

**2. Exceptions.** Title II of the ADA recognizes circumstances where the opportunity for participation by an individual with a disability may be limited. The authorized exceptions involve the following:

- The public entity is not required to take action that the public entity can demonstrate would cause (1) a fundamental alteration in the nature of the services, facilities, privileges, or accommodations involved or (2) undue financial and administrative burdens. 42 U.S.C. 12201(f); 28 C.F.R. 35.150(a)(3) and 35.164.
- The public entity is not required to allow an individual who poses a direct threat to the health or safety of others to participate in or benefit from services, programs, or activities. The criteria for making an individualized assessment of whether there is direct threat to health or safety of others is at 28 C.F.R. 35.139. A "direct threat" exists when there is a "significant risk to the health or safety of others that cannot be eliminated by reasonable accommodation." 42 U.S.C. 12111(3).

- A public entity may impose legitimate safety requirements that are necessary to operate its services, programs, and activities safely so long as the requirements are based on actual risks rather than speculation, stereotypes, or generalizations about individuals with disabilities. 28 C.F.R. 35.130(h).

**3. Application to abuse, neglect, dependency, and TPR proceedings.** The ADA is not a defense to a termination of parental rights (TPR) action. In a case of first impression, the North Carolina Court of Appeals held in *In re C.M.S.*, 184 N.C. App. 488 (2007), that the ADA did not preclude termination of parental rights of the respondent mother who had an intellectual disability (previously referred to as mental retardation). The court of appeals reviewed other state courts' treatment of the issue and adopted the rule followed by other states that TPR proceedings are not services, programs, or activities within the meaning of Title II of the ADA, and the ADA is not a defense to a TPR. *But see In re Hicks/Brown*, 893 N.W.2d 637 (Mich. 2017) (vacating and remanding order terminating parental rights of a mother with an intellectual disability; under Michigan law, TPR is improper without reasonable efforts finding; holding the department's efforts are not reasonable unless modified to accommodate a parent's disability and determining trial court erred when making the reasonable efforts finding by failing to consider that department's reunification efforts did not provide mother with specific services ordered by the court to accommodate mother's disability (based on request by mother's attorney in earlier proceedings regarding specific services that would provide such accommodations) and whether the department's efforts that were provided to mother nonetheless reasonably accommodated her disability). See Chapter 9 (discussing TPR).

At the same time that the court of appeals held the ADA was not a defense to the TPR, it also found that the requirements for and the trial court's findings about reasonable efforts to prevent or eliminate the need for the child's placement constituted compliance with the ADA. *In re C.M.S.*, 184 N.C. App. 488. Other states have noted that although the ADA is not a defense to a TPR, "[t]his is not to say that the ADA plays no role in child welfare proceedings." *In re Elijah C.*, 326 Conn. 480, 508 (2017). In a recent unpublished opinion, the North Carolina Court of Appeals relied on *In re C.M.S.* and held the trial court's findings that DSS made reasonable efforts was necessarily a finding that DSS complied with the anti-discrimination provision of the ADA in that the parent was not excluded from participation or denied the benefits of the programs or services of DSS. *In re S.A.*, 806 S.E.2d 81 (N.C. Ct. App. 2017) (unpublished). The court of appeals further determined that because the respondent parent did not object to the adequacy of the services offered by DSS before or during the permanency planning hearing (resulting in the order on appeal) as well as denying the need for services, she waived the argument that the services offered were inadequate under the ADA. *In re S.A.*, 806 S.E.2d 81 (unpublished).

**4. Notice of applicability.** Public entities must make available to applicants, participants, beneficiaries, and other interested persons information about anti-discrimination provisions and their applicability to the programs, services, and activities the public entity provides in a manner that notifies the persons of the ADA protections. 28 C.F.R. 35.106. *See* 28 C.F.R. 35.163 (information and signage for persons with impaired hearing or vision).

**Practice Notes:** A party to the proceeding may make a reasonable accommodation request. For example, if the parent knows he or she requires hands-on learning, he or she may request a reasonable accommodation as part of his or her full participation in a parenting education program, or if a parent needs an adaptive parenting program, he or she may make that request of DSS for inclusion in the case plan. An attorney for the parent may request an adaptive parenting capacity evaluation as a reasonable modification for his or her client. The child's guardian ad litem, parent, or placement provider may request a reasonable accommodation for the child, such as specialized transportation for the child. If a child is disabled and receiving special education services and/or reasonable modifications, the Individual Education Program (IEP) or 504 plan may provide information about the type of modifications the child will also need outside of the school setting. This may also apply to respondents who had an IEP or 504 plan when they were school age.

It may also be appropriate to raise a disagreement about whether modifications are reasonable such that they impact whether the efforts made by DSS are reasonable when the court hearing the abuse, neglect, or dependency action is determining whether DSS provided reasonable efforts. *See In re S.A.*, 806 S.E.2d 81 (N.C. Ct. App. 2017) (unpublished). The trial court has the authority to "order services or other efforts aimed at returning the juvenile to a safe home" at the nonsecure custody stage and to "specify efforts that are reasonable" at permanency planning hearings and in resulting orders. G.S. 7B-507(a)(5); 7B-906.2(b).

**AOC Form:**
AOC-G-116, Motion, Appointment, and Order Authorizing Payment of Sign Language Interpreter or Other Communication Access Service Provider (Oct. 2019).

**NC DHHS Form:**
DSS-5333, Americans with Disabilities Act - Did you know? (Jan. 2014).

**Resources:**
For federal guidance in a question and answer format with specific child welfare case examples, see Protecting the Rights of Parents and Prospective Parents with Disabilities: Technical Assistance for State and Local Child Welfare Agencies and Courts under Title II of the Americans with Disabilities Act and Section 504 of the Rehabilitation Act (Aug. 2015) by the U.S. Department of Justice Civil Rights Division and U.S. Department of Health and Human Services, Administration for Children and Families and Office for Civil Rights.

For guidelines by the American Psychological Association that address evaluations that may be used in a child welfare case, see
- Guidelines for Psychological Evaluations in Child Protection Matters.
- Guidelines for Assessment of and Intervention with Persons with Disabilities.

For information regarding accommodations for persons who are deaf or hearing impaired, see
- The North Carolina Administrative Office of the Courts (AOC) Guidelines for Accommodating Persons Who Are Deaf or Hard of Hearing in the Courts (March 2017).
- The Division of Services for the Deaf and the Hard of Hard of Hearing section of the

N.C. Department of Health and Human Services website, which includes a statewide interpreter directory.

For general information about access to services, programs, and activities for individuals with disabilities in the courts, see "Disability Access" under the "Help Topics" "Disability and Special Needs" section of the North Carolina Administrative Office of the Courts website.

For North Carolina Department of Health and Human Services Division of Social Services policy that specifically addresses issues related to children with disabilities (developmental delays, intellectual disability, motor impairment, sensory disability, learning disability, mental illness, and chronic illness) as well as consideration of a parent's disability, see DIV. OF SOC. SERVS., N.C. DEP'T OF HEALTH & HUMAN SERVICES, CHILD WELFARE MANUAL "Cross Function," available here. Use control F to search the terms "disability" and "disabilities."

For various resources of documents or websites that are useful to persons with disabilities, see the "Resources" section of the NC Statewide Independent Living Council website.

### E. Compliance

**1. Filing a complaint.** A person alleging a violation of Title II of the ADA may file a complaint with the appropriate federal designated agency within 180 days of the date of the alleged discrimination, unless the time is extended for good cause. 28 C.F.R. 35.170. The U.S. DHHS Office of Civil Rights and the U.S. DOJ both enforce Title II of the ADA as related to child welfare services and activities by DSS and the state courts. *See* 28 C.F.R. 35.190(b)(3) and (6). The complaint procedure is set forth at 28 C.F.R. 35.171 through 35.178. Title II utilizes the procedures and remedies set forth in the Civil Rights Act. 42 U.S.C. 12133 (referring to 29 U.S.C. 794a). See section 13.4.E, above (discussing violation procedures under Title VI of the Civil Rights Act).

A private lawsuit may also be filed in federal court, without the filing of a complaint with a federal agency. *See* 28 C.F.R. 35.172(d).

On a state and local level, when a public entity employs a minimum of fifty people, it must designate at least one employee to coordinate its ADA compliance efforts, which may include investigating complaints. The public entity must also adopt and publish grievance procedures regarding the resolution of any complaints. 28 C.F.R. 35.107.

**Resources:**
The grievance procedure and other information about disability access (including requesting a reasonable accommodation) in the North Carolina courts is available on the North Carolina Administrative Office of the Courts website under the "Disability Access" page of the "Help Topics" "Disability and Special Needs" section of the website.

The grievance procedure for the N.C. Department of Health and Human Services is available under the "About" "Department Initiatives" "ADA and Civil Rights Grievance Procedure" section of its website.

**2. Violations related to child welfare.** Violations of Title II of the ADA in the child welfare context have been found in other states based on a variety of different types of discriminatory practices. Some of the violations are as follows:

- A Voluntary Resolution Agreement between the U.S. DHHS Office of Civil Rights (OCR) and the Oregon Department of Human Services (Department) (Transaction Numbers 18-290275, 18-291152, and 18-291153) (November 2019). The agreement addresses the rights of parents with disabilities. OCR received complaints alleging children were removed from their parents who have disabilities, and that the parents were denied effective and meaningful opportunities for reunification due in significant part to stereotypical beliefs and discriminatory assumptions about the parents' abilities to safely care for their children because of the parents' low IQ scores. The OCR identified systemic deficiencies in the Department's implementation of disability rights policies, practices, and procedures. The agreement requires an individualized assessment of a parent with a disability rather a determination of safety risk based on stereotypes or generalizations about persons with disabilities or a specific diagnosis. The Department agreed to update its policies and procedures, implement a new disability rights training plan, and make assurances it will comply with the anti-discrimination disabilities laws, and OCR will monitor the Department's efforts and provide technical assistance.
- A letter of finding by the U.S. DOJ and U.S. DHHS to the Massachusetts Department of Children and Families, DJ No 204-36-216 and HHS No. 14-182176 (Jan. 29, 2015). The violation involved the removal of a newborn from her mother, Sara Gordon, who has a developmental disability. Findings were that the Department engaged in ongoing and extensive violations over a period of two years when it failed to reasonably modify its policies, practices, and procedures to accommodate Sara's disability and implement appropriate reunification services. The Department's actions were based on assumptions and stereotypes of Sara's disability and failed to consider appropriate family-based support services. The remedial measures imposed by the letter of finding include withdrawing the petition to terminate parental rights; implementing appropriate services and supports for reunification; paying compensatory damages; developing and implementing procedures on the ADA and Section 504 for assessments, services planning, visitation and safety requirements; and implementing a training program for staff.
- A letter of finding to the Florida Department of Children and Families, OCR Docket No. 05-36562 (Aug. 7, 2007) for failing to provide appropriate auxiliary aids of qualified sign language interpreters necessary for effective communication with persons who are deaf and hearing impaired.
- Settlement agreement between U.S. DHHS Office for Civil Rights and the State of Georgia Department of Human Services, OCR Transaction Number: 09-102792 (Dec. 17. 2015) regarding denial of an application to become a foster parent.

## 13.6 Servicemembers Civil Relief Act

### A. Introduction

The Servicemembers Civil Relief Act (SCRA), Pub. L. No. 108-189, sec. 1, Dec. 19, 2003, 117 Stat. 2835, was originally enacted in 1940 as the Soldiers' and Sailors' Civil Relief Act (SSCRA), ch. 888, 54 Stat. 1178. It is codified at 50 U.S.C. 3901 *et seq.* Prior to December 1, 2015, the SCRA and SSCRA were codified at 50 U.S.C. App. 501 *et seq.*

The SCRA's purpose is to protect servicemembers and strengthen our national defense. The law enables servicemembers to focus on defending the nation by providing for the temporary suspension of judicial and administrative non-criminal proceedings that may adversely affect servicemembers' rights during their military service.

Effective October 1, 2019, North Carolina enacted its own state Servicemembers Civil Relief Act (NC SCRA), which is codified at Article 4 of G.S. Chapter 127B. *See* S.L. 2019-161. The NC SCRA incorporates the rights, benefits, and protections of the federal SCRA and also extends those rights to members of a state National Guard who are acting under a state's order of active duty for more than thirty consecutive days and who reside in North Carolina. G.S. 127B-26 (purpose); 127B-27 (definitions); 127B-28 (incorporation and expansion of SCRA). The NC SCRA is not discussed in detail here.

In November 2019, the United States had over 1.3 million active duty military members and over 800,000 reservists. North Carolina was the fourth state (following California, Virginia, and Texas) with the most active duty members of the military.[5] In 2018, thirty-seven percent (37%) of active duty and forty-two percent (42%) of selected reserve members had children, the vast majority of whom were 11 years old or younger.[6] These numbers make it likely that some abuse, neglect, dependency, or termination of parental rights cases heard in the North Carolina courts will involve servicemembers who are parties in those actions.

---

**Resources:**
For more information about the SCRA, see
- Sara DePasquale, *The SCRA and Juvenile Proceedings*, UNC SCH. OF GOV'T: ON THE CIVIL SIDE BLOG (April 29, 2015).
- Cheryl Howell, *Servicemembers' Civil Relief Act Applies to Family Cases Too*, UNC SCH. OF GOV'T: ON THE CIVIL SIDE BLOG (Feb. 13, 2015) (note, do not use the hyperlink to the statute appearing in this blog; it is to former codified statutes).
- Search for "Servicemembers Civil Relief Act or SCRA" on the American Bar Association website to find "The ABA Military and Veterans Legal Center" pages discussing the SCRA.

---

[5] Statistical information was obtained from the Defense Manpower Data Center (DMDC), which collects data for the Department of Defense. See "Statistics & Reports" maintained under the DoD Data/Reports section of the DMDC website.

[6] Department of Defense, Office of the Deputy Assistant Secretary of Defense for Military Community and Family Policy. "2018 Demographics Profile of the Military Community," p. vi–vii, 2018.

- "Quick Reference Guide for Family Court Judges" by the Office of the Deputy Assistant Secretary of Defense for Military Community and Family Policy Office of Military Community Outreach (April 2014).

## B. Applicability

The SCRA applies to any non-criminal judicial or administrative proceeding that is commenced in a state (including a political subdivision), federal, or U.S. territory court or agency. 50 U.S.C. 3912. Child custody proceedings are specifically referenced in the SCRA. 50 U.S.C. 3931(a), 3932(a), 3938, and 3938a. Abuse, neglect, dependency, and termination of parental rights (TPR) proceedings are custody proceedings. *See* G.S. 50A-102(4); *In re E.J.X.*, 191 N.C. App. 34 (2008), *aff'd per curiam*, 363 N.C. 9 (2009); *see also In re A.K.*, 360 N.C. 449 (2006) (referring to abuse, neglect, or dependency proceeding as child custody proceeding).

The SCRA applies to abuse, neglect, dependency, and TPR actions even when a servicemember is not a party. The specific SCRA requirements and the number of SCRA provisions that apply to the proceeding will depend on various factors, such as whether a party has appeared in the case, when a judgment is entered, and whether a party is a servicemember.

**1. Servicemember defined.** A servicemember is a member of the Army, Navy, Air Force, Marine Corps, Coast Guard, and the commissioned corps of the National and Oceanic and Atmospheric Administration (NOAA) or the Public Health Service. 50 U.S.C. 3911(1) (referring to 10 U.S.C. 101(a)(5)).

The NC SCRA specifies that its definition of servicemember is a servicemember as defined by the federal SCRA who resides in North Carolina and adds a member of the North Carolina National Guard. G.S. 127B-27(4).

**2. Military service defined.** For purposes of the SCRA, a member of the Army, Navy, Air Force, Marine Corps, or Coast Guard is in military service when on active duty, which includes full-time training duty, annual training duty, and attendance while in active military service at a school designated as a military service school by law or the Secretary of the applicable military department. Active duty does not include full-time National Guard duty. A National Guard member is in military service when under a call to active service from the President or Secretary of Defense for at least thirty-one consecutive days for the purpose of responding to a national emergency that has been declared by the President and is supported by federal funding. A commissioned officer of NOAA or the Public Health Service who is in active service is in military service. Military service includes a period when a servicemember is absent from duty because of illness, wounds, leave, or other lawful reason. 50 U.S.C 3911(2); *see* 10 U.S.C. 101(d)(1).

Under the NC SCRA, military service also includes a member of a state National Guard who is under an order of *state active duty from the governor* of that state for more than thirty consecutive days. G.S. 127B-27(3).

## C. SCRA Requirements

**1. The SCRA affidavit.** In a proceeding where the defendant has not made an appearance, before the court may enter a temporary or final judgment for the plaintiff, the court must require the plaintiff to file an affidavit that states

- whether the defendant is or is not in military service and the necessary facts to support the assertion or
- the plaintiff is unable to determine whether the defendant is in military service.

50 U.S.C. 3931(a), (b); *see* 50 U.S.C. 3911(9) (definition of "judgment").

The SCRA does not define making an appearance and does not specify what constitutes "necessary facts" to support the assertion in the affidavit.

---

**Practice Note:** The petitioner should exercise diligence in determining whether each respondent in the action is in military service, which under the federal SCRA and the NC SCRA must include *both* federal military service and state National Guard service. Necessary facts to support the petitioner's assertion may be the petitioner's personal knowledge (e.g., the father told the DSS social worker he was not in the military), inquiries made to others (e.g., the father informed the DSS social worker that the child's mother works full-time, lives with him in the home, and is not in the military), or search results of the Department of Defense active duty status records for purposes of federal military service. Regarding military service under a state order of active duty, the NC SCRA requires that the servicemember provide a written or electronic copy of the military order within thirty days of when that military service terminates. G.S. 127B-28. Including a statement in the affidavit that the petitioner has/has not received a copy of a state military order from the respondent clarifies whether the NC SCRA applies to a member of the National Guard.

To obtain this information, the DSS social worker or the petitioner/movant in the TPR proceeding can ask the respondent and others that know the respondent about the respondent's military service and the basis for that person's knowledge or belief.

**Resource:** To conduct a search as to whether one or multiple individuals are on active duty status under a federal military order, access the Servicemembers Civil Relief Act (SCRA) Website. This website does not provide information on state orders of active duty for state National Guard service for purposes of the NC SCRA.

---

The SCRA affidavit is only required if the respondent does not make an appearance before the court enters a judgment for the plaintiff. A judgment means any order or ruling that is temporary or final, which includes a nonsecure custody order in an abuse, neglect, or dependency action. *See* 50 U.S.C. 3911(9); G.S. 7B-506(a), (e). When DSS requests an ex parte nonsecure custody order, no respondent makes an appearance. The SCRA requires that the affidavit be filed for each named respondent before the court enters the ex parte nonsecure custody order. If a respondent has notice of the nonsecure custody request but does not make an appearance, the SCRA affidavit is required before the nonsecure custody order is entered. In those cases where a nonsecure custody order is not requested or is not granted, the SCRA affidavit will be required for any respondent who has not appeared in the action before an order for the plaintiff is entered (e.g., an adjudication order). If the respondent appears in the action before an order is entered, an SCRA affidavit for that respondent is not required.

The form of the affidavit may be a written statement, declaration, verification, or certificate that is subscribed and certified to be true under penalty of perjury. 50 U.S.C. 3931(b)(4). In an abuse, neglect, dependency, or TPR case, the initiating petition (or TPR motion) must be verified. G.S. 7B-403(a); 7B-1104. The SCRA affidavit requirement may be satisfied by including the applicable statement and supporting facts in the verified pleading. It may also be a separate document, such as the form affidavit created by the North Carolina Administrative Office of the Courts (AOC).

**AOC Form:**
AOC-G-250, Servicemembers Civil Relief Act Affidavit (Nov. 2019).
Note the November 2019 edition of this form references the Servicemember Civil Relief Act Website to conduct a search of military service, but that search will not include information about a state's order to active duty for members of a state National Guard or a check/checkbox for whether the servicemember provided a copy of the military order issued by the governor of the applicable state.

**Practice Note:** A petitioner should be mindful of how much time passes between the filing of the affidavit (or verified petition/motion) and the entry of the judgment. Although the SCRA does not specify how soon the affidavit must be filed before the judgment is entered, if the facts support the possibility that a respondent may have entered military service since the filing of the affidavit, the court may require that a new affidavit be filed. If the affidavit shows that the respondent is not in military service, the court may enter the order and proceed with the case.

If the court is unable to determine whether the respondent is in military service, the court may enter a judgment. Before entering a judgment, the court may require the petitioner to file a bond in an amount approved by the court. The bond remains in effect until the time to appeal and set aside a judgment expires. The bond is available to indemnify the respondent against any loss or damage suffered by the respondent because of a judgment entered for the petitioner against the respondent that is later set aside in whole or in part. The court may also enter any order it determines necessary to protect the respondent's rights under the SCRA. 50 U.S.C. 3931(b)(3).

If the affidavit shows the respondent is in military service, additional SCRA protections apply.

**2. Additional SCRA requirements when respondent is in military service.**

**(a) Appointment of attorney.** If it appears that the respondent who has not made an appearance in the proceeding is in military service, the court may not enter a judgment until after the court appoints an attorney to represent him or her. 50 U.S.C. 3931(b)(2). The right to an attorney appointed under the SCRA is in addition to the right to appointed counsel provided to respondent parents under North Carolina's Juvenile Code. *See* G.S. 7B-602(a); 7B-1101.1(a). The SCRA right to an attorney continues even when the Juvenile Code requires that provisional counsel be dismissed if the parent does not appear at the hearing or does not qualify for appointed counsel. G.S. 7B-602(a)(1) and (2); 7B-1101.1(a)(1) and (2). The SCRA right to an attorney also applies to respondents who are custodians, guardians, or caretakers even though those parties do not have a statutory right to appointed counsel under the Juvenile Code. The SCRA does not address payment for the appointed attorney.

The attorney that is appointed should (1) try to locate a servicemember who was unable to be located prior to the attorney's appointment and (2) determine whether a stay is necessary and apply for a stay when appropriate. The SCRA attorney represents the servicemember, but the extent of that representation outside of locating the servicemember and requesting a stay is not addressed by the SCRA. *See* 50 U.S.C. 3931(b)(2), (d).

**(b) Stay of the proceeding**. There are two different stay provisions in the SCRA: 50 U.S.C 3931 and 50 U.S.C. 3932. The SCRA does not define a stay of the proceeding or address whether in a child custody proceeding a temporary emergency order that protects a child or temporary custody order that addresses the child's best interests is permitted during the pendency of the stay of the proceeding. The issue has not been addressed by the North Carolina appellate courts.

**The 50 U.S.C. 3931 stay**. A stay of the proceeding may be made pursuant to 50 U.S.C. 3931. The court, on its own motion or on the motion of the attorney appointed under the SCRA to represent a respondent, must grant a minimum ninety-day stay of the proceeding when

- the respondent is in military service and
- the court determines
    o there may be a defense but it cannot be presented without the respondent's presence or
    o after due diligence, the SCRA-appointed attorney has been unable to contact the respondent or otherwise determine if a meritorious defense exists.

50 U.S.C. 3931(d).

**The 50 U.S.C. 3932 stay**. A stay of the proceeding may also be made pursuant to 50 U.S.C. 3932. The court on its own or a party (a respondent or a petitioner/movant in a TPR) who is in military service and has received actual notice of the proceeding may apply for a stay of the proceeding at any stage before a final judgment is entered. The court must stay the proceeding for at least ninety days when the servicemember applies for a stay that includes

- a letter or other communication that sets forth the facts stating how the current military duty requirements materially affect the servicemember's ability to appear and states a date when the servicemember will be available to appear and
- a letter or other communication from the commanding officer stating the servicemember's current military duty prevents the servicemember from appearing and that military leave is not authorized for the servicemember at the time of the letter or communication.

50 U.S.C. 3932(b).

After the first mandatory 50 U.S.C. 3932 stay is granted, the servicemember may apply for another stay based on the continuing material effect of military duty on his or her ability to appear. An additional request for a stay must include the same information that was required for the first stay. 50 U.S.C. 3932(d)(1). The granting of an additional stay is not mandatory, but if the court denies the servicemember's request, the court must appoint an attorney to represent him or her in the proceeding. 50 U.S.C. 3932(d)(2). The scope of the representation and the costs for the attorney are not addressed by the SCRA.

**Practice Note:** The SCRA does not specifically address the servicemember's presence or ability to appear through alternative means such as videoconference, telephone, deposition, etc. The court and/or parties may want to inquire about the availability of such alternatives when requesting, objecting to, supporting, or deciding the motion to stay.

(c) **Reopen the judgment.** If a default judgment is entered against a servicemember during the servicemember's military service (or within sixty days after being released from such service), the servicemember may seek to reopen the judgment to allow the servicemember to defend the action. The application to reopen the judgment must be made no later than ninety days after the servicemember is released from military service. The court must reopen the judgment if it appears that the servicemember (1) was materially affected by the military service in defending the action and (2) has a meritorious defense to all or part of the action. 50 U.S.C. 3931(g). A default judgment is not defined by the SCRA but is referred to in the provision that applies when a defendant does not make an appearance. *See* 50 U.S.C. 3931. Note that default judgments under the North Carolina Rules of Civil Procedure are not permissible in abuse, neglect, dependency, or termination of parental rights proceedings, but orders may be entered in those actions when a respondent does not appear. *See In re Thrift,* 137 N.C. App. 559 (2000); *In re Quevedo,* 106 N.C. App. 574 (1992).

(d) **Child custody protection.** The SCRA addresses child custody orders when a parent is or will be deployed. Under the SCRA, deployment is defined as the movement or mobilization of a servicemember to a location for 61 to 540 days pursuant to temporary or permanent official orders that are designated as unaccompanied, do not authorize dependent travel, or do not permit the movement of family members to the same location. 50 U.S.C. 3938(e). When a court enters a temporary custody order based solely on a parent's deployment or anticipated deployment, the order must expire no later than the period justified by the deployment. 50 U.S.C. 3938(a). When a motion or petition is filed seeking a permanent order to modify a child custody order, the court may not consider the servicemember's absence because of a deployment or the possibility of a deployment as the sole determination of the child's best interests. 50 U.S.C. 3938(b). Note that 50 U.S.C. 3938 was added to the SCRA by Pub.L. 113-291, Dec. 19, 2014.

> **Practice Note:** In addition to the protections for deploying parents under the SCRA, North Carolina has the Uniform Deployed Parents and Custody and Visitation Act. *See* G.S. 50A-350 through -376. This Act is discussed briefly in Chapter 3.3.G.
>
> **Resource:** Additional information about the Act is available on the website of the Uniform Law Commission at "Deployed Parents Custody and Visitation Act."

(e) **Waiver of rights.** A servicemember may waive his or her rights and protections provided by the SCRA. 50 U.S.C. 3918(a).

## 13.7 Every Student Succeeds Act

### A. Introduction[7]

The Every Student Succeeds Act (ESSA), Pub. L. No. 114-95, 129 Stat. 1802, was enacted on December 10, 2015, and makes various amendments to 20 U.S.C. 6301 *et seq.* Implementing federal regulations are at 34 C.F.R. Parts 200 and 299; however, the regulations relating to state plans were disapproved by Congress and have no force or effect. Pub.L. 115-13, March 27, 2017, 131 Stat. 77.

ESSA reauthorizes the Elementary and Secondary Education Act (ESEA) and replaces the No Child Left Behind Act. ESSA is an education (as opposed to child welfare) law and conditions federal funding under ESEA on compliance with its requirements. The state educational agency, which in North Carolina is the Department of Public Instruction (DPI), must submit a state plan with the Secretary of the U.S. Department of Education (DOE) that contains criteria specified in ESSA. The DOE approved North Carolina's state plan on June 5, 2018.

> **Resource:** Information about ESSA and North Carolina's state plan is available on the "Every Student Succeeds Act" section of the Department of Public Instruction website.

Although there are several different components of ESSA, the discussion in this Manual is limited to those provisions that apply to educational stability for children in foster care. Although not defined in ESSA, foster care is defined for federal funding purposes under Titles IV-B and IV-E of the Social Security Act. Foster care is 24-hour substitute care for

---

[7] The content in this section discussing educational outcomes for children in foster care is sourced from the NATIONAL WORKING GROUP ON FOSTER CARE AND EDUCATION, "Fostering Success in Education: National Factsheet on the Educational Outcomes of Children in Foster Care" (April 2018).

children who are placed away from their parents and for whom the child welfare agency has placement and care responsibility and includes placements in family foster homes, relative foster homes, group homes, emergency shelters, residential facilities, child care institutions, and preadoptive homes, regardless of whether the foster care facility is licensed and/or foster care or adoptive subsidy payments are made. 45 C.F.R. 1355.20(a).

Compared to their peers, children in foster care are highly mobile and experience more unscheduled school changes. Children who change schools frequently make less academic progress than their peers and have difficulty developing and maintaining supportive relationships with adults and friendships with others. Children in foster care are more likely to be absent from school, receive special education services, experience a grade retention, receive a suspension or expulsion, and/or drop out of school. Children in foster care also have lower performance scores on academic assessments. Children in foster care take longer to graduate and have lower graduation rates than their peers. Sixty-five percent of youth in foster care complete high school or obtain a GED by age 21, with foster youth being more likely to complete high school with a GED as opposed to a diploma. Less than half of the foster youth who graduate from high school attend college. Only three to eleven percent of former foster youth attain a bachelor's degree compared to the national college completion rate of thirty-three percent.

ESSA seeks to improve educational outcomes for children in foster care by requiring state and local child welfare and education agencies to work together to assure the educational stability of children in foster care. Under ESSA, children in foster care must be allowed to remain in their school of origin when it is in their best interests to do so and when it is not, to immediately enroll in a new school when a school transfer is necessary. 20 U.S.C. 6311(g)(1)(E). These ESSA provisions became effective December 10, 2016. ESSA also requires states to annually report achievement and graduation rates for children in foster care. 20 U.S.C. 6311(h)(1)(C)(ii) and (iii).

There were 5,716 children in North Carolina who entered foster care during the 2016-2017 state fiscal year (July 1 through June 30).[8] Two out of three of those children experienced at least two placements and more than one out of four experienced four or more placements during their first year in care.

| 1 Placement | 2 Placements | 3 Placements | 4+ Placements |
|---|---|---|---|
| 35% | 21% | 13% | 28% |

Almost half of the children entering foster care in the 2016-2017 year were school age.

| Ages | 0-5 | 6-12 | 13-17 |
|---|---|---|---|
|  | 54% | 29% | 17% |

---

[8] Statistical information discussed in this section was obtained from D. F. Duncan, A. Flair, C. J. Stewart, J.S. Vaughn, S. Guest, R.A. Rose, and K.M.D. Malley, Jordan Institute for Families, University of North Carolina at Chapel Hill, School of Social Work, in "Management Assistance for Child Welfare, Work First, and Food & Nutrition Services in North Carolina" (v3.2, 2019) for "Child Welfare." Individual county and judicial district data are also available on this website. Last visited October 31, 2019.

Each placement, whether it is an initial or subsequent placement, may result in a child's relocation to a home that is located in a different school district than the school district the child was enrolled in at the time of his or her removal and/or change in placement. A change in placement may also result in a child being assigned to a different school located within the same school district.

A total of 16,752 children were in foster care at some point during the 2016-2017 fiscal year in North Carolina. Most children who enter foster care in North Carolina remain in care for more than one year. While a child is in foster care, he or she is at risk of experiencing a change in placement. Data about the length of a child's placement in foster care is collected at regular intervals with the longest data point being 1,080 days (essentially three years) in care. Statistics from the 2015-2016 state fiscal year capture the most recent long-term data. Children who came into foster care during that fiscal year stayed in foster care a median number of 477 days (or 1.3 years); one-third of those children remained in care for more than 720 days (almost 2 years), and one in six (16%) remained in care for more than 1,080 days. The majority of those children were school age.

| Ages | 0-5 | 6-12 | 13-17 | 18 and older |
|------|-----|------|-------|--------------|
|      | 39% | 32%  | 22%   | 7%           |

B. **Companion to the Fostering Connections Act.** Although ESSA was enacted in December 2015, the educational stability of children in foster care is an issue that a child welfare agency has been required to consider and address in a child's case plan since the Fostering Connections to Success and Increasing Adoption Act of 2008 (Fostering Connections). See Chapter 1.3.B.9 (discussing the Fostering Connections).

Fostering Connections requires DSS, as part of the child's case plan, to make an assurance that the child's foster care placement takes into account the appropriateness of the child's current educational setting and the proximity of the placement to the school the child was enrolled in at the time of the placement. 42 U.S.C. 675(1)(G)(i). In addition, DSS must make an assurance that it coordinated with the appropriate local school district(s) to ensure the child remains in the school the child was enrolled in at the time of each placement. 42 U.S.C. 675(1)(G)(ii)(I). Note that ESSA refers to this school as the "school of origin". *See, e.g.*, 20 U.S.C. 6311(g)(1)(E)(i). If remaining in the child's school of origin is not in the child's best interests, DSS and the new school district must assure the child's immediate and appropriate enrollment in the new school, with all the child's educational records being provided to that new school. 42 U.S.C. 675(1)(G)(ii)(II). For a discussion of access to and disclosure of educational records, see Chapter 14.5.

Best interest factors are not identified by Fostering Connections, but the child's case plan must be developed jointly with the child's parent(s) or guardian(s). 45 C.F.R. 1356.21(g)(1). As a result, the decision addressing the child's school placement and educational stability should be discussed with the child's parent or guardian. The U.S. Department of Health and Human Services (U.S. DHHS) issued Guidance on Fostering Connections that encourages child welfare agencies to develop a standard and deliberate process for determining best interests and gives examples of factors the agency may consider. Suggested factors include the child's preference, the child's safety, and the appropriateness of the educational programs in the current and new school and how those programs meet the child's needs.

Transportation to and from the child's school of origin is not specifically addressed by Fostering Connections, but the Act added to "foster care maintenance payments" payments to cover the cost of reasonable travel for the child to remain in the school in which he or she was enrolled at the time of placement. 42 U.S.C. 675(4). Additionally, the Guidance on Fostering Connections addresses payments for school transportation and states that the cost of transportation should not be a factor in determining best interests when making the school selection.

Fostering Connections places conditions on Title IV-E funding, which directly affects child welfare agencies. ESSA applies to state and local educational agencies and their applicable funding and thus complements Fostering Connections. ESSA also fills some of the gaps in Fostering Connections, such as transportation. These two laws together address school- and system-level issues to improve educational outcomes for school-age children who are placed in foster care.

### C. School Selection

ESSA requires that North Carolina's state plan include steps DPI will take to collaborate with North Carolina Department of Health and Human Services (the state agency responsible for supervising the state's child welfare system) to ensure the educational stability of children in foster care. Similar to Fostering Connections, there must be assurances that a child in foster care remains in his or her "school of origin" (the school the child is enrolled in at the time of the foster care placement), unless a determination is made that it is not in that child's best interest to do so. 20 U.S.C. 6311(g)(1)(E)(i). When a determination is made that it is not in the best interests of the child to remain in his or her school of origin, he or she must be immediately enrolled in the new school, even if the educational records are not available at the time of enrollment. 20 U.S.C. 6311(g)(1)(E)(ii). The new school contacts the former school to obtain the child's relevant educational records. 20 U.S.C. 6311(g)(1)(E)(iii). The educational stability provisions apply for the child's duration in foster care and not just to a specific placement or a school district's academic year. *See* 20 U.S.C. 6312(c)(5)(B).

**Practice Note:** School selection decisions are made at each placement change, starting with the child's initial removal. A decision as to whether it is in the child's best interests to remain in the school of origin may differ based on new circumstances created by the subsequent placement change. It is also possible that the child's school of origin will change during the time he or she is in foster care. For example, the child may transfer schools at the initial placement, making the new school the child's school of origin when a subsequent placement change is made.

Best interest factors regarding school selection include

- consideration of the appropriateness of the child's current educational setting and
- the proximity of the foster care placement to the child's school of origin.

20 U.S.C. 6311(g)(1)(E)(i).

Best interest factors are also discussed in the 2016 [Non-Regulatory Guidance: Ensuring Educational Stability for Children in Foster Care](#) that was jointly issued by the U.S. DOE and U.S. DHHS. Additional suggested best interests factors include

- the child's, the parent's, and if applicable the educational decision-maker's preferences;
- the child's attachment to the school or persons in the school;
- the placement of the child's siblings;
- how the school's climate impacts the child (including the child's safety);
- the availability and quality of the services that will meet the child's educational and socio-emotional needs, including when applicable the receipt and availability of special education and related services and/or English language services;
- the child's history of school transfers and the impact of those transfers on the child; and
- the length of the commute and its impact on the child.

ESSA does not specify the process for how the best interests determination is made or how to resolve a dispute. When read with the Fostering Connections Act, the decision is part of the child's case plan, which is developed by DSS in consultation with the parents and others. The jointly issued guidance from the U.S. DOE and U.S. DHHS states that absent a law to the contrary, the child welfare agency (DSS) should be the final decision maker given its unique position to access non-educational information that would be part of the decision, such as the child's safety, sibling placements, and permanency goals. According to North Carolina Department of Health and Human Services (NC DHHS) Division of Social Services child welfare policy, the decision should be made in a Child and Family Team (CFT) meeting and Best Interests Determination (BID) meeting, which are both part of the child welfare case. *See* DIV. OF SOC. SERVS., N.C. DEP'T OF HEALTH & HUMAN SERVICES, CHILD WELFARE MANUAL "Permanency Planning," available [here](#). [Joint guidance](#) issued by DPI and NC DHHS also addresses a dispute resolution process, which states DSS makes the final decision. However, a parent, child, or custodian may request an informal review by the DSS director in consultation with the DSS ESSA point of contact. The child remains in the school of origin with transportation provided while the dispute is being resolved.

---

**Practice Note:** Although not addressed in the federal statute or state policy, a parent or child who disagrees with the DSS decision regarding the child's best interests may raise that issue before the court hearing the abuse, neglect, or dependency action. The Juvenile Code requires the court to consider the child's best interests, including whether the child should remain in his or her community of residence. G.S. 7B-900; 7B-505(d); 7B-903(a1). The court is also authorized to delegate decision-making, including educational decisions, for a child who is in DSS custody to a parent, foster parent, or other individual. G.S. 7B-903.1(a).

---

### D. Transportation

ESSA requires that local school districts submit a plan to, and receive approval of the plan from, the state education agency (in North Carolina, DPI). 20 U.S.C 6312(a). These local plans must provide assurances that the school district will develop and implement written procedures that govern how transportation will be arranged for, provided, and funded for children in foster care who remain in their school of origin. 20 U.S.C. 6312(c)(5)(B). The plan must ensure that children in foster care needing transportation

- will promptly receive transportation in a cost-effective manner and in accordance with the provisions regulating foster care maintenance payments and
- that when additional costs arise, the school will provide transportation if either the local DSS agrees to reimburse the school, the local school agrees to pay for the cost, or the school and DSS agree to share the costs.

20 U.S.C. 6312(c)(5)(B).

If an agreement cannot be reached, ESSA does not designate a mandated dispute resolution process, but NC DHHS Division of Social Services child welfare policy does. ESSA does not allow for a child's delay in "promptly" receiving transportation to his or her school of origin because of a dispute over transportation between the school district(s) and DSS.

> **Resource:** For North Carolina guidance on the responsibility for and payment of transportation requirements under ESSA, see "Every Student Succeeds Act: Ensuring Educational Stability for Children and Youth in Foster Care in North Carolina" joint guidance issued by the North Carolina Department of Public Instruction and Division of Social Services.

### E. Designated Points of Contact

ESSA requires collaboration between the state education agency (DPI) and child welfare agencies as well as between local schools and child welfare agencies. As such, DPI must designate an employee who will serve as a point of contact for child welfare agencies and who will oversee the implementation of DPI's responsibilities under ESSA. The point of contact must be someone other than the State's homeless student coordinator designated under the McKinney-Vento Homeless Assistance Act. 20 U.S.C. 6311(g)(1)(E)(iv).

A county DSS may designate an employee who will serve as a point of contact to local school districts. If DSS gives written notice to the school district of its (DSS) local point of contact, the school district must also designate a point of contact. 20 U.S.C. 6312(c)(5)(A). The joint guidance from the U.S. DOE and U.S. DHHS discusses the role of the local points of contact. Some of the suggested responsibilities include serving as primary contacts for the respective agencies, ensuring compliance with ESSA provisions, documenting best interests determinations, developing transportation procedures including cost agreements, managing disputes, facilitating the transfer of needed records, and providing training to staff on ESSA provisions and the educational needs of children in foster care.

> **Resources:**
> Information about ESSA and the local points of contact for both DSS and local school districts are available through the SERVE Center at the University of North Carolina at Greensboro, here.

For more information about North Carolina's policies regarding educational stability for children in foster care, see
- "EVERY STUDENT SUCCEEDS ACT: ENSURING EDUCATIONAL STABILITY FOR CHILDREN AND YOUTH IN FOSTER CARE IN NORTH CAROLINA" joint guidance issued by the North Carolina Department of Public Instruction and Division of Social Services (Jan. 2017)
- DIV. OF SOC. SERVS., N.C. DEP'T OF HEALTH & HUMAN SERVICES, CHILD WELFARE MANUAL "Permanency Planning," available here.

For a discussion about ESSA and North Carolina's education and child welfare laws, see Sara DePasquale, *School Stability for Children in Foster Care*, UNC SCH. OF GOV'T: ON THE CIVIL SIDE BLOG (Sept. 21, 2016).

For a variety of resources and information discussing laws, regulations, guidance, strategies, and data regarding educational stability for children in foster care, see
- "Education Stability" on the Legal Center for Foster Care & Education website.
- "Educational Stability for Children and Youth in Foster Care" on the Child Welfare Information Gateway website.

For federal guidance, see
- The U.S. Department of Education and U.S. Department of Health and Human Services, Non-Regulatory Guidance: Ensuring Educational Stability for Children in Foster Care (June 23, 2016).
- The U.S. Department of Health and Human Services Administration on Children, Youth and Families, Guidance on Fostering Connections to Success and Increasing Adoptions Act of 2008 (July 9, 2010).

**NC DHHS DSS Forms:**
Forms are available on the SERVE Center website, here.
- DSS 5245, Child Education Status (Feb. 2017) and Instructions.
- DSS 5137, NC Best Interest Determination Form (Feb. 2017) and Instructions.
- DSS 5135, Foster Child Immediate Enrollment Form (Feb. 2017) and Instructions.
- DSS 5133, Foster Child Notification of Placement (Change) Form (Feb. 2017) and Instructions.

## 13.8 The Individuals with Disabilities Education Act

### A. Introduction

The Individuals with Disabilities Education Act (IDEA), Pub. L. No. 108-446, 118 Stat. 2647, was enacted in 1975 and was first known as the Education for All Handicapped Children Act (EHA), Pub. L. No. 94-142, 89 Stat. 773. IDEA is codified at 20 U.S.C. 1400 *et seq.* with accompanying regulations at 34 C.F.R. Parts 300 and 303. In addition to the federal law, North Carolina laws that comply with IDEA are codified at G.S. 115C-106.1 *et seq.*

IDEA is both an anti-discrimination and entitlement law. Its purpose is to protect the rights of children with disabilities and their parents and to improve educational results for such children. Through IDEA, children with disabilities must have access to a free appropriate public education that emphasizes special education and related services that are designed to meet such children's unique needs and prepare them for further education, employment, and independent living. IDEA also requires states to have a statewide, multidisciplinary, interagency system of early intervention services for infants and toddlers with disabilities and their families. 20 U.S.C. 1400.

The purposes, eligibility criteria, services, and procedural requirements under IDEA vary depending on the child's age. The differences are set forth in two separate parts of the law:

- Part B: children with disabilities, ages 3 through 21, and
- Part C: infants and toddlers with disabilities, under 3 years of age.

The role of a parent under IDEA is important. Under both parts, parents are involved in the process of determining their child's eligibility for services, the development of individualized educational or family service plans, and the provision of services to their children. Parents may utilize procedural safeguards that are available to them to protect their rights and the rights of their children.

IDEA allows for a parent to continue to assert his or her rights under IDEA even when the child is placed in DSS custody through a court order. Additionally, IDEA prohibits a DSS employee from acting as the child's parent under IDEA, even though the DSS social worker is often a decision-maker for other school related issues involving a child who is placed in DSS custody. *See* 34 C.F.R. 300.30(a)(3) and 303.27(a)(3), (b)(2). *See also* G.S. 7B-903.1(a) ("except as prohibited by federal law" language when authorizing DSS to make decisions for the child). Because the provisions of IDEA regarding the "parent" decision-maker differ from what is traditionally thought of when a court order in an abuse, neglect, or dependency action places the child in the custody of DSS or a third party, familiarity with the IDEA provisions regarding "parent" and "surrogate parent" are important. When understanding these provisions, DSS, the child's guardian ad litem, or the parent may raise the issue with the court hearing the abuse, neglect, or dependency action so that the court can enter an order designating who is the IDEA parent or when necessary, appointing a surrogate parent. See section 13.8.D, below (discussing parent and surrogate parent).

IDEA is a complex and comprehensive education law that consists of four parts (Parts A–D). The discussion in this Manual is limited to a general overview of selected portions of IDEA with an emphasis on those provisions that relate to children who have been substantiated for abuse, neglect, or dependency and/or have been placed in the custody of DSS as a result. The parties, attorneys, and the court involved in abuse, neglect, or dependency cases should be familiar with the IDEA provisions that specifically apply to children who are "wards of the state." *See, e.g.*, 20 U.S.C. 1401(36) and 1415(b)(2)(A)(i).

In addition, parties, attorneys, and the courts should be aware of the rights and protections under IDEA as children in foster care are 2.5 to 3.5 times more likely to receive special education services when compared to children who are not in foster care. Research studies also suggest that children in foster care who receive special education services are placed in more restrictive educational settings, have poorer quality educational plans, and experience significant delays in the receipt of special education and related services when compared to peers who are not in foster care.[9]

**Resources:**
The N.C. Department of Public Instruction maintains on its website a section for "Exceptional Children," which contains resources, policies, data, a directory of agency contact information by substantive area, model statewide forms, and other information about the implementation of IDEA in North Carolina. For the state policy, see Policies Governing Services for Children with Disabilities (Amended March 2018) under the "Policies" tab. The policy is cited as NC 1500–1508.

For additional information about IDEA and children in foster care, see the
- "Special Education" section of the Legal Center for Foster Care & Education website by the ABA Center on Children and the Law.
- "Special Education" page of the Child Welfare Information Gateway, U.S. Department of Health and Human Services website.

## B. Part B of IDEA: Children Ages 3–21

A child is eligible for the protections and services under IDEA if he or she is a "child with a disability" as that term is defined. Services and protections consist of

- comprehensive evaluations in all suspected areas of disability;
- the development and implementation of an individual education program (IEP), which provides special education and related services to a child with a disability, so that the child receives a "free appropriate public education" (FAPE) that meets his or her unique needs in the "least restrictive environment" (LRE); and
- procedural safeguards for parents and their children.

**1. Qualifying disability.** The definition of "a child with a disability" consists of two prongs. The child

- has at least one of the enumerated categories of disability and
- because of that disability requires special education and related services.

20 U.S.C. 1401(3); 34 C.F.R. 300.8(a); *see* G.S. 115C-106.3(1).

---

[9] NATIONAL WORKING GROUP ON FOSTER CARE AND EDUCATION, "Fostering Success in Education: National Factsheet on the Educational Outcomes of Children in Foster Care" (April 2018).

**(a) Categories of disability.** IDEA specifies fourteen categories of disability:

- Autism,
- Deaf-blindness,
- Deafness,
- Development delay,
- Emotional disturbance (also referred to as severe emotional disturbance),
- Hearing impairment,
- Intellectual disability (formerly referred to as mental retardation),
- Multiple disabilities,
- Orthopedic impairment,
- Other health impairment,
- Specific learning disability,
- Speech or language impairment,
- Traumatic brain injury, and
- Visual impairment including blindness.

20 U.S.C. 1401(3); 34 C.F.R. 300.8; *see* G.S. 115C-106.3(1), (2).

Each disabling condition has its own set of criteria under IDEA that can be found at 34 C.F.R. 300.8(b) and (c). *See also* 20 U.S.C. 1401(30) (definition of "specific learning disability"). States have discretion to determine the age range for children who qualify as having a developmental delay. 20 U.S.C. 1401(3)(B); 34 C.F.R. 300.111(b). In North Carolina, a developmental delay applies to children ages 3 through 7. G.S. 115C-106.3(2).

**(b) Need for special education and related services.** The existence of a condition (e.g., a mental health diagnosis or a clubfoot) does not in and of itself automatically qualify the child as a child with a disability under IDEA. IDEA requires that the child also need special education and related services because of the disabling condition. The need for special education, not the diagnosis (if there is one), is determinative. If a child only needs a related service without special education services, he or she does not qualify as a student with a disability under IDEA. 34 C.F.R. 300.8(a)(2)(i). However, if the related service for that particular child is considered special education for that child (e.g., a child with a speech impairment requires speech therapy as his or her specialized instruction), then that child qualifies a a child with a disability under IDEA. 34 C.F.R. 300.8(a)(2)(ii).

**Special education.** IDEA defines special education as specially designed instruction that meets the unique needs of the child with a disability. Specially designed instruction involves adapting the content, methodology, or delivery of instruction and includes adaptive physical education. Special education may be provided in the classroom, home, hospital, institution, or other setting. It is provided at no cost to parents, although parents may be charged incidental fees that are normally charged to nondisabled students or their parents as part of the regular education program. 20 U.S.C. 1401(29); 34 C.F.R. 300.39; *see* G.S. 115C-106.3(20).

**Related service.** A related service is a needed supportive service that assists a child with a disability in benefitting from special education. Related services include transportation; speech-language pathology and audiology services; interpreting services for children with hearing impairments; psychological, social work, and counseling services; physical and occupational therapy; recreation services; orientation and mobility services; and school nurse and certain diagnostic medical services that assist a child with a disability to benefit from special education. 20 U.S.C. 1401(26); 34 C.F.R. 300.34.

Parent counseling and training is also a related service. It is given to parents to assist them in understanding the special needs of their children by providing information about child development and helping parents acquire necessary skills to support the implementation of their child's individual education plan (IEP). 34 C.F.R. 300.34(c)(8).

> **Practice Note:** Services are determined on an individualized basis due to the child's unique needs. A child who is in foster care, which is a temporary placement, may require parent training for the foster parent who is currently caring for the child as well as for the parent, relative, guardian, or custodian with whom the child will be placed for his or her permanent plan.

**(c) The child's evaluation and disability determination.** The initial determination as to whether a child is an eligible child with a disability is based on a full and individual evaluation. 20 U.S.C. 1414(a)(1); *see* 34 C.F.R. 300.301(a). A child must also be reevaluated at least once every three years unless the parent and school agree an evaluation is unnecessary, and a parent or teacher may request that a child be reevaluated sooner than every three years. 20 U.S.C. 1414(a)(2); 34 C.F.R. 300.303. A child may not be determined to no longer qualify as a child with a disability without a reevaluation. 20 U.S.C. 1414(c)(5)(A); 34 C.F.R. 300.305(e).

The evaluation cannot be based on one single assessment but instead must use a variety of assessment tools, including information provided by the parent, a classroom observation, and observations by teachers and related service providers. 20 U.S.C. 1414(b)(2), (c)(1)(A); 34 C.F.R. 300.304(b), 300.305(a), and 300.310(a). When a child is out of school or not school age, there must be an observation of the child in an environment that is appropriate for children that age. 34 C.F.R. 300.310(c). The evaluation must assess the child in all areas of suspected disability and include if appropriate, health, vision, hearing, social and emotional status, general intelligence, academic performance, communicative status, and motor abilities. 20 U.S.C. 1414(b)(3)(B); 34 C.F.R. 300.304(c)(4). The evaluation must gather relevant functional, developmental, and academic information to assist in the determination of (1) whether the child is a child with a disability and (2) if so, the components of the child's individual education program (IEP). 20 U.S.C. 1414(b)(2)(A); 34 C.F.R. 300.304(b).

If a parent disagrees with a school's evaluation, he or she has a right to obtain an independent educational evaluation at public expense. 20 U.S.C. 1415(b)(1); 34 C.F.R. 300.502. A parent may also provide to the school or public agency an evaluation he or she obtained for the child, and that evaluation must be considered when determining whether the child qualifies as a child with a disability. 34 C.F.R. 300.502(c).

> **Practice Note**: As part of an abuse, neglect, or dependency case, a child may have received an evaluation that contains important information about his or her functional, developmental, or academic needs in addition to his or her social or emotional status. The information in the evaluation may be helpful in the determination of whether the child qualifies as a child with a disability under IDEA and if so, what services should be provided. Although confidentiality provisions apply to records obtained by DSS in an abuse, neglect, or dependency case, it is possible that the evaluation (or a redacted version) may be shared. Redisclosure by a parent who has obtained a copy pursuant to G.S. 7B-700 will be based on various factors that are specific to the case, including whether the parent is "acting responsibly" for the child (*see* 10A N.C.A.C. 69.0101(1)), local court rules, DSS policy, and any court orders. A clear avenue for sharing the evaluation (or a redacted version) is for DSS, on its own initiative or upon request by the school, parent, or other individual (e.g., foster parent), to provide a copy directly to the school pursuant to G.S. 7B-3100. Additionally, a court order may be requested by a party in the abuse, neglect, or dependency action that specifically authorizes the disclosure of the evaluation (or redacted version) to the school or public agency for the purpose of determining whether the child qualifies for special education services as a child with a disability, and if so, what services are needed.

The school-initiated evaluation requires informed parental consent and must be completed within sixty days of the school's receipt of that consent. Exceptions to that time limit are when (1) a parent fails to make the child available for the evaluation or (2) a child has transferred schools during this time period and the parent and new school agree to a different specific time period for the evaluation to be completed. 20 U.S.C. 1414(a)(1)(C)(ii); 34 C.F.R. 300.301(c), (d).

After the evaluation has been completed, the determination of whether the child is or continues to be a child with a disability is made by the "individual education program (IEP) Team," which includes the parent. 20 U.S.C. 1414(b)(4). See subsection 3, below, for a discussion of the IEP Team.

> **Practice Note:** A child who is diagnosed with a disability but does not qualify for special education services under IDEA may require reasonable accommodations and modifications under other federal anti-discrimination laws, such as Title II of the Americans with Disabilities Act or Section 504 of the Rehabilitation Act of 1973. See section 13.5, above, discussing the ADA.

**Resources:**
For more information about Section 504 of the Rehabilitation Act, see
- "Parent and Educator Resource Guide to Section 504 in Public Elementary and Secondary Schools" (Dec. 2016) by the U.S. Department of Education.
- "Protecting Student with Disabilities" on the "Office for Civil Rights" section of the U.S. Department of Education website.

**2. Services for children 3 to 21 years of age.** Children with disabilities must receive a "free appropriate public education" in the "least restrictive environment" through the provision of special education and related services as designated in their "individual education program." A free appropriate public education must be available to all qualifying children with disabilities, including those who have been suspended or expelled. 20 U.S.C. 1412(a)(1)(A); 34 C.F.R. 300.101(a); G.S. 115C-107.1(a)(3). In addition, a school cannot require that a child with a disability be prescribed medication to attend school, receive an evaluation to determine if the child has a disability, or receive services under IDEA. 20 U.S.C. 1412(a)(25); 34 C.F.R. 300.174. A child's eligibility for special education and related services ends upon the first of (1) a child's graduation from high school with a regular diploma or (2) the end of the school year in which the student turns 22. 20 U.S.C. 1414(c)(5)(B)(i); G.S. 115C-107.1(a)(1) and (2).

**(a) Free appropriate public education (FAPE).** A FAPE involves the provision of special education and related services that are set forth in the child's "individual educational program" (IEP). There are four components:

- **Free** - without charge to the parents. For children who receive Medicaid or other public benefits, a school may use the child's Medicaid or other public benefit to provide or pay for covered services under IDEA if the parent gives written consent to do so and receives a procedural safeguards notice of rights addressing the school's use of the benefit. 34 C.F.R. 300.154(d)(1), (d)(2)(iv) and (v). Any co-pay or deductible must be paid by the school. *See* 34 C.F.R. 300.154(d)(2)(ii). However, a school may not condition a child's receipt of a FAPE on a parent enrolling his or her child in a public benefit program. 34 C.F.R. 300.154(d)(2)(i). A school may not charge Medicaid or other public benefits if the school's use would decrease the child's available lifetime coverage, result in the family paying for services that would otherwise be covered and are required for the child when the child is not in school, increase premiums or discontinue benefits, or risk loss of eligibility for home and community-based waiver programs because of aggregated health-related expenditures. 34 C.F.R. 300.154(d)(2)(iii).

- **Appropriate** - receives an educational benefit. The educational services must meet the standards of the state board. 20 U.S.C. 1401(9)(B); G.S. 115C-106.3(4)b. The services should be reasonably calculated to enable the child to receive an educational benefit but do not require that the child receive the maximum or optimal benefit. *Bd. of Educ. of Hendrick Hudson Cent. Sch. Dist., Westchester County v. Rowley*, 458 U.S. 176 (1982). The core of IDEA is a focus on the particular child, which contemplates that child's individual levels of achievement, disability, and potential for growth. *Endrew F. ex rel. Joseph F. v. Douglas County Sch. Dist. RE-1*, 137 S.Ct. 988 (2017).

    For children who are integrated in the regular education classroom, an educational benefit includes services that are reasonably calculated to enable the child to achieve passing marks and advance from grade to grade. *Bd. of Educ. of Hendrick Hudson Cent. Sch. Dist., Westchester County*, 458 U.S. 176.

For a child who is not fully integrated in the regular classroom and is not able to achieve grade level, an educational benefit is progress appropriate in the light of the child's circumstances. The progress must be more than de minimis and appropriately ambitious to meet challenging objectives that are based on the child's unique needs. *Endrew F. ex rel. Joseph F. v. Douglas County Sch. Dist. RE-1*, 137 S.Ct. 988.

- **Public** - at public expense and under public supervision and direction. IDEA applies public schools including public charter schools. 20 U.S.C 1413(a)(5); 34 C.F.R. 300.209.

- **Education** – applies to preschool, elementary, and secondary school. Education includes academic and nonacademic programs to address a child's academic and functional needs. Children with disabilities must have available to them a variety of educational programs (e.g., art, music, industrial arts, and vocational education) that are available to children without disabilities and must have an equal opportunity to participate in nonacademic and extracurricular activities (e.g., athletics and special interest clubs). 34 C.F.R. 300.107 and 300.110.

20 U.S.C. 1401(9); 34 C.F.R. 300.17; G.S. 115C-106.3(4).

**(b) Least restrictive environment (LRE).** The LRE requires that a child with a disability is educated, to the maximum extent appropriate, with children who are not disabled. 20 U.S.C. 1412(a)(5)(A); 34 C.F.R. 300.114(a)(2)(i); G.S. 115C-106.3(10). The LRE addresses the setting or placement where a child with a disability receives educational services and consists of a continuum of placements, the least restrictive of which is the regular education classroom. The continuum of LRE placements include regular classes, special classes, special schools, home instruction, and instruction in hospitals and institutions. 34 C.F.R. 300.115. When an alternative setting outside of the school is required, the LRE is the setting that is as close as possible to the child's home. 34 C.F.R. 300.116(b)(3).

A child with a disability should only be removed from the regular education environment when the nature or severity of the child's disability is such that his or her education cannot be satisfactorily achieved in that setting with the use of supplementary aids and services. 20 U.S.C. 1412(a)(5)(A); 34 C.F.R. 300.114(a)(2)(ii); G.S. 115C-106.3(10). *See* G.S. 115C-107.2(b)(2). Although a child with a disability may not be able to remain in the regular education classroom for instruction, he or she may be able to participate with nondisabled peers in nonacademic settings and/or extracurricular activities such as meals and recess. 34 C.F.R. 300.117.

**(c) Individual Education Program (IEP).** The IEP is a written document for the child that is developed, reviewed, and revised according to the requirements set forth in 20 U.S.C. 1414(d), 20 U.S.C. 1401(14), 34 C.F.R. 300.22 and 300.320, and G.S. 115C-106.3(8). An IEP must be in place at the beginning of every school year and be reviewed at least annually. 20 U.S.C. 1414(d)(2)(A), (d)(4)(A)(i); 34 C.F.R. 300.323(a) and 300.324(b)(1)(i). Revisions may be needed as result of a lack of expected progress toward the annual goals, results of a reevaluation, information to or from the parent regarding the need for additional data about the child's needs, or the child's anticipated needs. 34 C.F.R. 300.324(b)(1)(ii).

The IEP details the student's educational program and includes the special education and related services and modifications that will be provided to the student. The IEP must consist of "an education program reasonably calculated to enable a child to make progress appropriate in light of the child's circumstances." *Endrew F. ex rel. Joseph F. v. Douglas County Sch. Dist. RE-1*, 137 S.Ct. 988, 1001 (2017).

IDEA requires that the IEP contain specific criteria, which are established in 20 U.S.C. 1414(d). Some of the required IEP content involve the identification of the student's problem areas, current level of academic and functional performance, annual academic and functional goals, and a description of how the child's progress toward meeting those annual goals will be periodically measured and reported (e.g., with quarterly report cards). The IEP must specify the LRE and when applicable, explain why the child will not participate with nondisabled peers in the regular education setting. *See* 20 U.S.C. 1414(d)(1)(A)(i); 34 C.F.R. 300.320(a)(5). When a child's behavior impedes his or her learning (or the learning of others), the IEP should include a positive behavior intervention plan and supports to address that behavior. 20 U.S.C. 1414(d)(3)(B)(i), (C); 34 C.F.R. 300.324(a)(2)(i) and (a)(3)(i). IEPs that are in effect when the child turns 16 years old and are developed or revised after the child is 16 years old must include transition services and postsecondary goals based upon age appropriate assessments related to training, education, employment, and where appropriate, independent living skills. 20 U.S.C. 1414(d)(1)(A)(i)(VIII); 34 C.F.R. 300.320(b).

**(d) Disciplinary action resulting in school removal.** A child with a disability is subject to the school's student code of conduct and may be subject to disciplinary action for a violation of that code of conduct. *See* 20 U.S.C. 1415(k)(1); 34 C.F.R. 300.530(b), (c). When the disciplinary action for a child with a disability results in a "change in placement," additional procedures and protections apply to that child. The purpose of the additional procedures is to ensure that students with disabilities are not disciplined because of their disability. North Carolina disciplinary policies and procedures for students with disabilities must be consistent with federal law. G.S. 115C-107.7(a).

A change of placement results from a child's removal from school for more than

- ten consecutive days or
- ten cumulative days during the same school year when the series of shorter-term removals constitute a pattern, which is determined by considering whether the behaviors resulting in the removals are substantially similar and the proximity between and length of each removal. The school or public agency determines whether the cumulative removals are a change in placement.

34 C.F.R. 300.536.

When there is a change of placement, the parent and relevant members of the IEP Team must hold a "manifestation determination" meeting to determine

- was the conduct in question caused by, or did it have a direct and substantial relationship to the child's disability, or
- was the conduct in question the direct result of the school's failure to implement the IEP.

20 U.S.C. 1415(k)(1)(E)(i); 34 C.F.R. 300.530(e)(1).

If the answer to either question is yes, a manifestation exists and the student cannot be disciplined. The student must be returned to the placement he or she was removed from unless the parent and school agree to a different placement. The student must also have a functional behavior assessment, and a behavior intervention plan (BIP) must be implemented or modified as necessary to address the child's behavior. 20 U.S.C. 1415(k)(1)(E)(ii), (F); 34 C.F.R. 300.530(e)(2), (f).

If the answer to both questions is no, there is no manifestation, and the student may be treated as any other student regarding disciplinary action. 20 U.S.C. 1415(k)(1)(C); 34 C.F.R. 300.530(c). A parent may appeal a manifestation determination by requesting a due process hearing. 20 U.S.C. 1415(k)(3); 34 C.F.R. 300.532(a).

Children who are suspended or expelled are entitled to a FAPE. 20 U.S.C. 1412(a)(1)(A); 34 C.F.R. 300.101(a); G.S. 115C-107.1(a)(3). As a result, educational and related services are required to be provided so as to enable the student to participate in the general curriculum (albeit in another setting) and to make progress on his or her IEP goals. 20 U.S.C. 1415(k)(1)(D)(i); 34 C.F.R. 300.530(d)(1)(i). The child should also receive a functional behavioral assessment and behavioral intervention services and modifications to address the behaviors in an effort to keep them from recurring. 20 U.S.C. 1415(k)(1)(D)(ii); 34 C.F.R. 300.530(d)(1)(ii). The IEP Team determines what services are appropriate. 34 C.F.R. 300.530(d)(5). Under North Carolina law, a student with a disability may not be placed on homebound instruction as a result of disciplinary action unless the IEP Team determines the homebound instruction is the least restrictive alternative environment for the student. If it is determined to be the least restrictive alternative environment, the homebound instruction must be evaluated by designees of the IEP Team on a monthly basis. G.S. 115C-107.7(b).

Regardless of whether there is a manifestation, a school may place a child in an "interim alternative educational setting" (IAES) for a maximum of forty-five school days when

- certain criteria involving weapons, drugs, or the infliction of serious bodily injury on another person at school or a school function exist or
- the school requests and proves at a due process hearing that the student remaining in his or her current placement is substantially likely to result in injury to self or others.

20 U.S.C. 1415(k)(1)(G), (k)(3)(A) and (B)(ii)(II), (k)(7); 34 C.F.R. 300.530(g), (i).

The IEP Team determines the IAES. 20 U.S.C. 1415(k)(2); 34 C.F.R. 300.531. If the parent disagrees with the IAES, he or she has a right to an expedited due process hearing. 20 U.S.C. 1415(k)(4)(B); 34 C.F.R. 300.532(a), (c).

All of these protections apply to a child who has not been determined to be eligible for special education and related services when the school had knowledge that the child was a child with a disability before the child engaged in the behavior that resulted in his or her removal. 20 U.S.C. 1415(k)(5)(A); 34 C.F.R. 300.534(a). Unless the child was determined to not be a "child with a disability" or the parent refused special education and related services for his or her child, a school is deemed to have knowledge when

- the parent wrote to the teacher or supervisory or administrative personnel about concerns that the child needs special education and related services;
- the parent requested an evaluation of the child; or
- the child's teacher or other school personnel expressed specific concerns to supervisory personnel about a pattern of behavior by the child.

20 U.S.C. 1415(k)(5)(B) and (C); 34 C.F.R. 300.534(b), (c).

North Carolina law also addresses "basis of knowledge." The school is deemed to have a basis of knowledge if prior to the behavior that precipitated the disciplinary action, the child's behavior and performance "clearly and convincingly" establishes the need for special education. Prior disciplinary infractions alone do not constitute clear and convincing evidence. G.S. 115C-107.7(c).

Children who are suspended or expelled may be referred for an evaluation to determine eligibility for services. 20 U.S.C. 1415(k)(5)(D)(ii); 34 C.F.R. 300.534(d)(2).

**(e) School transfer.** When a child with a disability transfers school districts or enrolls in a new school within the same school year, the new school must provide the child with a FAPE. The new school, after consulting with the parent, must provide services that are comparable to those described in the IEP that had been in effect at the previous school until

- the new school holds an IEP Team meeting and either adopts the IEP from the previous school or develops a new IEP in those cases where the school transfer is within North Carolina or
- the new school conducts an evaluation if it determines one is necessary and develops a new IEP when the transfer is from outside of North Carolina.

20 U.S.C. 1414(d)(2)(C)(i); 34 C.F.R. 300.323(e), (f).

---

**Practice Note:** The Every Student Succeeds Act and Fostering Connections Act (discussed in section 13.7, above) apply to children in foster care who, as a result of an initial removal or a change in placement, may now be living in a geographic area zoned to a different school or school district. Under those federal laws, a child remaining in the school in which he or she was enrolled at the time of an initial or changed placement is preferred. A school transfer should only occur after there has been a determination by the DSS social worker, parent, school district representative, child (if appropriate), and others that it is in the child's best interests to transfer schools.

**3. Decision-making by the IEP Team.** IDEA utilizes a team approach to decision-making. The team consists of a group of professionals and the child's parents and is referred to as the IEP Team. The IEP Team is responsible for

- reviewing the evaluations and determining whether a child is a child with a disability and if so, under what disabling condition (34 C.F.R. 300.306(a));
- developing, reviewing, and revising the child's IEP (34 C.F.R. 300.23 and 300.324); and
- conducting manifestation determinations and functional behavioral assessments, developing or modifying behavior intervention plans, and determining an interim alternative educational setting when there has been a change in placement resulting from disciplinary action (34 C.F.R. 300.530(e), (f) and 300.531).

20 U.S.C. 1414(b)(4)(A), (d)(3) and (4); 1415(k)(1)(E) and (F), (k)(2).

The IEP Team is composed of

- The child's parents;
- at least one regular education teacher for the child (if the child is or may be in the regular education setting);
- at least one special education teacher or provider for the child;
- a school district representative who knows about the general curriculum and the availability of the school's resources and is qualified to provide or supervise special education services;
- an individual who can interpret the instructional implications of the evaluation results (this may be someone who is a member of the team under different criteria);
- persons or agencies who have knowledge or special expertise about the child, including related services personnel, that are invited by the parent or school; and
- the child, when appropriate.

20 U.S.C. 1414(d)(1)(B); 34 C.F.R. 300.321.

**Practice Note:** Children in DSS custody have a team of professionals and support persons, such as the court-appointed guardian ad litem, current and former placement providers, the DSS social worker, other service providers, and relatives. A parent may determine that any of these individuals have knowledge or special expertise about the child and invite them to be members of the IEP Team. *See* 34 C.F.R. 300.321(c). Their participation as an IEP Team member may be especially helpful in situations where the child has experienced a number of placement changes or the need to transfer to a new school.

An IEP Team member may participate in the meeting by alternative means, such as video or conference calls. 20 U.S.C. 1414(f); 34 C.F.R. 300.322(c), 300.328, and 300.501(c)(3).

Parents are equal members of the IEP Team. IDEA requires that parents must be afforded an opportunity to inspect and review their child's educational records and to participate in meetings regarding the identification, evaluation, educational placement, and provision of a FAPE to their child. 34 C.F.R. 300.501 and 300.613; G.S. 115C-109.3(a). The school must take steps to ensure that one or both parents are present at each IEP Team meeting or afforded the opportunity to participate, and meetings should be scheduled at a mutually agreeable time and place. 34 C.F.R. 300.322(a). When a school is unable to convince a parent to attend, the IEP Team meeting may proceed without the parent, but the school must keep a record (e.g., notes of telephone calls made or attempted or visits to the home or workplace, copies of written correspondence) of its attempts to schedule a mutually agreed on time and place for the meeting. 34 C.F.R. 300.322(d) and 300.501(c)(4).

### 4. Procedural safeguards.

(a) **Prior written notice.** The school must provide parents with prior written notice of an IEP Team meeting. 34 C.F.R. 300.322(a)(1). Prior written notice must also be provided to a parent within a reasonable time before a school proposes or refuses to initiate or change a child's identification as a child with a disability, an evaluation, the educational placement, or the provision of a FAPE to the child. 20 U.S.C. 1415(b)(3), (c)(1); 34 C.F.R. 300.503; G.S. 115C-109.5. Parents of a child with a disability must also be given a copy of the procedural safeguards notice once per school year and at other times designated in 34 C.F.R. 300.504(a) and G.S. 115C-109.1.

(b) **Mediation.** A school must establish a mediation process to resolve disputes involving any matter under IDEA, even before a complaint or due process hearing is requested. 20 U.S.C. 1415(e)(1); 34 C.F.R. 300.506(a); *see* G.S. 115C-109.4(a). Participation in mediation is voluntary and cannot be used to delay or deny a complaint or due process hearing. 20 U.S.C. 1415(e)(2)(A); 34 C.F.R. 300.506(b); G.S. 115-109.4(b). The mediation must be held at a mutually convenient time and location and be conducted by a qualified and impartial mediator who is not an employee of the North Carolina Department of Public Instruction or the school district that is involved in the education or care of the child. 20 U.S.C. 1415(e)(2)(A)(iii) and (e)(2)(E); 34 C.F.R. 300.506(b)(1)(iii), (b)(5), (c); G.S. 115C-109.4(b)(3), (f).

(c) **Due process hearings.** Parents may appeal an IEP Team decision regarding eligibility, evaluation, services (FAPE), location of the program (LRE), and manifestation determination. 20 U.S.C. 1412(a)(6)(A), 1415(f) and (k)(3); 34 C.F.R. 300.507(a) and 300.536(b)(2); G.S. 115C-109.6(a). The appeal involves an administrative due process hearing before an administrative hearing officer. The request for a due process hearing is filed with the Office of Administrative Hearings and a copy must be provided to the designated contact at the North Carolina Department of Public Instruction (DPI) and the superintendent or director of special education for the school district or public agency. G.S. 115C-109.6(a); *see* 34 C.F.R. 300.508(a)(2). Absent a statutory exception, the request for a due process hearing must be filed within one year of when the parent knew or should have known of the alleged action that is the basis of the hearing request. G.S. 115C-109.6(b), (c). Specific procedures, including the notice, dispute resolution, and the hearing are set forth in 34 C.F.R. 300.508 through 300.512 and G.S. 115C-109.6 and 115C-109.7. The administrative hearing decision is final unless it is appealed to the Exceptional Children Division of DPI, where an impartial review of the decision is made by a Review Officer. G.S. 115C-109.9(a). *See* 20 U.S.C. 1415(g); 34 C.F.R. 300.514 The review officer may seek additional evidence and/or arguments from the parties. 34 C.F.R. 300.514(b)(2)(iii) and (iv). The DPI decision is final unless it is appealed to state or federal court. 20 U.S.C. 1415(i)(2) and (3)(A); 34 C.F.R. 300.516(a), (d); G.S. 115C-109.9(a), (d).

During the appeal process, unless the child is in an interim alternative educational setting under the disciplinary provisions of IDEA, the child remains in his or her then-current educational placement (commonly referred to as "stay put") unless the parties agree in writing to a different educational placement. 20 U.S.C. 1415(k)(4)(A), (j); 34 C.F.R. 300.518; G.S. 115C-109.9(e).

**(d) Complaint filed with the N.C. Department of Public Instruction (DPI).** A parent, individual, or organization may file a complaint with DPI alleging that a school district, a public agency, or DPI has violated the provisions of IDEA. *See* 34 C.F.R. 300.151 and 300.152. Complaint procedures are set forth in 34 C.F.R. 300.152 and involve an investigation of the allegation by DPI. The complaint must be filed within one year of when the alleged violation occurred. 34 C.F.R. 300.153(c). Possible remedies for a school district's failure to provide appropriate services include a corrective action plan that would address the individual child's needs (e.g., compensatory services) and the future provision of appropriate services for all children with disabilities. 34 C.F.R. 300.151(b).

**Practice Note:** DSS, a child's guardian ad litem, a parent, and others have standing to file a complaint alleging violations of IDEA related to a specific child or resulting from an observed systemic pattern of noncompliance by a school, school district, or public agency.

**Resources:**
The N.C. Department of Public Instruction has on the "Exceptional Children" section of its website
- "Parent Rights & Responsibilities in Special Education: Notice of Procedural Safeguards" (July 2016).
- Model Statewide Forms, which include "prior notice" forms and accompanying instructions.
- Procedures and Model Forms for Mediation, Due Process Hearings, and Complaints.

## C. Part C of IDEA: Children under 3 Years of Age

Part C of IDEA requires states to provide a coordinated multidisciplinary system of early intervention services for infants and toddlers with disabilities and their families to address the need to (1) minimize children's potential for developmental delay and need for special education and related services when these children become school age, (2) maximize the potential for individuals with disabilities to live independently, (3) enhance the capacity of families to meet the infants' and toddlers' special needs, and (4) enhance the capacity of the State and service providers to identify, evaluate, and meet the needs of all children, especially children who are minorities, low-income, live in rural or inner-city areas, or are in foster care. 20 U.S.C. 1431. *See* G.S. 143B-139.6A.

North Carolina's Early Intervention Branch (NCEI) is part of the state's Division of Public Health and is the lead agency for the Infant and Toddler Program (NC ITP), which is North Carolina's early intervention program. There are seventeen regional Children's Developmental Service Agencies (CDSA) in the Infant and Toddler program. The CDSAs accept referrals, contact families, determine eligibility, provide for services (including through contract agencies), and develop and review the "individualized family service plan" (IFSP).

---

**Resources:**
For more information about North Carolina's early intervention program, see
- The North Carolina Infant-Toddler Program website by the N.C. Department of Health and Human Services.
- "Special Needs" on the "Parents" section of the N.C. Department of Health and Human Services Child Development and Early Education website.
- "Early Intervention" section of the N.C. Department of Health and Human Services Medical Assistance website.
- N.C. Division of Medical Assistance, Medical and Health Choice Clinical Coverage Policy No. 8-J § 1.0 (Dec. 15, 2019).

For more information about IDEA Part C, see the Early Childhood Technical Assistance Center website.

For more information about Child Welfare and IDEA Part C, see
- CHILD WELFARE INFORMATION GATEWAY, "Addressing the Needs of Young Children in Child Welfare: Part C-Early Intervention Services" (Oct. 2018).
- The CHILD WELFARE POLICY MANUAL under the "Laws and Policies" section of the Children's Bureau, U.S. Department of Health and Human Services website, specifically "2.1I CAPTA, Assurances and Requirements, Referrals to IDEA, Part C."

---

**1. Children substantiated as abused or neglected.** Both the Child Abuse Prevention Treatment Act (CAPTA) and IDEA make specific references to the need for infants and toddlers in foster care to be referred for and, when eligible, receive early intervention services. *See* 20 U.S.C. 1431(a)(5), 1434(1) and 1437(b)(7); 42 U.S.C. 5106a(b)(2)(B)(xxi). CAPTA requires that states have procedures for referring children younger than 3 years old who have been substantiated as abused or neglected to early intervention services under Part C of IDEA. 42 U.S.C. 5106a(b)(2)(B)(xxi); *see* 20 U.S.C. 1435(c)(2)(G) and 1437(a)(6)(A); 34 C.F.R. 303.303(b). In North Carolina, referrals are made to the local Children's Developmental Services Agency (CDSA).

**2. Qualifying disability.** An infant or toddler with a disability is a child younger than 3 years old who needs early intervention services because he or she

- is experiencing developmental delays in at least one developmental area
    - cognitive,
    - physical,
    - communication,
    - social or emotional, or
    - adaptive; or
- has a diagnosed physical or mental condition that has a high probability of resulting in developmental delay (referred to in North Carolina as an "established condition").

20 U.S.C. 1432(5); 34 C.F.R. 303.21.

A child may be screened for or referred for early intervention services by parents, medical providers, social services staff, shelter staff, and others. 34 C.F.R. 303.303(c). Infants and toddlers must receive a timely comprehensive multidisciplinary evaluation of his or her functioning. 20 U.S.C. 1435(a)(3); 34 C.F.R. 303.321. No single procedure may be used as the sole determinant of whether the infant or toddler is eligible for services. Instead, the evaluation should include an evaluation instrument, information from parents and other sources, a record review, an observation of the child, and the identification of each developmental area level of functioning. 34 C.F.R. 303.321(b), (c); *see* 10A N.C.A.C. 27G.0903(1)[10]. There is also a family-directed assessment that is performed with those family members who are willing to participate. 34 C.F.R. 303.321(c)(2). The evaluation and assessment must be completed within forty-five days of when a referral is made unless an exception applies. Exceptions include the unavailability of the parent or child because of exceptional family circumstances or the parent not providing consent. 34 C.F.R. 303.310; 10A N.C.A.C. 27G.0903(1)(h), (i).

The lead agency determines whether the child is eligible. 34 C.F.R. 303.322. Criteria to meet either a developmental delay or an established condition is set forth in 10A N.C.A.C. 27G.0902. *See* 34 C.F.R. 303.10 and 303.111.

**3. Early intervention services (EI).** Eligible infants and toddlers receive early intervention services. EI are services that are provided by qualified personnel and are designed to meet the developmental needs of an infant or toddler with a disability in any of the following areas: physical, cognitive, communication, social or emotional, or adaptive development. 20 U.S.C. 1432(4)(C), (F); 34 C.F.R. 303.13(a), (c).

The services include early identification, screening, and assessment services; diagnostic and evaluative medical services; family training, counseling, and home visits; special instruction; speech and language pathology and audiology services; sign language and cued language services; occupational and physical therapy; psychological and social work services; vision services; nutrition services; assistive technology devices and services; health services that are

---

[10] Title 10A of the North Carolina Administrative Code, Chapter 27, subchapter G.

necessary to enable the infant or toddler to benefit from other early intervention services; transportation and related costs that are needed to enable the infant or toddler or family to receive another early intervention service; and service coordination. 20 U.S.C. 1432(4)(E); 34 C.F.R. 303.13(b), (d); G.S. 122C-3(13c); *see* 10A N.C.A.C. 27G.0902(3).

Early intervention services are provided under public supervision at no cost, except when federal or state law allows for a system of payments by families, such as a sliding fee. The services are provided to the maximum extent appropriate in a natural environment, including the child's home and community settings where children without disabilities participate (e.g., a child care center or Head Start program). 20 U.S.C. 1432(4)(A), (B) and (G); 34 C.F.R. 303.13(a).

If funding is available, the State Board of Education and the Secretary of the NC DHHS may enter into an agreement that allows early intervention services to continue for children with disabilities who are 3 years old until they enter or are eligible to enter kindergarten. While children are receiving continued early intervention services under Part C, they will not receive a free appropriate public education under Part B of IDEA. G.S. 115C-107.1(c); *see* 20 U.S.C. 1435(c); 34 C.F.R. 303.21(c).

**4. Individualized family service plan (IFSP).** An infant or toddler with a disability receives early intervention services through an IFSP. An IFSP includes (1) a multidisciplinary assessment of the infant's or toddler's unique needs and identifies the necessary services to meet those needs and (2) a family-directed assessment of resources, priorities, and concerns and the identification of family supports and services to enhance its capacity to meet the infant's and toddler's developmental needs. 20 U.S.C. 1436(a).

The IFSP must be in writing and include the contents specified at 20 U.S.C. 1436(d) and 34 C.F.R. 303.344. Some of the required components are the services that will be provided, the expected measurable outcomes for the infant or toddler and family, the natural environment where the services will be provided (or a justification for why the services will not be provided in the natural environment), and a designated service coordinator responsible for implementing the plan. *See* 10A N.C.A.C. 27G.0903(2). For toddlers about to age out of Part C, there must be transition planning from early intervention services to other appropriate services, including preschool services under Part B, and notice to the local school of the child's pending transition to Part B services. 20 U.S.C. 1436(d)(8) and 1437(a)(9); 34 C.F.R. 303.344(h).

When an infant or toddler is determined to be eligible for early intervention services, the IFSP meeting must be completed within forty-five days of the receipt of the referral, unless there are exceptional family circumstances or the parent does not consent. 34 C.F.R. 303.310 and 303.342(a); 10A N.C.A.C. 27G.0903(1)(h), (i). Before services may be provided, the parent must consent. 34 C.F.R. 303.342(e). A parent may decline any early intervention service for himself or herself, the infant or toddler, or other family members without jeopardizing the provision of other services. 34 C.F.R. 303.420(d); 10A N.C.A.C. 27G.0903(3)(i).

The family must be provided with a review of the plan at least every six months, and the plan must be evaluated annually. 20 U.S.C. 1436(b); 34 C.F.R. 303.342(b); 10A N.C.A.C. 27G.0903(3). The purpose of the review is to evaluate the child's progress and whether changes need to be made to the IFSP. 34 C.F.R. 303.342(b), (c).

**5. The IFSP Team.** The IFSP Team creates the IFSP. Members of the IFSP Team include

- the parent or parents,
- other family members as requested by the parent (if feasible),
- an advocate for the family if requested by the parent,
- the service coordinator designated by the local Children's Developmental Services Agency (CDSA),
- the person(s) directly involved in conducting the assessments, and
- persons who will be providing the early intervention services to the infant or toddler and family (as appropriate).

34 C.F.R. 303.343(a)(1); 10A N.C.A.C. 27G.0903(3)(c).

The IFSP meeting must be conducted at times and in settings that are convenient for the family and that are held in the family's language. 34 C.F.R. 303.342(d)(1); 10A N.C.A.C. 27G.0903(3)(j). Participants may participate through alternative means such as a telephone conference call, providing records to review at the meeting, or through an authorized representative. 34 C.F.R. 303.343(a)(2); 10 N.C.A.C. 27G.0903(3)(d).

**6. Procedural safeguards.** Required procedural protections are addressed at 20 U.S.C. 1439. *See also* 10A N.C.A.C. 27G.0905 (procedural safeguards). They include the right of parents to receive prior written notice of the proposed initiation of, change, or refusal to initiate or change the infant's or toddler's evaluation, identification, placement, or provision of early intervention services. 34 C.F.R. 303.421. Parents have the right to examine records related to screening, assessment, eligibility determinations, and the development and implementation of the IFSP and to confidentiality of personally identifying information with the right to notice of and consent to the exchange of information among agencies. 34 C.F.R. 303.401 and 303.405. Parents have the right to determine whether family members (including themselves) and/or their infant or toddler will accept or decline any early intervention services without jeopardizing other early intervention services. 34 C.F.R. 303.420(d). Parents also have the right to use the mediation procedure established under Part B of IDEA and a complaint resolution process where the parent may bring a civil action in state or federal court appealing the administrative hearing decision. 34 C.F.R. 303.430. See section 13.8.B.4, above. During the dispute resolution process, unless there is an agreement stating otherwise, the infant or toddler continues to receive the services that were being provided or that are not in dispute. 34 C.F.R. 303.430(e).

There must also be procedures to protect the infant's or toddler's rights when the parents are not known, cannot be located, or when the infant or toddler is a state ward. A surrogate parent may be appointed. 34 C.F.R. 303.422.

## D. Parent: Definition, Role, and Appointment of Surrogate Parent

**1. Parent's role.** The role of a parent under IDEA is important. A parent who suspects his or her child has a disability may make a referral for special education or early intervention services and request an evaluation. 20 U.S.C. 1414(a)(1)(B); 34 C.F.R. 303.303(c)(3). A parent's consent is required for evaluations and the initial provision of services. 20 U.S.C. 1414(a)(1)(D)(i)(I) and (c)(3), 1436(e); 34 C.F.R. 300.300(a), (b)(1), 303.342(e), and 303.420(a). A parent may also revoke consent to the continued provision of special education and related services or early intervention services. 34 C.F.R. 300.300(b)(4) and 303.7(c). A parent is a member of the IEP Team and may invite other participants the parent determines has specialized knowledge to be a member of the IEP Team. 20 U.S.C. 1414(d)(1)(B). *See* G.S. 115C-109.3(a). A parent is also a member of the IFSP Team and may invite other family members and an advocate to join the IFSP team. 34 C.F.R. 303.343(a)(1). A parent may exercise procedural safeguards, including the right to request an independent educational evaluation, mediation, or a due process hearing and to file a complaint.

Note that the rights of the parent transfer to the student when he or she turns 18 (unless the student has been determined to be incompetent). 20 U.S.C. 1415(m); 34 C.F.R. 300.520(a); G.S. 115C-109.2(a).

**2. Parent defined.** IDEA defines "parent" broadly. A "parent" is

- a biological or adoptive parent,
- a foster parent (unless state law or contractual obligations prohibit the foster parent from serving as a parent under IDEA; in North Carolina, the Department of Public Instruction policy states a therapeutic foster parent cannot act as a parent under IDEA. *See* NC 1500 2.23(a)(2) and 1504-1.20(d)(1)),
- a guardian authorized to act as the parent or make educational or early intervention decisions for the child (except for the State when the child is a "ward of the state"),
- an individual the child lives with who is acting in the place of a natural or adoptive parent (including a grandparent, stepparent, or other relative), or
- an individual who is legally responsible for the child's welfare.

20 U.S.C. 1401(23); 34 C.F.R. 300.30(a) and 303.27; G.S. 115C-106.3(14). Note that "guardian" is not defined by IDEA.

If the child does not have an IDEA parent, a surrogate parent is appointed and acts as the parent (discussed in subsection 4, below). *See* 20 U.S.C. 1415(b)(2) and 1439(a)(5); 34 C.F.R. 300.519 and 303.422; G.S. 115C-109.2(c), (d).

A child is a ward of the state when the child is in DSS custody but is not a child in foster care whose foster parent is a parent for purposes of IDEA. 20 U.S.C. 1401(36); 34 C.F.R. 300.45 and 303.37; NC 1500-2.37. Under North Carolina policy, therapeutic foster parents are not permitted to act as an IDEA parent. NC 1500-2.23(a)(2); 1504-1.20(d)(1).

**Practice Note:** A person who qualifies as an IDEA parent is not necessarily authorized to consent to educational services outside of the scope of IDEA (e.g., a school field trip) or other services outside of a school or early intervention program (e.g., medical services). Whether a person has the authority to consent to services or activities outside of IDEA identification and programming will depend on his or her legal relationship with the child, any court orders delegating or restricting that person's rights regarding the child, and applicable statutes for the presenting issue.

**3. Determining parent.** When there is more than one person who is qualified to act as the IDEA parent (e.g., the biological parent and the foster parent), a biological or adoptive parent who is attempting to act as the IDEA parent must be presumed to be the "parent." Examples of acting as an IDEA parent may be responding to prior written notices sent by the school and attending IEP Team meetings. There is an exception to this presumption when the parent does not have the legal authority to make educational decisions for the child (e.g., a court order limiting the parent's rights, a permanency planning order of guardianship or custody that does not authorize the parent to retain educational rights for the child, or a termination of parental rights order). 34 C.F.R. 300.30(b) and 303.27(b)(1); *see* 34 C.F.R. 300.300(a)(2).

When a biological or adoptive parent either does not have the legal authority to make educational decisions or in the absence of a court order addressing educational decisions, he or she is not acting as the IDEA parent, he or she is not the "parent" for purposes of IDEA. The foster parent or other person qualifying as an IDEA parent acts in that capacity.

The court hearing the abuse, neglect, or dependency action has the authority to decide who may make educational decisions for the child based on the child's best interests. The court may delegate the authority to make decisions for a child who is in DSS custody to a parent, foster parent, or other individual. G.S. 7B-903.1(a), (b). The court may also determine what (if any) rights and responsibilities remain with the parents when it is determining whether legal guardianship or custody to a third person should be established as the child's permanent plan. G.S. 7B-906.1(e)(2); *see In re M.B.*, 253 N.C. App. 437 (2017) (holding when a child's permanent plan places the child in guardianship or custody with a non-parent, the parent's rights and responsibilities, other than visitation, are lost if the court order does not provide otherwise).

If a court order identifies a person (e.g., the biological or adoptive parent, foster parent, guardian, custodian, or person the child lives with who is acting in place of the parent) to act as the IDEA parent or make educational or early intervention decisions for the child, that person must be determined to be the parent for purposes of IDEA. 34 C.F.R. 300.30(b)(2) and 303.27(b)(2). If the court appoints someone who does not meet any of the criteria of a "parent" under IDEA, the court is appointing a "surrogate parent," which is discussed further in subsection 4, below. Note, federal law prohibits a DSS employee from acting as the child's parent under IDEA. *See* 34 C.F.R. 300.30(a)(3) and 303.27(a)(3), (b)(2). *See also* G.S. 7B-903.1(a) ("except as prohibited by federal law" language when authorizing DSS to make decisions for the child).

**Practice Notes:** Absent a termination of parental rights order, a relinquishment, a court order limiting a parent's rights to make educational or early intervention services decisions for the child, or a permanency planning order that awards guardianship or custody to someone other than the parent without a provision delegating educational rights to the parent, the biological or adoptive parent has the authority to act as the "parent" for purposes of IDEA even when the child is placed in DSS custody.

A party in the abuse, neglect, or dependency case may raise the issue of the need for the court to address who has the authority to make special education or early intervention decisions for the child if the child receives or will be referred for services under IDEA. This is particularly important when a child is placed in a group home or therapeutic foster home. It may also be an issue when a child has experienced a number of placement changes that has resulted in a lack of consistency by any one person (e.g., a foster parent) or where the current foster parent has insufficient information about the child to meaningfully participate as the IDEA parent in the IEP or IFSP Team. The court may also consider the parent's role as the IDEA parent as part of the plan for reunification. Depending on who the court appoints and whether that person meets the criteria of "parent" as defined by IDEA, this person is considered to be either an IDEA parent or "surrogate parent."

Although the court may order someone other than one of the parents or the foster parent(s) to be the child's educational decision-maker for IDEA purposes, parents and current and former foster parents may still be invited to be a member of the IEP or IFSP Team by either the school or IDEA parent.

**4. Appointment of a surrogate parent.** The school or Children's Developmental Service Agency (CDSA) designated service coordinator must determine whether a surrogate parent is needed to protect the child's rights when the child's parent cannot be identified or located, the child is a ward of the state, or the child is an unaccompanied homeless youth. 34 C.F.R. 300.519(b) and 303.422(b); G.S. 115C-109.2(c); *see* 10A N.C.A.C. 27G.0904(b). A surrogate parent is needed when the child, infant, or toddler does not have someone who meets the definition of "parent" under IDEA to act on his or her behalf. Children who are placed in therapeutic foster homes or group homes are most likely to require a surrogate parent. Reasonable efforts to appoint a surrogate parent should occur within thirty days of when the school or CDSA determines the child needs a surrogate parent. 20 U.S.C. 1415(b)(2)(B); 34 C.F.R. 300.519(h) and 303.422(g); G.S. 115C-109.2(c).

**(a) Appointment by court or school.** When a surrogate parent is needed, one may be appointed by either

- the judge hearing the child's abuse, neglect, or dependency case or
- the school or CDSA (note that when the CDSA is making the appointment for a state ward, it must consult with the county DSS that has custody of the child, 34 C.F.R. 303.422(b)(2)).

20 U.S.C. 1415(b)(2)(A)(i); 34 C.F.R. 300.519(b)(2), (c) and 303.422(b), (c), (d).

> **Practice Note:** Although the school or service coordinator designed by the CDSA is required to determine whether a surrogate parent is needed, DSS, the child's guardian ad litem, or the parent may raise the issue with the court hearing the abuse, neglect, or dependency action so that the court can enter an order appointing a surrogate parent. This may result in a more expedient appointment of a surrogate parent and/or the appointment of someone who has a more substantial relationship with the child or understanding of the child's circumstances.

**(b) Criteria for surrogate parent.** A surrogate parent must not have a personal or professional conflict of interest with the child and must have adequate knowledge and skills to represent the child. 34 C.F.R. 300.519(d)(2)(ii)–(iii) and 303.422(d)(2)(ii)–(iii). The person appointed as a surrogate parent must not be an employee of the school district, the North Carolina Department of Public Instruction, the CDSA, or any other agency that is involved in the child's education, provision of early intervention services, or care. 20 U.S.C. 1415(b)(2)(A); 34 C.F.R. 300.519(d)(2)(i) and 303.422(d)(2)(i). *See* G.S. 115C-109.2(d); 10A N.C.A.C. 27G.0904. This means the surrogate parent cannot be the DSS social worker when DSS has custody (e.g., "care") of the child.

> **Practice Note**: DSS is involved in the child's care. As a result, a DSS employee, including the social worker assigned to the case, cannot be the child's surrogate parent. Under North Carolina policy, the same is also true for a therapeutic foster parent and an employee of a group home where the child is placed. NC 1504-1.20(d)(1). Although such an employee is not eligible to be the child's surrogate parent, he or she may be a member of the child's IEP Team as a person with knowledge or special expertise regarding the child who is invited by the surrogate parent or school.

> **Resource:** For more information about surrogate parents, see the "Special Education Surrogate Parents" section under "Policies" on the N.C. Department of Public Instruction website.

## 13.9 Special Immigrant Juvenile Status and Selected Immigration Resources

### A. Introduction and Selected Resources

Families involved in juvenile court proceedings may have immigration issues as a result of a parent's, potential caregiver's, or child's lack of legal status to stay in the United States. Immigration issues may impact the juvenile court proceeding (e.g., deported or detained parents), and the juvenile court proceeding may impact an individual's immigration issues. Immigration issues for these families are beyond the scope of this Manual, but resources are provided below.

One immigration issue that is directly and specifically related to a juvenile court proceeding involves undocumented noncitizen children and their potential for "special immigrant juvenile status" (SIJS). Undocumented noncitizen children who will not be reunified with their parent(s) may be eligible to achieve the lawful immigration status of SIJS if the juvenile court makes specific findings pertaining to the child, which are then included in a separate application for citizenship filed with the U.S. Citizenship and Immigration Services (USCIS). This section provides a general overview of SIJS as it relates to the juvenile court proceeding.

---

**Practice Notes:** Attorneys involved in juvenile proceedings in North Carolina should be familiar with any policies, procedures, or guidance relating to SIJS or other immigration issues promulgated by their respective agencies: the North Carolina Department of Health and Human Services Division of Social Services, the county department of social services, and the North Carolina Administrative Office of the Courts Guardian ad Litem Program and Parent Representation Division of the Office of Indigent Defense Services.

Local consulates may be able to provide assistance with various aspects of a juvenile case that involves a citizen of its country. It is important to determine which country the individual is from, so ask the question "what country are you a citizen of" or "where were you born."

In cases where language is a barrier, Title VI (as discussed in section 13.4, above) applies.

**Resources:**
The ABA Center on Children and Law maintains a section about "Child Welfare and Immigration," on its website, which includes information related to parents, children, and caregivers and Child Welfare and Immigration Quick Guides.

For general information including resources and toolkits for working with immigrant families, see
- The Center on Immigration and Child Welfare website.
- The Immigrant Legal Resource Center website
- The Child Welfare Information Gateway website, which includes pages addressing "Immigration and Child Welfare," "Immigration and Child Welfare Laws and Policies," "Working with Youth who are Immigrants and Refugees" and other resources available by searching the website using the term "immigration".

For information about parents and legal guardians who are detained or deported, see
- The "ICE Parental Interests Directive" (Aug. 29, 2017), a U.S. Immigration and Customs Enforcement (ICE) policy involving detained parents, legal guardians, and primary caretakers of minor children who are involved in child welfare proceedings.
- The CHILDREN'S BUREAU, U.S. DEP'T OF HEALTH & HUMAN SERVICES, Information Memorandum ACYF-CB-IM-15-02 (Feb. 20, 2015), addressing case planning and service delivery.
- Online Detainee Locator System on the U.S. Immigration and Customs Enforcement section of the Department of Homeland Security website.

For federal policy in a Q&A format discussing Titles IV-B and IV-E requirements related to citizenship, aliens and immigration, see the CHILD WELFARE POLICY MANUAL under the

"Laws and Policies" section of the Children's Bureau, U.S. Department of Health and Human Services website, specifically "7. Title IV-B" (see section 7.1) and "8. Title IV-E" (see section 8.4B).

In 2012, the U.S. Department of Homeland Security implemented the "Deferred Action for Childhood Arrivals Initiative," (DACA) under which certain people brought to this country as undocumented children may seek deferral of removal (deportation) and obtain work authorization if several criteria are met. An announcement that the DACA program is being phased out was issued on September 5, 2017. For information about the status of DACA, see "Deferred Action for Childhood Arrivals 2017 Announcement" and "Deferred Action for Childhood Arrivals: Response to January 2018 Preliminary Injunction" on the U.S. Citizenship and Immigration Services section of the Department of Homeland Security website.

When immigration issues arise, it is advisable to seek assistance from an immigration specialist. For representation and other information, see
- The "Immigrants and Refugees" section of the North Carolina Justice Center website.
- ImmigrationLawHelp.org, where you can select a state on the map for resources.
- The "Immigration Services" section of the U.S. Committee for Refugees and Immigrants website.

## B. Special Immigrant Juvenile Status and Obtaining Lawful Permanent Residency

**1. Introduction.** With Special Immigrant Juvenile Status (SIJS), an undocumented child who will not be reunified with his or her parent(s) due to abuse, neglect, or abandonment may be able to become a lawful permanent resident by applying for such status and permanent residency based on a SIJS petition. This is only possible once a juvenile court has made specific findings and orders meeting the requirements of SIJS. The juvenile court is not determining the child's immigration status but is instead making findings that are necessary for SIJS eligibility, which is determined by the U.S. Citizenship and Immigration Services (USCIS).

The status of "special immigrant juvenile" was created by section 153 of the Immigration Act of 1990, Pub. L. No. 101-649, 104 Stat. 4978. The federal regulations that implement the statute are contained in 8 C.F.R. 204.11. In 2008, the William Wilberforce Trafficking Victims Protection Reauthorization Act (TVPRA), Pub. L. No. 110-457, 122 Stat. 5044, changed some of the requirements and process for obtaining SIJS. Note that the federal regulations have not yet been amended to put the new TVPRA amendments into effect. Regulations were proposed and the comment period ended in November 2011 but was reopened for thirty days, ending November 15, 2019. *See* Special Juvenile Immigrant Petitions, 76 Fed. Reg. 54978 (proposed Sept. 6, 2011). The USCIS addresses the current requirements for SIJS in its POLICY MANUAL, specifically Volume 6 (Immigrants), Part J (Special Immigrant Juveniles). Three October 11, 2019 decisions from the Administrative Appeals Office are being relied upon for policy guidance There is no guarantee that the federal regulations will be changed to reflect the new laws or that USCIS will continue to proceed the same way. It is important to be aware of both the old and new requirements for

SIJS.

**2. Eligibility for SIJS.** Special immigrant juvenile is defined as

> an immigrant who is present in the United States (i) who has been declared to be dependent on a juvenile court located in the United States or whom such a court has legally committed to or placed under the custody of, an agency or department of a state, or an individual or entity appointed by a State or juvenile court located in the United States, and whose reunification with 1 or both of the immigrant's parents is not viable due to abuse, neglect, abandonment, or a similar basis found under State law; (ii) for whom it has been determined in administrative or judicial proceedings that it would not be in the alien's best interest to be returned to the alien's or parent's previous country of nationality or country of last habitual residence; and (iii) in whose case the Secretary of Homeland Security consents to the grant of special immigrant juvenile status....

8 U.S.C. 1101(a)(27)(J).

This definition requires specific findings by the juvenile court, which must then be included in a separate application for SIJS filed with the U.S. Citizenship and Immigration Services. *See* 8 C.F.R. 204.11(d)(2).

**(a) Court findings and orders.** To be classified as a special immigrant juvenile, the following requirements must be met and should be enumerated as specific findings in an order signed by a judge that will be submitted to USCIS with the SIJS petition.

- **Dependent or in custody.** The child must be declared a dependent of a juvenile court or placed in the custody of an agency or department of a state, *or an individual or entity appointed by either the state or a juvenile court* in the United States. *See* 8 U.S.C. 1101(a)(27)(J)(i); 8 C.F.R. 204.11(c)(3) and (4), (d)(2)(i). (The law prior to the TVPRA and current regulations do not include the language in italics regarding an entity or individual.) As long as the court has jurisdiction under state law to make determinations about the custody and care of juveniles, it falls within the term "juvenile court." *See* 8 C.F.R. 204.11(a).

- **Reunification not viable.** A court must find that reunification with one or both of the child's parents is not viable due to abuse, neglect, abandonment, *or similar basis found under state law*. *See* 8 U.S.C. 1101(a)(27)(J)(i); 8 C.F.R. 204.11(a), (c)(5), (d)(2)(ii). (The language in italics was added by the TVPRA and is not in current regulations.)

- **Best interest not to return.** There must be a judicial or administrative finding that it would not be in the child's best interest to be returned to the child's or parent's country of nationality or country of last habitual residence. 8 U.S.C. 1101(a)(27)(J)(ii); 8 C.F.R. 204.11(c)(6), (d)(2)(iii).

**(b) Additional requirements for eligibility.** In addition to the required court findings, the following requirements must be met to be eligible for SIJS:

- **Age.** The juvenile must be under 21, and documentary proof of age must be submitted with the application. 8 C.F.R. 204.11(c)(1), (d)(1).

- **Court jurisdiction.** The juvenile court must have jurisdiction over the child. Prior to the TVPRA (and still according to regulations), the person applying for SIJS had to remain under juvenile court jurisdiction throughout the immigration process. The USCIS has stated that for now it will approve petitions as long as the juvenile court had jurisdiction *when the SIJS petition was filed;* however, changed regulations may alter this policy. If jurisdiction does terminate due to the child aging out, an order that explicitly states that age is the reason for terminating jurisdiction could be beneficial in dealing with the tension between the regulations and the TVPRA.

- **Unmarried.** The juvenile must be unmarried at the time of filing and during the USCIS decision process. *See* 8 C.F.R. 204.11(c)(2).

---

**Resources:**
The U.S. Citizenship and Immigration Services section of the Department of Homeland Security website contains information about SIJS, including
- "Special Immigrant Juveniles."
- POLICY MANUAL, specifically Volume 6 (Immigrants), Part J (Special Immigrant Juveniles.

For more information about SIJS findings and North Carolina custody orders (including G.S. Chapter 50 orders), see Chery Howell, *Custody Orders Requesting Findings for Special Immigrant Juvenile Status*, UNC SCH. OF GOV'T: ON THE CIVIL SIDE BLOG (Sept. 30, 2016).

The Immigrant Legal Resource Center website contains various information on immigration issues. For issues particular to youth, see
- Practice Alert: SIJS Policy Updates and Proposed Regulations (November 2019).
- ANGIE JUNCK, SALLY KINOSHITA & KATHERINE BRADY, IMMIGRANT LEGAL RESOURCE CENTER, IMMIGRATION BENCHBOOK FOR JUVENILE AND FAMILY COURT JUDGES (2010).
- The "Immigrant Youth" section of the website.

---

**3. The application process.** The juvenile (or a person acting on the juvenile's behalf) applies for special immigrant juvenile status by filing the I-360 petition. 8 C.F.R. 204.11(b). The I-360 petition must include documentary evidence of the juvenile's age and a certified copy of the court order containing the required findings. *See* 8 C.F.R. 204.11(d). A juvenile may also file concurrently an application to become a lawful permanent resident, by filing the I-485 application. According to USCIS policy, the SIJS petition is adjudicated within 180 days after receipt of the filing of the petition. *See* USCIS POLICY MANUAL, Vol. 6, Pt. J, Ch. 4.

---

**Practice Note:** Before applying for SIJS, it is important to make a correct determination of eligibility because an ineligible child who is denied SIJS could be referred for deportation.

Before proceeding, attorneys involved in the child welfare action should refer the child to an immigration attorney, who should carefully consider with the child client the possible consequences or risks of applying for SIJS.

**USCIS Forms:**
I-360, Petition for Amerasian, Widow(er), or Special Immigrant with instructions.
I-485, Application to Register Permanent Residence or Adjust Status with instructions.

**Resources:**
The U.S. Citizenship and Immigration Services section of the Department of Homeland Security website contains information about SIJS, including
- "Special Immigrant Juveniles" page.
- POLICY MANUAL, specifically
  - Volume 6 (Immigrants), Part J (Special Immigrant Juveniles)
  - Volume 7 (Adjustment of Status), Part F (Special Immigrant-Based (EB-4) Adjustment, Chapter 7 (Special Immigrant Juveniles).

**4. Impact on parents.** Once SIJS is granted, the parents cannot derive any immigration benefit from the child. *See* 8 U.S.C. 1101(a)(27)(J)(iii)(II). The granting of SIJS, a court finding that reunification with a child is not viable, or an order for termination of parental rights does not cause a parent to become deportable or inadmissible. However, a criminal conviction for child abuse, neglect, or abandonment is a ground of deportability.

**Resource:** SEJAL ZOTA & JOHN RUBIN, IMMIGRATION CONSEQUENCES OF A CRIMINAL CONVICTION IN NORTH CAROLINA (UNC School of Government, 2017).

# Chapter 14

# Confidentiality and Information Sharing

# Chapter 14
# Confidentiality and Information Sharing

**14.1 Juvenile Records    14-3**
  A. Department of Social Services Information
     1. Public agency and public records law
     2. Disclosure prohibited for public assistance and social services information
     3. Disclosure prohibited for abuse, neglect, dependency information
  B. Court Records and Proceedings
     1. The juvenile court record
     2. Juvenile court hearings: open or closed to the public
     3. Adoption proceedings and records
  C. DSS Access to Information
  D. The Child's GAL Access to and Disclosure of Information
  E. Designated Agency Information Sharing
  F. Subpoenas

**14.2 Health Records and HIPAA    14-18**
  A. Covered Health Care Providers
  B. Protected Health Information
  C. Duty to Comply with HIPAA
  D. Impact on Abuse, Neglect, Dependency Laws
     1. Reporting child abuse, neglect, or dependency
     2. Assessment and protective services
     3. The child's GAL access to information
     4. Interagency information sharing
     5. Disclosure pursuant to a subpoena
     6. Disclosure pursuant to a court order
     7. Disclosure with patient authorization

**14.3 Mental Health Records and G.S. 122C    14-22**
  A. Covered Providers
  B. Confidential Information
  C. The Duty of Confidentiality
  D. Impact on Abuse, Neglect, Dependency Laws
     1. Reporting child abuse, neglect, or dependency
     2. Assessment and protective services
     3. The child's GAL access to information
     4. Interagency information sharing
     5. Disclosure pursuant to a subpoena
     6. Disclosure pursuant to a court order
     7. Disclosure with patient authorization

**14.4 Substance Abuse Records and 42 C.F.R. Part 2    14-25**
   A. Covered Programs
   B. Confidential Information
   C. Duty Imposed by Federal Substance Abuse Records Law
   D. Impact on Abuse, Neglect, Dependency Laws
      1. Reporting child abuse, neglect, or dependency
      2. Assessment and protective services
      3. The child's GAL access to information
      4. Interagency information sharing
      5. Disclosure pursuant to a subpoena
      6. Disclosure pursuant to a court order
      7. Disclosure with patient authorization

**14.5 Education Records and FERPA    14-31**
   A. Introduction
   B. Consent Required for Disclosure
      1. Consent required
      2. Personally identifiable information
      3. Education records
   C. Exceptions to Consent Requirement
      1. Overview
      2. Disclosure to child welfare agency responsible for child
      3. Disclosure to comply with judicial order or subpoena
      4. Disclosure for health or safety emergency
      5. Disclosure to school personnel and schools where child seeks to enroll
      6. Disclosure of directory information
   D. Documentation of Disclosure, Redisclosure, and Use of Information
   E. Complaints and Enforcement

---

**Resources:**
For a discussion of confidentiality and disclosure and the laws discussed in this Chapter, see AIMEE WALL, DISCLOSING PROTECTIVE SERVICES INFORMATION: A GUIDE FOR NORTH CAROLINA SOCIAL SERVICES AGENCIES (UNC School of Government, 2015).

For a searchable online database of statutes, regulations, cases, and guidance materials that apply to confidentiality requirements for protective services and public assistance programs, see the Social Services Confidentiality Research Tool (UNC School of Government, 2015).

For discussions of confidentiality in the context of social services programs, including a useful framework for analyzing confidentiality issues, see the following bulletin series from the UNC School of Government (formerly the Institute of Government):
- John L. Saxon, *Confidentiality and Social Services (Part I): What Is Confidentiality?*, SOCIAL SERVICES LAW BULLETIN No. 30 (UNC Institute of Government, Feb. 2001).

- John L. Saxon, *Confidentiality and Social Services (Part II): Where Do Confidentiality Rules Come From?*, SOCIAL SERVICES LAW BULLETIN No. 31 (UNC Institute of Government, May 2001).
- John L. Saxon, *Confidentiality and Social Services (Part III): A Process for Analyzing Issues Involving Confidentiality,* SOCIAL SERVICES LAW BULLETIN No. 35 (UNC Institute of Government, April 2002).

**NC DHHS DSS Form:**
DSS-5297, Consent for Release of Confidential Information (Dec. 2013).

## 14.1 Juvenile Records

Most information related to abuse, neglect, or dependency cases is confidential and has special protections under laws governing departments of social services, juvenile court proceedings, and adoption proceedings.

### A. Department of Social Services Information

**1. Public agency and public records law.** Each of North Carolina's 100 counties are political subdivisions of the state. Each county must provide social services programs pursuant to Chapters 108A (social services) and 111 (aid to the blind) of the General Statutes. G.S. 153A-255. The county board of commissioners creates agencies of the county government, which includes a department of social services (DSS). *See* G.S. 153A-76.

**Note,** for purposes of this Manual, "department of social services" or "DSS" refers to a department as defined by G.S. 7B-101(8a) regardless of how it is titled or structured.

The county DSS administers public assistance and social services programs. Public assistance programs relate to financial benefits that assist the county's indigent citizens (e.g., Food and Nutrition Services, Work First), and social services programs relate to the protection of the county's citizens (e.g., child welfare, public guardianship). *See* G.S. 108A-14; 108A-15; *see also* G.S. Chapter 108A, Articles 2 (Programs of Public Assistance), 3 (Social Services Programs), 6 (Protection of the Abused, Neglected, or Exploited Disabled Adult Act), and 6A (Protection of Disabled and Older Adults from Financial Exploitation).

A public record includes all documents, photographs, recordings, and other documentary materials made or received pursuant to law or ordinance in connection with the transaction of public business by any agency of the North Carolina government or its subdivisions. G.S. 132-1(a). Generally, records maintained by a county DSS are public records. People have a right to have access to public records. G.S. 132-1(b). However, a statutory exception may apply that limits and/or prohibits disclosure of a public record. The confidentiality of and access to DSS records are governed by several state and federal laws and regulations, some of which are discussed below.

**Resources:**
For a discussion about public records and disclosure, see
- Frayda Bluestein, *Is This a Public Record? A Framework for Answering Questions About Public Records Requests*, UNC SCH. OF GOV'T: COATES' CANONS: NC LOCAL GOVERNMENT LAW BLOG (June 9, 2010).
- DAVID LAWRENCE, PUBLIC RECORDS LAW FOR NORTH CAROLINA LOCAL GOVERNMENTS (UNC School of Government, 2d ed. 2010).

For further information about social services, see JOHN L. SAXON, SOCIAL SERVICES IN NORTH CAROLINA (UNC School of Government, 2008).

For information about consolidated human services agencies, see "Consolidated Human Services Agencies (CHSAs)" on the UNC School of Government website.

**2. Disclosure prohibited for public assistance and social services information.** One of the confidentiality statutes that applies to DSS is G.S. 108A-80, and it covers client (including applicant) information generally. Absent limited statutory exceptions, G.S. 108A-80(a) prohibits the disclosure of names or other information concerning persons applying for or receiving public assistance or social services that may be directly or indirectly derived from DSS records. Although the term "social services" is not defined, statutory context and usage indicate that child welfare is clearly encompassed within the scope of the expansive term. For example, child welfare services are specifically included in Article 3 of G.S. Chapter 108A, which is titled "Social Services Programs". Specific reference is also made to "grants-in-aid available for social services under the Social Security Act." G.S. 108A-71. Child welfare services and foster care and adoption maintenance payments are funded by Titles IV-B and IV-E of the Social Security Act. *See e.g.,* 42 U.S.C. 622; 42 U.S.C. 671; 45 C.F.R. Parts 1355, 1356, and 1357.

G.S. 108A-80(a) has broad application. It makes it unlawful for "any person to obtain, disclose or use, or to authorize, permit, or acquiesce in the use of" the protected information. This particular subsection, G.S. 108A-80(a), does not include a criminal penalty; however, a violation is likely a misdemeanor. *See* G.S. 108A-80(b), (c) (both stating a violation of "this section" is a Class 1 misdemeanor); *see also State v. Bishop*, 228 N.C. 371 (1947) (holding common law authorizes punishment by misdemeanor when a statute, in the interests of the public, forbids an act and does not expressly include a penalty).

In addition to the statute, state regulations (or Rules) based on G.S. 108A-80 that address confidentiality and access to client records are set forth in Title 10A of the North Carolina Administrative Code (N.C.A.C.) Chapter 69. The Rules consist of six sections:

- general provisions,
- safeguarding client information,
- client access to records,
- release of client information,
- disclosure of information without client consent, and
- service providers.

Under the Rules, the director of the state Division of Social Services or a county department of social services is required to disseminate written policy to and provide trainings for all persons with access to client information. 10A N.C.A.C. 69.0203(d); *see* 10A N.C.A.C. 69.0101(4) (definition of "director"). An employee who violates the confidentiality Rules is subject to disciplinary action including suspension or dismissal. 10A N.C.A.C. 69.0205.

The Rules specifically address conflict of laws with federal regulations or state statutes addressing confidentiality and require that DSS follow the statutes or regulations that provide more protection for the client. 10A N.C.A.C. 69.0201. The federal Child Abuse Prevention and Treatment Act (CAPTA), Titles IV-E and IV-B of the Social Security Act, and North Carolina's Juvenile Code (G.S. Chapter 7B) provide for additional restrictions on the disclosure of confidential information as it relates to information concerning a juvenile's abuse, neglect, or dependency. *See* 42 U.S.C. 5106a(b)(2)(B)(viii)–(xi); 42 U.S.C. 671(a)(8); 45 C.F.R. 1355.21(a); G.S. 7B-302(a1); 7B-2901(b); 7B-3100.

**3. Disclosure prohibited for abuse, neglect, dependency information.** In addition to the disclosure prohibition for social services client records under G.S. 108A-80, the Juvenile Code addresses the confidentiality and disclosure of DSS records related to abuse, neglect, or dependency in three different statutes: G.S. 7B-302(a1), 7B-2901(b), and 7B-3100. Additionally, the Rules regulating confidentiality of DSS child protective services information are found in 10A N.C.A.C. 70A.

G.S. 7B-302(a1) requires that all information received by DSS be held in "strictest confidence" unless a disclosure is authorized by statute. The requirement to maintain the information in "strictest confidence" starts when DSS first receives information about a child, typically from a report of suspected abuse, neglect, or dependency. DSS must maintain a case record for a child for whom protective services are initiated or who the court places in the custody of a DSS. 10A N.C.A.C. 70A.0112. The case record contains information about the assessment; family background information; safety responses; the case decision; notifications made to the family and others; the family services case plan and reviews of the case plan; and if applicable, court pleadings and reports, medical and psychological reports, and a summary of services. G.S. 7B-2901(b); 10A N.C.A.C. 70A.0112. The case record is confidential and information from it may only be disclosed in accordance with the Juvenile Code or other applicable law. 10A N.C.A.C. 70A.0112(a); *see* G.S. 7B-302(a1); 7B-2901(b); 10A N.C.A.C. 70A.0113.

> **Resource:** For information about DSS policies and procedures related to confidentiality in the child welfare setting, see DIV. OF SOC. SERVS., N.C. DEP'T OF HEALTH & HUMAN SERVICES, CHILD WELFARE MANUAL "Cross Function," available here.

- **(a) Exceptions authorizing disclosure.** There are a number of statutory exceptions to the requirement of confidentiality for DSS records and information.

    - **Circumstances affecting the reporter.** There is an extra layer of protection for the identity of the person who made the report of a child's suspected abuse, neglect, or dependency. A reporter's identity is confidential and may only be disclosed when authorized by court order or when the disclosure is to a federal, state, or local government entity or agent when that entity demonstrates a need for the reporter's name to carry out its mandated responsibilities. G.S. 7B-302(a1)(1a); 7B-303(e) (interference or obstruction petition); 7B-700(a) (reporter's identity may not be shared); *see Ritter v. Kimball*, 67 N.C. App. 333 (1984) (holding trial court did not abuse its discretion in limiting in a custody action the discovery of the reporter's identity based on (1) the statute requiring information received by DSS concerning reports of abuse or neglect be held in "strictest confidence" and the trial court's perception of the purpose of that statute as encouraging the reporting of abuse or neglect, and (2) G.S. 1A-1, Rule 26(c), which protects a person from "unreasonable annoyance, embarrassment, oppression, or undue burden").

DSS is required to disclose certain information to the reporter, specifically, whether the report was accepted for an assessment and/or referred to the appropriate law enforcement agency; whether there was a finding of abuse, neglect, or dependency; and whether and what action DSS is taking to protect the juvenile. G.S. 7B-302(f), (g).

**Resource:** Sara DePasquale, *A/N/D Reporting: Rights, Protections, and Prosecutor Review*, UNC SCH. OF GOV'T: ON THE CIVIL SIDE BLOG (June 21, 2017).

- **Discovery and parties sharing information.** The Juvenile Code addresses information sharing among the parties and discovery in abuse, neglect, dependency, and termination of parental rights proceedings. When a juvenile case is pending, DSS is authorized to share with any other party information that is relevant to the subject matter of the action. G.S. 7B-700(a). *See* G.S. 7B-302(a1)(2) and (5); 7B-2901(b)(1) and (4). There may be a local rule or administrative order that addresses information sharing among the parties (including the sharing of predisposition reports) and the use of discovery. G.S. 7B-700(b); 7B-808(c). Although G.S. 7B-700(c) permits parties to file motions for discovery, they may do so only if they have been unable to obtain information through information sharing authorized by G.S. 7B-700(a) and local rules (if applicable). *See* G.S. 7B-700(b). Motions for protective orders are a means by which any party can seek to protect information that he or she believes should not be disclosed. Requests for a protective order in a juvenile proceeding are governed by G.S. 7B-700(d). Information that is obtained through discovery or information sharing authorized by G.S.7B-700 may not be redisclosed if the redisclosure is prohibited by state or federal law. G.S. 7B-700(e).

  See Chapters 4.6 (discussing discovery) and 7.2.E.3 (discussing predisposition reports).

- **The child's guardian ad litem (GAL).** The Juvenile Code gives the child's GAL the authority to obtain any information or reports, whether or not confidential, that may in the GAL's opinion be relevant to the case. This includes information received and maintained by DSS. G.S. 7B-302(a1)(2); 7B-2901(b)(1). The only privilege that may be invoked to prevent the GAL from obtaining the information is the attorney-client privilege. G.S. 7B-601(c). Absent a court order or statutory authorization, the GAL is required to keep information confidential. G.S. 7B-601(c). Effective October 1, 2019, the GAL attorney advocate is authorized to disclose confidential information about the juvenile to an attorney who is representing the juvenile in a delinquency or undisciplined action. G.S. 7B-3100(c); *see* S.L. 2019-33. For a further discussion of a GAL's access to information and disclosures by a GAL generally, see section 14.1.D, below.

- **The child.** The child has a right to examine his or her DSS records, even after reaching the age of majority or becoming emancipated. G.S. 7B-302(a1)(2); 7B-2901(b)(1). This right to examine the records includes the child's attorney. 10A N.C.A.C. 70A.0113(a)(2).

- **Law enforcement and district attorney.** In certain circumstances, DSS will be required to notify law enforcement and the district attorney of a report or results of its assessment. If DSS receives a report that a child may have been physically harmed as a result of a crime that was not committed by the child's parent, guardian, custodian, or caretaker, the director must report that information to the district attorney (or designee) and the appropriate law enforcement agency so that the initiation of a criminal investigation and possible prosecution can commence. G.S. 7B-307(a).

    If, during the course of its assessment, DSS finds evidence that the child may have been abused, DSS must report those findings to the district attorney (or designee) and the appropriate law enforcement agency so as to coordinate the criminal investigation with the DSS assessment. G.S. 7B-307(a). In both situations, DSS must make an immediate oral report and a subsequent written report within forty-eight hours after receiving the information. G.S. 7B-307(a). If a report alleges that a child is abandoned, DSS must request law enforcement investigate through the North Carolina Center for Missing Persons and other national and state resources. G.S. 7B-302(a).

    Effective December 1, 2019, a new mandated universal reporting law requires any adult who knows or reasonably should have known that a juvenile has been or is a victim of a violent offense, sexual offense, or misdemeanor child abuse to immediately report that case to the appropriate local law enforcement agency in the county where the juvenile resides or is found. There is no exception for a DSS. G.S. 14-318.6; *see* S.L. 2019-245.

    If the person who reports the suspected abuse, neglect, or dependency requests a prosecutor review of a DSS decision not to file a petition, DSS must allow the district attorney (or designee) to access the case record. G.S. 7B-305; 10A N.C.A.C. 70A.0113(c).

**Resources:**
Sara DePasquale, *BIG NEW: S.L. 2019-245 Creates a New Universal Mandated Reporting Law for Child Victims of Crimes and Changes the Definition of "Caretaker,"* UNC SCH. OF GOV'T: ON THE CIVIL SIDE BLOG (Nov. 13, 2019).

Sara DePasquale, *A/N/D Reporting: Rights, Protections, and Prosecutor Review*, UNC SCH. OF GOV'T: ON THE CIVIL SIDE BLOG (June 21, 2017).

- **Government entity to protect a child.** DSS must disclose confidential information to any federal, state, or local government entity or its agent that needs the information to protect a child from abuse or neglect. G.S. 7B-302(a1)(1). The government entity may redisclose confidential information received from DSS if redisclosure is for purposes directly connected with carrying out the entity's mandated responsibilities. G.S. 7B-302(a1)(1).

  If DSS receives a report of a child's suspected maltreatment occurring in a child care facility, DSS must notify the North Carolina Department of Health and Human Services (NC DHHS) within twenty-four hours or on the next working day after receiving the report. G.S. 7B-307(a); *see* G.S. 110-105.3(a), (c).

  **Practice Note:** Effective January 1, 2016, investigations and responses involving protective actions and sanctions involving suspected child maltreatment occurring in a child care facility are part of the child care licensing system of the NC DHHS Division of Child Development and Early Education and are no longer regulated by the Juvenile Code. S.L. 2015-123.

  **Resources:** For more information about alleged child maltreatment occurring in a child care facility, including mandated reporting, investigations, and confidentiality of those records, see
    - SARA DEPASQUALE, *Suspected Child Maltreatment Occurring in a Child Care Facility* (UNC School of Government, 2016) supplemental Chapter 13a *in* JANET MASON, REPORTING CHILD ABUSE AND NEGLECT IN NORTH CAROLINA, (UNC School of Government, 3d ed. 2013).
    - Sara DePasquale, *The New Law Addressing Child Maltreatment in Child Care Facilities: It's the State's Responsibility*, UNC SCH. OF GOV'T: ON THE CIVIL SIDE BLOG (Jan. 6, 2016).

- **Military affiliation.** As part of its assessment of a report of abuse, neglect, or dependency, DSS should collect information about the military affiliation (if any) of the juvenile's parent, guardian, custodian, or caretaker. G.S. 7B-302(a). If DSS finds evidence that the juvenile may have been abused or neglected, DSS must (1) notify the appropriate military authority by making an immediate oral report and a subsequent written report within forty-eight hours after receipt of the information and (2) share information with that military authority. G.S. 7B-307(a); 7B-302(a); *see* S.L. 2019-201 (effective August 23, 2019).

- **Court order.** Confidential social services information may be disclosed pursuant to court order. 10A N.C.A.C. 70A.0113(a)(1). There are several different situations in which a court may order disclosure.

The court may order public agencies to share information regarding a child victim who is under DSS protective custody or placement by the court if the court finds that information sharing is necessary to reduce the trauma to the child victim. G.S. 7B-2901(c).

A district or superior court judge who is hearing a civil matter in which DSS is not a party (e.g., child custody) may order DSS to release confidential information if (1) DSS has reasonable notice and an opportunity to be heard and (2) the court determines the information is relevant and necessary to the trial and is unavailable from another source. G.S. 7B-302(a1)(3); 7B-2901(b)(2). The court may conduct an in camera review if needed to make that determination. G.S. 7B-302(a1)(3).

A defendant in a criminal action has a constitutional right to access third party information if that information is favorable and material to his or her defense. *Pennsylvania v. Ritchie*, 480 U.S. 39 (1987). In a criminal or delinquency action, the district or superior court judge presiding over that action must conduct an in camera review before releasing confidential DSS records to the defendant unless it is the child (who may now be an adult) who is the criminal defendant or alleged delinquent juvenile. G.S. 7B-302(a1)(4); 7B-2901(b)(3). The child (even upon reaching the age of majority) is entitled to examine the records without a court order. G.S. 7B-302(a1)(2); 7B-2901(b)(1).

> **Resource:** For a discussion on a criminal defendant's right to access, see Jessica Smith, *Defendant's Right to Third Party Confidential Records*, UNC SCH. OF GOV'T: NORTH CAROLINA CRIMINAL LAW BLOG (Oct. 2, 2014).

- **Provision of protective services.** In conducting its assessment or arranging for and providing protective services, DSS may consult with any agency or individual. G.S. 7B-302(e). DSS may share information and a "summary of documentation" from the case record without a court order with agencies or individuals that provide or facilitate the provision of protective services to a child. 10A N.C.A.C. 70A.0113(b). Protective services include screening reports, conducting assessments, and providing casework or other counseling services to the families to improve, preserve, and stabilize the family's life. G.S. 7B-300.

  DSS is required to identify and notify the child's relatives and other persons with legal custody of the child's siblings that the child is the subject of an abuse, neglect, or dependency action and, when applicable, is in nonsecure custody. G.S. 7B-505(b); 7B-800.1(a)(4); 7B-901(b). This notification is part of DSS efforts to explore the willingness and appropriateness of the relatives and other persons with legal custody of a child's siblings as potential resources for support or placement of the child. Under the Indian Child Welfare Act (ICWA), when the court knows or has reason to know the child is an Indian child, DSS, as the petitioner, is required to send notice to (i) the federally recognized tribe(s) the child is believed to be either a member of or eligible for membership of when a biological parent is a member of a federally recognized tribe, (ii) the regional director of the Bureau of Indian Affairs, (iii) the child's parents, and (iv) the Indian custodian (if any). 25 U.S.C. 1912(a); 25 C.F.R. 23.11(a) and 23.111. See Chapter 13.2 (discussing ICWA).

Foster parents and DSS (or the supervising agency) are required to exchange information about matters affecting the child's adjustment to the home, and the foster parent must agree to keep the information confidential and may only discuss it with DSS (or the supervising agency) or professionals designated by the agency. 10A N.C.A.C. 70E.0902(a)(4). Foster parents are also to be included in the child's decision-making team. 10A N.C.A.C. 70E.0902(b)(9). Foster parents must receive training on confidentiality. 10A N.C.A.C. 70E.1117(1)(n).

**(b) Disclosure in child fatality or near-fatality cases.** The Juvenile Code addresses a child's fatality or near fatality resulting from suspected abuse, neglect, or dependency, including the disclosure of information. A public agency (this includes but is not limited to DSS) that receives a request to disclose information related to a child fatality or near fatality must disclose the findings and information as defined by G.S. 7B-2901(a)(2) and limited by G.S. 7B-2902(c) through (f) if

- a person is criminally charged with causing the death or near death of a child or
- a district attorney certifies that a person would be charged but for that person's death.

However, not all confidential information is required to be disclosed, and there are circumstances under which the agency is permitted to deny a request for information. If a request is denied, the person seeking the information may go to superior court to seek an order compelling disclosure, and the court must conduct an in camera review to determine whether denial of the request was warranted. G.S. 7B-2902.

North Carolina has a Child Fatality Prevention System that consists of the

- North Carolina Child Fatality Task Force,
- North Carolina Child Fatality Prevention Team (State Prevention Team),
- State Child Fatality Review Team (State Review Team),
- local Community Child Protection Teams (CCPT) in every county, and
- local Child Fatality Prevention Teams in every county (note the local Child Fatality Prevention Team in a county may be blended with, rather than separate from, the local CCPT (*see* G.S. 7B-1406(b)).

Article 14 of G.S. Chapter 7B; G.S. 143B-150.20.

The Child Fatality Prevention System creates a multidisciplinary, community-wide approach to promote safe and healthy child development and to prevent future child abuse, neglect, and death by understanding the causes of childhood deaths, identifying gaps in services, improving coordination between state and local entities, and recommending changes to laws and policies. *See* G.S. 7B-1400 through -1414; 143B-150.20(b).

The State Prevention Team and local CCPTs review child deaths that are attributed to abuse or neglect or when a mandated report of suspected abuse or neglect was made before the child's death. G.S. 7B-1405(1), (6); 7B-1406(a), (b). The CCPT also reviews (1) selected active cases where children are receiving protective services and (2) cases that are brought to them for review by a member. G.S. 7B-1406(a)(1); 7B-1409(4). The local Child Fatality Prevention Team reviews all other child deaths (meaning those where the child's and family's involvement with DSS did not occur in the twelve months prior to the child's death, such as an accidental death or death resulting from a medical condition or illness). The State Review Team conducts in-depth reviews of any child fatalities where the child and family were involved with child protective services at some point in the twelve months before the child's death. The reviews by the State Review Team may include interviews with relevant persons and an examination of pertinent written materials. G.S. 143B-150.20(a). If necessary, the State Review Team may seek an order from the district court in the county where the investigation is pending that compels the disclosure of requested information that has not been received within thirty days of the request. G.S. 143B-150.20(d).

The various types of teams that make up the state's Child Fatality Prevention System have access to records, including medical, hospital, state, county, or local agency (including DSS) records. G.S. 7B-1413(a); 143B-150.20(d). Any confidential records that are acquired remain confidential and are not subject to discovery or introduction in evidence in any proceeding and may be disclosed only as necessary to carry out the purpose of the applicable team. G.S. 7B-1413(c); 143B-150.20(f).

The State Prevention Team, State Review Team, and local team meetings are not open meetings, although the State Review Team and/or a local team may hold periodic public meetings to discuss generally the findings and recommendations resulting from its reviews. G.S. 7B-1413(b); 143B-150.20(e). Members of any team or persons attending a team meeting may not testify about what happened at the meeting, the information presented at the meeting, or opinions the person formed as a result of the meeting. G.S. 7B-1413(c); 143B-150.20(f). Training on confidentiality requirements must be provided to team members. 10A N.C.A.C. 70A.0202(a)(2). Members and invited participants must sign a confidentiality statement. G.S. 7B-1413(d); 143B-150.20(g); 10A N.C.A.C. 70A.0203(b). However, nothing prohibits a person from testifying in a civil or criminal action about information within that person's independent knowledge. G.S. 7B-1413(c); 143B-150.20(f).

The NC DHHS Division of Social Services, after consulting with the appropriate district attorney to ensure the criteria for disclosure under G.S. 7B-2902(d) is satisfied, makes public the State Review Team's findings and recommendations for each fatality reviewed that relates to improving coordination between local and State entities. G.S. 143B-150.20(b).

**Resource**: For more information about child fatality reviews, see DIV. OF SOC. SERVS., N.C. DEP'T OF HEALTH & HUMAN SERVICES, CHILD WELFARE MANUAL "Cross Function" and "Child Fatality Prevention and Review," available here.

## B. Court Records and Proceedings

**1. The juvenile court record.** The clerk of superior court is responsible for maintaining all records pertaining to juvenile cases. The clerk's record includes the summons, the petition, custody orders, other court orders, written motions, other papers filed in the proceeding, and recordings of hearings. G.S. 7B-2901(a). All adjudicatory and dispositional hearings in abuse, neglect, or dependency proceedings are recorded; the court may order that other hearings be recorded. G.S. 7B-806. The recordings may be reduced to a written transcript only when notice of appeal has been timely filed. G.S. 7B-806; 7B-2901(a); *see* G.S. 7B-1001(appeal). Recordings may be erased after the time for appeal has expired with no appeal having been filed pursuant to a court order or the retention schedule that is approved by the Director of the Administrative Office of the Courts and Department of Natural and Cultural Resources. G.S. 7B-2901(a).

Records of juvenile cases alleging abuse, neglect, or dependency are withheld from public inspection and may be examined only by court order unless an exception applies. G.S. 7B-2901(a); *see* G.S. 1-72.1(f). The following persons may examine the court record and obtain copies of written parts of the record without a court order:

- the child who is named in the petition;
- the child's guardian ad litem;
- the county department of social services; and
- the child's parent, guardian, or custodian, or the attorney for the child, parent, guardian, or custodian.

G.S. 7B-2901(a).

For more information about the clerk's records and court administration, see Appendices 3 (JWise), 4 (Rules of Recordkeeping Procedures for the Office of the Clerk of Superior Court, Chapter XII), and 5 (Case Management). Note that Comment D. of Rule 12.5, Access to Files, of the Rules of Recordingkeeping states that "Entry of a TPR changes the legal relationship between a parent and child. The parent should not have access to documents filed subsequent to the TPR even if the TPR is on appeal unless the court has stayed the TPR order on appeal."

**2. Juvenile court hearings: open or closed to the public.** Federal law allows a state to determine its own policy related to public access to court proceedings that determine child abuse or neglect, but the state policy must ensure the safety and well-being of the child, parents, and family. 42 U.S.C. 671(c). In North Carolina, although court and DSS records related to abuse, neglect, or dependency are withheld from public inspection, the court hearings are open to the public. However, the court has the discretion to close a hearing or any part of a hearing so long as the child does not request that it remain open. G.S. 7B-801(a), (b).

When determining whether to close all or part of the hearing, the court considers the circumstances of the case, including but not limited to

- the nature of the allegations,

- the child's age and maturity,
- the benefit to the child of confidentiality,
- the benefit to the child of an open hearing, and
- the extent to which the confidentiality afforded the child's record pursuant to G.S. 132-1.4(*l*) (which addresses criminal investigations and refers to Article 29 of G.S. Chapter 7B) and G.S. 7B-2901 will be compromised by an open hearing.

G.S. 7B-801.

Even if a hearing is open, Rule 15 of the General Rules of Practice for the Superior and District Courts Supplemental to the Rules of Civil Procedure prohibits electronic media coverage and still photography of judicial proceedings.

**3. Adoption proceedings and records.** An adoption proceeding is a special proceeding that is heard before the clerk of superior court and is a separate proceeding from an abuse, neglect, dependency, or termination of parental rights proceeding. G.S. 48-2-100(a). However, when there is a question of fact, an equitable defense, or a request for equitable relief, the clerk must transfer the proceeding to district court. G.S. 48-2-601(a1). Judicial hearings related to an adoption must be held in closed court. G.S. 48-2-203.

Subject to very limited exceptions, all records related to an adoption, including those that are in the possession of the court, an agency, the State, a county, an attorney, or other professional, are confidential and may not be disclosed unless authorized by statute. G.S. 48-9-102(a). The only two exceptions to this strict confidentiality rule are the adoption decree and the entry in a special proceedings index in the office of the clerk of superior court. Records subject to this confidentiality rule include any documents, notes, pleadings, or other types of records that pertain to an adoption proceeding regardless of the physical form of the record, such as printed, written, microfilmed, audio- or video-tape recorded, and electronic materials. G.S. 48-9-101. During an adoption proceeding, records are not open to inspection by anyone without a court order that finds disclosure is necessary to protect the adoptee's interests. G.S. 48-9-102(b). When the adoption decree is final, all records except the Special Proceedings Index must be permanently retained and sealed. G.S. 48-9-102(c). Information may only be disclosed pursuant to the criteria set forth in Article 9 of G.S. Chapter 48. *See* G.S. 48-9-103 (release of non-identifying information); 48-9-104 (release of identifying information); 48-9-105 (written motion for release of information); 48-9-109 (certain disclosures authorized). The Indian Child Welfare Act (ICWA) requires certain disclosures that are not addressed in North Carolina law. See Chapter 13.2 (discussing ICWA, section K regarding adoptions).

## C. DSS Access to Information

When DSS is assessing whether a child is abused, neglected, or dependent and is subsequently providing services to that child and family, DSS will need to acquire information about the child and family from collateral sources. The Juvenile Code authorizes DSS to access information, including some confidential information, but that access to information is complicated by several factors, including federal laws that prohibit or limit access to certain types of records.

DSS may *demand in writing* any information or reports, whether or not confidential, that in the director's opinion may be relevant to an assessment of an abuse, neglect, or dependency report or to the provision of protective services. G.S. 7B-302(e). This authority does not extend to information protected by the attorney-client privilege. G.S. 7B-302(e). An agency or individual must provide access to and copies of the requested information to the extent the disclosure is permitted by federal law and regulations. G.S.7B-302(e). For a discussion of selected federal laws related to health, substance abuse, and educational records, see sections 14.2 (HIPAA), 14.4 (42 C.F.R. Part 2) and 14.5 (FERPA), below.

State laws restrict access to, or provide for the confidentiality of, some types of records and information. However, the broad access to confidential information DSS has under the Juvenile Code does not refer to state laws when limiting the authority of DSS to access confidential information. Additionally, some state laws explicitly make an exception to confidentiality for situations involving the reporting or assessment of abuse or neglect. *See, e.g.,* G.S. 122C-54(h) (although Mental Health, Developmental Disability and Substance Abuse Services providers are restricted from disclosing information, this provision states that providers are required to disclose confidential information for purposes of complying with Article 3 of G.S. Chapter 7B, which includes the mandatory reporting law and the DSS assessment).

A custodian of criminal investigative information or records may seek a court order preventing disclosure to DSS when a written request has been made for that information if the custodian believes that the disclosure would jeopardize an ongoing or future investigation, the rights of the state to prosecute a defendant, or a defendant's right to receive a fair trial. G.S. 7B-302(e). The custodian must prove by a preponderance of the evidence that one of these three criteria exists. G.S. 7B-302(e).

An agency or individual's refusal to disclose information sought by DSS might be considered interference with or obstruction of an assessment and subject him or her to an interference proceeding brought under G.S. 7B-303. See Chapter 5.1.G (relating to interference proceedings).

### D. The Child's GAL Access to and Disclosure of Information

Unless protected by attorney-client privilege, the child's guardian ad litem (GAL) has the authority to obtain any information or reports, whether or not confidential, that in the opinion of the GAL may be relevant to the case. G.S. 7B-601(c). Given the GAL's duties, the type of information that he or she considers relevant may be very broad. The GAL represents the child to assure the protection of the child's legal rights and protect and promote the child's best interests. G.S. 7B-601(a). A GAL's duties include making an investigation to determine the facts, the child's needs, and available resources within the family and community to meet those needs; exploring options with the court at dispositional hearings; conducting follow-up investigations to insure that court orders are being properly executed; and reporting to the court when the child's needs are not being met. G.S. 7B-601(a).

Although G.S. 7B-700(a) permits DSS to share with any other party information relevant to the juvenile proceeding, the same is not true for the GAL. The GAL is not generally authorized to share information he or she obtains unless ordered by the court, local rules provide otherwise, or if the sharing is pursuant to agency sharing provisions or disclosure to the juvenile's attorney in a delinquency or undisciplined action under G.S. 7B-3100. G.S. 7B-700(f); *see* G.S. 7B-601(c). However, the GAL must share with all parties reports and records before submitting the reports and records to the court. G.S. 7B-700(f). The AOC form Order to Appoint or Release Guardian Ad Litem and Attorney Advocate contains the following language related to this provision:

> The Guardian ad Litem has the authority to obtain any information or reports, whether or not confidential, that may in the Guardian ad Litem's opinion be relevant to the case. This order includes the release of confidential information subject to the Health Insurance Portability and Accountability Act of 1996 (HIPAA). 45 C.F.R. 164.512(a), (e). No privilege other than the attorney-client privilege may be invoked to prevent the Guardian ad Litem and the Court from obtaining such information. The confidentiality of the information or reports shall be respected by the Guardian ad Litem and no disclosure of any information or reports shall be made to anyone, except by order of the Court or unless otherwise provided by law.

**Practice Note:** Some custodians of records ask for a certified copy of the GAL appointment order before allowing access to or copies of records. Others accept a copy of a certified copy or simply look at the appointment order to verify the appointment before allowing access to records. Occasionally a records custodian will refuse to release information or records without a subpoena.

**AOC Form:**
AOC-J-207, Order to Appoint or Release Guardian Ad Litem and Attorney Advocate (June 2014).

### E. Designated Agency Information Sharing

The Juvenile Code provides for information sharing among agencies who work with children that are receiving protective services in abuse, neglect, or dependency cases. Specifically, G.S. 7B-3100(a) requires that "designated agencies" share with other designated agencies information that is in their possession (even if it is confidential) and has been requested and is relevant to

- any DSS assessment of a report of child abuse, neglect, or dependency;
- DSS's provision or arrangement of protective services in a child abuse, neglect, or dependency case; or
- any case in which a petition is filed alleging that a juvenile is abused, neglected, dependent, undisciplined, or delinquent.

Designated agencies must share information, however, only to the extent permitted by federal law and regulations (such as the Confidentiality of Substance Use Disorder Patient Records regulations and the Family Educational Rights and Privacy Act, discussed respectively in sections 14.4 and 14.5, below). G.S. 7B-3100(a). See also sections 14.2.D.4 and 14.4.D.4, below (discussing the Health Insurance Portability and Accountability Act and 42 C.F.R. Part 2 as related to G.S. 7B-3100). Designated agencies sharing information must document the name of the agency to which the information was provided and the date it was provided. 14B N.C.A.C. 11A.0302.

**Practice Note:** Information sharing is not defined. The applicable statute and rules do not explicitly authorize or prohibit the exchange of agency records. When determining whether copies of documents may be provided, the designated agencies should first look to any applicable federal laws. If a federal law prohibits the release of documents, that law must be followed. If there is no prohibition, absent a signed consent to release or court order that allows records to be released from one designated agency to another, the designated agencies will need to determine whether information sharing means releasing copies of records or disclosing information contained in the agency's records without providing copies of those records.

The purpose of the information sharing is limited. Designated agencies that receive information pursuant to these provisions may use the information only for the protection of the child and others or to improve the child's educational opportunities. G.S. 7B-3100(a).

Designated agencies must continue to share information until DSS closes the protective services case or, if a petition is filed, until the juvenile is no longer subject to the jurisdiction of the juvenile court. Designated agencies must keep shared information confidential and may not permit public inspection of the information. G.S. 7B-3100(a). Information shared with a local educational agency shall not be part of the student's official education record, and the principal must destroy the information when he or she finds that the school no longer needs the information to protect the safety of or improve the education opportunities for the student or others. G.S. 115C-404(a). The purpose of the information for use by the school, the sharing of that information to necessary school employees, and the sanction of the employee's dismissal for not maintaining the confidentiality of the shared information is addressed in G.S. 115C-404.

The Juvenile Code requires that the Division of Adult Correction and Juvenile Justice of the Department of Public Safety consult with the Conference of Chief District Court Judges and adopt rules that designate certain local agencies that are authorized to share information. G.S. 7B-3100(a). The applicable rules are 14B N.C.A.C. 11A.0301 and 11A.0302. The designated agencies include

- the Division of Adult Correction and Juvenile Justice of the Department of Public Safety (note the Division is still referred to as the Department of Juvenile Justice and Delinquency Prevention in the rules), which includes juvenile court counselors;
- GAL offices;
- county departments of social services;

- local management entities or area mental health, developmental disability, and substance abuse authorities;
- local law enforcement agencies;
- the district attorney's office in the district (however, while a district attorney (DA) may obtain information, the statute does not impose on a DA a requirement to disclose or release any information in the DA's possession);
- county mental health facilities and developmental disabilities and substance abuse programs;
- local school administrative units;
- local health departments; and
- any local agency that is located in the judicial district and is designated by an administrative order issued by the chief district court judge.

G.S. 7B-3100(a); 14B N.C.A.C. 11A.0301.

The court is not an "agency" and records maintained by the clerk of superior court are not subject to these provisions. The court records are governed by G.S. 7B-2901 (discussed in section 14.1.B, above).

**Practice Note:** In 2006, G.S. 7B-3100 was amended to expand its application to situations where DSS is assessing a report of or arranging for protective services for a child in an abuse, neglect, or dependency case. The rule governing information sharing among designated agencies, 14B N.C.A.C. 11A.0301, has not been revised since the statutory amendment and only authorizes information sharing between designated agencies in those cases where a petition is filed that alleges a juvenile is abused, neglected, dependent, delinquent, or undisciplined. Designated agencies may rely on G.S. 7B-3100. A chief district court judge may want to include in an administrative order authorized by G.S. 7B-3100 the language in that statute regarding the circumstances that allow for information sharing to occur between the agencies designated in that administrative order.

**Resource:** For more information about agency information sharing pursuant to G.S. 7B-3100 and the confidentiality laws that apply to health, mental health, and substance abuse services, see Mark F. Botts, LaToya B. Powell, Rachel Johnson, Jessica Jones, *North Carolina Juvenile Justice - Behavioral Health Information Sharing Guide* (UNC School of Government, 2015).

## F. Subpoenas

A subpoena may be served on a DSS, other agency, or person to acquire information through testimony or the production of records. *See* N.C. R. Civ. P. 45. Depending on state and federal laws related to confidentiality or privilege that apply to the agency or person served with a subpoena, the disclosure of the requested information may be prohibited or require a court order to disclose the information. In those cases, the service of a subpoena will not be sufficient to obtain the sought-after information. Additionally, agencies and attorneys sometimes may feel caught between the duty to protect information based on a belief that sharing the information would be damaging and a statutory authority to share the information. In situations where the recipient of the subpoena does not believe it has the statutory authority to disclose the information or it would be harmful to disclose the information, a written objection to the subpoena or motion to quash the subpoena may be necessary. *See* N.C. R. CIV. P. 45(c). The court will then resolve the dispute about whether the information should be disclosed, and if so, result in any necessary court orders for disclosure.

> **Resource:** For a discussion of subpoenas, see John Rubin & Aimee Wall, *Responding to Subpoenas for Health Department Records*, HEALTH LAW BULLETIN No. 82 (UNC School of Government, Sept. 2005).

## 14.2 Health Records and HIPAA[1]

The Health Insurance Portability and Accountability Act of 1996 (HIPAA) and its implementing regulations at Chapter 45 of the Code of Federal Regulations, Parts 160 and 164 (the "privacy rule") govern the use and disclosure of health care information. Generally, information acquired or created in connection with providing health care is confidential and may not be disclosed except as permitted or required by the privacy rule. *See* 45 C.F.R. Parts 160 and 164.

**Note,** mental health records are governed by both the privacy rule and the state law discussed in section 14.3. The use and disclosure of mental health records must comply with both laws. Substance use disorder treatment records are governed by the privacy rule, the state law discussed in section 14.3, below, and a federal law discussed in section 14.4, below. The use and disclosure of substance use disorder treatment records must comply with all three laws.

HIPAA is a complex federal law. For purposes of this Manual, this section focuses on disclosure of information by a covered health care provider when there is cause to suspect or a substantiation by DSS that a child is abused, neglected, or dependent. This section is an introductory overview of the relevant provisions of HIPAA and does not provide a comprehensive review of this federal law. Additionally, it does not address when DSS is subject to HIPAA requirements as a covered entity.

> **Resource:** For information about whether DSS is a HIPAA covered entity, see Aimee Wall, *Should a Local Government Be a HIPAA Hybrid Entity?*, UNC SCH. OF GOV'T: COATES' CANONS: NC LOCAL GOVERNMENT LAW BLOG (April 28, 2015).

### A. Covered Health Care Providers

The privacy rule applies to any "health care provider" that transmits health information in electronic form in connection with certain transactions, including the electronic transmission of information to a health plan for purposes of obtaining authorization or payment for health care services. *See* 45 C.F.R. 160.103, 164.500. While the transmission of information in electronic form for specified activities makes a health care provider a "covered entity" under

---

[1] This section was written by School of Government faculty member Mark Botts.

the privacy rule, once covered, the privacy rule protects health information maintained by the provider in any form, whether electronic or on paper. (Other covered entities include health plans and health care clearinghouses.) "Health care provider" is defined broadly to include any person or organization that, in the normal course of business, furnishes, bills, or is paid for care, services, or supplies related to the health of the individual. This includes services relating to the mental condition or functional status of an individual. *See* 45 C.F.R. 160.103 for definitions of "health care provider" and "health care".

### B. Protected Health Information

The privacy rule governs health information that is maintained in any form or medium (e.g., electronic, paper, or oral) that

- is created or received by a health care provider, health plan, employer, or health care clearinghouse;
- identifies an individual or provides a reasonable basis to believe that the information can be used to identify an individual; and
- relates to the past, present, or future physical or mental health or condition of an individual; the provision of health care to an individual; or the past, present, or future payment for the provision of health care to an individual.

### C. Duty to Comply with HIPAA

A covered entity, including a covered health care provider, may use and disclose protected health information only as permitted or required by the privacy rule. Any person or organization alleging a HIPAA violation may file a complaint with the U.S. DHHS Office of Civil Rights (OCR). Because OCR has the authority to impose significant civil monetary penalties for impermissible disclosures of protected health information, anyone seeking information from a health care provider will often be asked to point to a provision of the privacy rule that authorizes the provider to disclose the information. *See* 45 C.F.R. 160.402.

### D. Impact on Abuse, Neglect, Dependency Laws

**1. Reporting child abuse, neglect, or dependency.** Anyone who has cause to suspect that a child is abused, neglected, or dependent, or has died as a result of maltreatment, has a legal duty under state law to report the case to the department of social services in the county where the child resides or is found. G.S. 7B-301. The HIPAA privacy rule permits a covered health care provider or other covered entity to disclose protected health information to a government authority authorized by law to receive reports of child abuse or neglect. *See* 45 C.F.R. 164.512(b). Thus, the privacy rule does not prevent a covered provider from complying with North Carolina's reporting law nor does it bar the provider from disclosing protected health information when making a report required by G.S. 7B-301.

**2. Assessment and protective services.** The department of social services is required to assess every abuse, neglect, and dependency report that falls within the scope of the Juvenile Code. G.S. 7B-302. The director of social services (or the director's representative) may make a *written* demand for any information or reports, whether or not confidential, that in the director's opinion may be relevant to the assessment of a report or to the provision of protective services. G.S. 7B-302(e). Upon such demand, any agency or individual is required to provide access to and copies of confidential information to the extent permitted by federal law. The privacy rule permits a health care provider to disclose protected health information to the extent the disclosure is required by law. *See* 45 C.F.R. 164.512(a). Thus, the privacy rule permits a covered provider to disclose protected health information to DSS when DSS makes a written demand for the information pursuant to G.S. 7B-302(e).

**3. The child's GAL access to information.** G.S. 7B-601 authorizes the court to appoint a guardian ad litem (GAL) to represent children alleged to be abused, neglected, or dependent in juvenile court proceedings. The GAL has the authority to obtain "any information or reports, whether or not confidential, that may in the guardian ad litem's opinion be relevant to the case." G.S. 7B-601(c). Because the privacy rule says a health care provider may disclose protected health information to the extent that such disclosure is required by law, 45 C.F.R. 164.512(a), and because state law requires disclosure of information to a GAL appointed under G.S. 7B-601, the privacy rule permits a health care provider to disclose protected health information to the GAL as necessary to comply with G.S. 7B-601.

The form order used by courts to appoint a GAL includes the authorizing language of G.S. 7B-601(c) and adds that the authority includes the ability to obtain information protected by the HIPAA privacy rule. *See* AOC-J-207, Order to Appoint or Release Guardian ad Litem and Attorney Advocate (June 2014), quoted in section 14.1.D, above.

**4. Interagency information sharing.** As discussed in section 14.1.E, the Juvenile Code requires the adoption of rules designating local agencies that are *required* to share with one another, upon request and to the extent permitted by federal law and regulations, information in their possession that is relevant to

- any assessment of a report of child abuse, neglect, or dependency;
- the provision or arrangement of protective services in a child abuse, neglect, or dependency case by a local department of social services; or
- any case in which a petition is filed alleging that a juvenile is abused, neglected, dependent, undisciplined or delinquent.

G.S. 7B-3100.

To the extent that the rules designate health care providers or other HIPAA covered entities to disclose information pursuant to G.S. 7B-3100, the HIPAA privacy rule permits the information sharing because it authorizes a covered entity to disclose protected health information to the extent that such disclosure is required by law. 45 C.F.R. 164.512(a). The state law requirement to share information, combined with the privacy law's permission to disclose information when required by state law, requires the health care provider to disclose information in accordance with G.S. 7B-3100 if the health care provider is a designated agency by rule. *See* 14B N.C.A.C. 11A.0301 for a list of agencies designated to share information pursuant to G.S. 7B-3100.

**5. Disclosure pursuant to a subpoena.** The privacy rule permits a health care provider or other covered entity to disclose protected health information in response to a subpoena if the covered entity receives *satisfactory assurance* from the party seeking the information that reasonable efforts have been made by the party either to

- ensure that the individual who is the subject of the information has been given notice of the request or
- secure a qualified protective order.

*See* 45 C.F.R. 164.512(e).

*Satisfactory assurance of notice* means a written statement and accompanying documentation that the party requesting records has made a good faith attempt to provide written notice to the individual that includes sufficient information about the proceeding to permit the individual to raise an objection to the court and the time for the individual to raise objections has elapsed and either no objections were filed or all objections filed were resolved by the court and the disclosures being sought are consistent with such resolution.

*Satisfactory assurance of a qualified protective order* means a written statement and accompanying documentation demonstrating that the parties to the dispute giving rise to the request for information have agreed to a qualified protective order and have presented it to the court or tribunal, or the party seeking the information has requested a qualified protective order. (*See* 45 C.F.R. 164.512(e) for more information on protective orders.)

---

**Practice Note:** The HIPAA privacy rule does not preempt state and federal confidentiality laws that place greater restrictions on the disclosure of protected information. Because the state mental health confidentiality law and the federal law governing substance use disorder patient records do not permit the disclosure of protected information in response to a subpoena alone, information that is governed by those laws cannot be disclosed pursuant to a subpoena, notwithstanding the fact that the same information also may be subject to the HIPAA privacy rule. See sections 14.3 and 14.4, below.

---

**6. Disclosure pursuant to a court order.** A health care provider or other HIPAA covered entity may disclose protected health information in response to an order of a court or administrative tribunal, provided that the covered entity discloses only the information expressly authorized by the order. 45 C.F.R. 164.512(e)(1)(i). The privacy rule expresses no particular procedure or criteria for obtaining a court order to disclose protected health information.

**7. Disclosure with patient authorization.** A health care provider may disclose protected health information as authorized by the patient. The authorization must be voluntary and in writing. It also must be informed, which means that the individual signing the authorization must understand what information will be shared, with whom it will be shared, and for what purpose. Toward this end, the privacy rule specifies required content for a valid authorization. *See* 45 C.F.R. 164.508(c).

The patient's written authorization permits, but does not require, the health care provider or other covered entity to disclose information. Any disclosure made by a health care provider pursuant to a patient's authorization must be consistent with, and may not exceed, the terms of the written authorization. The patient may revoke the authorization at any time.

---

**Resources:**

For a detailed guide to HIPAA, see "The HIPAA Privacy Rule" section of the U.S. Department of Health and Human Services website.

For a sample patient-authorization-to-disclose form that meets the requirements of the HIPAA privacy rule, see Mark F. Botts, LaToya B. Powell, Rachel Johnson, Jessica Jones, *North Carolina Juvenile Justice - Behavioral Health Information Sharing Guide* (UNC School of Government, 2015).

---

## 14.3 Mental Health Records and G.S. 122C[2]

The Mental Health, Developmental Disabilities, and Substance Abuse Act of 1985, G.S. Chapter 122C, governs providers of mental health, developmental disabilities, and substance abuse services (MH/DD/SA services). G.S. 122C-52 through -56 govern the information relating to those services.

### A. Covered Providers

G.S. 122C applies to any "facility"—meaning any individual, agency, company, area authority, or state facility—at one location *whose primary purpose* is to provide services for the care, treatment, habilitation, or rehabilitation of the mentally ill, the developmentally disabled, or substance abusers. This definition includes public and private agencies, providers of outpatient as well as inpatient services, state-operated psychiatric hospitals, psychiatric residential treatment centers, and agencies and individuals who contract with area authorities to provide services to area authority clients.

An "area authority" is commonly referred to as a "local management entity/managed care organization" or "LME/MCO." Though these terms have distinct meanings in some contexts, for the purposes of this section of the Manual, the terms are interchangeable and refer to the public authorities responsible for contracting for the provision of publicly-funded MH/DD/SA services within a specified geographic service area. *See* G.S. 122C-3 for the definitions of these terms.

In addition to G.S. 122C, regulations at 10A N.C.A.C. 26B impose additional confidentiality requirements on a subset of MH/DD/SA facilities: area authorities, state facilities, and the individuals and agencies that contract to provide services on behalf of area authorities and state facilities.

---

[2] This section was written by School of Government faculty member Mark Botts.

## B. Confidential Information

Any information, whether recorded or not, relating to an individual served by a "facility" and received in connection with the performance of any function of the facility is confidential and may not be disclosed except as authorized by G.S. 122C-52 through -56 and, where applicable, 10A N.C.A.C. 26B. *See* G.S. 122C-3(9); 122C-52.

## C. The Duty of Confidentiality

No individual having access to confidential information may disclose it except as authorized by G.S. 122C and, where applicable, 10A N.C.A.C. 26B. The unauthorized disclosure of confidential information is a Class 3 misdemeanor (*see* G.S. 122C-52(e)) and could result in civil liability for the treatment facility or its employees. Further, because employees of area and state facilities are subject to disciplinary action if they disclose information in violation of G.S. 122C (*see* 10 N.C.A.C. 26B.0104), agencies subject to G.S. 122C will generally insist on identifying the legal authority for a disclosure before making the disclosure.

## D. Impact on Abuse, Neglect, Dependency Laws

**1. Reporting child abuse, neglect, or dependency.** Anyone who has cause to suspect that a child is abused, neglected, or dependent, or has died as a result of maltreatment, is required to report the case to the department of social services in the county where the child resides or is found. G.S. 7B-301. Under G.S. 122C-54(h), providers of MH/DD/SA services are required to disclose confidential information for purposes of complying with Article 3 of G.S. Chapter 7B, which includes 7B-301. Thus, the state law governing the confidentiality of MH/DD/SA services is not a bar to complying with the state's child abuse reporting statute, and providers of services must disclose confidential information when necessary to comply with the mandatory reporting law.

**2. Assessment and protective services.** The department of social services is required to assess every abuse, neglect, and dependency report that falls within the scope of the Juvenile Code. G.S.7B-302. The director or director's representative may make a *written* demand for any information or reports, whether or not confidential, that in the director's opinion may be relevant to the assessment or to the provision of protective services. Upon such demand, any agency or individual must provide access to and copies of confidential information to the extent permitted by federal law.

The state mental health confidentiality law requires individuals and agencies subject to the law to disclose confidential information for purposes of complying with Article 3 of G.S. Chapter 7B, which includes 7B-302. *See* G.S. 122C-54(h). Thus, even if DSS seeks information that falls within the scope of the confidentiality protections of G.S. 122C, providers of MH/DDSA services must provide access to and copies of the requested information, unless disclosure is prohibited by federal law and regulations.

**3. The child's GAL access to information.** A guardian ad litem (GAL) appointed under G.S. 7B-601 to represent children who are alleged to be abused, neglected, or dependent, has the authority to obtain "any information or reports, whether or not confidential, that may in the guardian ad litem's opinion be relevant to the case." G.S. 7B-601(c).

G.S. 122C-54(h) provides that facilities governed by G.S. 122C must disclose confidential information "as required by other State or federal law." Thus, when a court order appoints someone to be a GAL under G.S. 7B-601, the GAL must be granted access to any information, whether or not protected by G.S. 122C, that the GAL believes is relevant to the case.

**4. Interagency information sharing.** As discussed in sections 14.1.E and 14.2.D.4, above, the Juvenile Code requires the adoption of rules designating local agencies that are *required* to share with one another, upon request and to the extent permitted by federal law and regulations, information that is in their possession that is relevant to

- any assessment of a report of child abuse, neglect, or dependency;
- the provision or arrangement of protective services in a child abuse, neglect, or dependency case by a local department of social services; or
- any case in which a petition is filed alleging that a juvenile is abused, neglected, dependent, undisciplined or delinquent.

To the extent that the applicable rules, 14B N.C.A.C. 11A.0301, designate MH/DD/SA service providers among the agencies required to share information in accordance with G.S. 7B-3100, those service providers would be required to share information upon the request of another designated agency because G.S. 122C requires providers to disclose confidential information as required by other state law. *See* G.S. 122C-54(h).

The rules designate area mental health, developmental disabilities, and substance abuse authorities among the agencies required to share information pursuant to the statute, as well as any "local agency designated by an administrative order issued by the chief district court judge of the district court district in which the agency is located." 14B N.C.A.C. 11A.0301(j). Because the rules do not designate individuals and agencies who contract with area authorities to provide services to area authority clients, such providers of services do not come under G.S. 7B-3100 and, therefore, would not be permitted to disclose confidential information pursuant to the statute unless they are designated by an administrative court order as provided for in the rule. *See* 14B N.C.A.C. 11A.0301 for a list of agencies designated to share information pursuant to G.S. 7B-3100.

**5. Disclosure pursuant to a subpoena.** Unlike the privacy rule governing health records, discussed in section 14.2, above, G.S. 122C does not include a provision permitting a provider of MH/DD/SA services to disclose confidential information in response to a subpoena alone. A subpoena would compel disclosure of confidential information only if the confidentiality bar is removed by the client's written authorization to disclose, a court order requiring disclosure, or some other legal mandate, such as a statute or regulation, that requires disclosure under the particular circumstances.

**6. Disclosure pursuant to a court order.** A facility must disclose confidential information if a court of competent jurisdiction issues an order compelling disclosure. G.S. 122C-54(a). G.S. 122C-54(a) expresses no standard or criteria for the issuance of a court order. Presumably, the court should use a public interest test similar to the test articulated in the regulations governing substance abuse records, see section 14.4, below, which requires the court to balance the public interest and need for the disclosure against the potential injury to the patient, the patient-provider relationship, and the provider's on-going treatment services.

The evidentiary privilege statutes for mental health professionals may provide some guidance to the court. The privilege statutes for psychologists and other mental health professionals provide that a judge may order disclosure of privileged information when "necessary to the proper administration of justice" (e.g., in order that the truth be known and justice done). *See* G.S. 8-53.3 (psychologists); 8-53.5 (marital and family therapists); and 8-54.7 (social workers) and case annotations.

**7. Disclosure with patient authorization.** A facility may disclose confidential information if the client or his or her legally responsible person consents in writing to the release of the information to a specified person or agency. *See* G.S. 122C-53(a); 122C-3(28).

The state regulations that apply to area authorities and their contracted providers of services specify the required content for consent forms. *See* 10A N.C.A.C. 26B.0200. The consent must be voluntary, informed, and in writing. The client's consent is revocable, and it permits, but does not require, a facility to disclose confidential information.

Any consent form used for the disclosure of information that is confidential under G.S. 122C will probably need to conform to the HIPAA privacy rule requirements for patient authorization, as most MH/DD/SA providers also are healthcare providers covered by the privacy rule. The most effective way to ensure that you are using a consent form that meets the requirement of law is to have the patient sign and fully complete the treatment provider's own consent form.

**Resource:** For a sample patient-authorization-to-disclose form that meets the requirements of the HIPAA privacy rule and G.S. 122C, see Mark F. Botts, LaToya B. Powell, Rachel Johnson, Jessica Jones, *North Carolina Juvenile Justice - Behavioral Health Information Sharing Guide* (UNC School of Government, 2015).

## 14.4 Substance Abuse Records and 42 C.F.R. Part 2[3]

Federal law restricts the use and disclosure of patient information received or acquired by a federally assisted alcohol or drug abuse program. 42 U.S.C. 290dd-2; 42 C.F.R. Part 2.

---

[3] This section was written by School of Government faculty member Mark Botts.

## A. Covered Programs

The federal law governs federally assisted programs. A "program" is

- an individual or entity (other than a general medical facility) that holds itself out as providing, and provides, substance use disorder diagnosis, treatment, or referral for treatment;
- an identified unit with a general medical facility that holds itself out as providing, and provides, substance use disorder diagnosis, treatment, or referral for treatment; or
- medical personnel or other staff in a general medical facility whose primary function is the provision of substance use disorder diagnosis, treatment, or referral for treatment and who are identified as such providers.

*See* 42 C.F.R. 2.11 (definition of "substance use disorder").

A program is considered "federally assisted" if it participates in Medicare, has tax exempt status, is registered to dispense a controlled substance used in the treatment of substance use disorders, receives federal financial assistance in any form even if the financial assistance does not directly pay for substance use disorder treatment, and is a local government unit that receives federal funds that could be but are not necessarily spent for a substance abuse disorder program. *See* 42 C.F.R. 2.12(b). By participating in Medicaid and receiving federal block grant funding, area authorities (LME/MCOs) and the agencies that contract with them to provide substance use disorder diagnosis, treatment, or referral for treatment are federally assisted programs governed by 42 C.F.R. Part 2.

The federal regulations cover those treatment or rehabilitation programs, employee assistance programs, programs in general hospitals, and school-based programs who hold themselves out as providing and provide substance use disorder diagnosis, treatment, or referral for treatment. A private practitioner who specializes, and holds herself out as specializing, in diagnosing substance use disorders and referring patients elsewhere for treatment is covered by the regulations even though she does not treat substance use disorders.

However, as the three-part definition of "program" indicates, when it comes to general medical facilities, the regulations define "program" differently. The federal regulations would not apply to hospital emergency department personnel who refer a patient to the hospital's intensive care unit for an apparent drug overdose unless the *primary* function of such personnel is the provision of substance use disorder diagnosis, treatment, or referral for treatment and they are identified as providing such services. Alternatively, if the general hospital has promoted its emergency department or other identified unit, such as a detox unit, to the community as a provider of such services, the identified unit, but not the rest of the general hospital, would be a program covered by the regulations.

**Practice Note:** If a hospital emergency room treating a trauma patient performs a blood test that identifies cocaine or other drugs in the patient's blood, this alone would not make the hospital emergency room a "program" covered by the regulations and, therefore, the drug test results would not be protected by 42 C.F.R. Part 2. If, however, a substance abuse counselor evaluates the same patient for drug abuse and referral for treatment after the patient is admitted to a medical floor of the hospital, then the substance abuse counselor would be considered a "program."

## B. Confidential Information

The federal restrictions on disclosure apply to any information, whether recorded or not, that

- would identify a "patient" (defined as an individual who has applied for or been given substance use disorder treatment, diagnosis, or referral for treatment) as having or having had a substance use disorder and
- is alcohol or drug abuse information obtained by a federally assisted alcohol or drug abuse program for the purpose of treating substance use disorder, making a diagnosis for that treatment, or making a referral for that treatment.

The mere acknowledgement by program staff of the presence of an identified patient at a residential or inpatient facility would involve the disclosure of confidential information if the facility is publicly identified as a place where only substance use disorder diagnosis, treatment, or referral for treatment is provided. Acknowledging the presence of a patient in this circumstance would require either the patient's written consent or an authorizing court order issued in compliance with the regulations. For disclosures pursuant to a court order or patient consent, *see* section 14.4.D, below (discussing impact on abuse and neglect laws).

**Practice Note:** Suppose a child protective services worker investigating a report of child neglect requests access to a child's mental health record. The family/social history section of the child's record states that the mother, during the intake interview with the child's mental health counselor, disclosed that she abuses cocaine. This information is not covered by 42 C.F.R. Part 2 because it was not obtained for the purpose of treating or diagnosing the mother or referring her for treatment. The information also would not be covered because it does not identify the mother as a person who has applied for or received substance use disorder treatment, diagnosis, or referral for treatment.

A diagnosis that is made solely for the purpose of providing evidence for use by law enforcement agencies or officials is not confidential information because it is not obtained for the purpose of treating substance use disorder, making a diagnosis for treatment, or making a referral for that treatment. On the other hand, a diagnosis that is initially prepared by a program in connection with treatment or referral for treatment of a substance use disorder patient is covered by the regulations even if the diagnosis is not used for treatment because the patient does not follow up on the referral.

## C. Duty Imposed by Federal Substance Abuse Records Law

The regulations prohibit the *disclosure* and *use* of patient records except as permitted by the regulations themselves. Anyone who violates the law is subject to a criminal penalty in the form of a fine (up to $500 for first offense, up to $5,000 for each subsequent offense).

It is important for social services departments, guardians ad litem (GALs), and others who receive program information to understand that the duty of confidentiality imposed by the federal regulations may sometimes fall on them. The restrictions on disclosure apply to individuals and entities who receive patient information directly from a program or other lawful holder of information if they are notified of the prohibition on redisclosure in accordance with section 2.32 of the regulations. That section requires a program that discloses information pursuant to the patient's written consent to notify the recipient that the information continues to be protected by 42 C.F.R. Part 2 and may be redisclosed only as permitted by the regulations.

### D. Impact on Abuse, Neglect, Dependency Laws

If the federal law does not expressly permit the disclosure of confidential patient information in a particular circumstance, then the disclosure is prohibited. To understand the impact of 42 C.F.R. Part 2 on North Carolina's laws pertaining to child abuse, neglect, and dependency, we must start with the federal law's own rule regarding its relationship to state law: "no state law may either authorize or compel any disclosure prohibited by this part." 42 C.F.R. 2.20. Thus, where the Juvenile Code or other state law authorizes or compels a disclosure that is not permitted by 42 C.F.R. Part 2, the federal prohibition on disclosure must be followed. Conversely, the federal regulation does not preempt the field of state law. If the federal law permits a particular disclosure, but state law prohibits it, then state law controls. The federal law does not compel disclosure under any circumstance.

In addition to restricting the *disclosure* of information, the regulations also restrict the *use* of information to initiate or substantiate criminal charges against a patient. Generally, when a department of social services or guardian ad litem seeks information from programs for the purpose of carrying out their functions relating to child abuse, neglect, or dependency, the restrictions on program *disclosures* will apply to guide programs on how to respond to requests for information. Because the restrictions on *use* apply only to the use of information for purposes of criminal investigation or prosecution, those restrictions are not discussed here. *See* 42 C.F.R. 2.12 for the restrictions on use of information.

**1. Reporting child abuse, neglect, or dependency.** The federal restrictions on the disclosure of confidential information do not apply to the reporting of suspected child abuse or neglect under state laws mandating such reports. 42 C.F.R. 2.12(c)(6). Therefore, the federal law does not bar compliance with North Carolina's mandatory reporting statute (G.S. 7B-301), even if it means disclosing patient identifying information.

**2. Assessment and protective services.** Although substance use disorder programs (or third party payers who have received information from such programs) must make a report of suspected abuse, neglect, or dependency as mandated by G.S. 7B-301, they are not authorized to provide information beyond the initial report when DSS requests further information pursuant to its duty under G.S. 7B-302(e) to assess the report. The federal rules permit the disclosure of information for follow-up investigations or for court proceedings that may arise from the report only with the patient's written *consent* or a *court order* issued pursuant to Subpart E of the federal regulations. 42 C.F.R. 2.12(c)(6).

**3. The child's GAL access to information.** A guardian ad litem (GAL) appointed under G.S. 7B-601 to represent children who are alleged to be abused, neglected, or dependent, has the authority to obtain "any information or reports, whether or not confidential, that may in the guardian ad litem's opinion be relevant to the case." G.S. 7B-601(c). However, the federal regulations governing substance use disorder treatment records do not recognize this as a policy exception to the confidentiality of patient information. The federal rules permit the disclosure of information to a GAL only with the patient's written consent or a court order issued in compliance with Subpart E of the federal regulations.

**4. Interagency information sharing.** Although the HIPAA privacy rule and state mental health law permit the interagency sharing of confidential information as required by G.S. 7B-3100 and 14B N.C.A.C. 11A.0301 and discussed in sections 14.2.D.4 and 14.3.D.4, above, the federal drug and alcohol confidentiality law and its implementing regulations at 42 C.F.R. Part 2 do not permit the disclosure of confidential information pursuant to these state laws.

**5. Disclosure pursuant to a subpoena.** Unlike the privacy rule governing health records, discussed in section 14.2, above, and like the state confidentiality law governing MH/DD/SA services, 42 C.F.R. Part 2 does not include a provision permitting a provider of services to disclose confidential information in response to a subpoena alone. A subpoena compels disclosure of confidential information only if accompanied by the client's authorization to disclose, a court order to disclose, or some other legal mandate, such as a statute or regulation that requires disclosure under the circumstances.

**6. Disclosure pursuant to a court order.** Under Subpart E of 42 C.F.R. Part 2, a court of competent jurisdiction may authorize a use or disclosure that would otherwise be prohibited under the regulations. *See* 42 C.F.R. 2.61. Such an order does not compel disclosure; to compel disclosure a subpoena or similar mandate must be issued.

Subpart E sets forth the procedure and criteria for court orders authorizing

- disclosure for noncriminal purposes,
- disclosure and use of information to criminally investigate or prosecute patients,
- disclosure and use of information to investigate or prosecute a program or the person holding the records, and
- the use of undercover agents and informants to investigate employees or agents of a program in connection with a criminal matter.

The kind of order needed by a department of social services to obtain confidential information in the context of child abuse, neglect, or dependency proceedings is an order authorizing disclosure for noncriminal purposes. Any person having a legally recognized interest in the disclosure that is sought may apply for the order. The application may be filed separately or as part of a pending action and must use a fictitious name, such as John Doe, to refer to the patient unless the court orders the record of the proceeding sealed from public scrutiny. *See* 42 C.F.R. 2.64. When seeking a court order where there is no pending action, *see In re Albemarle Mental Health Center*, 42 N.C. App. 292 (1979) (where no civil or criminal proceeding has been commenced, the superior court has jurisdiction to hear a motion requesting an in camera hearing to determine whether information in the possession of a mental health center should be disclosed; the action is in the nature of a special proceeding.).

When the information is sought for noncriminal purposes, the patient and person holding the records must be given adequate notice and opportunity to file a written response or appear in person for the limited purpose of providing evidence on the legal criteria for issuance of the order. 42 C.F.R. 2.64. The judge may examine the records before making a decision. Any oral argument, review of evidence, or hearing on the application must be held in camera.

To order disclosure, the court must find "good cause" for the disclosure. For an order authorizing disclosure for noncriminal purposes, this means the court must find that

- other ways of obtaining the information are not available or would not be effective and
- the public interest and need for disclosure outweigh the potential injury to the patient, the patient's relationship to the program, and the program's ongoing treatment services.

Any order authorizing disclosure must (i) limit disclosure to those parts of the record that are essential to fulfill the purpose of the order, (ii) limit disclosure to those persons whose need for the information forms the basis for the order, and (iii) include any other measures that are necessary to limit disclosure for the protection of the patient, the patient-treatment provider relationship, and the program's ongoing treatment services (e.g., sealing from public scrutiny the record of any proceeding for which the disclosure of information has been ordered). *See* 42 C.F.R. 2.64.

The disclosure of certain information—the things a patient says to program personnel—requires additional findings by the court. A court may order the disclosure of "confidential communications" made by a patient to a program in the course of diagnosis, treatment, or referral for treatment only if the disclosure is

- necessary to protect against an existing threat to life or serious bodily injury, including circumstances that constitute suspected child abuse and neglect and verbal threats against third parties;
- necessary to the investigation or prosecution of an extremely serious crime; or
- in connection with litigation in which the patient offers testimony or other evidence pertaining to the content of the confidential communications. 42 C.F.R. 2.63.

**7. Disclosure with patient authorization.** A program may disclose confidential information with the consent of the patient. As with the HIPAA privacy rule and the state mental health law, patient consent must be voluntary and in writing. It also must be informed, which means that the individual signing the authorization must understand what information will be shared, with whom it will be shared, and for what purpose. Toward this end, the federal law governing substance use disorder programs specifies certain content that must be included in the written consent for it to be considered valid. *See* 42 C.F.R. 2.31.

Any consent form used for the disclosure of information that is confidential under 42 C.F.R. Part 2 will need to conform to the state law requirements for consent because G.S. 122C also applies to substance abuse treatment services. In addition, if the program is a covered entity under the HIPAA privacy rule, the privacy rule's requirements for patient authorization will apply. The most effective way to ensure that you are using a consent form that meets the requirement of law is to have the patient sign and fully complete the treatment program's own consent form.

**Resource:** For a sample consent-to-disclose form that meets the requirements of the HIPAA privacy rule, G.S. 122C, and 42 C.F.R. Part 2, see Mark F. Botts, LaToya B. Powell, Rachel Johnson, Jessica Jones, *North Carolina Juvenile Justice - Behavioral Health Information Sharing Guide* (UNC School of Government, 2015).

## 14.5 Education Records and FERPA

### A. Introduction

The Family Educational Rights and Privacy Act (FERPA), 20 U.S.C. 1232g, was enacted in 1974; the corresponding regulations are found at 34 C.F.R. Part 99. Amendments were made to FERPA by the Uninterrupted Scholars Act (USA) to address timely access to records. *See* Pub. L. No. 112-278, 126 Stat. 2480, effective January 14, 2013. Federal regulations have not been amended to include the USA provisions.

FERPA is a complex federal law that provides for access to education records by parents and "eligible students" while protecting the privacy of students and parents by governing the disclosure of education records by all educational institutions that receive federal funds. A parent includes a natural parent, guardian, or individual acting as a parent in the absence of a parent or guardian. An eligible student is a student who is 18 years old or attending a postsecondary institution. 34 C.F.R. 99.3. FERPA gives parents and eligible students certain rights with respect to inspecting, requesting changes to, and preventing disclosure of education records.

A county DSS that is providing child welfare (including an initial assessment) services to a child needs to access a child's education record. A DSS assessment of abuse, neglect, or dependency may require information from the child's school records. 10A N.C.A.C. 70A.0106(i)(4). A child's case plan with a county DSS includes the child's education records. 42 U.S.C. 675(1)(C); 10A N.C.A.C. 70G.0506(a)(5). Although state laws give certain individuals and agencies access to confidential information for the purpose of child protection and abuse, neglect, or dependency proceedings, access to and disclosure of education records in some circumstances are subject to FERPA requirements.

For the purposes of this Manual, this section focuses on consent to disclose information and certain exceptions to the need for consent. This section is an introductory overview of FERPA requirements most relevant to abuse, neglect, or dependency proceedings and does not comprehensively address FERPA.

**Resources:**
For more detailed information about FERPA, including regulations, explanations, fact sheets, and model forms, see
- "Student Privacy Policy Office" page on the U.S. Department of Education website.
- The "Protecting Student Privacy" website by the U.S. Department of Education: A Service of the Privacy Technical Assistance Center and the Student Privacy Policy Office.
- Areas of Focus, "Data & Information Sharing" section of the Legal Center for Foster Care and Education website.

## B. Consent Required for Disclosure

**1. Consent required.** Under FERPA, an educational agency or institution may not provide personally identifiable information from a student's education records without obtaining a *specific dated written consent* from the parent or eligible student, unless an exception to the consent requirement applies. 20 U.S.C. 1232g(b)(2)(A); 34 C.F.R. 99.30(a); *see* 20 U.S.C. 1232g(d) (student consent). The consent signature may be in an electronic form. 34 C.F.R. 99.30(d).

A consent to release records protected by FERPA must

- specify the records that may be disclosed,
- state the purpose of the disclosure, and
- identify the party or class of parties to whom the disclosure may be made.

34 C.F.R. 99.30(b).

Upon request, a parent or eligible student must also receive a copy of the records disclosed. 34 C.F.R. 99.30(c).

An educational agency must give FERPA rights and protections to a parent unless the school has been provided with evidence of a court order, state statute, or legally binding document that relates to divorce, separation, or custody that specifically revokes these rights. 34 C.F.R. 99.4.

**2. Personally identifiable information.** "Personally identifiable information" includes but is not limited to

- the student's name;
- the name of the student's parent or other family members;
- the address of the student or student's family;
- a personal identifier, such as the student's social security number, student number, or biometric record;
- other indirect identifiers, such as the student's date of birth, place of birth, and mother's maiden name;
- other information that, alone or in combination, is linked or linkable to a specific student

that would allow a reasonable person in the school community, who does not have personal knowledge of the relevant circumstances, to identify the student with reasonable certainty; or
- information requested by a person who the educational agency or institution reasonably believes knows the identity of the student to whom the education record relates.

34 C.F.R. 99.3. *See also* G.S. 115C-402.5(a)(4)a.

**3. Education records.** The term "education records" used in FERPA generally includes all records (which is information recorded in any way including handwriting, print, computer media, video or audio tape, film, microfilm, and microfiche) that are maintained by the agency or institution (or by a party acting for the agency or institution) and contain information directly related to a student. 20 U.S.C. 1232g(a)(4)(A); 34 C.F.R. 99.3. This means the records themselves and the information in them, wherever they are stored. Educational records are broadly defined. The health records of a student enrolled in elementary or secondary school, such as immunization and school nurse's records that are maintained by the school, are education records under FERPA. *See* Joint Guidance on the Application of the Family Educational Rights and Privacy Act (FERPA) and the Health Insurance Portability and Accountability Act of 1996 (HIPAA) to Student Health Records, (U.S. Department of Health and Human Services and U.S. Department of Public Education, Dec. 2019 Update).

North Carolina law identifies what information must be included in a student's official record. At a minimum, there must be adequate student identification data including a date of birth, attendance, grading and promotion, notices of long-term suspensions and expulsions and the conduct for which the suspension or expulsion was based, and other factual information deemed appropriate by the local board of education. G.S. 115C-402(b).

There are a number of exceptions in the definition of "education records." One narrow exception excludes personal notes kept in the sole possession of the maker, are used as a memory aid, and are not accessible or revealed to anyone except a temporary substitute for the person who made the notes. 20 U.S.C. 1232g(a)(4)(B)(i); 34 C.F.R. 99.3. Thus, a teacher's or administrator's personal notes that are not shared and are based on the personal knowledge and observations of the teacher or administrator are likely not subject to FERPA requirements.

Another exception involves "records of a law enforcement unit" of the education agency that were created and maintained by that unit for law enforcement purposes. 20 U.S.C. 1232g(a)(4)(B)(ii); 34 C.F.R. 99.3 and 99.8(b)(1). A law enforcement unit includes any individual, office, department, division, or other component of the agency such as a unit of commissioned police officers or non-commissioned security guards that is officially authorized by the agency to (1) maintain the physical security and safety of the agency; (2) enforce federal, state, or local law; or (3) refer to appropriate authorities a matter for enforcement of any federal, state, or local law against an individual or organization (that is not the education agency). 34 C.F.R. 99.8(a)(1). A law enforcement unit may also perform non-law enforcement functions, such as investigating incidents resulting in school disciplinary action. 34 C.F.R. 99.8(a)(2). Law enforcement records are not covered by FERPA. 34 C.F.R. 99.8(d). But, records that are not law enforcement records and are subject to FERPA are those records that (1) are created by the law enforcement unit for law enforcement purposes but are maintained by the educational agency and not the law enforcement unit and (2) are created and maintained by the law enforcement unit exclusively for a non-law enforcement purpose, such as school disciplinary action. 34 C.F.R. 99.8(b)(2).

**Resource:** For more information see School Resource Officers, School Law Enforcement Units, and the Family Educational Rights and Privacy Act (FERPA) (Feb. 2019) on the U.S Department of Education Protecting Student Privacy website.

### C. Exceptions to Consent Requirement

**1. Overview.** There are a number of exceptions to the requirement of written consent to allow disclosure to certain parties under certain conditions. Those most relevant to juvenile proceedings are disclosures

- to an agency caseworker or tribal organization authorized to access a student's case plan when legally responsible for the care and protection of the student;
- to comply with a judicial order or lawfully issued subpoena;
- to appropriate officials in cases of health and safety emergencies;
- of information that is "directory" information such as name, address, phone number, dates of attendance, etc.

*See* 34 C.F.R. 99.31, 99.36, 99.37, and 99.38 and the Uninterrupted Scholars Act, Pub. L. No. 112-278, 126 Stat. 2480.

**2. Disclosure to child welfare agency responsible for child.** The Uninterrupted Scholars Act allows educational agencies to release records without first obtaining written consent from a parent to a child welfare agency caseworker or other representative who has the right to access a student's case plan when the agency is legally responsible for the care and protection of the student. 20 U.S.C. 1232g(b)(1)(L). Note that this provision is permissive and not mandatory.

The child welfare agency may only disclose (or redisclose) the education record to an individual or entity that is authorized by the agency to receive the information and is engaged in addressing the student's education needs. The disclosure must be consistent with the applicable state law that protects the confidentiality of a student's education record. 20 U.S.C. 1232g(b)(1)(L).

**Resource:** NC DHHS Division of Social Services Dear County Directors Letter, CWS-07-2013: Family Educational Rights and Privacy Act (June 1, 2013).

**3. Disclosure to comply with judicial order or subpoena.** An educational agency or institution may disclose information to comply with a judicial order or lawfully issued subpoena. 34 C.F.R. 99.31(a)(9)(i). A juvenile court may order that the information be disclosed. The educational agency or institution must make a reasonable effort to notify the parent or eligible student of the order or subpoena before complying so the parent or eligible student may seek legal recourse. 34 C.F.R. 99.31(a)(9)(ii). However, notification to the parent is not required if

- the parent is a party to a court proceeding involving child abuse, neglect, or dependency and the order to disclose information is issued in that proceeding (this exception applies even if there is not an order removing the child from the home);
- the disclosure is in compliance with a federal grand jury subpoena or a subpoena issued for law enforcement purposes for which a court has ordered that the existence or contents of the subpoena or information furnished in response to the subpoena not be disclosed; or
- the disclosure is in compliance with an ex parte court order obtained by the U.S. Attorney General or that person's designee concerning certain investigations or prosecutions related to terrorism.

20 U.SC. 1232g(b)(2)(B); 34 C.F.R. 99.31(a)(9)(ii)(A)–(C).

**4. Disclosure for health or safety emergency.** An educational agency or institution may disclose personally identifiable information from an education record to appropriate parties in connection with an emergency if knowledge of the information is necessary to protect the health or safety of the student or other individuals. 34 C.F.R. 99.36(a); *see* 20 U.S.C. 1232g(b)(1)(I); 34 C.F.R. 99.31(a)(10). In making a determination as to whether this exception applies, an educational agency or institution may take into account the totality of the circumstances pertaining to a threat to the health or safety of a student or other individuals. If the determination is made that there is an articulable and significant threat to the health or safety of a student or other individual, disclosure may be made to any person whose knowledge of the information is necessary to protect the health or safety of the student or others. 34 C.F.R. 99.31(a)(10) and 99.36(c). When personally identifiable information is disclosed under the health and safety emergency exception, the education agency must record the articulable and significant threat to the health or safety of a student or other persons and the parties to whom the information was disclosed. 34 C.F.R. 99.32(a)(5).

Although FERPA does not include a specific exception for reporting child abuse or neglect, the health or safety exception may apply in the few cases in which it is necessary to consult school records to determine whether a report should be made. The exception also may apply when a social services director acting pursuant to G.S. 7B-302(e) makes a written demand for information or reports the director believes are relevant to an assessment or to the provision of protective services. It will depend on the education agency's determination, based on the totality of the circumstances, whether there is an articulable and significant threat to the child (who is the student whose record is sought) or others.

**5. Disclosure to school personnel and schools where the child seeks to enroll.** A student's school records may be shared with other school officials (including teachers) who the educational agency has determined has a legitimate educational interest in the information; the access should only be to those portions of the record in which there is a legitimate educational interest. 20 U.S.C. 1232g(b)(1)(A); 34 C.F.R. 99.31(a)(1). This provision limits who may access selected information contained in the student's record.

A student's educational record may be shared with other schools that the student seeks or intends to enroll in upon the condition that the student's parents are notified, receive a copy of the record if requested, and have an opportunity for a hearing to challenge the contents of the record. 20 U.S.C. 1232g(b)(1)(B). This issue may arise when children are moved to placements that result in a school transfer. School transfers should only happen when it is in the child's best interests to do so and is made in compliance with the Fostering Connections and Increasing Adoptions Act and the Every Student Succeeds Act as discussed in Chapter 13.7. In North Carolina, when a child transfers school systems, the receiving school shall obtain the child's record from the transferring school within thirty days of the child's enrollment. If a parent, custodian, or guardian provides the new school system with a copy of the child's records, the receiving school must request written verification of the records from the prior school. G.S. 115C-403(b).

**6. Disclosure of directory information.** Schools may disclose, without consent, "directory" information such as a student's name, address, telephone number, email address, photograph, date and place of birth, major field of study, grade level, enrollment status, honors and awards, dates of attendance (which does not mean specific daily records of attendance), participation in recognized activities and sports, and most recent educational agency attended. 20 U.S.C. 1232g(a)(5)(A); 34 C.F.R. 99.31(a)(11) and 99.37; *see* 34 C.F.R. 99.3 (definition of "directory information"). Directory information does not include a student's social security number or a student identification number that is used to gain access to education records (when not used in conjunction with other authenticating factors such as a PIN or password). 34 C.F.R. 99.3.

Parents and eligible students must be informed about directory information and their right to ask the school not to disclose it. 34 C.F.R. 99.31(a)(11) and 99.37(a); *see* G.S. 115C-402.5(a)(4)b.; 115C-402.15.

### D. Documentation of Disclosure, Redisclosure, and Use of Information

An educational agency must use reasonable methods to authenticate the identity of the person to whom it discloses personally identifiable information from the education record. 34 C.F.R. 99.31(c). An educational agency must maintain a record within each student's education record that indicates (1) all agencies and individuals (other than personnel within the agency) who have requested or obtained access to the student's record and (2) the person's or agency's legitimate interests in obtaining the information. 20 U.S.C. 1232g(b)(4)(A); 34 C.F.R. 99.32(a).

When an educational agency or institution is permitted to disclose personally identifiable information from an education record, it may do so only on the condition that the party to whom the information is disclosed will not disclose the information to any other party without the prior consent of the parent or eligible student. 20 U.S.C. 1232g(b)(4)(B); 34 C.F.R. 99.33(a)(1). The disclosed information may be used only for the purposes for which the disclosure was made. 34 C.F.R. 99.33(a)(2). This restriction on redisclosure does not include disclosure that is required by a court order or subpoena, for directory information, or when redisclosure has been authorized and documented by the education agency. 34 C.F.R. 99.33(b), (c); *see* 34 C.F.R. 99.32(b).

Note that redisclosure by child welfare agencies is also governed by G.S. 7B-302 and 7B-2901(b), which require information received by the department of social services to be maintained confidentially except for one of the enumerated statutory conditions.

**E. Complaints and Enforcement**

A parent or eligible student may file a written complaint regarding an alleged violation of FERPA with the

U.S. Department of Education
Student Privacy Policy Office
400 Maryland Avenue, S.W.
Washington, DC 20202

Or by email to FERPA.Complaints@ed.gov

34 C.F.R. 99.63; "File a Complaint" page of the U.S. Department of Education Protecting Student Privacy website.

The complaint contents, investigation procedures, and enforcement actions are explained in 34 C.F.R. 99.64 through 99.67. The United States Supreme Court has held that FERPA's nondisclosure provisions create no personal rights that are enforceable under 42 U.S.C. 1983. *Gonzaga Univ. v. Doe*, 536 U.S. 273 (2002).

# Appendixes

# Appendixes

**Appendix 1:** Resources and Organizations

**Appendix 2:** The Chief District Court Judge and Juvenile Court

**Appendix 3:** JWise: The Automated Information System for North Carolina Juvenile Courts

**Appendix 4:** Rules of Recordkeeping, Chapter XII

**Appendix 5:** Case Management for Abuse, Neglect, Dependency, and Termination of Parental Rights Cases in North Carolina Juvenile Courts

# Appendix 1
# Resources and Organizations

Resources that provide additional information about a discussed topic appear throughout this Manual. Some resources are referred to more frequently because they either provide (1) specific practical information for the legal professionals involved in abuse, neglect, dependency, and termination of parental rights proceedings in North Carolina or (2) information based on a national perspective on a variety of topics pertaining to child welfare. Those organizations offering several resources on numerous topics pertaining to child welfare are listed here.

## North Carolina Resources

- **The School of Government (SOG) at UNC-Chapel Hill**. The SOG is the largest university-based local government training, advisory, and research organization in the United States. Its values are nonpartisan, policy-neutral, and responsive. The SOG maintains a website (sog.unc.edu) that consists of information and resources addressing various fields of law, one of which is child welfare. Resources on the SOG's website that relate to abuse, neglect, dependency, and termination of parental rights proceedings in North Carolina include

    - this Manual, which is housed on the Abuse, Neglect, Dependency, and Termination of Parental Rights Manual microsite;
    - the juvenile law microsite, which offers a place to access materials and resources related to child welfare and juvenile justice;
    - the social services microsite, which contains publications, past course and conference materials, a DSS attorney roster, and upcoming trainings and conferences for social services, including child welfare;
    - the Indigent Defense Education microsite (IDE), which offers a place to access materials, resources (including the IDE reference manuals), and a calendar of training events;
    - the Child Welfare Case Compendium (CWCC), a categorized and online searchable database that consists of annotations of opinions addressing child welfare issues that have been published by the North Carolina appellate courts and the U.S. Supreme Court from January 2014 to present;
    - the Social Services Confidentiality Research Tool, an online searchable database that includes over 250 legal resources, including statutes, regulations, cases, and guidance materials addressing confidentiality in public assistance and protective services (including child welfare) programs;
    - Blogs (all of which are searchable by topic, keyword, and/or author)
        - On the Civil Side, focusing on civil legal issues including child welfare, juvenile justice, family law, civil procedure, estate proceedings, adult guardianship, small claims, etc.;

- - - North Carolina Criminal Law, which may have an occasional post that applies to child welfare; and
    - Coates' Canons: NC Local Government Law, which may have an occasional post that applies to child welfare as well as posts for departments of socials services;
  - Beyond the Bench Podcast by the North Carolina Judicial College at the SOG, specifically Season 2, which focuses on neglect and the child welfare system in North Carolina with a particular emphasis on homelessness; and
  - Publications written by SOG faculty, some of which are available for purchase and others at no charge, and searchable by type (bulletin, book, book chapter), author, topic, and/or keyword.

- **The North Carolina Administrative Office of the Courts (AOC).** The AOC is the administrative agency for the North Carolina Judicial Branch of state government. It provides services and resources to assist the unified state court system. The AOC has different divisions and programs, some of which relate directly to abuse, neglect, dependency, and termination of parental rights proceedings, including the following:

  - The North Carolina Court Improvement Program (NC-CIP) is a federally funded program with the purpose of improving court practice in child abuse, neglect, or dependency cases. The NC-CIP section of the AOC website contains various resources related to abuse, neglect, dependency, and termination of parental rights proceedings. NC-CIP also offers trainings for judges and attorneys involved in these proceedings. NC-CIP provided financial support for this Manual.
  - The North Carolina Guardian ad Litem (GAL) Program recruits, trains, and supervises GAL volunteers throughout the state, staffs local GAL offices, and serves as a member of the GAL team that represents the child's best interests in abuse, neglect, dependency, and related termination of parental rights proceedings. The GAL Program website contains numerous resources including a brief bank and other resources for GAL attorney advocates.
  - The North Carolina Office of Indigent Defense Services (IDS) has an Office of the Parent Defender, which coordinates, assists, and trains parents' attorneys at both the trial and appellate levels. IDS maintains a website that contains various resources for parent attorneys, including a brief bank, IDS policies, training materials, performance guidelines, and other information.

  In addition, the North Carolina Judicial Branch maintains a website (NCcourts.org) with various resources on different substantive topics for various audiences, including citizens, the courts, and employees. Some of the resources relate to child welfare, including

  - AOC Forms, searchable by form number, title, keyword, statute, and/or subject (one of which is "juvenile");
  - Court Rules,
  - Family Court; and
  - Information on Language Access in the courts.

- **The North Carolina Department of Health and Human Services Division of Social Services (NC DHHS DSS).** NC DHHS manages the delivery of health and human services to North Carolinians with a mission of providing essential services to improve the health, safety, and well-being of North Carolinians. It consists of thirty divisions, one of which is the Division of Social Services, which supervises the county administered child welfare system in North Carolina. The NC DHHS DSS website contains various resources that relate to child welfare including

    o NC DHHS DSS child welfare policy manuals, which can be found here;
    o NC DHHS DSS forms, which can be found here;
    o a Dear County Directors webpage; and
    o Child welfare statistics and reviews, including state plans and federal performance reviews.

## National Resources

A number of organizations operating on the national level provide information, resources, training, and even technical assistance related to child abuse, neglect, dependency, and termination of parental rights proceedings. Those that cover a variety of topics related to juvenile proceedings include (but are not limited to) the following:

- The Child Welfare Information Gateway is a service of the Children's Bureau, part of the Administration for Children and Families, U.S. Department of Health and Human Services. The Child Welfare Information Gateway website provides access to print and electronic publications, websites, and online databases covering a wide range of topics, including preventing and responding to abuse and neglect, permanency, foster care, adoption, and more. Its website is very comprehensive, and readers are encouraged to start here when researching most topics related to abuse, neglect, dependency, and juvenile court proceedings.

- The American Bar Association Center on Children and the Law addresses laws, policies, and judicial procedures affecting children. The Center has multiple projects focused on specific topics, generating publications with technical advice, standards of practice, and reports on research. The Center offers memberships and training, subscriptions, and listservs for attorneys and judges focused on specific topics and specific practice areas. The Center also offers a national conference on child welfare, as well as a parent attorney conference, every two years.

- The National Council of Juvenile and Family Court Judges (NCJFCJ) has a website with access to publications, training opportunities, and technical assistance, as well as membership opportunities, and covers a broad range of topics. The NCJFCJ website is a valuable resource for juvenile court judges.

- The National Association of Counsel for Children (NACC) addresses the legal protection and representation of children by training and educating child advocates and by effecting policy and legal systems change. The NACC offers training opportunities, memberships, and certifications and produces publications focused on the representation of children.

- The National Conference of State Legislatures (NCSL) website contains information on numerous substantive topics. There are various resources addressing child welfare, such as a child welfare legislation database searchable by topic and state, newsletters, toolkits, and more. The information can be found under "Human Services" and also by using the search box.

# Appendix 2
# The Chief District Court Judge and Juvenile Court*

## Leadership and Case Management

Time limits in the Juvenile Code (G.S. Chapter 7B) specify when certain hearings must be held and require that most orders in abuse, neglect, dependency, and termination of parental rights cases be entered within thirty days after the hearings from which they result. The timelines are aimed at avoiding undue delay in making decisions about children's placements and futures. Because juvenile cases may continue for years, require ongoing judicial oversight, and affect constitutionally protected family interests, the chief judge's role in the management of these cases is especially significant. The chief judge has a leadership role in determining how well statutory requirements are met, defining the priority juvenile cases receive, and conveying expectations for those who practice or participate in juvenile court.

## Local Rules

The Court Improvement Program, housed in the North Carolina Administrative Office of the Courts (AOC) offices, promotes the use of local juvenile court rules in abuse, neglect, and dependency cases. These rules establish uniform practice and procedure for abuse, neglect, and dependency court matters to achieve stable and secure homes for children who come within the court's jurisdiction. The purpose statement in the local rules should affirm that the overall objective of the juvenile court hearing abuse, neglect, and dependency proceedings is to move cases in a prompt and efficient manner toward a resolution that meets the permanency needs of the child while at the same time ensuring due process for all parties in the case. The chief district court judge and/or his/her designee should appoint a committee with representatives of all stakeholders in juvenile court to develop and/or periodically review and revise the local rules. Local rules are the foundation for accountability and should incorporate the time standards mandated by the North Carolina Juvenile Code.[1]

## Statutory References

1. **Permanency Mediation**

    G.S. 7B-202 directs the North Carolina Administrative Office of the Courts (AOC) to establish a statewide Permanency Mediation Program, consisting of local judicial district programs, to provide services for resolving issues in abuse, neglect, dependency, and termination of parental rights cases. Few such programs exist, and funding to phase the program in statewide has not been forthcoming. Should that change, the director of the AOC

---

*This Appendix includes only responsibilities that relate to abuse, neglect, dependency, and termination of parental rights proceedings.

[1] For more detailed information about local rules, see Best Practices For NC Juvenile Abuse, Neglect and Dependency Court Improvement Programs.

is authorized to "approve contractual agreements for such services as executed by order of the Chief District Court Judge of a district court district." G.S. 7B-202(b). The statute exempts the contracts from the competitive bidding procedures in G.S. Chapter 143.

## 2. Authority of Medical Professionals in Abuse Cases

G.S. 7B-308 establishes a procedure by which the chief district court judge (or the judge's designee) may authorize a medical professional to keep temporary physical custody of a child who may have been abused.

## 3. Delegation of Authority to Issue Nonsecure Custody Orders

G.S. 7B-502 authorizes the chief district court judge, by administrative order, to delegate the court's authority to issue nonsecure custody orders to persons other than district court judges. The administrative order (i) must specify the person(s) to whom the authority is delegated and (ii) must be filed in the clerk's office. Note that under G.S. 7B-506, entry of the order by someone other than a district court judge accelerates the time within which the first hearing on the need for continued nonsecure custody must be held. This delegated authority to make decisions about nonsecure custody should not be confused with the role of an official, usually a magistrate, who performs the ministerial act of entering a nonsecure custody order pursuant to a judge's order conveyed by telephone. *See* G.S. 7B-508. *See also* G.S. 7B-1902 (delegation of nonsecure custody in a juvenile delinquency or undisciplined proceeding to the chief court counselor (or staff)).

## 4. Discovery and Information Sharing

Pursuant to G.S. 7B-700(b), the chief district court judge may adopt local rules or enter an administrative order addressing parties' sharing of information and the use of discovery in juvenile cases.

## 5. Scheduling Adjudicatory Hearings

G.S. 7B-801(c) (abuse, neglect, and dependency cases) and 7B-1109(a) (termination of parental rights cases) state that adjudicatory hearings are to be held in the judicial district at the time and place the chief district court judge designates (which must be within the respective prescribed statutory time limits).

## 6. Rule or Order for Sharing Predisposition Reports

G.S. 7B-808(c) specifically authorizes a chief district court judge to make a local rule or enter an administrative order addressing the sharing of predisposition reports among parties. The rule or order may prohibit disclosure of reports to the juvenile. It may not prohibit a party entitled by law to receive confidential information from receiving it or allow disclosure of a confidential source protected by statute.

## 7. Transfer of Case to another Judicial District

Under G.S. 7B-900.1(d), before ordering a post-adjudication transfer of an abuse, neglect, or dependency case to a different judicial district, the transferring court must communicate with the chief district court judge or a judge presiding in juvenile court in the district to which the case is to be transferred. If the judge in that district makes a timely objection, the case may be transferred only if the court in the original district makes detailed findings of fact supporting a conclusion that the juvenile's best interests require that the case be transferred.

## 8. Guardian ad Litem Program

G.S. 7B-1201(a) requires the North Carolina Administrative Office of the Courts, in cooperation with each chief district court judge and other personnel in the judicial district, to implement and administer a guardian ad litem program.

## 9. Agency Information-Sharing Rules

G.S. 7B-3100(a) directs the Division of Adult Correction and Juvenile Justice of the Department of Public Safety, after consulting with the Conference of Chief District Court Judges, to adopt rules designating agencies that are authorized to share certain information about juveniles. The rules issued pursuant to that directive are 14B N.C.A.C. 11A .0301 and .0302. The designated agencies are identified and allow for the inclusion of "a local agency designated by an administrative order issued by the chief district court judge of the district court district in which the agency is located." 14B N.C.A.C. 11A.0301(j). Chief district court judges do not have authority to issue broad rules or orders regarding agency information sharing as they did under an older version of the statute. They may only add local agencies to the list set out in the administrative rule.

## 10. Community Child Protection Team

G.S. 7B-1407(c) provides that the membership of a Community Child Protection Team that also serves as the local Child Fatality Prevention Team must include a district court judge appointed by the chief district court judge in the judicial district.

# Appendix 3
# JWise: The Automated Information System for North Carolina Juvenile Courts[1]

JWise is an automated information system implemented by the North Carolina Administrative Office of the Courts (AOC) Technology Services Division in 2004. The primary purpose of JWise is to serve as the official index of juvenile cases and to improve outcomes for children in the child welfare and juvenile justice systems by providing case management tools. JWise is a unique computer application in that it is used by multiple court officials and court staff.

*Clerks* use JWise to record information that serves as the official court index for juvenile abuse, neglect, dependency; termination of parental rights (TPR); emancipation; delinquency; and undisciplined cases. The clerk enters codes in JWise based on information that appears in paper filings or is recorded in court minutes.

*Judicial staff,* such as Juvenile Case Coordinators, use JWise as their case management tool; they enter event data in JWise and use JWise to manage juvenile abuse, neglect, dependency, and TPR cases.

*Guardian ad Litem (GAL) staff* use JWise as their case management tool for juvenile cases and enter permanency codes so permanent plans can be tracked for each child.

*Judges* have access to view information in JWise but do not enter information into JWise.

## Official Court Index

Since JWise is the official court index for juvenile cases, clerks are exclusively responsible for entering and maintaining basic juvenile case information. This information includes

- demographic information on juveniles — name, address, telephone, race, gender, and date of birth;
- case related information — file number, initial filing date, names, and demographic information for parties related to the case (parents, attorneys, social workers, court counselors, victim/witness, caretakers, etc.); and
- information about legal allegations that are sworn in petitions—the date the allegation was entered and data on how the allegation was adjudicated and disposed. For example, a clerk would enter that a juvenile petition for neglect was filed on 1/1/09 and the juvenile was adjudicated neglected on 3/1/09.

---

[1] Information in this Appendix was provided by North Carolina Administrative Office of the Courts.

## Tracking Tool for Court Events

JWise is also a tracking tool for court events such as court hearings that are the basis for producing juvenile calendars, juvenile forms, and statistical reports. Events recorded in JWise are not the official court record for juvenile cases. All reports generated by JWise events contain the following disclaimer in the footer: *This Event Time Line is for informational purposes only and not the official court record.* In the future, JWise will contain a similar disclaimer on the event screen so that if court users print an event screen that contains the history of court activity, it will be clear from the disclaimer that the events are not the official court record.

JWise events are not the official juvenile record because they can be added to, edited, and deleted by multiple court employees — clerks, family court, and Guardian ad Litem staff. Although not an official record, JWise events are very important for the effective and efficient management of juvenile cases. JWise events serve as the basis for

- recording the nature of the court event (e.g., adjudication hearing), as well as the date, time, name of judge, and any notes related to that event;
- recording the outcome of the court event (e.g., resolved, continued);
- generating juvenile calendars; and
- generating all NC Key Time Standard Reports and CIP Federal Timeliness Measure Reports.

## GAL Management Tool

Since JWise is a shared tool for all Judicial Branch staff who work in juvenile court, Guardian ad Litem (GAL) staff benefit from having both current information on juvenile cases that is entered by clerks and by sharing information with other JWise users (e.g., GAL appointments).

## How Judges Can Use JWise

In order for JWise to produce accurate and complete calendars, forms, and reports, it must have accurate and complete data. Judges have a critical role in ensuring that meaningful and complete information about court hearings is entered into JWise about court hearings. It is important for judges to announce (or document) three things for the clerk at the conclusion of every court hearing:

1. outcome, or result of each hearing that appears on the court calendar;
2. date the judge's order is due if the court hearing results in an order; and
3. the future court event that should appear on the next court calendar.

## JWise Reports

As of July 2009, there are three abuse, neglect, and dependency time standard reports: adjudication hearings, disposition hearings, and the first permanency planning hearings.

All North Carolina Key Time Standard Reports contain the following data:

- the number of cases that met the statutory time standard,
- the number of cases that exceeded the statutory time standard, and
- the number of cases "in the queue" that have reached the time standard but have not had the hearing that is the subject of the report.

In addition to the time standard information, these reports also contain the following data on each juvenile case: file number, juvenile name, date of birth, age of juvenile (at time of report), gender, race, and case status (pending or completed). Because these reports are available in Microsoft Excel, court managers are able to sort the data in any number of ways to evaluate information such as

- the number of abuse, neglect, dependency petitions filed within any time period;
- the number of adjudication and disposition hearings a certain judge heard during a given time period;
- the time standard goals for juvenile cases per judge; and
- the average age of juveniles adjudicated.

In 2016, five new CIP Federal Timeliness Measure Reports were created.

**1. Time to First Permanency Hearing:** The median time from the filing of the original petition to first permanency hearing (how long it takes to complete the first permanency hearing).

**2. Time to All Subsequent Permanency Hearings:** The median length of time in days between each subsequent permanency hearing that occurs until final permanency is achieved. For example, the number of days between the first permanency hearing and the second permanency hearing, the second permanency hearing and third, etc., for each hearing that occurs while the child remains in care.

**3. Time to Permanent Placement:** The median time from filing of the original petition to legal permanency (how long it takes for children in abuse and neglect cases to achieve legal permanency, following the filing of the original petition). "Legal Permanency" means that there is a permanent and secure legal relationship between the adult caregiver and the child, including reunification, adoption, legal guardianship or placement with a fit and willing relative.

**4. Time to Termination of Parental Rights Petition:** Where reunification has not been achieved, the median time from filing of the original petition to filing the petition (or motion) to terminate parental rights (how long it takes from the date the original child abuse or neglect petition is filed to the date the termination of parental rights petition is filed).

**5. Time to Termination of Parental Rights:** Where reunification has not been achieved, the median time from filing of the original child abuse and neglect petition to the termination of parental rights (how long it takes from the date the original child abuse and neglect petition (or motion) was filed to the date the termination of parental rights proceeding is completed.

For additional information, the AOC's intranet site has a brief orientation and sample reports from JWise.

# Appendix 4
# Rules of Recordkeeping, Chapter XII

The North Carolina Administrative Office of the Courts (AOC) issues rules that govern recordkeeping in the offices of clerks of superior court. Only the rules applicable to juvenile records (Chapter XII) are reproduced here. These rules, effective November 18, 2019, could be revised at any time.

| STATE OF NORTH CAROLINA | Records of the Clerks of Superior Court |
|---|---|
| Rules of Recordkeeping | XII. Juvenile |

**Rule 12.1 - <u>CASE FILE FOLDER ESTABLISHED</u>:**

**Rule 12.1.1** - The clerk shall establish and maintain one case record for each juvenile who is the subject of one or more of the actions listed below. The case record shall consist of both a file folder, to house all original paper documents relating to the actions, and the electronic data entered into the automated JWise System as provided by the NCAOC. Electronic data shall be entered into the JWise System as prescribed by the user's manual.

1. An abuse, neglect, or dependency proceeding. [G.S. 7B-1000 through -1004]

2. A proceeding under the Interstate Compact on the Placement of Children. [G.S. 7B-3800 through -3806] (Example: placing a child from another state into foster care within this state)

3. A proceeding involving judicial consent for emergency surgical or medical treatment. [G.S. 7B-3600]

4. A proceeding to review a voluntary foster care placement. [G.S. 7B-910]

5. A proceeding in which a person is alleged to have obstructed or interfered with an investigation of abuse, neglect, or dependency. [G.S. 7B-303]

6. A proceeding to review an agency's plan for the placement of a child when one or both parents have surrendered the child for adoption or when a child returns to foster care after an adoption is dismissed or withdrawn. [G.S. 7B-909]

7. A delinquency or undisciplined juvenile proceeding. [G.S. 7B-1500 through -2706]

8. A proceeding under the Interstate Compact on Juveniles. [G.S. 7B-4000 through -4002]

9. A termination of parental rights (TPR) proceeding whether initiated by petition or motion [G.S. 7B-1100 through -1112] including any motions to reinstate the rights of a parent whose parental rights have been previously terminated. [G.S. 7B-1114]

10. An emancipation proceeding [G.S. 7B-3500 through -3509]

| Rules of Recordkeeping | XII. Juvenile |

The case file shall be divided into sub-folders:

- Subfolder A shall contain all documents relating to proceedings 1-6 above.
- Subfolder B shall contain all documents relating to proceedings 7 and 8 above.
- Subfolder T shall contain all documents relating to proceedings in 9 above.
- Subfolder E shall contain all documents relating to proceedings in 10 above.
- Subfolder P shall hold copies of newly filed petitions and other pre-adjudication documents, such as those relating to service of process. The file numbers on these documents should be "blacked out" before presenting the file to the judge. Upon adjudication or dismissal of the petition, all "blacked out" copies housed in Subfolder P should be discarded.

    The first petition filed involving a juvenile shall establish the case file, and all subsequent petitions or related documents for any of the proceedings listed above shall receive the same file number and be placed in the appropriate subfolder. The juvenile's name, date of birth, and case file number shall appear on the top tab of the juvenile file folder and subfolder(s), that are labeled "A", "B", "T", or "E" according to the type of documents they contain. Only the juvenile's name and date of birth shall appear on Subfolder P.

**Rule 12.1.2** -

A proceeding to review a voluntary foster care placement for a young adult. [G.S. 7B-910.1]

All documents filed in the proceeding shall establish a new case file and receive a new juvenile file number. The young adult's name, date of birth and case file number shall appear on the top tab of the file folder. (For file numbering see Rule 12.3.) There is no associated filing fee for these proceedings.

NOTE: Under no circumstances should any documentation relating to a Judicial Waiver of Parental Consent be placed in the juvenile file. (See Rule of Recordkeeping 18).

COMMENTS:

A. Subfolders may be held together in a larger folder or simply filed next to each other.

B. If a juvenile petition names several juveniles, each juvenile should have a separate case file. Copies of any petition, order, or other document that involves multiple juveniles, should be placed in each juvenile's file.

| Rules of Recordkeeping | XII. Juvenile |

C. A TPR petition should never be filed as a civil action. TPR should be initiated only by the filing of:

- a juvenile petition; or,
- a motion in the cause in a pending abuse, neglect, or dependency proceeding.

Normally, TPR documents should not be placed in a CVD case file. An order based on a TPR may be necessary to terminate a child support obligation, but the TPR order itself should not be placed in the CVD child support file.

If the Court does allow a party to pursue a TPR in a domestic relations or other civil (CVD) case, the clerk should place the original TPR documents in subfolder T of the existing juvenile file for the child; or, if there is no a juvenile file the Clerk shall create one.

D. The judge should only be provided the entire file on the juvenile after adjudication. Once the petition has been adjudicated the duplicate copy of the petition and supporting documents may be discarded, and any new orders or other filings shall be placed in subfolder A, B, T or E as appropriate. Once this is done, subfolder P may be retained in case another petition is filed.

E. Subfolder P should be used only for pending petitions and related documents, not for any documents filed subsequent to adjudication.

F. All documentary evidence offered and entered into evidence during a juvenile proceeding should remain in the file until the juvenile file is destroyed.

G. Fingerprint cards should not be accepted for filing. If these cards are submitted to the clerk, the clerk should return them to the agency responsible for taking the fingerprints. [G.S. 7B-2102(d)]

H. Parents may be ordered to appear and show cause why they should not be held in criminal contempt in a juvenile case. (G.S. 7B-904 and 7B-2706) The document finding the parent in criminal contempt should be used as the initiating document for establishing a criminal file. The file should be given the next available CR number and entered into the Automated Criminal and Infraction System (the ACIS system). (Note: Please see form AOC-CR-390 Direct Criminal Contempt/Summary Proceedings/Findings and Order as an initiating document to be used by the court.)

Parents who fail to appear in court for a juvenile proceeding, as required, may be served with a show cause order to appear in court on a certain date to show cause why the parent should not be held in indirect criminal contempt. If the parent is served with the show cause order, but fails to appear for the show cause hearing, the

Effective November 18, 2019

court may issue an order for the parent's arrest. A separate criminal file should be established using the original AOC-J-155 or AOC-J-344. A copy of the form should be retained in the juvenile file. All references to the juvenile should be removed from the original AOC-J-155 or AOC-J-344 before it is placed in the criminal file. If the court enters a criminal contempt order on AOC-J-156 or AOC-J-345, place the original form in the criminal file after removing all references to the juvenile and retain a copy for the juvenile file.

Parents may be ordered to appear and show cause why they should not be held in civil contempt for failing to comply with an order or directive entered by the juvenile court. The show cause order and any subsequent orders should be placed in the originating juvenile case file. This civil contempt information shall not be entered into the ACIS system or the VCAP system.

**Rule 12.2 - DATE STAMP ON FILINGS:** The clerk shall record the actual date of filing on all copies of the petition or any other filings in juvenile proceedings.

COMMENTS:

A. The best practice for the clerk in stamping the date and time of filing is to place his or her initials by the date and time stamp. While initialing the date and time stamp is not required, it is useful in tracking errors in filing and preventing the filing of papers without the clerk's control or knowledge.

B. When there is an emergency situation and the clerk's office is closed, magistrates may accept juvenile petitions for filing. [See G.S. 7B-404 and 7B-1804]. Petitions received by a magistrate must be delivered to the clerk's office as soon as the office is opened for business. The clerk shall record the date it is actually received in the office as the date of filing.

**Rule 12.3 - FILE NUMBERS:** The first petition filed relating to a juvenile shall be assigned the next available file number from the juvenile series for that year. The format for the juvenile series is: year of filing (*i.e.*, 06); court designation "J" for juvenile; and, the unique sequence number that begins with "1" at the beginning of each calendar year, (1, 2, 3, 4, etc.). Examples of complete file numbers are; 06J1, 06J2, 06J3, etc.

The format for the voluntary foster care placement of a young adult series (G.S. 7B-910.1) is: year of filing (*i.e.*, 2017); case type "JA"; and the unique sequence number that begins with "1" at the beginning of each calendar year, (1, 2, 3, 4, etc.). Examples of complete file numbers are 17JA1, 17JA2, 17JA3, etc.

COMMENTS:

A. The designation of A, B, T, E or P for the subfolders of the case file are not considered part of the case number. They are used only to separate different types of case documents within the file. When a file number is assigned to a voluntary foster care placement of a young adult case it receives a "JA" file number and there are no subfolders in these cases.

B. If a petition involves more than one juvenile, a number must be assigned to each individual juvenile. (See Comment B following Rule 12.1)

C. If using the JWise system, the file number will appear in the following format: 06JA1 (abuse, neglect, dependency), 06JB1 (undisciplined or delinquency) 06JT1 (TPR), or 06JE1 (emancipation).

**Rule 12.4 - INDEX TO JUVENILE CASES:** The clerk shall maintain an Index To Juvenile Proceedings. This index shall indicate the name of the juvenile, the nature of the case [*i.e.*, abuse, neglect, dependency, undisciplined, delinquency, emancipation or TPR], the file number, and whether the case has been appealed to the Court of Appeals. If a TPR or an adjudication of delinquency is contained in the file, this should be noted on the index. The Index to Juvenile Proceedings is not open to public inspection.

**Rule 12.5 - ACCESS TO FILES:** Abuse, neglect and dependency cases are not open to public inspection. The record includes the summons, petition, any custody order, court order, written motion, electronic or mechanical recording of the hearing, and other papers filed in the proceeding. (See G.S. 7B-2901). The following persons may review the record and obtain copies of the written parts of the record without a court order:

A. The person named in the petition as the juvenile;
B. The guardian ad litem;
C. The county department of social services; and
D. The juvenile's parent, guardian, or custodian, or attorney for the juvenile or the juvenile's parent, guardian, or custodian.

Undisciplined and delinquency cases are not open to public inspection. The record includes the summons and petition, any secure or nonsecure custody order, any electronic or mechanical recording of hearings, and any written motions, orders or papers filed in the proceedings. (See G.S. 7B-3000). In undisciplined and delinquency cases, the following persons may examine the juvenile's record and obtain copies of written parts of the record without a court order:

E. The juvenile or the juvenile's attorney;
F. The juvenile's parent, guardian, or custodian, or the authorized representative of the juvenile's parent, guardian, or custodian;
G. The prosecutor;
H. Court counselors; and
I. Probation officers in the Section of Community Corrections of the Division of Adult Corrections, as provided by G.S. 7B-3000(e1).

COMMENTS:

A. The court may direct the clerk to "seal" any portion of the juvenile's record. The clerk shall secure any sealed portion of a juvenile's record in an envelope clearly marked "SEALED: MAY BE EXAMINED ONLY BY ORDER OF THE COURT." The sealed information may be examined only by court order. [See G.S. 7B-3000 (c)]

B. Law enforcement officers are only allowed to review documents in subfolder B if accompanied by the prosecuting attorney. The district attorney may make copies of information contained in subfolder B, but law enforcement officers are not entitled to copies.

C. An electronic recording of the juvenile proceedings shall only be transcribed when notice of appeal has been timely given. The electronic recording can only be copied electronically or mechanically by order of the court. G.S. 7B-3000(d) (G.S. 7B-806 and 7B-2410).

D. Entry of a TPR changes the legal relationship between a parent and child. The parent should not have access to documents filed subsequent to the TPR even if the TPR is on appeal unless the court has stayed the TPR order on appeal. These documents should be bound together, placed within the appropriate sub-folder, and removed prior to providing the file to a parent for review. (See G.S. 7B-1112)

E. Orders Determining Parentage in Juvenile Proceedings. (see Rule 12.19 below)

**Rule 12.6 - EXPUNCTION OF RECORDS:** Certain records of juvenile delinquency/undisciplined proceedings can be expunged upon an order from the juvenile court in which the adjudication or proceeding occurred. G.S. 7B-3200 provides for expunction of these records in subsections:

(a) – expunction of adjudications of undisciplined status
(b) – expunction of certain adjudications of delinquency
(h) – expunction of dismissed allegations of delinquency or undisciplined status

This rule covers only the basics of filing and disposing of juvenile expunction petitions. For detailed procedures to carry out this rule, see the "Expunction Guide for Clerks" from NCAOC's Court Services, available on JUNO.

Filing: An expunction petition for juvenile records is to be filed in the "JB" subfolder containing the records of the allegation/adjudication addressed by the petition. If the JB subfolder already has been destroyed pursuant to the retention schedule, create a new JB subfolder for the expunction petition and related filings.

Effective November 18, 2019

**Expunction Order Appealed:** If the court's order granting or denying the expunction is appealed, retain all documentation related to the petition until final resolution of the appeal. If the order was granted and appealed by the State, treat the order as granted while the appeal is pending, unless the court orders otherwise, remove the expunged records from the primary juvenile file, keeping them in a secure location that is unavailable to persons who otherwise may have access to the juvenile files (e.g., court counselors).

**Petition Denied:** If the proceeding results in a denial of the petition, whether after an appeal or by the trial court and not appealed, place the denial order in the JB subfolder, but destroy all attachments (e.g., affidavits of good character). If the JB subfolder is later destroyed pursuant to the retention schedule, destroy the denied order with the subfolder. If the JB subfolder was destroyed pursuant to the retention schedule prior to the filing of the petition, then the petition (and its temporary subfolder) may be destroyed upon NCAOC approval.

**Petition Granted:** (Note: Detailed procedures for each of the steps below are provided in the "Expunction Guide for Clerks.")

1. Give notice of the granted order to the petitioner. If the petition was filed on the AOC-J-909 for dismissed allegations of undisciplined status or delinquency, notice of the granted petition may be given on the same form. If the petition was filed in any other format, use AOC-J-906 to provide notice to the petitioner.

2. Expunge only the allegations/adjudications specified in the expunction order.

    a. If records of other delinquency/undisciplined proceedings exist in the petitioner's JB subfolder, retain those other records.
    b. If the petitioner had no other delinquency/undisciplined proceedings, expunge the entire JB subfolder.
    c. If the JB subfolder is expunged and constituted the petitioner's only juvenile proceeding for the county, expunge the entire juvenile file and remove the petitioner's name from the Index to Juvenile Actions (*i.e.*, the JWise system).

3. Expunge the paper and electronic records as directed in the "Expunction Guide for Clerks."

4. Do not expunge civil records arising from the juvenile proceeding, such as civil judgments for attorney fees against a parent or guardian. (See Rule 12.17)

5. Notify State and local law enforcement agencies as directed in the "Expunction Guide for Clerks".

6. The clerk must send a certified copy of the expunction order to the NCAOC at the address in the guide. Note that if the expunction was for a dismissed allegation of delinquency or undisciplined status, provide a certified copy to the court counselor, also.

7. See the "Expunction Guide for Clerks" for "Other Cases & Special Situations" in juvenile expunction proceedings, such as juveniles whose names are recorded on the former, manual index to juvenile actions (the "green book"), expunging the verbatim recording of juvenile proceedings, and cases in which there was a change of venue to another county.

COMMENTS:

A. The NCAOC provides template forms for juvenile expunction proceedings. See AOC-J-903, J-904, J-906, and J-909. While parties are not required to use NCAOC forms for these proceedings, the forms cover all of the components of the expunction proceeding, so clerks should encourage petitioners to use them.

B. As custodian of the record, the clerk's function in the expunction process is to receive petitions for filing, schedule the petitions for hearing when required, and then file and carry out any order entered by the court. Questions such as whether or not a particular juvenile case qualifies for expunction, whether or not the correct form has been used, and whether or not any affidavits or other materials required by the expunction statute have been included are not of concern to the clerk's office. The court before which the petition is heard must determine any questions of its adequacy. Occasionally, a court may enter an order for expunction that appears questionable on its face. When such an order has been entered (*e.g.*, expunction of adjudication of a Class A - E felony, prohibited by G.S. 7B-3200(b)), the clerk may wish to confirm with the judge who entered the order that the order is what the court intended. If the judge indicates that the order is as intended, then the clerk should carry the order out.

## Rule 12.7 - CHANGE OF VENUE, OR TRANSFER OF CASE TO ANOTHER COUNTY OR TRIBAL COURT:

Transfer to Another County: The clerk shall ask the judge for instructions regarding whether the entire case or portions thereof are being transferred and what specifically the clerk should send to the other county. The clerk should transfer only those documents ordered transferred by the judge. Upon the filing of an order of the court transferring a case from one county (venue) to another, the clerk in the original county shall prepare a certified copy of the order of transfer and forward it along with all original papers in the file related to the juvenile proceedings specified in the order to the clerk in the receiving county by certified mail or other secure method. If the case has been scanned into EIMS, then it should be printed and certified to send to the transfer county. The clerk in the original county shall retain the original order of transfer along with photocopies of all the papers transferred.

Transfer to Tribal Court: The clerk may receive a request/order from a tribal court to transfer a juvenile case to the tribal court. The clerk shall ask the presiding district court judge for instructions regarding whether the case or portions thereof should be transferred to the tribal court. The clerk should transfer only those documents ordered transferred by the district court judge. Upon the filing of the district court judge's order to transfer the case, the clerk shall prepare a certified copy of the order of transfer and forward it along with copies of all papers in the file related to the juvenile proceedings specified in the order. If the case has been scanned into EIMS, then it should be printed and certified to send to the transfer county. The clerk in the original county shall retain the original order of transfer and the originals of all the papers transferred.

COMMENTS:

Transfers of abuse/neglect/dependency proceedings after adjudication shall occur within three business days of the entry of the order transferring venue (G.S. 7B-900.1). Transfers of other cases should be done as rapidly as possible.

No recording(s) of the juvenile proceeding(s) should be sent by the transferring county to the receiving county or the tribal court, unless ordered by a district court judge in the transferring county. If the case is appealed, the clerk in the hearing county shall submit the requested recording(s) to the transcriptionist.

Upon receiving a case that has been transferred from another county or a tribal court, the clerk shall promptly assign an appropriate file number to the case, ensure that any necessary appointments of new attorneys or guardians ad litem are made; and calendar the next court action as set forth in the order transferring venue and give appropriate notice to all parties.

## Rule 12.8 - TRANSFER OF A CASE TO SUPERIOR COURT:

**Rule 12.8.1 -** When the offense is a Class A felony committed by a juvenile who is 13 or older or a Class A-G felony committed by a juvenile at age 16 or 17, transfer to superior court is mandatory if the court finds probable cause. In such cases, form AOC-J-343, <u>Juvenile Order – Probable Cause Hearing</u>, is the initiating document in the superior court file. When transfer to superior court is ordered based on a transfer hearing, form AOC-J-442, <u>Juvenile Order Transfer Hearing</u>, is the initiating document in the superior court file.

The record of a juvenile case remains confidential even after jurisdiction over the juvenile is transferred to superior court. The initiating document, either form AOC-J-442 or AOC-J-343, is the only document from the juvenile file that may become part of the public record of the superior court proceedings, along with all documents made part of the record after transfer. A copy of the initiating document (AOC-J-442 or AOC-J-343) should be kept in the juvenile case file. Do not create a CRS file or enter information in the ACIS system for 10 days after entry of the transfer in order to allow opportunity for appeal.

<u>Appeals of a transfer:</u> When a transfer order is appealed, the appeal is heard in Superior Court. Notice of the appeal may be given in open court during the hearing or in writing within 10 days after the entry of the order. (Note: Entry means reduced to writing, signed by the judge, and filed

with the clerk.) The clerk shall also provide a copy of the written notice of appeal filed by the juvenile's attorney to the district attorney. The appeal should be included on the superior court calendar as an add-on hearing/case using the title "In the Matter of 06JB1492" and listing only the issue of "Appeal of Transfer". The offense or the juvenile's name may not be entered on the calendar. The clerk completing the case transfer shall add the case into the ACIS system only when the superior court judge denies the transfer appeal. If the appeal is granted, and thus the transfer does not move forward, all related documents are filed in the juvenile folder and no entry is made in the ACIS system.

**Rule 12.8.2** – Transfer to Superior Court (Indictment of 16- or 17- year old for Class A-G felony):

When the offense is a Class A-G felony committed at age 16 or 17, transfer to superior court is mandatory upon the return of a bill of indictment and notice to the juvenile. When transfer to superior court is based on the return of a bill of indictment, form AOC-J-444, Juvenile Order – Transfer After Bill of Indictment, is the initiating document in the superior court file.

The record of a juvenile case remains confidential even after jurisdiction over the juvenile is transferred to superior court. The initiating document, form AOC-J-444, is the only document from the juvenile file that may become part of the public record of the superior court proceedings, along with all documents made part of the record after transfer. A copy of form AOC-J-444 should be kept in the juvenile case file. Do not create a CRS file or enter information in the ACIS system for 10 days after entry of the transfer in order to allow opportunity for appeal.

Note: The court may enter a transfer order based on the return of a bill of indictment without a hearing. If form AOC-J-444 is entered without a hearing, the prosecutor or judge should forward a copy of the order to the juvenile clerk to process the transfer.

Appeals of a transfer: When a transfer order is appealed, the appeal is heard in Superior Court. Notice of the appeal may be given in open court during the hearing or in writing within 10 days after the entry of the order. (Note: Entry means reduced to writing, signed by the judge, and filed with the clerk.) The clerk shall also provide a copy of the written notice of appeal filed by the juvenile's attorney to the district attorney. The appeal should be included on the superior court calendar as an add-on hearing/case using the title "In the Matter of 06JB1492" and listing only the issue of "Appeal of Transfer". The offense or the juveniles name may not be entered on the calendar. The clerk completing the case transfer shall add the case into the ACIS system only when the superior court judge denies the transfer appeal. If the appeal is granted, and thus the transfer does not move forward, all related documents are filed in the juvenile folder and no entry is made in the ACIS system.

**Rule 12.8.3** – Remand to District Court After Transfer (Reverse Transfer):

Upon the joint motion of the prosecutor and the juvenile's attorney, the superior court must remand the charges back to district court for juvenile adjudication and order the expunction of the superior court charges. The superior court judge should use form AOC-CR-291, Motion and Order to Remand Case from Superior Court to District Court and Order of Expunction under G.S. 15A-145.8, to both remand the case and expunge the superior court charges. The criminal clerk should forward a copy of the AOC-CR-291, along with the original transfer order (*i.e.* AOC-J-343, AOC-J-442 or AOC-J-444) and any order assigning counsel for the juvenile, to the juvenile clerk for placement in the JB file. Once the original transfer order has been returned to the JB file, any copy of that order contained in the JB file may be destroyed.

Upon receipt of a copy of the AOC-CR-291, the juvenile clerk should calendar the case for adjudication, unless otherwise instructed by the prosecutor or juvenile court counselor and send notice of the hearing to all parties using form AOC-J-240A, Notice of Hearing in Juvenile Proceeding (Delinquent). The hearing should be scheduled for a date that provides the parties with at least 5 days written notice, as required by G.S. 7B-1807.

**Rule 12.9 - NOTIFICATION OF APPOINTED ATTORNEY:** Where an attorney is appointed by the court to represent a juvenile or parent(s) in a juvenile proceeding the clerk shall send the Notice of Appointment to the attorney in a sealed envelope. (Note: You may also place the sealed envelope in the attorney's mailbox located within the courthouse, if this is the established practice in your county.)

A. Court appointed attorneys may be appointed by either a District Court Judge or the clerk. If an abuse, neglect or dependency petition is filed, the clerk must appoint provisional counsel at the time of filing.

B. An attorney should not be appointed for a juvenile alleged to be undisciplined.

C. A juvenile does not need to prove indigence to receive a court-appointed attorney. However, parents seeking court appointed representation must go through the indigence screening process.

D. When the parents are eligible for court appointed attorneys, separate attorneys should be appointed for each parent.

E. In all TPR cases, a parent who is indigent is entitled to an appointed attorney unless the parent waives the right to counsel (Note: It does not matter whether the petition to terminate was filled by DSS or a private petitioner.)

F. When a juvenile in a delinquency or undisciplined action is placed in the custody or placement responsibility of DSS, a parent who is indigent is entitled to an appointed attorney for representation in hearings conducted pursuant to G.S. 7B-906.1 (review of placement), unless the parent waives the right to counsel. The court should address the issue of counsel with the juveniles' parent(s) at the dispositional hearing in which the juvenile is placed in custody to ensure that court-appointed counsel is assigned prior to the G.S. 7B-906.1 hearing. If counsel is appointed to represent a parent, the clerk should provide notice to the attorney, as provided in Rule 12.9.

| Rules of Recordkeeping | XII. Juvenile |
|---|---|

**Rule 12.10 - CALENDARS:** The clerk shall tightly control the distribution of juvenile calendars to ensure the confidentiality of the information listed on the calendar. In all juvenile proceedings, the presiding judge and the courtroom clerk shall each receive a copy of the juvenile calendar.

<u>Delinquency Sessions of Court</u>. One copy of the juvenile calendar shall be given to the district attorney, the chief court counselor and any attorney representing a juvenile on the calendar.

<u>Abuse/Neglect/Dependency Sessions of Court</u>. One copy of the juvenile calendar shall be given to the DSS attorney, the GAL Program Administrator, the GAL Attorney Advocate and any attorney representing a parent on the calendar.

A juvenile calendar shall never be provided to the juvenile or the juvenile's parents.

> COMMENTS:
>
> A. The clerk may want to write the name of the person receiving the juvenile calendar on the calendar provided to the person.
>
> B. If the calendar is not handed directly to the person authorized to receive the calendar, for example, the calendar is placed in the attorney's mail box located in the clerk's office, it should be placed in a sealed envelope.

**Rule 12.11 - MINUTES:** The clerk shall record the minutes of the juvenile court proceedings by making brief notations on the court calendar showing the disposition of each case heard during the session.

Juvenile court minutes shall be kept confidential.

**Rule 12.12 - AUTOMATED AUDIT REPORTS:** These reports are confidential and should not be distributed. The reports should be stored in a secured manner as any other juvenile record.

**Rule 12.13 –**
  A. **MICROFILM:** No part of the juvenile case file shall be microfilmed, including the attorney fee judgments.

  B. **SCANNING INTO EIMS** (Enterprise Information Management System): REPEALED EFFECTIVE APRIL 29, 2019 AND RESERVED FOR FUTURE USE.

**Rule 12.14 - EMANCIPATION ORDERS:** The certificate of emancipation shall be filed as a Registration and treated as any other filing of that type.

> COMMENTS:

Only the certificate of emancipation order shall be filed as a Registration. The petition and all other supporting documents shall remain in the juvenile file. Emancipation proceedings are as confidential as any other juvenile proceeding. However, where an order of emancipation has been entered the juvenile may receive a Form AOC-J-902M, <u>Certificate Of Emancipation</u>, at any time to verify that status.

**Rule 12.15 - RECORDING JUVENILE HEARINGS:** All adjudicatory, dispositional, probable cause, and transfer to superior court hearings shall be recorded. The court may order that other hearings be recorded.

COMMENTS:

A. The log of what is recorded is considered part of the minutes and should be physically attached to it.

B. When a case is heard out-of-county the recording should remain in the county of hearing.

C. If a case is heard out-of-county and later appealed, the clerk in the county where a recording exists must submit the recording to a transcriptionist. The juvenile clerk in the county where notice of appeal is given must notify the clerk in the originating county that the case has been appealed. The clerk must provide the name and contact information for the assigned transcriptionist to the clerk in the originating county.

**Rule 12.16 - PETITIONS FOR JUDICIAL REVIEW: DHHS LIST OF "RESPONSIBLE INDIVIDUALS":** The clerk shall establish a case file for each petition filed under G.S. 7B-323 seeking judicial review of a determination that the petitioner is a responsible individual. The clerk shall use one sequential number series for all responsible individual petitions filed. Each petition will be assigned the next available number from that JRI series. No index is to be maintained for these cases.

The format for the responsible individual series is: Year of filing and case type designator (*i.e.*, 07JRI); and the unique sequence number that begins with "1" at the beginning of each calendar year, (1, 2, 3, 4, etc.). Examples of complete file numbers are; 07JRI-1, 07JRI-2, 07JRI-3, etc.

JRI files are to be maintained by the Juvenile Department in the clerk's offices. However, they are to be kept separate from the juvenile files. Each hearing shall be recorded to a CD with no other cases or hearings on the same CD. (See RRS No. 7.11.1 for retention requirements.)

**Rule 12.17 - PROCESSING FEE APPLICATIONS WITH JUDGMENT ORDERED:** If the court enters a judgment on side two of the Fee Application/Judgment Order the original judgment shall be placed in a file titled, "Juvenile Fee Apps Reduced to Judgment", in case number order. A copy of this judgment shall be placed in the related juvenile file.

If the court did not enter a judgment on side two of the Fee Application/Judgment Order, the original judgment shall remain in the related juvenile file.

Periodically the clerk may compare the judgments in the Juvenile Fee Apps Reduced to Judgment file against the VCAP system to determine if any have been satisfied. If so they may be destroyed one year after the satisfaction date, without NCAOC approval. Fee Application/Judgment Orders held in the "Fee Applications Reduced to Judgment" folder continue to be maintained in as confidential a manner as any other documents filed in a juvenile proceeding.

**Rule 12.18 - NOTIFICATION OF FOSTER PARENTS:** The foster parent of a juvenile must be given 15 days' notice of all review hearings. The Department of Social Services must provide the clerk with the name and address of the foster parent providing care for the juvenile or provide written documentation to the clerk that the foster parent was sent notice of the hearing. If the clerk sends the notice, the clerk should not include the foster parent's name and address on the same notice sent to the juvenile's biological parents.

A notice to a foster parent should be housed separately from the juvenile file. The clerk should retain the notice in a suitable repository associated with the court calendar referred to in the notice. Access to this repository should be limited to the clerk of superior court.

**Rule 12.19 – ORDERS DETERMINING PARENTAGE IN JUVENILE PROCEEDINGS:** A juvenile proceeding may involve an adjudication affecting a child's parentage. When a judicial determination of parentage is entered in a juvenile proceeding, the court may issue a stand-alone Order that addresses the juvenile's parentage. The original stand-alone order should be placed in the new CVD file and a copy retained in the juvenile file. [See Rule 3.1, B,12(b)]

**Rule 12.20 – VICTIMS' RIGHTS MOTION IN DELINQUENCY CASES:**

In some delinquency cases, a victim (or a person acting on behalf of a victim) may assert his or her rights by filing a motion with the clerk of superior court in the same juvenile action that gave rise to the rights in question. Upon request, the clerk of superior court in each county shall provide form AOC-J-380, Motion and Order to Enforce Rights of Juvenile Delinquency Victim, to a person who seeks to file a victims' rights motion in a delinquency case. There are no filing fees for this motion.

Upon the filing of form AOC-J-380 with the clerk's office, the clerk shall forward copies of the motion to the prosecutor (if the prosecutor is not the elected district attorney), the elected district attorney, and the judge involved in the proceeding that gave rise to the rights in question. Upon receipt of the motion, the judge must review the motion in a timely manner. At the conclusion of this review, the judge must dispose of the motion or set it for a hearing.

If the judge sets the motion for a hearing, the clerk shall provide notice of the hearing to the person who filed the motion and the prosecutor (if the prosecutor is not the person filing the motion). The notice of hearing for this motion is included on side two of form AOC-J-380.

Note: A victim in a delinquency case is not entitled to examine or obtain copies of confidential juvenile records (see G.S. 7B-2057). When providing form AOC-J-380 to a victim, the clerk shall not acknowledge the existence of the juvenile's case or disclose any information from the confidential juvenile record, including the file number. The clerk should refer the victim to a prosecutor for any questions about the case or assistance completing the form. Once the motion is filed with the clerk, it becomes part of the juvenile's confidential record, and the clerk cannot provide a copy to the victim, unless ordered to do so by the court to provide notice of a hearing on the motion.

# Appendix 5
# Case Management for Abuse, Neglect, Dependency, and Termination of Parental Rights Cases in North Carolina Juvenile Courts[1]

Juvenile court case management is a primary responsibility of family court staff for abuse, neglect, dependency (AND) and termination of parental rights (TPR) juvenile cases. Judicial districts without family court or those that previously received Court Improvement Program (CIP) funds for a CIP Director position do not have case managers for juvenile cases but may have other staff, such as judicial assistants, who manage these cases. Juvenile clerks have an important role in juvenile court, but their role does not include case management.

While family court districts have staff to provide juvenile case management, these case managers work at the direction and supervision of the Chief District Court Judge (CDCJ). In addition, juvenile case management is directed by judges assigned to AND/TPR courts. Judicial leadership in juvenile court is the key to effective juvenile court case management. Therefore, judges in districts without family court can benefit from case management techniques described below; however, they will typically not have dedicated judicial staff to generate statistical reports so that the judge can analyze the data and develop recommendations to improve court efficiency and effectiveness. However, some judges, in an effort to make juvenile court a priority and as effective as possible for children and families, have designated other judicial staff (i.e., Judicial Assistants, Trial Court Coordinators, etc.) to review and maintain statistics.

The following are strategies for effective case management in juvenile court:

- **Court Schedule.** Inform the CDCJ about the amount of court time needed for the juvenile AND/TPR caseload. Case managers have various ways to assess whether there is sufficient bench time assigned for juvenile court. For example, keeping a Calendar Productivity Log for a period of time can track the number of cases resolved, continued, and not reached because of insufficient court time. In addition, case managers can monitor the number of juvenile petitions and motions filed and adjust the court schedule as needed.

- **Court Calendar or Docket.** Clerks are generally responsible for generating and producing the juvenile calendar in all judicial districts. However, in family court districts, case managers assume this function because the efficiency of juvenile court can be improved when a case manager organizes the cases, provides notes with important information to judges and other court partners on the calendar, and disseminates the calendars (sometimes in draft form first) to appropriate court partners.

- **Scheduling and Facilitating Child Planning Conferences.** Child Planning Conferences or Day One Conferences are a best practice for AND courts. These conferences help families and court partners identify issues, resolve problems, and develop action plans by sharing

---

[1] Information in this Appendix provided by North Carolina Administrative Office of the Courts.

information and making recommendations about child placement, visitation, health and education services, paternity, and child support. See Child Planning Conferences Best Practices and Procedures on the "Court Improvement Program" section of the North Carolina Administrative Office of the Courts website.

- **Entering and/or Monitoring JWise Data.** Case managers are local experts on JWise data since they are responsible for making certain that accurate and complete information is entered into the automated system in a timely manner. JWise is a unique computer application in that it is used by multiple court officials and court staff. Because reports generated from JWise are only as accurate as the data entered, case managers, on behalf of the judge(s), take the lead in monitoring data and troubleshooting any problems.

- **Generating and Sharing JWise Statistical Reports.** Case managers have the ability and knowledge to generate multiple reports from JWise. As of July 2009, there are three AND Time Standard Reports: Adjudication Hearings, Disposition Hearings, and the First Permanency Planning Hearing. In 2016, five new CIP Federal Timeliness Measure reports were created for users: Time to First Permanency Hearing, Time to all Subsequent Permanency Hearings, Time to Permanent Placement, Time to Termination of Parental Rights Petition, and Time to Termination of Parental Rights. More information on JWise is available in Appendix 3.

- **A Central Point of Contact.** Because juvenile court involves so many court partners that are required to be present in court, a juvenile case manager develops a good communication system where he or she is a central point of contact for judges and other court partners with pertinent information so court can proceed in a timely and efficient manner.

# Checklists

# Checklists

The following Checklists are intended to assist the attorneys and judges who are participating in the various hearings involved in abuse, neglect, dependency, and related termination of parental rights proceedings. Users are cautioned that these Checklists are not meant to be a comprehensive guide.

Users should refer to the statutes directly. Questions about the interpretation of a statute may be answered by referring to the applicable Chapter and section within this Manual.

Additionally, these Checklists reflect the laws and published appellate decisions through December 31, 2019 and will not reflect any changes that may result from legislative action or appellate court interpretation that occur after that date.

**Checklist 1:**  Nonsecure Custody Orders

**Checklist 2:**  Pre-Adjudication

**Checklist 3:**  Adjudication

**Checklist 4:**  Dispositional Findings and Options at Initial, Review, and Permanency Planning

**Checklist 5:**  Initial Disposition

**Checklist 6:**  Review

**Checklist 7:**  Permanency Planning

**Checklist 8:**  Termination of Parental Rights Hearing

**Checklist 9:**  Post-TPR Review Hearing

# Checklist 1
# Nonsecure Custody Orders

"Nonsecure custody" is a North Carolina specific term for a temporary emergency custody order that removes a child from his or her home before the court holds the adjudicatory hearing that determines whether the child is abused, neglected, and/or dependent. Nonsecure custody is not appropriate in every case but is available when certain statutory criteria exist that show a nonsecure custody order is necessary to protect the juvenile. Although the initial order for nonsecure custody may be entered ex parte when the notice provisions of G.S. 7B-502 do not apply, subsequent hearings on the need for continued nonsecure custody (as specified in G.S. 7B-506) are required.

**AOC Form Orders:**
AOC-J-150, Order for Nonsecure Custody (Oct. 2019).
AOC-J-151, Order on Need for Continued Nonsecure Custody (Oct. 2019).

**Initial Nonsecure Custody Order and Subject Matter Jurisdiction**

- ☐ A court action has been commenced by the filing of a verified petition alleging abuse, neglect, or dependency in district court by a county DSS. The petition was
    - ☐ filed with clerk's office during hours when court was open.
    - ☐ accepted by magistrate when the clerk's office was closed as authorized by G.S. 7B-404. G.S. 7B-402; 7B-403; 7B-405.
- ☐ The petition is properly signed by the department's director or authorized representative. G.S. 7B-101(10); 7B-401.1(a); 7B-403(a).
- ☐ The petition is properly verified. G.S. 7B-403(a).
- ☐ The petition requests relief. N.C. R. Civ. P. 7(b)(1).
- ☐ NC has jurisdiction under the UCCJEA pursuant to G.S. Chapter 50A (review the allegations in the petition or attached affidavit addressing criteria specified by G.S. 50A-209 regarding the child's status) (G.S. 7B-402(b)).
    - ☐ This is an initial child custody determination (G.S. 50A-201).
    - ☐ NC entered a child custody order prior to this action and NC has exclusive continuing jurisdiction (G.S. 50A-202).
    - ☐ NC has temporary emergency jurisdiction (G.S. 50A-204).
    - ☐ Another state has entered a child custody order but NC has jurisdiction to modify that order (G.S. 50A-203).
        - ☐ The child, the parents, and any person acting as a parent do not presently reside in the other state, or
        - ☐ The other state's court has relinquished jurisdiction to NC and there is a court order from that other state relinquishing jurisdiction.

## Compliance with Federal Laws

☐ *Servicemembers Civil Relief Act: 50 U.S.C. 3931–3932*
Before a judgment for petitioner (DSS) is entered,
  ☐ Each respondent has made an appearance in the case. No SCRA affidavit is required.
  ☐ For each respondent who has not made an appearance, there is an affidavit or allegation in the verified petition that addresses that respondent's military status.
  ☐ It appears that a respondent is in military service. When that respondent has not made an appearance, appoint an attorney to perform SCRA responsibilities.
  ☐ A respondent is in military service. When the criteria of 50 U.S.C. 3931(d), (f) or 50 U.S.C. 3932 is met, a stay of at least ninety days is required.
  ☐ Under the NC SCRA, a state national guard member has not provided a written or electronic copy of an order to active duty for more than thirty consecutive days that was issued by a state governor. G.S. 127B-27(3), (4); 127B-28.

☐ *Indian Child Welfare Act: 25 C.F.R. 23.107*
Mandatory inquiry as to child's status as "Indian child" (defined at 25 U.S.C. 1903(4)) must be made of all participants at the commencement of the proceeding, with responses on the record.
  ☐ The child is an Indian child. ICWA provisions apply.
  *Note*: If child resides or is domiciled on Indian land or is a ward of tribal court, tribal court has exclusive jurisdiction unless an exception applies. Provisions of "emergency proceeding" under ICWA must be followed.
  ☐ A participant has "reason to know" the child is an Indian child. Follow ICWA provisions unless and until court determines on the record that the child does not meet the definition of Indian child. Confirm that DSS or other party used due diligence to identify and work with all the tribes child may be member of (or eligible for membership of). Was ICWA notice sent?
  ☐ The child is not an Indian child and no participant has reason to know the child is an Indian child. Instruct the parties to inform the court if they later receive information that provides reason to know the child is an Indian child. ICWA does not apply.

## Required Determinations for all Nonsecure Custody Orders: G.S. 7B-503(a)

☐ There is a reasonable factual basis to believe that the matters alleged in the petition are true.
☐ One or more of the conditions in G.S. 7B-503(a) exist (see statute for exact language):
  ☐ abandonment;
  ☐ physically injury, sexual abuse, or serious emotional damage;
  ☐ exposed to substantial risk of physical injury or sexual abuse because of conditions created by parent, guardian, custodian, or caretaker;
  ☐ need for medical treatment to prevent serious physical harm that may result in death, disfigurement, or substantial impairment of bodily functions and parent, guardian, custodian, or caretaker is unwilling or unable to consent to treatment;
  ☐ consent by parent, guardian, custodian, or caretaker; or
  ☐ child is a runaway and consents.

- ☐ There is a reasonable basis to believe that there are no other reasonable means available to protect the juvenile.

All three criteria must be satisfied.

*Note*: For continued nonsecure custody, G.S. 7B-506(b) sets forth that
- DSS has the burden of proving by clear and convincing evidence that the juvenile's continued placement in nonsecure custody is necessary; and
- the court is not bound by usual rules of evidence but must receive testimony and allow parties to introduce evidence and cross-examine witnesses.

## Initial Nonsecure Custody and Execution of the Order

- ☐ Order authorizes law enforcement officer or other authorized person to take physical custody of the juvenile; leave copy of order with child's parent, guardian, custodian, or caretaker; and make due return of the order (G.S. 7B-504).
  Additionally, the court may determine
  - ☐ Based on the petition and request for nonsecure custody or petitioner's testimony that less intrusive remedy is not available, the law enforcement officer is authorized to enter private property to take physical custody of the juvenile.
  - ☐ There are exigent circumstances authorizing law enforcement officer to make forcible entry at any hour.
- ☐ The order may authorize the DSS director to consent to a Child Medical Evaluation (CME) if there are written findings demonstrating the director's compelling interest in having the CME before the first hearing on the need for continued nonsecure custody (G.S. 7B-505.1(b)).

## Continued Nonsecure Custody Preliminary Issues

- ☐ The parties have been properly served or waived service (G.S. 7B-406; 7B-407; 7B-200(b)).
- ☐ Venue is proper, or venue is transferred pursuant to G.S. 7B-400.
- ☐ Will one of the hearings on the need for continued nonsecure custody be combined with a pre-adjudication hearing? G.S. 7B-800.1(b), see Checklist 2.

*Representation (G.S. 7B-601; 7B-602):*
- ☐ Parent's provisional counsel is
  - ☐ confirmed.
  - ☐ dismissed.
- ☐ Does an unrepresented parent desire and is he or she eligible for appointed counsel (may be reconsidered at any stage in the proceeding)? If yes, appoint counsel.
- ☐ If the parent wants to waive the right to counsel, has the court examined him or her on the record and made findings to show that the waiver is knowing and voluntary?
- ☐ Parent is under age 18 and not emancipated. A Rule 17 GAL is appointed.
- ☐ There is a substantial question as to parent's competency and need for a Rule 17 GAL. A hearing on that issue is required.
- ☐ Abuse and/or neglect is alleged. A GAL and attorney advocate has been appointed for the juvenile.

☐ Only dependency is alleged. The court exercises its discretion to appoint a G.S. 7B-601 GAL and attorney advocate.

## Continued Nonsecure Custody Inquiries and Findings

At each hearing on the need for continued nonsecure custody, the court must determine the following (G.S. 7B-506):

☐ Is paternity at issue? If so, what efforts have been made to establish paternity? Order must include findings and may provide for specific efforts to be taken.
☐ If a parent is missing, what is known about the identity and location of that parent, and what efforts have been undertaken to locate and serve that parent? Order must include findings and may provide for specific efforts to be taken.
☐ What efforts have been made by DSS to identify and notify the child's relatives for potential resources for placement or support of the juvenile?
☐ Are there other juveniles remaining in the home? If so, what are DSS's assessment findings relating to those children? What if any actions has DSS taken and/or what services has DSS provided to protect those children?

Additional findings when a child is placed or remains in nonsecure custody with DSS (G.S. 7B-507):

☐ Whether continuation in or return to the child's own home would be contrary to the child's health and safety.
☐ Whether reasonable efforts have been made to prevent the need for placement (child's health and safety are the paramount concern) (finding may be that reasonable efforts were precluded by an immediate threat of harm to the child).
☐ A statement that the child's placement and care are the responsibility of DSS.

Required placement considerations (G.S. 7B-505(b), (d)):

☐ In making its order, the court must consider whether it is in the child's best interests to remain in his/her community of residence.
   ☐ Under Fostering Connections and the Every Student Succeeds Act (ESSA), is DSS considering the proximity of the placement to the child's school? Is the child remaining in his or her school based on a best interest determination made by DSS in consultation with others?
☐ Is a relative willing and able to provide care and supervision in a safe home? If so, placement must be ordered to that relative unless the court finds it is contrary to the child's best interests.
☐ Have reasonable efforts been made to place the siblings together absent DSS documentation that joint placement is contrary to the safety or well-being of any of the siblings (42 U.S.C. 671(a)(31))?
☐ Does the placement comply with the Interstate Compact on the Placement of Children (ICPC)?
☐ Does the placement comply with the Multiethnic Placement Act (MEPA-IEP)?
☐ When ICWA applies, does the placement comply with ICWA placement preferences?

Additional inquiries the court may make to address the following issues as appropriate:

- ☐ Has a petition been filed pursuant to G.S. 7B-302(d1) (caregiver with history of violence when abuse of child alleged)? If so, what are the results of any resulting mental health evaluation (G.S. 7B-503(b))?
- ☐ Does the order need to address consent for medical care for the child that is not routine or emergency care, including a CME? If so, provisions of G.S. 7B-505.1 apply.
- ☐ Is the child a member of a state-recognized Indian tribe? If so, the court may order DSS to notify the state-recognized tribe of the need for nonsecure custody for the purposes of locating relatives or nonrelative kin for placement (G.S. 7B-505(c)).
- ☐ Financial support.

## Outcomes

- ☐ Deny continued nonsecure custody, resulting in child's return home (the court must first consider the child's release to his or her parent, relative, guardian, custodian, or other responsible adult (G.S. 7B-503(a)).
- ☐ Continue nonsecure custody
    - ☐ Placement in nonsecure custody with (G.S. 7B-505(a))
        - ☐ DSS (the order must specify that placement and care are DSS responsibility and DSS must provide or arrange for the juvenile's placement unless the court orders a specific placement, G.S. 7B-507(a)(4)) or
        - ☐ a person designated in the order (after considering DSS recommendations, G.S. 7B-507(a)(4)).
    - ☐ Temporary residential placement may be in any of the following (G.S. 7B-505(a)):
        - ☐ the home of parent, relative, nonrelative kin, other person with legal custody of the child's sibling, or any home or facility approved by the court and designated in the order (see also G.S. 7B-505(b), (c));
        - ☐ a licensed foster home or home otherwise authorized by law to provide such care; or
        - ☐ a facility operated by DSS.
    - ☐ Order DSS to make diligent efforts to notify relatives and other persons with legal custody of the child's sibling that the child is in nonsecure custody, unless there is a finding that notification would be contrary to the child's best interests (G.S. 7B-505(b)).
    - ☐ Order visitation when custody is removed from a parent, guardian, or custodian or continues the child's placement outside of the home pursuant to G.S. 7B-905.1 (G.S. 7B-506(g1)).
    *Note:* When siblings who have been removed from their home are not jointly placed, reasonable efforts for visitation or other ongoing interaction between the siblings should be made absent DSS documentation that it would contrary to the safety or well-being of any sibling (42 U.S.C. 671(a)(31)).
    - ☐ May order services or other efforts aimed at returning the child to a safe home (G.S. 7B-507(a)(5)).
- ☐ Set next hearing date in compliance with time requirements of G.S. 7B-506(a).

*Note*: The court may not dismiss the petition or award permanent custody to a parent or other person without an adjudication on the merits.

# Checklist 2
# Pre-Adjudication

The court is required to consider criteria set forth in G.S. 7B-800.1 before the adjudicatory hearing. The pre-adjudication hearing may be combined with a hearing on the need for continued nonsecure custody or any pretrial hearing authorized by local rules. If nonsecure custody was not requested or granted, the pre-adjudication hearing is likely to be the first hearing in the action.

## Subject Matter Jurisdiction

- [ ] A court action has been commenced by the filing of a verified petition alleging abuse, neglect, or dependency in district court by a county DSS. The petition was
  - [ ] filed with clerk's office during hours when court was open.
  - [ ] accepted by magistrate when the clerk's office was closed as authorized by G.S. 7B-404.
  
  G.S. 7B-402; 7B-403; 7B-405.
- [ ] The petition is properly signed by the department's director or authorized representative. G.S. 7B-101(10); 7B-401.1(a); 7B-403(a).
- [ ] The petition is properly verified. G.S. 7B-403(a); 7B-800.1(a)(5a).
- [ ] The petition requests relief. N.C. R. Civ. P. 7(b)(1).
- [ ] NC has jurisdiction under the UCCJEA pursuant to G.S. Chapter 50A (review the allegations in the petition or attached affidavit addressing criteria specified by G.S. 50A-209 regarding the child's status) (G.S. 7B-402(b)).
  - [ ] This is an initial child custody determination (G.S. 50A-201).
  - [ ] NC entered a child custody order prior to this action and NC has exclusive continuing jurisdiction (G.S. 50A-202).
  - [ ] NC has temporary emergency jurisdiction (G.S. 50A-204) (*Note:* The court's authority is limited to entering temporary custody orders when it is exercising temporary emergency jurisdiction, impacting the court's authority to proceed to adjudication).
  - [ ] Another state has entered a child custody order but NC has jurisdiction to modify that order (G.S. 50A-203).
    - [ ] The child, the child's parents, and any person acting as a parent do not presently reside in the other state or
    - [ ] The other state's court has relinquished jurisdiction to NC and there is a court order from that other state relinquishing jurisdiction.

## Parties and Personal Jurisdiction: G.S. 7B-800.1(a)(2), (3), (5)

- [ ] Identify the parties to the proceeding (G.S. 7B-401.1):
  - [ ] DSS, the petitioner
  - [ ] Child
  - [ ] Parent 1

- ☐ Parent 2
- ☐ Putative father(s)
  - ☐ What efforts, if any, have been made to establish paternity, including identifying and locating missing parent?
  - ☐ Has paternity been established?
- ☐ Guardian
- ☐ Custodian
- ☐ Caretaker

☐ The parties have been properly served or waived service (G.S. 7B-406; 7B-407; 7B-200(b)).
☐ Have notice requirements been met?
☐ Any motions to intervene or remove a party as authorized by G.S. 7B-401.1(g), (h).

## Representation: G.S. 7B-601; 7B-602; 7B-800.1(a)(1)

☐ Parent's provisional counsel is
  ☐ confirmed.
  ☐ dismissed.
☐ Does an unrepresented parent desire and is he or she eligible for appointed counsel (may be reconsidered at any stage in the proceeding)? If yes, appoint counsel.
☐ If parent wants to waive the right to counsel, has the court examined the parent on the record and made findings to show that the waiver is knowing and voluntary?
☐ Parent is under age 18 and not emancipated. A Rule 17 GAL is appointed.
☐ There is a substantial question as to parent's competency and need for a Rule 17 GAL. A hearing on that issue is required.
☐ Abuse and/or neglect is alleged. A GAL and attorney advocate have been appointed for the juvenile.
☐ Only dependency is alleged. The court exercises its discretion to appoint a G.S. 7B-601 GAL and attorney advocate.

## Relatives: G.S. 7B-800.1(4)

☐ Has DSS identified and notified parents, relatives, or other persons with legal custody of the child's sibling(s) as potential resources for placement or support of the child?

## Other Pretrial Issues

☐ Venue is proper, or venue is transferred pursuant to G.S. 7B-400.
☐ Are there any motions to continue the adjudication hearing, which must be held within sixty days of petition being filed (G.S. 7B-801(c))? Continuances are limited by G.S. 7B-803 but permitted if there is
  ☐ Good cause to continue the hearing for as long as reasonably necessary to receive additional evidence, reports, or assessments that the court has requested or other needed information in the best interests of the child.
  ☐ Good cause to allow reasonable time for the parties to conduct expeditious discovery.

- ☐ Extraordinary circumstances that are necessary for the proper administration of justice or in the child's best interests (resolution of pending criminal charges arising from the same incident is not a sole extraordinary circumstance to continue the hearing).
- ☐ Are there discovery motions pursuant to G.S. 7B-700?
- ☐ Is DSS seeking to amend its petition as authorized by G.S. 7B-800?
- ☐ Is a writ requested for an incarcerated party?
- ☐ Is there a request for alternative means of participating? (see G.S. 50A-111).
- ☐ Is there a request for the hearing or part of the hearing to be closed (G.S. 7B-801(a))?
- ☐ Is there a motion for genetic marker testing regarding paternity (G.S. 8-50.1(b1))?
- ☐ Is a language interpreter needed?
- ☐ Are accommodations for a disability needed to allow for participation in the proceeding?
- ☐ Any other pretrial issue?
- ☐ Stipulations or Consent Order (see Checklist 3: Adjudication)

## Compliance with Federal Laws

☐ *Servicemembers Civil Relief Act: 50 U.S.C. 3931–3932*
Before a judgment for petitioner (DSS) is entered,
- ☐ Each respondent has made an appearance in the case. No SCRA affidavit is required.
- ☐ For each respondent who has not made an appearance, there is an affidavit or allegation in the verified petition that addresses that respondent's military status.
- ☐ It appears that a respondent is in military service. When that respondent has not made an appearance, appoint an attorney to perform SCRA responsibilities.
- ☐ A respondent is in military service. When the requirements of 50 U.S.C. 3931(d), (f) or 50 U.S.C. 3932 are met, a stay of at least ninety days is required.
- ☐ Under the NC SCRA, a state national guard member has not provided a written or electronic copy of an order to active duty for more than thirty consecutive days that was issued by a state governor. G.S. 127B-27(3), (4); 127B-28.

☐ *Indian Child Welfare Act: 25 C.F.R. 23.107*
Mandatory inquiry as to child's status as "Indian child" (defined at 25 U.S.C. 1903(4)) must be made of all participants at the commencement of the proceeding, with responses on the record.
- ☐ The child is an Indian child. ICWA provisions apply.
  *Note*: If child resides or is domiciled on Indian land or is a ward of tribal court, tribal court has exclusive jurisdiction unless an exception applies. Provisions of "emergency proceeding" under ICWA must be followed.
- ☐ A participant has "reason to know" the child is an Indian child. Follow ICWA provisions unless and until court determines on the record that the child does not meet the definition of Indian child. Confirm that DSS or other party used due diligence to identify and work with all the tribes child may be member of (or eligible for membership of). Was the ICWA notice sent?
- ☐ The child is not an Indian child and no participant has reason to know the child is an Indian child. Instruct the parties to inform the court if they later receive information that provides reason to know the child is an Indian child. ICWA does not apply.

# Checklist 3
# **Adjudication**

Prior to the adjudicatory hearing, the court should have held a pre-adjudication (or pretrial) hearing that addressed issues impacting the adjudication hearing (see Checklist 2). At the time of the adjudicatory hearing, the child may or may not be placed in nonsecure custody.

### Child's Status

An adjudication determines the child's status as abused, neglected, or dependent based on conditions alleged in the petition. It is not a determination of a parent's, guardian's, custodian's, or caregiver's culpability.

### AOC Form Order:
AOC- J-153, Juvenile Adjudication Order (Abuse/Neglect/Dependency) (Oct. 2013).

### Procedure

- [ ] Hearing (G.S. 7B-802; 7B-805)
  - No default judgment or judgment on the pleadings is permitted.
  - DSS must prove the allegations in the petition by clear and convincing evidence (G.S. 7B-807).
  - The rules of evidence apply (G.S. 7B-804).
  - Evidence is limited to that which relates to the allegations in the petition; however, two exceptions allow for post-petition evidence: (1) neglect is alleged and the parent and child have been separated for a period of time before the petition is filed and (2) the establishment of paternity.
- [ ] Stipulations of adjudicatory facts (G.S. 7B-807(a))
  Must comply with one:
  - [ ] be in writing, signed by each party stipulating to the specific facts, and submitted to the court.
  - [ ] be read into the record, followed by an oral statement of agreement from each party agreeing to the stipulated facts.
- [ ] Consent order (G.S. 7B-801(b1))
  All three are required:
  - [ ] All parties are present or represented by counsel who is present and authorized to consent.
  - [ ] The child is represented by counsel (if a GAL has not been appointed to a juvenile who has been alleged to be a dependent juvenile only, this provision is not satisfied and a consent cannot be taken).
  - [ ] The court makes sufficient findings of fact.

## Findings and Conclusions

The order shall (G.S. 7B-807)
- ☐ contain appropriate findings of fact (supported by competent evidence in the record);
- ☐ contain appropriate conclusions of law (supported by the findings of fact);
- ☐ if adjudicating the juvenile abused, neglected, or dependent, state that the allegations have been proved by clear and convincing evidence; and
- ☐ be entered (reduced to writing, signed by the judge who presided over the hearing, and filed with the clerk) no later than thirty days following completion of the hearing.

*Note*: If the petition alleged more than one condition (abuse, neglect, dependency), the order should make findings and conclusions about each condition alleged.

## Outcomes

The court adjudicates the existence or nonexistence of the condition(s) alleged in the petition based on a clear and convincing evidence standard (G.S. 7B-805; 7B-807).
- ☐ DSS failed to meet its burden of proof. Petition dismissed with prejudice. If child was placed in nonsecure custody, child must be released to his or her parent, custodian, guardian, or caretaker. (G.S. 7B-807(a)).
- ☐ DSS met its burden of proof by clear and convincing evidence. Child is adjudicated as one or more of the conditions alleged in the petition:
  - ☐ abused, and/or
  - ☐ neglected, and/or
  - ☐ dependent.

If the child is adjudicated abused, neglected, and/or dependent, the court proceeds to an initial dispositional hearing to be concluded within thirty days of completion of the adjudicatory hearing (G.S. 7B-901). Pending entry of the initial dispositional order, the court should address the following in a temporary order:
- ☐ custody, placement, and visitation.

# Checklist 4
# Dispositional Findings and Options at Initial, Review and Permanency Planning

**HOW TO USE THIS CHECKLIST: USE TOGETHER WITH A CORRESPONDING CHECKLIST FOR THE PARTICULAR DISPOSITIONAL HEARING (Initial, Review, Permanency Planning)**

There are different types of dispositional hearings: initial, review, and permanency planning. Each hearing requires the court to examine certain specified factors and make certain findings. Some of those factors and findings apply to every initial, review, or permanency planning hearing, and others are specific to the hearing type. The court is also authorized at every dispositional hearing to order a dispositional plan that addresses issues related to placement, custody, services, and conditions that are imposed on the parties. This Checklist addresses those factors, findings, and dispositional options that apply to all the dispositional hearings and is meant to be **used together with the corresponding Checklist** that identifies additional factors, findings, and options that apply to the specific hearing type.

**Procedure**

- ☐ Hearing (G.S. 7B-901; 7B-906.1)
- ☐ Consent order (G.S. 7B-801(b1))
  All three are required:
  - ☐ All parties are present or represented by counsel who is present and authorized to consent.
  - ☐ The child is represented by counsel (if a GAL has not been appointed to a juvenile who has been alleged to be a dependent juvenile only, this provision is not satisfied and a consent cannot be taken)
  - ☐ The court makes sufficient findings of fact.

**Evidentiary Issues**

- The standard is the child's best interests, and there is no burden of proof on any party.
- The court considers evidence that is relevant, reliable, and necessary to determine the needs of the juvenile and most appropriate disposition, which may include hearsay testimony and written reports (G.S. 7B-901(a); 7B-906.1(c)).

**Required Placement Considerations**

G.S. 7B-903(a1), (b):
- ☐ When placement is not with a parent, the court must consider whether a relative is willing and able to provide care and supervision in a safe home. If there is such a relative, placement must be ordered to that relative unless the court finds it is contrary to the child's best

interests.
- ☐ In making its order, the court must consider whether it is in the child's best interests to remain in his/her community of residence.
    - ☐ Under Fostering Connections and the Every Student Succeeds Act (ESSA), is DSS considering the proximity of the placement to the child's school? Is the child remaining in his or her school based on a best interest determination made by DSS in consultation with others?
- ☐ Does the placement comply with the Interstate Compact on the Placement of Children (ICPC)?
- ☐ When the court has found the child has been physically abused by an individual, if that individual has a history of violent behavior against people, the court must consider the opinion of the mental health professional who performed an evaluation required by G.S. 7B-302(d1) before returning the custody of the child to that individual.

G.S. 7B-903.1(c):
- ☐ Before *DSS recommends* a return of the child's physical custody to a parent, guardian, custodian, or caretaker *from whom the child was removed*, DSS must provide the court with documentation of at least two observations of visits between the child and removal parent, guardian, custodian, or caretaker, where each visit was at least one hour and the visits were at least seven days apart. Note that the DSS observation is not required before DSS recommends placement with the non-removal parent or when another party in the case seeks placement with the removal parent, guardian, custodian, or caretaker.

Other considerations:
- ☐ Does the placement comply with the Multiethnic Placement Act (MEPA-IEP)?
- ☐ When ICWA applies, does the placement comply with ICWA placement preferences?
- ☐ Have reasonable efforts been made to place siblings together absent DSS documentation that a joint placement is contrary to the safety or well-being of any of the siblings (42 U.S.C. 671(a)(31))?

---

**Dispositional Alternatives (Placement and Custody): G.S. 7B-903(a); 7B-906.1(i), (j), (*l*)**

The court may combine any of the applicable alternatives when it finds the disposition to be in the child's best interests.
- ☐ Dismiss the case (appropriate when no purpose would be served by continuing to exercise jurisdiction; legal status of the child and parents reverts to the status that existed prior to the filing of the petition, G.S. 7B-201(b)).
- ☐ Continue the case to allow the parent, guardian, custodian, caretaker, or others to take appropriate action.
- ☐ In-home supervision by DSS in the child's county or by another individual available to the court, subject to any conditions placed on the parent, guardian, custodian, or caretaker.
- ☐ Custody ordered to
    - ☐ Parent;
        - ☐ Court must consider whether jurisdiction in juvenile proceeding should be terminated and custody ordered pursuant to G.S. Chapter 50 (G.S. 7B-911).

Custody ordered to (continued)
- ☐ relative, other suitable person, or private agency offering placement services;
    - ☐ Court has verified the person receiving custody
        - ☐ understands the legal significance of the placement (this applies to each person) and
        - ☐ will have adequate resources to care appropriately for the child.
    - ☐ Court must consider whether jurisdiction in juvenile proceeding should be terminated and custody ordered pursuant to G.S. Chapter 50 (G.S. 7B-911).
- ☐ DSS in the county of the child's residence (or, if the child's residence is in another state, in the county where the child is found for return to appropriate authorities in the child's home state);
    - ☐ Decision making authority when DSS has custody of the child: G.S. 7B-903.1
        - ☐ Court may delegate any part of DSS authority to make decisions that are generally made by a child's custodian to the child's parent, foster parent, or other individual.
        - ☐ Court may set out alternative parameters for who approves normal childhood activities for child after finding it is not in the child's best interest to allow the child's placement provider (e.g., foster parent) to make such decisions without court or DSS approval.
        - ☐ Court must find there will be proper care and supervision in a safe home before DSS may allow unsupervised visits or return physical custody of the child to the parent, guardian, custodian, or caretaker from whom the child was removed.
        - ☐ If the order needs to address consent for medical care for the child that is not routine or emergency care, provisions of G.S. 7B-505.1(c) apply.
- ☐ Appointment of a guardian pursuant to G.S. 7B-600.
    - ☐ Court has verified the person being appointed guardian
        - ☐ understands the legal significance of the appointment (this applies to each person) and
        - ☐ will have adequate resources to care appropriately for the child.

---

**Required Findings when Child Placed or Continues in Out-of-Home Care**

G.S. 7B-903(a2), (a3):
- ☐ Continuation in/return to the child's own home would be contrary to the child's health and safety.
- ☐ Whether DSS has made reasonable efforts made to prevent the need for placement (child's health and safety are the paramount concern) (finding may be that reasonable efforts were precluded by an immediate threat of harm to the child).

G.S. 7B-905.1
- ☐ Visitation order that is in child's best interests and consistent with his or her health and safety. The visitation order must include either
    - ☐ Minimum outline
        - ☐ minimum duration,
        - ☐ minimum frequency, and
        - ☐ whether visits must be supervised. If court is ordering supervised visitation, court must find parent has the ability to pay before ordering a parent to pay for the cost of

supervision. When visitation is order, the plan may specify conditions under which visitation may be suspended.
- ☐ No visitation. There must be a finding that visitation is not in the child's best interests consistent with his or her health and safety 7B-905.1(b) or a parent forfeited his or her right to visitation
- ☐ All parties must be informed of the right to file a motion for review of the visitation plan.

## Order Addressing Child's Evaluation and Treatment: G.S. 7B-903(d), (e); 7B-904

The court may order the following:
- ☐ Evaluation of the child by a physician, psychiatrist, psychologist, or other qualified expert, to determine the needs of the child.
  - ☐ When evaluation ordered and after its completion, the court must conduct a hearing to determine the treatment needs of the child and payment for the treatment.
  - ☐ Notice of the hearing must be given to the county manager or person designated by the chair of the board of county commissioners of the child's county of residence.
  - ☐ Payment of cost of evaluation or treatment by the parent or other responsible parties or, if the parent is unable to pay, by the county.
- ☐ DSS to coordinate with the appropriate representative of the area mental health, developmental disabilities, and substance abuse services (or LME/MCO) to develop a treatment plan for a child the court determines is mentally ill or developmentally disabled.
- ☐ Participation in child's treatment by a parent, guardian, custodian, stepparent, adult member of the child's household, or an adult relative caring for the child, if found to be in the child's best interest.

The court may not order the child's commitment directly to an institution (that order is void).
- ☐ Although not an order, the court may sign and consent to a child's admission to a hospital or developmental center for persons with intellectual or developmental disabilities if such admission is required and the parent, guardian, or custodian refuses to consent.

## Order Directed to Parents or Others: G.S. 7B-904

The court may order a parent, guardian, custodian, or caretaker who has been served with a summons (or has otherwise submitted to the court's jurisdiction) to
- ☐ attend and participate in parenting classes if available in the judicial district where the parent, guardian, custodian, or caretaker lives;
- ☐ provide transportation for the child to keep appointments for any treatment ordered by the court (if the child is in the home and to the extent the person is able to provide transportation);
- ☐ take appropriate steps to remedy conditions in the home that led or contributed to the adjudication or to the court's removal of the child from the home;
- ☐ upon finding it is in the child's best interests, to participate in psychiatric, psychological, or other treatment or counseling directed towards remedying the behaviors or conditions that led or contributed to the child's adjudication or court's removal of the child from that person's custody, and may

- ☐ require compliance with treatment plan approved by the court or
- ☐ condition legal custody or physical placement of the child on compliance with that treatment
- ☐ order the individual to pay the cost of the treatment and if unable to do so, may
  - ☐ order the county to pay when the compliance with treatment is a condition for legal custody or physical placement of the child with that parent or other adult.
  - ☐ order treatment currently available from a local mental health program.
☐ A parent over whom the court has personal jurisdiction may be ordered to pay a reasonable portion of the cost of the child's care based on the parent's ability to do so when legal custody of the child is vested with someone other than the parent.

**Additional Components of Order: G.S. 7B-905; 7B-906.1(h)**

The order shall
- ☐ contain appropriate findings of fact (supported by competent evidence in the record);
- ☐ contain appropriate conclusions of law (supported by the findings of fact);
- ☐ be entered (reduced to writing, signed by the judge who presided over the hearing, and filed with the clerk) no later than thirty days following completion of the hearing.
- ☐ Complete
  - ☐ Checklist 5 for initial dispositional hearing,
  - ☐ Checklist 6 for review hearing, or
  - ☐ Checklist 7 for permanency planning hearing.

# Checklist 5
# Initial Disposition

This Checklist includes those factors, findings, and options that are specific to the initial disposition conducted pursuant to G.S. 7B-901(c). **USE TOGETHER WITH CHECKLIST 4,** which contains additional required factors, findings, and options that apply.

**AOC Form Order:**
AOC- J-154, Juvenile Disposition Order (Abuse/Neglect/Dependency) (Oct. 2015).

**Required Evidence**

- [ ] DSS must submit a predisposition report or the court must make a written finding that the report is unnecessary (G.S. 7B-808).

**Required Inquiries and Findings: G.S. 7B-901(b)**

- [ ] Is paternity at issue? If so, what efforts have been made to establish paternity? Order must include findings and may provide for specific efforts to be taken.
- [ ] If a parent is missing, what is known about the identity and location of that parent, and what efforts have been undertaken to locate and serve that parent? Order must include findings and may provide for specific efforts to be taken.
- [ ] What efforts have been made to identify and notify the child's relatives, parents, or other persons with legal custody of the child's sibling(s) as potential resources for the child's placement or support?

**Order and Required Findings for Ceasing Reunification Efforts: G.S. 7B-901(c)**

When a child is placed in DSS custody, the court must order (unless exception below applies) that reasonable efforts are not required if it makes written findings that

- [ ] A court of competent jurisdiction determines or has determined that an aggravated circumstance exists because the parent committed or encouraged or allowed any of the following on the child:
    - [ ] sexual abuse;
    - [ ] chronic physical or emotional abuse;
    - [ ] torture;
    - [ ] abandonment;
    - [ ] chronic or toxic exposure to alcohol or controlled substances that causes impairment of or addiction in the child; or
    - [ ] any other act, practice, or conduct that increased the enormity or added to the injurious consequences of the abuse or neglect.
- [ ] The parent's rights to another child were involuntarily terminated by a court of competent

jurisdiction.
- ☐ A court of competent jurisdiction determines has determined that the parent
    - ☐ committed murder or voluntary manslaughter of another child of his/hers;
    - ☐ aided, abetted, attempted, conspired, or solicited to commit murder or voluntary manslaughter of this child or another of the parent's children;
    - ☐ committed felony assault resulting in serious bodily injury to this child or another of the parent's children;
    - ☐ committed sexual abuse against this child or another of the parent's children; or
    - ☐ has been required to register as a sex offender on any government-administered registry.

Despite making a written finding of one of the above factors,
- ☐ the court finds there is compelling evidence warranting continued reunification efforts.

### Additional Components of Order: G.S. 7B-905

The order shall
- ☐ state the precise terms of the disposition, including the person(s) responsible for carrying out whatever is required in the disposition, as well as the person or agency in whom custody is vested;
- ☐ direct that a review hearing be scheduled within ninety days from the initial dispositional hearing when the child is removed from the custody or a parent, guardian, custodian, or caretaker
    - ☐ Exception: when reunification efforts have been ceased, a permanency planning hearing must be scheduled within thirty days (G.S. 7B-901(d)).

☐ **Complete Checklist 4 for additional requirements.**

# Checklist 6
# Review

This Checklist includes those factors, findings, and options that are specific to a review hearing conducted pursuant to G.S. 7B-906.1. **USE TOGETHER WITH CHECKLIST 4,** which contains additional required factors, findings, and options that apply.

### Required Notice: G.S. 7B-906.1(b)

- ☐ The clerk provided fifteen days' notice of the hearing and its purpose to the parents; child (if 12 or older); the child's GAL; if applicable, the guardian or custodian (including agency with custody); and any other person or agency the court specifies.
- ☐ The clerk provided fifteen days' notice of the hearing to the person providing care for the child or DSS filed written documentation with the clerk that it sent notice to the person providing care for the child.

### Required Factors and Findings: G.S. 7B-906.1(d)

At every review hearing, the court must consider the following criteria and make written findings of those that are relevant:

- ☐ Services that have been offered to reunite the child with either parent, regardless of whether the child resided with the parent at the time of removal, or with the guardian or custodian from whom the child was removed.
- ☐ Reports on visitation and whether there is a need to create, modify, or enforce an appropriate visitation plan in accordance with G.S. 7B-905.1.
- ☐ Whether efforts to reunite the child with either parent clearly would be unsuccessful or inconsistent with the child's health or safety and need for a safe, permanent home within a reasonable period of time. The court must consider reunification efforts regardless of whether the child lived with the parent, guardian, or custodian at the time of the removal.
    - ☐ If the court determines efforts would be unsuccessful or inconsistent, the court must schedule a permanency planning hearing within thirty days to address concurrent permanency planning under G.S. 7B-906.2. (The court does not have the authority to order that reunification efforts cease at a review hearing).
- ☐ Reports on placements the child has had, the appropriateness of the child's current placement, and the goals of the child's foster care plan, including the role the current foster parent will play in the planning for the child.
- ☐ If the child is 16 or 17 years old, a report on an independent living assessment and, if appropriate, an independent living plan.
- ☐ Whether termination of parental rights should be considered and if so, when.
- ☐ Any other criteria the court deems necessary.

- ☐ **Complete Checklist 4 for additional requirements.**

# Checklist 7
# **Permanency Planning**

The court is required to make numerous statutory findings at the permanency planning stage. However, the statutory findings are not applied universally to all permanency planning hearings but instead are conditioned on specific circumstances (e.g., a permanency planning hearing involving a child who is 14 years old or older, or what is ordered). This Checklist addresses the various circumstances and the different factors, findings, and options that apply to permanency planning hearings. **USE TOGETHER WITH CHECKLIST 4,** which contains additional required factors, findings, and options that apply.

**Required Notice: G.S. 7B-906.1(b)**

☐ The clerk provided fifteen days' notice of the hearing and its purpose to the parents; child (if 12 or older); the child's GAL; if applicable, the guardian or custodian (including agency with custody); and any other person or agency the court specifies.
☐ The clerk provided fifteen days' notice of the hearing to the person providing care for the child or DSS filed written documentation with the clerk that it sent notice to the person providing care for the child.

*Note*: If an objection to a deficient notice is raised (e.g., less than fifteen days' notice provided), the court may not proceed with a permanency planning hearing. If no objection is raised, the party waives the issue of insufficient notice.

**Required Findings and Conclusion at Every Permanency Planning Hearing**

G.S. 7B-906.1(d)
The court must consider the following criteria and make written findings of those that are *relevant*:

☐ Services that have been offered to reunite the child with either parent, regardless of whether the child resided with the parent at the time of removal, or with the guardian or custodian from whom the child was removed.
☐ Reports on visitation and whether there is a need to create, modify, or enforce an appropriate visitation plan in accordance with G.S. 7B-905.1.
☐ Whether efforts to reunite the child with either parent clearly would be unsuccessful or inconsistent with the child's health or safety and need for a safe, permanent home within a reasonable period of time. The court must consider reunification efforts regardless of whether the child lived with the parent, guardian, or custodian at the time of the removal.
☐ Reports on placements the child has had, the appropriateness of the child's current placement, and the goals of the child's foster care plan, including the role the current foster parent will play in the planning for the child.
☐ If the child is 16 or 17 years old, a report on an independent living assessment and, if appropriate, an independent living plan.

- ☐ Whether termination of parental rights should be considered and if so, when.
- ☐ Any other criteria the court deems necessary.

### G.S. 7B-906.2(c): Required Findings
- ☐ The court must make a finding about whether the department's efforts toward reunification were reasonable. The finding is not required when reunification efforts have been previously ceased.
- ☐ The court must make findings of the efforts the department made toward
  - ☐ the primary permanent plan in effect before the hearing and
  - ☐ any secondary permanent plans in effect before the hearing.

### G.S 7B-906.2(c): Required Conclusion
- ☐ The court must make a conclusion as to whether efforts to finalize the permanent plan were reasonable to achieve timely permanence for the child.

### G.S. 7B-906.2(d)
The court shall make written findings as to *each* of the following, which demonstrates the degree of success or failure toward reunification:
Whether the parent
- ☐ is making adequate progress under the plan within a reasonable period of time;
- ☐ is actively participating in or cooperating with the plan, the department, and the child's GAL;
- ☐ remains available to the court, department, and child's GAL;
- ☐ is acting in a manner that is inconsistent with the child's health or safety.

### G.S. 7B-906.1(g)
At the conclusion of *each* permanency planning hearing, the court
- ☐ shall make specific findings of the best permanent plans to achieve a safe, permanent home for the child within a reasonable period of time;

---

**Any Permanency Planning Hearing Where Child Not Placed with Parent: G.S. 7B-906.1(e)**

Additionally, the court must consider the following criteria and make written findings about those that are *relevant:*
- ☐ Whether it is possible for the child to be placed with a parent within the next six months and, if not, why such placement is not in the child's best interests.
- ☐ Where placement with a parent is unlikely within six months, whether legal guardianship or custody with a relative or some other suitable person should be established and, if so, rights and responsibilities that should remain with the parents.
- ☐ Where the child's placement with a parent is unlikely within six months, whether adoption should be pursued and, if so, any barriers to the child's adoption.
- ☐ Where the child's placement with a parent is unlikely within six months, whether the child should remain in the current placement, or be placed in another permanent living arrangement and why.

- ☐ Whether the department, since the initial permanency planning hearing, has made reasonable efforts to implement the permanent plan.
- ☐ Any other criteria the court deems necessary.

### Juvenile Is 14 or Older and in DSS Custody: G.S. 7B-912(a), (b)

Additional findings are required when the juvenile is 14 and older. At every permanency planning hearing, the court must inquire about and make written findings of *each* of the following:
- ☐ The services provided to assist the teen in making a transition to adulthood.
- ☐ The steps the department is taking to ensure that the foster family or other licensed placement provider follows the reasonable and prudent parent standard.
- ☐ Whether the teen has regular opportunities to engage in age- or –developmentally appropriate activities.

At or before the last permanency planning hearing that is at least ninety days before the juvenile turns 18, the court must
- ☐ inquire as to whether the juvenile has a copy of his or her birth certificate, social security card, health insurance information, driver's license or other identification card, and any educational or medical records the juvenile requests and
- ☐ determine the person or entity that should assist the juvenile in obtaining these documents before he or she turns 18.

### Special Circumstances and Additional Findings Delaying or Relieving DSS's Initiation of TPR: G.S. 7B-906.1(f), (m)

When the court finds a TPR is necessary to perfect the primary permanent plan, the department shall file a TPR petition (or motion) within sixty days from the entry of the order unless
- ☐ the court makes written findings regarding why the petition (or motion) cannot be filed in sixty days and specifies a time frame in which the TPR petition (or motion) must be filed.

The requirement that the department file a TPR petition (or motion) applies when either
- ☐ the department has custody or placement responsibility of child who has been placed outside the home for twelve of the most recent twenty-two months or
- ☐ a court of competent jurisdiction has determined a parent has abandoned the child; committed murder or voluntary manslaughter of another child of the parent; or has aided, abetted, attempted, conspired, or solicited to commit murder or voluntary manslaughter of this child or another child of the parent.

The department is not required to initiate a TPR if the court finds *any* of the following:
- ☐ the primary permanent plan is guardianship or custody with a relative or other suitable person;
- ☐ the court makes specific findings as to why filing the TPR petition is not in the child's best interests; or
- ☐ the department has not provided the child's family with services it deems necessary when reasonable efforts are still required to enable the child's return to a safe home. G.S. 7B-906.1(f).

## Required Findings to Waive Further Hearings: G.S. 7B-906.1(k), (n)

The court may waive further permanency planning review hearings, may require written reports to the court by the person or agency with custody of the child in lieu of permanency planning review hearings, or order that the hearings be held less often than every six months if the court finds *each* of the following by *clear, cogent, and convincing evidence*:
- ☐ The child has resided in the placement for at least one year or the child has resided in the placement for at least six consecutive months and the court enters a consent order pursuant to G.S 7B-801(b1).
- ☐ The placement is stable and continuation of the placement is in the child's best interests.
- ☐ Neither the child's best interests nor any party's rights require that review hearings be held every six months.
- ☐ All parties are aware that the matter may be brought before the court for review at any time by the filing of a motion for review or on the court's own motion.
- ☐ The court order has designated the relative or other suitable person as the child's permanent custodian or guardian of the person.

*Note:* When custody is placed with a parent, the court is relieved of the duty to hold periodic review hearings.

## Order for Permanent Plans: G.S. 7B-906.2(a)–(b)

The court must adopt one or more concurrent permanent plans
- ☐ it finds are in the child's best interest G.S. 7B-906.2(a)

and must identify
- ☐ the primary permanent plan and
- ☐ the secondary permanent plan G.S. 7B-906.2(b)

unless
- ☐ concurrent planning is not required because a permanent plan is or has been achieved G.S. 7B-906.2(a1) (so a secondary plan is no longer necessary).

The court
- ☐ must order the department to make efforts toward finalizing the primary and secondary permanent plans and
- ☐ may specify efforts that are reasonable to timely achieve permanence for the child.

There are six permanent plans, some of which require specific findings.
- ☐ **Reunification** must be a primary or secondary plan unless the court makes written *findings of one of the following:*
    - ☐ The court made findings at initial disposition under G.S. 7B-901(c) that reunification efforts are not required.
    - ☐ The court made findings under G.S. 7B-906.1(d)(3).
    - ☐ The permanent plan is or has been achieved so there is no concurrent (secondary) plan.
    - ☐ Reunification efforts clearly would be unsuccessful.
    - ☐ Reunification efforts would be inconsistent with the child's health or safety.

- ☐ **Adoption**
- ☐ **Guardianship**
    - ☐ The court finds by clear and convincing evidence that the parent has waived his or her constitutional parental rights by being unfit, neglecting the child's welfare, or acting inconsistently with his or her constitutionally protected status.
    - ☐ The court must verify that the person receiving guardianship
        - ☐ understands the legal significance of the appointment (applies to each person) and
        - ☐ will have adequate resources to appropriately care for the child. G.S. 7B-906.1(j).
- ☐ **Custody** to a relative or other suitable person
    - ☐ The court finds by clear and convincing evidence that the parent has waived his or her constitutional parental rights by being unfit, neglecting the child's welfare, or acting inconsistently with his or her constitutionally protected status.
    - ☐ The court must verify that the person receiving custody
        - ☐ understands the legal significance of the placement (applies to each person) and
        - ☐ will have adequate resources to appropriately care for the child. G.S. 7B-906.1(j).
    - ☐ Under G.S. 7B-911, the court must determine whether jurisdiction in the juvenile action should be terminated and custody ordered pursuant to G.S. Chapter 50. If the answer is yes, the court must follow the requirements of G.S. 7B-911 and make findings that
        - ☐ are required under G.S. Chapter 50,
        - ☐ there is not a need for continued state intervention on behalf of the juvenile through a juvenile court proceeding, and
        - ☐ at least six months have passed since the court determined the child's placement with the person to whom the court is awarding custody is the permanent plan for the child.
            - ☐ This finding is not required when custody is being awarded to
                - ☐ a parent or
                - ☐ a person with whom the child was living when the petition was filed.
- ☐ **Another Planned Permanent Living Arrangement (APPLA)** under G.S. 7B-912(c), (d)
    - ☐ The court must find *each* of the following:
        - ☐ The juvenile is 16 or 17 years old.
        - ☐ The department has made diligent efforts to place the teen permanently with a parent or relative or in a guardianship or an adoptive placement.
        - ☐ There are compelling reasons that it is not in the teen's best interests to be placed permanently with a parent or relative or in a guardianship or adoptive placement.
        - ☐ APPLA is the best permanent plan for the teen.
        - ☐ After questioning the teen, addresses the teen's desired permanency outcome.
- ☐ **Reinstatement of Parental Rights** pursuant to G.S. 7B-1114.

---

☐ **Complete Checklist 4 for additional requirements.**

# Checklist 8
# Termination of Parental Rights Hearing

This Checklist addresses preliminary matters, the adjudication of grounds, and the disposition for termination of parental rights proceedings related to an abuse, neglect, or dependency action.

## Subject Matter Jurisdiction

- ☐ The TPR action is initiated by a person with standing as authorized by G.S. 7B-1103(a).
- ☐ The petition or motion is properly verified (G.S. 7B-1104).
- ☐ The petition or motion requests relief. N.C. R. Civ. P. 7(b)(1).
- ☐ The petition or motion is filed in the judicial district where the juvenile resides in, is found in, or is in the county where a department (or licensed child-placing agency) with legal or actual custody of the juvenile is located at the time the petition or motion is filed (G.S. 7B-1101).
- ☐ NC has jurisdiction under the UCCJEA pursuant to G.S. Chapter 50A (review the allegations in the petition or attached affidavit addressing criteria specified by G.S. 50A-209 regarding the child's status) (G.S. 7B-1101):
  - ☐ This is an initial child custody determination (G.S. 50A-201).
  - ☐ NC entered a child custody order prior to this action and NC has exclusive continuing jurisdiction (G.S. 50A-202).
  - ☐ Another state has entered a child custody order but NC has jurisdiction to modify that order (G.S. 50A-203).
    - ☐ The child, the child's parents, and any person acting as a parent do not presently reside in the other state or
    - ☐ The other state's court has relinquished jurisdiction to NC and there is a court order from that other state relinquishing jurisdiction.
- ☐ For a nonresident parent, process was served pursuant to G.S. 7B-1106 (G.S. 7B-1101).

## Preliminary Issues

- ☐ The pretrial hearing required by G.S. 7B-1108.1 has been conducted or is combined with the adjudicatory hearing.
- ☐ Do any pretrial motions need to be decided?
- ☐ Is paternity an issue? If so, has a motion for genetic marker testing been made (G.S. 8-50.1(b1))?
- ☐ Has the court found reasonable cause exists to order, pursuant to G.S. 7B-1109(c), that
  - ☐ the child be examined by a psychiatrist, licensed clinical psychologist, physician, public or private agency, or any other expert to ascertain the child's psychological or physical condition or needs or
  - ☐ the parent be examined by a psychiatrist, licensed clinical psychologist, physician, public or private agency, or any other expert to ascertain the parent's ability to care for the

child?
- ☐ For the unknown parent, the court held a hearing pursuant to G.S. 7B-1105 to determine the parent's name or identity.
- ☐ The parties have been properly served or waived service (G.S. 7B-1106; 7B-1106.1; 7B-1102).
  - ☐ Before service by publication on a known parent was made, the court made findings that the respondent could not otherwise be served despite diligent efforts made by the petitioner, and the court approved the form of the notice (G.S. 7B-1106(a)).
- ☐ An answer or response was filed denying material allegations in the petition or motion. A GAL and attorney advocate have been appointed for the child as required by G.S. 7B-1108(b).
- ☐ No answer or response denying material allegations has been filed, but the court exercised its discretion to appoint a GAL and attorney advocate as permitted by G.S. 7B-1108(c).

*Parent Representation: G.S. 7B-1101.1; 7B-1109(b)*
- ☐ Court must inquire as to whether respondent is present and represented by counsel. If not represented, court must inquire as to whether respondent wants counsel and is indigent.
- ☐ If provisional counsel was appointed, has the appointment been confirmed or should provisional counsel be dismissed pursuant to G.S. 7B-1101.1(a)?
- ☐ If respondent wants to waive the right to counsel, has the court examined the respondent on the record and made findings to show that the waiver is knowing and voluntary?
- ☐ The parent is under age 18 and is not emancipated. A Rule 17 GAL is appointed.
- ☐ There is a substantial question as to parent's competency and need for a Rule 17 GAL. A hearing on that issue is required.

*Timing of Hearing: G.S. 7B-1109(a), (b), (d)*
- ☐ Are there any motions to continue the hearing, which must be held within ninety days of the petition or motion being filed (G.S. 7B-1109(a))? Continuances are limited (G.S. 7B-1109(b), (d)).
  - ☐ Is there good cause to continue hearing for up to ninety days from the date of the initial petition to receive additional evidence, reports, or assessments that the court has requested, to allow the parties to conduct expeditious discovery, or to receive any other needed information in the best interests of the child?
  - ☐ Continuance beyond ninety days may be granted when a written order states the grounds for the continuance based on extraordinary circumstances that are necessary for the proper administration of justice (see G.S.7B-803, resolution of pending criminal charges arising from the same incident is not a sole extraordinary circumstance to continue the hearing).
  - ☐ If the court appoints an attorney to a parent who was unrepresented at the hearing, the court must grant the parent an extension of time as is reasonable to permit appointed counsel to prepare a defense.

## Compliance with Federal Laws

☐ *Servicemembers Civil Relief Act: 50 U.S.C. 3931–3932*
Before a judgment for petitioner (DSS) is entered,
  ☐ Each respondent has made an appearance in the case. No SCRA affidavit is required.
  ☐ For each respondent who has not made an appearance, there is an affidavit or allegation in the verified petition that addresses that respondent's military status.
  ☐ It appears that a respondent is in military service. When that respondent has not made an appearance, appoint an attorney to perform SCRA responsibilities.
  ☐ A respondent is in military service. When the requirements of 50 U.S.C. 3931(d), (f) or 50 U.S.C. 3932 are met, a stay of at least ninety days is required.
  ☐ Under the NC SCRA, a state national guard member has not provided a written or electronic copy of an order to active duty for more than thirty consecutive days that was issued by a state governor. G.S. 127B-27(3), (4); 127B-28.

☐ *Indian Child Welfare Act: 25 C.F.R. 23.107*
Mandatory inquiry as to child's status as "Indian child" (defined at 25 U.S.C. 1903(4)) must be made of all participants at the commencement of the proceeding, with responses on the record.
  ☐ The child is an Indian child. ICWA provisions apply.
  *Note*: If child resides or is domiciled on Indian land or is a ward of tribal court, tribal court has exclusive jurisdiction unless an exception applies. A TPR does not meet the exception for an emergency proceeding.
  ☐ A participant has "reason to know" the child is an Indian child. Follow ICWA provisions unless and until court determines on the record that the child does not meet the definition of Indian child. Confirm that petitioner/movant used due diligence to identify and work with all the tribes child may be member of (or eligible for membership of). Was the ICWA notice sent?.
  ☐ The child is not an Indian child and no participant has reason to know the child is an Indian child. Instruct the parties to inform the court if they later receive information that provides reason to know the child is an Indian child. ICWA does not apply.

## Adjudication: G.S. 7B-1109; 7B-1111

☐ The petitioner or movant proved by clear, cogent, and convincing evidence at least one of the alleged grounds.

*Note:* The evidence must support findings of fact sufficient to support a conclusion of law that the alleged ground exists. The rules of evidence apply to adjudication hearings. There must be a hearing; no default judgment or judgment on the pleadings is permitted (G.S. 7B-1107).

## Dispositional Determination of Best Interest: G.S. 7B-1110(a)

When one or more grounds are adjudicated, the court must determine whether it is in the child's best interest to terminate parental rights by considering the following factors and making written findings of fact about those that are *relevant*:
- ☐ the child's age;
- ☐ likelihood of the child's adoption;
- ☐ whether termination will aid in the accomplishment of the child's permanent plan;
- ☐ the bond between the child and the parent;
- ☐ the quality of the relationship between the child and the proposed adoptive parent, guardian, custodian, or other permanent placement;
- ☐ any other relevant consideration.

*Note:* At disposition, the court may consider any evidence, including hearsay, that it finds to be relevant, reliable, and necessary to determine the child's best interests.

## Order: G.S. 7B-1109(e); 7B-1110

- ☐ The court must find facts and adjudicate (i.e., make a conclusion of law regarding) the existence or nonexistence of each ground alleged in the petition or motion.
- ☐ The order must be entered (signed by the judge presiding over the hearing and filed with the clerk) within thirty days following completion of the hearing.

*Outcomes:*
- ☐ Dismiss the petition/Deny the motion.
  At least one of the following must apply:
  - ☐ None of the alleged grounds have been proved by clear, cogent, and convincing evidence.
    - ☐ Make appropriate findings of fact and conclusions of law.
  - ☐ At least one alleged ground was proved but it is not in the child's best interest to terminate parental rights.
    - ☐ Must include the facts and conclusions on which the dismissal/denial is based.
- ☐ Grant the petition or motion.
  - ☐ The order that adjudicates a ground must state that the findings are based on clear, cogent, and convincing evidence.
  - ☐ The order must include findings of fact about the factors that were relevant to the determination of the child's best interests.
  - ☐ If the juvenile was not in the custody of DSS or a child-placing agency at the time the TPR petition or motion was filed, the order may place the juvenile in the custody of the petitioner/movant, some other suitable person, DSS, or a child-placing agency as may appear to be in the child's best interests (G.S. 7B-1112(2)).

## Findings Relating to Particular Grounds

Following are reminders of *some* of the necessary findings of fact relating to five of the most frequently alleged grounds involving a TPR with an underlying abuse, neglect, or dependency proceeding.

### Neglect or Abuse: G.S. 7B-1111(a)(1)

For this ground, neglect and abuse are defined by G.S. 7B-101(15) and (1) respectively. This ground requires findings of
- ☐ current neglect or abuse or
- ☐ if the child has been separated from the parent for a long period of time,
  - ☐ past neglect or abuse and
  - ☐ a likelihood of repetition of neglect or abuse if the child were returned home.
- ☐ Neglect under either prong above requires a finding of harm or substantial risk of harm to the juvenile.

### Willfully leaving the child in foster care or other placement for more than a year without making reasonable progress under the circumstances to correct conditions that led to the child's removal: G.S. 7B-1111(a)(2)

This ground has two prongs:
- ☐ the child has willfully been left in foster care or placement outside the home for over twelve months before the filing of the TPR petition or motion (removal must be due to a court order) and
- ☐ at the time of the TPR hearing, the parent has not made reasonable progress under the circumstances to correct the conditions that led to the child's removal.

Poverty cannot be the basis for the TPR.

There must be findings
- ☐ sufficient to support a conclusion of willfulness, which requires findings about what the parent did in relation to what the parent was capable of doing;
- ☐ that address a parent's failure to make reasonable progress in relation to the conditions that led to the child's removal from the home; and
- ☐ that show that the child's placement outside the home for at least a year has been pursuant to a court order.

### Willfully failed to pay a reasonable portion of the child's cost of care although physically and financially able to do so: G.S. 7B-1111(a)(3)

If the child has been placed in the custody of DSS, a licensed child-placing agency, child-caring institution, or a foster home, there must be findings that show
- ☐ the nonpayment of a reasonable portion of the cost of the child's care for at least six months before the filing of the TPR petition or motion;
- ☐ the parent's ability to pay some amount greater than what he or she paid during the relevant six-month time period; and
- ☐ the parent's failure to pay was willful.

**Dependency with a reasonable probability it will continue for the foreseeable future: G.S. 7B-1111(a)(6)**

For this ground, dependency is defined by G.S. 7B-101(9). This ground requires findings that
- ☐ the parent does not have an ability to provide care or supervision to the child (based on any cause or condition, e.g., mental illness, substance abuse, incarceration);
- ☐ the parent lacks an available alternative child care arrangement for the child; and
- ☐ the parent's incapability is likely to continue for the foreseeable future (but is not required to be permanent, throughout the child's minority, or for a known precise duration).

**Abandonment**

A TPR based on abandonment can be based on two different grounds:
- ☐ G.S. 7B-1111(a)(1), neglect, as the definition of neglect in G.S. 7B-101(15) includes a juvenile who has been abandoned;
- ☐ G.S. 7B-1111(a)(7), a parent has willfully abandoned the child for at least six consecutive months immediately preceding the filing of the TPR petition or motion.

Under G.S. 7B-1111(a)(7), findings must address
- ☐ a parent's willful intent to forego all parental duties and relinquish all parental claims (e.g., no financial support for, contact with, or inquiries about the child)
- ☐ during the relevant six-month time period.

# Checklist 9
# Post-TPR Review Hearing

The post-TPR review hearing is governed by G.S. 7B-908. Its purpose is to ensure that every reasonable effort is being made to provide for permanent placement plans for a child who has been placed in the custody of a department (DSS) or licensed child-placing agency (agency), which are consistent with the child's best interest.

## When Required: G.S. 7B-908(b)

The post-TPR review hearing must be held within six months from the date of the termination hearing when the child is in DSS (or agency) custody and
- ☐ parental rights have been terminated by an action brought by DSS or an agency with custody of the child, the child's GAL, the child's guardian of the person, or the person with whom the child has lived continuously for at least two years immediately preceding the filing of the TPR action, or
- ☐ one parent's parental rights have been terminated and the other parent's rights have been relinquished under G.S. Chapter 48.

Post-TPR hearings are held every six months until the child is adopted.

*Note:* When there has not been a relinquishment of the child by a parent, G.S. 7B-908 does not clarify whether the requirement for this post-TPR hearing applies when one or both parents' rights have been terminated. The statute governing post-TPR review hearings does not authorize the court to waive holding these hearings. If a concurrent permanent plan other than adoption is achieved (e.g., the secondary plan), under G.S. 7B-908, post-TPR review hearings continue to be conducted every six months. Additionally, permanency planning review hearings should also occur unless the court made G.S. 7B-906.1(n) findings and waived those hearings.

## Required Notice: G.S. 7B-908(b)(1)

The clerk must give notice no more than thirty days and no less than fifteen days prior to each post-TPR review hearing to
- ☐ the child if 12 or older;
- ☐ the child's GAL, if any;
- ☐ the child's legal custodian or guardian;
- ☐ the person providing care for the child (DSS may send the notice and file written documentation with the clerk that is has done so); and
- ☐ any other person or agency the court specifies.

## Appointment of GAL for Child: G.S. 7B-908(b)(2)

If the child was unrepresented by a GAL at the TPR hearing, the court may
- ☐ appoint a GAL at the first post-TPR review hearing and
- ☐ continue the case for as much time as is necessary for the GAL to become familiar with the facts of the case.

## The Hearing: G.S. 7B-908(a), (b)(1)

- Unless the court directs otherwise, the child, child's GAL, legal custodian, guardian, and person providing care for the child may participate in the hearings.
- A parent whose rights have been terminated is not a party to the proceeding unless there is a pending appeal of the TPR order and the order is stayed pending the appeal.
- The court may consider any evidence, including hearsay evidence, that it finds to be relevant, reliable, and necessary to determine the child's needs and most appropriate disposition.

## Required Inquiries and Findings: G.S. 7B-908(c)

The court must consider the following factors and making written findings of those that are *relevant:*
- ☐ the adequacy of the permanency plans developed by DSS (or the agency) for permanent placement relevant to the child's best interests and DSS's (or the agency's) efforts to implement the plans;
- ☐ whether the child has been listed for adoptive placement with NC Kids Adoption and Foster Care Network or any other child-specific recruitment program or whether the court finds, based on the child's best interests, that there is an exemption to the listing;
- ☐ efforts previously made by DSS or the agency to find a permanent placement for the child;
- ☐ whether the current placement is in the child's best interests.

## Order: G.S. 7B-908(d), (e1)

The court must
- ☐ make findings of fact (supported by competent evidence),
- ☐ adopt concurrent permanent plans in accordance with G.S. 7B-906.2(a)(2)–(6), and
- ☐ identify
  - ☐ a primary plan and
  - ☐ a secondary plan.

The court may
- ☐ specify efforts that are necessary to accomplish the permanent placement that is in the child's best interests,
- ☐ order a placement it finds to be in the child's best interests, if the child is not placed with prospective adoptive parents as selected in G.S. 7B-1112.1 and the court has considered DSS's recommendations.

The order must be entered (signed by the judge presiding over the hearing and filed with the clerk) within thirty days following completion of the hearing.